The Moneywise Guide to No

This uniquely informative guide first appeare
New World', and contained just 64 pages! Since then, tens of thousands of users and contributors later, it has become the most sought-after guidebook for the serious, economy-minded traveller who wants to see and experience all that the North American continent has to offer.

The *Moneywise Guide* remains the only guidebook to cover all three countries of North America in one sensible-size volume. It remains the only guidebook which treats not only all the usual cities and tourist areas of North America, but also those lesser-known cities, towns and communities which form natural waypoints on the major travel routes.

Ideal for the traveller just passing through or staying a while, the *Moneywise Guide* will inform you, entertain you and, above all, save you money.

Where to stay—budget accommodation tested, assessed and updated by the users, checked by the editors. Small downtown hostels, economy motels, YMCAs, youth hostels, bed and breakfasts, tourist homes.

Where not to stay—'no-go' areas, seedy spots, and places to avoid.

Where to eat—the latest in 'mean cuisine' for those who still buy their meals with cash, not plastic.

What to see—the sights you'll want to see, from Disneyland to national parks, the things you'll want to do, throughout the continent. Updated entrance fees. Hundreds of *free* attractions.

General information—the most comprehensive 'General' section of any guide to North America. How to get there to visit or to work, what to take, what to wear. Visas, insurance and other paperwork. Immigration, people and customs. Driving, hiking and other forms of low-budget travel. And where to get further information.

About the authors: **Anna Crew** has a background in journalism and has edited this Guide for many years. She is British but lives at present in Connecticut, from where she directs BUNAC'S camp counselor programme, BUNACAMP. **Nicholas Ludlow** is also British, but based in Washington DC. An inveterate traveller throughout North America, he is a freelance writer and editor and specialist in the economics of developing countries.

Richard Jolly from Cambridge, has a degree in International Business from the University of Plymouth and is fluent in French; has travelled throughout Canada and the US. Co-revised the US and Canada sections of this edition.
Anette Kaminski, raised in Sao Paulo, Brazil, now based in Washington DC, fluent in both Portuguese and Spanish, has a masters degree in international relations from Johns Hopkins School of International Studies (SAIS). Revised the Mexico section of the guide.
Tom Ridgway from Sherbourne, Dorset, is taking an honours degree in English Literature at Queen Mary & Westfield College, University of London, and is film editor of the University newspaper *London Student*. He is widely travelled in the US and Canada and has worked in the UK at the Birmingham *Post & Mail* and *Western Gazette*. Co-revised the US section of the book.

☆ ☆ ☆ ☆ ☆ ☆

The Moneywise Guide to

NORTH AMERICA

USA

Plus Canada and Mexico

Editors: Anna L. Crew and
Nicholas H. Ludlow

Research and Revision 1994 Edition:
Richard Jolly, Anette Kaminski,
Tom Ridgway

BUNAC

THE MONEYWISE GUIDE TO NORTH AMERICA
26th Edition

Published by BUNAC Travel Services Ltd,
16 Bowling Green Lane, London EC1R 0BD

British Library Cataloguing in Publication Data

Moneywise Guide to North America: USA,
Canada, Mexico. – 26 Rev. ed
I. Crew, Anna II. Ludlow, Nicholas H.
917.04

ISBN 0-9511066-8-6

General Editors: Anna L. Crew and Nicholas H. Ludlow.

Research and Revision: Richard Jolly, Anette Kaminski,
Tom Ridgway.

Additional editorial assistance: Justine Edwards, Daniella Finn,
Philippa Howe, Khashif Khan, Ruth McMurdo, plus the many readers who
sent in corrections and additions.

Special thanks to Jim Buck and Sarah Eykyn.

Cover design: Randak Design Consultants Limited
Cover pictures: Chris Mileham, Robert Harding Picture Library
Design and maps: Vera Brice; Randak Design Consultants Limited.

Set in Compugraphic Palacio by Create Publishing Services Ltd, Bath.
Printed and bound in Great Britain by The Bath Press, Lower Bristol Road,
Bath BA2 3BL.

Contents

THE FUTURE OF THIS GUIDE

Quoted comments throughout the *Guide* are genuine remarks made by travellers over the years. Comments from present readers—the more descriptive the better—will add to the colour and usefulness of the next edition.

For brief comments, and most importantly for correcting or adding information about accommodation, fares and so on, please use the **Correction and Addition** slips at the back of the *Guide*. Hotel brochures, local bus schedules, maps and similar tidbits are gratefully received. Also welcome are longer accounts, so feel free to send in letters.

In all cases, please write only on one side of each sheet of paper. Thank you for your help.

☆ ☆ ☆ ☆ ☆ ☆

The Undiscovered Continent

The most amazing thing about North America is that after a spell of travelling you find it so different from what you expected it to be. Everyone thinks they have a good idea of what it is all about. American technology, politics, media and entertainments daily make their mark the world over. North America is the most publicised continent on earth.

But the projected image hides, both from foreigners and North Americans themselves, a largely undiscovered continent. The polyglot of peoples out of which Canada, the United States and Mexico are each differently formed can make Europe, for example, look comparatively homogeneous. Just a ride on the New York City subway is enough to convince anyone of that.

There are huge tracts of magnificent landscapes, unsettled and hardly explored: forests, glaciers, deserts and jungles; mountains, canyons, prairies, vast lakes and seashores; orchards in Oregon, farming valleys in Vermont, pre-Columbian Indian settlements, many of them unchanged and still inhabited, in Mexico and Arizona, totem poles in British Columbia, fishing villages in Nova Scotia.

Then there are the cities, the hubs of late 20th century North America: Los Angeles an exploding star, San Francisco riding on a sea of hills, New York a concrete canyon, Chicago scraping the sky with the longest fingers in the world, Houston a port and rocket centre, New Orleans blowing jazz across the Mississippi, Québec only geographically in the New World, its soul still back across the Atlantic, Vancouver, Canada's golden gateway to the Pacific, and Mexico City a brilliant mosaic of Spanish and Aztec design. In between is the 'heartland', thousands of small communities each with its own distinctive character and way of life.

The variety and complexity are more than a lifetime of sitting in front of a television set will even remotely convey to you. And there is the discovery too of the instant, of even the future, for North America is always reaching ahead and you have to be there, in the running, to get a glimpse of tomorrow.

☆ ☆ ☆ ☆ ☆ ☆

This edition is dedicated to the memory of Max—a true lover of exploring and the great outdoors.

About The Moneywise Guide

This is a Guide to most of the usual and many of the unusual places in North America and should prove of service to anyone, but most of all the moneywise traveller. North America can be an expensive continent if you let it. But part of its great variety is the many places to eat and sleep and the many different ways of moving about from which you can choose to suit your pocket, and with the help of this Guide it can be a real bargain. Anyone who is happy about spending more money will easily find a $90 hotel bed and a $30 meal, in which case this Guide is content with showing you the way to the Statue of Liberty or the Grand Canyon. But for people really on a budget, this is also a Guide to thousands of inexpensive places to rest your head and fill your belly *and* to get you to the Grand Canyon on a shoestring.

In separate sections this Guide covers the USA, Canada and Mexico. General introductions precede detailed coverage of each country. Make a point of first reading these background chapters: here you will find general information on each country, facts about visas, currency, health and other things, money-saving tips on eating, accommodation and travel. *Note that much of the information found in the US Background section will also be of value for travel to Canada and Mexico.*

Each country is then divided into regions, e.g. The Midwest, and in the case of the USA and Canada, states and provinces within each region follow *alphabetically*. There is also an Index at the back of the Guide.

Hotel and restaurant listings are the result of the first-hand experience of the Guide's authors and its thousands of readers since the preceding edition. Prices quoted are usually the lowest available. Within the same month at the same hotel, one traveller might spend more on a room than another. This is usually because the rooms were of different standards, but never be afraid to question room rates or even to bargain over them. **You should also allow for inflation when budgeting for the trip. It is therefore probably advisable to allow more for the overall cost of accommodation than the rates printed here would indicate. Similarly it should be remembered that all travel/vacation costs rise each year in North America and so it is quite possible that prices will change after the Guide has gone to print. Sorry!**

Please remember that the **maps in this Guide are only intended to give you a rough orientation**—an artist's impression—when first arriving in the city. They are not, nor are they intended to be, fully comprehensive. If staying anywhere for any length of time, buy a good street map, though first see if you can get one free from the local Chamber of Commerce or tourist office.

Accommodation Listings Abbreviations:
S = single; D = double; T = triple; Q = quad; XP = extra person in room; Bfast = breakfast; facs = facilities; AC = air conditioning.

1. USA

BACKGROUND

BEFORE YOU GO

Unless you plan to enter the USA under the *Visa Waiver Program*, before departing you must obtain an entry visa (main categories listed below). Currently citizens of France, Germany, Italy, Japan, The Netherlands, Sweden, Switzerland and the U.K. are eligible to participate in the Waiver Program under which visitors to the US for less than 90 days can apply for entry permission on arrival. Check with your airline or travel agent about this. If not applicable to you, you will have to apply for one of the following:

Visitors (B) Visa. This allows you to remain in the US for a maximum of six months, the period to be determined on arrival by immigration officials based on how long they think your money will hold out. When you first obtain your visa abroad it may be stamped 'valid indefinitely'. This means it may be used repeatedly; but each stay is limited to the six-month maximum. You may not work on a Visitors Visa.

In Transit (C) Visa. This allows you to go from A to B via the US and to stay in the US a maximum of 29 days. It can be issued for multiple entries.

Student (F) Visa. You must pursue a fulltime course of study for one year minimum at a school that is identified and approved in advance. Sometimes you have to post a money bond before entering the US. It allows you to work, but only under certain, limited, circumstances.

Temporary Workers (H) Visa. Issued only if you offer specialised skills or qualifications, and requires a written offer from your prospective employer. It's very difficult to obtain.

Exchange (J) Visa. For non-immigrant exchange visitors, J-1 visas are obtainable only through an approved, sponsoring organization. The terms are usually very specific. J-1 participants can work, study, train, research or

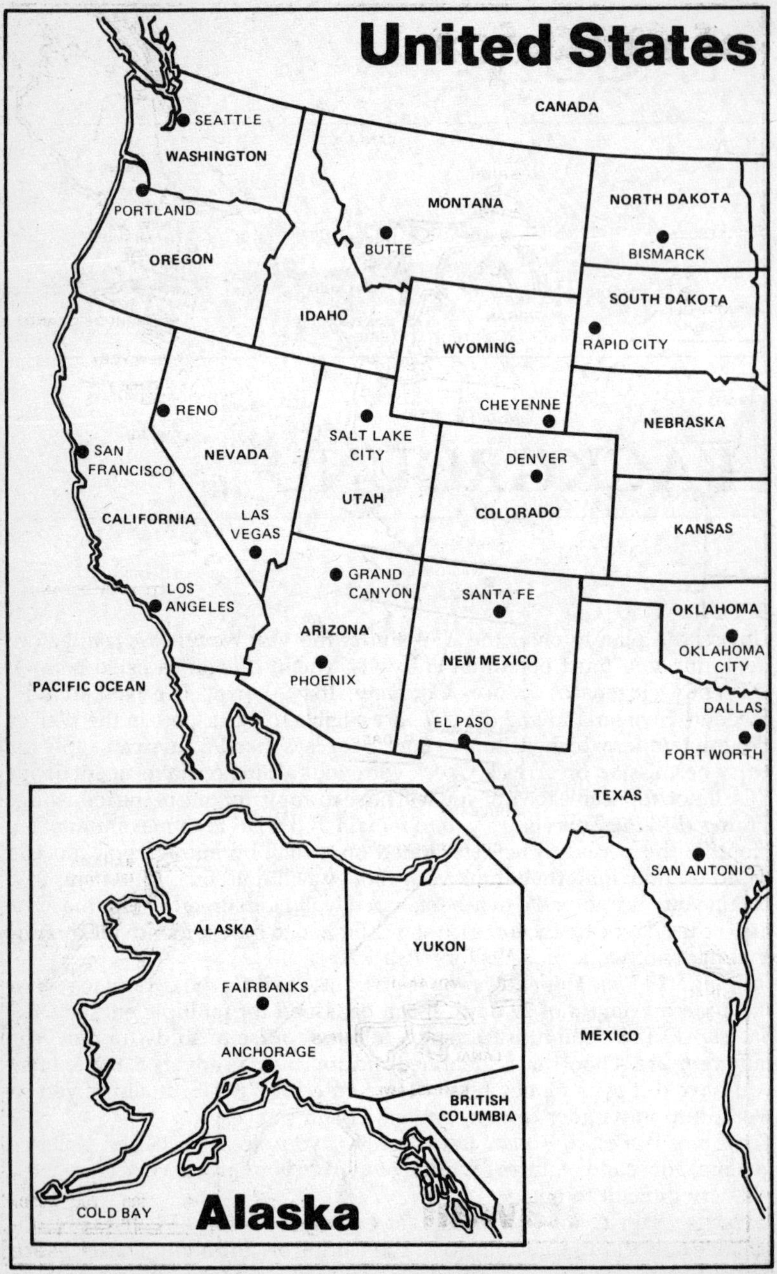
United States
CANADA
SEATTLE
WASHINGTON
PORTLAND
OREGON
MONTANA
BUTTE
NORTH DAKOTA
BISMARCK
SOUTH DAKOTA
RAPID CITY
IDAHO
WYOMING
CHEYENNE
NEBRASKA
RENO
NEVADA
SAN FRANCISCO
SALT LAKE CITY
DENVER
UTAH
COLORADO
KANSAS
CALIFORNIA
LAS VEGAS
GRAND CANYON
LOS ANGELES
SANTA FE
OKLAHOMA
OKLAHOMA CITY
ARIZONA
PHOENIX
NEW MEXICO
PACIFIC OCEAN
DALLAS
FORT WORTH
EL PASO
TEXAS
SAN ANTONIO
MEXICO
ALASKA
YUKON
FAIRBANKS
ANCHORAGE
BRITISH COLUMBIA
COLD BAY
Alaska

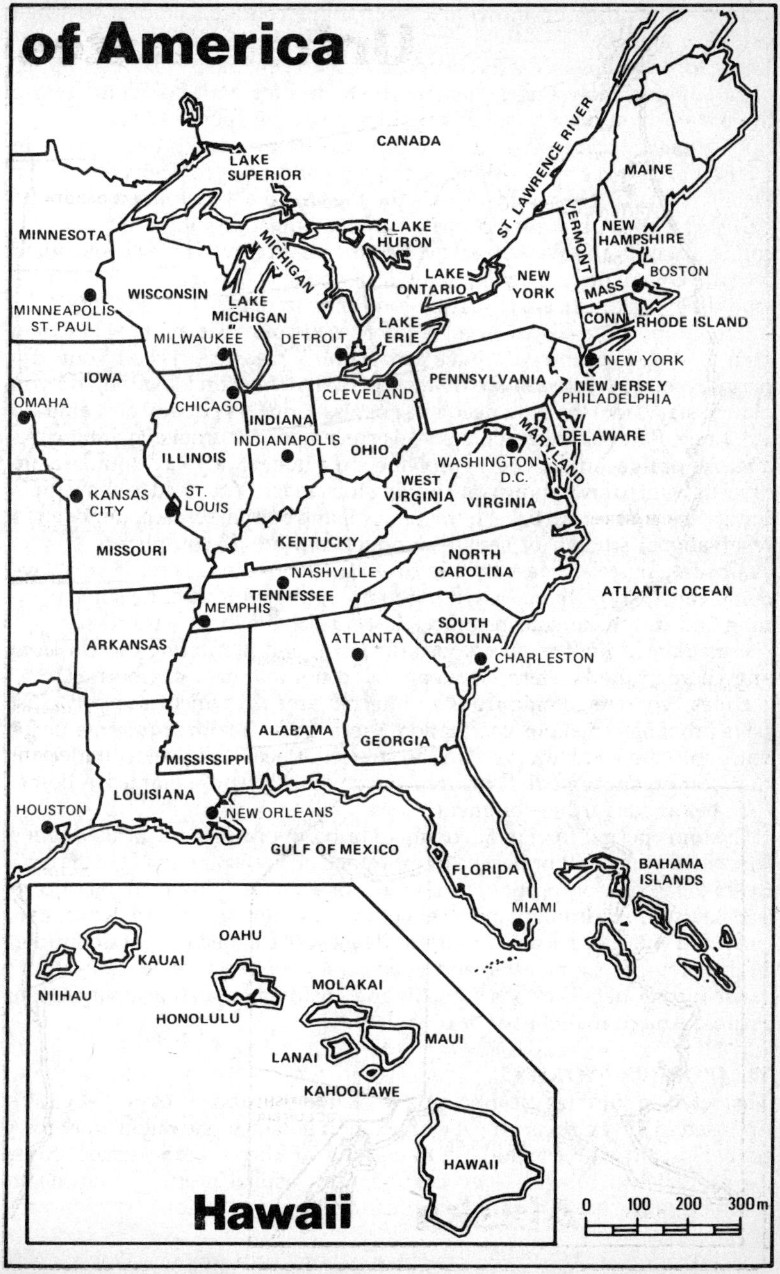
of America
CANADA
LAKE SUPERIOR
MINNESOTA
LAKE HURON
MICHIGAN
ST. LAWRENCE RIVER
MAINE
VERMONT
NEW HAMPSHIRE
BOSTON
LAKE ONTARIO
NEW YORK
MASS
CONN
RHODE ISLAND
WISCONSIN
LAKE MICHIGAN
MINNEAPOLIS ST. PAUL
MILWAUKEE
DETROIT
LAKE ERIE
NEW YORK
IOWA
PENNSYLVANIA
NEW JERSEY
PHILADELPHIA
OMAHA
CHICAGO
CLEVELAND
INDIANA
INDIANAPOLIS
OHIO
MARYLAND
DELAWARE
ILLINOIS
WASHINGTON D.C.
KANSAS CITY
ST. LOUIS
WEST VIRGINIA
VIRGINIA
MISSOURI
KENTUCKY
NORTH CAROLINA
NASHVILLE
TENNESSEE
ATLANTIC OCEAN
MEMPHIS
SOUTH CAROLINA
ARKANSAS
ATLANTA
CHARLESTON
ALABAMA
GEORGIA
MISSISSIPPI
LOUISIANA
HOUSTON
NEW ORLEANS
GULF OF MEXICO
FLORIDA
BAHAMA ISLANDS
MIAMI
OAHU
KAUAI
NIIHAU
MOLAKAI
HONOLULU
MAUI
LANAI
KAHOOLAWE
HAWAII
Hawaii
0 100 200 300m

lecture—depending on individual programme conditions—for a specified period of time.
Fiancé (K) Visa. Given for the purpose of marrying a US citizen within 90 days. Unfortunately it doesn't allow you to look for 'Mr/Miss Right' during the first 89; you have to show a petition from the spouse-to-be.
(Q) Cultural Exchange Visa. A new programme for certain participants in cultural exchanges eg. working at Disneyworld or Epcot Centre.
Immigrants Visa. (*Green card.*) This is the Big One that lets you remain in the US *ad infinitum*. It's subject to the quota limitations imposed on your country of origin. It also subjects you to the possibility of being conscripted into the US military, an eventuality designed to cool the ardour of many a would-be (male) citizen. It takes a long time to obtain.

Immigration officials ask you the purpose of your visit and how long you plan to stay. Probably you have arrived on a pleasure visit. If your visa permits you to work, say so. In answer to the question How long do you plan to stay? note that you need not possess X dollars per day or X amount of money. Rather immigration officials are looking for proof of planning. As a reader of this Guide, you're probably on a budget anyway. Immigration officials want to know how you're going to manage. You need to show them things like your return ticket home; rail, air and bus passes; accommodation reservations; student or senior identification; etc. If you plan to stay in campsites, hostels, guest houses or with friends, tell them. If you have credit cards, show them. Anything to prove that you've done some planning and can make your resources last for the time you wish to stay.

Canadians do not require a visa (to visit), and if entering the US from anywhere in the Western Hemisphere do not require a passport either.

Unless you are coming from an infected area, in which case you must have proof of a smallpox vaccination, there are no **health requirements** for entry into the US. However, on the subject of health, it is most important that you organise medical **insurance** for yourself before you leave home. (See below for further comment.)

Customs permit foreign residents to bring in one litre of spirits or wine (provided you are 21 or over); 200 cigarettes or 100 cigars (not Havana) or 3 lbs of tobacco or proportionate amounts of each (an additional quantity of 100 cigars may be brought in under your gift exemption), $100 worth of gifts provided you stay at least 72 hours and have not claimed the gift exemption in the previous six months, and your personal effects free of duty.

For further details on visa, health and customs regulations, contact the nearest American embassy or consulate.

TEMPORARY WORK

This refers to summer vacation type work under the auspices of a J-1 visa as opposed to the more career-type of position in which one might work for a limited period of time in the USA under, say, an H visa. J programmes cover a great variety of categories: everything from hospital interns to counsellors working with children on summer camps. The regulations for each programme vary.

In Britain, BUNAC (the British Universities North America Club) organises educational work travel exchange programmes to the United States and

Canada. The 'Work America' programme is for full-time students studying at a British university or college, and provides the student with a work permit for the duration of the summer. Participants can take any job other than that of camp counselling. In Ireland, USIT operate a similar programme for Irish students.

If you are interested in working with children on an American summer camp, then the BUNACAMP programme may be for you. BUNACAMP will place you as a counselor on a camp and loan you the round-trip fare across the Atlantic. All you pay to register on the programme is £59. You would also have to pay for insurance once you get a definite place. You repay the loan for your airfare etc. out of your salary and are still left with about $390–$450 pocket money at the end of camp.

For details on these programmes contact: BUNAC, 16 Bowling Green Lane, London EC1R 0BD. Tel: (071) 251-3472.

Doubtless many people do work in 'underground jobs' such as in casual labour, fruit harvesting, farm work, restaurant work etc., but if you are contemplating this you should be aware of the risks involved. The penalties you would be likely to incur would be deportation and the knowledge that you would have to face an extremely uphill task should you ever want to return to America again. You should also be aware that the new Immigration Act means that an employer hiring an illegal alien faces stiff penalties if caught. This of course acts as a deterrent should an employer be contemplating the possibility and lessens the chances of employment for someone without a work visa.

GETTING THERE

This Guide is used by readers all over the world, and the best and least expensive way of reaching the United States will vary according to where you're starting out. Check advertisements, ask friends and travel agents—including the 'bucket shop' variety. Be alert. Fares are constantly changing.

For the budget traveller, the choice is basically charter, economy, APEX, inclusive package and, possibly, standby. If you are travelling to North America from Britain a group charter fare will probably be cheapest. Watch the press for ads. or ask a travel agent about such fares. Of the scheduled airlines Continental Airlines, flying from Gatwick Airport to Newark, NJ (New York), and Virgin Atlantic flying from Heathrow to JFK and Newark Airports, offer fares from about £420 to £490 return, depending on when you travel and when you book. Virgin also fly to Boston, Miami and Orlando, FL, and to Los Angeles, (San Francisco service is scheduled to begin May 1994); while Continental can connect the traveller on to various US cities (and Mexico) through their domestic network from Newark.

However, don't overlook carriers like British Airways or American Airlines. They will sometimes come in with good deals and are worth investigating. BA also offer regional departures.

Economy fares are pretty expensive; if you're willing to accept a few restrictions you can save a lot of money on other types of fare.

APEX (Advance Purchase Excursion) tickets are sold by the scheduled airlines themselves and must be purchased at least 21 days before departure. At the time of purchase you must fix your date of departure and return; if you later decide to change either of these dates you'll have to pay a penalty charge.

Advanced Booking Charters (ABCs) have roughly the same restrictions as APEX tickets and you may find yourself either travelling on a plane wholly chartered by the travel operator or else on a scheduled airline from whom the operator will have bought a block of seats at a special charter rate. For the tourist or budget traveller this is probably the most popular method of getting to America. From Britain expect to pay about the same or a little less than the fares quoted above for Virgin and Continental.

Standby fares, if available, are probably the cheapest; you buy the ticket when you like, but space is allocated only on the day of departure. Summer weekends are the most difficult times to get space; midweek departures are usually easier. These tickets are bought directly from the airline, which can advise you of your prospects a day or so before your intended date of departure.

It may be possible to get yourself hired as a *courier* for a one-off flight. Using this method you pay a reduced price on a scheduled flight and in return you carry with you and deliver a package at the other end. Check directly with the many courier operations which make their living shipping business packages back and forth across the Atlantic.

Inclusive packages abound, offering considerable flexibility. Some, however, treat America as a substitute for two weeks on the Costa del Sol—there was never much excuse for fish and chips at Torremolinos when there was all of Spain to see, and there is even less excuse for two weeks of fish and chips in Miami when an entire continent awaits you.

Fly-drive packages including air fare, unlimited mileage car and accommodation vouchers are a good bet, especially if you're travelling as a family or with friends. Prices vary according to size of car, standard of accommodation and the number of people travelling together.

At the same time that you consider how to get to North America, you should be considering how to travel around once there. Certain discounts and travel passes may only be available to non-residents purchasing their tickets abroad. Also, when you buy your tickets outside the US you save the sales tax.

CLIMATE

Remember that you are not travelling over a country but across a vast continent and that the climate varies accordingly. Consider that the distance from New York to Miami is equivalent to that from London to Tangier, and that New York and Los Angeles are as distant from each other as London and Baghdad, and you get a good idea of what this can mean.

Indoors, these differences are minimised by central heating and air conditioning, but outside, winters can be very cold in Washington DC (for instance) and even further south, and summers extremely hot everywhere.

Temperatures approaching 90°F (32°C) day after day, sometimes accompanied by a suffocating humidity, are not unusual in the summer. New York, Washington DC, New Orleans and the Deep South can be particularly unpleasant. As early as September, however, nights can be cool everywhere, and freezing in mountainous areas.

Some generalisations on climatic regions:
New England, the Northeast, Mid-Atlantic and Midwest. Cold in the winter, often humid in the summer and as hot as anywhere else in America including Florida and southern California.
The Southwest. Warm to hot throughout the year, and nearly always dry.
The Pacific States. Washington, Oregon and northern California have moderate climates: not too cold in the winter—though often wet, not too hot in the summer. San Francisco is often bathed in summer afternoon fogs. Southern California is warm to hot the year round, and nearly always dry.
The South. Hot in summer, mild in winter though agreeably warm in Florida.
The Mountains. In summer, days are warm but nights can be cold. Very cold throughout the winter.
The Deserts. Very hot and dry throughout the year, but can be cold at night.

WHAT TO TAKE AND HOW TO TAKE IT

Take as little as possible, choose clothes for their use in a variety of situations and when you have made your final selection, halve it!

It is always a nuisance to have too much, and anyway if necessary, you can purchase what you need in America. The present exchange rate means that American stores offer many shopping bargains for visitors. In particular items like jeans, shirts, T-shirts and casual clothes are good buys in the US. If you hunt around you can usually find something on sale.

Laundromats are often open 24 hours a day. The cost of a wash is usually $1 (in quarters); drying machines usually take 25¢—you just keep feeding in the quarters, total per load is about $1.25.

Whatever luggage you take, make sure it's easy to handle. Getting on and off buses and trains, even just changing planes, can be an ordeal if your bags are too heavy or too many. The best solution is to take one hold-all, be it a suitcase or a backpack, and then a smaller bag which you can sling from your shoulder. Even when you have to check in your hold-all at the airport or bus station, you can keep all your documents, travellers' cheques and your paperback novel safely and conveniently by your side. It is also a good idea to keep a change of clothing in your shoulder bag in case your suitcase/backpack gets lost by an airline or bus company.

For extra security many travellers also wear a neck (or belt) wallet/pouch for passport, cash, travellers cheques and other valuables. It is also a good idea to photocopy your passport and other important documents and keep the copies SEPARATE from the originals. Should you lose your passport you should immediately contact your nearest national consulate (British consulates in Atlanta, Boston, Chicago, Houston, Los Angeles, New York, San Francisco and Washington DC).

Some tips: at bus stations in particular, make absolutely certain that your bag is going on your bus and that you get a check-in ticket for it. You would be amazed at the number of times bag and body go off in different directions. And if you're a backpacker just arrived in a big city, you can usually

City temperatures (in Fahrenheit).		Jan–Feb	Mar–Apr	May–June	Jul–Aug	Sep–Oct	Nov–Dec
CHICAGO	Low	20°	35°	56°	67°	53°	28°
	High	34	51	74	83	69	42
	Average	27	43	65	75	61	35
DENVER	Low	18	29	58	43	43	22
	High	46	57	88	73	73	50
	Average	32	43	73	58	58	36
HONOLULU	Low	68	69	72	74	73	69
	High	74	75	80	84	83	79
	Average	71	72	76	79	78	74
HOUSTON	Low	48	58	71	75	67	50
	High	64	74	89	93	87	68
	Average	56	66	80	84	77	59
LAS VEGAS	Low	35	47	64	76	61	47
	High	57	73	84	102	87	61
	Average	46	60	79	89	74	54
LOS ANGELES	Low	46	50	57	62	59	49
	High	64	66	71	76	75	69
	Average	55	58	64	69	67	59
MIAMI	Low	59	64	72	75	73	61
	High	77	82	88	89	87	79
	Average	68	73	80	82	80	70
NEW ORLEANS	Low	49	59	71	76	68	52
	High	67	75	87	92	84	68
	Average	58	67	79	84	77	60
NEW YORK	Low	26	38	58	68	54	34
	High	40	54	76	84	72	44
	Average	33	46	67	76	63	39
SAN FRANCISCO	Low	43	46	51	54	52	45
	High	57	64	65	72	72	61
	Average	50	55	58	63	62	53
ST LOUIS	Low	24	38	58	67	52	30
	High	42	60	80	89	76	50
	Average	33	49	69	78	64	40
SEATTLE	Low	24	39	47	54	47	37
	High	46	55	69	76	65	49
	Average	35	47	58	65	56	43
WASHINGTON DC	Low	29	41	61	68	56	35
	High	45	61	79	86	74	51
	Average	37	51	70	77	65	43

leave your pack at one of the museums for free and then skip off to look for a room, or do a little sightseeing unencumbered.

TIME ZONES

The continental US is divided into four time zones, Eastern Standard Time, Central Standard Time, Mountain Standard Time and Pacific Standard Time. Exact zone boundaries are shown on most road maps.

Noon EST = 11am CST = 10am MST = 9am PST. Standard time in Hawaii is two hours earlier than PST, ie 9am PST = 7am HST. Daylight Saving Time occurs widely though not universally throughout the United States; from the end of April to the end of October clocks are put forward one hour. Carefully check air, rail and bus schedules in advance.

THE AMERICAN PEOPLE

Keeping in mind the vastness of the United States and the thought that this is a continent you are visiting rather than a country, it becomes a little easier to appreciate the diversity of the land and its people. America is an incredibly cosmopolitan society. Glance at the names in the telephone book of almost any town anywhere in America for evidence of this. Every nationality on earth, speaking scores of the world's languages, every creed, every race is represented here.

The only true native peoples of the USA, of course are the Indians, who are thought to have arrived in America by way of the Bering Strait from Asia several thousands of years before the Pilgrim Fathers made landfall in Massachusetts. Since the time of the European migration the lot of the 'Native American' (as the Indian is now called) has not been a happy one. Harried and hounded by the westward moving white man, Native Americans were eventually pushed into their own 'reservations', inevitably on the poorest and most infertile land around. In more recent times the position of the Native American has improved a little but there is still a long, long way to go. Having Indian blood is a matter for fierce pride and many Indians still harbour great resentment towards the white man. Be aware of this should you visit a reservation and be respectful towards the people and their laws and customs.

Cosmopolitan America may be, but not yet a melting pot. National groups tend to stick together—you will see bumper stickers reading 'Irish-American', 'Proud to be Polish' for instance. At the top of the social heap are still the WASPS (White Anglo Saxon Protestants) represented by the British, Germans and Scandinavians, and followed by the Irish and other European groups. Next come Asians, then Blacks and the fast-rising Hispanics. It is estimated that Hispanics will soon outnumber the black population and become the largest minority group. As immigration continues and fortunes around the world turn this way or that so will American society continue to evolve in order to cope with new national groupings and social trends.

It is to this constantly changing society, the moving frontier, that one can perhaps trace the roots of the violence present in American society. Where tradition is scarce, where the future is always being built anew, there is often a sense of rootlessness and self-doubt in which violence, crime, drug or alcohol dependency, religious, political or social fads and fancies can easily flourish. There is a great deal of poverty in the land of opportunity, contrasting sharply with the material splendours of those who have in abundance.

That is the dark side. On the brighter side, American people in their own land are more hospitable, kind and generous than any other nation. Even the newest immigrants take great pride in their new land. Everywhere there is a flag flying, on private homes as well as on public buildings; allegiance to America is constantly recited and renewed. Despite economic recession it remains on the whole an optimistic land, always reaching to the future, always trying to be best, and proud of its role in the world. Americans are therefore demanding, enthusiastic; living hard, playing hard; conforming, yet individualistic; still hopeful that they can have the best of everything.

MEETING PEOPLE

Americans are naturally outgoing and hospitable, more so when they detect a foreign accent. Don't be surprised if you are invited to dinner, taken places and shown round the local sights. Staying at a private bed and breakfast place is a prime way to mingle with Americans—the services you get and the friendliness you'll receive go far beyond the monetary exchange. State fairs and other such special events—rodeos, clambakes, New England autumn fairs, etc—are an essential slice of the American pie and another way of meeting people informally.

If you want a more organised approach for meeting Americans, we suggest a number of organisations within our listings and also the following (most of which require making advance arrangements):

1. Contact the **National Council for International Visitors** (NCIV), 1420 K St NW, Suite 800, Washington DC 20005, (202) 842-1414. Ask for their booklet called *Where to Phone,* a complete rundown of local organisations willing to extend hospitality.
2. Enquire at the local **Chambers of Commerce** and Visitors Bureaux about their 'Visit a local family' programmes, if any. Some of them are very active in this area. A number have volunteer language banks also, if you're having difficulty communicating.
3. Contact the **US Travel and Tourist Admin (USTTA)** and ask about the Americans at Home programme, US Dept of Commerce, Washington DC 20230. Also offices in Canada, the British Isles, Europe, etc.
4. **Servas.** An organisation of approved hosts and travellers that arranges homestays. Charges membership fee plus $15 for host list. Guests then make their own contacts. US Servas Committee, 11 John St, Rm 407, New York, NY 10038, (212) 267-0252.
5. Also recommended for arranging homestays is **The Experiment in International Living**. You can contact them at PO Box 676, Brattleboro, VT 05302, (802) 257-7751.

HEALTH AND WELFARE

There is no free or subsidised national health service in the United States for anyone under retirement age. For most people, therefore, medical, dental and hospital services have to be paid for and they can be expensive. However, the emergency room of any public hospital provides medical care to anyone who walks in the door, (and is prepared for a long wait) and only charges those who have insurance or are otherwise able to pay, the government reimbursing them for the rest.

The 'emergency' doesn't have to be a car crash or the like—it can be a high fever or stomach pains, anything of a reasonably acute nature or which you feel needs immediate attention. Teaching hospitals—medical and dental—are other possible sources of free, or cheaper, treatment. Women may find help through the local women's centre.

Nevertheless, it is essential to be insured (ask your travel agent), and a good idea to get a dental checkup before going. If you wear glasses or contact lenses take spares, or at least prescriptions.

MONEY

Dollars and cents are of course the basic units of American money. The back of all dollar bills are green (hence 'greenbacks'), no colour distinctions being made for different denominations. The commonly used coins are: one cent (penny), five cents (nickel), 10 cents (dime), and 25 cents (quarter). 50¢ pieces (half dollars) and silver dollars (not really silver anymore) are gaining in usage, while there has been talk of phasing out the penny—that's inflation for you. 'Always carry plenty of quarters when travelling. Very useful for phones, soda machines, laundry machines, etc.'

There is generally no problem in using US dollars in Canada, albeit with a loss on the exchange rate; but this is never possible vice versa.

It's useful always to carry small change for things like exact fare buses, but do not carry large sums of cash. Instead keep the bulk of your money in travellers cheques which can be purchased both in the US and abroad and should be in dollar denominations. The best known cheques are those of American Express, so you will have the least difficulty cashing these, even in out of the way places. (You can also have your mail sent to American Express offices—ask for a complete list.) Thomas Cook travellers cheques are also acceptable, especially as lost ones can be reclaimed at any Hertz Car Rental desk. Dollar denomination cheques can be used like regular money. There's no need to cash them at a bank: use them instead to pay for meals, supermarket purchases or whatever. Ten or 20 dollar cheques are accepted like this almost always and you'll be given change just as though you'd presented the cashier with dollar bills. Be prepared to show I.D. when you cash your cheques.

Credit cards can be even more valuable than travellers cheques as they are often used to guarantee room reservations over the phone and are accepted in lieu of a deposit when renting a car—indeed *without* a credit card you may be considered so untrustworthy that not only a deposit but your passport will be held as security too. Or, you may not be able to rent at all without a credit card. The major credit cards are VISA, Master Charge and Access (each with the other's symbol on the reverse), Diners Club and American Express. If you hold a bank card (eg VISA), it could well be worthwhile to increase your credit limit for travel purposes—you should ask your bank manager.

Banks. Bank hours are usually 9am–2pm or 3pm Monday to Friday. Many banks stay open until 6pm on Fridays but hardly ever on Saturday mornings.

If you ever receive a cheque, it is important to cash it in the same area—i.e. at a branch of the bank on which it is drawn. Without a bank account to pay into, it will be impossible to cash it elsewhere—the American banking system is not as integrated as elsewhere in the world. Some form of identification (eg passport) is necessary when cashing a personal or company cheque.

Tax. There is usually a three to eight percent sales tax on most items over 20¢ and meals over $1. This is never included in the stated price and varies from place to place according to whether you are being charged state or city sales tax. There is also a 'bed tax' in most cities that ranges from five to ten percent on hotel rooms. 'Bed tax' does not generally apply to bed and breakfast places. *Note that unless stated, accommodation rates in this Guide do not include tax.*

Tipping. It is customary in the US to tip the following: taxi drivers, waiters, hotel bellboys, airport luggage porters. Ten to 15 percent is the accepted amount. Some restaurants do include service in the menu price so make sure you don't tip them twice.

COMMUNICATIONS

Mail. Post offices are infrequent, but since the alternative is a commercial stamp machine which in the spirit of free enterprise sells stamps but only at a considerable profit, it is advisable to stock up at post offices when you can. As of going to press, first class letters within the US are 29¢; the air mail rate for post cards to Europe is 40¢, aerogrammes 45¢, air mail letters up to 1 oz 50¢.

Mail within the US travels at a snail's pace: allow a week coast to coast or to Canada, and four days for any distance more than around the corner. For guaranteed overnight delivery you have to use Express Mail which has a minimum rate of $9.95! You must always include the zip code on a US address. To mail a letter without a zip code is to invite considerable delay if not everlasting loss!

It is possible to have mail sent General Delivery (Poste Restante) for collection (also to American Express offices if you use their travellers cheques). The post office will usually keep it for 10 days before returning it to sender.

American post offices deal *only* with mail.

Telegrams. Internal telegrams are sent by Western Union and not from the post office. Telegrams abroad are cheaper by night rate. You hand or telephone in your message anytime and ask for second class treatment. But it may take 48 hours before the telegram is delivered.

Telephone. Phones in North America are easy to use. All numbers have an Area Code (3 digits), an Exchange Code (3 digits) and a number (4 digits). You do not dial the Area Code if you are within that dialling area (eg omit the 202 when calling Washington D.C. numbers from within Washington).

When calling from pay phones in most areas of North America, you dial the whole number preceded by 1 (if you have enough coins to pay for the call), or by 0 (zero, not the O in MNO) if you are making a collect call. Before dialling, you insert the minimum amount of money as instructed on the pay phone (eg 25¢). When you have dialled the complete number, the operator will come on the line and tell you how much to put in (if you dialled 1 first). If you dialled 0 first, a recorded message may ask you to 'please dial your card number or zero for an operator now'. Press 0, wait, and the operator will ask how he/she can help you. You then say: 'I'd like to make a collect call, please. My name is . . . .'

Whenever the operator answers, your money is refunded to you. Don't forget to take it out of the machine! You may find that you are being spoken to by a recording which says something like 'Deposit 40 cents, please'. Obey the voice . . . .

If calling at peak time, you may need to have ready up to $3.50 a minute in 25¢, 10¢ and 5¢ coins. The cheapest time to make a long distance call is between 11pm and 8am. Between 5pm and 11pm and at weekends the next cheapest time; 8am–5pm is the most expensive time. Remember to allow for time zone differences when phoning.

If making calls from your hotel, remember that it is cheaper to use the phone in the hotel lobby rather than the one in your bedroom. It's always cheaper to dial direct and not through the operator. In many areas local calls are free from private phones. If you make a pay call from a private phone you can get the operator to tell you how much the call cost. A reverse charges call is called a collect call.

Look for pay telephones in drug stores, gas stations, highway rest areas, in transport terminals and along the street. Phone cards are not readily available in North America. You can buy an AT&T version in Europe before you go, or, better value, is the Telekey Card sold by BUNAC in the U.K. and in America. The Telekey Card also has a 'mail box' system allowing callers to leave messages for the card holder which the card holder can dial in for at any time.

ELECTRICITY

Voltage is 110–115V, 60 cycles AC. American plugs have two flat pins. Try to get an adaptor before you go. Even if you have a dual voltage appliance you will still need an adaptor. You will not be able to use your home hairdryer, shaver or whatever, unless it is dual voltage.

SHOPPING

Major stores often have long opening hours, eg from 9am or 10am to 9pm or 10pm—on one, several or even all days of the week. Smaller shops in cities are sometimes open all night: you should have no trouble getting a meal or a drink, or shopping for food and other basics, 24 hours a day—though you'll pay more for the privilege.

Large American supermarkets and department stores can make their foreign equivalents look like they're suffering from war-time rationing. The variety of goods on offer—and at relatively low prices—is amazing. The American consumer is a keen and well practised shopper with an eye for a bargain, seldom in fact, buying anything when it's not on sale. Almost every town has at least one shopping mall (pronounced 'maul') on the outskirts where you can observe the credit card culture in action and brouse to your heart's content from about 10 am to 9 pm.

Good buys in the US include cameras, CDs, electronic goods, sound equipment, denims, winter clothes, and casual clothes, in particular western gear. Just how good a bargain will of course depend upon the exchange rate at the time of your visit. Even if it is not in your favour, if you do as all Americans do and shop only when the item you want is on sale, you will still be able to net some bargains.

THE METRIC SYSTEM

The US still uses feet and miles, pounds and gallons, Fahrenheit instead of Centigrade/Celsius, and it appears as though it will for some time to come. The only things that have gone metric are liquor and wine bottles, some gasoline pumps and the National Park Service. A conversion table is to be found in the Appendix.

DRINKING

Although nationwide Prohibition ended in the US in 1933, you will still find places in which you cannot get a drink at all, or where you cannot stand to drink, or must bring your own bottle—one anomaly after another. This is because each state decides whether it will be 'dry' or 'wet', and sometimes this is left to counties on an optional basis.

American beer (which as a legacy of Prohibition has a relatively low alcohol content) is of the lager variety—Knickerbocker, Miller, Schaeffer, Budweiser, Pabst, Rheingold, etc. Bottled beer is always more expensive than draught. America is the home of the cocktail. Spirit concoctions are excellent and a major part of American ingenuity is devoted to thinking up new ones—and extraordinary names for them! Bars never close before midnight, stay open sometimes till 4am, or even 23 hours a day. Try to sample local wines, New York and California turn out the best. Visit a winery in these states too.

The minimum drinking age is now 21 in almost every state in the US and the federal government is threatening to cut highway funds to those states which do not comply. A strong anti-drink climate of opinion exists in the US at present, and the under-age drinking rules are strictly enforced. Someone under 21 may not be able to drink alcohol at all during their stay in the USA. You will need to carry I.D. when ordering a drink or buying liquor in a store just in case you are asked—even if you think you look much older than 21!

TOBACCO

Cigarettes are about $2.25 for a pack of 20, five big cigars for about the same price. Pipe tobacco is heavily flavoured—imported brands are better and not much more expensive. Unless you learnt to chew tobacco at the same time as you were breast-fed, forget it. Tobacco addicts should stock up on cartons at supermarkets for substantial savings.

Smoking is increasingly frowned upon and many restaurants (even McDonald's) and other public places now have 'non-smoking' sections. Smoking is banned on all US internal flights except those of more than 6 hours.

DRUGS

A great deal has been written about the 'drug culture' of the US. Probably most of it is absolutely true. The best advice is the obvious— stay away from it. Reject all advances made to you on the street, in bus terminals, airports, wherever. It is illegal to possess or sell narcotics. Penalties can be severe.

PUBLIC HOLIDAYS

New Year's Day (1 January)
Washington's Birthday (third Monday in February)
Memorial Day (last Monday in May)
Independence Day (4 July)
Labor Day (first Monday in September)
Columbus Day (second Monday in October)
Veterans' Day (11 November)
Thanksgiving (fourth Thursday in November)
Christmas (25 December)

Though many smaller shops and almost all businesses close on public holidays, many of the biggest stores and multiples will make a point of being open—often offering sales. Outside of cities, supermarkets are open during at least part of a public holiday. On days of all primary and general elections all bars are closed. There are numerous other public holidays that are not nationwide, eg Lincoln's Birthday, St Patrick's Day. Jewish New Year brings New York to a standstill.

The summer tourism and recreational season extends from Memorial Day to Labor Day. After Labor Day you can expect some hours or days of opening to be reduced, or some attractions to be closed altogether. The same may apply to related transport services. Unless otherwise specified, times and days of openings in this guide refer to the summer season. Outside this period, you should phone in advance.

INFORMATION

A multitude of resources exist in the US both to make your stay more informed and enjoyable and to help you out if you encounter problems. Among the most useful:

1. *Libraries.* One in almost every town, often open late hours and on weekends, libraries and librarians are a traveller's best friend. Besides reference works, atlases, local guidebooks, they offer transit schedules, local and other newspapers, magazines, free community newspapers, phone books, brochures on helping organisations and are unfailingly kind about answering questions and making phone enquiries for you. They also have toilets, comfy chairs and often a social calendar of free evening events.
2. *Travelers Aid.* Their kiosks are found at bus, train and plane terminals across the country—invaluable for cheap lodging and other suggestions, helpful with free maps and brochures, and solid support if your trip runs into a snag (whether it's a medical, financial or practical problem).
3. *Chambers of Commerce and Visitors Bureaux.* Found almost everywhere, with lots of free materials, maps (although you usually have to purchase the really good maps) and advice. Big-city offices have multilingual staffs, are open longer hours and sometimes weekends. Smaller places are open

9am–5pm, Monday to Friday; many have recorded events messages for local activities when they are closed. A major drawback is that they are primarily member organisations; few of them will even recognise much less recommend non-member hotels, restaurants, etc. That means that you won't hear much about low-budget places from them and some bureaux will even try to warn you off such places. Don't buy it. If driving, look out for State highway 'welcome stations'. They are a good source of free maps and local information and often provide free juice or coffee.
4. Many communities have a *volunteer clearinghouse phone service* designed to answer a variety of needs, from real emergencies to simple orientation. Usually listed in both the white and yellow pages of the phone book, and variously called Hotline, Helpline, Crisis Center, People's Switchboard, Community Switchboard, We Care, or some such. Their well-trained volunteers can steer you to the resources available in the community—free, cheap and not-so-cheap.
5. *Women's Centers and Senior Centers* provide the same kind of clearinghouse info and friendly support on a walk-in basis; you will also find them in nearly every US town and listed in the phone book. The Centers also make excellent places to meet people, and often sponsor a range of free and interesting activities. You might also try the Free Clinics, which still exist in a number of big cities. Many of them operate hotlines, referral services, crash pad recommendations and other services besides free health care.
6. *Maps.* Besides the free ones from Visitor Centers, State Tourism Offices and so forth, you may be interested in specialty maps, such as Greyhound's excellent 'United States of Greyhound', a monster which shows all of the US and Canadian routes clearly marked, plus major parks and monuments. Free. An organisation called DATO, 1100 Connecticut Avenue NW, Washington DC 20036, publishes a series of maps that show the routes of Lewis and Clark, the pioneer trails such as the Oregon, Santa Fe and Mormon, and Pony Express routes, allowing you to trace portions of them for yourself. Write for details and prices.

EMERGENCIES/SAFETY

Many towns and cities have '911' as the emergency telephone number—for police, fire, ambulance. Otherwise you would dial '0' for operator. The emergency number is always indicated on public telephones. The previously mentioned Travelers Aid, to be found at major bus and rail stations and airports, will also help in emergency situations.

Yes, the USA can be a dangerous place, but then so can your own home town if you happen to be in the wrong place at the wrong time. In other words chance or fate alone may determine what may or may not happen to you. This is not to say that you should not take reasonable, sensible, standard precautions to protect your safety.

Don't wander into parks or dark alleys alone or late at night; carry your valuables in a neck or waist pouch; don't leave your belongings unattended; stay in what you know to be safe areas of towns and cities—if it feels 'wrong', get out; don't hitchhike or drive alone; and stay alert to what is happening around you. Remember, although crime rates are high, most Americans *never* encounter crime in their daily lives.

THE GREAT OUTDOORS

One of the most exciting things about North America is the great tracts of unspoilt land. The most superlative examples have usually been specially preserved as National Parks. There are 41 National Parks in the United States, all of which offer the visitor beautiful scenery; everything from fantastic seascapes, deep canyons, spectacular volcanoes, to pure lakes and craggy mountains. Many parks are somewhat off the beaten track and although the roadways in all are excellent, the parks are best seen more slowly on foot, by bicycle, horse, or canoe. Most offer camping facilities (see under Accommodation) and some, cabin or hotel accommodation.

Some parks are free but in general the entrance fee will be $3–$5. Should you intend to use the National Park system extensively, purchase a Golden Eagle Passport on sale at all parks, or from the National Park Service, Office of Public Inquiries, PO Box 37127, Washington DC 20013. The Pass costs $25 and gives you, and anyone accompanying you in a private vehicle, access to all the parks for a year at no further expense. Also, visitors arriving before 7am sometimes get in free. Camping, of course, costs extra.

There are also numerous National Seashores, Monuments and Forests, and other federally administered preserves which should not be overlooked. In addition there are thousands of state parks across America, many of which provide facilities for swimming, camping, walking etc. for a modest entry fee.

Almost all the National Parks are included in this Guide. For more information write directly to the Park, asking for details and brochures. A list of the major National Parks in the US follows.

Acadia, Maine.
Arches, Utah.
Badlands, South Dakota.
Big Bend, Texas.
Bryce Canyon, Utah.
Canyonlands, Utah.
Carlsbad Caverns, New Mexico.
Crater Lake, Oregon.
Denali, Alaska.
Everglades, Florida.
Glacier, Montana.
Grand Canyon, Arizona.
Grand Teton, Wyoming.
Great Basin, Nevada.
Great Smoky Mountains. Tennessee/North Carolina.
Guadalupe Mountains, Texas.
Haleakala, Island of Maui, Hawaii.
Hawaii Volcanoes, Island of Hawaii, Hawaii.
Hot Springs, Arkansas.
Isle Royale, Michigan.
Kings Canyon, California.
Lassen Volcanic, California.
Mammoth Cave, Kentucky.
Mesa Verde, Colorado.
Mount Rainier, Washington.
National Reef, Utah.
North Cascades, Washington.
Olympic, Washington.
Petrified Forest, Arizona.
Platt, Oklahoma.
Redwood, California.
Rocky Mountain, Colorado.
Sequoia, California.
Shenandoah, Virginia.
Theodore Roosevelt, North Dakota.
Virgin Islands, St John, Virgin Islands.
Voyageurs, Minnesota.
Wind Cave, South Dakota.
Yellowstone, Wyoming/Montana/ Idaho.
Yosemite, California.
Zion, Utah.

SPORT AND RECREATION

At times on your travels across America it may seem as though every man, woman, child, and dog, jog, run or otherwise 'keep fit' at least four times a week so many people will you see doing just that. Certainly as a nation Americans tend towards the active, outdoors existence. After all they have the climate and the country to make it all possible.

In summer there's swimming, sailing, 'surfin', waterski-ing, fishing, diving and all the other water-based activities, plus tennis, baseball, athletics, camping, hiking, cycling . . . the list is endless. Then just when you begin to get tired of all that, along comes the football (American) season, followed by basketball, and ice hockey. Then it snows and do Americans sit at home and watch it? Silly question. Now it's time for ski-ing (downhill or cross-country), skating, hunting, ice-fishing, more ice hockey and so on. In short if it exists as a sport you will find it somewhere in America—yes, even rugby and croquet.

On the professional scene the biggies are football (American) and baseball. The latter goes from April through until October and football starts at the end of the summer and finishes in January when finally overtaken by the weather. Try and go to a professional game in either sport—it's a real slice of American pie. There is a major league team in almost every large city. Soccer is played but still hasn't really caught on to anything like the level of the European game. Basketball, athletics, ice hockey, tennis, horse/motor racing and wrestling, are other major spectator sports.

One interesting point about the US sport scene is the attention given nationally to the, often near-professional, college/university teams. This is especially the case with basketball and football where the college teams are often followed with equal enthusiasm to that given to the pros.

MEDIA AND ENTERTAINMENT

In these days of cable and satellite TV it is not unusual to be able to tune into 50 or 60 channels on your **television** set. Network television can be condescending, boring, total rubbish—an insult to the intelligence. Best programmes feature old movies (squeezed in between commercials), news coverage, reruns of old sitcoms which always offer an interesting look at bygone America, and the public television channels which show British imports—*Are You Being Served?*, *All Creatures Great and Small*, *Blackadder*, *Yes, Prime Minister* etc—and offer excellent current affairs, science and nature programmes as well as live theatre and music.

At whatever time of night or day there is always something to watch! The proliferation of cable has brought more specialist viewing to the small screen. Sport, religion, local events, movies, Spanish/Japanese/Cuban/whatever, and music videos (MTV) are just a few of the offerings. You will not be able to resist!

And there's even more **radio**, and here the overkill holds promise for in amongst the top-40 musical pop stations there are first-rate classical, jazz, blues, bluegrass, country, R&B, progressive and regional music stations, as well as some solid all-news stations. Radio is also an excellent way of finding out about an area you're visiting or just driving through.

Every city with any claim to consequence will have its theatres and its own **orchestra** and **opera company**, with performances often to a very high standard. In this respect, Americans arguably enjoy a greater access to culture than Europeans with their brighter but more centralised cultural traditions.

Hollywood still turns out more **movies** than anywhere else in the world except India, and with the decline of the studios there has been more freelancing, more opportunity for outsiders with new ideas to hit the big screen. In writing, directing and acting, America easily holds its own as one of the four or five great film-making nations.

If you're interested in concerts, plays, etc, one easy solution is to look up **TICKETRON** in the local phone book. They are nationwide agents, but have information on what's on in the particular city you're in—they publish a free monthly list of all events, though take a percentage on any tickets you buy from them.

The *New York Times* is one of the most respected of American **newspapers** and in content comes closest to being the country's national newspaper. The mammoth Sunday edition of *The Times* should keep you going at least until Thursday. There is, of course, an actual, coast-to-coast, national newspaper—*USA Today*. Published weekdays, across America, and using full colour throughout, it manages to a large extent to overcome the problems of time zones, and the diversity of life in the US. In general people still buy their local papers and all towns and cities have at least one. Among the best are the *Los Angeles Times*, the *Washington Post* and the *Wall Street Journal*. The latter is a good read for the considerable insight it offers into a great variety of topics both inside and well beyond the world of finance. Wherever you are of course, the local paper is your best resource for local events as well as adding to your picture of American life.

Magazines proliferate, covering every conceivable interest and point of view. Sample the offerings on hot rods, sex, flying saucers, sport, computers, snowmobiles, collectibles and so on if you want to appreciate the American appetite for every sort of information. Also there are growing numbers of magazines for business women and the environmentally aware, plus large circulation black publications. Some of the best writing is found in *The New Yorker*, *The Atlantic Monthly*—which grew out of the Transcendentalist and anti-slavery movements—*Esquire* and *Playboy*, though the last ministers as much to the senses as to the mind. *Rolling Stone* is still the voice of pop, *MS* is for the socially aware ladies who are not yet so socially aware that they read the *Wall Street Journal*, and there's always *Time* and *Newsweek* to read on the loo.

Last but not least there are the **comics**, including that whole stable of Marvel heroes (Captain America, Spiderman, The Hulk) who express the variety of American neuroses, or those old standbys from a more innocent, confident age, principally Superman and Scrooge McDuck.

ON THE ROAD

ACCOMMODATION

Let's face facts: accommodation in North America is going to absorb at least one-third of your travel money. So how can you keep that figure to a minimum while enjoying your trip to the maximum? Here are eight pointers:

1. *Learn your accommodation options.* You'll constantly hear about the visible and well-advertised options: chain hotels and motels, lodgings close to freeways and tourist attractions, National Park accommodation and the conventional rock-bottom suggestions—YMCAs and youth hostels. But a wealth of inexpensive and almost invisible alternatives exist in North America. Examples: guest and tourist homes; bed and breakfast in private residences; farms and ranches; resorts and retreats; residence clubs, *casas de huespedes* and other pension-style lodgings; free campsites on Indian lands; non-hostel accommodations which honour hostel rates and philosophies; university-associated places to stay, many open to the general public; and self-catering digs, from apartments to rustic cabins to housekeeping/efficiency units in standard hotels/motels. (We will give you lots of specific examples of these choices throughout this edition of the Guide.)
2. *Choose a lodging that also gives you a taste of North America.* Want to stay in a New York City brownstone, a San Francisco painted Victorian, a Maui condo, a solar-heated A-frame near a ski slope? How about spending a few days on a Mississippi River houseboat or riding through Kansas prairies with a covered wagon train? Maybe you'd rather tent-camp in a Sioux teepee, explore a Mennonite farm, visit a Southern plantation, sleep in a goldminer's cabin, gain a few pounds at a Basque boarding-house, beachcomb near a lighthouse hostel or stay in a 400-year-old Mexican mansion. It's all here. And by integrating your sleeping (and sometimes eating) arrangements with an offbeat experience, you'll receive double value. In the process, you'll get acquainted with everyday North Americans from many walks of life.
3. *Rent a room the way you shop for a car.* If tourism is down and vacancy rates are up, you'll have added leverage and bargaining power. Use it! Don't be afraid to haggle—hotel/motel rates in the US are extremely fluid and based on what the market will bear. (Unlike Mexico, where they are government regulated.) Rooms within a building are never identical—ask to see the cheapest. It may be small, viewless or noisy. It may also suit your needs very well. If you're willing to share a bath, sleep in a dorm, or take a room without air-conditioning or TV, *say so*. Most clerks (in the US anyway) will assume you require a private bath and colour TV to sustain life, and won't mention other accommodation. 'Ask for a room that is out of service and then offer a price for the night. You may be lucky.'
4. *Use impeccable timing.* Plan ahead to take advantage of special offers and slow times. Do your travelling on weekends so you arrive to catch the midweek (Sunday through Thursday) rates. Alternatively, look for higher-priced hotels at your destination that offer low-cost weekend or 'getaway' packages—often very good value. If you can possibly swing it, travel in May or September: best weather, fewest crowds and significantly lower offseason prices. Another timing tip: the later in the evening it gets, the more likelihood you have of a reduced rate on a room. You may be tired and worried about a place to lay your weary head but remember: the hotel/motel owner is even more worried about filling that room, which goes on costing him money whether empty or full. But caution, in resort areas and big cities at peak holiday times desirable accommodation fills by 4–5pm.
5. *Always ask about discounts and special rates.* You'd be amazed at the dis-

count categories that exist in North America. A partial list: senior, student, youth hostel card-holder, bus/train/plane passholder, rental car user, member of AAA or other auto club, YMCA/YWCA member, Sierra Club or other environmental club members, military, family, group, foreign visitor, government employee, airline employee and commercial rate. Incidentally, hotel/motel people sometimes grant 'commercial rates' as a face-saving way to fill rooms, so it pays to flash your company identification or business card and ask for them. Throughout this edition, you'll notice we've indicated specific discount offers where known. 'Being a British student was worth a $2 discount to many motel owners.' Being a *Moneywise Guide* holder sometimes gets you a better deal too!

6. *Ask other travellers for accommodation leads.* When travelling in the US most Americans tend to stay with families/friends, at chain motels/hotels, or in campgrounds or RV (recreational vehicles). Thus they are often oblivious to the unsung lodging opportunities around them.

7. *Double up. Better yet, triple up.* US lodging (with the exception of hostels, YMCAs and a few hotels/motels that give the lone traveller a break) has a Noah's Ark, two-by-two mentality. Your best bet is to travel with one or more companions. Relish your independence? Then split up and rendezvous with friends every couple of days—you'll still save money. 'Five of us crammed into a $60 double room with owner's consent. Try any motel.'

8. *Learn about local variants and accommodation nomenclature.* Lodging traditions vary around North America. For instance, the best bargains in Hawaii are called hotel apartments—Honolulu is full of them. In Colorado, ski lodges with dorms (ask for 'hiker' or 'skier' rooms) are popular. San Francisco is a mecca for congenial residence clubs which offer superlative weekly rates for room and board. Parts of the South and New England are full of small guest houses. In Canada, low-priced B&B digs are called tourist homes. When you enter an area, ask the Visitors Centre or librarians, or look in the Yellow Pages; if there's a local variant, you should spot it. Second, learn what lodging descriptions really mean. In the US, the cheapest and simplest accommodation is variously described as 'economy', 'budget', 'no frills', 'rustic', 'basic' or 'European-style rooms'. The breakfast portion of bed and breakfast may vary from a continental roll-and-coffee to a full meal; ask. Unlike Europe, many US B&Bs offer (for a modest fee) other meals, transportation, tours and worthwhile goodies from free bike loans to use of libraries, saunas and tennis courts. Beware of lodging descriptions that include the words 'affordable', 'quaint', 'Old World charm' (evidently it costs a fortune to drag charm from the Old World to the New), and 'standard' or 'tourist class' (travel agenteese for mid-price range).

Hotels and motels. Thanks to the great success of the Motel 6 chain, the American travel industry has reluctantly concluded that no-frills lodging is not just a ploy for the pathologically frugal. Thus dozens of budget chain motels have emerged in the last decade. Except for Motel 6, however, they tend to be regional in scope and with prices that vary from unit to unit and season to season. To be fair: many of them offer more for the money (eg pool, larger rooms, bath, phones, TV, etc). See the Appendix for a list of budget hotel chains in the US.

Budget motels work out cheapest with three or more people. Unfortunately, they are often difficult to reach without a car, but do call to ask about bus connections, if any. As a rule, cheapie motels (chain or non-chain) provide better, cleaner and safer accommodation for the money than do cheap downtown hotels.

Finding a hotel with the ideal mix of low price and reasonable quality is an art. Besides the suggestions in this Guide, you could try: (1) comparing notes with other travellers; (2) asking the Greyhound bus driver and at the terminal—but be careful with this; in small towns or out west maybe, but in New York, Detroit etc, forget it; and (3) check at the Travelers Aid kiosks in transit terminals. It's also wise to leave your luggage in a locker so you can check out your prospects. Ask to see rooms and don't settle for bad-news facilities (eg doors that don't lock or that have signs of forced entry, unclean linen, etc). If you are a woman, we strongly advise you to arrive in big cities during daylight hours.

YMCAs and YWCAs. Most YMCAs offering accomodation are located in the often run-down heart of big city downtowns. Y lodgings have no membership or age restrictions and the use of rec facilities is often free. Two-thirds of them are coed; the rest, men only.

The economics of desperation bring in a mixed clientele; that, coupled with the grimy streets outside and steadily rising prices sometimes make the YMCA less and less of a bargain especially if there is more than one of you. For the single traveller the Y can still be the best bargain in town. You may do even better with prepaid reservations (valid at 124 YMCAs in the US, Canada and Mexico), and better still with an AYH card—many Ys give hostel rates. Contact the Y's Way, 224 E 47th St, New York NY 10017 or call (212) 755-2410 for their brochures.

The women-only YWCAs are concentrated in the Northeast, the Midwest and Texas. They tend to be smaller, more cheerful and better bargains than their YMCA counterparts—if you can get in.

Hostels. American Youth Hostels (AYH) has just adopted the new International Youth Hostel Federation blue triangle symbol and become Hostelling International—American Youth Hostels. Some 200 US hostels are already re-affiliated to the reborn HI-AYH, and members can now make reservations through the International Booking Network (IBN) for a $2 fee. Most major USA gateway hostels are part of the network.

All in all, the hostel situation in the USA is pretty good and is especially bright in the Northeast states and in Ohio, Michigan, Minnesota, Colorado, Arizona, California, Oregon, Washington and Alaska (along the ferry route) but pretty thin elsewhere. There are hostels near Yellowstone and Yosemite, and in expensive cities like Chicago, Houston, Los Angeles, New York City, San Francisco, Minneapolis, Miami Beach and Washington DC. Mexico has 20 hostels in Mexico City, Acapulco, Cancun and elsewhere. Canada recently opened hostels in Montréal and Toronto, and there are many others in major cities as well as in recreation areas.

If you belong to an overseas Youth Hostel Association, you're entitled to use HI-AYH and AAIH (see below) facilities. Annual fees in the US are $25 (age 18–54) and $35 family. Write AYH, Membership Dept., 733 15th St NW, Washington DC 20005, or phone: 202-783-6161. Overseas visitors who are not members in their own country can buy a Hostelling International card for $20. Many hostels also sell an introductory pass so you can try it on a one-time basis. Other hostels will allow non-members to stay at a higher, non-member, rate. It is recommended that if you plan to do a lot of hostelling you get the handbook published jointly by HI-AYH and the Canadian Hostelling Association which lists all hostels in both countries. If you join in the US it comes free. Otherwise send $7 to the AYH to get your copy.

In addition to AYH-affiliated hostels there are a growing number of independently run hostels in the US. The American Association of Independent Hostels (AAIH) has hostels, or else provides hostel-type (i.e. dorm.) accommodation within large hotels in several cities. Aimed primarily at the young, international traveller, they are generally located in downtown areas near to the bus terminal. Then there are many other smaller independents which seem to spring up like mushrooms, mostly in the large cities such as Los Angeles (a prime hostel spot) and New Orleans. In some cases they last one season and then disappear! So be careful.

The accommodation provided by independent hostels in general can be a bit of a mixed bag. Some are very good, but others aim simply to cram in as many people as possible regardless of standards of cleanliness, safety or sanitation. If you are on a budget, of course, you may feel you don't really have a choice. The majority of the hostels listed in this book have been recommended by previous users.

Pluses of North American hostelling: often in locales of great scenic beauty; a growing number are housed in buildings of historic or architectural interest (from decommissioned lighthouses to adobe haciendas); many offer special activities free or at low cost, from wilderness canoe or cycling trips to hot-tubbing. Reader comments show that US hostels are generally more relaxed and friendly than their European counterparts. 'I found youth hostels most convenient places to stay. Full of young people of all nationalities, the hostels were a nucleus of information and I met many travelling partners. Whilst not boasting of exceptional comforts, the hostels generally proved to be very good value and certainly took a lot out of the loneliness of travelling on one's own.'

Drawbacks? Uneven distribution make hiking or biking itineraries impractical, except for certain regions. Remote locales make it tough to use public transport to get to many of them. And hostel curfews and customs can cramp your style, particularly if you plan to do much urban or nighttime sightseeing. 'Most US hostels insist on your having (or renting for 50¢) a sheet sleeping bag.' 'On the whole American hostels were very good indeed.'

University-associated lodging. Over 230 universities in the US and Canada offer on-campus housing in dorms and residence halls. Points to consider: usually available summer only (exceptions noted in listings); rates vary widely and definitely favour doubles and weekly stays; facilities often heavily booked; campuses can be far from city centres. But it's always worth trying the local student union or campus housing office when in the vicinity. Many of these offerings are open to the general public.

You can also find off-campus residences, fraternity and sorority houses with summer space to rent, all of which tend to be looser, friendlier and cheaper than on-campus options. Fringe benefits: use of kitchen facilities (sometimes) and entree into the thirsty social life of local students, including the infamous TGs or kegger parties.

Camping. Camping provides the cheapest and one of the most enjoyable means of seeing the best parts of North America, the National and State Parks and other preserves. Your choices are almost infinite—free campgrounds in the US alone total over 20,000! State Park camping fees range from zero to $8 and are indicated with the state listings. National Parks (same price range) are given considerable attention in this Guide; for further information, write to the National Park Service, US Department of the Interior, Washington DC 20240. Other excellent sources for campgrounds info are the AAA books, Rand McNally's *Campground and Trailer Park Guide* (17,000 US and Canada listings) and the tourism offices of each state.

You should be aware that the biggest drawback for the on-foot traveller is access. Ironic as it sounds, you really need a car to get to numerous campgrounds and trailheads to backcountry camping, especially those sites located on National Forest or Bureau of Land Management property. Once you have wheels it is possible to zig-zag your way across America camping in some of the loneliest, loveliest spots in the world. It might even be worth investigating hiring a camper vehicle (VW or the dreaded RV) for an extended trip. For a group of 3 or more it could be worth the extra expense.

Campground facilities vary from fully developed sites with electricity, bunk-equipped cabins and hot showers to primitive sites where you're expected to bury your wastes and pack out your rubbish. Tent campers are advised to avoid RV-oriented campgrounds. They may offer a pool, laundromat, store and other amenities but the noise, asphalt and vehicle fumes sadly dilute the 'wilderness' experience. Although more expensive, private campgrounds can be good. A number of readers have recommended KOA (Kampgrounds of America). In general, while their sites are not always the most scenic, their facilities are luxurious in camping terms. 'We used the KOA campgrounds the whole time—they have the best facilities available. And get a KOA discount card; this allows a 10 percent reduction on the cost of a campsite, plus gives a "free" guide.' Sites cost $12–$16. For the hiking/biking camper, many State Parks offer a few sites designated as 'hiker/biker' for 50¢–$1 per night on a first-come, first-served basis.

In the north, the camping season lasts from mid-May to mid-September or less, depending on weather. In the Rockies and other mountainous areas, temperatures drop dramatically in the evening, making warm clothing vital. In the warm dry Southwest, you probably won't have to put up a tent. At Yellowstone and other northern parks, you may encounter bears who roam the campground for food. These bears are not interested in campers as nourishment and will not harm you as long as you leave them well alone. Do not leave food in the tent, in ice chests, on picnic tables or near your sleeping bag. Lock it in the trunk of your car, or use park-recommended 'bear cables'. Bring along a generous supply of insect repellant and calamine lotion to combat mosquito bites, chigger (a maddening insect that burrows beneath your skin) attacks and poison ivy/poison oak (glossy three-leaved plants).

Popular National and State Parks get very crowded from Memorial Day through to Labor Day, making May and September the ideal months for visits. In summer, you may want to book through TICKETRON, the national ticketing service, to ensure a place. To get the best site, try to arrive by 5pm or earlier. Beware that some campgrounds keep the 'No Vacancy' sign up all summer so always ask. At the most popular parks queuing all night for space is not unheard of.

Native American campgrounds and other Indian-run lodging facilities are a first-rate way to get acquainted with North America's first people. Most sites are located on reservation land which, if you remember your history, has traditionally been located about a million miles from nowhere. Although the whites did their best to fob off nothing but marginal lands on the Indians, what they ended up with is often superbly scenic. A car is nearly imperative as you'll find little public transit to and from reservation land. Besides campgrounds, Native American owned facilities range from simple motels to sumptuous resorts. Some offer traditional dancing, crafts and native food. For a detailed and loving look at the Indian nations, read Jamake Highwater's *Indian America* (Fodor). The American Indian Travel Commission, 1133 21st St NW, 8th Fl, Washington DC 20036, phone (202) 293-1433 can also give you information.

Bed and breakfast. An old concept in Europe, B&B crossed the Atlantic a few years ago and has now hybridised in several directions. Most visible are the 'too cute to be true' B&B Inns, widely written about and gushed over and punitively expensive in most cases. Least visible but most moneywise are the private homes in the US, Canada and Mexico which only rent rooms through an agency intermediary. (This is partly for security reasons, partly because of US zoning laws.) Most agencies concentrate on a given city or state; you'll find their names and addresses under the appropriate listing. Their rates run from $35–$45 single and from $45–$90 double. (NB: higher rates are for incredibly lavish digs.) Booking procedures, type of breakfast, length of stay and other conditions vary from agency to agency. The common denominator is the need to book ahead. If in the US, this can often be handled with a phone call. Only rarely can you breeze into town and get same-day accommodation.

If you are planning to do a lot of B&Bing you should consider buying one of the many books on the market which list hundreds of guest houses or tourist homes on a national or regional basis. A good guide will also list the various reservation services, their rates and how they work.

Is the lack of flexibility worth it? Most people think so. Foreign visitors who want to meet locals, see American homes and eat home cooking are particularly enthusiastic. Private home B&Bs are an inexpensive, warm and caring environment for women travellers on their own, too. Bonuses: many B&Bs serve meals other than breakfast and a large number are willing to pick up and deliver guests (sometimes a small fee). Hosts often speak other languages, so make your needs known at booking time. Canadian B&Bs are called hospitality homes. In Mexico, the B&B programme is known as Posada Mexico.

There are several B&B umbrella agencies which cover a number of states (and countries) and which cater to foreign and US travellers. They can book you into one B&B or work out a whole itinerary of B&Bs for you. Write for details and brochures. A few of the better known agencies:
1. B&B International, PO Box 282910, San Francisco, CA 94128-2910, call (415) 696-1690. Outstanding host and guest matchups; fees from $50 up single or double; full breakfast; many homes throughout California and Nevada.
2. Northwest B&B Inc, 610 SW Broadway, Suite 606, Portland OR 97223. Call (503) 246-8366. As the name implies, homes in Washington, Oregon, British Columbia, California, and Hawaii. Full breakfasts; $15 membership fee (which includes detailed 160-page book of listings); rooms are $20–$30 single, $35–$55 double. Also: Pacific B&B, 701 NW 60th, Seattle, WA 98107; (206) 784-0539. Rates from $45 single.
3. B&B League Ltd, PO Box 9490, Washington DC 20016. Phone: (202) 363-7767. Recommended primarily for travellers in pairs, since rates are $40–$115 single, $50–$135 double plus $10 booking fee. Continental breakfast. Homes in DC and area.

Like every other business in America, new organisations mushroom all the time. Some of them are very localised so it is always worth checking in the immediate vicinity (e.g. Yellow Pages) for local listings.

Other accommodation possibilities. If you're planning to bicycle around the US, it makes sense to contact Bikecentennial, a national non-profit organization, on PO Box 8308, Missoula, Montana 59807. Tel: (406) 721-1776. The American Youth Hostels Association (AYH) offers special tours for cyclists and of course accommodation. Also recommended is a series published by Ballantine—*Cyclist's Guides to Overnight Stops*.

Two mutual hospitality exchange programmes also exist. The Globetrotters' Club, BCM/Roving, London WC1N 3XX (postal address only; there is no office) and in the US, Box 9243, North Hollywood CA 91609, has a $10 membership fee, magazine and directory. Members have the option of choosing to offer hospitality or not. The Traveler's Directory, 6224 Baynton St, Philadelphia PA 19144: an informal, mutual hospitality exchange system listing people worldwide who can stay in each others' homes free of charge when travelling. To be listed, you must complete an application form, giving a brief summary of your interests and what hospitality you can offer. Only those who have been listed can obtain a copy of the directory.

Should you decide to (or be reduced to) crash out it is a good idea to ask locally whether or not your chosen spot is safe. The local police, or students, are probably the best people to ask but it's not a good idea to just crash out by the side of the road or on the beach without checking first. Some readers have suggested highway rest areas as good sleeping places but sometimes this is not allowed and you should only do this if other people are clearly doing so already—never alone.

If you're totally stranded and penniless then Travelers Aid or the Salvation Army may help.

FOOD

To eat cheaply and well in America is easy once you realise that menu prices have more to do with restaurant decor and labour costs than with food quality. Everyone will quickly develop his or her own game plan depending on available funds and taste. However you should plan to get at least some of your meals from non-restaurant sources: supermarkets, open-air farmers markets, roadside stands and farms.

When possible, avoid higher-priced outlets like 24-hour stores, bus station canteens, street vendors, beach stands, airport restaurants and liquor stores. 'Many supermarkets, especially 7–11s, have microwaves, so a hot stew can be eaten for the price of the can.' In general the food you buy and prepare yourself will always be the cheapest. At least one meal a day should fall into this category.

Keep away from endless soft drinks; even at supermarkets, they're 75¢ and up, double that elsewhere. Accompany your dining-out meals with ice water or lower-priced multiple refills like coffee or tea.

If you can eat a good meal in the morning then you'd be wise to start with a big breakfast (best food bargain in the US) and/or to stay in bed and breakfasts, hotels, hostels and other lodgings which include it as part of the price. Everywhere you will find excellent breakfast 'specials' for as little as $1.25 for eggs, toast etc. At lunchtime, again look for daily 'specials'—usually the tastiest/freshest and cheapest choice available.

In the evening, plan to eat early (to take advantage of lower-priced 'sunset' or 'Early Bird' specials) or eat in a non-restaurant setting.

Wherever you are, check out the Happy Hour situation. States and cities with liberal liquor laws often honour a daily discount period (usually 4–7pm) with cheap drinks and free food, sometimes a stunning array of it. Fittingly, California is the Happy Hour paradise.

No matter where you are, ethnic restaurants are invariably the cheapest. Chinese, Mexican and Italian can be found in profusion. In larger areas, look for Vietnamese, Greek, German, Indian and other specialties. Cafeterias offer cheap if sometimes insipid food; besides downtown, look for them on campuses, around hospitals, in large museums, in department stores and at YMCAs. 'Anyone can eat in university cafeterias—all you want for the price of a burger, fries and soft drink at McDonalds.' The good old American diner is another reasonably inexpensive option, usually with an amazing choice of dishes on the menu and enormous portions.

Regional and local specialties are usually wonderful, or at the very least a worthwhile cultural experience. As you work your way around the country sample Key lime pie, Virginia ham and redeye gravy, Chicago-style deep-dish pizza, California guacamole dip, Southern grits, Hawaiian poi and roast pig, Wisconsin bratwurst, Maryland crabcakes, Navajo tacos.

In the West, salads and salad bars are generally excellent. Large sandwiches (often with local nomenclature like grinder, submarine, po' boy, blimp, hero, hoagie, etc) on rolls with meatballs, sausage, corned beef, you name it, are available everywhere for a couple of dollars.

Many readers have suggested the salad bars now available in some fast food chains or as sold by the pound in supermarkets and grocery stores. For about $3 you can eat as heartily as any well-to-do rabbit. Those on a budget will inevitably find themselves eating from time to time at McDonald's, Burger King, Pizza Hut, Kentucky Fried Chicken and the rest. At least you know what you're getting. Coast to coast it's always the same! The Taco Bell chain has been recommended for a good, filling, cheap vegetarian meal e.g. 79¢ for bean burritto. And there's always pizza!

Americans are ice cream fanatics and eat it year-round in more flavours and combinations than you've ever dreamed of. Lots of the ice cream parlours will give you free samples until you hit on the one you want most.

Wherever you eat, portions are invariably enormous—you'll soon understand why Americans invented the doggie bag for leftovers! 'Forget doggie bags—nobody objected to our ordering one portion and two plates and sharing—portions still bigger than at home.'

'Nowhere have I found it difficult, and usually I've found it fun, hunting out a place to suit my quite small pocket. I do feel that discovering food, rather than following a map to it, is part of the holiday.'

TRAVEL

The means you choose to travel around North America will depend on your budget, your time, your adventurousness and a number of other factors. Since there are certain discounts available to travellers who buy their tickets outside North America, it is a good idea to give careful consideration to travel plans *before* you go. Also, when you buy your tickets outside the US, you save the eight percent sales tax. Basically, travel is like everything else in America—you have to shop around for the best buys. Never be afraid to ask for the cheapest fare. There are always variations and the clerk selling you a ticket is not necessarily about to offer you the cheapest one.

'Canada and the US cater for wheelchairs much better than the UK does. Theatres, museums, pavements, airports, bus stations, even buses are all usually equipped with either lifts or ramps.'

Bus. Travelling long distances cross-country by bus has become a part of American mythology and for natives and overseas visitors alike bus remains the most popular method of cheap travel in North America. Despite competition from comparatively inexpensive air fares which has resulted in the cutting back on bus routes and facilities in recent times, the major nationwide company, Greyhound, and the many regional, smaller companies, survive and flourish and will no doubt still be the chief means of inter-city transportation for most budget travellers to North America for the forseeable future.

It is possible to travel comfortably all over North America whether it be on Greyhound or one of the many other bus lines. Bus terminals provide restaurants, ticket, baggage and parcel services, travel bureaux, restrooms and left-luggage lockers, although you should be aware that bus stations are often in the seediest areas of downtown and therefore not a place to actually plan on spending a lot of time. Periodic rest stops are made every three to four hours enroute and if you are on a very tight budget you can save by travelling at nights and sleeping on the bus.

At the time of writing, Greyhound are in the process of switching to a national, computerised reservation service. This could mean that there will be dramatic changes in the way bus riding works. Effectively, this ends the days when you can just turn up and get on a bus. Now you will have to phone ahead and make a reservation.

When travelling by bus from point A to point B, always ask about the cheapest available fare. Fare reductions are made and usually depend on the time of travel, how long away, when returning etc. Available to overseas visitors are the various Greyhound Ameripasses. These are the 7-day Pass for £90; 15 days for £135 and 30 days at £180. You can buy extra days at £12 per day both at the original time of purchase and while on the road although only up until the day before the pass expires. A 4-day Pass is available in the U.K. for £50. It is non-refundable and valid for travel only on Monday to Thursday. The Ameripass is not valid for travel in Canada except for direct journeys from Seattle to Vancouver, Fargo to Winnipeg, Buffalo/Detroit to Toronto, and Boston or New York to Montreal. (*For further information on Greyhound fares in Canada, please see the Background Canada section of this book.*) It is also possible to buy the Ameripass from Greyhound International (only) office in New York City, Port Authority Bus Terminal. The 7-day pass is $135, the 15-day pass $199 and for 30 days, $270.

Time on all the passes starts ticking away when you start your journey. The passes offer unlimited travel on Greyhound routes (and those of participating carriers) for the duration of the pass. They represent excellent value for the cross-country traveller.

Some Tips. Whenever possible, take your bags on to the bus with you, otherwise get a check-in ticket, make sure they are labelled and watch them like a hawk—it is not uncommon for you and your bags to set off in different directions, and without the check-in ticket you may never get them back. If you have to put your bag underneath the bus it is recommended that at each stop en route to your destination you get off the bus and watch to make sure that your bag stays there and continues with you—on the same bus. 'If all lockers are taken, luggage can be stored for up to 24 hours at a cost of $1.50 per piece, in the bus depot luggage store.'

'Bus pass coupons have to be validated each time for further travel. As ticket lines can be very long, it's good to have your ticket stamped for the next journey as soon as you arrive.'

If planning to sleep on the bus, get a cheap inflatable pillow. It can make all the difference to your comfort, though some readers say a sleeping bag is better 'and doesn't puncture'. Malleable wax ear plugs are also a good idea for lighter sleepers. Always have a sweatshirt or pullover with you. Bus drivers seem to be impervious to cold. 'Even at 3am on a chill night the air conditioning is set to combat the climate of Alice Springs.'

The bus passes often entitle you to discounts at station restaurants, nearby hotels and on various sightseeing tours. It's in fact cheaper to eat away from the stations, but you might not always have the time to do so.

Most bus routes are meant solely to get you from A to B; scenic considerations rarely come into it.

The Green Tortoise. A kind of alternative bus/tour combo designed to get the budget traveller across country cheaply, but in a fun, laid-back way.

Time is not of the essence here. No effort is made to get there fast. The idea is to meander gently with the route changing at the request of the passengers. The coast to coast trips begin and end in either New York or Boston and San Francisco, depart weekly, last 11 days and at present cost $279. You will need extra money for meals en route. Other tours are available—to Yosemite, the Grand Canyon, Mexico, Alaska and New Orleans for Mardi Gras. Green Tortoise also provides a cheap way of travelling down the West Coast—Seattle to LA, $89; San Francisco to LA, $30.

Buses accommodate 28 to 44 people and have most of their seats removed and replaced by wooden platforms covered with foam rubber padding. They also have stoves and refrigerators. Often cross-country tours are accompanied by a cook. Passengers can put $9 or so a day into a kitty and get two full meals cooked on the bus but often eaten at some scenic place such as a Louisiana bayou or the banks of the Rio Grande. Smoking is banned on the buses.

'A wonderful trip. I made many new and lasting friends and saw many places I might otherwise have missed.' 'Don't do it if you're an insomniac, a loner, need a shower more than once every three days, or a moaner.'

Reservations should be made through Green Tortoise, PO Box 24459, San Francisco CA 94124. Or for information phone San Francisco (415) 821-0803, Seattle (206) 324-RIDE, Portland (503) 225-0310, Eugene (503) 937-3603, Los Angeles (310) 392-1990, New York (212) 431-3348, or Boston (617) 265-8533, or (800) 227-4766 outside California, for all general enquiries.

Car. The car overwhelmingly remains the most popular form of travel and the vast system of super-highways—'monuments to motion'—enable you to cover great distances at high average speeds, despite the nationwide imposition of a 55mph speed limit (65 mph on some rural interstates). 'The National System of Interstate and Defence Highways is designed for maximum efficiency. For enjoyment, try state and country roads, even for a lengthy trip. The additional time spent will be more than compensated for by the increased intimacy with American culture and scenery.'

Buying a car. For a group of three or four it can be worthwhile buying a second-hand car. Try to buy and sell privately, utilising the notice boards of universities, and the local press.

Be sure to obtain a 'title' or, in states such as New York, a notarised bill of sale. If stopped by the police, 'proof of ownership' will be required. (In some states it is illegal to drive without this.) Allow for a delay while the title comes through. If you buy from a dealer he can issue temporary licence plates on the spot.

You can have your car checked over at a gas station at a very low cost. If you have to buy new parts get them at one of the nationwide stores like Montgomery Ward or Sears, or from major gas stations like Shell and Mobil. They will give you guarantees and have the advantage of being readily available all over the continent. Garages are efficient and friendly, and if you are from out-of-state, will usually do repairs, however major, on the spot.

Prices of second-hand cars vary very much from place to place and tend to be higher on the West Coast. Prices fall in September when the next year's new cars come on to the market. Leave several days for selling your car and if possible try not to do it in New York. Automatic cars are easier to sell.

'Two of us bought a large station wagon for $800 and drove it 12,000 miles in two months. We slept in it often, and sometimes ate in it too. We sold it back to the dealer we bought it from at half-price. Worst problems: two $50 repair bills and finding places to park.' 'We bought a car. It cost $400 among seven. I personally paid $50 and to travel 5000 miles it cost me $60 in gas. Well worth it and it gave us freedom to visit so many places.'

Insurance. Although insurance cover is not obligatory in every state, you are strongly advised to take out at least third-party cover—and full comprehensive coverage is preferable—as insurance claims can be very high and inadequate insurance can lead to financial ruin. Expect to pay at least $450 for six month's coverage. 'State Farm Insurance, found in all states, offers good service and very good short-term policies.'

Insurance premiums are generally high, particularly for males under 25. Women are considered better risks and their premiums are lower. Premiums are lower if you are resident outside large urban areas. Allow time for your policy to come through.

In states where insurance is compulsory it is necessary to have it before you can register your car. 'We bought a car in Colorado and had trouble insuring it with an International Drivers' License. So be prepared to take a test and get a state license!'

Licences. All states and provinces of the US and Canada now officially recognise all European licences and those of Japan, Australia and New Zealand among others. However, an International Driving Licence is recommended since it provides you with photographic ID. Also police are more familiar with them and this could save you time and embarrassment (but don't forget to bring your *original* licence too—you may not be able to hire a car or get a drive-away without it). In addition, your own licence can be validated by the AAA office in the USA. Although not a legal requirement, it's a good idea to have it done particularly if your licence is not in English. You won't encounter many multi-lingual patrolmen along the way. You must always have your insurance certificate, car registration certificate and driving licence with you in the car—there is no grace period; you will simply be done for driving without the legally required documents.

Road Tips. Traffic regulations vary from state to state, so familiarise yourself with them in each. The 55mph speed limit is standard, however, except on some rural interstate highways, (mainly in the west), where it is 65 mph. Many readers recommend buying the Rand McNally *Interstate Road Atlas,* useful even for non-drivers. Maps from gas stations cost around $2.

'Most truck drivers have CBs. When driving, follow the example they set. If they adhere to the speed limit it means they've picked up the police lurking in the locality. If the truckers exceed the limit it means there are no cops around and it is safe for you to exceed the limit too.'

If you have a breakdown, raising the hood is the recognised distress signal. Also switch on your flashing warning lights.

Never pass a stopped and flashing school bus (they are usually yellow) no matter which side of the road it is on: it is not only against the law, but could easily result in death or injury to young children.

AAA Membership. Benefits: Towing service, $5000 bail if arrested, excellent and free maps and regional guide books, and a comprehensive information and advisory service. For example, the AAA will plan your journey for you, giving the quickest or most scenic routes, and provide detailed maps of the towns you will pass through.

Touring membership costs $70 the first year, $60 thereafter and entitles you to full membership rights. Apply to: AAA, 1000 AAA Drive, Heathrow, FL 32746, or to AAA, Broadway and 62nd St., in New York, 212-586-1166, or to the Club in whichever State you happen to be.

Membership of your own national automobile association entitles you to AAA benefits.

Gasoline. Depending on which part of the country you are in, expect to pay as much as $1.65 per gallon, or as little as about $1. (The American gallon is one-fifth smaller than the imperial gallon used in Britain and Canada and is equivalent to 3.8 litres.)

When driving in remote areas, always keep your tank topped up. Gas stations can be few and far between. Keep a reserve supply in a container for emergencies. Shop around and use self service pumps for cheapest gas.

Automobile Transporting Companies. Americans change homes more often than any other people, and may live for a few years in New York and then move off to California. When they do move they sometimes put their car (or one of them) into the hands of an automobile transporting company which does no more than find someone like you to drive the car from A to B.

Most movements are from east to west, major starting points being New York, Detroit and Toronto. 'East–west is the easiest route to get; otherwise New York–Florida or New York–Atlanta. The cheapest way to travel bar hitching.' Even on the popular routes you may have to wait a couple of days for a car, particularly in summer.

Conditions regarding age limitation, time schedules, routing, gas and oil expenses, deposit, insurance and medical fitness vary considerably and should always be carefully checked. And another thing: 'The car trunk may be full of the owner's belongings, leaving no room for yours.' A fair example would be for a driver 21 years or over, with character references, to be charged a $100–$200 deposit, refundable on safe delivery. 'A superb and cheap way of travelling. I went with three others in a van and it only cost us $70 each in gas to get from New York to San Francisco via the Grand Canyon.' 'Beware. We had a series of bad experiences. Each office acts independently and sometimes against what the same company's office elsewhere tells you.' 'You have to take a reasonably direct route, but the time limit (after which you are reported to the FBI) allows a fair amount of sightseeing. I was given nine days for the coast-to-coast trip and made it in six. It's certainly a great way to see America.'

'I drove a new Cadillac with only two thousand miles on the clock. It was air conditioned, everything electric—really unbelievable, and we slept in it at night. Good places to sleep are truck-stops run by Texaco, Union 76, etc. They have 24-hour restaurants and free showers, and the truckers themselves, though rough-looking, are often interesting people to talk to.'

'When asking for your deposit back and before handing the keys over, hold out for cash. American cheques are a bugger to cash.' And a word of warning: 'It is essential to check the car thoroughly for dents and scratches before taking it. We lost $135 because the owner complained about scratches and we could not prove they were there before we took it.'

The names of companies can be found in the *Yellow Pages* under 'Automobile and Truck Transporting'. It is a good idea to shop around, go to the office in person, and make sure you do not sign away your insurance rights—ie make sure you personally are covered and not just the vehicle. One company recommended in the past is Dependable. The largest of the companies is probably AAACON, but exercise caution with them. Some readers have indicated problems with the company. The addresses of a few of the plethora of companies are listed under many towns and cities below.

Car Rentals. The biggest national firms are Hertz, Avis, National, Budget, Thrifty and Dollar. The last two are generally cheaper, but even Hertz can offer some amazing deals. It's important to phone around. Always compare costs per day against costs per mile and other variations, such as unlimited mileage or so many miles free, within the context of your specific needs. Many rental companies offer discount rates to foreign visitors, though sometimes only when bookings are made abroad.

The renter must usually be 21 or over, sometimes over 25 (Sears has been mentioned as one hire company which may rent to someone under 21). If you don't have a credit card then a hefty cash deposit will be required, and for foreigners a passport may also have to be deposited as security. 'It's very difficult to rent a car without a major credit card, and in many cases it's not possible to leave a deposit.' 'Small companies generally ask drivers to be 25 or over; large companies usually accept drivers from 18 provided they have a major credit card.'

Insurance is not usually included in the cost, or often it's only third-party. It's essential that you take out full coverage; the alternative may be a lifetime of paying off someone's massive hospital bills.

Greyhound operates one of the cheapest rental companies, though it concentrates mostly on Florida and California. Alamo and Amerex are also recommended. Then there are the companies renting out older cars, eg. Rent-a-Wreck, Rent-a-Heap, Rent-a-Junk and Ugly Duckling. But they are not always the cheapest or most flexible, eg in some instances you must stay within a 50- or 100-mile radius of the point of rental. Worth checking out, though. 'Phone the national company number as well as the local agent's number. One may well offer a better deal than the other.'

'Ask a travel agent for good deals; I found them to be in the know.' 'It's a good idea to check with the airline you're travelling on for special arrangements. Sometimes these can only be booked before the flight.' 'Don't entertain a firm that charges for mileage and drop-off; there are plenty that don't.' 'If you want unlimited mileage you must usually go to a large company.'

'We found car rental easiest, most convenient and, for groups of three or more, the cheapest way of getting to see National Parks and other areas where transport, other than tours, is minimal.'

Air. The vast distances of the North American continent have resulted in the popularity and relative cheapness of domestic air travel, and since government deregulation there has been a bewildering and ever-changing scramble to offer more for less. There are air travel bargains to be had but it is often hard to keep track of what is available. If you plan to fly check with a travel agent, phone around the airlines and keep an eye on newspaper and television advertising—and always ask for the cheapest available fare.

Some possibilities: night flights are sometimes cheaper than day flights; some airlines from time to time offer off-peak, cheaper, fares. Other airlines make discounts if you travel on a flight making stops en route and, if planning to travel great distances, it may pay to investigate the air passes (see below). There may be considerable price competition on major routes such as New York to Florida and New York to the West Coast. Once again, the clear message is shop around!

Additionally there are two Visit USA bargains available only to non-US residents and offering incredible value for cross-country travel. The terms and prices vary from airline to airline, but the principles are the same and the tickets have to be purchased BEFORE leaving for America.

The first (VUSA fares) offers a discount on all flights on the airline's system though the itinerary must be worked out and paid for prior to departure for the US. Reservations can be made at any time. This scheme may be preferable if you know in advance where you want to go and if you're not stopping at many places. Discounts are usually up to 40 percent.

The second is more like a bus pass: for a fixed all-in price you can cover an unlimited number of miles on the airline's route system within a certain period of time. There may be a few limitations, eg making only two coast-to-coast flights, or being able to make only one stopover at any one city. The validity period varies. At the time of writing Delta Airlines offer a 30-day 'space available' (ie standby) pass for $499. This can only be bought in conjunction with a transatlantic flight, and before you go. The pass does not include Canada & Mexico.

The Delta Pass has been highly recommended by previous users. Delta have an extensive route network covering the USA and getting on a flight is hardly ever a problem. However, the pass does not cover Canada, Mexico, Alaska or Hawaii.

Northwest Airlines have several pass-type options, but only in conjunction with a transatlantic journey on Northwest, British Airways or Virgin Atlantic. The available options range from a 30-day standby, unlimited travel pass for use within the continental USA and Canada for $399, to a

60-day confirmed seat basis pass for travel to four cities in the continental USA and Canada for $379. Coupons for travel to additional cities can be purchased before departure. These schemes will be preferable if you want to keep your travel arrangements flexible and cover a lot of ground. One of the advantages of travelling by air is that careful timing can get you free meals and night flights save on accommodation expenses. Air passes can be bought from most travel agents.

Rail. The railroads played a major role in the history of the United States, but over recent decades declined in service, increased in price, lost money and saw much of their former business go to cars and airlines. Part of the reason for this may have been the great number of competing railways and the inability of the individual companies to undertake the new investment necessary to improve service and efficiency. But then in 1971 Amtrak was established. All the major lines now operate under the one Amtrak board, and though the railways remain privately owned, losses on passenger services are made up for by government subsidy.

On long-haul Western routes, outdated equipment has been replaced by new double-decker Superliners, variously fitted up as lounges, dining cars (restaurant upstairs, kitchen below), sleeping cars (with bedrooms) and open-plan coaches. On shorter routes and generally in the East, cylinder-shaped Amcoaches are used, their interiors like luxury airliners.

In the East, frequency, time-keeping and the large number of destinations served permit comparison with European railways. From Chicago westwards it is the trans-Siberian railway that comes to mind. There are only six east-west routes, but all except one operate daily. Delays are common. But for the traveller that should not matter: the scenery is often spectacular, the service is better than on any railway in the world, you can eat and drink well and inexpensively, and the company is congenial. The Western railways are the last stronghold of graceful travel in America and many readers have written in to praise Amtrak and the standard of its services. 'Ideal for the student traveller going from city to city.' 'Very comfortable.' 'The best way to see a wide variety of scenery. On occasions we felt less worn from 20 hours on a train than four hours on a bus.' 'A wonderful window on to the USA.'

A rundown on some of the more interesting routes:

The Empire Builder runs between Chicago and Seattle via Milwaukee, Minneapolis/St Paul, Fargo in North Dakota, Glacier National Park and Spokane. Majestic scenery. Takes about 46 hours; operates daily.

The Coast Starlight, between Los Angeles and Seattle, offers superb coastal, forest and mountain scenery. 'Attracts many young people. A highly social train: spontaneous parties and lust.' Takes 33 hours; operates daily.

The San Francisco Zephyr runs between Chicago and Oakland via Omaha, Denver, Cheyenne and Reno—prairies, plains, and best of all the mountains between Reno and Sacramento. Takes 48 hours, operates daily.

The California Zephyr, formally operated by The Denver & Rio Grande Western Railroad, is now operated by Amtrak three times a week. The journey, between Denver and Salt Lake City, takes 14 hours, almost all in daylight, and climbs 9000 feet over the Rockies for what is considered the greatest railway ride in America. It then runs on to Las Vegas and LA.

RIDING SCENIC RAIL

North America, especially the Rockies, is full of scenic narrow gauge railways, where restored steam locomotives backtrack to bygone days. These are some of the more interesting rides.

Cumbres & Toltec Scenic Railroad in Antonito, CO, is North America's highest narrow-gauge steam railroad. Full-day, 64-mile tour, $50; (719) 376-5483. **Great Smoky Mountain Railway**, Bryson City, NC (near Asheville). Trips through Nantahala Gorge and Fontana Lake, 9am & 2pm Wed-Sun; $16 for 4-hr round trip. To reserve call: (704) 586-8811. **Mt Washington (NH) Railway Co**, (800) 922-8825. Historic route with steep grade, highly scenic trip to highest point in Northeast; 3-hour trip, $32. **Royal Hudson Steam Train**, Vancouver, British Columbia, (604) 68-TRAIN, follows the coast of Howe Sound to small mining town; $24 for full day. **Narrow Gauge Railroad**, Durango, CO, (303) 247-2733. Along Animas River Valley to Silverton. Old fashioned. $37 round trip, 4 trips daily. **Pikes Peak Cog Railway**, Colorado Springs, CO, (303) 685-5401. Several trips daily from Manitou Springs to Pikes Peak, the highest route in the US. **Skunk Train**, Ft Bragg, CA, (707) 964-6371. Half day $21, full day, $26. Scenic route through Redwoods. **Strasbourg Railroad**, Strasburg, PA, (717) 687-7522. 45-min route through Amish country several times a day, $6.50. America's oldest short-line steam locomotive.

Also special are the *Pioneer* between Seattle and Salt Lake City, the *Adirondack* between New York and Montréal, and the crack *Broadway Limited* between New York and Chicago with the best onboard dining service.

USARAIL passes for 30/15 days unlimited travel are available to overseas visitors outside the US and in some US cities eg, New York, Los Angeles, Washington DC, Miami. High season rates (May 30–August 28th) are: $399/$318 Nationwide, $299/$238 Western region, $239/$188 Eastern region and Far Western region. For the 30-day Coastal Pass (east or west) it's $209. Once you have bought the pass you can make reservations by phoning (800) USA-RAIL. 'Excellent value, great way to travel. Trains spacious and comfortable. Staff friendly and helpful.' 'Disadvantages—trains slow and often late.' It is essential to make reservations as far ahead as possible for the busy East Coast routes to Florida. 'One drawback is the early morning (4 am!) arrival time at some mid-west stations.'

In Britain contact: Long Haul Leisurerail, PO Box 113, Peterborough PE1 1LE; 0733 51780. BUNAC members can get passes from BUNAC in London. In the US: Amtrak Travel Center, PO Box 311, Addison, Illinois 60101.

Boats. 'If you want to take a longer trip on the Mississippi, you can try to get on a towing boat. But you'll have to work hard. Look in the *Yellow Pages* under "Towing—Marine".'

How about paddling your own canoe? The Appalachian Mountain Club publishes three books of interest to canoeists and kayakers: *AMC River Guide I: Northeastern New England; AMC River Guide II: Central and Southern New England;* and *AMC White Water Handbook for Canoe and Kayak*. They're available by mail from AMC Books, 5 Joy Street, Boston MA 02108.

The Chicagoland Canoe Base Inc, 4019 N Narragansett Avenue, Chicago IL 60634, can provide you with all the information you need on canoes, kayaks, rafts, accessories, rentals, books and maps.

Hitchhiking. Hitchhiking in the United States can vary from state to state, but generally it can be 'superb, simply due to the long rides'. However, we strongly recommend that women, or even men, do not hitch alone.

'A sure way of getting long rides in relative comfort and at speeds in excess of the general 55mph limit is to ask for rides at truck stops. At Union 76 truck stops there will often be hundreds of trucks going to all parts of America. Just ask the drivers in the canteen. By using this method I managed to cover over 1000 miles from Mexico to New Orleans with only two rides'. 'Don't try truck stops unless on your own. Even then, due to new insurance regulations, it's difficult.' 'I had better luck at truck stops at night when drivers like passengers to keep them awake.' 'Truck stop directories can be obtained free at truck stops.'

Hitching is forbidden on freeways and interstates, so get your rides on the ramps, at rest areas, or at service areas. With regard to other roads, the laws vary from state to state, but even when hitching is technically illegal you can usually still get away with it if you are standing on the shoulder or sidewalk, and sometimes even if you are walking with the traffic, regardless of the fact that you might be walking backwards. 'I had no problems except the usual ones. The police are okay, though they may ask to see your identification.' 'Police in New York warned me, "Ten days in jail if we see you again". The next day I was given a ride by a policeman.'

Never carry any dope. Display your national flag. Always carry a sign saying where you want to go. 'We carried two signs: one stating our destination, the other saying PLEASE. Fantastic results.' 'Female hitchhikers should not use destination signs; that way you have a chance to look over the driver before accepting.' Avoid getting off in cities if you don't want to stay there. 'People who gave us lifts often gave us meals and even a bed for the night.'

'Warning to female hitchhikers: don't hitch overnight trucks unless willing to satisfy the driver. No malice intended but "payment" is expected. At least that's what I found, and I was hitching with my boyfriend.' 'I often got rides with truckers and found them nice and helpful people. I slept in a cab of a truck three times without having to grant any favours, and I was a female alone. I'm not recommending overnight rides with truckers nor hitching alone for that matter, but I had no bad experiences.'

Holidays, especially Labor Day, are good times to travel as there are millions of cars on the road. If you don't want to thumb, try radio stations or look in the local (especially the freaky) papers. 'For hitching long-distance, or if you're prepared to share the driving, try the ride boards at universities—either advertise yourself or go to see what's offered. I got from Chicago to San Francisco this way in one car.'

'When crossing the US–Canadian border do not say you're a hitchhiker.' 'Beware the heat in the Southwest, ie anywhere between LA and mid-Texas. In this area hitchers should carry a large container of water and some salt tablets. Hitchers have been found dead on the side of the road due to dehydration.' 'People are usually very congenial and offer accommodation and food.' 'I hitched from San Francisco to New York in four and a half days and could have done it in less. I experienced no more hassles than I have in Europe. The Southern states are populated by a different breed of people who are proud to be rebels and consider the Civil War to be still on, but they are still cool for hitching, especially if you are European. By the way, they call you Euro-penises.' 'I hitched 9500 miles with over 130 lifts and all but two were very friendly and helpful. I got beds, showers, endless meals, and made friends while hitching. Far more rewarding than bus travel.'

Hitching by air is another possibility. America is dotted with thousands of *small airfields* (ie not JFK or LA International) located outside most towns from which people fly in *small aircraft* for pleasure or business. Those are the people you ask. 'Difficult across US/Canada border.' 'Air hitching is really difficult but saves so much time it's worth a try.' 'I walked into an air freight company office in San Francisco and got a free ride back to New York with the overnight packages.' Not a good idea to carry much luggage though—*small*, light, aircraft remember.

Bicycle. There's a 4450-mile TransAmerica Trail stretching from Virginia to Oregon, divided into five shorter routes. Five sectional booklets are available, with detailed maps and details of flora, fauna, campsites, eateries, bike shops and gradients enroute. Free leaflet from Bikecentennial, PO Box 8308, Missoula, Montana. Tel: (406) 721-1776. Also, HI-AYH does bicycle tours; information is available from their headquarters.

A strong bicycle lock is advisable for security when parking in towns, plus a helmet (US drivers are not attuned to looking out for bikes). Bicycles are cheaper in the US than abroad. It's possible to ship a bike around the US with Amtrak or the bus companies provided it's dismantled and boxed. Bikes can sometimes be taken free on flights to and from the US as part of your baggage allowance and again must be boxed. The cost, if any, varies from airline to airline.

Walking. Yes it is done. Mostly by mad dogs and Englishmen. Like John Lees of Brighton, England, who in 1972 walked from City Hall, Los Angeles, to City Hall, New York, a distance of 2876 miles, in 53 days 12 hours 15 minutes, averaging 53.75 miles per day.

'When asking for directions, remember that most people think you are on wheels. I was directed to one place along a roadway that took me 15 minutes to negotiate in the boiling hot sun, an excursion I could have avoided by cutting—in one-third the time—through a leafy forest. Unfortunately, the guy I asked thought I was a Chevy, so I had to go the long way round.'

A list of more than 25 hiking clubs along the East Coast can be obtained by writing to the Appalachian Trail Conference, Box 236, Harpers Ferry WV 25425. The Conference manages the 2000-mile Maine to Georgia Appalachian Trail in conjunction with the National Park Service. For 50¢ they'll send you information about the trail, membership, etc. Be sure to ask specifically for the list of clubs.

On the West Coast there's the Sierra Club. They can provide information about the Pacific Crest Trail, 2400 miles along the Pacific Coast from Canada to Mexico, plus other walks: 530 Bush Street, San Francisco CA 94108.

Tours. If young and on your own and looking for fun and adventure, consider perhaps TrekAmerica's camping expeditions: 25 days up the Alaska Highway, for example, or six-week coast-to-coast journeys, stopping at the most interesting cities, towns and national parks enroute. During July and August a 14-day tour costs about £490 plus $35 per week for food. The four week tour is about £700, plus $30 per week for food. Extras such as riding and sailing are available at extra cost.

In Britain, contact TrekAmerica, Worldwide Reservation Admin, Trek House, The Bullring, Deddington, Oxford. Tel: 0869 38777. In the USA: TrekAmerica, PO Box 470, Blairstown, NJ 07825. Tel: (908) 362–9198 or (800) 221–0596. 'An excellent way to see America if you don't mind camping and long drives. For a girl travelling on her own who didn't want to Greyhound or hitch, it enabled me to see a terrific amount in three weeks.'

Hostelling International-AYH also organise hiking and biking tours. Ask for their 'Discovery Tours' booklet for information.

Urban Travel. City buses and subway systems generally offer good services throughout North America. Usually, a flat fare is used which can make short hops expensive but long rides very reasonable. Many cities have a transfer system allowing you to change from one bus line to another, or even from bus to subway, without paying extra. Stick-ups have meant that bus drivers will not carry any more money than is absolutely necessary, so you must always have the exact fare.

Taxis can be pretty expensive unless shared. The ubiquitous Gray Line company ensures that nearly every city has its bus tour, and some have boat tours as well.

For further details on all forms of urban travel, see under city headings throughout the Guide.

THE WORLD CUP IN 1994–WHERE THE ACTION IS

On July 4th 1988, when FIFA announced the USA as host to the 1994 World Cup, there was consternation. It was thought that the unique atmosphere of the Cup would be lost on a country that didn't like, or even know, about soccer. However, in reality the US loves the game. Soccer lags only behind basketball in popularity among American youth and there are now more university soccer teams than football teams. The trouble is that there is nowhere for talented players to parade their skills after college, there being no real professional soccer leagues. The fact that the game does not keep stopping and starting like football has kept TV away. There is just not enough time to show commercials thus making it an uneconomical proposition for the networks. The World Cup however, will be shown on TV without the commercials—thanks to a deal with the sponsors.

The competition will run for a month from June 17th 1994 until the final on July 17th and will start with group games. The top teams from each group and four third placed teams will go through to the Round of 16. From this round it will be knockout, leaving two teams to battle it out for the biggest prize in world sport. The nine venues are:

BOSTON, Foxboro Stadium, capacity 61,000. The site of England's infamous loss to the US in June 1992. The stadium is easily accessible by commuter train from Boston. Will host six matches including one of the quarter-finals.

CHICAGO, Soldier Field, cap. 66,814. The home of the Bears, not far from downtown on the shores of Lake Michigan. Will host the opening ceremony and game on June 17th, featuring reigning champions, Germany, and four other matches.

DALLAS, Cotton Bowl, cap. 72,000. Situated in Fair Park on the east of Dallas. Another six match and quarter-final venue.

DETROIT, Pontiac Silverdome, cap. 76,000. Located in Pontiac, about 18 miles NE of Detroit. A world first: soccer on real grass—indoors. About $600,000 has been spent developing a special blend of grass that will grow indoors, banks of halogen lamps giving the grass the light it needs between games. Will see four games.

LOS ANGELES, Rose Bowl, cap. 102,083. In Pasadena, 7 miles from downtown LA. Host to the 1993 Superbowl, this huge stadium will host eight matches including one of the semi-finals, and the final itself on July 17th.

NEW YORK, Giants Stadium, cap. 76,891. In East Rutherford, NJ, it was here that the famed New York Cosmos, Pele *et al*, played between 1977 and 1984. Will stage seven games, including the other semi-final.

ORLANDO, Citrus Bowl, cap. 70,188. One mile west of downtown. Nearby is Lake Sylvan, headquarters of the US national team. Five game stadium.

SAN FRANCISCO, Stanford Stadium, cap. 86,019. Situated on the campus of Stanford University in Palo Alto, 27 miles south of SF, six games will be played here, including a quarter-final.

WASHINGTON DC, RFK Stadium, cap. 56,500. Easily accessible by Metro, RFK is home to the Redskins and once to the Diplomats soccer team whose star attraction was the legendary Johann Cruyff. Five games will be played here.

Tickets will be available through **World Cup Tickets**, (800) 769–1994, for individual games—that is if any are still around. There are 1.1 million 'Category III' tickets. These are the cheapest and prices range from $25 for first round matches to $180 for the final. It looks as though there will be very few tickets left, so the only option may be to go through 'scalpers' (touts), or keep an eye out in ticket agencies and newspapers for spares. If you just can't manage to get a ticket, then the cable TV network **ESPN** will show 41 games and **ABC** will televise 11, including the final.

NEW ENGLAND

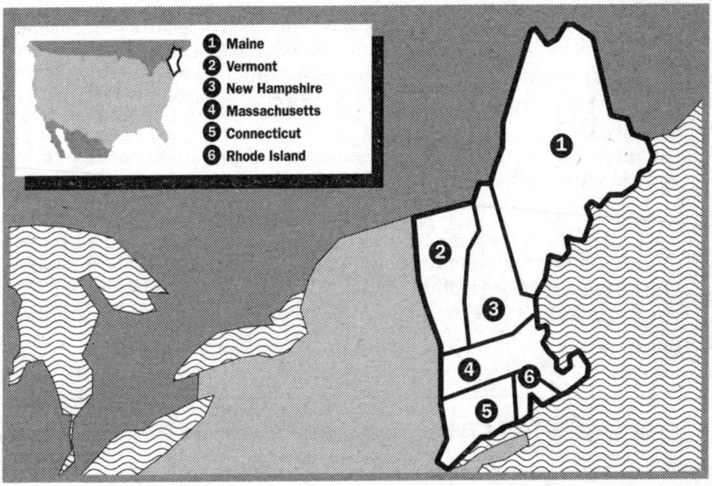

The upper northeast corner of the United States is sometimes called the nation's attic. This was one of the first areas in the New World to be colonised by Europeans, in the persons of the Pilgrim Fathers, and it is the old historical ties, more than any other, which bind these New England states together. It was also here that American independence was born, embodied by such patriots as Paul Revere and Sam Adams. New England's size does not match its great historical significance—its six states are together smaller than Oklahoma.

New England is a melting pot, spiced with a rich diversity gained from the British, Irish, Italians, French Canadians, Portuguese, Jews and many others who now make up the majority of the population. To the rest of the United States, however, a New Englander is still a Yankee, and a whole series of myths and legends has grown up around him. The Yankee is well known for his canniness, thrift, industry, a taciturn nature and natural suspicion of strangers. The lovely white picket fences often seen around New England homes are pointed out to the newcomer as proof of this last characteristic.

Hesitant hospitality aside, New England is always a delightful area to visit, offering the tourist a great variety of scenery from the rugged White Mountains of New Hampshire to the rolling green hills of Vermont, Massachusetts and Connecticut, and the often spectacular coastline, varying in its moods from state to state. Cultural contrasts abound: contemporary, cosmopolitan Boston stands alongside revered reminders of early American society.

New England was once known for textiles, shoes and paper. At the time of the Revolution, this was where American machinery was manufactured.

The Colt arms factory was here, Eli Whitney developed the cotton gin here. New England is now best known for expertise in electronics, advanced technology and education.

Politically, New England is important; the world's first written 'constitution'—the Mayflower Compact—was signed by the Pilgrim Fathers here in 1620. The American revolution was hatched in Boston, and in modern times, ex-President Bush and the Kennedys hailed from the area. The all-important first primary in the election of presidential candidates is held in New Hampshire.

The seasons are distinct in New England—a long, cold, winter followed by a short blossom-filled spring, a hot, often humid summer, and best of all for the visitor, a glorious autumn when the leaves turn the hillsides gold, scarlet and amber.

Hard-core hikers may like to tackle the 2000-mile long Appalachian Trail. This, the longest marked trail in the world, begins north of Bangor in Maine and winds more than 2000 miles from Baxter State Park to the mountains of Georgia.

CONNECTICUT

Known as the Constitution or Nutmeg State, Connecticut has historically regarded itself as part of New England, although in reality the area abutting New York State along Long Island Sound has far stronger ties with New York City than it has, say, with Burlington, VT, or even with the state capital, Hartford. Many people commute daily to New York from such places as Greenwich, Stamford and Bridgeport, and look to the New York media for their news and entertainment.

Away from the coast, Connecticut is a state of broad rivers, farms, forests, rolling hills and placid colonial villages. In particular, the Litchfield Hills in the northwestern part of the state offer pretty scenery and have several excellent state parks good for camping and walking.

Connecticut is the third smallest state in the Union and one of the most densely populated.

The submarine was invented here in 1776 and Connecticut is also the birthplace of the lollipop and the payphone. The insurance industry has its roots in Connecticut, and the Constitution State is home to America's first law school, and some of the oldest university art collections are at Yale, in New Haven.

The telephone area code for the entire state is 203.

HARTFORD The state capital, Hartford is known also as 'the insurance capital of the United States'—the headquarters of 40 insurance companies are located here. With this dark-suited image, Hartford has not been noted for its sparkling social life. More recently, however, efforts are being made to turn the city into a livelier regional attraction. The Civic Center and State House Square, providing shopping, restaurants, and entertainment, should be added to the visitor's list of more antique sights, such as Mark

Twain's House, the pre-World War One carousel in Bushnell Park, and, in the nearby suburbs of Wethersfield and Farmington, some of the oldest colonial houses in the US.

While here, pick up a copy of the *Hartford Courant*, founded in 1764 and the newspaper with the oldest continuous name and circulation in the nation, possibly in the world.

ACCOMMODATION

Country Inns, 100 Weston St, 5 min drive from downtown, 724-4667, $55.
Days Inn, 207 Brainard Rd, 247-3297, D-$48.
Susse Chalet Inn, 185 Brainard Rd, about 5 mins from downtown, exit 27 off I-91 South, 525-9306. Pool. S-$45–$50. Most hotels downtown are $50 and up for doubles.
Windsor Home Hostel, 126 Giddings Ave, Windsor (north of Hartford on I-91), 683-2847. $10 AYH; $13 non-AYH, $1 linen charge. Call ahead—only fits four people, and reservations are required.
YMCA, 160 Jewel St, 522-4183, $17, men and women.
YWCA, 135 Broad St, 525-1163. Women only. S-$16, shared bath, $23 private bath, dorm-$10. Laundry, kitchen, lounge.

FOOD/ENTERTAINMENT

Brown, Thompson & Co, 942 Main St, 525-1600. Lunch $4–$8; Dinner $5.95–$15. Very popular with the locals. Live comedy on weekends with $8 cover.
Russian Lady, 191 Ann St, 525-3003. In a wonderful old building topped with a statue of a royal Russian lady, hence the name. Tue–Sat: live bands. Drinks special offered every night. Check out the rooftop garden!
The Municipal Cafe, 485 Main St, 278–4844. Open from 7am–2.30pm for good meals, this popular cafe then re-opens at 7pm with a cheap bar menu and Weds–Sat there's live local music too.

OF INTEREST

Old State House, 800 Main St, 522-6766. Formerly the State Capitol, now restored and refurbished back to its 1796 appearance. Has information centre, Mon–Sat 10am–5pm, Sun noon–5pm.
State Capitol, Capitol Ave and Trinity St, 240-0222, exit 48 off I–84. Contains lots of Connecticut historical memorabilia. Tours available Mon–Fri, 9.15am–1.15pm; open Sat 10.15am–2.15pm; free.
Bushnell Park, adjacent State Capitol, 246-7739, has a 1914 carousel; you can ride one of its 48 horses or a chariot to the tunes of a Wurlitzer Band Organ for 50¢.
Mark Twain & Harriet Beecher Stowe Houses, Nook Farm, 351 Farmington, 525-9317. MT lived here for almost 20 years, publishing his major works from his Victorian-Gothic style home, with Mrs Stowe as his next-door neighbour. Twain spent more time in Connecticut than he did in Hannibal, his boyhood home, which gets all the fame and has more tourist traps, to boot. Summer Mon–Sat 9.30am–4pm, Sun 12pm–4pm, in winter closed Mon; $10 for both.
Wadsworth Atheneum, 600 Main St, 247-9111. One of New England's best art collections with 45,000 works; it is the country's oldest public art gallery. Tue–Sun, 11am–5pm; $3, $1.50 students. Free all day Thurs & Sat 11am–1pm.
Hartford Jai-Alai, 89 Weston St, 525-8611. First jai-alai in northeast US, top players. Seats $4. Eves Mon–Fri, matinee & eve Sat, matinee Sun.

INFORMATION

Convention and Visitors Bureau, Civic Center Plaza, 728-6789. Mon–Fri, 8.30am–4.30pm.
Travelers Aid, 30 Asylum St, Suite 4, 522-2247, Mon–Fri 9am–5pm.

TRAVEL

Greyhound/Bonanza Bus Lines, 800-231-2222 and AMTRAK, (800) 872-7245 (USA-RAIL) at Union Place.
NB. Only regular transport available from downtown to Bradley International Airport is via shuttle service from downtown hotels. Cost: about $8.

LITCHFIELD HILLS In the northwestern corner of the state, this is an area of rolling hills, with woods, rivers, streams and lakes. The town of Litchfield is a movieman's epitome of New England, with its white wooden churches, fine colonial houses, and of course, picket fences. The town centre itself is a National Historic Site. Harriet Beecher Stowe and Ethan Allen were born here: the **Litchfield Historical Society**, 567-4501, has all the facts, and historical and art exhibits. Those of a judicial frame of mind may wish to stop at the **Tapping Reeve House**, South St, 567-4501. America's first law school, it produced a vice-president, numerous supreme court justices and scores of congressmen. Tues–Sat 10am–4pm, Sun noon–4pm.

Nearby is **Bantam Lake**, good for water sports, including ice yachting in winter. The **White Memorial Foundation**, a wildlife sanctuary and museum, takes up about half of the lake's shoreline.

Southwest of the lake via Rte 109 and Rte 47 is the village of **Washington**, another 'jewel of a colonial village', home to many artists and writers, including, for the summer of '89, the Rolling Stones who chose this unlikely place to rehearse their US tour. Even older than the Stones are the artefacts at the **American Indian Archaeological Institute**. To get there take Rte 47 to Rte 199, 868-0518. Open Mon–Sat 10am–5pm, Sun noon–5pm. West of Washington is **Kent** and the **Sloane-Stanley Museum**, 927-3849, which displays Americana donated by Connecticut artist Eric Sloane. Open Wed–Sun 10am–4pm. $3.

The Litchfield Hills are a good area for walking and camping. Three of the nicer state parks, where you can do both, are **Housatonic Meadows, Lake Waramaug** and **Macedonia Brook**, none of which are far from Kent. For more information on parks, historic sites, accommodation and restaurants in the area contact **Litchfield Hills Visitors Commission**, P.O. Box 177, New Preston, CT 06777, 868-2214. For camping permits in the State Parks write to the **Bureau of State Parks and Forests**, 165 Capitol Avenue, #265, Hartford, 06106 or call on 566-2304.

BRISTOL One time clock-making capital of the US, Bristol is now primarily an industrial centre and not an ideal spot to overnight. But, three whimsical museums in and around town make it a worthwhile day-trip from Hartford or a memorable lunch stop between Litchfield and New Haven.

OF INTEREST

American Clock and Watch Museum, 100 Maple St, Bristol, 583-6070, $3. Open March–Nov, 10am–5pm. A horologist's delight, brimming over with timepieces past and present, comic and stately, grand and miniature. Over 3500 pieces in all. A must at noon!
Lock Museum of America, in Terryville just west of Bristol, 130 Main St (Rte 6), 589-6359. Open 1.30pm–4.30pm, Tue–Fri, $3. Over 22,000 locks, keys and related hardware dating back as far as 2000 BC.

New England Carousel Museum, 95 Riverside Ave, Bristol, 583-9441, Mon–Fri, 1pm–5pm, Sat 10am–5pm, Sun noon–5pm, $4. Some 300 carved horses, cats, elephants, chariots, etc., of intricate and occasionally bejeweled design. Guided tours include 2 hurdy gurdy organs, and a workshop restoring working carousel figures and parts. Magical.

FOOD
Farmington Ave offers a plethora of burger, pizza and taco joints, but if home cooking is what your heart and stomach desire try **Bardell's Family Restaurant**, 99 Farmington Ave, 585-7009; breakfast specials from $1.50, lunches and dinners from $2.

NEW HAVEN The city grew up around its harbour and Yale University (boola, boola). This Ivy League university, one of the best and oldest in the United States, currently enjoys recognition for graduating President Bill Clinton, Hillary Clinton, *and* former president George Bush.

Sadly, however, New Haven has failed to uphold its 19th-century reputation as one of America's most beautiful cities. While some areas are undergoing renovation, the nicest parts by far are still found on and around the Green. On the credit side, however, theatre and music thrive in New Haven, and there are numerous enjoyable bars, cafes, and restaurants patronised by the student population.

Going east along Long Island Sound, you come to New London, from where you can catch a ferry to Long Island and Block Island. Further still, there's Mystic, enroute to Newport, RI, and the Massachusetts seacoast.

ACCOMMODATION
Duncan Hotel, 1151 Chapel St, 787-1273. Downtown, right next to Yale, well-appointed for the price. Colour TV and use of pool next door. S–$45–55, D–$60–65.
Regal Inn, 1605 Whalley Ave, (Exit 59 off rte 15), 389-9504. S-$35, D-$38. TV.
Three Judges Motor Lodge, 1560 Whalley Ave, 389-2161. S–$33, D–$45.

FOOD
Archie Moore's, 188½ Willow St, ½ mile north of Peabody Museum, 773-9870. Named 'best watering hole in state', great buffalo wings, nachos, burgers, pasta, baseball on the tube, popular with grad students and locals, moderately priced. Plus bangers and mash, and mushy peas—especially for homesick British students!
Cha Da Thai, 1151 Chapel St, 776-9802. Appetizers $4.95 upwards, main courses $7.25 upwards. 10% discount for students. Downstairs from Duncan Hotel. 'Happens to be extremely good.'
Louie's Lunch, 263 Crown St, 562-5507. Enjoy breakfast cooked in 250-year-old frying pan under shadow of stones from Taj Mahal, Leningrad Tsar's palace, the Potomac, etc. Lunches good too, at this reputed birthplace of the hamburger. Unique, antique, friendly atmosphere.
Pepe's Pizzaria, 157 Wooster St, 865-5762. Good pizza.
Yankee Doodle Coffee Shop, 260 Elm St, 865-1074. The 'Doodle' serves good breakfasts, cheeseburgers, steak sandwiches, BLT's. 'One of the best deals in America' (Yalie recommendation).

OF INTEREST
Shore Line Trolley Museum, Branford, 5 miles from New Haven, 467-7635. Open daily Memorial Day–Labor Day, 11am–5pm. Admission and 3-mile ride, $5.

The Green, once a wild, swampy forest trodden by Indians, is now a shaded park. This was the central sector of the original nine town squares laid out in 1638. Despite encroaching modern buildings, the Green still retains much of its original flavour, flanked as it is on the north side by the impressive, ivy-clad halls of Yale.
Peabody Museum of Natural History, 170 Whitney Ave, 432-5050. Dinosaurs and Connecticut flora and fauna. Open Mon–Sat 10am–5pm, Sun noon–5pm; $3.50.
Yale University Art Gallery, 1111 Chapel St, 432-0600. The first gallery to be connected with an American university and the home of the Morgan Collection of American Miniatures. Also a good collection of French Impressionists. Open Tue–Sat 10am–5pm, Sun 2pm–5pm; free.
Yale Center for British Art, 1080 Chapel St, 432-2800. Hogarth, Constable, Turner. Most comprehensive collection of British works outside Britain. Open Tue–Sat 10am–5pm, Sun noon–5pm; free.
Yale University. Highlights include the Old Campus through Phelps Gate off College St, **Connecticut Hall** (the oldest building), the **Art of Architecture Building** designed by Paul Rudolph and the **Beinicke Rare Book Library**. Free 1-hr guided tours in summer, 432-2300, start at Phelps Gate.

ENTERTAINMENT
Be sure to pick up a copy of the *Yale Daily News*: the *After Hours* section has listings of concerts, parties, bands, drama, films, etc. In summer try the *New Haven Advocate*, a free paper that can be found throughout town.
Toad's Place, 300 York St, 624-8623. Dance club and concert venue where the Rolling Stones played unannounced prior to their 1989 tour. Here in 1990, Bob Dylan made his first club appearance in 25 years (a five-hour, four-set concert!).
Look for current productions at the **Long Wharf Theater**, 222 Sergent Dr, 787-4282. Tony award-winning theatre which has played host to pre-Broadway productions. Discount tickets available for students on day of performance.
The excellent **Yale Repertory Theater**, 222 York St, 432-1234, boasts Meryl Streep, Henry Winkler and many others as alumni.

INFORMATION
Maps and guides from the University Information Office, 344 College St, 432-2300.
Traveler's Aid, 1 State St, 787-3959.
New Haven Visitors and Convention Bureau, 195 Church St (on the Green), 787-822. Mon-Fri 9am–5pm.

TRAVEL
Amtrak, Union Ave, (800) USA-RAIL.
Connecticut Limousine Service, 10 Brewery St, 800-472-5466, has frequent runs to JFK, Newark and La Guardia Airports. $32 to JFK and LGA, or if you're under 22, $26; $35 to Newark, under 22, $27. Also runs from other CT towns.
Greyhound, 45 George St, 772-2470.
Metro-North Commuter Railroad, Union Station, fares are cheaper to New York than Amtrak, $9.50 off-peak, $13 rush-hour.

CONNECTICUT RIVER VALLEY The lower river valley, where river meets sea between New Haven and New London, is one of the state's loveliest, most unspoilt and peaceful areas. Once an important seafaring commercial centre, this is now an area for gentle sailing, pottering around the small towns, or watching the wildlife at Selden Neck State Park or out on the salt marshes around Old Lyme.

ACCOMMODATION
Unless you feel like treating yourself to a night at one of the expensive old inns

here—the **Griswold** or the **Copper Beech Inn** at Essex, or the **Old Lyme**—you will have to search out a motel or campground somewhere off I-95.

OF INTEREST
Essex Main St is lined with white clapboard homes of colonial sea captains. America's first warship, *Oliver Cromwell*, was built here. At the **Ivoryton Playhouse**, Katharine Hepburn 'found out what theatre was all about'.
Valley Railroad, Exit 3 off Rte 9, 767-0103. Scenic 2-hour combined train/boat ride along the Connecticut River, $14. Train only, $8.50. Runs daily in summer, Wed–Sun rest of year; closed winter except for special Xmas trains.
Gillette Castle State Park, across the river from Essex, off Rte 82, 526-2336. Once the estate of actor William Gillette who made his name playing Sherlock Holmes. The castle was built and furnished like a Victorian stage-setting. 'Weird.' Open daily spring & summer 10am–5pm, Sat & Sun in fall, 10am–5pm; $2. Reached by the **Chester-Hadlyme ferry**, which has been in service since 1769. The trip across the river costs $2 for a car and driver, 50¢ additional people.
Old Lyme, Rte 156. Summer artists' colony and home of the **Nut Museum**, 434-7636, dedicated to a greater awareness of nuts. Owner Elizabeth Tashjian, artist and visionary, collects art, music, and lore on the nut and has appeared on the Johnny Carson and David Letterman shows singing her 'nutty' songs. Open between May 1 and Oct 31 Wed, Sat, Sun 1pm–5pm, otherwise call for appointment; admission is $3 plus one nut (no, your friend doesn't qualify). 'Indescribably bizarre.'
A one-time boarding house and centre of the Old Lyme art colony is now the **Florence Griswold Museum**, 96 Lyme St, 434-5542. The bohemian antics of Miss Griswold and her fellow impressionists were considered somewhat shocking by the locals. You can see their work Tue–Sat 10am–5pm, Sun 1pm–5pm; Nov–May, Wed–Sun 1pm–5pm; $3.

NEW LONDON Off I-95, on the River Thames (pronounced as it looks), the town, once an important whaling port, had the distinction of being burnt to the ground by Benedict Arnold and his troops in 1781. Today it is the home of Connecticut College and the US Coast Guard Academy. There are some well-restored houses on Star Street and on Green Street is the Dutch Tavern frequented by Eugene O'Neill. 'The best bar in the US; unique atmosphere.'

ACCOMMODATION
Susse Chalet Motel, west of New London, exit 74 off I-95, 739-6991. S–$38, D–$44.

OF INTEREST
Groton, across the Thames, on Rte 12. The first nuclear-powered sub was launched from the Electric Boat Shipyard here in 1954. **Nautilus Memorial**, 449-3558, open Wed–Mon 9am–5pm. Tues 1pm–5pm.
Connecticut College Arboretum, Williams St, 447-1911, 425 acres of hiking trails and ponds, open daily early am 'til dusk.
Lyman Allyn Art Museum, 625 William St, down the street from arboretum, 443-2545, specializing in New London furniture and silver, also includes outstanding collection of dolls and dolls houses. Open 1pm–5pm Sun–Fri, 11am–5pm Sat, $3 donation. Guided tours $1 with student ID.
Monte Cristo Cottage, 325 Pequot Ave, 443-0051, boyhood home of Eugene O'Neill, inspired sets for *Ah, Wilderness* and *Long Day's Journey Into Night*; named after the Count of Monte Cristo, his actor-father's most famous part, $1 with student ID. April–Dec, Mon–Fri, 1–4pm.
Ocean Beach Park, foot of Ocean Ave, 447-3031. Recreation area offering swimming, water slide, jetskis, windsurfing, paddleboats, miniature golf, food

concessions. Open daily in summer 9am–midnight, 8am–midnight at w/end. Parking $7–$9, rides extra.
Mystic Marinelife Aquarium, just off I-95, 536-3323. Whales, sea lions, dolphins, seals. Open daily 9am–6pm, gates close at 4.30pm; $9. Call the aquarium collect if you see a marine mammal stranded on the beach.
Mystic Seaport, 572-0711. A re-created mid-19th century coastal village and maritime museum on Rte 27. Some of the fastest clipper ships were built in Mystic and the last of the wooden whaling ships, the *Charles W. Morgan* (which celebrated its 150th anniversary in 1991) awaits inspection. Open daily 9am–8pm in summer; $15. Can return next day for free. Seasonal events include a lobster festival over Memorial Day weekend, Labor Day Weekend Fish Fry and October Chowderfest.

FOOD
In New London:
James's Gourmet Deli, 181 Bank St, 445-8577.
Two Sister's Deli, 300 Captain's Walk, 444-0504, both for good sandwiches and salads.
Bangkok City, 123 Captain's Walk, 442-6970, Thai food at cheapish prices.
In **Groton** there is **Paul's Pasta**, 223 Thames, 445-5276, a favourite with local students.

MAINE

More than one hundred years ago, Maine was a comparatively wealthy state—inland it can be a sadly poor place now—with huge farms, significant ports and fine houses. Since then time has stood still; that, and just a charming touch of decay, is what makes Maine a great place to get away from it all.

Especially recommended is the drive 'down east' (northeast) along the rocky coastline of the Pine Tree State. On a straight line, the coast of Maine is 250 miles long, but all the bays, harbours and peninsulas lengthen the shoreline to some 2400 miles. Inland are acres of unexplored, moose-filled forests and huge lakes, remote and seldom visited, 2,500 in all. While in Maine, look out for blueberry festivals, clambakes, and lobster picnics. The state annually harvests millions of pounds of fish and shellfish. By far the most valuable part of the catch is lobster. If you enjoy eating lobster, this is undoubtedly the place to do it. You're bound to have potatoes served on the side—Maine is among the top spud producers in the US.

In addition to hiking, boating, and swimming, Maine offers great opportunities for biking and white water rafting. Thousands of miles of safe and lovely secondary roads—good for biking—wind through the interior and along the shore of Maine. Many bike stores offer reasonably priced rentals, and two guidebooks provide scenic routes and travel tips for bikers: *25 Bicycle Tours in Maine*, by Howard Stone (Back Country Publications, P.O. Box 175, Woodstock, VT 05091), and *Bicycling*, by DeLorme Publishing Company.

White Water Rafting in Maine is an adventure not to be missed. You'll find both water and outfitters to be plentiful at **The Forks** (named for the confluences of the Dead and Kennebec Rivers in the upper Kennebec Valley) and the **West Branch of the Penobscot** between Moosehead Lake and Baxter State Park in the Katahdin/Moosehead Region. *Great Rivers of the East*, P.O. Box 442, Jim Thorpe, PA 18829, (800) 828-7238 provides recommendations and a brochure on reputable East Coast outfitters including those in Maine. Canoeists should head for the **Allagash Wilderness Waterway** in northern Aroostook County.

For more information on camping and access rules write to the **Bureau of Parks and Recreation**, Maine Department of Conservation, State House, Station #22, Augusta, 04333, or call on 207-289-3821.

If all that exercise is not for you, then Maine has one other main attraction: factory outlet stores 'headquartered' in the Kittery area. There are real bargains to be found with products often having up to 50% off.

National Park: Acadia

The telephone area code for Maine is 207.

SOUTH COAST If you're in a hurry to head 'down east', hop on I-95, but if you have the time to meander try coastal Route 1. This winding road, which can be busy during the summer, provides easy access to a variety of sea-side towns and attractions.

Though actually beginning further south, the Maine version of Route 1 begins in **Kittery**. Known historically for its shipbuilders, this town currently hosts numerous factory outlets offering everything from designer fashions to household tools at discount prices. If relaxing on a long, sandy beach is more appealing, head for **Ogunquit** about 10 miles north. Centuries after the Indians named this 'beautiful place by the sea', it is still an attractive and popular shore resort. You'll find a quieter spot a few miles off Rte 1 on Rte 9 at the **Rachel Carson National Wildlife Refuge** in **Wells**, 646-9226. Here, solitude and rare birds among 1600 acres of shady wetlands combine to delight ornithologist and picnicker alike.

Continuing up Rte 9 brings you to **Kennebunkport**, vacation residence of former president, George Bush. Though beautifully maintained, this one-time ship-building village is sadly falling victim to 'quaint disease'. Avoid downtown at rush hour, and to miss the crowds, make the trek up Ocean Ave to Bush's Walker Point only before breakfast.

Try **Dixon's Campground**, 2 miles south of Ogunquit on **Cape Neddick**, 363-2131, free shuttle to beach 3 times daily, one person $21, $25 with hook-up, two people $25, $29 with hook-up, $8 each additional person, reservations accepted.

PORTLAND The gateway to northeast Maine, Portland is the largest city (pop. 64,000) in a state where cities and towns are few and far between. Here the coast changes from long sections of beach to a hodgepodge of islands, bays and inlets. Portland had an early history of Indian massacres and British burnings. The city has recently been revitalised and restored and is now a commercial and cultural centre, as well as being home to the University of Southern Maine. The attractively preserved Old Port Exchange on the waterfront has a pleasingly 19th Century atmosphere.

Take a ferry to one of the hundreds of islands in Casco Bay. Inland there is vast Sebago Lake for summer swimming, sailing, waterskiing and sunning.

ACCOMMODATION

Hotel Everett, 51A Oak St, 773-7882. S–$38, D–$48. Off-season rates lower. 'Clean and only 5 minute walk from scenic Old Port area.'
South Portland Motor Inn Wandlyn, jnct Maine Turnpike and exit 7 and Maine Mall Rd, 772-3450. D–$60. 'Massive room, shuttle service to airport and bus station.'
Susse Chalet Motor Lodge, 1200 Brighton Ave, at Turnpike (I–95), exit 8, 774-6101. S–$50, D–$63. Off-season rates about 40% cheaper.
YMCA, 70 Forest Ave, 874-1105. S–$22, week. Single rooms, men only. Hard to reserve a room, but worth a try.
YWCA, 87 Spring St, 874-1130. S–$27, D–$44. Women only. Free use of pool in morning. 'A clean, friendly place, very handy for Old Portland.'

FOOD

Carburs Restaurant and Lounge, 123 Middle St, 772-7794. 26-page menu. *Huge* sandwiches from $4–$10. 'I have never eaten so well so cheaply.'
Good Egg Cafe, 705 Congress St, 773-0801. Wholegrain pancakes, corned beef hash, creative omelettes. Around $12 for two.
Great Lost Bear, 540 Forest Ave, 772-0300, chili, burgers, veggie specials.
Magic Muffin Restaurant, 551 Congress St, 773-6957, breakfast all day, 2 daily specials under $2.95; soups, salads, sandwiches for lunch. Mon–Fri 6am–4pm, Sat 7am–3pm, Sun 7am–2pm.
Raffles Cafe Bookstore, 555 Congress St, 761-3930. Granola, pastries, sandwiches, Middle Eastern salads. Breakfast $6 for two, lunch $14 for two. Plus two floors of books.
Three Dollar Dewey's, 446 Fore St, 772-3310, pub style, 10 beers on tap, 50-plus bottle beers, three alarm chili, burgers, etc, nothing on menu over $6.

OF INTEREST

Boat trips. Casco Bay Lines, CBITD Ferry Terminal, Commercial and Franklin Sts, 774-7871; year round service to Peaks, Chebeague, Long, Great and Little Diamond and Cliff Islands. $4.50–$9. Also offers narrated cruises of Casco Bay, $7.50–$13.50.
House Island Cruises, Long Wharf, Commercial St, 799-8188, 1 hour scenic cruises of Casco Bay, $6.
Farmers Market: sells local produce; some organic food. 8am–2pm in fair weather, Mon, Wed, Sat; check with Visitor's Bureau for locations.
Henry Wadsworth Longfellow House, 485 Congress St, 772-1807. Was the poet's childhood home. Open June–Sept, Tue–Sat 10am–4pm; $3.
Old Orchard Beach, south of Portland. 'Maine's answer to Blackpool. Large water slides, good beach. Lots of French Canadians frequent this place.' Biddeford/Saco Shuttle Bus, 282-5408, leaves Portland for Old Orchard Beach four times daily from corner of Elm and Congress on Monument Sq; $3 one way.
Higgins, **Crescent** and **Scarborough** beaches are also good, and **Prout's Neck** is where artist Winslow Homer did much of his painting.
Old Port Exchange, on the waterfront. Reconstructed in Victorian style with cobblestone streets, gas lamps, boutiques and restaurants. Favourite haunt for locals as well as visitors.
Portland Museum of Art, 7 Congress St, 775-6148. Painting, sculpture and decorative arts, including works by Homer and Wyeth. Tues–Sat 10am–5pm, Thurs till 9pm, Sun noon–5pm; $5.
Portland Head Coastguard Station and Lighthouse, follow road to Cape Elizabeth south from Portland, off US 1. Follow signs to Portland Head. Commissioned by George Washington and built in 1791, Portland head light is Maine's oldest lighthouse. Small museum and picnic facilities. 'Great views.'
Maine Arts Festival takes place during the second week in August and features international music, dance and performance art, as well as folk arts, workshops and local foods. Advance purchase discounts available. Contact WCSH TV, 828-6666.

INFORMATION
Greater Portland Convention and Visitors Bureau, 305 Commercial St, 772-4994. Sells maps for self-guided walking tours; $1.

TRAVEL
Greyhound, St John and Congress Sts, 772-6587. Be careful at night.
Prince of Fundy ferry to Yarmouth, Nova Scotia, 775-5616. Runs nightly May–Oct, 11 hour trip. Peak season (from mid-June), $75 per person one way, $98 for car. Tues & Wed, car goes for $49.

Continuing on up the coast will bring you to **Freeport**, a haven for over 100 factory outlets, chief of which is *THE* sporting and outdoor goods store, L.L. Bean. Open 365 days a year, 24 hours a day, Bean's is a Mecca to preppie America, and the pilgrims come here at all hours. 'It was really strange to be shopping at 3 o'clock in the morning.' In case you're feeling overly verdant, there's relief just around the corner at the **Desert of Maine**, Desert Rd, Freeport, 865-6962, $4.75 includes guided tour (8.30am–6pm daily) and tram rides (9am–4pm) through the dunes. There are 100s of acres of sandy glacial (not ocean) remains creating dunes up to 80 feet high. You have to feel it to believe it.

MID-COAST **Brunswick** is home to small, but lovely **Bowdoin College**, alma mater of writers Hawthorne and Longfellow and explorers Peary and MacMillan among others. Currently the college hosts Bowdoin Summer Music Festival featuring nationally renowned artists and low-priced concerts. Also on campus are the Peary-MacMillan Arctic Museum, Hubbard Hall, 725-3416, polar exploration, ecology and Inuit culture. Tues–Sat 10am–5pm, Sun 2pm–5pm; and the Museum of Art, Walker Art Building, 725-3275, featuring Baskins as well as old masters and Greek and Roman artefacts. Hours as above.

Dipping off Rte 1 onto Rte 27 takes you into **Boothbay Harbor**, a bit touristy perhaps but a good taking off point for quiet, isolated **Monhegan Island** where cars are prohibited, and artists take refuge. This is not an island for wild nights (no bars or discos in town), but if you're in the mood for rocky cliffs, ocean spray, and hiking amid 600 varieties of wildflowers it's worth the 1½ hour ferry ride into Muscongus Bay. Daily from Pier 8, 63 Commercial St, 633-2284, $26 per person RT, resvs recommended.

Getting back onto Route 1 and continuing north you hit **Rockland**, which hosts an annual Maine Lobster Festival the first weekend in August. Generations of artists have found this coast an inspiration; Andrew Wyeth spent much of his life in nearby Cushing, and the **William A. Farnsworth Museum and Library** in **Rockland**, 596-6457, $5, has a large collection of paintings by the Wyeth family on permanent display. Just north of Rockland is **Camden**. Picturesquely situated with a busy little harbour, the town has a Cornish-like charm, despite the tourists, and although the trash-trend emporia fast encroach, there are still genuine and attractive local craft shops. If it's not foggy, the observatory atop **Mount Battie** affords a spectacular view of Camden harbour, the sea and the surrounding hills. It's an enjoyable two-mile hike from the town. Try camping at **Camden Hills**

State Park, 1¼ miles north of town on Rte 1, sites are $13 per night. Reservations are recommended, apply to the Park Bureau in Augusta but arrive between 10am and 2pm and you'll probably get a pitch.

At **Lincolnville**, sample great fish and chips right by the sea, and in **Belfast**, stop at Perry's Nut House, Sears Port Ave, 338-1630, to get 'hugged by a Maine bear'. Sample homemade fudge and candy made in Perry's kitchen. For tourist information contact Rockport, Lincoln, **Camden Chamber of Commerce**, P.O. Box 919M, Camden, Maine 04843, 236-4404.

With a name said to be derived from an old hymn tune, **Bangor** is socially about that exciting. The best time to be in Bangor is during the Bangor Fair, one of the oldest in the country, held annually during the first week in August. The town claims famous lumberjack, Paul Bunyan, as its own and has a statue to prove it. This mythical figure was the subject of many a tall story in timber country, like the one about him digging the Grand Canyon.

Otherwise, by-pass the town and continue on your way to **Bar Harbor** via the coastal route, or else head inland where thousands of lakes make this a popular area for canoeists. **Moosehead Lake**, 40 miles long and 10 miles wide, is the largest.

P.S. Fans of *Murder She Wrote* should note that there is no Cabot Cave in Maine; the TV series is shot in Mendocino, California.

ACADIA NATIONAL PARK/BAR HARBOR The park encompasses a magnificent wild, rocky stretch of coast and its hinterland. The granite hills of Acadia sweep down into the Atlantic where the ocean has carved out numerous inlets, cliffs and caves. At every twist and turn of the roads around the coast a new and spectacular view of the sea becomes visible.

For the best view of all, it is an easy walk or drive to the summit of **Cadillac Mountain** (1530 ft), the park's highest point and the highest place on the Atlantic coast north of Rio. Beneath the 'mountain' lie lakes, cranberry bogs, quiet spruce forests, and the Atlantic itself. Driving the dramatic Loop Road, $5, from the Park Visitor Center takes about 1½–3 hrs (depending on the number of stops you make) and offers incredible scenic views. A stop right on the Loop, and not to be missed, is tea and popovers at Jordan Pond House, 276-3610, (also serves lunch and dinner). The House is an easy drive from Seal or Bar Harbor and accessible by several hiking trails. The Park Visitors Center, off Rte 3 near Hull Cove, is open from 8am–8pm and offers audio-cassette tours.

Bar Harbor is the most popular resort on the **Mount Desert Island** part of Acadia National Park. This was a town of spacious, fashionable summer homes owned by the wealthy, until 1947 when a great fire burnt most of them to the ground. More recently, chi-chi boutiques and quiche luncheon restaurants have invaded, driving prices up. The Bar Harbor Music Festival presents concerts through July and August. The less-frequented **Isle au Haut** is the other half of Acadia; a good place for walking, it can be reached by ferry from Stonington on the southern tip of Deer Isle.

ACCOMMODATION

Bass Cottage in the Field, off Main St, downtown, 288-3705. S–$38 up, D–$69 up, reservations needed, esp. in summer.

Mt Desert Island Youth Hostel, Kennebec St, 288-5587. Summer only (mid-June–Labor Day). $8 AYH, non-AYH $11, adv resv recommended.
YWCA, 23 Mt Desert St, 288-5008. Women only. S–$25, D–$20.
Camping. Within the park there are sites at Black Woods and Seawall, 288-3338. Black Woods can be reached by car, costs $12/night, and reservations are accepted. Seawall can be reached by car; sites are $10/night, on a first-come-first-served basis. Walk-ins at Seawall are $7/night. There are also more expensive private campgrounds near the park.

OF INTEREST

North-East Whale Watch, Municipal Pier, Northeast Harbor, 276-5803, full day research trips leave 8.30am return 5.30pm, provide your own food and drink and help researchers catalogue finback and humpback whales, $30. Resvs recommended. 'We saw four species of whale, an enormous school of porpoise, and about a thousand seals basking in the sun.'

INFORMATION

Army–Navy Surplus Store, 70 Main St, 288-3084. Sells complete camping gear.
Chamber of Commerce, 93 Cottage St, 288-5103. 'Extremely helpful.'
Park Visitors Center, 288-3338, just off Rte 3 at Hulls Cove. Short film about the park shown every hour, and has all the information you'll need.

TRAVEL

Bar Harbor Bicycle Shop, 141 Cottage St, 288-3886. Sells, rents and repairs.
Acadia Bike and Canoe, 48 Cottage St, 288-5483. Sells and rents mountain bikes and canoes.
Private bus tours of Acadia National Park. Call Richard Cough at 288-4728.
Marine Atlantic Ferry to Yarmouth, Nova Scotia, 288-3395. 6-hr crossing, leaves daily at 8am, mid-June–mid-Sept. $54 per car, $44 per adult.
Greyhound Bus runs a limited service to Bar Harbor or Ellsworth, 20 miles away.

THE APPALACHIAN TRAIL About 100 miles north of Bangor is **Baxter State Park**, where **Mount Katahdin** (5267 ft) marks the northern starting point of the Appalachian Trail. This is wild, remote country where moose out-number humans. (Best time to see a moose: early morning/late afternoon, late spring to early summer. Best place: near bogs and ponds, keep yourself unobtrusive.) The park, which can be reached via **Millinocket** or **Greenville**, was a gift from Percival Baxter, one of the state's former governors.

He bought all 201,000 acres and then donated it all to be kept as wilderness. The peak of Katahdin is named in his honour. There are ten campgrounds in the park, only two of which are inaccessible by car. For all information on camping and for detailed area maps call in or write to the **Baxter State Park Headquarters**, 64 Balsam Drive, Millinocket, 04462, phone 723-5140.

Just to the north of Baxter lies the **Allagash Wilderness Waterway**. This is a canoeist's paradise, a 100-mile-long stretch of lakes and rivers preserved in their primitive state to provide white-water and backwoods experience for the modern canoeist.

INFORMATION

Write to the Appalachian Trail Conference, PO Box 807, Harper's Ferry, WV 25425; or the Appalachian Mountain Club, 5 Joy St, Boston, MA 02108.

MASSACHUSETTS

The Bay State is rivalled only by Virginia in the richness of its history. Massachusetts was the colony where the loudest and most open protests were raised against the British prior to 1777. After the initial skirmishes, the war switched to the other colonies, yet Massachusetts contributed the largest number of troops to the war: 20,000 militia, 67,907 regulars in the Continental Army.

Presidents John Adams, John Quincy Adams, John Kennedy and George Bush all came from Massachusetts, as did Daniel Webster; in the field of literature Robert Frost, John Whittier, Emily Dickinson, Louisa May Alcott, Nathaniel Hawthorne, Henry David Thoreau and Ralph Waldo Emerson were either born or came to live here. Just to show that there is a lighter side to the Bay state, Massachusetts is also the birthplace of sewing machines, frozen food and roller skates.

Massachusetts takes its name from the Massachuset Indians who occupied the Bay Territory, including Boston, in the early 17th century. An annual Indian pow-wow is still held at Mashpee in July.

The telephone area code for the eastern part of the State is 617, for mid-Massachusetts and the Cape it's 508, and in the west it's 413.

BOSTON Capital of Massachusetts and, undeniably, of New England, Boston is a proud Yankee city and seaport thick with reminders of its past. Bostonians are fiercely loyal, regarding their city as the hub of New England, and in colonial times of the whole New World. Boston was the spiritual heart of the Revolution, the birthplace of American commerce and industry, and leader of the new nation in the arts and education. These days, the original WASPs (White Anglo Saxon Protestants) have been joined by successive generations of Blacks, Irish, Poles and Italians, and the city has developed a more cosmopolitan touch.

Boston has a cosier feel to it than most major American cities, and also something of a European flavour. It's compact and therefore a great place to walk (or jog). Within a comparatively small area you can stroll through 18th century cobbled streets, or on the Common where the colonists grazed their cattle, down by the harbour or river, or around such fine examples of modern architecture as in the Back Bay or the impressive Government Center.

For all its historical associations, Boston is a city of youth and vitality and many of the city's businesses and amenities cater to the young and diverse population. In addition to prestigious Harvard and MIT, there are 70 accredited colleges in Greater Boston, enrolling over a quarter of a million students.

Boston acquired its nickname, 'the Athens of America', by the 19th century and continues to earn it as a centre for music, literature and the arts. At any time it is possible to see good theatre, modern dance, and hear classical, jazz, folk or new wave music. Sport too has its place. In summer, when the Boston Red Sox baseball team is battling it out in the race for the

American League title, the only real place to be is at Fenway Park, eating hot dogs and guzzling coke, but never on any account cheering for the opposition. In winter the mania transfers itself to basketball with the Celtics, football with the New England Patriots, and to ice hockey with the Boston Bruins.

One of the nation's finest examples of creative urban renewal is Faneuil Hall Marketplace. Its revitalization became Boston's bicentennial gift to itself and to everyone. Twenty years ago historic Faneuil Hall stood as a rundown building on the blighted waterfront. The Rouse Company, well known for its many impressive urban revitalization projects, transformed it into a permanent festival, with over 150 shops, boutiques, and food stalls and 23 restaurants. Over 15 million visit the complex each year, and you'll feel sure that they all chose the same day you did.

An estimated 3 million spectators turned up when Boston hosted the Grand Regatta Columbus '92 Quincentenary to commemorate the 500th anniversary of the discovery of America. A fleet of tall ships visited Boston harbour for a week in July after the parade around New York harbour on July 4th weekend.

The natural centre for journeys around Massachusetts, Boston is particularly convenient for visits to nearby Cambridge, Concord, Lexington, Saugus, Salem and Gloucester.

The telephone area code for Boston and Cambridge is 617.

ACCOMMODATION

Accommodation in Boston is generally expensive, especially the hotels. We list a few 'cheaper' hotels first, but suggest you consider the guest houses and hostels mentioned if you want to keep your costs down to what it would be in most other cities. The Information Center at the Tremont St side of the Boston Common provides a list of low-cost accommodation.

Beacon Inn, (two locations) 1087 or 1750 Beacon St, Brookline, 566-0088, on Green Line C Car. S–$46, D–$52–$82 depending on size of room. Fans, b/w TV. Both 100-year-old Victorian brownstones. Reservations suggested. Small and in a quiet neighbourhood.

Beech Tree Inn, 83 Longwood Ave, Brookline 277-1620, near MBTA Beacon St stop, 12 mins from downtown. S–$49–$60 (dep. on shared or private bath), D–$53–$58, T-$64. All prices include tax and continental breakfast. 'Excellent.'

Boston International Youth Hostel, 12 Hemenway St, 536-9455, in Back Bay. Opens 7am–midnight (dorms closed 11am–2pm). Sun–Thur midnight curfew; Fri, Sat 2am. $14 AYH; non-members can join for $18. Sheet deposit $2. 'Superb kitchen facilities. Very friendly staff.' 'Excellent hostel, launderette, clean, good value, maximum stay 3 nights (we stayed for 4), take subway to "Hynes Convention Center" then 2 blocks.' 'Good for meeting people. Go early in the morning to reserve a bed.'

Greater Boston YMCA, 316 Huntington Ave, 536-7800. S–$36, D–$48, plus $5 returnable key deposit; includes breakfast. Mixed reviews. 'Clean, friendly, safe.' 'Unpleasant clientele, be careful, seems to have a bad atmosphere.'

International Fellowship House, 386 Marlborough St, 247-7248. S–$20 for dorm rm. $2 sheets and $3 breakfast. $5 dinner available. 'Full of friendly, foreign students.'

Susse Chalet Motor Lodges and Inns locations in nearby Dorchester, Braintree, Cambridge and Newton. Cambridge prices range from S–$65, D–$55–$76. Phone (800) 258-1980 for reservations, directions.

Towne House Motor Inn, 100 N Beacon in Watertown, 926-2200. D–$70.

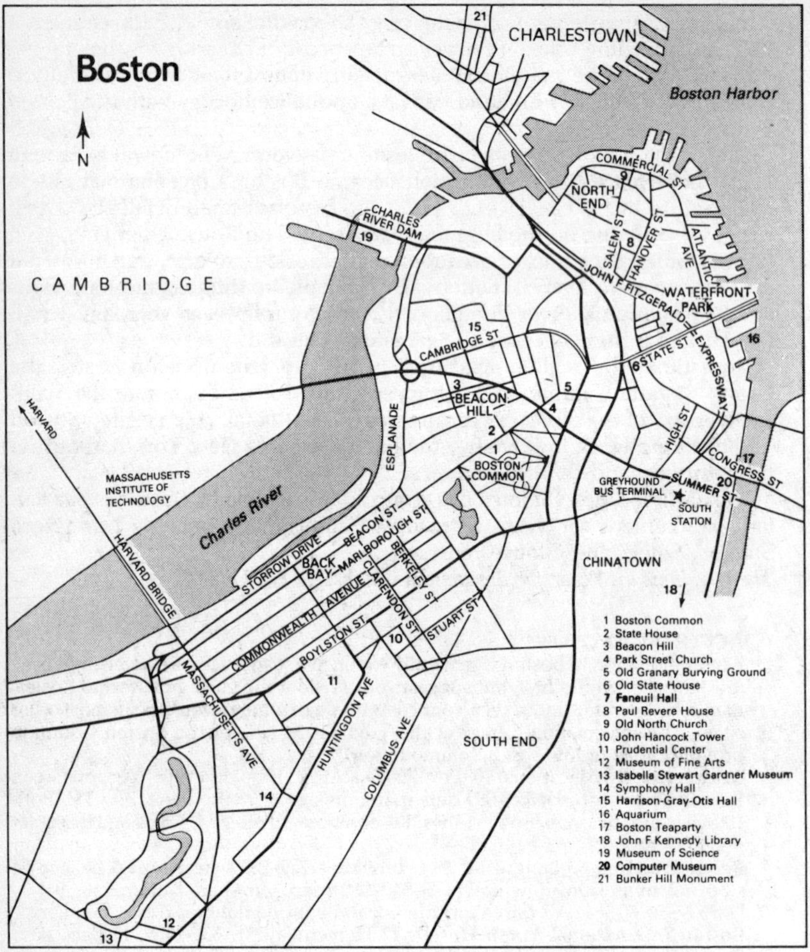

YWCA, Berkeley Residence Club, 40 Berkeley St, 482-8850. Women only, 2-week maximum stay. S–$29, D–$42 plus $2 temporary membership. 'Safe and clean.'

HOUSING INFORMATION

Boston's Preferred Properties Inc, 54 Westland Ave, 859-3838. Studios, apts for rent. Prices start at $425/month. 'Well recommended.' 'Very helpful.'

Meegan Services, 569-3800, will help you find accommodation (has long lists of hotels, guest houses, etc). Work 8am–11.30pm. Free.

Roommate Connection Referral Agency, in Boston, Brookline and Cambridge, 262-4679 for 24-hr info line. 'Shared accommodation, short/long term Boston & suburbs. $65 fee, housing $400–$500/month depending on location. Private homes or apartments.

Townhouse Realty Co, 272 Newbury St, 267-1344. 'Friendly guys. Rent one-room studio apts, about $150/week.

FOOD

Bull & Finch, 84 Beacon St, 227-9605, by the Public Garden. An English pub; serves burgers, sandwiches, etc at moderate prices. Only the exterior has anything to do with *Cheers* (the series was filmed in LA), but at least you can imagine that Sam or Rebecca are going to walk in the door.

Country Life, 112 Broad St. 350-8625 'Excellent veggie restaurant. Eat as much as you want, $7.'

Durgin Park, 390 Faneuil Hall in Quincy Market, 227-2038. Known for its good food, great prices, long bar, and wisecracking waitresses: 'They throw food in front of you, spill water on your head and insult you. Hilarious. An excellent act.' An *act*? Family-style eating. Ribs, seafood; famous for its prime rib. Go for lunch for the best buys. Great Chowder. Open 7 days a week, 11.30am–10pm.

Legal Seafood, at Park Plaza Hotel, 35 Columbus, 426-5526, and various locations in the Boston area; large and well-known for excellent seafood; prices are moderate.

No-Name Restaurant, 15½ Fish Pier, near southeast end of Northern Ave, 338-7539. In old warehouse. Fish meals at $5 and up; expect queues. 'Vibrant atmosphere.' 'Hard to find; a bit of a walk, but the best seafood for the price in Boston.' 'A shouting match and a shoveling session, but great.'

Pizza Pad, 540 Commonwealth Ave, Kenmore Sq, 720-0692. $7.50 and up. 'Cheap and cheerful.'

Quincy Market has plenty of foodstalls of great variety: Chinese, Italian, Greek, health foods, etc.

Warburton's Bakery and Cafe, Government Center (and other locations). 'Great muffins; politicians eat here for breakfast.' Also good sausage rolls and pasties.

OF INTEREST

The Freedom Trail is a walking tour through the heart of old Boston, beginning in the Boston Common at the Visitors Center. On it you can visit nearly all Boston's associations with the American Revolution. The Trail is clearly marked by a path of red bricks set in the sidewalk; few visitors to Boston escape it. The Trail tends to be a tad dull, and unless you have a passionate interest in American revolutionary history, forget it. Old Town Trolley shuttle bus, $14, 269-7010, goes everywhere of historical note; you get on and off and on again when you like—tickets from Boston Common Visitors Center, 536-4100. National Park Service tours leave from Visitors Center at 15 State St, lasts 1½ hrs. From 10am–4pm—Old South Meeting House, Old State House, Paul Revere's house, and Old North Church.

Boston Common. Boston is the only large American city still to have its common. The Common and Public Gardens are agreeable places for a leisurely stroll, but not at night.

State House, with its large gold dome, is the seat of the Massachusetts State Government. Charles Bulfinch, greatest American architect of the late 18th century designed the central part of the building. Free guided tours weekdays 10am–4pm. Enter on Beacon St, 727-3676.

Beacon Hill, especially Louisburg Square, is Boston's old residential section to which every visitor must make a pilgrimage. Louisa May Alcott, William Dean Howels, the Brahmin Literary Set and many other famous Bostonians lived here.

Park St Church, Brimstone corner. Built 1809. Scene of William Lloyd Garrison's first anti-slavery address, also where *America* was first sung, in 1832. Open daily in summer 9am–4pm, 523-3383.

Old Granary Burying Ground, in the location of a 17th century granary, is an interesting graveyard with many 18th century heroes including Paul Revere, Sam Adams and John Hancock. A grave marked 'Mary Goose' is supposedly the final resting place of Mother Goose.

Old South Meeting House at School and Washington, built 1729, was where Samuel Adams gave the signal that launched the Boston Tea Party in 1773. Has interesting exhibit of Phyllis Wheatley, a former slave from Senegal, who was the first published black poet (in 1765).

Old State House, corner of Washington and State Sts. Built 1713 as the seat of British colonial government; the *Declaration of Independence* was read from the East Balcony in 1776. Has an important display of Americana. Open daily 9.30am–5pm; recently renovated.

Faneuil Hall, Merchants Row, Faneuil Hall Sq, 242-5642. Built in 1742 and given to the city of Boston by Peter Faneuil. Known as the 'Cradle of Liberty' the hall was the scene of mass meetings during the pre-revolutionary period. Open daily 9am–5pm. And what is that up there? A bird, a plane, superman? No, it's a weathervane in the form of a grasshopper that sits atop Faneuil Hall, placed there at the request of Peter Faneuil himself. 'Grasshopper' was the symbol of the Boston port and during the War of 1812, was the password used to weed out spies: if you couldn't identify it as the symbol of Boston, you were in trouble. You'll see grasshoppers everywhere here—on every shopping bag and many restaurant menus—a handy reminder in case anyone takes you for a spy.

Faneuil Hall Marketplace includes a floor of Faneuil Hall and the adjacent Quincy Market. The whole is a revitalized complex of eating places, small shops and produce stands. Open Mon–Sat 10am–9pm, Sun noon–6pm (restaurants open later).

Paul Revere House, in the North End on the Freedom Trail. Paul Revere lived here from 1770 to 1780 and set out from here on the famous ride. Probably the oldest wooden structure in Boston; built 1670s. Open daily in summer 9.30am–5.30pm, in winter 10am–4pm; $2.00, 523-2330.

Old North Church, Salem St, in the north end, near the end of the Freedom Trail. Built 1723, gave Revere the signal to ride. 'Perhaps the most elegant and historic church in the USA.'

Back Bay, southwest of the common is a lively, beautiful 19th century development project built on land reclaimed from the Charles River. In this area is **Trinity Church**, Copley Square, 536-0944. Open daily 8am–6pm. Designed in 1877 by HH Richardson, this church is French Romanesque style on the outside. Inside its highly decorated walls and flamboyant mosaics give it more the feel and look of Greek Orthodox. The IM Pei designed **John Hancock Tower** stands right behind the church. This is the tallest building in New England and there is an observatory on the 60th floor from which there are excellent views of the surrounding city. Open 9am–10pm Mon–Sat, 10am–10pm Sun; $3. 'A must. Sets you up for the whole city.' 'There are two interesting audio-visual presentations in the observatory on the city and its history.' There is one small problem with the building, however, hundreds of the 10,344 panes of tempered glass have fallen out onto the street below. Pei has had to replace them all, costing millions of dollars. The problem has never been solved but fortunately up to now no one has been hurt.

Prudential Center, 236-3318, or The 'Pru' as it is known locally, was a daring, $150 million urban renewal project of the 1960s, with apartments, offices, and countless shops. Boston mayor, Raymond L Flynn, jumped police lines to help evacuate office workers in Jan 1986, when a fire broke out in the building. Flynn, aka 'Raybo,' 'Captain Marvel' and 'The Human 911', has developed a penchant for battling pit bull terriers and rushing into burning buildings—no doubt a relief after all those boring administrative duties. On the 50th floor is an observatory, **SkyWalk**, which while it has been overshadowed by the Hancock Tower, has the only 360 degree viewing deck. Skywalk is open Mon–Sat, 10am–10pm, Sun noon–10pm; $2.75, $1.75 w/student ID. Two floors up is the 'Top of The Hub', popular at night, where you can have a drink while enjoying a great view of the area.

Christian Science Center, 175 Huntington Ave, 450-2000, world headquarters of the Christian Science religion, is a conglomerate of stunning buildings including the Mother Church; the Publishing Society, which produces among other literature the highly respected *Christian Science Monitor*; and the **Mapparium**, a beautiful 40-foot stained glass, walk-thru globe with unusual acoustics. 'You walk *into* the world! Tremendous visual and sensory delight.' Call for info on free guided tours. Open 9.30am–4pm.

Museum of Fine Arts, 465 Huntington Ave, 276-9300. One of the finest art collections in the US, with outstanding Asiatic and 'marvellous Egyptian' sections. Also some fine American watercolours, wonderful Gaugins and Degas and the largest collection of Monets outside of France. Entire museum open Tues, Sat, Sun 10am–4.45pm, Wed–Fri 10am–9.45pm; West Wing only open Thurs–Fri, 5pm–9.45pm. $7, $6 with student ID; West Wing only, $5, free Wed 4pm–9.45pm. 'Well worth the money; allow at least a whole day.'

Isabella Stewart Gardner Museum, 280 Fenway, 566-1401. Italianate villa built by the eccentric Mrs Gardner to house her art collection in 1903. It lost many fine works in a 1989 robbery but still a lot to see, including the house itself. Open Tue–Sat, 11am–5pm, $6, $3 with student ID. 'Excellent.'

On the waterfront

New England Aquarium, Central Wharf, off Atlantic Ave, 973-5200. World's largest collection of sharks and 2000 other specimens in a 187,000 gallon tank. Dolphin and sea lion shows daily. 'Excellent! Could spend the whole day there.' Open Mon–Fri 9am–5pm, Thur till 8pm, Sat and Sun, 9am–6pm; $7.50. 'One dollar less after 4pm but you miss all the shows.'

Boston Teaparty Ship & Museum, Congress St Bridge, 338-1773. *Beaver II*, replica of ship whose dumped cargo brewed rebellion in 1773. Ship and museum open daily 9am–dusk. $5. 'A rip-off. Makes you feel proud to be British.'

John F Kennedy Library and Museum, Columbia Point, overlooking harbour, 929-4523. Another IM Pei building it houses momentoes and memorials to not only JFK but also his brother Robert. Open daily 9am–5pm; $5. Take T to U Mass then take free shuttle bus (runs every 20 mins).

Museum of Science, on the Charles River Dam in Science Park, 723-2500. The $10 million large-screen theatre is worth a visit—so big it can project a lifesize image of a whale. 'Could spend 2 days here and still not see it all.' Open daily 9am–5pm, Fri till 9pm; combination tickets to theatre, planetarium and museum vary from $10–$14, students $4.50.

Computer Museum, Museum Wharf, 300 Congress St, 423-6758 (call even if you don't need info—the museum's hilarious computer answers the phone). The world's first computer museum was opened in 1984, it is still the only one. Open Tue–Sun 10am–6pm; $7, $5 with student ID; Sun 3pm–5pm, half-price. 'Hands-on.' 'Hats off.'

USS Constitution, a frigate from the war of 1812, preserved in Charleston Navy Yard, 242-0543. Open to the public 9.30am–3.50pm, free. Interesting tours conducted by members of Navy. Nearby is the **Bunker Hill Monument** commemorating the first set battle of the Revolution. The battle was actually fought on a different hill, but all the good stuff is here; **Bunker Hill Pavilion**, 241-7575; $3, $2 with student ID with an audio-visual programme, *The Whites of Their Eyes*, giving the background to the battle with dramatic effects (every ½ hour from 9.30am–5pm).

Boston Harbour Cruises, leaving from Long Wharf, 277-4320. 1½ hrs around the Boston Harbour, $8; $5 for a cruise to the *USS Constitution* and St. George's Island; sunset cruises, 1½ hrs, $8. Take a sweatshirt.

Bay State Cruise Co (723 7800) runs **ferries** to Boston Harbor Islands State Park, 30 islands with colorful names such as Grape, Bumpkin, and Gallops, including Little Brewster, site of the Boston Light, the oldest continuous aid to navigation in the US. Free concerts on Georges Island in the summer.

Whale-watching trips, 973-5200, organised by the Aquarium April–Oct, $23, $18.50 students. Guaranteed to see at least one whale or you get a 'rain check'.

ENTERTAINMENT

Read *Boston Phoenix* or check the Thursday edition of the *Boston Globe* for '*Calendar*' section. The **Bostix** booth in Faneuil Hall has half-price tickets on day of performance and lots of other tickets and information.

Look for free jazz concerts in Copley Square, lunchtimes, in summer.

Symphony Hall, 301 Massachusetts Ave, 266-1492. Discount available Fri 9am and Sat 5pm for evening performances in the fall/winter. Home of the Boston Symphony and the popular 'Pops'. During the first week in July, the 'Pops', which were for many years led by John Williams, of movie music fame, play at the **Hatch Memorial Shell** by the Charles River. The outdoor concerts are all free, so get there early if you want to get good places. The concerts begin at 8pm. 'Take a picnic, lots of fun'. All kinds of free events such as jazz concerts at Hatch Shell most summer evenings.
Sevens, 77 Charles St, 523-9074, 'Authentic British pub atmosphere; serves both local and imported beer. Friendly.' Most expensive item on the menu is $4.25!
Axis, 13 Lansdowne St, near Fenway Park, 262-2437. Punk, new wave, great place for dancing, dress down. Cover varies $5–$20 with the band, often British. Videos; gay Sun. Closed Mon.
Next door to Axis is **Avalon Club**, 15 Lansdowne St, 262-2424. Boston's most popular dance club; Top-40/progressive format. Open Wed–Sun, gay Sun, $5.
Top of the Hub, 800 Boylston St, 536-1775. Bar-drinking and dancing atop Prudential Center with Boston at your feet. You can get away with paying less than $4.
Tune into WGBH, the city's non-commercial TV channel and reputed to be one of the best in America.
Closest beach is Revere. 'Scruffy but only 75¢ on the Blue Line.'

SPORT
Despite its cultural pretentions Boston loves sport and the teams inspire devotion in the city. In the summer there are the **Boston Red Sox**, who play at **Fenway Park**, 267-8661, one of the most beautiful ball parks in the States. The fall and winter see the **New England Patriots** play American football at **Foxborough**, (800) 543-1776, an easy train ride from South Station. 'A fantastic day out,' The **Boston Garden** is the home of both the **Celtics** for basketball, 523-3030, and the **Bruins**, 227-3200, for ice-hockey.

SHOPPING
Filene's Automatic Bargain Basement, 426 Washington St. A Boston institution. Amazing bargains to be had—everything from designer clothes to luggage.
The **Boyleston Street** area in Back Bay, is good for books, records and lively in the evenings.

INFORMATION
National Park Service Visitor Center, 15 State St, 242-5642, centrally located. Has 8-min slide show of Freedom Trail, lots of books, pamphlets and brochures on Boston and surrounding areas, very helpful Park Service guides. Free guided tours of the trail in the summer. Daily 9am–5pm.
The Greater Boston Convention and Visitors Bureau runs two info centers: **Boston Common Visitors Center**, the Common on Tremont St, 536-4100; and **Greater Boston Convention and Tourist Bureau**, west side of Prudential Plaza, 536-4100. Both provide an abundance of free brochures on places to go and things to do, as well as 'T' guides and bus info. For $2.95 you can purchase the *Official Guidebook to Boston*, 100-plus pages with numerous maps of city.
Massachusetts Office of Travel and Tourism, 100 Cambridge St, 13th floor, 727-3201.

TRAVEL
Public transport, buses and subways, is operated by the Massachusetts Bay Transit Authority (MBTA). Flat fare subway-85¢, bus-60¢, no transfers. The '**Boston Passport**' allows unlimited travel on bus, trolley and subway lines and is available for 3 days ($9) or 7 days ($18). Note that bus and subway services shut down around 12.30am, check schedules to avoid strandings. For information phone 722-3200.

The **subway**, known as the 'T' (hence T-stations) comprises four intersecting lines: the Blue, Green, Orange and Red. Maps are posted in stations, or you can pick up a free colour-coded map at any station or visitors centre. 'A joy after the NYC subway.'

Logan Airport is across the bay from downtown: take the Blue Line subway to Airport station from where there's a linking bus to the terminals. You can take the water shuttle from Logan to Rowe's Wharf for $8. Leaves about every 15 mins 6am–8pm, except Sat. Call (800) 235-6426 for details.

Amtrak trains depart from South Station (Red Line, main station) and Back Bay Station (Green Line, Copley; Orange line, Back Bay) For resv and sched info phone (800) USA-RAIL. MBTA commuter trains, servicing the Boston region, are also run by Amtrak and depart South Station and North Station (Green and Orange lines); for info call 227-5070.

Bonanza Bus Lines, Back Bay Railway Station, 145 Dartmouth Street at Copley Square, 720-4110, buses to Portsmouth, Newport, etc.

Plymouth and Brockton Street Railway Co. (a bus service) operates from the Greyhound terminal, 773-9400, to Plymouth, Hyannis and Provincetown.

Greyhound, at South Station, ticket info, 423-5810. Red Line.

Peter Pan Bus Line, 555 Atlantic Ave, near South Station (on the Red Line), 426-7838, serves New England except Maine, Vermont and Rhode Island.

Green Tortoise, (800) 227-4766. Camper bus touring company which sponsors interesting, economical 1–4 week trips all over North America.

American Auto Transporters, Inc, 120 Jackson St, Canton, Mass, about 19 miles south of Boston, 821-4660. Minimum age: 21. Must have good driving record.

CAMBRIDGE The most famous of the Boston metropolitan area's universities, MIT and Harvard, are in Cambridge. The lifestyle of the concentration of students here sets the pace for both sides of the Charles River, and Harvard Square is where it all happens. You will be amazed at the diversity of life, entertainment and action to be found in such a small area. On Mt Auburn St at Club 47, Joan Baez began mesmerizing the world. From 1958–1968 Club 47 was host to the folk revolution (Bob Dylan, Maria Muldaur, Jim Kweskin Jug Band, Judy Collins, etc.) The huge green bird atop the nearby Harvard Lampoon building is the petrified ship of fools, courtesy of the creators of *Animal House*. For something completely different, stroll through Harvard Yard or visit one of the historic houses.

You can take the 'T' to Harvard Square from Boston, but it's better to walk across Harvard Bridge, taking in the cityscapes, and the sailors, windsurfers and rowers on the river below.

ACCOMMODATION

Cambridge Family YMCA, 820 Massachusetts Ave, Central Sq, 661-9622. S–$32, Men only, no private baths, no doubles. 'Lots of life here.' 'Tatty rooms.'

Cambridge YWCA, 7 Temple St, Center Sq, 491-6050. Women only. Members $30 per night; non-members $35; all shared baths. 'Friendly, and good location.'

The Irving House, 24 Irving Street, 547-4600. S–from $36; D–$50–$80, includes continental breakfast. 'Quite small rooms but clean and quiet.'
Reservations required.

FOOD

Pick up the free *Square Deal* newspaper for lots of discounts and special offers at the local eateries.

Acropolis, 1680 Mass Ave, 492-0900. 'Good, inexpensive, Greek.'

Café of India, 52A Brattle St, Harvard Sq, 661-0683. Good, hearty indian food. Lunch $4–$6.50, dinner $8–$15.

Elsie's, 71 Mt Auburn St, 354-8781. A real Harvard institution. Superb, cheap sandwiches. Open 7am to 8pm.
Hong Kong, 1236 Mass Ave, 864-5311. Chinese restaurant, closed Mon. 'Excellent drinking establishment (lounge upstairs). A Harvard/Tufts hangout.'
Pizzeria Uno, 22 Harvard Sq, 497-1530. 'Lively Italian restaurant. Good value.'
Upstairs at the Pudding, 10 Holyoke St, 864-1933. Fixed price, $42 covers gourmet four course meal for big-eaters and big-spenders; otherwise, a la carte menu available. Above the famous 'Hasty Pudding,' Harvard's oldest club, which boasts such alumni as John Quincy Adams, Teddy Roosevelt, FDR and JFK.

OF INTEREST
Harvard University, founded 1636, is the oldest university in North America. Massachusetts Hall (1720) is the oldest building still standing. The **Harvard University Visitors Information Center** is at 1350 Massachusetts Ave, 495-1573 (in the Holyoke Center). Daily conducted tours; free. Walk from Harvard Square up Brattle St past **Radcliffe**, previously a women's college, now fully merged with Harvard, to **Longfellow's house**, 876-4491, where the poet lived between 1837 and 1882. The house is open to the public and is furnished with Longfellow's furniture and books. In earlier times George Washington used this house as his HQ. Open daily 10am–4.30pm; $2. Also in the campus area is the **Fogg Art Museum**, Quincy and Broadway, 495-9400. Has the largest collection of Ingres outside of France. Tues–Sun 10am–5pm, $4, $2 student. **Le Corbusier's Carpenter Center of the Visual Arts** and **Houghton Library** (housing the Keats collection), 495-3251, are opposite **Memorial Church**; the **Harvard Museums of Natural History**, contained in one building with entrances at 11 Divinity and 26 Oxford St include: **Peabody Museum of Archeology and Ethnology**, **Museum of Comparative Zoology**, **Botanical Museum and Mineralogical and Geological Museum**. 'It takes all day to see most of it.' 'There's a spectacular collection of glass flowers by Theopold and Rudolph Blaschka in the Botanical Museum. The **Fogg Art Museum** is especially good on things Chinese, but does not open on weekends during the summer.' For information on all Harvard museums call 495-1910. All museums (except Fogg) open Mon–Sat 9am–4.30pm, Sun 1pm–4.30pm; students $2, free Sat 9am–11am.
Old Burying Ground, corner of Church and Garden. Graves go back to 1635 and many Revolutionary War heroes and several Harvard presidents are buried here.
Mt Auburn Cemetery on Mt Auburn St, contains the graves of Longfellow, James Lowell, Oliver Wendell Holmes and Mary Baker Eddy, founder of Christian Science. Both a cemetery and a park, with ponds, hills, footpaths, arboretum. 'Quiet relaxing place, great for birdwatching in spring.'
MIT tours, 253-4795, include a look at the lovely chapel designed by Eero Saarinen. Student conducted tours Mon–Fri begin at 10am and 2pm at the information centre, 77 Massachusetts Ave. 'It's probably just as worthwhile to get a map and wander around yourself.'
Cambridge Discovery Tours, begin at info booth in centre of Harvard Sq, 497-1630, general intro to historic sites of Cambridge and Harvard Yard, $10 for coach tour, $5 for walking tour, or $1 for self-guided tour map.
Book Stores. It's not surprising, perhaps, that America's academic capital plays host to one of the world's greatest collections of book stores. If you can't find a title within the 25–30 shops clustered in and around Harvard Square, chances are it's not been published. A few of the more intriguing shops:
Asian Books, 12 Arroe St, 354-0005, one of the largest collections of Asian and Islamic literature.
Grolier Bookshop, 6 Plympton St, 547-4648, oldest continuously operating poetry bookshop in US, more than 9000 titles from Dickinson to Ginsberg, hosts readings and prizes.
Harvard Co-op, 1400 Mass Ave, 499-2000, books, posters, records, and more.
Revolution Books, 38 John F Kennedy St, 492-5443, anything you could want by Marx, Lenin, Stalin, Mao, etc.

Words Worth, 30 Brattle St, 354-5201, over 50,000 titles in 110 categories.

ENTERTAINMENT

Watch *Boston Phoenix* for details of concerts and lectures. Also, *The Harvard Gazette, Crimson* and *Independent* are good, though the latter is not published in summer. The active music scene is closely tied to Harvard and MIT; summer is therefore quieter.

Boathouse, 56 JFK St off Harvard Sq, 491-6476. 'Best Cambridge bar.'
TT The Bear's Place, 10 Brookline St, Central Square, 492-0082, hard rock, beer.
Ryles, 212 Hampshire St, Inman Sq, 876-9330, $5 cover. Not cheap, but good jazz.

CONCORD Near Concord's old North Bridge on 19 April 1775, local farmers took aim at advancing British redcoats and fired the 'shot heard round the world'. The British detachment successfully confiscated the rebels' ammunition dump in the village, but suffered 272 casualties before returning to Boston. The bridge is part of the **Minuteman National Historic Park**, 369-6993; park rangers give excellent historical talks here on request. Battle re-enactments are staged throughout Concord and Lexington on Patriot's Day (closest Monday to April 19), and a special 'Colonial weekend' in early October includes militia muster, firing drills, colonial music, hay rides and food.

Concord is also the home of the literary transcendentalist movement. Interestingly, all of the best-known transcendentalists, Ralph Waldo Emerson, Henry David Thoreau, Nathanial Hawthorne, Amos Bronson Alcott and his daughter, Louisa May, at one point lived within blocks of each other in this tiny, pristine town. Also in town is Sleepy Hollow Cemetery, where some of them have been laid to rest. Not far away is Thoreau's Walden Pond.

The telephone area code for Concord is 508.

ACCOMMODATION

Accommodation here is rather expensive. The best bet may be to contact **Bed and Breakfast in Minuteman Country**, PO Box 665, Cambridge, Mass 02140, (617) 576-2112. They maintain a list of about 35 bed & breakfast homes in the Concord and Lexington area, S-$50-$90, D-$65-$95. All include at least continental breakfast.

FOOD

Different Drummer, 86 Thoreau St, 369-8700, 1 block from town centre. Open Mon-Sun for lunch ($5-$8), Tues-Sun for dinner ($9-$16).
Walden Station, 24 Walden St, 371-2233, in town centre, lunch from $7, dinner from $10.

OF INTEREST

Thoreau Lyceum, 156 Belknap St, 369-5912. The Lyceum includes a research library and collection of memorabilia, as well as a furnished replica of the writer's house at Walden. Open Mon-Sat 10am-5pm, Sun 2pm-5pm. $2, $1.50 for students.

INFORMATION/TRAVEL

Concord Chamber of Commerce Information Center, call 369-3120, or write One-half Main St, Concord, Mass 01742.
MBTA Station, (800) 392-6099. 20 miles north of Boston, Concord is served by commuter trains from North Station.

LEXINGTON Lexington shares with Concord the distinction of being the site of the first skirmish in the American Revolution, though when Paul Revere galloped through this 'Birthplace of American Liberty', it was not the depressing and urbanised satellite of Boston that it is today.
The telephone area code for Lexington is 617.

ACCOMMODATION

See Concord Accommodation section for Bed and Breakfast information.
Battle Green Motor Inn, 1720 Massachusetts Ave, 862-6100, is the cheapest hotel in town. S-$56-$59, D-$64.

OF INTEREST

Lexington Green, where it all happened two centuries ago (and is re-enacted every year on Patriot's Day, the Monday closest to 19 April). The Green is lined with lovely colonial houses; on the east side, facing the road by which the British approached, is the famous **Minuteman Statue**. Over in the southwest corner of the green is the Revolutionary Monument erected in 1799 to commemorate the 8 minutemen killed here.
Near the Green is **Buckman Tavern**, the oldest of the local hostelries and gathering place for the local minutemen on drill nights.
Hancock-Clarke House, 36 Hancock Street, 861-0928, is where Sam Adams and John Hancock were staying when Paul Revere came galloping by to warn them. Open mid-April to Oct, Mon-Sat 10am-5pm, Sun 1pm-5pm; $2.50 ($5 combo ticket gets you into Buckman and Monroe taverns nearby, otherwise $2.50 for each building).
Monroe Tavern, 1332 Mass Ave, was headquarters and hospital for British troops. 862-1703. Fri-Sun 10am-5pm.

INFORMATION

Chamber of Commerce Information Center, 862-1450, near Buckman Tavern at 1875 Massachusetts Ave, has details and literature. In summer guides give lectures on the Green.

THE NORTH SHORE Just north of Boston on Hwy 1 is **Saugus**, founded in 1646 and the birthplace of the American iron industry. The restored ironworks with turning waterwheels, massive hammers and wheezing bellows clanks away at **Saugus Iron Works National Historical Site**, (617) 233-0050. Open daily 9am-5pm all year, guided tours Apr-Oct; free.

Beyond Saugus on Hwy 1 lies **Salem**. In 1692 at the **Witch House**, 310½ Essex St, 744-0180, was the home of the famous witch trials in which Puritan judges sent 19 suspected witches to the gallows and ordered a man to be crushed to death under millstones. The whole horrific turn of events was used by Arthur Miller in his play *The Crucible*, as a metaphor for the 1950's McCarthy communist 'trials'. The **Salem Witch Museum**, 19½ Washington Sq North, 744-1692, has an audio-visual programme with life-sized dioramas which tell the story of the witchcraft hysteria. Open daily 10am-7pm in July and August; till 5pm the rest of the year; $4. For a slightly more sensational rendition of history, visit the **Witch Dungeon**, 16 Lynde St, 744-9812. A witch trial is re-enacted for the audience's edification. Afterwards, visitors tour the horrific lower dungeons. Open daily 10am-5pm; $4. 'A rip-off. Lasts about 15 minutes and not very realistic.'

Nathaniel Hawthorne worked at the **Old Customs House**, and the **House of Seven Gables**, 54 Turner St, 744-0991, made famous in his novel still stands, complete with secret stairways and hidden compartments. Open daily, in July and August; 9.30am–5.30pm; 10am–4.30pm $6.50.

A prominent port in colonial days, Salem is a veritable museum of American architecture of the 17–19th centuries. Chestnut St, considered the most beautiful street in town, is lined with the lovely homes of Salem Clipper captains and owners. The **Pioneer Village** off West Ave in Forest River Park just outside Salem historic district, 745-0525, shows typical homes of the Puritan community, *circa* 1630.

On **Cape Ann**, about 30 miles north of Boston, **Gloucester** was once a major fishing centre. This oldest of American seaports retains its salty atmosphere as a summer resort. Four miles north of Gloucester, off Rte 127A, is the typical fishing village of **Rockport**, now an artist colony and full of arty-crafty stores. 'Great for browsing and getting broke.'

On your way north from here to New Hampshire and Maine, there's the small town of **Newburyport**, a lovely old port town, which has 'the most beautiful "Y" in the USA' in a restored colonial house at 13 Market St. This YWCA has one small problem, you can't stay for less than six weeks. $55 per week, women only, 465-0981.

'While you're here, go whale watching; from Hilton's Fishing Dock, 462-8381. $23 for whole day; money goes to finance research.'

The telephone area code for Salem and the North Shore is 508.

PLYMOUTH Plymouth Rock marks the spot where the Pilgrims landed on 26 December 1620, established the first English colony north of Virginia and celebrated the first Thanksgiving Day the following fall. A few 17th-century houses still stand, and on Leyden St markers indicate where the very first houses stood. The Pilgrims who succumbed to the initial bitter winter are buried on Cole's Hill. Moored by the Rock is ***Mayflower II***, a full-size replica of the original. 'Worth a quick visit, but it's really for Americans.'

The telephone area code for Plymouth is 508.

ACCOMMODATION

Guest houses are the cheapest places to stay here, but they are more coveted and more expensive every year. Try looking in the area behind the Tourist Information Center.

Blue Anchor Motel, 7 Lincoln St, 746-9551. Rooms $50–$65.

Camping: Indianhead Campground, 1929 State Rd, 12 miles south of Plymouth, 888-3688. Tough it out with a laundromat, showers, groceries, fishing and swimming and miniature golf, boat rentals, amusement arcade. Tent sites $20 for 2 people, $4 each addtl person.

Plymouth Rock KOA Kampground, Middleboro, 15 miles from Plymouth, 947-6435. 2 laundromats, showers, pool, game room, food store. $19 for two in a no-hook-up tent, $29 for a cabin. 'Friendly; great place.'

FOOD

There are many reasonably priced sub shops and good greasy spoons in Plymouth. Generally, the farther away from the water, the cheaper.

Cap'n Harry's Deli & Sandwich Shop, 25 Water St, 747-5699. Sandwiches $3.50–$5. 9am–8pm.

Mug & Muffin Restaurant, 22 Main St, 746-9741. Breakfast special $2.49. Open 6.30am–4pm daily.

OF INTEREST

Plymouth Rock, on the harbour, supposedly the first stepping stone of the pilgrims in Plymouth. Good for a chuckle, but don't make a special trip for it.

Mayflower II, 746-1622. The replica of the original, built in England and sailed to America in 1957. Admission $5.75 (but see below).

Plimouth Plantation. Rte 3 & Warren Ave, 746-1622. Replica of original settlement, 3 miles south of town square. Open daily, 9am–5pm. It's cheaper if you visit *Mayflower II* and Plimouth Plantation with a combined ticket ($18.50). Both are staffed by American students dressed as Pilgrims and speaking with 'English accents', pretending they are still in the 17th century. 'Less pro-American bias than elsewhere on the East Coast. Characters very knowledgeable.'

Cranberry World Visitor Center, Water St near *Mayflower II*, 747-2350. Run by the Ocean Spray Company, makers of cranberry drinks. Open daily 9.30am–5pm; free. 'Nice facility and tour.' 'More than you ever wanted to know about cranberries.' Free samples.

Pilgrim Hall Museum, 75 Court St, 746-1620. Personal possessions and records of the Pilgrims. Open 10am–4pm; $5, $4 students.

INFORMATION

Plymouth Information Center, North Park Ave, just east of Hwys 44 & 3A, 746-4779. General information on historical attractions available here.

Chamber of Commerce, 91 Samoset St, 746-3377.

CAPE COD A 65 mile long hook jutting out into the Atlantic, the Cape is a narrow string of sand from where, atop a dune, you can gaze over the ocean on one side and Cape Cod Bay on the other. It's a blustery, chilly spot out of season, but in summer delightfully sunny with a refreshing tang of salt in the air.

The Cape, which has no less than 77 beaches, is home to many scientists who come to study the ocean's mysteries. The **Woods Hole Oceanographic Institute**, at the southern point of the Cape, is the most famous research group here. Be sure to see the **National Marine Fisheries Service's Aquarium**, 548-7684, home to many rare New England species of sea life. At the other end of the Cape, near the northeast tip, is the **Wellfleet Bay Wildlife Sanctuary** in South Wellfleet, a 1000-acre area operated by the Massachusetts Audubon Society.

Although the Cape is an extremely popular summer resort, it is still possible to avoid the crowds and escape to deserted sand dunes or down beautiful, sandy New England lanes leading to the sea: simply avoid Hyannis and the coast south of Cape Cod National Seashore.

Hyannis and environs is the part of the Cape most exploited by tourism and free enterprise, but over in the lower Cape, small towns like Sandwich, Barnstaple, Catumet and Pocasset remain relatively quiet, even in the high season. After Labor Day you can have the whole Cape to yourself. (Well, sort of; Cape Codders let you know in no uncertain terms, that it belongs to them. However, high unemployment in recent years means that the Cape's commercial community are depending on tourists more than ever for their livelihood.)

On the Cape you will come up against numerous private beaches, or public ones which extract heavy parking fees. The Chamber of Commerce booklet *Cape Cod Vacationer*, free and available everywhere, lists all beaches and their status and has other useful information. There is plenty of camping near Sandwich where there is also a free public beach. State run and private sites can also be found in Bourne, Brewster, and Truro. Near Brewster is Orleans—a favourite beach for surfers.

Aside from the tourist, the Cape's great source of revenue is the cranberry. Nearly three-quarters of the world's cranberry crop is produced here and in neighbouring Plymouth County.

The telephone area code for Cape Cod is 508.

ACCOMMODATION

Can be expensive, but there are several camping sites and also 3 youth hostels. For other listings, see Hyannis or Provincetown, or else consult *Yankee Magazine's Guide to New England* or the *Cape Cod Vacationer*.

Bed and Breakfast, Cape Cod, Box 341, West Hyannisport, MA 02672; 775-2772. Reservation service for the Cape. Can arrange in-season S–$45 up, D–$60 up, $5 one-time booking charge with 25% deposit.

Mid-Cape Hostel, Goody Hallet Dr, Eastham, 255-2785. Open mid-May to mid-Sept; $10-AYH, $13-non-members. July and Aug reservations necessary. Bike rentals, $8 per day. Open 7.30am–9.30am and 5pm–10.30pm. 'Very strict.'

Camping: recommended sites are the **Shawme Crowell State Forest** at Sandwich, 888-0351, and the **Roland C Nickerson State Forest** at Brewster, 896-3491; but be warned: 'Campsites are often full right up to Labor Day and you may need to drive right out to North Truro to find a vacancy.' Plan your summer Cape Cod accommodation as early as you can.

TRAVEL

Bonanza Bus Lines, 59 Depot Ave (old train depot), Falmouth, 548-7588. Services to Boston, New York, Bourne. $39 to New York. $11 to Boston.

Plymouth & Brockton Street Railway, 17 Elm, Hyannis, 775-5524. Serves Provincetown, $7.50 from Hyannis.

Cape Cod Scenic Railroad, Hyannis to Sandwich, 866-4526, Tue–Sun, $10.50.

HYANNIS The metropolis of the Cape, Hyannis is the main supply centre for the area; shops, schools, hospital, harbour and airport (flights and sailings to Nantucket). Main Street is almost the typical all-American strip; for charm you want the outlying areas like Hyannisport and Craigville with its excellent beach for swimming.

More upper crust than most of the other Cape Cod towns, Hyannis is the home of wealthy trendies and is bathed in the aura of the Kennedy family sequestered in their Hyannisport compound.

ACCOMMODATION

Hyland Youth Hostel, 465 Falmouth Rd, 775-2970. Open Mar–Nov. $10 AYH, $13 non-members. Opens at 5pm daily. Reservations advisable, especially in July and Aug. 1½ miles to ferry and beaches. To get to hostel, walk 1 mile down Barnstable Rd to Airport Rotary and turn left on Rte 28 north; hostel is ¾ mile on left. 'Excellent—clean, friendly, homely.'

FOOD

East End Grill, 247 Main St, 790-2898, is a local favourite. Good prices and giant servings.

Hearth & Kettle, 412 Main St, 771-3737. $2 and up. 'Recommend the Early Bird Specials 12pm–6pm daily.'

Mooring, 230 Ocean St, on the harbour, 775-4656. Open into the wee hours, depending on the crowd. $5–$8. 'Good food.'

Perry's, 546 Main St. 775-9711. Breakfast, sandwiches $2.75 upwards.

INFORMATION
Cape Cod Chamber of Commerce, Rtes 6 & 132, 362-3225. Offers information on the entire Cape area. Accommodation information, *The Vacationer* booklet, *Resort Directory*, *Current Events* booklet, maps, camping, tenting, whale watching. A good place to start learning about the Cape highlights. Summer hours Mon–Fri 8.30am–5pm daily, weekend 10am–4pm.
Hyannis Area Chamber of Commerce, Rte 132, Hampton Rd, 775-2201. Open Mon–Sat 9–5pm, Sun 11am–3pm. Offers accommodation information and maps and tour information.

TRAVEL
During the summer, boats leave 6 times daily from Hyannis South St Dock for Nantucket, and 15 times daily from Woods Hole, Railroad Ave, for Martha's Vineyard. Round trip to Nantucket is $19.50, to the Vineyard, $9. Contact the Steamship Authority, 540-2022 for schedule. Trips around the Hyannis Inner Harbour to gape at the Kennedy compound are also available for $8. Contact the Hy-Line Harbour Cruises, on the Ocean St docks, 775-7185.

PROVINCETOWN P-town, as it's known locally, is at the very tip of the Cape, thus giving it its other nickname: Land's End. The Pilgrim Fathers' first landfall in North America was actually here. They stayed for four or five weeks before moving on to Plymouth. It's a sore point with the town, P-towners believing that they, not Plymouth, should have the fuss and fame. Pilgrim references are therefore much encouraged here.

In summer the town is jam-packed with artists, playwrights and craftsmen (including a large gay community), and the tourists and hangers-on who come to watch them. P-town is an attractive spot with old clapboard houses, narrow streets and miles of sandy beaches. Commercial St, appropriately named, is the main drag, so to speak. In the summer months, it's a perpetual street fair. For a special evening's entertainment, take a beach taxi ride over the sand dunes.

ACCOMMODATION
Alice Dunham's Guest House, 3 Dyer St, 487-3330. Old, Victorian sea captain's house. $38–$52 per night. One night free for each fortnight stayed. 10% discount before 30 May and after Labor Day. 'Nicest place in town.' 'Friendly, interesting proprietress.' Only four rooms so reserve early.
Joshua Paine Guest House, 15 Tremont St, in the west end (quiet, non-commercial part), 487-1551. June 15–Sept 15. S–$35, D–$45. 'Friendly; nice place.'
The Outermost Hostel, 28 Winslow St, 487-4378. $14 per night. 'Consists of cabins, own shower, shared kitchen.'

FOOD
Stormy Harbor, 277 Commercial St, 487-1680, serves great Portuguese food. Open April–Oct. $2.50 and up.
Surf Restaurant, 315 Commercial St on MacMillan Wharf, 487-1367. A drafthouse with jug band, washboard, and kazoos! Full seafood menu. $5–$15.

OF INTEREST
Provincetown Museum, at the base of the Pilgrim Monument, 487-1310. 'The Treasures of the pirate ship, *Whydah*. Displays artifacts from the ship of the pirate Samuel (Black Sam) Bellamy sunk in 1717 and identified in 1984.' Open daily 9am–5pm until Sept; closes earlier in winter. $5 admission to monument, museum and exhibit; $3 for museum and monument only.

INFORMATION

Province Land's Visitors Center in Cape Cod National Seashore, 487-1256, off Race Point Road. Tour information, maps of seashore. Open daily in summer 9am–6pm.

Provincetown Chamber of Commerce, 307 Commercial St, 487-3424, offers maps and an accommodation listing. 9am–5pm daily.

Shuttle bus starts in June from the centre of town to the beach; $1. Art's Dune Tour, Commercial and Standish Sts. April–Oct. $7 for standard tour, $8 for sunset tour (need resv.) Dune Tours go continually throughout the day from 10am.

Whale Watching from MacMillan Wharf, $16 for 3½ hrs at sea. 'Naturalist on board gave good, interesting commentary; we saw several, including one that swam under and around the boat; incredible and not to be missed.'

NANTUCKET 'The Little Grey Lady of the Sea', as the island is known, provided inspiration for Melville's *Moby Dick*. A salty place with cedar shingles, lobsters bought right off the boats, old anchors and whale oil vats, and miles of open sand beaches terrific for swimming, surfing, fishing and all-night bonfire parties.

The cobblestoned Main Street of Nantucket town and fine colonial homes testify to the past prosperity built on the blubber of the hunted whales. Today the money flows in with the flood of 'off-islanders' in summer; a crowded place then, but a lot of fun. For the pristine scene, come out of season when there's nobody there but the 'on-islanders', some of whom brag that they have never seen the mainland. Best to browse the isle by bike. *The telephone area code for Nantucket is 508.*

ACCOMMODATION

The island is generally a very expensive place to stay, and to maintain premium hotel rates any riff-raff caught camping will be fined $50, i.e., what you would have paid for a bed. But all is not lost:

Nantucket Accommodations Bureau, 4 Dennis Dr, P.O. Box 217, Nantucket, MA 02554, 228-9559. Lists most of the island's guest houses and inns. Charges $12 for service. Call or write early for best bargains.

Nesbitt Inn, 21 Broad St, 228-2446 in centre of town. S–$46, D–$71; T/Q–$93–$104. Continental breakfast included.

Star of the Sea Youth Hostel, Surfside, Nantucket, MA 02554. 3 miles from Nantucket town at the end of Atlantic Ave, 228-0433. Open 1 April–10 Oct. $10 AYH, $13 non-members. Book in advance during July.

FOOD

Captain Tobey's Chowder House, Straight Wharf, 228-0836. 'Good seafood.' Pricey.

Downeyflake, Harbour View Way, 228-4533. 'Excellent homemade things.'

Henry's, on Steamboat Wharf, 228-0123, has the biggest, and some say the best, sandwiches on the island.

OF INTEREST

Whaling Museum, Broad St, 228-1736. In the 18th and early 19th centuries, Nantucket was the best known whaling town in America. You can recapture something of the flavour of those times here. Has a good scrimshaw collection. Open 10am–5pm; $4.

Whale Watching. Call 1-800-WHALING for details. About $65 for a day trip (9.30am–5pm). 'Saw more than 20 whales. Best part of our trip.'

ENTERTAINMENT

Rose and Crown, S Water Street, 228-2595. 'Packed out but has a dance floor.'

The Muse, 44 Atlantic Ave (2 miles out of town), 228-9716. Best live entertainment on the island: rock and roll, reggae, blues. Don't miss the lipsynching contest on Sundays!
Gaslight Theatre, N Union St, 228-4435. Cinema showing mainstream and art films.

INFORMATION
Chamber of Commerce, Pacific Club Building, Main St, 228-1700, maps, restaurant and accommodation information. 8.30am–6pm, Mon–Fri.
Hub Board, Main St, very useful for ads of jobs and rooms. 'We found 2 rooms from it on the first day.'

TRAVEL
During the summer there are daily sailings from Hyannis to the island. The trip takes about 2 hrs and costs about $20 or $166 if you bring a car. Check times and prices with Hy-Line, 775-7185, or the Steamship Authority, 771-4000.

MARTHA'S VINEYARD To this day the question remains: was Bartholomew Gosnold basking in thoughts of his 5-year old daughter or fearing the wrath of his mother-in-law when he named this grape-covered island Martha in 1602? Though we'll never know, it's a pleasure to visit this quiet, beautiful haven 5 miles off the Cape.

Surfing, swimming and sailing are the attractions, though it's going to cost you your tiller arm to hire a boat. Settle instead for a bicycle (rentals widely available) and peddle around Edgartown, the sailing centre, where you can admire the fine old houses of the whaling captains, or make the more strenuous trip out to Gayhead to watch the setting sun do its light show against the coloured cliffs. For a quieter time, visit the peaceful fishing village of Menemsha.

If you long to ditch people for the gentler company of swans, lesser terns and mergansers, pay a visit to one of the Vineyard's three wildlife refuges: **Cedar Tree Neck** on the North Shore run by Sheriff's Meadow Fdn., 693-7233; **Long Point** on the South Shore, or **Wasque Point** on Chappaquiddick, both managed by Trustees for Reservations, 693-7662. Massachusetts Audubon Society runs natural history tours to bird haven **Monomoy Islands**. Reservations are required so call in advance for dates and rates, 349-2615.

The island is dry (no alcohol sold) except for Edgartown and Oak Bluffs. *The telephone area code for Martha's Vineyard is 508.*

ACCOMMODATION
Accommodation lists and maps are available from the Chamber of Commerce, 693-0085. Open Mon–Fri, 9am–5pm, Sat 10am–2pm. One-stop job shop locates housing and jobs in the early summer months. Continuation of project is contingent upon funding.
Manter Memorial YH, Edgartown Rd, PO Box 158, W Tisbury, MA 02575, 693-2665. Open 1 April–30 Nov. $10 AYH, $13 non-members. Reservations essential for July and August; include SASE with first night deposit for confirmation. 'A long way from anywhere.'
Camping: Martha's Vineyard Family Campground, Edgartown Rd, Vineyard Haven, 693-3772. $21/site for 2. **Webb's Camping Area**, Barnes Rd, Oak Bluffs, 693–0233. $23 for 2. $8 per additional person.

TRAVEL
See under Hyannis for ferry information.

NEW BEDFORD/FALL RIVER On Rte 6 on the way from the Cape to Providence, RI, **New Bedford** was once the whaling capital of the world. In the past decade it's undergone massive renovation and has been transformed from a dismal, rundown place to a cross between Mystic Seaport and Nantucket. There is a fascinating whaling museum, well worth visiting, and known for its exceptional collections of scrimshaw, 18 Johnny Cake Hill, 997-0046, open Mon–Fri 9am–5pm, weekends 11am–5pm, $3.50. Scrimshaw, perfected by New England sailors in the 19th century, involves carving and etching the surface of the teeth or jawbone of the whale. You'll find several old houses and small craft stores, which sell, among other things, fine scrimshaw.

Further west is the port town of **Fall River**, where the *Battleship Massachussetts*, veteran of WWII Pacific and North African battles, is moored. Open daily 9am–5pm, 9am–8pm in July/Aug; $8; 678-1100.

THE BERKSHIRE HILLS Running north to Vermont and south to Connecticut along the western border of Massachusetts, the Berkshires are gracious, tasteful, subdued, holding on to the values of a bygone age. **Williamstown** (famous for its college), **Lenox** and **Stockbridge** nestle among the hills, and this is a good area to get off the beaten track and explore the quiet villages, or hike some of the trails around **Mount Greylock**, at 3491 feet the highest peak in the state. The summit offers splendid views of the Hudson Valley and the Green Mountains of southern Vermont. The Berkshires are also a cultural centre in summer, the musical and theatrical events being based around Lenox, Lee and Stockbridge. The free *Berkshire Eagle* will keep you abreast of current happenings.
The telephone area code for the area is 413.

PITTSFIELD Named after the same Pitt who tagged Pittsburgh, PA, this was the birthplace of writer Herman Melville. The Atheneum has a room devoted to his effects, and you can visit his house, Arrowhead, just on the edge of Pittsfield on Holmes Road 442-1793. Open Mon–Sat, 10.30am–4.30pm, Sun 11am–3.30pm; $4. Nathaniel Hawthorne and Oliver Wendell Holmes also lived or summered around Pittsfield.

Five miles west is **Hancock Shaker Village**, well worth a visit. A religious sect who got nearer my God to Thee by doing an early form of boogalloo, earning their name from their early nickname 'Shaking Quakers', the Shakers originated in the late 18th century in Manchester, England and flourished for two centuries. Today the handful who remain live in Maine and New Hampshire; their decline surely, at least in part, has something to do with their avowal of celibacy. They are best known for their simple yet exquisite architecture, furniture and handcrafts. The Hancock Shaker Village, founded in 1790, displays many fine examples of their primitive but beautiful craftsmanship. Alas the Shakers abandoned their village to the tourists in 1959. Often 9.30am–5pm daily. $10. 443-0188.

ACCOMMODATION
Tanglewood Motor Inn, Pittsfield Lenox Rd, 3 miles south of town on Rtes 7 and 20, 442-4000. S–$58, upwards.
YMCA, 292 North St, 499-7650. All rooms are singles; $22 daily, $57 weekly.

INFORMATION/TRAVEL
Berkshire Visitors Bureau, Berkshire Common, 443-9186. Mon–Fri 8.30am–4.30pm.
Amtrak's *Lake Shore Limited,* Boston-Chicago, stops here: Depot St between North & Center. Call (800) USA-RAIL.

LENOX The **Tanglewood Music Festival** is held here for 10 weeks late June–Aug, with thousands of visitors, outdoor prom style, listening to the Boston Symphony Orchestra. The main shed holds 6000 people, but many prefer to sit out on the lawns with a blanket and picnic. For tickets and information call 637-1940. All kinds of music are performed during the season, and there are many other fringe activities in the area. Accommodation available at the Susse Chalet Motor Lodge, Massachusetts Turnpike, exit 2, on Rtes 7 & 20, 637-3560. Summer S/D–$70 up, special weekend package available.

Lee is the scene of one of the other main Berkshire festivals, the **Jacob's Pillow Dance Festival**, 243-0745, with ballet, jazz and contemporary dance, held at the Ted Shawn Theater off US 20 east of Lee, late June–August. North of Lee is the **October State Forest**, with the Appalachian Trail running through it.

Situated on Rte 20 at the junctions of I-84 and Massachusetts Turnpike, **Old Sturbridge**, (508) 347-3362, a preserved and restored early 19th century village, is enroute from Boston (56 miles to the east) and the Berkshires. It is meant to show the visitor life in a rustic Yankee village. Many traditional crafts and trades such as tinsmithing, broom making, or milling are carried on here and demonstrated daily. On less of a grand scale than Williamsburg and perhaps nicer for that. In winter there are old fashioned sleigh rides through the snow. Open 9am–5pm Daily. Entrance: $15. 'Worth it if you have a whole day.'

NEW HAMPSHIRE

Many people consider the Granite State the most scenic state east of the Mississippi. The only state named after an English county, New Hampshire has a short but sandy Atlantic coastline, hundreds of lakes (the biggest is 72-square-mile Lake Winnipesaukee), the impressive White Mountain range, more than 60 covered wooden bridges and a 90 percent tree cover. The countryside, warm and green in the summer, seems to catch fire when the leaves change colour in the Fall Foliage Show. The long, cold, snowy winters make the state a popular and fashionable skiing centre.

Notice the granite walls everywhere. Built by the early settlers to enclose their fields, the walls remain even though most of the fields are forest again.

New Hampshire was the first state to declare its independence and also the first to adopt its own constitution. Nowadays it is regarded as a political barometer, the results of its early primary elections strongly influencing the choice of candidates in the presidential elections.

The inhabitants are mostly genuine, laconic Yankees, and the state motto 'Live Free or Die' reflects the tough Yankee spirit behind the Revolutionary War. A good way to find cheap lodgings is to call New Hampshire Bed & Breakfast, PO Box 146, Ashfield, MA 01330, 279-8348. They book reservations at more than 60 small Bed & Breakfasts across the state and 150 establishments throughout New England, S/D-$35-$80. A hearty New England breakfast is included at most establishments.

The telephone area code for New Hampshire is 603.

PORTSMOUTH Global politics took place here in 1905 when the treaty ending the Russo-Japanese War was signed under the interested eye of President Theodore Roosevelt. Apart from being a footnote in history, Portsmouth, as New Hampshire's only seaport, has numerous old and well-preserved homes, many of them built by ship captains. Nearby, on New Hampshire's tiny 18-mile coastline, there are several fine, sandy beaches, including those at Wallis Sands and Rye Harbor.

ACCOMMODATION

Anchorage Inn, 417 Woodbury Ave, 431-8111. $75 for two or $65 if reserved in advance. TV, indoor pool.

Pine Haven Motel, 6½ miles south of town on US 1, 964-8187. S–$56 upwards, D–$65. Coffee. Open year-round.

OF INTEREST

John Paul Jones House, Middle and State Sts, 436-8420. Built 1758, house of the US Naval hero. Jones obtained the surrender of a British warship in 1779, as his own ship was sinking. Later, he became a Russian contra-admiral and died in Paris during the French Revolution. Mon–Sat 10am–4pm, Sun 12–4pm; $4.

Old Harbor Area, Bow & Ceres Sts, once the focus of the thriving seaport, is now an area of craft shops and eateries.

Strawberry Banke (sic), 10-acre preservation project in Old South End. From this site, starting in 1623, grew the town of Portsmouth. Buildings date from 1695 to 1820, some now house exhibits and craft shops.

INFORMATION

Portsmouth Chamber of Commerce, 500 Market St, PO Box 239, 436-1118.

CONCORD Capital of New Hampshire, on the Merrimack River, and famous in the 19th century for the Concord stagecoach, used throughout the old West. More recently, this is where Christa McAuliffe, chosen to be the first teacher in space, lived and taught until the shuttle disaster in 1986.

If you're about to tour the state, this is a reasonably central place to start, and it's on the main highway from Boston. About 55 miles to the southwest is 3500 foot high Monadnock Mountain, with a splendid view of the Northern Appalachians. North of Concord lie the lakes of central New Hampshire, and further north still are the alpine-like White Mountains.

ACCOMMODATION

Barwood Manor Motel, 300 S Main St, I-93 Exit 15W to Rte 3N, 753-4867. Rms $39 up.
Brick Tower Motor Inn, 414 S Main St, I-93 Exit 12S, 224-9565. Rms $55 up. Swimming pool, sauna, TV.

FOOD

Thursday's Rest and Lounge, 6 Pleasant St, 224-2626. 'Creative, homemade cuisine.' Open Mon–Sat 7am–9pm. Sunday brunch 7–9am. Live entertainment.

OF INTEREST

Pierce Manse, 14 Penacook St, 224-7668. Restored home of President Franklin Pierce. Open mid-June to mid-Sept, 11am–3pm; $2.
State House, 107 N Main St, 271-1110. The Hall of Flags is worth seeing. Open year-round, Mon–Fri, 8.30am–4.30pm; free.

INFORMATION

Greater Concord Chamber of Commerce, 244 N Main St, 224-2508.
New Hampshire Office of Vacation Travel, PO Box 856, Concord, NH 03302, 271-2666. Open 8am-4pm daily.

THE WHITE MOUNTAINS are dominated by **Mount Washington**, at 6288 ft the highest peak in the Northeast, where wind velocity has been recorded at 231 miles per hour! Climbing the mountain is quite a feat, but it can be done in summer, and the view is well worth the effort. Be warned: the weather can be nasty, even in July and Aug. Take warm clothing. Most visitors ride the cog railway to the top, with six states and Canada visible on a clear day. It's not cheap, though; the 3-hr round trip costs $32. For more info, call 466-2222. The auto (toll) road to the summit is equally costly, too: $14 per car plus $5 for each passenger. $18 per person for a tour.

At the base of Mt Washington, along Rte 302, is the resort of **Bretton Woods**, where Western leaders meeting towards the end of World War II to reorganize Europe's shattered economy, founded the World Bank and International Monetary Fund. Now it has a cosy ski resort.

Visit **Franconia Notch** and its 700-foot flume chasm with the **Old Man of the Mountains**, a natural stone profile, rising at the northwest end. **Cannon Mountain** in this area can be conquered by an aerial tramway. The **New England Ski Museum** is on Rte 3 in Franconia Notch State Park, 823-7177. Ancient skiing artifacts, from New England and elsewhere. Open daily exc. Wed, noon–5pm; free.

Cranmore and **Wildcat Mountains** to the southeast of Mt Washington are more sheltered than most, with the best skiing facilities in the White Mountains.

During fine summer weekends, the area attracts crowds of people; anyone seeking a bit of peace and quiet is strongly advised to search elsewhere. Accommodation and all facilities are generally expensive.

ACCOMMODATION

Hikers may want to consider staying at one or several of the **Appalachian Mountain Club's 8 huts**, spaced a day's hike apart; rates run from $20–$50, depending on the amenities and meals provided. Reservation and deposit required. Call 466-2727 or write for brochure and to make reservations at AMC Pinkham Notch Camp, PO Box 298, Gorham, NH 03581. 'Clean, friendly and helpful. Hearty meals.'

Bowman Base Camp, Rte 2, Randolph (north part of national forest), 466-5130. Bunks–$10.80 AYH, $11.80 non-members; tent site $7.50.
Crawford Notch Youth Hostel, Rte 302, 846-7773, run by AMC. $10 AMC members, $15 non-members. Open year round. 'We went midweek after Labor Day and the hostel was almost empty. Avoid Fridays and Saturdays.'
Wildcat Inn, in Jackson, 383-4245. S–from $54, D–$76, includes breakfast. Live entertainment on weekends.
Camping is available at 20 state parks in the White Mountain National Forest, as well as at numerous other private campgrounds.

INFORMATION
White Mountain National Forest Information, 466-2713. Crawford Notch State, Park, 374-2272. Trail & weather info, 466-2725. Franconia Notch State Park, 823-5563.

LAKE WINNIPESAUKEE Lying just south of the White Mountains, this is New Hampshire's largest body of water and a popular summer spot for visitors. Come here for sunning, swimming and sailing against a backdrop of tree-covered hills. **Center Harbor**, **Laconia**, **Wolfboro** and **Meredith** are the main centres for accommodation and sightseeing. There are several campgrounds around the lake.

HANOVER Fifty-nine miles northwest of Concord, Hanover is the home of **Dartmouth**, the northernmost Ivy League college, and probably the most conservative. Founded in 1769 by one Eleazar Wheelock as an experiment in 'spreading Christian education to the Indians and other youth', Dartmouth ranks as the nation's ninth oldest college, and has on its campus several lovely old colonial buildings.

ACCOMMODATION
Occom Inn, 35 N Main St, 643-2313, S–$46 up, D–$52 up with shared bath.
At Dartmouth get information on rooms at fraternity houses, and shelters along the nearby Appalachian Trail.

RHODE ISLAND

'Little Rhody' is the smallest state in the nation. With 400 miles of shoreline, it is dominated by the sea, and the Narragansett Bay, which cuts the state almost in half.

A colony founded by Roger Williams who dissented from the Puritan theocracy of Massachusetts, Rhode Island successfully developed by smuggling, slaving and whaling and for a while hesitated to sacrifice its post-Revolutionary War independence by joining the United States.

Little Rhode Island is home to some of America's biggest music events—the Newport Jazz and Folk Festivals.
The area code for the entire state is 401.

PROVIDENCE After being expelled by the Puritan Massachusetts Bay Colony for his liberal beliefs, Roger Williams fled to his friends among the

Narragansett Indians in 1636. On land purchased from them, he established the settlement which he named 'in commemoration of God's providence'.

Rhode Island's state capital and New England's fourth largest city, Providence is enjoying a renaissance as a modern industrial city and port, fiercely proud of its success, its traditions and its historic past. Many fine houses and commercial buildings survive from earlier times; and these, along with the prestigious Brown University, are the main points of interest for the casual visitor.

ACCOMMODATION

International House, 8 Stimson Ave, 421-7181. S-$25, D-$30 for students; S-$45, D-$50 for non-students. $20/$40 for addtl night. 'Clean, friendly, and cheap.'
Susse Chalet Inn, 341 Highland Ave, Seehonk, MA. (½ mile south of I-95, exit 1, 5 miles east of town), (508) 336-7900. S-$54, D-$58, T-$70, Q-$75.

FOOD

Luke's Luau Hut, 59 Eddy St, near Westminster Sq behind City Hall, 621-9770. Upstairs dining room serves inexpensive Chinese food and infamous 'orgie bowls'—communal drinks with a punch. Popular with students. Serves lunch Mon–Fri, 11am–2pm, dinner Fri–Sat only, 5pm–9.30pm (10.30pm—at w/end).
Meeting St Cafe, 220 Meeting St, on College Hill, 273-1066. Pastries, soups, salads, etc, 7am–11pm. Moderate prices.
Murphy's Delicatessen, 55 Union St (behind the Biltmore), 621-8467. Sandwiches as big as Rhode Island. Open daily 11.30am–1.15am.
Smith's Restaurant, 1049 Atwells Ave, 861-4937. Excellent Italian food (and lots of it) for great prices. Open Mon–Thur 11am–9.30pm, Fri till 10.30pm, Sat 4pm–10.30pm.
Wes's Ribs, 38 Dike St, Olneyville Sq, 421-9090, ribs, sandwiches. Open 11.30am–2am Sun–Thur, till 4am Fri–Sat.

OF INTEREST

Arcade, between Westminster & Weybosset Sts, a Greek Revival Building, the first enclosed shopping mall in America. Shops, fast food stalls, restaurants. 'Very small and expensive.'
Beneficient Congregational Church, 300 Weybosset St, dates from 1810 and is one of the earliest examples of Classical Revival in the country. The interior is patterned after New England meeting houses.
Benefit Street also known as 'mile of history,' has a collection of meticulously restored Colonial and Victorian houses, many open to the public.
Brown University, College Hill, 863-1000. A member of the Ivy League, has been here since 1764; interesting libraries and exhibitions (eg pre-16th century books, and Renaissance through 20th century paintings in the **Annmary Brown Memorial**). For tours, stop by Admissions Office, 45 Prospect St, 863-2378.
First Baptist Church, 75 N Main St, dates from 1775 and stands where Roger Williams founded the first Baptist church in America in 1638.
Providence Athenaeum, 251 Benefit St, 421-6970, a Classical Revival structure chiefly interesting because here Edgar Allen Poe wooed Sarah Helen Whitman, his prototypical Annabel Lee. Open Mon–Fri 8.30am–5.30pm, Wed till 8.30pm.
Rhode Island School of Design, 224 Benefit St, contains a first-rate **Museum of Art**, 454-6500. 19th century French and modern Latin American painters, 18th century porcelains and oriental textiles, and classical art; also the **Pendleton House**, faithfully furnished replica of an early Providence house. Open Wed–Sat noon–5pm in summer, longer hours in winter, $2, students 50¢.
State House, Smith St, 277-2726. Has the second largest unsupported marble dome in the world (St. Peter's in Rome is the largest). Inside is the 1663 charter granted by Charles II and a full-length Gilbert Stuart portrait of George Washington. Open Mon–Fri 8.30am–4.30pm.

INFORMATION/TRAVEL

Providence Preservation Society, 21 Meeting St, 831-7440. 1772 publishing house; plenty of info here on historical Providence. Sells booklets (80¢) and rents cassettes ($5) for walking tours. Open Mon–Fri 9am–5pm.
Visitor Information Center, 30 Exchange Terrace, 4th floor, 274-1636. 'Very helpful.'
Bonanza Bus Lines/Greyhound, 102 Fountain St, 454-0790.
Rhode Island Public Transit Authority (RIPTA), 265 Melrose, 847-0209.

PAWTUCKET If you're in the mood for a side trip of historic and contemporary dimensions, make the short (5–10 min) drive up I–95 to Pawtucket. **Slater Mill Historic Site**, Roosevelt Ave, 725-8638 features an 8-ton water wheel operating a 19th-century machine shop as well as exhibits of local history and fibre artists. $4 for a tour.

Travelling east across town on Armistice Blvd takes you to **Slater Memorial Park**, a fine place for a picnic and a tour through **Daggett House**, 333-1268, the Colonel's home built in 1685, which has an impressive collection of 17th and 18th century memorabilia. Open weekends only in summer, 2pm–5pm. The park has no less than 9 baseball fields, tennis courts and a merry-go-round; open 10am–9pm daily. Wind down your day as the pitchers wind up at **McCoy Stadium**. Eat hot dogs, drink beer and watch the **AAA Pawtucket Red Sox** play their hearts out to make the major league. 724-7300 for ticket and schedule information.

NEWPORT Thirty miles away from Providence on Narraganset Bay, Newport is a lively summer resort and home of such enchanting events as the Newport Bermuda Race, a tall ships regatta, and the famous Newport Folk, Jazz and Music festivals.

Although a rival of Boston and New York in colonial times, Newport really came into its own only around the turn of the century when the town became the place for millionaires to build their summer 'cottages'. Many of these ridiculously ornate relics of the Gilded Age are now open to the public. Find them close by Newport's fabulous beach and on Bellevue Avenue.

ACCOMMODATION

Hotels here are above average in price and tend to fill up quickly, especially in summer, so make plans for Newport as early as possible.
The **Newport County Chamber of Commerce**, 45 Valley Rd in Middletown, 847-1600, provides a list including budget and rock-bottom accommodation; guest houses usually offer the best deal.
Seaman's Church Institute, 18 Market Square, 847-4260, $10 per night or $65 per week. First come, first served with preference to sea faring folk, but 'if you're here and there's a vacancy, we'll take you'.
University of Rhode Island Youth Hostel, in **Kingston** 25 miles west of Newport on Rte 138, 789-3929. $6 AYH, $9 non-members. Inexpensive, but a good drive out of Newport and public transport not frequent. Check-in 6.30pm–10pm; Check-out 8.30am.

FOOD

Dry Dock Seafood, 448 Thames St, 847-3974, 11am–10pm Sun–Thurs; 11am–11pm Fri–Sat. Bring your own beer, inexpensive.
Shore Dinner Hall, Waites Wharf, 848-5058, casual, family, picnic setting, inexpensive chicken and seafood with great view of Newport harbour.

OF INTEREST

Cruising by ship or sailboat, around Narragansset Bay is a pleasant introduction. **Harbor Cruises**, departing Newport Harbor Hotel, 49 Americas Cup Ave, 849-3575, offer daily one-hour narrated cruises of the Bay, $6.50; **Newport Sailing School and Cruises Ltd**, departing Goat Island, 683-2738, offer 2-hour or half-day cruises aboard 23′–30′ sloops, $20–$40 per person, by reservation only; **Viking Boat Cruises**, depart Goat Island Marina, 847-6921 or 847-1340, and offer daily 1-hour cruises, $7, as well as a cruise that stops and tours Hammersmith Farm $13.

The Newport Preservation Society, 118 Mill St, 847-1000, maintains 7 of the mansions: **The Breakers, Marble House, Rosecliff, Chateau-sur-Mer, Kingscote, Hunter House**, and **The Elms** plus **Green Animals**, a topiary garden. **The Breakers**, Cornelius Vanderbilt's, is unquestionably the most opulent. **Marble House** is thought to have been inspired by the Petit Trianon at Versailles. **Rosecliff** is where the *Great Gatsby* was filmed. The Breakers are $7.50; all others are $6. Special combination tickets available. All open daily in summer, 10am–5pm. The Breakers open till 8pm, Jul–Sep.

Other privately owned mansions of interest:

Mrs Astor's Beechwood, 589 Bellevue Ave, 846-3772, is the most enjoyable to visit, with actors as servants and hangers-on of Mrs Astor leading you as her personal guests in a tongue-in-cheek tour of her home. (Most of the characters portrayed are British.) Open daily, 10am–4pm. $7.75.

Hammersmith Farm, on Ocean Dr, next to Ft Adams, 846-0420, was the summer residence of Mrs Hugh Auchincloss, mother of Jacqueline Kennedy. This was the setting for Jack and Jackie's wedding reception, and the presidential hideaway during the early 60's. Kennedy memorabilia abounds. Open daily until end October 10am–7pm; $6.50.

Belcourt Castle, Bellevue Ave, 846-0669, has a staggering collection of antiques and treasures from all over the world. Open daily, 9am–5pm, $6.50, $5 students.

Newport Folk Festival. Joan Baez and Arlo Guthrie made their career debuts here, joining folk-greats Bob Dylan, Doc Watson, Pete Seeger, etc., to make this *the* folk festival of the sixties. Recently revived by Ben and Jerry of ice cream fame, it once again provides a forum for top talent. Held every year at Fort Adams State Park over two days in August, phone 847-3700 for exact dates and ticket information.

Newport Jazz Festival. The oldest, and considered by many the finest, jazz festival in the world. Held in mid-August. For information write Jazz Festival, PO Box 605, Newport, RI 02840, (847-3700), or ask at the Chamber of Commerce.

Block Island 12 miles south of the mainland and a peaceful summer resort with wonderful beaches, first settled in 1661; classified by the Nature Conservancy as one of the '12 great places in the Western hemisphere'. Has two interesting restored lighthouses, one featuring a 19th century newspaper story that tallied the value of ships wrecked around the island as greater than that of the island itself. Ideal for biking; plenty of bike rentals from $9 day up. Day trips recommended since food and lodging prices tend to gouge the unwary.

Try lobster rolls at **Smugglers Cove**; **Cappizanos** for pizza; clam chowder at **Harborside**. There are ferries run by Interstate Navigation, tel (401) 783-4613, and Nelseco (same number) to the island from New London ($13.50 one way), Newport ($6.45), Port Judith (Galilee) ($6.60) and Providence ($7.40). The four hour trip from Providence is recommended. 'Great getaway.'

INFORMATION/TRAVEL

Newport Chamber of Commerce, 45 Valley Rd, in Middletown, 5 min drive from Newport, 847-1600. Very helpful.

Newport Preservation Society, 118 Mill St, 847-1000.

Bonanza Bus, 23 Americas Cup Ave, 846-1820.

VERMONT

Vermont, which celebrated its bicentennary in 1991, is a state of firsts: it produced the first constitution to outlaw slavery in 1777 and was the first state to offer troops in the Civil War; the first US patent was issued to a Vermonter, and the first boy scout group was started in Barre in 1909—by a Scottish immigrant!

Vermont has always been known for its fiercely independent people, from the colonial days when it asserted its own independence in the form of a republic. The state remained that way for 14 years, operating its own post office and minting its own money. Vermonters have retained their independent spirit and protective sentiment for the state. They cherish the beauty of their Green Mountains, banning billboards and imposing the toughest anti-pollution laws in the US. An ardent defender of state rights, Vermont has supported only one Democratic presidential candidate and elected only one Democratic senator in over a century.

Vermont is famous for maple syrup, Cheddar cheese and the magnificence of its autumn foliage and winter ski trails. The autumn colours are at their best toward the end of Sept; this is also the time for foliage festivals and get-togethers. March is the season for syrup festivals, but there are a number of museums open year round devoted entirely to the history and manufacture of this state institution.

The state has many small, progressive schools and has always attracted artists, craftsmen and writers, including the painter Norman Rockwell who lived in Arlington, and Rudyard Kipling, who wrote *The Jungle Book* in Dummerston.

The area code for the entire area is 802.

BURLINGTON This small city of approximately 40,000, a metropolis by Vermont standards, is set on the eastern shore of Lake Champlain, the beautiful 120-mile-long lake (the sixth largest in the US) which divides the New York Adirondacks from the Green Mountains of Vermont. Home of the University of Vermont, Burlington in 1981 became the first city in the US to elect a socialist mayor: Bernard Sanders won by the slim majority of 10 votes. The town's economy boomed as a result, and Sanders, a charged character who champions a national health scheme for the US, now represents Vermont in the US Congress. Burlington hosts a number of festivals each year, the craziest of which has to be the 'Fools-a-Float' challenge each September.

ACCOMMODATION

Eaton House B&B, RR 1 Box 139, Browns Trace, Jericho, VT 05465, 899-2354. S-$30, D-$50-$70. Kitchen and laundry facs.

Haus Kelley B&B, Old West Bolton Rd, Underhill Center, VT 05490, 899-3905. D-$22.50 per person. Price includes 'big breakfast'.

Howden Cottage B&B, 32 North Champlain St, VT 05401, 864-7198. S-$39, D-$49 inc. continental breakfast.

Midtown Motel, 230 Main St, 862-9686. S-$38.50, D-$44, XP-$5.50.

Susse Chalet, 590 St George Road, Williston, 10 min south of Burlington, take exit 12 off I-89, 879-8999. S-$49, D-$60.
YWCA, 278 Main St, 862-7520. Women only. Call for reservations. No short stays. Monthly rate $265-$345/mth

FOOD
Ben & Jerry's, 169 Cherry St, 862-9620. 'Best ice cream in the world', according to *Time* magazine. A Vermont original; destined to reach the far ends of the earth.
Burlington Bagel Bakery, 139 St Paul St, 658-0563, open 7am-6pm Mon-Fri, 5pm Sat, 4pm Sun. Filling and inexpensive; from 40¢.
Chicken Bone Cafe, 43 King St, 2 blocks from the lake, 864-9674, serves lunch and dinner, popular with students and locals. Open 11.30am-2am.
Daily Planet, 15 Center St, 862-9647, good, moderately priced bar food, lunch and dinner, Bass and Guinness on tap, student and yuppy hang out.
Henry's, 155 Bank St, 862-9010. In the heart of Burlington, a local hangout serving 'Americana', burgers and 'blue-plate specials'.
Oasis, 189 Bank St, 864-5308. Homemade food, sandwiches. Open 5.15am-4.30pm. Mon-Sat.

OF INTEREST
Boat tours of Lake Champlain aboard *Spirit of Ethan Allen*, replica of a vintage paddlewheeler. 4 daily cruises around the lake, $7.50, sunset trips also available.
Ethan Allen Homestead Trust, off Rt 127 N, 865-4556, home of Ethan Allen, Revolutionary War hero who with the Green Mountain Boys took Ft. Ticonderoga without a shot. Features multi-media show, exhibits, gift shop and 200-acre park with picknicking, fishing, canoeing. $3.50, open 10am-5pm daily.
Robert Hull Fleming Museum, U of Vermont, Colchester Ave, 656-2090. European, decorative and Native American art. Open Tue-Fri, noon-4pm in summer; 9am-4pm in winter. Sat-Sun 1-5pm. Suggested donation $2.
Shelburne Museum, 7 miles south on Hwy 7. Outdoor museum of early New England life. 45 acres of Americana. 'Worthwhile if you have a whole day.' Open 10am-5pm; $15. 985-3344.

INFORMATION
Chamber of Commerce, 209 Battery St, 863-3489.

MIDDLEBURY This small and beautiful New England town which borders on the Green Mountains has miles of hiking trails, including the Appalachian itself, with overnight shelters and various state parks for camping. One of the nicest state parks is not far from Middlebury, on beautiful **Lake Dunmore**.

The town is built around a village green and Otter Creek, flowing right through the middle of Middlebury. This is the home of the UVM Morgan Horse Farm, where the first American breed of horse is bred and trained. Picturesque, stone-built Middlebury College, founded in 1800, is famous for its excellent 'total-immersion' summer school of foreign languages, and gives a lively flavour to the town.

ACCOMMODATION
Accommodation in Middlebury itself is expensive but elegant and friendly. Call ahead as most have limited availability.
Cream Hill Farm, near Shoreham, 20 mins southwest of Middlebury, 897-2101. 1100-acre sheep and cattle farm. Renovated 18th-century farmhouse, family atmosphere; S-$40, D-$50, inc. breakfast.

Homestead Bread and Breakfast, off Rte 125 in Weybridge, 2½ miles north west of Middlebury, 545-2263, contemporary home, traditional hospitality, S–$40. Double-bed rooms.
Shoreham and Country Store, Rte 74, Main St, Village Green, Shoreham Village, 897-5861. S–$44, D–$75. Prices per room, inc. breakfast.
Camping: **Branbury State Park** on east side of Lake Dunmore, 10 miles south of Middlebury on Rte 53, 247-5925, swimming, fishing, boating, bath house. Tent site $12 for 4 people, $3 per extra person; lean-to $16 for 4 people, $4 per extra person. **Lake Dunmore Kampersville**, south of E Middlebury on Rte 53, 352-4501; $16.50–$22 site, depending on facilities.
Rivers Bend Inc Camping Area, 3 miles north of Middlebury, 1 mile off Dog Team Rd, 388-9092; $12.60 site.

FOOD

Fire and Ice, 26 Seymour St, 388-7166. Friendly. Seafood, steak. Great salad bar. Locals, students, and travellers. Lunch 11.30am–4pm, dinner 5pm–9pm. Closed Mon.
Woody's Restaurant, 5 Bakery Lane, 388-4182. Outdoor dining. Fresh seafood, steaks, pasta. Open 11.30am–11pm; Sunday brunch 10.30am–3pm.

OF INTEREST

Vermont State Craft Center at Frog Hollow, Mill St, 388-3177. Craft gallery featuring the work of over 250 Vermont craftsmen, studios open to the public.

INFORMATION

Middlebury Chamber of Commerce, 2 Court St, 388-7951.

MONTPELIER This smallest capital in the nation is also surely one of the most beautiful, with its stunning 14-carat gold-leaf State House dome dominating the city. It was the granite industry which built Montpelier and nearby Barre. Today the economy is based on the state government and the insurance business; although a granite revival is afoot.

Montpelier is also a thriving centre for threatre, music, crafts and antiques, and boasts its own museum and Historical Society. If you want to get away from it all, wander the back roads and admire the scenery. 'Come here for a slice of 50s rural village community life!'

ACCOMMODATION

Econolodge, 101 Northfield St, ½ mile from downtown, 223-5258. S–$45, D–$51.
Montpelier Guest House, 22 North St, 229-0878, $32–$60 per room. Victorian house and cottage, 10 min walk to downtown, no smoking. 15% discount for those with bikes; also for stays exceeding 2 nights. Owner Karen Kitzmiller is a well-qualified tour guide—she represents Montpelier in the State Legislature!
Vermonter Motel, Barre-Montpelier Rd, 3 miles from Montpelier and Barre, 476-8541. S–$36, D–$39 inc. tax.
Wayside Restaurant and B&B, US 302, RD 2, VT 05602, 223-6202 (or 223-6611 during day.) Rooms $30–$35. Price includes breakfast at the restaurant.

FOOD

Montpelier is home to the **New England Culinary Institute**, so quality, low-priced restaurants abound. It is also the home of Ben and Jerry, ice cream giants.
Ben & Jerry's Ice Cream Factory, Hwy 89 north to Waterbury, 1 mile north on Rte 100, 244-5641. The genesis of the ice cream made by two guys from Vermont. Taste for yourself during factory tours—ice cream cold off the dasher! Open Mon–Sat 9am–8pm, tours every ½ hr; $1. Ask about their interesting management philosophy.

Horn of the Moon Cafe, 8 Langdon St, 223-2895. All-natural, vegetarian food. Open 7am–9pm Mon–Sat, Sun 10am–2pm (brunch), 5pm–8pm.
Hunger Mountain Co-op, 403 Barre St, 223-6910. 1½ miles from Montpelier. 'Fantastic selection at great prices. Good place to stock up on food.'
Julio's, 44 Main St, 229-9348. Good Mexican food. 'The cheapest eats in town.' Mon–Sat 11.30am–10pm, Sun 4–10pm.
Thrush Tavern, 107 State St, 223-2030. Lunch, dinner, seafood, burgers, sandwiches. Open 11am–11pm Mon–Fri, 4pm–12 midnight Sat.

OF INTEREST

Morse Farm, Country Rd (3 miles from Montpelier; follow signs on Main St), 223-2740. Watch maple syrup being made, and sample the end product! Cheese is also produced here. Open 8am–5pm, 8pm in summer.

INFORMATION

Montpelier Chamber of Commerce, Granger Rd, 229-5711.

STOWE At the foot of Vermont's highest peak, Mt Mansfield (4393 ft), sits Stowe, one of New England's most popular resorts. Although predominately a skiing town, Stowe is gaining popularity in all seasons for its variety of outdoor activities—hiking, biking, canoeing, hang-gliding. It is also the home of the von Trapp Family, of *Sound of Music* fame, who operate a lodge and ski touring centre.

ACCOMMODATION

Anderson Lodge, 3430 Mountain Rd, 253-7336. Rooms $32 per person. Price includes full breakfast.
Baas' Gastehaus B&B, 180 Edson Hill, 253-8376. Only two double rooms; book well in advance. S–$50, D–$58, includes continental breakfast.
Golden Kitz, 1965 Mountain Rd, 253-4217. Rooms $20–$28 per person. A la carte breakfast menu available.
Ski Hostel Lodge, PO Box 58, Waterbury Center, VT 05677, 7 miles from Stowe, off 89 on Maple Street across from fire station, 244-8859. Call for reservations S–$25, kitchen facilities.
Vermont State Ski Dorm, on Rte 108, 8 miles from the centre of Stowe, 253-4010. 'The best in town.' A hostel in summer only; $11 AYH.

FOOD

Angelo's Pizza, Mountain Road, 253-8931. Open 11.30am–late. Calzones, pizzas, grinders, pasta, chicken dishes. Popular with locals.
Fox Fire, Route 100, 253-4887. Open 5.30–9pm. Northern Italian home-style cooking.
McCarthy's, Mountain Rd, ½ mile from centre of town, 253-8626. Serves breakfast and lunch only. Sandwiches, grinders, soups. 'Lots of homemade goodies.' Daily specials. Open 7 days, 6am–3pm.
Ye Olde England Inn/Mr Pickwick's Pub, Rte 108, 253-7558. English-style pub with pints of ale and darts. 'Great place.'

INFORMATION

Stowe Chamber of Commerce, Main St, 253-7321, has local accommodation and travel information.

THE NORTHEAST

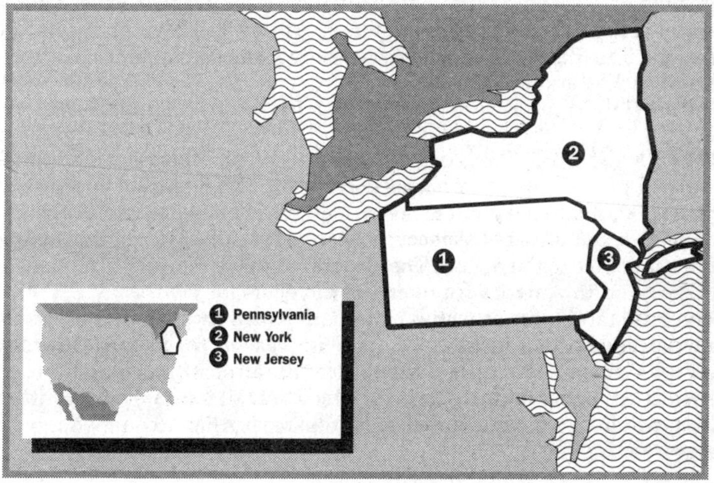

Through the Northeastern region runs most of the 400-mile strip of that megalopolis known as 'Boswash' (Boston to Washington). This rates as the nation's most crowded urban concentration, containing the nation's largest city, New York, and heaviest industry. The region has been called the headquarters for Enterprise America for from the time of the industrial revolution much of the impetus for commercial and industrial expansion has stemmed from these states.

You would be cheating yourself if during your tour of the Northeast you did not veer away from the nasty highway of I-95 to visit parts of the large tracts of unspoiled countryside within easy reach of the cities. Make it a point to see the mountainous Adirondacks in northern New York State and the rolling farmlands of western Pennsylvania; and there is greater variety still. It's also a region rich in historical and cultural associations with a wealth of places to visit and things to do. The climate varies as much as the geography. Winters are very cold and snow can be expected everywhere, while summers are marked by great heat and humidity.

NEW JERSEY

Sandwiched between industrial Pennsylvania and New York, New Jersey when first glimpsed after crossing the Hudson River from Manhattan seems an incredible wasteland, a lunar cesspool not to be missed. Riding the **New Jersey Turnpike** (toll road) between New York and Delaware and seeing mile after mile of refinery pipes, gasoline storage tanks and smelly smokestacks, you may well ask yourself what happened to America The Beautiful!

What is hard to believe is that there really is some truth to the state's nickname, the Garden State. West from the New York suburbs and interstate highways that bisect the state lies the bucolic **Delaware River Valley** in a corner of the Appalachian mountains. To the east are a virginal pine forest called the **Pine Barrens** and the **Jersey Shore** along the Atlantic, 150 miles of sandy beaches and boardwalks.

There are three telephone area codes for New Jersey: 201, 609 and 908.

NEWARK In truth, this is one of America's most unpleasant cities, with a history of physical decay, political corruption, racial tension and plain old ugliness. Manhattan's poorer cousin, Newark even *sounds* like a corruption of *New York*, but the city has recently been redeveloping as its airport draws more commerce to the region. The airport has made Newark a frequent first and last stop in America for overseas travellers.

The busy (and quite attractive) international airport is in fact as much as the traveller need ever see. There is no reason to go into downtown Newark. Accommodation is available near the airport but it is on the expensive side. It's better to catch the New Jersey Transit bus ($7) into Manhattan and stay there. (See New York City section for further accommodation and travel information.)

INFORMATION/TRAVEL

Travel and Tourism, Gateway Center, (201) 624-4462.
Greyhound, Penn Station and Market St, (800) 231-2222.

THE PALISADES are a 15-mile long line of granite cliffs rising as high as 500 feet above the Hudson. The most impressive view is from the George Washington Bridge when riding over from Manhattan, but on the New Jersey side you can enjoy the **Palisades Interstate Park** with its picnic grounds and beautiful woods.

West from Newark, in an area of dense suburbs, is the residence and laboratory of American inventor Thomas A. Edison, creator of the phonograph, incandescent light bulb and other harbingers of modernity. From the Garden State Parkway (toll) take Exit 145 to I-280 West, then Exit 10, right at light, go through two more lights, left at second one on to Main St, site is ¾ mile down at corner of Main St and Lakeside Ave. Edison's home, Glenmont, was rehabilitated in 1987. $2. (201) 736-0550.

Just across the Hudson river from lower Manhattan is the gritty port town of **Hoboken**, famous as the place where *On The Waterfront* was filmed, and where Frank Sinatra was born. PATH commuter trains from New York will get you there, and as you pass through the station, marvel at its intricate marble construction. One of the better technological universities, **Stevens Institute**, also calls Hoboken home, as does an aromatic Maxwell House coffee plant.

Two fine universities lie just off the New Jersey Turnpike (toll) southwest of Newark. **New Brunswick** is the home of **Rutgers University**, and 30 miles further is **Princeton**, a beautiful New England town that ran away to New Jersey. Both Albert Einstein and Thomas Mann lived here, while

F. Scott Fitzgerald and Eugene O'Neill are among the more luminous alumni of **Princeton University**. Woodrow Wilson, former US president and international do-gooder, was president of the university 1902–10. Free tours of the campus start at the yellow Maclean House; (609) 258-3603, Mon–Sat 10am–3.30pm and Sun afternoons. Highlights include Nassau Hall, built in 1756, where the Continental Congress met in 1783, and which was used as barracks during the Revolution by both American and British soldiers.

FOOD IN PRINCETON

PJ's Pancake House, (609) 924-1353, Nassau St adjoining main campus. Specializes in pancakes and waffles—*the* place to go for breakfast, $3–6.00.
Winbury's, Nassau St and Palmer's Sq, (609) 921-0700. 'They do a good brunch.'

Fifteen miles west from Princeton is the point where General Washington crossed the Delaware River on a bone-chilling Christmas night in 1776 to deliver a special Christmas present to the British troops at Trenton. Eight days later he stormed the garrison at Princeton.

THE JERSEY SHORE begins south of Newark. Drive along the **Garden State Parkway**, which follows the contour of the coast. Gritty **Asbury Park**, where it seems everyone works in a garage, is Bruce Springsteen country. Forty miles further south is the road to **Long Beach**. 'A great place to relax and enjoy sea, sun and sand. No usual boardwalk, but no usual commercialism.'

ATLANTIC CITY Once the best loved seaside resort in America and the original model for the game of Monopoly, Atlantic City saw its glamour wilt when better-off bathers made for hotter climes in the South and the West. The home of salt water taffy and the Miss America contest, the town took out a new lease on life in 1977 when casino gambling was legalised here.

With the arrival of the gambling resorts, a new game of monopoly has ensued (Donald Trump heading the list of players), with speculators razing entire city blocks in hopes of profit, and investors raising a dozen garish, neon-lit pleasure palaces. The result is an urban desert spotted with the casinos and linked to the rest of the world by hundreds of buses bringing the hopeful from Philadelphia, New York and Washington. Special Amtrak trains, with connecting buses to the casinos, go there too.

The beach was nearly washed away by hurricane 'Gloria' in 1985, but rebounded as crowded as ever. To escape the crowds and gaudy joie de vivre of Atlantic City, go north to the 2700 acres of **Island Beach State Park**, (908) 793-0506.

The telephone area code is 609.

ACCOMMODATION

Atlantic City is more expensive than the rest of the Jersey shore, especially during the summer season. If you're stranded and have to stay in town, **Ameriroom Hotline**, (800) 888-5825, provides a free reservation service ($10 cancellation fee only) for hotels, condos and casinos throughout the city; pricey, but efficient.
Shamrock Hotel, 133 St James Pl, 348-9832. S–$100 per week, D–$110 per week.
Camping is the cheapest alternative: **Casino Campground**, Hwy 575 and Moss Mill Rd, 12 miles west of Atlantic City, 652-1577, $18.75 per tent site for 2 people, $2.50 per extra person.

Pleasantville Campground, 408 N Mill Rd, 8 miles west of Atlantic City, 641-3176. $24 for tentsite for 4 people, free showers. $3 per extra person.
Inexpensive, family run motels can be found on the Whitehorse Pike in Abescon, Rte 30.

FOOD/ENTERTAINMENT

Maloney's Bar and Restaurant, 43 S Washington Ave, 823-3546. 'A wild and enjoyable bar.'
White House Sub Shop, Mississippi & Arctic Ave, 345-1564. World famous since 1946. $6–8, half-subs $3–4.

OF INTEREST

Convention Hall on the Boardwalk, 348-7000, is the largest in the world, seating 70,000 in the main auditorium. It also has the world's largest pipe organ to match. Watch the Miss America Pageant here mid-Sept.
Lucy the Margate Elephant, 9200 Atlantic Ave, 823-6473. A building in the shape of an elephant, originally built of wood and tin in 1881. Tours $2; high season daily, 10am–8.30pm.

INFORMATION/TRAVEL

Chamber of Commerce, 1301 Atlantic Ave, 345-5600.
Convention and Visitors Bureau, 2314 Pacific Ave, 348-7111.
Many of the casinos run free or low-priced buses to Atlantic City from New York and Philadelphia. Check the *Yellow Pages* under 'Casinos' for information or look for billboard advertisements. The Greyhound 'Lucky Streak' service from Philadelphia costs about $12.
Greyhound is at Arctic and Arkansas Aves, 345-6617. (Tel 215-931-4014 for 'Lucky Streak' tickets).
Also, New Jersey Transit, same location, (800) 582-5946.

OCEAN CITY, 8 miles south, is as sober as Atlantic City is hedonistic. Alcohol cannot be bought on the island. Beaches are crowded, but there is plenty of work in the summer resorts, and though one's pleasures must be 'imported' from the mainland, the young students working there make the nightlife a lively one. Rooms in the numerous boarding houses and old resort hotels are plentiful and inexpensive.
The area code is 609.

ACCOMMODATION

Commodore Guesthouse, 701 Plymouth Place, 399-4761. Talk to Jane Hill. D-$34, twin-$36.
The Ocean Call, 1412 Central Ave, 399-4215. $70 pp per wk; use of kitchen. 'Full of students.' 'Highly recommended.'
Ocean City Guest House Association, PO Box 356, Ocean City, NJ 08226, 399–8894. $35–$145 a night for rooms that often hold more than one person. Brochure available.

INFORMATION

Ocean City Information Center, on 52 South between Somers Point and Ocean City, 399-2629 or (800) BEACHNJ, has info on beaches, hotels, restaurants. Help and information also available at bus station.

WILDWOOD is a smaller, perhaps more wholesome, version of Atlantic City, practically at the tip of the southern peninsula of the state. The beach is 1000 ft wide in some places and there are 2 miles of boardwalk, six amusement parks, and plenty of wild nightlife. It's also a resort where families come for their traditional week by the sea. 'Lots of American students work here. Everyone works hard and plays hard. We had a fabulous time.'

ACCOMMODATION

'Accommodation easily found by walking around and asking. Wildwood Crest is the nicest area to live.'

Beachwood Hotel, 210 E Montgomery Ave, 729-0608, swimming pool, TV, refrigerators. 1 block from boardwalk and beach. D–$60–$80. 'Small, no AC, but friendly.'

Overbrook Apts, 216 E Roberts Ave, 729-2775. 'Reasonable rates, family atmosphere. Likes overseas students.' Also recommended: **Clearview Hotel**, E. Poplar Ave, **Holly Beach Hotel** on Spicer Ave, and **Mount Vernon Hotel** 124–126 E. Lotus Rd.

FOOD/ENTERTAINMENT

Recommended are the **Harbor Inn** on Lincoln Ave for 'reasonable prices and live bands', and **Razzles** on Schellenger Ave for 'good music'.

Also recommended for its 'good food and atmosphere' is **Ernie's Diner** on Atlantic Ave, 522-8288.

CAPE MAY is a remarkably well-preserved beach resort in the Victorian style. Most of the buildings date from the 1870s–80s, so the town is free of much of the chintz afflicting the rest of the shore. There is an interesting light-house. The beaches are clean due to a massive clean-up operation since 1988. Beach tags must now be displayed, $3 per day from beach vendors. Beach Tag Office 884-9520. Certainly worth a look. If you're heading south, you may want to take the Cape May Ferry to Lewes, Delaware. Frequent daily sailings, costing $18 car and driver, $4.50 each passenger. Foot passengers, $4.50 one way; same-day round-trip, $8.50. Bikes, $8. Call 886-2718 for schedule.

INFORMATION

Welcome Center, 405 Lafayette St, 884-9562, has info on restaurants, accommodation, tours, etc. Free phones for calling guest houses. Open Mon–Sat 9am–4pm.

DELAWARE WATER GAP This is in the area that most justifies the 'Garden State' tag. Here the mountains diverge dramatically to make way for the Delaware River; a haven for canoeists, hikers and other outdoor enthusiasts.

ACCOMMODATION

AYH, Old Mine Road, Delaware Water Gap National Recreation Area, (201) 948-6750. Reservations advisable. $8.

NEW YORK

Everything about New York State is big. It has the biggest industrial, commercial and population centre in the United States all rolled into one great metropolis, which together with the vast upstate area contributes mightily to the nation's manufacturing and agricultural output.

In colonial times New York was one of the most sizeable chunks of land in North America, hence its nickname, the Empire State. Although New York state was technically discovered in 1524 by Giovanni da Verrazano sailing for France, Henry Hudson (an Englishman employed by the Dutch) sailed through the Lower Bay of New York in 1609, and on up the river which now bears his name. The river was later fought over by the British and the Dutch, whilst the Brits also wrested the Northern area from the French.

Peter Minuit founded the Dutch Colony of New Amsterdam (renamed New York City by its conquerors in 1664) after buying Manhattan from the Indians for $24 worth of trinkets. Yet it says something about the vastness of the state, much of it still wilderness even today, that as late as 1700 the most formidable empire in New York was that of the Iroquois Confederacy of the Five Nations based in Syracuse and controlling the water routes to the coast and therefore trade. Their power was broken only in the middle of that century when the British defeated the Indians and their French allies at Ticonderoga, Niagara and Montreal.

NEW YORK CITY The nation's largest city, New York is also the business, entertainment and publishing capital of the United States, its busiest port, and host to the United Nations. More than 18 million people, as diverse as the peoples of the United Nations, live and work in the New York metropolitan area stretching out into New Jersey and Connecticut. It isn't possible within this book to give more than the merest introduction to New York, so, if you plan to spend some time here, we recommend you buy the excellent *Michelin Guide* or *Access* guides.

Though the city is composed of five boroughs, Queens, Brooklyn, the Bronx, Staten Island and Manhattan, it's the last of these that you're really talking about when you say New York: that long stretch of stone lying between the Hudson and East Rivers, the place where skyscrapers tower over an intense mangle of social extremes.

New York's explosive variety and its appeal to so many different types of people make it an exciting place to visit. Chances are that whatever you are looking for, you will find, and so much more besides. In the words of President John F Kennedy, 'Other cities are nouns. New York is a verb.' New York offers the finest in theatre, cinema, music, museums, shopping, restaurants and general tourist attractions, as well as a riveting study in social contrast. Just watch the bag ladies huddle over a steam grating across the street from a row of limousines. It can be hot and humid in the summer, cold and windy in winter; it can be filthy, or dangerous, flashy, or funny, but it is a city which is always outrageous, alive, enthusiastic and, above all, resilient.

The city, commonly called The Big Apple (originally jazz musician slang for the 'big time'), tottered on the brink of bankruptcy in 1975, sprang back, underwent something of a renaissance, and is now going through another transitional phase. Tired of the drug problem, the homeless throngs on the streets, the filth and high crime levels, New Yorkers have just thrown over the city's first black mayor, democrat David Dinkins. The new mayor, republican Rudolph Guiliani, has promised a safer, cleaner city. New Yorkers have heard *that* before.

The telephone area codes are 212 for Manhattan and the Bronx, 718 for Brooklyn, Queens and Staten Island.

MANHATTAN NEIGHBOURHOODS

The Financial District: This is the oldest part of the city, a maze of narrow winding canyons that stand where Peter Stuyvesant once erected his wall to keep the Indians out. That's where Wall Street gets its name. The New York Stock Exchange is here on Broad St, and the American Stock Exchange is on Trinity Place. George Washington was inaugurated first President of the United States at Federal Hall, Wall and Nassau Sts, in 1789. From Battery Park you can take the ferry to Staten Island and the Statue of Liberty. Towering over everything are the second tallest buildings in the world—the 1,350-foot twin towers of the World Trade Center, at West St. **Battery Park City**: situated near Battery Park is literally a land-fill. Water was pumped out and the *roads dropped* to create this waterfront community. The district is a necropolis on Sundays, thus great for cycling or a picnic on the steps of City Hall. The thriving South Street Seaport area combines a museum, tall ships and a cluster of seafood restaurants that collectively bear witness to New York's origins as a port.

Chinatown: The public telephones are housed in miniature pagodas, and the local grocery shops are great for snow peas or bok choy (Chinese lettuce). Restaurants are good, plentiful and cheap. Chinese New Year is celebrated with the explosion of firecrackers the first full moon after 21 January. Mott and Mulberry are the major streets.

Little Italy: Just northwest of Chinatown, in the area of Mulberry and Grand St. Good restaurants, bakeries and grocery shops, and a lively place in June with the Feast of St. Anthony, again in September with the feast of San Gennaro, when you can ride ferris wheels in the middle of the street, eat lasagne and zeppoles, and buy large buttons that beckon, 'Kiss me, I'm Italian.'

SoHo: Formerly a warehouse and trading district, SoHo, the area south of Houston (pronounced HOW-ston) St and, increasingly, **Tribeca** (stands for triangle below canal), the area between Soho and the World Trade Center, shelter the struggling artists and musicians chased out of more expensive neighbourhoods. Their artwork, music and theatre fill the old industrial lofts with the avant-garde of American culture. Restaurants and excellent cheap clothing and electronic stores abound. Tribeca is also home to a wealth of nice restaurants (buy your coffees and brunches here) and, like Soho, there are many cast-iron buildings, dating from the turn of the century. Movie star Robert De Niro moved here in 1982 and opened his own film centre and grill restaurant (the TriBeCa Grill). Other celebrity residents include Dan Ackroyd and Bette Middler.

The Lower East Side: Orchard and Delancey Streets have attracted waves of immigrants, Eastern European Jews in the early part of this century, Puerto Ricans and Haitians today. Some older Jews still remain and Sunday is their big market day, a good time to swoop in for bargains. Note that many stores are closed on Saturdays—the Jewish Sabbath. Word has it the Lower East Side is slowly growing more fashionable, with poor immigrants being chased out by galleries and restaurants.

The East Village: St Marks Place and Second Avenue took the overflow from increasingly pricey Greenwich Village to become the hang-out for students, artists and writers. It's also home to some of the more wasted punks and drop-outs, who in need of a fix might rob you at night, so tread carefully. Former inhabitants of the East Village include WH Auden and James Fennimore Cooper.

Greenwich Village: New York's original bohemian quarter and one-time home of such figures as Edgar Allan Poe, e e cummings, Eugene O'Neill, Allen Ginsburg and Dylan Thomas, the Village is not what it used to be. Lots of expensive plastic cafes now cater to the tourists, but 10th, 11th and 12th Sts remain calm, lined with brownstones for the chi-chi rich. New York University faces onto Washington Square, with its version of the Arc de Triomphe. In the square listen to the live music, everything from casual guitar strumming to classical violin; watch the jugglers and break dancers, and compare strategy with the hustlers working the chess boards. During the summer, street fairs are common up and down the Village streets. The area of the Village centered on Christopher Street is also home to New York's large gay community, though the AIDS scare has slowed the nightlife there.

Chelsea: Home to the garment district, where one-third of all the clothes worn in the US are made or handled, Chelsea is a vast stretch of warehouses and lofts that is starting to gentrify under the pressure from Greenwich Village. The flower district is dug in around 27th St. To forget the grime of the city, walk along here among the ferns, tropical plants and examples of every imaginable flower in season. To the west stand the crumbling remains of the docks where the great steamships used to call. Better known as **Hell's Kitchen**, the hope is that the waterfront will revive now that the giant space-age Jacob K Javits Convention Center is complete. Further uptown, around Herald Square and 34th St, things are bustling around the large department stores like Macy's and A&S, as well as inside the new nine-storey Herald Center shopping mall. Just a block away in either direction stand the Empire State Building and newly revamped Madison Square Garden. The Garden is where sports events, exhibitions and pop concerts happen; beneath it is **Penn Station** where you can catch trains out to Long Island, or Amtrak to Boston, Washington or Chicago.

Midtown: The core of the Big Apple. East and West, between 42nd and 59th Sts, is the heart of the theatre district, cinema district, shopping district and porno district, to name a few.

Fifth Ave splits midtown down the middle, marking the border between East side and West side. The swankiest shops in the city elbow for space along this justifiably famous street. Rockefeller Center and St Patrick's Cathedral are here, and when Britain decides to pawn the crown jewels, they'll be on sale at Tiffany's, corner of 57th St. The impressive Trump Tower, ritziest building in New York, packs five floors of astonishingly expensive boutiques around a rose marble waterfall. 'You won't be able to afford anything, but definitely worth a look.' The brotherhood of mankind fulminates daily in the United Nations Building on 44th St, by the East River. **Grand Central Station**, with trains to upstate New York and Connecticut dominates E 42 St. **Times Square**, now home to pimps and tarts as well as the Broadway theatres, dominates W 42nd. Despite City Hall's attempts to clean up the area, junkies, peep shows, porn cinemas and all manner of sleaze still flourish. Renovation work is currently underway and several hotels and office buildings have sprung up: an indication that the area is gradually becoming more respectable. Well policed, it's not as dangerous as it seems, but be on your guard—the action here goes on all night. Pleasant places in which to picnic or relax are the 'pocket parks' in Midtown: 57th St east of Fifth Ave, and 47th St between 2nd and 3rd.

Central Park: An enormous and enjoyable expanse of grass and schist rock outcroppings scratched by the last retreating glacier, the park extends from 59th to 110th St with ponds, gardens, tennis courts and zoo. On Sundays the streets are blocked off, and the park fills with New Yorkers walking, sailing model boats, jogging, riding, cycling, roller skating, skate boarding, playing baseball, necking, reading the *Sunday Times* or, annoyingly, playing huge boombox radios unbelievably loudly, although there are several 'quiet' zones where ghettoblasters and the like are banned. Look for free concerts, plays and opera in the summer, ice skating in the winter. And don't forget to clear out at night; the park is unsafe after sundown.

The Upper East Side: The 60s, 70s and 80s in this area are among the most coveted addresses in New York. The vast Metropolitan Museum of Art and the spiralling Guggenheim anchor Museum Mile along Fifth Ave. East 86th St is the heart of Yorkville, the German part of town, with beer and Gemülichkeit on draught. Beginning at 96th St and running north to 145th is East Harlem, the largely Puerto Rican section called El Barrio. A sprinkling of Irish and Italian families remain, desperately trying to learn Spanish.

The Upper West Side: At the intersection of Columbus and Broadway lies the cultural hub of Manhattan, The Lincoln Center, which includes the Metropolitan Opera House and the New York State Theatre. At night it's pretty crowded; by summer's day it's a pleasant place to sit and eat ice cream. Around 72nd St and on Columbus Avenue is a young, semi-posh and lively neighbourhood; on Central Park West is the impressive victorian Dakota building where John Lennon lived and died. Across the street, in the park, is the memorial to Lennon, Strawberry Fields. Further north on Central Park West is the Natural History Museum, and still further, in the Morningside Heights area, is Columbia University at Broadway and 116th St.

Harlem: This is the centre of New York's black community, stretching from the top end of Central Park up to 155th, and encompassing everything from miserable tenements to fashionable residential rows. 125th St is where it all happens, where some amazing gaits and pink Cadillacs are still to be seen. But money for drugs is in short supply and the night visitor particularly may find himself broke in the gutter. With the reopening of the famous Apollo Theatre, a springboard of many great black artists and jazz musicians a generation ago, Harlem could be poised for a possible rebirth.

ACCOMMODATION

For very cheap accommodation read the classified ads in *The Village Voice*, published every Wednesday, Section 812, Furnished rooms, and the notice boards at the Loeb Student Center, Washington Square. Shops near Columbia U are sometimes good for sub-lets. Also try the fraternity houses around NYU and Columbia. Single accommodation is expensive in NYC but rates for doubles and triples go down markedly, so travel in herds where possible.

Allerton House Hotel, 130 E 57th St, 753-8841. For women only. Excellent location, tight security, whistle-clean rooms. S–$42 up, with bath, $62. D–$77 with bath.

Big Apple Hostel, 109 W 45th St, 302-2603. $17 dorm, $45 for private room. Good location. Same building as St. James Hotel. 'Don't recommend.'

Broadway American Hotel, 2178 Broadway, 362-1100. A newish 'economy' hotel, conveniently situated. Refrigerators and shared baths. S–$45 and $55, D–$65.

Carlton Arms Hotel, 160 E 25th St (at 2nd Avenue), S–$40 or $53 with bath, D–$53 or $61 with bath. 'Amazing artwork in rooms. Phone ahead to reserve.'

Chelsea Hotel, 222 W 23rd St, 243-3700. D–$89 to $99, triples from $95. Pay in advance for 6 nights, get the seventh free. TV $3 extra. AC in some rooms, ask! A once and future haven to artists, writers and other fringe elements. See where Thomas Wolfe wrote, Dylan Thomas drank, and Sid Vicious offed his honey.

Chelsea International Hostel, 251 20th St, 647-0010. $16 dorm; linen provided plus free coffee.

Chelsea Center, 339 W 19th St, 243-4922. $20 dorm style, breakfast incl. Kitchen, hot showers. 'Very cramped.' 'Safe, friendly, personal atmosphere.' German, French spoken. Closed 11am–5pm. No curfew, book ahead.

Fashion Institute of Technology, 210 W 27th St, 760-7885. Empty dormitory space to let between mid-June to end of July. Priority to FIT students. One week stay minimum, at $16 a day for dorm room plus $10 registration fee. $21 per person for apartment shared by 1 or 2. Talk to housing director. Price varies each summer.

Gershwin Hotel, 7 E 27th St, 545-8000. $17 mixed dorms, $59 private room with bath. Nr. Empire State Building. Recently opened. 'Basic, but clean and good security.' 'Nice, friendly staff.'

International AYH-Hostel, 891 Amsterdam Ave, btwn 103rd and 104th Sts, 932-2300. Take #1 or #9 subway to 103rd St and walk 1 block east. Largest hostel in the USA. Self service kitchen. Garden. $22 members, $25 non. BUNAC office is here.

International Student Center, 38 W 88th St, 787-7706. $12 in dorms of 5–10 persons with attached bathroom. Kitchen, sheets available. Limited to foreigners. Five night limit in summer. 'Friendly place in heart of big city.' Closed Jun–Jul.

International House, 500 Riverside Drive, 316-8400. S–$25. Close to Columbia University and subway. 'Clean. Excellent and cheap canteen.'

Mansfield Hotel, 12 W 44th St, off Fifth Ave, 944-6050. D from $90. Vincent Price lived here for 3 years. 'A definite feeling of warmth here, like a small European hotel.'

Martha Washington Hotel, 30 E 30th St, 689-1900. Women only. S from $42 a day, $167 per wk, Twin bedded room with running water from $60 a day, $130 per wk, per person.

Pickwick Arms Hotel, 230 E 51st St, 355-0300. S–$48, $55, $65, D from $100. 'Excellent central location; small basic rooms, slightly shabby.'

Remington Hotel, 129 W 46th St, 221-2600. S from $60, with bath $84. D–$72, with bath, $90. AC and TV.

Roger Williams Hotel, 28 E 31st St, 684-7500. An extra 15% discount for BUNAC-ers. T–$25, D–$30 per person (students only), S–$46. Kitchenette, bath.

Travel Inn Motor Hotel, 515 W 42nd St, 695-7171. S from $88, D from $105. Bath, TV, AC, use of pool included. Free parking. 'Can be quite inexpensive if several share a room—the floors are comfortably carpeted.'

YMCA—McBurney, 206 W 24th St, 741-9226. Men and Women. S–$32, for colour TV, D–$48. $94.50 per wk. Max. stay 25 days. 'Reasonable rooms, but mainly frequented by older people; handy for Washington Sq and Greenwich Village.'

YMCA—Vanderbilt, 224 E 47th St, 755-2410. Men and women. S–$42, D from $52, $10 key deposit. TV in rooms.

YMCA—West Side, 5 W 63rd St, 787-4400. Men and women. S–$42, D–$52.

Hotel Wolcott, 4 W 31st St, just west of Fifth Ave, 268-2900. Renaissance-style mansion with crystal chandeliers and wrought-iron staircases. S–$40, D–$45, T–(with bath) $65. 'Very nice.'

FOOD

Manhattan, home to 13,000 places serving food, is truly the restaurant goer's paradise. Since three-quarters of them will go out of business in the next five years, hundreds of replacements open in Manhattan every year, so New Yorkers never lack for new, interesting places to visit. A lot of them are expensive, but if you look hard, ask the local people where they eat, and have some luck, you'll be able to find cheap, good places that serve any of dozens of ethnic and American specialties. Below you'll find two lists, one containing some tried-and-true favourites, the other, a list of neighbourhoods known to have a lot of cheap, good restaurants.

Burger Joint, Broadway at 76th St, 362-9238. 'The best burgers (& pizzas next door) plus Greek-style food.' Inexpensive, veggies catered for.

Carnegie Deli, Seventh Ave at 55th St, 757-2245. Sandwiches large enough to feed two people start here at $8.95. Other Jewish specialties. This was the restaurant featured in Woody Allen's *Broadway Danny Rose*. World's best cheesecake here, and their corned beef and pastrami are rated no. 1 in the country.

Christine's, 44 Lexington Ave, and 2nd Ave and E 26th St, 953-1920. Polish and standard American with Eastern European flavour. 'Good pierogi.' Filling, tasty food, $7 up.

Cucina Della Fontana, 368 Bleecker, 242-0636. Italian garden restaurant (downstairs). 'Reasonable prices and unusual place.'

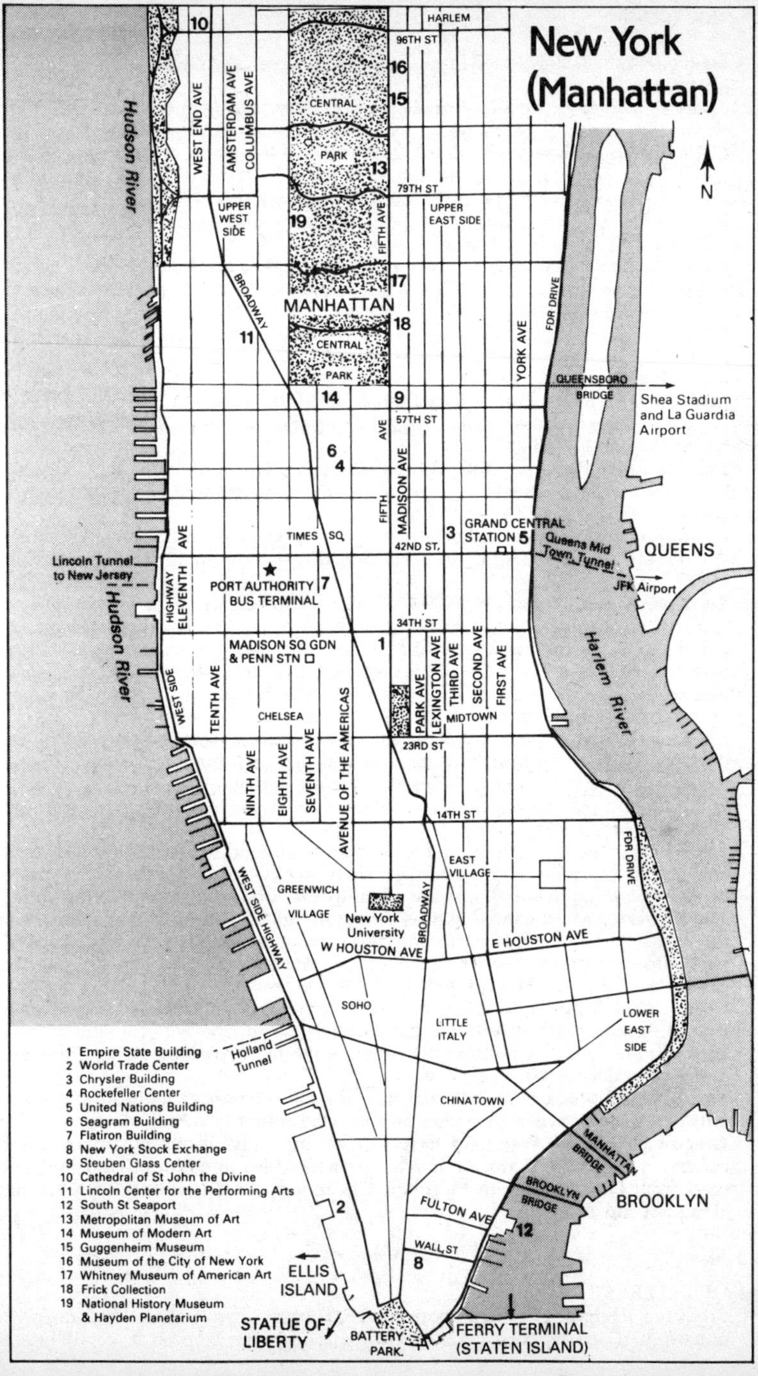
New York (Manhattan)
N
HARLEM
96TH ST
79TH ST
57TH ST
42ND ST.
34TH ST
23RD ST
14TH ST
WEST END AVE
AMSTERDAM AVE
COLUMBUS AVE
CENTRAL PARK
UPPER WEST SIDE
UPPER EAST SIDE
FIFTH AVE
BROADWAY
MANHATTAN
CENTRAL PARK
FDR DRIVE
YORK AVE
QUEENSBORO BRIDGE
Shea Stadium and La Guardia Airport
MADISON AVE
TIMES SQ
GRAND CENTRAL STATION
Queens Mid Town Tunnel
QUEENS
JFK Airport
Lincoln Tunnel to New Jersey
Hudson River
ELEVENTH AVE
HIGHWAY
PORT AUTHORITY BUS TERMINAL
MADISON SQ GDN & PENN STN
WEST SIDE
TENTH AVE
CHELSEA
NINTH AVE
EIGHTH AVE
SEVENTH AVE
AVENUE OF THE AMERICAS
PARK AVE
LEXINGTON AVE
THIRD AVE
SECOND AVE
FIRST AVE
MIDTOWN
Harlem River
EAST VILLAGE
WEST SIDE HIGHWAY
GREENWICH VILLAGE
New York University
W HOUSTON AVE
E HOUSTON AVE
SOHO
LITTLE ITALY
LOWER EAST SIDE
Holland Tunnel
CHINATOWN
MANHATTAN BRIDGE
BROOKLYN BRIDGE
BROOKLYN
FULTON AVE
WALL ST
ELLIS ISLAND
STATUE OF LIBERTY
BATTERY PARK
FERRY TERMINAL (STATEN ISLAND)
1 Empire State Building
2 World Trade Center
3 Chrysler Building
4 Rockefeller Center
5 United Nations Building
6 Seagram Building
7 Flatiron Building
8 New York Stock Exchange
9 Steuben Glass Center
10 Cathedral of St John the Divine
11 Lincoln Center for the Performing Arts
12 South St Seaport
13 Metropolitan Museum of Art
14 Museum of Modern Art
15 Guggenheim Museum
16 Museum of the City of New York
17 Whitney Museum of American Art
18 Frick Collection
19 National History Museum & Hayden Planetarium

Dallas BBQ, 21 University Place, 674-4450. 'Great early bird specials.' ($7.95 for two.)
Eddie's, Waverley Pl and Broadway, 420-0919. NYU student eatery. 'Very cheap and enormous portions.'
El Cantinero, 86 University Place, 255-9378. Authentic Mexican food. Fajitas a speciality. Lunch for $6, dinners start at $9. On Monday, all you can eat for $7.95. 5–8pm every night—FREE food if you buy a drink.
Jackson Hole, 232 E 64th St, 371-7187, or 91st St and Madison Ave, 427-2820. 'Manhattan's finest half-pound hamburgers, $3.75.'
Katz's Delicatessen, 205 E Houston St, 254-2246, Lower East Side. You can sample the meat before deciding which sandwich. Have been in business for 103 years. A New York Jewish institution.
Luna, 112 Mulberry St, 226-8657. Cheap, tasty Italian food in the heart of Little Italy. Mafioso Crazy Joe Gallo was gunned down in the intersection not far from here.
Mee Sum Mee Tea House and Pastry, 48 Mott St, 233-8155. 'Only Chinese people; waiter didn't speak English.' Prices for lunch $2.50–$6.50. 'Try "shrimp lo mein" $3.75.'
Famous Ray's Pizza, 319 6th Ave, 645-8404, or 11th St and 6th Ave, 243-2253. Greenwich Village. One slice of pizza the size of Luxembourg costs less than $3 and is a filling meal. 'This is the best.'
Ukrainian Restaurant, 140 Second Ave at 8th St, 529-5024. Several Ukrainian restaurants in the neighbourhood, but this is the best. Bowl of borscht for $2.
Ye Waverly Inn, 16 Bank St, 929-4377. American cuisine, with chicken pot pie featured attraction. Cozy atmosphere with fireplaces and backyard garden.
For cheap, spicy **Indian** food, visit Madison Ave around 27th St, also E Sixth St between First and Second Avenues and other nearby streets. The number of hole-in-the-wall restaurants here has exploded recently. Dinner for $5 isn't a fantasy, but bring your own booze if you want a drink with dinner.
Chinatown justifies its reputation as a haven for good, inexpensive Chinese cooking. Walk along Mott, Bayard and Pell Sts, read menus, and look for the restaurant where the most Chinese people are eating.
For oom-pah-pah bands and the wurst in **German** cooking, stroll through **Yorkville**, along E 86 St.
Little Italy, next to Chinatown, has a number of good Italian restaurants, cafes and groceries, with waiters surlier than Rocky ready to push the pasta. Mulberry and Lafayette Sts, south of Houston, are especially fertile territory.
The Bowery, east of Chinatown, is more famous for its bums (that's American for derelict) than for places to eat. But if your budget is rock bottom, walk along Bowery St by day for some of the lowest food prices in the city. Be careful at night. Try **MacDougall's**, 89 MacDougall, 477-4021.
Upper West Side, between 60th and 90th Sts has an endless succession of trendy restaurants. Try **Victor's Cafe**, 236 W. 52nd, 586-7714 for Cuban food. Lots of new, trendy cafe-type places are opening, especially along Columbus and Amsterdam Aves.
SoHo, south of Houston to Canal, has a large number of interesting restaurants squeezed between the galleries and second-hand clothing stores.
Greenwich Village West and **East Village** are probably the most varied and exciting places to look for food. Walk between 14th St south of Houston, and west from First Avenue to the river. Cheaper spots cluster around NYU and along Second Ave.

OF INTEREST

Brooklyn Heights. A neighbourhood of brick, brownstone and wooden houses, high up overlooking New York harbour. New York as it was 100 years ago. You can walk here across the **Brooklyn Bridge**, a hundred-year-old suspension bridge, from South Street Seaport, for a fine view of lower Manhattan.

Cathedral of St John the Divine, 112th St and Amsterdam Ave, 316-7540. Otherwise known as St John the Unfinished. Work began in 1892, was suspended in 1941 when America entered the war. Enthusiasm waned, funds dried up and Americans forgot how to build Gothic cathedrals. Even unfinished (with 100 years' work still to go), it is the largest Gothic cathedral in the world. Free tours at 11am (Sun-service at 11am; tour at 12.45. Closed Mon). $2 donation. Open 7am–5pm. 'Weird, wonderful, memorable.' Also, don't miss the **Peace Park** and its amazing fountain right next door.

Chrysler Building, 405 Lexington and 42nd St. Lovely example of 'art deco' architecture incorporating auto parts among other things. Was the world's tallest building for one whole year.

Coney Island, containing the famous amusement park, **Astroland**, W 10th St and Surf Ave, (718) 372-0275. A gaudy, fun place for generations, with crowded beach. Admission $12.99. While here visit the **NY Aquarium**, (718) 265-3400, open 10am–5pm daily; till 7pm weekends. $5.75 adults. 'Fantastic.' Both the BMT and IND subways will get you there. (See Beaches).

Ellis Island. Once the landing point for 15 million European immigrants entering the US between 1892 and 1924, and consequently a place of enormous significance and poignancy for many Americans. Re-opened late 1990 as a wonderful museum. 'Highly recommended.' 9am–4pm weekdays, 9am–5pm Sat, Sun. For info call (212) 363-6304. **Circle Line** is the only way to get from Manhattan to Ellis Island. Ferries leave Battery Park every half hour, 9.30am–4pm.

Empire State Building, Fifth Ave and 34th St, 736-3100. The office at the bottom will give a report of the atmospheric conditions at the top. Make sure it's a clear day. $3.75 to go up, no discounts for students. Not the tallest building any more, but the view, night and day, is still fantastic. 'Go up at night, unforgettable views and less crowded.' Open 9.30am till 11.30pm. On the Concourse level downstairs you'll find the **Guinness World Records Exhibit Hall**, 947-2335. Daily 9am–10pm. $7 entry. 'Not worth it. Buying the book is a better investment.'

Flatiron Building, Madison Sq at 22nd St. The first iron-framed building and progenitor of New York's skyscrapers. An ornate wedge shaped building, it's still worth seeing.

Liberty Island, $6 round trip. Info: 269-5755. Beware of hours of heated queueing with no shade: go to the dock early (arrive by 8.45am; first boat leaves for Ellis Island directly, 9.15am). Consider going by way of New Jersey (from Liberty State Park—75% of visitors leave from Manhattan.)

Lincoln Center for the Performing Arts, 62nd–65th Sts and Columbus Ave, 875-5000. Largest performing arts centre in the world, containing opera house, concert hall, theatre, museum, Juilliard School. Hour long tour $7.50, students $6.50. Times vary so call same day you want to go after 9.30am to reserve a place. Lincoln Center Performance Hotline for current shows: 875-5400. The **Metropolitan Opera House** has its own backstage tours, but closes early in the summer. Call 769-7020 for details. Look for free concerts and other happenings during the summer.

New York Stock Exchange, 20 Broad St at Wall St. Free admission to the observation gallery and Visitors Center, open weekdays 9.15am–4.00pm. Arrive early to get a ticket.

Radio City Music Hall, 50th St and 6th Ave, 632-4041. Tours of the world's largest movie theatres in an art deco palace cost $8 and run daily from 10.15am to 4.45pm starting from the lobby.

Seagram Building, 375 Park Ave, between 52nd and 53rd St, 572-7000. Designed by Mies Van Der Rohe and Phillip Johnson as first 'anti-bourgeois' modern building. Brief free tour, Tue, 3pm.

South Street Seaport, 669-9400, by Fulton St Fish Market. A five-block restoration of New York 200 years ago, undertaken for the Bicentennial. The ship museum costs $6, students $4. Evening entertainments include Cocktail Cruises ($15) and live Music Cruises ($18). Also—craft centre and 19th century printing store. Tours noon and 7pm. Open 10am–5pm.
Staten Island Ferry, (718) 390-5253. Nobody should miss what is certainly the best travel bargain to be found anywhere. It costs just 50 cents round trip. Frequent departures from Battery Park, at the tip of Manhattan. Passes close to the Statue of Liberty. Superb view of the Manhattan skyline, many people's (among them poet Walt Whitman's) favourite view of New York.
Statue of Liberty National Monument, Liberty Island, 269-5755. After getting the world's largest facelift, Lady Liberty is again open to the public. $6 admission, open 7 days a week. Take Circle Line boats from Battery Park. Free **American Museum of Immigration** in statue's base. 'Best time to go is 9.30am.'
Steuben Glass Center, Fifth Ave and 56th St. Too expensive to buy but always superb to look at.
United Nations Building, First Ave and 46th St, 963-7713. Hour-long tours are run every 30 minutes, 9.15am–4.45pm. Adults $6.50, students $4.50, children $3, not under 5 yrs. Expect an hour-long wait. The General Assembly usually meets between 10.30am and 1.00pm and after 3.00pm, Sept–Dec. Free tickets for these and other official meetings during the year are issued at the admission desk in the main lobby no earlier than 30 min before the meeting, and are given on a first-come, first-served basis. Be sure to arrive early.
Woodlawn Cemetery. In the Bronx, and the last stop on the subway. The last stop for much of New York's high society, too. 400 landscaped acres of opulent mausolea and monuments to men who started from nothing and worked their way to a spot of turf at Woodlawn. Cast includes Westinghouse, Bat Masterson, associate of Wyatt Earp, Fiorello La Guardia, F W Woolworth, J C Penney, and A Bulova, the watch tycoon.
World Financial Center, across from the World Trade Center, Battery Park City, Hudson River and West St, Manhattan. Take the subway #1 or #9 to Courtland St. A gathering place of shops, restaurants and entertainment. Particularly relaxing (and free!) on a hot day is the **Winter Garden**, one of the most beautiful indoor spaces around. Tall, elegant palm trees and AC, a superb view of the harbour and a flowing monumental staircase. Info: 945-0505.
World Trade Center, Church, Vesey, West and Liberty Sts, 435-7000. The views from the 107th floor glassed-in observation deck and 110th floor open air promenade—more than a quarter mile high—are spectacular. Open 9.30am–11.30pm, $4.

MUSEUMS AND ART GALLERIES

American Museum of Natural History, Central Pk W between 77th and 81st Sts, 769-5000. Huge, scattered over 22 buildings. Natural history collection from all continents and seas, though especially strong on Africa and North America. Open daily, incl holidays. Sun–Thur 10am–5.45pm, Fri–Sat 10am–8.45pm. Entry by donation, suggested $5 adult, $2.50 students. In the same complex, the **Hayden Planetarium**, 81st between Central Park West and Columbus, 769-5920. 45 min shows, Mon–Fri at 1.30pm and 3.30pm, Sat and Sun at 1, 2, 3, 4. Closed holidays. Adults $5, students $4. Fri–Sat eve. Laser-light shows, $8.50.
The Cloisters, Fort Tryon Park, off Henry Hudson Parkway, call 923-3700 for bus and subway info. A branch of the Metropolitan devoted to medieval European art. On top of a hill overlooking the Hudson, the museum gives the impression of a 12th-century monastery. One of the lesser known but more enjoyable galleries. Open Mar–Oct, Tue–Sun 9.30am–5.15pm, closed Mon; rest of year closes at 4.45pm. Adults $6, students $3 (includes admittance to Metropolitan Museum of Art). Tours for individuals at 3pm, Tue–Thur.

The Frick Collection, 1 E 70th St at Fifth Ave, 288-0700. Walk in to this Italianate villa, once Henry Frick's home, and there is a peaceful hush in the small courtyard. Walk round the rooms and see works by Titian, Velázquez, Whistler and a searing Rembrandt self-portrait; plus wonderful furniture and interiors. A small delight. Tues–Sat 10am–6pm, Sun 1am–6pm; $3, $1.50 students. 'Unsuspected highlight of New York.'

Solomon R. Guggenheim Museum, 1071 Fifth Ave at 88th St, 423-3500. After restoration the fantastic building is finally as architect Frank Lloyd Wright wished it. The spiral winds down taking you past the contemporary art collection. Now with a new wing for more permanent displays. Open daily except Thurs 10am–8pm; $7, $4 students. Also has second location downtown at 575 Broadway at Prince St, combination tickets $10, $6 students, with its Impressionist, Surrealist and Minimalist collection.

Intrepid Sea–Air–Space Museum, W 46th St and 12th Ave, Pier 86, 245-2533. Restored aircraft carrier with planes, also space exhibit and submarine. Open daily 10am–5pm, $7.

Metropolitan Museum of Art, Central Park, Fifth Ave and 82nd St, 879-5500. One of the world's greatest collections and the largest of its kind in the Western Hemisphere. There are over 3 million works tracing the evolution of art from the 13th century to the present day, plus the largest Egyptian collection outside Egypt. Particularly restful on a blistering summer's day is **Astor Court**, the Ming scholar's retreat. Stone, flora and a miniature waterfall are arranged in a yin and yang relationship, installed by 27 Chinese engineers in 1980. Tue–Sun 9.30am–5.15pm, Fri–Sat 9.30am–8.45pm, closed Mon. Suggested donation, $6 adults, $3 students.

Museum of Modern Art, 11 W 53rd St, 708-9480. Set up in 1929 because the Met refused to acknowledge the existence of modern art, this is the place to see Picasso, Monet, and just about any other modern painter you can care to think of, plus superb photography. Rest those weary feet in the restful and heavily stocked sculpture garden. Open Fri–Tues 11am–6pm, Thurs 9pm, Closed Wed; $7.50, $4.50 students, pay as little as you want from 5pm Thurs. Films at 2pm and 5pm.

Museum of the American Indian (in the National Smithsonian Institute), Broadway at 155th St, 283-2497. One of the finest collections of native American artifacts in the world. Open Tue–Sat 10am–5pm, Sun 1–5pm, closed holidays. $3 adults, $2 students. 'A treasure house.' This is part of the Audubon Terrace Museum Group which includes the **Hispanic Society of America** with Spanish and Portuguese sculpture, painting, and decorative arts, 690-0743. Open Tue–Sat 10am–4.30pm, Sun 1pm–4pm, closed Mon. Free, visits by appt only (926-2234). Library closed Aug.

Museum of TV and Radio, 25 W 52 St, 621-6800. The computer library here holds over 40,000 TV and radio programs, commercials for listening and viewing. Popular, so reserve on arrival. Also special exhibits and screenings. Open Tue–Sun 12–6, Thurs 12–8. Closed Mondays. $5, students $4.

American Numismatic Society with more than 1 million coins, 234-3130. Open Tue–Sat, 9am–4.30pm, Sunday 1pm–4pm, closed Mon.

Museum of the City of New York, Fifth Ave at 103rd St, 534-1672. Fascinating story of city's growth from a small Dutch community. Free, although donations suggested, $5 adults, $3 students. Open Wed–Sat 10am–5pm, Sun and holidays 1pm–5pm.

Whitney Museum of American Art, 945 Madison Ave, corner of 75th St, 570-3636. Devoted exclusively to 20th-century American art. Wed–Sat 11am–6pm, Sun 11am–6pm, closed Mon and Tue. Adults $6, students $5.

TOURS

Since the city is best explored on foot, and bus tours are very expensive, the authors consider that the only tours really worth taking are the boat trips around Manhattan and the bus and foot treks around Harlem.

Circle Line, Pier 83, 12th Ave and W 42nd St, 563-3200. 3 hr boat trips around Manhattan leave regularly beginning at 9.30am, last tour at 4.30pm. Call for harbour light cruises (7pm every evening). Adults $18, children under 12, $9. 'Make sure you sit on left side of boat.' 'Can get chilly.' 'Great value.'
Grayline Tours, 900 Eighth Ave between 53rd and 54th Sts, 397-2600. Offers 2 hr tours of Harlem and Manhattan. Lower Manhattan, at $14.75 adults, and a 4½ hr combined, $24.50 adults. The Grayline tours are probably not worth taking unless you're only in New York for a brief time.
Island Helicopters haul you aloft from their pads at 34th St on the East River, 683-4575. Tours start at $47 per person for 10 minutes of booming and zooming over the UN and East River. Other longer, costlier tours available. 'A real experience if you've never been up in a helicopter before.' 'Try to sit next to the pilot.'

ENTERTAINMENT

No other American city can offer such a variety of amusements. Entertainment, however, can be expensive for the stranger who does not know his way around. Broadway theatres, most night clubs and some cinemas will put a strain on modest budgets. At the same time, free entertainment abounds.
Read the *New Yorker, Village Voice, Where Magazine, Seven Days, New York Magazine*'s *Cue Magazine* section, or look for a free copy of *NY Talk*, for complete details of shows, jazz and cinemas. The New York Convention and Visitors Bureau, 2 Columbus Circle, 397-8222, can also provide useful information regarding shows, events and entertainments.
There are free orchestral, pop, operatic concerts, dance groups, and theatrical performances in **Central Park** throughout the summer. These are popular, so try to arrive at least 2 hours before the performance to stake your claim. Also, look out for local street festivals.
Greenwich Village and **SoHo** are two of the most interesting entertainment areas. Good jazz and folk music, as well as eating places, can still be found among the many tourist traps in the Village, although SoHo is definitely where New Yorkers go now. Go to the better places, even if there is an admission charge; you will find the best music. Beware of places that do not advertise an admission or cover charge but extract large sums for a required drink and offer inferior entertainment.
Washington Square is infested with pseudo folksingers on weekend afternoons. The **Loeb Student Center** on the south side of the Square presents a series of excellent free concerts on Weds in July.

JAZZ

Check the *Village Voice, New York Magazine*'s *Cue Section* and *Jazz Interactions* news sheet for all the gigs. Jazz remains one of New York City's biggest sounds and the action takes place all over town.
Apollo Theatre, 253 W 125th St, 749-5838 or 864-0372, nearest subway stop: 125th St station on Eighth Ave line. Historic jazz cabaret and theatre. Now has shows at $15 and up. Try the famous Wednesday Amateur nights at 7.30 for $5–15. Book ahead at Ticket Masters, 307-7171. Look for some of the biggest names in contemporary music to play here. Amateur night once gave so many their first big break. Remember to be careful in Harlem at night.
Cajun, 129 Eighth Ave at 16th St, 691-6174. Come here for the classic New Orleans sound.
Blue Note, 131 W Third St, 475-8592. Serves food and hot jazz. 'Small, but attracts some big names.' 'Jazz capital of the world.' Music $20, $5 min at table or $15 min at bar.
Fat Tuesday's, 190 Third Ave, 533-7902. A lively place.
Greenwich Village Jazz Festival. In Washington Sq. Free. 'Great atmosphere and big names, including Dizzy Gillespie.'

Sweet Basil, 88 Seventh Ave S, 242-1785. Smallish room with nice atmosphere and pleasant food; attracts the best bands; a steep $15 cover.
Village Gate, 160 Bleecker St, corner of Thompson St, Greenwich Village, 475-5120. Good trad jazz, 10pm onwards.
Village Vanguard, 178 Seventh Ave S, 255-4037. Sleazy, unkempt, chaotic and cramped; the perfect jazz club, always worth going to, whoever's playing.

BLUES
Dan Lynch's, 221 Second Ave at 14th St, 677-0911. A melting-pot of blues music in an atmospheric, faded dive.
Manny's Car Wash, 1558 3rd Ave at 87th St, 369-2583. Mostly local bands playing upbeat blues-rock. Interior is like *Budweiser* commercial; 45 rpm singles, photos and beer signs adorn the walls.
Tramps, 45 W 21st St, 727-7788. The *New York Times* bills it 'the most comfortable and refined place in the city to hear genuine blues'.

ROCK
CBGB's, 315 Bowery at Bleecker, 473-7743. Starts new rock bands off on the route to fame and fortune. Blondie and Talking Heads both had their debuts here.
Palladium, 126 E 14th St, 473-7171. 'The best and flashiest disco in town.' Very state of the art; includes 50 banks of TV monitors! Doors open 9pm.
Ritz, W 54th btwn 8th and Broadway, 956-3731. The hottest of the hot, this gets most of the big names. Wed–Sat 10pm–4am, 'Clubland'. Wed–Thur $10, Fri $12, Sat $15.

COUNTRY/WESTERN
Lone Star Roadhouse, 240 W 52nd St btwn Broadway and 8th, 245-2950. The 'official' Texas Embassy in the Big Apple. Offers an authentic Western experience, with 'the best in modern country-music', R&B, rock, Texas beer, hot chili, and a dance floor just right for two-stepping the night away.
Rodeo Bar/Albuquerque Eats, 375 Third Ave at 27th St, 683-6500. Authentic Southwest cuisine with late night country & western entertainment.

COMEDY
In the past few years, the number of comedy clubs across America has exploded, led by New York City. Since these clubs are popular, call at least a day before to reserve a table and check out prices.
Caroline's, 1626 Broadway between 49th and 50th, 956-0101, light snacks, cabaret.
Catch a Rising Star, 1487 First Ave betwn 77th and 78th Sts, 794–1906. Well-named. Tomorrow's famous names get up and practise their routines. The place really comes alive in the late hours when today's stars return to help them out. Sun–Thur $8 cover charge, Fri–Sat $12. 2 drinks min.
Improvisation, 358 W 44th St, 765-8268. Stand-up comics and some good, short theatre. Mon before 9pm no cover charge.

THEATRE
Broadway prices are high, but tickets go on sale at half price ($2.50 service charge) on the day of performance at the **TKTS** booth, 47th St at Times Sq, 354-5800. 'Be prepared for very long queues.' Wed, Sat matinee sales 10am–2pm, Sunday 12–2pm, evening sales 3pm–8pm. Get there at least 45 minutes before sale time for best pickings. Same day tickets are also available at 2 World Trade Center, where the lines are shorter (Mon–Fri 11am–5.30pm, Sat 11am–1pm, travellers' cheques accepted).
There is also always something interesting happening 'Off-Broadway' and prices are lower. Read the *Village Voice* for 'Off-off-Broadway' plays, the best theatre buy. Keep a look-out in hotels, drugstores, coffee shops, news-stands and

Visitors Bureau at 2 Columbus Circle for 'Two Fers' (two tickets for the price of one). If you hang around the outside of a show that is not sold out, right before it begins, and timing is critical, you can bargain your way into very cheap theatre seats. Standing room is often available at the most popular shows.

CINEMA

Movie houses around Times Square and along the Upper East Side start around $7. There are many other smaller and cheaper neighbourhood cinemas, however. Look them up under 'Other Movies' in the *Village Voice*.

Radio City Music Hall, the largest cinema in the world, in an art deco palace. Guided tour $8. Home of the famous, spectacular Rockettes. For tour info call 632-4000.

Info on tickets to TV shows being taped in Manhattan can often be obtained from the Convention and Visitors Bureau at 2 Columbus Circle. Or just call the TV stations.

SHOPPING

Department Stores: Macy's, Broadway at 34th St. New York's biggest; Bloomingdale's, Lexington and 58th, mais c'est chic! Sak's Fifth Avenue, and Lord and Taylor are the epitome of American Style.

Book Stores: Strand Bookshop, Broadway and 12th St. Huge second-hand bookstore. Barnes and Noble, 600 Fifth Ave, and 17th St and Fifth Ave, reductions on best sellers and others. Science Fiction Bookshop, 163 Bleecker St, 473-3010. Stocks virtually every SF book in print. Rizzoli Books, 57th St off 5th Ave, beautiful, coffee table books. Coliseum Books, Broadway at 57th St, 757-8381; a BUNAC favourite, open until 11pm (10pm Mon).

Records: Downstairs Records, 35 W 43rd St, 354-4684. A great place to look for that lost Deanna Durbin single. J&R Music World, 23 Park Row, 732-8600. Enormous stocks of records and tapes. Venus Records, Sixth Ave at 8th St. 'Good for old records, collector's items. Tower Records at 67th St and Broadway and 692 Broadway.

Clothing: Canal Jean Co, 304 Canal St and 504 Broadway at Spring St. Jeans, etc. (Canal St is good for everything.) Orchard St Market, Lower East Side, off Canal St, Sun mornings. 'Traditional Jewish street market, lots of bustle and colour.'

OUT OF DOORS

The Bronx Zoo, properly the New York Zoological Park, Fordham Rd and Southern Blvd, (718) 220-5100. Take the #5 or #2 to E 180th St. Open daily, 10am–5pm, $5.75 adults, $2 kids, Tue–Thurs, free. Shorter hours in winter. New York's biggest zoo: children's zoo, animal rides and safari monorail $1.50 extra. New baboon reserve.

Central Park Zoo, 830 5th Ave, north of Plaza Hotel. The shining star of zoos with exquisite rainforest, arctic and other exhibits.

Central Park offers so much to the visitor and resident alike—a zoo, skating rinks, pools, playgrounds, horse paths, and even a maze garden—that it is impossible to conceive of life in New York without it. Visit the information center at the Dairy, west of the zoo near 64th St, 794-6564, for an excellent map and orientation to one of the world's great parks.

Beaches: Coney Island and **Brighton Beach**, Brooklyn, reached by D Subway. **Jones Beach**, by car, or Long Island Railroad from Penn Station to Freeport, then local bus to beach. $8.

Spectator sports: baseball in summer: the Mets at Shea Stadium in Queens, the Yankees at Yankee Stadium in the Bronx. Basketball, the Knicks at Madison Square Garden, the Nets across the Hudson in the Meadowlands. The Islanders ice hockey team plays at the Coliseum, Uniondale on Long Island, and the Rangers skate in Madison Square Garden. For tennis devotees, the US Open takes place at Flushing Meadows in Queens in early September. The Jets and Giants American football teams play in the Meadowlands.

AMERICA'S AMAZING THEME PARKS

America's incredible amusement parks have evolved from trolley company-sponsored carnivals, a ploy to attract passengers, to the present megaparks that entertain over 129 million visitors annually in hundreds of versions of derring-do, spine-tingling, and otherwise. If you're looking for thrills, try these:

THEME PARKS: Coney Island, New York City. Indulge in nostalgia, of the sort featured in Woody Allen's *Radio Days* and countless other films. **Disney World**, Orlando, FL. The largest and most visited in America features The Epcot Center, Magic Kingdom, Typhoon Lagoon Waterpark, Pleasure Island nightclub extravaganza. **MGM Studios** park is nearby (407-824-4321) currently featuring *Star Tours* ('A ride to the moon of Endor') and *Here Come the Muppets!* Planned for 1994: *Roger Rabbit's Hollywood*, and *Tower of Terror Hotel*. **Disneyland**, Anaheim, CA. The original Disney park and 2nd most visited, includes Space Mountain Rollercoaster, Michael Jackson's amazing 3-D movie *Captain Eo*, Star Tours. **Universal Studios** (407-363-8000) Already well-established in LA, the Orlando branch opened in 1990 with 444 acres of rides, shows and attractions from the movie world. Rides include *the virtual reality Back to the Future, ET* and *Confrontation* and there is an *Alfred Hitchcock—the art of making movies* show.

ROLLERCOASTER PARKS: The fastest, highest and biggest US rollercoasters are in the flat Midwest. Among the most well-known: **King's Island**, Mason OH, (513) 398-5600. Eight banked turns and 70 mph speeds make this wooden rollercoaster *The Beast*, the world's longest with 7400 feet of tracks (lasting a death-defying 3 mins 40s). Their *King Cobra*, a stand-up looping coaster, is described as 'the ultimate elevator nightmare in forward motion'. New here in '93 was *Top Gun*, based on the film, a 2 mins 30 secs suspended adrenelin rush. Even more terrifying, according to the *New York Times*, is the Magnum XL-200 at **Cedar Point**, Sandusky OH, (419) 626-0830. This coaster climbs 20 stories only to hurtle down a 60-degree drop with curves at 70 mph. Cedar Point's most recent addition is Snake River Falls, with 80 ft drops at 50 degree angles, this is the world's tallest, steepest and fastest water-ride. For true rush-junkies, ther is also the horrifying 65 mph *Meanstreak*. **Six Flags Great America**, Gurnee IL (708) 249-1776, offers the double-track triple helix wooden *American Eagle* which reaches speeds of over 66 mph; *Batman*, a 2 min suspended outside looping thrill-of-a-lifetime; and the triple looping *Steel Shockwave*. **Six Flags over Mid-America**, Eureka MO, (314) 938-5300. The park's newest coaster, the *Ninja*, has spirals, drops, a sidewinder and 360 degree loop. **Worlds of Fun** (and Oceans of Fun water park next-door), Kansas City MO, (816) 454-4545, has two equally thrilling coasters, the *Timber Wolf* is faster but the *Orient Express* has twists and coils and even doubles back on itself. In the south, **Six Flags in Arlington** TX, (817) 640-8900, features *Flashback*, a sky coaster that zips you forward and backwards in corkscrew spirals; the *Texas Cliffhanger* drops a sickening 128 in a free fall. The *Texas Giant* drops 137 ft at 62 mph and is the second in size only to the 166 ft drop *Rattler* at the **Texas Fiesta**, San Antonio (210) 697-5050. At **Astroworld**, Houston TX, (713) 799-1234, try the *Texas Cyclone*, a long-time favourite and the *Sky Screamer*, an elevator car simulates a free fall from 10 stories. Their newly-imported *Ultra Twister* is described as 'like riding inside a giant slinky, with a 9-storey free-fall to start'. At **Six Flags over Georgia** near Atlanta, (404) 739-3400, the *Free Fall* slowly climbs 10 stories but descends at 50 mph. Here also is the world's first triple-loop roller coaster, the *Mind Bender*. **Six Flags Magic Mountain**, Valencia, CA, (805) 255-4111. The world's largest looping rollercoaster, the *Viper*, reaches 70 mph and achieves 7 inversions – 'The initial drop is truly heart-stopping!' 'They even have cameras mounted on the cars.' Other rides include *Colossus*, one of the largest double-track, wooden coasters in the world; and the *Revolution*, who's track threads through tunnels 'A knee-wobbling experience.' The next biggest adrenalin-high sought by American Coaster Enthusiasts is a 100 mph-ride necessitating a drop of 40 stories!

WATER PARKS: Of growing popularity and ingenuity, especially in America's warmer states, are America's 136 waterparks. In Florida, **Typhoon Lagoon** in Orlando, (407) 560-4100 has the largest wave pool in the US; **Adventure Island**, Tampa, (813) 987-5660 is home of the *Tampa Typhoon*, a slide that shoots down from a height of seven stories. **Waterworld's** *Tidal Wave*, in Denver CO, (303) 427-7873, releases mammoth waves. **Water Country U.S.A.**, Williamsburg VA, (800) 343-7946, boasts *Double Rampage*, a nearly-vertical water slide of 75 feet. On the body flume, *Jet Stream*, you'll reach up to 25 mph as you round a curve—on your back. New here is *Malibu Pipeline*, a totally enclosed (dark tunnel) flume ride over 3 stories high. **Wet and Wild** parks are located in Orlando FL, Las Vegas NV, and Dallas TX and feature, among other rides, fast, helical rides on water mats (Mach 2) and sensational seven-story free fall. Professional surfing competitions can be witnessed at **Wild River Park**, Laguna CA.

INFORMATION

New York Convention and Visitors Bureau, 2 Columbus Circle, 397-8222. Free maps, list of tourist attractions. Offers pamphlets with walking tours of the city. The International Center, 7th floor of 50 W 23rd St betwn 5th and 6th, 255-9555, gives parties, cultural events and English lessons.
Traveler's Aid, 944-0013, 158 W 42nd St.
Post Offices: dozens around the city. Major ones are, Eighth Ave at 33rd St (open 24 hrs), 340 W 42nd St, Lexington Ave and E 45th, in Macy's, Herald Square, beneath Rockefeller Center (enter at 620 or 610 Fifth Ave), 62nd and Broadway.

TRANSPORTATION–WITHIN MANHATTAN

Subways. You should not be deterred by the infuriating topography of New York's subway. Although dirty, noisy, and sometimes unpleasant, the subway is one of the cheapest and best means of transport around the city. The fare is now $1.25 and may be $1.50 by summer '94. Buy subway tokens at the kiosk near the turnstiles. A new cleaning solution has done away with most of the graffiti that once covered the cars—an 'improvement' that many find quite sad. There are express and local trains; it is very important to know which you have to take to reach your destination. Since the whole system is very badly marked, alertness and a venturesome spirit are prerequisites. To be avoided by lone women late at night. Free maps are obtainable from the booking offices. For information on subway trains and city buses, call Transit Authority at (718) 330-1234. There are information centres at Penn Station, Grand Central and the Port Authority.
PATH trains link several subway stops with points in New Jersey.
City Buses, (718) 330-1234. Exact fare, $1.25 (may be $1.50) in change, required. Transfers available. Your ISIC card may get you a student discount.
Taxis. Ride only in the ones painted bright yellow, others are imposters. Learn the meaning of fear, as your certifiable driver squeezes the cab between two buses at 45mph. Tip driver 15 percent if you arrive alive. Expensive for one, but for three or four, economical over short distances.
Bike Rental. 'An original and dangerous way to see New York.' Companies come and go, so check yellow pages in phone book. Rental places usually require credit card or $50 deposit.
Roller Skates. Look around in Central Park on weekends to find roller skate or roller blade rental places.

ARRIVING IN/LEAVING MANHATTAN

Buses. All inter-city bus lines including merged Greyhound behemoth, (800) 231-2222, use the Port Authority Terminal, Eighth Ave and 41st St. Arrive at least one hour early to purchase tickets. Though the building is new, the inhabitants late at night are a bit run down. Be careful.
Green Tortoise, 431-3348 or (800) 227-4766. 11 day trip Westbound buses to SF, LA for $289 and $76 for food.
Trains: Penn Station, 33rd and Eighth, under Madison Sq Garden. Amtrak service, (800) USA-RAIL, between Boston, Washington, Chicago and further south and west. Amtrak north towards Montreal and Toronto. Also Long Island Railroad, (718) 217-5477, and PATH, (800) 234-7284. Tickets also at Amtrak Rockefeller Plaza Office, 12 W 51st St, (800) 872-7245.
Grand Central Station, 42nd and Park. Handles Metro-North Commuter Railroad (532-4900) to NY suburbs and Connecticut.
New Jersey Transit trains, (201) 762-5100, can also take you to Princeton, and Philadelphia.
Car Rental. Difficult if you're under 25, or don't have a major credit card. Try bargaining and arguing. See *Yellow Pages* for companies. Thrifty, National and Rent-a-Wreck among the cheapest. 'Most companies want driver to have licence and credit card with a sufficiently large credit limit; they won't allow splitting the cost between several people. Cash is generally useless except at international airports in conjunction with a passport.'

Car Driveaways. Automobile transporting companies, e.g. Auto Driveaway, 967-2344 abound, but the best is Dependable Drive-Away, 801 East Edgar Rd, Linden NJ, (800) 626-2505. No credit card required (age 21). 'Call in person, rather than phone.' For **maps** try the Rand McNally Map Store, 150 E 52nd St btwn Lexington and 3rd Ave, 758-7488, or AAA, 586-1166.

Car Rides. For rides with college students, check the bulletin boards at NYU, Loeb Center, Washington Sq, or at the Columbia University Bookshop, near Columbia U. Hitchhiking is dangerous. Single women absolutely mustn't do it, single men are taking their chances.

J. F. Kennedy Airport. Allow at least 1½ hrs travel. The cheapest way: subway to Howard Beach, $1.25 (or $1.40?), then free shuttle bus to airport terminals. Otherwise: take the 'E' subway train to Union Turnpike/Kew Gardens, then catch the Q10 bus to JFK. Total cost, $2.50 (or $2.80), (718) 995-4700 for info. You can also take the Long Island Railroad train from Penn Station to Jamaica, $3.50, then the Carey bus to JFK, $5. Another quick, easy way: Carey Transportation, (718) 632-0500—$11 from 125 Park Ave near Grand Central Station and also Port Authority. Carey also has buses connecting to LaGuardia and Newark airports. For general info: (800) AIR-RIDE.

LaGuardia Airport. Allow at least 1 hr travel. The cheapest way in and out: Q47 or Q33 bus to Roosevelt Ave/Jackson Heights subway station, then E train to Manhattan. Easier: Carey Transportation—$8.50 to 125 Park Ave near Grand Central Station and Port Authority.

Newark Airport. Allow at least 1 hr travel. Olympia Airport Express to Penn Station, Grand Central Station, or World Trade Center, $7. (212) 964-6233. NJ Transit Express Bus #300 to New York Port Authority—$7.

LONG ISLAND 'The Island', as New Yorkers call it, is a 150-mile-long glacial moraine, the terminal line of the last encroachment of the Ice Age. Extending eastwards from Manhattan, it includes two of the New York City boroughs, Brooklyn and Queens, and the built-up suburban county of Nassau, though more than half its length is occupied by the more rural county of Suffolk.

Long Island Sound quietly laps against its North Shore where hills, headlands, fields and woods have attracted some of the great houses of the wealthy. Scott Fitzgerald's Gatsby partied here, and **Sagamore Hill**, outside of Glen Cove, Nassau, was the home of President Theodore Roosevelt. In **Huntington**, further east, poet Walt Whitman spent his childhood (you can visit the house) and, nearby, the Vanderbilts had an estate which they connected to New York City with their own private motorway.

The South Shore, protected by Fire Island, receives a surprisingly gentle Atlantic breeze. Its beaches are generally flat and sandy. Except right out at the **Hamptons** (Southampton and East Hampton), this shoreline has always been less exclusive than the north, but it has certainly attracted those in search of magnificent beaches which stretch in a virtually unbroken line 100 miles out from the city.

All areas of Long Island are easily accessible from Manhattan via the Long Island Railroad from Penn Station, or via the Northern State and Southern State Parkways, and the Long Island Expressway, which at the city end is so often jammed with traffic that it's known as 'the longest parking lot in the world', but which eventually sweeps beyond the pandemonium towards the remoteness of Montauk Point's majestic lighthouse.

Long Island is fraught with social experiments, and **Jones Beach** is one of the nicest of them. With millions unemployed during the Depression,

President Franklin Roosevelt found work for many and fun for more by developing this four-mile stretch of the South Shore into an excellent sandy beach. On a hot summer's weekend, or the Fourth of July, up to half a million people and their cars join the seagulls for a good splash in the sun and water. Go there during the week if you want more of the beach to yourself. The Long Island Railroad, (718) 454-5477, offers train/bus service between the beach and Manhattan.

Fire Island, on a long sandbar further east than Jones Beach, is nicer yet, being not so much developed as preserved as a National Seashore for its natural beauty and bird life. Here is an excellent place for swimming, surfing, sunbathing, fishing, cooking over an open grill and getting up to no good in the sand dunes.

Facing the calm waters of Gardiners Bay, **Sag Harbor**, once a whaling port, is now a pleasant town where John Steinbeck chose to end his days, and where those wealthy enough to own sailing boats moor them. The **Sag Harbor Whaling Museum**, (516) 725-0770, is on Main St. Open daily 10am–5pm, Sun 1pm–5pm. Admission $3.

There are in fact several such salty and tranquil spots at the end of the island, as well as an Indian Reservation. A few days wandering is well worth it.

Many of the place names on Long Island derive from the Indians who once lived here fishing, planting or hunting deer: the Wantaghs, Patchogues and Montauks were a few of the tribes. **Montauk Point** marks the eastern extremity of Long Island where a towering lighthouse, built in 1796 by order of George Washington, looks over three sides of water and offers magnificent views of the rising sun.

Curiously enough, the oldest cattle ranch in the United States is also located out here.

HUDSON RIVER VALLEY Though not the key to the Northwest Passage that many early explorers hoped it would be, the Hudson has gouged a considerable valley from the mountains of upstate New York past the chalk cliffs of the Palisades to the granite slab of Manhattan, and onwards even from there, forming a great underwater trench several hundred miles long out to the edge of the continental shelf.

Much of the scenery along the valley is very beautiful and contains many historical towns such as **Tarrytown**, **West Point**, **Hyde Park** and electrifying **Sing Sing State Prison** in **Ossining**.

About 16 miles north of the George Washington Bridge on the eastern side of the Hudson, **Tarrytown** was the home of Washington Irving and Rip Van Winkle, the model for his story *The Legend of Sleepy Hollow*. His books, manuscripts and furniture are still here, the house, on West Sunnyside Lane, open to visitors. Both he and Andrew Carnegie, the American Steel magnate, are buried in Sleepy Hollow Cemetery. Also worth a visit are two restored (with Rockefeller money) Dutch colonial manors, the **Philipsburg** and **Van Cortlandt Manors**. The Philipsburg Manor has a working gristmill and, operating it, a miller from Staffordshire, England. Entrance to the Washington Irving House, **Sunnyside**, and each of the manors is $6. For information call (914) 631-8200.

Not an Indian reservation but a military reservation, **West Point** is the site of the US Military Academy, founded in 1802 to train military officers. The Academy is the alma mater of such architects of victory as Robert E Lee, General Custer and William (sue the media) Westmoreland.

If you like brass bands and cadets walking in straight lines, this is the place for you. Museum and grounds open daily. Parade schedules can be obtained by calling the information officer at 938-2638. Close by is the 5000-acre **Bear Mountain State Park**, good for camping and hiking. Park office, 446-4736.

Hyde Park, a small village 80 miles north of New York City, lies on scenic Route 9 overlooking the Hudson River. It was the home of President Franklin D Roosevelt and both he and Eleanor lie buried in the Rose Garden of the FDR Library and Museum. Nearby is the **Frederick W Vanderbilt mansion**, a Beaux-Arts-style house with elaborate furnishings. See how the big-time millionaires lived. For information call (914) 229-9115, open 9–5 daily April–October. $2.

Just a little further up the Hudson is the quaintish city of **Kingston**, founded as a Dutch trading post in 1614. In 1777 it became the first state capital and you can visit the restored Senate House on Fair St, 338-2786, where the senators met before fleeing for their lives in the face of a British attack. There are several Colonial buildings in the area, including the Old Dutch Church on Main St.

Woodstock, a magic name from the 1960s, is nearby off Route 28. Many an aging hippy can be seen making a nostalgic pilgrimage to the village which came to symbolise the Age of Aquarius youth movement after the rock concert to end all concerts in 1969. Imagine their suprise upon learning that the festival was actually held 57 miles south on Rte 17-B in the town of Bethel! Promoters intended to hold the festival in Woodstock but as its popularity became more apparent were forced to move it to a more spacious location. Today Woodstock, the town, is as it has long been, an arts colony with lots of boutiques and summertime craft and theatrical festivals.

The Catskill Mountains, just to the west of Kingston, is reputedly the spot where Rip Van Winkle dozed off for 20 years. It's an area of hills, streams, hiking paths and ski trails. The Catskills used to be the place where wealthy New Yorkers took their holidays and there is just a touch of decay and nostalgia at the resorts, an air of having seen better days. The resorts still operate, catering to a more Eastern European Jewish clientele, hence the nickname for the area, the Borscht Belt. The area remains a marvellous retreat for walking and getting away from it all.
The telephone area code is 914.

ALBANY Capital of the State of New York and named after the Duke of York and Albany who later became James II of England. Not the greatest place for the casual visitor but downtown does have some interesting new architecture in the shape of the Rockefeller Empire State Plaza, a massive shopping, office and cultural complex that cost a billion dollars to build.

Situated near the juncture of the Hudson and Mohawk Rivers, and on a line with the boundary between western Massachusetts and southern Vermont, the city is a convenient halting place before visiting these states, or

before exploring the local New York attractions of Saratoga, Lake George and Ticonderoga, the Adirondacks and Ausable Chasm.
The telephone area code is 518.

ACCOMMODATION
The most inexpensive accommodation during the summer is likely to be at the residence halls of the **State University of New York at Albany** (SUNYA), 442-5875, the **College of St Rose**, 454-5295. Call ahead to see if a room is available.
Days Inn, 16 Wolf Rd, take I-87 to exit 2E (Rte 5), 3 miles from downtown, 459-3600. D–$82. AC, cable TV, pool, and continental breakfast incl.
Econo Lodge, 300 Broadway, 434–4111. S–$61, D–$68, bath and TV. 'Expensive but convenient.'
YMCA, 13 State St and Connecticut, 374-9136. Men only. $21.50 per night, $60 + $5 key deposit.

OF INTEREST
Albany Institute of History and Art, 125 Washington Ave, 463-4478. Oldest museum in the state, some say the country. Dutch period and Hudson River School landscape paintings, 18th and 19th century furniture, etc. Open Tue–Fri 10am–5pm, Sat–Sun noon–5. Free.
Gov Nelson A Rockefeller Empire State Plaza, between Madison and State Sts, centre of town, 474-2418. 12-building complex housing 30 state agencies and cultural facilities. The most striking feature of this ultra-brute-modern affair is the 44-storey state office tower with **observation deck** up top, panoramas 9am–3.45pm, free.
New York State Museum, Empire State Plaza, 474-5842. Geology, history, Indians and natural history. In the New York Metropolis Hall is a vast display of the NYC urbanisation process, including a 1940 subway car, 1929 Yellow Cab, 1930 Chinatown import–export shop and mock-up of Sesame Street stage set. Daily 10am–5pm. Free. 'Superb.'
Schuyler Mansion State Historic Site, 32 Catherine St, 434-0834. Built in 1762, home of Gen Philip Schuyler, revolutionary luminary. Gentleman Johnny Burgoyne was a prisoner and Schuyler's daughter Betsy married Alexander Hamilton here. Free tours Wed–Sat 10am–5pm, Sun 1–5pm, Apr–Dec and every winter weekend.
State Capitol, northern end of Empire State Plaza, 474-2117. Free 1-hr tours 9am–4pm daily. Begun in 1867, the building includes the Million Dollar Staircase. The stonecarvers of the staircase reproduced in stone not only the famous, but also their family and friends. Also Senate and Assembly Chamber.

INFORMATION
Visitors Assistance, #106 on the Concourse, Empire State Plaza, 474-2418, 8am–5pm daily.
Traveler's Aid, 200 Green St, 463-2124.
Chamber of Commerce, 540 Broadway, 434-1214.

TRAVEL
Greyhound, 34 Hamilton St, 434–8095 or (800) 231 2222.
Amtrak, Albany-Rensselaer station, East St, (800) USA-RAIL or 462-5763. The scenic *Adirondack* train passes through between NYC and Montreal.

SARATOGA SPRINGS About 30 miles north of Albany, this favourite resort with its mineral springs bears a Mohawk name meaning 'place of swift water'. The waters, high in mineral content, are on tap at the Spa State Park. Abraham Lincoln's son, Bob, came here to celebrate his graduation from Harvard and found a town agog with its new racecourse. Now the nation's oldest thoroughbred racing track the **Saratoga Race Track** (called America's Ascot when it opened 100 years ago) runs races every August. The **National Museum of Racing** is located in town on Union Ave and Ludlow St. During August, accommodation is therefore more expensive and less available than at other times of the year. However, the **Saratoga Downtowner** (584-6160) at 413 Broadway is a good deal at $65 for a double room incl. breakfast and indoor pool. Read Damon Runyon's short stories before you go.

Saratoga Springs is also the summer home of the **New York City Ballet** in July, the Philadelphia Orchestra in August, and various transient rock and roll bands, all of which play at the outdoor **Saratoga Performing Arts Center**, 587-3330. Lawn seats cost between $10–12, depending on event.

Saratoga claims to have more restaurants per capita than any other American town, so finding good food won't be hard. Finding cheap food may be harder, so to savour the essence of Saratoga cuisine, buy a bag of crisps called *Saratoga Chips*, which were invented here 100 years ago. Try also the new **Hobo's** (587-7764) at 423 Broadway. A bowl of jambalaya, with rice, chicken, shrimps and home smoked sausage costs $5.75.

The telephone area code is 518.

LAKE GEORGE Another 25 miles north of Saratoga Springs is the town of Lake George and the lake itself, running to Fort Ticonderoga where it constricts before opening out again as Lake Champlain.

Lake George is billed as the resort area with 'a million dollar beach', but that refers less to the shore's quality and more to how much it probably costs to clean the place up after the tourist hordes have been by. Best to keep going through the area and on to the Adirondack Park.

Fort Ticonderoga at the other end of the lake is accessible by road or by boat from Lake George town, and is of interest to those who would know the methods by which the British Empire grew great. Constructed by the French in 1755, the British waited just long enough for it to be made comfortable before taking it over in 1756. Perhaps requiring some repairs to be made, the British then let rebel Ethan Allen grab it in 1775, and when suitable again for officers and gentlemen, Burgoyne took it back in 1777. The Yanks got the place in the end and now conduct guided tours for $6. Call 585-2821 for information. Open mid-May to mid-Oct. There is a car ferry service from Ticonderoga to Vermont.

The telephone area code is 518.

THE ADIRONDACKS This 101 year old state park encompasses the year round resort area of the Adirondack Mountains, an enormous expanse of mountains (incl. the state's highest peak, Mt Macy at 5344 ft), forests and lakes stretching thousands of square miles west of Lakes George and Champlian.

Lake Placid is the sporting centre of the area. After having been promoted by Melvil Dewey (of Decimal Library Classification System fame) as a summer resort in 1950, the site previously hosted the first Winter Olympic Games in 1932 and again in 1980. The landscape, with cross-country and downhill ski trails, large lakes and chairlifts is equally suitable for summer and winter excursions. The best view of the area is from the Olympic ski jump platform, 523-2202, $5. 'Worth it for the view alone.'

Ausable Chasm lies on the western shores of Lake Champlain where the Ausable River has cut a vast canyon through the rock. Boats, bridges and footpaths allow the visitor to explore it. Angling fanatics can obtain **fishing licences** for the river from the Town Hall on Main St (523-2162). $6 for a 5 day pass. $28 for the season.

ACCOMMODATION

Lake Placid is generally expensive. These are the best deals:
Hotel St Moritz, 31 Saranac Ave, 523-9240. D–$38 Sun–Thurs, $55, Fri–Sat, incls breakfast.
Northway Motel, 5 Wilmington Rd, across from junction of Rts 73 and 86, 523-3500. S–$49, D–$65.

OF INTEREST

Ausable Chasm, 834-7454. The tour by foot, boat and return bus costs a whopping $12.95. Available daily mid-May to mid-Oct. 'Not worth the effort. Big tourist trap full of little English grannies.'
Blue Mountain Lake, about 40 miles southwest of Lake Placid enroute to Utica and Syracuse. Lake and mountain scenery, and the **Adirondack Museum**, 1 mile north, (518) 352-7311. Shows life in the Adirondacks since colonial times, with 1890 private railroad car, log hotel, 1932 Winter Olympics memorabilia. Open daily 9.30am–5.30pm, $10. 'Allow 2–3 hrs to see it all.' 'Excellent.'
Lake Placid: **John Brown Farm State Historic Site**, 2 miles out of town on Rte 73; 523-3900. This is where he lies amouldering in the grave (see Harpers Ferry, West Virginia). Late May through late Oct: Wed–Sat 10am–5pm, Sun 1–5pm; admission free.

THE FINGER LAKES These slender lakes, splayed like the fingers of an open hand across midwestern New York, were formed by receding glaciers of the last Ice Age. Their names—Canandaigua, Seneca, Cayuga, Owasco and Skaneateles, still speak of the Indian legend that the lakes are the impress of the Great Spirit who here laid his hand upon the earth.

The lakes extend through a lush area of farmlands and vineyards, and are home to a number of wineries where you can sample the product. 'Very pleasant area. Go to wineries for short tour and a booze up on terrible wines.' But first, and enroute, perhaps make time for a stop at **Cooperstown**, a charming summer resort and home to the **Baseball Hall of Fame** (607-547-9988).

Syracuse, to the east of the Finger Lakes, was the site Chief Hiawatha chose about 1570 as the capital for the Iroquois Confederacy. Around the council fires of the longhouse met the Five Nations which for two centuries dominated northeastern North America. Salt first brought the Indians and later the French and Americans to the shores of Lake Onondaga. Syracuse was founded in 1805 and for many years most of the salt used in America came from here. The New York State Fair is held annually in Syracuse from late August through Labor Day. Well-regarded Syracuse University was founded here in 1870. Try staying at the **Downing International Hostel, AYH,** 535 Oak St, (315) 472-5788. Members $9, non-members $12.50 'Arrive early.'

ITHACA As the bumper sticker saying goes 'Ithaca is gorges'. Situated at the southern end of Cayuga Lake, Ithaca has within its boundaries many deep river gorges and spectacular waterfalls as well as hills that rival those of San Francisco in their steepness.

Perched high atop a hill overlooking Cayuga Lake is Ivy-Leaguer Cornell University (on a campus considered by many to be the most beautiful in the US) and also in town is well regarded, liberal arts Ithaca College. This high concentration of students (18,000 or so at Cornell) make the campus and town a fun, lively place to visit.

The telephone area code is 607.

ACCOMMODATION

Elmshade Guest House, 402 S Albany St, 273-1707. S–$39, D–$50, with shared bath.

Hillside Inn, 518 Stewart Ave, 272-9507, S–$35, D–$50. AC, colour TV.

Super 8 Motel, W Clinton St at Rte 13, 273-8088. S–$37–$42, D–$46–$48.

Trumansburg—Podunk Home Hostel (AYH), Podunk Rd, (at the Ski Centre), 387-9277. $5 members, $7 non-members. 10 miles from Ithaca by Greyhound or local bus, 2 mile walk from bus stop. On a Finnish homestead.

Camping: Buttermilk Falls State Park, 273-5761, 1 mile south on Rte 13, $11.50 first night, $10 extra nights.

FOOD/ENTERTAINMENT

Cornell is reputed to have the best campus food in the US. **The Ivy Room, Willard Straight Hall**, is open to all. Cornell also makes its own ice cream. The **Collegetown area** on the edge of campus is also good for eating and is the place to be when the sun goes down. Try **The Nines**, 311 College Ave, for live bands, beer and cheap pizza.

Ithaca Commons downtown has various eateries including **Heart's Content**, 156 State St. Soup, salads, 'great cheesecake and huge cookies' and sandwiches. Inexpensive. Here too are **Plums** and **The Haunt**, two recommended student bars. The Haunt has live music on Sat.

Hal's Delicatessen, 115 N Aurora, 273-7765. Old fashioned, but cheap, filling sandwiches etc. 'Well fed for $5.'

Moosewood Restaurant, Seneca and Cayuga Sts, 273-9610. Famous vegetarian restaurant. The owners have written three very popular vegetarian cookbooks, to be found on the kitchen shelf of every self-respecting college student. $4–$8.

The Other Side, 110 N Aurora, 273–2115. 'Good buffalo wings', chicken and burgers. $5 up. Homemade soups.

OF INTEREST

Hiking and biking are the ways to get around the area. There is a 30-mile hiking trail which loops around Ithaca and this may be a good way to start.

Cornell University. On the northeast side of town and can be reached by local bus from downtown. Take a guided tour (255-6200) or just wander. Climb the **McGraw Tower** (162 steps) for a glorious view of the lake and hills. Further vistas can be had from the **Herbert F. Johnson Museum of Art** (255-6464). Designed by I M Pei and dubbed 'the sewing machine', the museum also offers excellent collections of Asian, graphic and modern art. Tues–Sun 10am–5pm. Weds till 8pm. Free.

Cornell Plantations. The campus covers some 4000 acres including the main campus buildings, experimental farms, nature trails, Beebe Lake and **Sapsucker Woods**, a bird sanctuary. The Plantations are one of the nicest things on campus and comprise an arboretum, specialised plant collections in the botanical gardens, and a network of forest trails. Nice to wander and picnic. Off Judd Falls Rd, 255-3020.

Taughannock Falls State Park, 10 miles N on Rt 89. A mile-long glen with 400 ft walls and 215 ft high falls (higher than Niagara).
Buttermilk Falls State Park, south on Rte 13. Waterfalls and quiet pools are the main features. Good for swimming, hiking and a picnic.

INFORMATION/TRAVEL
Ithaca Chamber of Commerce, 904 East Shore Drive, 273-7080.
Tompkins County Tourist Info, 272-1313.
Greyhound, W State and N Fulton Sts, 272-7930.
Local Ithaca Transit, 277-7433, and Cornell Uni Transit around campus, 255-RIDE.

Still within the Finger Lakes region is **Corning**, 50 miles southwest of Ithaca. Corningware and Steuben Glass originated here, and it's well worth spending several hours at the amazing **Corning Glass Center**, watching glass being cut, moulded, blown into any shape for every conceivable use. For information phone 974-8271. Open daily 9am–8pm. Adults $6, student discount. Midway between Ithaca and Corning is **Elmira** where Mark Twain wrote *Huckleberry Finn*. He is buried here—in Woodlawn cemetery.

North of Corning at the extremity of Seneca Lake is **Watkins Glen** famous for a lovely park, motor racing and discount shopping. For info on international motor racing events phone 535-2481. Various car and go-kart meets are held throughout the summer. The small town of **Hammondsport**, at the southern end of Keuka Lake, has its own salute to another form of high speed travel—flying. This is the birthplace of pioneer aviator, **Glen H. Curtis** and you can visit the aviation museum named after him here.

Northeast of the Finger Lakes, on the shores of Lake Ontario, **Rochester** is a grimy, crowded city encircled by insipid flowery suburbs. But one mile east of downtown is the **George Eastman House**, (716) 271-3361, abode of the founder of Kodak and now the **International Museum of Photography**, 900 East Ave, sure to fascinate amateur and professional alike. Open Tue–Sat 10am–4.30pm, Sun 1pm–4.30pm. Admission $6, $4.50 students.
The telephone area code for the whole region is 607.

NIAGARA FALLS A traditional destination for honeymoon couples in search of the awesome, and including Marilyn Monroe in *Niagara*. Mere tourists also flock to Niagara to see one of the most outstanding spectacles on the continent.

On the US side are the American Falls and the Bridal Veil Falls with a drop of 190 feet and a combined breadth of 1060 feet in a fairly straight line; the Horseshoe Falls, belonging half to the US and half to Canada, describe a deep curve 2200 feet long though with a slightly lower drop of 185 feet. About 1,500,000 gallons of water would normally plummet over the three falls each second, but the use of the river's waters to generate electricity reduces that flow by half in the summer and by three-quarters in the winter.

The Canadian side offers the better view (see Niagara Falls, Ontario), but (or therefore) it's more commercialised.
The telephone area code is 716.

ACCOMMODATION
Coachman Motel, 523 Third St, 285-2295. Rates vary, weekends in summer are the most expensive times, S-$57, D-$69 during week. 'Very good location near falls.'

Envoy Motor Inn, 102 Niagara St, 282-5584. $64 double bed, 2 doubles $76. 'Excellent location for Aquarium, Theme Park and 3 minutes from Rainbow Bridge, the Falls and Canada.'
Frontier Youth Hostel (AYH), 1101 Ferry Ave, corner of Memorial Parkway, 282-3700. $11 members, $15.50 non-members. Advance booking suggested in summer, must give security deposit. 'One of the friendliest and most helpful hostels in America; clean small dormitories; 15 minutes from falls.' 'Very cramped.' Closed 9.30am–5pm. Check in 5pm–11pm. Will collect from Amtrak, $2.
Olde Niagara House, 337 Buffalo Ave, 285-9408. S–$45, D-$55. Incls bfast. 'Brilliant.'
Rainbow Guest House, 423 Rainbow Blvd S, 282-1135. D–$45 incls bfast. 'Friendly.'
Thundering Water Motor Inn, 5919 Niagara Falls Blvd, 283-1100. D-$73 with bath, shower, cable TV, pool. $5 taxi from falls. 'Clean, bright and friendly . . . some rooms have waterbeds.'
Tibbett's Point Lighthouse, on Lake Ontario, St Vincent, (315) 654-3450. A 67-foot (working) lighthouse provides innovative hostel accommodation; a short ferry ride away from Ontario. $10 AYH, $13 non-members.
YMCA, 1317 Portage Rd, (716) 285-8491. $10 for men and women with a sleeping bag on a dorm room mattress, private room $20 for men only, sleeping hours 10pm–7am. 'Wonderful showers, incredible security.' 30 minute walk to the falls.

FOOD

'**Rainbow Blvd N**, variety of quite cheap places to eat—Chinese, Italian, American, etc.'

OF INTEREST

Aquarium, 701 Whirlpool St, 285-3575. World's first inland oceanarium, using synthetic seawater. Dolphins, sharks etc; $6.25. Open 9am–7pm.
Cave of the Winds Tour, on Goat Island is not really a cave. Don oilskins for a trip to the base of Bridal Veil Falls, $4.50. 9.30am–7.30pm.
Helicopter Flights, suspended from US side at time of writing. See Niagara Falls, Ontario for more info.
Niagara Power Project Visitors Center, 285-3211. Self-guided free tour of how hydroelectric power is made.
Old Fort Niagara. About 6 miles north in Fort Niagara State Park, 745-7611. The fort saw service under three flags—British, French and American, and contains some pre-revolutionary buildings. Displays of drill musket firing, etc. $5.75.
Prospect Point Observation Tower, 50¢.
Seeing the Falls. Walk from the US to Canada via the **Rainbow Bridge**. Cost 25¢ each way, and don't forget your passport. If you have a restricted visa, check in with the customs people on the US side to make sure you won't have any problems returning. On either side you can don oilskins for a trip on the **Maid of the Mists** boat, 284-8897, which will carry you within drenching distance of the Falls. Cost $7, open mid-Apr to mid-Oct until 8pm. Boat leaves every 15 minutes. 'Youth Hostel provides people staying there with a discount voucher.'

INFORMATION

Niagara Falls Convention and Visitors Information Line: 285-2400.
Visitors Center at 4th and Niagara Sts, 284-2000, open daily 8.30am–8.30pm.
Travelers Aid, 826 Chilton Ave, 285-6984.

TRAVEL

Amtrak, twice daily, (800) USA-RAIL or 683-8440. NB: station is two miles out of town.
Greyhound, 343 4th St, not actually a Greyhound stop, but you can get Greyhound tickets and a bus to Buffalo Greyhound Station for $1.75 (in exact change).
From/to Buffalo Airport: bus to downtown ($7), then #40 to Falls.

BUFFALO is better known for its cold snowy winters than for its tourist attractions. This is not a city to dawdle in, but it is near enough to the Falls, and is an important travel centre. If fate should cast you into the city, be sure to enjoy one nice thing Buffalo is famous for—spicy chicken wings, $3 and up for 10 at many restaurants, especially along the Elmwood strip.
The telephone area code is 716.

ACCOMMODATION

Airways Hotel, 4230 Genesee St near the airport, 632-4315. S–$54, D–$60, TV, AC and Irish pub with frequent live entertainment in the Hotel.

FOOD

Anchor Bar, Main and High Sts, 886-8920. Where the chicken wings originated.
Skaros Family Restaurant, 3003 Walden Ave, 687-9465. Nr Amtrak station. 'Cheap, good food. Dinner $4.'

INFORMATION/TRAVEL

Convention and Tourism Division of Greater Buffalo Chamber of Commerce, 107 Delaware Ave, 852-0511.
Amtrak, 75 Exchange St, (800) 872-7245. Bus to Falls from here is $15.
Greyhound Station, 181 Ellicott St, 855-7531. Bus 40 to Falls, $1.75.
Buffalo Bus and Metro Information: 855-7211.

PENNSYLVANIA

The 'Keystone State' seemed at one time destined to become one of the most powerful states in the nation, bridging the gap between North and South. The Civil War, one of the worst battles America has known was fought in the centre of the state. During the Industrial Revolution, Pennsylvania retained its prominence, with Pittsburgh as the steel-producing capital of the country. Today, as industry has migrated south, Pennsylvania's economy and population have shifted. Pittsburgh and Philadelphia, the two major cities, are enjoying a renaissance and renewed economic growth, and tourism in all parts of the state is now second only to health services in contribution to Pennsylvania's economy.

Pennsylvania is also known for its lush scenery: rolling hills; rich, meticulously cultivated farmlands; and the Appalachian Mountains, which provide good hunting, hiking, and camping.

PHILADELPHIA At the time of the American Revolution the City of Brotherly Love was the second largest in the English-speaking world. Both the Declaration of Independence and the federal Constitution were signed here, and for visitors interested in pursuing the Liberty Trail, Philadelphia rivals Boston in historical reminders.

In the early 1800's, when the commercial and political power moved to New York City and Washington DC, Philadelphia's stature began to wane. The early 1900s were dreary for the city, which gained the nickname 'Filthy-delphia' and became the brunt of jokes by W C Fields, who quipped that he

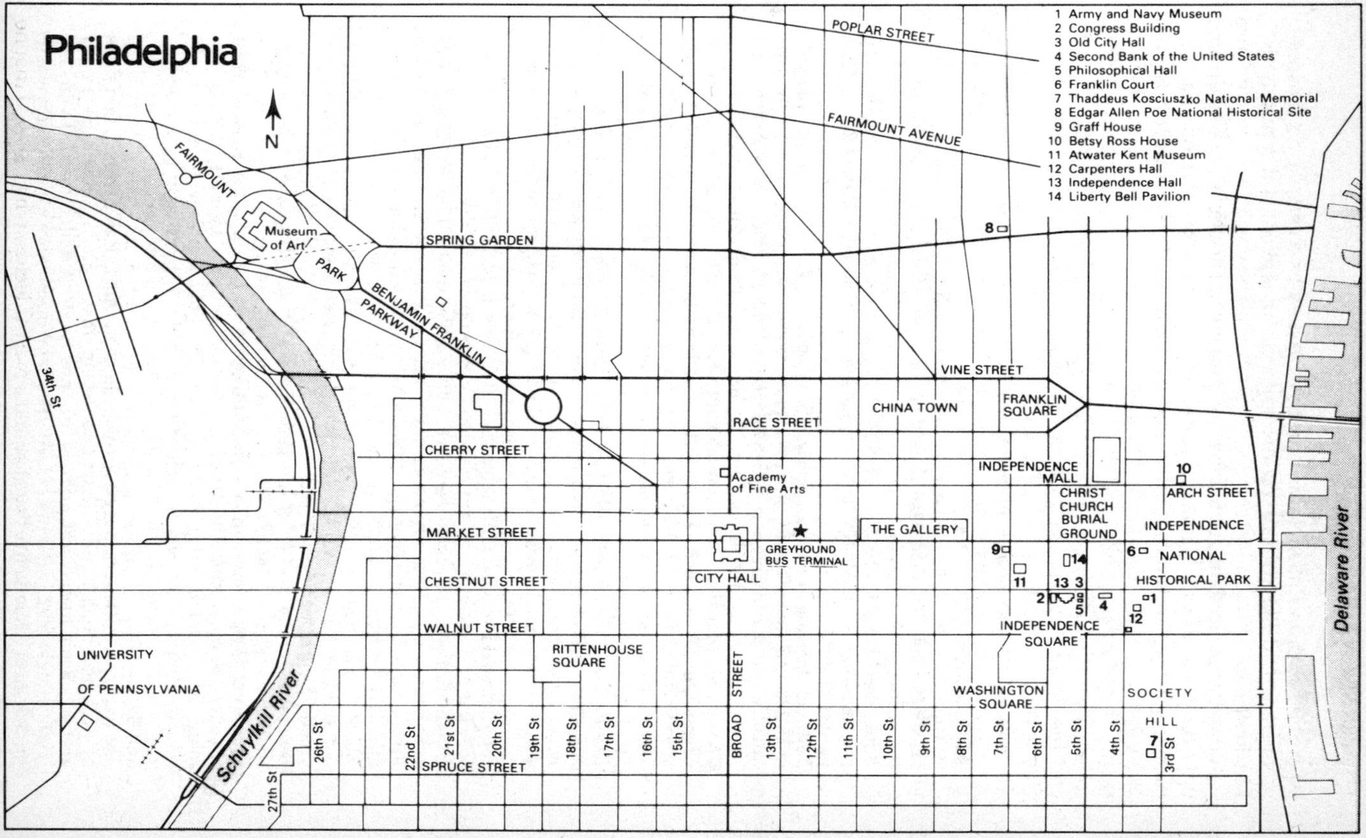
Philadelphia
N
1 Army and Navy Museum
2 Congress Building
3 Old City Hall
4 Second Bank of the United States
5 Philosophical Hall
6 Franklin Court
7 Thaddeus Kosciuszko National Memorial
8 Edgar Allen Poe National Historical Site
9 Graff House
10 Betsy Ross House
11 Atwater Kent Museum
12 Carpenters Hall
13 Independence Hall
14 Liberty Bell Pavilion
POPLAR STREET
FAIRMOUNT AVENUE
FAIRMOUNT
Museum of Art
PARK
SPRING GARDEN
BENJAMIN FRANKLIN PARKWAY
VINE STREET
CHINA TOWN
FRANKLIN SQUARE
RACE STREET
CHERRY STREET
Academy of Fine Arts
INDEPENDENCE MALL
CHRIST CHURCH BURIAL GROUND
ARCH STREET
INDEPENDENCE NATIONAL HISTORICAL PARK
THE GALLERY
MARKET STREET
GREYHOUND BUS TERMINAL
CITY HALL
CHESTNUT STREET
WALNUT STREET
INDEPENDENCE SQUARE
RITTENHOUSE SQUARE
WASHINGTON SQUARE
SOCIETY HILL
BROAD STREET
SPRUCE STREET
34th St
27th St
26th St
22nd St
21st St
20th St
19th St
18th St
17th St
16th St
15th St
13th St
12th St
11th St
10th St
9th St
8th St
7th St
6th St
5th St
4th St
3rd St
UNIVERSITY OF PENNSYLVANIA
Schuylkill River
Delaware River

'spent a month in Philadelphia one day'. Asked by *Vanity Fair* magazine what he would like to have on his epitaph, he replied, 'I'd rather be in Philadelphia.'

Today Philadelphians are having the last laugh. The city is once again an important manufacturing and cultural centre, and some glamour has returned, the result of a recent urban and riverside face lift. There are numerous universities and colleges in the area, hence plenty of students, hence plenty of restaurants, bars and discotheques; and the black ghettoes, the Italian Market and Chinatown provide a special ethnic flavour. Valley Forge and the Pennsylvania Dutch Country lie just to the west, and New York City is only an hour and a half away.
The area code for the Philadelphia area is 215.

ACCOMMODATION

Antique Row Bed & Breakfast, 341 South 12th Street, 592-7802. S–$45, D–$55 incl breakfast, cable TV, shared bath. 'Best possible price for the best possible B&B in the best possible location.'

Bank Street Hostel, 32 S Bank St, 922-0222. $14 dorm, plus $2 for sheet sleeping bag (must use one). AC, TV, laundry, kitchen facs. Closed 9.30am–4.30pm. 'The perfect hostel.'

Bed and Breakfast of Philadelphia, 1530 Locust St #K, 735-1917 (in Philly) or (800) 220-1917 (out of Philly). Rooms in and around Philadelphia, numerous hosts fluent in European languages. S–$30–$60 , D–$40–110. Deposit of one night's rent, plus 6% required at booking. Be sure to ask about cancellation fees.

Chamounix Mansion International Youth Hostel, W Fairmount Park at end of Chamounix Dr, 878-3676. $9.50–AYH. 'Excellent, but out of the way.' 'I cannot speak highly enough of this place.' 'Ten minute walk through woods, but trolley service in and out of town available on weekends.' Take No. 38 bus from Market St. 'Take food with you.'

Divine Tracy Hotel, 20 S 36th near U of Penn, 382-4310. Long list of rules: no smoking, no alcohol, no meals in rooms; women required to wear dresses or skirts w/stockings, and shorts are prohibited for either gender. But if the limitations don't bother you, the price is right: S–$23–$29, D–$34–$42, shared bath, for rooms on single-sex floors. Cash or travellers cheques only.

International House of Philadelphia, 3701 Chestnut St, 387-5125. Students only. $52. Laundry facilities. 'Good place to meet people.'

LaSalle College, 20th and Olney Ave, Office of Residential Life, 951-1550. S–$23 with bath, D–$28. Reservations essential; call 5 days in advance (ask for Mrs Jeri Brockington, Housing Manager). No bookings after Aug 15th.

Old First Reformed Church, 4th and Race Sts, smack in the middle of downtown, 922-9663. $11, mats and pillows provided—sheets $1. Open 2nd week in July to 3rd week in August. 'Clean, very friendly, peaceful and quiet; breakfast provided.' Doors open 5pm–10pm.

Several fraternity houses at the **University of Pennsylvania** offer housing to transient students. Call 898-5263 for information.

Camping: West Chester KOA, in **Embreville** on Rte 162 (just west of West Chester), 30 miles from Philadelphia, 486-0447, laundry, showers, store, swimming, fishing, miniature golf, daily van trips into Philadelphia with minimum of 5 people. Tent site, $18.50 per night; camper cabin, $34 per night for 2 people.

FOOD

The local specialities are 'hoagies', cold subs of all kinds; 'Philly steaks', thin slices of steak on an Italian roll with onions, catsup, mayo, green peppers, cheese ... and you name it; and soft pretzels, gigantic twists of dough freckled with salt crystals, zigzagged with mustard. All these and many more are sold everywhere on the street, especially in neighbourhoods filled with fast food stalls.

The Bourse, 21 S 5th St, 625-0300, certainly the most convenient collection of eateries, in the heart of the historical area. A restored building full of interesting shops and a large variety of food stalls, including a good one for your mandatory Philly Cheesesteak.
Brass Rail, 3942 Chestnut St, 222-4250, has good pub style food; a favourite with locals.
Gold Standard Cafeteria, 3601 Locust Walk, 387-3463, on U Penn campus and near the International House. Good prices and a good place to meet people.
Gulf Coast, 3701 Chestnut St, 387-8813. Open 12pm–10pm. Good seafood and sandwiches from $4.50.
Old City Pizza, 3rd and Arch St, 574-9494. 'Big portions, low prices.'
Reading Terminal Market, 12th and Arch, 922-2317, has a variety of shops. Here you can get shoo-fly pie, a heavy, molasses-packed Pennsylvania Dutch concoction.
Salad Alley, 1720 Sansom St and 4040 Locust St, The Bourse, 349-7644. International gourmet soups and the best, unlimited salad bar in town, $6.
Southeast China Restaurant, 1000 Arch St, 629-1888. In the centre of Chinatown. 'Good for vegetarians.'

OF INTEREST

The best way to begin a tour of Philadelphia is to go first to the **National Parks Service Visitors Center**, 3rd and Chestnut, 597-8974, in the 'Most Historic Square Mile in America'. Here you can arm yourself with the *Visitors' Guide Map of Philadelphia* and other free maps and literature on the city and surrounding area. The staff is generally quite knowledgeable and helpful. Open daily in summer, 9am–6pm.
In the heart of the heritage city is the **Independence National Historical Park**, the four-block area near the Delaware River. It includes: **Carpenters Hall**, home of the first Continental Congress, and **Independence Hall**, Chestnut between 5th and 6th Sts, is where the Declaration of Independence was signed. Here also is the **Liberty Bell Pavilion**, at Market between 5th and 6th. Admission to colonial buildings in the area is free. Independence Hall and the Liberty Bell Pavilion are open daily in summer 9am–8pm; Carpenters Hall Tue–Sun 10am–4pm; the other buildings are open daily 9am–6pm. After Labor Day, all buildings are open daily 9am–5pm.
Other historic sites within or close to the park include: **Army Navy Museum**, at Chestnut between 3rd and 4th, depicts origin of the US Army and Navy, 597–2458.
Atwater Kent Museum, 7th between Market and Chestnut, 922-3031. Depicts Philly's growth through the centuries. Open Tue–Sat 9.30am–4.45pm; free.
Betsy Ross House, 239 Arch St. Betsy Ross is said to have put together the first American flag from strips of petticoats. 10am–5pm daily.
Near this house, off 2nd Ave is **Elfreth's Alley**, 574-0560. The oldest continuously occupied residential street in America, lined with Georgian homes. House No 126 is a museum, open daily 10am–4pm. 50¢.
Christ Church, on 2nd St above Market St, 922-1695, is open daily Mon–Sat 9am–5pm, Sun 1pm–5pm. Franklin and 6 other signatories to the Declaration of Independence are buried at **Christ Church Burial Ground**, 5th and Arch Sts, open daily Apr 15–Oct 15.
Congress Hall, Chestnut and 6th next door to Independence Hall, is where the legislature met when Philadelphia was the nation's capital.
Franklin Court, at Market between 3rd and 4th, 592-1289. Interesting collection of buildings. A working print shop, showing Franklin's trade; a post office open 7 days a week, where you can get your letters hand cancelled with a colonial style stamp; an underground museum which features a diorama of Franklin's life and inventions and a phone bank (you can call up Thomas Jefferson and find out what he thought of Ben).

Graff House, 7th & Market Sts, is a reconstruction of the house where Thomas Jefferson drafted the Declaration of Independence.
Old City Hall, 5th & Chestnut, was the first home of the US Supreme Court.
Philosophical Hall, the home of the American Philosophical Society, founded by Benjamin Franklin in 1743.
Second Bank of the United States, Chestnut between 4th and 5th, a beautiful Greek Revival building looking somewhat out of place here, has an interesting portrait collection.
Society Hill, restored colonial town houses around Spruce & 4th Sts. The name comes from the Free Society of Stock Traders, a company formed here by William Penn.
Thaddeus Kosciuszko National Memorial, 3rd & Pine Sts, where Mr K, who helped the colonists win the revolution, stayed 1797–98.
Todd House, 4th and Walnut Sts. A house that figured prominently in Philadelphia society of the 1790s and the home of Dolley Pane, who later married James Madison. Sign up at the Visitors Center, 3rd St btwn Walnut and Chestnut Sts for a tour. Free.
United States Mint, 5th & Arch Sts, 597-7350. Small museum, self-guiding tour along viewing balcony, free unless you want to mint your own souvenir coin for $2. Open daily, 9am–4.30pm.
Elsewhere in Philly: **Academy of Natural Sciences**, 19th St and Benjamin Franklin Parkway, 299-1000, big dinosaur exhibit. Mon–Fri 10am–4.30pm, Sat–Sun 10am–5pm; $6.
Edgar Allen Poe National Historical Site, 532 N 7th St, 597-8780, where Poe lived when his short stories *The Black Hat*, *Gold Bug*, and *The Telltale Heart* were published, 1843–1844.
Fairmount Park, west along Benjamin Franklin Pkwy towards the Schuylkill River. A beautiful riverside park of 1000s of acres, the site of the Centennial Exposition of 1876. Walks, bike and bridle paths, outdoor concerts, and a 90-minute ride on a recreated turn-of-the century trolley to see it all. Within the park are several colonial mansions, and other attractions:
Japanese House and Gardens on the grounds of the Horticultural Center, 878-5097. $2.50, visitors required to wear socks and no shoes. Open Wed–Sun 11am-4pm.
Rodin Museum, 22nd and Benjamin Franklin Pkwy, 787-5476. Somehow, they prised *The Thinker* and *The Burghers of Calais* away from the French. Open Tue–Sun 10am–5pm.
Philadelphia Museum of Art, in the centre of Fairmount Park, 763-8100, ranks as one of the world's greatest, with more than 500,000 works of art. (It's the third-largest museum in the US). See the arms & armour collection. Open Tue–Sun 10am–5pm; $6, $3 w/student ID. Sun free till 1pm. 'Worth every penny.'
Philadelphia Zoo, 34th and Girard, 243-1100, America's first, open daily 9.30am–5pm (weekends and hols, 9.30am-6pm). $7. Treehouse $1 extra.
Fairmount Water Works, right next to the art museum, 581-5111, home of **Philadelphia Ranger Corps Visitors Center** with info on all the sights in the park as well as trolleys and shuttles to get you there.
Franklin Institute Science Museum and Fels Planetarium, 20th and Benjamin Parkway, 448-1200. Worth a visit. Open daily, 9.30am–5pm; planetarium show 2pm daily. $9.50 for museum and planetarium (cheaper 5pm–closing). The complex now includes the **Mandel Future Center** and the **Omnibus Theater**, one of the world's most modern cinemas with a 4-storey screen and 3D sound, $7.
Germantown, in northwest Philadelphia and originally settled by German folk. Many old houses and fine mansions, some of distinctive German design. The best are **Cliveden**, dating back to 1763, and **Stenton Mansion**, built by Penn's secretary, James Logan. Cliveden is open Tue–Sat 10am–4pm, Sun 1pm–4pm; $4, $3 with student ID. Stenton is open Tue-Sat 1pm–4pm; $3.
Mummers Museum, 2nd and Washington Aves, 336-3050. Open Tue–Sat 9.30am–5pm, Sun noon–5pm (Sun closing Jul & Aug), $2.50, students $2.

Hypnotic and hilarious, the Mummers—a Philly original—are hard to explain; you just have to *see*. Their New Years Day parade is legend. They also hold outdoor string band concerts Tue at 8pm.
Pennsylvania Academy of the Fine Arts, Broad and Cherry Sts, 972-7600. Nation's oldest art museum and school. Good collection of American art dating from 1750. Tues-Sat 10am-5pm, Sun 11am-5pm. $5, $2 with student ID; free Sat 10am-1pm.
University Museum of Archaeology/Anthropology, University of Pennsylvania Campus, 33rd & Spruce Sts, 898-4000. Outstanding archaeological exhibits. Open Tue-Sat 10am-4.30pm, Sun 1pm-5pm, closed Sun during summer; $4.
Tours: Audio Walk and Tour of Historic Philadelphia, 6th and Sansom Sts, inside the Norman Rockwell Museum, 922-4345, rents light-weight headsets for nicely narrated walking tour through the Independence National Historical Park, from 10am daily; from 11am Sun. Buy tapes for $10.95 or rent tapes for $9 person, $18 for 2 or more. Includes discount coupons to major museums.

ENTERTAINMENT
Check the *Weekend* section of the Friday *Philadelphia Inquirer* or phone the Philadelphia Tourist Center, 636-1666, or the Cultural Affairs Council, 972-8500, for information.
South St, from Front to 7th and from South to Market, the old city area, is the funky end of town, with many restaurants, pubs and clubs. The area around Walnut and 38th Sts is also good for pubs.
Khyber Pass, 54 S 2nd St, 440-9683. Featuring live rock n'roll, imported beers are cheaper during happy hour.

INFORMATION
Visitors and Tourist Information Center, 16th and JFK Blvd, 636-1666.
Philadelphia Convention and Visitors Bureau, 1515 Market St #2020, 636-3300.
National Parks Service Visitors Center, 3rd & Chestnut, 597-8974.
Philadelphia Council for International Visitors, Civic Center Museum, 34th & Civic Center Blvd, 823-7261.
Travelers Aid, 311 S Juniper St, 546-0571. Also at airport and 30th St Station.

TRAVEL
Amtrak, for intercity trains, 30th St Station, 824-1600.
To and from New York City: SEPTA to Trenton, NJ, to connect with NJ Transit to Penn Station, NY, ($14).
Greyhound, 1001 Filbert St, 931-4001.

VALLEY FORGE/BRANDYWINE RIVER VALLEY Just east and south of Philadelphia, this is a region steeped in history and art. **Valley Forge National Historic Park**, 783-1000, one of the nation's most solemn memorial grounds, is 20 miles west of Philadelphia. (Inquire at Visitors Bureau about buses, tours.) General Washington hibernated here along with his half-starved troops through the bitter winter of 1777-78. Loaded with Americana, including Washington's headquarters, cabins modelled after those in which the troops were billeted, and a few museums. Dogwoods blooming in spring enhance the pastoral air.

South of Valley Forge, the **Brandywine River Valley** has inspired three generations of Wyeths—NC, Andrew and Jamie—to produce a uniquely American brand of art. The **Brandywine River Museum** in **Chadds Ford**, 388-2700, holds the world's largest collection of Wyeth paintings. The museum is open daily 9.30am-4.30pm; $5, $2.50 w/student ID. 'Highly recommended.'

PENNSYLVANIA DUTCH COUNTRY While most of the original settlers of Lancaster County have long since been absorbed into modern society, the Amish and Mennonites have retained their traditional identities in this stretch of country west of Philadelphia. Eschewing electricity and modern machinery, the 'plain people' still speak a form of Low German ('Dutch' is a derivation from 'Deutsch', the German word for 'German'). The women in their long dresses and small caps and the bearded menfolk in sombre black suits and broad-brimmed hats continue to live as simply and contentedly as they did centuries before in southern Germany.

The Pennsylvania Dutch have always fascinated visitors, and the 1984 award-winning film *Witness* has only increased the interest. In order to really understand what you are seeing, try reading *The Amish*, by John A. Hostetler, and *A Quiet Peaceable Life*, by John L. Ruth, which provide an excellent introduction to the area and its people. Both are available at the **Peoples Place**, Main Street, Intercourse, 768-7171. *Note:* Restrain your cameras; the plain people consider photographs to be 'graven images', a no-no as you'll understand.

The area lies on Hwy 30, but to avoid an excess of tourists, take to the sideroads. One good excursion is the 3 mile jaunt from **Paradise** to **Strasburg**, equally enjoyable on foot or via the old railroad. **Lancaster**, US capital-for-a-day (the day was 27 September, 1777), was a prominent city in the late 18th century; the well-preserved downtown reflects the town's colonial heritage. If you're looking for **Intercourse**, you'll find it signposted at the junction of Hwys 772 & 340 east of Lancaster.

Keep an eye out in late June and early July for the **Kutztown Folk Festival**: soap making, sauerkraut shredding, pewtering, square dancing and folklore sessions. 'The festival is a real hoe-down, straw-in-the-hair fun affair.'

The telephone area code is 717.

ACCOMMODATION

Accommodation is relatively inexpensive here, but in summer the hotels and motels can be expensive, and the best deals go quickly. The best places to stay are the farm homes: they're cheaper, serve hearty breakfasts, and you'll learn more about your hosts. For the best information on accommodation, contact the **Mennonite Information Center**, (see below).

Countryside Motel, 134 Hartman Bridge Rd, on Hwy 896 6 miles east of Lancaster, 687-8431. S–$37, D–$40.

Quiet Haven, 2556 Siegrist Rd, on Hwy 896 7 miles east of Lancaster, 397-6231. D–$52.

Shirley's AYH, Geigertown, off Rte 82, (215) 286-9537. $8.25. Conveniently located for visits to Dutch Country and the French Creek State Park. Reservations essential.

Kountry Manor, on Highway 625, 25 miles northeast of Lancaster, near Bowmansville, (215) 445-9570. Up to 10 beds available for $10 a night per person. Contact Jim or Ruth. Good to phone in advance.

FOOD

Amish austerity does not extend to eating. Many restaurants in the area serve bountiful communal feasts of sausage, scrapple, pickles, beef, chow-chow, schnitz and knepp, noodles, homebaked bread, apple butter, funnel cakes and molasses shoo-fly pie.

Lancaster's **Central Market**, King & Queen Sts, 291-4723, sells produce and goodies; it's one of the best places to see what Pennsylvania Dutch food is all about. Open Tue and Fri 6.30am–4.30pm & Sat 6am–2pm.

OF INTEREST

Amish Village Inc, on Hwy 896, 7 miles southeast of Lancaster, 687-8511. See the Amish way of life, and tourists seeing the Amish way of life. Open daily 9am–6pm. $5.

Ephrata Cloister, a dozen miles north of Lancaster on Hwy 272, 733-6600, was founded and later forsaken by a German community of Seventh Day Baptists. Living as sisters and brothers, they stooped through low doorways to learn humility and walked down narrow hallways to assure themselves of the straight and narrow path. Many of their original structures of unpainted wood, now gloomy-grey with time, still stand. Open Mon–Sat, 9am–5pm, Sun noon–5pm (last tour at 4pm); $5. There are now candlelit tours on Fri and Sat evenings 6.30 and 7.30pm. $5; call 733-4811.

Historical Lancaster Walking Tours, 100 S Queen St, 653-8225. Interesting walking tour of colonial Lancaster. Tours Mon–Sat 10am and 1.30pm; Sun 1.30pm only. $4. Tours last an hour and a half, with a preceding 10 min presentation.

Pennsylvania Farm Museum, in Landis Valley on Hwy 272, 3 miles north of Lancaster, 569-0401. A museum village with the buildings, homes, trades and tools of three centuries. Open Tue–Sat 9am–5pm, Sun noon–5pm; $7, students free.

People's Place, Main St, Intercourse, 768-7171. Open Mon–Sat 9.30am–9.30pm. The self-guided tour, 'Amish World', $3. Award-winning 25-min slide documentary, *Who are the Amish?*, shown every 30 mins, 9.30am–6.45pm, also $3 combo ticket for tour and slide show, $5.50. 'Worth every penny.' Evenings at 7.30pm *Hazel's People* is shown, $4.

Railroad Museum of Pennsylvania, Rte 741 east of Strasburg, 687-8628. Historic locos and rolling stock. Open Mon–Sat 9am–5pm, Sun 11am–7pm; $6.

Strasburg Railroad, Rte 741 east of Lancaster, 687–7522, goes to and from Paradise, 45 minutes. America's oldest short-line steam locomotive. Runs in summer Mon–Sat 10am–7pm, Sun noon–7pm (different hrs in winter); $6.50.

INFORMATION/TRAVEL

Mennonite Information Center, 2209 Millstream Rd, 4½ miles east of Lancaster off Hwy 30, 299-0954. Go here first. Very helpful and friendly staff who can assist you in finding accommodation, tours and background on Mennonites and Amish. See the film introducing the area and people. The center also has the most non-commercial tour of the area, which is a treat in this overly exploited area. Here you can hire a local Mennonite guide for $5 plus $8.50 per hour (2 hour min) for a fascinating country tour of homes, barns, factories. 'Not to be missed.'

Pennsylvania Dutch Visitors Bureau, 501 Greenfield Rd, Lancaster, 299-8901. Brochures and maps. Mon–Sat 8am–6pm, Sun 8am–5pm.

Amtrak, McGovern Ave, (800) 872-7245.

HARRISBURG The undistinguished capital of Pennsylvania has two outstanding features: heading west, the landscape becomes beautiful, even dramatic, where the broad Susquehanna River cuts a gap through granite bluffs and green forests; and the city is crowned with a stunning Italian Renaissance capitol dome modelled after St. Peter's in Rome (and built on graft; get the scandalous scoop from a local resident). Rockville Bridge, 4 miles west of Harrisburg, spanning the Susquehanna, is the longest and widest stone arch bridge in the world.

The Harrisburg area sprang to international attention in 1979 after the nuclear accident at nearby **Three Mile Island**, which brought into question the safety of nuclear reactors. The accident didn't scare away tourists, of course not. Tourism, in fact, increased fourfold in the area. The **TMI Visitors Center**, across from the plant near **Middletown** on Rte 441 south, 367-0518, has a fascinating description of what happened and what steps have been taken to keep it from happening again. Open Thurs–Sun 12pm–4.30pm.

Further north up the Susquehanna River lies the **Pine Creek Gorge**, otherwise called the Grand Canyon of Pennsylvania, and said to be one of the last and most extensive wilderness regions between New York and Chicago. This once industrial area has been reabsorbed into nature and, with its free-flowing river and creek-side track, is now a haven for hikers, bikers, canoeists and horseback riders alike. **Wellsboro** is the nearest town for the area and a good base for activities. Call Pine Creek Outfitters, (717) 724-3003, for more info.

East of Harrisburg, in **Hummeltown**, are the **Indian Echo Caves**, 566-8131, with impressive natural formations. Open daily 9am–5.45pm; $6.50 for a 45 min guided tour. You can pan for gems at Gem Mill Junction, $4 a bag. There are also carriage rides for $2.
The telephone area code is 717.

HERSHEY A company town built in 1903 by a Mennonite candy bar magnate of the same name who came up with the inspired concept of milk chocolate. The air is thick with the aroma of chocolate and almonds; the two main streets are Chocolate and Cocoa Aves, and even the streetlamps are shaped like Hershey's famous 'kisses'. A beautiful Spanish-style resort hotel, the Hotel Hershey, sits atop the town; luscious gardens surround it. **Hershey's Chocolate World** near the park entrance takes you on a 12-min ride from the cocoa bean to the candy shop (but not into the factory—those tours were discontinued in 1973, after they had become too popular). Open daily 9am–7.45pm. Free, but no free samples, and you never leave without spending money on chocolate (there are worse fates). Call 534-4903 for more information.

Also here is **Hersheypark**, (800) 437-7439, an English, German and Pennsylvania Dutch theme park with 50 rides and enough entertainment to keep you occupied all day. Open daily until 25th Aug, 10.30am–10pm. $22.95 for the day; cheaper after 5pm.

GETTYSBURG The quiet peaceful town that Gettysburg is today belies its history as the site of 51,000 casualties in 3 days in the most significant battle of the worst war America has ever known, the Civil War. On 3 July, 1863, General Robert E Lee was defeated here, and the tide turned irrevocably against the South. Lincoln came later to give his famous Address at the dedication of the National Cemetery. The battlefield is now preserved as a national military park where visitors may follow the struggle of both sides on maps and displays.
The area code is 717.

ACCOMMODATION

Gettysburg has many 'Ma and Pa' motel/guest house operations, so with a little bit of searching you can find good, central, and relatively inexpensive accommodation even in the summer, the peak season.

Gettysburg International Youth Hostel, 27 Chambersburg St, 334-1020. In a restored historic building. $8 AYH, check-in 5pm–9pm. $11 nm. $1 sleeping sheet.
North of Gettysburg: Ironmonger's Mansion Youth Hostel, on Rte 223 in Pine Grover Furnace State Park, 486-7575, $8, $11, $1 sleeping sheet. Check-in 5pm–10.30pm; reservations essential. Built in 1762, the original Ironworks manufactured cannonballs during the Revolutionary war. Don't miss Bob Beard's special candlelit tour of the mansion.
Round Top Campground, south on Rte 134, 334-9656. Showers, riding stable, laundry, pool and mini-golf. $10 for 2 people, $15 with water and electricity hookup.

OF INTEREST
Go directly to the **National Park Visitors Center**, on Business Rte 15, 334-1124, for complete introduction and information. Park staff are extremely knowledgeable and helpful. Here you can make arrangements for touring. You can hire a local licensed battlefield guide for $20 for 2 hours (AutoTour cassettes, $10.50 for 4 hrs, are available from the Wax Museum in town). Here also you can see the **Electric Map**, showing troop movements during the battle; open daily 8am–5pm, $2. The **Cyclorama**, next door to the Visitors Center, is probably the most dramatic rendition; view this dioramic painting of Pickett's charge, augmented by a sound-and-light show, daily from 9am–5pm, $2.
A. Lincoln's Place Theater, 213 Steinwehr, 334-6049. Here James Getty, a Lincoln scholar and look-alike, gives an intimate talk in which he, as Lincoln, recounts memories, describes events and answers any question you could possibly have about the man. Not to be missed. 'Unbelievable!' (As far as anyone knows, Getty is not related to J Gettys, the town's founder.) Shows Mon–Fri 8pm; $5.50.
Eisenhower National Historic Site (take shuttle bus from Visitors Center), 334-1124 (same number as Gettysburg), is a farm where the President retired and died. Open daily, 8.30am–4.15pm; $3.60.
National Tower, 334-6754. Open daily 9am–6.30pm. $3.85. Let the high speed elevators whisk you up 300ft to the top for a spectacular view of the area.

INFORMATION
National Park Visitors Center, Business Rte 15, 334-1124. Open daily 8am–6pm.
Gettysburg Travel Council, 35 Carlisle St, 334-6274. Open daily 9am–6pm. Very helpful; has accommodation information. (Park gardens open 6am–10pm).

PITTSBURGH When Rand McNally named Pittsburgh 'the nation's most liveable city' in 1985, everyone was surprised but the Pittsburghers, for they have always had fierce pride in their city. Famous for steel and home of much of the nation's industry, Pittsburgh coughed its way through the Industrial Revolution in a perpetual cloud of smoke. After World War II it began a clean-up campaign and in recent years has emerged, blinking, into the sunlight. And an amazing transformation it is: Pittsburgh's skyline of blast furnaces, open hearths, steel mills and dramatic bridges is imposing, and the city's air is reportedly now cleaner than that of any other American Metropolis. There is some exciting architecture down at the Golden Triangle, where the Allegheny and Monongahela Rivers join to form the Ohio River. Pittsburgh's terrain is an appealing mix of plateaux and hillsides, narrow valleys and rivers; with elevations ranging from 715 to 1240 ft, expect to do some climbing.

As a bizarre footnote, the former nation of Czechoslovakia was founded in Pittsburgh, of all places. In 1918, the leaders of the Czechs and the

Slovaks met in the Moose Club (now the Elks Club) at Penn & Scott Place to hammer out the Pittsburgh Agreement uniting these peoples.
The telephone area code for Pittsburgh is 412.

ACCOMMODATION

Hotel and motel accommodation is expensive in the Pittsburgh area; if you have a car, you would do better to stay on the outskirts in the Monroeville and Green Tree areas. Wherever you stay in Pittsburgh reservations are advisable, particularly at the guest houses.
Envoy Inn/Pittsburgh West, I-79 & Steubenville Pike, 922-0120. S–$47, D–$49.
St Regis Residence for Women, 50 Congress St, 281-9888. Women only. S–$75 week. Week-long stays include breakfast & dinner.
Point Park College Youth Hostel, 201 Wood St, 391-4100. $10, check-in 2pm–12am.
Wood Street Commons, 301 3rd Ave, 765-2532. D–$35–$52 a week, on a monthly basis. Would-be residents are interviewed and moving-in takes about a week. Interviews on Mon, Tue, Thu and Fri, 8.30am–10am.

FOOD

The local brew is Iron City Beer, available at any bar that knows it's in Pittsburgh.
Benkovitz Seafood, 23rd and Smallman, 263-3016. A market and one-time truckers' joint in the wholesale district, now moved up several pegs but keeping down its prices.
Big Z Hamburgers, 961 Liberty Ave, 1½ blocks from Greyhound (turn right out of terminal), 566-2600. 'Not cheap, but plenty, and colourful surroundings. Relief to get away from bus terminal fare if just passing through.'
Parmanti Brothers, 3 outlets in Pittsburgh on Cherry, Forbes and 18th (open 24hrs), 263-2142. Unique recipe grilled cheese sandwiches served with fries and coleslaw. $3.25–$5. Also soup and chilli.

OF INTEREST

Pittsburgh culture was once severely neglected by the city's big-money steel magnates, who couldn't wait to get out of town to the refined air of Europe and New York's Fifth Avenue. The cultural life has picked up considerably since then, and Pittsburgh now boasts several fine museums and universities as well as the world-class Pittsburgh Symphony Orchestra.
Carnegie Institute, 4400 Forbes Ave, Oakland, 622-3131. Encompasses 2 internationally-known museums: the **Museum of Art** includes masterpieces of the French Impressionists and contemporary works as well as decorative arts of the ancient world; and the **Carnegie Museum of Natural History** tells the story of the earth and man in hundreds of displays of arts, crafts and natural history, including minerals, gems and Egyptian mummies. An impressive herd of prehistoric monsters towers over strange skeleton birds. The institute is open Tue–Sat 10am–5pm, Sun 1pm–5pm; $5, $3 w/college ID. Open Mondays Jul–Aug.
Carnegie Science Center, 1 Allegheny Ave, W of Three Rivers Stadium, 237-2400. This is a new development and includes the former Buhl Science Center and Planetarium. Don't miss the Van de Graaf generator which spits indoor lightning several times a day (announced over loudspeakers). The new **Henry J. Buhl Jnr Planetarium** gives sky shows daily, and the **Omnimax Theater** has just opened with shows on the 79 ft domed ceiling drawing the audience into the action. There are also tours around the WW2 *Requin* (meaning 'shark') submarine in front of the Center. Open Sun–Thur 10am–6pm, Fri and Sat till 9pm. $5.75 to $12 depending on what you opt to see.
Duquesne Incline, 1220 Grandview Ave, 381-1665, a vertical trolley from 1877 carries you 400 feet into the air for a bird's eye view of the city and its three rivers, open every day until 1am, $1 each way.
Fallingwater, southeast of Pittsburgh, 329-8501. This futuristic home-over-a-waterfall is a paragon of Frank Lloyd Wright design. Take Hwy 51 South to

Uniontown, Rte 40 East to Farmington, 381 North for 12 miles (through Ohio Pyle Park) to Fallingwater on left. Tours every half hour, Tue–Sun 10am–4pm; $6, hols and wkends $8. Reservations essential.

Fort Pitt Museum, Point State Park, 281-9284. Recreated bastion to tell the story of the struggle between Britain and France for Ohio county. Also history of Fort Duquesne and early Pittsburgh. Open Tue–Sat 10am–4.30pm; Sun noon–4.30pm (hours subject to change), $4.

Frick Museum, 7227 Reynolds St, Pt Breeze, 371-0600. French, Italian and Flemish Renaissance paintings. Open Tue–Sat 10am–5.30pm, Sun noon–6pm; free. Free jazz and chamber concerts Oct–April, offers free lectures on temporary exhibits. Also the recently-restored **Clayton House** (call 371-0606 for reservations), $5, $3 with student ID and **Clayton Greenhouse** and **Carriage Museum**.

Nationality Classrooms at University of Pittsburgh, in the Gothic masterpiece, the Cathedral of Learning, 624-6000. Impressive conglomeration of 23 classrooms designed in different international designs with authentic furnishings from all over the world. 'Worth a visit.' Open Mon–Fri 9am–4pm, Sat 9.30am–3pm, Sun 11am–3pm. Classrooms are locked on weekends, but tape-recorded tour includes key; during week they are empty and quiet in the afternoon. $2.

Pittsburgh Zoo, Hill Rd, Highland Park, 665-3640. 55 acres of natural habitat show off animals that include 16 species of endangered primates. A new tropical rain forest exhibit covers 5 acres inside and 5 acres open air. Open 10am–6pm, $5.75.

White-Water Rafting on the Youghiogheny River. Day trips last 5–6 hours and cost $26–S40 during the week and up to $52 at the weekend. Contact **Laurel Highlands River Tours** (329-8531) or **White Water Adventurers Inc** (329-8850) for more info. 'A spectacular experience.'

ENTERTAINMENT

For students, **Oakland** is the place, although the **Shadyside** area still has its fair share of swing. Read *Rock Flash* and *In Pittsburgh* free from around town, to find out what's going on.

Rock and pop concerts, ice shows, sports events at the **Civic Arena**, Center and Bedford Aves, downtown at Washington Plaza, 642-1800. The arena has a vast, retractable, dome-shaped roof.

Heinz Hall, 600 Penn Ave, downtown, 392-4900. Elegant hall named after the ketchup king. Home to the Pittsburgh Symphony Orchestra.

Shakespeare in the Park. Three Rivers Shakespeare Festival offers free outdoor performances in various city park locations throughout the summer, call 624-0102 for details.

Three Rivers Stadium is home turf for the Pirates (baseball) and the Steelers (football); 321-0650 for schedule info.

INFORMATION/TRAVEL

Convention and Visitors Bureau, 4 Gateway Center, 281-7711, (800) 366-0093.
Amtrak, Liberty Ave and Grant St, near bus terminal, 471-6170.
Greyhound, 11th and Liberty Ave, (800) 231-2222.

TITUSVILLE The oil well business got off to a picturesque start out here in northwestern Pennsylvania. In 1859, Col Edwin Drake, right here in Titusville, sunk the first oil well in the world. The site is now **Drake Well Memorial Park**, with a working reconstruction of the original rig and a museum containing photos and artifacts of the early boom days, (814) 827-2797, open daily May–Oct, 9am–5pm, $4. Park open daily 8am–dusk.

THE MID-ATLANTIC

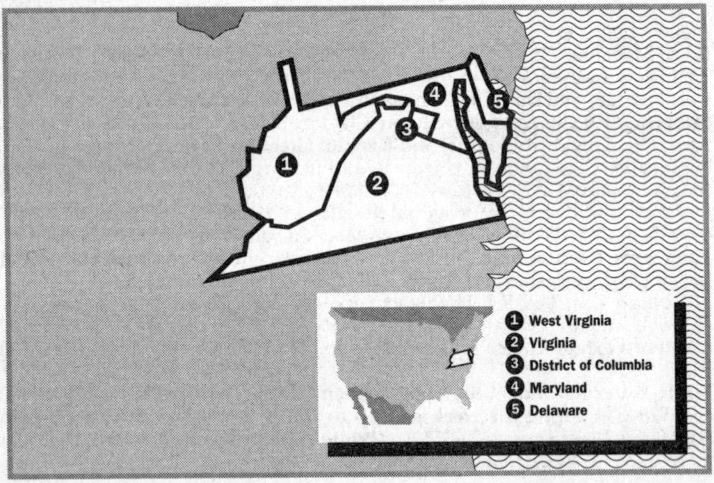

A visit to this region, where North meets South historically and climatically, reveals not only America's past but the shape of its future: decisions made here are the stuff from which history books are written. Focused on Washington DC, the area features politics, colonial and civil war history, legions of lawyers, and growing federal research. The nation's governmental heart has spawned technology, research and information industries in neighbouring Maryland and Virginia where there are such notable federal establishments as NASA's Goddard Spaceflight Center, the National Cancer Institute at Frederick, the Agricultural Department Research Center at Greenbelt, the National Security Agency at Fort Meade, the National Institute of Health in Bethesda, and the Smithsonian Institution in Washington. The I-270 'Technology Corridor' from Washington to Frederick now outpaces growth in California's 'Silicon Valley'.

The region has a varied climate (snowy in winter, almost monsoonal in July), brilliant springtime flora (azaleas, dogwoods, flowering cherries), and its natural resources offer recreation in all seasons. You can sail and fish on the Chesapeake Bay, hike, raft and ski in the Appalachians of Virginia and West Virginia.

DELAWARE

This skinny triangle of a state should have been named, in all fairness, 'du Pont': it was built on the success of the du Pont empire. (The family traces its roots in Delaware soil back 200 years when Pierre Samuel du Pont de

Nemours, a counselor to Louis XVI at the time of the French Revolution, decided to visit his friend Thomas Jefferson and take an extended vacation in the US for his health.) The state is instead named for the British Lord de La Warr, who never set foot on his namesake's soil. The second smallest state in the Union, Delaware is known fancifully as the Diamond State because of its value in proportion to its size. And Delawareans proudly call it the First State, as it was the first to ratify the US Constitution.

If you're like most travellers, you will probably only pass through the northern tip of the triangle—across the Delaware Memorial Bridge (the world's largest twin span bridge) and on to Baltimore, Philadelphia, or New York City. Between the state's northern metropolis, Wilmington, and the southerly Fenwick Island lie miles of sandy coastline. Flat coastal plain covers 94 per cent of Delaware's 3 counties (2 at high tide, residents say); there's even a cypress swamp, the most northerly in the US. Ponds and tidy farms are sprinkled across the wooden backbone of the peninsula, which levels out towards the Maryland border.

A former slave-holding state, Delaware sided with the North in the Civil War, and ran an 'underground railway', a clandestine escape route from house cellar to house cellar that brought 3000 blacks to Northern freedom. It was then, too, that the du Ponts, reckoned to be the richest family in the world, made their first multi-millions by manufacturing explosives for the cause.

The telephone area code for the entire state is 302.

WILMINGTON The 'Chemical Capital of the World', and the lucky spot where Eleuthere du Pont decided to build his powder mill in 1802. Wealth, labs, factories and eyesores followed, though downtown renewal has restored the Grand Opera House. There are several other imposing or otherwise interesting historical relics to see before pushing on to Dover, 45 miles south.

ACCOMMODATION/FOOD

Gateway Motor Inn, 1515 N du Pont Hwy, New Castle, 328-3500. S–$35, D–$42. Outdoor olympic-size pool.

YMCA, 10th & Walnut Sts, 571-6935. Men only. S–$63–$73 weekly, $275–$390 monthly (no daily rates). Advance reservations necessary.

YWCA, 225 King St, 658-7161. Women only. S–$65–$75 weekly. Advance reservations necessary.

The Fox, 900 N Market, Wilmington, 654-9700. Cafeteria-style breakfasts and lunches. Call for daily specials.

OF INTEREST

Brandywine Park, along the river between Augustine and Market St Bridges, 571-7713. Playground, zoo and landscaped gardens with 118 Japanese cherry trees.

Grand Opera House, 818 Market St Mall, 652-5577. Built in 1871 with an ornate cast iron facade, it now houses the **Delaware Center for the Performing Arts**.

Hagley Museum, Barley Mill Rd & Brandywine Creek, 658-2401. 225-acre complex on the site of the original du Pont black powder works, with restored granite buildings amidst wooded hillsides and huge trees; pleasant walks along the Brandywine. Exhibits, demonstrations and museum. Open daily 9.30am–4.30pm. Admission $9.75; $7.50 w/student ID. 'Very interesting and worthwhile.'

Holy Trinity (Old Swedes) Church, 606 Church St, 652-5629. The oldest (1698) Protestant church still active in North America. Once severely Swedish Lutheran, now more ornately Episcopalian.
Longwood Gardens, 12 miles west of Wilmington at US 1 and Rt 52 near Kennett Square, PA, (215) 388-6741. Yet another du Pont hangout, formerly the country estate of industrial magnate Pierre S du Pont (a descendant of the first Pierre S). Outdoor gardens open 9am–6pm, Tue, Thur & Sat till 10.30pm; conservatories open 10am–5pm, Tue, Thurs & Sat till 10.30pm. $10, Tue. $6. Admission includes many concerts and choreographed fountain displays. 'Beautiful.'
Nemours Mansion and Gardens, 3½ miles northwest on Rockland Rd, 651-6912. 102-room Louis XVI chateau look-alike with all the gear: furniture, tapestries, French gardens, etc, built 1910 by Alfred I duPont. Note spelling is different from other 'du Ponts'. Alfred spelled his name *this* way. 2-hr tours Tue–Sun by reservation, $8, May–Nov.
New Castle, 6 miles south of Wilmington on Rte 9, is a small town full of the atmosphere and architecture of the colonial and early republic periods. Near Strand and Delaware Sts, William Penn, of Pennsylvania fame, entered his vast colonial lands. Here, a round border separates the states of Pennsylvania and Delaware; the spire of the New Castle courthouse was used as the compass point to create this odd configuration.
The Rocks, at the foot of 7th St, 1 block south of Church St. A monument marks the site of **Fort Christina**, built by the Swedish-Dutch expedition which landed here in 1638. Also an 18th century log cabin survives. Free.
Winterthur Museum, 6 miles northwest on Rte 52, 888-4600. Once the home of Henry Francis du Pont, Winterthur now houses one of the world's greatest antique collections—nearly 200 period rooms display American decorative arts from the 17th–19th centuries. 1 hr tour, $10; 2 hr tour, $20.

INFORMATION/TRAVEL

Visitors Bureau, 1300 Market St, Suite 504, 652-4088.
Amtrak, Martin Luther King Jr Blvd & French St, (800) USA-RAIL.
Greyhound, Wilmington Bus Station, 101 N French St, 655-6111 or (800) 231-2222. Open 24 hrs.

DOVER

DOVER One of the oldest state capitals in the nation, Dover was founded in 1683 when William Penn decided to build those amenities of civilised life on the site—a prison and county courthouse.

ACCOMMODATION

Budget Host, 246 N du Pont Hwy, 678-0160. Pool, AC, cable TV, coin laundry. S–$38, D–$50.
Howard Johnson's, 561 N du Pont Hwy, 678-8900. Pool, AC, cable TV, coin laundry. S–$43, D–$50.

OF INTEREST

Legislative Hall, capitol building on Court St.
Old State House, the Green, 739-2466. Built in 1792, a fine example of American Georgian architecture with portraits of Delaware celebrities inside. Open Tue–Sat 10am–4pm, Sun 1.30pm–4pm.
Delaware State Museum, 316 S Governors Ave, 739-4266. Three galleries house fascinating range of Americana. Open Tue–Sat 10am–3.30pm. Closed Sun & Mon.

INFORMATION/TRAVEL

Dover Information Center, 406 Federal St, 739-4266, provides information on accommodation, restaurants and museums. 'Very helpful.'
Greyhound, 650 Bay Court Plaza, 734-1417. Open Mon–Fri 9am–4pm, w/ends 11am–4pm.

THE DELAWARE COAST Much of the coastline follows Delaware Bay out towards the Atlantic, but even the southern shore is protected from the open ocean by Fenwick Island. **Lewes** (pronounced 'Lewis') is one of the earliest European settlements in the New World. First inhabited by the Dutch, Lewes is now the traditional home of pilots who guide ships up Delaware Bay—and a charming town to explore by foot. Further south near Delaware Seashore State Park, **Rehoboth Beach** is popular with Washingtonians fleeing the US capital's beastly summer heat. 'Rehoboth', Hebrew for 'enough room' will seem ironic to anyone visiting the body-blanketed beach on a hot weekend. Nearby **Dewey Beach** and **Bethany Beach** are nearly as popular.

ACCOMMODATION

In Rehoboth in the summer, rates are very high. Try searching on foot away from the ocean or contact the Chamber of Commerce, 501 Rehoboth Ave in the Train Station, 227-2233, for room listings.

Camping:

Near Lewes, **Cape Henlopen State Park** on Rte 9, 645-8983. $14 sites for 4 people; XP-$2.

Between Dewey and Bethany Beaches, **Delaware Seashore State Park** on Rte 1 at the Indian River inlet, 227-2800. $13 sites for 4 people; XP-$2. 'Friendly proprietors.'

FOOD

Rehoboth Beach is paradise for junk-food junkies, e.g. pizza at **Nicola's** on 1st St, and french fries at **Thrasher's**.

DISTRICT OF COLUMBIA

WASHINGTON DC The Federal Capital lies on the Potomac River between North and South. This was Thomas Jefferson's idea, a seat of government free of regional interest, while Congress, which oversees the district, entrusted the design to Frenchman Pierre L'Enfant. In 1791 L'Enfant began work on a city he envisioned would rival the capitals of Europe, at the same time reflecting the bold qualities of the new America.

Washington today does indeed have a monumental quality, with its broad avenues, magnificent memorials, and great granite buildings in the classical style. It is only in recent, years, however, that Washington has overcome its backwater past, progressing from the days when John F Kennedy wryly described it a city of 'Northern charm and Southern efficiency', to become the nation's focal point as it is today.

A formerly transient town, which once changed populations with every new presidential administration, DC has become a highly desirable place to live. This is particularly evident in Georgetown, whose quaint brick houses, once quarters for slaves, poor labourers and free blacks, now command million-dollar sums. Georgetown's M and Wisconsin Streets buzz with cosmopolitan diners, flutter with art galleries and expensive boutiques; its quiet townhouse-lined neighbourhoods are best explored on foot.

While Georgetown caters increasingly to well-heeled tourists and suburbanites, another section of town known as Adams-Morgan attracts a more diverse, local crowd. 'Flavour' is the password to this buzzing, international community just a few minutes walk from Dupont Circle. From Cajun to Caribbean, Ethiopian to Hispanic, you name it and you're likely to find it (at bargain prices) along 18th St at Columbia Rd. Primarily a night-time neighbourhood, things change every September on Adams-Morgan Day when the streets explode with music, dance, ethnic food and thousands of Washingtonians who, for one day at least, exchange their pinstripes for T-shirts and let it all hang out.

Indeed, despite its bureaucratic image, DC is surprisingly youthful, due in part to a large student population (Georgetown U, George Washington U, American U, Catholic U and Johns Hopkins) and a probably larger international community that includes, besides embassies, the 6000-person World Bank, its sister the International Monetary Fund (IMF), the Inter-American Development Bank, and the Organization of American States (OAS), plus sizeable immigrant groups. Crime in DC is concentrated in the northeast, southeast and southwest quadrants. Fortunately for the traveller, the majority of attractions, accommodation, and restaurants are located in the northwest quadrant, an area that is unusually safe for a city. Even so, it is always advisable to travel with caution, especially at night.

Washington is a pleasant city to visit. There is a tremendous amount to see (mostly free), and it's cleaner and greener than most US cities, with a subway system which is graffiti-proof, efficient and safe. Some parts of the city now buzz with recently revitalized activity around the Old Post Office, the Georgetown waterfront and 18th St in Adams-Morgan. During the summer there is a constant stream of interesting events on the Mall and other locations, but beware the great heat and humidity. The most agreeable times to visit are spring, when daffodils, cherry trees, tulips, azaleas, and magnolias bloom in orderly succession; and autumn, when the air is crisp and clear, and the museums are not overflowing with tourists.

The telephone area code for Washington is 202.

ACCOMMODATION

Housing, like most things in DC, is more expensive than in other US cities and less abundant for the budget traveller. For longer, summer, stays, be prepared to search long and hard as you will be competing with the hoards of interns that descend on the Capital from May to September.

George Washington University Off-Campus Housing Office, Harvin Center, 800 21st St NW, 994-7221. Advertises apartments and shared houses available for the summer period. Rooms in fraternity houses are also usually vacant for the summer. **Georgetown University** publishes a weekly listing of accommodation for rent. In general, university dorms are only available to students taking summer courses at those universities—and these are usually full by the end of May. Try the notice boards at local cafes (**Chesapeake Bagel Bakery** and **Food for Thought**, both on Connecticut Ave, have boards brimming with ads), and at Union Station.

Connecticut Woodley Guest Home, 2647 Woodley Rd NW, 667-0218. S–$45, D–$62, shared bath. Nearest Subway stop: Woodley Park Zoo.

Davis House, 1822 R St NW, near Dupont Circle, 232-3196, is run by Quakers and has limited, bare accommodation (no private rooms or private baths) at $30. No smoking or drinking.

Harrington Hotel, 11th and E NW, 628-8140. Downtown, between Capitol and White House. $79 for 4. 'Crowded.' 'Clean, safe & central location, near all tourist attractions, self-service cafeteria downstairs.' 'Brilliant.'
International Guest House, 1441 Kennedy St NW, 726-5808. 4 miles from downtown. D–$25 (per person), includes breakfast and tea and cookies at 9pm. 'Very kind people; you can meet travellers from all over the world here.'
Kalorama Guest House, 1854 Mintwood Pl NW, 667-6369. D–$74, shared bath. 'We were very well looked after.' XP $5.
Meg's International Guest House, 1315 Euclid NW, 462-0284. S–$25, D–$45.
University Inn, 2134 G St, 342-8020. S-$42, D–$47. 'Clean, efficient, friendly.' In Georgetown.
Washington International AYH Hostel, 1009 11th St NW, 737-2333. $15 AYH, $18 non-members. $2 sheet rental. Open all day; 10 bedrooms; organises tours and outings. Clean, even a little sterile, plus 'some obnoxious staff'.
Washington International Student House, 2452 18th St NW, 265-5575. In the heart of lively, trendy, Adams Morgan, this is the place to stay for the newly arrived foreign traveller. $15 per night for clean and 'cozy' dorms (10 per room). Kitchen facilities, free linen, alcohol permitted. 'Cheapest, best place in DC. Friendly management, great atmosphere.' 'Unhelpful, crowded and hot.'
William Penn House, 515 E Capitol St, 543-5560. A Quaker Seminary Center open to travellers when there are no conferences. $25 (for students), $40 (for non-students) per night for dorm-style room includes a hearty breakfast. 'Clean and friendly, no smoking or alcohol.'
Camping: Greenbelt Park, Greenbelt, MD, (301) 344-3944. 6 miles north of Washington along I-95, off at exit 23. Sites $8, no showers.
HOUSING INFO:
Bed & Bread, 3918 W St NW, north of Georgetown, 338-8163. Information and referral service for women and their families only (couples OK). From $15 a night for a shared room; can find you a room immediately in safe neighbourhood (Glover Park, above G'town). 'Excellent, people very friendly and kind.'
Foreign Student Service Council, 2337 18th St NW, 232-4979, has a directory of local families willing to lodge foreign students for the cultural exchange—they are not hotels! Free telephones for enquiries. 'Worth a try.' Office open Mon–Fri 9.30am–5pm.
For bed and breakfast listings: **The Bed & Breakfast League**, and **Sweet Dreams and Toast**, PO Box 9490, DC 20016, 363-7767, S–$45 up, D–$55 up.

FOOD

NEAR THE MALL: Restaurants are scarce around the Mall, and the distance between them can be daunting to a hungry stomach-on-legs. Most museums have a (crowded, noisy, smoky) cafeteria with some awful, overpriced, plastic food. A few government cafeterias are open to the public during working hours: '**Dept of Commerce** building cafeteria—good food at reasonable prices.' Here are some inexpensive eating alternatives, but be aware that, in the summer, all the other visitors to the nation's capital are going to head for them, too.
The Cascades Cafe, in the basement of the **National Gallery of Art** between the old and new wings. Open Sat 11.30am–4.30pm, Sun noon–3.30pm. Buffet (right next to the cafe) open Mon–Sat 11am–4.30pm, Sun noon–4pm. 'Tourist food, tourist prices, but it's beside a fabulous waterfall—it's like being a part of a sculpture. Worth a cup of coffee.' (The gallery also contains another good cafe, and an unusually decent, though crowded, cafeteria.)
International Square, 19th and K, 223-1850, French, Italian, Chinese, US, etc. Sit next to indoor fountain. Open Mon–Fri 7.30am–6.30pm, Sat 10am–6pm.
Old Post Office Pavilion, 1100 Pennsylvania Ave. 'Large selection of reasonably priced places to eat—American, Greek, Indian, Chinese, etc,' plus entertainment. Open Mon–Sat 10am–9.30pm; Sun noon–8pm.
Scholl's Colonial Cafeteria, 1990 K St NW in the Esplanade Mall, 296-3065, is THE place to eat for those on a budget. Good, homecooked food at unbelievably

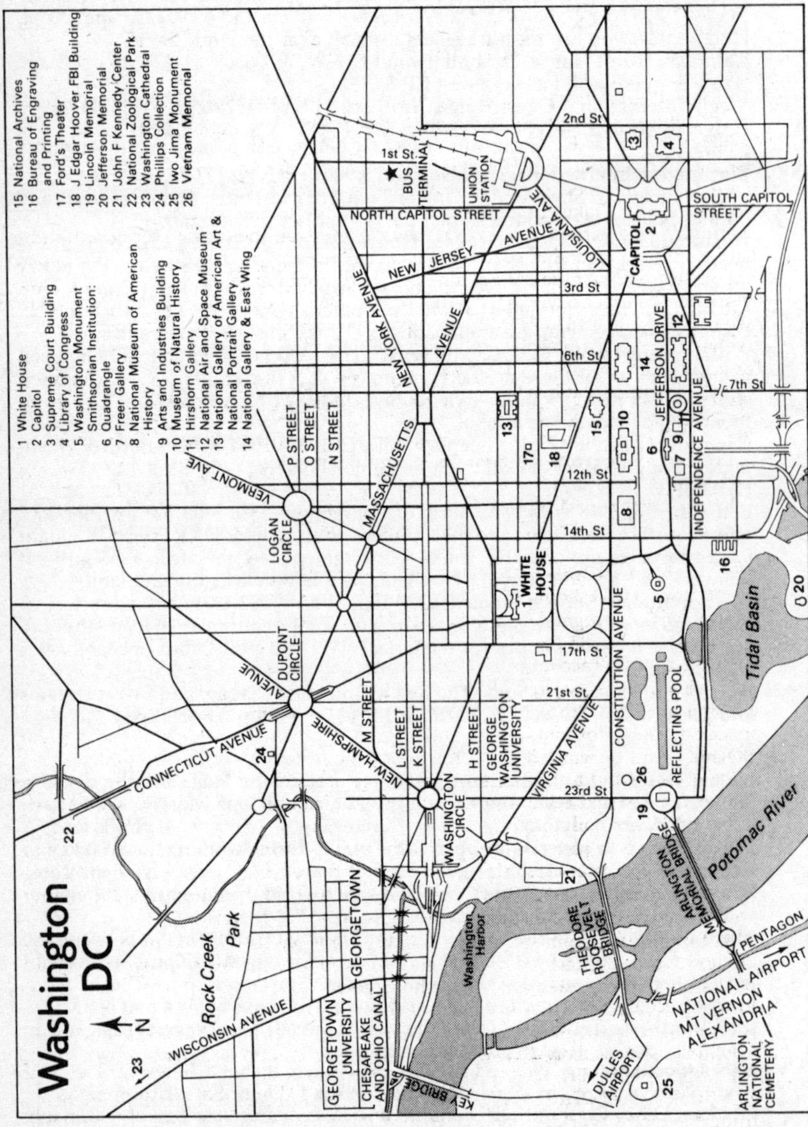

Washington DC
N
1 White House
2 Capitol
3 Supreme Court Building
4 Library of Congress
5 Washington Monument
Smithsonian Institution:
6 Quadrangle
7 Freer Gallery
8 National Museum of American History
9 Arts and Industries Building
10 Museum of Natural History
11 Hirshorn Gallery
12 National Air and Space Museum
13 National Gallery of American Art & National Portrait Gallery
14 National Gallery & East Wing
15 National Archives
16 Bureau of Engraving and Printing
17 Ford's Theater
18 J Edgar Hoover FBI Building
19 Lincoln Memorial
20 Jefferson Memorial
21 John F Kennedy Center
22 National Zoological Park
23 Washington Cathedral
24 Phillips Collection
25 Iwo Jima Monument
26 Vietnam Memorial
Rock Creek Park
WISCONSIN AVENUE
CONNECTICUT AVENUE
DUPONT CIRCLE
LOGAN CIRCLE
VERMONT AVE
P STREET
O STREET
N STREET
M STREET
L STREET
K STREET
H STREET
NEW HAMPSHIRE
MASSACHUSETTS
NEW YORK AVENUE
AVENUE
NEW JERSEY AVENUE
NORTH CAPITOL STREET
SOUTH CAPITOL STREET
LOUISIANA AVE
1st St.
2nd St
3rd St
6th St
7th St
12th St
14th St
17th St
21st St
23rd St
BUS TERMINAL
UNION STATION
CAPITOL
WHITE HOUSE
GEORGE WASHINGTON UNIVERSITY
WASHINGTON CIRCLE
VIRGINIA AVENUE
CONSTITUTION AVENUE
JEFFERSON DRIVE
INDEPENDENCE AVENUE
REFLECTING POOL
Tidal Basin
Potomac River
GEORGETOWN
GEORGETOWN UNIVERSITY
CHESAPEAKE AND OHIO CANAL
Washington Harbor
KEY BRIDGE
THEODORE ROOSEVELT BRIDGE
ARLINGTON MEMORIAL BRIDGE
PENTAGON
NATIONAL AIRPORT
MT VERNON
ALEXANDRIA
DULLES AIRPORT
ARLINGTON NATIONAL CEMETERY

low prices. 'Try the rhubarb pie, in fact, any pie!' Open daily except Sundays, 7am–8pm. Closed between meal times.

Shops at National Place, 13th & Pennsylvania, 783-9090. Plenty of inexpensive cafes. Open Mon–Sat 10am–7pm, Sun noon–5pm.

US Senate Cafeteria, 224-4249, in the basement of the Dirkson Bldg, Capitol Hill. Famous for its Bean Soup. 'Try it—you'll know where they get their wind.' Open to public 7.30am–noon & 1.30pm–3.30pm; noon–1.30pm is feeding time for congress people alone.

Union Station, 1st Ave and Massachusetts, houses a wide variety of eating places, everything from bagels to rice bowls to gourmet frozen yoghourt.

ETHNIC FOOD: DC excels at cheap, authentic ethnic restaurants—whether begun by diplomats who outlive their governments or not, no one can say for sure. Generally speaking, look for **Vietnamese** food in the Vietnamese enclave in Arlington, VA (take the blue/orange metro line to the Clarendon stop); good **Ethiopian** and various types of **Hispanic** eateries in the Adams-Morgan 18th St and Columbia area; and **seafood** at Eastern Market (7th St) at the Capitol South metro stop on the blue/orange line, especially for crab cakes, and on Maine Ave along the Potomac River in SW Washington. If you're feeling spontaneous, go to Adams-Morgan and look around; it would be hard to go wrong, no matter which restaurant you stumble into. Unless otherwise noted, assume Georgetown restaurants are a rip-off.

Some recommendations:

Burrito Brothers, 332-2308, 1524 Connecticut Ave. Carry-out your quesadillas, tacos, etc, a few southward steps to Dupont Circle for a Mexican picnic amid an ever-changing crowd of bike messengers, chess players, musicians, protesters. Delicious and filling for a good price. Open 11am–11pm, Sun, 8pm.

Cactus Cantina, 3300 Wisconsin Ave, 686-7222. the best value Mexican in DC, find it by the big plastic cacti outside. Open daily 11.30am–10.30pm 'till late on Saturdays.

City Lights of China, 265-6688, 1731 Connecticut Ave. Absolutely the best Chinese food in Washington; even the fortune cookies are delicious! Try pan-fried dumplings and vegetable curl to start. 'Moderately expensive and worth it.'

El Tamarindo, 1785 Florida Ave NW, 328-3660. Salvadorean and Mexican dinners, \$6–\$9. By all accounts the cheapest and best in Adams-Morgan. Free tortillas and salsa to start; wash it all down with a Mexican beer.

Meskerem, 2343 18th St NW, 462-4100. Ethiopian restaurant renowned for quality cuisine and affordable prices. Eat upstairs sitting on floor cushions, and soak in the ambience. Be warned, though; you'll struggle to your feet after filling up on a plate of *injera* and *wats*! Friendly staff and bright decor. Vegetable combination platter for 3, \$9.50 each. Worth it: 'You won't have to eat for a week!' Open noon–midnight daily.

Paru's, 2010 S St just north of Dupont Circle, 483-5133. Informal setting, tasty Indian food; specials \$6. Bring your own beer or wine.

Spaghetti Garden, 2317 18th St, 265-6665, inexpensive, filling, roof-top dining with view of Adams-Morgan.

Thai Room, 5037 Connecticut Ave NW at Nebraska, 244-5933. Mingle with overlanders over real Thai food. Don't get this mixed up with the more expensive and not-as-good Thai restaurant down the street.

PLAIN OLD AMERICAN: Plenty of these in DC, too.

Au Bon Pain, in the mall behind GWU at 20th and Penn Ave, 887-9215 and other locations. Choose from a variety of different breads and design your own sandwich. Open Mon–Fri, 6am–9.30pm, w/ends 8am–8pm.

The Brickskellar, 22nd St NW, btwn P and Q, 293–1885. Over 600 different beers from all over the world. Good, cheap food includes (genuine) buffalo. 'Tastes like beef.' Beers from US microbreweries more potent than US domestic beers—you have been warned! Open Sun–Thur 11.30am–2am, Fri–Sat 'til 3am.

Lindy's Bon Apétit, 2040 Pennsylvania Ave, near Tower Records, 452-0055. The

best burgers in DC. Choose from the 22 different varieties of burgers and lots of sandwiches, $2–$6. Also has sit-down in the Red Lion upstairs.
Safeway Town House Food Store, 2060 L St NW and 20th and S Sts, 659-8784. 'Substantially cheaper than People's Drug if shopping for meals. Good salad bar.'
Trios Restaurant, 17th & Q NW, 232-6305. 'Very friendly little restaurant, serving good food. Frequented by lots of local people. About $10 per head.'
BREAKFAST: Chesapeake Bagel Bakery, CT Ave just above Dupont Circle, and at several locations throughout DC area, for great coffee and bran muffins, as well as 60¢ bagels (also open for lunch and supper).
Sherrill's Bakery, 233 Pennsylvania Ave SE, Capitol Hill, 544-2480, bee-hive coiffed waitresses are pros at moving food and people. Don't cross them!
ATMOSPHERE: American Cafe, 1211 Wisconsin Ave NW, in Georgetown, and 19th and M Sts, 944-9464, is the flagship restaurant of this ever-expanding chain. Moderately expensive.
Au Pied de Cochon, 1335 Wisconsin Ave, NW, 333-5440, Georgetown. Site of real-life spy hi-jinks involving KGB defector (or not?) and flabbergasted CIA agent. Ask a bartender for a commemorative 'Yurchenko shooter' and for the *true* tale behind the events of 4 Nov 1985. Open 24 hrs, in case anyone needs to come in out of the cold.
Food for Thought, 1738 Connecticut Ave NW, 797-1095. Vegetarian food included; whole-earth music nightly. Bargain prices for substantial meals.
Kramerbooks and Afterwords Cafe, 1517 Connecticut Ave NW, 387-1400. Bookshop and cafe with jazz, folk and bluegrass music; the place to book-browse or people-watch. Order margueritas and split the atomic nachos, or chill out with a smoothie (blended ice-cream, fruit and liqueur—delicious!)
Old Ebbitt Grill, 675 15th St NW, 347-4800. Actually, not so old—the renovated building was opened in 1984. Seafood, Italian and American specialities in this warmly ornate establishment near the White House, populated by movers, shakers and watchers thereof.
SWEET TOOTH: The best ice cream in DC is **Bob's Famous Homemade Ice Cream**, 2416 Wisconsin Ave NW. 'Inventor of Oreo ice cream and other exotic flavours—try the ridiculously large sundae.'
Winners in the variety stakes are: **Ben & Jerry's**, Columbia and 18th, 667–6677. Flavours include environmentally-conscious *Rainforest Crunch*. A cool place to hang out. Open daily 8am–11pm, weekends 'til 1pm.
Thomas Sweets, Wisconsin and P St, Georgetown, 337-0616. Their 'Skinny Dip' is recommended, among others. Try their Cinnamon ice cream also, if you like 'Cheerios'!

OF INTEREST

GOVERNMENT BUILDINGS:
Botanic Garden, 1st and Maryland, between Air and Space Museum and Capitol, 225-7099. Tired feet will enjoy a respite as their owners lounge on benches amid 500 varieties of orchids and other tropical flora. Open 9am–5pm. Free.
Bureau of Engraving and Printing, 14th and C Sts SW, 622-2000. Manufactures money—not only all denominations of paper bills, but government bonds and stamps as well. Guided tours 9am–2pm Mon–Fri; free. Hour-long wait for a 25-min tour. No free samples.
Folger Library, at corner of 2nd and East Capitol Sts, behind the Jefferson Building, 544-4600. Here you'll find America's finest Shakespeare collection, including 79 copies of the First Folio (the first published edition of Shakespeare's collected works)—more copies than anyone else has. At least 1 of the 79 is always on display. Open 10am–4pm. Mon–Sat.
J Edgar Hoover FBI Building, Pennsylvania Ave between 9th & 10th Sts NW, 324-3447, named after the man they couldn't get rid of because he had the goods on them all, even though, as it turns out, the Mafia had the goods on *him*. The only way to enter the building is to go on the free 1-hr guided tours which run every 15

mins, Mon–Fri 8.45am–4.15pm starting from the E entrance. See various FBI labs, a fire-arms demo and mildly impressive displays of riches recovered from bad guys. 'Ugliest building in DC.' 'Disappointing.'

Library of Congress, 1st & Independence SE, opposite Capitol, 707-5000. The largest library in the world is made up of three buildings, but the one you'll want to see is the astounding **Jefferson Building**: walls, ceilings and floors are covered with inspiring, allegorical scenes representing such popular subjects as 'Truth, Beauty', etc.' The cumulative effect is overwhelming. Among the library's holdings are a perfect copy of the Gutenberg Bible (1450), first book to be printed from moveable type; Jefferson's rough draft of the Declaration of Independence; Lincoln's drafts of the Gettysburg Address; a vast folk music collection you can listen to (by appt); and a major portion of the books published in the US since the Civil War. Open Mon–Fri 8.30am–9.30pm, Thurs, Fri & Sat 8.30am–5pm, free. Tours hourly 9am–4pm. A slide show 'America's Library' is shown hourly on weekdays in the **Orientation Theatre**, Jefferson Bldg; tours leave hourly 10am–3pm from the theatre. 'Fascinating—read the newspaper of the day after Kennedy's assassination.'

National Archives, 8th & Constitution NW, 501-5402. Open daily 8.45am–9.45pm, Sat 'til 5pm. Free. Preserves and makes available government records of enduring value, e.g. Declaration of Independence, Bill of Rights, Constitution and Watergate Tapes; listen to latter at archives branch on 845 S Pickett St in Alexandria, (703) 756-6498, 8.30am–4.30pm Mon–Fri (pick up a shuttle from the archives).

Supreme Court Building, on 1st St, between Maryland Ave & E Capitol St NE, facing the Capitol, 479-3000. Where the country's highest judicial body holds its sessions. You can see the court in session by waiting in line, but the court is usually adjourned from the last part of June until the first Monday of October. Open Mon–Fri 9am–4.30pm; tours 9.30am–3.30pm.

The Capitol, 224-3121, on Capitol Hill, the central point of Washington, from which the city is divided into quadrants. The city's most familiar landmark, it holds the chambers of the Senate and the House of Representatives. Of particular note are the works of Brumidi in the Great Rotunda and corridors. Introductory tour covers only the Rotunda and the Crypt, then you're left to your own devices. 'Queues not very long, very interesting tour, certainly worthwhile.' Most interesting part is the Senate Chamber-much smaller than you'd expect.' Open to visitors 9am–8pm daily Easter–Labor Day; 9am–4.30pm rest of the year; closed 1 Jan, Thanksgiving and 25 Dec. Free guided tours are available from the Rotunda daily, 9am–3.45pm. When the Senate or House are in session, you need a pass to enter. Passes for the Senate Gallery can be obtained from the Appointment Desk, Senate side; for the House apply to the Doorkeeper's Office on the House side of the Capitol. Passports or other ID are required. The underground train linking the Capitol and the Senate Office Buildings is available to all.

White House, 1600 Pennsylvania Ave, 456-7041. Although he chose the site, George Washington is the only president never to have slept here. The White house has been rebuilt or redesigned inside and out many times, most memorably in 1814, courtesy of the British Army. The structural integrity may have been most severely tested 15 years later, during Andrew Jackson's inaugural carouse (the new president's backwoods buddies nearly destroyed the place). On a tour you'll be shuffled through a few of the well-proportioned rooms and furnishings supplied by successive Mrs Presidents. Free tours Tue–Sat 10am–noon. 'Long, slow lines.' Be at the Ellipse by 8am; even at that time the queue is huge, though it moves fairly quickly. Pick up a same-day ticket at the visitor's waiting area there; come back at the time printed on your ticket, but expect further waits before actually getting in.

Voice of America, 330 Independence Ave, 619-4700. Watch and listen to live broadcasts. 'Fascinating; not just another radio station.'

MONUMENTS:

Lincoln Memorial, at the foot of the Mall, open 8am–midnight, free. The large brooding figure, sculptured with mastery and affection, flanked by two Lincoln addresses, is an impressive sight which no visitor to the city should miss. Rather than becoming an overgrown tombstone, this memorial has evolved into a living symbol of freedom and human dignity. It has an enviable history: in 1939, the Daughters of the American Revolution barred black singer Marian Anderson from performing in the DAR's Constitution Hall; Anderson sang at the memorial instead, at Eleanor Roosevelt's request. Civil rights marches began at its steps, crowned in 1963 by Martin Luther King's 'I Have a Dream' speech. Anti-Vietnam War marchers also made the memorial their staging ground; ironically (or perhaps appropriately), the **Vietnam Veterans Memorial** is just next door, a sombre granite slash in the ground that, by listing the names of all 58,000 American dead on its walls has a shockingly direct power. The faces of the visitors tell more than the memorial does.

Jefferson Memorial, on Tidal Basin south of Mall. The dome, based on Jefferson's home at Monticello, and the quiet serenity of the ionic columns add to a smaller and more intimate monument than Lincoln's. See it at night, floodlit, for best effect.

Washington Monument, on the Mall at 15th, 426-6839. A 555-ft obelisk, by law the tallest structure in DC. The view at the top is splendid, but the observation room is grungy, and you have to jockey for position in the crowds for the privilege of peeking through gunhole-slit sized portals. There is always a queue to take the ride up, even on the coldest winter day. Don't believe anyone who tells you that the line about ⅓ of the way up the side of the monument is the 'high water mark' from spring floods (it's the point at which construction was halted during the Civil War and later resumed with a different colour of stone), and don't let anyone sell you an 'elevator pass' (it's *free*). 'Closes during thunderstorms!' 8am–midnight summer; 9am–5pm rest of year.

SMITHSONIAN INSTITUTION. The world's largest collection of museums was begun by a British scientist, James Smithson, who left his entire fortune (105 bags of gold) to finance it. Today the Smithsonian comprises 15 museums plus the National Zoo. Most of these museums are on the Mall between the Capitol and the Washington Monument. There are millions of catalogued items ranging from Lindbergh's plane to Glenn's capsule, from fossils to the Hope Diamond, from moon rocks to the First Ladies' gowns. Admission to all museums is free (there is a nominal charge for films shown). Generally open 10am–5.30pm (some museums extend their evening hours in summer). For recorded info on new displays and the day's events at the museums, phone 357-2020; for general info 357-2700.

The **Arthur M. Sackler Gallery** and the **National Museum of African Art**, both 357-1729, 10th & Independence SW. Opened in 1987, these two museums sit underground, behind the Smithsonian Castle. The former houses a collection of Asian art and artifacts, while the latter is the only museum dedicated to the African arts in the US. The **Freer Gallery**, 12th & Jefferson Dr SW, reopened after renovation in 1993 to show its wonderful collection of Asian and Asian-inspired art, with a new underground link to the Sackler.

The **Smithsonian Castle**, the museum's original building, houses a Visitors Center with info on all there is to see and do.

Arts and Industries Building, 9th & Jefferson, has the Centennial collection from the World Exposition in 1876. Funky old place, full of old machinery, trains and stuffed stuff.

Hirshhorn Museum and Sculpture Garden on the Mall at Independence, has a modern art collection not to be missed. The upper floors of the controversial, donut-shaped Hirshhorn display a fine permanent collection of 20th century art (1930–1970ish); the lounge has a nice view of the Mall. But the changing exhibits in the basement are where the avant-garde action is. The theatre in the basement occasionally screens free cutting-edge films.

National Air and Space Museum, 357-1686, next door to the Hirshhorn, is the world's most popular museum, with everything from space capsules to U2 photographs of Soviet missile sites, to the earliest planes. 'Best thing we did in Washington, take a tape-recorded tour for most benefit.' 'A must.' See the 'mind-blowing' films such as *To Fly* and *The Dream is Alive* on a 5-storey screen that gives you the impression you are riding through a forest in a coach, zooming over the desert in your fighter jet or hovering outside your space capsule above the earth; films are highly recommended by readers; $3.25, $2 students.
National Museum of American History, across the Mall at 12th & Constitution, has all sorts of Americana including Dorothy's ruby slippers, Fonzie's leather jacket, and Archie Bunker's chair. The original 'Star-Spangled Banner', immortalized by Francis Scott Key, comes out to the blare of trumpets every hour on the half hour. 'A delve into the realms of American culture!' Don't miss the Information Technology exhibit—see how faxes began!
The National Postal Museum, City Post Office Building, Massachusetts Ave & North Capitol St NE, 357-1729. The newest addition to the Smithsonian empire is a paeon to not only the lowly stamp, but also the way the postal system has helped to define the country.
Museum of Natural History, 10th & Constitution, is truly 'the nation's attic'—some 118 million artifacts—it even *smells* like mothballs and formaldehyde. Among warrens where you could wander for ever are wildlife dioramas, dinosaur bones, the Hope Diamond, a scale model of a blue whale, a functioning coral reef, live insects, Indian skulls with partially-healed holes in them (one has 7), a perfect crystal ball and the world's largest stuffed elephant.
National Museum of American Art & National Portrait Gallery, in the Old Patent Office Bldg, bounded by 7th & 9th, G and F Sts NW. Greek Revival architecture with beautiful vaulted galleries. The building served as a Civil War hospital and was the scene of Lincoln's 2nd inaugural ball. The permanent collections include 200 years of American art, plus portraits of famous Americans by such artists as Charles Wilson Peale and Gilbert Stuart. Photography, too: past exhibits include the work of Rolling Stone photographer Annie Leibovitz.
National Gallery of Art, 737-4215, sprawls magnificently along Constitution at the upper end of the Mall. The old wing houses one of the world's great collections of Western European painting and sculpture, from the 13th century to present, and American art from colonial times. Rembrandt, French Impressionists, Flemish, Spanish, German and British artists are all represented, plus one proudly-displayed Da Vinci, the sole work by that artist on the North American continent. Connected via an underground walkway, **IM Pei's east wing** is a work of art in itself. This modern structure, formed by unexpected juxtapositions of triangles, displays the gallery's modern art. Appropriately enough, Picasso, Mondrian, Rothko, Motherwell and O'Keeffe line the walls, and magnificent changing exhibitions keep things lively. Open Mon–Fri, 10am–5pm, w/ends 11am–6pm.
National Zoological Park in Rock Creek Pk, entrances along the 3000 block of Connecticut Ave NW, 673-4800. Giant pandas are the pride of the zoo, along with Golden Lion, Tamarinds, and a fabulous wetlands exhibit. Open summer 8am–8pm, winter 8am–6pm (animal houses close earlier). Get off at the Woodley Park stop on the metro red line and follow the trail of families pushing prams.

MORE OF INTEREST

Corcoran Gallery of Art, 17th St between E St and New York Ave NW, 638-3211. Extensive collection of 18th–20th century American art; European paintings, sculpture, tapestries and pottery; changing exhibits of modern art, photography and local artists. Open Wed–Mon 10am–5pm, Thur till 9pm. Closed Tue.
Ford's Theater, 511 10th St NW, 347-4833. Where Lincoln was shot by John Wilkes Booth, 14 April 1865. Beautifully restored, and still putting on plays; phone to avoid rehearsals and performances if just looking. Open daily 9am–5pm, free.

Interesting talks on the half hour. Excellent museum in basement. Opposite is the house where Lincoln died the next day, open daily 10am–5pm, free.

Georgetown, west of Rock Creek Park and north of K St NW. A small town of beautiful houses, shady streets and expensive shops and restaurants, or a yuppie toytown nightmare, the choice is yours. Even though it has now lost the 'trendy' title to Adams-Morgan, it is still popular especially at weekends when M St becomes a strip for 'cruising'. The **harbour front**, a collection of expensive restaurants and bars, is interesting for its architecture and for people watching. The 'living' statues are always a talking point and access to the Potomac is most welcome, especially lovely at night, when the orchestrated fountain gushes in a colourful symphonetta.

Dumbarton Oaks, 32nd St between R and S, 338-8278. Hidden away above Georgetown sits a discrete wonder. The museum is a great collection of Byzantine and Mayan art, some of it in a Phillip Johnson-designed extension with truly bizarre acoustics. The gardens are simply heavenly, the design making every corner private, romantic and relaxing. 'The one real "must-see" in DC.' Museum open Tue–Sun 2pm–5pm, donation asked for; gardens open daily 2pm–6pm, $2.

The **Chesapeake & Ohio Canal** passes through Georgetown, and the towpath makes for good cycling, walking or jogging. Free folk and jazz concerts at the **Foundry Mall** alongside the canal on alternate Sundays at 1.30pm, 866-6984. Barge trips from Georgetown June–Sept, (301) 299-2026, or (301) 413-0024. Upriver the **Great Falls of the Potomac**, (703) 285-2966, are worth a look from either the MD or VA side. $5, 3 trips daily.

John F Kennedy Center for the Performing Arts, at the bottom of New Hampshire Ave on the Potomac, 467-4600. The finest music, drama, dance and film from the US and abroad. Students get half-price tickets for some performances. Tours daily 10am–1pm, free. Terrace views of the Mall, Georgetown and Rosslyn across the Potomac are gorgeous, especially at night. 'Excellent tours.'

National Geographic Society, Explorer's Hall, 17th and M Sts, 857-7588. The world famous magazine displays some of its work with interesting exhibits showing some breathtaking photography and the world's largest free-standing globe—brings geography to life. Open Mon–Sat 10am–5pm, Sun 10am–5pm. Free. 'Quality museum.'

National Museum of Women in the Arts, 1250 New York Ave, 783-5000. One of the few museums devoted entirely to art created by women, incl. Mary Cassat, Georgia O'Keeffe. Open Tue–Sat 10am–5pm, Sun noon–5pm. $1 donation. 'Worth seeing.' Free concerts at special times. Call for info.

Old Post Office Pavilion, 1100 Pennsylvania, 523-5691, has a 20-min tour that includes a free ride up an interior glass elevator to a tower overlooking the city. Not as high as the Washington Monument—but the lines are not as long, and the breezy arches afford a much less obstructed view. Daily 8am–10.30pm. Entertainment at the Pavilion daily. Also free jazz, dance and other entertainment at **Freedom Plaza** across Penn Ave, call 724-9091 for times. Reggae, rap & classical.

Phillips Collection, 1600 21st NW at Q St, 387-2151. In an unprepossessing house and gallery extension sits a treasurehouse of art. While its centerpiece of Renoir's *Luncheon of the Boating Party* attracts all the tourists, go and see the Cezannes, Picassos, Delacroixs, Goyas, and a room of Rothko. Open Mon–Sat 10am–5pm, Sun noon-7pm. $4.50, $3.25 students at w/ends, suggested donations during the week. 'Beautifully designed; superb collection.' 'A wonderful surpise.'

Washington Cathedral (Cathedral Church of St Peter and St Paul), Massachusetts and Wisconsin Aves NW, 537-6200. Take the best from all the Gothic cathedrals you have every seen, mix, stirring occasionally, and you have Washington Cathedral. Teddy Roosevelt laid the cornerstone in 1907 and it was finally completed in September 1990. It *is* beautiful despite being close to architectural pastiche; and it dominates the skyline from wherever you are in DC, perched as it is on one of the city's highest points. It has gargoyles of Washington lawyers and a moonrock embedded in one of its stained glass windows. Woodrow Wilson, Admiral

Dewey, and Helen Keller are interred here. Carillon concerts and organ recitals weekly; tours Mon–Sat 10am–3.15pm, Sun 12.30–2.45pm. Tower is open until 9pm in summer.

Wilderness Society – Ansel Adams Collection, 900 17th St NW, 833-2300. Permanent exhibition of almost 70 Adams prints. Open Mon–Fri 9am–5pm. Closed hols. Free. 'A must.'

Nearby in Arlington, VA:

Arlington National Cemetery, 697-2131, where more than 218,000 people are buried, including JFK and his brother Robert. Changing of the Guard Ceremony at the **Tomb of the Unknown Soldier** takes place every half hour, May–Oct; once on the hour rest of the year. 'Impressive!' 'Beautifully serene—hard to believe Washington could be this peaceful.' **The Arlington House** (or Curtis Lee Mansion), overlooking the cemetery, was home to Robert E. Lee until the Civil War, when he left and never returned. It's preserved in its original state. Provides a dramatic view of the city.

Iwo Jima Memorial is a sculpture of 5 marines and a sailor hoisting an American flag on to Mt Surabachi on the island of Iwo Jima, modelled after a famous World War II photograph by Joe Rosenthal. 'Stunning, as is the view from here to Washington.'

The Pentagon, (703) 545-6700, nearby, gives desperately dull tours of its gargantuan facility.

Alexandria, a few miles down the George Washington Memorial Parkway, is a mini-Georgetown, a delight with over 100 18th century buildings. Follow King Street east toward the water to get to the heart of the Old Town. Don't miss the unique **Torpedo Factory**, whose original purpose has been subverted by artists in search of studio space. A modern addition to the building has expanded browsing opportunities.

Mount Vernon, 8 miles south of Alexandria via the George Washington Parkway, (703) 780-2000. Home of George Washington and a fine example of a colonial plantation house, built 1740. Original furnishings, plus key to the Bastille, etc. George and Martha are buried here, too. Open daily 9am–5pm 1 March–31 Oct, 9am–4pm rest of year; $7.

Potomac River Rides are run by Spirit Harbour Cruises and provide an alternative way to view the city. Two hour cruises depart twice daily from Pier 4, 6th at Water St, and cost around $22. There is also a pleasant cruise to **Mount Vernon**. Call Spirit on 554-8000.

North of DC:

Mormon Temple, 9900 Stoneybrook Dr, in Kensington, MD, (301) 587-0144. Looms like an apparition from the Emerald City as you drive east on Hwy 495, the 'beltway'. Local jokesters routinely enscribe 'Surrender Dorothy' on an overpass nearby. Open 10am–9pm daily.

RFK Memorial Stadium is the home of the Washington Redskins, '88 & '92 Superbowl Champs, who play here from August (pre-season) until January. Tickets around $40 available from Ticketmaster. Call (800) 432-7328 or go to Hecht's dept store. 'Skins fever hits the city in early August', 'fans are fiercely proud'.

SHOPPING

Potomac Mills, 20 miles south of DC off I-95 near Woodbridge, (703) 490-5948. An enormous shopping mall filled with 'outlet' stores of all the major chains. Levi Strauss, Calvin Klein, Nike, Macy's, Nordstrom, Ikea and others are all here offering you their merchandise at warehouse prices. 'Don't be sucked in—prices are not that low.' 'Hi-tack.' 'Levis 501's for $25.' Open Mon–Sat 10am–9.30, Sun 11pm–6pm.

Woodward and Lothrop, at Metro Center, 347-5300. One of the best department stores. Watch out for frequently held 'sales' with selected items at 50% off. 'They seem to have a permanent sale'; 'I made my best buys in DC here.'

Pentagon City, easily accessible on the metro. State of the art, multi-level mall. 'Worth it just to see the building—amazing.'
Georgetown is the place to be seen shopping. Levis and Timberland have stores here on Wisconsin Ave but the real bargains will be elsewhere. Try further along M St. There are other malls accessible by metro such as **Mazza Galleria** (Friendship Heights) and **Ballston Commons** (Ballston).

TOURS

Gray Line, Union Station, bus parking level, 289-1995, offers a variety of sightseeing tours of Washington and surrounding areas. You can catch them at the major hotels. Around $18 for a 4 hr tour.
Scandal Tours, 783-7212, see where Ollie and Fawn shredded, Gary and Dawn 'visited', and Nixon's cronies eavesdropped as you laugh your way through this tour of Washington's more infamous sights. Saturdays, 1pm. $27, from Hilton hotel.
Tourmobile, 554-5100 or 554-7950 (recording), offers Washington and Arlington Cemetery tours for $8.50 and Mt Vernon in the spring and summer for $16.50. Combo tours for $25.50, admission included. Passes are good for a day of unlimited reboarding and you can begin at any sight. Look for Tourmobile Sightseeing Shuttle Bus Stop sign; buses run every 20 min. 'Convenient and easy to use.'
A tour is not really necessary; most Washington sights are easily reached on foot or metro, and Arlington is an easy walk across the Potomac.

ENTERTAINMENT

For the best, most comprehensive listings and reviews of what's going on in the area, pick up a free copy of the *City Paper* issued Thursdays (in shops and from street-corner boxes); the *Weekend* section of Friday's *Washington Post* and the NW neighbourhood paper, *The InTowner*, the free NW paper published monthly and available in shops and restaurants around Dupont Circle and Adams-Morgan.
Festivals: 2 major yearly events, the **Smithsonian Folklife Festival**, held around 4 July on the Mall; and **Adams-Morgan Day** (mid-Sept) on 18th St, 332-3292, with ethnic music, dance and food plus blues and gospel sounds. DC's most prominent park, a huge village green known as **the Mall**, is the grassy stage for all manner of summer entertainment. Over July 4, fireworks and fun concerts are held there (best viewing of fireworks from Kennedy Center Terrace; pick up free tickets two Sundays preceding the 4th, or barge in at the last minute, 254-3760.) Weekends on the Mall see sports events, including polo.
Nightlife: In DC, much of it centres on drinking in dingy bars. Actually, such establishments can be good places to meet people and sample the character of Washington. **Childe Harold**, 1610 20th NW, 483-6702, a centre of activity in DuPont Circle; **Holiday Inn**, 2101 Wisconsin Ave NW, 338-4600, upper Georgetown, 'loads of food Mon–Fri 5–7pm. 1 block from 'Social Safeway' where senators and social climbers dress up to shop.' **Sign of the Whale**, 1825 M St NW, 785-1110, 'ladies night (Wed) – $7 for as much as you can drink!'; **Tune Inn**, 331½ Pennsylvania Ave SE, 543-2725, is a 'sleazy bar where waitresses have biceps & insult you—the hip place to go'.
Eclectic music/spectacles abound:
Birchmere, 3901 Mt Vernon Ave, Alexandria, VA, (703) 549-5919, draws the nation's best bluegrass and country bands to its stage, including the 'Seldom Scene' every Thurs.
Blues Alley, off Wisconsin between M & K, Georgetown, 337-4141, showcases best jazz artists in the country. Expensive and reservations necessary, but worth the entrance charge of $10–$30. Also serves Creole cuisine.
Cafe Lautrec, 2431 18th St, 265-6436. Chic, French-style cafe/bar, easily located by the huge Lautrec painting outside. Always busy; often queues to get in.
Comedy Cafe, 1520 K St NW, 638-JOKE, attempts to provide laughs and often succeeds. $5–$10.

Dance Place, 3325 8th St NE (2 blocks from Brookland stop on the metro red line), 269-1600. Innovative modern dance performances.
The Front Page, 19th St NW, 296-6500. 'Popular bar for Happy Hour.' (Mon–Fri 4pm–7pm). Cheap beer and free food. 'Good atmosphere, especially on Fridays.'
The Irish Times, 14 F St NW, 543-5433. The place to go for those feeling homesick—full of Brits and Irish! A fair number of Americans too: fraternity boys ('sigma chi till I die!'), marines, firefighters . . . the world is here. Live music; place your requests and sing along—but keep your eye on the bill. Has downstairs pub theatre.
La Nicoise, 1721 Wisconsin Ave NW, 965-9300. No lie–French waiters serve you on roller skates. Dinner $20–$25, cabaret show every night.
One Step Down, 2517 Pennsylvania Ave NW, 331-8863. Great jazz just over the bridge from G'town. No cover for jam sessions on weekend afternoons. Much cheaper than Blues Alley and more intimate, too. Cover $5–$15.
For dancing:
Cities, 2424 18th St NW, 328-7194. Restaurant/bar on first floor, night club with live music and/or DJ on second. Changes menu to represent different city every few months.
Café Heaven & **Café Hell,** 2327 18th St NW, 667-HELL. In the heart of Adams-Morgan, this two tier club/bar is heaven upstairs, hell down.
Fifth Column, 915 F St NW, 393-3632. Huge converted bank with two dance floors and open air bar in between. A poseurs' paradise; come here to see and to be seen. Mon $5 entry, under-21s admitted. Thurs–Sat cover varies from $6–$8. Expect to queue if you come late (club opens at 10pm). House, 'industrial' and European dance music.
15 Minutes, 1030 15th St NW, 408-1855. Bar/club with lots of live shows, good music, and a wild and groovy atmosphere. Some evenings 18+; mostly, however, 21+; cover varies.
Kilimanjaro, 1724 California St NW, 328-3838. African dance music, calypso, reggae—with some rap thrown in. Live music at weekends; cover jumps to $10 or more. Strict dress code; no shorts, caps, etc.
9.30 Club, 930 F St NW, 244-3189. It smells, it's dark, dingy and small but if indie's your thing, then this is it. Has great live music, local bands like Unrest, $5; out-of-town bands, $7–$10.
Trax, 80 M St SE, 488-3320. Great club, horrific area. Indie/Euro-dance. Open Thurs–Sun, $5 cover; 18+.
Theatre in Washington gets better and better.
The Arena Stage, 6th & Maine Ave SW, 554-9066, has one of the finest repertory companies in the nation.
John F. Kennedy Center for the Performing Arts on the Potomac River south of Georgetown, 254-3600, has several theatres: the Opera House (ballet, plays, opera); the Eisenhower Theater (plays); the Terrace Theater; the Concert Hall, home of the world-class National Symphony; and the movie house of the American Film Institute (AFI). Even if you can't afford the steep ticket prices, don't miss the astounding views of the Potomac River, Georgetown and the Mall from the outside terrace, particularly at night.
National Theater, 1321 E St NW, 628-6161, also has some of the best performances in the city, direct from—or heading for—Broadway.
Source Theatre Company, 1835 14th St NW, 462-1073, does some powerful productions on small stages. Prices are reasonable, but careful in this area at night.
Wolf Trap Park, 1624 Trap Rd, Vienna, VA, (703) 255-1868, the only US national park devoted to the arts. You can sit on the lawn or in the open-air theatre for top-notch ballet, symphonies, opera or popular music. Lawn tickets are cheaper, and you can picnic during the performance, but come early and bring a blanket. Ride the metro orange line to West Falls Church and pick up a shuttle to Wolf Trap for $3.50. For ticket information call **Ticketplace**, 12th & F Sts NW, 842-5387, to purchase discount tickets on the day of a show or on Sat for a Sun show. You must pay cash.

AMERICAN MUSIC—THE SOUND OF SURPRISE

BLUEGRASS: Washington, DC is called bluegrass capital, but this very ethnic American music is heard throughout the Midwest too. **The Birchmere**, a premiere showcase of folk music, bluegrass, country. Catch *Seldom Scene* Thur night in **Alexandria, VA**, (703) 549-5919. **The Station Inn, Nashville, TN**, (615) 255-3307, plays bluegrass six nights a week. Among bands to catch: *Bill Monroe and the Blue Grass Boys* or *Jim & Jesse and the Virginia Boys*; for progressive style, hear the *New Grass Revival*. Most bluegrass action happens at some 400 + festivals across the country. For a listing refer to *Bluegrass Unlimited*, Box 111, Broad Run, VA 22014, (703) 349-8181.

BLUES: There are good local blues bands all over the US, but **Chicago** is the blues centre. Pick up a copy of *The Reader* for info. Don't miss **B.L.U.E.S.**, (312) 528-1012, with low-down blues, fresh acts; hot, smoky, and cramped. Try also **Rosa's**, (312) 342-0452, small, not as well known, but great music. Don't miss the free **Blues Fest** in early June, (312) 744-3315. If appearances count for anything, **Benny's, New Orleans, LA**, a bare-bones shack, wins hand-down for inspiring the blues. For general current info, read *Living Blues*, published by the University of Mississippi. Charlie Sayles (you'll know him by his eye patch) is DC's best 'Blues Harp' player. Catch him at Kramerbooks Afterwords. Oakland, CA is also filled with blues bars.

COUNTRY: Branson, MO, has become the new centre for country, with the **Andy Williams Theater**, (417) 334-7263, the **Grand Palace**, 334-7263, with its Special Star Sunday shows with Kenny Rogers for example, and the **Wayne Newton Theater**, 336-3986, where Johnny Cash is a regular—to name but three of the town's 34 clubs. The legendary **Broken Spoke, Austin, TX,** (512) 442-6189, once frequented by Willie Nelson and Ray Price, is one of the last honky-tonks. Continues to showcase bands just on the edge of hitting big time. **Crazy Horse, Santa Ana, CA**, (714) 549-1512, is billed as the top country and western entertainment spot; top names perform here. For two-stepping and hot chilli, go to **Lone Star Cafe , New York City**, (212) 245-2950. **Jimmy Driftwood Barn, Mountainview, Ark**, (501) 269-8042, hosts the best Ozark country bands. You never know what legend will turn up next at the **Bullpen Lounge**, (615) 255-6464, in **Nashville, TN**. For reading, try *Music City News*.

FOLK: Smithsonian Folklife Festival, Washington, DC, late-June to early July, has authentic folk and ethnic music, dancing. Excellent performers grace the back room of this guitar shop at weekends: **McCabe's, Santa Monica, CA**, (310) 828-4403. Try the **New Orleans Heritage Fest** for an eclectic mix of gospel, zydeco, progressive rock, jazz and more. The **Aspen Music Festival, Aspen, CO**, late June–Aug, 9 weeks, (303) 925-3172. As good as **Tanglewood Music Festival** in Lenox, MA, in terms of prestige and importance. Open rehearsals and other free events.

GOSPEL: Two million people fill the streets of **Harlem** during its massive week-long fest of gospel, rhythm & blues, and jazz. To hear gospel at its best, go to church in Detroit, Chicago or Harlem. In Washington DC, superb, uplifting gospel music can be heard each Sunday at **St Augustine's Catholic Church**, 15th and V Sts NW, 265-1470.

JAZZ: There are good jazz clubs in most North American cities. **The Baked Potato** near Universal Studios in **LA**, (818) 980-1615, is the oldest major jazz club in the US and launching pad for many famous performers. **Preservation Hall**, hub of **New Orleans** jazz, hosts pioneers of Dixieland, (504) 523-8939. In **Washington, DC, Blues Alley**, (202) 337-4141, you can see such people as Wynston Masalis and a lineup of other greats. There's no place like **New York City** for jazz: try **Blue Note,** (212) 475-8592; **Fat Tuesday's**, 533-7902; **Sweet Basil's**, 242-1785, 'Village temple of jazz'; the venerable **Village Vanguard**, 255-4037; or newer **Visiones**, 673-5576. Don't miss **JVC Jazz Festival, NYC**, June 23–July 1, (212) 397-8222. More than 40 events and 1000 performers at different locations including Lincoln Center and Carnegie Hall. All the best including Ella Fitzgerald, Ray Charles and many others. Other excellent festivals: **Chicago Jazz Fest** is exceptional, Labor Day weekend, (312) 744-3315; **Monterey, CA, Jazz Fest**, mid-September, (408) 373-3366; and **Montreux/Detroit Fest**, in Michigan, early Sept, (313) 259-5400. More than 100 performers play their licks in **Burlington, VT**, June 7–12; call DISCOVER JAZZ, (802) 863-7992. See magazines *Jazz Times* or *Downbeat* for the latest on the jazz scene nationwide.

RHYTHM & BLUES; The tradition rooted in Bo Diddly, Jerry Lee Lewis, Chuck Berry, Carl Perkins and others still survives at the **Rum Boogie Cafe, Memphis, TN**, (901) 528-0150. Danny Gatton is not strictly R&B (he plays in every style from blues to country to jazz, and every combination in between, including Les Paul and bottlenecked Thelonious Monk), but he's brilliant nonetheless. Hear him at **Club Soda, Birchmere,** etc, if you're in **Washington, DC**.

During the summer there is always **Lollapalooza**. Originally conceived in 1991 by Perry Farrell as an alternative music and political travelling roadshow, the 27-odd shows are now as mainstream as Genesis. However, it's still a great day out and the music will always be loud, yes, that's *loud*.

INFORMATION

For current information on events around the city, the following numbers are useful:

Dial-an-Event, 737-8866, for an exhaustive rundown of general events.

Dial-a-Park, 619-PARK, gives info on activities at the memorials and park areas.

Dial-a-Museum, 357-2020, gives current info on exhibits at the Smithsonian.

Tourist Information Center, 1455 Pennsylvania Ave, opposite the Department of Commerce building and between the Washington and Willard Hotels. Tel: 789-7038. Stop here first for free brochures, maps, and information on the city. Open Mon–Sat, 9am–5pm.

Travelers Aid, 1015 12th St NW, 347-0101. Also at National Airport, 684-3472, and Dulles Airport, 661-8636.

TRAVEL

Confusion over the street lay-out here is forgiveable. The same address mayua have four different locations, one in each quadrant. Just remember that N–S streets are numbered, E–W states are lettered, and the Parisian-style diagonal avenues are named after US states, one of the focal points being the Capitol.

Metro, 637-7000, Washington's space-age subway system is an experience in itself. Never-ending escalators descend below ground to reveal cavernous, museum-like vaults—'something out of 2001'. It whisks you in minutes to shopping and other developments now springing up around town e.g. Mazza Gallery (Friendship Heights). The system is clean, efficient and safe; platform walls are protected from grafitti by deep dry-moats and trains are carpeted (vacuumed daily). Cynics claim that everyone in DC could have been given a car for the money! Most places are within easy reach of a station which are identified (rather obscurely) by brown posts marked with a white 'M'. Lines are denoted by colour and end-of-line destination. Farecards cost $1 (more during rush hours and for longer journeys) obtained from machines before you reach the platform. One-day pass $5. Dollar bills are accepted, change given, and transfers to buses are free. Trains run Mon–Fri 5.30am–midnight; Sat 8am–midnight; Sun 10am–midnight.

Metrobus is a complex but extensive system integrated with the Metro—practically every block in the city is reachable by bus, call 637-7000. When stuck, ask any bus-driver for assistance, they are willing to help. All buses stop every couple of blocks on their route. #30, 32, 34 & 36 are very useful for Penn Ave, Georgetown and Wisconsin Ave. Exact fares are required—'carry a wad of $1 bills'.

Taxicabs are relatively inexpensive, but the system is complicated, based on a 'zone system'. For that reason, visitors are vulnerable to the small minority of cabbies who may try to overcharge. Be savvy. Ask the driver to tell you how much a ride will be, especially from the airport. By law, rates and zone information must be posted in the cab—study this to learn the system. There's a surcharge at afternoon rush-hour (4pm–6.30pm). Also, be sure the driver understands English before you get in the cab. Shared rides are cheaper.

Airports:

Baltimore Washington International Airport (BWI), one hour north of Washington, is served by Amtrak, (800) USA-RAIL, $10 o/w.

National, (800) 221-1111, is close to the city—too close for comfort, many locals will say—and easy to get to on the Metro blue and yellow lines. Domestic flights only.

Washington Dulles International Airport, (703) 471-7838, is located about 26 miles from downtown Washington. Flights are generally cheaper here. Sharing a cab out may be cheaper than the shuttle, about $40, (703) 661-8230.

Washington Flyer is a shuttle service which serves National and Dulles airports. It runs every 30 minutes 6.30am–9.30pm Mon–Fri, every hour at the w-end. Arrival terminal to 16 & K St NW downtown, $16 from Dulles, $8 from National (cash only).

Greyhound, 1005 1st NE, (800) 231-2222. New terminal behind Union Station. Open 24 hrs. Not an area to be alone in at night.
Union Station, 1st & Massachusetts NE, 484-7540, serves Amtrak, B&O, Virginia Express and metro. 8 mins from downtown. Day trips and overnights from here to Baltimore, Harpers Ferry, Fredericksburg, etc. Open 24 hrs. Beautifully renovated, lots of eateries, shops and multiplex cinema.
Look in the *Washington Post* for *shared expense rides*, especially late August/early Sept when students are returning to college.

MARYLAND

That Maryland is 'America in miniature' is the local boast. The state's first inhabitants came in search of religious toleration. They landed in southern Maryland on territory granted to the Catholic Lord Baltimore by Charles I from whose wife, Henrietta Maria, the state takes its name. Perched precariously on the Mason-Dixon line, Maryland shows northern influences in its western mountainous area, settled heavily by British and Germans, and southern character along the eastern shoreline famous for hunting, old antebellum mansions, and delicious Chesapeake Bay crab and oysters. Maryland credits itself with the second largest steelworks in the world, the Bethlehem Steel Corporation at Sparrow's Point.

If you have time, visit the tobacco auctions in Hughesville, La Plata, Upper Marlboro, Waldorf or Waysons Corner; the auctioneer's patter is riveting. Or, attend a tournament of the official state sport—jousting!
The telephone area code in the west of the state is 301, in the east it's 410.

BALTIMORE Baltimore is one of the nation's major seaports, and the eastern terminus of the first railroad in America, the Baltimore & Ohio. Not long ago, Baltimore was considered the ugly step-sister to Washington, DC and other major cities on the east coast. Today it sparkles from one of the most successful urban renewal programs in America. The city's Inner Harbor, the centrepiece of Baltimore's rebirth, was designed by the prolific Rouse Company, also responsible for Fanieul Hall in Boston and the entire city of Columbia, Maryland, a pleasant stopover near Baltimore.

On Baltimore's seafront, recently re-discovered (though trying hard not to be) **Fells Point** offers an unpretentious step back into the city's colonial and sea-faring history. The country's oldest, continuously working waterfront has for the most part avoided both development and tourism, resulting in a setting strikingly unchanged for some 200 years. But don't think this is a staid, museum-like area. 'Real' people live and work here, and in addition to history, the Point has a great food market, bars, restaurants and summer ethnic festivals.

Although Baltimore is only recently earning recognition, Baltimoreans have always taken great pride in their city. Indeed, there are many reasons to love Baltimore. Though often compared unfavourably with nearby Washington in the sophistication department, Baltimore definitely wins on the coziness scale. Working class city that it is, Baltimore has more ethnic flavour, and more texture (as the movies *Diner, Avalon* and *Tin Men* suggest). It is a city that is fiercely proud of its baseball team, the Orioles, and of its heroes, which include baseball star Babe Ruth, journalistic curmudgeon H L Mencken, and author and poet Edgar Allen Poe. While you're here, don't miss tasting fresh crab; and use correct pronunciation when referring to city or state: 'Bawlmer, Merlind' is quite acceptable.

ACCOMMODATION

Baltimore International Hostel, 17 W Mulberry St, 576-8880. $10 AYH, $13 non-members. 'Close to Inner Harbor area; 4 blocks from Greyhound. Clean; nice staff.' Closed 12pm–5pm every day.
Schaefer Hotel, 723 St Paul St at Madison, 332-0405. S/D-$40 with shared bath, $40–$45 with private bath. 'Clean, adequate rooms; fairly central.'

FOOD

People have gone to amazing lengths to eat in this, the 'gastronomic capital of America'. The story is told, that marching on Baltimore after burning Washington in 1814, British General Ross declared that he would dine that evening 'in Baltimore or in Hell'! Picked off by a sharpshooter in an ensuing battle, he didn't dine that night on Cheasapeake Bay crab. Modern invaders are luckier: crab, Baltimore's speciality, is available anywhere there's salt water. The scrumptious crustaceans are served by the dozen hot from the pot, peppered with volcanic Old Bay seasoning. Your only implements will be a mallet and a newspaper. Soft shell crabs are delicious too. Also, try **Phillip's** crab cakes at **Harbor Place**, Pratt & Lombard, a giant Inner Harbor pavilion with countless fast food stalls and a few restaurants. Don't miss **Ostrowski's** Polish kielbasa there, either. 'Beautiful view of harbor.'
Lexington Market, Lexington & Eutaw, is a little United Nations of people, languages and food, food, food in endless display.
Breakfast: Jimmy's, 801 S Broadway, Fell's Point, 327-3273. Good, solid breakfasts at low prices. Usually crowded, especially Sun am.
Atmosphere: Mencken's Cultured Pearl Cafe, 1114 Hollins, 837-1947. The neon sign in the window says, 'EAT ART'. Jokes about starving artists aside, you eat the food and look at the art. The latter is a revolving show of local artists' essays into the avant-garde, the former is some truly great Tex-Mex eats that got lost and went to Baltimore.
Cafe Tattoo, 4825 Belair Rd, 325-RIBS. Four-star ribs/world-class chili.
Bertha's Dining Room, 734 S Broadway, Fell's Point, 327-5795. The restaurant's catchphrase is 'EAT BERTHA'S MUSSELS!' and you can for about $7. Wash it down with one of 90 different beers.
Ikaros, 4805 Eastern Ave, 633-3750. Greek.
Louie's Bookstore Cafe, 518 N Charles, 962-1225. Seafood and literature.
Pete's Grille, 3130 Greenmount Avenue, 467-7698. A real diner with good, cheap food and a great atmosphere.

OF INTEREST

Babe Ruth Birthplace and Maryland Baseball Hall of Fame, 216 Emory, 727-1539. Memorabilia of America's favorite slugger and other Maryland heroes. Open summer 10am–5pm; winter 10am–4pm; $4.50.
Baltimore Museum of Art, Charles & 31st Sts, 396-7100. Owes its wonderful Matisse collection to the shrewd purchases of the Cone sisters from the artist himself. Plus good Modernism section. Open Wed–Fri 10am–4pm; Sat–Sun 11am–6pm. $5.50, $3.50 students, free Thurs.
Edgar Allen Poe House, 203 N Amity, 396-7932. Winding staircase leads to the tiny garrett where Poe wrote 1832–1835. Sporadic hours: open some months

Wed–Sat noon–4pm, others Sat only; closed mid-Dec to March; $2. Phone to check. NB: Poe was never wealthy, and his former home is in a rundown area. Use caution.

Fell's Point, a revamped harbour area around Aliceanna, Lancaster, Ann and Thames Streets. Shops and good places to eat. Can be reached by the water taxi which ferries people around the harbour.

Flag House, Pratt & Albermarle Sts, 837-1793. The house where Mary Pickersgill who sewed the flag that inspired Francis Scott Key to write the *Star Spangled Banner*. Open Tue–Fri 10am–4pm, Sat 9am–4.30pm; and the **Maryland Historical Society**, 201 W Monument St, 685-3750, has the original manuscript of that poem which was later (1931) adopted as the national anthem.

Fort McHenry, end of Fort Ave, 962-4290. The fort was bombarded for 25 hrs by the British during the War of 1812. Detained by the British, Francis Scott Key, seeing at the end of the bombardment that the Star Spangled Banner was still flying over the fort, felt moved to write what was to become the national anthem. After trying to sing it, you will wish the British had either not captured Key or had been better shots. Today, the fort's ancient cannons still cover the harbour. Open daily, 8am–8pm. $2. 'Catch the boat across to the fort, leaves every ½ hour from Inner Harbor; very worthwhile.'

Maryland Science Center and Davis Planetarium, 601 Light St on the harbour, 685-2370. Computer games, Chesapeake Bay and Baltimore City displays, geology, 5-story IMAX theatre, star shows in planetarium. $8.50. 'Not worth it.'

Mount Clare Station, Pratt and Poppleton Sts, 237-2387. The first railroad station in the US. Erected 1830. From here Samuel FB Morse sent the first telegraph message 'what hath God wrought'. Tues–Sun 10am–5pm, $5.

National Aquarium, Pier 3, E Pratt St, 576-3810. Take the elevator to the 4th flr, then the escalator to the rain forest where piranhas glower, sloths dangle, and free-flying birds practically land on your head. Then walk along a spiraling aquarium tank to the friendly, schmoo-like Beluga whales, who laugh at the crowds around their 1st-floor tank. 'Expensive, but worth it. Modern and interesting design; the shark tank is amazing.' Summer: Mon–Thurs 9am–5pm, Fri–Sun 9am–8pm; Winter: Sat–Thur 10am–5pm, Fri 10am–8pm; $11.50.

Peale Museum, 225 N Holiday St, and the **Walters Art Gallery**, 600 N Charles St at Center, 547-9000. One of the largest private collections in the world with something of everything from across the ages. With a new floor to house the Oriental decorative arts. Open Tues–Sun 11am–5pm, $4, students free with ID, free Wed.

Poe's Grave at Westminster Hall, Fayette & Green, 706-7228. The tombstone marking his grave (and those of his cousin/wife and aunt/mother-in-law, buried with him) is near the front gate. Take a fascinating tour (1st & 3rd Fri & Sat of each month) of the church's catacombs and grounds for $3 (reservations required). Cemetery is open daily during daylight hours, free. On Halloween the local historical society hosts a weirdly funny party in the graveyard, during which 'Frank the Body-Snatcher' lectures on the perils of his profession. On Poe's birthday, Jan 19, fans come from around the world for a midnight celebration that began in 1949, 100 years after Poe's death. It continues to this day unchanged: a mysterious man clad in black appears after midnight to offer a toast of French cognac to Poe's memory; after the ceremony he leaves roses and the open bottle at the grave and vanishes into the night.

Top of the World at the top of the **World Trade Center**, 401 East Pratt St, Inner Harbor, 837–4515, the world's tallest pentagonal building, designed by I M Pei, is an excellent place to start seeing the city. Exhibits on Baltimore's history and exceptional view, $2.

US Frigate Constellation, Constellation Dock, 1 E Pratt St, 539-1797. A 1797 frigate and America's oldest warship. Open 10am–7.30pm daily, $3.50.

Washington Monument, Charles St and Mt Vernon Pl. 178 feet high, the monument was built between 1815 and 1842, long before the one in DC.

ENTERTAINMENT

Harbor Place may seem the logical hot spot, especially the enormous factory here converted into an adult Disneyland with corresponding steep tariff, but it's best avoided. Instead head for **Fell's Point**, east of Harbor Place, where the real fun is. Around 9pm or 10pm, serious drinking and dancing get underway in the numerous little bars filled with local rowdies, yuppies, bohemians, unrepentant pirates and assorted lowlifes, all in good fun. Most places here charge a buck or two cover, if that, on weekends. Tourists invariably get lost trying to find it, not because it's difficult to find—just take the trolley from Inner Harbor or follow Broadway toward the harbour till you run out of street—but because locals intentionally give them the wrong directions, ha ha.

SPORT

Baltimore Orioles, Orioles Stadium, Camden Yards, 685-9800. 'Great baseball in an electric atmosphere. The highlight of my stay in Baltimore. I cannot recommend this highly enough. THE place to go for a good time. Watch out for 'Wild Bill' the beloved taxi driver/cheerleader.' The beautiful new stadium was opened in 1992. Has wonderful roast beef sandwiches made on outdoor grills. Amtrak and MARC run special trains from DC to Camden Yards on game days, $9 return, from Union Station, (202) 484-7540. Return train leaves Camden 20 minutes after last out. 'Great value and a real Oriole atmosphere even before you reach the ground.'

INFORMATION

Baltimore Area Convention and Visitors Association, 1 East Pratt St, 837-4636, information on accommodation, restaurants, attractions.
Travelers Aid, 204 N Liberty, 685-3569 or 685-5874, and at Baltimore-Washington International Airport.

TRAVEL

Amtrak, Penn Station, 1515 N Charles St, (800) 872-7245.
Baltimore Trolley Works, 396-4259, makes round trip up Charles St from Hyatt Regency, Mon–Sat 11am–7pm or to Fells Point from Pratt St Pavilion daily 11am–7pm. 25c.
Greyhound, 210 W Fayette St, 744-9311.
Water Taxi service, Constellation Dock, Pratt St, 547-0090. Calls at 14 points around the harbour. $3.25 all-day unlimited use.
Baltimore/Washington International Airport, 10 miles south of Baltimore. Take the #230 Mass Transit bus from downtown, $1.95, during the week; at weekends take #240. Call Mass Transit, 539-5000, for schedule information, and for information on light rail system for downtown and suburbs; $1.10.

ANNAPOLIS Situated on Chesapeake Bay, the city of Queen Anne is the capital of Maryland and was briefly capital of the young Republic from November 1783 to August 1874. At the State House, George Washington resigned his command of the Revolutionary Army after his victory over British forces. The waterfront is 18th century and clustered behind it is one of the most beautiful of America's colonial towns.

Annapolis is synonymous with sailing and the United States Naval Academy; now coed, it's still 'where the boys are' and acts as a magnet for young women, especially on weekends. The bars on the wharf are good for a beer and overhearing the fish stories of Chesapeake Bay. Treat yourself to a basket of hot crab, delicious and cheap, and catch the Clam Festival in late August. A trip round the harbour is a must. The movie, *Patriot Games,* was shot here.

ACCOMMODATION

Accommodation tends to be expensive in this trendy little town.
Capital KOA Campground, 11 miles from Annapolis on Rt. 3 north in Millersville, 923-2771. April–Nov; sites for two $20, with hook-up $25, $4 each additional person.

FOOD

Chick and Ruth's, 165 Main, 269-6737. Down the street from the state capitol, this delightful deli has politically-named specials in a homey, memorabilia-crammed atmosphere.
Market House, Market Space, City Dock. Restoration of an 1858 building with tons of fresh seafood and various other foods. 'Best value, tastiest seafood in town!' 'Best oysters in the east!'
Maryland Inn, Church Circle, 263-2641. Well-known early 18th century inn, houses **King of France Tavern**, 'excellent' jazz. Charlie Byrd's home base.

OF INTEREST

Maryland State House, State Circle, 974-3400. Oldest US State House in continuous legislative use. 'Interesting tour.'
US Naval Academy, bordered by King George St & Severn River, 263-6933. Large, beautiful chapel has sarcophagus of John Paul Jones. Guided walking tours depart from Ricketts Hall. Free admission to grounds; charge for tours. 'Excellent, interesting tour.'
Walking Tours, Historic Annapolis Tour, 267-8149, covers major sights. Mon–Fri meet at Old Treasury, State Circle; Sat–Sun at Victualling Warehouse, Maritime Museum, foot of Maine St. $7 for 1½ hr. tour of colonial Annapolis.
A **Boat trip** round the harbour is the pleasantest way to experience the many facets of Annapolis; **Chesapeake Marine Tours**, Slip 20, City Dock, 268-7600, have 40 minute cruises for $5.

ASSATEAGUE ISLAND Situated off Maryland's Atlantic coast, the island is the home to the threatened peregrine falcon and the snow goose. Roaming the island are the Chincoteague wild ponies, descendants of shipwrecked horses. Assateague is a 37-mile long narrow barrier island. Maryland's **Assateague State Park** sits at the northern end, 641-2120, **Assateague Island National Seashore** is in the middle, 641-3030 and **Chincoteague National Wildlife Refuge**, belonging to Virginia, is in the south, (804) 336-6122. Limited camping is available in both Maryland parks, $9–$18 site, reservations required. The refuge has hiking trails. 'Delightful area.'

OCEAN CITY Maryland's only major oceanside resort, and summer vacation spot for Washingtonians and Baltimoreans. The town has a lively boardwalk and a wide beach, but gets quite crowded in the summer. This is the place to go if you want a wild time. Plenty of boarding house accommodation and good for summer jobs. 'Packed with British and Irish students. Anticipate bumping into your arch enemies from England here.'

ACCOMMODATION

Accommodation can be reasonable here during the off season; as with many summer resorts, in June, July and August, even the tackiest dives can get away with outrageous rates. A rule of thumb is the farther away from the boardwalk, the better. Accommodation is available—you just have to walk around to find it. 'Beware of those selling 'cheap' accommodation at the bus terminal and realtors who are out to make money out of summer student employees.'

Harbor Lights Townhouse Apartments, PO Box 622, Ocean City, MD 21842, 289-6626. Furnished, well equipped apartments. Long-term only.
Jarman House, 105 Talbot St, 289-7678. 'Low weekly rates. Great for working students.'
Ocean City Convention and Visitors Bureau, 4001 Coastal Highway, 289-8181, can provide accommodation information.
Whispering Sands Aptmts, 45th St, Ocean City, MD 21842, 289-5759. 'Reasonable; friendly.' 'Ace.'

FOOD
Food, food everywhere, especially in summer months. Many restaurants close after Labor Day, but even so, you'll never starve here.
Bull on the Beach, 12th at Boardwalk, 289-3744. 'Excellent sandwiches.'
La Hacienda, 80th St at Coastal Hwy, 524-8080. 'Great Mexican food.'
Trader Lee's, over Rte 50 bridge, opp Mall, 213-2000. 'Great for drinking and dancing, Friday nights only.'

ANTIETAM BATTLEFIELD Its overwhelming defeat at the second battle of Bull Run in 1862 marked the nadir of the Union's military fortunes. Robert E Lee crossed the Potomac and advanced north into Maryland. British Prime Minister Lord Palmerston, expecting further Southern victories, was prepared to intervene on the side of the Confederacy. General George B McClellan, Commander of the Army of the Potomac, met Lee in battle at Antietam Creek, 45 miles west of Baltimore, northwest of Harper's Ferry. McClellan halted the Southern advance after the bloodiest battle of the Civil War, which resulted in 23,000 casualties on 17 Sept, 1862, more than on any other single day of the war. With Lee back in Virginia licking his wounds, all foreign thought of intervention was postponed. Five days later, on 22 Sept, a more confident Lincoln issued his *Emancipation Proclamation*, freeing only those slaves in the rebellious states.

The scene of the battle is now a National Park, with an excellent museum and diorama at its Visitors Center near Sharpsburg, off Rte 65 (Hagerstown Pike), open daily except Thanksgiving, Christmas and New Year. The park can be reached via Rt 65 or Rt 34. $2 entrance fee; call 432-5124 for more information.

CHESAPEAKE & OHIO CANAL Until the advent of the railways, America made use of a considerable system of canals throughout the Northeast and Midwest, one of these being the Chesapeake & Ohio, running along the Maryland border from Washington, DC to Cumberland via Harper's Ferry. The canal was opened by President John Quincy Adams in 1828 and is now a National Historic Park extending for 185 miles, the longest of all national preserves. Disused but leafy and beautiful, the banks of the canal are well worth a hike or bicycle ride (bikes can be rented in DC).

VIRGINIA

The Old Dominion State is famed for its colonial heritage, for the statesmen it has produced, its historic homes and estates, and the great battlefields on which the fate of the nation was decided in both the 18th and 19th centuries. Seven of the 15 pre-Civil War Presidents were born in the state.

Named after Elizabeth, The Virgin Queen, the colony was the first to be permanently settled by the English, and by 1619 had the first representative legislature in the New World. The American Revolution ended with the surrender of Cornwallis at Yorktown, while the Civil War closed with Lee's surrender to Grant at Appomattox. That event marked the end of Virginia's rivalry with New England for political, cultural and intellectual supremacy.

Virginia is the least southern, both geographically and in attitude, of the old Confederate states and suffers least from their usual social problems. It is a state that has a great deal to offer both from the scenic and the historic point of view. In the east, sandy beaches and the amazing 17½ mile Chesapeake Bay Bridge Tunnel linking Virginia to Maryland, in the west, the Skyline Drive and the Shenandoah National Park, while everywhere there are countless well-preserved links with the past.

National Park: Shenandoah.

RICHMOND As Mathew Brady's famous photographs clearly tell, this capital of Virginia and of the old Confederacy was largely destroyed by retreating southern troops. Today, modernization and restoration have rendered an attractive, bustling city with plenty of history and entertainment. Richmond also makes a good base for visiting nearby landmarks, but—'it's dead at weekends'.

The telephone area code is 804.

ACCOMMODATION

Bensonhouse of Richmond, 2036 Monument Ave, 353-6900. B&B agency, offering rooms in the Richmond area and other major cities in central Virginia. S-$45 up, D-$55 up, 355-6900.

Massad House Hotel, 11 N 4th St, 648-2893. S-$35, D-$40. Recommended by YMCA, which does not have overnights. 'Good accommodation.'

FOOD

Aunt Sarah's Pancake House, 4205 W Broad St, 271-1070, and other Virginia locations. Real old-time Virginny cooking.

Farmer's Market, on 17th St in Richmond's old town Shockoe Bottom near Shockoe Slip, 780-8597. Oldest continuously operating farmer's market in the country. Mon–Sat 6am–9pm.

Infantry Blues Café, 6th St Market Place, 649-1803. Burgers, salads and a bar. 'Food delicious and reasonably priced.'

OF INTEREST

City Hall Skydeck, 9th & Broad, for a view of the city.

Hollywood Cemetery, Albemarle and Cherry Sts, US Presidents James Monroe and John Tyler, and Confederate President Jefferson Davis, are buried here, along with some 18,000 Confederate soldiers.

John Marshall House, 648-7998, 1790 home of the third Chief Justice of the US Supreme Court. Tue–Sat 10am–5pm, Sun 1pm–5pm, $3.

Science Museum of Virginia, 2500 W Broad St, 367-0000. Has 'hands-on' exhibits and 3–5 shows daily in the excellent Universe Space Theater, where films are shown on a large planetarium dome. Open daily, 9.30am–8pm. $3.50.

St John's Church, 24th & Broad. Built 1741, this is where Patrick Henry made his famous 'Give me liberty or give me death' speech. Edgar Allan Poe's mother is buried in the graveyard here. Nearby is a '**Poe Museum**' in a house Poe never lived in. You would be well advised to skip it. The museum's only attraction is that it is across the street from a cigarette company—Poe would have been amused.
The State Capitol, Capitol Square, 786-4344, the building was designed by Thomas Jefferson. Daily 9am–5pm.
Valentine Museum, 1015 E Clay St, 649-0711, on the life and history of Richmond. Open Mon–Sat 10am–5pm; Sun noon–5pm. $3.50.
Virginia Museum of Fine Arts, Boulevard and Grove Sts, 367-0878. One of the finest art galleries in the US. Entry by donation. Open Tues–Sun 11am–5pm; Thur 11am–8pm; Sun 1pm–5pm.
White House and Museum of the Confederacy are at 1201 E Clay St, 649-1861. Mon–Sun 10am–5pm, $7.
There is a block ticket available for all the city's main museums—$11.

ENTERTAINMENT
King's Dominion, north on I-95, (804) 876-5000, $25 all day. 'Great rides—don't miss the Anaconda.'
Richmond Raft Company, 4400 E Main St, 222-7238, the only urban whitewater run in the country rages right through the heart of historic Richmond.
Shockoe Slip, Carey St between 12th and 14th Sts, old warehouses now store hip restaurants, bars, and nightclubs.
Sixth St Market, btwn Coliseum and Grace St, live music, beer and dancing every Friday afternoon in summer.

INFORMATION
Visitors Information Center, 1710 Robin Hood Rd, exit 14 off I-95, 358-5511. Has 6-min video on Richmond and Virginia and info on accommodation, restaurants, travel, and attractions. Open daily, summer 9am–7pm, winter 9am–5pm. Also Visitors Center at Sixth Street Marketplace.

TRAVEL
Amtrak, 7519 Staples Mill Rd, 266-4996. About five miles from downtown, no buses available. Taxi fare $10–$12.
Greyhound, 2910 N Blvd, (800)-231-2222. Then take #24 bus to town.
Richmond International Airport, 226-3052. Buses to and from the airport are few and far between; phone Grooms Transportation, 222-7222, for pick-up service, $12 one person, $17 for two, $20 for three, after that $6 a head.

FREDERICKSBURG North of Richmond off the I-95, the place where four great Civil War battles were fought. You can tour the Fredericksburg Battlefield where Lee's army fought off wave after wave of charging Federals from Marye's Heights.

The town itself has several interesting old houses standing, among them the home of Mary Washington, George Washington's mother; **Kenmore**, the home of George's sister, Betty Washington Lewis; and the **Rising Sun Tavern**, owned by George's brother, Charles, and meeting place for Jefferson, Patrick Henry and other patriots.
The telephone area code is 703.

INFORMATION
Fredericksburg Battlefield Visitors Center, Lafayette Blvd, 373-6122. Museum exhibits, guided walking tours (in summer), and 12-minute slide show describe the four battles of Fredericksburg. 8.30am–6.30pm; 9am–5pm in winter.

WILLIAMSBURG As state capital between 1699 and 1780, Williamsburg played a significant role leading up to the American Revolution. Washington, Patrick Henry and Jefferson were among the men who served here as members of the House of Burgesses and began uniting with Boston in opposition to the British Crown. Nowadays there is Colonial Williamsburg, hundreds of houses painstakingly restored to create the look of earlier times with actors dressed up to give an air of reality. It even tries to address the subject of slavery—Virginia was the first slave state—with the actors 'living' a slave's life. Even so this is, as one reader put it, 'a sort of colonial Disneyland'.

ACCOMMODATION

Williamsburg is loaded with hotels; but even the modest ones charge high rates. The **Colonial Williamsburg Visitors Center**, 229-1000, has a list of tourist homes from about $50.

The **College of William and Mary** fraternities and sororities sometimes have rooms. Check at the housing office, 221-4314.

Johnson's Guest Home, 101 Thomas Nelson Lane, 229-3909. S–$32, D–$45. Kind, friendly landlady will pick up from train or bus station. 'Excellent place.'

The cheapest accommodation around may well be **Sangraal By-The-Sea Hostel**, in **Wake** (south of Urbanna, VA), 776-6500. Actually, it's by the Rappahannock River where it meets the Chesapeake Bay, but a lovely location all the same. Urbanna is almost due north of Williamsburg; take Hwy 17. $10 AYH, $15 non-members; reservations recommended.

Camping: Fort Cherokee Campground, 8758 Pocahontas Trail, 220-0386. $11 per site for two, $1 per extra person. Reached by 'Grove Route' bus.

FOOD

A Good Place to Eat, 410 Duke of Gloucester St, 229-4370. A wide variety of good food, reasonably priced.

College Deli, opp. William and Mary College, 229-6627. 'Best place in North America for sandwiches.'

Sal's Pizza, 1242 Richmond Rd, in the commercial part of town, 220-2641. 'Best pizza in town.'

OF INTEREST

Colonial Williamsburg. Perhaps the best buildings are the Capitol, jail, Raleigh Tavern, Governor's palace, and various colonial craft shops.

Tickets are priced according to the number of buildings and craft shops visited—basic admission, 12-bldgs, $24. 'Royal Governors Pass', covering all buildings and good for 7 consecutive days, $29; 229-1000 for more info. Finally, you can just wander for free without going into the houses at all. Go first to the **Visitors Center**. You can see a documentary film here which may make the visit more meaningful. Vis Ctr open daily 8.30–8pm; historic area open 9am–5pm.

College of William and Mary. Founded 1693, the second oldest in the nation.

In the vicinity is **Jamestown**, first permanent English settlement in America. Not that much has been restored: the visitor must often content himself with looking at foundations. Plagues, Indians, starvation and fires hindered its development, and when finally the penninsula became an island, Williamsburg and Yorktown prospered in its stead. The original settlement is about a mile from the more recent **Jamestown Settlement Park**, 229-1607, opened by Elizabeth II in 1957. In the park are replicas of the three ships, *Susan Constant*, *Godspeed* and *Discovery*, a re-creation of the first fort, an Indian village and a museum. Open daily 9am–5pm; $7.50.

Yorktown is the least restored of the James River historical areas. The battlefield and 6–7 18th century structures remain. The French navy blockaded and bombarded the town while the Franco-American allies, outnumbering the British 2 to 1, pressed in overland. The surrender of the British at Yorktown ended the War of Independence, although the final peace treaty wasn't signed until 2 years later. **The Yorktown Victory Center**, in Yorktown on Rt 238, 887-1776, sits on a 21-acre tract overlooking the York River. Built for the Bicentennial, it is a permanent museum dramatising the military events of the Revolution. Open daily 9am–5pm; $3.75.

James River Plantations. Take Rte 5 along the river to visit several plantation homes of early American leaders; take Hwy 60 to **Carter's Grove** (also to Busch Gardens), often called 'the most beautiful colonial home in America'.

Busch Gardens, 3 miles east of Williamsburg on Hwy 60, 253-3350. A European-themed amusement park operated by the Anheuser Busch Brewing Company. Unlimited rides and entertainment all day; evening discount. Also has a monorail that takes you to the bewery where free samples await, but have your ID ready if you wish to taste! Summer: open 10am–10pm, Fri–Sat till midnight. $26.50. 'Loads of fun. Don't miss the Big Bad Wolf.'

INFORMATION

Williamsburg Chamber of Commerce, 201 Penniman Rd, 229-6511. Open Mon–Fri, 8.30am–5pm.

Colonial Williamsburg Visitors Center, on State Hwy 132-Y, (800) HISTORY. Runs shuttle bus to Historic section, free with admission ticket 8.50am–10pm, also has info on food, accommodation, etc.

TRAVEL

Greyhound, 229-1460; and Amtrak, 229-8750, at 468 N Boundary.

VIRGINIA BEACH Continuing southeast from Williamsburg and past Norfolk, you come to this fast-growing resort with a 28-mile beach running from the landing dunes of America's first permanent colonists on Cape Henry to Virginia's Outer Banks. From here you can get on the amazing Chesapeake Bay Bridge Tunnel for the northern drive up the Atlantic coastline, stopping off to visit Assateague National Seashore (see also Maryland).

ACCOMMODATION

All prices skyrocket from June to Labor Day. $59 for a double passes for 'economy' at the tackiest hotel or motel. It's cheaper to rent an 'efficiency apartment' and cram everyone you know into it. For starters, go to or call **Angie's Guest Cottage**, 302 24th St, 428-4690; $11 AYH, $14 non-members. B&B D–$38 up, camping $8 AYH, $10 non-members. If they don't have space, they'll recommend others that might, although no one's prices come close to matching Angie's. The **Visitors Center**, 2100 Parks Ave, 425-7511, is also very helpful.

FOOD

The Jewish Mother, 3108 Pacific Ave, 422-5430. Burgers, sandwiches, etc. 'Friendly place, and while waiting you can crayon on the walls and menus!'

OF INTEREST

Poe wasn't the only Edgar around these parts with a finger on the pulse of the paranormal: the work of Edgar Cayce, the 'best documented psychic of modern times' is explained in exhibits, lectures, movies and tours at his **A.R.E. Library and Conference Center**, 67th & Atlantic, 428-3588. You can learn about life after death and have your ESP tested too. Open Mon–Fri 9am–8.00pm, Sat 8.30am–5.00pm, Sun 11am–8pm. Free.

CHARLOTTESVILLE Located in central Virginia and surrounded by beautiful dogwood-laden countryside and old estates, Charlottesville is one of the most interesting and charming places in the state. The homes of Jefferson, Madison, and Monroe are nearby, as are the birthplaces of Lewis and Clark. Recent converts to the gentleman-farmer lifestyle, for which the area is renowned, include Sissy Spacek, Sam Shepherd, Jessica Lange and Mohammad Ali. Much of the architecture is either directly Jefferson's or influenced by his example. The elegant University of Virginia is testimony to his humanism and architectural genius.
The telephone area code is 804.

ACCOMMODATION

Econo Lodge, 2014 Holiday Dr, 295-3185 and 400 Emmett St, 296-2104. S-$42, D-$50.
Town and Country Motor Lodge, Rte 250E, 293-6191. S-$34, D-$36. 'Very friendly and clean.'

FOOD

Big Jim's Barbeque, 2104 Angus Rd, 296-8283. Huge burgers that you can't finish, Cajun-style.
Macado's, 1505 University Ave, across the street from the University Lawn, 971-3558. Downstairs it's wonderful sandwich time; upstairs it's the bar.
White Spot Restaurant, 1407 W Maian St, 972-9746. Try the GUS, an egg-cheese-cholesterolburger, with fries and a soda for $3.50 in this basic and small diner. Friendly, helpful staff.

OF INTEREST

Ash Lawn, 2½ mi beyond Monticello on Rt 53, 293-9539, 535-acre estate of the 5th US president, James Monroe. The site was chosen by his close friend Thomas Jefferson. Open daily 9am–6pm. $6.
Historic Court Square, E Jefferson St, self-guided tour info available free at visitors center and historical society.
Michie Tavern, ½ mile from Monticello on Rt 53, 977-1234. Re-creates 18th-century tavern life. Story had it that Jefferson, Monroe, Madison and Lafayette met here. Converted log-house next door serves all-you-can-eat 18th-century southern-style lunch 9am–5pm. $5 museum. Have lunch and museum entry is $3.
Monticello, 3 miles southeast of the town on Rte 53, 979-7346. The architectural masterpiece where Thomas Jefferson lived and experimented. Built from his own design, this Palladian villa has many ingenious extras such as the clock that sits over the front door. Recently renovated, including a $1 million new roof, it now 'looks more like it did when he lived there than it has at any time since his death', according to *The New York Times*. Open daily 8am–5pm, $8. Tours of the house leave every five minutes. 'Magnificent, with fine views of the surrounding countryside.

ENTERTAINMENT

Friday After 5.00, on the mall, live entertainment, festive atmosphere, every Friday during summer.
Millers, 109 W Main St near the mall, 971-8511, bar with live music every night but Sunday (when they're closed). $2–$4 cover for some shows.

INFORMATION

Albemarle County Historical Society, 220 Court Square, 296-1492, brochure on historic sites, museum features law in Virginia and local history.
Charlottesville Visitors Center, at intersection of Rt 20 and I-64 on the way to Monticello, 293-6789, has info on places to eat and stay, and things to do in Charlottesville; also has exhibit 'Thomas Jefferson at Monticello'.

TRAVEL
Amtrak, 7th and W Main, 296-4559.
Greyhound, 310 W Main, 295-5131.

APPOMATTOX South of Charlottesville on US 460 and just outside the town proper is Appomattox Court House, 352-8987, where Lee surrendered to Grant and Grant responded as the friend and gentleman he was. The date was 9 April 1865.

SHENANDOAH NATIONAL PARK Though only 80 miles from Washington DC, the park remains a wilderness area. The 105-mile long Skyline Drive runs along the crest of the Blue Ridge Mountains, following the old Appalachian Trail, and with an average elevation of over 3000 ft. The southern end of the drive meets the Blue Ridge Parkway which takes the traveller clear down to the Smokies.

The route affords a continuous series of magnificent views over steeply wooded ravines to the Piedmont Plateau on the east, and across the fertile farmlands of the Shenandoah Valley to the west. Check the weather before doing the Skyline Drive. If it's bad, you'll just drive through clouds.

There are over 500 miles of foot trails for every grade of hiker. Campgrounds, lodges and shelters can be found throughout the park (see below). Look out for pioneer dwellings and homesteads.
Skyline Drive Entrance: (North to south) Front Royal off Hwy 340; Thornton Gap near Luray off Hwy 211; Swift Run Gap near Elkton off Hwy 33; Rockfish Gap near Waynesboro off Hwy 250 or Interstate 64. $5 per vehicle.
The area code is 703.

ACCOMMODATION
Bear's Den AYH-Hostel, just off Rte 601 S, near Bluemont, 554–8708. A stone lodge that sits on the Appalachian Trail, overlooking the Shenandoah River. Office hours 5pm–9pm, front gate locked at 10pm. $9, $11 non-AYH. Camping available at $4 per person.
Campgrounds: Mathews Arm at Skyline Drive milepost 22.2 (no showers); **Big Meadows** at milepost 51; **Lewis Mountain** at milepost 57.5; **Loft Mountain** at milepost 79.5. Tent sites $10 per night. All on first-come, first-served basis, except Big Meadows which requires reservations—(800) 452-1111.
Lodges: Skyland Lodge, milepost 41.7 or 42.5. Room with 2 D beds $79; **Big Meadows Lodge**, milepost 51. D–$60. Restaurants, easy access to hiking trails. Reservations required (must book months in advance for fall), ARA Virginia Skyline Company, Inc, 743-5108.
All campgrounds and lodges have rangers-in-residence who provide info on trails, natural history, etc. Shelters for day hikers, and huts for backpackers with *3-night* or *Appalachian-Through-Trail-Permits* only are scattered throughout the park. Be sure to talk to rangers about location, availability and permits.

INFORMATION
Shenandoah National Park Visitors Centers: Byrd Center at Big Meadows, milepost 51, 999-2243; Dickie Ridge Center at mile post 4.6, 635-3566.

OF INTEREST
Luray Caverns, 743-6551, with stalactites and -mites, and organ. Open daily 9.00am–7pm; $10.75. 'Excessive.' 'Worth every cent.'

WHITEWATER

North America is home to some of the worlds most beautiful and spectacular rivers making it ideal for whitewater rafting: a mind-blowing experience you'll remember for years. These are some of the most fun whitewater rivers:

EAST: Chattooga, Long Creek, SC. 50 ft/mile drops through most inaccessible canyons in Southeast, site of movie *Deliverance*. Day trips $50, call Wildwater Outfitters (803) 647-9587. **Cheat, Albright, WV.** Try 'Big Nasty' and 'Coliseum' rapids, part of largest natural watershed in East; rafted mainly April–May. Half-day trips from $45; for more info call WV Visitors Center, (800) 225-5982. **Gauley, Summerville, WV.** 2-day autumn trip rated 'the best', experience or deathwish needed for Upper section. Day trips from $75, for more info call (800) 225-5982. **James, Richmond, VA.** Raft past commuters in metropolitan Richmond. $40 day trip includes nature refuge, or raft through evening rush hour for $25. **New, Beckley, WV**, is the world's second oldest river after the Nile. Lower section is known as 'Grand Canyon of the East', with spectacular view of the longest, highest single-span bridge on earth. Day trips from $72, for more info call (800) 225-5982. **Youghiogheny** (The 'Yough', pronounced (Yock'), **Ohiopyle State Park, PA**, (412) 329-8591. Splendid, challenging rapids for $40 half day, full day recommended. **Upper Yough, Friendsville, MD.** Ranks among most challenging in world with rapid names including 'Meat Cleaver' and 'Double Pencil Sharpener' (!); an experienced rafter's dream,a beginner's night-mare. **Penobscot, Maine**, through the steep-walled granite Ripogenus Gorge, one of the most scenic whitewater stretches in east US. But no time for the view if you ride the 'Exterminator' Class V rapid—'intense'. Call Wilderness Rafting Expeditions, (207) 534-2242, $75 w-end trips. **Appalachian Wildwaters, Rowlesburg, WV** (304) 454-2475 covers most of the popular rivers.
WEST: Colorado, Grand Canyon, AZ. Over 150 world-class rapids between Badger Creek and Lava Falls, surrounded by canyon walls a mile high. Arizona Tourist Board (602) 542-8687. **Middle Fork of Salmon, Boise, ID.** Whitewater of unforgettable intensity and beauty, natural hot springs and waterfalls. Idaho Outfitters and Guides Association (208) 342-1438. **Snake, Boise, ID**. Rafting through Hell's Canyon, the deepest gorge in the world, on 'reorganizer' rapids and warm water. Idaho Outfitters and Guides Association (208) 342-1438.
For more information on Eastern whitewater, consult *Whitewater Rafting in Eastern North America* by Lloyd D Armstead, Pequot Press, Chester, CT. For extended trips on Western rivers, contact the *American Wilderness Experience*, Boulder, CO, (800) 444-0099.

Tips: Wherever you decide to go, bear in mind the following: look for an established outfitter that has been in business for a number of years and has a current licence. Decide what you want and know the level of ability required (Class I–III for first-timers, IV–VI more advanced, difficult rapids). Plan ahead—deposits may be required; w-ends are more expensive than weekdays; find out what the price includes, meals, equipment, etc. Finally, if you fall out of the raft, point your feet DOWNstream.

WEST VIRGINIA

A common image people have of West Virginia is of a poor but proud population struggling to make a living from coal mining and enduring a hard life between business cycles as up-and-down as the Appalachian mountains that cover the state.

Though this image is partly accurate, 50 years of federal programmes, a growing tourist economy, and industries flourishing in other, less mountainous parts of the state have combined to alter the economic picture of West Virginia. The most striking aspect of the Mountain State, however, remains its natural beauty. Tree-covered mountains, raging rivers, caves, waterfalls and gorges offer the visitor a variety of scenic vistas and wilderness adventures.

The state was formed during the Civil War when people in the western part of Virginia refused to join the rebels and seceded from the Confederacy and not from the Union. The mountain people, who still speak a form of Elizabethan English, are authentic hillbillies and local bluegrass musicians can be heard in small town and big city alike.

The telephone area code for the entire state is 304.

CHARLESTON Not to be confused with Charleston, South Carolina. This is the state capital and an industrial town; not much to look at, but there are nice hills nearby, and the city is a good base for a more interesting visit to the countryside.

ACCOMMODATION

Night's Inn, 6401 MacCorkle Ave, I-77 exit 95, 925-0451. S–$38, D–$45.

Red Roof Inn, 4006 MacCorkle Ave, at junction with I-64 exit 54, 744-1500. S–$41, D–$49.

OF INTEREST

Cultural Center, corner of Greenbrier and Washington Sts, 558-0162. Free exhibits of West Virginia arts, crafts and history. Mon–Fri 9am–5pm, Sat & Sun 1pm–5pm.

State Capitol, Main rotunda, Washington St E, 558-3809, free tours daily 9am–3.15pm, Sat 9am–4pm, Sun 12pm–3.30pm. (Mon–Sat in winter.)

INFORMATION/TRAVEL

Convention and Visitors Bureau, 200 Civic Center Dr, Suite 2, 344-5075.
Amtrak, 350 MacCorkle Ave SE, (800) USA-RAIL.
Greyhound, 300 Reynolds St, (800) 231-2222.

NEW RIVER GORGE In the southernmost part of the state, the New and Gauley rivers churn some of the most exciting rapids anywhere. The Gauley, in fact, is billed as one of the top ten whitewater rivers in the world. The major city serving the region is **Beckley**, where motel accommodation, hiking equipment and warm food can be found. The area can be reached by following I-77, the West Virginia Turnpike (toll).

ACCOMMODATION

Charles House Motel, 222 S. Heber St, 253-8318. S–$33, D–$38–44, colour TV and bath. 'Convenient.'
Days Inn, off I-77 exit 44, 255-5291. S–$45, D–$50.

OF INTEREST

Exhibition Coal Mine, New River Park in Beckley, 256-1747. Learn about coal mining by going down into a real coal pit. Adults $5. April–Nov, 10am–5.30pm daily. 'Take a sweater.'
Honey-In-The-Rock Theater, in Grandview State Park near Beckley, 256-6800. Classic and modern drama by local repertory companies, Jun–early Sept, daily except Mon, 8.30pm. Includes play about Hatfield/McCoy feud. Tickets $12; Fri/Sat–$15.
New River Gorge, every Friday, the Amtrak *Cardinal* between Chicago and New York, offers a narrated trip through the gorge between White Sulphur Springs and Montgomery.
Whitewater Rafting. The Chamber of Commerce in Beckley, 500 N Valley Dr, 252-7328, has brochures of more than 25 organisations that run whitewater rafting tours along the New and Gauley Rivers at various prices. $66 buys you the thrill of a lifetime.

MONONGAHELA NATIONAL FOREST Sounding like the name of a monster from a Japanese sci-fi flick, the Monongahela is actually a charming and beautiful forest covering much of eastern West Virginia. Unusual geological formations beneath the mountains have resulted in the creation of some of the largest caverns in the world, as well as warm mineral springs that bubble up in several valleys. There's coal under the mountains too, and many of the back roads are made bumpy by the giant coal trucks that roll in convoy all day and all night.

White Sulphur Springs, across the border from Virginia, is home to a stately resort and spa, the Greenbrier, 536-1110. Though accommodation is expensive, free afternoon tea and chamber music is available in the lobby daily at 4.15pm for well-dressed looking folks. 'Beautiful place to visit and relax.' Within a few miles of the town are the **Lost World Caverns** and the **Organ Cave**, both filled with amazing rock formations and bats. Lost World, in Lewisburg, 645-6677, costs $6 for a self-guided tour. Organ Cave, on Hwy 219, 647-5551, costs $5 for a guided tour. Both 9am–7pm. Also along Hwy 219 is the **Droop Mountain State Park**, site of a Civil War battle.

Two hours northeast of White Sulphur Springs is **Cass Scenic Railroad**, 456-4300, where a coal-fired locomotive hauls visitors along old logging railways through the remote corners of the National Forest late May–through early Oct. 1½ hr rides at 11am, 1pm, 3pm; $9; 4½ hr trip at noon, $12.

Green Bank National Radio Astronomy Observatory, on Rte 28, 456-2011, is 10 miles away from the Cass Railroad. This is a major radio telescope which American scientists are using to map the universe and study its chemical composition. Free daily tours from mid-June–Aug between 9am–4pm.

ACCOMMODATION

Allstate Motel, Hwy 60, 1½ miles east of White Sulphur Springs, 536-1731. S–$31, D–$43.
Colonial Court Motel, Hwy 60, 536-2121. S–$39, D–$44.

Camping. There are no camping restrictions in the forest, so if you want some of that pioneer spirit, just find a spot and camp down. State parks with campgrounds: **Greenbrier**, near White Sulphur Springs, 536-1944, has cabins that can be rented by large groups. **Watoga**, near Hillsboro, Rte 28, 799-4087.

NORTHERN PANHANDLE The section of the state that sticks up between Ohio and Pennsylvania, has two things worth visiting: **Grave Creek Mounds**, at Moundsville, 843-1410, the largest pre-historic, conical Indian burial site in the US. Indians of another sort inspired **Prabhupada's Palace of Gold** in New Vrindaban, south of Wheeling on Hwy 250, 843-1600. This glittering gold complex is a Hare Krishna tribute to their departed leader. Future plans include a theme park called 'City of God', proving that it's not *all* spirituality, after all. Open daily 9am–8pm.

HARPERS FERRY The National Park Service preserves this small, historic town where in 1859 John Brown raided the government arsenal, freed a few blacks and hoped to spark a general slave uprising. He was captured the following evening by Col Robert E Lee and two months later was tried and publicly hanged in neighbouring Charles Town.

Harper's Ferry was once the site of an army arms factory and arsenal, and was largely destroyed at the start of the Civil War when the two armies fought each other to carry off as much weaponry as possible. Highly recommended for Civil War buffs—Harpers Ferry changed hands 17 times during the war—the area also appeals to nature lovers for the view from Jefferson Rock. Park Service tours throughout the day, 8am–6pm in summer; in winter, talks are few and far between, but exhibits and orientation films are open 'till 5pm. Phone 535-6223 for more info. Pedestrian bridge connects into C&O Canal Towpath over the river.

At the confluence of the Shenandoah and Potomac Rivers, and bordered by three states, Harpers Ferry is readily accessible by car from Washington DC, Baltimore, and Harrisburg. By train, ride B&O and Amtrak from Washington (three trains daily), $13 o/w. You might also want to pass through here if you're on your way to Antietam battlefield or the Skyline drive through Virginia's Shenandoah National Park.

Nearby **Shepherdstown**, the oldest town in West Virginia, home of Shepherd College, offers shops, higher priced accommodation and restaurants (**Betty's, Mecklenburg Inn, Yellow Brick Bank**). **Charles Town** has a race track with nearby motels and cheap eats (**Sadler Cafe, Stuck and Alger**, both on W Washington St) as well as country fairs, carriage rides and charming old houses. The first rural postal delivery service in the US began here.

ACCOMMODATION

Bear's Den, 25 miles south of Harper's Ferry in Bluemont, VA, (703) 554-8708. $9 AYH, $11 non-members. See also 'Virginia'.

Harpers Ferry AYH Hostel, on Sandy Hook Rd, in MD, (301) 834-7652. $8–$9 AYH, $12 non-members; $4 AYH camping.

OF INTEREST

Whitewater Rafting on the Shenandoah, a gentler ride than the New River Gorge. Blue Ridge Outfitters, Hwy 340, 2 mi from the Harpers Ferry National Park, (304) 725-3444, offers raft and canoe trips, Mar–Oct $45. Reservations.

THE MIDWEST

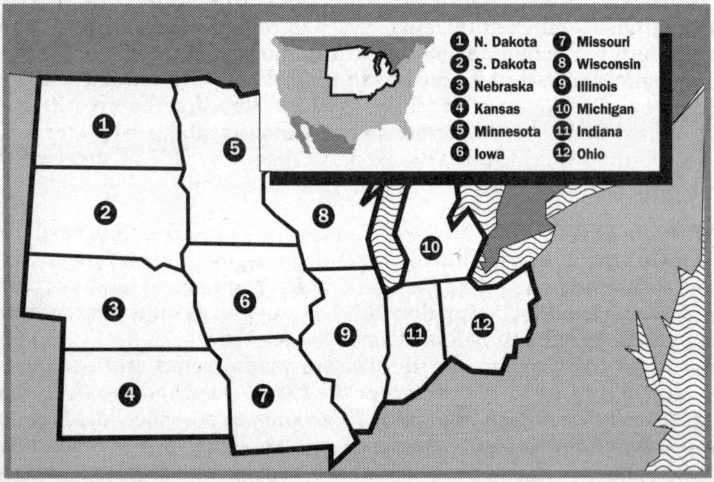

The Midwest (defined here as the 12 states from Ohio west to the Dakotas) is the rich, flat underbelly of the US, its glacier-scoured fertile lands yielding massive quantities of corn, soybeans, hay, wheat and livestock. It's also the manufacturing, transportation and industrial heart of America; the Chicago-Gary area alone once poured more steel than all of France. The region boasts the world's most powerful and fastest computer, CRAY-2 (in Minneapolis), the highest-energy particle accelerator (near Batavia, Illinois), and the largest manufacturer of farm equipment (in Moline, Illinois).

But the recession of the early 1980s hit the Midwest hard. From some it earned the nickname 'the rust belt' for its deteriorating and closed-down factories. Falling prices and excessive debts trapped many farmers in a downward spiral toward bankruptcy, causing unprecedented suicides that tore at the fabric of a settled life. However, industry has recently revived somewhat; farm prices and the value of land have also risen.

The essential quality of Midwestern life is its smalltown character, and that's where you should seek it out. Take time to meet its friendly and generous people, to get to know the prairie villages and the slow drawl of fields between them. Listen to the charming Scandinavian brogue of the northern states. And try to find time to read the novels of Nobel Prize winner Sinclair Lewis (*Babbitt*, *Main Street*, *Elmer Gantry*), each of which was carefully mapped out by Lewis in quintessential midwestern cities.

Mother Nature provides much of the drama here, from tornados in spring–summer to the fantastic electrical storm displays that light up summer evenings. The area is also seismically active: in 1811–1812, the biggest quakes in recorded history rolled through one million square miles, causing the Mississippi and Ohio Rivers to flow backwards.

The region's mighty rivers and Great Lakes serve as liquid highways for its products, just as they did in paddlewheeler days; they also create liquid disasters such the great floods of 1993 that caused way over $10 billion in damage and left millions of people homeless and (ironically) without water. Itself once 'the West', the Midwest in turn became the staging area for pioneer trails like the Santa Fe, Oregon and Mormon. With the advent of the railroad, the region became the distribution link between cattle ranch and consumer, a role it continues to play today.

ILLINOIS

Illinois takes its nickname from the prairie, the original ground cover for the vast region lying east of the Mississippi River. On it, the grasses grew nine feet or more, which is why Illinois' corn can get as high as an elephant's eye today. West of the Mississippi, the land gradually turns from prairie to plains which are just as flat but receive less rain, more sun, and have thinner soil—prime wheat-growing land.

The Prairie State has a tradition of plain-spoken eloquence, from Lincoln, Sandberg and Hemingway to the Grange Movement farmers of the 1870s, who took as their slogan: 'Raise less corn and more hell!' Its premier city, Chicago, is also the birthplace of the only truly American architecture and the earthy Chicago blues. In the countryside, you'll taste Midwestern hospitality at its best, as sweet and honest as an ear of young corn.

CHICAGO In the aftermath of the Great Fire of 1871, a Chicago realtor put up a sign that read: 'All gone but wife, children and energy!' That unquenchable jauntiness is still Chicago's trademark. The place hurls superlatives at you: tallest buildings, largest grain market, greatest distribution point, busiest airport and train terminal, biggest Polish populace outside Warsaw, highest concentration of practicing psychics—the list is endless.

Chicago, which is where Ferris Bueller took his day off, has two popular nicknames, Second City and The Windy City. For decades it was the nation's second most populous region, after New York, but that title has since passed to Los Angeles. It's the politics, not the breeze sweeping in off Lake Michigan, that explains Chicago's other nickname.

Volatile is the word for Chicago's politics, particularly for the periods following the deaths of Mayor Richard Daley and more recently, of the much admired black mayor, Harold Washington. The ruthless Mayor Daley ran one of the last great political machines in America for a generation after World War II. He made Chicago 'the city that works'. His son, Richard M Daley, elected in 1988, is a man of the 90s. He's captured the affection and trust of Chicago's crazy quilt of ethnic and political groups.

Built on a swamp the Indians called 'place of the stinking wild onions', Chicago is the fount of architectural innovation in the United States, a vital communications and trading centre, and the hub for both industry and agriculture in the Midwest. Both the true skyscraper, where the stress falls

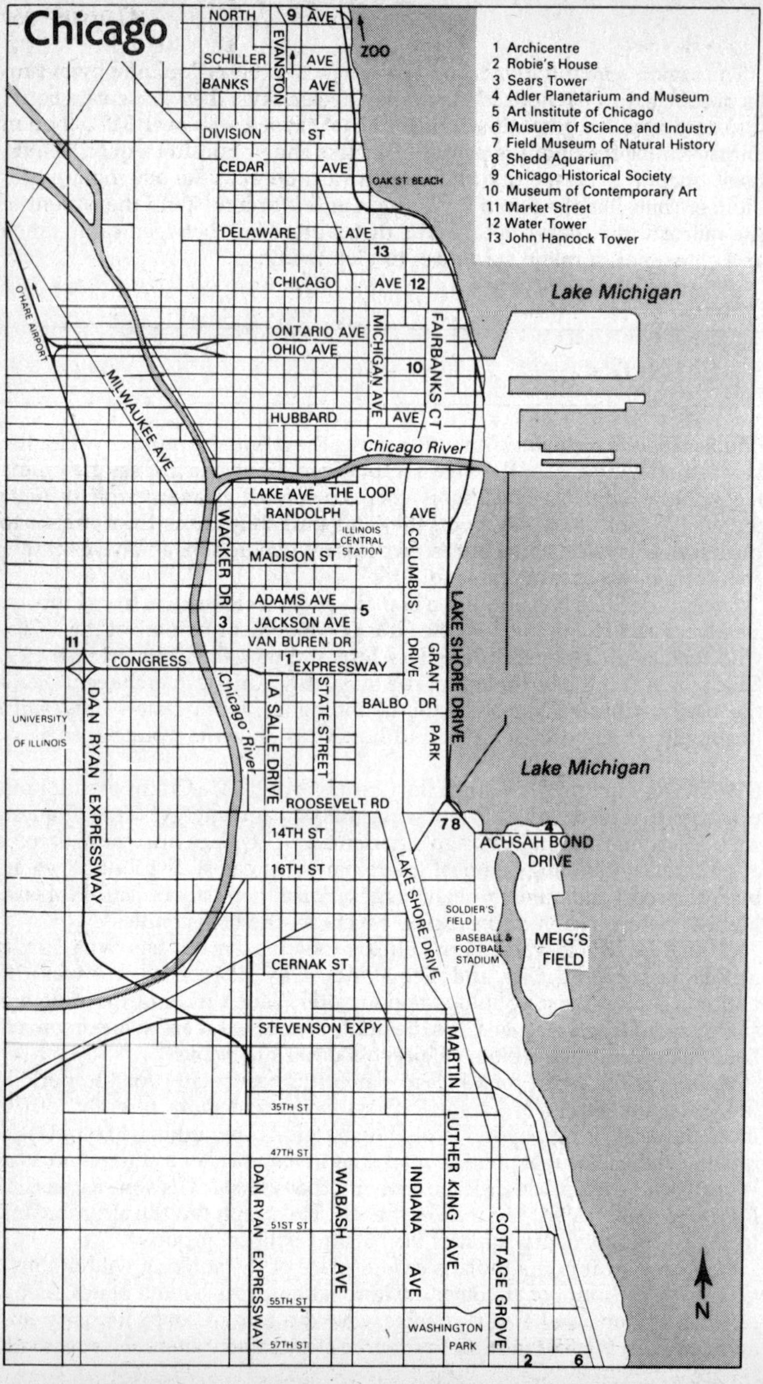
Chicago
1 Archicentre
2 Robie's House
3 Sears Tower
4 Adler Planetarium and Museum
5 Art Institute of Chicago
6 Musuem of Science and Industry
7 Field Museum of Natural History
8 Shedd Aquarium
9 Chicago Historical Society
10 Museum of Contemporary Art
11 Market Street
12 Water Tower
13 John Hancock Tower
Lake Michigan
Lake Michigan
NORTH AVE
SCHILLER AVE
BANKS AVE
DIVISION ST
CEDAR AVE
EVANSTON
ZOO
OAK ST BEACH
DELAWARE AVE
CHICAGO AVE
ONTARIO AVE
OHIO AVE
MICHIGAN AVE
FAIRBANKS CT
HUBBARD AVE
O'HARE AIRPORT
MILWAUKEE AVE
Chicago River
LAKE AVE
THE LOOP
RANDOLPH AVE
ILLINOIS CENTRAL STATION
MADISON ST
ADAMS AVE
JACKSON AVE
VAN BUREN DR
WACKER DR
COLUMBUS DRIVE
GRANT PARK
LAKE SHORE DRIVE
CONGRESS EXPRESSWAY
BALBO DR
DAN RYAN EXPRESSWAY
UNIVERSITY OF ILLINOIS
Chicago River
LA SALLE DRIVE
STATE STREET
ROOSEVELT RD
14TH ST
16TH ST
ACHSAH BOND DRIVE
LAKE SHORE DRIVE
SOLDIER'S FIELD
BASEBALL & FOOTBALL STADIUM
MEIG'S FIELD
CERNAK ST
STEVENSON EXPY
MARTIN LUTHER KING AVE
35TH ST
47TH ST
51ST ST
55TH ST
57TH ST
DAN RYAN EXPRESSWAY
WABASH AVE
INDIANA AVE
COTTAGE GROVE
WASHINGTON PARK
N

on the metal skeleton rather than the walls, and balloon framing, a cheap breakthrough in housing construction, were born here. At various times Chicago was the home of Louis Sullivan, Frank Lloyd Wright, Daniel Burnham, Helmut Jahn and Mies van der Rohe. The city possesses the finest architectural tradition in the country and had the good sense to preserve its lakeshore as recreational land, giving it an extraordinary skyline along 27 miles of parklands and clean beaches.

Always pugnacious, Chicago in its gangland heyday (1920s–1940s) had wide-open criminal activity and hundreds of unsolved mob murders. The 1988 movie, *The Untouchables*, reveals the morbid underworld of the infamous criminal, Al Capone, and his gang. One public official tried to divert attention from his Capone connections with an anti-British Empire campaign. He periodically offered to punch King George V 'in the snoot' if the monarch ever ventured near Chicago. Mob action may be gone, but the city still has an exceptionally high murder rate. As a natural corollary, Chicago also has more practising lawyers than all of England. With this in mind, visitors should remember that the Loop and lakeshore areas are the safest. After dark, stay clear of parks and poorly-lit streets. These cautions hold particularly true for women. The South Side is very risky at night.
The telephone area code is 312.

ACCOMMODATION

AAIH-Chicago International Hostel, 6318 N Winthrope Ave, 262-1011. $13 members, $15 non-members. El train to Loyola. '30 minutes from downtown and El right next to hostel so very noisy.' Closed 10am–4pm, midnight curfew weekdays. 'Hire a bike from the hostel and cycle through the waterfront park. It takes you all the way downtown. An interesting and different way to see the city.'

Arlington House Hostel, 616 W Arlington Pl, 929-5380. $13 AYH, $16 non-members. 'Excellent hostel, but dirty bathrooms.' 'Friendly, in good area.'

Avenue Motel, 1154 S Michigan Ave, 427-8200. S–$55, D–$59. Good area; shower, colour TV, beach nearby. 'Although quite expensive, clean, central and easy to find.' 'Area not safe at night.'

Blackstone Hotel, 636 S Michigan Ave, across from Grant Park, 427-4300. S/D–$66 for students during non-convention days (Fri, Sat & Sun). Near museums, State St shopping.

Cass Hotel, 640 N Wabash Ave, 787-4030. S–$46 up, D–$52 up. 2 blks off Michigan Ave. 'Central location but not great rooms.'

Harrison Hotel, 65 E Harrison, 427-8000. S/D–$50 per night, $250 a week.

International House, 1414 E 59th, 753-2270. Take Illinois Central RR to 59th St, walk 2 blks west. Open mid-June–August. $16 AYH card, $29 non-members. Cheap in-house cafeteria. Near science museum. 'Good place.'

Lawson YMCA, 30 Chicago Ave, 944-6211. Coed, S–$31 + $5 key deposit. Pool. 'Convenient and safe neighbourhood, if squalid.'

Ohio East Hotel, 15 E Ohio, 644-8222. Month: $315. No AC or TV but clean and with excellent views. 'Full of weirdos.'

Parkway Eleanor Club, 1550 N Dearborn Pkwy, 664-8245. $25 per night incl. bfast, plus $3 membership, $1 linen deposit, and $1 key deposit. Women only. 'Full of American students and by Lake Michigan.'

Tokyo Hotel, 19 E Ohio St, 787-4900. S/D–$25 + $2 key deposit. Good locale. 'Rather seedy, bath mouldy and lots of cockroaches and bed bugs.' 'Fantastic views from back rooms.' 'Clean, bright.'

Also try **Northwestern University**, Accom. Office, Geo. McClellan Bldg, 850 Lakeside Dr, 908-8514. $15–$19 per night, June & July only. Call for application.

FOOD

Local specialties: Chicago-style deep-dish pizza, stuffed pizza, kosher all-beef hotdogs and el-cheapo hamburgers called sliders.

Ann Sathers, 929 W Belmont, 348-2378, take the El to Belmont. Homemade cinnamon rolls, pies and bread.

Berghoff's, west of State at 17 W Adams, 427-3170. German menu, a Chicago tradition, big helpings. Closed Sun.

Billy Goats, 430 N Michigan, 222-1525. Cheap rib-eye steaks. 'Run by Greeks who holler your order across the Midwest: Cheezebooga, Cheezebooga, Pepsi, Pepsi! No fries, Cheeps!'

Ed Debevic's, 640 N Wells at Ontario, 664–1707. 50's-style diner. 'Great American food. The most fun you can have eating out.'

Edwardo's, 8 locations including 1212 N Dearborn, 337-4490, on the near North Side; 521 S Dearborn, 939-3366, downtown; and 1321 E 57th St, 241-7960, in Hyde Park. Pizza, pasta & salads.

Gino's East, 160 E Superior, 943-1124. 'Most well-known pizza house in Chicago.'

Giordano's, 747 N Rush St, 951-0747, and about a dozen other locations. Voted best pizza by *Chicago Magazine*.

John Barleycorn Memorial Pub, 658 W Belden Ave at Lincoln Ave, 348-8899. Free slide show set to classical music. An English-style pub with artsy intellectuals.

Miller's Pub, 134 S Wabash Ave. 'Good for breakfast, with friendly service, moderate prices and a good atmosphere.'

Rocky's, south of Navy Pier. 90 yrs of tradition behind this restaurant on the riverfront, w/ mural of the late Rocky looking out over the water.

Thai Star, 660 N State, 951-1196. Charming, inexpensive, one of the first of its kind in Chicago.

White Castle, several locations around Chicago. Home of the slider, so called because its grease content helps it slide down the throat easily. Order 4 or more for a meal.

For ice-cream lovers: try the luscious 'frango mint' at **Marshall Fields** 3rd floor ice-cream parlour, State and Randolph.

For breakfast try: **Lou Mitchell's**, 565 W Jackson, 939-3111, 1 blk from Union Station. A family operation since it opened in 1923, this venerable eatery gives free Milk Duds to the 'ladies', donut holes and a prune to all. Fresh-ground coffee, baked goods, Greek toast. 'Wonderful atmosphere.'

Mitchell's Original, 101 W North at Clark, 642-5246. Good filling breakfasts for under $5.

West Egg on State, 1139 N State, 951-7900. Wide variety, excellent.

OF INTEREST

The Loop, a 5- by 7-block city core, is defined by the steel tracks of the elevated subway ('El'), a transit system with a voice like a giant trash compactor yet strangely lovable. Besides being fast and cheap, this dotted line of noise gives free rein to voyeurism, letting you virtuously peep at a thousand fleeting tableaux as you flash past. Within the Loop are theatres, smart hotels and shopping districts, including the once pre-eminent **Marshall Fields** department store (still has the best Christmas windows anywhere).

State Street, running north-south, and **Madison**, east-west, bisect within the Loop at what's called the world's busiest intersection. (At 1 S State, take a peep at the delicate ironwork, by Louis Sullivan, F L Wright's mentor.) All street numbers in Chicago begin here, each block representing increments of 100. One block east of the Loop is Michigan Ave; its most elegant stretch, the **Magnificent Mile**, gives a glittering, often windy view of Lake Michigan.

Archi Center, 224 S Michigan, 922-3431, offers tours of outstanding Chicago architecture. 2-hr walk around the Loop costs $9, Mon–Sat at 10am & 1.30pm, Sun

1.30pm. 'Good way to see a variety of Chicago architecture. Wear comfortable shoes.' Bus tour departs Sat at 9.30am in spring, summer and fall, for 4-hr tour including Frank Lloyd Wright's **Robie House**, $25.

For a panoramic view of the city you can ascend **Sears Tower**, 875-9447, the tallest and one of the ugliest buildings in the world, at Wacker Drive and Adams. On a clear day you can see across the lake to Michigan—60 miles. Go at night for a truly spectacular view of the city but forget the audio-visual show beforehand, it's a waste of time. Open 9am–10.30pm, $6. Or take a **boat trip**—Chicago is at its best from the lake. 'Best thing I did in Chicago.' Mercury, 332-1353, and Wendella, 337-1446, boats leave from opposite sides of the Chicago River at Michigan and Wacker Dr: 1½-hr trip, $9; 2-hr trip, $11. The longer the better as you sail further and proportionately less of your time is taken up with passing through the locks into Lake Michigan (which is 8ft higher than the river). Best of all is the 2-hr night-time trip (7.30pm departure) for the dazzling lights. 'Boat stops in front of Buckingham Fountain—spectacular lights and colour show.'

Marina City, 300 N State St, a prototype self-contained 'vertical city' of residences, offices and spiral car port; resembles two upended corncobs.

John Hancock Center, 875 N Michigan, 751-3680. Tallest residential building in the world. Cocktail bar skywalk. Views of the city at night; $6, observation hall. Open 9am–midnight.

Adler Planetarium and Museum, 1300 S Lake Shore Dr, 322-0329. $4 sky shows. 'Good show, interesting photos.' 9am–5pm daily, 9pm Fri.

Art Institute, Michigan & Adams St, 443-3500. A magnificent collection of Impressionism, post-Impressionism—great Cézanne and Gaugin, modern American art and the Thorne Rooms: a series of minutely detailed period rooms—in miniature. Open Mon–Fri 10.30am–4.30pm, Tues 'til 8pm, Sat 10am–5pm, Sun 12pm–5pm. Tues free, $6.50 adults, $3.25 students with ID other days. Good basement café. 'Wonderful, well worth six bucks.'

Frank Lloyd Wright houses. There are 25 in the suburbs; the Art Institute bookshop has good guidebooks. You need a car to see many of them, but FLW's own house and studio at Chicago and Forest Aves in Oak Park is reachable by El—to Harlem. From here, some of the houses are within walking distance.

Museum of Science and Industry, E 57th St & Lake Shore Dr, 684-1414. 'Magnificent place.' Free; fees for coal mine, U-boat sub. Open daily 9.30am–5.30pm in summer, shorter hours in winter. $5, plus extra for Omnimax Theatre. Free Thurs. 'Best I've ever been to—easily spend a whole day here.'

American Police Center and Museum, 1700 S State St, 431-0005. Mon–Fri 8.30am–4.30pm; $3. 'Death masks, including Dillinger's.'

Field Museum of Natural History, Roosevelt Rd & Lake Shore Dr, 922-9410. Anthropology, botany, zoology, geology. Open daily 9am–5pm; $5, $3 students with ID, free Thur. 'There are interesting exhibits on American Indians and Eskimos.'

Shedd Aquarium, next to Field Museum, 939-2426. Open daily 9am–6pm year-round; $4, free Thur. Also an oceanarium with dolphins, penguins, etc. $8 combo.

Chicago Historical Society, Clark St & North Ave, 642-4600. Outstanding on Lincoln with notebooks, letters, fashions, photos, manuscripts, furnishings. Open Mon–Sat 9.30am–4.30pm, Sun/hol noon–5pm; $3, free Mon. Library open Tue–Sat only.

Chicago Board of Trade, 141 W Jackson Blvd, 435-3500. 'This is the commodities exchange, there is a free visitors' gallery with an audio-visual presentation.' An incredible $25 billion change hands here each day, in grain contracts, treasury bonds and other commodities. Open Mon–Fri, 9am–2pm. Free.

Chicago Mercantile Exchange, 30 S Wacker St, 930-1000. The largest financial futures exchange in the world handles over 400,000 contracts each day, including those of pork bellies and other livestock. From the visitors centre, you can observe the colourful, madcap behaviour on the floor below. Open Mon–Fri, 7.30am–3.15pm, main floor; 8th floor for foreign currency, 7.15am–2pm.

Museum of Contemporary Art, 237 E Ontario St, 280-2660. Open Tue–Sat 10am–5pm, Sun noon–5pm; $4, $2 students ID, free Tue. Good cafe.

University of Chicago, 5 miles south on the Midway. Fermi and colleagues first sustained a nuclear chain reaction on 2 Dec, 1942, under seats of an abandoned football stadium at 57th & Ellis. Henry Moore's sculpture 'Nuclear Energy' marks the site. One of America's best universities.

Water Tower Pumping Station, 806 N Michigan Ave at Pearson St. This fanciful Gothic Revival station conceals a very utilitarian pump—it distributes over 72 million gallons of water each day. One of the few public buildings to survive the 1871 fire, consequently revered by Chicagoans. Mon–Thurs 9.30am–5.00pm, 7pm Fri. **Here's Chicago**, 467-5304, offers tours of the station, plus films and exhibits about the fire and gangster era. Open 10am–5pm daily, $5.75, $4.50 with student ID. **Visitors Center** with maps, discount coupons in booklet 'Chicago's Got It' in the lobby, 9.30am–5pm daily.

Maxwell Street Market, 8 blks SW of Loop, 1300 South Ave at Halsted. Incredible variety and colour but *caveat emptor* and watch your wallet. Vendors like to pretend the merchandise is hot but what's hot is the live music and blues licks on Sun. 'Don't walk here. Take a taxi.'

State Street, now converted to an attractive pedestrian and public transit mall.

Michigan Ave, 20s and 30s facades, mortared with money, opulent restraint, shops for ogling only.

Outdoor art. There is enough to see without having to spend a dime: the skyscrapers are amazing and there is plenty of outdoor art. The Standard Oil building, 200 E Randolph St, the world's fourth tallest; the Hancock Tower; the Chicago Tribune Tower with its ornate faux-Gothic design, 435 N Michigan Dr, and the Wrigley building opposite; the elliptical, mirrored offices that look out onto the river, 333 W Wacker Dr; the wedge-shaped Illinois State Center, 100 W Randolph St, with its light, airy atrium; and, of course, the black monolith that is Sears Tower. **Sculpture** fills the city. Outside the State Center sits Alexander Calder's *Flamingo*, a huge set of pink interconnecting girders; *The Picasso*, Daley Center Plaza at Washington and Dearborn, is a 63 ft steel woman with typical abstraction; *Untitled Sounding Sculpture* by Bertoia outside Standard Oil; *Batcolumn*, Claes Oldenburg's huge baseball bat in full erection at 600 W Madison; Joan Miro's *Chicago*, a smaller homage to the city than most, Brunswick Plaza, 69 W Washington; and finally Marc Chagall's *Four Season*'s 70 ft mosaic wall that looks like graffiti, First National Bank Plaza.

Beaches. 18 sandy miles of 'em—free! Try **Oak St** beach just NE of John Hancock Center, or **Lincoln Park** beaches. 'Makes Chicago seem like the seaside.' 'Quite pleasant walking along waterfront—a park all the way to Museum of Science.'

Tomb-hopping. Al Capone has two graves, one at Mt Olivet ('qui reposa'), another at Mt Carmel ('My Jesus mercy').

Great Ape House, Lincoln Park Zoo, 2200 N Cannon Dr, 294-4660; open daily 9am–5pm, free. Ingenious glass cylinder arrangement lets you see monkeyshines at close hand. NB: Keep out of park after sunset.

Buckingham Fountain: set in Grant Park along Chicago's lake front, the fountain is outlined against the skyscrapers of the Loop. At night a light show transforms the fountain into a dazzling, many-coloured sculpture.

The industrial Chicago suburb of **Des Plaines** is the birthplace of that most American of eateries, McDonald's. The original is now the **McDonald's Museum**, 400 Lee St, (708) 297-5022, open Tues–Sat, 10am–4pm. Lots of 50's McDonald's memorabilia—but you can't eat here! Go to the *operating* McDonald's across the street for your Big Mac instead. In Oak Brook, the nation's only **Hamburger University** trains McDonald's managers.

ENTERTAINMENT

Chicago is the centre of the blues world, has one of the strongest folk scenes in America and boasts an impressive amount of jazz activity. Pick up a free copy of

The Reader, published Fri and available at record shops, to find out where it's happening. Also check the listings in *Chicago Magazine* or buy Hargrove and Snooks' *500 Things to Do in Chicago for Free*. NB: Stick to Old Town, the Rush Street area, and the North Side at night, even if you are in an armoured car.

Avalon, Belmont and Sheffield, 472-3020. El stop is Belmont. Local bands. $3–$6 cover. 'New wave.'

B.L.U.E.S., 2519 N Halsted, 528-1012. 'The people—exhilarating. The blues—totally overpowering.' 'Crowded, small, hot.' $5–$7 cover. Opens 8pm.

Club 950, 950 Wrightwood, 929-8955. Alternative and new wave. $2 cover after 10pm weekends. 'Lots of English music.'

Experience 'slam' poetry at the **Green Mill Lounge**, 4802 N Broadway, 878-5552. Every Sun at 7pm, local poets recite their work, one-on-one, for up to $50 in winnings at this 80-year-old mobster hangout.

Hot Tix, 24 S State St, 977-1755. 'Half-price tickets for same day performances—theatre, dance, the arts.'

Jazz Andy's, 11 E Hubbard, 642-6805. A great place to hear jazz. Free shows at noon Tue–Fri; daily shows at 5pm, $3 Sat/Sun 9pm.

North Pier Chicago, a restored warehouse on the Chicago River with shops, restaurants and **Dick's Last Resort**, a large jazz bar. Close by is **Navy Pier**, stretching into Lake Michigan. If it's still untouched by redeveloper's hands, have a pleasant, uncommercial walk.

Second City Comedy Revue, 1616 N Wells, 337-3992. 'The place to see great comedians with a twisted sense of humour.' John Belushi, Jim Belushi and Bill Murray are among the egregious graduates of this wellspring of irreverent American comedy. Two sets of revues Fri & Sat, one show Tue, Wed, Thur & Sun.

Sluggers World Class Sports Bar, Inc., 3540 N Clark, 248-0055. Has acres of screens with all sports and a games room with an indoor baseball batting cage! Cheap beer too. 'A right laugh.'

Wise Fools Pub, 2270 N Lincoln, 929-1510. Blues and jazz greats, $4–$8 cover.

Chicago Blues Festival (in early June) and **Chicago Jazz Festival** (in late August), Grant Park, 744-3315. Largest free blues and jazz festivals. To hear who's playing, call 744-3315. Afterwards there's more jamming at the clubs.

SPORT

Chicagoans are sports mad. After the Chicago Bulls basketball team won the NBA title for the second time in 1992, the celebrations became a riot. See the Bulls and their all-star team at the Chicago Stadium, 1800 W Madison, 943-5800, in the summer. The Blackhawks play ice-hockey there in the winter, 733-5300. NFL action can be viewed at Soldier Field, McFetridge Dr and S Lake Shore Dr, 663-5408, with the once mighty Bears now struggling. Wrigley Field, 1060 W Addison, 404-2827, is the home of the Cubs and one of the most beautiful base-ball parks in the country. Intimate and packed to the rafters with people and atmosphere, it was the last park in the leagues to introduce floodlights: night games didn't arrive until 1988. An ideal way to taste the most American thing this side of apple pie. The White Sox play at Comiskey Park, 924-1000, and have equally fervent supporters.

INFORMATION

Visitors Center: 806 N Michigan at Pearson, 9am–5pm daily, 280-5740. Good map of the Loop.

State of Illinois Tourism, 310 S Michigan, (800) 882-0292, Mon–Fri, 9am–5pm.

Travelers Aid, 327 S LaSalle, 435-4543; at Greyhound, 435-4537; and airport, terminal 2, 686-7562. Maps, brochures. 'Extremely helpful.'

TRAVEL
Greyhound, 630 W Harrison St, 781-2900. 'Public library nearby, with free art exhibits—good place to go if between buses.'
Local bus CTA/RTA, 836-7000. Fare for buses and El: $1.25.
Amtrak, Union Station, Canal and Adams Sts, 655-2354. Hub of the Amtrak intercity system. Think *The Untouchables*. Think Kevin Costner standing atop of a set of steps, gun in hand. Think pram going down the steps between bullets. Now walk up the steps in the station and relive it.
O'Hare International Airport. The busiest airport in the world. The Northwest El line takes you directly to the airport for $1.50. There are buses, but congestion is horrific, it'll take forever.
Auto Driveaway, 310 S Michigan, 939-3600. 'Friendly.' 'Very helpful.'

SPRINGFIELD The pleasant state capital has one main attraction: Abraham Lincoln. At the age of 28, 'The Great Emancipator' arrived in the city to practice law and stayed for twenty years. See the only house he ever owned, 426 S 7th St, 789-2357. Recently beautifully restored, it has a useful visitors bureau; you can also visit Lincoln's old **law offices**, 6th & Adams, 785-7289; the **Lincoln Depot**, Monroe & 9th, 788-1356, where he boarded the train to go to DC for his inauguration; the **family tomb**, Oak Ridge Cemetery, 782-2717; and the **Old State Capitol**, Capitol Plaza, 785-7960, where he was a member of the Illinois House of Representatives.
There are other 'highlights' such as walking the same route as Abe did when he worked at the post office, the family pew in the church, and his bank ledger. Northeast of the city on Rte 97 is **New Salem Historic Site**, 632-7953, a reconstruction of the 1830's village where Lincoln lived as a young man. All this is free.
The state's other adopted golden boy, Frank Lloyd Wright, is also on show in Springfield. The **Dana-Thomas House**, 301 E Lawrence, 782-6776, was built in 1903 for a local socialite. This prime example of the 'Prairie Style' that Wright pioneered also has furnishings by the man himself. Opening times vary, so call ahead.
The telephone area code is 217.

ACCOMMODATION
Best Rest Inn, 700 N Dirksen Pkwy, 522-7966. Laundry, colour cable TV, fridge available. S–$26, D–$35.
Capitol City Motel, 1620 N 9th, 528-0462. Nr the fairgrounds and with kitchenettes. S–$28, D–$35.
Motel 6, 3125 Widetrack Dr, 789-1063. S–$28, D–$35.
All-Star 8 Inn, 2224 E Cook, 789-0361. S–$29, D–$29–$35.

FOOD
Biggies and Bubbas, 530 N 1st St, 525-1818. American food and brunch.
Try around the **Vinegar Hill Mall**, 1st and Cook Sts, for cheap-eats, there are lots of places to quell those hunger pangs.

INFORMATION/TRAVEL
Springfield Convention and Visitors Bureau, 109 N 7th, 789-2360. Open Mon–Fri 8am–5pm.
Greyhound, Dirksen Parkway, reachable by #6 bus.

GALENA Once an opulent riverboat and lead-mining town in northwest Illinois, Galena is now a beautiful backwater of stately homes and small-town friendliness. Galena produced a clutch of Civil War generals, including Ulysses S Grant; each year, the townspeople re-enact a battle or two.

If you have a car, by all means take the Great River Road south from Galena, which follows the Mississippi all the way to New Orleans. A lovely drive.

METROPOLIS It's a bird, it's a plane, it's Clark Kent's 'home town' in southern Illinois on the Ohio River. Giant mural of Superman in the park, free kryptonite from the Chamber of Commerce, and for entertainment and the comics—the *Daily Planet*. No, this isn't where Superman was invented, or even where he was supposed to have lived ('Metropolis' in the comic book was a big city; this Metropolis is a small town of a few thousand friendly souls). Nonetheless, locals hold a 'Superman Celebration' each year on the 2nd weekend of June, complete with bank robbery foiled by you-know-who; (618) 524-2714 for more info.

INDIANA

The Hoosier State has a wholesome, almost cornball ingenuousness about it, so it's not surprising to learn that it's the home of Notre Dame, Johnny Appleseed, Orville Wright (Wilbur was born in neighbouring Ohio), Studebaker, Cole Porter, Amish villages of *Friendly Persuasion* fame and David Letterman of late-night TV show notoriety. The rural portions have most to offer: rustic landscapes of country roads, covered bridges (notably in Parke County west of Indianapolis), round barns (in Fulton County) and even a 'Steamboat' Gothic mansion (in Vevay on the Ohio River).

Indiana cranks out lots of steel and more band instruments than any place on earth. Most of the heavy industry is in the northwest corner of the state, near Chicago, so don't let the atrocity called Gary colour your opinion of the rest of the state.

Several rebels, with and without causes, are buried here: Eugene Debs in Terre Haute, and James Dean in Fairmont (whose gravestone behind Friends Church is walking away in ghoulish bits and pieces). For a more mundane type of rebellion, check out Sunny Haven Recreation Park, a 20-acre nudist camp and site of sunbathing conventions.

INDIANAPOLIS Foursquare in the centre of the state, Indianapolis is state capital, national headquarters for the American Legion, home of the Indy 500 auto race and crossroads of America, so-called because a dozen or so major routes meet here. The city is as exciting as mashed potatoes except during the month of May, when the '500' Festival, the Indy time trials and other pre-race madness stir things up a bit. It's almost impossible to get seats for the race itself on Memorial Day Sunday (you must write for them a year in advance), but standing room and scalpers' tickets are available closer to race day. Time trials and qualifying runs begin 2–3 weeks before the main event and provide nearly the same level of thrills, decibels and mayhem as the big race, so bring beer, lunch and make a day of it. At night, party with the racing fans along Georgetown Ave. Call 241-2501 for prices and schedules, or write to: Tickets, Indianapolis Motor Speedway, PO Box 24152, Speedway, IN 46224.

During spring, summer and fall, folk festivals take place by and around the Monument Circle area downtown.

The telephone area code is 317.

ACCOMMODATION

Basic Inn, 5117 E 38th St, 547-1100. S–$24, D–$28.
Indianapolis Motor 8, 3731 Shadeland, 545-6051. S–$28, D–$36.
Motel 6 Inn, 5241 W Bradbury St at Lyndhurst, 248-1231. S–$28, D–$35.
Skyline Motel, 6617 E Washington St, 359-8201. S, D both $28.
YMCA, 860 W 10th St, 634-2478. S–$25, $66 weekly. Higher during 500 Festival. 'Raunchy area.' Take #13 or 6 bus to get there.

FOOD

Between Bread, 136 N Delaware, 638-4174. Great sandwiches.
Broad Ripple Village, north of city centre at 62nd St, is a mall full of ethnic restaurants and quaint shops.
Renee's French Restaurant, 839 E Westfield Blvd, 251-4142. 'Cheap, friendly with a really pleasant atmosphere.'
Shapiro's Deli, 808 S Meridian, 631-4041. Cheap and good cafeteria style food.

OF INTEREST

Benjamin Harrison House, 1230 N Delaware, 631-1898. Home of the 23rd President of the US. Mon–Sat 10am–4pm, Sun 12.30–4pm. $2.
Children's Museum, 3000 N Meridian, take 29th St exit off I-65, 924-5431. Mon–Sat 10am–5pm, Thurs 'til 8pm, Sun noon–5pm; $6. World's largest kiddie museum: puppets, films, mummy, Tyranosaurus Rex, huge toy and antique train layout.
Harrison Eiteljorg Museum, 500 W Washington, 636-9378. A private collection of American art, both Native and Western, in a lovely atmosphere. Mon–Sat 10am–5pm, Sun noon–5pm; $3, $1.50 students.
Indiana State Fair, Meridian St and Rt 37. Two weeks of Hoosier hoopla in Aug. 'Huge, mad, big name groups.'
Indianapolis Zoo, 1200 W Washington, 630-2030. One of the newest and therefore well planned. $8.50, open 9am–5pm daily.
Museum of Art, 1200 W 38th St, 923-1331. Open Tue–Sat 10am–5pm; Sun, noon–5pm, free.
Union Station, 200 S Illinois St. Built in 1888, one of the finest examples of Romanesque Revival architecture in the US. Galleries, restaurants, boutiques and passenger trains.
Conner Prairie Pioneer Settlement, 6 miles N of Indianapolis, is a restoration of a 30-building pioneer village *circa* 1836. Visit typical homes and workplaces of the era, eat frontier cooking, celebrate various festivals and meet inhabitants. Allisonville Rd exit off I-465, 773-0666. Open Tue-Sat 10am–5pm, Sun noon–5pm, $8.
Indianapolis Motor Speedway, 4790 W 16th St, 241-2500. Tickets for the time trials are sold at the gates the day of the trials. Gates open at 7am the opening day; 9am other days. You can park in the infield.
Speedway Museum, located in the infield of the Speedway, has a collection of Indy racers and memorabilia. Open daily 9am–5pm, $2.
The Circus Hall of Fame, 472-7553, in **Peru**, a town on US 31, 70 miles north of Indianapolis. Peru was once the winter home for travelling circuses, and young

amateur performers put on 10 free shows in July, Tues–Sat, 10am–5pm, Sun 1.30pm–5pm. Nearby accommodation at two state campgrounds: Frances Slocum and Miami, at Lake Mississinewa.

ENTERTAINMENT

City Taproom, 28 S Pennsylvania St, 637-1334. Live jazz, no cover. Closed Sun.
The Chatterbox, 435 Massachusetts Ave, 636-0584. Divey bar but good jazz.
Crackers Comedy Club, 8207 Keystone Crossing, 846-2500. Tue–Fri, shows at 8.30pm, extra show Fri at 10.30pm, Sat at 8pm, 10pm, Sun at 8pm.
Ike's and Jonesy's, 717 W Jackson, 632-4553. 50s and 60s music. Open until 3am, no cover. Closed Sun.
The Slippery Noodle, 372 N Meridian, 631-6968. Good music across a broad spectrum.
Sports Bar and Grill, 231 S Meridian, 631-5838. Nr Union Station, famous for its 'lingerie lunches'.
The Vogue, 6259 N College, 255-2828. Music for the masses.

INFORMATION

Visitors Information: Indianapolis City Center at Pan American Plaza, 201 S Capitol Ave, 800-323-INDY. Open Mon–Fri 10am–5.30pm, Sat until 4pm.
Greyhound, N Capital Ave & E Ohio St, 635-4501. Open 24 hrs.
Amtrak, 350 S Illinois St, 263-0550.
Metro Bus, 36 N Delaware, 635-3344. Runs the city buses; off-peak rate 75¢, rush hour $1.
Indianapolis International Airport, 7 miles SW of downtown; hop on the #9 'W Washington' bus to get there, basic fares apply.

AMISH COUNTRY Another hour north and east from Peru lands you in the heart of Amish country in the counties of LaGrange and Elkhart. The town of **Shipshewana**, SR 5 off US 20, is a centre of Amish culture, with an auction and fleamarket every Tuesday and Wednesday in the summertime. Yoder's Department store also carries Amish crafts and foods for those who miss the market days. For info about Mennonite and Amish history visit **Menno-Hof** across from the flea market on SR 5, 768-4117. At the **Buggy Wheel Restaurant and Bakery** try German sausage or roast pork and for dessert eat outrageous wet-bottom shoo-fly pie.

In the town of **Nappanee** on US 6, tours of an Amish farm and buggy rides are available, 773-4188. Nappanee is also home to the **Pletcher Art Festival** in early August and the **Apple Festival** in late September. The **Essenhaus Restaurant** in Middlebury, at the intersection of SR 13 and US 20, serves up Amish cooking.
NB: Watch out for slow-moving Amish buggies on back roads.
The telephone area code is 219.

BLOOMINGTON is a pleasant college town, home of Indiana University, an hour's drive southwest from Indianapolis on Rt 37. The movie *Breaking Away* was filmed here, and featured a bike race called the little 500. The race is an annual event in mid-April. Look too for the numerous abandoned stone quarries, also featured in the movie, which now serve as swimming holes on hot summer days.

An hour southwest from Bloomington takes you to the Wabash River town of **Vincennes**, site of **Grouseland**, the home of the shortest-lived US president—William Henry Harrison. At his inauguration, doubtless ignoring his mother's advice, Harrison gave a two-hour speech in freezing rain, contracted pneumonia and died 31 days later, never having made a major decision as president. His 32-day term lasted from 4 March–4 April, 1841.

Seventy-five miles downstream from Vincennes lies the town of **New Harmony**, where two Utopian communities were set up in the early 19th century. In 1814 a grumpy Lutheran named George Rapp quit Germany to found New Harmony and await the coming of the Lord. Being delayed for some reason, the Lord never appeared, and Rapp departed after having waited ten years. Rapp left his village to expatriate Robert Owen, a Welshman, who founded a community of equality based on education. Kindergarten, coed public education and other new ideas in education were first tried here, and what remains is an historic district of 20 buildings and a dramatic 'roofless church' designed by Philip Johnson.

The telephone area code for the region is 812.

FOOD

Garcia's Pizza, 114 S Indiana Ave, 334-0404. Good pan pizza by the slice.
Nick's, 423 E Kirkwood Ave, 332-4040. Cheap hamburgers and beer.

TRAVEL/INFORMATION

Visitors Bureau, 2855 N Walnut, 334-8900.
Greyhound, 535 N Walnut St, 332-1522.

IOWA

Imagine this: a state that produces unthinkable quantities of corn, soybeans and cattle and quarter of the nation's porkers and generates over $10 billion annually from its agriculture, is hit by the worst flood in history; a flood that leaves the whole state a National Disaster Area and hundreds of thousands of people homeless and without water. This was Iowa's fate in 1993 when heavy rains and already full rivers combined to leave the Hawkeye State as one huge muddy pond.

The weather has always been famous in Iowa—with its nature of instant changes (such as the freak blizzard that resulted in the serendipitous development of the Golden Delicious apple) and amazing electrical storms. Herbert Hoover, 31st President, is the most well-known of the strong Quaker community that resides here and which was a vital link in the underground railway that was the road to freedom for thousands of slaves. It was to Iowa that black scientist and inventor George Washington Carver fled to escape persecution. Every four years Iowans are remembered by the rest of the country when they have first shot in the choice of the next President.

DES MOINES Trisected by rivers, Iowa's capital (population 193,000, excluding hogs) is a green and friendly place to catch your breath and take advantage of good food and lodging. Like Minneapolis, the city has a (carpeted) skywalk connecting major downtown buildings. 'A really beautiful city.' Worth seeing is the **Living Farms** complex, whose visitors

have included Nikita Krushchev and Pope John Paul II (the latter delivered mass—shades of *Animal Farm*).
The telephone area code is 515.

ACCOMMODATION
Motel 6, 4817 Fleur Dr, 287-6364. Close to airport. S–$32, D–$38.
YMCA, 101 Locust, 288-0131. Men only. $19.50 includes use of facs; $5 key deposit.
YWCA, 717 Grand, 244-8961. Women only. Large, grand. S–$8 nightly.

FOOD
Bishop's Cafeteria, in the Merle Hay Mall (largest shopping mall in Iowa), off I-80, 276-1534.
To eat **downtown**, go to the Court Ave district: **Julio's**, Tex-Mex, 244-1710; **Kaplin Hat**, a renovated hat factory with inexpensive steaks, 243-1414; and **Stella's Blue Sky Diner**, 4th and Locust, 246-1953, with cheese frenchies and vintage rock and roll.

OF INTEREST
Adventureland, east of city, 142A exit off I-80, 266-2121. Thrill rides include the Tornado rollercoaster: 'largest and fastest in the Upper Midwest'. Daily, Memorial Day–Labor Day, 10am–10pm; $18.
Iowa State Fair, 12 days in late Aug. Top-notch. Camping at fairgrounds at Dean Ave, 262-3111. Huge, good amenities, wooded area; $8–$10 site.
Living History Farms, I-35 and I-80 at Hickman Rd exit, 278-5286. Four operating farms: 1700s Indian, 1850s pioneer, 1900s farm and farm of the future; also 1870 town of Walnut Hill. Lots of special events, exhibits. Open May–Oct, Mon–Sat 9am–5pm, Sun 11am–6pm; $7.

INFORMATION/TRAVEL
Visitors Bureau, 309 Court Ave, 242-4705, in Saddlery Bldg, 2nd Floor, and at Des Moines International Airport, 286-4960.
MTA city bus, 283-8111. Serves downtown, the fairgrounds. 75¢.
There is a bus service to the aiport, but it is rather erratic and takes a tortuous route; take a cab to be sure, $8–9.

EFFIGY MOUNDS NATIONAL MONUMENT In northeast Iowa, 1500 acres along Mississippi River bluffs, dotted with prehistoric burial mounds shaped like birds and bears, some of which date back to 1000 BC. In the north unit, 'Great Bear' stretches 120 ft from head to tail. Museum with artefacts, interpretive history 3 miles north of Marquette on H-76, open daily 8am–7pm summers, 873-3491. 'The March of Bears' lies in the south unit, where ten bear mounds and three bird mounds are strung together in one line. Most impressive when outlined by snow; area has lovely autumn colours also. Greyhound goes no closer than Dubuque, IA or LaCrosse, WI, so car rental or hitching a must. 12 miles SW of Dubuque, the Trappist monastery of **New Melleray Abbey** allows free overnight stays (offering encouraged) Sun–Thur, a nice counterpoint to mound exploration. Often full, call to make reservations, 588-2319.
The telephone area code is 319.

AMANA Settled by German mystics in 1854, the Amana Colonies (7 villages located one hour apart by oxen) became the longest-lived commune in the US. Reorganised along corporate lines in 1932, Amana residents no longer practice communal living but instead produce microwave ovens and other appliances along with woollens, wine and other hand-crafted goods. You can walk past the houses, factories and workshops (built along traditional German lines) and visit museums but the main attraction is the solid food (heavy on pork and carbohydrates).

The telephone area code for Amana, Williamsburg, Brooklyn and Iowa City is 319.

ACCOMMODATION/FOOD

Super 8 Inn, Rt 2, Box 179H, Williamsburg, 668-2800. S-$34, D-$37, T-$44, Q-$48.

Wesley House Hostel, 120 N Dubuque St, Iowa City, 338-1179. Open year-round except Thanksgiving and Christmas-New Year. $10 AYH member, $20 non-member.

Colony Inn, downtown in Amana, 622-6270. 'Great breakfast—$6 for fruit salad, pancakes, eggs, sausage, hashbrowns and more.'!

KANSAS

Kansas is America's heartland. Although a prairie state in quintessence (think of *Little House on the Prairie*) with all the home sweet homeyness you could want, there's still a wildness in the air here: namely, the wind. For all its landlocked glory, Kansas seems mysteriously powered by oceanic forces—full of wheat fields rippling under the caress of constant breezes.

This same, unceasing wind has played a hand in the Sunflower State's history—kicking up deadly dust storms and twisters (one of which sucked up poor Dorothy in *The Wizard of Oz*), driving lonely pioneer women insane with its howling. The survivors, however, must have been of good stock, for Kansas boasts the first woman mayor (1887), the first female US senator (Nancy Landon Kassebaum), the most famous aviatrix (Amelia Earhart) and the most fanatical and annoying prohibitionist, Carry Nation.

Carry began by singing hymns to saloon idlers, but soon found it more effective to turn saloons into kindling with a hatchet. Besides being anti-booze, Carry's vendetta encompassed tobacco, corsets, barroom paintings and foreign foods. Her last 'hatchetation' ended in ignominy: she unwisely took on a female saloonkeeper, who thrashed her soundly. Carry's zeal kept Prohibition alive in Kansas until 1948.

Kansas' bid for statehood was the fuse for the outbreak of the Civil War, and ferocious anti- and pro-slavery factions gained it the epithet 'Bleeding Kansas'. In the riproaring cattle and railroad era of mid/late 1800s, cowhands drove one million cattle a year to Abilene, and 'blew' their $1-a-day wages on cards, rotgut and fancy 'wimmin'. The cow capital eventually moved west from Abilene to Wichita and Dodge City. As the 'breadbasket to the world', Kansas sells much of its surplus wheat to needy Russia. Ironically, the original seeds for 'Turkey Red', a hard winter variety, were brought here from Russia in 1874 by Mennonite settlers.

'A remarkable state, well worth making an effort to discover.' 'At night, a magnificent and fulfilling stillness falls over the plains.'

ABILENE Considering its associations with the Chisholm Trail, Wild Bill Hickok and all, Abilene's lack of westernness disappoints. Abilene is really Ike's Kansas—grain elevators, porch swings and funky little cafes; and is the unlikely subject of the affectionate chorus, 'prettiest town I've ever seen'. The Eisenhower buildings are pompous but do stop for a look at Ike's simple boyhood home.
The telephone area code is 913.

ACCOMMODATION
B&B Country, 206 6th St in Wakefield, 20 miles from Abilene, 461-5596. Folksy, friendly—just like Kansas. S-$25, D-$35, includes a hearty breakfast with original, prize-winning homecooked pancakes. Reservations required.
Best Western, 2210 N Buckeye, 1 mile from downtown, 263-2050. S-$34, Q-$47.

OF INTEREST
The Garden of Eden—yes, you read it here first—is in **Lucas**, 22 miles east of Paradise, west of Abilene on I-70. An eccentric by the name of S. P. Dinsmoor built this statue garden in the 1920s in his front yard, using 113 tons of concrete, among other things. A Civil War veteran, Dinsmoor held a cynical and rather prophetic view of the 20th century, particularly toward crooked bankers and lawyers. 16 miles N of I-70, off Hwy 272. Open daily 9am–6pm in the summer, (913) 525-6395. $4. 12 miles from the geodetic centre of the US.

WICHITA Meaning 'painted faces' in Indian, Wichita has Kansas' most worthwhile cowboy mockup in its Cow Town ('authentic, much better than Dodge City'), with five original and 32 replica buildings. Boeing, Cessna and Beech—three major aircraft producers—make Wichita the 'Air Capital of the World'. 'Great place to hitch-hike by air.'
The telephone area code is 316.

ACCOMMODATION
Motel 6, 5736 W Kellogg St, 945-8440. S-$31, D-$37.
Town Manor Motel, 1112 N Broadway at 10th, 267-2878. S-$25, D-$29.

OF INTEREST
Old Cowtown Museum, 1871 Sim Park Dr, 264-6398. A 'living' historic village. Open Mon-Sat 10am–5pm, Sun noon–5pm; $3.50.
There are several good (free!) art museums, including the **Ulrich Museum** at the University of Wichita, 689-3664, which has on its outside wall an exquisite Miro mosaic with over one million pieces of glass. Closed summers, open Wed-Sun during school year.
Kansas skyscrapers hold wheat, not people, and you'll find the tallest **grain elevators** in the world in **Hutchinson**, 45 miles northwest on SR 96. They hold 20 million bushels of grain.

INFORMATION
Visitors Bureau, 100 S Main, #100, 265-2800. Stop here first for map and information.

THE SANTA FE AND OTHER TRAILS Because of its geographic position, Kansas was crosshatched with trails: the Santa Fe, Chisholm, Oregon, Smoky Hill and others. Whether travelling across Kansas, or settling it, pioneers needed grit and resilience. South of Colby (60 miles from Colorado), near I-70, you can examine an authentic sod house at the Prairie

Museum. **Fort Larned** (6 miles from Larned off Highway 154) and graffiti-covered **Pawnee Rock** (northeast of Larned on 156) still stand as trail markers. Along US 50, 9 miles west of Dodge City, wagon ruts of the Santa Fe trail can be seen.

MICHIGAN

Which state has 3000 miles of shoreline and the nation's largest sand dune yet touches no ocean? Which state has more than 10,000 lakes and isn't Minnesota? Michigan, that's who. Rich soil and surprisingly friendly climate (considering it's Canada's neighbour) make the Wolverine State tops in cherry, blueberry and other fruit growing. The wine country is centred around Paw Paw in southeast Michigan.

A campers' and hikers' dream, Michigan has youth hostels, thousands of campsites (including the unspoiled northern pleasures of Isle Royale National Park) and a rich network of farm trails and roadside produce markets on its two peninsulas.
National park: Isle Royale.

DETROIT Forget car manufacturing, Motown and race riots—as elsewhere, you can still get mugged in Detroit but auto assembly lines and good soul music are both disappearing. A bustling inland port, the city is working to revitalise a decaying downtown (with emphasis on flashy complexes like the Renaissance Center to snare those lucrative convention gigs). However, parts of downtown still look like bomb sites and it is a desperately sad place to be. The natives of course live out in the suburbs and that's probably, if you have to come here at all, where *you* should stay too!

The Motor City came by its name and fame quite by accident, and largely because Henry Ford, Ransom Olds and other auto innovators happened to live and work in the area. The auto industry brought thousands of blacks to Detroit; one of them was Berry Gordy, founder in 1959 of the Motown sound (Smokey Robinson, the Supremes, the Temptations, etc), who used to make up songs on the Ford assembly line to relieve the monotony.
The telephone area code is 313.

ACCOMMODATION
American Ft Wayne Hotel, and **AAIH International Hostel**, 408 Temple, 831-7150. Private rooms with AC, TV; S–$21, D–$32 for AYH members, + $2 key deposit.
Americana Motel, 1999 East Jefferson Ave, 567-8888. 5 blks from the Renaissance Center. S–$30, D–$40 + $5 key deposit.
Bali Hi Hotel, 10501 E Jefferson Ave, 822-3500. A short drive from downtown. S–$26, D–$34, plus $3 key deposit.
Cabana Motel, 12291 Harper Ave, 371-1220. Located near Connor off I-94. S–$30, D–$35.
Country Grandma's Home Hostel, 22330 Bell Rd, New Boston, MI 48164, 753-4901. $9 AYH.
Falcon Inn Motel, 25125 Michigan Ave, Dearborn, near Telegraph on US 12, 278-6540. Convenient for the Henry Ford Museum and Greenfield Village. S–$25, D–$32.

Mercy College of Detroit, 8200 W Outer Dr, 592-6170, 11 miles from downtown off Southfield Fwy (Rt 39). S–$24, D–$22 per person.
Tea House of the Golden Dragon Home Hostel, 8585 Harding Ave, Center Line, MI 48015, 756-2676; $5 AYH. 'Amazing place.'
Village Motel, 21725 Michigan Ave at Oakwood Blvd in Dearborn, off Southfield Fwy, 565-8511. Near the Henry Ford Museum and Greenfield Village. S–$42, D–$47.
YMCA, 2020 Witherell, 962-6126. $21 + $10 key deposit. Men only. Pool; book ahead. 'Very clean rooms. A bargain.'

FOOD

Strong ethnic communities here, so head for Greektown, Chinatown and the Polish community (called Hamtramck—actually an independent city within Detroit).
Doug's Body Shop, 22061 Woodward Ave, Ferndale, 318-1940. Done in late and early American cars. Check for your favourite Chrysler.
Elias Brothers Big Boy, 400 Renaissance Center, 259-0606. Try the sandwiches and homemade desserts.
Jacoby's, 624 Brush St, 962-7067. Nr Greyhound, 2 blks N of RenCen, has landmark status.
Markets: **Hart Plaza** between the RenCen & Civic Center holds weekend ethnic festivals all summer long. **Eastern Market** on Russell St has produce bargains. Open year round.
Pizza Paplis Tavern, 553 Monroe in Greektown, 961-8020. Deep-dish Chicago pizza, fresh pasta and large sandwiches.
Soup Kitchen Saloon, 1585 Franklin, 259-2643. Known as 'Detroit's home of the blues'. Pasta, creole and fresh fish specials. Cover of $5–$15 for gigs.

OF INTEREST

Renaissance Center, the 'RenCen' on the river, 568-5600, is a mirrored fortress of four 39-story towers protecting an 83-story hotel. The glass-fronted elevator ride is certainly worth it for the view ($3), if the costly drinks at the top are not. 'Fantastic views of Detroit, Windsor, the river.' 100+ shops, restaurants. Across the street is **Mariner's Church**, 1848 shrine for lake sailors, whose bells still toll each time a life is lost on the lake.
Cobo Hall and the **Joe Louis Arena**, where sporting events, ice capades, concerts and the circus come to town. 600 Civic Centre Dr, 567-7444.
Detroit Institute of Art (DIA), 5200 Woodward Ave, 833-7900. Open Wed–Fri 11am–4pm, w/ends 11am–5pm. $4. From fine primitives to Andy Warhol, plus Diego Rivera's famous and scathing mural on factory life. Also: *Quilting Time*, a mosaic by black modern artist Romare Bearden. Cafe in Renaissance decor.
Greenfield Village and adjacent **Henry Ford Museum** in **Dearborn**, west of Detroit. Greenfield Village is 240 acres containing 100+ genuine historic buildings amassed by Henry Ford and set up in sometimes curious juxtaposition: Abe Lincoln's courthouse, Wright Brothers' cycle shop, Edison's lab (complete with vial said to contain Edison's dying breath). Almost everything runs or ticks or does something—a stunning microcosm of the roots of technological Americana. Fee rides for horse carriages, steam trains, Model-T Fords, steamboats, horse-drawn sleighs. The fantastic 12-acre Ford Museum has huge transportation collection, antique aircraft. Open daily, 9am–5pm; admission of $11.50 each to village and museum, 2-day pass to both for $20; 271-1620.
Belle Isle, an island park in the Detroit River (bridge at E Jefferson), has 5 sections: an aquarium (free), conservatory, a safari-like zoo, and the **Dossins Great Lakes Museum** (donation).
Royal Oak Zoo, N of Detroit, 398-0903. Open daily 10am–5pm; $6.
Motown Museum, 2648 W Grand Blvd, 875-2264. It all began here, Hitsville USA, as Berry Gordy called it. OK, so the company's now based in LA but you can still see where it all *used* to happen, Studio A. Also the piano Diana Ross and The

Supremes used, lots of gold discs and other assorted memorabilia. Open Mon noon–5pm, Tues–Sat 10am–5pm, Sun 2pm–5pm, last tour at 4.30pm; $3.
Windsor, Canada: this city which gets mixed reviews is *south*, yes south, of Detroit. It is reached via bridge or tunnel and recommended, but with a few warnings: 'I was given a difficult time because I was backpacking and had only $100 plus ticket home. Plenty of trucks outside immigration to ask for a ride though.'
Detroit Grand Prix, Indy Cars World Championship race takes place in mid-June. The course follows the city streets by the RenCen.
Detroit Kool Jazz Festival, 259-5400. This is the US half of the Swiss Montreux International Jazz Festival, one of the most prestigious and widely recognized festivals. Most of the concerts are free. In early Sept.

INFORMATION
Visitors Bureau, Hart Plaza on E Jefferson St, 567-1170, or 100 RenCen, Suite 1950, 259-4333. Both are centrally located and quite helpful.
Michigan Travel Bureau, (800) 543-2937.
Visitor Hotline, 567-1170.
Travelers Aid, at Greyhound and 211 W Congress, 962-6740; at Metro Airport, 941-3943.

TRAVEL
Amtrak, 2601 Rose St, 964-5335. Not the best station or area to be stuck in at night.
Greyhound, 1001 Howard St, 961-8011.
Detroit Department of Transportation (DOT), 933-1300. Runs buses in the downtown area. $1.
Southeastern Michigan Area Regional Transit (SMART), 962-5515. For buses to the 'burbs.
Metropolitan Wayne County Airport, 942-3550. Detroit's main airport, about 21 miles from downtown. To get there by bus, take a SMART bus #200 from Michigan Ave to Middlebelt, change there and take the #285 to the airport, takes about 90 mins–2 hrs, $1.60. Alternatively, Commuter Transportation, 941-3252, runs a shuttle bus from major downtown hotels; reservations required, $13 o/w. Taxi about $30.

FLINT midway between Detroit and Lake Huron's Saginaw Bay, has what Motor City lacks nowadays: **auto plant tours**. Buick City has hi-tech and robotics tours on Tue & Thur. You'll need to book tours far in advance during summer. Call the Flint Area Convention & Visitors Bureau, (800) 288-8040, for more information.
Mott Lake Hostel, 4 miles NE of Flint, 736-5760. $8 AYH, $11 non-members. Phone reservations OK up to 2 wks in advance.
The telephone area code is 313.

ANN ARBOR An hour's bus ride west of Detroit, Ann Arbor is thoroughly dominated by the University of Michigan and loves it. As a consequence, lots of good hangouts, live music including excellent bluegrass, cheap eats, support services, and events like the July Art Fair.
The telephone area code is 313.

ACCOMMODATION
Ann Arbor YMCA, 350 S 5th Ave, 663-0536, downtown at William St. Clean dorm rooms for men and women, S–$23.
Lamp Post Motel, 2424 E Stadium Blvd, 971-8000. S–$50, D–$53. Same friendly management as the **Arbor Lodge**.

U of M, Conference & Catering Services, 603 Madison, 764-5325. Summer dorm rooms; S–$28, D–$36. Reservations required.

FOOD/ENTERTAINMENT

Afternoon Delight, 251 E Liberty St, 665-7513. This place has all natural muffins and pitta sandwiches. Try the yoghurt shakes.

Rick's American Cafe, 611 Church St, 996-2747. Reggae and blues bands, $3–$6 cover, closed Sun. Serves burgers, burritos, nachos and more; dinner only. Best bar in Ann Arbor, according to the town's citizens.

OF INTEREST

Ann Arbor Summer Festival, in July. Offers a variety of performances and exhibits every day.

Gerald R. Ford Presidential Library, 1000 Beal Ave, 741-2218. Open Mon–Fri 8.45am–4.45pm.

Museum of Art in Alumni Hall, S University, 525 State St, 764-0395. First-rate collection of Asian and Western art. Open Tue–Sat 11am–4pm, Sun 1–5pm; free.

Nichols Arboretum and Gallup Park are next to the Huron River on the city's northeastern edge. You can canoe, fish and swim. Open daily 6am–10pm. Call the Ann Arbor Recreation Dept, 994-2326, or Park and Recreation Dept, 994-2780.

INFORMATION/TRAVEL

Ann Arbor Convention and Visitors Bureau, 211 E Huron, Suite 6, 995-7281.
Amtrak, 325 Depot St, 994-4906. Services to Detroit and Chicago.
Greyhound, 116 W Huron St, 662-5511, at Ashley St, 1 blk off Main St.

NATIONAL LAKESHORE/UPPER PENINSULA Michigan has two special wilderness areas, the **Upper Peninsula** and the **Sleeping Bear Dunes National Lakeshore**. The Upper Peninsula is above Wisconsin. This multi-million acre forest is bordered by three of the Great Lakes. It provides a rare retreat into untouched wilderness; hiking, cross-country skiing, fishing and canoeing are available. For more information, contact the Upper Peninsula Travel and Recreational Association, PO Box 400, Iron Mountain, MI 49801, 774-5480. Also, the US Forestry Service, Hiawatha National Forest, 2727 North Lincoln Rd, Escanaba, MI 49829, 786-4062, can supply you with guides and maps.

Sleeping Bear Dunes, 45 minutes from **Traverse City**, is known for its magnificent sand dunes and polar-bear swimming (Lake Michigan never seems to warm up). In Traverse City, catch the **Bing Cherry Festival** in mid-July, an excellent festival.

The telephone area code for the Upper Peninsula is 906; for Sleeping Bear Dunes, 616.

ACCOMMODATION

Northwestern Michigan Community College, East Hall, 1701 E Front St, Traverse City, 922-1406. About a mile from the bus station. Summer on weekends only. S–$20, D–$30 + $15 extra for private bath.

MACKINAC ISLAND An island in time as well as space, Mackinac (pronounced Mackinaw) permits no motor vehicles—your choices are horseback, bicycle, surrey or shank's mare. Restful, beautiful Victorian, especially nice during the June Lilac Festival. Chocoholics Note: island speciality is homemade fudge. Boat runs every hour in summer.

Don't miss at least a look at the elegant 1880s Grand Hotel, which starred in the movies *This Time for Keeps* and *Somewhere in Time*. It has a porch that never ends, the longest in the world.
The telephone area code is 906.

ACCOMMODATION
Unfortunately, accommodation is rather expensive here and no camping is allowed on the island. Also, there are few lockers to be found here, or on the mainland at St Ignace and Mackinaw City, so you will be carrying your rucksack with you—'an exhausting bind if you go over to the island intent on walking'. The moral of this is: if you plan to go here, plan ahead. The Chamber of Commerce is helpful, 706 S Huron, 436-5574.
Bogan Lane Inn, PO 482, Mackinac Island, ¾ mile E of the boat docks, (906) 847-3439. $55 night, incl bfast. Reservations required. Open year round.
There are the usual motel chains along I-75; they are probably your best bet.

TRAVEL/INFORMATION
Arnold Mackinac Island Ferry, Box 220, Mackinac Island, MI 49757, 847-3351 or 643-8275. Departures from Mackinaw City and St. Ignace, $11 round trip.
Mackinac Island Chamber of Commerce, 847-3783.
Shepler's Mackinac Island Ferry, Box 250, Mackinaw City, MI 49701, (616) 436-5023. Serves Mackinaw City and St Ignace, also $11 round trip.

ISLE ROYALE NATIONAL PARK This is the roadless, wild and beautiful 'eye' in Lake Superior's wolfish head. Free camping by permit only, including use of screened shelters around the island. 'Boil surface water at least 5 minutes.' Carry salt along—inland lakes on the island have leeches. Island closed in winter.

MINNESOTA

Driving through Minnesota, you may well wonder if you took a wrong turn somewhere and wound up in Scandinavia. The countryside, fertile farmland in the south, covered with pine forests in the north and dotted with 15,000 glacier-scoured lakes, almost duplicates the Nordic landscape. Doubtless this is why so many immigrant Swedes and Norwegians moved here earlier this century; to them, the state looked like home and had frigid winters so everyone could keep their skis on.

Vikings may have learned of Minnesota's Nordic delights early on, if a Viking runestone dated from AD 1000 proves authentic. Much of the population still appears Nordic, and the countryside and cities are among the cleanest and most well-preserved in the US.

The land also seems to attract giants, both literal and figurative. It's the birthplace of J Paul Getty, Bob Dylan, Charles Lindbergh, F Scott Fitzgerald, Sinclair Lewis and the Mississippi River, as well as the home of Paul Bunyon the woodsman and the Jolly Green Giant of canned pea fame.

The state is especially lovely during Indian summer; highway markers often point out the most vivid colour displays. Free maps of the fall colour routes are obtainable from the Minnesota Tourism Bureau, 375 Jackson, Rm

250, St Paul, MN 55101. Or call toll-free within the state, (800) 652-9747, for guidance. Any time of year, North Shore Drive (US 61) along Lake Superior north to Canada is a top contender for the most beautiful camping and gawking route in America. Miles of well-kept biking paths criss-cross the state. The Heartland Trail, a 27-mile paved bike trail in north-central Minnesota, is one of the loveliest. Call (800) 657-3700 for more information. While here be sure to go canoeing, a peculiarly Minnesotan tradition passed down from Chippewa Indians and French–Canadian trappers to present day. You can disappear into the north country wilderness and not see another person for days on end. Fishing is the other biggie sport up here. **National Park:** Voyageurs.

MINNEAPOLIS/ST PAUL Laced together by the curves of the Mississippi River, Minneapolis and St Paul are 'Twin Cities' only in geographic terms. It's said that Minneapolis was born of water, St Paul of whiskey.

Minneapolis is young, Scandinavian, modern, relaxed, a working-class city freckled with lakes and home base of 15 Fortune 500 companies, headed by electronics. As in San Diego and Seattle, residents here sensibly take advantage of their versatile setting; many spend their lunch hour sailing in summer. Minneapolis was and is Mary Tyler Moore territory, as bouncy and clean as the Pillsbury doughboy, another local product.

St Paul began as an outpost with the uncouth name of Pig's Eye, described in 1843 as 'populated by mosquitoes, snakes, Indians and about 12 white people'. Perhaps to compensate for these rough beginnings, St Paul has become a conservative capital city of Irish and German Catholics, doting on history and Eastern refinement. F Scott Fitzgerald is St Paul's native son. (So is Charles 'Peanuts' Shultz, but he was evidently too brash for St Paul; in high school his cartoons were rejected by the school yearbook.)

To the south is the younger sibling of **Bloomington**, where lurks the gigantic "Mall of America" (#7 bus). Out of the three metropolitan areas, Minneapolis offers most for the visitor: friendly, outgoing locals, a handsome downtown with mall, skyways, parks, a meandering waterfront and swimmable lakes. Stick to downtown, however: 'I am astonished—could other US downtowns be like this, given a chance? The rest of Minneapolis that I've seen is as ordinary and soulless as anywhere else in America.'
The telephone area code is 612.

ACCOMMODATION

Fraternities in the 16-1700 block of University Ave can sometimes offer room to travellers. 'Very cheap and plenty of lovely half-naked men wandering around—just what you need after two months in camp.'
Hall Home Hostel, 1361 Lafond Ave, St Paul, 647-0611. $8. 'Small but very friendly.'
Hillview Motel, Highways 169 & 41, 445-7111. S–$35, D–$45.
Student's Coop, 1721 University Ave SE, 331-1078. $10/night, available only in summer. Kitchen, laundry, colour TV. 'Smashing place to live—full of friendly lunatics. Great social life.'
Super 8 Motel, 7800 S 2nd Ave, exit at Nicollet Ave off I–494, 888–8800. S–$36, D–$42. Close to airport, shops, zoo. Several around the twin cities. Call 738-1600.
Camping: Lebanon Hills Regional Park Campground, 12100 Johnny Cake Ridge Rd, Apple Valley, (612) 454-9211. Tent site $10.

FOOD

Be sure to try Minnesota specialties: wild rice, walleyed pike, sweet corn and Fairbault blue cheese. St Paul's soul dish is *boya*, a Hungarian stew served on the slightest pretext. For cheap munchies try some of the downtown and college bars during happy hour.

Cafe Latte, 850 Grand Ave, St Paul, 224-5687. Located in Victoria Crossing. The most decadent chocolate desserts. Bring a friend so you can try more than one. Also, good soups and so-so sandwiches.

Ediner, Calhoun Square, Mpls, 925-4008. Trendy '50s-style diner.

Green Mill, 2626 Hennepin Ave, Mpls, 374-2131. Excellent burgers, good pizza.

It's Greek to Me, 626 W Lake St, Mpls, 825-9922. Gyros are cheap and even moussaka is reasonably priced.

Lotus, 313 SE Oak St, Mpls, 331-1781, and 3037 Hennepin Ave, near Calhoun Square, 825-2263. Vietnamese food in a stylish setting.

Mudpie, 2549 Lyndale Ave, Mpls, 872-9435. Natural food.

New Riverside Cafe, 329 Cedar Ave S, Mpls, 333-4814. This is a West Bank hang-out. Vegetarian. Also has live music.

North Country Co-op, 2129 Riverside Ave, 338-3110. Full grocery with fresh produce and bread—even pickled Japanese vegetables.

Swatdee, 607 Washington Ave, S Mpls, 338-6451, and 289 E 5th St, St Paul, 222-5859. The one in St Paul is the older and better restaurant. Some of the best Thai food.

Seward Community Cafe, 2129 Franklin Ave, Mpls, 332-1011. The Sunday breakfast is very cheap and filling.

OF INTEREST—MINNEAPOLIS

Besides being the longest pedestrian walkway in the US, the **downtown mall** along Nicollet Ave is one of the most agreeable and attractive. It's full of flowers, fountains, friendly conversation, strollers, sandwich-eaters, bus stop shelters, wafting classical music, boutiques and smart shops. Overhead an enclosed **Skyway system** (designed for Minnesota winters) lets pedestrians cross in comfort from building to building across 45 downtown blocks.

Focal point of the Mall and Skyway complex is the 57-storey **IDS Center** at Nicollet and 8th St. The **Crystal Court**, a 3-level arcade within the IDS complex, has a 'ceiling' of crystal pyramids and shapes which nicely diffuse the sunlight, creating a dappled effect as though one were strolling beneath trees. Both the lighting and the vivacious cafe/meeting-place ambiance are best absorbed mornings until lunchtime. Cafe has reasonable lunch specials, and there's an info center in the Crystal Court. Suggestions of scenic walks around the Twin Cities can be found in free leaflets from the info center in the IDS Complex and Minnesota Convention and Visitor Commission, 1219 Marquette Ave, Suite 300, Mpls, MN 55403; 348-4313. Recommended: cross the Hennepin Ave bridge to the far side of the Mississippi and then return to downtown via the 3rd Ave/Central Ave bridge. The area immediately across the river is called **Riverplace** & **St Anthony Main**, restored warehouses on the original cobblestone Main Street of Minneapolis. The 3rd Ave bridge takes you across to St Anthony Falls; the Minneapolis side is lined with fine old warehouses and flour mills (walk along S 1st St to Portland Ave), e.g. the Crown Roller Mill built in 1879. Between these mills and S Washington Ave is the **Milwaukee Road Station**, a handsome complex which the city has decided to preserve. A favourite walk or bike ride is along the Mississippi on either side. Others are around Lake of the Isles, Cedar Lake, Lake Harriet or Lake Calhoun, all in south Minneapolis. This is a city with 153 parks and 45 continuous miles of bike paths.

American–Swedish Institute, 2600 Park Ave, 871-4907. Shops, fine art, 33-room mansion with exhibits on Minnesota's Scandinavian heritage. Open Tue–Sat noon–4pm, Wed 'til 8pm, Sun 1pm–5pm; $3.

Walker Art Center, 725 Vineland Pl, 375-7600, a modern collection, open Tue–Sat 10am–8pm, Sun 11am–5pm; $3. Free on Thurs. On the grounds is the **Sculpture Garden**, including the enormous Spoonbridge and Cherry.
Hennepin County Historical Museum, 2303 3rd Ave S, 870-1329. Early days of Hennepin County. Open Tue–Sun noon–5pm; $1.50, 50¢ students.
Historic Fort Snelling, junction of Hwys 5 and 55 near airport, 726-1171. Open daily May–Oct noon–5pm. Reconstruction and preservation of 1827-era fort. Film, exhibits, fort tours; $3.
Lake Harriet, W 44th St, 348-4825. Paddlewheel boat tours & concerts, summers only; $2.50.
MC Gallery, 400 1st Ave N, 339-1480. One of 9 galleries located in the Wyman Building. Features good contemporary American arts.
Minneapolis Institute of Arts, 2400 3rd Ave S, 870-3046. Tue–Sat 10am–5pm, Thur 10am–9pm, Sun 12–5pm; free, special shows $3, $2 students.
Minnehaha Falls and Park, south of city. 144-acre woodland with 53-foot cataract popularised (though never seen) by Longfellow in his *Song of Hiawatha*.
Festivals, summertime noon concerts throughout downtown Mpls, esp Nicollet Mall. Peavea Plaza has Thur night jazz in June, 5pm–7pm; 338-3807 for more information. Activities of the lakes are featured in the **Aquatennial** in July, and the **Minnesota State Fair** is held in Aug at Snelling Ace, St Paul; 642-2200.

OF INTEREST—ST PAUL
Alexander Ramsey House, 255 S Exchange St, 296-0100. Victorian home of early Minnesota governor, run by Minnesota Historical Society. Tours Tue–Sat 10am–3pm, $3.
Indian Mounds State Park, Dayton's Bluff, east of downtown. A pleasant picnic spot overlooking the Mississippi, believed to be a Sioux burial site.
James J Hill House, 240 Summit Ave, 297-2555. 45-room Romanesque mansion and private art gallery that once belonged to the builder of the Great Northern Railway. Tours every ½ hour Wed–Sat 10am–4pm, $3.
Jonathan Padelford Packet Boat Co, 227-1100, Harriet Island, downtown St Paul. Paddlewheel boat tours of Mississippi River. 3 daily 1½-hr cruises in summer, less often in May & Sept, $8.
Landmark Center, 75 W 5th St, 292-3225. The old Federal building, now an art gallery. Worth going for the architecture alone. Open Mon–Fri 8am–5pm, Thurs until 8pm, Sat 10am–5pm, Sun 1pm–5pm; free.
Science Museum, 10th St and Wabasha Ave, 221-9488. Mon–Sat 9.30am–9pm, Sun 10am–9pm. Omnitheatre, a huge, domed screen, 221-9400. Buy ticket for $5.50 and enter the museum for $1.
State Capitol, near the Science Museum, 297-3521. Tour building, governor's quarters, golden horses on top and base of dome for panoramic view. Tours Mon–Fri 9am–4pm, Sat 10am–3pm, Sun 1pm–3pm; free.
Summit Avenue District. The Victorian mansions get grander as you work your way up Laurel, Holly, Portland and Summit Aves—just the way the family of F Scott Fitzgerald did. Born at 294 Laurel, FSF and family lived in 4 successively posher homes before ending up at 599 Summit, where he wrote his first novel in 1919.
On the **University of Minnesota campus** is the **Goldstein Gallery**, MacNeal Hall; displays on fashion, housing, and interior design.
Nearby: Minnesota Zoo, in Apple Valley south of St Paul, 432-9000. Buses from Twin Cities' downtowns. 5 zones, from tropics to oceanic, with Siberian tigers, wolves and caribou. Open daily 9am–6pm during the 6 warm (relatively) months, 10am–4pm during the Ice Age; $4.
Mall of America, 60 E Broadway, Bloomington, 883-8850, about 15 mins from St Paul; take MTC bus #54 or #7. The largest shopping mall in the States with the usual feast for shopping gastronomes and also for added piquancy: a seven acre indoor theme park with a rollercoaster and Golf Mountain—a two level 18 hole 'golf course'!

Tailor's Falls, located on the St Croix River near Wisconsin border. Spectacular falls and great rock climbing. On your drive up, stop in Stillwater.
Lake Pepin, 1 hr south of the Twin Cities on Hwy 61. Good swimming beaches.
Sauk Center. Sinclair Lewis' hometown and the setting for his book, *Main Street*. Located 2 hours NW of St Paul on 94 West. Interpretative Center and museum Mon–Sun 8.30am–5.00pm, June–Aug; Mon–Fri 8.30am–3.00pm, Sept–May, free. Lewis' boyhood home open June–Aug only, 9.30am–5pm, Sun 10.30am–5pm, $2.50. (612) 352-5201.

ENTERTAINMENT—MINNEAPOLIS

Glam Slam, 110 N 5th St, 338-0632. $5–$8 cover. 'Great nightclub.'
Hayes' City Stage Theater, 1430 Washington Ave S, 338-5534. Excellent satires and stand-up improvs.
First Avenue and **7th St Entry**, 701 1st Ave N, 332-1775. First Avenue was made famous by Prince in the movie *Purple Rain*. You probably won't see Prince, but you can see good rock groups. 7th St Entry is around the corner: cheaper, lesser-known groups.
Guthrie Theater, 725 Vineland Pl, 377-2224, was founded in the 1960s by Sir Tyrone Guthrie and has one of the finest repertory companies in the US. Excellent discounts for students week nights and Sunday. Low cost previews; enquire.
Orchestra Hall, 1111 Nicollet Mall, 371-5656. Home of Minneapolis Orchestra. Cabaret in summer; jazz, pop and other concerts.
U of Minnesota. 17th and University Ave SE, 627-4430. The **Dinkytown** area near campus on the east side of the river is liveliest at night. On campus: 'the Film Society often has free or cheap screenings of recent flicks. See notice board in Student Union'.
Good country rock groups perform at many bars in the metropolitan area.

ENTERTAINMENT—ST PAUL

Jerome Hill Theatre, 5th & Jackson, St Paul, 646-6104. Shows high-quality, non-Hollywood films, $5.50.
Ordway, 345 Washington St, near Landmark Center, 224-4222. The St Paul Chamber Orchestra and Minnesota Opera perform here.
World Theatre, 10 E Exchange St, 290-1221. Once home of *A Prairie Home Companion*, now hosts a Saturday night radio show featuring some of the finest in American folk music. Call for times & ticket prices.

INFORMATION

Arts Resource and Information Center, hotline telephone with up-to-date information about exhibits in Twin Cities, 870-3131.
Minneapolis Convention and Visitor Commission, 1219 Marquette Ave, #300 348-4330, or Info Center at Crystal Court in IDS complex. Get free 'Do It Yourself' brochure, map of downtown and Skyways from either source.
Travelers Aid, 726-5500. Located at airport on upper level.
Minnesota Tourism Bureau, 375 Jackson St, St Paul, 296-5029.
St Paul Chamber of Commerce, 101 Norwest Center, 55 E 5th St, St Paul, 223-5000.

TRAVEL

Amtrak, 730 Transfer Rd, 633-1127 or 800-USA-RAIL. On the 'Empire Builder' route that connects Chicago and Seattle/Portland.
Greyhound, in Mpls: 29 N 9th St; in St Paul, 25 W 9th St, both on 371-3325.
Metropolitan Transit Commission (MTC), 827-7733, runs the two cities integrated bus systems. Basic fare 85¢, $1.10 rush hour.
Minneapolis/St Paul International Airport, about 9 miles from both downtowns. Take the #7 C,D,E, or F bus from 6th St, Mpls, basic fares on boarding and then 25¢ on disembarking; Airport Express runs a limousine service to downtown hotels, $7 o/w, $11 rtn to St Paul; $9 o/w, $13 rtn to Mpls.

DULUTH Situated on a steep hillside overlooking Lake Superior, the city is the world's largest fresh-water port and is known for its unbelievably cold winters, with the wind whipping off the lake. The mines that used to provide the city with much of its income have all but disappeared and now it's you, the happy tourist, who helps keep the place moving. It's access to the lake that most people come for; there is a beautiful new 1-mile walkway that takes the visitor along the shore of the lake and across the harbour. Accommodation can be a problem in the summer when it's busier and the motels bump up their prices, but try **Best Western Downtown Motel**, 131 W 2nd St, 727-6851, S–$50 and up, D–$52 and up, up. Visit the **Convention and Visitors Bureau**, 100 Lake Shore Dr, 722-4011, for information on the best current deals.

HIBBING Famous for three things: Mesabi Range iron ore, the birthplace of Greyhound buses and also of Bob Dylan. The US Hockey Hall of Fame is nearby, on US 53 one hour north of Duluth. For those interested in digging up more knowledge about mining, the Minnesota Museum of Mining in Chisholm and the Iron Range Interpretive Center may be worth visiting. Hwy 73 takes you through a multicoloured mini-Grand Canyon, the mined-out maw of the Pillsbury open pit. Along the way are several vista points for viewing other gaping holes, some as much as four miles long and two miles wide.

NORTHERN MINNESOTA is known for the beauty of its wild areas. Among the best: **Chippewa National Forest**, a 650,000 acre wilderness that contains nearly 500 lakes and rivers with broad vistas of beautiful large and small lakes. Hiking trails have been developed and maintained for visitors. Bald eagles are the star attractions. For information call (218) 547-1044.

North Shore, Lake Superior. If you have about a week, you can drive all the way around Lake Superior into Canada and Wisconsin. Otherwise, go to Duluth to see this beautiful shore line.

Superior National Forest stretches across Minnesota's northeastern area from the Canadian border to the north shore of Lake Superior. It is especially known for the **Boundary Waters Canoe Area**, a million-acre protected wilderness area honey-combed with rivers. There are bugs, bears and a lot of portaging, but, if you come prepared, this adventure is well worthwhile. For information write to the Forest Supervisor, PO Box 338, Duluth, MN 55801, or call the Minnesota Tourism Bureau in St Paul, 296-5029.

VOYAGEURS NATIONAL PARK On the Minnesota-Canadian border, this 219,000 acre expanse of forested lake country is just beginning to be developed for public use. The park takes its name from the French Canadians who plied this network of lakes and streams in canoes, transporting explorers (some seeking the Northwest Passage), missionaries and soldiers to the West, and returning by Montreal with vast quantities of furs. You can reach the park by car, but inside there are only waterways and you'll need to rent a boat. Free primitive camping in designated area. Other lodgings at nearby private resorts. No park entrance fee. A new visitors center is located 11 miles east of International Falls on Black Bay off County

Road 96. Houseboats can be rented on **Rainy Lake, Crane Lake** or the **Ash River**. For more information write Voyageurs National Park, Box 50, International Falls, MN 56649 or call (218) 283-9821.

MISSOURI

Mix equal parts of the Old South, the Wild West and the modern Midwest and you've got the flavour of the Show Me State: shrewd, salt of the earth, slightly cantankerous—nobody here believes anything unless they see it with their own eyes. The flat landscape is dominated and divided by the Big Muddy, the Missouri River, a wilful, sediment-laden powerhouse. Missouri produces more tents, lead, Missouri mules, corncob pipes and space vehicles than anyone else. Missouri has also produced Harry S Truman, Mark Twain, TS Eliot, Jesse James and Generals Pershing and Bradley.

In the southwest begins the Ozark Plateau, wooded, full of springs, unspoilt rivers and caverns like Fantastic near Springfield, which has seen service as a speakeasy and a KKK meeting place. Other interesting caves include Meramec (55 miles southwest of St Louis), a five-storey cave variously used as a Civil War gunpowder mill, an underground railway station, and a hideout for Jesse James' gang. A portion of the Cherokee Trail of Tears runs through northeast Missouri and has been made into a scenic camping and recreational area.

ST LOUIS Founded in 1764 by French traders, its associations are as American as apple pie. Home of both the ice cream cone and the hot dog, the latter first devoured in 1893 by hungry St Louis Browns baseball fans. St Louis is where W C Handy wrote and sang the blues, where slave Dred Scott sued for freedom, where one-time resident Tennessee Williams set his *Glass Menagerie* and where Charles Lindbergh got the bucks for his trans-Atlantic venture.

Huge, humid, full of unsavoury slums and heavy industry from meat-packing to beer-brewing, the city nevertheless has a vital cultural life, lots of free attractions and the elegant Gateway to the West arch.
The telephone area code is 314.

ACCOMMODATION

Huckleberry Finn Youth Hostel, 1904-1908 S 12th St, 241-0076. $12 AYH. 'Oldest facilities but good place to stay.' Get there on #73 bus.

Lewis and Clark Intl AYH, 1500 S 5th St, St Charles, MO 83303, (314) 946-1000. In Noah's Ark Motor-Inn across the river on Lewis & Clark Trail.

Washington University, 6515 Wydown, 935-4637. 1 June–7 Aug, open to public. S-$18, D-$32.

To reserve a **Bed & Breakfast** place write: Bed & Breakfast of St Louis, River Country, MO & IL, 1900 Wyoming, St Louis, MO 63118, 771-1993. Over 40 B&Bs. Willing to work within budget restraints and they'll also pick you up at the rail and bus stations.

FOOD

Jimmie's Deli & Restaurant, 415 N 9th, 241-8760. Any kind of meal, 24 hrs a day. A favourite with truck drivers.
McDonald's, on riverboard along the Mississippi. Built along lines of a riverboat, complete with Mark Twain at the helm!
Noah's Ark, 1500 S 5th St, St Charles (across the river from St Louis), 946-1000. 'Dinner is pricey, but the restaurant is a scream—all they need is a good storm, and it's a cruise ship!'
Old Spaghetti Factory, 727 N 1st St, 621-0276. 'Massive helpings, good atmosphere, spaghetti dinners with dessert, coffee from $4–$8.'
There are also many inexpensive ethnic restaurants around **Laclede's Landing** and on the 4th flr of **St Louis Center**, Locust & 6th St.

OF INTEREST

Gateway Arch, 425-4465. A unique 40-person tram ('don't go if you get seasick') mounts the core of each leg of this 630-ft stainless steel arch designed by Eero Saarinen. Once there, you overlook the city and the Mississippi. 'Awesome.' Get there before 11am to avoid long lines. Open daily 8am–10pm during summer; 9am–6pm, winter. $2.50 for tram ride; $2 to enter the grounds of the arch and the **Museum of Westward Expansion** complex beneath the arch. 'The museum is very atmospheric, giving vivid impressions of frontier life.' $1 for film depicting the construction of the arch. **The Old Court House**, west of Arch at 11 N 4th St, was scene of slavery auctions and the unsuccessful attempt by slave Dred Scott to win his freedom in court; the ramifications of his case helped ignite the Civil War. Trial room no longer exists, but you may see **Dred Scott's** grave in Section 1, Calvary Cemetery.
Forest Park, midtown, 5 miles west of Gateway Arch. A large and well laid-out park with numerous attractions; in 1904 the site of the centennial Louisiana Purchase Exposition and World's Fair. An electric signal from the White House simultaneously unfurled 10,000 flags, while fountains flowed, bands played, 62 foreign nations exhibited, and 19 million people visited, there to sample iced tea and ice cream cones for the first time. Of the 1576 buildings erected for the fair, only one was permanent; it's now the **St Louis Art Museum**, one of the most impressive in the US. Nearby, the **St Louis Zoo**, 781-0900. Open daily 9am–5pm, free. **Outdoor Municipal Opera** (1500 free seats at the back of the 12,000-seat amphitheatre) holds operettas, ballets, musical comedies and concerts most nights in summer. Call 361-1900 for schedule. **The Jewel Box** is a floral conservatory. **St Louis Science Center**, southeast corner of Forest Park, 289-4444. Open Mon–Thur 9.30am–5pm, Fri–Sat till 9pm, Sun 11am–5pm; free.
Union Station, recently completed restoration of 19th century Gothic train station. Now full of—surprise!—shops and restaurants and old railroad cars.
Anheuser-Busch Brewery, 13th and Lynch St, 577-2626. World's largest brewery gives free tour with beer, pretzels and a look at Clydesdale horses. Mon–Sat 9am–5pm.
Missouri Botanical Gardens, Tower Grove & Shaw Ave, 577-5100. 479 acres. See the Climatron, first geodesic-domed greenhouse with computer-controlled climates maintained within. Summer hours: 9am–8pm daily; closes at 5pm in winter. $2 admission; free Wed and Sat mornings.
The Magic House, 516 S Kirkwood Rd, 822-8900. Mon–Thur + Sat 9.30am–5.30pm, Sun 11.30am–5.30pm. $3. 'Illusions, tests and games meant for children. Just as many adults go.'
Grant's Farm, Gravois Rd at Grant Rd (outskirts), 843-1700. Free look at the largest group of lovably huge Clydesdale horses anywhere, with a few deer, buffalo & birds thrown in. Reservations a must. Tue–Sun 9am–3pm June–Aug; Thur–Sun, spring and fall.

ENTERTAINMENT

Gateway Riverboat Cruises, below Gateway Arch, 621-4040. The oldest excursion company on the Mississippi offers sightseeing trips of varying duration and price on one of its three boats, *Huck Finn, Tom Sawyer* and the *Belle of St Louis;* $7–$30 for the cruise, including dinner.
Laclede's Landing, a 1-blk area of redeveloped mills and warehouses along the river just north of Gateway Arch, is focus of nightlife.
Paddlewheel steamboat trips are easy to find in St Louis, most of the boats dock in front of the arch. Check out the last authentic showboat, the *Lt Robert E Lee,* 241-1282.

INFORMATION

Try the Visitors Center at Gateway Arch, 425-4465.
Fun Phone, 421-2100, gives a roundup of events, entertainment.
St Louis Convention and Visitors Commission, 10 S Broadway, Suite 300, 421-1023 or (800) 247-9791.
Travelers Aid, 809 N Broadway, 241-5820.

TRAVEL

Amtrak, 550 S 16th St, (800) 872-7245 or 331-3300. Service to Chicago, New Orleans, Dallas, Denver and Kansas City; station closes at midnight.
Greyhound, 801 N Broadway, 231-7800. Open 24 hours.
Bi-State Transit, 231-2345, runs the city buses with basic fare of $1.
Metrolink, also run by Bi-State, is the new light railway that can take you to most of the major sights. $1 basic fare, 10¢ transfer; day pass valid for both bus and Metro, $3.
Lambert/St Louis International Airport, 426-2955. About 10 miles from downtown and serviced by Bi-State buses and Metrolink: the easiest way is to take the Metro to the new airport station that is to open in Spring '94 or catch the 'Natural Bridge' #4 bus on Broadway and Locust, journey time of about 1½ hrs, $1 for both. Greyhound also runs buses from their terminal, $6, taking about 20 mins.

HANNIBAL Although born down the road a piece, Mark Twain (*neé* Samuel Clemens) spent his boyhood in Hannibal, and this is the place that flogs Twainiana for all it's worth. It's good-natured hucksterism for the most part. The old rogue would no doubt approve, being no stranger to exaggeration himself: 'Recently someone sent me a picture of the house I was born in. Heretofore I have always stated that it was a palace but I shall be more guarded now.'

Eschew Tom Sawyer's cave (2 miles out of town and decidedly unspooky) and take a 1-hr boat trip on the Mississippi: departures at 11am, 1.30pm and 4pm (boards ½ hr before), $7; 221-3222. **Mark Twain's home and museum**, 206 Hill Street, is worth a look-in especially if you like Norman Rockwell.

Twilight Zone time: MT's birth coincided with the appearance of Halley's Comet. Throughout his life, Twain predicted he would go out as he had come in. In 1910, right on cue, the comet reappeared and Twain snuffed it.
The telephone area code is 314.

KANSAS CITY Envelope-maker for the world, international headquarters for Hallmark, and home base of the baseballers, the Kansas City Royals, Kansas City is also an important cattle market, which leads us unerringly to Arthur Bryant's, the Holy Grail of barbequedom and a reason for visiting the city. Once part of a great blues and jazz triangle with New Orleans and

Chicago, KC nurtured the careers of Count Basie, Duke Ellington, Charlie 'Yardbird' Parker. KC's sister city is Seville, Spain, which explains the preponderance of Moorish arches, Spanish tiles and ornamental fountains around town. The effect may not look like Spain to a Spaniard, but it sure does to a Missourian.
The telephone area code is 816.

ACCOMMODATION
Super 8 Motel, 6900 NW 83 Terrace, NW Kansas City, 587-0808. S-$38, D-$45. 5m from airport. One of several Super 8s in the area.
Rockhurst College, 926-4125, has cheap digs June–July, open to the general public. Available only by the week: S-$21, D-$18 per person. Call or write for an application, 1100 Rockhurst Rd, KC, MO 64110.

FOOD
Arthur Bryant's, 1727 Brooklyn at 17th, 231-1123. It's the sauce, which you'll see aging in the window. Get lots of sauce. World class BBQ ribs and $5 brisket sandwiches. Go on, stuff yourself.
Dixon's Chili, many locales in KC. Harry Truman loved KC chili—cheap and savoury.

OF INTEREST
Museum of History and Science, 3218 Gladstone Blvd, 483-8300. Tue–Sat, 9.30am–5.30pm, Sun noon–5pm; $2.50. Housed in the 72-room mansion of lumber king RA Long, are exhibits on natural, regional history, and anthropology. Crawl-through igloo, other good native American stuff.
Nelson Atkins Museum of Fine Art, 45th Terrace & Oak Sts, 561-4000. Huge variety, especially of oriental art and crafts. Outdoor sculpture garden is great with its fine Henry Moore collection. Open Tues–Thurs 10am–4pm, Fri 10am–9pm, Sat 10am–5pm, Sun 1pm–5pm; $4, $1 students w/ID.
The Livestock Exchange and Stockyards are at 12th & Genessee. If the smell doesn't remove your appetite, the **Golden Ox** next door has good if somewhat pricey steaks.
Country Club Plaza, between Main St and SW Expressway. Oldest shopping mall in the US. Huge Spanish-style plaza with fountains, genuine Iberian art, beautiful night lighting, interesting food and shops (200 of 'em). At 47th & Nicholas, a copy of the Giralda Tower in Seville. 47th and Central: Spanish murals, exquisite sevillano tilework depicting the bullfight. Splendid display of lights at Christmas.
Crown Center, Main and Pershing Rd. 'City within a city,' built by those friendly people at Hallmark Cards. Hotel, shops, 5-storey waterfall, indoor gardens, restaurants, etc. 'Go Sat mornings when woodcarvers, artists, etc are at work.' Attached to it is the **Hallmark Visitors Center**, 274-5672, open Mon–Fri 9am–5pm, Sat 9.30am–4.30pm. Lots of exhibits showing how the company grew big, peddling sentiment and gushing rhymes.
Independence, a few miles east of KC and one-time home of that well-known haberdasher Harry Truman. The library and museum contain presidential papers; his grave is in the courtyard. Free 30-minute slide and sound show, *The Man From Missouri,* hourly at the Jackson County Courthouse.

ENTERTAINMENT
Westport, original city heart between 39th and 45th Sts, is famous for good taverns and nightlife. Or try **Grand Emporium**, 3832 Main St, 531-1504; good bands. With luck, you may catch the **Jazz Pub Crawl** in May or Sept, a night of hopping in and out of 30 clubs with hot live jazz. Shuttle buses transport you safely from one to the next at your leisure.
Jazz hotline, 931-2888, gives the lowdown on what's playing all around town.

Kansas City Riverboat, River City Drive on the Kansas side, (913) 281-5300. Missouri River's largest and newest riverboats feature 1-hr daytime excursions, Sunday brunch and moonlight cruises; $6–$17.

INFORMATION/TRAVEL
Visitors Bureau, 1100 Main, 221-5242 or (800) 767-7700.
Chamber of Commerce, 920 Main, 221-2424.
Amtrak, 2200 Main St, 421-3622. For trains for St Louis, Chicago, and even LA.
Greyhound, 1101 Troost St, 221-2835.
Kansas City Area Transportation Authority (Metro), 221-0660.
Kansas City International Airport, 243-5237, about 18 miles from the city. Take the #29 Metro bus from downtown, 90¢ or $1.10 for express, about an hour. The KCI Shuttle picks up from major downtown hotels and costs $10 o/w; a taxi will cost you about $30.

ST JOSEPH 'Wanted: young skinny wiry fellows, not over 18. Must be expert riders willing to risk death daily. Orphans preferred. Wages $25/week. Apply Central Overland Express.' Over 100 young masochists applied and thus on 3 April 1860, began the Pony Express, a 2000-mile Missouri to California mail delivery system. Only in operation 18 months, it left a lasting impression on the world. The museum at 914 Penn Street, (816) 232-8471, preserves the original stables and other interesting memorabilia, well worth a visit; open Mon–Sat 9am–5pm, Sun 1pm–5pm, $1. Same day, different year in St Joe, Bob Ford shot Jesse James for a $10,000 reward. The house where the shot was fired is now the **Jesse James Home Museum**, 12th & Penn, (816) 232-8206, which is full of original Jamesabilia and even has the hole left by the bullet in the wall; open Mon–Sat 10am–5pm, Sun 1pm–5pm, $2, $1 students.

CAVES Of all things, Missouri is blessed with more known caves than any other state, many with guided tours to keep you from getting lost and driving up the owners' insurance premiums. For more information, write Missouri Division of Tourism, PO Box 1055, Jefferson City, MO 65102, or call (314) 751-4133. Some examples: **Bluff Dwellers' Cave**, 2 mls S of Noel, (417) 475-3666. A 45-min tour includes stalactite curtains, corals, 10-ton balanced rock, as well as a 54-foot rimstone dam; $5. **Fantastic Caverns**, 4 mls N of Springfield, (417) 833-2010. They are as good as their name implies, and you don't even have to walk! Propane-run jeeps transport visitors through the caves in modern comfort; $11.50. **Marvel Cave,** Branson, (417) 338-2611, has a huge waterfall at a depth of 500 ft and a main chamber that is 20 storeys high. Back on the surface is **Silver Dollar City**, an 1880's theme park. $24 gets you into the park and Marvel Cave.

NEBRASKA

A huge, tilting plate of a state, Nebraska rises from 840 feet at its Missouri River eastern border to nearly 5000 feet as it approaches the Rockies. Through it runs the feeble Platte River, 'a mile wide, a foot deep, too thick to swim and too thin to plow', along which countless buffalo roamed until done in by kill-crazy Buffalo Bills. As shallow as 6 inches in places, the Platte nonetheless made an excellent 'highway' and water supply for the 2.5 million folks who crossed Nebraska in Conestoga wagons, 1840–66. Even today, the most worthwhile things to see in the state are those connected with the pioneer trails west.

Like other plains states, Nebraska has perfectly miserable weather summer and winter. Its speciality is hailstones, which occasionally reach the size of golfballs. A leading producer of beef cattle, TV dinners and popcorn, Nebraska specialises in silos, both grain and ICBM missile.

OMAHA Once a jumping-off place for pioneers, Omaha is the Union Pacific train headquarters and has taken over the noissome title of 'meat packer for the world' from Chicago. Friendly yes, but about as lively at night as a hog carcass, except around Old Market.

Hometown of Fred Astaire and Malcolm X, Omaha nowadays is site of Boys Town and also the underground Strategic Air Command (SAC) headquarters.

The telephone area code is 402.

ACCOMMODATION

Motel 6, 10708 M St, 331-3161. S–$32, D–$39.
Satellite Motel, 6006 L St, 733-7373. S–$33, D–$45.
YMCA, 430 S 20th, 341-1600. S–$10, D–$12. Pool, 5 minutes from Greyhound. 'New, clean, pleasant.'

FOOD/ENTERTAINMENT

Bohemian Cafe, 1406 S 13th St, 342-9838. 'Czech food and atmosphere—the duck is superb.' Lunches for $4, dinners $6–$8.
The Diner, 12th & Harney Sts, 341-9870. For a true diner experience for under $3 for lunch.
Dubliner Pub, 12th & Harney, 342-5887. A good place to shoot darts. 150 imported beers.
Spaghetti Works, 502 S 11th St in Old Market, 422-0770. $4.50 lunch, $6 dinner buys pasta, garlic bread and salad bar. Also one in suburban Ralston, off I-80 at 84th St and Park Drive
Garden Cafe, Old Market Place, 'wholesome breakfast' for $3 and dinners for $6.

OF INTEREST

Boys Town, 136th St and W Dodge Rd, 498–1140. Incls Hall of History, stamp and coin museum. Tours daily 8am–5.30pm; free. 'Very interesting.'
Joslyn Art Museum, 2200 Dodge St, 342-3300. Housed in Art Deco building, Indian and other art; pictures painted during the Maximillian Expedition up the Missouri River in 1833–4 are worth seeing. Free jazz Thur eves in July. Open Tue–Sat 10am–5pm, Thur until 9pm, Sun 1–5pm; $3.
Western Heritage Museum, 801 S 10th St, 444-5071. Housed in the wonderful Art Deco old Union Station, worth a look in itself, this museum has displays on Omaha and Nebraska history. Open Mon–Sat 10am–5pm, Sun 1am–5pm, $3.
Orpheum Theatre, 409 S 16th St, 444-4750. An ornate theatre featuring concerts, ballet, plays.
Union Pacific Historical Museum, 1416 Dodge, 271-3530. Lots of Lincoln memorabilia including replica of his funeral car with original furnishings, plus oddments. Open Mon–Fri 9am–3pm, Sat 9am–noon; free.
Union Stockyards, 29th & O Sts, 734-1900. Pig and cattle auction on Wed.
Old Market, 10th & Howard. Cobbled streets, warehouses recycled into smart shops, galleries, restaurants. 'Most interesting place in Omaha.'

See where oft eulogised and misrepresented black leader **Malcolm X**—neé Malcolm Little—was born, 3448 Pinkey St. Then see the wider picture, **Great Plains Black Museum**, 2213 Lake St, 345-2212, has extensive exhibits on the black experience, including black cowboys, athletes and soldiers; open Mon–Fri 8.30am–5pm, $2.
Strategic Air Command Museum, 2510 Clay St, Bellevue, 10 miles S of Omaha, off Hwy 75, 292-2001. Bombers, missiles, a *red phone* (hear the end of the world!) and the *Red Alert* slide show, shown in winter only. 'Nuclear nightmare at its *finest*! A must-see!' 8am–8pm summer; 8am–5pm winter; $4.
Henry Doorly Zoo, 10th and Dear Park Blvd, 733-8400. Contains rare white Bengal tigers and a 4½ acre aviary, the world's second largest, and 'Lied Jungle', a simulated tropical rainforest with the accompanying wildlife. Open 9.30am–5pm daily summers; until 6pm Sun/hol. Visitors can remain in the park for two hours after the park has closed; $6.25.
General Crook House, 30th & Fort, 455-9990, Italianate brick mansion, with beautiful Victorian gardens stands on the site of Fort Omaha; built in 1879 by the outpost's first commander, General George Crook. Mon–Fri 10am–4pm, Sun 1pm–4pm, $3.50. Tours of city arranged from the house.

INFORMATION/TRAVEL
Visitors Bureau, 1819 Farnam, Suite 1200, 444-4660.
Events Hotline, 444-6800.
Student Center, U of Nebraska, 60th and Dodge Sts, 554-2383. Helpful with accommodation, rides, general info.
Greyhound, 16th & Jackson, 341-1900.
Amtrak, 1003 S 9th St, 342-1501.

LINCOLN The Nebraska State Capitol dominates this cow town and many miles of surrounding plains. This is home of the Unicameral, Nebraska's unique one-house, non-partisan legislative body—an improvisation made during the Depression to save money.

The capitol, 'Tower on the Plains', was not blown in by tornado, despite what its incongruent appearance may suggest, but architect Bertram Goodhue did come all the way from New York City in 1920 to design this early 'skyscraper'. The broad base of the building represents the plains; the tower the aspirations of the pioneers.

Lincoln was home to William Jennings Bryan, a populist who three times was the Democratic Party's presidential candidate around the turn of the century, and who finally made a monkey of himself at the notorious Scope's Monkey Trial in Tennessee. His house stands at 4900 Summer Street.
The telephone area code is 402.

ACCOMMODATION/FOOD
Cornerstone Youth Hostel, 640 N 16th St, on U of Nebraska campus, 476-0355. $8 AYH members, $10 non-members. 11pm curfew.
P.O. Pears, 322 S 9th St, 476-8551. A college hangout with cheap beer, good burgers, and live music.

OF INTEREST
Sheldon Memorial Art Gallery houses a fine collection of 20th century American art and sculpture garden. At 12th and R Sts, 472-2461. Open Mon–Sat 10am–5pm, plus 7pm–9pm Thur–Sat; Sun, 2pm–9pm; free.
State Capitol. In Art Deco style with a bit of everything inside. Open Mon–Fri 9am–5pm, Sat 10am–5pm, Sun 1pm–5pm; guided tours on the hour; 471-2311.

Roller-Skating Museum, 4730 South St, 483-7551. See the world's largest collection of roller skates, including skates on stilts and skates worn by dancing bears, horses. Free; Mon–Fri 9am–5pm.

INFORMATION/TRAVEL
Tourist Information Center, 301 Centennial Mall S, 471-3796.
Chamber of Commerce, 1221 N St, #320, 476-7511.
Greyhound, 940 P St, 474-1071.
Amtrak, 201 N 7th, 476-1295.

ALONG THE PIONEER AND PONY EXPRESS TRAILS The Oregon, Mormon and other pioneer trails plus the Pony Express routes followed the Platte River, which today is paralleled in large part by Interstate 80 and by Hwys 30 (east) and 26 (west).

The land outside of Omaha lies flat and covered with farms. If you like corn, you should be in heaven here. Two and one-half hours west from Omaha, in the town of **Grand Island** on Hwy 34, is the **Stuhr Museum of the Prairie Pioneer**, (308) 381-5316, a preservation of a small frontier village of the late 1800s. $6. Picnic area.

Going east to west: at **Gothenburg** in midstate, you can see two original Pony Express stations (one at 96 Ranch St) and an old stagecoach stop with bullet holes still in the walls. At **Lafayette City Park**, free camping. **North Platte**, long-time home of scout and show biz personality Buffalo Bill Cody, offers a free look at his ranch house—a pretty but prissy-looking Victorian affair. At **Scout's Rest Ranch State Park**, $2 per vehicle entrance fee, (308) 535-8035. Nightly rodeos are held across from the park at 8.30pm in the summer; B Bill got his nickname for killing 4280 buffalo in 17 months while employed by the railroad to supply meat for its crews.

At **Bayard** further west, the Oregon Trail Wagon Train company offers 1- and 4-day treks which circle **Chimney Rock**. Meals (including pioneer items like vinegar pie and hoecakes), wagon driving or riding, and other activities from an Indian 'attack' to prairie square-dancing for about $150 a day. They also do 3-hr covered wagon tours to Chimney Rock and back, for $7.50 per person. Book through Oregon Trail Wagon Train, Rt 2, PO Box 502, Bayard, NE 69334 or call (308) 586-1850.

Scotts Bluff and **Chimney Rock**, off US 26 in western Nebraska, are two rock formations that served as landmarks for the frontier families. Both are climbable with poignant pioneer graves and clearly defined wagon ruts. The park rangers at Scotts Bluff give daily lectures in summer and the pioneer campsite can be visited. Spectacular views from the bluff.

NORTH DAKOTA

Virtually border to border farmland, interspersed with missile sites, North Dakota grows lots of wheat, sugar beets and cattle. Its superlatives aren't exactly the kind to make you rush up here: it has the world's largest concrete buffalo (in Jamestown), concrete Holstein (in New Salem) and steel turtle with movable head (40,000 lbs in Dunseith). Not to mention the

longest road without a curve—110 miles of tedium on Rte 46. But do explore the Badlands and the simple pleasures of what Teddy Roosevelt called 'the roughrider country', in the west, accessible by bus to Medora.
The telephone area code for the state is 701.

BISMARCK Capital and craftily named by the Northern Pacific railway after Otto von B in the hope of getting German marks to capitalise railroad construction (it worked).

OF INTEREST
State Capitol Building, 224-2000. Famous sons and daughters in the Roughrider gallery: Eric Sevareid, Peggy Lee, Lawrence Welk, Roger Maris. Take the elevator to the 19th floor to the observation deck and see for miles and miles over the plains. Open daily in summer Mon–Fri 8am–5pm, Sat 9am–4pm, Sun 1–4pm; free.
North Dakota Heritage Center (on Capitol grounds), 244-2666, has an Indian collection called one of the finest in the world. Many personal effects of Sitting Bull. Not to be missed: the Indian crafts store—outstanding and authentic artifacts for sale. Mon–Fri 8am–5pm, Sat 9am–5pm, Sun 11am–5pm; free.
United Tribes International performs a **pow-wow** in early Sept, where you can see native Americans dance, play drums and chant in full costume. Others take place sporadically at Indian reservations, check with tribal offices at Ft. Totten, Turtle Mountain and others.

INFORMATION/TRAVEL
Bismarck Visitors Bureau, 523 N 4th St, 222-4308.
North Dakota Tourism Dept, Liberty Memorial Building, near the state capitol, 224-2525.
Amtrak, 400 1st Ave SW, Minot, 852-0358. The nearest station to Bismarck, it lies on the 'Empire Builder' Chicago–Seattle route.
Greyhound, 1237 W Divide Ave, 223-6576.

LEWIS AND CLARK TRAIL By auto or on foot, you can retrace the explorers' route of 1804 south along the Missouri River. Points of interest include: **Ft Yates** (Sioux national headquarters), **Ft Lincoln** (from which Custer and the 7th Cavalry rode out to defeat), **Ft Mandan** (where Sakakawea joined Lewis and Clark), buffalo wallows, **Knife River Indian Village**, and **Sitting Bull Historic Site**, where the leader was originally buried. Great hunters, 600 Sioux braves once killed over 6000 buffalo in three days in 1882. An excellent Indian campground one mile west of Ft Yates at Long Soldier Coulee Park, open year-round.

BADLANDS AND ROOSEVELT NATIONAL PARK There are three units, spread over 75 miles of rough terrain. Described as 'grand, dismal and majestic', the Badlands formations are best seen early morning and late afternoon. (Not to be confused with South Dakota's Badlands, which are bigger and badder.) The south unit near Medora has a 36-mile loop with scenic overlooks, buffalo and prairie dogs, and a campground at Cottonwood. Teddy's **Elkhorn Ranch** is very remote; the ranch ultimately showed a net loss of $21,000 but he loved the area, saying: 'I owe more than I can ever express to the men and women of the cow country'. Sully Creek Campground, two miles from Medora: 'Primitive, can get cold but very convenient to Roosevelt if one has a car.'

INTERNATIONAL PEACE GARDENS On the US/Candian border—the world's longest unfortified border. The formal gardens commemorate years of peace between the countries. Enter via **Dunseith**. Open daily 7.45am–9.30pm; $7. Tel: 263-4390.

OHIO

Ohio makes everything and more of it than anybody else: comic books, coffins, Liederkranz cheese, bank vaults, vacuums, false teeth, playing cards, rubber, jet turbine engines, soap, glassware—you name it. Small wonder that Ohio also produced America's first billionaire: John D Rockefeller. They're always tinkering in Ohio, birthplace of the cash register, the fly swatter, the menthol cigarette and the beer can, not to mention one of the Wright brothers, Thomas Edison, John Glenn and Neil Armstrong.

Get out of its highly industrialised cities and you'll discover a surprising amount of green and gentle countryside, full of lakes, wineries (50 of them), farms with roadside produce and local colour from Amish villages to oddities like Hinckley, buzzard capital of the world (where you can satisfy that craving for a buzzard cookie). Sinclair Lewis used Ohio as his model setting for small town America in *Babbit*, a novel written in 1922 about a businessman whose individuality is eliminated by Republican pressures to conform.

The state also has some of America's best roller coasters and amusement parks, the largest state fair in the US, over 1000 festivals (including Twinsday at Twinsburg) and is birthplace of eight presidents. No wonder Ohio ranks third in tourism, behind New York and California.

CINCINNATI Probably unique in being a place which grew to cityhood on steamboat traffic, as many as 8000 boats a year docked at Cincinnati to take on passengers, lightning rods and lacy 'French' ironwork destined for New Orleans bordellos. Besides their practical value, steamboats were raced incessantly, causing huge sums of money to change hands and equally astonishing losses of life—in one five-year period, 2268 people died in steamboat explosions. Settled by Germans, the 'City of Seven Hills' became a leading producer of machine tools, Ivory soap, beer, gin and a variety of ham favoured by Queen Victoria, all without losing its livable, likeable essence.
The telephone area code is 513.

ACCOMMODATION
Anna Louise Residence for Women, 300 Lytle St, near the Taft Museum, 421-5211. S-$15, $42/week if you stay 30-days or longer. Call to reserve weekly rooms.
Cincinnati Home Hostel, 2200 Maplewood Ave, 651-2329. Long walk to downtown. S-$8 AYH.
College of Mount St Joseph, 5701 Delhi Pike, 244-4327, 8 mls W of downtown off Rte 50 on Fairbanks St (it turns into Delhi Pike). Clean rooms in quiet location. S-$15, D-$20. Call for reservations.

University of Cincinnati, Calhoun Residence Hall, Calhoun St, 556-8596. Near Clifton Ave, south side of campus, 2–3 mls N of downtown. Take buses # 17, # 18, # 19, from downtown. AC rooms available; call ahead. S–$24, D–$28, discounts for longer stays.
Camping: Camp Shore Campgrounds, Rte 56 Aurora, (812) 438-2135, 30 miles west of Cincinnati on the Ohio River. $14/site, includes swimming and tennis.

FOOD
Cincinnati's Germanic tradition means it has a number of **beer gardens**. It's also noted for local chili, served '3-, 4-or 5-way'; eg with spaghetti, beans, meat, onions, Cheddar cheese. Chili parlours abound, each with a secret recipe. It's accepted that they all contain cinnamon; rumour has it that **Skyline Chili** adds chocolate too. Here are just a few around town (meal average $4 with soft drink): **Skyline Chili**, 643 Vine St, 241-2020 and at 6th & Walnut, 381-4244; **Gold Star**, 8467 Beachmont Ave, 474-4916; **Hartwell's Empress Chili**, 8340 Vine St, 20 min N of downtown, 761-5599. For a filling $2 breakfast, try **Reba's Diner**, 588 Cheviot Rd, 385-4833.
Also: **Findlay Market**, Findlay & Elm St, 352-3282. Produce and picnic items. Open Mon–Wed 7am–1.30pm, Fri–Sat 7am–6pm.
Izzy's, Elm & 9th, 721-4241. A Cincinnati tradition.

OF INTEREST
Cincinnati Art Museum, Eden Park Dr, 721-5204. Open Tue–Sat 10am–5pm, Sun 1pm–5pm; $5, $4 with student ID & free Sat.
Meier's Winesellers, 6955 Plainfield Pike, 891-2900. Ohio's oldest and largest winery. Free tours of wine making and wine aging, ending with wine tasting. Mon–Sat 10am–3pm; bar and garden open until 5pm.
Taft Museum, 316 Pike, 241-0343. Federal 1820 mansion houses collection of paintings, Chinese porcelains, French enamel, portraits. Mon–Sat 10am–5pm, Sun 12–5pm; $2, $1 students. 'Exquisite. Marred only by poor taste in carpets.'
Tyler Davidson Fountain Square. The centre of downtown activity is around here. Lunchtime concerts, pre and post-ballgame celebrations; shops and businesses.
Union Terminal, 1301 Western Ave, 287-7000. The newly renovated building, an Art Deco gem with the world's highest unsupported dome, now houses 'Museum Center', which includes **Museum of Natural History** where a cavern full of bats and the Ice Age (simulated) awaits; the **Cincinnati Historical Society** has a mock-up of a 1860's street to wander in; and finally pop over to the **Omnimax** to see those films on the big screen. Museums open Mon–Sat 9am–5pm, Sun 11am–6pm; to one museum $5, to two $8 and for everything $12. Call to check Omnimax showtimes.
Krohn Conservatory, Eden Park, 352-4086. One of the largest public greenhouses in the world. Seasonal floral displays. Open daily 10am–5pm; donation encouraged.
Carew Tower, 5th and Vine Sts. From the 49th floor, take a gander at Cincinnati, the Ohio River and Kentucky opposite.
Cincinnati Zoo, 3400 Vine St, 281-4701. Called 'the sexiest zoo in the US' for its successful breeding programme: lots of gorillas, rare white Bengal tigers, an insectarium. Daily 9am–6pm, gates close at 8pm; $6.50.
Contemporary Arts Center, 115 E 5th St, 721-0390. Open Mon–Sat 10am–6pm; Sun 1pm–5pm, $2, $1 with student ID, free Mon and Sun.
Riverboats. At public landing, foot of Broadway. Revitalised riverfront area, including seating at the Serpentine Wall for pleasant boat-watching. Cruises heavily booked and rather pricey, but you can take in arrivals, departures and attendant hoopla and steam calliope-playing for free.

Cincinnati is home base for the *Delta Queen*, genuine relic on the National Register of Historic Landmarks. This is a real paddlewheeler as opposed to the ignoble beasties that ply the waters in hundreds of US cities and towns. *Showboat*

Majestic also docks here, with live theatre nightly; $10, $9 students. On the Covington, KY, side is the *Mike Fink*, a riverboat restaurant with a delectable New Orleans-style seafood bar. Not cheap but you may feel like splurging on catfish, crab legs and chocolate chip pecan pie. For information about year-round cruising, sightseeing, lunches and dinners aboard boats here contact BB Riverboats, at the foot of Greenup St, (606) 261-8500. 1-hr cruises start at $6. Located at **Covington Landing**.
King's Island, in Mason, off I-71, 398-5600. The Midwest's largest and often busiest theme park and the world's longest coaster, 'The Beast'. Over 100 rides and live shows; fireworks nightly. Open daily Memorial Day–Labor Day; $24. 'Need a car to get there.'
The Beach, 2590 Waterpark Dr in Mason, 20 mls N of Cincinnati on I-71, 398-SWIM. One of the ten largest water parks in the US, with a 25,000 sq ft wave pool, as well as speed, giant inner-tube and body slides, $15.

ENTERTAINMENT
Mt Adams, Cincinnati's answer to Greenwich Village, is where the yuppies are. The students hang out in the **Clifton area**, where the University of Cincinnati is. The place to go in this college town is **Calhoun St** or **Short Vine** (1 blk off Vine St). Many bars and clubs, ranging in musical style, dress code, and price in the U district. Try to time your visit for the **Oktoberfest** in mid-Sept; lots of dancing, eating, and beer drinking in downtown area.
Arnold's, 210 E 8th St, 421-6234, between Main and Sycamore downtown. Has jazz, ragtime and swing music along with sandwiches and dinners. Cincinnati's oldest bar.
Blind Lemon, 936 Hatch St, Mt Adams, 241-3885. Old-fashioned decor. Pop, acoustic guitar music at 9.30pm, no cover.
Music Hall, 1241 Elm St by Lincoln Park Dr, 721-8222. Classical music; discounted student tickets 10 min before performances. Call **River Bend**, 348-2229, for ticket info on these concerts; pop, rock and more.
Playhouse in the Park, 962 Mt Adams Circle, 421-3888. A theatre in the round with plays Oct–June, cabaret in the summer. Student rush tickets on sale 15 min before performances.

SPORT
Cincinnati Reds games, 421-REDS, at Riverfront Stadium. America's first professional baseball team. The Bengals football team also play at Riverfront Stadium, 621-3550.

INFORMATION/TRAVEL
Visitors Information Center on Fountain Square, in the heart of town, 421-INFO.
Greyhound, 1005 Gilbert, (800) 231-2222. A long walk from city centre.
Amtrak, 1901 River Rd, 651-3337.
Metro Buses, 6 E 4th, 621-4455. Rush-hour fare of 80¢, 65¢ off peak.
Greater Cincinnati International Airport is actually in Kentucky, about 13 miles away. Jetport Express, (606) 283-3702, runs shuttle buses there from downtown hotels for $10 o/w every half-hour.

COLUMBUS Writer O Henry once did three years for embezzlement in a Columbus cell, while in confinement he produced some of his best stories. Local humorist James Thurber attended Ohio State University briefly and set his play *The Male Animal*, there. This capital city sits in a region intriguingly called Leatherlips, the name of a Wyandot Indian chief who was executed by his people for siding with palefaces.
The telephone area code is 614.

ACCOMMODATION
Heart of Ohio Hostel, 95 E 12th Ave, 294-7157. $10 AYH, $13 non-members. 'Superb. Highly recommended.' Take #2 bus.
YMCA, 40 W Long St, 224-1131. Men only; S-$16.25 + $5 key deposit.

FOOD/ENTERTAINMENT
Blue Danube, 2439 N High St, 261-9308. Good, cheap restaurant with generous portions.
The French Market/Continent, 6076 Busch Blvd. All kinds of European restaurants and foodstalls.
Good eating places in the **German Village**, bus from High St. Also at **North Market**, 29 Spruce, a century-old centre for produce.
For nightlife, try **North High St**, 2 mls N of downtown. This is where the Ohio State University students go.

OF INTEREST
Center of Science and Industry (COSI), 280 E Broad St, 228-2674. 4 flrs of science, health, industry and history exhibits. Open Mon–Sat 10am–5pm, Sun noon–5.30pm; $5, $3 with student ID. 'Worth it.'
Columbus Zoo, 9990 Riverside Dr, 645-3550. Exit 20, Sawmill Rd, off I-270 outer belt. 100-acre zoo. Impressive collection of great apes, including the first gorilla ever born in captivity; only zoo in the world housing four generations of gorillas. Open daily 9am–6pm. $5.
German Village, 624 S Third St, 221-8888. Open daily. Restored 19th century community containing private homes, shops, restaurants.
Ohio State University library: largest collection of Thurber's works, drawings.
Ohio Theatre, 55 E State St, 469-0939. A 1930s cinema with wonderful Titian red, gold-spangled baroque interior. 'Amazing decor; organist rises through the floor.'
State Capitol, Broad & High, 466-2125. Open daily until 5pm. Free tours of this historic Greek Revival structure.
Wyandot Lake Amusement Park, adjacent to the zoo, 889-9283, has 43 rides. Open Mon–Thur 10am–8pm, Fri–Sun 10am–9pm, $13.

INFORMATION/TRAVEL
Visitors Bureau, 10 W Broad St, Suite 1300, 866-4888.
Greyhound, 111 E Town St, 221-5311.
Central Ohio Transit Authority (COTA), 228-1776, runs the local buses; $1.35 express routes, $1 basic fare.
Port Columbus International Airport, east of downtown. Take the COTA bus #16 'Long St' from Broad & High, takes about 30 mins, $1.

CLEVELAND Superman was born in Cleveland in 1933, brainchild of 2 teenagers who in 1938 sold all rights for $130 and commenced upon a lifetime of generally fruitless litigation. This earthly urban version of Krypton, like the doomed planet, is an entirely suitable birthplace for the 'Man of Steel'—at once an industrial powerhouse, but looking like Dresden after the war. Iron and steel were once the big money-earners; also shipbuilding, for Cleveland is on Lake Erie—the Great Lakes a great fissure through the core of America—with ocean-going ships tied up along its waterfront. John D Rockefeller spun his oil business here into one of the largest personal fortunes the world has ever known. Downtown is thick with corporate headquarters, while the symphony orchestra and municipal art museum and other cultural endeavours rank amongst the finest in the US.

Cleveland will be site of the Rock and Roll Hall of Fame designed by

IM Pei, an honour won after an arduous battle with Philadelphia and San Francisco. It will open in late 1995. It has good credentials: one of its disc jockeys coined the phrase 'rock & roll' and the city hosted the very first rock concert in 1952.
The telephone area code is 216.

ACCOMMODATION
Brooklyn YMCA, 3881 Pearl Rd (W 25th St), 749-2355; $28 nightly, $77 per week.
Knight's Inn, I-90 at SR 306, exit 193, 953-8835. D–$47.
Red Roof Inn, I-90 & Crocker Rd, exit 156, Westlake, 892-7920. D–$57.
Camping: Woodside Lake Park, 2256 Frost Rd, 626-4251. 35 miles east of downtown, off I-480, in Streetsboro. Campsite $15.

FOOD
Hungarian restaurants are Cleveland's pride: various along Buckeye Rd; the best is **Balaton**, 921-9691. Cleveland is also the home of the **'National Rib Burn-off'** held Memorial Day weekend, bringing in best ribs from all over the world. As one would guess, a restaurant in this host city has even won the competition; **Geppetto's**, 3314 Warren Rd, 941-1120. And the prices are reasonable.
The gastronomic cross-section at the **West Side Market**, 25th and Lorain Ave, has old world vibes, inexpensive and mouth-watering selection.
The Arcade, Euclid Ave, east of Public Square. 5-level mall, filled with a wide variety of ethnic restaurants.
Coventry Road area in Cleveland, interesting stores and food shops.

OF INTEREST
Museum of Art, 11150 East Blvd at University Circle, 421-7340. Free and first-rate, second only to the NY Metropolitan. Open Tue, Thur, Fri 10am–6pm, Wed 10am–10pm, Sat 9am–5pm, Sun 1pm–6pm.
Museum of Natural History, Wade Oval University Circle, 231-4600. Open Mon–Sat 10am–5pm, Sun 1pm–5.30pm; $5, $3 w/student ID, free Tue & Thur 3pm–5pm.
NASA-Lewis Research Center, 21000 Brookpark Rd, adjacent to Cleveland Hopkins Airport, 433-4000. Exhibits of NASA work. Mon–Fri 9am–4pm, Sat 10am–3pm, Sun 1pm–5pm.
Shaker Historical Museum, 16740 S Park Blvd, Shaker Heights, 921-1201. Open Tue–Fri 2pm–5pm, Sun 2pm–5pm. Once the site of a rural commune begun by the Shakers, a religious sect who turned their backs on industrialization for 10 minutes—and along came Cleveland! Today's Shaker Heights is a ritzy suburb with good (and not always expensive) restaurants.
Sea World, a 90-acre marine life park with only Tsunami wave pool in Midwest. $21, $14 after 7pm in summers. Take Solon Exit off I-480 east from downtown, 995-2121.

ENTERTAINMENT
Cleveland Ballet, 1375 Euclid Ave, 1 Playhouse Sq, 621-2260. Professional repertory ballet, featuring modern and classical work.
Cleveland Orchestra, Severance Hall, 11001 Euclid Ave, 231-7300. World-famous symphony orchestra established in 1918, presenting a variety of concerts.
Cleveland Playhouse, 8500 Euclid Ave, 795-7000. 3-theatre complex. The season runs Jan–June, Oct–Dec.
The Flats, NW of Public Square, where the Cuyahoga River meets Lake Erie. Many rock bars and good eating establishments including **Fagan's**, 996 Old River, 241-6116 ('live music and excellent food').

INFORMATION/TRAVEL
Visitors Information Center, 3100 Tower City Centre on Public Square, 621-4110.
Greyhound, 1465 Chester Ave, (800) 231-2222. 'High crime area—take extreme care, especially at night, even in restrooms.'
Amtrak, Lakefront Station, 200 Cleveland Memorial Shoreway, 696-5115.
Regional Transit Authority, 621-9500, runs buses and the rapid rail system. Basic fare on buses, $1.25; express buses and rail, $1.50.
Cleveland Hopkins International Airport, 265-3729. About 11 miles from downtown, the easiest, cheapest and quickest way to get there is to take the #66X—Red Line train; $1.50 o/w.

TOLEDO A must-see in Ohio is the **Toledo Museum of Art**, 2445 Monroe Street at Scottwood Avenue, Toledo, (419) 255-8000. Houses the finest collection of glass in the US; founded by Edward Libbey, who brought the glass industry to Toledo in 1888. Open Tue–Sat 10am–4pm, Sun 1pm–5pm; free. A good day trip from Cleveland or Detroit—or stay at **Toledo AYH Hostel**, 4027 McGregor Lane, (419) 474-1993; $6 AYH, $9 non-member.

SERPENT MOUND STATE MEMORIAL and MOUND CITY NATIONAL MONUMENT South of Chillicothe near Locust Grove and 3 miles north of Chillicothe are these two Indian sites in south central Ohio. The first is the largest Indian effigy mound in the US, built by the Adena culture *circa* 1000 BC. 'Unforgettable, majestic and truly amazing that it's still around at all.' In summer, green grass covers the enormous coils, making them even more sinuous. The Mound City group dates back 2000 years; the 23 burial mounds are described as 'the city of the dead'. One contains a window through which you can view a mica grave, four cremation burials and numerous artefacts. Open mid-June until Labor Day 8am–7pm, $2 per person entrance fee, $4 per car load.

SOUTH DAKOTA

The Coyote State is living proof that bad weather (from 40 below zero to a blazing 116 degrees) can't be all bad. To look at its tourist brochures, you'd think the place was full of nothing but jolly Anglo hunters, ranchers and fishermen. It has, however, a large (mostly Sioux) Indian population on nine reservations, regarded as 'uppity Injuns' (and worse) for their quixotic determination to win back more of their traditional lands. It was the discovery of gold in the Black Hills (verified by that catalytic figure, General Custer) that spelled doom for the fierce Sioux nations: today gold continues to be South Dakota's leading mineral.

Concentrate on the scenic western section: Mt Rushmore, the Black Hills, the Badlands. Because of distances and lack of public transit, it's difficult to sightsee without a car. Wyoming's Devil's Tower is only 35 miles from the South Dakota border, but you'll need a car to reach it as well.

The state's newest tourist attraction is what Kevin Costner left behind, namely the sets from his earnest and politically correct epic, *Dances With*

Wolves. It's possible to visit Ft Hays, a whole faux fort, through Prairie Adventures, 342-4578; the camp by the river where the tribe celebrates its buffalo hunt and where Costner gets married, Dakota Vistas, 347-3138; the Sioux winter camp that ends the film is in Little Spearfish Canyon in the Black Hills National Forest.

National Parks: Wind Cave
Badlands.

The telephone area code is 605.

RAPID CITY A strategic spot for exploring the Black Hills and Badlands, itself a hodgepodge of tourist claptrapery.

ACCOMMODATION/FOOD

Bunkhouse Lodge in nearby Custer, 673-3029. $9.

College Inn Motel, 123 Kansas City St (part of National College), 394-4800, (800) 752-8942 within the state. D–$65. 6 blks from bus depot. 'Clean, well furnished.' Pool, laundry, cafeteria.

YMCA, 815 Kansas City St, 342-8538. $10 AYH. Summer only. 12 singles (no bedding) in coed room. You can reserve by postcard, zip code 57701, or phone ahead. **JB Big Boy Restaurant** around the corner.

Tally's, 530 6th St, 342-7621. Downtown; good food for not much money. 'Nice food and good locale.'

OF INTEREST

Sioux Indian Museum and Crafts Center, West Blvd between St Joe and Main Sts, 348-0557. Wonderful collection of historical objects, excellent crafts, all the contemporary Sioux artists from Oscar Howe to Herman Red Elk. Sioux are noted for beadwork, stone pipes, quillwork. Open winter Tue–Sun 10am–5pm, Sun 1pm–5pm; in summer Mon–Sat 9am–5pm, Sun 1pm–5pm. 'A waste of time.'

Caves in the Rapid City region: Sitting Bull Crystal Caverns, 9 mls S on Hwy 16 (heading toward Mt. Rushmore), has calcite dog-spar crystals. Open daily 7am–7pm, $5.50. **Diamond Crystal Cave** is closest: 'Quite long but very pleasant walk.' '**Bethlehem Cave Drive** is superb though bumpy. Best cave in Black Hills.'

INFORMATION

Chamber of Commerce, Rushmore Plaza Civic Center, 343-1744. Useful maps. Ask for the South Dakota Vacation Guide, with a dandy section on panning for gold and rockhounding. 'Very helpful people.'

TRAVEL

Gray Line Tours, 342-4461 or (800) 456-4461 (out of state). Different itineraries of Black Hills, Rushmore, Devil's Tower, Custer Game Refuge: June–mid-Oct. Leaves daily at 9am, returns 5pm, pickup from various hotels. $28 and up for the day. The fully narrated 9-hr Black Hills tour is 'quite extensive; well worth the money'.

Stagecoach West, 343-3113. An alternative to Gray Line for tours to the Black Hills and Mount Rushmore.

DEADWOOD Twenty-eight miles northwest of Rapid City via I-90, Deadwood calls itself 'where the West is fun!' but 'where the West is wax' might be more like it. Once the stomping ground for Calamity Jane, Wild Bill Hickok, Deadwood Dick and the rest, but amazingly ordinary today.

ACCOMMODATION

Super 8 Motel, Hwy 85 S, 578-2535. Reasonable for groups of 4 or 5; around $80 nightly. Discounted after Labor Day. 'Pool, sauna, friendly, very clean.'

OF INTEREST

Number 10 saloon, Main St. See the chair where Wild Bill Hickok was gunned down while holding a poker hand of 2 aces and a pair of eights—still called 'a dead man's hand'. Hickok was never punished for any of his killings, several of which were clearly murders; *his* killer was hanged, however.

Adams Memorial Museum, 578-1714, Sherman St in downtown. 'Interesting.' Gold-mining train, Wild Bill's marriage certificate and a sea of other nonsense. Open summer, 9am–6pm; free.

The Ghost of Deadwood Gulch, 678-3583. A wax museum where a play called *The Trial of Jack Mcall* is performed every night except Sun in summer. Starts with dramatic capture of Hickok's killer, continues with trial in town hall. 'A laugh.'

Mt Moriah 'Boot Hill' cemetery. Good place to do gravestone rubbings: Calamity, Wild Bill are here.

Nearby: Lead (pronounced Leed), a steep little mining town with the largest gold mine in the western hemisphere, the **Homestake**, 584-3110. Surface tours May–Sept, $3. Half a million ounces of gold are mined each year; about 13 million tons remain. 'Free ore sample.' Open Mon–Fri 8am–4pm in May, Sept 10am–5pm w/ends. 8am–5pm in summer.

Spearfish, for 56 years home of the *Black Hills Passion Play*. June–Aug. At 8.15pm on Tue, Thur & Sun; $5–$12. Huge cast in outdoor setting.

THE BLACK HILLS They are poorly named: picture instead high and ancient mountains cloaked with spectacular pine forests, a green citadel above the vastness of tawny plains and considered sacred ground by the Sioux.

OF INTEREST

Wind Cave National Park, 11 miles N of Hot Springs, 745-4600. 28,000 acres. Discovered in 1881, the cave, some 10 miles deep, is named for the winds that whistle in and out of it, caused by changes in barometric pressure. Open daily, 45 mins to 90 mins tours; $2–$5. Dress warmly. Above ground and free, superb animal watching and photographing: deer, buffalo, antelope, prairie dog towns. Dawn and dusk are the best times. 'The candlelight tour is great.'

Custer State Park, 255-4515. Free if you drive through on Highway 16A, otherwise $8 for a 5-day vehicle permit; $5–$10 per site to camp. Over 1600 buffalo, around which you can take a thrilling 1½-hr jeep ride for $15, daily in summer, by appointment otherwise; horseback riding, $13.50 an hr. Any tour through the Black Hills should include **Needles Highway**, past spectacular vulcanic pinnacles. Someone once wanted to carve these into Wild West heroes, the genesis of the Rushmore idea. There are two concessions here: the **State Game Lodge**, 255-4541; and the **Blue Bell Lodge**, 255-4531. Check with them for jeeps or horses.

Jewel Cave National Monument, 673-2288. Dog-tooth crystals of calcite sparkle from its walls in the 2nd longest cave system in the US. Park hours and tours are decided each season depending on available federal funds; take the historic tour for $4, more strenuous but fun, if it's offered.

Mt Rushmore, 574-2523. Free including a 12-min film, evening amphitheatre programmes at 9pm. It took 14 years to create the 60-ft-high granite faces of Washington, Jefferson, Teddy Roosevelt and Lincoln, carved by Gutzon Borglum and partly paid for with South Dakota schoolkids' pennies and it is still not finished. Most beautiful in morning light and when floodlit, summer eves. Visitors Center, 8am–10pm. Sculptor Studio, where models and tools are displayed, 8am–7pm, summer only.

Crazy Horse Monument, N of Custer on Route 385. A great Oglala Sioux leader, Crazy Horse resisted white encroachment on Indian lands and at 33 was stabbed in the back by an American soldier under a flag of truce. If ever finished, this completely 3-dimensional monument to him will dwarf Rushmore, ultimately standing 563 ft high and 641 ft long. Korczak Ziolkoski logged 36 years and blasted away some 7 million tons of rock before dying in 1982. His family has carried on and you can see work in progress between 7am–8.30pm, daily. Check with Gray Line tours or drive through, $6 a person, $15 per car load.

BADLANDS NATIONAL PARK Like hell with the fires put out, as the locals used to say, 207 square miles of weird and beautiful buttes, canyons and brilliantly coloured rock formations of clay and sand washed from the Black Hills. At sunset the sandstone slopes turn all shades of pink and purple. Bones of sabre-toothed tigers, three-toed horses and Tyrannosaurus Rex have been found in this arid land once covered by swamps. 'Absolutely amazing—the surprise package of our tour. Come into it at dawn with the sun at your back—it'll blow your mind, it's that good.' 'Well worth the 10-mile hike along rough track to watch the sunset and spend the night at Sage Creek primitive campground. No water on site.'

OF INTEREST

Kodoka, an authentic Western backwater town east of the Badlands on I-90, is the best place to stay overnight to make the favoured dawn drive through the Badlands, emerging at **Wall**. Excellent visitor centre at the **Cedar Pass Badlands entrance**, includes video. To stay, **West Motel**, Hwy 16 and I-90 Business Loop, 837-2427; S–$36, D–$45. 'Clean rooms, friendly staff.'

Wall, notorious for **Wall Drug**, 279-2175, a drug store that mutated into a tourist-trap-run-wild. Roads leading to and from Wall are peppered with some of the 3000 billboards hawking the place; other signs can be found at the North and South Poles, a Kenyan rail station and in the Paris Metro, informing potential customers of the number of miles it is to Wall Drug. Sip free ice water and nickel coffee, buy a rattlesnake ashtray and puzzle over a jackalope, a cross between a jackrabbit and an antelope.

MITCHELL If passing through, take time to see the **Corn Palace**, a vaguely Russian fantasy of onion domes, dazzling pointillistic murals formed of 3000 bushels of coloured corn cobs. Watch artists construct new murals each summer on the outer wall of the civic auditorium. Extraordinary. In Mitchell also, the **Oscar Howe Art Center**, housing work by the most noted Sioux artist of present times. Open Tue–Sat 10am–5pm; donation. Area lodging: **Skoglund Farm** near Canova off I-90, 247-3445. They will pick you up from bus depot at Salem. $30 a night includes two full meals plus coffee at a friendly family operation. Horses to ride, animals to pet on a working cattle ranch.

WOUNDED KNEE 'I did not know then how much was ended. When I look back from this high hill of my old age, I can still see the butchered women and children lying heaped and scattered all along the crooked gulch as plain as when I saw them with eyes still young. And I can see that something else died there in the bloody mud, and was buried in the blizzard. A people's dream died there. It was a beautiful dream. The nation's hoop is broken and scattered. There is no centre any longer, and the sacred tree is dead.'—Black Elk.

The symbolic end of Indian freedom came at Christmastime, 1890, at the so-called Battle of Wounded Knee when the US Cavalry opened fire with rifles and field guns on 120 Indian men and 230 Indian women and children.

Most were murdered instantly; some wounded crawled away through a terrible blizzard. Torn and bleeding, many did not crawl far: a returning army burial party found numerous bodies frozen into grotesque shapes against the snow.

A shabby monument marks the spot 100 miles southeast of Rapid City, a few miles off Route 18 near Pine Ridge.

But their unquiet mass grave nearby continues to serve as a rallying point for this century's Indians. In 1973, at the second battle of Wounded Knee, two Indians died in the 71-day siege of the American Indian Movement, and the chapter is far from over.

NB: although the reservation has a motel, museum and other tourist facilities, don't expect uniformly friendly attitudes toward white faces.

MOBRIDGE On a high hill across the Missouri from Mobridge in north-central South Dakota is Sitting Bull's grave. One of the events preceding the massacre at Wounded Knee was the murder of Sitting Bull, the great Sioux leader, organiser and victor at Little Bighorn. It was carried out by Indian policemen under the eye of the US Cavalry.

The authorities always felt uncomfortable with Sitting Bull alive, regarding him as a subversive figure. In death, however, he became something of a commodity. Originally buried in North Dakota, Sitting Bull's body was snatched by South Dakotans, who planted him in Mobridge. A large stone bust was placed over the grave, just to be sure Sitting Bull stays put. Mobridge has a sculpture of Sitting Bull by Korczak Ziolkowski and ten fine murals by Sioux artist Oscar Howe in the municipal auditorium.

WISCONSIN

A liquid sort of place, Wisconsin: famed for beer, milk and water of all sorts—Wisconsinites gave names to 14,949 of their inland lakes before giving up in despair. On Lakes Michigan and Superior, the state sports no less than 14 ocean-going ports. Other places had gold rushes: Wisconsin had a 'lead rush'.

Politically, the Badger State has swung from the rapaciousness of early lumber barons to the progressive decades of the 'fighting LaFollettes', from Commie witch-hunter Joseph McCarthy to present-day liberal Gaylord Nelson.

Unlike other Midwest states, the cities here are clean, amiable and altogether charming. Of course, so is the countryside, but watch out for mosquitoes the size of aircraft carriers (the price you pay for all those lakes).

Many old railroads have been converted into trails for bicycling, running, hiking and skiing.

MILWAUKEE There's a comfortable, old-shoe feeling about Milwaukee, enhanced by its reputation for good beer, 'brats' and baseball. Remarkably short on grime and slums, long on restaurants and festivals, the city is a

good-natured mix of ethnic groups, especially Germans, Poles and Serbs. In quantity of beer produced, Milwaukee has now been aced out by, gasp, Los Angeles, but for quality this is still Der Platz.
The telephone area code is 414.

ACCOMMODATION

Excel Inn, 115 North Mayfair Rd, Wauwatosa, 257-0140. S–$42, D–$47.
Halter Home Hostel, 2956 N 77th, 258-7692; $10 AYH.
Red Barn Youth Hostel, 6750 W Loomis Rd, 10 miles SW of downtown, 529-3299. $8 AYH.
Red Roof Inn, 6360 S 13th St, Oak Creek, 764-3500. S–$39 up, D–$47–$52.

FOOD

Besides Wisconsin's famous cheeses, Milwaukee is noted for 'beer and brats', the latter a particularly succulent variety of German bratwurst, served boiled in beer and tangy with sauce. If you don't go to a Brewers baseball game and gorge in the sun on beernbrats, you've blown it. Also try local frozen custard at places like Kopps and Gilles. German and Serb restaurants are best bets ethnically, but also check to see if Milwaukee is celebrating one of its ethnic feasts at the lakefront.

OF INTEREST

Miller Brewery Tour, 4251 W State, 931-2337. Open Mon–Sat 10am–3.30pm. Free tour, ending with courtesy suds.

TAKE ME OUT TO THE BALLGAME

Baseball may be more American than apple pie. First played in modern form, it's said, by Abner Doubleday in Cooperstown, New York, 155 years ago (in 1839), America's national sport is an inexpensive ($5 and up) treat not to be missed. The pleasure of watching a game on a warm summer evening, beer and hot dogs in hand, cannot be beaten. Along the way, brush up on your ballgame terms, such as steal, chopper, pop-up, fly, walk, bunt, line-drive, slider, RBI, ERA, ball four, bottom-of-the-ninth, watermelon, strikeout, etc. These are the two leagues, both including a Canadian team, the winners of which meet in the end-of-the season World Series every year:

NATIONAL LEAGUE (est 1876): **East**—Chicago *Cubs*, Montreal *Expos*, New York *Mets*, St Louis *Cardinals*, Pittsburg *Pirates*, Philadelphia *Phillies*, Florida *Marlins*.
West—San Francisco *Giants*, Houston *Astros*, San Diego *Padres*, Cincinnati *Reds*, Los Angeles *Dodgers*, Atlanta *Braves*, Colorado *Rockies*.
The National gained, as part of the 1993 'expansion', two new teams—the Marlins (based in Miami), and Rockies (based in Denver).

AMERICAN LEAGUE (est 1900): **East**—Baltimore *Orioles*, Toronto *Blue Jays*, Boston *Red Sox*, Milwaukee *Brewers*, Cleveland *Indians*, New York *Yankees*, Detroit *Tigers*.
West—Oakland *Athletics*, California *Angels*, Kansas City *Royals*, Texas *Rangers*, Minnesota *Twins*, Seattle *Mariners*, Chicago *Whitesox*.

BALLPARKS: Candlestick Park/San Francisco Giants, where 60,000 fans were rocked by the October '89 earthquake as they waited for the start of Game Three of the World Series against the Oakland 'A's. **Comisky Park/ Chicago Whitesox,** (312) 924-1000. Has craziest fans who staged 'Disco Sucks Night' in 1979 and craziest organist Nancy, a jokester who cranks out an appropriate song for every situation and player. As host to the 'Black Sox Scandal', this is where the World Series was fixed in 1919. 'Say it

TAKE ME OUT TO THE BALLGAME (contd)

ain't so, Joe,' they asked of Joe Jackson, one of the eight players involved. See the movie *Eight Men Out*. **County Stadium/Milwaukee Brewers**, (414) 933-9000. Known for the best stadium food and beverage including bratwurst, barbecued chicken and steak with secret sauce. Hank Aaron wound up his career here in 1976 with the major league lifetime home run record of 755. **Dodger Stadium/Los Angeles Dodgers**, (213) 224-1301. Most palatial of the stadia, and probably the only one with as many celebrities in the bleachers as on the field. 1988 World Series opened here, during which Kirk Gibson of LA hit a 2-run homer in the final inning with two outs, giving the Dodgers a 5–4 victory over the Oakland Athletics. **Fenway Park/ Boston Red Sox**, (617) 267-8661. Home of the 'Green Monster' in left field, intimate atmosphere lets you be a part of the game like in the good ol' days. The Red Sox were the first team to win the World Series when it was established in 1903. **Jack Murphy Stadium/San Diego Padres**, (619) 283-4494. Baseball à la California, complete with sunny skies, warm temperatures, and fans in their bathing suits tossing giant beach balls. **Orioles Stadium**, Camden Yards/**Baltimore Orioles**, (410) 685-9800. The new, $105 million, 48,000-seat ballpark downtown opened in 1992. Only 4 blocks from Baltimore's inner harbour, and the newest stadium in baseball, it has a wonderful barbecue-soaked atmosphere. **Oakland Coliseum/Oakland Athletics**, (510) 638-0500. Here baseball combines with the finest sound and video system in the league to create baseball-rock. The team isn't half bad either, though they lost the 1988 World Series to Dodger neighbours. **Royals Stadium/Kansas City Royals**, (816) 921-8000. More than one baseball player has conceded that this is their favourite away stadium. KC barbecue, baked beans and baseball make for a great game. **Toronto Skydome/Blue Jays**, (416) 341-1111. New in 1989, this space-age ballpark has the largest retractable roof in the world, and the first non-US world champions. They won in 1992 and again in 1993. **Wrigley Field/Chicago Cubs**, (312) 404-2824. Oldest in league, and most traditional with ivy-covered walls and hand-turned scoreboard. Join legendary Ronnie in shouting 'Go Cubs, Go Cubs'. **Yankee Stadium/New York Yankees** (718) 293-6000. Wellspring of many baseball legends, including Yogi Berra who, once when a game was poorly attended, is reported to have said, 'If the people don't want to come out to the park, nobody's gonna stop them'. Fans voted unfriendliest by baseball players. The 1927 'Murderers' Row Team' included Lou Gehrig, Bob Meusel, Tony Lazzeri, and Babe Ruth who hit a home run every nine trips to the plate that year. Catch Yankees fans at their most partisan during a game with arch-rivals Boston Red Sox.

Milwaukee County Zoo, 10001 W Bluemound Rd, 771-3040. Open daily 9am–5pm; $6.

Discovery World Museum, 818 Wisconsin Ave, 765-9966. Open Mon–Sat 9am–5pm, Sun 11am–5pm; $3.50, $1.75 w/student ID, Tues 3pm–5pm free. Science and technology exhibits.

Washington Park, NW from downtown, *Music Under The Stars* concerts in July & Aug; free. Call 278-4391 for details.

Public Museum, 800 W Wells St, 278-2700. Walk-through European village of Milwaukee's 33 ethnic groups—charming. The Polish and Serbian houses are beautiful. Also a huge hand-made Costa-Rican rain forest, constructed with wood and other natural materials. Remarkable effect. Open daily 9am–5pm; $4.50, $3 students.

Milwaukee Art Museum, 750 N Lincoln Memorial Dr, 224-3200. Open Tue–Sat 10am–5pm, Thur noon–9pm, Sun noon–5pm; $4, $2 students. Strong in Haitain primitives, 19th century German and American contemporary works, such as some Warhol soup cans.
Mitchell Park Conservatory, 524 S Layton Blvd, 649-9800. Three 7-storey glass domes with different luxuriant botanical gardens: arid, tropical and a seasonal display. Open daily 9am–5pm; $2.50.

ENTERTAINMENT
Fun Line, 799-1177.
Sample the 6000+ taverns—most are rollicking, unpretentious good fun. **Summerfest**, 2-week festival June & July, by lakefront. 'Groups, beer, funfair, massive.' **Festa Italiana** in July, one of the biggest pastafazools anywhere: 'delicious'. Jul–Aug: **German, Irish, Polish Feasts.**
Bombay Bicycle Club, 509 W Wisconsin Ave, 271-7250. Music videos.
Performing Arts Theater, 929 W Water St, 273-7206. The Milwaukee Symphony.
Milwaukee Repertory Theater, 108 E Wells St, 224-9490. First-class plays; $6 and up. Season runs Sept–May.

INFORMATION/TRAVEL
Visitors Bureau, 510 W Kilborn, 273-7222 & 747-4808 at airport.
Amtrak, 433 W St Paul Ave, (800) 872-7245.
Milwaukee County Transit System, 344-6711. Runs the metro area buses, $1.10 basic fare, $8.75 weekly unlimited use pass.
Greyhound, 606 N 7th St, (800) 231-2222.
General Mitchell International Airport, 5300 S Howell Ave. Take the #80 bus from 6th & Wisconsin, $1.10. Takes about 30 mins.

MADISON To some, Madison, wrapped picturesquely around two lakes, is the bastion of enlightened civilization. A famous college town; it is similar to Ann Arbor and Berkeley in its radical activism. It probably has the highest under-employment anywhere; your taxi driver no doubt has a PhD in Medieval Philosophy and your waiter one in Set Theory Topology. The east side has the alternative community, the west side has all those liberal democrats who belong to the ACLU and the Women's Political Caucus. There's a lot packed into this pretty town, plus cheap eats starting at 2 open-air farmers' markets. Rent a bike to get around.
The telephone area code is 608.

ACCOMMODATION
Excel Inn, 4202 E Towne Blvd, 241-3861. S–$40, D–$46.
Wisconsin Center Guest House, 610 Langdon, 256-2621. S–$35, D–$39. On fraternity row. Great frat parties in the vicinity. In **Dodgeville**, 40 miles west of Madison on Hwy 18: **Folklore Village Farm**, Rt 3, 924-4000. $8 AYH, $3 one-time memb. fee.
Spring Valley Trails Home Hostel, RR 2, PO Box 170, Dodgeville, WI 53533, 935-5725. A-frame house available, $10 per person. Write for reservations.

FOOD
Best eateries are on or near campus.
Brat Und Brau, 1421 Regent, 257-2187. Good, cheap burgers, brats and salad bars.
Cafe Palms, in the Club de Washington, 256-0166. After hours, has killer muffins and amusing waiters.
Ella's Kosher Deli, 425 State St, 457-8611. A real deli, standby of natives; sit and shmooze for hours.
The Fess, 123 E Doty, 256-0263. Sat and Sun brunch will leave you stuffed for a week. Never-ending stream of fresh baked goods.
Gino's, 540 State St, 257-9022. Known for its stuffed pizza.

Saturday's Farmers' Market, Capitol Sq, 6.30am–12pm. Beautiful local produce with a festival atmosphere.

Sunprint Cafe and Gallery, 638 State St, 255-1555. Original photographs in cafe setting. Specialities are coffee, soups, sandwiches and pastries.

Willy St Co-op, 1202 Williamson St, 251-6776. A well-run co-op on Madison's east side. You'll be at the heart of Madison's alternative culture while you buy veggies. Open daily 8am–9pm.

OF INTEREST

It all revolves around the campus—a must for briefing yourself on social action, people, and activities throughout the town. Pick up a copy of *Isthmus*, be sure to read 'Dear Ursula'.

American Players Theater, in Spring Green, 45 mls W of Madison, 588-7401. Quality Shakespearean and classical drama performed in the open air. Bring a picnic and enjoy the beautiful countryside. Performances on Tues–Sun evenings mid-June–Oct; $14 and up.

Lakeshore path, start behind the Union terrace and walk out to Picnic Point. You'll meet many joggers and Madisonians talking over their problems.

State Capitol, 266-0382. The story goes that it is just a foot shorter than the one in Washington, DC. Open Mon–Sat 9am–4pm, Sun 1pm–4pm.

Vilas Park Zoo, Drake & Grant. This is not the world's greatest zoo, but Vilas Park has lovely beaches and is a nice place to take a walk. Open daily 9.30am–8pm.

Nearby: Wisconsin Dells, 53 miles north of Madison. 'Magnificent rock and river scenery but terribly commercialised. Only visible by boat.' Inexpensive all-you-can-eat at the **Paul Bunyan Lumberjack** restaurant, 254-8717.

Baraboo, about 40 miles north of Madison. In May 1884, the five Ringling Brothers began their world-renowned circus in a modest way, behind the Baraboo jail. Their former winter quarters is now the site of the excellent **Circus World Museum**, 426 Water St, 356-8341. Daily 1-ring performances, 152 rococo circus wagons, 19th century sideshow, calliope. Open daily 9am–10pm; $11.

Taliesin, the workshop, architecture school and home of Frank Lloyd Wright is west of Madison on Rte 23, 588-2511. There are three different tours: the workshop tour runs daily 9am–4pm, $8; the workshop and gardens can be seen Mon–Fri, same times, $20; and the house itself can be seen at the exorbitant rate of $40, Thurs–Sat, at 10.30am and 12.30pm. Call 588-7948 to reserve tickets. FLW may have been more famous, but the prize for sheer originality has to go to Alex Jordan for his spectacular **House on the Rock**, south of Taliesin in Rte 23, 935-3639. Described by *Roadside America* as 'the Palace of Versailles converted into a Tussaud wax museum by a Kuwaiti sheik', House on the Rock is a mind-boggling conglomeration of mermaids, angels, antiques, enormous things (fireplace, steam locomotive, carousel, theatre, organs), catwalks, bisque dolls, and the heart-stopping 'Infinity Room', a horizontal glass-enclosed needle stretching 140 feet out into the clear Wisconsin air with no visible means of support. *See it*! Open daily 9am–5.30pm for tickets, closes 7.45pm; $14.

LAKE SUPERIOR REGION In northwestern Wisconsin, 2 areas to explore: **Indian Head Country**, extending from the shore of Lake Superior to the Mississippi River; and the **Apostle Islands**, a national lakeshore known for its peaceful beauty. Call 266-2621 or write Wisconsin Dept of Natural Resources, PO Box 7921, Madison, WI 53707, for more information.

In these parts, fishing has become a sort of pagan religion. See a testimonial to Wisconsin fish-worship at the **National Fresh Water Fishing Hall of Fame**, on Hwy 27 in **Hayward**, (715) 634-4440. Icons include gigantic fibreglass statues of beloved sports fish, including a muskie the size of a blue whale (in which you can be Jonah—observation deck inside the muskie's mouth). Open daily 15 April–1 Nov, 10am–5pm; $3.50.

THE MOUNTAIN STATES

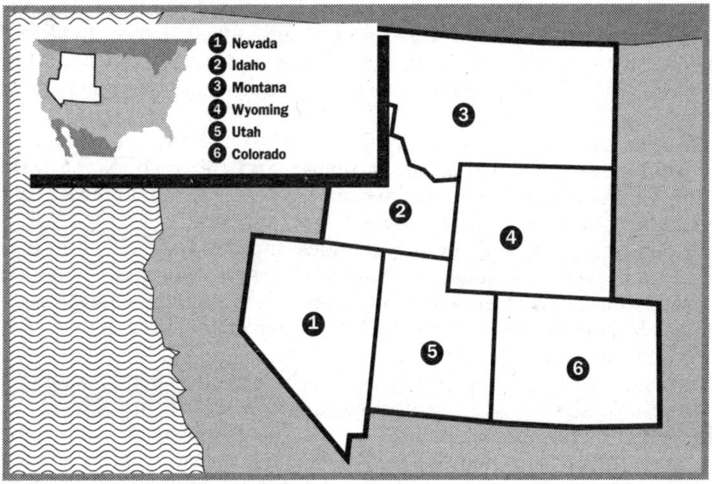

After the endless horizontality of the Midwest, the carefully manicured patterns of fences and townships and agriculture, the landscape of the Mountain States bursts upon you, young and rangy and wild as a colt. These are exuberant mountains, still in their teens: the Rockies, the San Juans, the Grand Tetons. Even now, crossing them is a pilgrimage, an event; just imagine how their sharp white beauty must have made pioneers' hearts sink into their boots.

The topography doesn't limit itself to mountains, either. In this six-state cluster, you are treated to geysers, glaciers, buttes, vast river chasms, vivid canyons in paintbrush colours. The greater portion of this beauty is protected in National Parks and Monuments, among them: Rocky Mountain, Yellowstone, Craters of the Moon, Glacier, Devil's Tower, Zion and Bryce Canyon. Counterpoint to all this natural grandeur is provided by Las Vegas, Reno and Hoover Dam/Lake Mead, without a doubt the most wondrously artificial trio of spots on earth.

Organized outdoor adventures are one way to explore the area. Llama trips, white-water rafting and trekking can be compared and booked at no extra cost through American Wilderness Experience (AWE). Write PO Box 1486, Boulder, CO 80306 or call (303) 444-2632 for a catalogue, which lists various outfitter agencies and trips in the Mountain States, Arizona, New Mexico, California, Oregon, Hawaii, Alaska, Canada, Mexico, Minnesota and West Virginia.

Las Vegas excepted, weather throughout the region is dry and hot in summer, cold and snowy in winter. Even summer evenings can be cold, so plan accordingly.

COLORADO

Horace Greeley, the newspaper editor famous for his advice 'Go West, young man', in truth found the West a bit raw for his tastes. In 1860, he described what he saw on the frontier: 'They had a careless way of firing revolvers, sometimes at each other, at other times quite miscellaneously—so I left'.

Like other mountain states, Colorado had a lusty, shoot-em-up past filled with gold seekers, gold diggers, cattlemen and con men. Many former mining towns remain, some recycled into ski resorts, others tarted up for tourism but still in settings of unparalleled grandeur.

Although manufacturer of mundanities such as luggage and second largest employer of federal government workers, Colorado is a prime tourist destination with good reason. Known as the nation's backbone, the state has 54 peaks over 14,000 feet. Over 75 percent of US land over 10,000 feet is concentrated in Colorado.

The eastern section up to the Rockies has little to offer, being a monotony of rangeland, strewn with dun-coloured tumbleweeds and fenced 'hog-tight, horse-high and bull-strong', as the cowpokes put it. Concentrate instead on the western half, where you find two national parks, awesome scenery and an extraordinary display of summer wildflowers (some 5000 species).

Colorado's many youth hostels, among the best in the US, include ranches, historic hotels and ski lodges.

National Parks: Rocky Mountains
Mesa Verde

DENVER Impressively situated against a backdrop of snowy peaks, Denver has grown to be the single most important metropolis in an area larger than Western Europe. Much of the unpleasant urban sprawl, crime and pollution that plague other American cities has arrived in Denver. Despite this and an ugly decade of rapid development, Denver now sports a modern, well-finished look, befitting its role as banking, government, and industrial capital for the Rocky Mountains.

People pour into Denver by the million each year, many in transit. Since December 1993 many of them have been arriving at the first major, new aiport in the US for 20 years—Denver International Airport. The largest in the world (53 acres), it can handle around 32 million people a year. In 1858 you couldn't see Northern Colorado for dust as thousands of miners left in search of a different kind of dust—gold. As a result, Denver—complete with Colorado's first saloon—emerged and became the state's capital.

With a median age of 30, over 200 parks and more days of sunshine (300) than San Diego or Miami Beach, the 'Mile High' city is teeming with sports-mad enthusiasts. Denver boasts the world's largest sporting goods store (where you shop in golf carts). Its undying love of the Broncos football team has reached saturation point; games are sold out for an undetermined number of years.

The Colorado Rockies, one of baseball's 'expansion' teams of 1993, sell out all of their home games. At present they share Mile High Stadium with the Broncos but from 1995 they will have their own stadium downtown. There is one problem, however: they are drawing crowds of 55,000 plus and the new stadium will only hold 45,000.

Denver was also once a centre of counter-culture, a mecca for spiritualists, faith healers and radical thought. Though the politicized coffeehouses that populated Jack Kerouac's *On the Road* are gone, a lively cultural life still throbs in Denver when the sun goes down. Most likely you'll find the nation's most educated downtown workforce at the movies, as the city leads the nation in attendance.

Downtown Denver revolves around 16th St Mall, a mile-long promenade lined with up-market shops. The building of so many office blocks around the city centre has meant that the Mall is very lively around lunchtime but virtually devoid of activity after 6pm. 'Denver is dead after 7pm. Not the sort of place to walk alone at night.'

The telephone area code is 303.

ACCOMMODATION

Big Al's Youth Hostel, 1714 Humboldt, 393-7165. $10. 'Laid back.' Who is Al?

Denver International Youth Hostel, 630 E 16th Ave at Washington St, 832-9996. Houseparents are good guides to the area. No curfew. $7, must do a chore in the morning ($10 otherwise!), laundry facilities.

Franklin House B&B, 1620 Franklin St, 331-9106. S-$24, D-$35-$45, incl bfast.

Motel 6, Wadsworth Blvd, 232-4924, S-$30, D-$36.

Motel 6, 3050 W 49th Ave, 455-8888. S-$31, D-$37. AC, pool, TV, phones. Bus stop 1 blk away. 'Friendly staff, good service.'

Melbourne Hotel and Hostel, 607 22nd St, 292-6386. S-$18 ($15 w/AYH card), D-$22 ($20 w/AYH card), hostel $8, $9 non-members. 6 blocks from bus stn. 'Brilliant.' 'Good, clean rooms. Staff very helpful.'

Standish Hotel, 1530 California St, 534-3231. S-$18, D-$29. XP-$2. 'Quiet, pleasant, simply furnished. Staff and clientele obviously regarded young people as quite a curiosity.' 'Not for a woman alone.'

YMCA, 25 E 16th Ave, Denver, CO 80202, 861-8300. Coed. Across from city bus stn. Write to make reservations. S-$20-$26, D-$40, $12 key deposit. 'Very limited bathroom facilities.'

FOOD

Try Rocky Mountain trout, the local specialty. This is also the home of 'Rocky Mt oysters', an indelicate dish made of French-fried bull testicles.

Denver Magazine lists dozens of places to eat in Denver, and includes an extensive ethnic restaurant guide. 'Larimer & 17th Sts, variety of quite cheap places to eat—Turkish, Greek, Chinese, French, pizza.'

Casa Bonita, 6715 W Colfax, 232-5115. The all-you-can-eat Mexican platter for $8.29 is not the half of it. This isn't a restaurant, it's a Mexican carnival—with gun fights, cliff divers, mariachi bands. Watch out for other Casa Bonitas (this is a chain) in Tulsa and Oklahoma City. 'Disappointing.'

Duffy's Shamrock, 1635 Court Place near YMCA, 534-4935. 'Good service, excellent value.' 'A godsend for the traditional boozer. Longest bar west of Mississippi. Red and green chili.' 'All-American food.'

The Market, 1445 Larimer St, 534-5140. 'A trendy place to sit and drink coffee, buy health foods, watch people.' $4-$6, self-service.

Observatory Bar and Cafe, El Rancho and Evergreen, (take exit 252 off I-90 West), 526-1988. Open-air dining overlooking the Continental Divide. Free use of telescopes on weekends (but need to check in advance—ask for Bob Randel).

The Old Spaghetti Factory, 18th & Lawrence St, 295-1864, dinners with drink and dessert, $5–$8 in colourful surroundings.
20th St Cafe, just behind Greyhound bus station at 1123 20th St, 295-9041. 'Good cheap breakfast and lunch in clean and friendly surroundings.'

OF INTEREST

Art Museum, 100 W 14th Ave Pkwy, 575-2793, $3, $1.50 w/student ID. Striking, fortresslike building covered with a million sparkling tiles. Six floors of well-displayed art from totem poles to Picasso. Second floor, Native American art collection. 'Exhibits on Indians more interesting and paintings better than in many small US galleries.' Tue–Sat 10am–5pm, Sun noon–5pm.
Black American West Museum, 3091 California St, 292–2566. Black pioneer history. Founded by Paul Stewart, now in his 60s, who as a child was told he could only play the Indian—'there are no black cowboys'. Wrong again, as his museum proves. Also pays homage to western black women. Open Wed–Fri 10am–2pm, Sat noon–5pm, Sun 2pm–5pm or call for an appointment. $2. (Be sure to meet Paul if you get a chance, he tells great stories.)
Colorado History Museum, 13th and Broadway, 866-3682. The 112-ft time line spans 150 years of Colorado history, with documents, maps, photos, and artifacts. Open Mon–Sat 10am–4.30pm, Sun noon–4.30pm; $3; $1.50 w/student ID.
Larimer Square, 14th to 16th Sts. Denver's restored Victorian and highly commercial 'heart', with gaslit lamps and horse-drawn carriages. Bring brass or take a pass. Larimer Square runs into **16th Street Mall**, Denver's $76 million pedestrian path with more shops and eateries and free shuttle buses. Nearby is the glittering new **Tabor Center**, a completely glass-enclosed shopping complex, named after an 1890s gold rush bonanza king.
Denver Center for Performing Arts, 2 blks southwest of Larimer Square, 839-4000. High-tech acoustics here: sound is controlled by dozens of 'floating' discs suspended from the ceiling of the nation's first symphony in the round. Free tours.
Museum of Natural History, Colorado & Montague Sts in City Park, 322-7009. Recommended for its detailed dioramas, meteorite and mineral collections, dinosaur displays. Laser and rock shows at planetarium, $5. IMAX giant screen cinema, $5. 'Exhilarating experience.' Open 9am–5pm.
Museum of Western Art, 1727 Tremont Place, 296-1880. Tue–Sat 10am–4.30pm; $3, $2 students w/ID. Russell's classic cowboy sketches, sculpture and paintings by Remington, O'Keeffe and many other western artists are housed in this former gambling hall and brothel. An underground tunnel connected this house of ill repute to **Brown Palace**, a beautiful grand dame hotel with stained-glass roof.
The Molly Brown House Museum, 1340 Pennsylvania St, 832-4092. The Titanic sunk, but Molly didn't, earning her fame & the name 'unsinkable Molly Brown'. 'Interesting story, uninteresting museum.' $3. In summers, open Mon–Sat 10am–4pm & Sun noon–4pm; in winter, closed Mon & at 4pm other days.
State Capitol, 14th St and Broadway, 866-2604. This dome has been gold-leafed 3 times since 1907, but of true value is the Colorado onyx (the world's entire supply) used in the interior of the Capitol. As you ascend to the top, pause at step 13—it's exactly 5280 feet above sea level. On the deck, a brass marker identifies surrounding peaks. Free 30-min tours Mon–Fri 9am–3.30pm, Sat 9.30am–2.30pm, closed Sun.
US Mint, 320 W Colfax Ave, 844-3582. Free 20-min tours Mon–Fri 8am–3pm. Production stops for two weeks at end of fiscal year, late June/July, though tours continue. Long queues, get there early. Stamps out 35 million coins a day; 'no free samples'.
Nearby: Coors Brewery, 13th and Ford, Golden, 277-2337. Free 30-min tours and suds, Mon–Sat 8.30am–4.30pm. Bring proper ID. 'Very nice people.' From Denver, take bus #16, marked Golden. Overlooking Coors, high above on Lookout

Mt, is **Buffalo Bill Grave and Museum**, 526-0747. Open daily 9am–5pm. Lots of Wild West show and Pony Express artifacts of this flamboyant figure who symbolised the make-believe West. Among other things, you learn here that scalping was unknown to most Plains Indians until introduced by white scalp hunters. $2.

ENTERTAINMENT

Pick up a copy of *Westword*, a free weekly, for info about the arts in Denver.
Buckhorn Exchange, 1000 Osage St, 534-9505. Pricey downstairs restaurant with buffalo and elk entrees. Stick to upstairs, Denver's oldest western bar. Outdoor covered patio Fri–Sat, live music in cocktail lounge (incl folk music and 'old ballads').
El Chapultepec, 20th and Market, 295-9126. 55-year-old jazz bar. 'A real dive, but good jazz.'
Glendale is Denver's 'singles scene' with over a dozen discos, saloons and restaurants crammed into a small area. Bars with discos, outdoor volleyball courts, saddles for bar stools ... you name it.
Red Rocks Amphitheater, SW edge of Greater Denver in Morrison. Listen to summer rock, country & western, pop and classical concerts surrounded by 440-ft red sandstone bluffs. 'Any concert here is a must—the most beautiful setting in the world with spectacular views over the prairies and Denver.' For tickets, phone 640-7334. Park admission is free; shows up to $25.
Top of the Week at the Denver Art Museum, 100 W 14th Ave Pkwy, 575-2793. Live bands in winter, $3. Call to confirm.
Wazee Supper Club, 1600 15th St, 623-9518. Great pizza and downtown neighbourhood bar. No cover. 12 beers on tap, $1.50–$2.25 per glass.
Wyncoop Brewing Company, 1634 18th St, 297-2700. Six beers on tap at all times, all brewed on premises. Stout, porter, light and medium ales, bitter beers. Tours of brewery Sat 1pm–5pm.

SHOPPING

Tattered Cover, 2955 East 1st Ave, 892-1505. Reputedly one of the nation's most outstanding bookshops (so says the *NY Times*). Four storeys with reading lamps and comfy chairs to aid browsers. Will mail books anywhere in the world. Open Mon–Sat 9.30am–10pm, Sun 10am–6pm.

INFORMATION

Visitors Bureau, 225 W Colfax Ave, 892-1112. Also at airport. Summer, Mon–Sat 8am–5pm, Sun 10am–2pm; winters, Mon–Sat 9am–5pm.
Travel Info desk at bus station, run by *the* man, John Shrant. A former hostel owner, Big John can help with nearly anything—check here first, 292-6111. 'The best.'
State Tourism Dept, 1625 Broadway, (800) 433-2656, or 592-5510.

TRAVEL

Greyhound, (800) 231-2222, 1055 19th St & Curtis. Bus service to Salt Lake City is one of the most scenic routes in America. 'The best part is the first 3 hours out of Denver.' 'Do not do it at night, fantastic scenery, too great to sleep through.'
City Bus, RTD, 299-6000, $1 during rush hours, 50¢ mid-day and evenings. $2.50 to Boulder.'
Amtrak, Union Station, 17th and Wyncoop Sts, 534-2812. The 'Sunset Limited', Chicago-LA route runs through Denver and the stretch to Salt Lake City is one of the best in the US, with the train running slowly up into the mountains, through one of the longest tunnels in the US, into beautiful gorges otherwise inaccessible to humanity.
Car rental: Cheap Heaps, 393-0028.
Auto Driveaway, 757-1211. Continental Transportation Inc, 232-1522.

HEADING NORTH TO THE ROCKIES Leaving Denver on I-70 west, one of the most scenic routes north—the Peak-to-Peak Highway—begins near **Central City**, a well-preserved Victorian town with honky-tonk saloons. The discovery of gold in Central City in 1859 turned fledgling Denver into little more than a revolving door, when everyone cleared out overnight to strike it rich. You can still pan for gold in what was 'the richest square mile on earth'.

The final leg of this road, Highway 7, leads to the east entrance of the Rocky Mountain National Park. An alternate route to this entrance at Estes Park, Highway 36, passes through Boulder.

BOULDER Although it's become too popular for its own good, Boulder still makes a scenic and lively alternative to Denver for explorations in northern Colorado. A student mecca, at its grooviest along the Pearl Street Mall: 'fun on Sundays, clowns, magic shows, good eats, lots of young people'. 'Quite a magical place and altogether more interesting than Denver.' 'One of my favorite places in the whole USA. A medium-sized university town, full of life and young people.'
The telephone area code is 303.

ACCOMMODATION
Boulder International Youth Hostel, 1107 12th St, 442-9304. $11, with $5 deposit. Kitchen. 20 mins to mountains. 'Friendly, relaxed.' 'Ill-equipped kitchen.' 'Rather cramped.'

FOOD
Boulder is the only city in the US to own its own glacier, which once served as a delicious water supply.
Alfred Packer Memorial Grill, U of Colorado, University Memorial Bldg, 16th and Broadway, 492-6578. Named after the only man ever convicted of cannibalism in the US. Alf's orgy took place in 1886, when he and 5 others were trapped by blizzards at Slumgullion Pass for 60 days. Alf got 17 years from the judge, who said: 'There were only 6 Democrats in Hinsdale County and you, you son-of-a-bitch, ate 5 of them!' Postscript: Packer became a vegetarian after his release from prison.
Baby Dee's Coffee Shop, University Memorial Blding, 16th and Broadway, 938-1816. A student hang-out; gourmet ice-cream and coffee shop.
Colacci's, 816 Main, 673-9400. Excellent Italian food, huge portions—shared.
New Age Foods, 1122 Pearl St Mall, 443-0755. Cheap, good veggie cafeteria upstairs from health food store. Nice variety and large helpings for $2.50.
Old Chicago Pizza Parlour, 1102 Pearl, 443-5031. Huge selection (110) of beers. Beer monsters can try the 'World Tour of Beers Special' in the bar: drink 25 or more and become a member of the *Foamers* club. Prizes! But don't forget the food: 'Best pizza I've ever tasted.'
Potter's Restaurant, Broadway and Pearl, 444-3100. Large array of soups, sandwiches and salads. Dancing at night.
Village Coffee Shop, 1605 Folsom Ave at 24th St, 442-9689. Massive breakfasts for under $3.

OF INTEREST
Arapaho Glacier, 28 miles west. 1 mile long and 100–500 ft thick, the Arapaho moves at a sedate 11 to 27 inches per year. Nothing to worry about.
U of Colorado, 492-1411, ersatz Spanish architecture, big party place. **Fiske Planetarium**, 492-5001, on campus: 'Worth a visit, especially the laser show'. Open Mon–Fri 8am–5pm, some Sat eves, year-round, varying prices. Laser show $3.50.

ENTERTAINMENT
The Mall, along Pearl St. 'Superb spectacles any summer evening—all free.' Near the mall is **The Walrus**, 1911 11th St, 443-9902. 'Meet lots of students. Cozy, friendly atmosphere.'
On University Hill, **Tulagi**, 442-1369, has cheap eats and drinks, occasional music, and more students.
Colorado Shakespeare Festival, at U of Colorado. Rates 3rd in nation. Call 492-8181 for tickets, $10.

ESTES PARK A hairbreadth away from the park entrance to Rocky Mountain National Park, Estes may be the most convenient place to lodge if you're without wheels. Commercial campgrounds here have showers and are nearer to everything.

ACCOMMODATION
H-Bar-G Ranch Hostel (AYH), 6 mls from Estes Park at the head of Devil's Gulch, 586-3688. $8 per night. Memberships for sale at hostel for $18 to foreign nationals. Former dude ranch with splendid views. 'Lou, the warden, takes hostelers into town every morning at 7.30am and picks people up from the Chamber of Commerce at Estes Park at 5pm.' 'Lou will rent out cars.' 'Best hostel I stayed at.' Open 25 May to 12 September.

FOOD/ENTERTAINMENT
The Lariat, Grand Lake, 627-9965. Western bar.
The Wheel Bar, downtown Estes Park, 586-9381. Cheap liquor, steaks under $10.

ROCKY MOUNTAIN NATIONAL PARK To the Indians and early trappers, these were the Shining Mountains, gleaming with silvery lakes, golden sunrises, blue-white glaciers and snowpacks. Later settlers prosaically dubbed them 'Rocky', but there is nothing prosaic about this wildlife-rich range of mountains and valleys crowned by a cross-section of the Continental Divide. Over 70 peaks in the park are 12,000 feet or more and even the untrained eye can see the clear traces of glacial action and the five active glaciers that remain. **Longs Peak** at 14,255 feet is highest.

Be sure to take the **Trail Ridge Road** (Hwy 34), which follows an old Ute and Arapaho trail along the very crest of a ridge. Along its 50 miles, you actually overlook 10,000ft peaks, alpine lakes, spruce forests and wildflower-spangled meadows. Particularly delightful when the flowers are at their peak, June–July; indeed, snow keeps this and other park roads impassable until the end of May and from late October on.

Other routes lead hikers to a variety of long and short trails. One excellent trail is the 5.6 mile hike from **Glacier Gorge Junction** to **Bear Lake** and **Lake Haiyaha**. At the end of the hike, catch the park bus back to Glacier Gorge. Horseback riding is also popular; horses can be rented at Estes Park and Grand Lake. (Also at Glacier Creek and Moraine stables in the National Park.) The $5 per car entrance fee is valid for seven days. The park has hundreds of trails; for good maps visit the main visitors' centre 2 miles west of downtown Estes Park. Open daily summers, 8am–9pm. Other centres are scattered throughout the park. For info, call Rocky Mountain National Park Office: 586-2371.
The telephone area code is 303.

ACCOMMODATION

Campgrounds near east entrance cost $10 per night: **Moraine Park, Glacier Basin** require booking (through Ticketron, call (800) 365-2267). **Aspen Glen, Longs Peak** and **Timber Creek** are first-come, first served and cost $7. Free back country camping permits for the entire park are available at Back Country Office, Rocky Mtn National Park, Estes Park, CO 80517, 586-4459. 'Glacier Basin has a free bus to the main hiking area. Campsites have no shops or showers so it is difficult without a car.'

Near southwest entrance. Excellent lodging at **Shadowcliff AYH, Grand Lake**, 627-9220. $7.50 AYH, $9 non-members. 'Brilliant Scandinavian-style hostel on cliff overlooking lake.'

South of Grand Lake off Hwy 40 is **Winter Park Hostel**, 726-5356, behind Conoco gas station in town. $7.50 AYH, $9.50 non-members. 1 blk from Greyhound stop; free shuttle transportation from Amtrak stop to Winter Park. Exceptional skiing in winter; hiking/biking in summer. Sat evenings, Jul–Aug, owners will truck you to rodeos, $5 admission. Owner Polly Cullen can help with ideas, info, directions, etc. Hostel receipt entitles you to 25% off bike rentals ($9 a day) and ski rentals ($8 a day), and 10% discount at 4 restaurants (meals then $5–$10); also rafting $35 a day. For pastries, homemade bread and more, go to the British-owned **Carver's Bakery**.

TRAVEL

The best way to get to the park is by car; see car rentals under Denver. **Gray Line** offers daily 10-hr tour of the park for $36, leaving from Denver, 289-2841. Hitching to the park is described as 'very easy'.

COLORADO SPRINGS Founded by bonanza kings and intended as a resort and retirement centre, the Springs grew to become second largest city and a military headquarters for the US Air Force Academy, NORAD and Ft Carson. Trash features like motel sprawl cannot dim the glory of its setting at the base of Pike's Peak. Constant winds at the Peak blow the snow like a banner, an exhilarating sight. The city makes a good base to explore Garden of the Gods, Cripple Creek and Royal Gorge.

The telephone area code is 719.

ACCOMMODATION

B&B Rocky Mountains, 906 S Pearl, Denver, CO 80209, (800) 733-8415. A tad expensive, but a few places for $25–$35. 'Friendly and really helpful people. Recommended for that family feeling.'

Buffalo Lodge, 2 El Paso Blvd, 634-2851. D-$32–$39, T-$44. AC, pool, TV, telephones, laundry facilities, continental bfast, bus stop 2 blks. Trolley to Colorado Springs every hour.

Garden of Gods Campground (AYH), 3704 W Colorado Ave, 475-9450. Summers only; pool. Cabins: $10 AYH. Camping: $18 for 2, members or not; $22 w/hook-up.

Motel 6, 3228 N Chestnut St, 520-5400. S-$35, D-$41. AC, pool. View of Pike's Peak from rooms.

Outlook Lodge, off Hwy 24, west from Colorado Springs, 684-2303. S/D-$49–$60. Includes bfast.

ENTERTAINMENT/FOOD

Poor Richard's Feed & Read, 324 N Tejon St, 632-7721. Part of an entertainment complex with espresso bar, theatre and bookstore as neighbours. Poor Richard's has an art gallery and excellent vegetarian dishes for $5.

OF INTEREST

North American Air Defense Command Headquarters (NORAD), sits 1800 ft below Cheyenne Mountain in its own cavern designed to withstand even a direct

nuclear hit. Tours of the base are very popular and have to be booked months in advance through the tour scheduler, 554-2241, write to Air Force Space Command Public Affairs, attn: Tours Program, Peterson AFB, CO 80914-5002. Cancellation places are available, call for more info; passport number needed.
US Olympic Complex, 1750 E Boulder St, 578-4618. Home of the US Olympic Committee HQ, 14,000 potential Olympians come and train here every year. Free 1½ hr-long tours from the Visitor Center (includes a film). The velodrome is in Memorial Park, 4 blks from main complex. Open Mon–Sat 9am–5pm, Sun 10am–5pm.
Pike's Peak, Lon Chaney of horror movie fame was once a guide to this 14,110-ft peak. Hike the Barr National Recreation Trail or take the 18-mile auto highway that climbs 7039 ft—nearly to the top of the mountain. For experienced mountain drivers only. This is the course of one of the most harrowing and oldest car races in the world, held in July. At the top is the view that inspired Katharine Lee Bates to write *America the Beautiful* in 1893.
Pike's Peak **cog railway**, 685-1045, open May–Oct is $21 to the summit. Follow one of the trails for as long as you like and then walk down. 'The view is breathtaking.' 'Take a sweater.'
Garden of the Gods, NW of Colorado Springs off Hwy 24. 940 acres of stunning red sandstone formations, especially striking at sunrise or sunset. Free. 'Outstanding scenic beauty—next thing to Grand Canyon.' 'Well worth a visit.'
Nearby: Canon City and **Royal Gorge**, the town from which Tom Mix launched his cowboy career and also known through the films *Cat Ballou* and *True Grit*. Little of interest except the art shop at the Colorado State Penitentiary and Royal Gorge, site of the highest suspension bridge in the world, an acrophobe's nightmare. Lousy with tourist claptrap of all sorts (including the sickening aerial tram), but the viewpoint is stupendous. $9.50 for either tram ride or train ride to bottom of the gorge, open daily. You can also find the **Prison Museum** along Rte 50—free admission.
Cripple Creek, on the opposite side of Pike's Peak. The picturesque, but difficult route is via Gold Camp Road (follow Old Stage Road then join up with Gold Camp to avoid the tunnel cave-in)—3 to 4 hrs of gravel and curves (Teddy Roosevelt called it 'the trip that bankrupts the English language'). Far easier is the route by Hwys 24 and 67 (about an hr). In its heyday, Cripple Creek yielded more than $25 million in gold in one year and had the honour of being called a 'foul cesspool' by Carry Nation for its brothels and 5 opera houses. Despite tourism the place has considerable charm. Don't miss the salty cemetery (wry epitaphs, heart-shaped madame's tombstone, wooden headstones, etc) and the superlative melodrama, twice daily Tue–Sun, June–Aug. Stay overnight at the Victorian relic **Imperial Hotel**, 689-2922, with shared bath, w/days D–$49, w/ends $71, to partake of the melodrama downstairs and the excellent buffet dinners. The **Mollie Kathleen Gold Mine**, 689-2465. $7—'very worthwhile—free gold ore' and takes you 1000ft down. Open daily 9am–5pm.

INFORMATION
Colorado Springs Chamber of Commerce, (800) 888-4748.
Cripple Creek Chamber of Commerce, (800) 526-8777.
Greyhound, 120 S Weber St, Colorado Springs, 635-1505. $9 o/w to Denver.

ASPEN 210 miles west of Denver on Highway 82, Aspen is a tasteful, beautiful ski resort and classical music festival site, set amid National Forests and more recently the multi-million spreads of Jack Nicholson, Don Johnson, Melanie Griffith, Cher and others. Most things cost the earth in Aspen but reasonable accommodation can be found here, unlike the case with its patrician sister resort, Vail.
The telephone area code is 303.

ACCOMMODATION

NB: rates are highest in winter, lowest in spring and autumn.

Alpine Lodge, 1240 E Cooper Ave, 925-7351. Summer rates: S/D-$43–$49 with shared bath; bfast incl.

Alpen Hutte, 471 Rainbow Dr, PO Box 919, Silverthorne, (on I-90; get off bus at Silverthorne), 468-6336. $12. Nr Breckenridge ski area.

St Moritz Lodge, 334 W Hyman, 925-3220. Dorms $22 summer ('till Nov), $30–$45 winter, shared bath. Partial kitchen. Sauna, pool.

In nearby Breckenridge:

Fireside Inn, Wellington & French Sts, 453-6456. Summer dorms: $15 AYH, $17 non-members. Hot tub, cable TV.

Camping, free wilderness camping w/running water in **White River National Forest**, which covers nearly all of Pitkin County. Closest: E Maroon, 1 mile NW of Aspen on Hwy 32.

FOOD

Recommended: **Pour la France**, 411 E Main, 920-1151: 'Sit on street and watch the world go by'; **Hickory House** on W Main, 925-2313. 'Good breakfast, lunch, reasonably priced.' $4.95 specials.

OF INTEREST

Aspen Music Festival, 9 weeks late June–Aug, 925-3172. Rivals Tanglewood's Berkshire Festival, in prestige and importance. 'The combination of setting, fresh air and music blew my mind.' Many open rehearsals and other free events.

Gondola up Aspen Mt to 11,000 ft, 925-1220; $11.

INFORMATION

Aspen Resort Association Visitors Center, 328 E Hyman, 925-5656.

The airport lies 5 miles from town; take the county bus from the highway that runs outside the airport, 50¢; it will take you downtown.

ACROSS WESTERN COLORADO The northernmost route will take you through **Steamboat Springs**, an expensive ski resort ('fun and friendly—great skiing'), and ultimately to **Dinosaur National Monument**, which overlaps into Utah. The monument presents striking and lonely canyon vistas (used by Butch Cassidy and Co as a hideout) and the fossil remains of stegosaurus, brontosaurus and other big guys, exposed in bas relief on the quarry face, with more being excavated before your eyes. 'Not at all gimmicky; fascinating to anyone even vaguely interested in paleontology or geology.' NB: quarry, visitor centre is in Utah; see that section.

The major route west is the Interstate 70, which passes through the Eisenhower Tunnel, Eagle and **Glenwood Springs**, an invigorating place to pause for a dip in the world's largest open-air thermal pool. Wyatt Earp's sidekick at the OK Corral, Doc Holliday, lies buried here, his headstone reading: 'He died in bed.' The Interstate continues its scenic paralleling of the Colorado River all the way to Grand Junction, the last town of any size in Colorado and gateway to the towering spires and canyon wilderness of **Colorado National Monument**, 858-3617, $4 per car, $2 on foot, camping available, $7 a site.

Further south is the **Black Canyon** of the **Gunnison National Monument** ('a very special place—deer wander regularly through campsites') near Montrose, and the high adventure of the journey through Ouray and Telluride to Silverton and well south to Durango. **Ouray**, the 'Switzerland of America', is noted for the Camp Bird Mine, which produced $24 million for the Walsh family and remains productive today. With some of the loot, papa Walsh bought his daughter the Hope Diamond.

'Try getting a ride in the back of a pickup truck between Ouray and **Telluride**. The views are spectacular, the road, hair-raising.' Dizzy Gillespie once said, 'If Telluride ain't paradise, then heaven can wait,' as wait it did for Butch Cassidy, who pulled his first bank job here. Interesting buildings from the mining era have earned Telluride national historic landmark status. Telluride is also well-known as a ski resort (inexpensive, too) and festival centre, including the remarkable Labor Day Film Festival (now ranked second only to Cannes) and summer music events from bluegrass and jazz concerts.

The telephone area code is 303.

ACCOMMODATION

Camping at **Dinosaur National Monument**, 374-2216, $5 entrance fee, $8/site with bath and running water; motels at nearby Dinosaur, CO and Vernal, UT. See also *Utah*.

Glenwood Springs Hostel, 1021 Grand Ave, Glenwood Springs, CO 81601, 945-8545. $10.25 members and students. Large record collection and taping facilities. Will pick up from bus or train with advance notice. Kitchen, laundry, free bedding. 'Comfortable'. Rent mountain bikes for $10.

At Grand Junction: Melrose Hotel, 337 Colorado Ave, 242-9636. With shared bath, S–$18, D–$30, $10 AYH. Walking distance to bus and rail stns. Also have 4 day accommodation and hiking tours package, $8.

At Montrose: Mesa Hotel, 10 N Townsend, 249-3773. D–$47. Discounts for multiple night stays. Run by friendly, multilingual Basque couple. Bus station in same blk.

At Telluride: New Sheridan Hotel, 231 W Colorado Ave, 728-4351. S/D–$39. Restored hotel with a bar that appeared in *Butch Cassidy and the Sundance Kid*.

At Silverton: French Baker Teller House, 1250 Greene St, 387-5423. S–$27, D–$36. 'Town worth visiting, price incl. b'fast.'

OF INTEREST

Glenwood Springs Hot Pool, Glenwood Lodge, 945-6571. 'Exhilarating.' 'Especially superb at night.' $6 for all-day pass, 7.30am–10pm.

Million-dollar highway, between Ouray and Silverton. A 6-mile stretch, numbered among the most spectacular in the US.

TRAVEL/INFORMATION

Amtrak: Glenwood Springs, 413 7th St, 872-7245; Grand Junction, 339 S 1st St, (800) USA-RAIL. Both stops on the beautiful 'California Zephyr' route.

Greyhound: Glenwood Springs, 118 W 6th Ave, 945-8501; Grand Junction, 230 5th St, 242-6012.

Grand Junction Tourist Information Center, 759 Horizon Dr, 243-1001. Info, maps.

Glenwood Springs Chamber Resort Association, 1102 Grand Ave, 945-6589.

Dinosaur National Monument. No direct transit, but take bus or Frontier Airlines to Vernal, Utah, where you can rent a car or hitch.

Glenwood Springs: 'Day trip from Denver; take 7.45am bus service to Glenwood Springs. Glorious Rocky Mt scenery along the way. If the bus is not late, you arrive at noon. Swim, eat strawberry waffles at the Pancake House behind bus station and catch 4.20pm bus back to Denver, arriving at 8.10pm. A long day, but worth it.'

Ouray and south: bus route from Grand Junction to Durango passes through

Montrose, Ouray and Silverton. 'Unparalleled scenery; exceeds the Denver-Salt Lake City run. Canyons through 11,000 ft red rock mountains. Best from mid-Sept when aspens have changed to gold.' 'Wrecked cars 500 ft below, left as warning to other motorists.'
Telluride: jeep trail to Ouray over 13,000-ft Imogen Pass. 'Astounding' in a jeep, a truly remarkable accomplishment when covered on foot—as many people do each summer in a 19-mile race.

DURANGO Located in the southwest corner of the state, Durango is as authentically western as a Stetson hat (which incidentally was invented in Colorado in 1863). Billy the Kid and other outlaw types used to make Durango their headquarters; before that, the Spaniards came looking for gold, found it and lost it again when local Ute Indians got fed up with them.

Western hospitality is common currency here, markedly so at the local youth hostel. Durango's location 40 miles east of Mesa Verde makes it a natural base for sightseeing.

ACCOMMODATION

Youth Hostel, 543 E 2nd Ave, 247-9905. $10 AYH and non-members. 'Olsons very friendly, willing to help.' 'Without a doubt the best hostel I've seen—clean, well-equipped, nice garden and BBQ.'

OF INTEREST

The main local attraction is the circa 1882 **narrow-gauge railway to Silverton**, 247-2733. The train runs 45 miles one way and climbs 3000 ft through the sawtoothed San Juan Mts. Round trip takes all day, costs $37 (more if you reserve seat in the elegant parlour car). Runs 2–4 times daily, early May through mid-Oct. It is recommended that you book 'at least 6 weeks in advance'. Others say arriving at 7.15am suffices, but the odds are against you. Alternatively, take the am bus to Silverton and then catch the train back to Durango. 'Plenty of seats on south-bound journey.' 'Beautiful scenery, worth every dollar.'

FOOD/ENTERTAINMENT

'If you're feeling flush, try fresh trout at the **Palace Restaurant**,' 3 Depot Place, 247-2018.
Farquharts, 725 Main, 247-2861, is recommended for boozing and live music.
Diamond Belle Saloon, in the Strater Hotel, 699 Main Ave, 247-4431. 'Authentic saloon atmosphere with ragtime piano.' Also in hotel: **Diamond Circle Theater** has melodramas in the summer every night but Sun, $10.

MESA VERDE NATIONAL PARK 'Far above me, set in a great cavern in the face of the cliff, I saw a little city of stone, asleep.'—Willa Cather.

No matter how limited your tourist plans for the West might be, a visit to Mesa Verde, the finest of the prehistoric Indian culture preserves, is a must. The 80-square-mile area rises 2000 feet above the surrounding plain, gashed by many deep canyons. On the surface of the tableland now covered in junipers and piñon trees, the Indians once tilled their squash, beans and corn, while from the depths of the canyon they drew their drinking water from springs. Originally they built their pueblos on the surface, but later for security dug their homes into the sheer canyon walls.

There are two loops to the park: one leads to **Cliff Palace** built by the Anasazi tribe in 1100–1275 AD, which is a large medieval-looking town containing 220 living rooms, 23 kivas and eight floor levels, all within a single cave. You can climb on parts of it. The other loop, to **Mesa Wetherill**, provides good vantage points for viewing the hundreds of ruins scattered throughout the canyons. The dwellings were occupied for about a century beginning in 1200 and were vacated for unknown reasons, though probably due to drought.

To really enjoy the park, read the park service pamphlet on the centuries of human habitation here. A visit to the museum, with its extensive exhibits of tools, clothing, pottery and dioramas depicting the Anasazi way of life, is also a must for understanding the culture. Admission to park, $5.

ACCOMMODATION

In Cortez: El Capri Motel, 2110 S Broadway, 565-3764. S/D–$46. Cheaper in winter. AC, pool, TV.

In Mesa Verde Park: Mesa Verde Campgrounds, 529-4400, $8, $16 w/hook-up. Showers, store, snack bar, laundry. 'Gets very cold at night; need warm sleeping bag as well as tent.'

TRAVEL

ARA Tours from Farview Lodge in the park, saving non-drivers the 6-mile hike to Cliff Palace. Buses leave at 9.30am and cost $12 for a 3-hr tour; $15 for 6 hrs. Call 529-4421. A free mini-train can also take you part way to Wetherill Mesa. Check all timetables for the park in advance.

Hitching is not allowed in the park, though you can discreetly ask for rides in parking lots.

OF INTEREST

Four Corners. The meeting of Colorado, Utah, Arizona and New Mexico is commemorated with a slab of inscribed concrete where you can sprawl to have your picture taken performing the amazing feat of being in 4 states at once! In summer, Indians from Navajo and other tribes come in their pickups and sell their handcrafted wares, often at much better prices than you'll find in the tourist centres or trading posts.

IDAHO

Rugged with mountains (50 peaks over 10,000 feet), slashed with wild rivers and deep chasms (including the Snake River and Hell's Canyon, deepest in North America), dappled with fishing lakes and hot springs, Idaho is like Colorado without the people or the public transit.

The state was settled by French trappers, later by a mix of Basques, Mormons and WASPS who came to run livestock, mine silver, log timber and grow lots of delicious Idaho spuds. Idahoans are a taciturn lot; interesting, then, that the most famous figures associated with the state were noted for eloquence. One was Chief Joseph of the Nez Perce Indians, who surrendered by saying: 'From where the sun now stands, I will fight no more forever'. The other, writer Ernest Hemingway, was an adoptive Idahoan who chose to live, write (parts of *For Whom the Bell Tolls*), commit suicide and be buried in Idaho.

The most scenic section is the panhandle, located along the northern route taken by Greyhound and crowned by the shattering beauty of Lake

Coeur d'Alene—well worth a stop. The southerly route takes you within 80 miles of the Craters of the Moon and near Sun Valley, but is minimally interesting otherwise.
National Park, Yellowstone (though this is mostly in Wyoming). For main entrances to park, see Montana.
The telephone area code for Idaho is 208.

CRATERS OF THE MOON NATIONAL MONUMENT A grotesque grey landscape of extinct cones, gaping fissures and cave-like lava tubes, the most extravagant of which can be seen from one 7-mile loop road in the 83-square-mile preserve. US moon astronauts spent a day in training here, rockhounding. **Camping**: $8/night on loose rock, mid-April to mid-October only recommended, 527-3257. No public transport to park; Salmon River Stages runs to **Arco**, 19 miles outside the park.

This chilling region, which looks like the day after an atomic attack, is appropriately the home for much nuclear testing and tinkering. 30 miles east is the Idaho National Engineering Laboratory. Nearby **Arco** was the first town lit by atomic power. The area has more nuclear reactors per citizen than anywhere else in the world, and Atomic City needs no introduction. Keep within park limits!

TWIN FALLS Set on a pretty stretch of the Snake River, Twin Falls is near sights of interest and a starting point for a journey into Sun Valley and Sawtooth National Forest. West off US 30, the **Balanced Rock** rests on a base only a few feet in diameter. No sneezing. Five miles northeast of town are thundering **Shoshone Falls**, 52 feet higher than Niagara Falls. Most spectacular in winter. As you head north to Sun Valley on Rte 75, cool off at **Shoshone Ice Caves**, a lava tube spanning three blks, with naturally frigid temperatures and fascinating ice formations. Open daily 8am–8pm; $4.50, 886-2058. 'Bring your coat.'

ACCOMMODATION
Gooding Hotel and AYH, 112 Main St, Gooding, 934-4374. Head west from Twin Falls, exit Hwy 46. Dorms (AYH members only) $10, D–$24. B&B rooms: S–$32, D–$37. Full kitchen and lounge. Located near Snake River—rafting, boating, waterskiing, rock-climbing.

OF INTEREST
Hell's Canyon, on the Snake River, stretches 50 miles and is the deepest chasm in North America (up to 7,900ft deep). To see it by car, Rim View Drive (Rd 241 out of Riggins) is one of the rough roads cut through Hells Canyon Nat. Recreation Area. NB: Some areas are restricted by the Forest Service. White Water tours are available, but are generally expensive. Contact Idaho Outfitters and Guides Association, PO Box 95, T-9, Boise ID 83701, (208)-342-1919 for information.

SUN VALLEY/KETCHUM World-class skiing on ol' Baldy has attracted world-class spenders, their thirst for ultra-resort fare in tow. So for fun go to nearby Ketchum, more congenial and much less ostentatious—but still expensive.

ACCOMMODATION

Ski View Lodge, 409 S Hwy 75, 726-3441. 8 individual cabins, each containing 3 double beds, showers, cable TV, gas heating. D–$49, Q–$71. Cheap camping by the creek.
Pitch a tent free anywhere in **Sawtooth National Recreation Area**, north on Rt 75.

FOOD/ENTERTAINMENT

Desperado's, 4th & Washington, 726-3068. Tacos for $2 and a selection of 15 Mexican beers.
Louie's, 331 Leadville St, 726-7775. In remodeled church building, serving 20 kinds of pizza. Extremely popular.
Pioneer Saloon, 308 N Main, 726-3139. Prime ribs, fresh fish and hefty prices. But cheap beer and *the* place to go in town.

OF INTEREST

You're in one of the best kept secrets of the West, so spend some time hiking in **Sawtooth**. The Chamber of Commerce, 4th & Main St, 726-3423, has maps and info as does Redfish Visitors Center, 774-3376, at the northern end of Stanley Lake. After hiking, relax in one of the many hot springs in the area; the closest is **Warm Springs**, near Baldy Mt ski lift.

BOISE If you've spent the last few hours rendered comatose by the serial passing of small farmhouses either east or west of Boise, you'll probably experience a jolt of hope upon arriving here. Boise, capital of Idaho, is a very pleasant and liveable town, and a good place to plan a white-water rafting trip on the Salmon River.

ACCOMMODATION

Boulevard, 1121 S Capitol, 342-4629. S/D–$27–$37 for room w/ continental bfast.
Cabana Inn, 1600 Main St, 343-6000. S–$29, D–$34.
Capri Hotel, 2600 Fairview, 344-8617. S–$30, D–$35.

FOOD

Noodles, 6th & Main, 342-9300. Slice of pizza and salad for $2.95; $5–$7 pasta dishes w/salad and garlic bread.
At **8th Street Marketplace** are several small cafes and shops, such as **Cafe Ole**, 344-3222, with $5 Mexican lunch specials.

TRAVEL/INFORMATION

Amtrak, 2601 Eastover Terrace, 336-5992. Lies on the 'Pioneer' Chicago-Denver-Seattle route.
Greyhound, 1212 W Bannock St, 343-3681.
Idaho Travel Council, 700 W State St, (800) 635-7820.

COEUR D'ALENE This utterly lovely lake, whose depth and fire remind one of sapphires, is considered one of the most beautiful in the world. In the keeping of such glamorous company, the city of Coeur d'Alene inevitably went for a facelift, in 1988 tastefully revamping downtown and building a huge resort and the world's largest floating boardwalk.

ACCOMMODATION

Down motel row (Sherman Ave) are several similarly-priced rooms: **Alpine Inn**, 664-5412, S/D–$38–$42; **Bates Motel**, 667-1411, S–$38, D–$44; **Lakedrive Motel**, 316 S 24th (end of Sherman Ave), 667-8486, S–$36, D–$38.

FOOD

Idaho Rubys, 206 N 4th St, 664-8522. Homemade bread, soups, salads. 'Half' sandwiches are filling enough in themselves—$2.75. Specials (sandwich and soup)—$4.50.

Rustlers Roost, 819 Sherman, 664-5513. Good food all day long. Serves the city's only barbeque at dinner.

OF INTEREST

Be sure to take the 1½ hr **lake excursion**, $10, leaving from Independence Point near the resort.

Fishing permits are $6 per day, available at any marina or tackle shops.

Digging for rare star garnets at Emerald Creek south of St Maries ranks somewhere between gardening and an Indiana Jones adventure. (Follow Hwy 3 south 25 miles to Rd 447; SE 8 miles to Parking Area, then ½ mile hike to 81 Gulch.) All-day digging permits are issued here for $5. They have very limited equipment, bring a container and shovel if possible! Guides will show you what to do. These black and blue garnets are found only in Idaho and India. Wear old shoes and clothes—it's wet and muddy.

Coeur d'Alene Visitors Information, 1st & Sherman, (800) CDA-4YOU.

MONTANA

Touted as the 'Big Sky' country, Montana is an immense, Western-feeling state, rich in coal, sapphires and chrome, a grower of wheat and cattle, and a regular record-breaker when it comes to the hottest, coldest, windiest and snowiest weather in the lower 48 states. And wouldn't you know it—Gary Cooper was born here. Yup.

Its only sizeable minority are the Indians—about 30,000 Crows, Northern Cheyennes, Blackfeet, Flatheads, Grox Ventres, Chippewas and Crees. And Montana's the place where the Indians put paid to the whites, not only at the Little Bighorn but at the Battles of Big Hole and Rosebud as well. Indians on the seven reservations offer numerous events and facilities to non-Indians and are generally very friendly.

While in Montana, try to catch a rodeo, and don't overlook the work of artist Charles M Russell, whose cowboy days are brilliantly depicted in oils and bronze at Great Falls, Helena and other towns.

One of America's great train journeys is the *Empire Builder* route across northern Montana, especially the portion that loops around Glacier National Park—both east and westbound trips are in daylight or at dusk.

National Parks: Glacier, Yellowstone (mostly in Wyoming). For information on guided walks in the parks and other wilderness areas, contact the Montana Wilderness Association, Box 635, Helena, MT 59624, or call 443-7350.

Important note: while most of Yellowstone lies in Wyoming, three of the main entrances and the gateway towns of West Yellowstone and Gardiner are in Montana and are best reached via Greyhound from Montana cities or from Idaho Falls, Idaho. Read *both* Montana and Wyoming sections when trip planning for the park.

Telephone area code for the whole state is 406.

BUTTE A company town one mile above sea level, dominated by a giant copper mining company. Its locale in southwestern Montana makes it a good base to explore the ghost towns and Indian battlefields roundabout. 'Road from Butte to Helena is great—lots of cliffs, narrow canyons, etc.' The white madonna-like figure of 'Our Lady of the Rockies' stretches 80 feet upward, adding watchful presence to the Continental Divide and Butte.

ACCOMMODATION
Capri Motel, 220 N Wyoming St, 723-4391. S-$34, D-$39, incl tax and continental bfast. Cable TV, AC.
Finlen Motor Inn, Broadway & Wyoming, downtown, 723-5461. S-$34, D-$36.
Kings, 307 S Main, Twin Bridges, (Hwy 41 S from Butte), 684-5639. S/D-$32.

OF INTEREST
Visit the **mining museum at Montana Tech** or the **World Museum of Mining**, on a shaft-mining site, Park St. Plenty of antique mining equipment. At the same location, **Hell's Roaring Gulch** is a replica of pioneer village including a sauerkraut factory, Chinese laundry and general store at same location; both museums and village are free.
Copper King Mansion, 219 W Granite, 782-7580. 34-room mansion of copper baron W A Clark. Open daily 9am-5pm; $5. Or visit his son's home, **Arts Chateau**, 723-7600, at 321 Broadway, for more art and antiques, $3.50.
Ghost Towns. About 60 miles SE of Butte is **Nevada City**, a restored village of 50 buildings and a museum. 'Don't miss the deafening collection of organs, pianolas, etc, and the old RR carriages.' To pan for gold in nearby streams, visit the **River of Gold** in Nevada City, 843-5526, $10.50 for a bucket of 'dirt' to pan for gold with. 'Takes lots of patience to pan for gold outside RR station to end up with a few tiny specks of the yellow stuff.' Hop on the **Alder Gulch Short Line train** for a two-mile transit to Virginia City, a 'working ghost town,' more restored buildings, shops, restaurants, daily Western shootouts, etc.
Our Lady of the Rockies, an 80ft statue on East Ridge overlooking Butte. Finished in 1985, it was built by volunteers from many religious sects, with donated materials.
Between Virginia City and **Bannack** (Montana's first boom town and territorial capital) was the 'Vigilante Trail'. In 6 months, 190 murders were committed here and gang activity got so notorious that miners secretly formed a vigilante committee; when they caught up with the gang leader, it turned out to be their sheriff, who was duly hanged on his very own gallows. 'Bannack: the best old Western town I've seen. Still has gallows, jail. View from top of Boot Hill unbelieveable.'
Castle (Calamity Jane's home town) and **Elkhorn** (300 old buildings still standing) are other interesting destinations.
Big Hole National Battlefield. Site of the Nez Perce victory over US troops in 1877. Chief Joseph and his band were in flight to Canada, having refused to accept reservation life. Pursued by troops, they fought courageously and intelligently under Joseph's masterful military leadership. Despite their win, they were pursued and ultimately beaten at Bear Paw, less than 30 miles from the Canadian border.

TRAVEL/INFORMATION
Greyhound, 105 W Broadway, 723-3287.
Chamber of Commerce, 2950 Harrison Ave, 494-5595.

BILLINGS Montana's largest and most sophisticated city, Billings is on the Yellowstone River and makes a good stopover point for travellers from North or South Dakota en route to Yellowstone. This is a good route to the park, via the scenic Cook City, Hwy 212. 'A spectacular mountain view—

pass 10,000 feet up & lots of elk & buffalo along the way! Don't go before mid-June, though—otherwise, snowed in.'

ACCOMMODATION
Billings Inn, 880 N 29th St, 252-6800. S–$42, D–$46, incl continental bfast.

FOOD
King's Table, 411 S 24th St W, 656-7290. Take exit 446 off I-90. Enormous buffet of salad, homemade soups, roast beef, ham, breads and much more; $6 dinners, $5.50 lunches. There are several Chinese and Mexican restaurants in town, some with reasonable lunch specials.

OF INTEREST
Foucault Pendulum, First Citizen's Bank Building, 1st Ave N and Broadway. Two storeys tall, this pendulum is modelled on the same principles that account for the earth's rotation. Free.
Western Heritage Center, 2822 Montana Ave, 256-6809. Exhibits change twice a year, but the theme in general is an 'Interpretive program reflecting on the history of the Yellowstone Valley River region'. Open Tue–Sat 10am–5pm, Sun 1–5pm; suggested donation.
Yellowstone Art Center, 401 N 27th, 256-6804. Museum of modern and Western art housed in 1916-vintage jail. Tue–Sat 10am–5pm, Thurs 11am–8pm, Sun noon–5pm in summer; free.
Chief Black Otter Trail. N of the city: spectacular views, Indian scout grave, and a monument to settlers. **Sacrifice Cliff**, on the trail, is said to be the place where Indian braves, distraught over the loss of their families to smallpox, rode their ponies and themselves into oblivion. In **Pictograph Cave State Park**, you can also see Indian drawings. $3 per vehicle.
Pompey's Pillar, 30 miles east of Billings. A National Landmark along the Lewis and Clark trail. Huge sandstone formation 'signed' by Capt William Clark in 1806 and named by him in honour of Sacajawea's son Pompey.

TRAVEL/INFORMATION
Greyhound, 2502 1st Ave N, 245-5116.
Chamber of Commerce, 815 S 27th St, 252-4016.

CUSTER BATTLEFIELD NATIONAL MONUMENT Here on the Little Big Horn River, just under 60 miles east of Billings, General George Custer imprudently attacked the main camp of the Sioux, Hunkpapas and others. The date was 25 June 1876. 'I did not think it possible that any white man would attack us, so strong as we were,' said one Oglala chief. A Cheyenne recalled that after he had taken a swim in the river he 'looked up the Little Big Horn toward Sitting Bull's camp. I saw a great dust rising. It looked like a whirlwind. Soon a Sioux horseman came rushing into camp shouting: 'Soldiers come! Plenty white soldiers!'

Before they could be moved to safety downstream, several women and children were killed, including the family of warrior Gall. 'It made my heart bad. After that I killed all my enemies with the hatchet.' Brilliantly led by Sitting Bull and Crazy Horse, the Indians routed the soldiers and surrounded Custer's column, killing them all. Who killed Custer is not known. Sitting Bull described his last moments: His hair 'was the colour of the grass when the frost comes. Where the last stand was made, the Long Hair stood like a sheaf of corn with all the ears fallen around him.'

GREAT FALLS Home base for Charles M Russell and an outstanding collection of his work; also home base for a fearsome array of Minuteman missiles at Malstrom AFB. This is a likeable hick town, home of the state fair in August and a useful stopover if heading north towards Canada or Glacier National Park. (Kalispell, the western gateway, is actually a better way to the Glacier.)

ACCOMMODATION
Super 8 Motel, 1214 13th S, 727-7600. S–$42, D–$49.

OF INTEREST
C M Russell Museum, 400 13th St N, 727-8787. Outstanding collection of his Western paintings, bronzes and wax models. Other famous painters on show include Remington and George Montgomery. Mon–Sat 9am–6pm, Sun 1pm–5pm, $4, $2 w/student ID. Russell's **house and studio** are at 1300 4th Ave N, open in summer, free.

TRAVEL
Greyhound, 326 1st Ave S, 453-1541.

GLACIER/WATERTON NATIONAL PARK 'Nothing that I can write can possibly exaggerate the grandeur and beauty of their work.' So wrote naturalist John Muir about glaciers, and nowhere are his words truer than here, surely one of the contenders for the title of 'most beautiful place on earth.' The joining of Glacier in Montana and Waterton in Alberta created this 'International Peace Park', the first in the world to cross national boundaries.

The Glacier section is traversed east to west by the **Going-to-the-Sun Highway**. Open mid-June to mid-Oct (snowed in the rest of the year), these 50 miles of remarkable beauty are most impressive coming from the west: hugging the side of a cliff for dear life, the road grinds its way up a dizzy precipice along a fantastic hanging valley backed by angry peaks to **Logan Pass**. From the visitors center at the pass, there are day hikes—either along the **Garden Wall** to the north, or up **Mt Oberlin**, an easy peak by Glacier standards that pays off with an eagle's eyrie-view of the park. Nearly 1000 miles of trails wind among rugged mountains and cirque glaciers, leading to encounters with wildflower-scattered alpine meadows, trout-splashed lakes and quizzical mountain goats. Glacier's dangerous and unpredictable grizzlies are *not* one of the tourist attractions; wear bells on your toes (or boots) to avoid surprising a browsing bear. Park naturalists lead parties to **Grinnell** and **Sperry Glaciers**; one trail goes over the **Triple Divide**, a unique point from which water trickling through tiny streams must choose its ultimate destination: west to the Pacific; southeast to the Gulf of Mexico; or northeast to Hudson Bay.

When it comes to scenery, the Canadian side is no slouch, either. To reach **Waterton**, you must leave Glacier Park at the east entrance (**St Mary**), and re-enter just at the US-Canada border. The Canadian park, much smaller than its sister to the south, centres on Waterton Lake. The cruise from the north shore to the south is wonderful, and the hike around the lake's east side has been called Canada's best.

Generally warm in summer with occasional storms and invariably cold nights; by Oct, some of the park is liable to be snowed in. Excellent trout fishing; if you don't fancy catching your own, **Eddy's**, in **Apgar**, 888-5361, (at the foot of Lake McDonald), is famous locally for good $12 trout dinners.

ACCOMMODATION

Glacier Park makes reservations at the 4 hotels and 3 motels within the park. They recommend reservations 6 months in advance, but last minute cancellations may make available rooms that start at $18 for a basic wood cabin. Local number is 226-5551, toll-free within Montana is (800) 332-9351.
Brownie's Grocery and AYH Hostel, 1020 Montana Hwy 49, 226-4426. (800) 662-7625 reservations. 6 blks from Amtrak stn—will pick up. $10, $13 non-members, rooms $20–$23 non-members. Check-in 7.30am–10pm. Kitchen and laundry facs, linen and info provided.
North Fork Hostel, 862-0184, in Polebridge on the western border of the park. In old log house, no electricity, $10 AYH. Many lodges at **East and West Glacier**, just outside park. Best prices for doubles, triples or quads, so it pays to bunch up.
Park Campsites cost $10. If you are in a car, $5 buys you a 7-day pass. Back country camping free with permit from park office. Watch out for bears. Call the park office, 888-5441, for information.
Super 8 Motel,1441 1st Ave E, (800) 800-8000 or 755-1888, D–$55.

TRAVEL

In summer Amtrak stops at Glacier Park. The railtracks through the park have no joints and so the ride is silent, except for the park ranger who gives a commentary about the sights and history of the park.
Greyhound only serves as far as Great Falls.
There is no bus service to the park, but the hitchhiking is easy and safe.
Horses can be rented in East and West Glacier. If you enjoy exotica, the Great Northern Llama Company offers llama pack trips. Cost is $145 per person per day and includes meals. Call 755-9044 or write 1795 Middle Rd, Columbia Falls, MT 59912. River rafting trips by Glacier Raft Co and others, 888-5541, cost $29 for a half-day, $57 for a whole day.

GATEWAY CITIES TO YELLOWSTONE: BOZEMAN, GARDINER, WEST YELLOWSTONE Of *Zen and the Art of Motorcycle Maintenance* fame, Bozeman is a college town and agricultural centre. It lies on the Butte to Billings Greyhound route; south from Bozeman, Hwy 191 dips in and out of Yellowstone Park, coming at length (90 miles) to West Yellowstone.

Gardiner, a small village on Yellowstone's central north border, has the only approach open year-round. West Yellowstone, a few blocks from the western entrance to Yellowstone, has numerous lodgings, shuttlebus service to Old Faithful, bike rentals, car rentals and other amenities for exploring the park. Hitching is also good and relatively safe.

ACCOMMODATION

In Bozeman: Rainbow Motel, 510 N 7th Ave, 587-4201, S–$36, D–$46, outdoor htd pool. **Royal 6 Motel**, 310 N 7th Ave, 587-3103, S/D–$42.
Sacakawea International Backpackers Hostel, 405 W Olive St, 586-4659. $8.
In West Yellowstone: Madison Motel, 139 Yellowstone Ave, 646-7745. S–$26–$50, D–$35–$62, shared bath. Hotel part circa 1912, reflects early, pre-auto days of Yellowstone. 'Romantic old loghouse.' 'Very friendly'.
Wagon Wheels RV Campground, Gibbon and Faithful Sts, 4 blks from Greyhound, 646-7872. $19 per camping site XP–$3. 'Very generous host. Shower block is palatial.' 5-min walk to **Running Bear Pancake House**.

TRAVEL
Gray Line bus tours, 646-9374, of the park leave from West Yellowstone and cost $30, plus $4 first time park entry if not already paid. 'A fascinating day tour. Lots of chances to get out and view the sights.'
Car rental: 'If traveling from Bozeman and returning, try hiring a car for a round trip in 24 hours. Four of us did and it worked out cheaper than busing.'
Karstage, 586-8567. Runs shuttle service from West Yellowstone to Old Faithful geyser, $9. Leaves West Yellowstone 11.30am; takes 1½ hours.
Greyhound, 127 Yellowstone Ave, West Yellowstone, 646-7666.

NEVADA

'Stark' describes the Silver State. It's a flat and monochrome universe of sagebrush, raked with north-south mountain ranges that rise like angry cat scratches from the dry desert floor.

Nevada's the place for misanthropes. About 800,000 people rattle around in a state that measures 110,000 square miles, and 50 percent of them live in and around Las Vegas. Despite its small population, Nevada became a state in 1864 on the strength of the gold and silver from the Comstock Lode, which helped finance the Union side of the Civil War. After several boom-and-bust cycles, Nevada got on a permanent roll when three things happened: the building of Hoover Dam in 1931, which drew thousands of workers into the state; the legalisation of gambling the same year, which grew to become the largest single source of revenue; and government nuclear testing in the 1950s, which provided good jobs (and generous amounts of irradiation).

Nevada's trademarks may be glitter, fallout and quickie marriages, but it's also a land of ranches, Basque and Mormon communities and natural wonders like the Valley of Fire, weirdly beautiful Pyramid Lake, and (unofficially) the oldest tree in the world, in Great Basin national park.
National Park: Great Basin.
The telephone area code for the state is 702.

LAS VEGAS There is a point at which overwhelming vulgarity achieves a certain grandeur, and Las Vegas is living proof. Just remember to see it at night. In the blue velvet hours, it's an opulent oasis of neon jewels, endless breakfasts and raucous jackpots, a snug clockless world that throbs with totally unwarranted promise and specious glamour. As daylight approaches, the mirage wavers and melts away and the oasis becomes a banal forest of overweight signs, tacky and oppressive.

Best approaches for nighttime views: coming from Boulder City, through Railroad Pass gives you a brilliant view of the entire city, as does the *Desert Wind* train from Los Angeles.

The splashiest casino-hotels are along The Strip, where it all began in 1941 with El Rancho Vegas. The denizens of the city are keen to point out that it did *not* all start with gangster Bugsy Siegel and 'The Pink Flamingo' as Hollywood said in the movie *Bugsy*. Three miles from The Strip lies 'Glitter

Gulch', the downtown area, a high-wattage cluster of 15 casino-hotels where Dustin Hoffman played his special trick in *Rainman*. The Gulch tries harder with looser slots, cheaper eats and a more tolerant and friendly attitude towards newcomers and low-rollers. However: lots of cheap lodging and food deals on The Strip, so it's a toss-up. A word of warning for those under the magic State-side age of 21, the casinos will let you in, will let you gamble, will let you lose but if you win they'll dispatch the security guards to 'card' you. So if you're under 21, say adieu to that money. Finally, a little advice from *Fear and Loathing in Las Vegas* and the Doctor, Hunter S. Thompson: '. . . this is not a good town for psychedelic drugs. Reality itself is too twisted'.

ACCOMMODATION

Since the casino owners want to encourage visits by unwary tourists, cheap lodging is the rule in Las Vegas. Lodgings are cheaper in winter than summer, cheaper midweek than on weekends. Avoid public holidays if you can. Sometimes there are some astonishing bargains, even at big flashy hotels on The Strip on Las Vegas Blvd. 'Don't be afraid of bargaining.' If you find it difficult to get a room on a summer weekend, try one of the big places—more likely to have vacancies and it can still work out cheaply for 2 or more people. Beware of booking agents, 'they tell you the city is fully booked, just one free room. They then charge you $20 to book it. Don't be fooled by the free fun books they offer—you can get them anywhere'.

Also, compare freebies (eg coupons for gambling, shows, meals) between hotels—they can make a big difference to your overall expenses. Local radio and giveaway papers advertise the latest bargains, as do the *LA Times'* classified ads.

Downtown (close to bus, train stations):

Budget Inn, 301 S Main St, 385-5560. Across the street from Greyhound. 'Spotless.' S/D–$27 weekdays, $29 weekends.

Crest Motel, 207 N 6th near Fremont, 382-5642. S–$32, D–$37 ($15–$20 more on weekends). VCRs in rooms. Free breakfast at the El Cortez. 'It's one of the best deals in Vegas.'

Las Vegas Airport Inn, 5100 Paradise Rd, 798-2777. S/D–$38 weekdays, $65–$104 weekends.

Las Vegas Independent Hostel, 1208 S Las Vegas Blvd, 385-9955. $9 + $5 key deposit. TV, video, free coffee, tea and lemonade. Also organise 3-day tours leaving Mon and Fri to Grand Canyon, $115, 'Real friendly.'

Lee Motel, 200 S 8th St, 382-1297. S–$23, D–$25 incl key deposit. 'Clean.'

Victory Hotel, 307 S Main St, 384-0260. 1–2 blks from Greyhound. S/D–$46. 'Cheap, helpful.'

On the Strip:

The Aztec Inn Casino, 220 Las Vegas Blvd S, 385-4566. D-$32 weekdays, $54 w/ends. 'In easy reach of all casinos, safe, with brilliant rooms.'

Circus Circus, 2880 Las Vegas Blvd S, 734-0410. Hundreds of AC rooms, TV, pool, amazing themed amenities including 3-ring circus. S/D–$42 weekdays (up to 4 people per rm), $54 weekends. Payment of first night req in advance; phone (800) 634-3450 for reservations. 'Excellent.'

King Albert, 185 Albert Ave, 732–1555. Behind Maxim Hotel. S/D–$38 weekdays, $53 weekends.

Sahara Hotel, 2535 Las Vegas Blvd S, 737-2111. D–$31–$114. 'First class. Amazing pool.'

Stardust Hotel, 3000 Las Vegas Blvd, 737-6111. Possibly the most garish on The Strip (what an honour), with 1,034 AC rooms and a motel annex, S–D–$24–$250(!) weekdays, $40–$250 w/ends, with frequent specials advertised in newspapers and elsewhere. 'Sparkling room.'

FOOD

As a ploy to keep you gambling, many casinos dish up cheap and/or free meals to keep your strength up. You don't have to gamble to take advantage, either. Do read the fine print, however; some of the largesse has strings attached. Free or cheap breakfasts are commonplace. Many of the cheapie 'lunches' and 'dinners' actually serve breakfast food, so be prepared to like eggs and toast. The local paper prints a list of the all-you-can-eat buffets and other cheap deals at all hotels and casinos; you shouldn't spend more than $4 at breakfast, $4–$8 at lunch/dinner. Don't expect quality (some of it is barely edible), just quantity. Most frequently mentioned: **Freemont Hotel; Circus Circus**, the Strip, 734-1410, with buffet breakfast for $2.50, brunch for $3, dinner for $4. 'Best you could want.' Also, **The Horsehoe**, the Strip, 382-1600, $2 steak meal after 10pm; **Holiday Casino**, the Strip, 359-5000, $4 for buffet breakfast, $5 for lunch, $5 for dinner. Free or cheap drinks are another casino attraction. If you are gambling, waitresses are glad to serve all manner of libation. 'To get free drinks, go to casinos where they are playing 'Keno'. Sit down and pretend to play by marking sheets provided. The waitresses then come and take your drink order for free!'

OF INTEREST

Vinon's Horseshoe, 128 Freemont, 382-1600, has glass elevator to Skye Rm, worth a ride for the views of Glitter Gulch, The Strip, the desert and mountains beyond.

Caesar's Palace, The Strip, 731-7110. Outrageous fixtures—Cleopatra's Barge, a Temple of Diana with moving sidewalk, etc. Superb Omnimax theatre next door. If nothing else, visit the **Liberace Museum**, 1775 E Tropicana Ave, 798-5595, a memorial to an entertainer who personified the Las Vegas way of life. Open Mon–Sat 10am–5pm, Sun 1pm–5pm, $6.50, $3.50 students to look at all 3 bldgs full of glitz (the world's largest rhinestone is here as well).

Red Rock Canyon, about 12 miles west of Vegas. Gray Line, 384-1234, has an all-day tour Tues–Thur. Leaves at 10am from downtown hotels, returns at 5pm; $26.50 incl lunch. 'Very beautiful.'

ENTERTAINMENT

Las Vegas is famous for big-name superstar shows featuring comedians such as Bill Cosby, George Carlin and Joan Rivers, as well as entertainers such as George Burns, Diana Ross and Frank Sinatra. Championship boxing matches, golf tournaments and other sporting events also take place here. Paris-style revues, soft-core sex shows and lounge singers are all Las Vegas standards. Few shows are free, but like the restaurants and lodgings, they are less expensive here than most places, and the drinks are usually cheap.

Wet 'N Wild Water Park, Las Vegas Blvd S, 734-0088. $18.

For a simple, free way to relax in Las Vegas, hop into any of the fancy pools in the hotels along the strip. Several readers have written to say that no one asked if they were guests at the hotel. The key is to look like you belong there.

INFORMATION

Las Vegas Convention and Visitors Bureau, 3150 Paradise Rd, in the Convention Center, one block from the Strip, 892-0711.

Nevada Visitors Bureau, 687-3636, info on state attractions.

Chamber of Commerce, 2301 E Sahara, 457-1467.

Las Vegas Events Hotline: 731-2115.

TRAVEL

Greyhound, 200 S Main St, downtown, (800) 231-2222. Also at the Tropicana and Rivieria Hotels.

Amtrak, Union Plaza, 1 Main St, (800) USA-RAIL. Daily service. LA-Salt Lake City/Ogden, Utah, via the *Desert Wind*. Highly social train; recommended.

Auto Driveaway, 252-8904, 3355 Spring Mountain Rd.

McCarran International Airport, 5 miles south of downtown. Lavish, carpeted. 'Large couches, ideal for dossing.' Don't play slots here. Take the CATRIDE #1 'Maryland Pkwy' bus from 300 N Casino Ctr, $1, takes about 45 minutes. Many of the big hotels also have free airport shuttles.
Scenic Airlines, 739-1900 or (800) 634-6801, does 4 different trips from Las Vegas to the Grand Canyon. Best value probably the 7-hr air-ground tour over Hoover Dam and all along the Canyon in a small plane. Expensive at $191, but well worth it for a unique experience. Or skip the organized ground tour and just fly there for $161. Book in advance.
Las Vegas, according to one traveller, is 'hell to hitch out of'.

HOOVER DAM and LAKE MEAD Proof that engineering can be elegant as well as massive, Hoover's 726-foot vaguely Art Deco wall holds back miragelike Lake Mead, irrigates over one million acres, and keeps the lights on in LA and elsewhere. 'You can see the best of it by just driving past.' 'Fantastic value. Don't just drive past!' Tours 9am–4.15pm, $1; 293-1081. 'Tour goes right inside the workings of the dam.' 'Probably absorbing for the student engineer but not for the artistically inclined.' An oasis of trees and shade by the shore of Lake Mead is the **Boulder Beach Campground**, 293-8906, $6 a night for a tent space. NB: do *not* stay here in summer, when the temperature is 100°F at 4am and the air is wall-to-wall insects! 'You'd have to camp in the lake to get a decent night's sleep.'

RENO Although it tries hard to peddle greed, instant gratification (eg quickie marriages/divorces) and fantasy like Big Brother Las Vegas, Reno doesn't quite make it. Despite the worst of intentions, little glimpses of culture, humanity and scenic beauty keep peaking through: its treelined parkway along the Truckee River; its friendly university; its jazz festivals; its good Basque restaurants. Close to the beauties of Lake Tahoe and a day's drive from San Francisco, 'the Biggest Little City' makes a pleasant base to explore Virginia and Carson Cities.

ACCOMMODATION/FOOD
El Cortez Hotel, 239 W 2nd St, 322-9161. S/D–$26 weekdays, $30 weekends.
Senator Hotel, 136 W 2nd St, 322-2125. S–$17, D–$22 + $5 key dep. Hard to get a room. Clean, quiet, friendly. Near casinos. Laundrette.
Windsor Hotel, 214 West St, 323-6171. S–$22, D–$26–$29. Higher on weekends. A clean little hotel 2 blocks from casinos.
As in Las Vegas, cheap food is available at most casinos.

OF INTEREST
National Automobile Museum, 333-9300. 10 S Lake St in downtown. $7.50. Daily 9.30am–5.30pm. Mind-boggling collection of over 200 classic autos: Bugattis, 1886 Riker electric, an 1938 Phantom Corsair Coupe, entertainers' custom vehicles, plus rail cars, boats. Watch restoration of cars in progress.
Nevada Historical Museum, 1650 N Virginia St, near campus, 688-1190. Washoe Indian Dat-So-La-Lee was one of the finest weavers of Native American baskets in the country. Her work, as well as mining history and the development of casino industry, is on display Mon–Sat 10am–5pm. Free.
Nearby: Virginia City. A $25/week reporter for the local *Territorial Enterprise*, Mark Twain wrote of this semi-ghost town in its boisterous prime: 'It was no place for a Presbyterian, and I did not remain one for very long'. The **Territorial Enterprise Building** (54 S C St), 847-0525, still owns the original printing and editorial rooms of the paper where Samuel Clemens first used his pen-name in 1863. Open

10am–4pm daily, $1. The Sundance Saloon, now a T-shirt shop, still houses the city's oldest bar; the Union Brewery Saloon has a brewery downstairs and an untouristy watering hole (a rough crowd) upstairs. The city also has a melting pot of **cemeteries**, from Masonic and Catholic to Chinese and Mexican. Explore also the museums on C St—one of the best being **The Way It Was**, full of mining and local history and don't miss the annual camel races, held on the weekend following Labor Day. The Chamber of Commerce can tell you more, 847-0311.

Carson City. Loaded with Victorian gingerbread and refreshingly situated in the green Sierra foothills, this is the smallest capital city in the lower 48. Mark Twain lived at 502 N Division St with his brother, who was the first territorial secretary of state. Free sights include a rare collection of natural gold formation at the **Carson Nugget**; the former mint (now the **State Museum**); and the **Nevada State RR Museum** on 600 N Carson St, 687-4810. $3, students free. 8.30am–4.30pm daily.

TRAVEL

Amtrak, E Commercial Row & Center, (800) 872-7245. The run from Sacramento via Truckee is dazzling.

Greyhound, 155 Stevenson St, 322-4511. Limited bus service to Ely, 70 miles west of Great Basin National Park on Trans-Nevada-Stages bus at the Greyhound stop. Leaves Mon and Thur at 12.15pm.

GREAT BASIN NATIONAL PARK Opened in 1987, Great Basin was the first new national park in the lower 48 in 15 years. The youngest of the parks is also the least-visited, due mainly to its location near Route 50, the 'loneliest road in the county', and 300 miles east of Reno, with Salt Lake City a further 250 miles to the east. The nearest town to the 77,100-acre Great Basin is the miniscule **Baker** whose population of 50 boasts half a dozen houses, a gas station, a two-room school, post office, two bars and a convenience store.

Scenery within the park varies from spectacular mountains topped by the 13,063 ft **Wheeler Peak**, to sagebush-studded desert, alpine lakes, deep limestone caves, lush meadows and groves of gnarled bristlecone pines, the oldest living trees. The vistas are said to be 'unbelievable, absolutely outstanding'. Explorer John C. Fremont, who travelled through the area in the early 1800s is credited with the name Great Basin for the region. The idea for a national park here is more recent, however, having been under consideration for a mere 50 years. $4 entry fee to park.

Park headquarters and visitor centre is at **Lehman Caves**. To camp free, go to Wheeler or Baker Parks; other campgrounds with drinkable water cost $5/site. For park information phone 234-7331.

UTAH

Although the US government owns 70 percent of Utah's land, the Beehive state is, for all intents and purposes, under Mormon control, a unique situation indeed considering the American insistence on separation of church and state.

The Church of Jesus Christ of the Latter-Day Saints began in 1827 when New Yorker Joseph Smith was led by an angel named Moroni to some gold tablets. Translated (with Moroni's help and two seer stones called Urim and Tummim) into English, the writings became the scriptures of the *Book of Mormon*. The fledgling sect was pushed from New York westward but didn't encounter any significant antagonism until Smith introduced polygamy at Nauvoo, Illinois. A hostile mob promptly killed Smith and his brother. The mantle fell to Brigham Young, who ably led his band west to the bleak wilds of northern Utah, in which no one, not even the local Ute Indians, seemed terribly interested.

The industrious Mormons established their new state of Deseret and applied repeatedly to the US government for admission to the Union but were turned down over the issue of polygamy, which was still going strong. (Brigham himself ultimately had 27 wives and 56 children.) After years of wrangling, in 1890 the Mormons gave in and banned polygamy among themselves. A number of dissenters left and their descendents can be found living quietly and polygamously in Mexico, Arizona and elsewhere.

The importance of Mormonism makes Utah—especially Salt Lake City and environs—sharply different and in many ways better than other states. Hardworking Mormons have built clean, prosperous, humanistic cities and settlements. On the negative side, it's hard to find a drinkable cup of coffee anywhere. Mormons discourage the use of coffee and stimulants and apparently feel the same way about seasonings. Liquor laws, once extremely stringent, have eased somewhat but getting a drink in a restaurant can still be a baroque procedure.

All of Utah's five National Parks are in the south, an area studded with magnificent monuments of the greatest historical, geological and scenic importance. Take a tour or rent a car, allowing yourself ample time for exploration and reflection. Utah makes a good point from which to explore attractions on the Utah-Arizona border and further south, such as Monument Valley, the Navajo reservation and the north rim of the Grand Canyon (via Kanab). A boat trip through the flooded canyons of the Glen Canyon National Recreation Area is also an unforgettable (albeit pricey) experience.

National Parks: Zion
Bryce Canyon
Canyonlands
Capitol Reef
Arches

The telephone area code for the whole of Utah is 801.

SALT LAKE CITY Not just a state capital but the Mecca/Vatican/Jerusalem for Mormons worldwide, Salt Lake City has a joyful, almost noble air about it. Founder Brigham Young had a sharp eye; the city is cradled by the snowy Wasatch Mountains, a setting of remarkable grace. Add to that streets broad enough for a four-oxen cart to turn in, a tree for every citizen, clean air and ecclesiastical architecture that succeeds in being impressive without being dull, and you have quite a place.

'The beauty of this city is that nearly everything worth seeing is within ten minutes walk of the Greyhound terminal. I managed to see a great deal in the four hours' break I had between buses. I found Mormonism really interesting but it's easier to stomach if taken with a pinch of salt.'

Not hard to do, since the Great Salt Lake lies just 18 miles west of the city. The lake is a mere remnant of Lake Bonneville, a vast prehistoric sea that covered much of Utah and parts of Nevada and Idaho. The outline of the ancient sea is still visible from the air.

ACCOMMODATION

Avenues Residential Center, 107 F St, Salt Lake City, UT 84103. 363-8137. Dorm-$10-$14, non-AYH members; S-$21, D-$32, T-$40, Q-$50. No telephone reservations. 1 night's cash in advance req (at least 3 days notice). 'Spacious, well-equipped, kitchen, launderette.'

Carlton Hotel, 140 East South Temple St, 355-3418. Shared bath: S-$28, D-$34; private bath; S-$59; D-$65; Nr bus depot. 'Super place with lovely bathrooms, restaurant.'

Colonial Village Motel, 1530 S Main, 486-8171. S-$21, D-$24. Colour TV.

Deseret Inn, 50 W 500 South, 532-2900. S-$39, D-$43. As many in a room as is possible!

Salt Lake City International Hostel, at Kendell Motel, 667 N 300 W, 355-0293. 9 blks from bus stn. Dorms $15, private rms D-$35. Kitchens, linen $1; check in any time if call first.

FOOD/SHOPPING

Marianne's Deli, 149 West 200 South, 364-0513. Genuine ethnic servicing SLC's German population. Good salami, sausages, sauerkraut, meals from $3.50, sandwiches $2.95.

Lotsa Hotsa Pizza, 50 South Main (basement of Crossroads Plaza Mall), 363-0353. 'Succulent pizza slices $1.75, other specials around $3-$4.'

Union Cafeteria, 581-5888, on the university campus is about the cheapest place in town with good choice.

OF INTEREST

Visitors Centers in Temple Square, in the north and south parts of the square, 240-2534. Run by the Mormon church, the visitor centers offer a number of free tours to various church-related attractions. Excellent walking tour maps are also available. 'Guided tour conducted by Mormons who must have been trained to sell insurance. Intimidating.'

LDS Church office building, 50 East North Temple, 240-2531. Free guided tours Mon-Sat 9am-4pm plus 'fantastic view from 26th floor'.

Genealogical Library, 35 NW Temple, 240-2331. Because Mormon doctrine recommends the baptism of adherents' long-dead ancestors, the church has been accumulating and organizing genealogical records from all ages and all corners of the earth. With more than 2 billion on record, the library has become a major world centre for genealogical research. If you know the birthdate and birthplace of an ancestor before 1900, the library can probably help you trace your family tree back for generations (they have a separate section for British ancestry). Open Mon 7.30am-6pm, Tue-Fri till 10pm. Free tour and help.

Mormon Temple on Temple Square. This monumental structure in Mormon Gothic took exactly 40 years and $4 million to build. Notice the golden statue of the angel Moroni on one of the towers; according to LDS doctrine, this was the being who appeared to church founder Joseph Smith. 'Even if you're only passing through, go to see the temple. Fantastic the way it's lit up.' Not open to non-church members.

Mormon Tabernacle, 240-3221, home of the Mormon Tabernacle Choir. To witness the weekly radio and TV broadcasts, be in your seat by 8.30am Sun morning to be sure of a place, or watch the choir rehearsal at 8pm Thurs eve. 'An acoustic wonder.' This is one place where if you stand in the back you can still hear a pin drop in the centre.

NATIONAL PARKS—SOME TOP CHOICES

It can take a lifetime to visit all of North America's National Parks, and a bulging wallet. If you're planning to go to several, think about buying a *Golden Eagle Pass* ($25, valid for a year) from any one of the parks charging entrance fees. If you only have time to see a few, here are some of the best: **Acadia/Maine**, (207) 288-3338. America miniaturized with beaches, forests, lakes, and Mt Cadillac, the highest point on the Eastern seaboard. **Banff and Jasper/Alberta**, (403) 762-4256/852-6161. Banff, Canada's oldest park, offers mountain grandeur and hot mineral springs. Alongside is Jasper with more mountains, glaciers and lakes. Colombia Icefields, between the two, is the place to spot various big-horned sheep, moose, elk, bears and wapiti. Breathtaking. **Everglades/Florida**, (305) 247-6211. 2nd largest in US, with panthers, bobcats and alligators; a 50-mile wide river that's only 6 inches deep. Bug spray essential. **Fundy/New Brunswick**, (506) 887-2000. Has the highest tides in the world. **Glacier National Park/ Waterton Lakes/Montana and Alberta**, together making the **International Peace Park**, (406) 888-5441/(403) 859-5105. 10,000 years ago glaciers carved peaks, valleys, ripples here. 50 glacier crumbs remain. **Grand Canyon/ Arizona**, (602) 638-7888. Deeper, wider and more colourful than thought possible; you cannot prepare yourself for this one. **Great Smoky Mountains/Tennessee**, (615) 436-1200. Highly accessible. Home of Clingman's Dome, highest point in the Smokies. Try any of the 900 miles of trails along the Appalachian Trail. **Olympic/Washington**, (206) 452-4501. Boasts rain forest, Mt Olympus at 7,965 ft and Grey Whales along coast; best seen in Sept–Oct or Mar–Apr. Isolated from the mainland for so long, the park has several unique species of plant and animal, eg Roosevelt elk and Olympian chipmunk. **Yellowstone/Wyoming**, (307) 344-7381. World's 1st national park and largest in Lower 48. Its myriad attractions include Old Faithful and other geysers, wildlife, mudpots and much more. **Yosemite/California**, (209) 372-0200. Home of the superlative El Capitan, Half Dome, Bridalveil Falls, Glacier Point, redwoods you can drive through and more.

Additional Mormonabilia: 'This is the Place' monument at Pioneer Trail State Park, Emigration Canyon, at east edge of city. Also restored pioneer settlement, etc. 'Mormons are obsessed with the pioneers but they don't try to convert you—in fact, I found Mormonism quite fascinating.'
Brigham Young's grave in the cemetery on 1st Ave between State and A Sts.
Beehive House, 67 E South Temple, 240-2671. BY's first residence. Free tours Mon–Fri 9.30am–6.30pm, Sat 9.30am–4.30pm, Sun 10am–1pm. The adjoining **Lion's House** was home for 19 of BY's wives, where they lived in tiny dorm rooms in the upper hall and main floor. Legend has it that after supper the great man would climb the stairs and chalk an X on the door of his lady for the night. Sometimes a rival would erase the X and chalk another on her door before the absent-minded stud came back upstairs. In this fashion, BY brought 56 new Mormons into the world.
Symphony Hall, at **Salt Palace Center**, 533-5626. Glorious glass wedge of a place; SW of Temple Square. The Salt Palace itself also houses the **Capitol Theater** and is home to the Utah Jazz (NBA basketball!) and Salt Lake Golden Eagles (hockey) teams. 128,000 crowd capacity—free self-guiding tours of both the Palace and the Symphony Hall are available.
Utah Museum of Fine Arts and Utah Museum of Natural History are on the campus of University of Utah, 581-6927, or 581-7332, $3.

Shopping: Brigham Young established the first department store in the US, the Zion Cooperative Mercantile Institution (ZCMI). Now a huge affair, and at one time it was the biggest covered mall in the country. Also good browsing at Trolley Square and Crossroads Plaza.
Great Salt Lake, 18 miles west. 1500 square miles and 10 percent saline, the Mormons used to put joints of beef in the water overnight, retrieving them tolerably well pickled. Then the lake was saltier, but more fresh water is added each year when the snow melts off the mountains.

ENTERTAINMENT
Days of '47 Festival, 3rd week in July. Rodeo, parades, free concerts, dances, and a sunrise service by the Mormon Tabernacle Choir. 'Fun.'
Raging Waters, 1200 W 1700 S, 973-9900. Utah's largest water theme park. Open Mon–Sat 11am–8pm, Sun 11am–6pm. Avoid visiting Aug 14th. $13 ($8 after 4pm).

INFORMATION
Salt Lake Convention and Visitors Bureau, 180 South West Temple, 521-2868.
Utah Travel Council, Council Hall on Capitol Hill, 538-1030. Info on attractions in rest of Utah.

TRAVEL
Amtrak, 320 S Rio Grande, 364-8562. The trip on the *Desert Wind* from here to LA is a great trip through the desert. 'Timetable is confusing—there are through carriages to SLC, no need to change at Ogden as we did.'
Greyhound, 160 W South Temple, (800) 231-2222. Not a good area.
Gray Line Tours, trip to Bingham Canyon and the Greta Salt Lake, $22. Leave 2pm, about 4 hrs. Tickets at Shilo Inn, 206 SW Temple, or call 521-7060. 'Bus to San Francisco drives along the lake anyway.'
Utah Transport Authority (UTA), 287-4636, runs the buses; 65¢ basic fare.
Salt Lake City International Airport, 776 N Terminal Dr, about 4 miles west of downtown. Catch the #50 bus from Main St outside the ZMCI Center, 65¢; goes straight there.

PROMONTORY About 80 miles north of Salt Lake City is the **Golden Spike National Historic Site**, 471-2209, marking the spot where North America's first transcontinental railroad was completed in 1869. After a symbolic gold-spike ceremony, Leland Stanford and Thomas Durant, the heads of the railroads thus joined, attempted to pound in the final iron stake. Both missed, and a professional spike-pounder standing nearby was called on to do the job. Each 10 May and on the 2nd Sat of August, the gold-spike ceremony is reenacted (hopefully without mishaps).

DINOSAUR NATIONAL MONUMENT This park overlaps two states (see also Colorado) but the major attractions lie mostly in Utah. **Vernal** has a superb **Field House of Natural History**; nearby is dinosaur quarry, where you are on eye level with half-exposed brontosaurus and other remains. See Indian Petroglyphs as you look down into the gorge beside the quarry. The road from Vernal to Daggett is called 'the Drive through the Ages' for the billion years of earth's history that lie exposed on either side. Numerous campgrounds in and around the Dinosaur National Monument, emphasis on RVs though. **Dinosaur Gardens**, 235 E Main, 789-4002. Educational explanations of ancient fossils plus 14 life-sized dinosaurs, mineral hall, et al. Open summer 8am–9pm, winter 9am–5pm; $1.50, $1 students. $3 per carload (up to 8 people).

ZION NATIONAL PARK Though not as famous as Yosemite or the Grand Canyon, tiny Zion ranks with those giants in outstanding landscapes. Zion has a huge, painted gorge of magnificent and constantly changing colours, its floor is an oasis of green. At one point the North Fork of the Virgin River pours over the 2000-foot drop of the **Narrows Abyss**, whose walls are just 20 feet apart. Cottonwoods grow on the lush canyon floor, where you can camp. So delightful was the sight that the first Mormons called it Zion, later corrected by Brigham Young, who proclaimed 'It is not Zion', and 'Not Zion' it remained for some years.

An 8-mile road winds along the canyon floor for starters, but for a better look you are advised to walk. There are numerous short trails, sometimes dotted with guide boxes containing leaflets on local flora and geological features. You can do any of these on your own, though a ranger leads hikers along the **Gateway** to the **Narrows Trail** in summer. Before setting off on any trail, long or short, check with rangers for advice on availability of drinking water in certain areas, sudden summer cloud-bursts with attendant flash flooding, and rockfalls.

'We liked the **Emerald Pools footpath**, a gentle stroll for a hot day—beautiful waterfall, a cool and welcome swim.' 'Try walking up to **Angels' Landing**, 5-mile round trip rising 1488 feet. Incredible views.' 'Angels' Landing walk—strenuous but very rewarding.' (NB: sheer drops along path—*not* for acrophobes.) The best view of the **Great White Throne**, a colossal multicoloured butte, is from the **Temple of Sinawava**. $5 park entry fee, good for 7 days.

ACCOMMODATION
Park HQ: 772-3256. **Camping**: 375 sites, unreserved; arrive by noon to snag one, $7 each. Fuel, running water, toilets. No showers.
Motels, groceries, and gas station at **Springdale**, 2 miles from south entrance.
Cedar City, 40 miles north of Zion, 16 miles from Cedar Breaks National Monument (called 'Little Bryce' for its spires, perhaps more intensely coloured than anywhere else—good camping) makes a good base.
Astro Budget Inn, 323 S Main, 586-6557. S–$42, D–$44, XP–$5. AC, cable TV.
Economy Motel, 443 S Main St, 586-4461. S/D–$35. AC, TV.
At Kanab: Canyonlands International Hostel, 143 E 100 South, (801) 644-5554. $9 dorm, kitchen, TV, launderette. Camping $9 when house is full. Also good for Grand Canyon, AZ. 'Great.'

TRAVEL
Greyhound, 355-4684, from Salt Lake City and Las Vegas to Cedar City.
Within Zion: 45 mins tram rides into main canyon, 772-3213. $2.75, daily 9am–5pm.
Hitching between Cedar City and Zion is slow.
Car rental: National Car Rental, Town and Country Inn. 50 W 200 N, Cedar City, 586-9900.

BRYCE CANYON NATIONAL PARK Bryce's landscape belongs to God's Gothic period—delicately chiselled spires, colonnades and crenellated ridges in vivid to pastel pinks, madders, oranges, violets. Most stunning when seen against the sun: west rim in morning, east rim in afternoon. Named for Ebeneezer Bryce, an unpoetic soul who described the canyon as 'a hell of a place to lose a cow'. From the pine-covered clifftops (site of the visitors centre and other facilities), the horseshoe-shaped amphitheatres reveal surreal formations that have been likened to houses, sunburned people and pertrified sunsets. For hiking, descend the canyon to the **Peekaboo Trail** or for a short trip along the **Navajo** and **Queen's Garden trails** which link at the bottom. About 1½ hours for a quick trot. There is a 16-mile auto road but the views are less spectacular. On full-moon nights, take the free 'moon walks' down Navajo Trail. 'Wall Street is more spectacular than Queen's Garden.' Park HQ: 834-5322. Entrance fee, $6.

ACCOMMODATION
Bryce Canyon Pines Motel, outside Panguitch on Rt 12, 6 miles from Bryce entrance, 834-5441. T-$77, Q-$83; lower in winter. AC, pool, cafe, homey dining room with good home cooking. Horseback riding. State liquor store.
Camping in park, $7/night for up to 7 people per site.

TRAVEL
Bryce Zion Trail Rides, 834-5219, has horseback trips in both Bryce and Zion National Parks. Make reservations at lodges or on phone.

MOAB A former uranium mining town on US 163 in east-central Utah, Moab makes a convenient centre from which to visit Canyonlands, Arches and Capitol Reef National Parks.

It's also a place to book a tour to one of these parks. Lin Ottinger's land tours are recommended: 137 N Main, Moab, 259-7312. Other operators in town offer bike rentals and tours, horseback riding and white-water rafting. The Visitors Center at Center and Main can help you sort out options. Open daily 8am–10pm summers, (800) 635-6622. For rafting ($38 per day) contact Tag-A-Long Tours, 425 N Main St, Moab (801) 259-8946.

ACCOMMODATION
Inca Inn Motel, 570 N Main, 259-7261. S-$38, D-$41, XP-$3. Cable TV, AC, pool.
Lazy Lizard Hostel, 1213 S Hwy 191, 259-6057. Dorm-$7, S/D-$22. Separate bath/shower room and hot tub in the back; kitchen and laundry facs. Not affiliated w/AYH, same prices for all. 'Nice atmosphere.'
The Virginian, 70 E 200 St S, 259-5951. S-$30, D-$42, XP-$4. Fridges, cable TV, AC, reservations essential.
Camping in Arches National Park, a mere 2 mls from town, 259-8161. $7 Apr–Oct; otherwise free.

ARCHES, CANYONLANDS, CAPITOL REEF Arches contains water-hewn natural bridges and over 90 arches of smoky red sandstone carved by the tireless wind. 'Our most memorable national park.' $4 entrance fee. **Natural Bridges** is noted for three rock bridges, the foremost a 268-foot span; less well-known features are the hundreds of Anasazi cliff ruins and the world's largest photovoltaic solar generating plant (free viewing), which runs the park's electrical system.

The outstanding characteristic of **Canyonlands** is its variety of colour and forms: towering spires, bold mesas, needles, arches, intricate canyons, roaring rapids, bottomlands and sandbars. The park is rich in petroglyphs, pictographs and ruins: the Maze district with its Harvest Scene and the Needles district south of Squaw Springs campground are particularly good.

If you enter Canyonland Park at the **Maze** Visitors Center, 259-2652, and entrance in the south-eastern corner, then there is no admission fee. 'Superb view from **Dead Horse Pt**, just outside park.'

Capitol Reef, rising 1000 feet above the Fremont River and extending for 20 miles, is the most spectacular monocline (tilted cliff) in the US. The bands of rock exposed along its length are luminous, rich and varied in their colour, and often cut with petroglyphs of unusual size and style. Its formations were named 'sleeping rainbows' by the Navajos. For lodging, try **Rim Rock Resort Lodge**, 7 minutes from Capital Reef on Hwy 24, 425-3843. Summer: D–$49. Book horse tours, fishing trips, other expeditions here; 'Good restaurant.'

GLEN CANYON, MONUMENT VALLEY The soaring pink sandstone arch of Rainbow Bridge and the beauties of boating in Glen Canyon can be undertaken from Moab, but closer bases would be **Page**, Arizona, and **Kanab**, Utah.

On Navajo land, **Monument Valley's** landscape of richly-coloured outcroppings was the scene of many a John Ford western. Two campsites: 'the best is in the Tribal Park among the mesas—quiet, hot showers'.

WYOMING

'The foothills of heaven' to Buffalo Bill, who first saw this land in 1870, 'Wyoming' means 'wide prairie place' in an Indian tongue, Algonquin Indian, paradoxically, for Algonquin-speaking tribes lived thousands of miles away on the East Coast. The name, in fact, was first given to a valley in Pennsylvania, later re-applied much more appropriately to this section of the continent.

Cowboy machismo and women's rights might seem an odd mixture, but Wyoming is nicknamed the Equality State for good reason: it had the first women's suffrage act, the first female voter, governor, justice of the peace and director of the US mint. (Buffalo Bill was among the early feminists of Wyoming, declaring 'if a woman can do the same work that a man can do and do it just as well, she should have the same pay').

A horsy, folksy, gun-totin' state, home of the notorious Hole-in-the-Wall Gang in the 1890s, Wyoming has ranches so huge they're measured in sections instead of acres. Everyone knows about the twin treasures of Yellowstone and Grand Teton National Parks, but Wyoming also contains Devil's Tower, now imprinted on the world's retina as an extra-terrestrial landing pad; and Salt Creek, world's largest light oil field and site of the infamous Teapot Dome scandal in 1927.

National Parks: Grand Teton
Yellowstone (largely in Wyoming but slivers of the park are in Montana and Idaho; see Montana section for additional information).

The telephone area code for the whole of Wyoming is 307.

CHEYENNE Once fondly called 'hell on wheels' for its volatile mix of cowpokes, cattle rustlers and con men, capital city Cheyenne now contents itself with having the purest air and the most frequent hailstorms in the US. A little of the old buckaroo flavour returns each July during the week-long Frontier Days rodeo, largest in the US.

ACCOMMODATION
Big Horn Motel, 2004 E Lincolnway, 632-3122. S-$24, D-$28, TV, AC.
Home Ranch Motel, 2414 E Lincolnway, 634-3575. S-$28, D-$37 summers.
Lariat Motel Ltd, 600 Central Ave, 635-8439, S-$27, D-$36, TV.
Motel 6, 1735 Westland Rd, 635-6806. S-$35, D-$41.
Super 8 Motel, 1900 W Lincolnway, Hwy 30 West, 635-8741. S-$39, D-$45.

FOOD
Albany Cafe and Restaurant, 1506 Capitol Ave, 638-3507. Good lunch counter; dinner from 5pm. Bar is good for meeting people. 'Not a pickup bar, not gay, not expensive, good music. Can this be true?'

OF INTEREST
Frontier Days, 'Daddy of 'em All' rodeo, last full week in July. 778-7200. 4 parades, chuckwagon race, free pancake breakfasts, and perhaps the best rodeo in the US. Tickets are pricey: $8-$20. 'During rodeo, the whole town goes wild on Saturday night but forget it at other times'; 'Cheyenne is dead as a doorpost on Saturday night'. However, there are planned entertainments every evening, eg country music, Indian dancing at an Indian village.
State Museum, Central Ave & 23rd St, 777-7024. Worthwhile cowboy, Indian and pioneer museum. Free tours available on request (48 hrs notice req). Open Mon–Fri 8am–5pm, Sat noon–4pm, free.
Also the **Old West Museum**, Frontier Park, 778-7200, has splendid collection of horse-drawn vehicles, Oglala Sioux beadwork. Open Mon–Sat 8am–7pm, Sun 10am–6pm; $3.

TRAVEL/INFORMATION
Greyhound, 634-7744, at 1503 Capitol Avenue.
Cheyenne Area Convention and Visitors Bureau, 309 Lincoln Way, 778-3133.

DEVIL'S TOWER NATIONAL MONUMENT Accorded inter-galactic notoriety in *Close Encounters of the Third Kind,* Devil's Tower was declared the nation's first national monument in 1906 in recognition of the special part it played in Indian legend. A landmark also for early terrestrial explorers and travellers, the monolith is a fluted pillar of sombre igneous rock rising 865 feet above its wooded base and 1280 feet above the Belle Fourche River. Open year-round, $4 entrance fee per vehicle.

NB: 'Tower can be climbed safely *only* by experienced rock-climbers and takes about 4 hours. Descent 1 hour.'

The scene is 'creepily impressive, much more so than the movie.' In the park are prairie-dog villages, an outdoor amphitheatre and ranger programmes in summer (talks, demos and guided walks on the subject of wildlife, rockclimbing or the monument, 9.30am–4.30pm). Park Visitors' Center: 467-5501; open 8am–7pm.

ACCOMMODATION
Campsites at the monument open year-round; $7 per night.
Arrowhead Motel, 214 Cleveland St in **Sundance**, 283-3307. S/D-$49. 'Most clean and attractive. Friendly, helpful and bright.'

YELLOWSTONE NATIONAL PARK Established in 1872, the oldest and perhaps the most well-loved of the national parks, Yellowstone comprises 2.2 million acres, covering the northwest corner of Wyoming and dribbling over into Idaho and Montana. Three of the five entrances are in Montana; they and the gateway cities of Gardiner, Bozeman and West Yellowstone are discussed in the Montana section. Wyoming park entrances are from the east via Cody, from the south via Jackson/Grand Teton National Park.

Drought and 40- to 70-mile-per-hour winds set the stage for the uncontrollable forest fires of 1988. The fires burned a mosaic pattern throughout nearly 800,000 acres, but only half of this acreage was blackened, and much of this is quickly rejuvenating. None of the major attractions were disturbed.

Yellowstone is one of the world's most impressive thermal regions. Besides Old Faithful (which blows over 100-foot, dispelling 5,000 gallons of water every 79 minutes or so), there are some 10,000 geysers, hot springs, colourful paint pots and gooey mud pools—an uncanny array of colours, temperatures, smells, disquieting sounds and eruptions. Old Faithful is the most famous, but many others erupt more frequently nearby and also in the **Norris Junction area**. There you can see hundreds of geysers and pools on a walk of less than two miles.

Another priority should be the **Grand Canyon of the Yellowstone River**, whose 1,500 foot gorge is 'one wild welter of colour', as Rudyard Kipling put it. 'Breath-taking—even better than the Arizona one.' The river tumbles into the canyon through the **Lower Falls**, twice the height of Niagara Falls. **Artist Point** gives possibly the most scenic view of Yellowstone—look over the sheer drop of 700 feet to the canyon below. Also do not miss **Yellowstone Lake**, famous for its trout, and 110 miles of shoreline and sublime scenery, nor '**Morning Glory**', a deep turquoise lake rimmed with gold along the Firehole River.

A wildlife sanctuary, the park is filled with deer, moose, bison, bear and other creatures. Because so many people fed the bears (often being hurt in the process, besides perverting the animals' way of life), the park has removed many of them to remote areas. Over 100 who had become real menaces over the years had to be shot—all due to human meddling. If you do sight bears, do not feed them, get close to them, or come between an adult and cubs. The bears are wild, and meant to stay that way.

Cars were not admitted to the park until 1915; today, about 800,000 of them enter, with attendant traffic jams, accidents, pollution and parking problems. But as in other parks, visitors tend to congregate in the same places, leaving the rest of the park refreshingly empty.

Challenging hikes include the 3½-mile walk to the summit of **Mt Washburn** (but stay on trails, don't take shortcuts). If you have more time, rent a canoe at West Yellowstone and canoe/camp the **Lewis River** to the **Shoshone Lakes**—a pristine, wildlife-filled journey. Many campsites (free permit required) along route and at the lake. 'Don't forget Canyon and Upper Falls—on a par with Grand Canyon!'

The park is open year-round ($10 per car, good for 7 days), but the official season runs May to September, after which bus service and other facilities cease and there is a real chance of snow. Offseason months, the only roads and entrance open are via Gardiner. However, you can take a snow coach from West Yellowstone. Yellowstone in winter is enchanting: the wildlife move in close to the warmth of the geysers and thermal springs—awesome to see them in the swirling mists. You can actually ski or snowshoe close to bison and elk.

ACCOMMODATION
Lodging outside the park is discussed under West Yellowstone and Gardiner, Montana. See also Cody.
Within the Park:
9 different lodges and cabin clusters are available for individuals and small groups. Prices range from $16 a night for a cabin without linens or running water up to $88 for fully equipped lodges. **Roosevelt Lodge** is the cheapest, $20–$50, 'only place worth the money'. Other bargains are **Old Faithful Snowlodge**, $50–$73, and **Old Faithful Lodge and Cabins**, $20–$35. Lodges open and close at different times in spring and fall. Call 344-7311 to reserve space.
Camping: 11 campgrounds with more than 2300 sites are available for $6–$10 a night. Usually filled before noon in summer, first-come first-served. 'If you are prepared to sleep in the car, you can use the high bear-risk campsites.' 'Arrive before 8pm if you want a shower—or use hotel as we did.' Camping can be very cold, even in July, so bring a warm sleeping bag. To camp outside the developed sites and away from all the RVs, obtain a free permit at one of the park's visitor centres, where you can also buy a necessary hiking map. Do not sleep with food near you. At night some bears can't distinguish between bags of crisps and bags of people! Winter camping at Mammoth Campground only.

FOOD
Six concessions in the park, none particularly cheap. If you can manage, bring in groceries from West Yellowstone.

TRAVEL
TW Services, 344-7901, tours of Lower and Upper Loops of the park, around $24–$25. 'Clerks at West Yellowstone very helpful with advice.' 'You can make your own combinations.'
Hitching within the park is rated 'very easy'.
Greyhound: see W Yellowstone, MT.

GRAND TETON NATIONAL PARK Twenty miles due south of Yellowstone lies the totally different world of the Grand Teton Mountains. As awe-inspiring as Yellowstone, this park reminds one of Alpine Europe rather than the American West. The Tetons rise without preliminaries from a level valley to sharp pinnacles more than 13,000 feet high, separated by deep glaciated clefts. On their crags and flanks, you see remnants of the last great glaciation that once covered North America, 10,000 years ago. Besides peaks, valleys like Jackson Hole, the lakes and the winding Snake River add up to a stirring environment. Jackson Hole, Jenny Spring and Solitude Lakes make good if icy swimming.

Warm clothes and tough shoes are essential here. There are many excellent hiking trails and this is mountaineering country; several schools have their headquarters in the area. Permits for climbing must be obtained from a park ranger, and it's not for novices.

One of the best ways to absorb the Tetons is to float down the Snake River on a large rubber raft steered by boatmen. In the forests at river's edge you may see some of the elk which form the largest herd in America. Commercial river rafting tours abound, but depending on your karma you may meet up with a group of locals who are already going. Join in—but remember Snake River rapids require skillful handling.

Accommodation both in the park and in nearby Jackson tends to be more costly than at Yellowstone and vicinity. However, **Colter Bay Village Cabins** in the park, nr Jackson Lake, are very reasonable. One room (1–2 people) in a log cabin, shared bath—$27. The tent cabins are cheaper and more 'adventurous', constructed of canvas and logs, with outdoor grill and woodburning stoves. Bring own bedding for bunks; 1–2 people $22, XP–$2.50.

JACKSON A cross between Aspen and Boulder, pretty and gentrified Jackson draws crowds of boisterous tourists in summer, but in winter the tiny village entices gentler, more noble visitors when 10,000 elk come to graze at the edge of town. Capture some of this magic on a sleigh ride through the elk refuge, 733-9212, $7.50. In the spring, local boy scouts collect and sell antlers, some of which end up as aphrodisiacs in the Far East.

ACCOMMODATION

Bunkhouse, 733-3668, 2 blks N of town square, 215 N Cache St, PO Box 486, WY 83001. $20/dorm bed. The hostel has lounge with TV, kitchen facs.
The Hostel 'X', Box 546, Teton Village, 12 miles north of Jackson, 733-3415. $13.50 AYH, $34 non-members. Game room, pool, lounge with fireplace.
Grand Teton Lodge Co. has tent cabins, with canvas-covered patio, double-deck bunks, outdoor grill, picnic table, woodburning stove, $22 for two, XP-$2.50. 45 miles N of Jackson on Hwy 89. Write to reserve: PO 250, Moran, WY 83013; 543-2811.

FOOD

Bubba's, 515 W Broadway, 733-2288. Good home cooking, lunch specials from $3.95 up and a build-your-own breakfast, $3.25. Sandwiches $2.55.
Mountain High Pizza Pie, 120 W Broadway, 733-3646. Traditional, deep-dish and whole wheat crusts, $5–$10. Outdoor seating; plays Dead music.

ENTERTAINMENT

For good reading, pick up a copy of *Jackson Hole News* or *Jackson Hole Guide*. Both have been awarded 'best weekly in the nation' over the years, and the competition continues. Try **JJ's Silver-Dollar Bar**, with 2,000 silver coins embedded in the counter; or the recently-remodelled **The Rancher**, 733-3886, facing the town square. Live music 6 nights a week; packed out with locals Wed–Sat 5–8pm when comedian Kit Attaway takes the floor.
Mangy Moose, in Teton Village, 733-9779. Live bands with $1–$5 cover.
Jackson Hole Llamas, 733-1617. 5-hr trek with llamas (by group request only) includes lunch and a spectacular view of the Tetons, $500 an outing (ie 10 people—$50 each). Also available: longer guided trips in Teton, Yellowstone, and Wind River areas, but they're expensive. It's cheaper to take llamas alone, without a guide, but you must first win the llama's and owner Lou Centralla's confidence.

TRAVEL/INFORMATION

Morning Star Buses, 733-4521, runs a service between Jackson and Teton Village twice a day, $2. (The bus turns north to the village about a mile from Wilson, you may be able to talk the driver into letting you off there.)

AMERICAN BEACHES

From the rugged and lonely north Pacific shoreline to the crowded, hedonistic playgrounds of Florida's coasts, America's beaches have something for everyone. Even to the landlocked, the scent of coconut oil strikes a deeper chord than that of traditional apple pie. For a truly American experience, try these beaches:

WEST COAST—The best: Redondo Beach, south of Los Angeles. Hawaiian George Freeth introduced the Polynesian art of surfing to the mainland here. **Most beautiful:** 17 miles of seals and sea lions, pink and purple ice plants between **Pacific Grove** and **Carmel**. See the surfers at sunset. **Most fashionable: Malibu**, with its bleached sandy beaches, celebs' homes dotting the hills above. A close second is **La Jolla**, near San Diego, CA, a ritzy, cove-lined beach frequented by upscale beachcombers, divers and surfers. **Strangest: Venice Beach**, near LA, has rollerskating grannies, graffiti, and a lot of muscle. **Snorkelling: Hanauma Bay**, Oahu, Hawaii. The best. **Surfing: Maui Island** in Hawaii boasts incredible surfing. NB: all the beaches in Hawaii are public. Try the local sport of 'Boogie-boarding', so-called because participants 'boogie' down the beach on rectangular boards, riding on the tail end of the surf. **Windsurfing: Hookipa Beach Park, Maui**—unrivalled as the world's No. 1 location due to constant trade winds and exceptional wave conditions. 'Fun just to watch.' 'If everybody had an ocean, across the USA, then everybody'd be surfing, Californ-I-A,' sang the Beach Boys, most likely with **Long Beach** in mind, *the* place for surfing and site of Howard Hughes' *Spruce Goose*. **Most forgotten: Santa Catalina Island**. Accessible by ferry. No cars, just scuba diving and swimming.

Most peaceful: Long Beach, on Vancouver Island's west coast, BC 12 miles of sea, sand and solitude.

THE EAST COAST—Hampton Beach, New Hampshire, has boardwalk, arcades, and waterslides. **Virginia Beach**, Virginia, fast growing resort with 28 m beach. **Brunswick**, Maine, hosts excellent Beach Bluegrass Festival over Labor Day weekend. **Ocean City**, Maryland, crowded with Washingtonians, wild. **Myrtle Beach**, South Carolina, 3rd most-visited spot on East Coast behind Disneyworld and Atlantic City. Nearby **North Myrtle** becomes a student mecca in early mid-May. **Atlantic City**, New Jersey, birthplace of salt water taffy and showplace of Miss America. **Asbury Park**, decaying but still can lay claim to Bruce Springsteen.

FLORIDA—Sanibel Island, for the best seashells, starfish; **Cocoa Beach** has cosmic surfing and the added attraction of being the blast-off site for Space Shuttle flights. **Fort Lauderdale**, midway between Palm Beach and Miami is a glut of beer, raw lust and sports cars.

Jackson Hole Airport, about 8 miles from town. Jackson Hole Transportation runs a shuttle service from the town's hotels to the airport, $6, or a taxi for $8. Phone ahead to request service.

Jackson Hole Chamber of Commerce, 532 N Cache St, 733-3316. For all local information and help.

Hitching is described as 'very easy'.

CODY It may look like endless motels, but be not dismayed. Cody possesses a superlative, four-in-one museum complex and an Old Trail Town that are well worth your attention. About 60 miles east of Yellowstone, Cody is of course the namesake of William F, also known as Buffalo Bill, bison hunter/Army scout/Pony Express rider turned showman. His Wild West show was one of several that earned their players a living by touring the US, Canada and Europe with a mawkish morality play of brave cowboys and savage redskins—very popular at the time. Royalty loved it; Queen Victoria gave Cody a diamond brooch, saying his show was so exciting she found it 'almost impossible to sit'. Annie Oakley and Sitting Bull were among Buffalo Bill's prize 'exhibits'; the mythology created thereby was later recycled by Hollywood.

East of Cody, the vividly coloured strata of **Shell Canyon** along the winding stretch of Highway 14 between Shell and Sheridan is highly scenic; to reach Custer's Last Stand in Montana, turn north at Sheridan.

ACCOMMODATION

Irma Hotel, 1192 Sheridan Ave, 587-4221. Luxurious and expensive, S–$47–$70, D–$54–$82, but a grandly historic place built by Buffalo Bill and named after his daughter. If you don't stay, at least stop by for a drink at the incredible French cherrywood bar, a gift from Queen Victoria after BB's command performance in England. Merchants' lunches ($4.25-$6) and even dinners are very good value at the Irma Grill.

Pawnee Hotel, 1032 12th, 587-2239. S–$30, D–$36–$41.

OF INTEREST

Buffalo Bill Historical Center, 720 Sheridan, 587-4771. Daily 7am–10pm, June through August, 8am–8pm thereafter; $7 (students, ages 13–21, $4). Contains 4 museums: The **Buffalo Bill Museum** holds Cody memorabilia, BB's boyhood home. The **Plains Indian Musuem** is huge, imaginative and head-and-shoulders above most Indian collections. The **Whitney Gallery of Western Art** has bluechip Western painters: Remington, Catlin, Russell and Bierstadt's work on Yellowstone. Recently opened in a new gallery is the **Cody Firearms Museum** (formerly the Winchester Gun Museum), with over 5,000 firearms from America and Europe.

Old Trail Town, 587-5302, 2 miles west in Shoshone Canyon. A well-conceived collection of historic buildings and relics from all over Wyoming from Cassidy and Sundance's hideout to Jeremiah Johnson's grave. 'Non-gimmicky.' Open mid-May to mid-Sept, $3. Open 8am–7pm.

Rodeos early June–Aug, nightly 2 miles west of town. Enquire locally. The **Cody Stampede** is held annually around 4th July.

THE PACIFIC STATES

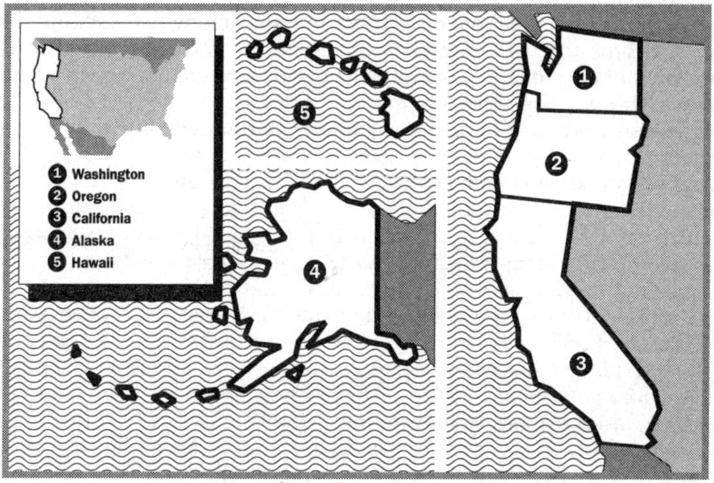

The Pacific states have everything and more. From ancient redwoods to modern cities, from lumbermen to film stars, from Polynesian huts to Arctic igloos, and in every state much of the most exciting scenery in America. The Russians, British, French, Spanish and Mexicans have all had claims here, and though Americans swept west under the conquering banner of Manifest Destiny, some of the old influences survive.

But the Pacific is also where the rainbow ends, where expectations must finally prove themselves. Enthusiasm reigns, and that is probably the region's most enjoyable quality—though the final results are still awaited.

ALASKA

Aleut for 'great land', Alaska has a penchant for superlatives: biggest, coldest, costliest, highest peak, longest coastline, richest animal life, longest *and* shortest days.

Alaskans are proud people who are Alaskans first, and, by the way, Americans. The contiguous states, known as the 'Lower 48' are far, far away, and Alaskans seem quite glad about that.

The state was jeered at as 'Seward's Folley' when President Lincoln's Secretary of State bought it from the Russians for 2¢ an acre in 1867. But no one laughed for very long, for gold was discovered only a few years later, inspiring a deluge of opportunists and virtually creating such towns as Skagway, Fairbanks and Juneau.

In 1968 one of the world's richest caches of petroleum was discovered in Prudhoe Bay, and a consortium of oil companies financed the 800-mile Trans-Alaska Pipeline, which brings 1.5 million barrels daily to Valdez, on Prince William Sound.

In an attempt to spread the oil profits equitably among native people and other Alaskans, the 1971 Alaska Native Claims Settlement Act puts emphasis on money and land ownership, concepts foreign to the state's native peoples. The Act has consequently had a devastating impact: you'll see many downtrodden and misplaced Indians, particularly in Fairbanks and Anchorage.

Alaska is breathtakingly beautiful and well worth visiting, particularly in summer when daytime temperatures are surprisingly warm and there's plenty of daylight. Campers and hikers be forewarned however: the unofficial state bird here is the mosquito. And watch out for the wildlife: humans are expected to give way to bears on trails and pathways. According to travel writer Erik Sandberg-Diment of the *Washington Post*, 'that part is easy. The part about doing it slowly, without running, is more difficult'.

The land route of the Alaska Highway from British Columbia to Fairbanks and Anchorage is an adventure, but the finest approach is by boat from Seattle or Prince Rupert. State-run, inexpensive ferries ply the Inside Passage year-round, allowing closeup looks at glaciers, islands, fjords, whales and stopover privileges at the various ports of call.

Prices in Alaska range from 'tolerable' in the southeastern panhandle to double those in Seattle, San Francisco and elsewhere. 'Some things are not much more than the lower 48, but be prepared for some nasty shocks.' Bus passes aren't valid in Alaska, but various tours are available. Gasoline prices are on par with or slightly higher than California. Conventional lodging is very costly, but spartan youth hostels do exist, and there are campgrounds everywhere. (Come prepared for plummeting temperatures at night, although one reader notes that the American tourists simply wear their shorts over thermal underwear during the day.) Stick to locally grown produce and seafood to keep food costs down.

National Park: Denali (formerly Mt McKinley).

The telephone area code for the state is 907.

THE INSIDE PASSAGE and THE PANHANDLE Warmed by the Japanese Current and protected from the open sea by a necklace of islands, this southeastern waterway enjoys the state's mildest weather (a relative term meaning it rarely gets below zero in winter). Besides access by cruise ships, the state operates an eight-ferry system called the Alaska Marine Highway, an appropriate name since five of the seven ports in the Panhandle have no overland highway access to the outside world. 'Just the sight of a humpback whale breaching is enough to make the journey a memorable one.' 'Good vessels, interesting places to stop over, many opportunities to meet people.' 'In summer, Tongass Forest interpreters give free talks, film shows, on board. An imaginative and interesting service.'

First port of call is **Ketchikan**, still a salmon centre, now more dependent on cruiseship traffic. Weatherbeaten houses on stilts and the harbour give it a New England flavour, but it never rained like this in Massachusetts. The record here is 223.8″ a year.

Sitka, once capital of Russian America and beautifully sited at the foot of Fuji-like Mt Edgecumbe, has a reconstructed Russian cathedral full of icons, plus interesting gravestones from this period. There is also a large and well-preserved collection of totems. James Michener spent much time here researching his book, *Alaska*.

Capital city, **Juneau**, climbs steep wooded hillsides with wooden stairways and a kaleidoscope of architectural styles. It's a great irony and a bone of contention among many Alaskans that the capital city is not reachable by highway, only by air or water. The once impassioned-campaign to move the capital city is on hold because of the expense involved. **Mendenhall Glacier**, 14 miles away (and accessible by car) has camping. From Haines, the old Dalton Trail leads off to the **Klondike**, several ghost towns and the amazing overhang of Rainbow Glacier.

In its sourdough heyday, **Skagway** was big-city size. Now down to a population of 704 (most up-to-date figure available, i.e. 1988), it's reaping a new gold rush of tourists to photograph its well-preserved wooden sidewalks, false-front buildings and memorials to Soapy Smith, the local bad guy. 'On his birthday, locals urinate on his grave.' Best during the oldtime fervour of Sourdough Days, celebrated in September.

ACCOMMODATION

Alaskan Hotel, 167 Franklin, **Juneau**, 586-1000 or (800) 327-9347. S–$44, D–$55 with shared bath, cheaper in winter. Rooms with private bath: S–$61, D–$72. Sauna, jacuzzi, some kitchenettes. One of the oldest in state, on National Register of Historic Places, built 1913, Victorian decor.

Bear Creek Camp & Hostel, PO Box 1158, **Haines**, AK 98827-1158, 2 miles out of Haines, 766-2259. $10 AYH, $12 non-members, wood-heated. Cabins (with electricity) also for rent, $30 for 4. Hot showers, kitchen facs. Free shuttle from ferry, call ahead.

Eagles Nest Motel, 1183 Haines Hwy, **Haines**, 766-2891. S–$63, D–$84, T–$90, Q–$92. Colour TV.

Gilmore Hotel, 326 Front St, **Ketchikan**, 225-9423. S/D–$65. Next door to **Annabel's Keg and Chowder House**, open 7am–10pm (lunch $5–$10, dinner $20–$50).

Juneau Youth Hostel, 614 Harris St, 3 blks from downtown, 586-9559. $10 AYH. Kitchen, showers, large common room with fireplace. Open year round, 7am–9am, 5pm–11pm daily. Reservations requested. First night's payment in advance to book.

Ketchikan Youth Hostel, First United Methodist Church, Grant and Main Sts, PO Box 8515, 225-3319. Open Memorial Day–Labor Day. $7 AYH, $10 non-members. 3-night limit, extendable by manager. Kitchen, piano, hot showers, open for late-arriving ferries if call beforehand.

Sitka Youth Hostel, United Methodist Church, 303 Kimsham St, 747-8425. Open 1 June–31 Aug. $7 AYH, $10 non-members.

Skagway Inn, 7th and Broadway, 983–2289. Bed and bfast. S–$57, D–$69, shared bath. Also in Skagway: **Irene's Inn**, on Broadway and 6th St, in historic district, 983-2520. S–$39, D–$54 w/shared bath.

Camping: $10 at all state parks, or buy a $50 camping pass good for one year. In **Ketchikan**, 225-2148, US Forest Service manages **Ward Lake** area campgrounds, $20; 2-week limit June–Aug. Also: $5 at **Mendenhall Glacier** near **Juneau**, beautiful views of glacier. For reservations call (800) 280-CAMP. Free camping on steep **Chilkoot Trail** from Skagway no permit needed, but check-in with the Klondike

Gold Rush National Park office, Broadway, 983-2921, first. Historic and breathtaking route—one of the most beautiful passes in Alaska—worth lingering.

OF INTEREST

Ketchikan: Salmon Capital of the World: see **Deer Mountain Fish Hatchery**, next to the Totem Heritage Center (see below). **Historic Creek Street** is the old red-light district with renovated stores and galleries.

Tlingit (pronounced Klinkit!) **Totems** at Saxman Totem Park (2 miles south by bus) have a woodcarver on site; Totem Bight State Park (10 miles north), and Totem Heritage Center, 601 Deermont St, 225-5900.

Ketchikan Museum, 225-5600, 629 Dock St, downtown, with displays on local history, art, native heritage and fishing. Open Mon–Sat 8am–5pm. $1 (free on Sun).

Sitka: Sitka National Historical Park, Lincoln St, at the other end of which is **Castle Hill**, the actual spot where the sale of Alaska from Russia to US occurred; open 8am–6pm daily, free.

Southeastern Alaska Indian Cultural Center, 747-6281, in the park, 106 Metlakatla St. Tlingit Indian craftsmen and artists at work. Open daily, 8am–5pm in summer, Mon–Fri 9am–5pm in winter.

Sheldon Jackson State Museum, 104 College Dr, 747-8981. Impressive collection of artefacts, representing all four native groups of Alaska: Eskimos, Aleutians, Athabaskans and NW Indians. Jackson began the Indian Trading School, a boarding school for natives in Alaska. Building itself is a National Historical Site, the first concrete building in Alaska. Open daily in summer, 8am–5pm; Tue–Sat 10am–4pm after Sept 15, $2.

Russian Bishops' House, Lincoln St, 747-6281. Largest and last remaining Russian-built home in Alaska. Open daily, 8.30am–5pm summer; by appointment only in winter.

St. Michael's Cathedral, 747-8120, Russian Orthodox, in middle of street in centre of town. Stunning, built during Russian period, burned in 1966 and since restored. Open Mon–Sat 11am–3pm, closed Sun.

Juneau: Alaska Historical Society and Museum, 4th and Main. Exhibits on mining and city history. Also see the **State Museum**, 465-2907, on Whittier St for good artefacts; $2, students free. In summer, nightly salmon bakes, self-guided walking tours of historic Juneau, through the Visitors Bureau at 3rd and Seward, 586-2201.

Alaskan Brewing Co., 524 Shaune Dr (in Lemon Creek), 780-5866. The beer has been awarded prizes galore and been featured in *Northern Exposure*. Tours of the brewery: Tues–Sat, 11am–4.30pm summer; Thurs–Sat 11am–4.30pm winter.

Glacier Bay National Park, 50 miles NW of Juneau. Beautiful and untouched wilderness of seals, whales, bears and 20 glaciers. Access by boat or plane only; expensive. 'Awesome.'

Haines: Old Ft Seward, 766-2202, now a centre for the Chilkat dancers. Don't miss Indian artists at work on totems, masks, and soapstone, Mon–Fri 9am–5pm, Memorial Day–Labor Day. Near Haines is the world's largest concentration of **bald eagles**; best months Oct & Nov.

Skagway: Klondike Gold Rush National Park, 983-2921. The 7-block historic Broadway Street contains many restored private and park-owned structures, leftovers from the Gold Rush days. Open 8am–6pm.

Trail of '98 Museum, 983-2420, upstairs in City Hall, 7th and Spring. Gold Rush and Native artefacts on display. Fascinating stuff. Open 9am–5pm daily. $2 adults, $1 students.

INFORMATION

Ketchikan: Visitors Bureau, at the City Dock, 131 Front St, 225-6166. Open 30 May-30 Sept daily, 8am–5pm; Oct–May, Mon–Fri 8am–5pm.

Sitka: Visitors Bureau, 330 Harbor Dr, 747-5940.

Juneau: Visitors Bureau, 134 3rd St at Seward, 586-2201. Mon–Fri 8am–5pm; and Sat & Sun in summer. Also Visitors Center at State Office Building, Mon–Fri, 8am–4.30pm, 465–2010.
Skagway: Visitors Bureau, 2nd & 3rd at Broadway, 983-2854. Open 8.30am-noon and 1–5pm daily.

TRAVEL

Alaska Marine Highway, PO Box R, Juneau, AK 99802-5535. (800) 642-0066 or 465-3941. Contact for reservations, schedules and other info. Bellingham, WA-Skagway, $236; Juneau–Haines $18; Juneau–Sitka, $24. Meals, staterooms cost extra, run at or below hotel prices. 'Tolerates camping out and sleeping bags on top-deck solarium for those who have the gear and can't sleep on reclining seats.' 'Board early if you want a place on the solarium.' 'Boat deck is heated, has camping beds, showers, lockers provided free.' 'Cafeteria good value, but taking your own food definitely advisable.' Only one ferry makes the complete Bellingham–Skagway run, once a week in summer. 'Very crowded.' 3 ferries work Prince Rupert–Skagwag, runs Sun, Tues, Thurs & Sat, $118. 'Winter service much reduced due to maintenance.' (See also Seattle.)
Gray Line, (800) 544-2206. Runs buses from Haines to Anchorage, Tues, Wed, Fri and Sun at 8.15pm, takes two days, $189. Also Skagway-Whitehorse daily at 7.30am, $52. Both services only run until mid-September.
Allstar Rent-a-Car, 9104 Menden Hall Mall Rd, 790-2414. Provides shuttle from airport or ferry terminal to their office.

THE ALASKA HIGHWAY For years nearly all gravel or dirt-surfaced, the highway nowadays is paved from top to bottom. Beginning at Dawson Creek, British Columbia, it's 915 miles to Whitehorse in the Yukon and a total of 1,420 to its official end in Delta Junction. To reach Fairbanks, take the Richardson Hwy, a continuation of the Alaska Highway. The Glenn Highway out of Tok leads to Anchorage.

ACCOMMODATION

Plenty of expensive motels along the way. Also numerous campgrounds; bring a tent. In and near Tok:
TOK International Youth Hostel, PO Box 532, Tok, AK 99780, 883-3745. Summer only; $7.50 AYH + non-AYH. Kitchen, beds, all in a big tent.

TRAVEL

'Make sure your car is in good running order and carry a few of the more essential spare parts. Garages charge what they like for spares.' Gas stations are every 20–50 miles, occasionally as far apart as 100 miles.
Hitching: long waits. Don't get let off at Tok Junction (which gets below-zero temps in Sept): 'horror stories abound of people getting stuck'. Alaskan law requires motorists to pick up hitchhikers when it is very cold out, but we don't recommend you put this to the test.
Greyhound bus service: year-round, fewer schedules in winter. Informative drivers; informality reigns.

INFORMATION

Tok Information Center, Alaska Public Lands Info Center, PO Box 359, Tok, AK 99780, 883-5667. 'Friendly, helpful.'
Milepost ($16.95 + $4.50 shipping in US, more for UK), is an essential mile-by-mile guide to the Highway, both Alaska and Canada portions. To order: Vernon Publishing, 300 Northrup Way #200, Bellevue, WA 98004 or call (800) 331-3510.
Free, useful literature about Alaska from Division of Tourism, PO Box E, Juneau, AK 99801, 465-2010.

ANCHORAGE Largest city (226,000) in Alaska and unremarkably modern since its rebuilding after the 1964 earthquake, Anchorage makes a good excursion base for Mt McKinley, the peninsula and the islands of southwestern Alaska. The quake sunk some of the land around here below sea level, inundating the ground with salt water. The result is an eerie vista of sodden, sterile land and skeletal trees.

Besides its transportation links and a fairly rambunctious nightlife, Anchorage also dabbles in the business of love: its *Alaskamen*, published every two months, provides profiles and photos of eligibles for women in the Lower 48, and is so far credited with 150 engagements and marriages. Single men outnumber single women in Alaska by 30–1, ripe conditions for matchmaking.

ACCOMMODATION

Anchorage International AYH Hostel, 700 H St, 276-3635. Open 8am–noon, 5pm–12am. $10 AYH, $15 non-members. Laundry, kitchen. 'Good place, easy to meet people.' 'Very crowded July–Aug.' Reservations recommended; out by noon.

Inlet Inn, 539 H St, downtown; other locations, 277-5541. No-frills budget chain; S-$60, D-$65, cheaper in winter.

South of Anchorage on the New Seward Hwy, in **Girdwood**: **Alyeska Home Hostel**, PO Box 10-4099, Anchorage, AK 99510, 783-2099, $8 AYH, $11 non-members. Wood-burning stove; 6 bunks, no laundry or bathing facilities. Reservations required. NB, All hostel reservations may be booked through the Alaska AYH Council on 562-7772.

North of Anchorage on Hwy 1 (btwn Palmer and Glennallen): **Sheep Mountain Lodge**, HC03 Box 8490, **Palmer**, AK 99645. Summer only; $8 AYH, $11 non-members. Cabins also available, D-$60, incl sauna. Free showers with both. Hot-tub, jacuzzi extra. Restaurant with home-cooked meals. Hiking.

In **Seward: Snow River International Home Hostel**, HCR 64, Box 425, Seward, AK 99664. $10 AYH, $13 non-members. Kitchen, bathroom. Must have sleeping bag.

FOOD/ENTERTAINMENT

Mr Whiteky's Fly-by-Night Club, 3300 Spenard Rd, 279-SPAM. Even in darkest Alaska, you can satisfy that unquenchable craving for Spam! This 'sleazy' place has Spam entrees in every imaginable configuration, as well as great nightly entertainment ('adult' musical show 'Whale Fat Follies', from $10, pokes fun at Alaska and its tourists, 8–10.30pm). Menu has now been 'expanded' to include desserts, sandwiches and seafood. Also serves fine champagnes, the recommended accompaniment to spam. (Your spam is free when you order Don Perignon.) Open Tue–Sat, 4pm–2am.

OF INTEREST

Museum of History and Art, 121 W 7th Ave, 343-4326. Historic and ethnographic art from all over Alaska. Open 9am–6pm Mon–Fri in summer, 10am–6pm Tues–Sat, Sun 1–5pm, from Sept 14. $4 adults.

Alaska Zoo, on O'Malley, off Seward Hwy, 346-3242. Open daily 9am–6pm, $6.

Nearby: Ekoutna Burial Grounds, 26 miles north on Glenn Hwy. Indian cemetery with spirit houses that look like doll houses, interesting gravesites. Get info from visitors bureau. 'Fascinating.'

There are still regular earth tremors—'one of 5.5 while we were here'—but nothing to compare with the 1964 monster quake—yet.

Must-see: the magnificent **Columbia Glacier**, 440 square miles of ice over a half-mile thick surging into Prince William Sound east of Anchorage. No overland access, but West Grey Line Tour, 547 W 4th Ave, 277-5581, operates the expensive **Glacier Queen** to the glacier's edge, where the Columbia 'calves' (breaks off) into the sea. Incipient icebergs are born with a thunderous roar and fountains of salt water and ice; the seals sunning themselves on ice floes nearby remain unperturbed. '*Go*—you'll never forget it.'

Portage Glacier, 53 miles south of Anchorage. Gray Line, 277-5581, offers several tours: 1-hour cruise leaving from dock on Portage Lake, $20; 7½-hour tour including transport to Portage Glacier and 1-hr cruise, $51. Gray Line and other tours available from Anchorage call at Alyeska Ski Resort, 40 miles south, on the way. Award winning film *Voices of the Ice* shown at Portage Glacier Visitors Information Center (end of Portage Hwy), 783-2326, 9.30am–6.30pm daily, by donation. 'Superb.' 'A must.'

INFORMATION

Visitors Bureau, 546 W 4th St, 274-3531. Open daily, in summer 7.30am–7pm; from Sept 8.30am–6pm.

Alaska Public Lands Information Center, 605 W 4th Ave, 271-2737. Open daily 9am–6pm. (Camping and shuttle reservations for Denali National Park stop at 6pm.) Info on state and federal recreational lands. 'Helpful; friendly people.'

TRAVEL

Alaska Airlines, Northwest, United, Western and MarkAir, 243-6275, in-state airline, fly to cities in Alaska.

The 80-yr-old Alaska RR runs between Anchorage and Fairbanks via Denali National Park ($120 one-way); call 456-4155, daily 7am–5pm. One train daily each way. Anchorage to Seward train ($70 return) passes within 800 ft of a glacier. Also daily bus from Anchorage to Portage, 278-5776 (take $16 train, dep 11am and 3pm, to Whittier, then $20 bus to Portage); several times weekly to Seward. 'Not a good town to be without a car.'

DENALI NATIONAL PARK Mount McKinley has twin peaks, the south being higher at 20,306 ft. Although Indians named it Denali (meaning 'the tall one'), the mountain was renamed for the US president while he was campaigning. A later president, Jimmy Carter, had it officially renamed Denali in 1979, but locals and the enlightened have always called it—both the park and the mountain—Denali.

This giant, tallest in North America, surveys a vast kingdom of tundra, mountain wilderness and unusual wildlife (caribou, Dall sheep, moose, grizzlies). The highway over **Polychrome Pass** into the valley of Denali is astonishing: a huge bowl, rimmed with frozen Niagaras of clouds tumbling over the encircling cliffs, spreads out before you. And in the distance, Denali itself, shrouded in cloud cover 75 per cent of the time in summer.

Eighty-six miles of gravel road allow you to see much of the park by bus (you can go into the park only 12 miles by car, unless you have a campsite reserved), but hiking one of the trails radiating from McKinley Park Hotel is the best way to enter into the spirit of the place. Best views of the mountaintop at **Wonder Lake**—'have to go at least 8 miles into the park to see the mountain'. Free shuttle buses to Wonder Lake, Eielson Visitors Center and other points. (Visitors Center ½ mile up Park Rd, 683-1266/1267, open daily 8am–8pm until late September, then 7am–6pm. Pick up coupons for free shuttle buses here. 'Fantastically situated; caribou come right up to the centre.') No food or gas in the park except at Park entrance. Don't overlook a trip to **Yentana**, the 'Galloping Glacier'—most beautifully coloured on earth. $3 entrance fee good for 7 days.

ACCOMMODATION
Denali Hostel, PO Box 801, Denali Pk, 683-1295, about 9 miles north of park entrance. Friendly hosts will pick up from park if you call ahead, $22.
The National Park Service, 683-2294, has several sites available in summer, one open year-round, on a first come, first served basis. $12/night. At the time of writing, Alaska was switching to the MISTIX system to reserve campsites.
If you're willing (and able!) to pay: **Denali National Park Hotel**, 276-7234, inside the park. S/D–$72.
Grizzly Bear Cabins, 6 miles south of main entrance, 683-2696. Tent cabins, D–$22, bath with showers with hot water nearby. Other cabins $51–$104 (subject to change). Reservations recommended (by VISA only), summer only.
Salmon Bake Hotel, 1 mile north of Park Entrance, 683-2733. S/D–$60, T/Q–$65, shared bath. Electricity, restaurant.

TRAVEL
Free and frequent shuttle bus service to all 7 campgrounds in park till Labor Day, reduced after that. Shuttles book up quickly but stand-bys available from 5.30am. Wildlife coach tours from the hotel recommended; $45 with box lunch; lasts approx. 7 hours. Open mid-May to mid-Sept. 'Interesting—*the* way to see wildlife and the park.' Rail, bus and air service from Anchorage and Fairbanks.

FAIRBANKS Warmest place in Alaska in summer and one of the coldest in the winter, Fairbanks was once a frontier town with 93 saloons in one three-block stretch. Today the second largest city, a direct result of the Pipeline and oil boom, it is 150 miles south of the Arctic Circle. Try to time your visit for one of its many festivals: the Eskimo/Indian Olympics (dancing, blanket toss, etc) each July and the Solstice Festival, 19–21 June, are among the wildest. Play or watch midnight baseball at the latter. 'Definitely the rough frontier town—drunken Indians everywhere.' 'Surprisingly nice—lots of trees.'

ACCOMMODATION
College Bunkhouse, 1541 Westwood Way, 479-2627. $15 a night. Within walking distance of university.
Cripple Creek Resort Hotel, Ester City, 6 miles from U of Alaska, 479-2500. Open June–Labor Day. Group transport available from major downtown hotels. S–$46, D–$60. Former mining camp with traditional, family-style meals, saloon, nightly entertainment. Unusual and popular. Home to the Malemute Saloon, notorious in Alaska. 'Awesome Northern Lights show here.'
Fairbanks Backpackers Hostel, 2895 Mack Rd, 479-2034, near the University of Alaska. $13.50 a night, will pick up from train station or airport.
Fairbanks Hotel, 517 3rd Ave, downtown, 456-6440. S–$45, D–$50 with shared bath; D–$60 w/private bath. Bus stop nearby. Small, clean, no frills.
Fairbanks International Youth Hostel, 1641 Willow St, 456-4159. At time of going to press, owner Paul Schulz was putting people up in his own home; call for current arrangements, about $6 AYH, $10 non-AYH.
Fairview Manor, 1260 Airport Way #3A2, 452-2662. Apartments rented by the week. $200 for 1-bedroom, can fit 3 persons; $250 for 2-bedroom, $350 for 3-bedroom, can fit up to 6, includes pots, pans and linen, $50 deposit.
Many bed and breakfasts including **Ah! Rose Marie**, 302 Cowles St, 456-2040. S–$43 up, D–$60 up. 'Loves to have students.' Close to bus line, centrally located.
Alaska's 7 Gables, 4312 Birch Lane, 479–0751. S/D–$45–$70, new beds. Inclusive: 'gourmet' breakfast, bikes, canoes, jacuzzis, cable TV, phones.
Delta Junction Youth Hostel, between Tok and Fairbanks (from Fairbanks take milepost 272 on Richardson Hwy), PO Box 971, Delta Junction, 99737, 895-5074. $7; sleeping bags required, no smoking.

OF INTEREST

U of Alaska Museum, 4.5 miles NW of city, 474-7505. Over 125,000 items; Eskimo arts and crafts. Open 9am–7pm summer; 9am–5pm September. $4, students $3. 'Superb, don't miss it.' 'Definitely one of Alaska's highlights.'

Alaskaland, Airport Way and Peger Road, 2 miles outside city near airport, 459-1087. The 44-acre site, developed to commemorate the Alaska Centennial in 1967, portrays state history with gold rush cabins, a sternwheeler, Indian and Eskimo villages and a mining valley. Free, closes Labor Day. Pricey, but gets praise: 'Alaska Salmon Bake—all you can eat; salmon, halibut, ribs, etc—lovely!' New 36-hole miniature golf course—the farthest north in the world! Old-fashioned carousel and train; various nightly shows. Also: **Fairbanks Summer Folk Fest** is held here in July, 457-6939.

Eagle Summit, 108 miles along the Steese Highway, from where you can watch the sun fail to set on 21 and 22 June.

INFORMATION

Alaska Public Lands Information Center, 250 Cushman, Suite 1A, 456-0527. Open 8.30am–9pm daily, w/ends 10am–6pm. Has free info films.

U of Alaska Student Union: info board for digs, rides, etc.

Visitors Information Center, 550 1st Ave, next to Golden Heart Park, 456-5774. 8am–8pm daily summer; Mon–Fri 8am–5pm, w/ends 10am–4pm.

TRAVEL

Air (see Anchorage)

Train to McKinley and Anchorage, call 456-4155 for reservations, open daily 7.30am–4pm. One train each way daily (once a week from mid-Sept, i.e. Sun to Anchorage; Sat return journey to Fairbanks.) $120 to Anchorage, $45 to Denali.

Local bus, 459-1011. 'Very limited, most journeys $1.50.' Daily 6.45am–7.45pm. 'Fairbanks very difficult without a car.'

CALIFORNIA

California. The word beckons, like an incantation: the Far West inspires images of sun, sand, surfing, Hollywood, adventure, health foods, healthy people and easy life. But California is much more complex than its popular image implies. You could spend a lifetime in the Golden State and still not see it all. It has the natural beauty of several states combined: rich redwood groves containing the tallest trees on earth; the stark superlatives of Death Valley; and the dizzying glacier-carved heights of Yosemite Valley. Like Shangri-La, California is cut off from the rest of the world by uninviting terrain: the volatile Trinity Alps in the north and the Sierras in the east; the Mojave Desert in the south; and to the west, over 100 miles of sunny beaches and rocky precipices on the Pacific Ocean coast.

When pioneers crossed the prairie to California, they found a land with potential for riches beyond mere gold, a promise that has since been fulfilled. There's more of everything in California—more people (over 30 million) more money (it's the world's 6th largest economic power), and more science activity (a disproportionate share of the US's pure science research and more Nobel laureates than the former Soviet Union). A key partner in the emerging Pacific Basin economy, California leads in both agricultural and industrial output, from avocados to aerospace, from Silicon Valley to Sunset Strip.

Recently, however, the golden image has begun to look a little tarnished. As unemployment figures rise, crime rates climb, LA riots and burns and is then hit by a killer earthquake. All the while the state gets more and more crowded, a certain disillusionment is apparent. The result: a *reverse* immigration trend, as Californians head *east* to seek the wide open spaces of states like Montana and Wyoming.

National Parks: Kings Canyon, Lassen Volcanic, Redwood, Sequoia, Yosemite

The major regions and cities of California are listed below, roughly from north to south.

ACCOMMODATION OVERVIEW

Perhaps in response to its popularity, California offers a great variety of lodging options, many of them dead cheap. This is but a brief summary to supplement specific information listed under *ACCOMMODATION* for each region or city.

Youth Hostels. Operating hostels number about 35, and new ones open all the time. Others are in a state of flux because of precarious funding. Always enquire locally—even the AYH handbook cannot keep pace with developments.

Motel 6. The chain began here, in the state that invented the motel. This 150-unit+ chain offers basic rooms at very reasonable rates. Call (505) 891-6161 (Albuquerque, NM) to reserve a room anywhere in California. No pampering: their 6pm 'show up or lose your reservation' policy is extremely firm; if you book ahead, be sure you'll be able to arrive on time. If you pre-paid and can't get there, you need to cancel the reservation before 6pm or no money back. If you're stuck, **E–Z Motels**, have been recommended as a similar budget alternative.

University lodgings. Many universities throw their dorms open to travelling students in the summer; also, most have housing offices that may list information on temporary housing. Accommodation in university towns is often easy to get in the summer, when all the students are gone; it may be more difficult if the university town is also a resort town (e.g. Santa Barbara, Santa Cruz, San Diego).

Camping. National Park and monument fees are from $6–$12 (in addition to an entrance fee of around $5 per vehicle.) Primitive campsites are often much less, sometimes free; most require permits for back country use. 'State campsites are a good deal if you have a carload of people. Very good facilities.''Police will allow sleeping on Southern Cal beaches (for foreign tourists anyway) but be careful—many are hangouts for gays with attendant queer-bashers.' Also, be advised that some coastal communities respond with hostility to car- or beach-sleepers—even those who are just passing through. Some local ordinances actually prohibit sleeping in any sort of vehicle within the city limits.

To reserve campsites: For reservations and campsite availability in CA state parks: call (800) 444-7275, $4–$30 per site plus $4 service charge, sites can accommodate up to 8 people. For national forests throughout the West Coast, call (800) 280-CAMP, $5–$20 per site plus a ghastly $6 service charge. Most campsites at national parks are first come, first served; however, sites at Yosemite and Sequoia can be reserved 8 weeks in advance in person through MISTIX, call (415) 556-4122 for info.

NORTHERN COAST Redwoods were plentiful on the American continent around the age of the dinosaurs. During the Ice Age, these trees barely escaped the fate of their old contemporaries. A narrow 400-mile-long strip was all that survived of the coastal species of *sequoia sempervirens,* and this remnant was further depleted by logging early in this century.

You can see these majestic survivors in the very northwesternmost corner of the state along two stretches of Hwy 101: **Humboldt Redwoods State Park** (take a detour off the highway north of Garberville to see the **Avenue of the Giants**); and **Redwood National Park**, which stretches from Orick to Crescent City and encompasses three state parks. In this park—a 'UNESCO World Heritage Site'—are the world's tallest trees, two over 367 feet tall. *The telephone area code is 707.*

ACCOMMODATION

This area is saturated with pricey bed and breakfast inns, which you should avoid in favour of inexpensive local motels. Camping fees for the parks are pretty stiff, considering you don't have a roof over your head, unless you are splitting the expense among several people.

Humboldt Redwoods State Park, 946-2409. 3 campgrounds, $14 per night for up to 8 people per camp.

Klamath Redwood Hostel, at Wilson Creek Rd (12 miles south of **Crescent City**), 482-8265. Newly restored 19th century home; $9 AYH or non-members. Close to beach and Redwood Forest. Greyhound will stop here, local buses will not.

Prairie Creek Motel, 488-3841, 2 miles north of **Orick** on Hwy 101. Charges by the person: 1 for $28, 2 for $34. 'Friendly Swiss and German couple. Can't recommend highly enough.'

Redwood National Park, 464-6101, encompasses 3 state parks that offer campsites with showers, $12-$14 per night.

FOOD

Chocolate Mousse, corner of Alban and Kasten 937-4323, in **Mendocino**, has excellent black-out cake; great for late-night coffee. Open 11.30am-9.30pm Mon-Thurs, Fri & Sat till 10.30pm, Sun 10am-9.30pm.

Prairie Creek Park Cafe, 2 miles north of **Orick** on Hwy 101, take Fern Canyon exit, 488-3841. Chow down on elk, buffalo and boar at the only gourmet restaurant in the area; $7-$16 dinners, closed Mon. Serves breakfast and lunch also.

Samoa Cookhouse, west of **Eureka**, across the Samoa Bridge spanning Humboldt Bay; turn left on Samoa Rd, take 1st left turn, 442-1659. This, the 'last of western cookhouses', is worth searching for. Loggers ate here once, and food is still served lumberjack-style: dish after dish arrives at long, communal tables, and everyone digs in. You'd have to be a lumberjack to finish it all. One price per meal for adults: B-$6, L-$6, D-$12.

OF INTEREST

Carson Mansion, 2nd & M Sts, **Eureka**. You can look at the exterior of this classic example of Victorian architecture, but you can't go inside (it's a men's club). Both Eureka and nearby Arcata have many other stately homes of this era.

Skunk Train, 964-6371, Laurel St, **Ft Bragg**. Steam engine (diesel in winter) takes you through tunnels and trees on an old logging run between Ft Bragg and Willits. $26 for full day, $21 for half, June-Sept.

Pygmy Forest, between Navarro and Noyo Rivers on Hwy 1; particularly visible around Jug Handle Creek, south of Ft Bragg. Impoverished and acidic soil has produced dwarfism in native cypress, manzanita and pine.

The town of **Mendocino** on Hwy 1, an artists' colony by the sea, is a wonderful place to stop, stretch and stroll. Artisans show & sell at Gallery Faire (crafts) and Studio 2 (jewellery), among others. The town appears as Cabot Cove in the TV series *Murder, She Wrote*. Be sure to visit **Mendocino Headlands State Park** while you're there. When they shot the movie, *The Russians are Coming* along the Mendocino coast, they were wrong: the Russians have been here and gone. See the well-restored proof at **Ft Ross**, a 19th century seal-hunting outpost, and the only genuine Russian military installation in the lower 48 states.

TRAVEL/INFORMATION
Redwood Information Center at Orick Ranger Station, PO Box 7, Orick, CA 95555, 488-3461. Open 8am–6pm summer, 9am–5pm rest of year. Greyhound passes through the park, stopping near park entrance. Tall Trees Shuttle from ranger station to grove is a 40-minute ride each way with 3 miles of walking through the trees; count on 4–5 hrs total. 'Superb walks through the redwood forest.'

MOUNT SHASTA and LASSEN VOLCANIC NATIONAL PARK Some 160 miles northwest of Sacramento stands 14,162-ft **Mt Shasta**, the white-haired patriarch of Northern California. Sharing the crest of the mountain is Shasta's slightly smaller mate, **Shastina**. Nearly overwhelmed by the massive pair is baby **Black Butte**, a pile of volcanic ash that attests to its parents' vigour.

Younger, shorter, hotter-headed sister to Mt Shasta is **Lassen Peak**, which last erupted in 1917—a wink of the geologic eye. Brilliantly bizarre moonscape, nasty mudpots, pools of turquoise and gold, sulphurous steam vents reveal volcanic activity, especially in the **Bumpass Hell** area. You are free to climb the 2½ miles to the three craters of Lassen: main road takes you near, trail is easy, fine views of Shasta and the devastation to the northeast. Excellent summer programmes: Ishi, the last Stone Age man in America, was found near Lassen, and the Manzanita Lake info centre has photo displays of him. Open year-round but snows keep most sectors inaccessible from late Oct to early June. $5 per car, $3 on foot. 'Yosemite is tame by comparison.' Park Info, 595-4444.
The telephone area code is 916.

ACCOMMODATION
Pine Needles Motel, 1340 S Mt Shasta Blvd, 926-4811. S–$37, D–$42.
Swiss Holiday Lodge, 2400 S Mt Shasta Blvd, 926-3446. Pretty chalet, tremendous view of Mt Shasta. S–$44, D–$46.
Camping at Lassen: Juniper is free, most sites open May–Sept; call 445-8828.

TRAVEL
Greyhound, 305 Mt Shasta Blvd, 241-2531, serves Redding.
Amtrak serves Redding and Dunsmuir, (800) 872-7245.

SACRAMENTO The capital of California is also an agricultural centre. Tomatoes are a big crop; the city is known affectionately as 'Sack O' Tomatoes'. It is also known by less affectionate (and unprintable) names by those Californians who apparently resent having such a hick town heading up such a sophisticated state.

Nothing more than a one-man barony until 1848, Sacramento mushroomed into prominence as a supply dump for Gold Rush miners. Today the city, at the confluence of the Sacramento and American Rivers, has a pleasant, midwestern feel. All its sights are downtown; the best way to see them is on foot.
The telephone area code is 916.

ACCOMMODATION
Berry Hotel, 729 L St, 442-2971. S-$28, D-$38. 'Threadbare but friendly.' Weekly & monthly rates available. $2 key deposit.
Capitol Park Hotel, 9th & L Sts, 441-5361. 1½ blocks from Greyhound. S-$31, D-$39. 'Very central, very clean.'
Motel 6, 1415 30th St, 457-0777. Close to Sutter's Ft, reachable by bus. S-$30, D-$40. Pool, AC, noisy (freeway nearby).

FOOD
Fanny Ann's Saloon, 1023 2nd St, 441-0505, Philly, turkey sandwiches, salads. 'A pleasant change from burgers.' Open 11.30am–2am.
Fox and Goose, 1001 R St, 443-8825. Real British pub fare. Open 7am–12am.

OF INTEREST
Old Sacramento, 28-acre historic district on Sacramento River. Over 100 renovated buildings, 41 of them 19th century originals. Especially evocative at night. Includes **Sacramento History Center, Old Eagle Theatre, Pony Express Monument** and **State Railroad Museum**, the last open daily 10am–5pm, $5; 445-4209.
Sutter's Ft, 2701 L St, 445-4422, the bane of Sacramento schoolchildren, should fascinate anyone interested in history. **State Indian Museum**, on the same park-like grounds, displays examples of an Indian sweathouse and a teepee. Both daily 10am–5pm; $2.
State Capitol, 10th St at Capitol Mall. Magnificently restored to its 19th century grandeur. Eat lunch in the reasonably-priced basement cafeteria (a pleasant enough dungeon) or picnic on the lawn under massive deodar cedars (the species originated in the Himalayas). Open Mon–Fri 9am–5pm; Sat/Sun 10am–4pm; hourly tours.
Old Governor's Mansion, 16th & H Sts, 323-3047. Charming wedding-cake Victorian, open 10am–4pm, $2. 'Best sight in city,' 'good tour and stories'.
Crocker Art Museum, 216 O St, 264-5423. Stately old mansion with staid old paintings; catch the sometimes-wild modern art exhibits upstairs. Wed–Sun 10am–5pm, Thurs 'til 9pm, closed Mon & Tue. $3.50.
Nearby: Mother Lode country, with its vivid gold and ghost towns and Sierra scenery: **Coloma**, where James Marshall found the nugget that set off the Rush, **Nevada City** and **Folsom** are served by Greyhound and (in patchwork fashion) by local buses.

INFORMATION
Visitors Bureau, 1104 Front St, Old Sacramento, 442-7644. Open 9am–5pm Mon–Sat.
Travelers Aid, 717 K St, Suite 217, 443-1719.

TRAVEL
Greyhound, 715 L, (800) 231-2222. 'Gambler's buses ($17) to Tahoe, Reno—if you can afford to lay out the fare. On arrival Harrah's Casino gives you money in chips and food voucher. Details in local papers—a great day out.'
Regional transit: buses and a new light rail system, 321-2877. $3 day pass. You can walk from 6th and K to Old Sac (3 blks).
Amtrak, 4th & I, 444-2280 or (800) 872-7245.
Cars R Us, 500 N 12th St, 448-4074. From $25/day. Open 9am–5pm, Mon–Fri.
River City Queen, 921-1111, has 2-hr boat trips up and down the Sacramento River, $24, w-ends only.
Sacramento Airport is located 8 miles NW of town and is served by numerous shuttle bus companies who will pick you up from any downtown area. The journey takes 20–30 minutes o/w and will cost $9–$15, depending on where you are picked up from. Call in advance to reserve: Gold Dust Shuttles (944-4444) or Sacramento Metro (962-1222).

LAKE TAHOE For two adjacent states, California and Nevada seem worlds apart: one is verdant, varied and mellow; the other, desiccated, monotonous and frantically on the make. Nowhere is the contrast greater than on the shores of the lake the states share, Lake Tahoe, a sapphire in a mountain setting two hours east of Sacramento. On the California side, South Lake Tahoe is a ski-bum village in winter, a granola filling station for hikers in summer. Across the border in Stateline, Nevada, casino-dwellers pump the one-armed bandits year-round, rarely venturing out into the light of day. Both sides have natural beauty to spare, although the area gets ridiculously crowded in mid-summer and during the ski season.
The telephone area code is 916 in California and 702 in Nevada.

ACCOMMODATION
Econolodge, 3536 S Lake Tahoe Blvd, 544-2036. S–$31, D–$39 during the week. More expensive at w-ends and during the ski-season.
Shenandoah Motel, 4074 Pine Blvd, **South Lake Tahoe**, 544-2985. Summer rates: S/D–$38, XP–$5. Colour TV, 4 blocks from Nevada casinos.
Tahoe Mountain Lodge, 3868 Hwy 50, **South Lake Tahoe**, 541-6380. Weekdays: S–$20, D–$31; 'variable' on weekends, which means they stick it to you.
Value Inn Motel, 2659 S Lake Tahoe Blvd, 544-3959. S–$31, D–$37 during the week.
Camping in state parks and forests around Lake Tahoe, from $10–$12. See *Accommodation* overview for info on reserving campsites.

OF INTEREST
Truckee near Donner Pass on Hwy 80: wooden buildings and a frontier atmosphere. 2 miles west of Truckee is **Donner State Park**, where in the winter of 1846–47, the 89-member Donner party was trapped by 22-ft snows (memorial statue there is as tall as the snow was deep that year). Only 47 survived the ordeal, many of them resorting to cannibalism.

INFORMATION
Visitors Bureau and Chamber of Commerce, Hwy 50, South Lake Tahoe, 541-5255. Open Mon–Fri 8.30am–5pm, Sat–Sun 9am–4pm.

TRAVEL
Greyhound, 1099 Park Ave, South Lake Tahoe, 544-2241. Open 7.30am–6.30pm. LTR busline also in terminal. Train rides from Truckee to Reno provide magnificent views of the lake.

WINE COUNTRY Both **Napa Valley** and its less-famous neighbour **Sonoma Valley** are noted for superlative viticulture; these areas produce everything from world-class cabernets to sassy jug wines. Just two hours by car from San Francisco, the scenery alone is worth the trip. Bus service to both valleys is good, but renting a car is a capital way to tour. That way, you can alternate wine-tasting with stops at farms, roadside stands, cheese factories, delis and other tasty locales.

Besides wine, you can taste the sparkling mineral water that bubbles out of the ground at **Calistoga** and visit the spas there; watch gliders and hot air balloons over the vineyards; visit Jack London's Beauty Ranch near old-worldly **Glen Ellen**; and maybe even pause a moment at the Tucolay Cemetery near Napa, where Mammy Pleasant is buried. A 19th century black civil rights advocate who owned a string of San Francisco brothels,

Mammy Pleasant gave more than $40,000 to finance John Brown's raid on Harper's Ferry and travelled around the South to raise sentiment for Brown among the blacks. Her headstone reads: 'Mother of civil rights in California, friend of John Brown.'
The area code here is 707.

ACCOMMODATION
Budget accommodation in the wine country is hard to find; B&B prices hover around $50–$100 per night, tending towards the high end of the scale.
Bothe-Napa Valley State Park, 3801 St Helena Hwy, 942-4575. Sites $12 for 1 vehicle, $5 each additional vehicle; hot showers available. Open 8am–dusk.
Calistoga Spa Hot Springs, 1006 Washington St, Calistoga, 942-6269. D–$78, weekdays. Discounts for 4 days (10%), 7 days (15%). Reservations advised.
Triple-S Ranch, 4600 Mountain Home Ranch Rd, Calistoga, 942-6730. These all-wood cabins are a good deal: 2 people for $49. Reservations recommended on weekends.

FOOD
Restaurant fare tends to be dauntingly expensive in most instances, but there are numerous delis and stores with picnic makings, and many wineries have pleasant picnic areas. Get suggestions for good grocery stores and bakeries from the locals. Some good ones are the Sonoma and Vella Cheese Factories; the Sonoma French Bakery (San Franciscans come *here* for sourdough bread); the Twin Hill Ranch near Sebastopol (applesauce bread); and the Oakville Grocery in Oakville. Calistoga has at least 7 all-different breakfast places. Affordable restaurants with good food include:
Curb Side Cafe, 1245 1st St, **Napa**, 253-2307. $5–$7 sandwiches.
The Diner, 6476 Washington St, **Yountville**, 944-2626. Good breakfasts, Mexican food. Try the flautas.

OF INTEREST
Wineries: Over 250 in Napa Valley alone. The tiny ones tucked away on side roads are informal and fun, but you need a car to get to them. The big 7 wineries, from north to south, are: **Christian Brothers**, housed in a castle with catacomb-like cellars where the wine ages in gargantuan barrels; **Mondavi**, Cliff May building, 'technical tour,' picnics on the lawn; **Inglenook**, mix of old and new buildings (the winery in back is owned by Francis Ford Coppola); **Beaulieu**, good tours; **Martini**; **Beringer**, whose Gothic Rhine House is a landmark; and **Krug**, the oldest in the valley. Other good wineries: **Sterling**, 1111 Dunaweal Ln, 942-3000, near Calistoga. Open 10.30am–4.30pm daily, $6 tram to 'spectacular view'. **Stag's Leap**, 5766 Silverado Tr, Napa, has superb wine that measures up to the Continent's best; 944-2020 to arrange a tour. For champagne, hit **Kornell Brothers** in Calistoga. Around Sonoma are 4 more standouts, from **Sebastiani** to **Buena Vista**. The latter is the original winery of Agoston Haraszthy, the Hungarian 'count' who brought European vinestock to the US. Green Hungarian is good; Mozart Festival here in summer. Most wineries have tasting at the end of tours, 10am–4pm or so. 'Christian Brothers' last tour of the day is more like party-night than wine tasting-you get half glasses to taste!' 'Christian—one of the best—lets you try as many wines as you like.'
Jack London State Historic Park, off Hwy 12 in **Glen Ellen**, 938-5216. Contains ruins of Wolf House, built by author of *Call of the Wild*. Museum open 10am–5pm, Park open 9.30am–7pm, $5 admission per vehicle.
Robert Louis Stevenson Park, in **St Helena**, 7 miles northeast of Calistoga on Hwy 29. Free, day use only, wonderful picnicking and hiking (new trail leading to former site of RLS house). Bring your own water or wine.
Sonoma is still centred around its lush plaza, where in 1846 Yankee rebels raised a grizzly-bear flag and established the short-lived Republic of California. The

republic gave way 40 days later to US control, but the flag, and its symbol, stuck. Remnants of Spanish control still exist here, including the **mission** and **Lachryma Montis**, home of General Vallejo, who once govered much of California. If you have the chance, take the highway from Sonoma to Hwy 80; it's a beautiful drive any time of year.

INFORMATION
The local Chambers of Commerce are helpful. Be sure to pick up their farm trails brochures: Napa Chamber of Commerce, 1556 1st St, Napa, 226-7455. Open 9am–5pm Mon–Fri; Sonoma Chamber of Commerce, 645 Broadway, 996-1033. Open Mon–Fri 9am–5pm; St Helena Chamber of Commerce, 1080 Main St, 963-4456. Open Mon–Fri 10am–4pm.
Wine Institute, 425 Market St, Ste 1000 (1½ blocks east of Union Sq in San Francisco), (415) 512-0151. Offers free guide to Napa Valley. Open Mon–Fri 9am–5pm.

TRAVEL
Greyhound serves Napa to St Helena, Calistoga twice daily; but the trip requires an overnight stay. If you get off at St Helena, it's an easy walk to 3 wineries immediately north of town. Service also to Sonoma.
Golden Gate Transport (544-1323) to Santa Rosa (about $5) and then #30 bus to the vineyards.

MARIN COUNTY Linked to San Francisco by the slender scarlet bracelet of the Golden Gate Bridge is Marin County, whose predominant hues are two shades of green—green hills and green money. The western edge, facing the Pacific, is wild, windblown, solitary and beautiful. Among its treasures is the 70,000-acre **Pt Reyes National Seashore**, which has an earthquake trail along the San Andreas Fault. At the very point of Pt Reyes is a lighthouse; from December to February, migrating gray whales can sometimes be seen from here. Further up the peninsula is **Tomales Bay State Park. Drake's Beach** is another gem, where Sir Francis may have landed when he claimed all of Nova Albion for Elizabeth I.

Near Pt Reyes are other public wilderness sanctuaries, among them popular **Stinson Beach** (closest swimming beach to San Francisco, enquire locally about the sea serpent) and **Muir Woods**, 6 miles of cool trails through a hushed and fragrant cathedral of *sequoia sempervivens*, some as tall as 240 feet. **Mt Tamalpais**, favourite of hikers and bicyclers, commands fantastic views; its trails link up with Stinson's, Muir Wood's and others.

Inner Marin is stuffed with plush communities that line the northwest shore of San Francisco Bay. From **Tiburon** you can take a ferry to nearby **Angel Island**, which has seen several incarnations as a duelling field, military staging ground for three wars, quarantine station for Asian immigrants and a missile site. The island is now a state park with campsites, friendly deer, bicycling trails and the ghostly ruins of Civil War officers' houses to explore. Former whalers' harbour **Sausalito** has the best view of San Francisco, lots of costly, cutesie bars and boutiques, and a houseboat colony, the last vestige of its bohemian past. 'A fantastic way to get a feel for the area is to take a ferry to Sausalito and walk back across the Golden Gate Bridge. Once across, you can catch a bus back to downtown.'
The telephone area code for Marin County is 415.

ACCOMMODATION
The hostel and camping situation in Marin:
Angel Island camping, $9 per camp (8 people per camp max). To stay in one of the island's 9 camps, you must reserve in advance by phone, (800) 444-7275, or by mail, MISTIX, PO Box 85705, San Diego, CA 92138-5705. Reservations are accepted up to 8 weeks in advance by phone, 9 weeks by mail, which is just about how far ahead you'll have to reserve a place if you want to stay on Sat night. Fireplaces, water, chemical toilets.
Also see San Francisco section *Housing Information*.
Golden Gate Hostel, 941 Fort Barry, **Sausalito**, CA 94965, 331-2777. Open year-round, 3 miles from bus stop near tunnel. $9 for both AYH members and non-members. Handsome former officers' quarters, rec room, well-equipped kitchen, laundry, bicycle storage. Bring food. 'Very spacious hostel.' Check-in 4.30pm–11pm; out by 9.30am. Runs shuttle to downtown SF some summers, call ahead. Otherwise, you'll need a car to get into the city. 'Popular but far from centre of town.'
Point Reyes Hostel, Box 247, Point Reyes Station, CA 94956, 663-8811. $9. Check-in 4.30–9.30pm; out by 9.30am. Write to reserve beds.

FOOD/ENTERTAINMENT
Gray Whale Pizza, 669-1244, off Hwy 1 in **Inverness**, enroute to Pt. Reyes. 'Huge, excellent pizzas.'
Greater Gatsby's, 39 Caledonia, **Sausalito**, 332-4500. Come see Marin mellow out in this restaurant/bar. Bar opens at 11am, food served from 11.30am, closes midnight.
Mayflower Inn, 1533 4th, near Shaver, **San Rafael**, 456-1011. Genuine British pub with darts on Tue & Wed and raucous singing at any time. Bangers, pasties, fish & chips, and pints of Guinness in front of a blazing fire. Guaranteed to cure any case of homesickness. Open Mon–Fri 11.30am–2am, Sat–Sun 9am–2am.

OF INTEREST
Rainbow Tunnel, Hwy 1 northbound from Golden Gate Bridge to Marin County. A monument to a CalTrans engineer's whimsy. You'll know it when you see it.
San Francisco Bay Model, 2100 Bridgeway, 332-3871. Constructed by the Army Corps of Engineers, the hydraulic model simulates tides, oil spills, etc. Tue–Fri 9am–4pm, Sat, Sun & hols 10am–6pm.
Ferries from Tiburon to Angel Island, 435-2131.
Marin County Civic Center, San Rafael. Reminiscent of a Roman aqueduct, the civic center is a riot of pink and turquoise against emerald hills and azure California sky. Some people love this Frank Lloyd Wright structure; some call it the Bay Area's biggest sore thumb. Whatever your opinion, you shouldn't miss seeing it—and if you travel through Marin County on Hwy 101, you won't. Tours on request.

SAN FRANCISCO Big, beautiful Baghdad-by-the-Bay, San Francisco is a city that flows like a magic carpet of images: hills, bridges, cable cars, fog, ferryboats, gays, painted Victorians, earthquakes, movie car chases. Known to all simply as 'the City' ('Frisco' warrants the death sentence), San Francisco occupies a peerless setting on the tip of a green and hilly thumb separating ocean from bay. A narrow strait, fraught with dangerous under-tows, is spanned with a sense of drama by a shimmering Golden Gate Bridge. Seen from afar, the city is by turns a citadel shining in the sun, a bank of diamonds glittering in the night, a coquette peeking over a ruff of fog, heartbreakingly lovely. Closer examination reveals imperfections: slums, cold corporate canyons, porno districts and boxy tract homes and, with memories of the 1989 earthquake still fresh, the ever-present fear of the 'big one'. Never mind; even with its flaws, San Francisco is still way ahead of whoever's in second place.

History and geography have conspired to make San Francisco a city of neighbourhoods in the European manner. Ethnic differences are not assimilated but encouraged, imparting a cosmopolitan flavour that comes as a welcome relief after the monotony of much of urban America. This westernmost of Western cities, paradoxically, is America's door to the East—to China, Hong Kong, Japan, and the rest of Asia—with which California does more business than with Europe.

It's hard to have a bad time here. The wealth of things to see and do, the diverse and delicious foods, and most of all, the San Franciscans themselves, make visiting a delight. People migrate here not to be successful but to be (or learn to be) happy and human. Their efforts make San Francisco a city of good manners, full of little kindnesses and occasional gallant acts, whether saving whales or cable cars, that speak of altruism and love.

Temperatures are mild year-round. Spring and autumn offer the most sunshine, but come prepared for brisk winds and chilly weather at any time. Unexpectedly, summer is when the city's famous fog crosses the line into infamy. Mark Twain, it is said, once complained that the 'coldest winter I ever spent was a summer in San Francisco'.

San Francisco's central location is perfect for daytrips to nearby attractions. Berkeley, Santa Cruz, Marin County and the Napa and Sonoma wine country can be reached within two hours by public transport. It's more likely that, when it comes time to leave, you'll have to tear yourself away. When in San Francisco, remember three things: wear strong shoes, watch for seagulls and keep an eye on your heart at all times; otherwise as the song says, you'll probably leave it here.

The telephone area code is 415.

SURVIVAL

San Francisco's Greyhound depot is located in a scruffy-to-rotten district, predictably worse at night. When seeking accommodation, bear in mind that the large triangle formed by Market, Divisadero and Geary is a high crime area which spills over to the other side of Market, where the Greyhound depot is. The worst section is the Western Addition, bounded by Geary, Hayes, Steiner and Gough. Stay out, day or night (no reason to visit, anyway). Other dicey streets at night are the first four blocks of Turk, Eddy and Ellis. That doesn't mean you shouldn't stay here—just be aware and exercise caution, particularly after dark.

ACCOMMODATION

NB: The best accommodation goes quickly, especially in youth hostels, so check in early. If arriving late, phone ahead. Accommodation info also available at Greyhound. See also hostel listings for Marin County.

AYH Travel Services, 425 Divisadero, Suite 301, 863-9939, provides hostel information, travel services, books and supplies. Mon–Sat noon–6pm.

AYH Hostel at Union Square, 312 Mason St, 788-5604. $14 members, $17 nonmembers. New 200-bed hostel right in the centre of things. Open 24 hrs, 14 nights max stay.

to Sausalito past Alcatraz, the infamous prison; locally known as 'hills' while dangling from the on a MUNI tram for a tour of the peninsula; or the Golden Gate Bridge in the evening, San Francisco is fairly com-

AAIH San Francisco European Guest House International Hostel, 761 Minna St, 861-6634. $13/night for shared dorms, 3 to 6 per room. Run by former Greyhound driver and 15 mins walk from Greyhound. Kitchen, TV rm, lockers. No curfew. 'Very friendly; totally mixed.' 'Don't seem to turn anyone away so very hot and crowded.' 'Not a safe area at night.' 'Excellent staff.' 'We arrived at 7.15am and it was already full (for males).' 'Shared a bathroom with 20 others.'

Adelaide Inn, 5 Isodora Duncan, 441-2261. S–$36, D–$47, XP–$6. Shared bathroom facs. Continental breakfast incl.

Amsterdam Hotel, 749 Taylor, 673-3277. S–$51, D–$56 shared bath. 'Clean and friendly.' Continental bfast incl.

Ansonia Hotel and Residence Club, 711 Post St, 673-2670. S–$42 hall bathroom. Rates include breakfast and room phones. International clientele. 'Very clean.'

Castor Hotel, 705 Vallejo St, 788-9709. S–$20. 'Central location. Given outside key so no curfew.'

Central YMCA, 220 Golden Gate Ave, 885-0460. S–$32.

Gates Hotel, 140 Ellis St, 781-0430. S–$39, $28 shared bath; D–$47, $32 shared bath +$5 key deposit. 'Handy location. Always has beds.'

Geary Hotel, 610 Geary St, 673-9221. 'Helpful, clean, will give student discount.' S–$41, D–$47.

Golden Gate Hotel, 775 Bush, between Powell and Mason, 392-3702. S/D–$61, shared bath. Excellent location, within walking distance to just about everything; safe and clean. 'Very friendly and helpful staff.' 'We got 4 in a room for $48.' Continental bfast and tea.

Harcourt Residence Club, 1105 Larkin St, 673-7720. Weekly rates only; $130 shared bath, $150 private bath. Incls breakfast and dinner, maid service. Sundeck, lounge with 40″ colour TV, $20 key deposit. 'Excellent for meeting friends.'

Hotel All Seasons, 417 Stockton St, 2 blks N of Union Square, 986-8737. S–$45, D–$51 with private bath. 'Very friendly, ideal for Chinatown and Fisherman's Wharf.' 'Excellent, safe, clean if dull.'

Hotel One, 587 Eddy St, 775-5934. 5 min from Greyhound. S–$39, D–$43 shared bath; $5 extra with private bath. Colour TV, newly remodeled. 'Clean.' 'Rough area.' Price includes brkfst.

Interclub Globe Hostel, 10 Hallam Pl, 431-0540, on Folsom between 7th & 8th. From Greyhound take bus #14 or 15 min walk. $15 shared dorms, in nightclub district, no curfew. $10 key deposit. 'Brilliant atmosphere—best hostel I stayed in'. 'Druggy area.'

Olympic Hotel, 140 Mason, 982-5010. S–$28 without bath, D–$35 with bath. Half a block from bus stop, near Hilton. 'Very nice, friendly.' 'Clean rooms, excellent value.' 'In an area of sex shops and prostitution.'

Pacific Tradewinds Guest House, 680 Sacramento St, 433-7970. Converted apartment owned and run by two former backpackers. $14 per night in clean, comfortable dorms. Centrally and conveniently located in Chinatown, close to Market St and all public transport. 'Very friendly and homely atmosphere.' 'Best accommodation I stayed in.'

Pensione International, 875 Post St, 775-3344. S/D–$45. 'Central, comfortable and friendly.' Continental bfast incl. $5 discount for AYH members.

San Francisco International Hostel, Bldg 240, Ft Mason, on Bay & Franklin, 771-7277. Take 42, 47 or 49 bus from Van Ness. $13 per night, 3 nights max. Dorm overlooking the bay, kitchen, laundry. Ft Mason itself has many attractions and is close to others. 'Arrive early—fills very quickly.' 'The abundance of British students makes it a good place to head for if you're alone and want to share costs.' 'Full by 8am.' Open 7am–2pm, 4.30pm–midnight.

Hotel Verona, 317 Leavenworth St, 771-4242. S–$30, D–$40. 'Great location.'

The Original San Francisco Roommate Referral Service, 610A Cole St, 558-9191. A $24 fee gets you lists of rooms to rent—shared housing only. 'Very helpful, found somewhere straight away.'

FOOD

Food is one of the things San Francisco does best; sampling the amazing variety of local cuisines is a top priority. The city grew as a seaport, so eat like a sailor: Dungeness crab and sourdough bread, Irish coffee and Anchor Steam, the local beer. Move on to other cultures in one of the many excellent and cheap ethnic restaurants—Persian and Basque, Salvadorean and Greek, Szechuan and Russian, Italian and Vietnamese.

Atmosphere: **Buena Vista Cafe**, 2765 Hyde, 474-5044. Go on a foggy night and listen to foghorns moan and cable cars clang while you nurse an Irish coffee (introduced to the US in 1953 by SF newspaperman Stanton Delaplane). 'Extremely crowded'. **Hamburger Mary's**, 1582 Folsom, 626-5767. 'Best hamburgers, good music, friendly atmosphere, run by gays'. **Specs' 12 Adler Museum Cafe**, 12 Adler St, off Columbus, 421-4112. Finding this seedy and wonderfully authentic North Beach bar can be a challenge, but its location (down an obscure alley called Saroyan) keeps it safe from the hordes of conventioneers swarming along Columbus. Don't bring your little dog, Dorothy; **Tommy's Joynt**, Van Ness and Geary, 775-4216. 'Great decor, huge buffalo stew.' Open 11am–1.45am.

Breakfast: **Brother Juniper's**, 1065 Sutter St, 771-8929. Homemade breads, muffins, peaceful atmosphere. 'Best breakfast in town, original dishes, $6 or less.' Proceeds go to family shelter behind restaurant. Lunch also: **Doidges**, 2217 Union, at Filmore, 921-2149, serves lunch as well until 1.45pm weekdays and until 2.45pm weekends. Need reservations. **Pinecrest Restaurant**, Mason and Geary. 'Dinner and breakfast served, all day. Open 24 hrs. **Sears Fine Foods**, 439 Powell. Try French toast made from sourdough bread. 'Excellent breakfast, go extra early'. **Economy Restaurant**, 18 7th St, 552-8830. '2 eggs, 3 sausage, hash browns, toast—$2.37.' Breakfast all day. Open daily 6.30am–8pm.

Burritos: **La Cumbre**, 515 Valencia, near 16th, 863-8205.

Greek: **Athens Greek Restaurant**, 39 Mason. Open daily, 11am–midnight.

Hamburgers: **Hot 'N Hunky**, 4039 18th, 621-6365. Just like it sounds. **Original Joes's**, 144 Taylor, between Turk & Eddy, 775-4877, serves 12-ounce burgers—regular or charbroiled (after 5pm)—for under $6 (European soccer teams eat here). Open Mon–Fri, 10.30am–1am.

Italian: **Little Joe's**, 523 Broadway, 982-7639. Spectacular chefs, huge portions—ask to split spaghetti con pesto or roast chicken. Open daily 11am–11pm. **Tommasso** 1042 Kearny, 398-9696, for pizza. Open daily 10am–10pm.

Oriental: Best tempura at **Sanppo**, 1702 Post, 346-3486; best Szechuan at **Tsing Tao**, 3107 Clement, between 32nd & 33rd, 387-2344.

Indian: **Sirtaj Indian Cuisine**, 48 5th St, 957-0140. All-you-can-eat lunch buffet $6. 'Mildly spicy; veg & non-veg. Full of local people.'

Sourdough bread: **Boudin Bakery**. Several locations (Pier 39, Fisherman's Wharf, Ghiradelli Square), 928-1849. Best sourdough outside Sonoma, CA.

Steaks: **Tad's Steak House**, 120 Powell, 982-1718. Steak, salad and bread for $6. 'Excellent food.' Open daily 6.30am–11pm.

Sweet tooth: **Gelato Classico**, 576 Union. The standard of excellence in Italian ices. **Ice Cream Delight**, 2205 Clement, serves Lappert's ice cream. Born on the Hawaiian island of Kauai, Lappert's is considered by some to be the best ice cream in the free world. At 16%–18% butterfat, you can't get ice cream richer than this, unless you want to eat frozen butter. **Just Desserts**, four locations. 'Best cheesecake, chocolate cake in the city.'

Vegetarian: **Green's at Fort Mason**, Bldg A, Laguna St at Marina Blvd, 771-6222. 'Culinary experience for vegetarians. View of the bay very beautiful.'

OF INTEREST

Don't go looking for 'sights' and miss the best one: San Francisco itself. The best way to take it all in is to alternate walking with cable car or bus riding. Spend at least half your time away from the tourist ghetto of Fisherman's Wharf, The Cannery, Pier 39, Ghiradelli Square, etc, all of which are aimed squarely at your wallet. You've missed an essential part of the city's heart if you don't do one or

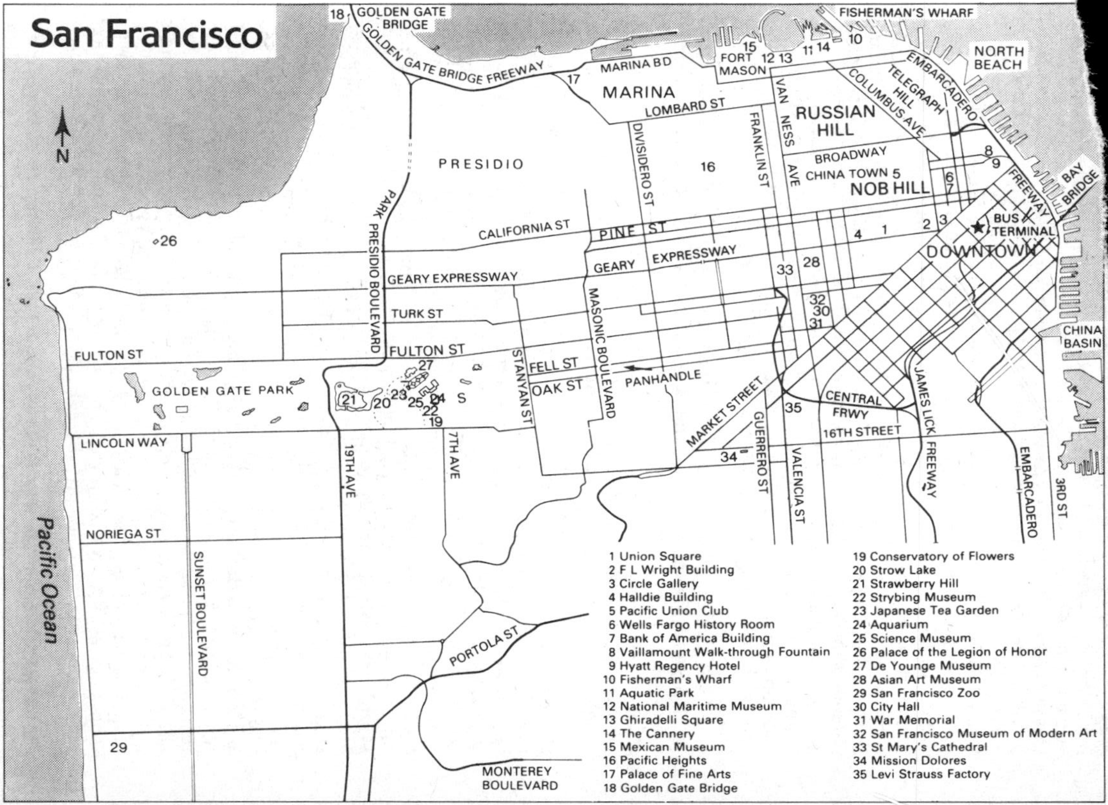
San Francisco
N
GOLDEN GATE BRIDGE
GOLDEN GATE BRIDGE FREEWAY
FISHERMAN'S WHARF
NORTH BEACH
FORT MASON
MARINA BD
MARINA
LOMBARD ST
RUSSIAN HILL
TELEGRAPH HILL
COLUMBUS AVE
EMBARCADERO
BROADWAY
CHINA TOWN
NOB HILL
VAN NESS AVE
FRANKLIN ST
DIVISIDERO ST
PRESIDIO
PARK PRESIDIO BOULEVARD
CALIFORNIA ST
PINE ST
GEARY EXPRESSWAY
GEARY
EXPRESSWAY
TURK ST
FULTON ST
FELL ST
OAK ST
STANYAN ST
MASONIC BOULEVARD
PANHANDLE
MARKET STREET
GUERRERO ST
VALENCIA ST
CENTRAL FRWY
16TH STREET
JAMES LICK FREEWAY
FREEWAY
BAY BRIDGE
BUS TERMINAL
DOWNTOWN
CHINA BASIN
EMBARCADERO
3RD ST
GOLDEN GATE PARK
LINCOLN WAY
19TH AVE
7TH AVE
NORIEGA ST
SUNSET BOULEVARD
PORTOLA ST
MONTEREY BOULEVARD
Pacific Ocean
1 Union Square
2 F L Wright Building
3 Circle Gallery
4 Halldie Building
5 Pacific Union Club
6 Wells Fargo History Room
7 Bank of America Building
8 Vaillamount Walk-through Fountain
9 Hyatt Regency Hotel
10 Fisherman's Wharf
11 Aquatic Park
12 National Maritime Museum
13 Ghiradelli Square
14 The Cannery
15 Mexican Museum
16 Pacific Heights
17 Palace of Fine Arts
18 Golden Gate Bridge
19 Conservatory of Flowers
20 Strow Lake
21 Strawberry Hill
22 Strybing Museum
23 Japanese Tea Garden
24 Aquarium
25 Science Museum
26 Palace of the Legion of Honor
27 De Younge Museum
28 Asian Art Museum
29 San Francisco Zoo
30 City Hall
31 War Memorial
32 San Francisco Museum of Modern Art
33 St Mary's Cathedral
34 Mission Dolores
35 Levi Strauss Factory

stand on the Marin headlands north of
watching the lights of the city come on. Unlike LA, Sa
pact, easy to comprehend and well equipped with public transport to give
legs a much-needed break on its 43-plus hills.

Union Square: City centre, named on the eve of the Civil War. In 1906, the square served as emergency camp for earthquake refugees. Nearby is **Maiden Lane**, once a red-hot red-light district, now a charming cul-de-sac with the only Frank Lloyd Wright building in the city—the **Circle Gallery**. A striking tunnel entrance and interior ramp leads to this art gallery, the prototype for the Guggenheim Museum in New York City. The Gallery is at 140 Maiden Lane, 989-2100, Mon–Sat 10am–6pm, Sun noon–5pm, free.

North at 130 Sutter is the progenitor of the modern glass skyscraper, the 1917 **Hallidie Building**. Superb stores abound; even Woolworth's is nice, although **Gump's** is the local landmark among them. You'll also find **theatres** on Geary and **cinemas** on Market. At Market and New Montgomery is the **Sheraton-Palace Hotel**, whose lacy skylighted garden court was the sole remnant in this luxurious structure after the 1907 earthquake. Singer Enrico Caruso was staying in the Palace when the quake hit; he rushed out, said 'Give me Vesuvius!' and left SF in haste.

Nob Hill: Cable car lines criss-cross here; transfer point. **Cable Car Museum**, Washington & Mason, 474-1887: 'The cable cars are powered from here, see how they work, very interesting.' Open daily 10am–6pm; free. North of Union Square is the grande dame of SF hills; prior to the quake it was crowded with mansions, of which only the **Pacific Union Club** was left standing. If you're dressed for it, take the elevators to the view bars atop the **Fairmont** and **Mark Hopkins Hotels**. (The Fairmont features in the TV soap *Hotel.)*

Chinatown: more Chinese live here than in any other Chinatown in the states. Inhabiting Grant and Stockton between Bush and Broadway, SF's Chinatown can be a crowded confusion of sights, smells and sounds. 'Do yourself a favour and spend a couple of hours just wandering around taking it all in, especially the seafood shops.' All the tourists go to Grant; you should explore Stockton, Washington and little side streets to see: herbal shops at 837 and 857 Washington; fortune cookies being made at Mee Mee, 1328 Stockton; and t'ai chi practiced in the morning at Portsmouth Sq, RL Stevenson's old hang-out between Clay and Washington, where the City began.

Financial district: **Montgomery St** is the 'Wall Street of the West'. **Wells Fargo History Museum**, 396-2619, 420 Montgomery. The bank whose symbol is a stagecoach pays homage to its worst enemy, Black Bart, who robbed Wells Fargo 28 times in 7 years (successfully all but once). Also includes other mementoes of the Old West. Free, Mon–Fri 9am–5pm.

Bank of America Building. This building, the second tallest in the city, is pretty obvious, but for the record it's at 555 California St. The Carnelian Room, a posh restaurant on the 52nd floor, offers an excellent view along with prices you can't afford. Plebs are tolerated 3pm–6pm, but don't wear shorts. Restricted viewing is also possible from the 27th floor of the **Transamerica Pyramid**, a $34 million corporate symbol that has, amazingly, given the Golden Gate Bridge a run for its money as the City's symbol as well. The view of the Bay and hills beyond is nice, but it's more fun to go right up to the edge of the plate glass window—a plate glass wall, really—and just look down.

Embarcadero: **Vaillancourt walk-through fountain**, a 710-ton assemblage of 101 concrete boxes, unveiled in 1971 to cries of 'loathsome monstrosity,' 'idiotic rubble', etc. A must-see.

Hyatt Regency Hotel, Embarcadero Plaza, 788-1234. Glittering seven-sided pyramid, its lobby filled with trees, birds, flowers, fountains and Sat–Sun, free music. Ride the twinkly elevators to the 18th floor for costly drinks in Equinox, a restaurant that revolves, with a magnificent view of the Bay Bridge. 'Romantic, delightful—$9.50 cocktails.' 'Required to buy drink.'

North Beach: This, the birthplace of the beat movement, fends off Greenwich Village's claim to the same by maintaining even now a certain junkyard style. Once the centre of the riproaring Barbary Coast, the area now hosts topless, bottomless, seemingly endless clubs along Broadway's 'mammary lane'. Clashing crazily with this gaudy neon fleshpot are clubs, coffeehouses and bookstores that reek of intellectual prestige or pretense, depending on your point of view. Among the greatest (and not the latest) are **City Lights Bookstore**, 261 Columbus, still owned by Lawrence Ferlinghetti, still stocked with Alan Ginsberg. Look for **29 Russell St**, where Jack Kerouac wrote *On the Road*. Get *triste* at **Cafe Trieste**, 609 Vallejo, at Grant, 392-6739, to the tune of an aria from a tragic Italian opera (Sat 1pm), and drown your sorrows in a cafe latte; 'the highlight of my trip'! Pay your respects at **Vesuvio Club**, 255 Columbus, 362-3370. When the beat movement bit the dust, the detritus gravitated here. Once, Kerouac and Dylan Thomas bent elbows at Vesuvio; the drinks are still cheap.

Telegraph Hill/Russian Hill: Romantic **Telegraph Hill** is topped by **Coit Tower**. Does it look like the nozzle of a firehose to you? $3 for the elevator to the top. **Russian Hill** was the gathering place for bohemian writers, artists and poets, from Ambrose Bierce to George ('cool grey city of love') Sterling. It boasts not 1 but 3 steep streets that make it the most vertical district in SF: famous **Lombard**, with its 8 switchbacks and 90-degree angles (almost impossible to photograph but featured in movies such as *What's Up Doc?* and *Foul Play*); **Filbert** between Hyde and Leavenworth; and **Union** between Polk and Hyde.

Fisherman's Wharf/Pier 39: Minuscule amount of wharf, surrounded by a frightening quantity of souvenir rubbish, overpriced seafood, dreary wax museums and bad restaurants. The working wharf is a series of 3 finger piers, just past Johnson and Joseph Chandlery. A fair walk from the Wharf is **Pier 39**, a carefully hokey construct of carnival and commerce.

Aquatic Park, 3 blocks left of Fisherman's Wharf. The 6 vessels moored here as well as the nearby **National Maritime Museum** (daily 10am–5pm), 929-0202, are charming, 'especially the restored ferry'. $3 to enter **Hyde Street Pier**, where you can board 3 of the ships, including the 1886 *Balclutha*. Elsewhere is docked the liberty ship *Jeremiah O'Brien* and the WWII sub *Pompanito*, all with boarding fees. Also at the Aquatic: free swimming beach, cold but fairly clean, with free showers. Nearby is open-air seating where wonderful conga and jam sessions take place on fine Sat–Sun afternoons. Between Aquatic and the Wharf are **Ghiradelli Square** and **The Cannery**, both mazes of specialty shops, restaurants and contrived street colour with a thin veneer of history overall.

Mexican Museum, Bldg D, Ft Mason, 441-0445. $3, $2 with student ID. Don't pass up this rich panorama of folk, colonial and Mexican-American works, from masks to pottery to Siquieros lithos. Outstanding special exhibits. Get in free 1st Wed of every month. Open Wed–Sun noon–5pm.

The Marina/Pacific Heights: The flat Marina district gives way to hills, climbing to Union St, now a trendy shopping and social district. From here on up is **Pacific Heights**, with its surpassing collection of **Victorian mansions**, many of them colourfully painted. Webster, Pine and the 1900 to 3300 blocks of Sacramento contain many charming examples.

Marina Safeway, 15 Marina Blvd, 563-4946. Locally infamous pick-up joint and grocery store. Visit the produce department for proof that San Franciscans love their fog so much that they create it artificially indoors, too.

Palace of Fine Arts, 3601 Lyon St, 563-7337. Built for the 1916 Panama-Pacific Exposition out of plaster of Paris, the palace was not expected to hold up, as it did, for fifty years. It was restored with cement in 1967 and now houses the **Exploratorium**, a carnival of science and art that explains principles of physics and human perception through hands-on exhibits. Reserve in advance to see the super-popular Tactile Dome: 1 week in advance for weekdays, 4–6 weeks in advance for weekends. Admission to the rest of the Exploratorium is free the first Wed of

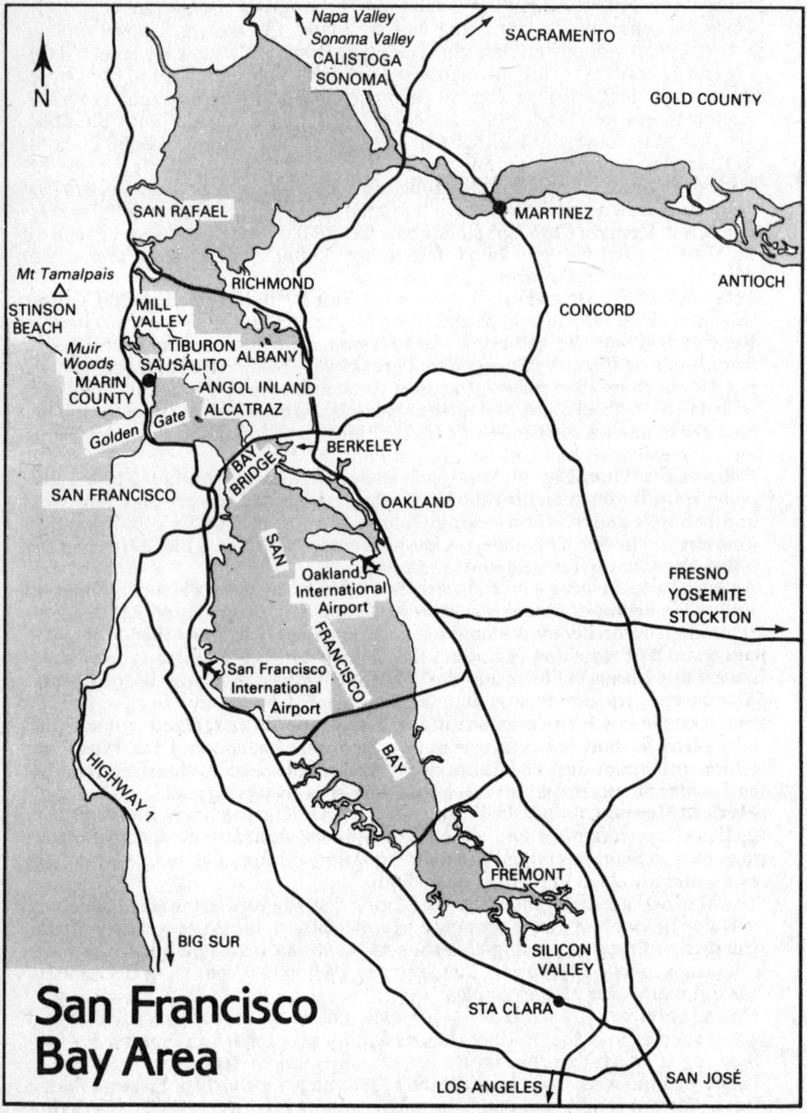

San Francisco Bay Area

every month, otherwise $8, $6 students. Open Sat–Sun, 10am–5pm, Wed 10am–9.30pm, Thur–Fri 10am–5pm. Closed Mon & Tues. 'Don't miss it!'
Golden Gate Bridge: It's painted orange-red but glows gold in the afternoon sun. Perhaps the most famous suspension bridge in the world, the 1½ mile Golden Gate links SF with the green Marin headlands (honeycombed with war fortifications). You can walk or bike across for free (dress warmly); pedestrian walk closes at sunset. At midpoint, you'll be 220 ft above the water, a drop that has drawn over 700 suicides. By car, the bridge is free northbound, $3 southbound. 'Take bus to bridge, then walk down through wooded area with lovely plants, stroll along beach all the way back to Fisherman's Wharf. Lovely way to spend a day.' Other ways to do the bridge: walk from SF to Marin on the Bay side, and once across, keep going down Alexander Dr to Sausalito (about a mile, downhill all the way) and catch the ferry back to SF—the best of both worlds.
Golden Gate Park and West SF: An exceptional park of 1017 acres, filled with a vast array of plantings, foot and bridle paths. Lots of free events and admissions, especially on first Wed of every month; Sunday concerts on music concourse; lovely **Conservatory of flowers; Stow Lake** and **Strawberry Hill**; scruffy buffalo in the west end; occasional outstanding Sunday jugglers in the park near Conservatory; **Strybing Arboretum**. Get to the enchanting **Japanese tea garden** early or late to miss tour bus hordes. For info on places and events within the park, call the San Francisco Recreation and Parks Department, 666-7106. Within the park: The **California Academy of Sciences**, $7, includes admission to the **Aquarium**, 221-5100, which has huge, open tanks, and the **Science Museum**, with its Hall of Man; the **de Young Museum**, $5, 750-3600, 'not worth the price or time'; and **Asian Art Museum**, $5, 668-8921. All free 1st Wed of the month, closed Mon, Tue. 'Don't walk to the park from the bus station unless you want to find out what it is like to be mugged or raped (local police advice).'
Haight-Ashbury, south of the Golden Gate panhandle, was famous in flower-power days, now being spiffed up in what is sometimes called the 'creeping gentrification' of the City. Take a stroll down Hashbury Lane: **Janis Joplin's pad at** 112 Lyon, now home of a charitable organization, and **Jefferson Airplane's hangar** at 2400 Fulton. South and east of Haight is **Noe Valley**, a sunny version of Greenwich Village, whose main drag, **Castro St** is synonymous with gaydom. **Twin Peak** provides (on clear days) a fine view of San Francisco.
Seal Rocks area: Cliff House, a spooky, Gothic-style reconstruction of a seaside resort on a cliff above the crashing sea. It offers a panorama from a walk-in *camera obscura*, and on the lower level, the **Musee Mechanique**, a droll collection of vintage arcade machines, from Fatty Arbuckle to zee French flasher! Free, but bring dimes and quarters. Daily 11am–7pm, 10am–8pm on w-ends, 386-1170.
San Francisco Zoo, Sloat and 45th, 753-7061. $6.50, 10am–5pm daily.
Civic Center: Between Franklin, Larkin, McAllister and Hayes. Its centre is **City Hall**, unhappy scene in 1978 of the dual murder of the mayor and gay supervisor by a former supervisor; both the crime and minimal punishment provoked rioting, outrage, and jolted SF's image as a tolerant mecca for gays.
War Memorial Opera saw the signing of the UN charter on 25 April, 1945.
San Francisco Museum of Modern Art, Van Ness and McAllister, 863-8800. All the bluechips: Miro, Klee, Jasper, Pollock, etc. Free 1st Tue of every month, 10am–5pm, otherwise $4. Sat–Sun 11am–5pm, Wed & Fri 10am–5pm, Thur 10am–9pm ($2 if you come after 5 pm). Closed Mon. $2 students w/ID.
St Mary's Cathedral, Geary & Gough. Almost extra-terrestrial in feeling, with a free-hanging meteor shower over the altar. 'Well worth seeing.' Free.
SoMA (South of Market): **Anchor Brewing Company**, 1705 Mariposa, 863-8350. See how SF's own Anchor Steam Beer is created. Tasting follows 30–40 min tour. One tour per day, Mon–Fri, in early pm. Call 1 week in advance for reservation, max of 10 people per group. Free.
The Mission district: weekend evenings, Chicano youth strut their mechanical stuff with their highly customised vehicles in the phenomenon known as low

riding. On Mission between 16th and 24th or so; enquire locally. The area is rich in **murals**. See for yourself at the minipark between York and Bryan on 24th; in Balmy Alley between 24th and 25th; and on Folsom at 26th. **Mission Dolores** at 16th and Dolores is a simple, restored structure with an ornate basilica peering over its shoulder. Open May–Sept, daily 9am–4pm, $1 donation. Interesting cemetery; drop in any time for free. The first **Levi Strauss Factory**, 250 Valencia, 565-9153, gives good tours every Weds. Ten people min in group. Call on Tues if individual to join school group.

The Bay: **Cruises** around the Bay: from Piers 39 and 41, the Red and White fleets, 546-2829, and the Blue and Gold fleet, 781-7877, for $15. Lasts about an hour, no student discounts. 'Not recommended.' Frequent departures. Dress warmly and wait for clear weather. Better still, ride the Red and White ferries to Sausalito and Tiburon, departing from Fisherman's Wharf; Golden Gate ferries to Sausalito and Larkspur, departing from the Ferry Building on Embarcadero, 332-6600.

Helicopter flights over the Bay, Alcatraz, Golden Gate Bridge, leave from Oakland SF Helicopter Tours, (800) 400-2404. $70 for 15 min, $120 for 30 mins. 'Go in morning for best photos.' 'Phenomenal.' Worth it on a clear day.'

Alcatraz, Pier 41, 546-2805, ferry is $8.50 (includes audio tour) whether you buy at the Pier or through TELETRON, 392-7469. Day trip to 'the Rock', where the likes of Al Capone, Machine Gun Kelley and the 'Birdman' were incarcerated from Civil War times to 1963. 'Dress warmly.' Tours year-round, 9am–5pm, every ½ hour. 'Buy tickets the day before—or weeks before through TICKETRON.' 'Long queues—get there early.' 'Best tour I went on in whole of US.'

City Lights Bookstore, 261 Columbus Ave, 362-8193. It's not the best bookstore in the city but not every store has the history of this one. This was the mecca for the Beat writers, such as Jack Kerouac, to come and be arty, and the owner published Alan Ginsberg's seminal poem, *Howl*. The alley next to the store is named in honour of Kerouac.

ENTERTAINMENT

Whatever your sexual proclivities, it takes quite a bit of cash (and often a smart appearance) to explore the singles bars, meat-rack taverns and gay watering holes of SF. Some tips: go at happy hour, when drinks are cheaper and hors d'oeuvres available; Union St is hetero, Castro-Polk is gay. A better tip: SF has a high VD and herpes rate, and the action has calmed down considerably since the advent of AIDS. Emphasis is now on 'safe sex', but sex that's safe hasn't been invented. In unfamiliar environs, your best tip is to relax, enjoy the atmosphere and music, and save your hunting for your home turf.

The City's 'happening' nightlife scene is constantly changing due to fashion and nightclubs changing names or going bust (as in any city). The area south of Market is usually quite lively. The best sources of info for events, clubs, music are the BAM monthly, the free *Bay Guardian* (comes out Weds) and the *Pink Datebook* section of the Sunday *Chronicle Examiner*. Also, you can call the City Guide Hotline, 332-9611, for answers to questions on entertainment as well as dining, accommodation, shops and services.

Cadillac Bar, 1 Holland Court, 543-8226. Mexican restaurant and bar with live Latin music. 'Great atmosphere and good fun.' Open 11am–11pm, Mon–Thurs, Fri & Sat till 12, Sun till 10.

DNA Lounge, 375 11th St, 626-2532. Subterranean disco-club open for all-night dancing.

Johnny Love's, 1500 Broadway, 931-8021. Live music nightly—jazz, dance. Where the baseball players hang-out. Open 7 days 5pm–2am. Also has a restaurant.

Pier 23 Cafe, The Embarcadero, 362-5125. Newly remodeled cafe/nightclub has Bay view, funky atmosphere. Open 11.30am–midnight Mon–Fri, 11am–1.30am Sat.

Plowshares, Ft Mason Center, Laguna St at Marina Blvd, 681-7966. Traditional, modern folk music.

Rasselas Jazz Club and Ethiopian Restaurant, 2801 California St, 567-5010. Jazz, blues and cabaret-style evenings. Restaurant opens at 5pm, live music 8pm–midnight.
Rock & Bowl, 1855 Haight St, 826-BOWL. Combine disco and bowling, add 12 ft video screens, and there you have it. the young and hip place to be on a Thurs, Fri or Sat night. Fri and Sat operate on a shift system—2 per evening, $7–10. Call ahead to reserve. Thursday action starts at 9pm. 'Good for a laugh.'
Slim's, 373 11th St, 255-0333. No age limit, over 21's get a stamp entitling them to a drink. 'Good for local bands.' Cover $3.20 depending on the band.
Sigmund Stern Grove Concert Series, 19th Ave and Sloat Blvd, 252-6252. Bring a picnic and listen to opera/jazz/classical in a bower of eucalyptus and redwood trees. Free, Sun 2pm, mid-June–mid-Aug. Serious music, dance, theatre offerings are abundant; see the *Datebook*. The symphony has inexpensive (around $11.50) open rehearsal seats; enquire at 431-5400. Also: 'You can usually get a standing ticket for $7.50 at the Opera House; after 1st act, grab a free seat. Productions of a high standard.'

SHOPPING
Tower Records, Columbus and Bay, 885-0500. Vast selection, open until midnight daily. For deeply discounted records and rare stuff, go to Rasputin's in Berkeley; for second-hand records try Reckless Records, 1401 Haight St.
Vintage clothing and factory overruns: many marvellous shops. Try along Clement, at the Thrift Town on Mission, and in Haight-Ashbury.
'Ragsamatazz, 254 Clement, good quality factory outlet for designer clothing.'
'In Hispanic shops, be prepared to bargain. Never pay until you get the goods.'

SPORT
For professional baseball lovers: the SF Giants in Candlestick Park, Gilman Ave, and the Oakland A's at the Coliseum. Later in the year, football action takes over, with the SF 49ers at Candlestick.

INFORMATION
Visitors Bureau, 900 Market at Powell, 391-2000. Multilingual, helpful, open daily. Events message on 391-2001.
Redwood Empire Association, 785 Market St, floor 15. 543-8334. Helpful organisation, friendly staff with info on all 'Redwood' counties—SF and north. Free guide. Open Mon–Fri, 9am–5pm.
San Francisco Convention and Visitors Bureau, Hallidie Plaza, Market Pound St, 974-6900. Open Mon–Fri 8.30am–5pm.
Travelers Aid, 1049 Market St, Suite 500, 255-2252, and at Greyhound, 50 7th St.
Haight-Ashbury Switchboard, 1338 Haight. Information on emergency shelter, a ride board, mail and message service, backpack storage and general information. Free survival guide.
General: SF is a Moonies mecca; they are friendly, may invite you to their camp, 120 miles north, or to dinner. Nip their overtures in the bud with a forthright, 'piss off'. 'Very convincing, hard to get away from.' 'Also watch out for hit artists around North Beach.'

TRAVEL
Pick up BART or Golden Gate Transit maps for free, or a MUNI map for a fee. 'Wonderful but incomprehensible, even with regional transport guide; e.g. trains become street cars. Transfers and cheap deals exist. Ask. Even the natives kept asking us questions in BART stations.'
Local transit: MUNI city transit, 673-MUNI. 700-mile network of buses and trains with frequent service, friendly drivers and good transfer system; $1 to go anywhere on system, part of which is underground. MUNI also runs the fabled cable cars; $1 with bus transfer, $2 for 120 min, $6 all day, $10 for 3 consecutive days. With the 1- or 3-day pass, discounts are available at museums and other

attractions. Pick up passes at the Visitor Information Center at Hallidie Plaza, and the cable car ticket booth at Pier 39; Victoria Park.
BART, 788-BART in SF, (510) 465-BART in East Bay. Sleek, carpeted, comfortable Bullet-Beneath-the-Bay, connecting SF with Oakland, Berkeley, etc. Fares 80¢–$3.00. Long waits during rush hours and on Sun. Transfers valid between BART and MUNI. 'Worth it just for the experience.' Open Mon–Sat 6am–midnight, Sun 9am–midnight.
San Mateo Transit (Samtrans), Burlingame, (800) 660-4287 or 508-6200, SF to Palo Alto, San Mateo. Some runs do not accept luggage. $1.75 **to airport** from 5th and Mission—bus #7F.
Express Airporter bus, 923 Folsom, 673-2433. Daily service from 5.20am–11pm, every 20 min in daytime. $8 one way; $14 round trip. Also leaves from various hotels in the financial district and Fisherman's Wharf.
Golden Gate Transit, 332-6600. Operates bridge, ferries to Sausalito and Larkspur from Ferry Bldg, about $4 one way, and buses to Marin and Sonoma counties from Transbay Terminal, at 1st and Mission.
A/C Transit services East Bay from Transbay Terminal, (510) 839-2882. Often faster than BART in rush hours.
Amtrak, (800) 872-7245, free shuttle from Transbay to Oakland depot where you get daily service on *Coast Starlight* and *San Joaquins* (to Merced, Fresno, near National Parks). Also commuter train, 700 4th St at Townsend, 495-4546. Frequent trains, SF–San Jose only. Open 5am–8pm.
Greyhound, 50 7th St, 495-1569. Open 5am–12.30am.
For tours: **Gray Line**, 558-7300. City tours, Muir Woods, Sausalito, cruises. From 3½ hours to all day; from $25, open daily 9am–3.30pm.
Green Tortoise Bus, 285-2441 or from outside CA, toll-free (800) 227-4766. Counterculture service to East Coast, Baja, Alaska, Seattle, New Orleans, the Grand Canyon, Yosemite and just about anywhere, in diesels with sleeping platforms. To everything there is a season—and the Tortoises migrate accordingly: Mexico in winter, Alaska in summer, California anytime.
Rental cars: Thrifty, 928-6666, seems to offer best value. From about $62 (incl insurance, free mileage) for a week within CA; 25 and over, reservations a week in advance.
San Francisco International Airport, 12 miles south. 761-0800; customs information, 876-2816. Moonie-infested. For airport bus service see above.

BERKELEY and OAKLAND Like Siamese twins, these two neighbour cities blend imperceptibly into one another physically, while each demonstrates a personality of its own. Easily reached by BART or bus, this area—the East Bay—offers good day trips; Berkeley for its university and accompanying cultural and social dividends, Oakland for its Jack London Square, excellent lakeside museum, blues clubs and baseball team known as the 'Athletics'. Both cities are short on cheap lodgings and long on streets that are unsafe to walk at night.

Concentrate on the area in and around the university, the closest you'll come to the fabled Berzerkley of free speech, anti-war, radical fame. 'Rather bohemian atmosphere, good for buying secondhand rare books, homemade trinkets or discussing Marxist ideology with a stranger in a coffeehouse.'
The telephone area code is 510.

ACCOMMODATION

Easily the greatest challenge to visitors is trying to find somewhere cheap to sleep in the East Bay. One source is housing advertised in the *Daily Californian*, the newspaper of the University of California, Berkeley. Also, try UC Berkeley fraternities—easy access to city and inexpensive if not free. 'Filthy but at the price who

cares?' Each fraternity determines for itself whether or not to accept guests, and policies are subject to change. If the frats turn you down (or vice versa), here are some more possibilities:
Berkeley Hotel, 2001 Bancroft, Berkeley, 843-4043, S/D-$34.
Motel 6, 8484 Edes, Oakland, 638-1180, S-$36, D-$42.
YMCA, 2001 Allston Way, 848-6800. $23/day, includes use of facilities. $2 key deposit, 14-day max stay.

FOOD

Blondie's Pizza, 2340 Telegraph, 548-1129. 'Slice for $1.25–$1.75.'
Brennan's, 720 University Avenue, Berkeley, 841-0960. Downtown bar with Guinness, cheap and simple foods—a local hangout. Open 11am–9.30pm (food), bar 'til 12.30am. Fri and Sat 'til 2am.
Cafe Mediterranean, 2475 Telegraph, near Dwight, Berkeley, 841-5634. Intellectual/political crowd. Open daily 7am–midnight.
Cafe Milano, 2522 Bancroft, 644-3100. Nicknamed 'Cafe Pretentious'. 'This is a must if you're going to sample the atmosphere of Berkeley properly.' Open daily 7am–midnight.
Flint's Barbecue, 3114 San Pablo Ave, Oakland, 658-9912, and 6609 Shattuck, Oakland, 653-0593. 'Best ribs in town.' Open daily 11am–2.30am.
Pasand, 2286 Shattuck, Berkeley, 549-2559. Indian food, excellent and cheap.
Spenger's, 1919 4th, Berkeley, 845-7771. Forget Fisherman's Wharf, this is THE Bay Area institution for seafood. Open 6am–midnight Thurs–Sat, 'til 11am Sun–Wed. $7–$17.
University cafeterias on campus ('except the main one—expensive'), open until 3pm in summer. **International House** is also recommended.

OF INTEREST

On campus: both the **Campanile (Sather Tower)** in the centre of campus and the **Lawrence Hall of Science** on the hill above (take bus) have excellent views of Berkeley and the Bay.
Main Library (where Mario Savio and Joan Baez addressed the first major student demonstration against the Vietnam War in 1964) has world's largest collection of Mark Twain materials. 'Try the browsing room (Morrison Rm)—British newspapers, headphones to listen to records.' **Phoebe Hearst Museum**, corner of Bancroft and College, 643-7648. Excellent Indian costumes and crafts, $1.50. Open Mon–Fri 10am–4.30pm, Sat & Sun noon–4.30pm. Free on Thur. **University Art Museum**, Bancroft Way, 642-1207. Video, performance art, modern works, $5. Wed–Sun, 11am–5pm; free Thur 11am–noon. 'Not worth it.' Located in the museum building is **Pacific Film Archives**, 2625 Durant, 642-1124. Nightly showing, more at term time. $5.50 for the first show, $1.50 for additional features. Runs gamut from Japanese samurai flicks to vintage 1930s classics. **Lawrence Hall of Science**, Centennial Dr, 642-5132. Open Mon–Fri 10am–4.30pm, Sat–Sun 10am–5pm, $5, $4 with student ID. 'Top of the mountain, excellent view, amazing museum, spent whole afternoon playing computer games.' The football stadium sits directly on the Hayward fault, a branch of the San Andreas; a large vertical crack may be seen through the upper tier. **Black Oak Books**, 1491 Shattuck, 486-0698. Open 10am–10pm daily. New and used books on all subjects. The best part is the Sunday night reading, often given by some very well-known authors and poets. Readings don't happen every Sunday, though, so check first. 'A gem. Go!'
Off campus: Tilden Park, free, above city in the Berkeley Hills.
Moe's Bookstore, 2476 Telegraph, 849-2087. Huge and politically hip—4 floors of books. Open daily 10am–11pm.
Sake Takara USA Inc., 708 Addison at 4th, Berkeley, 540-8250, 15-min slide show and free tastings of wine and sake, every hour on the hour, noon–6pm daily.

Oakland: Jack London Sq, 10 minutes from BART City Center station. Visit Jack London's cabin from his Klondike days, have a drink at the First and Last Chance Saloon, where London and RL Stevenson used to tipple. 'Village is excellent reconstruction of the wharf area.'
Lake Merritt, downtown Oakland, is the largest saltwater lake within a US city; overlooking it is the **Oakland Museum** at 1000 Oak, 238-3401. Art, history and natural science of California—free and good. Wed-Sat 10am-5pm, Sun noon-7pm. Closed Mon & Tue.

ENTERTAINMENT
Ashkenaz, 1317 San Pablo, 525-5054. Multi-ethnic folk dancing. 'Cheap fun.'
Cafe Bistro, 2271 Shattuck, 848-3081. Bar with live jazz.
Freight and Salvage, 1111 Addison St, 548-1761. Mixed bag of country, bluegrass, ethnic groups and comedy, free.
Larry Blake's, 2367 Telegraph, 848-0886. Big-name blues bands. 'Lively restaurant/bar with good local bands.' 'Lively part is downstairs.' Open 11.30am-2am. Food served until 10pm.
Triple Rock, 1920 Shattuck, 843-2739. Great bar with a redwood deck. Beer brewed on premises. For punk, go to Berkeley Square. Open daily 11am-12.30am or 1.30am.

SURVIVAL/INFORMATION/TRAVEL
Berkeley Support Services, 2100 Martin Luther King Way, 848-3378, has info, plus rough and ready crash pad, emphasis on rough. Not recommended for women. 'This is designed for the truely homeless, so use only in emergency.'
Berkeley Free Clinic, 2339 Durant, 548-2570 (24-hr). Open from 7pm (Mon-Thu), call at 6.45pm.
UC/Berkeley bus service, 642-5149, free shuttle buses from Berkeley BART stations to campus, Botanical Gardens, Hall of Science, etc.
Oakland International Airport. Take the AirBART bus from the Colosseum station. Leaves every 10 mins from 6am-midnight, $2. Call 465-BART.

SANTA CRUZ-MONTEREY This stretch of coast rivals the section north of San Francisco in its scenic beauty. Not nearly so unpopulated, though—tiny hamlets and larger towns line Hwy 1 (also known in this area as the Cabrillo Highway). The first major city, **Santa Cruz**, is 90 miles south of SF and similarly suffering considerable damage in the October '89 earthquake. Jumping nightlife, lots of movies and bookstores, surfers aplenty and a rowdy beach and boardwalk scene earn the town its name, as pronounced by natives: 'Sanna Cruize'. The **University of California campus**, home of the 'Battling Banana Slugs', is a special jewel. Eight colleges, independent of one another are hidden in the redwoods on a hill above the town; can you find them all?

Nearby is **Capitola-by-the-Sea**, a doll's village of Victorian houses and beach bungalows; its name comes from the days when this sleepy seaside resort was California's capital. Catch the Begonia Festival if you're here in September. Further south are the towns of **Soquel**, **Aptos**.

Around the curve of the **Monterey Bay**, the towns of **Pacific Grove**, **Monterey**, **Pebble Beach** and **Carmel-by-the-Sea** cluster on a knob of land jutting out into the Pacific. Here, the cheap glitz of the Santa Cruz boardwalk gives way to much more expensive glitz, and the soft warm beauty of the coast turns angular, dramatic and cold. You don't need to shell out $5 for the **17-Mile Drive** to see it, though—bike it for free, or just

north of the drive is an even more beautiful stretch, beginning at Ocean View Blvd and 3rd St in Pacific Grove: **Sunset Drive**, which also happens to be the best time to see it. And it's also free.
The telephone area code is 408.

SURVIVAL

This is a resort area, which means the necessities of life—food and shelter—tend to be treated as luxuries here: you can spend exorbitant amounts on either. Fortunately, Santa Cruz has a culture that generally welcomes students, transients or people who combine both qualities at once; the Monterey and Carmel area can be hostile to same.

ACCOMMODATION

Montara Lighthouse Hostel, Hwy 1, 25 miles south of San Francisco, (415) 728-7177. Restored lighthouse in an exceptionally beautiful place; includes an outdoor hot tub. $9 AYH members, $12 non-members.
Pigeon Point Lighthouse Hostel, Hwy 1, 50 miles south of San Francisco, (415) 879-0633. Modern bungalows; tidepools to the north. $9 AYH, $12 non-members; $5 extra for twin rooms.
Santa Cruz Hostel, 511 Broadway, Box 1241, Santa Cruz, CA 95061, 423-8304. 5-min walk from Greyhound; 11pm curfew. $12 AYH, $15 non-members.
Townhouse Motel, 1106 Fremont, Seaside, 394-3113. 1 blk from Monterey, close to beach, aquarium. S–$39, D–$41. 'Good accommodation.'
Big Sur Campground and Cabins, 667-2322. $20 a night for two, XP–$3. Cabins S/D–$38. 2 miles north of Pfeiffer-Big Sur State Park.

FOOD

Generally, be wary of any restaurant that caters too obviously to the tourist trade. Plenty of places, particularly in Santa Cruz, have a reputation with the locals for serving overpriced, mediocre food; the restaurants in Monterey and Carmel are merely overpriced. Here are some eateries that are more in line with a hungry student's needs:
Georgiana's, behind **Bookshop Santa Cruz**, 1520 Pacific Avenue, 423-0900, **Santa Cruz**. In a Mediterranean-style courtyard that becomes the town square on Sunday afternoons.
Each of the 8 colleges of the **university** has its own coffee house, where you can mix and mingle with the students; the best is **Banana Joe's** at Crown College. Closed summers.
Mike's Seafood Restaurant, at the Fisherman's Wharf in **Monterey**, 372-6153. 'Cheap for the area, good seafood.' Open daily 9am–10pm.
Mr Toots, 221A Esplanade, **Capitola**, 475-3679. Grab a bran muffin and watch the seagulls from the outside deck. Open daily 8am–1am.
Seychelles, 313 Cedar, **Santa Cruz**, 425-0450. 'Quintessential Californian vegetarian meals.' Open daily 11.30am–3.30pm, 5.30pm–11.30pm.
Village Corner, Dolores & 6th, **Carmel**, 624-3588. Greek food, good breakfasts, informal setting. Open daily 7.30am–10pm.
Whole Earth Restaurant, UC Santa Cruz campus, 426-8255. An oversized treehouse with politically-conscious cuisine. Closed weekends in summer.
Zachary's, 819 Pacific, **Santa Cruz**, 427-0646. Huge, good breakfasts for cheap. Go early unless you're keen on queues. Open Tue–Sun, 7am–2.30pm.

OF INTEREST

Coming down Hwy 1 from SF, you get to **Pt Ano Nuevo** (pronounced 'An-yo Noo-ey-vo') **State Beach** before Santa Cruz. If it's winter, you may be able to see breeding elephant seals lazing in the rookery there.
Critters of another sort romp on the area's nude beaches; best known is the 'red,

white and blue' beach, marked by a mailbox sporting stripes of those colours 4 miles south of Davenport on Hwy 1.

Coming into town, glimpse **UC Santa Cruz** on the swelling green hills to your left; from roads leading to its colleges nestled in the trees, you can get spectacular views of Monterey Bay. The vista from **Cowell College** is particularly good.

Of the Coney Island-type boardwalks that once lined California's coast, only one remains, and here it is: the Santa Cruz **beach and boardwalk**. The municipal wharf is also worth a stroll.

If you get weary of squishing discarded hot dogs between your toes, wander over to the **Pacific Garden Mall**, which has organic restaurants, organic clothing stores and organic people roaming the streets.

Just north of the boardwalk is **West Cliff Drive**, which leads to **Natural Bridges State Beach** ($3 car); though only one of the sandstone bridges still stands.

If you have time and transportation, take Hwy 17 (drive carefully) to San Jose to see the **Winchester Mystery House**, 525 S Winchester Blvd, 247-2101. Tours $12.50. Sara Winchester, the story goes, was directed by the ghosts of people killed by Winchester Rifles to build additions onto her home haphazardly and continuously. The resulting jumble of 160 skewed rooms, staircases that go up and down, and doors leading to nowhere is seen by some as the architectural analogue to development in the surrounding Silicon Valley. Open 9am–5.30pm.

Cannery Row, Monterey. Rows of defunct sardine canneries immortalized by John Steinbeck make wonderful homes for little shoppes. Open 8am–7pm. **Kalisa's Cosmopolitan Gourmet Restaurant**, 851 Cannery Row, 372-8512, is a reformed brothel, with belly dancing on 2nd Sat of the month; across the street, the more cerebral **Monterey Bay Aquarium**, 375-3333, displays species native to the Monterey Bay in huge tank settings so natural that visitors get the impression that they are the ones behind glass. Open daily, 9.30am–6pm in summer; $7.75 students, $10.50 adults. 'Great value for money. Fantastic for biologists and non-biologists alike.'

Carmel is an acquired taste. The town draws hordes of curiosity seekers, all of whom want to catch a glimpse of actor and one-time mayor, Clint Eastwood at his **Hog's Breath Inn**, at San Carlos and 5th. You won't, but stop by anyway for a look, maybe a drink—in a setting that would make Bilbo Baggins feel right at home. Carmel has been accused of calculated cuteness but is worth seeing, if only for the experience of wandering down an alley and discovering a greenhouse in a hidden courtyard. **The Mission**, ½ mile from downtown, has a star-shaped window framed by vines, fountains and flowers. It's free (donations are 'nice'). The white sand beach nearby is great for running barefoot on; don't attempt to swim in the cold and treacherous surf, though.

Point Lobos State Reserve, 624-4909, 2 miles south of Carmel. Monterey-Salinas Transit stops here several times a day, on its way to Big Sur. $6 per car, walkers get in free. (You can park your car on the highway and walk in to avoid the fee.) 450 acres of natural beauty: coves, islands, fearless animals and birds. Best of all are China Cove and the beach beyond (take lunch). Open daily 9am–7pm.

Pfeiffer-Big Sur State Park, 667-2315, is only one tiny part of the 90-mile stretch of scissored coastline between Carmel and San Simeon known as 'Big Sur'. The stretch is almost pristine and wholly soul satisfying. Free with ticket from Point Lobus, otherwise $6. Do stop for the obligatory open-air quaff and sea-gazing at **Nepenthe**, 667-2345; Cafe Amphora on the lower deck actually has the better view. Big Sur was home to the beats and Henry Miller and today continues to be inhabited (sparsely) by rugged individualists.

INFORMATION

Santa Cruz Convention and Visitors Center, 701 Front St, 425-1234, open Mon–Sat 9am–5pm, Sun 10am–4pm.

Monterey Convention and Visitors Bureau, 380 Alvarado, 649-1770, has a self-guiding walk brochure for the city's old buildings.

Carmel Tourist Information Center, 624-1711. Open Mon–Fri 7am–4pm.

TRAVEL
Greyhound has service from SF to Monterey, 423-1800 or (800) 231-2222. Open 7.30am–7.45pm.
Santa Cruz Metro, 425-8600. Lots of routes, runs late. $1, $3 day pass, for bus or summer shuttle to Santa Cruz beach; free shuttle to Capitola beach also runs in the summer.
Monterey-Salinas Transit, 899-2555 or 424-7695. $1.25 per zone, free transfers. All downtown routes stop at Munras/Tyler/Pearl St triangle. Serves Monterey, Pacific Grove and Carmel; spring and summer service to Big and Little Sur as far as Nepenthe ($2.50 one way).

SAN LUIS OBISPO and SANTA BARBARA COUNTIES Called the central coast, this region stretches from Big Sur south to Santa Barbara. Among its highlights are **San Simeon**, site of **Hearst Castle**, built by William Randolph Hearst, newspaper magnate and the *Citizen Kane* of Orson Welles' film. This Spanish-style castle houses Hearst's $75 million art collection, which includes now-priceless tapestries, rugs, jade, statuary, even entire antique ceilings and fireplaces and assorted loot from all over Europe, including Cardinal de Richelieu's bed. 'A two-hour trip into paradise.'

Further down the coast, **Morro Rock** makes a monolithic landmark at water's edge, the first in a series of volcanic peaks that march picturesquely through San Luis Obispo County. You can follow them along Hwy 1 (also the bus route). Beaches and camping opportunities abound; the amiable character of the inland town of **San Luis Obispo** adds to the area's appeal.

Ninety miles south of Morro Bay on Hwy 101 is **Solvang**, a charming coastal replica of a Danish town, 'worth a visit with its reasonably priced accommodation and restaurants'. Further south, **Santa Barbara** beckons. Far and away the loveliest of coastal cities, from its setting against the Santa Ynez Mountains to its beautiful Spanish adobe architecture. Despite its wealth, Santa Barbara is a non-stuffy, youthful city, with a big UC campus, sophisticated nightlife and the best sidewalk cafe idling anywhere in the US. 'Beautiful unspoilt beaches.' 'Elegant little town with a lot happening.'
The telephone area code is 805.

ACCOMMODATION
For Hearst Castle, **camping** is possible at San Simeon and further south at Atascadero Beach.
Bill's Home Hostel, 929-3467, in Nipomo, 50 miles NW of Santa Barbara just off the I-101. Get a map from the Mobil Station in Nipomo for directions. 12 beds, non-smoking, $10 per night.
Geranda B&B, 1056 Bay Oak Dr, **Los Osos**, 30 miles south of Hearst Castle, 528-3973. Say 'Eric' sent you. $12 per night.
Morro Bay State Park camping info line: 772-2560.
Hotel State Street, 121 State St, Santa Barbara, 966-6586. S/D–$40 and up, shared bath. 'Excellent; staff very nice and helpful.'

OF INTEREST/FOOD
Hearst Castle, State Hwy 1, 927-2000 for other info. Book at least a day in advance through MISTIX, (800) 444-7275. $14 for 1 of 4 tours covering different aspects of the castle; $25 for evening tours. 'Take Tour 2 or 3—smaller groups, more personal and informative.' Each tour lasts about 1½ hours. Tours from 8.20am–3.20pm.
Morro Bay State Park, Hwy 1, 772-7434. Bird sanctuary, heron rookery. Open 8.30am–10.45pm.

Giant Chessboard, Embarcadero at Front, Morro Bay, 772-1214. The local chess club plays each Saturday, noon–5pm, on a 16′ × 16′ board with redwood pieces that weigh as much as a small child. Possible to rent other days.

Old Mission Santa Barbara, upper end of Laguna St, Santa Barbara, 682-4713. Noble facade with columns and towers, many unusual touches, from Moorish fountain to Mexican skulls in the 1786 'Queen of the Missions'. Open daily 9am–5pm. More beautiful still is the **County Courthouse**, 1120 Anacapa St: a 1929 Hispano-Moorish treasure, inside and out.

Nearby is the **Presidio Cafe**, 812 Anacapa St, 966-2428. One of SB's great places for lolling on the patio. Also try **Joe's Cafe**, 536 State, 966-4638: 'bustling atmosphere, lashings of food at low prices; a favourite students' meeting place.' Open Mon–Thurs 11am–10.30pm, Fri and Sat 'till midnight, Sun 4pm–11pm.

McConnell's Ice Cream, 1213 State St, 965-5400. 'Best ice cream in America—and we sampled quite a few!' 17% butterfat. Open Sun–Thurs 11am–11pm, Fri & Sat 'til midnight.

YOSEMITE An Oxford don once said, 'Think in centuries'. In Yosemite, it's inescapable. Cut in jewel facets by a glacial knife, the park encompasses nearly 1,200 square miles of incredible beauty—luminous lakes and dashing streams; groves of redwood elder statesmen and aged incense cedar; salt- and pepper boulders comically abandoned in boggy alpine meadows by the retreating glaciers of past millennia.

People bemoan the popularity of Yosemite, but not even 3 million visitors per year can ruin it. One-third of them choose to jam the park between July and August, and 80% of those content themselves with a stay in Yosemite Valley (just call it 'nature's parking lot'), leaving vast areas untrampled. Despite its congestion, you shouldn't miss Yosemite Valley's supreme vistas of **Bridalveil Falls** and **Glacier Point**, as well as the steel-blue shoulders of **Half Dome** and **El Capitan**. A mountaineers' mecca, Half Dome is the sheerest cliff in America (the back way up isn't exactly flat, either), and El Capitan, the biggest block of exposed granite in the world, so huge you need binoculars to see the climbers scaling it.

A fine way to see the park is to travel up Hwy 41 from Fresno to the south entrance near **Mariposa Grove of Big Trees**; the exit from Wawona Tunnel into the valley is absolutely spine-tingling. If you have the time, don't leave the park right after seeing the valley; instead, take the high road, Hwy 120, over **Tioga Pass** to shimmering, endangered **Mono Lake**. Continue south on Hwy 395 through **Owens Valley**, a neglected gem in a dusty corner of the state; **Mt Whitney** is visible from the highway.

Open year-round, Yosemite Valley is at its best in spring and early autumn; in summer visitors pay for the balmy weather by watching the spectacular waterfalls fade to a trickle. But winter is the time hardy souls and true Yosemite afficionados love best. With the season's first dusting of snow, the valley becomes a stark, eerie, white-on-black tableau—a living Ansel Adams photograph.

The telephone area code is 209.

ACCOMMODATION

Within the park: More than any other spot in California, you must book cabin, lodge or camping accommodation in advance to avoid disappointment. Campsites can be reserved through MISTIX, (800) 365-2267.

Tent cabins at **Curry Village**, $38 for 2 persons. 'Pay for 2, fit 6 in.' 'Was too cold to get undressed when I was there in Sept.' Showers nearby, often overtaxed. For

reservations: 252-4848. Also at **Housekeeping Camp**, 1 mile south of Yosemite Village, $42 for 4 persons, $3–XP. Summer only. Other **cabins** at **Curry Village, Yosemite Lodge, White Wolf Lodge**. Housekeeping units have a stove (sometimes outside), cost a little more. No bedding or utensils.
Campsites: $2 for **Sunnyside**, a walk-in, and your only hope if you haven't booked in advance. Call 372-8502.
Also possible to take the shuttle to **Backpacker's Camp**, a quiet retreat behind North Pine's campground, $2. Maximum stay is 1 day.
Outside Park: **Motel 6**, 1983 E Childs Ave at Hwy 99, **Merced**, 384-3702. S–$27, D–$34. **Tree House Hostel**, Box 173, **Midpines**, CA 95345, 742-6318. $7.50 AYH, $10.50 non-members. This hostel was damaged by fire in August '93 and is to be rebuilt for 1994. Call for advance reservations and directions.
Yosemite Gateway Home Hostel, Merced, 725-0407. $10. Will pick up from Greyhound and Amtrak. Reservations essential.

FOOD
Food is costly and often poor in the park. Readers recommend Yosemite Valley's burger shop and pizza house. Grocery stores, restaurants, cafeterias are located at Yosemite Valley, Curry Village, Wawona, Tioga Lake, White Wolf, Fish Camp, El Portal and Tuolumne Meadows.

OF INTEREST
Everything. If you're adventurous, climb Half Dome by hiking around to the *back* via a 17-mile round-trip trail and hauling yourself up a cable-and-slats 'stairway' to the top. The payoff is the view: the panorama of Yosemite Valley and beyond, and the dizzying drop-off from the cliff. 'Hike Yosemite Valley, Glacier Pt, Illilouette Falls, Panorama Trail, Nevada Falls, Vernal Falls, Happy Isles for best photos. 14 miles, 3200-ft ascents and descents. Walk up to Nevada Falls via John Muir Trail and then down by Mist Trail. Take a swimsuit—icy mountain pools. (Do not swim above waterfalls.) Good for those with less time. Met a bear—terrifying.'

INFORMATION
Park open year-round except Hwy 120 at Tioga Pass. $5 cars, $2 per hiker or bus passenger. 'Keep your ticket—checked on exit for it.'
Visitors Center, 372-0299 at village mall in Yosemite Valley.

TRAVEL
Round-trip service to Yosemite from Merced: Via Bus Line, from the Greyhound Depot, 722-0366, $29 round-trip.
Greyhound, 710 W 16th St, 722-2121, serve all cities along Hwy 99.
Hitching: 'a bit slow between Merced and Yosemite'. Yosemite is 67 miles east of Merced.
Yosemite Park Tour Co. Various tours 2–8 hrs, $13.75–$37.

SEQUOIA-KINGS CANYON NATIONAL PARKS These two parks, established around 1890 and administered jointly since WWII, straddle a magnificent cross-section of the high Sierras, including 14,495-ft **Mt Whitney**, highest peak in the lower 48 states. Here you'll find the beautiful and impetuous **Kings River**, remnants of Indian camps, and wildlife that may venture into view in early morning or at dusk. Here, too, are stands of giant sequoia; like their redwood cousins along the coast, these trees are survivors of the Ice Age and lumber companies both. One of their number, the 2500-year-old **General Sherman**, is the world's most massive living thing, in all his 275-foot-high, 2145-ton glory. The two-mile **Congress Trail** into the heart of the **Great Forest** begins at the Sherman tree.

Access to the parks is by road from the west and southwest or by foot from the east. Bus service is available from Visalia to trailheads on both sides of the Sierras. 'Road to Owens Valley gives very pretty views and climbs to about 4000 feet above sea level.'
The telephone area code is 209.

ACCOMMODATION

Dow Villa Hotel, 310 S Main, **Lone Pine**, (619) 876-5521. Hospitable place, good rooms with and without bath, $58 for 2 people, XP–$4. Use of jacuzzi, pool.
Hotel Burgess, 1726 11th St, **Reedley**, 638-6315. About 57 miles from park entrance. Wildly furnished hotel, no 2 rooms alike. Single or double $35 and up.
Motel 6, 933 N Parkway Dr at Hwy 99, **Fresno**, 233-3913. S–$25, D–$32.
Willow Motel, 138 Willow St, **Lone Pine**, (619) 876-5655. S/D–$49, more in summer. Colour TV, shower, kitchens $7 extra.
Camping in parks: $10–$12 per site, no reservations, but getting a site 'shouldn't be a problem', according to rangers. Free backcountry camping with permit. Also free camping on Sequoia National Forest lands near park. '**Buckeye Flat** campground— pleasant, rustic. We saw a bear in camp.' Rustic cabins without baths from $35 for 2, XP–$7, at **Giant Forest**, in Sequoia, and at **Grant Grove**, in Kings. Book ahead; reservations line for both: 561-3314. Also costlier cabins, cottages.

INFORMATION/TRAVEL

Sequoia and Kings Canyon National Park Information, 565-3541, gives general information for both parks. Recordings on weather: 565-3351; and on backpacking: 565-3708. 'Helpful and informative.' Open 8am–6pm.
Parks open year-round. $5 per vehicle covers both. $2 per person. Access in winter via highways 198 and 180.
In summer: park bus tours; horse rentals available.

DEATH VALLEY Covering two million acres, most of them about a million miles from nowhere, Death Valley has cornered the market on hottest, driest and lowest (282 feet below sea level) place in the US (ironically, less than 100 miles from Mt Whitney, highest point in the lower 48 states). High peaks ringing the valley prohibit moisture, and white sand and hills reflect light in a blinding glare. But the definition of Death Valley is heat: one July day in 1972, Furnace Creek lived up to its name with a ground reading of 201 degrees (that's not a typo), while the air was a balmy 128 degrees.

Death Valley lies 300 miles northeast of Los Angeles and 135 miles northwest of Las Vegas; the only bus is from Las Vegas. Park lodging boils down to **camping** for $5 per site (western campsites are free in summer to escapees from mental institutions), the costly **Furnace Creek Ranch**, 786-2345 ($76 and up a night), and the **Stove Pipe Wells Motel**, 786-2387 (not much better at S/D–$58). 'During summer, arrive by 6pm. Otherwise no key.' A better bet is the gas station/motel at **Panamint Springs**, 10 miles west of the park. 'A welcome relief in the middle of nowhere.'

Late October to early May is the sanest time to gaze at the tortured landscapes of **Zabriskie Point** and **Dante's View**, climb the **Ubehebe Crater**, explore **Scotty's Castle**, and slide on the sensuous sand dunes at **Stove Pipe Wells**. Scotty's Castle is no prospector's shack but a $2 million, 18-room Spanish fortress with an 1100-pipe organ, a large waterfall in the living room and other astonishing features built by colourful con-man Walter Scott. Always dramatic, the desert can bring forth storms of wildflowers in March and April as suddenly as it does storms of water or sand.

Park headquarters at **Furnace Creek**, 786-2331, has a museum, descriptive literature, food and a cool oasis of date palms. Free rangers' hikes and programmes daily, less often in summer. Open daily 8am–6pm.
The telephone area code is 619.

PALM SPRINGS A flat desert town hugging snow-capped mountains, Palm Springs is a class act—from artfully weathered New Mexican adobes to its view of 10,831-foot Mt San Jacinto. Even the Indians are millionaires here, but don't let that put you off. During the hot, dry summer, prices melt like ice cubes and swimming pools can be reached within microseconds from air conditioned rooms.
The telephone area code is 619.

ACCOMMODATION

Each hotel seems to set its own dates for low season, very approximately June through Sept. Rates always lowest Sun–Thurs. To find the best deal, check newspaper specials, ask the Visitors Bureau, call around and don't be afraid to haggle. Except for Motel 6, winter rates are generally shocking.
Carlton Hotel, 1333 N Indian Ave, 325-5416. S/D–$28 in summer. Weekly rates available, $110–$140.
Motel 6, 595 E Palm Canyon Dr, 325-6129 and 660 S Palm Canyon Dr, 327-4200. Lush setting, pools, book ages ahead. Summer rates: S–$33, D–$38.
Sunbeam Inn, 291 Camino Monte Vista, 323-3812. 15 June—15 Oct, S/D–$39 and up; winter rates from $54. 'Cheerful, small, with pool.'

FOOD

In summer, they practically give the food away; check local paper, giveaway tabloids for 'early bird' brunch and other specials.
Las Casuelas, 222 S Palm Canyon, 325-2794. 'Great Mexican food.' Open daily 11am–10pm.
Nate's Deli, 100 S Indian Ave, 325-3506. 'Dinner specials good if you're hungry. A local institution.' Open daily 8am–8pm.

OF INTEREST

Aerial Tramway, off Hwy 111, 325-1391. 18 minutes, 8516 ft, and 5 climatic zones later, you're on **Mt San Jacinto** and it's 30–40 degrees cooler (in summer); you may even need a jacket. At the top: restaurant ('ride and dine' for $20), mule rides, backpacking, events and free camping. 'Can see part of San Andreas fault from top.' Open 8am–9pm weekends, from 10am on weekdays, $15.95.
Desert Museum, 101 Museum Dr, 325-7186. Open Tue–Fri 10am–4pm, Sat–Sun 10am–5pm, $5. Impressive modern art, Indian basketry. Closed July–Sept.
Living Desert Reserve, 47900 Portola Ave, Palm Desert (east of Palm Springs off Hwy 111), 346-5694. 1200 acres of native plants, gazelles, Bighorn sheep and other desert denizens. 'After sundown' room displays with nocturnal beasties. Open Sept 1-June 15; daily 9am–5pm, $7, seniors $6.
Cabot's Indian Pueblo Museum, 67616 Desert View Ave, in Desert Hot Springs (north of I-10 on Palm Drive), 329-7610. Eccentric 5-storey pueblo, built of found objects by Cabot Yerxa. Inside are the prospector/packrat's mementos of the Battle of Little Bighorn and Eskimo and Indian relics. Open weekends only in July & Aug; otherwise Wed–Sun 10am–4pm, $2.50.

INFORMATION

Chamber of Commerce, 190 W Amado Rd, 325-1577; and at airport, Palm Springs Convention & Visitors Bureau, off Hwy 111 in the Atrium Design Center, Ste 201, 770-9000. Pick up the *Palm Springs Desert Guide* and the Calender of Events, put out by the city, and the *Desert Weekly* and *Palm Springs Magazine*: all are free and packed with info, special offers.

TRAVEL

Greyhound, 311 N Indian Ave, 325-2053. On the Phoenix–LA route. Open 6am–5pm (daily).
Sun Bus Transit, 343-3451. Local buses; also has cheap shuttle (75¢) around town. Open daily 8am–5pm.
Desert Stage Lines, 367-3581. Buses to Joshua Tree and Twentynine Palms. Open daily Mon–Fri 9.30am–6pm.
Gray Line, 325-0974. Open daily 8am–2pm.
Take bus #21 to Palm Springs Airport, leaving from Boristo and Indian every 15 mins, 75¢.

JOSHUA TREE NATIONAL MONUMENT In the high desert 54 miles east of Palm Springs is this 870-square-mile sanctuary of startling rock formations, mountain lions and kangaroo rats, colourful cacti and giant 50-foot agave trees with manlike arms and twisted bodies. These odd plants were named in the 1850s by Mormon pioneers, who recalled a line from *The Book of Joshua*: 'Thou shalt follow the way pointed for Thee by the trees'.

Entrance to the monument and all **campsites** is free in the summer until Aug 31st (two charge $5 in the winter, reserve through TICKETRON); you need to bring food, water and firewood. Good exhibits, museum and ranger-guided tours from park headquarters at **Twentynine Palms**, (619) 367-7511, and the visitor centre at **Cottonwood Springs**. From 5185-foot **Salton View**, you get a splendid panorama of the Coachella Valley, the Salton Sea and Palm Springs. On a clear day you can see Signal Mountain in Mexico.

LOS ANGELES Everything you have ever heard about LA is true. The place is so large and diverse that it will become whatever you wish to make it. There is urban angst and alienation downtown, and sun-seeking hedonism at Zuma beach. There is Greek sculpture in Malibu and a Cadillac stuck into a Beverly Hills roof. There is the film director sipping Perrier in Venice and the Vietnamese fisherman angling for dinner off the Santa Monica Pier. Remember that this city specializes in creating fantasy. The only way to find your own LA is to jump in with both feet.

Whatever you find, you'll be in good company. Thirteen million Angelenos speak 100 languages, and it's true—most do say 'have a nice day', some even mean it. Its part climate, and part culture—LA has always drawn more from the Far East and Latin America than from New York and the grimy East Coast. The pace is a bit slower here, and the attitudes more tolerant. Easterners may deride LA as shallow and vain, but there is little doubt among Angelenos that theirs is a city struggling with social, economic and artistic questions difficult for outsiders to appreciate.

Most difficult to grasp is the great fear that one day the California Dream may be over. The place where people came to live a dream is slowly becoming less than that. The freeways are clogged, the air is smoggy and there is a constant worry about water. When in May 1992 four white police officers were acquitted of beating black motorist Rodney King, the riot that ensued did not just leave more than 50 people dead but left the city with a

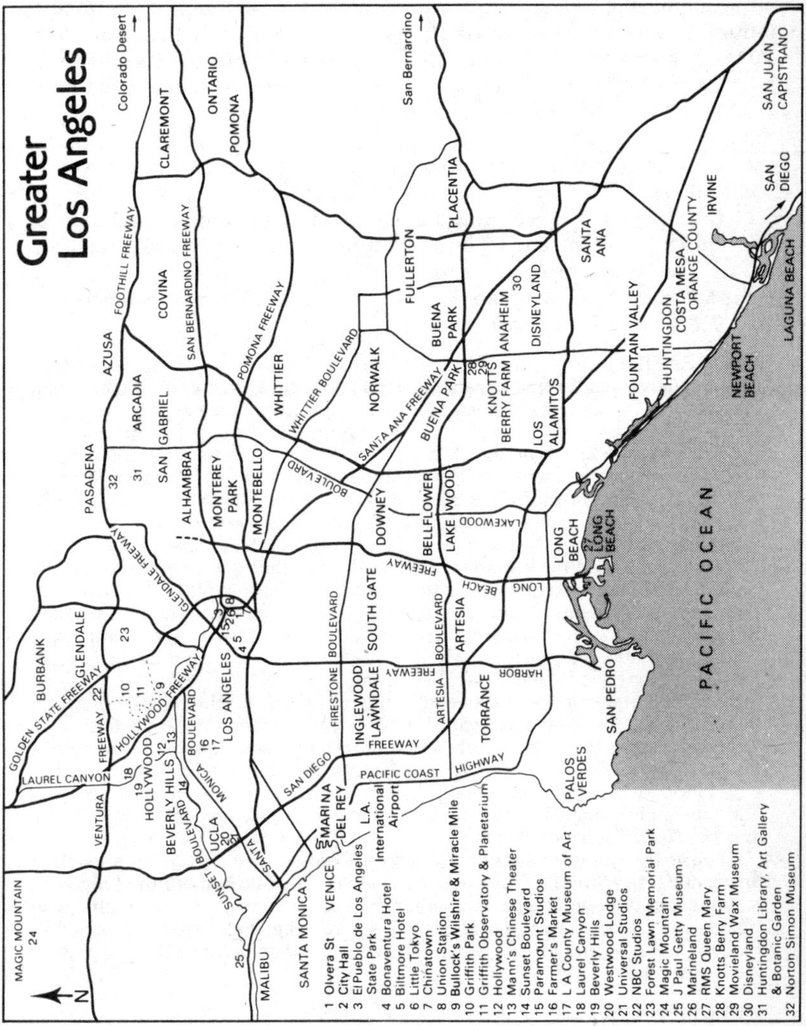
Greater Los Angeles
N
MAGIC MOUNTAIN 24
25
MALIBU
SANTA MONICA
VENICE
MARINA DEL REY
L.A. International Airport
SUNSET
BOULEVARD
SANTA
MONICA
UCLA 20 21
BEVERLY HILLS 14
HOLLYWOOD 19 18 12 13
VENTURA FREEWAY
LAUREL CANYON
HOLLYWOOD FREEWAY
BOULEVARD 16 17
LOS ANGELES
10 11 9
22
GOLDEN STATE FREEWAY
BURBANK
GLENDALE
23
GLENDALE FREEWAY
4 5 15 3 2 6 8 1 7
SAN DIEGO FREEWAY
PACIFIC COAST HIGHWAY
INGLEWOOD
LAWNDALE
FIRESTONE BOULEVARD
SOUTH GATE
ARTESIA BOULEVARD
ARTESIA
TORRANCE
HARBOR FREEWAY
LONG BEACH FREEWAY
PALOS VERDES
SAN PEDRO
LONG BEACH
LONG BEACH 27
LAKEWOOD
BELLFLOWER
DOWNEY
MONTEBELLO
MONTEREY PARK
ALHAMBRA
SAN GABRIEL
PASADENA 32 31
ARCADIA
AZUSA
FOOTHILL FREEWAY
COVINA
SAN BERNARDINO FREEWAY
POMONA FREEWAY
WHITTIER
WHITTIER BOULEVARD
BOULEVARD
NORWALK
SANTA ANA FREEWAY
BUENA PARK
KNOTTS BERRY FARM 28 29
LOS ALAMITOS
ANAHEIM 30
DISNEYLAND
FULLERTON
PLACENTIA
SANTA ANA
FOUNTAIN VALLEY
HUNTINGDON
COSTA MESA
ORANGE COUNTY
IRVINE
NEWPORT BEACH
LAGUNA BEACH
SAN DIEGO
SAN JUAN CAPISTRANO
CLAREMONT
POMONA
ONTARIO
Colorado Desert
San Bernardino
PACIFIC OCEAN
1 Olvera St
2 City Hall
3 El Pueblo de Los Angeles State Park
4 Bonaventura Hotel
5 Biltmore Hotel
6 Little Tokyo
7 Chinatown
8 Union Station
9 Bullock's Wilshire & Miracle Mile
10 Griffith Park
11 Griffith Observatory & Planetarium
12 Hollywood
13 Mann's Chinese Theater
14 Sunset Boulevard
15 Paramount Studios
16 Farmer's Market
17 L A County Museum of Art
18 Laurel Canyon
19 Beverly Hills
20 Westwood Lodge
21 Universal Studios
22 NBC Studios
23 Forest Lawn Memorial Park
24 Magic Mountain
25 J Paul Getty Museum
26 Marineland
27 RMS Queen Mary
28 Knotts Berry Farm
29 Movieland Wax Museum
30 Disneyland
31 Huntingdon Library, Art Gallery & Botanic Garden
32 Norton Simon Museum

profound sense of identity crisis. Then came the massive earthquake on the 17th January, 1994. More than 50 died and many people were left homeless and stranded. The dream had become a nightmare.

Despite the growing congestion, the youthful LA sense of unlimited possibilities is easily restored with a trip among Mulholland Drive. Named for the engineer of LA's first aqueduct, Mulholland twists along the spine of mountains separating LA from the San Fernando Valley. A drive here offers sweeping vistas out over the enormous possibilities of the LA basin. At night the city lights stretch down to the sea, covering a seemingly limitless expanse. Clearly this was a city meant to dream dreams.

If you haven't acquired a car, it is surely now or never. You will no doubt get lost, spend countless hours looking for parking, but there's a sly exhilaration to driving LA freeways. It's like urban surfing. Once you've experienced the silken pull of seamless traffic, conquered a complex exchange as cars confidently curl on and off into new trajectories, and got a taste of life in the fast lane, you'll probably agree.

Area code for LA is 213, for Santa Monica and Venice 310, for the San Fernando Valley 818, and for Long Beach and Orange County 714.

GEOGRAPHY

LA is immense and the first thing you need to do is get a sense of how to find your way round. For convenience sake, we'll assume that you have landed at the airport, and you're looking at a map. The airport is on the coast, in the middle of the **Santa Monica Bay**. Moving south along the coast you come to **Long Beach** (the *Queen Mary* is moored here, and Disneyland is about 10 miles inland from here in Anaheim) and then the resort areas of **Huntington Beach**, **Newport Beach**, **Laguna Beach** and finally **San Diego** about 125 miles south of LA.

Moving north along the coast from the airport, you first come to **Marina Del Rey**, the largest man-made marina in the world, and then to the beach community of **Venice**, a bohemian hang-out on the beach. When LA people let it all hang out, this is where it hangs. Moving along, you come to **Santa Monica**, also called Soviet Monica for its liberal leanings. This area is a pleasant beach community with a large British population. **Malibu Beach** is about a 25-minute drive north from here along the Pacific Coast Hwy. Moving inland from Santa Monica along **Sunset Blvd** you come to **Westwood**, home of UCLA. Further along Sunset, in **Beverly Hills**, the feeling is decidedly posh, and anything but collegiate.

Sunset passes through Beverly Hills and **Hollywood** and into **Downtown**. Below Hollywood is the **Melrose/West Hollywood** area, the cutting edge of LA chic. Hopping over the Hollywood Hills to the north, you enter **North Hollywood** and the **San Fernando Valley**. The TV and movie studios are located in Burbank and the North Hollywood area.

If you arrive by train or bus you will come into downtown. By bus it is possible to arrive at Santa Monica, Hollywood, Pasadena, Glendale and North Hollywood stations, but by train you have no other choice. Of course, LA is a tough city in places, particularly Downtown and East LA—'Never go near, especially at night'. Sticking to the West Side—Beverly Hills, Westwood and parts of Hollywood—is generally safe.

ACCOMMODATION

Getting around LA can be a battle, so you should choose lodging near where you will want to spend the most time. Beverly Hills, Westwood, and the West Side are centrally located to many sights. Do not stay downtown just because it sounds as though all the sites are there. They're not. Downtown has many cheap lodgings, but unless you want a concentrated urban and ethnic mix with some artistic trappings, you'll be better off elsewhere.

Downtown (close to Union train station, bus station):
Motel de Ville, 1123 W 7th St, 624-8474. S–$40, D–$45, $2 discount per day with student ID if you stay 4 nights or longer. Colour TV, AC, pool. Busy street. 'Good value.' 'Terrible area.' 'Don't hesitate to bargain.'
Rosslyn Hotel, 112 W 5th St, 624-3311. Close to Greyhound. S–$25, D–$33, Weekly S–$125, D–$160; $5 key deposit. 'Spartan, but convenient.'
Beverly Hills/Hollywood/West Side (close to entertainment, shopping, movie sites): **Hollywood Vine Motel**, 1133 Vine St, near Santa Monica Blvd, 466-7501. S/D–$45 up. 'Friendly and near to Hollywood Greyhound.'
Hollywood International Hostel, 6561 Franklin Ave, (800) 750-6561 (in-state) or (213) 463-0797. 3–4 bed dorms, $15. Weekly rate $80. Private rooms D-$30 with bath & shower. Price includes breakfast, TV room, kitchen facs, linen, free coffee. Call for free rides to/from/airport/Universal Studios. Hostel is actually on Hollywood Blvd.
Orchid Hotel, 819 S Flower St, 624-5855. In the heart of downtown. S–$34, D–$40. 'Gave us a student discount. Bargain breakfast at the Gaslighter Restaurant.'
Hollywood YMCA-Hostel, 1553 N Hudson Ave on the corner of Selma, 467-4161. 4 blks from Greyhound. Hostel: $11. Non-hostel: S–$23, D–$26. Cafe.
Hotel del Flores, 409 N Crescent Dr, south of Santa Monica Blvd, 274-5115. S/D–$47 and up, shared bath. 'Very clean, pleasant management.'
Hotel Howard, 1738 N Whitely Ave, 466-6943. Reserve at least a week in advance, especially in the summer. Rentals on per-week basis, but occasionally lets for 3 days. Clean linen, maid service, hall phones, refrigerators, coin-op laundry and generally nice apartments. S–$32, D–$40; weekly rates: S–$158, D–$180, $10 refundable advance deposit. 'Very modern and clean. Staff very friendly.'
Banana Bungalow, 2775 Cahuenga Blvd, W Hollywood, 851-1129. $15 dorm, D-$45. TV, bath, pool. Free shuttle to airport and beach. 'Fantastic.'
The Valley *(Area code: 818)*: **El Patio Motel**, 11466 Ventura Blvd, corner of Tujunga, nr studios, 760-9602. D–$67. AC, TV.
La Tura Motel, 11745 Ventura Blvd, in Studio City nr Universal Studios, 762-2260. S–$30. 'Need a car.'
Along Coast, Near Airport: Airport Interclub Hostel, 2221 Lincoln Blvd, (310) 305-0250. Closest hostel to the airport. $14 per night plus $5 deposit, passport required. Open 24 hrs. Take shuttle bus C from airport to Lot C, then blue bus #3 (50¢) to Victoria Ave.
Cadillac Hotel, 401 Ocean Front Walk, Venice B, 399-8876. S/D–$63 up; dorm–$19 up. Will pick-up from airport. Free coffee. 'Really friendly.'
Colonial Inn Hostel, 421 8th St, Huntington Beach, about 20 miles south of Airport, (714) 536-3315. From airport take the #232 bus to the Long Beach Transit Center, board the #95 to the Hostel, not far from the Huntington Beach Pier. Run by a self-described 'funky old lady having a good time'. $12 hostel, $14 p.p. double.
LA International Hostel, 3601 S Gaffey St, Bldg 613, San Pedro, 831-8109. $10.50 AYH, $13.50 non-members. 'Clean and friendly.' #446 bus to Korean Bell from 6th and Los Angeles Sts. Last bus leaves downtown at 2.45pm.
Santa Monica International AYH-Hostel, 1436 2nd St, Santa Monica, 90401, 393-9913. $16 members, $19 non-members. Largest, and newest, hostel on west coast. Library, kitch facs, TV room, 2 blocks from beach. 'Fantastic facilities, but too many rules.' No. 33 bus from downtown.
Share-Tel International Hostel, 20 Brooks Ave, (310) 392-0325. $17 per night, $110 per week. After Labor Day, $15 per night, $90 p/wk. Show passport or student ID. Kitchen facs, linen, no curfew, safe area.
Tradewinds Hotel, 4200 W Century Blvd, Inglewood, 419-0999. Free shuttle from airport. Q–$73. Pool, restaurant.
Venice Beach Cotel, 25 Windward Ave, Venice, 399-7649. $50 up, $15 up dorm. 'Great.' On the beach.
Venice Beach Hostel, 701 Washington St, (310) 306-5180. Take bus #33 from Spring St nr Greyhound terminal, $1.50. $12 per night or $70 p/wk in a relaxed

atmosphere. Kitchen, cable TV lounge. 'Very sociable hostel.' 'Staff have lots of info on what to do in LA, just ask.' Close to beach, bars and nightclubs. Surfboard rental.
Venice Marina Hostel, 2915 Yale Ave, Marina Del Rey, (310) 301-3983. $13, kitchen, lockers, laundry, nr beach. Will pick up from airport.
Nr Disneyland: Fullerton Hacienda AYH Hostel, 1700 North Harbour Blvd, Fullerton, (714) 738-3721. $13.20 members, non-members $3 more. 15 minutes car drive from Disneyland. 3 dorms, 8 beds in each, 2 bathrooms, shared kitchen, linen rental $1. Take the 'Golden Star' or 'Airway' shuttles from airport to the door, $15.

FOOD
The greater LA area has over 25,000 eating establishments. Does this city love to eat out, or what? In fact, during the 1982 recession, people in Los Angeles ate out more often than they had before the downturn. One reason for this obsession may be the mobile lifestyle, and the rich mix of ethnic cultures. Don't be surprised to find kosher burritos, Thai Tacos and more.
Downtown: Clifton's Cafeterias, 648 S Broadway, 627-1673; 515 W 7th St, 485-1726. Vast array of cheap dishes, soothing decor from a redwood forest with real waterfall to the Art Deco touches at 7th St. Open 7am–7pm.
El Tepayac, 812 N Evergreen, 268-1960, is home to the *Manuel Special*, an enormous burrito requiring two people to finish. This barrio hang-out draws an unusual mix of police, locals and Mexico food junkies. Closed Tue. Open 6am–9.45pm. Til 11pm Fri & Sat.
Kosher Burrito, 1st St, 626-0998, cleanest burritos in town.
La Luz Del Dia, W 1 Olvera St, 628-7495. Mexican food mecca. Cheapest deal going. Open 11am–10pm, Tue–Sun; closed Mon.
Mandarin Deli, in the food center, 727 N Broadway in Chinatown. 623-6054. You know its authentic because no-one here speaks English. Try the *jiao tzi* (fried dumplings). Open 11am–9pm.
Pantry Cafe, 877 S Figueroa, 972-9279. Huge helpings of basic meat and potatoes fare. The Pantry is famous, not for its food, but because it is so unassuming and has been here forever. An anomaly in trendy LA. Open 24hrs.
Pho Hoa, 640 N. Broadway, 626-5530. 'Good Vietnamese restaurant. Large portions, reasonably priced.' Open 7am–7pm.
West Side: Apple Pan, 10801 W Pico Blvd, 475-3585. Unassuming burger and apple pie shop. Great food with the locals lining up behind the counter stools (no tables) waiting for a spot at the trough. Open 11am–12am, closed Mon.
Barney's Beanery, 8447 Santa Monica Blvd, 654-2287. Things haven't changed too much since Janis Joplin used to hang out here. The pool tables still need new felt, the vinyl in the booths is still bright, and the action at the bar is still pretty fierce. The chili is worth the price of admission. A great place to meet locals.
Canter's Deli, 419 N Fairfax, 651-2030, open 24hrs. In LA's old Jewish section close to CBS Television City. There is no better deli or bakery in town, especially at 3am.
CC Brown's Hot Fudge Shop, on Hollywood Blvd near Mann's Chinese Theater, 464-9726. Pressed tin roof, dark-wood booths, this ice cream store takes you back to the days when ice cream was still made by hand. Claims to be the originator of the hot fudge sundae.
Dolores' West Restaurant, 11407 Santa Monica Blvd at Purdue, 477-1061. Offers the bottomless coke. An old-fashioned burger joint. Open 24 hrs.
Ed Debevic's, 134 N La Cienega at Wilshire, 659-1952. '50s-dressed staff dance on tables—totally wild.' Open 11.30am–11pm, Fri–Sat 'til 1am.
Farmers' Market, 6333 W 3rd St, 100 block of Fairfax, 933-9211. California is an agricultural engine, and this farmers' market is an impressive cornucopia. Stop here for Bob's coffee and donuts on your way to the big time at nearby CBS TV City or the county museum (LACMA). Gray Line Tours of Hollywood leave near here.

Musso And Franks, 6667 Hollywood Blvd, 467-5123. This old bar and grill is a regular for film industry types. It offers a touch of the golden era of Hollywood elegance.
Nate 'n' Al's, 414 N Beverly Dr, 274-0101. Opens 7.30am every day. The Beverly Hills power schmooze takes place here early in the am.
Tail O' the Pup, 329 N San Vicente at Beverly, 652-4517. A hot-dog shaped stand complete with bright yellow mustard oozing out of the sides.
The Valley: Adam's Restaurant, 17500 Ventura, 990-7427. Great for ribs. Open 5pm–11pm.
Dupar's, 12036 Ventura Blvd, (818) 766-4437, great pies and one of the best coffee shops in town. 'This is a real hang-out late on a Friday or Saturday.'
Along the Beach: Alice's Restaurant, Malibu Pier, 23000 Pacific Coast Highway, (310) 456-6646. Right on the beach. Good place to stop for brunch or dinner on a trip up the coast to Malibu. Open 5pm–11pm for dinner.
Patrick's Roadhouse, 106 Entrada just off Corner of Pac Coast Hwy and Entrada Dr, across the street from Will Rogers State Beach, 459-4544. Open 8am–3pm weekdays; 9am–3pm weekends. Make reservations for the weekends. Arnold Schwarzenegger had his bachelor party here. 'Good homemade fish and chips.'
Rose Cafe, 220 Rose Ave in Venice, 399-0711. Pretty place serving healthy food to beautiful people. Visitors are greeted by a mural of a bright red rose. Open 7.30am–11pm, Mon–Fri.
Wildflour Pizza, 2807 Main St in Santa Monica, 392-3300. *LA Times* says its the best pie in town. Open Mon–Thur, and Sat 'til 10.30pm.
Ye Olde King's Head Pub, 116 Santa Monica Blvd, 451-1402, a real ghetto for expatriate Brits, complete with darts, chips, everything.

OF INTEREST
For convenience, sites have been grouped geographically. It would be wise to plan day trips around one important site, rather than, say, attempt to get from Universal Studios to Disneyland, 2 hours away by car, in one day. The RTD has an excellent self-guided tour booklet for people using the bus.
Downtown: Despite rumours to the contrary, downtown LA does exist. In fact, film producers use it as a double for Manhattan. Old and graceful structures survive, especially around the beautiful **Pershing Square Park**, but the area is dominated by soaring skyscrapers. To get oriented take DASH, (213) 972-6000, a private bus system which covers all of downtown, 25¢ each time you board.
City Hall, 200 Spring St. was until quite recently the tallest building in LA. It features an eclectic style of Babylonian and Byzantine architecture, and has an observation deck on the 27th floor. The ***Los Angeles Times*** is across the street and offers free tours at 11.15am and 3pm on weekdays. You can see the editorial offices, press and production rooms of this major newspaper. You'll also get a free replica of the first edition in 1881. Just a few blocks from City Hall around 1st and San Pedro Sts, is **Little Tokyo**, a bustling area which has grown like mad in the last few years. LA has had an important Japanese community since the 1880s, although they were unconstitutionally rounded up during WWII and herded into camps. The community has rebuilt since that shattering experience. This is a good place to walk around. Be sure to visit the **Japanese American Cultural And Community Center gardens**, 244 S San Pedro, the koi pool at the **New Otani Hotel** and the many Japanese speciality shops.
Walking along Broadway away from Little Tokyo towards **Pershing Square**, you would think you were in Mexico. This bustling Hispanic area becomes the garment and diamond districts near 7th St. If you turn west on 5th St off Broadway you come to Pershing Square—a graceful park in the middle of downtown. On the site of an Indian (later Spanish) trail, the **Biltmore Hotel**, 506 S Grand, is the square's most charming and sumptuous hotel complete with a fountain and wood-beamed ceiling in the Spanish-style entrance. JFK stayed in the $2400-a-day suite when he won the Democratic presidential nomination in 1960. A graceful architectural counterbalance to the skyscrapers is the Byzantine style **Los Angeles**

Central Library, 433 S Spring St, 612-3200. Open Mon–Thur 10am–8pm, Fri–Sat 10am–5.30pm.

Each of the enormous skyscrapers surrounding the Library—the **Arco Towers**, the **Citicorp Center**, and the **Bonaventure Hotel**—are small cities in themselves. They house underground shopping, parking and restaurants and are connected to one another by skywalks and underground passages. LA was the first city in the country to develop the concept of such skyscrapers, that function as self-contained shopping, entertainment and office complexes. The idea fits LA well, for it provides a centralized environment in a very decentralized city. The Bonaventure in particular offers a stunning atrium and impressive glass elevators that whisk you along the outside of the building to a restaurant at the top. On clear days the view is remarkable.

Hop on the DASH bus, or walk north along Broadway to get to **Chinatown and Olvera St**. Just off Main St, in the preserved Olvera St area, is the original Spanish settlement of Los Angeles, now the **El Pueblo de Los Angeles State Historic Park**, 628-7164. The small original Mexican settlement lead by Felipe de Neve adopted that big name of El Pueblo de La Reina de Los Angeles de Porciuncula. Olvera St, and the **Iglesia de Nuestra Senora** across the street are the oldest and most colourful reminders of LA's Spanish roots. This is a good area to have a Mexican lunch (try **La Luz Del Dia**) and to shop among the colourful Mexican and Central American stalls. Since the Spanish-style **Union Train Station** is nearby on Alameda St, you may want to save Olvera St until your last day in LA.

Walk up Main St to Ord and head left to Broadway, and Mexico gives way to China, and **Chinatown**—not as classy as Little Tokyo, but full of good places to eat. The street life is perhaps a bit more old-fashioned here. Between crates of live chickens stacked helter skelter on the sidewalk, merchants still hold live birds upside down while old Chinese women poke the breast bones to check for tenderness. Your best orientation to the rest of LA is to take **Sunset Blvd** west away from Downtown (RTD #2). Beginning in El Pueblo Park, Sunset shoots out towards Hollywood, banks in to the **Sunset Strip**, wends through the posh areas of **Beverly Hills** and **Bel Air**, and finally dips down to the Ocean. Sunset Blvd cuts a grand path through LA's many attractions. It is central to the city, and indeed, people measure their success in life by whether or not they have managed to acquire a home on the fashionable 'North Side' of 'The Boulevard'.

Hollywood: At Sunset and Los Feliz Blvd, head north to **Griffith Park**. The largest city park in America, Griffith offers trails, bridle paths, a zoo, the Greek Theater, three golf courses, and an observatory and planetarium. Performances in the Greek Theater from June through September; for info call 480-3232. The park observatory is free, and the 65' long, 12' wide refractor telescope is open to the public, from sundown til 9.50pm. The ocean breeze generally blows the smog away, and visibility is good. There is also a free **Hall of Science**, a **Planetarium** $4, and **Laserium** ($6) featuring shows about different topics in astronomy. For hours and information call 664-1191, for astronomical information dial Sky Report, 663-8171. From the Planetarium you will not need a telescope to see the famous Hollywood Sign. The 50 foot letters were built by a real estate developer, and originally spelled out Hollywoodland, the name of his development.

Not far from the observatory you'll find the stars are on the street along **Hollywood Blvd**. Over 2500 names of stars are laid into the terrazzo sidewalk above bronze symbols of microphones, cameras, television sets or records denoting the craft which brought them fame. Do not expect Hollywood to glitter as brightly as her sidewalks. The area has been a somewhat shabby, red-light district since the 50's. Children who run away from home for the glamour of Hollywood are often suckered into prostitution and worse. The Art Deco **Pantages Theater**, recalls the glamour of by-gone days. Built in 1929, the Pantages for many years housed the Academy Awards, and today draws many Broadway musicals. **Fredericks of Hollywood**, 6608 Hollywood Blvd, 466-8506, is LA's original, and uninhibited, sexual image-maker. Open Mon–Thur 10am–8pm, Fri 'til 9pm, Sat 10am–6pm, Sun noon–5pm.

The most popular Hollywood attraction is **Mann's Chinese Theater**, 6925 Hollywood Blvd, 464-8111. The theatre opened in 1927 with the premiere of DeMille's *King of Kings*, and was christened by Norma Talmage who accidentally stepped in wet cement that night, the birth of a Hollywood tradition. Some of the world's most famous anatomy is imprinted here, including Michael Jackson, Donald Duck, R2-D2, Trigger and Marilyn Monroe. The building itself is a strange blend of Polynesian and Chinese Imperial architecture. Mann's offers one of the best sound systems, and largest screens in LA. Open 11am–8pm, Mon–Fri $4.50–$7.60

Hollywood offers several other architectural styles than the bizarre Chinese at Mann's. Frank Lloyd Wright designed two homes near here—**Hollyhock House**, open to the public, 662-7272, and **Sowden House**. **Hollywood Bowl**, 2301 N Highland Ave, a large ampitheatre with near-perfect acoustics. The bowl hosts major jazz, classical and rock concerts. Call 480–3232 for tickets. Open Mon–Fri 8am–9pm, Sat–Sun 8.30am–7pm. Off Hollywood, on Vine St is the **Capitol Records** office, designed to look like a stack of 45s with a huge 92′ needle on top. The red beacon on the needle spells out Hollywood in morse code.

After leaving Hollywood, but just before Beverly Hills, Sunset Blvd banks into the famous **Sunset Strip**—an exciting night spot lined with inventive, hand-painted billboards, and the best rock clubs in LA. At the other end of the frenzied Sunset Strip, Beverly Hills is as calm as a bank vault on Sunday. Everyone who has seen *Beverly Hills Cop* knows how rich and bizarre the residents are here. Actually, there are more attorneys and businessmen than Arabs, movie stars and drug lords. **Rodeo Drive** (pronounced Row-DAY-o) near Wilshire Blvd is the most expensive retail strip in the world. The Gucci side is the most fashionable. If you want to see the nearby homes of the stars—Gene Kelly lived at 725 Rodeo, Carl Reiner at 714—you'll need to rent a car, take the bus or a Gray Line tour.

For a more affordable shopping experience head to the massive **Beverly Center**, corner 3rd and La Cienega. Next to the center, the Cadillac sticking out of the roof marks the spot of the **Hard Rock Cafe**. Be sure and stop in at the **Beverly Hills Hotel**. The bright pink decor is hard to miss. The film industry does its business at the Hotel bar called the Polo Lounge. Bring your wallet and don't forget to have yourself paged.

Sunset continues on past the Polo Lounge along the northern edge of **Westwood Village** and **UCLA**. Tucked in with the campus, Westwood Village is a huge and handsome mall, one of LA's few walking districts, and chockful of cinemas, shops, street buskers and socialising places. 'Fri and Sat nights are like a circus with sword-swallowers, dancers, musicians, and even fortune-telling cats!' Celebs also frequent Westwood. The campus area is a live party spot. 'Frat parties along Gayley from 21 Sept on. Free beer, spirits, food, entertainment and the best-looking women in the world.' 'On a quieter note, **Westwood Village Cemetery**, 1218 Glendon, has the most visited grave in LA, that of Marilyn Monroe; Natalie Wood is also buried here.

Continuing past Westwood, Sunset winds through miles of exclusive **Pacific Palisades** real estate (Ronald Reagan lived here) finally reaching Pacific Coast Highway just above Santa Monica.

The Valley: Made famous by the song *Valley Girl*, the **San Fernando Valley** is primarily a bedroom community for kids who drive Camaros. The shopping is excellent at the **Sherman Oaks Galleria**, just over the hill from Westwood. The most interesting part of the valley is near the studios in the North Hollywood area. Other than the studios, the most major sites are the **LA Zoo** in **Glendale**, and the famous **Forest Lawn Memorial Park**, 1712 S Glendale Ave, Glendale, open 8am–5pm, 254-3131. Also friendly branches in the Hollywood Hills, near Artesia and in West Covina, each with its own artwork, patriotic themes and style. This is the American way of death as depicted in Evelyn Waugh's *The Loved One*: odourless, spotless, artistically uplifting, almost fun, at least for the survivors. It's hard to keep from giggling at the crass wonder of it all, from repros of the Greatest Hits of Michelangelo and Leonardo de Vinci to the comic-book approach on the 'Life of

Jesus' mosaics. Take a copy of Ken Schessler's *This is Hollywood* along (but keep it out of sight—park officials won't allow the book on the grounds) to find where the notables are planted. Free, open daily 8am–5pm.

Museums and art galleries:
Downtown: Exposition Park, corner of Exposition & Figueroa Blvds, was built in the early 1900s and houses LA's oldest museums and a beautiful rose garden.
Museum of Science and Industry, 744-7447, contains the Halls of Economics & Finance and of Health. Admission is free, except for the IMAX theatre, 744-2019. Adults $6, students $4.75. The airplane collection is impressive. Open daily 10am–5pm.
Natural History Museum of LA County, 744-DINO, 744-3414. Open 10am–5pm Tue–Sun. Admission $5, students $3.50. Main exhibits include 'battling dinosaurs', habitat halls with stuffed animals placed in natural settings, and the American History Halls covering the Revolutionary War to 1914. Also impressive are the California and Southwest History Halls and the Pre-Columbian—Meso American Hall covering Maya, Inca, and other civilisations. The Hall of Gems and Minerals includes the 102-karat Ashberg Diamond, thought to have been a part of the Russian crown jewels.
Nearby is the **Coliseum**, site of the 1932 and 1984 Olympics, and **USC**. Best known for its football team, USC is affectionately called the University of Spoiled Children, although its real name is the University of Southern California.
LACE, Los Angeles Contemporary Exhibitions, 6522 Hollywood Blvd, (213) 957-1777, is devoted to artists who are still alive. The primary alternative space to the burgeoning traditional museum scene, LACE offers everything from performance art to video art. If there is an avant-garde in LA, it stays one step ahead by coming here. Free. Call for hours and extra info.
MOCA, Museum of Contemporary Art, 250 S Grand between 2nd and 4th, 62-MOCA-2. Closed Mon; open Thur 11am–8pm and 11am–5pm other days; $4, $2 students. Thurs after 5pm is free. Famous Japanese architect Arata Isozaki designed this newest museum on the LA scene. The building itself is a work of art, integrating primary shapes into abstract patterns. The prime materials are rough finished red sandstone, gray granite and green panelling with a pink diamond pattern. The trim is in polished granite. Most impressive is the large polished onyx gable window above the ticket booth. The collection includes many modern artists from the 1940s to the present—Louise Nevelson, Robert Rauschenberg, David Hockney and others. MOCA's second building is the **Temporary Contemporary**, 152 N Central Ave. Tickets can be used for both buildings on the same day. This is under renovation at time of writing and is due to re-open in the fall of '94.
West Side: Los Angeles County Museum of Art, mercifully abbreviated to **LACMA**, 5905 Wilshire Blvd, 857-6111. LACMA has grown impressively in the last few years. A recent building houses the collection of 20th century works by Picasso, Braque and Matisse. The older Armand Hammer Building houses an impressive collection of Far Eastern works. LA has been developing the good sense to look west, to Japan and Asia for its artistic inspiration. The proof is found in the new **Pavilion for Japanese Art** which opened in mid-1988. The pavilion houses the Shin'enkan collection of Edo period screens and scrolls. Widely regarded as the most outstanding collection of its kind, the 32,100-square-foot pavilion instantly became a world-class centre for Japanese art. $4 students.
La Brea Tar Pits are nearby. An ancient source of natural tar, the pits were often covered with a light layer of dust and water. Ice Age animals seeking water became ensnared in the tar and their bones were preserved for history, making the Tar Pits the single richest fossil find in the world. The **George C. Page Museum of La Brea Discoveries** exhibits of fossils in atrium. Open pit to watch excavating in summer months. Still millions of fossils. Open Tue–Sun 10am–5pm, $3.50 students.

Beach: J. Paul Getty Museum, 17985 Pacific Coast Highway, (310) 458-2003. The richest man in the world never lived in the painstaking reproduction of a Roman Villa at Herculaneum he built overlooking the Pacific to house his stunning art collection. Apparently Getty was afraid of flying from London across the Atlantic. The Getty houses a strong collection of French 18th century art. The museum is free, but you will hear many different rumours about the difficulty of getting in. Parking space is limited and cars need reservations which are hard to get in the summer. Tue–Fri you can park at the nearby Charthouse Restaurant for $4 and take a shuttle bus to the Museum. RTD bus #434 stops nearby and you can walk up to the museum—but you must ask the bus-driver for a pass to enter. If you are on a bike or motorcycle, you can get in without a reservation. Open Tue–Sun 10am–5pm.

Pasadena: The Norton Simon Museum of Art, Colorado and North Orange Blvd, 681-2484. Adults $4, Students $2. Thur–Sun noon–6pm. The worst day in the history of the LACMA was the day that Norton Simon got mad and decided to take his ball and go and start his own game. Simon had been on the museum's board, but decided to open his own museum in Pasadena. Simon's extensive collection includes Degas and Rodin (the *Burgers of Calais*) and a garden graced by Henry Moore's sculptures arranged along a fountain.

Huntington Library, Art Gallery and Botanical Gardens, 1151 Oxford Rd in San Marino, (818) 405-2275. An impressive and well-housed collection of Gainsborough and Guttenburgs. English tea is offered every Friday afternoon. 'The gardens are mind-blowing.' Open Tue–Fri 1–4.30pm, Sat 10.30am–4.30pm. Suggested donation $5, $3 students.

Amusement Parks: Disneyland, 1313 S Harbor Blvd, Anaheim, (714) 999-4000. This is the original **Magic Kingdom** and the culmination of Walt Disney's dream. Disney designed the 57 attractions to provide wholesome entertainment for adults & children in this flawlessly clean park. Attractions are grouped into 7 theme parks: you enter the park through Main Street, a re-creation of an old American town. New Orleans Square houses one of the most elaborate rides, the *Pirates of the Caribbean*. Adventureland is devoted to the explorer spirit of African safaris. Fantasyland recreates the magic of the animation classics; the entrance is through Sleeping Beauty's castle, right next to the Matterhorn roller coaster. In Frontierland, you can journey through the old west on an incredible mining train roller coaster. A visionary himself, Disney took special interest in the future. You can do this at Tomorrowland, which includes the legendary Space Mountain roller coaster, the 3-D *Captain EO*, starring Michael Jackson; and newest thriller, Star Tours, a flight simulator. Finally, Critter Country features the popular Splash Mountain, a water flume attraction themed around *Song of the South* adventures.

There is year-round entertainment (e.g. Big bands, the Videopolis Dance Club) but the Electric Light Parade (9pm) with hundreds of light-bedecked floats and fireworks, is only available summer evenings. Since all this is available for the $30 admission fee ($55 2-day pass), you really have to ask yourself why you should see any of the other parks in town. Open 8am–1am daily in summer; 10am–6pm weekdays, 9am–midnight weekends in winter. For specific hours call (714) 999-4000. RTD, 635-6010, from downtown: take #460 East on 6th—$2.90. Runs as late as 1.20am in summer. Local Orange County Bus from Greyhound Terminal at corner of Harbor and Orange Wood, Orange County Transit: (OCTD) (714) 571-5800. #43 on Harbor, every 15 min. 'Get there as early as possible. Lines for good rides become enormous by noon.' 'Avoid Saturday!' 'Take a full day.' 'Don't miss the parade of Disney Characters.' 'Don't leave luggage at Greyhound—station closes at 9pm, Disneyland at midnight.' Greyhound—Anaheim, 999-1256, $5 o/w. 'Tomorrowland is best—see it first.' 'Don't miss *America the Beautiful* 360-degree film.'

Knott's Berry Farm, 8039 Beach Blvd, Buena Park, (714) 220-5200. The gift shops outnumber the rides and attractions 10 to 1 but its Montezooma's Revenge (with 360-degree upside-down loops) is nauseatingly effective, allowing you to meet

yourself (and possibly your lunch) coming back. 'Hurts, but must be tried.' New rides: The Boomerang, a 54 second reverse looping roller coaster; XK-1, where you are launched as from an aircraft-carrier and you do the steering in a cockpit seven stories up; the Whirlpool, an indoor ride with sound and light show. Great waterworks show at lake. Lots of special celebrations, rock concerts, discount promotions. Check the papers. 9am–midnight, $25.95. 20 mins to Disneyland.
Movieland Wax Museum, 7711 Beach Blvd, Buena Park, one block north of Knott's, (714) 522-1154, 200-plus movie and TV stars captured (not always successfully) in wax. The big event is the Chamber of Horrors, based on 13 scary movies, including *Werewolf in London, Dracula, The Exorcist* and *Psycho*. Here you can also be fooled by moviestar look alikes of Clint Eastwood, Michael Jackson, Marilyn Monroe, Bette Davis. Box office open daily 9am–7.30pm, $12.95.
RMS Queen Mary On Pier J, Long Beach, #7 at south end of Long Beach Freeway. Open daily 10am–6pm; $5.
Six Flags Magic Mountain, Valencia, north of LA, (805) 255-4111. Alton Towers has nothing on this place. Experience some of the biggest rollercoaster rides in the world: The Viper, Collossus, The Revolution and the Ninja are all here. 'Thrilling to the extreme'. 'Arrive early, by the afternoon 2 hour queues are not uncommon'. Accessible only by car (remember where you parked—huge car park) or shuttle—Magic Line, (213) 653-1090, from any downtown hotel, $58 return including admission.
Universal Studios Tour, 100 Universal City Plaza, (818) 508-9600. $29 for a 2½ hour tour taken by tram through the 420 acre lot. Shows include *Conan the Barbarian*, a *Star Trek* adventure (you'll be in the show), *Jaws* and a 30' King Kong attempting to derail the tram. Tours leave from 9am–7pm summers; varying hours in off-season. Get there early to avoid crowds. 'Get right-hand seat on tram—most scenes, Jaws, etc, to the right.' 'More recent attractions include *Back to the Future*, a virtual reality ride through time in a DeLorean, and *Backdraft*, a scorching sensation based on the movie. 'Not on a par with Disneyland'. 'Better than Disneyland.' Take RTD # 424 from downtown heading north on Broadway.
Near Universal is the 18-theater **Cineplex Odeon Universal City Cinema**, (818) 508-0588. If a movie isn't playing there, it isn't playing. Hard-core movie fans will head to **Eddie Brandt's Saturday Matinee**, 6310 Colfax, (818) 506-4242 home to 4 million movie stills priced from $5–$6. Open Tue–Fri 1–6pm. Sat 8.30am–5pm.

The Industry: —what the cognoscente call the movie business. To get a feel for it, read the trade magazines *Hollywood Reporter* and *Variety*. More hands on experience can be gained by hanging out at the Polo Lounge, or Ma Maison Restaurant, but for those without the necessary wallets, TV shows are free, and you can watch them being taped at any of the major studios. Tickets are available from the Visitors Center ('We got tickets to Jay Leno') or from the TV reps in front of Mann's Chinese Theater in Hollywood.
ABC Television, 4151 Prospect St, (310) 557-7777, Mon–Fri 9am–5pm. Taping only, no tours. Only morning talk shows. Tickets (818) 506-0067.
CBS TV City, 7800 Beverly Blvd, 852-2455. Ticket office open 6.30am–5pm daily. Pat Sajak talk show, Bob Newhart, game shows. Arrive before 8am. Take your passport.
NBC Studio Tour, 3000 W Alameda, (818) 840-4444. To see a show taped, arrive early at the ticket office on the west side of the NBC complex off California St. Open 8am–5pm weekdays, 9.30am–4pm on weekends.

ENTERTAINMENT

BAM, free monthly paper, lists gigs up and down the West Coast. Also pick up *The Reader* and *LA Weekly*, free, full of entertainment listings. All available at record/bookstores, newstands. New issues on Thursdays.
Anti-Club, 4658 Melrose, 661-3913. Everything from cow-punk, video poetry and South African. Cheap beer.

The World Famous Baked Potato, 3787 Cahuenga Blvd, near Universal, (818) 980-1615. Oldest major contemporary jazz watering hole. Tiny, but Lee Ritenour, Larry Carlton, among others established themselves here. Get there early for enormous spuds stuffed with whatever you want. Showtimes 9.30pm and 11.30pm.
Club Lingerie, 6507 Sunset, 466-8557. New bands and chic nighttime crowd.
The Palace, 1735 N Vine St, (213) 467-4571. Rock out in a restored old theatre. Famous LA club owner Filthy McNasty's lastest is called **FM Station**. A living room ambience from which to watch LA rock, and dance. 11700 Victory near Universal Studios, (818) 769-2220.
The Troubadour, 9081 Santa Monica Blvd, 276-6168. Aging but legendary launching pad for top rock acts; small and smoky. Cover plus 1-drink minimum, cheaper on Mon hoot nights. Cover $4 Sun-Thur; Fri–Sat $8 and up.
Whiskey a Go Go, 8901 Sunset Blvd, (310) 652-4202. Cream of rock triumvirate. Cover, naturally.
The Palomino, 6907 Lankershim Blvd, near Universal Studios, (818) 764-4010. The place for country music since the 50s. Now has blues, rock; country on Tue only. The Pal serves BBQ and bands in a ranch-like atmosphere.
Theatre/Comedy: The Improv, 8162 Melrose Ave, 651-2583. The one-liners at the bar rival those on stage.
The Comedy Store, 8433 Sunset, 656-6225. A comedy mall with large stage and turns out many comics.
Los Angeles Theater Center, 514 S Spring, 627-6500. LA's major regional theatre for new playwrights. At 5.30pm, before a show, you can get half-price tickets. Student prices are $19, Saturday night $25. Tickets (213) 660-TKTS.
LA has an enormous number of larger theatres, including the **Mark Taper Forum**, the **Shubert** and **Ahmanson**. The best theatre is often at the small equity-waiver houses where struggling actors hone their skills while waiting for the big break. Check the *Reader* and *Weekly* for listings. Best bets are usually the **Group Repertory** or **Odyssey**.
Cinema: As you would expect from the world's film capitol, there are a lot of movies around town. NB: *DO NOT CALL MOVIES 'FLICKS'!* It brands you an outsider. Westwood is the place where most films premiere.
The Nuart, 11272 Santa Monica Blvd, 478-6379. Revival/art house par excellence.
Pacific Cinerama Dome, 6360 Sunset Blvd, 466-3401. This large-screen geodesic dome-shaped theatre housed the premiere of *Apocalypse Now*, among others. Open 12.30pm. $7.50 admission fee. Call 466-3347 for programme info.
The Beverly Cineplex, in Beverly Center, Beverly and La Cienega, 652-7760. 13 theatres featuring popular first-runs as well as art films.

OUT OF DOORS

Catalina Island, 26 miles off Long Beach. A romantic green hideaway, 85% in its natural state. Well worth a trip to see the perfect harbour of Avalon and its delightful vernacular architecture, plus the natural beauties of the place. Snorkelling is best at Lovers Cove, but look out for sharks. 'Beautiful.' Ships cost $32.50 round trip, depart from Balbon Pavilion. Phone Catalina Passenger Service, (714) 673-5245 (Newport). Reservation required. Departs at 9am daily.
Rent a Sail, 13560 Mindanao Way, Marina Del Rey, 822-1868. Rents sailboats from 14 to 25 feet for between $16 and $35 per hour. $20 deposit required. Accepts only cash or traveller's checks. Takes about 25 minutes to sail out into the open ocean. Advance reservations for large boats suggested on weekends.
Malibu Canyon, just north of Malibu offers one of the most stunning day trips in Los Angeles. Take this canyon road to the Malibu State Creek Park for trails into the rugged Santa Monica Mountains. Campground with hot showers, bathroom, biking/hiking trails. First come, first served, $14–$16/site. Call (800) 444-PARK for hiking and camping information. Park info, (310) 457-1324.

SPORT

Southern California is a paradise for sports lovers. In professional sport you can catch the **Dodgers** baseball team at Dodger Stadium, 1000 Elysian Park Ave (224-1400) or, also in major league baseball, the **California Angels** at Anaheim Stadium, 2000 Gene Atuzy Way, Anaheim (714) 937-6700. Open Mon–Sat 9am–5.30pm, $7–$11. Anaheim Stadium is home too to the National Football League team the **LA Rams**, 937-6767, while the city's other football team, **The Raiders**, play at The Coliseum, 3939 S Figueroa, (213) 748-6131. The Coliseum hosted the Olympic Games in 1932 and more recently in 1984. For tickets to the famous **LA Lakers** (basketball), call (310) 412-5000.

INFORMATION

Visitors Information, Greater LA Visitors Bureau, 685 S Figueroa St, by the Hilton Hotel, 689-8822. Open Mon–Fri 8.30am–5pm. Very helpful multilingual staff. Offers free maps, bus and rail information, TV taping tickets, and run-downs of special events. Also has a small branch in Hollywood in Jane's House, 6541 Hollywood Blvd, 461-4213. Open Mon–Sat 9am–5pm.
Travelers Aid, 453 S Spring St, (213) 468-2500, #901, Mon–Fri 8.30am–5pm.
Human Services Hotline, 24 hr, 686-0950, locates doctors, emergency medical help.

TRAVEL

Greyhound, 208 E 6th St at Los Angeles St, (213) 629-8402. Inside, a huge, clean but cheerless terminal with no cafe; outside, the meanest streets anywhere—a zoo. Don't plan any overnights here. 'Friends twice approached by vicious druggies and tramps outside station—be careful.' 'Stay on the upper level.'
Amtrak, (800) 872-7245, 800 N Alameda, also stations in Fullerton, Santa Ana, San Juan Capistrano, San Clemente and San Diego. The *Coast Starlight* to Seattle is highly recommended for socializing and scenery.
RTD Rail System. Info: 972-6235. 20 mile Blue Line light rail south from 7th & Figueroa downtown to Long Beach, 22 stations, $1.10; 16-station Red Line E-W subway has 5 of its planned 16 stations open from Union Station/Civic Center downtown to Wilshire and Western to Hollywood and N Hollywood (completion due late '94); Orange and Green lines, latter from airport to Norwalk to open in 1995.
LA Bus System (RTD) bus info: 626-4455. Bottom level of Greyhound terminal. Basic fare $1.30, $1.55 with transfers. Monthly pass ($42) can be purchased at RTD centres, a convenient one is at 6249 Hollywood Blvd, Mon–Fri 10am–6pm. 'Excellent value.' 'From the airport, change buses at Broadway.'
Santa Monica City Bus, Big Blue Bus, 451-5444. Open Mon–Fri 8am–5pm.
Orange County Transit District, (714) 636-7433.
Gray Line Tours, 856-5900. Picks up at Farmers' Market. $62 to Disneyland includes admission, $26 tour of stars' homes. Open Mon–Sat 9am–4pm.
Hollywood Fantasy Tours, 469-8184. Mon–Sun 9am–4pm.
Car Rentals: Avon Rent-a-Car, (800) 822-2866 in-state, rents convertibles for $59.95 per day, 200 free miles, 18c per mile.
Alamo also recommended from $99.99 and up per week, unlimited free mileage, (800) 327-0400.
Thrify Car Rental, (800) 367-2277. '$116 a week, unlimited mileage.' Reservations req 7 days in advance.
EZ Rent-A-Car, 4730 W Century Blvd, (310) 673-3844, Inglewood.
Midway Rent-A-Car, 8420 Sunset Blvd, 650-5823, $139/wk (1000 miles free). 'Can bargain with them over rate and mileage.'
Auto Driveaway, 3407 6th St, #525, 666-6100, 9am–5pm, Mon–Fri.
Ride board, Floor B, Ackerman Union, UCLA.
Los Angeles International Airport (LAX), is located on the west side of town, just south of Venice. Transportation to and from downtown is fastest and least com-

plicated using one of the numerous shuttle companies. Many accommodations offer free airport pick-ups so check beforehand. In general, shuttle companies will take you/pick you up to/from any major hotel, operate 24 hrs, require a days notice and cost $9–$12. Take your pick: Super Shuttle, (310) 782-6600: USA Shuttle (310) 204-3100; Airway Shuttle, (800) 660-6042. Venice Beach is a $15 cab ride from LAX. Airport information (310) 646-5252.

THE COAST TO SAN DIEGO: Huntington Beach. Surfer capital, a famed party beach. 'The local surfers love to take a complete novice in hand so don't hesitate to ask how it's done.'

Newport Beach. Terribly yachty and formal except on **Balboa Island**, a mecca for boy/girl-watching. 'Try the Balboa bars and the frozen bananas at the icecream kiosks.' **T-K Burgers** at 2119 W Balboa Blvd is the most popular hangout for the non-deckshoe set.

Laguna Beach, 30 miles south of LA, buffered against urban sprawl by the San Joaquin Hills, has a decided Mediterranean look, from its indented coves to its trees and greenery right down to the waterline. The long white sand beach has superb snorkelling, surfing (for experts) and safe swimming at **Aliso Beach Park**. In winter, whale watching and tidepooling are likewise excellent. Long a haven for artists, Laguna is famous for its 7-week Pageant of the Masters each July–Aug, but the accompanying Sawdust Festival (crafts, live music, jugglers, food) is more accessible and more fun. While here, plan to eat at **The Cottage**, 308 N Coast Hwy, or **The Stand** on Thalia St, recommended by a Lagunian for its 'great Mexican food, smoothies and tofu cheeseless cake'. 'Laguna has excellent atmosphere, very picturesque.'

Orange County/Anaheim (Area code: 714): **San Juan Capistrano**, 12 miles inland from Laguna and 22 miles south of Santa Ana. This mission town is well served by Greyhound, Orange County buses and Amtrak, so you have little excuse for passing up its mission, easily the best in California. The chapel, oldest building still standing in the state, is almost Minoan in proportions, feeling and colour. Also on the grounds are the romantic ruins of the great church tumbled by an 1812 earthquake and now a favoured nesting place for the famous swallows. Indian graveyard, jail, various interesting buildings. Well worth your dollar. Take a lunch.

SAN DIEGO One glimpse of San Diego, and it's hard to believe that when Juan Cabrillo first landed here in 1542, he found not a single tree or blade of grass. Today, this desert-defying city is green, green, green by a blue, blue sea. Developed as a naval port, San Diego is strategically (for the tourist) located 100 miles south of Los Angeles and as close to Tijuana as any sane person should want to get.

The town is breezy and casual, famous for top-notch Mexican and seafood restaurants, monstrous 'happy hour' spreads, a historic old town, and great beaches accessible by bus from downtown. Lavish sunshine and its citizens' personal wealth haven't entirely eliminated the small-town flavour of San Diego.

The telephone area code is 619.

ACCOMMODATION

Armed Services YMCA Hostel, 500 W Broadway, 232-1133. Coed, $29, $5 key deposit. Mixed reviews: 'clean, friendly', 'lots of weirdos, unsafe area at night'. Also has cheap AYH dorm, $10. Check in after 4pm; no curfew. 'Helpful staff.'

Banana Bungalow, 707 Reed Ave, Mission Beach, 273-3060. Dorm $11–$15, S–$45 up. Incls b'fast; laundry. On the beach.

Capri Hotel, 319 West E St, 232-3369. S–$29, D–$34. 'Clean, friendly, TV, kitchen, washing facilities.'

Clarke's Flamingo Lodge, 1765 Union St, 234-6787. S–$30, D–$40, 10% discount with student ID. 9 blocks from Greyhound. 'Very clean; very friendly', 'excellent value.' In-room coffee, colour TV, free phone. Coffee shop and swimming pool, free tourist info and map; free pickup on request from bus or train station or from airport.
Golden West Hotel, 720 4th Ave, 233-7596. S–$15, D–$31 with private bath. Near Horton Plaza. Plus $2 key deposit.
Imperial Beach Hostel, 170 Palm Ave, Imperial Beach (south of San Diego), 423-8039. $10 AYH, $13 non-members. 5 miles from Tijuana.
Jim's, 1425 C St, 235-8341. $13. 'Best place—brilliant easy going atmosphere.' 'Shared, mixed, rooms and communal kitchen—crazy people.' 'Ask for DAN.'
Maryland Hotel, 630 F St, 239-9243, S–$24, D–$34. Nr Gaslamp District. $5 key deposit.
Pickwick Hotel, 132 W Broadway, 234-0141. Next to Greyhound. $44, $10 key deposit. 'Clean.' 'Dangerous area.'
Pt Loma Hostel, 3790 Udall St, 223-4778. 6½ miles from downtown; take 35 bus to Ocean Beach. $12 AYH, $15 non-members. 'Well equipped, near cheap markets, 20 min walk from beach.' '2am curfew but $1 late pass available.' Closed 11am–4pm.
San Clemente Hostel, 233 Avenida Granada, San Clemente (Hwy 5 north of San Diego), (714) 492-2848. Nr fishing pier and beach; $9 AYH, $12 non-members.
YWCA, 1012 C St, 239-0355. Women 18+ only. AYH dorms, $10; $5 key deposit, $1 linen charge. 7-day maximum. Single (non-AYH), $20. Close to transit, out of worst area. 'Good, clean, laundry and cooking facilities.' 'Excellent.'

FOOD

It's here that you're likely to find some of the best Mexican food in the US, and plenty of places to choose from. Some of the best are:
Chuey's Cafe, 1894 Main St, 234-6937. String beef tacos, other outstanding Mexican dishes $2–$11. Nearby murals at Chicano Park on the Coronado Bay Bridge make a fitting post-comida stroll. Open Sat 'til 3.30am; closed Sun.
El Indio Tortilla Shop, 3695 India St, an artists' district, 299-0333. 'Heavenly chicken burritos, 50 takeout items, park across the way.' $6.50/dish, open daily 7am–9pm.
Roberto's, many locations in and around the city, wonderful greasy-spoon dives, popular with the locals; among the best for Mexican food. 'Great place. Try the rolled tacos.'
Non-Mexican: Boll Weevil Restaurants, 17 locations around San Diego. Excellent, inexpensive burgers. 'More flavour than any other burger I had in three months.'
Big Kitchen, 3003 Grape St, 234-5789. A breakfast-and-lunch place with characters. Look for comedienne Whoopi Goldberg's graffitti contribution on the kitchen wall. Open Mon–Fri 6am–2pm, Sat–Sun 7am–3pm.
Chicken Pie Shop, 2631 Oklahoma Blvd, 295-0156. Scrumptious chicken & turkey pies for $1.10 to go, $1.75 sit-down with side dish. Open daily 10am–8.30pm.
Filipe's Pizza, 4 locations in San Diego. 'Best Italian food in San Diego. Try the lasagne; really superb.'
Old Spaghetti Factory, 275 5th St, 233-4323. 'Eat in a train, a change from Greyhound.' Around $7/dish, open daily 11.30am–2pm and 5–10pm.

OF INTEREST

Old Town, a snippet of the city's original heart, along San Diego Ave. Free walking tours from the Plaza make the few historical remnants come to life. Up the hill is **Presidio Park**; its **Serra Museum**, 2727 Presidio, houses documents, maps, archaelogical finds from the nearby dig.
Balboa Park. Take the bus or bike to this superlative 1074-acre park, whose pink-icing Mexican Churrigueresque buildings were designed by Bertram Goodhue for the 1915–16 Panama-California International Exposition. 'Beautiful.

Worth going to just for the architecture.' The park has 11 museums and galleries (free on the 1st Tue of each month), a world-class zoo, a carousel complete with brass ring, pipe organ and other concerts, free sidewalk entertainment, free facilities for everything from volleyball to frisbee golf. Info Center: 1549 El Prado, 239-9628.

Inside the park: Museum of Art, 232-7931. Open Tue–Sun 10am–4.30pm Thurs 8pm. $5, $2 with student ID; **Natural History Museum**, 232-3821. Open 9.30am–4.30pm daily, $6; **Aerospace Museum**, 2001 Pan American Plaza, 234-8291. Open 10am–4pm, $4; **Museum of Man**, 1350 El Prado, 239-2001. Open 10am–4.30pm, $4; **Space Theater/Science Center**, science portion is smallish, no great shakes, but the 360-degree films are exhilarating. 'Worth it if addicted to OMNI-Max films.'

San Diego Zoo, in Balboa Park, 234-3153, is one of the world's best—a luxurious setting for the 3200 animals. General admission $12 up—includes the 45-min bus tour, aerial tram and children's zoo as well. Open 9am–6pm; gates close at 4pm. Don't miss the walk-through hummingbird aviary, the koalas and the primates. 'Good zoo but not quite as good as expected.' 'Need 5 hours to see it all.'

Also at Balboa: summer light opera at the **Starlight Bowl**, free Sunday afternoon music at the organ pavilion, and the Pacific Relations cottages.

Sea World, 1720 S Shores Rd, 222-6363, on Mission Bay north of downtown. Expensive at $26, so you'd better like performing whales, dolphins, seals. Best part is the new **Penguin Encounter**, with 300 penguins in their beloved refrigerated setting. 'Don't miss the seal and otter shows.' 'An all-day affair.' Daily 10am–6pm.

Wild Animal Park, 30 miles north of San Diego off Hwy I-15 near **Escondido**, 234-6541. 1800 acres of animals freely roaming in their natural habitats; view from a 50-minute ride in a monorail. Spanish architecture. 'Lots to see—don't miss bird shows. Best monorail run is 4.30pm for most animal activity.' 'Amazing.' $17.50 includes entrance, monorail, all live shows. Open 9am–5pm daily; gates close at 4pm. Parking $3.

Cabrillo National Monument, Pt Loma, 557-5450. Take a # 6 bus from downtown San Diego. Splendiferous view of the site where Juan Cabrillo first touched land at San Miguel Bay. Excellent tidepools, nature walks, films on whales, exhibit hall. Open summer 9am–7.30pm, winter until 5.15pm. Fee $4.

Southern California Exposition, Del Mar Fairgrounds, north of San Diego, 755-1161. Some of everything: outdoor flower and garden show, arts, gems, minerals, hobbies, crafts, jams, jellies, 4600 animals and a carnival for 20 days in late June and early July. $6.

Mission Bay Park, 2581 Quivira Ct, 221-8900. 4600-acre marine park, the largest facility of its kind in the world. Sailing, fishing, water skiing, wind surfing on 27 miles of beaches.

La Jolla, the jewel of San Diego, from sculptured rocks at Windansea to the St Tropez-like La Jolla Shores and limpid La Jolla Cove. On La Jolla Bvld, rent snorkels and roam in this fabulous underwater park and wildlife preserve.

ENTERTAINMENT

Beachcomber, 539-9902, 2901 Mission Blvd. '2-minute walk to Pacific Ocean.' Frequented by British and Australians. Open 7am–2am. Margaritas $2.50.

Billy Bones, 959 Hornblend St, Pacific Beach, 272-2780. Cheap food. 'Good atmosphere, worth the queue to get in.'

Blarney Stone Pub, 5617 Balboa Ave, Clairemont, 279-2033. Happy hour Mon–Fri, 4–9pm. Traditional Irish music Wed–Sun.

Confetti, 5373 Mission Center Rd, Mission Valley, 291–8635. 'Always a party! Something cookin' every day of the week.' Popular nightclub. Thurs–Sat, dancing to good rock 'n' roll with DJ's. Margaritas 95¢, $1 per plate. Reservations: 291-1184.

Diego's Club and Cantina, 860 Garnet Ave, Pacific Beach, 272-1241. 'THE action spot at the beach.' Open 11am–10pm Mon–Sat, Sun 11am–8.30pm.

Humphrey's, 2241 Shelter Island Dr, 224-3577. Great happy hours. Open 7am–3pm and 5pm–11pm.
The Princess of Wales, 1665 India St, downtown, 238-1266. Thur–Sat piano from 7pm. '*Real* beers on tap. Biggest surprise is when you walk out of the door and back into California.'

SPORT
San Diego's baseball team, the **Padres**, plays at Jack Murphy Stadium, 9449 Friars Rd, 283-4494; National League football at the same place in autumn and winter with the **Chargers**, 280-2121.

SHOPPING
Seaport Village, 14-acre shopping complex at West Harbor Dr and Kettner Blvd; 75 shops and restaurants. Opens 10am.
Bazaar del Mundo International Marketplace in Old Town, 10am–10pm.

INFORMATION
San Diego Convention and Visitors Bureau, 1st & F, 236-1212. Open 8.30am–5pm.
Balboa Park Info Center, House of Hospitality, Balboa Park, 239-0512. Open 9.30am–4pm.
Small info centres also in Old Town, at airport, and along the highway.
Travelers Aid, 1122 4th Ave, Suite 201, 232-7991. Open Mon–Thurs 8.30am–4.30pm. Also at airport, 231-7361. Open 8am–11pm.

TRAVEL
Amtrak, 1050 Kettner Blvd at Broadway, 239-9021. Romantic 1915 depot with twin Moorish towers. Around 8 runs a day to LA, takes about 2 hrs 45 mins.
Greyhound, 120 W Broadway, 239-3266. Open 24 hours.
San Diego Regional Transit, 233-3004. Runs a 'very efficient and easy to understand' bus system. Basic fare $1.50; 'Daytripper' one-day pass, $4. Also operates **San Diego Trolley**, making breaks for the US border near El Cajon and Tijuana every 15 mins from Amtrak; $3.50 rtn. 'Buy a return ticket to Tijuana, you won't want to stay long.' 'Quick, comfortable' and cheaper than Mexicoach and Greyhound.
San Diego International Airport (Lindbergh Field) lies slightly northwest of downtown. Take #2 bus from Broadway downtown to reach it, $1.50. Last bus into downtown, 1am.
Auto Driveaway, 396 Park Blvd, 295-8060. Open Mon–Fri, 9am–4.30pm.

ANZA-BORREGO DESERT and EASTERN SAN DIEGO COUNTY The 600,000-acre state park is in San Diego's back yard, at the end of a scenic 90-mile climb through forests, mountains and the charming gold-mining village of **Julian**, ultimately spiraling down 3000 feet to the Sonoran Desert floor.

The route can be traversed by bicycle (tough) or car, but there's also a cheap bus service via the Northeast County Bus Service, 765-0145, several times weekly from **El Cajon**, east of San Diego, to Julian, Borrego Springs and other points. Open Mon–Fri 7am–noon and 2–5pm.

At once desolate and grand, the Anza-Borrego Desert embraces sandstone canyons, rare elephant trees, pine-rimmed canyons, oases and wadis. Springtime brings wildflowers, which you can see year-round at the excellent sound and light presentation at the visitors center, 767-5311. Open only at w/ends during summer 9am–5pm. For reservations: (800) 444-7275. Camping in the park is free at primitive sites, $10 at developed campgrounds. Best months are Nov–May; it's terribly hot thereafter. If you don't

want to camp, stay in Julian at one of the 30 bed and breakfasts or cottages rather than in expensive Borrego Springs. Either way, don't miss out on the spectacular apple pie and chicken pie at the **Julian Cafe**, 765-2712.
The telephone area code is 619.

HAWAII

When your plane touches down, congratulate yourself—you've made it to paradise. But, as the song says, they've 'paved paradise and put up a parking lot'—particularly in Oahu, likely to be the first place you see. Japanese investors have fuelled real estate price increases, and prices in general are quite high. Hawaii has its poor and its homeless, but paradise still exists in this tourist-trampled state, if you know where to look.

For the real Hawaiians, this is actually Paradise Lost. Hawaii is the northern tip of the 'Polynesian Triangle'—a four-cornered triangle(!) with Fiji in the west, Easter Island in the east and New Zealand in the south. The spread of the Polynesian peoples (polynesia = many islands) can be charted, by archaeologists and philologists, from Malayan and Indonesian roots. It is believed that Hawaii was first inhabited sixteen hundred years ago by Polynesians setting out in their canoes from the Marquesas Islands in what is now French Polynesia. For centuries they grew their taro, hunted their pigs, and occasionally had each other over for dinner (one-way tickets only), undisturbed by 'civilisation'. Captain Cook, when he arrived at Kona in 1778, inadvertently brought an end to that, but the Hawaiians brought an end to him, which was irony, if not justice. Not for nothing did he name Hawaii the 'Sandwich Islands'; he had inside knowledge!

Polynesian-blooded Hawaiians now number about 250,000, and are well outnumbered by the descendants of the immigrants brought in to expand the sugar industry in the late 19th century: Europeans/Americans, Chinese, Japanese, Koreans, and, lately, Filipinos, Samoans and Vietnamese. The indigenous Hawaiians were powerless when American missionaries-turned-opportunists stole their lands and then their kingdom during the last century, just as they were when the US Government completed the process in 1959.

Just west of Kauai lies Niihau, the 'forbidden isle'. The family that owns Niihau, the western-most island of the archipelago, has prohibited outsiders in an attempt to preserve the culture of old Hawaii. Elsewhere in Hawaii the pure Hawaiian is almost, as Mark Twain put it, "a curiosity in his own land". The 'missionaries' also banned the teaching of the Hawaiian language (as well as removing some letters from the alphabet!), so that by 1987 fewer than 2,000 people spoke the native tongue. Now, though, children can be taught in Hawaiian if they wish. There is a small but committed movement of Hawaiians still trying to regain their stolen sovereignty.

Hawaii's eight island chain has been formed (and is still being formed) by volcanic activity (mythically, Pele, the goddess of fire). The islands are actually the tips of the tallest volcanic mountains on earth (Mauna Kea on the Big Island is 13,796′ above sea level, and over 19,000′ below!). The oldest sizeable island (Kauai) is to the west, but the newest island (Hawaii itself, the Big Island) is still growing in the east as tectonic plate movement pushes the islands westward from the faultline. As of 1993, lava bubbling and sizzling into the sea sometimes adds metres per day to the eastern coastline. The Big Island is becoming the Even Bigger Island, and you can stand and watch it happen beneath your feet.

The main islands (from left to right: Kauai, Oahu, Maui and Hawaii) are readily accessible by air and are all worth visiting for their differing flavours, scenery and beaches. All beaches in Hawaii are public and most are excellent. They are home to obsessive hordes of young, tanned hedonists with sub-bleached hair, whose life is the surf, the board they ride on, and the beaten up old campervans they live in. Hippie-dom with a sporting purpose. (Many of those who 'dropped out' in the '60's found their way to Hawaii. The hair is still long, but it's turned grey.) The Big Island is not noted for its beaches, but it has its own spectacular volcanic scenery and "13 different climates".

From **Oahu**, with its cosmopolitan capital, Honolulu, you can island-hop via the reasonably-priced local airlines to **Hawaii**, the Big Island, for its rural and volcanic scenery, and **Maui** or **Kauai** for beaches and tranquility. Don't be discouraged by the astronomical prices of the big resort hotels. Good, cheap motels and bed & breakfasts abound. (Pacific-Hawaii B&B, 970 N Kalaheo, #218A, Kailua, HI 96734, offers rooms on the four main islands starting from $45 and up: call 262-6140 or (800) 999-6026 from the mainland). County, state and national campsites are available for overnight stays for a minimal fee; most require an advance permit. Rustic cabins are available as well, but book way ahead.

National Parks: Haleakala
Hawaii Volcanoes

The telephone area code is 808.

OAHU Most urbanised and brutalised of the islands, but don't write Oahu off entirely. It absorbs the brunt of nearly 4 million visitors a year. In doing so, it's won a few battles (billboards are banned, flowers are planted everywhere) and lost a few (highrise forests in Waikiki, plastic leis for tour groups).

Honolulu is the state capital, legally and touristically. But don't come looking for miles of beaches, Hawaiian village charm or quiet. You'll find Waikiki a postage-stamp sized beach covered with bodies in various shades of red. Honolulu's pace, while not quite the gallop of hypertensive Los Angeles, is nonetheless brisk. Crowded with traffic on foot and wheel both, Honolulu is a place to act the tourist, to shop at the International Market, to sip maitais and eat puupuus (Hawaii's hors d'oeuvres) and have a good time when the sun goes down.

For cheap food, the city offers huge and colourful produce and seafood markets as well as Japanese box lunch takeouts and noodle stands. If you like, join in the on-going debate over the merits of *poi*, a Hawaiian staple made of taro root. Packaged in plastic bags and sold in local stores, the squishy grey stuff looks remarkably like wallpaper paste. Some people say it tastes like it too, but be open-minded and decide for yourself. Although they are somewhat buried in the barrage of tourist ballyhoo, Honolulu's cultural attractions (from museums to Chinatown) are worth finding, and the city's historical sites, Pearl Harbor and Punchbowl Crater in particular, are tasteful and moving. Get a fantastic view of Honolulu from old war fortifications atop **Diamond Head**, a volcanic crater overshadowing the city. Local teens hang out in the smelly bunkers; note an eerie inscription memorialising a murder committed there. Go early—the hike up is as tiring as the view is rewarding, and the parking lot closes at dusk.

Good bus transit on the islands allows you easy access to the beautiful country outside Honolulu. Following Hwy 72 east, you come to **Koko Head State Park**; here, **Hanauma Bay** is snorkelling heaven. Coral reefs form tunnels and pools through which you can chase elusive, colourful fish and sea turtles. To the northeast of Honolulu on Hwy 61 lies the **Koolau Range**, which, like most Hawaiian ranges, is formed by steep, grooved ridges dripping with lush foliage. Cutting through the mountain, **Nuuanu Pali Pass** offers splendid views of the ocean. It was here that King Kamehameha the Great defeated the Oahuans in 1795, literally forcing them over the cliffs; the victorious king became the first ruler of the united Hawaiian Islands.

Near Hauula on the northeast coast, a tough one-mile climb along a rough mountain ravine brings you to the **Sacred Falls**, one of the loveliest sights on the island: 2500-foot cliffs form a splendid backdrop to the falls, dropping 87 feet into the gorge. Oahu's northern side boasts incredible beaches—**Sunset** and **Waimea Bay** among them—as well as some of the best surfing on earth (the infamous **Banzai Pipeline** is here). Further on is the **Puu O Mahuka Heiau**, where humans were once sacrificed to the gods (the practice has since been discontinued).

ACCOMMODATION

Waikiki is crowded with low-cost digs, many with kitchens, most a couple of blocks from the beach. Reservations advised year-round. NB: city buses take backpacks 'at the discretion of the driver'. Anything you can hold on your lap or load under your seat is fine. Otherwise, be prepared to take a cab to your hostel or hotel.

Big Surf Hotel, 1690 Ala Moana Blvd, nr boat harbour, 946-6525. S–$37, suites $50 and up (1–4 people).

Central YMCA, 401 Atkinson Dr, across from Ala Moana Shopping Center, 941-3344. S–$30 + $10 key deposit men, 18+ only. First come, first served; pool, weight room, 4 racquet ball courts. 'Convenient for all buses.'

Edmunds Hotel Apartments, 2411 Ala Wai Blvd, 923-8381. S–$35, D–$38. B/W TV; homey, recommended.

Hale Aloha AYH Hostel, 2417 Prince Edward St, Honolulu, 2 blks off beach; for reservations, 926-8313. Dorm–$15 AYH members only. Must reserve in advance. Kitchens.

Honolulu International AYH Hostel, 2323A Sea View Ave, Honolulu, 96822, 946-0591. Across the street from U of Hawaii; take #19 or #20; transfer to bus #6 to University, $12 AYH, $15 non-members. Must reserve ahead. ($10 deposit guarantees room for 3 nights.) Kitchen, patio under coconut trees, laundry. 'Very busy.'

Interclub Hostel 'Waikiki', 2413 Kuhio Ave, 924-2636. Dorm–$16, private room–$49. Laundry, BBQs, cable TV.

Waikiki Prince Hotel, 2431 Prince Edward St, 922-1544. S–$30, $34 up with kitchen. TV, A/C. S–$35–$48 w/bath.
YWCA Fernhurst Residence, 1566 Wilder Ave, Honolulu, 96822, 941-2231, is recommended for women. Shared rooms: $20 YWCA members, $25 + $5 key deposit non-members (NB: if staying less than 3 nights, members pay full price.) Private rooms: S–$33 ($28 YWCA), D–$25 per person ($20). Breakfast and dinner Mon–Fri. Reservations with one night's deposit (money order or traveller's cheques) required. Bus to downtown, Waikiki.
NB: Camping is not recommended on Oahu; locals like to gather at campsites and may feel you are encroaching on their turf. Check out the grounds; if they are obviously being used by tourists, camping probably OK, particularly if the site seems to be patrolled regularly.

FOOD

In the local parlance, Hawaiians don't eat, they 'grind'. If it's a luau or all-you can eat smorgy, they 'grind to da max!' Grinding episodes usually start with puupuus (Hawaiian munchies), which reflect the state's ethnic diversity, from egg rolls to falafel. This is the home of the maitai, a nobly-proportioned ration of rum, pineapple juice, chunks of fruit and a baby orchid. Another local poison is the blue Hawaii, a toxic-looking concoction made from blue curacao and who knows what else? Good ethnic eating at Japanese delis, Chinese takeaway counters and noodle shops. If you're still not stuffed, tap into Honolulu's lavish happy hour spreads, or better still, a luau. When it comes to luaus, choices are plenty, but prices are high. Read the free *Waikiki Beach Press* and other local papers for Church luaus, generally cheaper and friendlier, with better food and entertainment, than those at the big hotels. Be sure to sample shave ice, Hawaii's better answer to the snowcone. And before you leave Oahu, don't miss the **McDonald's** in **Laie**. Regular old fast food, but the restaurant was constructed to resemble a Hawaiian longhouse, complete with tropical flowers and an indoor grotto.
Helena's, 1364 N King, Honolulu, 845-8044. Inexpensive Hawaiian specialties—butterfish, laulau, poi.
Queen Kapiolani, 150 Kapahulu Ave, Honolulu, 922-1941. Buffet lunch Thurs–Sat only, 11am–2pm, $11.95 all-you-can-eat.
Chuck Machado's luau on the beach outside the Waikiki Beachcomber Hotel at 2300 Kalakaua Ave, 823-0249, $24.50 covers everything (except alcoholic drinks), tax, tip, Polynesian show, and all da pig you can grind! Tue, Thur and Sun, 6.30pm. Also '$5 off 2nd adult' coupons in *This Week*.

OF INTEREST

In Honolulu: Bishop Museum and Planetarium, 1525 Benice St, 847-3511. 9am–5pm daily, $7.95 includes gallery tours, dance performances, craft demonstrations and planetarium shows. Incredible feather cloaks (treasured as booty by the ancient kings), Hawaiian and Polynesian artifacts.
Foster Botanical Garden, 50 N Vineyard Blvd, 522-7065. Daily 9am–4pm. $1. Cool oasis of rare trees, orchids and flowers.
Honolulu Zoo, 151 Kapahulu Ave, 971-7171. Open 9am–5pm daily. $3. World's finest group of tropical birds.
Iolani Palace, King and Richards St, 522-0832. Open 9am–2.15pm Wed–Sat; 45 min tours begin every 15 mins. Only royal palace on American soil, used just 11 years by the Hawaiian monarchs. Queen Liliuokalani wrote *Aloha Oe*, easily the most famous Hawaiian song, while imprisoned here. $4. Very popular; reservations necessary.
Kodak Hula Show, Waikiki Shell by Kapiolani Park, 833-1661. Tue–Thur 10am–11.15am. Free; array of Hawaiian, Tahitian dancing, costumes to blow colour film on; get there early for seats (sometimes is filled by 9.30am). More free shows at: **King's Village**, on Kaiulani across from the Hyatt Regency, 944-6855, Sun, Tues, Thurs at 6.15pm.

Academy of Arts, 900 S Beretania, at Ward (take #2 bus from Waikiki), 532-8701. Open Tue–Sat 10am–4.30pm, Sun 1pm–5pm; closed Mon. Free; 30 galleries surrounding six garden courts. From Polynesian to avant-garde, including one of the finest collections of Asian Art in America. James Michener collection of Ukiyo-e woodblock prints is one of world's best. Academy also shows 'alternative' and foreign films ($4), and has concert and theatre programmes; call 532-8768.
Outside Honolulu: USS Arizona Memorial at **Pearl Harbor**, 422-2771. Departures from Halawa Gate. 20-minute film on Japanese attack on Pearl Harbor at the Visitors Center, followed by free Navy boat tours of the harbour and memorial. You can look down through the limpid water to see the ghostly outline of the Arizona, wherein lie 1000 of the sailors (some have been removed) who died on 7 Dec, 1941. Shivery. Take #20 bus from Waikiki, 1-hr bus ride, or shuttle bus (see TRAVEL). Open daily 8am–5pm; tours 8am–3pm. Free; arrive early, queue forms at 7am for same-day tickets.
USS Bowfin, next to Arizona Memorial, 423-1341. Self-guided tour (w/hand-held receiver) of this WW2 submarine. Open 8am–5pm daily (last tour 4.30pm), $6.
Sea Life Park, Makapuu Point, 259-7933. 16 miles east of Waikiki on Hwy 72. $16, cheaper than mainland aquatic parks and better, too. The huge reef tank gives you skindiver's view of brilliant fish, coral, sharks. Various shows. Sat–Thur 9.30am–5pm; Fri 'til 10pm. Bus service Fridays back to hotels after Hawaiian entertainment at 10pm.

ENTERTAINMENT
Dirty Mary's, 2109 Kuhio, Honolulu, 922-6722. Co-ed gay bar with no cover. In same building as **Hamburger Mary's**, a restaurant with weekend barbeques (ave. plate $1.50). Building open 8am–2am.
The Wave, 1877 Kalakaua, Honolulu, 941-0424. Live rock music every night, 8.30pm–4am; free entry 'til 10pm, then $5 cover. Mondays (DJ only, no live music); everyone wearing lipstick gets in free 'til 1am! 21+.

INFORMATION/TRAVEL
Visitors Bureau, 7th flr, 2270 Kalakaua, Waikiki Business Plaza, Honolulu, 923-1811. Open Mon–Fri, 8am–4.30pm.
24-hr surf report, 836-1952.
MTL, 848-5555, offers good bus service around the island; 60c gets you anywhere; free transfers. Runs airport bus also.

MAUI Twenty-five flying minutes southeast of Honolulu is Maui, trendiest of the islands and famous for sweet onions, potato chips, humpback whales and Maui wowie, a potent variety of local marijuana. Formed by two volcanic masses linked by a wasp-waisted isthmus, Maui is marked by an extraordinary variety of terrain and climate, from the cold dryness of 10,023-foot **Haleakala volcanic crater** to the lush wetness of **Hana** (to describe it would require a new vocabulary for hues of green). The former whaling port of **Lahaina** is touristy and social; the upcountry eucalyptus land around **Makawao** is rural and mellow. Once past the endless condos of Kihei and Wailea, there are superb beaches and camping opportunities at **Makena** and further south.

At **Haleakala National Park**, 572-9306, $4 per car, the 'House of the Sun' has the largest dormant (for the last 200 years, anyway) volcano in the world, 21 miles in circumference. If you go there, you will be told repeatedly that the crater is big enough to swallow all of Manhattan (you might as well hear it here first). The terrain is magnificent: graceful cones and curves of deep red and purple punctuated by ethereal silversword plants. Huge

cumulus clouds sometimes pour over the crater lip and pile up like whipped cream. At dawn and dusk you may see the Spectre of Brocken effect, where your shadow is projected gigantically against the clouds and encircled by rainbow light. Sunrise at Haleakala is like a slow-motion fireworks display, best seen near the Puu Ulaula observation centre. NB: Dress warmly!
Hookipa Beach Park, on Maui's north shore, is the Mecca of the windsurfing world—a sport that is taking over the island and as much fun to watch as it is to do—well, almost.

ACCOMMODATION/FOOD
Flown-in food is costly on Maui, so stick to local products: seafood, pineapple, lettuce, tomatoes, fabulous sweet onions like nowhere else on earth (it's the soil), potato chips ('Maui Kitch'n Cook'd Potato Chips' is the one you want, accept no substitutes), and 'Maui blanc' (pineapple wine). While on the west side of Maui, seek out cheap hotels; on the east side, try the campgrounds.
Banana Bungalow, 310 N Market St, Wailuku, 244-5090. $15 dorm, $-$32. Cheap meals, airport and beach shuttles.
Camp Keanae, on East side of Maui, 36 miles east of airport, 242-9007. Mailing address and reservations through YMCA: 250 Kanaloa Ave, Kahuluihi, 96732. Isolated, beautiful setting. 100 beds (no linens). Bring your own food. 1-2 people $8 per person. Kitchen. Reserve in advance. Check-in 4pm-6pm; out by 9am.
Pioneer Inn, 658 Wharf St, **Lahaina**, 661-3636. With AC and private bath, D-$66.
At Haleakala: A small amount of free **tent camping** plus 3 **hiker cabins**, $22 per night for 2 people or fewer; cabins are so popular they're booked by lottery. Access by foot or on horseback only. Worth enquiring about cancellations when you get there, 572-9306. Reservation attempts at PO Box 369, Makwao, 96768.
Other **camping cabins**, from $10 for 1 person to $30 for 6 people. Free **tent camping** at **Waianapanapa State Park**, near Hana, 243-5352, or at **Oheo Gulch**, 15 miles from Hana, no drinking water, 572-9306. Book in advance (call 243-5354), then pick permit up at office on 54 S High St, Wailuki.

OF INTEREST/TRAVEL
Lahaina: viewing for **humpback whales** who mate and calve in the channel Dec-Mar; lots of whale-watching tours from the harbour. Also see the **whaling museum** on the brig *Carthaginian*, 661-3262, at the harbour, $3; its A/V show has whale songs and birth of a whale. Open daily 9am-4.30pm.
In Kaanapali: Whalers Museum, Village on the Beach, 661-5992. Open 9.30am-10pm daily, free. Whaling artifacts, photographs, and antiques from 19th C. 'Small but stunning and poignant.'
Hana area: 54 miles of bad but beautiful road keep Hana private; Charles Lindbergh loved it, lived and is buried here. Lodging is exclusive, so day trips or camping near Seven Pools is just about it. 'Don't miss the **Oheo Gulch and Stream**; crystal clear, just like paradise.'
The Shuttle runs between Lahaina and Kaanapali every 25 mins, with stops at Royal Lahaina, Sheraton, Marriott, Kaanapali Beach and Hyatt, free.
Visitors Bureau, 250 Ala Maha St, Suite N16, Kahului, 871-8691. Open Mon-Fri 8am-4.30pm.

HAWAII Called the Big Island for its size (and to distinguish it from Hawaii, the state, which encompasses all of the islands). Also known as the Orchid Island for the 22,000 varieties that grow wild and in nurseries, this is the youngest and firiest of the archipelago. Unlike its sister isles, which draw crowds to their beaches, Hawaii's main attraction is inland—**Hawaii Volcanoes National Park**, a cracked and crumpled moonscape created by the living volcano Mauna Loa. Each day the volcano adds to the island's real estate, dumping 650,000 cubic yards of red-hot lava into the ocean, enough to pave a thin sidewalk from here to New York. Nearby **Mauno Kea** recently earned new fame. From its peak scientists discovered a galaxy 12 billion light years away, that began forming much sooner than was thought possible after the 'Big Bang'. This and **Kilauea** are two of the world's most active volcanoes. Mark Twain (when it was fashionable for 19th century writers, such as Somerset Maugham, Jack London and Robert Louis Stevenson, to visit the islands) wrote of Kilauea, 'The smell of sulphur is strong, but not unpleasant to a sinner.'

But there are other facets to the Big Island: the jungley mystery of the east side; the desert bleakness of the south; the commercialised carnival of the Kona Coast to the west, wafted with coffee-laden breezes; and the rolling hills of the north, Hawaiian cowboy country. Best of all is the comparative lack of crowding; the Big Island is big enough to comfortably accommodate all comers. This is a place where the aloha spirit hasn't frayed too much, and people still get together to 'talk story' and watch the sun set. 'Twenty years behind the times!'

ACCOMMODATION

The **Kona Coast** on the western side is where the high-priced hotels are; **Hilo** on the east retains an unspoiled, if dilapidated charm. Cheap rooms can be found on either side of the island, however.

Arnott's Lodge, 98 Apapane Rd, Hilo, 96720, 969-7097. $17 bunk, S–$29, D–$40, D–$20 (semi-private). Kitchen, TV lounge.

Dolphin Bay Hotel, 333 Iliahi, Hilo, 935-1466. S–$41, D–$49, XP–$10. Wonderful garden with pick-your-own breakfast. Kitchen.

Hilo Hotel, 142 Kinoole St, 961-3733. S/D–$43 and $50. Coffee in the morning.

Hotel Honokaa, PO Box 185, Honokaa, 96727, 775-0678. S–$32 up, D–$35 up, reservations required. 'Very simple.' Has been going over 80 years.

Kona Tiki Hotel, 75-5968 Alii Dr, 329-1425, on the **Kona Coast**. D–$59, XP–$8. 3-day min. Pre-payment required. Fridges, ocean views, freshwater swimming pool. ($64 w/full kitchen.)

The county runs **beach parks** where you can **camp** for $1 p/person per night; permits required, pick up from County Parks offices—4 on island. Call County Parks on 961-8311 for info.

FOOD

Kona coffee and macadamia nuts are the indigenous items on the menu; restaurants seem to put the nuts in everything. Free samples and self-guided tours at, among others:

Hawaiian Holiday Macadamia Nut Company in Haina off Hwy 19 near Honokaa, 775-7743, daily 9am–5.30pm.

Kona Hawaiian Macadamia Nut and Candy Factory, 20 miles south of Kailua-Kona off Hwy 11, 328-8141, Mon–Fri 8am–4.30pm, Sat 8am–4pm.

Royal Kona Coffee Mill and Museum, Hwy 160 on the way to Captain Cook's Monument, 328-2511, daily 9am–5pm.

OF INTEREST

Only in America—drive-in-volcanoes at **Hawaii Volcanoes National Park**, $5 per car, good for 7 days, via Hwy 11 from Hilo, 967-7311. Crater Rim Drive takes you through the **Kilauea Caldera**, almost into the gaping maw of the **Halemaumau Firepit**. Here lives Pele, the notoriously bad-tempered Hawaiian fire goddess. If you're lucky, you may see a sacrifice to appease Pele at the edge of the firepit. Nowadays, food, cookies, pineapples, whole dressed chickens, is what gets tossed over the edge (park regulations prohibit virgins), with the result being something of a rubbish bin, as plastic bags and bottles are chucked in with the food.

Pele makes her presence known at nearby **Mauna Loa** as well. Being a shield volcano (so-called because of its characteristic shape), Mauna Loa erupts in a relatively controlled manner, allowing the curious to get a closer look.

Going south on Hwy 11, the magnificent vista of the island's desert south comes into view. You can visit the legendary **black sand beaches** at Kaimu and Punaluu, but be warned, the 'sand' is really volcanic rubble. Walking on it is a little like walking on broken glass, so bring shoes.

The sand is green at **Ka Lae** (that is, if you can find any sand among the huge boulders that cover most of the shore). This is the most southerly point in the US, and the Hawaiian Plymouth Rock; here, Polynesian explorers first beached their canoes and established Hawaii's oldest known settlement, *circa* AD 750. Ka Lae is not developed for tourists and most car rental agencies prohibit customers from travelling this road.

Further north on the island's western side is **Captain Cook's Monument**, accessible only by sea. Here the European discoverer of the Hawaiian Islands, once regarded by natives as a god, suffered a massive drop in popularity in 1779. The marker showing where he was killed (while intervening in a dispute) is under water.

Kahaluu Park Beach, just south of Disappearing Sands Beach on Alii Drive. Amazing snorkelling among flashy fish, none of which is bigger than you are. It's like swimming through an aquarium. If you've forgotten your mask and fins, rent them from the park or at Jack's Diving Locker at the Kona Inn Shopping Village in Kailua-Kona, 329-7585, for $7.50/24hrs.

Manta ray watching, Kona Surf Hotel. Nightly, the hotel spotlights the ocean where huge rays come to feed; free and thrilling.

Taking Hwy 19 from Kailua-Kona, you pass through the verdant hills of northern Hawaii. Turn onto Hwy 24 at Honokaa to see the dreamlike **Waipi'o Valley**, a little green world captured by steep cliffs. The road goes all the way down to the valley, but the last part is too steep for cars. Jeep transport is available for a fee. Spare yourself the expense and the gear-grinding heart-attack ride down by hoofing it; if you're in reasonably good shape, you'll make it back up, too. Your reward: playing in the surf at the wonderful beach.

NB: A road to avoid is Hwy 200, the 80-mile saddle road with a high fatality rate between the twin behemoths Mauna Kea and Mauna Loa. Once you're on it, there's no turning back: attempting a U-turn on the narrow road lined with lava rock guarantees a flat tire or worse. Not to mention the debilitating fog. If you choose to traverse this or other questionable roads in a rented car, you must do so at your own risk. Check the contract for the company's policy.

INFORMATION/TRAVEL

Visitors Bureau, 75-5719 W Alii Dr, 329-7787. Open Mon–Fri, 8am–noon & 1pm–4.30pm.

Hele-on-bus takes you from Hilo to Kailua-Kona, Hawaii Volcanoes National Park, Pahoa and other points for 75¢–$6 one way; 935–8241.

Car rentals: Dollar Rent-a-Car, 961-6059, 845 Kanoelehua Ave.

Avis Rent-a-Car, 935-1290, at Hilo Airport.

KAUAI Once the 'Garden Island' was known as the 'undiscovered isle', but no more. Now Kauai has its share of supermarkets, condos, huge resorts and canned tours. A constant stream of rent-a-cars flows along the highway that almost-girdles the island; crossing the street can be an adventure in itself. The landscape that lent the backdrop for the filming of *South Pacific* in the 1950s still endures: **Lumahai and Haena beaches** on postcard-perfect **Hanalei Bay**. But other patches of paradise are gone: the heavenly waterfall where France Nuygen cavorted with her GI beau has been closed due to tourist overload.

ACCOMMODATION
Hotel Coral Reef, 1516 Kuhio Hwy, **Kapaa**, 822-4481. S/D–$70 in Ocean Front section. Continental breakfast and car rentals.
Garden Island Inn, 3445 Wilcox Rd, **Nawiliwili** (2 miles from Lihue), 245-7227 or (800) 648-0154. S/D–$52–89, ocean views.

FOOD/OF INTEREST
Kauai is the proud birthplace of **Lappert's ice cream**, available at not 1 but 6!!! Lappert's locations, including the Coconut Marketplace, the Coco Palms Hotel and the Princeville Shopping Center. Now you know you're in paradise.
Green Garden, 13749 Kaumualii Hwy, Hanapepe, 335-5422, for mahi-mahi (dolphin fish) and lilikoi (passionfruit) pie.
National Tropical Botanical Gardens, end of Hailima Rd (past 'Dead Entry' sign), 941-6650. Research centre and various collections of tropical, native and international plants, including award-winning Allerton Estate Garden, leading up to Ocean (palms, gingers, lilies and bamboo grove). Their Native Hawaiian Plant Project protects endangered species. Tours only; 9am and 1pm daily, 2.5 hours + 2 mile walk, $15. Book in advance.
North from Lihue on Hwy 56: Turn off the road for a panoramic ocean view from **Kilauea Lighthouse**. Further north is the aforementioned Hanalei Bay; don't let its beauty distract you from the oriental splendour of **Hanalei Valley**, inland from the highway. Wet and dry caves are right on the road; pull off and explore!
Hwy 56 ends at **Ke'e Beach**, where the cliffhanging trail along the gorgeous **Na Pali Coast** begins. An easy hike takes you through some of the best scenery in the Hawaiian Islands: as you round one crucial corner, you get your first breathtaking view of a series of precipices plunging into the sea. The beach at the end of the hike is not for swimming, but that will be obvious. Breakers pound continually onto the boulder-strewn shore, sucking back with vacuum force.
South from Lihue on Hwy 50: Two historic sites of European contact with Hawaii: the **Old Russian Fort** (Ft Elizabeth), now a brush-covered rocky ruin; and **Captain Cook's Landing** (Jan 1778) at Waimea Bay.
Take a side trip to see the **Menehune Ditch**, an ancient aqueduct built, some say, in a single night by Menehunes—Hawaiian leprechauns! All archeologists know is that *someone* built the aqueduct years before the first Polynesian explorers arrived in Kauai.

INFORMATION
Visitors Info Office, Suite 205, Lihue Plaza Bldg, 3016 Umi St, Lihue, 245–3971. Open Mon–Fri, 8am–4pm.

OREGON

In 1804–1806, Lewis and Clark explored this region, following the mighty Columbia River to its mouth. Their favourable reports brought pioneers along the 2000-mile trail—at first a trickle, swelling by the 1840s into a flood. A remarkably homogeneous bunch they were, too: farmers from the Midwest and South running from the economic depression of 1837–1840, looking for good soil, rainfall and an environment with neither malaria nor snow. Later, Astoria was founded near the mouth of the Columbia River to promote trade with China.

Oregon became a US territory the year of the California gold rush and promptly lost two-thirds of its males to the gold fever. A few struck it rich; more returned home and started selling wheat and lumber to the miners. At one point, Oregon wheat was actually made legal tender at $1 a bushel.

The heavily-forested Beaver State has suffered in recent years from a decline in the demand for lumber but still produces half the plywood in the US, the process having been invented here. Tourism is now the third-largest industry. Fortunately Oregonians work hard to preserve the state's natural beauty and like Vermonters, they have banned the construction of new billboards and kept crass tourist traps to a minimum (with noticeable exceptions along the coast). In 1991, Oregon was judged 'Greenest state in the US' by environmentalists.

The biggest magnet for visitors is the 400-mile coastline, protected as an almost-continuous series of state beaches. At times cold, foggy and windy, this region offers a kaleidoscope of magnificent sights: offshore rocks, driftwood-piled sands, cliffs, caves, twisted pines and acres of rhododendrons. Coastal villages seem to specialise in weatherbeaten charm.

Picturesque barns, covered bridges and historic villages make the area from the coast to the east Willamette valley fun to explore. Unless you're bent on speed, avoid the dull ribbon of interstate freeway that unseams the valley north to south.

Both the youth hostel and the bed and breakfast networks are alive and well in Oregon. Biking is extremely popular here; just remember that it, like other outdoor activities can be rained out at any moment. Most of the time, it's a slow mournful drizzle, the kind that drove Lewis and Clark nearly crazy during their winter sojourn at Fort Clatsop.

Though many east coasters have drifted west to this state and find it much more beautiful that its more-popular neighbour to the south, Oregon has not drawn nearly the number of converts as California has. This makes Oregonians happy: while there you may spot one of the bumper stickers that define the 'Oregon attitude': 'Don't Californicate Oregon'. Furthering the wry underselling of the state, another slogan warns: 'In Oregon, you don't tan; you rust'. Travellers are welcome, however, as long as they're passing through. The most popular bumper sticker reads, 'Welcome to Oregon. Now go home.'

National Park: Crater Lake

The telephone area code for the state is 503.

PORTLAND In 1843, a couple of canoeists enroute to Oregon City liked what they saw here and staked a 'tomahawk claim' by slashing trees in a 320-acre rectangle. The naming of the town was similarly impromptu: settlers flipped a coin (the losing name was Boston).

Portland modestly revels in its sparkling mountain and riverside setting, its luxuriant rose gardens (two-week Festival of Roses in June) and its low-key neighbourliness. Opportunities abound for good eating and social action in this city of booklovers, art lovers and ardent joggers.

Portland makes an ideal base to explore the Columbia River Gorge: take Hwy 84 east along the river to Troutdale and turn off onto the Columbia River Scenic Highway. The old highway stops south of Bonneville Dam (its fish hatcheries are nice), but the scenic beauty doesn't. Further east on Hwy 84, the surrounding land dries up. Towns and farms line the river like oases, in stark contrast to the surrounding high desert cliffs. This is a drive that shows the state at its best.

ACCOMMODATION

Portland International Hostel, 3031 SE Hawthorne Blvd, 236-6281. $12 AYH, $14 non-AYH. Catch #5 bus from 5th St. Open 5–11pm and before 10am only. Baggage storage available if arrive before 10am. New downtown hostel planned for 1994.

Portland Rose Motel, 8920 SW Barbur Blvd, 244-0107. Rooms $33 up. TV, laundry facilities.

YWCA, 1111 SW 10th Ave, Portland, OR 97205, 223-6281. 'Excellent YWCA—clean, helpful, quiet.' S–$23, D–$30 (communal bathroom); private bath S–$28, D–$33. Must reserve with deposit.

FOOD

The tastiest thing in Oregon is free—the drinking water. Grocery prices are high in town, even for local produce. You'll do better at the roadside produce stands, particularly along the Columbia River, where the peaches are huge and drip all over your shirt when you bite into them. Don't miss local specialties: blackberry and boysenberry pie, razor clams (hideously expensive, but with a licence you can dig your own), scallops, smelt and Dungeness crab.

Bijou Cafe, 132 SW 3rd, 222-3187. 'A must for visitors. Great value for money with a friendly and relaxed atmosphere.' Open daily for breakfast and lunch.

Bread & Ink, 3610 SE Hawthorne, 239-4756. Local favourite for lunch. 'Best burgers.' Also pasta, fish specials. Mon–Sat 8am–late, Sun 9am–2pm.

Dan and Louis Oyster Bar, 208 SW Ankeny, 227-5906. Outstanding oysters, stew, marine atmosphere. Open daily 11am–10pm, midnight weekends.

Old Wives' Tales, 1300 E Burnside, 238-0470. Multi-ethnic vegetarian, chicken and seafood; also soup and salad bar. 'Tiny browsing library, and New Age, classical and jazz music round out the eclectic atmosphere.' Open daily for breakfast, lunch and dinner.

Papa Haydn's at two locations, 5829 SE Milwaukee, 232-9440 and 701 NW 23rd St, 228-7317. A Viennese coffeehouse with dynamite pastries. 'Milwaukee location hard to find.' Open Tues–Thur 11.30am–11pm, Fri, Sat midnight, Sun 10am–3pm.

Saturday Market, under west end of Burnside Bridge, in Skidmore, SW 1st and Ankeny. 'Original buyers market.' Stalls with homemade everything. 'Wonderful.' 222-6072. Sat 10am–5pm, Sun 11am–4.30pm.

OF INTEREST

Washington Park, west of town, has **Japanese Gardens**, 223-1321, with 5 traditional styles, especially lovely with the white cone of Mt Hood framed by maple leaves and pagodas. $5; $2.50 with student ID. Open 10am–6pm till Sept; 10am–4pm after Oct. Also in the park is the **Rose Test Garden**, free, with over 8000 rosebushes. From here you can take 'the world's smallest railroad', $2.50, through the forest to the **Zoo-OMSI** complex. The Zoo, 4001 SW Canyon Rd, 226-1561, open daily 9.30am–7pm (last admission 6pm), $5, has a huge chimp collection and large elephant herd. The **Oregon Museum of Science and Industry (OMSI)**, 4015 SW Canyon Rd, 797-4000, is open daily 9.30am–5.30pm, Fri 'til 9pm, Sat & Sun 'til 7pm. $6.50. Cheap planetarium shows. Don't miss 'state of the heart', a human heart preserved through plastination; software that checks your cardio-vascular health; and a biofeedback train that goes faster as you get warmer. Bus #63 stops at these and other locations in the park; pick it up on Washington St downtown.

South Park Blocks, a 12-block corridor of green grass, statues and tall trees, with Portland State University campus at the south end.
Portland Art Museum, 1219 SW Park Ave, at the South Park Blocks, 226-2811. $4.50, $2.50 students with ID. Tue–Sat 11am–5pm, Sun 1pm–5pm. European, 19th and 20th century American, pre-Columbian, West African, Asian and Pacific Northwest Indian art.
Portland Building, between Main and Madison, 4th and 5th, Architect Michael Graves, knowingly or not, has taken a page from Frank Lloyd Wright's notebook by designing a controversial pink and blue public building for a mid-sized American city (cf 'Marin County' in *California* section). Outside on the 5th Ave side is the *Portlandia* sculpture, a giant lady with hammered copper skin like the Statue of Liberty; she holds a trident instead of a torch.
Skidmore Old Town Historic District, New Market Block, SW 1st and Ankeny. Interconnected townhouses with open plaza, colonnade, outdoor stands.
Pioneer Square, 701 SW 6th is an open-air city centre square paid for by the sale of 65,000 bricks used to build the square. The benefactors' names are inscribed on each one. Free performances and activities year-round. See the 'weather ball', a meteorological glockenspiel. 'Silly noon-time fanfare.'
With a name like Portland, it's got to have a . . . you guessed it—the **Port of Portland**, 231-5000. A free 2 hr bus tour takes you by bulk cargo operations, ship repair yards, 2 marine terminals, and international airport. Very popular; reservations required. Write to: PO Box 3529, Portland, OR 97208. Tours every Sat during summer for groups of 6 or less.
The Grotto, NW 85th & Sandy Blvd, 254-7371. Natural grotto in huge cliff, resembling grotto at Lourdes. Lower grounds are free, but it's worth $1.50 to see the monastery above (take elevator) for rose gardens, Marian art and one of the best views you can get of Portland, the Columbia River and Washington state beyond. Open 9am–8pm daily.
Some of Portland's most pleasant features are its **fountains**: the **Lovejoy**, SW 3rd & Harrison; the **Rose Ftn**, at O'Bryant Sq, 408 SW Park; **Ira Kellar Ftn**, 3rd & SW Clay and the **Skidmore Ftn**, 1888 SW 1st & Ankeny.
Outside Portland: The Columbia River Gorge, stretches east from Portland to The Dalles and offers truly magnificent scenery. Sailboard enthusiasts will know this place to be the most 'radical' location outside Hawai due to the constant wind funnelled between the high cliffs. Take a car up and along the Historic River Highway which parts with I-84 at Troutdale to enjoy spectacular views of the Gorge and see some of the numerous waterfalls en-route (**Multnomah** is the biggest and most impressive). For real escapism, go up to the tranquil setting of **Lost Lake** and a close-up of **Mt Hood**, the state's tallest mountain. 'Spectacular, picture-book scenery.' Greyhound and Amtrak both serve the area (around $25 rt to the Dalles from Portland), 'Amtrak is best for views.' **Bonneville Dam**, with its salmon farms and fish ladders is also worth a look.
Hwy 30, west. A beautiful 100-mile drive to **Astoria** that romps up hill, down dale, beside the Columbia and its wooded islands, and past roadside stands, houseboats, picturesque backwaters, juicy blackberries—there's even a pulloff to see **Mt St Helens**. **Westport**, with its Wahkiakum ferry across the river, makes a good lunch stop.

ENTERTAINMENT

There are 16 microbreweries in the state, many in Portland. A favourite, **Bridgeport Brew Pub**, 1313 NW Marshal, 241-7179, offers several cask-conditioned ales. Or watch free movies at **Mission Theatre and Pub**, 17th & Gleason NW, as you sample seasonal brews. 223-4031.
Bagdad Pub, 3702 SE Hawthorne, 236-9234. Great pizza, beer and movies.
Check the *Willamette Weekly* for listings of good local blues and rock bands. **Key Largo**, 223-9919, 31 1st Ave, between Couch and Burnside, has rhythm & blues, rock & roll, jazz. $3–$6 cover. Portland hosts excellent festivals: the **Blues Fest** in

June, **The Bite** in mid-August, **Art Quake** in early September and others. 'Saw excellent African ballet for $2.'

INFORMATION
Convention & Visitors Association, 26 SW Salmon, 222-2223. Open Mon–Fri 8.30am–5pm, Sat 9am–3pm. 'Maps and a bounty of info.'
Chamber of Commerce, 221 NW 2nd St, 228-9411.

TRAVEL
Tri-Met city bus and Max rail, 231-3198 for rates and info. Free downtown zone, 95¢–$1.25 to other areas.
Greyhound, 550 NW 6th Ave, (800) 231-2222.
Amtrak, 800 NW 6th Ave, 273-4865.
Gray Line, 4320 N Suttle Rd, 285-9845. Lots of tours: Mt Hood, the Columbia River, coast, around town. Pickup at local hotels.
Rent-a-Wreck, 9785 SW Shady Lane, 624-1804.
Green Tortoise, 225-0310 or (800) 227-4766. $15 to Seattle, $59 to San Francisco, $79 to LA. Departs from SW 6th and College, outside the university deli.
Portland Airport is located about 13 miles east of the city. To get there take bus # 12 labelled 'Sandy Blvd to Airport' from SW 6th and Main. This will take around 20 minutes and costs $1.25. Dash Airport Shuttle runs daily services every 30 minutes from various downtown hotels and the Greyhound Depot. $7 o/w, 246-4676. A taxi will cost around $25, call 227-1234.

THE OREGON COAST Hwy 101 runs along the Pacific coast from the southernmost tip of California to the Canadian border, but the Oregon stretch, especially the pristine 225-mile section from the California boundary to **Newport**, is surely the loveliest. It's also the driest part of the Oregon coast (it gets about half the amount of rain as the stretch north of Newport), a definite attraction for those camping out. 'Best way to see this is by camping, buy a tube tent, light, compact, about $12.' The coast offers driftwood hunting, whale watching, clamdigging and rockhounding, from agates to jasper. While you're on the beach, nose-to-sand, look for glass floats, the ultimate beachcombing prize. The powerful combo of the Japanese Current and westerly winds wash these green, amber and turquoise buoyancy balls from Japanese fishing nets all the way across the Pacific. December through March is the best time to search; look for non-rocky beaches with moderate slope and go early to beat other float-hunters. Swimming is dangerous in many areas and cold everywhere; enquire locally.

Going north-to-south, the Oregon Coast starts at **Astoria**, a miniature San Francisco at the mouth of the Columbia River. Founded in 1811 by John Jacob Astor as a base for the Pacific Fur Company, the town survived as the first permanent US settlement on the Pacific Coast due to successful trading with China. While there, check out the rococco Flavel House and Shallon Winery; try scallops at Pier 11 and Finnish limpa bread at local bakeries. Also of interest is **Ft Clatsop**, where Lewis and Clark spent the winter of 1805. If you're in a car, cross the Megler Bridge to Washington, spanning 4.6 miles and barely skimming the surface of the water. Back on Hwy 101, turn west to **Ft Stevens**, a historic park with a picturesque shipwreck. **Seaside**, with its boardwalk, arcades and popular swimming beach, is a candyfloss sort of town, noted for cheap seafood at Norma's. **Cannon Beach** merits a pause: monolithic Haystack Rock, a charming art-mad village, and great windy walking at Ecola State Park are some of its pluses. Its annual **Sand Sculpture Derby** in spring is one of the most inventive anywhere.

Near **Tillamook**, take the **Three Capes Rd**, a 39-mile loop through a succession of scenic vistas, villages and lighthouses to **Three Arch Rocks National Wildlife Refuge**, with its herd of Steller sea lions. Tillamook provides tasting of its namesake cheese and others, along with wine, at the Blue Heron and Tillamook Cheese Factories. The lively little fishing and beach town **Newport**, on a sheltered and beautiful bay, is a good place to eat Dungeness crab and browse with other holiday makers. 'A friendly young community on NW cliff, where there are quaint wooden summer cottages facing the ocean.' Of interest here is the **Oregon Coast Aquarium**, 2820 SE Ferry Slip Rd, 867-3123, next to the Science Center. Recently opened in 1992, the aquarium offers various exhibit galleries of Oregon marine-life, including an outdoor animal park and sea-bird aviary. Open daily 9am–6pm (10am–4pm in winter), $7.35 admission. Neighbouring **Depoe Bay** is noted as an excellent whale-watching spot, Nov–March; along its seawall, geyser-like sprays of ocean water often arch over the highway. **Beverly Beach** to the south is the nearest campground and has hiker/biker spots.

South of Newport is a likeable tourist trap called **Sea Gulch**, a village of antic lifesize figures. The carving is done freehand—with a chainsaw!—and you can watch. **Yachats** (that's *Yah*-hots) is worth a stop, especially in smelt season May–Sept, or better yet, during the annual Smelt Fry in early July. It's nothing to eat a dozen of the silvery mini-fish and fun to watch the catch, too. Good non-fish offerings at the Adobe Hotel and others. Between rhododendron-happy Florence and Yachats are the **Sea Lion Caves**, 547-3111, reached via elevator and reeking of perennial, fishy sea lion halitosis. Open daily 9am until dusk, $5.50; you can also see the huge creatures more distantly from various points near the caves.

Oregon Dunes, some as high as 600 ft, stretch for 40 miles to Florence; duneside camping is possible but crowded at **Honeyman State Park**; the **Umpqua Lighthouse State Park** (hiker/biker section), 6 miles south of Reedsport, is better. Biggest town in SW Oregon, **Coos Bay** is a fishing and lumber port good for a night's stopover, with a grimy bar, good meals at the Blue Heron Bistro, and myrtlewood factories.

Hwy 101 turns inland at Coos Bay, but you can follow secondary roads nearer the coast to spectacular scenery at **Sunset Bay** (camping) and **Shore Acres State Park**. At cranberry-growing **Bandon** you have a cheese factory, the makings of an art colony, a youth hostel, and natural beauty all around. Further along, the panorama of **Humbug Mountain** and the rock-strewn coast are a worthwhile stop; 3-mile hike to the top. Excellent campground with low-cost hiker/biker section. **Gold Beach** is on the banks of the Rogue, an officially-designated wild river and prime spot for rafting and fishing. Good smoked salmon here.

ACCOMMODATION

Adobe Motel, 1555 Hwy 101 N, **Yachats**, 547-3141. D–$90 with ocean view, $58 without. Fireplace, sauna, excellent breakfasts and dinners, agate hunting and smelt fishing on their beach.

Sylvia Beach Hotel, 267 NW Cliff, 265-5428. $22 dorm (incl breakfast), S/D-$65 and up depending on view. 'Superb location, excellent value.'
Sea Star AYH Hostel, 375 2nd St, **Bandon**, 347-9632. Open year round. AYH members $9, non-members $12. 'Couples' rooms $21–$26. B&B accommodation also available with ocean view, $60 up. Hostel has bistro with everything made on premises frо́m organic ingredients (they make their own pasta dough, smoke their own meats—even roll their own sausages). Open 8am–3pm Mon–Wed, 8am–10pm Thur–Sun.
City Center Motel, 538 SW Coast Hwy, Newport, 265-7381. Rooms $41 up.
Camping: There are over 50 campgrounds in Oregon's state park system; $10 for tent, $11 for water/electricity. Many sites have hiker/biker sections for $2. **Tugman State Park**, $13, near Lakeside, 759-3604, open mid-April–Labor Day, comes highly praised: 'Best campsites in the US'. Greyhound will drop you where you like. Warm sleeping bag and tent advised, also food as parks are usually distant from shops. Free camping near **Florence** in the dunes—or try **Siuslaw National Forest**, $6–$10 night, and **Sunset Bay State Park**, 888-4902, sites from $14.
Call (800) 283-CAMP to reserve sites in national forests; (800) 444-PARK for sites in state parks.

CRATER LAKE NATIONAL PARK Mt St Helens was a minor firecracker compared with **Mt Mazama**, which exploded some 6800 years ago to form **Crater Lake**. This inky blue well, in a densely forested part of southern Oregon's Cascade Range, cannot be bettered for dramatic settings: approached through a moonlike landscape and rimmed by 500 to 2000-ft cliffs (all that is left of 12,000-ft Mazama), Crater Lake descends to depths of 1932 feet, making it one of the deepest lakes in the world. Poking through the surface are **Phantom Ship Island** and **Wizard Island**, itself an extinct volcanic cone. Boat excursions visit Wizard, where you can hike to its 760-ft summit and down into its 90-ft-deep crater. The 33-mile **Rim Drive** is open mid-July to October; also recommended are the 1-mile hike down to the lake from Cleetwood Cove and the 1½-mile **Discovery Pt Trail**. From high points in the park, you can see Mt Shasta, 100 miles to the south. Wonderful bird-watching, wildflowers and nature programmes. Crater Lake is even more beautiful in winter, when snowcapped conifers are reflected in the deep blue iris of the lake.

ACCOMMODATION AND FOOD

Ft Klamath Lodge in **Ft Klamath**, Hwy 62, about 22 miles south of Crater Lake, 381-2234. S–$32, D–$37. Restaurant and grocery nearby.
Mazama Campground, 594-2511, at the junction of West and South Entrance Roads, open mid-June to Oct, depending on snow conditions: $11. Campsites in the backcountry free and for $5 at **Lost Creek Campground**, on Pinnacles Rd, open July–Sept. The Nature Trail begins here. Grocery store at Rim Village; also excellent fishing.
Lodging also at **Klamath Falls** and **Medford**; try **Motel 6**'s—884-2110 in Klamath Falls, and 773-4290 in Medford, $32 up, XP–$6.
Oregon Motel 8 and RV Park, Hwy 97 N, 3½ miles N of Klamath Falls, 882-0482. Sites $10.60.

INFORMATION/TRAVEL

National Park information, 594-2211. $5 entrance fee per car, $3 for cyclists and hikers. Rim Drive is closed in winter; enter the park via Hwy 62 south or west. Greyhound, 1200 Klamath Ave, Klamath Falls, 882-4616.

SOUTHERN OREGON South and west of Crater Lake are a cluster of worthwhile destinations, made more appealing by well-placed hostels and other good lodging. **Ashland**, America's answer to the Old Vic, has three theatres (including a pleasant one outdoors) and an 8-month play schedule that specialises in Shakespeare but draws on other sources as well. Not far away is **Jacksonville**, an intelligently-restored gold mining town. Stagecoach rides are offered to the cemetery and 80-odd homes there. Nearby also are the **Rogue River** and **Oregon Caves National Monument**; the latter are set deep in the marble heart of **Mt Elijah** and full of stalagmites & stalactites, flowstone formations and strenuous hikes. Near **Cave Junction** is **Takilma**, a former hippy mecca which still has a hippy hospital. Nowadays the area is populated with 'survivalists'; apparently the natural convection of the land would eliminate the danger of radiation in the event of nuclear attack.

ACCOMMODATION

Ashland AYH Hostel, 150 N Main St, **Ashland**, 482-9217. Open year round $11. AYH, $13 non-members. 3 blks to Shakespeare Festival. Large kitchen, laundry; in historic home.

Fordson Home Hostel, 250 Robinson Rd, **Cave Junction**, 592-3203. $8 AYH, $10 non-members. More adventurous types might opt for the $6 motor home, $5 trailer, $4 summer bunkhouse, or $3 camping (with pit toilets). Solar showers (great fun), river swimming and free berries in season. 13 miles to Oregon Caves, close to wineries (one is being built next door), bikes for use. Owner Jack Heald is a mine of information about the area and gives his guests 40-minute tours covering sights from antique tractors to Douglas Firs. If you stay on a weekend he'll even take you rock' n' roll' dancing!

Manor Motel, 476 N Main St, **Ashland**, 482-2246. S/D–$58, XP–$2. Colour TV, AC. Rooms with kitchen also available. Downtown. Reservations required in advance, with 1-day deposit.

WASHINGTON

A persistent legend has it that the original name proposed for Washington was 'Columbia'; the idea was dropped to avoid confusion with the nation's capital. True or not, Washington has always been haunted by its name, to the extent that the state once advertised itself to tourists as 'The *Other* Washington', thereby selling itself short.

Like neighbouring Oregon, the 'Evergreen State' is mountainous, rainy and green in the west, and flat, dry and tawny in the east. Likewise, it has but one pre-eminent city, Seattle, which enjoys a pugnacious rivalry with Portland. Once a stronghold of the radical labour movement (the Wobblies were here in the 1930s), Washington now builds more Boeings, raises more apples, processes more seafood and stores more nuclear waste than just about anyone else.

This is also David Lynch country. *Blue Velvet* and *Twin Peaks* were both filmed here, and there does seem to be a strange atmosphere invoked by the countryside that just might explain the bizarre nature of his work.

A large share of the state's scenic beauty is within reach of Seattle: **Puget Sound** and its hundreds of islands; the still, dark **Olympic rain forest**; omnipresent **Mt Rainier**; and the obtrusive upstart, **Mt St Helens**, 75 miles south. Other sights are further flung. **North Cascades National Park**, an expanse of alpine loveliness, with canyons, glaciers, peaks and grizzlies, lies along the British Columbia border. In the eastern part of Washington are **Grand Coulee Dam**, the Palouse River Canyon and the 'Scablands', a weird, scarred landscape left thousands of years ago by a glacial flood that inundated much of the Columbia Plateau. The Long Beach peninsula, though part of southwest Washington is more conveniently reached from Astoria, Oregon.

Rain is endemic to the Northwest, but Seattle gets most of its 34 inches per year between October and May; the Olympic rain forest gets up to 150 inches annually.

National Parks: Olympic
Mount Rainier
North Cascades

The telephone area code for all places listed is 206.

SEATTLE Long befeore the advent of 'grunge', before Nirvana, Soundgarden *et al*, the 'Emerald City' was a place to be. With becoming arrangements of hills, houses, water and mountains Seattle has long been a mecca for those who like life with a more laid-back attitude.

To the southwest, the skyline is dominated by snowy Mt Rainier. To the west, the city's great deepwater harbour opens onto island-studded Puget Sound and the Olympic Mountains. Urbanisation is further subdivided by lakes and parks, from tiny to massive, girding the downtown district into a compact and pleasing shape. The look is an idiosyncratic mix of sleek and traditional, of contemporary ranch houses and bohemian houseboats. All this adds up to a city that feels similar to another great Pacific metropolis whose initials are 'SF'. Don't tell Seattlites that; they defend their city's individuality. And rightly so, Seattle does have a certain flair. It's not every city that would make a Wagnerian opera cycle (sung in German and English) its major cultural event, or outfit its waterfront with vintage 1927 Australian streetcars and its airport with a meditation room?

Considering that it's a major gateway to, and trade partner with, the Orient, Seattle shows few Asian influences of non-gustatory kind. Rather, at its core the city is boisterous, adventurous and optimistic, no doubt a legacy of its logging and Klondike gold rush past.

If coffee is your amour then Seattle is the place to get in some serious drinking. The city seems to run on caffeine, supplied by some of the strongest espressos you will ever taste. There are coffee bars and cafés everywhere all serving 'damn fine cups of jo', as Agent Cooper would say. You'll be wired for weeks.

ACCOMMODATION

College Inn Guest House, 4000 University Way NE, 633-4441. S–$42, D–$60, all shared bath. Continental breakfast plus all-day coffee, tea. Antique; registered as a historical landmark.

Commodore Hotel, 2013 2nd Ave, 448-8868. S–$43, D–$45 w/bath. Hostel: $12 + $3 linen AYH.
Downtown YMCA, 909 4th Ave, 382-5000. S–$39, $31 AYH; D–$44, $37 AYH, TV–$2 extra. Jacuzzi and gym. Excellent, very clean. '5th floor more comfortable, better facilties than 4th floor at same price.'
International Hostel, AYH, 84 Union, 622-5443. Nr Pike Place Market. $15 summer, AYH members only; membership–$18. Laundry. Old building but modern interior. Take bus #174 from bus station to Union and 4th Sts.
Moore Hotel, 1926 2nd Ave, 448-4851. S–$45, D–$50. 'Clean, modern, spacious—offered us the best deal.'
Nendel's Valu Inn, 139th and Pacific Hwy, 244-0810. S–$47, D–$52, T–$56. AC, colour TV, transport to/from airport.
St Regis Hotel, 116 Stewart at 2nd, 448-6366. S–$32; $41 w/bath, D–$41; $47 w/bath. 'Basic but comfortable.' Laundry and restaurant.
Vashon Home Hostel, Rt 5, Box 349 (168th & 121st), **Vashon Island**, WA 98070. $8 AYH, $11 non-members. Check-in 3.30pm–10.30pm, out by noon. Reservations required, 463-2592. A ferry ride from downtown. Stay in a log cabin, a Sioux teepee or a covered wagon.
B&B's: lots of options including B&B International, Northwest B&B, addresses and numbers in *Accommodation Background*. Also: Pacific B&B, 701 NW 60th, Seattle, WA 98107 or call 784-0539; Traveller's B&B, Box 492, Mercer Island, WA 98040 or call 232-2345. Rates S–from $40, D–from $48 (luxurious accommodations command the higher rates–$75 double). Traveller's reference service covers Seattle and most of the Northwest, including Puget Sound, Tacoma, Olympia, Spokane, Victoria and Vancouver Island, BC.

FOOD

Washington is famous for superb fruit (especially peaches, apples and berries), Dungeness crab, Olympia oysters, razor and littleneck clams, and the indigenous candy, 'Aplets' and 'Cotlets,' a sort of jellied fruit bar covered with powdered sugar and guaranteed to be addictive. Seattle is a prime place to sample them all. Excellent Chinese, Thai, Japanese and Vietnamese restaurants, too.
Cafe Loc, Seattle Center, 728-9292. 'Good Vietnamese food.'
Elliott Bay Book Company, 1st and Main, 624-6600. Cafe and literary gathering place, with over 100,000 titles. Open Mon–Sat 10am–11pm, Sun noon–6pm.
Emmet Watson's Oyster Bar, 1916 Pike Place, behind the Soames-Dunn bldg, 448-7721. Best oysters anywhere, also good ceviche (marinated fish). Inexpensive, $4–$8.
Gravity Bar, 415 Broadway East, 325-7186. A trendy, stainless steel decked juice bar serving things like 'Ginger Rogers', a fruit and vegetable drink containing carrots, apple and ginger, $2.
Iron Horse, 311 3rd Ave S, ½ block from King St Station, 223-9506. 'Burgers delivered by model trains! Great railroading atmosphere.' Open Mon–Sat 11am–9pm, Sun 11am–8pm.
Ivar's Acres of Clams Restaurant, Pier 54, 624-6852. Seattle seafood tradition since 1938. Great old photos and waterfront view.
Pike Place Market is *the* place to purchase fresh produce, meat, fish and walk-away items; it's a warren of ethnic treats from Filipino lumpia to Spanish tapas.
Old Spaghetti Factory, Elliot and Broad, near Pier 70, 441-7724. Meals $5–$8, daily specials.
Streamliner Diner, 397 Winslow Way, Bainbridge Island, 842-8595. Breakfast and lunch only; American and Mexican food $5–$6; reach the island via ferry from Seattle.

OF INTEREST

Mt St Helens. The Indians called it 'Loowelit-klah', or 'smoking mountain', and they knew what they were talking about. On 18 May, 1980, the mountain erupted, blowing away a cubic mile of earth, killing 57 people and 2 million mammals, birds and fish, and exhaling smoke and ash to 72,000 feet to circle the globe. Since then, Mt St Helens has erupted sporadically but on a smaller scale; quakes and ominous rumblings are commonplace. Plan on spending all day on your trip, whether from Seattle or Portland. 'A beautiful place.'

To experience the mountain, options include: **Air flyovers** from nearby Toledo, Cougar or Randle, which give the best views of flattened trees, debris-choked rivers and devastated landscape slowly regenerating itself. **Bus tours** run from Seattle through a loop road leading to the mountain, also accessible by **car**. Check in with the Forest Service info center, turn west off I-5 on exit 49, or call 274-2100 to enter the volcano zone. **Hikers** can make a difficult but worthwhile trek from **Meta Lake** to **Independence Pass**, which overlooks ruined **Spirit Lake**, chilling views of desolation and crumpled human artifacts. The Norway Pass trail is also excellent. If you'd like to keep a respectful distance, you can take in the eruption and aftermath on the 100-ft screen of the **Omnidome**, Pier 59, in Seattle, 622-1868. $5.95. 'It's as if you're flying round the mountain during its eruption.' 'Do not on any account miss this extraordinary 30-minute film.' Next to **Aquarium** (see below): combo tickets available $8.95.

The Space Needle, 443-2111, a 605-ft relic of the 1962 Seattle World's Fair, has stunning views, best at night when the city is lit up. $6 for glass elevator ride to the top. 'Kitschiest souvenir shop in Seattle on top.' Revolving restaurant at 500 feet. On the grounds of **Seattle Center**, 90-second ride for 60¢. **Fun Forest** amusement park is there, too.

Pacific Science Center, next to Space Needle, 443-2001, includes 6 buildings: spacerium, planetarium, computer rooms, seismograph, Indian longhouse, lots of science toys. Open Mon–Fri 10am–5pm, w/ends 10am–6pm. $5.50 entrance fee; $6.50 incls IMAX or laser shows. IMAX info line: 443-IMAX. 'Laserium *Rock It* is an exciting presentation.' The Center also has many shops, eateries and entertainment from opera to rock to folk festivals.

Museum of Flight, 9404 E Marginal Way S, 764-5720. Over 40 aircraft from the beginnings of aviation to an Apollo command module. Newest exhibit is a full-scale F-18 mock-up where you can sit in the cockpit. Open 10am–5pm daily (Thur 'til 9pm). $6 adults.

International District, between Main and Lane, 4th and 8th. Culturally-neutral official name for Seattle's Chinatown, bright with Buddhist temples, restaurants, herbal shops and the Bon Odori Festival in Aug.

Pike Place Market, Pike and 1st, 682-7453. Begun in 1907, this multi-level maze of regional colour boasts over 250 permanent businesses (and a reserve of 200 arts and crafts and 100 farmers), including dozens of restaurants, standup bars and takeaway places, plus local produce and seafood. Also bookshops, coffeehouses, bars, second-hand shops, crafts and 'excellent free entertainment by buskers and street musicians'. Daily 9am–6pm Mon–Sat; some vendors open Sun 10am–5pm as well.

The waterfront is the soul of any port town, and Seattle is no exception. The working piers for the Alaska halibut and salmon fleet and the large freighters are remote, but the tourist's waterfront is front and centre. Piers 48 through 70 have steamships to Victoria and also the Victoria Clipper Catamaran, a **waterfront park**; **Ye Olde Curiosity Shop**, a delightfully macabre melange of shrunken heads, mummies, fleas wearing dresses, etc ('must be seen'); a **firefighting museum**; and the **Seattle Aquarium** at Pier 59, 386-4320, a fishbowl where you are in the bowl, and the fish swim overhead. 'Marvellous.' Open daily 10am–7pm; $6.50. Watch out for the 'Coconut Crab' exhibit.

Harbour ferries to Bainbridge Island, Pier 51, 464-6400, $3.30 without car, round trip. Pubs and art galleries on the island, even a winery: **Bainbridge Island Winery**, 682 State Hwy 305 NE, 842-WINE. Free informal tours in Washington's second smallest winery, every Sun at 2pm. Otherwise open Wed–Sun noon–5pm for winetasting and self-guided tour around vineyards.

Pioneer Square, around 1st and Yesler, heart of old downtown. The original 'skid road', so-named because logs were 'skidded' along the road in lumberjack days, gave rise to 'Skid Row', a term widely imitated in several cities from LA to NYC. Nicely restored, but still a gathering place for bums and blots-on-the town; good walking tour map available.

Klondike Gold Rush National Historical Park, at 117 S Main, 553-7220. Exhibits, free films and gold panning demos. 'Watch Chaplin's *The Gold Rush* free on 1st Sun in every month.' Open daily 9am–5pm, free.

'Dirt! Corruption! Sewers! Scandal!' Sound good? Then take an **underground** tour, 610 1st Ave at **Doc Maynard's Public House**, 682-4646. When Seattle burned down in 1889, the city simply built the new on top of the old. What's left below is an odd warren of storefronts, brothels, speakeasies and tunnels where sailors are popularly supposed to have been shanghaied. Tour ends (naturally) at a gift shop. 'Highly amusing account of Seattle's early sewage system. Never thought crap could be so funny.' 'Interesting rip-off.' Tours last 1½ hrs; $5.95, $4.50 with college ID. Booking required.

Lake View Cemetery, next to **Volunteer Park**, at 14th Ave and E Prospect. Divided by nationality—Chinese, Japanese, Polish, etc. Also **Bruce Lee's grave**, covered with letters to him, martial arts trophies, mementoes, flowers, etc, left by devotees.

Seattle Art Museum, 100 University St, 654-3100. Newly-designed museum designed by Robert Venturi (the man who gave us the National Gallery extension in London) and it is his usual post-modern joke of differing styles from Egyptian to Neo-Classical. The building is better than its contents. Open Tues–Sun, 10am–5pm, until 9pm Thurs; $6, $4 students. First Tues of every month open 10am–7pm, free.

University of Washington, 15th Ave NE. Info centre on NE 40th. 'Beautiful, like Berkeley.' On campus, an arboretum and Japanese tea garden, gift of Seattle's sister city, Kobe.

Government locks, connecting Puget Sound, Lake Union and Lake Washington, were built in 1916 and at that time second only to the Panama locks in size. 'Best free sight in Seattle. Boats and leaping salmon passing through all day.' 'Some salmon nearly jump onto the footpath!' 'Interesting historical/ecological display in building.'

Nearby: Boeing Aircraft Factory, 3303 Casino Rd S, **Everett**, 30 miles north of Seattle, exit 189 west off I-5. Call 342-4801 for tour info. See jumbo jets in the making in the building where the world's largest jetliners are manufactured. Very heavily booked in summer; free 90-min tours Mon–Fri 9am–4pm. Tickets available beginning at 8am for the day but beware—can be sold out by 9am.

ENTERTAINMENT

The 5th Avenue, 1308 5th Ave, *circa* 1926 vaudeville house patterned after Imperial Chinese architecture of the Forbidden City, renovated in 1980 for $2.6 million, now hosts Broadway shows. Free tours for groups of 6 or more; call 625-1468. 'Absolutely smashing place.'

Seattle Opera, 389-7676, at the Seattle Center. Get there 20 minutes before curtain up for 'student rush': leftover tickets sold at half-price, as low as $15. Occasionally, on selected performances, any leftover tickets are sold for $15, regardless of original price. Also performing at the Center, the **Seattle Symphony**, 443-4747. Rock and pop acts as well as legitimate theatre at the **Paramount Theater**, 911 Pine, 682-1414. Not cheap but good acoustics.

The Seattle Arts Festival, Bumbershoot, takes place at the Seattle Center annually over Labor Day weekend. $8 admission in advance; $9 at gate. Bands, food, art, etc. 'Amazing, very popular.' Hotline 441-FEST.

Pioneer Square, **Volunteer Park** and the **campuses of U of Washington and Seattle University** (downtown at E Cherry and Broadway) are all nuclei for daylight and after-dark activities. Read the *Post-Intelligencer* and the *Seattle Times'*

Tempo mag for listings. *Tempo* has a 'Hot Tix' column with discount and free stuff.

INFORMATION
Visitors Bureau, 800 Convention Place, enter Union St side, 461-5840. Open 8.30am–5pm Mon–Fri.
Travelers Aid, 909 4th (inside YMCA building), 461-3888.
Free and useful maps from Dept of Transportation, Transportation Bldg, 420 Maple Park E, Olympia, WA 98504.

TRAVEL
Amtrak, King St Station, 3rd Ave & Jackson, (800) USA-RAIL. The *Pioneer* goes to Ogden/Salt Lake City, the *Coast Starlight* to Oakland/SF and LA, a beautiful ride down the coast, and the *Empire Builder*, a mammoth 42 hour trip to Chicago via Minneapolis.
Greyhound, 8th and Stewart, (800) 231-2222. Serves Bellingham for ferry services north, $19 o/w, 3 a day and Vancouver, BC, $22 o/w, $39 rtn.
Metro, 553-3000, runs the local buses. Within the 'Magic Carpet' downtown area all buses free; 85¢–$1.60, depending on zone and rush-hour restrictions. All-day unlimited passes available only at w/ends and holidays, $1.70.
Seattle-Tacoma International Airport (Sea-Tac), about 12 miles south of the city. From downtown take #194 from the Metro Tunnel, Mon–Sat, $1.60 peak times, $1.10 off-peak; on Sundays take M from 2nd and Union, $1.10.
Gray Line, from the Westin Hotel, Space Needle and other points, 624-5813.
Ferry to Alaska and the Inside Passage: Alaska Marine Highway System, departs 7pm Fri (time may vary) from port in Bellingham, WA, 89 miles north of Seattle. Call 676-8445 for info; rates vary (cheapest: $154 to Ketchikan).
To islands, Olympic peninsula, Bremerton, Vashon Island and other points: Washington State Ferries, Pier 52, 464-6400. 'Excellent way to see the Sound and the islands around Seattle.' Ferries for the **San Juan Islands** departs from Anacortes (north of Seattle), 293-8166. See San Juan section.

OLYMPIC NATIONAL PARK Sparkling mountains and lush forests occupying 1400 square miles in the centre and along the coastline of the Olympic peninsula, making this a crown jewel of US national parks. Hwy 101 circles the park, but only a few roads penetrate inward; its wilderness is further fortified by vast tracts of national forest around it. A hikers' park indeed.

Massive glacier-cut peaks are the park's signature. The highest at 7965 feet, was named **Mt Olympus** by an English sea captain in 1788. Use the **Port Angeles** entrance to get here. 'Don't miss the 18-mile drive from sea level to one mile high at Hurricane Ridge—what views of Mount Olympus and its glaciers!'

The park proves that rain forests are not solely a tropical phenomenon. West of Olympus in the Bogachiel, Hoh, Quinault and Queets river valleys is the great **Olympic rain forest**. Jewelled with moisture, tree limbs cloaked in clubmoss, this cool Amazon suffused by primordial light gets 150 inches of rain in an average year. Best access is via the 20-mile drive up the Hoh River. Don't overlook the intelligent displays at the visitor centre and the views along Quilcene River.

Dense forest runs almost into the sea along the pristine, rocky coastal strip. The best view is at the southern end where Hwy 101 passes close to shore, but the best part is **Lake Ozette**, reached only by trails. Here the undergrowth is extravagant and the ground is boggy; much of the trail is bolstered by boards. Bears sometimes lumber down to the water in search of a meal. About 4 miles from the lake is beautiful **Cape Alava**, especially when silhouetted at sunset. 'Make every effort to see this park—fantastic.'

Admission to the park is $4 per vehicle at most entrances, good for 7 days. **Campgrounds** in the park are $8 per night, but primitive sites are free. No food stores in the park, so purchase beforehand in Port Angeles.

INFORMATION/TRAVEL

Olympic National Park Headquarters, 600 E Park Ave, Port Angeles, and Visitors Center, 3002 Mt Angeles Rd, both 452-4501. Summer hours 8am–6pm, winter 9am–4.30pm. Information on self-guided trails.

Greyhound, 1315 E Front, Port Angeles, (800) 231-2222. Greyhound does one trip from Seattle to Port Angeles, departing 10.45am Mon–Fri, $14 single, from $28 r.t.

PORT TOWNSEND and THE SAN JUAN ISLANDS Port Townsend shows you that western Washington isn't uniformly soggy; it lies in the 'rain shadow' of the great Olympic Mountains, and gets a mere 18 inches a year. Sunny weather, a vital cultural life, ebullient Victorian architecture and two nearby hostels make Port Townsend an excellent place to base for exploration. Seek out good food and friendly faces at the Lighthouse Cafe and occasional music at the Town Tavern.

In 1859 the US gained the 192-island chain of the **San Juans** in the great 'Pig War', precipitated when a British pig recklessly invaded an American garden and was shot. The resulting squeal of outrage had US and British troops snout to snout on island soil, but diplomacy won out. With Kaiser Wilhelm the unlikely mediator, the US got the San Juans and the British got bangers, one supposes.

Connected by bridges to the mainland and each other are the islands of **Whidbey, Fidalgo** and **Camano**. The city of **Anacortes** on Fidalgo is a major ferry terminus. Despite their accessibility, these islands are quite rural. Further north and well served by ferry are **Orcas, Lopez** and **San Juan**. All have excellent camping, unsurpassable shorelines and scenery with good clamming and some fine beaches. Lopez is best for bicycling and has a good swimming beach at Spencer Spit, though water temperatures averages a chilly 55 degrees. Call island information, 468-3663.

ACCOMMODATION

Fort Flagler AYH Hostel, Ft Flagler State Park, Nordland (on Marrowstone Island), 20 miles from Port Townsend, 385-1288. $8.50 AYH, $11.50 non-members, + $3 linen charge. Open May–Sept, rest of year by reservation. (Reservations advisable through Sept.) Bikes to borrow. Not very well insulated, rural, and only 14 beds. 'The place to ebb out for a while.'

Palace Hotel, 1002 Water St, 385-0755. S–from $53, D–from $58. TV, brass beds, antique decor. Bus stops 1 blk up street.

Port Townsend AYH Hostel, Ft Worden State Park, Port Townsend, 385-0655. $8.50 AYH, $11.50 non-members, couple rooms available. Near the town and a sandy beach, in the place where they filmed *An Officer and a Gentleman*.

On the San Juans: Doe Bay Village Youth Hostel, Star Rte 86, Olga, **Orcas Island**, 376-2291 or 376-4755. No longer in AYH association, but still gives members a discount; $12.50, $14.50 non-members, $10.50 camping. 'Used to be a '70s love-camp and is still like one in many ways. Not recommended.' Showers, fully-equipped kitchen, hot tubs $3/24hrs. 'Wonderful view over Otter coast.'

Palmer's Chart House, PO Box 51, Deer Harbor, **Orcas Island**, WA 98243, 376-4231. $49, D–$65, homecooked breakfast included. Open year-round, warm place

with private baths and entrances, decks and lots of amenities & pampering. Overlooks Deer Harbor. 1-hr ferry ride to Orcas from Anacortes; from Orcas, 1 hr to Sidney. Morning or afternoon sailing for $30 per person on the Palmer's 33-ft yacht, *Amante,* weather permitting; reservations needed. Highly recommended for an unusual American experience.
State Park Camping, Star Rte Box 22, Eastsound, WA 98245, 376-2326. $11 + $5 for reservation for **Moran** on **Orcas**. Reservations before Labor Day and by writing 2 weeks in advance only.
San Juan Island Camping: Snug Harbour Resort, $20/site up to 4 people, call 378-4762 to reserve; **Lakedale Campground**, $5 site, 378-2350. NB: a reader warns that San Juan island camping is crowded and full of American tourists, whereas the other islands are booked up in August. Reserve early.

OF INTEREST
San Juan Island: Whale Museum, 62 First St N, Friday Harbor, 378-4710. Exhibits of whale skeletons, brains; reading materials. 10am–5pm daily in summer. Includes videos on Orcas and other whaling subjects. $3 adults, $2.50 students. 'Small but very good.'
Whale watching at Lime Kiln Point, no entrance fee. From the cliff above the water you can see both Orcas and Minke whales come close to the rocks to feed on salmon. 'Usually arrive in afternoon.'

TRAVEL
Greyhound, 1329 N State, Bellingham, 733-5251. Take Greyhound from Seattle to Port Angeles & connect with Jefferson County Transit to P.T. $1.10.
Ferries from Anacortes daily to Shaw, Lopez, Orcas, San Juan and Sidney, BC. Westward journey to any island $4.65/foot passenger, then inter-island travel free. Orcas island to Sidney, BC, $2.25. Ferry and land combinations are extremely numerous; you'll do best to study the free ferry schedules and maps: call 464-6400 or (800) 542-7052 (in Washington).

MOUNT RAINIER NATIONAL PARK It was the enterprising 18th century British Admiral Rainier who got this 14,410-foot mountain named after himself. Today Mt Rainier, 80 miles south of Seattle and clearly visible from there, is surrounded by a national park that should interest the most jaded peak peeker. With 575 inches of snow piling up in an average year, little of the mountain shows beneath the glittering whiteness. More than 40 glaciers crown Mt Rainier, and lush conifer forests line its lower slopes, interrupted by meadows bright with wildflowers in July and August.

The **Wonderland Trail** wanders for 90 miles around the mountain, passing through snowfields, meadows and forests, with shelter cabins at convenient intervals. The full walk can take 10 days, but there are lesser trails for those with lesser ambitions. Near the park's southeast corner is the **Trail of the Patriarchs**, leading through groves of massive red cedar and Douglas fir. The best place for seeing wildflowers is to march up from **Paradise Valley**. In the northeast, excellent hiking trails branch out from **Sunrise**, the highest point in the park that can be reached by road.

July through September are often warm and clear, sunsets and sunrises over the mountain are unforgettable. It rains even in summer, and cloudy, rainy or foggy weather is the rule the rest of the year. Always dress warmly and bring raingear. Entrance to the park is $5 per car, $3 for hikers or bicyclers, or by bus.

A reader suggests the **Cascade foothills** north of Rainier as a closer alternative: 'Drive 30 miles east to North Bend, then follow south fork of the Snoqualmie River for 15 miles. Take dirt track marked Lake Talapus to car park. From there, a 2-mile hike to the lake. Gorge yourself on blueberries, swim and dive off rocks, kill bugs—on a sunny day, this beats any city tour. This is the real America.'

ACCOMMODATION

Campgrounds: Ohanapecosh $8; **Cougar Rock and White River**, $6; **Sunshine Point Ipsut Creek**, $5. Open summers only except for Sunshine Point. Come equipped for cold. At higher altitudes, there will be snow on the ground, maybe some from the sky even in the dead of summer.

Mt Haven Campground & Cabins at Cedar Park, 569-2594. $10 per site with shower, laundry. Cabins: D–$48–$61, Q–$74–$81, kitchens, bath, shower, fireplace.

Paradise Inn, 569-2413, at 5400ft. Open mid-June to early Oct. S/D–$64. To reserve rooms at Paradise, write to Mt Rainier Guest Services, Attn: Reservations, PO Box 108, Ashford, WA 98304, 569-2275.

INFORMATION/TRAVEL

Mount Rainier National Park Headquarters, 569-2211. Open Mon–Fri 8am–4.30pm. For recording on weather and road conditions, food, lodging, camping, hiking, visitors centres and more.

Henry M Jackson Memorial Visitors Center (largest centre in the park), ½ blk from Paradise Inn, open daily 8am–7pm.

Greyhound, 1319 Pacific Ave, Tacoma, 383-3629.

NORTH CASCADES NATIONAL PARK Spectacular scenery in the Cascade Mountains: razor-backed peaks, plunging waterfalls, high snowfields and deep lakes. From Seattle, take Hwy 5 north to Hwy 20 east. No entrance fee to park; most areas are wilderness, inaccessible by road. You can, however, drive to three **campgrounds** in the park: **Colonial Creek** and **Newhalen**, each $7 per night; and **Goodell**, $5 per night. Forest Service info at 856-5700. Visitors Center on left side of Hwy 20.

LONG BEACH PENINSULA On its long sandy finger of land in extreme southwest Washington, the Long Beach peninsula harbours an immense clam and driftwood-filled beach, covered with huge dunes (great for escaping the wind) and backed by pines hiding hundreds of old-fashioned beach cottages. Besides the windswept beauty of the area, visit the free **Lewis and Clark Interpretive Center**, 642-3029, 10am–5pm daily mid-May through mid-September, near **Cape Disappointment Lighthouse**, a superb audio-visual evocation of the hardships and wonders of the explorers' epic journey. The display ramps lead you to the same magnificent ocean overlook that climaxed Lewis and Clark's trip in 1805.

ACCOMMODATION

Ft Columbia AYH Hostel, Box 224, **Chinook**, 777-8755. $8.50 AYH, $11.50 nonmembers. Open April–Sept; at other times of year, send reservation a month in advance. 7 miles from Astoria, Oregon, across a toll bridge ($1.50 each way for cars, 50¢ bicycles, hitchhikers free). The hostel is in an old army hospital in a lovely, isolated site in Ft Columbia State Park overlooking Columbia River in park with museum, old fort. Near Chinook Indian village. Good bathing.

THE SOUTHWEST

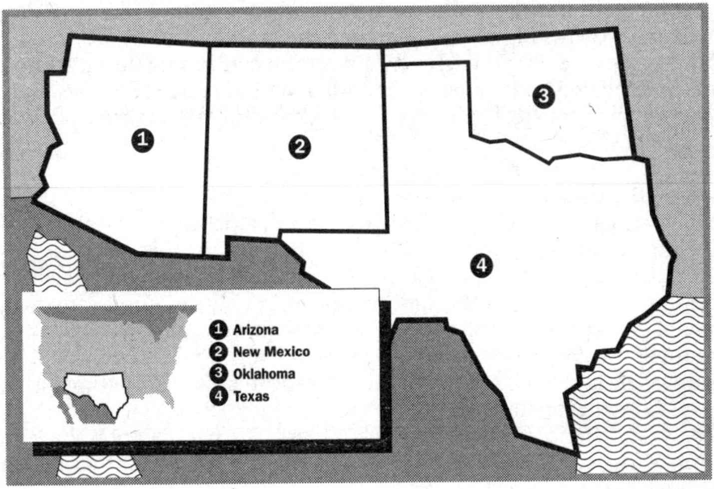

Much of this area is exactly as you would expect from seeing Westerns—whether shot in Spain or elsewhere. Purple mountains, searing deserts, cactus, cowboys and Indians inhabit Arizona, New Mexico and west Texas. Contrasting with this region are the lush farmlands of east Texas and Oklahoma and northern Arizona's and New Mexico's parks and ski resorts on the tailbone of the Rocky Mountains.

Hardly passing through an intervening industrial stage, the Southwest since World War II has leapt from a simple economy into the nuclear-industrial-aerospace age and is now the bright buckle of the Sun Belt. But the past has not been lost—old Indian and Spanish influences remain.

For several decades after it was blazed in 1822, the Sante Fe Trail served emigrants and traders between Missouri and the Southwest. Now the major thoroughfares are I-40 (the legendary 'Route 66') to the north and the cross-country I-10 to the south. To enjoy the natural splendour of the region and get a sample of day-to-day life here, stay off I-40 as much as possible.

ARIZONA

Once called the 'Baby State' (the words of one of the state's first senators) because it is the youngest of the lower 48, Arizona has slid comfortably into its mature role as a mecca for retirees and families on vacation. The low cost of living and unique quality of life are now also drawing younger residents in large numbers. A land of vast silences and arid beauty, the Grand

Canyon State (its new moniker) also contains sharp and sometimes troubling contrasts. One-quarter of Arizona is Indian land, containing the incredibly ancient and artistically advanced cultures of the Hopis, Navajos and others, and one in twenty inhabitants is a Native American. Yet Indians in this state were not allowed to vote until 1948.

Arizona's works of nature are among the grandest in the US, if not the world, beginning with the Grand Canyon and continuing through 17 other highly variegated national parks, monuments and recreation areas. But the works of man range from banal to short-sightedly destructive: water-greedy cities, a borrowed London Bridge, and dam-drowned canyons (even the upper portion of the Grand Canyon—the Marble Canyon—was threatened with a dam at one time!).

The southern section from Tucson east is the richest historically. It was once the stomping ground of Wyatt Earp, Billy the Kid, Apache chiefs Geronimo and Cochise and assorted prospectors, padres and gunslingers. Northern Arizona, with its stark mesas and richly coloured canyons (all could be called 'Grand') offers the greatest scenic drama. Glen Canyon and Monument Valley, both spilling over into Utah, and Canyon de Chelly should all be high on the visitor's list, after the mandatory pilgrimage to the Grand Canyon, of course.

The vast distances between cities and parks—not to mention the sprawl within Phoenix and Tucson themselves—make a car a smart acquisition.

National Parks: Grand Canyon
Petrified Forest.

The telephone area code is 602.

PHOENIX Huge, hot and horizontal, Phoenix is quite possibly the world's worst city for pedestrians. The city isn't a convenient gateway to anywhere—although at the rate it's sprawling, Phoenix may one day ooze right up to the lip of the Grand Canyon.

Actually the suburbs can be more interesting than the metropolis itself. **Tempe** is home to Arizona State U, with the largest student body in the west. **Scottsdale**, the destination for the moneyed traveller and the rich, boasts some decadent resorts.

ACCOMMODATION

NB: In general, expect much higher rates Oct–May in large Arizona cities like Phoenix and Tucson. If travelling in summer, check the rates at the posh resorts—opulence can be had for less than $50 nightly.

In Phoenix: Econo Lodge, 5050 Black Canyon Hwy, 242-8011. S–$40, D–$46. Off I–17 in downtown. Free coffee.

B&B in Arizona, PO Box 8628, Scottsdale, AZ 85252, 265-9511, (800) 266-7829. Rooms in private homes in Phoenix and many other locations in Arizona. S–$45 up, D–$50 up.

Mi Casa-Su Casa, PO Box 950, Tempe, AZ 85281, 990-0682, (800) 456-0682. Rooms in 135 homes statewide, and also in Utah and New Mexico. S–$35 up, D–$45 up. Loves foreign travellers.

Metcalf House AYH, 1026 N 9th btwn Roosevelt and Portland, 254-9803. AYH $10, non-members $12. 'Good for help and information.'

YMCA, 350 N 1st Ave, 253-6181. Co-ed, 1 floor for women. S–$18; $10 key deposit. Pool, athletic facs. 'Clean.'

In Tempe: Tempe University Travelodge, 1005 E Apache Blvd, 968-7871. S–$37 up, D–$42 up, incl. b/fast.

FOOD

Essentially an expensive gringo resort area, with fast food and a 24-hour convenience store seemingly on every corner. In **Tempe**, near the university, are low-cost bars and nosheries where students congregate. Most are along Mill Ave at University Ave. Hot spots include the **Dash Inn**, 731 E Apache at Rural, 966-0775. Cheap Mexican food and pitchers of margaritas. Also the **Club Rio**, 430 N Scottsdale Rd, 894-0533. 'Huge burgers.' (Thursday burgers $3.30.) For a splurge, try steaks cooked Indian-style, over mesquite, a technique that originated here. **Pinnacle Peak Patio**, 10426 E Jomax Rd in Scottsdale, 585-1603, is where locals go for cheap and excellent mesquite-broiled fare. Open generally 4pm–11pm.

OF INTEREST

Always phone first or check with visitors bureau; sights are far apart and the summer heat will make you believe that Phoenix has, like its namesake, risen from the ashes of some still-smouldering inferno.

Camelback Pt Park, take Echo Canyon Park Rd. Phoenix' most visible landmark offers scenic views, picnicking, good trails.

Desert Botanical Gardens, 1201 N Galvin Parkway, 941-1225. On the border of Phoenix and Scottsdale in Papago Park, by the zoo. Carefully maintained garden of 10,000 plants that shows how desert ecosystem works. Open 9am–sunset, 7am–sunset in July & Aug. $5.

Heard Museum, 22 E Monte Vista Rd, 252-8848. Outstanding silverwork, weavings, basketry, plus most of former Sen Barry Goldwater's collection of 450 Hopi Kachina dolls. Open Mon–Sat 9.30am–5pm, Sun noon–5pm. $5, $4 students.

Mystery Castle, 800 E Mineral Rd, 268-1581. Bizarre mansion built by a man who felt guilty about deserting his wife and child. Tour the 18-rooms (none on the same level or in the same shape) for $3, students $2. Closed July, August and Sept.

Paolo Soleri's gallery/studio, 6433 Doubletree Ranch Rd, Scottsdale, 948-6145. Open daily 9am–5pm. **Arcosanti**, 632-7135, Soleri's futuristic vertical city in the making, is 65 miles north of the studio off I-17. Tours from 10am–4pm, $5 donation. Must have a car.

Phoenix Art Museum, 1625 N Central, 257-1222. Art from medieval to Western. Open Tue–Sat 10am–5pm, Wed till 9pm, Sun noon–5pm. $4, $1.50 students.

Phoenix Zoo, Galvin Parkway and E Van Buren St, 273-1341. Specializing in Arizona wildlife; recently refurbished Arizona Trail is a 'zoo within a zoo', covering indigenous species from the state. Open daily 7am–4pm. $6.

Pueblo Grande Museum, 4619 E Washington, 495-0900. The Hohokam people—the ancestors of modern-day Pimas and Papagos—are thought to have built this irrigated city about 200 BC and disappeared about AD 1450. Visit both museum and dig site here. Open Mon–Sat 9am–4.45pm, Sun 1pm–4.45pm. 50¢.

Taliesin West, at the end of 108th St, Scottsdale, 860-8810 (call for exact directions). Frank Lloyd Wright's winter home and workshop. June–Sept 1hr tour, 8 & 11am daily, $8, $6 students; 2½ hr tour at 7.30am & 10am, $20, Thurs only. Reservations essential.

The Annual Paysan Rodeo, Rodeo Ground, 474-4515. Said to be the world's oldest continuous rodeo (over 170 yrs old). 3rd weekend in August. $12.

In Scottsdale: Rawhide's 1880s Western Town, Scottsdale Rd, 563-1880. Arizona's largest western theme attraction. Includes Old West shootouts, saloon, a steam powered locomotive *c.* 1880, a steakhouse (with deep-fried rattlesnake on the menu), rodeo country music and stage coach rides. Open 5pm–10pm daily; free.

In Tempe, the **Nelson Fine Arts Center**, 965-2787, built in 1989, is an avant-guarde showcase housing a Dance Lab, Playhouse and ASU Art Museum. The Museum has 4 galleries of changing exhibits, open Tue–Fri 8.30am–4.30pm, Sat

10am–4pm, Sun 1pm–5pm. Free admission. **Gammage Center for Performing Arts**, designed by Frank Lloyd Wright, is also here, 965-5062 (free ½ hr tours in winter, begins end Sept); student discount on tickets. Elsewhere on campus: the **Matthews Center** (off Forest Mall) houses permanent collections including African and Latin American art, American crockery and ceramics, and a sculpture zoo and aviary. Open Tue–Fri 8.30am–4.30pm, Sun 1pm–5pm, free. **Matthews Hall**, next door, is a museum of photography with changing exhibitions. Open Mon–Thur 10.30am–4.30pm, Sun noon–4.30pm, 965-6517. **Anthropology Museum**, 965-6213, **Planetarium** (reservations req), 965-6891, and **Memorial Union** (SU) art gallery, 965-6822, are also free.

About 55 miles southeast of Phoenix lies **Casa Grande Ruins National Monument** a 4-storey structure built by the Pueblo Indians AD 1300 and protected from further erosion by a hilarious 'umbrella', courtesy of the US government AD 1936.

Far more spectacular are the ruins at **Tonto National Monument**, 60 miles east. 'The **Apache Trail** follows Route 88 to Tortilla Flats and Roosevelt Lake through superb desert scenery with views of Superstition Mountains and Weavers Needle. Make a day trip of it.'

ENTERTAINMENT

Big Surf, 1500 N McClintock Rd, Tempe, 947-2477. The surf reaches 5 ft on this 2½-acre body of water; no surfing any more but swimming still permitted. 300 ft water slide and waving palms complete the oasis illusion. 'Most indulgent moment of my holiday; drinking Pepsi, watching girls surfing on machine-made waves in the middle of the desert.' Open mid-March through Sept, Tue–Thur 10am–6pm, Fri–Mon 10am–6pm. $12.25 plus $4 for raft rental. Discount coupons at 'Smithy's.'

INFORMATION

Phoenix & Valley of the Sun Convention & Visitors Bureaux, 505 N 2nd St, 254-6500. Also at 2nd St and Adams and at airport.
Tempe Chamber of Commerce, 51 W 3rd St, 894-8158.
Scottsdale Chamber of Commerce, 7343 E Scottsdale Mall, 945-8481.
Casa Grande Chamber of Commerce, 575 N Marshall, 836-2125.

TRAVEL

Amtrak, Union Station, 401 W Harrison St, 253-0121.
Greyhound, downtown, 5th St & E Washington, (800) 231-2222. Be careful in this area. Also at 2647 W Glendale near freeway, 246-4341.
Phoenix Transit, 253-5000. $3 for all day pass, otherwise $1. No service Sundays.
Sky Harbor International Airport, south-east of downtown. There are showers and lockers available. To get there from downtown, Mon–Fri take the 'Red Line' bus from Jefferson, opposite the American Arena and go east, 75¢; on Sat, take the 'Zero' bus from Jefferson until you reach Buckeye and then transfer to the # 13 airport bus, 75¢, remember to pick up a transfer; on Sun and public holidays, call Dial-a-Ride, 271-4545, trip about $3.
Car rental: Admirals, 402 S 24th St, 275-6101. $26 + insurance per day, used cars to let.
AAA Driveaway, 4814 S 35th St, 468-1733. 'Good availability of driveaways both east and west. Cheap way to travel.'
Horseback trail rides into the Superstition Mt Wilderness: Gold Canyon stables, 982-7822. 2hr $27, 4hr $43; and Peralta Stables, 982-5488, both in Apache Junction.

TUCSON Once capital of the Arizona territory and now a university town, Tucson retains a Western informality as it grows past the half-million mark. Folksiness notwithstanding, Tucson is, like Phoenix, a big, tough town with its share of crime, poverty and drugs. Watch your step in downtown, particularly at night and especially if you are female.

Most worthwhile sights are well away from downtown: the Desert Museum, Mission San Xavier del Bac, Saguaro National Monument, Old Tucson and the interesting Yaqui Indian tribe. The Yaquis have been immortalised in the books of Carlos Castaneda, a renegade anthropologist who claims that members of this tribe possess ancient knowledge of true sorcery. Whether or not you buy this view, the Yaquis are a highly spiritual and musical people, whose rites combine native and Catholic traditions. Their public performances (around Pascua, a village south of Tucson) are especially magnificent during Holy Week and at Christmas.

Both Tucson and Phoenix are in the Sonora Desert, surrounded by giant saguaro forests, cacti and mountains—all within driving (not walking) distance. Tucson is 65 miles north of Nogales, an agreeable town on the Arizona–Mexico border.

ACCOMMODATION

Congress Hotel and AAIH Hostel, 311 E Congress St, 792-1197. $13 hostel; w/student ID: S–$35, D–$39, for private rooms. 'Best value in USA.' 'Wild progressive club in lobby. Great fun.'

FOOD

Tucson is the place to get great Mexican food, especially *chimichangas*, reportedly invented here. *Chimichangas* are essentially fried pastry stuffed with beef, chilies, onion, cheese and salsa.

Caruso's, 434 N 4th Ave, 624-5765. 'Great lasagna, $6 and up.'

El Minuto Cafe, 354 S Main, 882-4145. 'Excellent and cheap Mexican food, basic decor.'

Food Conspiracy Co-op, 412 N 4th, 624-4821. Closes 7.30pm, 6pm Sun.

Mamas, Park and University, 882-3993. Pizza, subs, beer and jazz. 'Very popular student joint.'

Sanchez Burrito Co, 2539 N 1st Ave, 747-8960. Huge helpings, low prices, eg $2.99–$3.99 burritos, dinners $4.99. 'Authentic and excellent.'

OF INTEREST

Mission San Xavier del Bac, 9 miles southwest on Papago reservation, 294-2624. Completed in 1797 and called 'the white dove of the desert' for its cool beauty, the mission has weathered 3 political jurisdictions, 2 explosions and 1 large earthquake and still serves as church and school for the Papagos, known formally as the Tohono O'dham nation. Open Mon–Fri 8am–6pm, donation.

If you have come in search of the Old West, you won't find it here. But if you're looking for old John Wayne flicks, you'll see them come to life at **Old Tucson**, 12 miles west of the real thing, 883-6457, a 1939 movie set where hayburners from *Rio Bravo* to *High Chaparral* were filmed. Lots of corny family fun—$12 ($7.50 after 5pm) gets you gunfights, bank raids, museums and unlimited rides on antique trains, cars and a carousel. Stagecoach rides $1 per person. New last year: 'Wizard of the West Magic and Illusion act.' Daily 9am–9pm. 'Low-budget tourist trap.'

Just past Old Tucson (a spectacular drive) is the **Arizona-Sonora Desert Museum**, 14 miles west of the city. Detailed look at Sonoran desert, from tunnels that let you peer into snake and prairie-dog households to outdoor habitats of Gila monsters and mountain lions. Plants and rock of the desert are represented as well, in a museum that has been called 'the most distinctive in the US'. 'Don't miss this place.' Visit early am or late afternoon to see maximum animal activity, 883-1380. At same site: **Congdon Earth Sciences Center** with a manmade limestone cave showing subterranean rock and life forms, and explanations of volcanic activity. 7.30am–6pm daily, $8 for both (rates subject to change).

Saguaro National Monument, 2 sections, one east and one west of Tucson, 670-6680. Found naturally only in southern Arizona and Sonora, Mexico (although pirated plants may be seen as far away as LA), giant saguaro cacti grow to 50 ft tall and live for as much as 200 years. In late May, waxy white flowers sprout from the tips of cacti arms—a charming and improbable sight. East Park, 3693 S Old Spanish Trail, has the oldest stands; $4 to drive the loop, gates close at 7pm. West park is free, always open, 2700 N Kinney Rd.

Sabino Canyon and Seven Falls, two of the area's most popular and breathtaking hiking areas. At end of Sabino Canyon Road, 12 miles northeast of downtown. Either take a tram up the canyon ($5) or walk. The falls can be reached only by a 4½-mile hike. No overnight camping, 749-3223.

Kitt Peak National Observatory, 56 miles SW of Tucson, on Rte 86, 620-5350. Centre for astronomical research. Open daily 9am–3.45pm. Film at 10.30am and 1.30pm. Guided tours at weekends and on weekdays after films. Free. 'Fascinating.'

Titan Missile Museum, exit 69 on I-19 in Green Valley, 791-2929. Don a hardhat and see the only ICBM silo in the world open to the public. Nov–April open daily 9am–4pm, May–Oct closed Mon–Tues. $5. 'A chilling, frightening and all-powerful must see.' Reservations recommended.

Pima Air Museum, 6000 E Valencia Rd near airport, 574-9658. Huge airplane cemetery. Tour plane used by Presidents Kennedy and Johnson. Open daily 9am–5pm, $5.

Tucson Museum of Art, 140 N Main, 624-2333. Outstanding collection of Pre-Columbian artefacts. Open Tue–Sat 10am–4pm, Sun 12pm–4pm. $2, $1 student, free Tues.

Worthwhile museums on UA campus: **Center for Creative Photography**, 621-7968, magnificent new museum that houses 50,000 fine art photos, incl the Ansel Adams archives. Three galleries with changing exhibits and a photo library; make appt to view archives. **Arizona State Museum**, Park Ave at Uni gates, 621-4895, free daily with archaeology, Navajo, Apache, Pueblo artefacts. Open Mon–Sat 9am–5pm, Sat 2pm–5pm. The **Historical Society**, 628-5774, Park and 2nd. 'Free excellent displays of Southwest history.' Donations appreciated. **Flandrau Planetarium**, free exhibits on space, astronomy. 'Part of tracking system for Voyager mission and space shuttle. Also laser shows with Pink Floyd, others, $5, Wed–Thurs $1 off.' 621-7827 for programme info. Students $4 ($4.50 theatre admission).

ENTERTAINMENT

Bum Steer, 1910 N Stone, 884-7377. Good lunch specials. 'A must. Good luck lads and don't forget Happy Hour.'

Green Dolphin Bar, 622-6099. A student hang-out, cover charge occasionally. 'Cheap and friendly.' 'Very cheap beer.'

Near UA Campus: The Shanty, 401 E 9th, 623-2664. 'Good friendly pub and student watering hole'; **Gentle Ben's**, 841 N Tyndall, 624-4177.

INFORMATION

Metropolitan Tucson Convention and Visitors Bureau, 130 S Scott, 624-1817. Mon–Fri 8am–5pm, w/ends 9am–4pm.

TRAVEL

Greyhound, 2 S 4th Ave, (800) 231-2222. 'Girls near depot should stay on the move. This is the local prostitutes' pitch—clients are very persistent and extremely unpleasant.'

Amtrak, 400 E Toole St, 623-4442. On the *Sunset Ltd* LA–Miami route.

Local bus, Suntran, 792-9222, basic fare 75¢ exact change. Weekend pass $1.50.

Car Rental: Budget, 3085 E Valencia, 889-8800; Rent-a-Ride, 294-4100.

Tucson International Airport, 573-8000; south of downtown on Valencia Rd. Take the #8 bus east on Broadway as far as Alvernon, transfer to #11 'Tucson Airport' and go south, 75¢ and free transfer. After bus hours, call Arizona Stagecoach, 889-1000, pick-up or drop-off at downtown hotels, $13.

TOMBSTONE, BISBEE and APACHE COUNTRY This rugged terrain, once subject to the raids of Mexican revolutionary Pancho Villa, was originally Apache territory. Cochise, who fought the US Cavalry until 1886, was never captured and lies buried somewhere in the **Coronado National Forest**, about 60 miles east of Tucson. (Fellow Apache chief Geronimo was imprisoned in Oklahoma and died there in 1900.)

Tombstone, was named as a bit of death-defying bravado by the prospector who founded the town. Told that in this wild Apache country, he would find 'only his own tombstone', he struck silver instead. The silver was short-lived (1877–90), but the tombstones survive, in this city that lives off the tourists it traps. **Boot Hill Cemetery** (closes at dusk), one of the few sights in town that is free, displays the epitaph of the Clanton Gang, 'Murdered on the Street of Tombstone'—by Marshal Wyatt Earp, Earp's brothers and Doc Holliday at the shootout at OK Corrall. The shootout is re-enacted for visitors 2pm on the 1st and 3rd Sundays, $3.50, (on the 2nd and 4th Sundays, you can see the 'vigilantes and vigilettes' have it out in downtown). 'Whole place is a little false but great fun.' The **Bird Cage Theater** where Lola Montez danced, is still standing and houses a museum.

South of Tombstone by 25 miles, **Bisbee** clings to the sides of steep hills—a mining town of great character and considerable charm. Over $2 billion in silver, gold and copper came from these hills, but today Bisbee is famous for a special variety of turquoise, on display at Bisbee Blue Jewelry. Don't miss the delightful Art Deco courthouse or the nearby 'Lavender Pit Queen Mine'. If you're here in the summer, take heart: Bisbee is 5500 feet above sea level, making it much cooler than Tombstone.

ACCOMMODATION
Cochise Hotel and Waterworks, Cochise, AZ 85606, 384-3156. S–$22, D–$30. Booking mandatory for this authentic relic of the Old West: brass beds, quilts, chamberpots (plus modern plumbing) and chicken or steak dinners homecooked by the irascible proprietress. No AC, bring your own booze.
Camping: free in **Coronado National Forest**, 826-3593.
In Bisbee: Copper Queen Hotel, 11 Howell Ave, 432-2216. S/D–$72 up. Beautiful, regal, once the headquarters for everyone from Teddy Roosevelt to 'Black Jack' Pershing, hot on Pancho Villa's trail. Good sidewalk cafe, pool, saloon. 'Many rooms with antique furniture—a trip back in time when this was a bustling mining town.'

OF INTEREST/INFORMATION
Copper Queen Mine in Bisbee, 118 Arizona St, 432-2071. Daily tours, 1 hr, $8 at 9am, 10.30am, noon, 2pm and 3.30pm. 'Cold, so dress warmly.' 'Extensive, informative, good value.'
Tombstone Epitaph, the town local newspaper. Saved from bankruptcy by U of Arizona, now published by students. Pick up a copy or call 457-2211 for Tombstone info.
Visitors Center, 457-3729.

FLAGSTAFF Gateway to the Grand Canyon, a college town with character, Flagstaff is home of 'NAU' (Northern Arizona University, or otherwise, 'Not A University'). Other scenic splendours nearby are Oak Creek Canyon and Montezuma Castle to the south; Meteor Crater, Petrified Forest and Canyon de Chelly to the east; and Sunset Crater and Wupatki to the north. Somewhat closer to the Grand Canyon is **Williams**, which has some lodgings and good camping.

ACCOMMODATION

'Worth getting into a casual conversation with a Northern Arizona University student. Tell them of your exploits and ask for a bed for the night. It worked for me and some others.' Rates begin falling after Labor Day and are cheapest Nov–May. Summer rates given below.

Americana Motor Hotel, 2650 E Santa Fe Ave, 526-2200. S–$39, D–$52. Pool.

Chalet Lodge, 1919 E Santa Fe, 774-2779. S/D–$38 up.

Downtowner Hostel, 19 S San Francisco St, 774-8461. 1 blk from Amtrak. Dorm-$9, semi-private rooms $11, no curfew. Free coffee and doughnuts in morning. 'Helpful staff.' Only until Aug.

Hotel du Beau Hostel (AAIH), 19 W Phoenix, 774-6731, directly behind Amtrak. $11 dorm, $25 for private double room. Situated in a once famous motel, this friendly and fun hostel has free coffee, fruit and doughnuts all day. Runs shuttle to the Canyon, $22. 'The best hostel I stayed in.' 'Looked after our rucksacks as we visited the Canyon.' 'Best night in America.'

Flamingo Motel, 560 W Hwy 66, 779-2251. From $37, bath, TV. Next to bus station. 'Basic, but convenient.'

Weatherford Hotel and Hostel (AYH), 23 N Leroux, 774-2731. $10. Near Amtrak, buses. 'Lively area at night.' 'Excellent bar with good entertainment, English beer on draught.' Reservations advisable.

Western Hills, 1612 E Santa Fe Ave, 774-6633. S–$33, D–$41. Pool.

In Williams: try the **Red Lake Hostel**, Hwy 64, 635-4122. $10.

FOOD

Alpine Pizza, 7 N Leroux, 779-4109, praised for its Italian food. Open 11am–11pm.

Choi's, 7 E Aspen, 774-3492. 'Excellent', 'best value'. 6am–3pm.

Grand Canyon Cafe, 110 E Santa Fe, 774-2252. 'Superb value; 3-course meal under $6.' 7am–9pm.

Mary's Cafe, N Hwy 89, 526-0008. 'Huge homemade cinnamon rolls.'

OF INTEREST

Flagstaff Festival of the Arts, NAU, 774-7750. June through Aug. A variety of performing arts, incl poetry readings, dance, theatre, concerts (orchestral, chamber, pop, jazz), film classics, and dinner theatres and brunches.

The Festival of Native American Arts, Coconino Center for the Arts, Fort Valley Rd, 1 mile before Museum of Northern Arizona, Hwy 180, 779-6921. Mid-June to early August. Free (donations accepted), 9am–5pm. Contemporary art exhibits, dance, demonstrations, films, outdoor markets.

Lowell Observatory, 1400 W Mars Hill Rd, 774-3358. Tour (donations), includes telescope through which Percivall Lowell 'discovered' canals on Mars; here also where Pluto was first sighted in 1930. 'Worth it if only for view over Flagstaff.' Tours 10am, noon, 2pm & 4pm (Sat no 10am tour); telescope Mon, Wed, Fri 8pm.

Walnut Canyon, 10 miles east. Lush canyon filled with cliff-hanging ruins. The day-use trail is strenuous in places (involving 240 steps over 185 ft). Visitors' Center open 7am–6pm daily, 526-3367. 'Wildlife and Indian relics, very worthwhile and not crowded.' Trail closes at 5pm.

TRAVEL
Amtrak, 1 E Santa Fe Ave, 774-8679. *Southwest Limited* between LA and Chicago stops here. USA Rail Pass holders can use free shuttle to Canyon, leaves 8am.
To get to Grand Canyon:
Greyhound, 399 S Malpais Lane, 774-4573. 1 trip/day, 8.45am to Grand Canyon; $25 return.
Nava Hopi Tours, 401 S Malpais Lane, 774-5003. Dep 8.30am, $37 circular.
Lloyd Taylor Tours, 4836 E Halfmoon Dr, 526-2501. 7-person van tours to various points in Arizona. $40 to Canyon.
'If using a Delta pass, we suggest you fly to Flagstaff rather than Canyon airport. Difficult to get on the small commuter planes. Hire a car from Flagstaff, or hitch!'
Hitching: reported as 'easy' to and from the Canyon. 'Just as quick as the bus trip.' Elsewhere, best to rent a car.
Budget Car Rentals, 100 N Humphries; 774-2763. $30 per day +$12 insurance; 100 free miles, 25¢ after that. Must be 21, with credit card. Probably the best way to see the Canyon, if you can round up three other people to split the cost.

OAK CREEK CANYON and SEDONA Going down Hwy 89A from Flagstaff, the road makes a switchback descent into this brilliantly tinted canyon carved by Oak Creek. From the **Oak Creek natural area**, a footpath takes you along the floor, through a dense growth of pines, cypresses and junipers, crossing repeatedly the swift-running brook. After the 16-mile descent you come to **Sedona**, a pretty artists' colony and setting for many of Zane Grey's Western novels. Take Hwy 179, south of Sedona, and the landscape opens up into striking vistas punctuated by mesas and serrated sandstone cliffs of red, pink, ochre and buff. Spend some time at the Frank Lloyd Wright Church of the Holy Cross, a stunning concrete shadowbox set against rust-coloured cliffs. The view from inside is nearly as moving, often accompanied by Gregorian chants.

ACCOMMODATION
Star Motel, 295 Jordan Rd, Sedona, 282-3641. Summer rooms S/D–$54. 'Clean, neat.'
Cave Spring Campgrounds, 12 miles N of Sedona on Hwy 89A. A busy campground, $8 for unreserved sites so get there early. For reservations call (800) 280-CAMP but there is a reservation fee of $6.

OF INTEREST
Sedona Arts Center, N on US 89A, Art Barn Rd, 282-3809. Free. Centre of the performing as well as visual arts. Touring exhibitions which change every 5 weeks; very diverse media and subject matter. Tue–Sat 10.30am–4.30pm, Sun 1.30pm–4.30pm.
NB: Sedona is itself a centre for contemporary and traditional arts; galleries located throughout the city.

INFORMATION
Sedona-Oak Creek Canyon Chamber of Commerce, 89A & Forest Rd, 282-7722.

MONTEZUMA CASTLE NATIONAL MONUMENT Further south on I-17 is **Tuzigoot National Monument**, a pueblo ruin atop a mesa overlooking the Verde River. But for a better example, cut across to Hwy 279 for **Montezuma Castle** (AD 100–1400), far more picturesque and intact. Neither a castle nor connected with Montezuma, this was a cliff dwelling inhabited by Sinagua farmers. 'Ask at visitors centre for directions to Clear Creek campground. Friendly owners. You can swim in the nine-foot pool formed by the stream nearby.'

PETRIFIED FOREST NATIONAL PARK This 94,000-acre park actually contains the varicoloured buttes and badlands of the **Painted Desert** as well as Indian petroglyphs at **Newspaper Rock**, pueblo ruins, two museums and a large 'forest' of felled and petrified logs. The trees date back to the Triassic period and were probably brought here by a flood, covered with mud and volcanic ash, preserved by silica quartz and laid bare once again by erosion. Most of the fossilised remains are jasper, agate, a few of clear quartz and amethyst. Like the red, yellow, blue and umber tones of the Painted Desert, these vivid colours are caused by mineral impurities. An excellent road bisects the park north to south. Park fee is $5 per car; camping for hikers only (with permit) at two spots. The museum-restaurant at the north end contains murals by noted Hopi artists.

ACCOMMODATION
No lodging in the park.
Arizona Rancho Motor Lodge Hostel (AYH), Tovar and Apache Dv in **Holbrook**, 524-6770. 19 miles from park. $7 winter, $8 summer. 'Friendly, clean, comfortable.' 'Mrs Taylor is very helpful.' Son Henry Taylor runs the Weatherford Hostel in Flagstaff.
Brad's Motel, 301 W Hopi Dr, **Holbrook**, 3 blocks from Greyhound, 524-6929. S–$20, D–$24.

TRAVEL
Greyhound operates along I-40 to Holbrook. Roy Baker's Tours of the area have been criticised by readers; enquire at the Holbrook Hostel instead.

NAVAJO and HOPI RESERVATIONS The **Navajo** nation occupies the northeast corner of Arizona (plus parts of Utah and New Mexico), an area the size of West Virginia. On it dwell a shy, dignified, beauty-loving people, the largest and most cohesive of all Native American groups. Nearly all Navajos are fluent in their native tongue, a language of such complexity that Japanese cryptographers were unable to decipher it during the Second World War, when the US military used Navajos to send secret information. Originally a nomadic culture, the flexible Navajos adopted sheepherding and horses from the Spanish, weaving and sandpainting from the Pueblo Indians, and more recently such things as pickup trucks from the whites. The reservation, while poor, is a fascinating mix of traditional hogans and wooden frame houses, uranium mines and trading posts, all in a setting of agriculturally marginal but scenically rich terrain, anchored by the four sacred peaks of Mounts Blanca, Taylor, Humphrey and Hesperus.

Amidst the 150,000 Navajos is an arrowhead-shaped nugget of land upon which sit the three mesas of the **Hopis**, a strenuously peaceful and traditional tribe of farmers and villagers. The 6500 Hopis have planted corn and ignored Spaniards, Navajos and Anglos alike for nearly a thousand years, their religion and culture still poetically and distinctly non-Western.

Route 264 crosses both reservations, allowing you access to the Hopi mesa villages and the Navajo settlements and capital at **Window Rock** on the Arizona–New Mexico border. Neither group is particularly forthcoming with whites, but you can bridge their suspicion by respecting their strong feelings about photographs, alcohol, tape recorders and local customs. Always ask permission to take pictures; if you are allowed, expect to pay for it and live up to your bargain. If you are lucky enough to witness dancing or healing ceremonies, behave as the Indians do to avoid giving offence.

Oraibi on the Third Mesa vies with the Pueblo Indians' Acoma as the oldest continuously inhabited settlement in the US. To enter the village, you must ask permission of the chief and pay a fee—absolutely no cameras, however. One of the most intriguing Hopi villages is **Walpi**, high atop the narrow tip of the Second Mesa. Dating from the 17th century, this classic adobe village of kivas and sculptured houses remains startlingly alien. 'Hire a four-wheel drive to get up very steep roads, dirt tracks.'

Monument Valley, scene of countless John Ford films and full of Navajo sacred places, sprawls across Arizona-Utah state lines and can be reached via Hwys 160 and 163 from the south. Perhaps easier is the access from the Utah side. Page, Arizona (also site of Lake Powell and its 90 flooded canyons) makes a good base for Monument Valley exploration. A car is almost a necessity, both here and elsewhere on the reservations. There is some bus service via Nava-Hopi from Window Rock to Tuba City, which stops at Kearns Canyon in Hopiland.

Besides looking at the masterful rugs, pottery, jewellery and other crafts, be sure to sample Indian food. Navajo specialties include fried bread, mutton stew and roast prairie dog. Interesting Hopi dishes are *nakquivi* or hominy stew and the beautiful blue cornmeal bread served with canteloupe for breakfast. The Hopi Cultural Center has a restaurant, 734-2401, on Rte 264; open daily.

ACCOMMODATION

Greyhills Inn, 160 Warrior Dv, Tuba City, 283-6271. On a Navajo reservation; near Pature Canyon and several dinosaur tracks. 'Easy access' to Grand Canyon. $10.50 dorm with AYH membership, D–$21. Check-in 1pm–10pm. Tennis courts. Reservations advisable.

CANYON DE CHELLY NATIONAL MONUMENT Surrounded by Navajo land, Canyon de Chelly (about 30 miles north of Hwy 264 and pronounced 'Canyon de *Shay*') has the powerful beauty of a bygone Garden of Eden. Occupied successively by the Basket Makers, the Hopis and the Navajos, the canyon was just one of the targets in the 1863 US Army campaign to subdue or annihilate the Navajos. Kit Carson and his men eventually overwhelmed the stronghold at Canyon de Chelly, killing livestock and Indians, destroying hogans and gardens, even cutting down the treasured peach trees, a move which shattered the Navajos. Canyon de Chelly is again inhabited by Navajos, who live among 800-year-old pueblo buildings. Both are upstaged by the fantastic walls of the canyon itself, 1000 feet of sheer orange verticality.

A road runs along the rim with several lookouts to view **White House Ruin** and **Spider Rock**. The only descent you're allowed to navigate solo is the White House Trail; all others require a Navajo guide.

ACCOMMODATION

Free camping: 100 sites in Cottonwood Campground ½ mile from visitors centre.

INFORMATION
Visitors Centre, near Chinle, 674-5213, open 8am–7pm year-round. Although a National Monument, Canyon de Chelly is on Navajo land and is therefore subject to certain restrictions designed to limit intrusion into Navajo privacy.

TRAVEL
No public transport to either the monument or Chinle. Inside the monument, jeeps tour the canyon floor for a good look at ruins and pictographs, $31 half day, $50 full day, through Thunderbird Lodge, 674-5841. As mentioned earlier, except for White House Trail, all hikers must have park ranger or an authorised Navajo guide; about $8 hr.
Justin's Horse Hire, 674-5678. $8 per hr ride along the canyon floor +$8 for obligatory guide. 'My best experience in America—just like in the movies!'

SUNSET CRATER and WUPATKI NATIONAL MONUMENTS Hwy 180, the most direct route from Flagstaff to the Grand Canyon, is also the dullest. A better choice is to travel US 89 past Sunset Crater and Wupatki, turning off for the Canyon at Cameron.

Long a volcanic region, **Sunset Crater** erupted most recently about AD 1064, leaving a colourful cone on a jet black lava field. The crater rim makes an interesting hike although trips into the crater are no longer allowed. From the rim, over 50 volcanic peaks, including the San Franciscos, can be seen. Camping; lava tubes to explore. The volcanic ash from Sunset made good fertiliser, and a number of Indian groups built pueblos nearby at **Wupatki**. There are over 800 ruins on mesa tops, a ball court, dance arena, and a museum to interpret the finds at this long since abandoned settlement. $3 admission per car, $1 if on foot, includes entry to both monuments, 8am–5pm.

THE GRAND CANYON According to legend a Texas cowboy riding across the Arizona desert came to the edge of the Grand Canyon unprepared for what he would see, 'Good God,' he exclaimed, 'something happened here'.

This astonishment is probably repeated daily. Approached from a flat, sloping plain on all sides, the Grand Canyon is a startlingly abrupt gash. Wind, frost and the Colorado River have gnawed a magnificent, 217-mile-long canyon from the landscape, filled with 270 animal species and containing four of the seven known life zones. To the visitor on the rim, the colourful buttes amid early-morning mist appear as a dreamlike valley of palaces. The proportions of the 1-mile-deep canyon are deceptive; most people find it difficult to believe that it is never less than 4 times wider than it is deep. The cross-sectional prospect from **Grandview Point** helps set matters straight.

The Grand Canyon has 3 parts: the **South Rim**, open year-round, access via Hwy 64/180 from Williams and Flagstaff; the **North Rim**, open mid-May to mid-Oct, access via Hwy 67 from Jacob Lake; and the **Inner Canyon**, open year-round, access from the rim by foot, mule or boat only. To get from the North to the South Rim or vice-versa is 215 miles by car or an arduous 20-mile hike down and up. If you're not able to take your time in the park, you should choose early on which rim you want to visit.

The South Rim is easy to reach and has the best views as well as the lion's share of the lodgings and amenities. The North Rim boasts cooler temperatures, special autumn colours, an abundance of animal life and uncrowded serenity (a quarter-million tourists per year here versus 3 million on the south side).

If you're at all fit, you'll want to hike to the **canyon floor**, or at least part of the way. If you make it to the bottom, don't forget to touch an outcropping of black Vishnu Schist; this metamorphic rock, the lowest layer in the canyon, was formed when the Earth was half the age it is now. 'Hard work, but an awesome and breath-taking spectacle.' 'Do read the hiking tips under *Of Interest* before setting out; the heat, the stiff 4500 foot climb, the high altitude of the entire area and the need to carry large amounts of water are all factors you must prepare for.' 'No 2-D picture could ever do justice to this scene of nature at her most imposing form. Even if you have to go to great lengths to get here, that first sight of the canyon . . . you'll have no regrets.'

Park entrance fee is $10 per car. It's $4 for someone on foot or on a bus!

ACCOMMODATION

Sadly the Grand Canyon youth hostel has closed, leaving no budget accommodation here other than camping.

Grand Canyon Lodges, 638-2631, for the South Rim, books accommodation for 7 lodges and hotels within or near the park. Prices start at $30 for a room without a bath, $45 for one with a bath. **Bright Angel Lodge and Cabins** is usually the least expensive. **Maswik** and **Original** and **New Yavapai** are also reasonable. Book well ahead, even after Labor Day. Failing that, be on hand 3.30pm–4.30pm for no-shows; the lodges always hold a few rooms for people on the last buses from Flagstaff and Williams.

Camping: Mather, 638-7851, in Grand Canyon Village, is open year-round, $10 a site. 'Always places reserved for people without own transport.' Reserve through MISTIX, (800) 365-2267. NB: Tent not needed in June and early July; later in summer, monsoons deluge the area. Campsites fill quickly June through Sept, so get there *very* early (ie. before 9am). Other campsites on the south side at **Trailer Village** in Grand Village by entrance of park, 638-2631, $18 for 2 people, XP–$1.50. Also: 'Free camping allowed on National Forest land. Go 6 miles south on South Entrance Rd, turn at forest track on left opp Squire Inn. OK as long as you remain within ½ mile of public telephone.'

Down the Canyon: Free camping at one of the 4 hike-in sites requires both an overnight wilderness permit and a trailhead or campground reservation. 'As soon as you arrive, go to the Backcountry Office by 7am for a chance at unclaimed permits.' Keep in mind that there's a heavy fine for those caught camping without a permit.

Phantom Ranch, on canyon floor, 638-2401. Rustic cabins: D–$53; dorms $19. Booked up *long* in advance. 'Now air conditioned, very comfortable.' NB: Anything you buy down here is bound to be expensive, and that includes food. Leave excess luggage on the rim for a fee.

North Rim: Grand Canyon Lodge, 638-2611. Late May to mid-Oct only. Cheapest are **Pioneer Cabins**, 4 people for $62. **Western Cabins** are $75 for 2 people, but have more comfort and unbelievable views. Can also reserve in Cedar City, UT, (800) 586-7686. Campsite reservations and trail info at Lodge, but no place to check luggage.

North Rim Campground, 638-7872, $10 per site. NB: Often necessary to camp outside park on National Forest land the night before, arriving at North Rim early am to nab site. Reservations through MISTIX (800) 365-2267; $5 handling fee.

Outside park to the north: Jacob Lake Inn, 44 miles north, 643-7232. Open year-round: cabins: S/D–$45–$55.
See also under 'Utah' for hostel accommodation at **Kanab**.

FOOD

Expensive and generally poor everywhere in the park, even at cafeterias. Best bets: **Babbitt's General Store**, 638-2262, (across from Visitors Center; 8am–8pm daily); **Bright Angel Restaurant**, 638-2631, especially their specials; and **Grand Canyon Lodge** at the North Rim, 638-2611, (6.30am–9pm; lunch $3 up, dinner $8–$18).

OF INTEREST

Tips: Whether you descend the canyon or not, guard against heat exhaustion and dehydration by drinking the park-recommended juice mixture. Water alone will not satisfy your body's requirements, as the rangers will tell you. Other hiking tips: wear a hat, don't wear sandals, always check beforehand to make sure your trail is open. For hiking into the Canyon, plan to carry 4 litres of water per person per day. Also carry food, permit, pocket knife, signal mirror, flashlight, maps, matches and first-aid kit. Calculate 2 hrs up for every hr going down. (If you do get lost or injured, stay on the trail so they can find you.) The park service warns against hiking to the Colorado River and back in one day. Readers add: 'Do take notice of time estimates.' If you plan to camp at the bottom, you need a minimum of equipment—it reaches 100 degrees in summer. 'Hardly worth the effort to carry tent.' A final recommendation: 'When camping at the bottom, start the ascent at 3am, escaping the midday heat, seeing sunrise over the Canyon, and catching the 9am bus back to Flagstaff.'
Along the South Rim, the most remarkable views are from Hopi, Yaki, Grand View and Desert Views points. A 9-mile trail from Yavapai Museum to Hermit's Rest follows the very edge of the Canyon. Pick up relevant leaflets from the visitors centres before setting out. The South Rim is also the starting point for the South Kaibab and Bright Angel Trails to descend into the canyon.
Bright Angel Trail has water at 3 points (May–Sept only) and is 8 miles to the river. 'A good one-day hike—Bright Angel to Plateau Point and back, 12 miles. Great scenery.' 'Try to leave yourself 8 hrs for comfort.' 'Water is essential.'
South Kaibab Trail is 6 miles down, no campgrounds, no water and little shade: don't attempt in summer. 'Colorado River is nice to paddle in—too strong for anything else.'
From the North Rim, the North Kaibab Trail is 14 miles with water at 4 points. A good day hike would be to Roaring Springs and back, about 6–8 hrs. The entire Kaibab Trail is 21 miles and connects North and South Rims. Views from the North Rim include Cape Royal (nature talks in summer), Angel's Window, overlooking the Colorado River, and the much-photographed Shiva's Temple, a ruddy promontory of great beauty.
Ranger programmes, 638-7888, are highly recommended; they conduct guided hikes, do evening slide shows, etc. In winter, programmes are inside the Shrine of Ages building. Also recommended: the sunrise and sunset photo walks by the Kodak rep.
Mule Rides into the Canyon: from South and North Rims (summer only). Outrageously popular and booked up for 6 months in advance, but many no-shows so try anyway. 1-day trips $80 per person including lunch, and overnight trips with 3 meals, cabin accommodation, 1 person–$243, 2–$433, XP–$200. The following restrictions apply: you can't be pregnant or handicapped or weigh more than 200 pounds, and you must be at least 4′7″ tall, speak fluent English (the mules don't like people who talk funny), and not to be afraid of heights. To reserve, write to PO Box 699, Reservation Dept, South Rim, Grand Canyon National Park, AZ 86023, or call 638-2401. Guaranteed reservations require pre-payment. For **whitewater boat trips** down the Colorado, the park office has list of companies. Rewarding trip but costs around $100 a day.

Air tours depart from LA, Las Vegas, Phoenix, Flagstaff and Williams. Dozens of small companies offer tours; by day the sky above the canyon is filled with buzzing planes (much to the disgust of environmental groups and visitors who value serenity). Check Chambers of Commerce and *Yellow Pages* in those cities under Airline Tours. At the park, call 638-2407 to reserve a seat; $55 for 45 minutes in an airplane. Helicopter tours, 638-2419, cost $80 for 30 min, higher for longer tours. Until recently, copters and planes flew below canyon rim. This practice was banned after a 1986 crash in the canyon.
Grand Canyon Caverns, on Rte 66, 422-3223. Descend 21 storeys into the welcome 56-degree caves of coloured minerals, by elevator. 45-min tours, daily 8am–6pm, $7.50.
For a special experience that few park visitors get to enjoy, hike in to **Havasupai Falls** from the Havasupai Indian Reservation adjacent to the park on the southwest side. The heavy calcium content of Havasu Creek has resulted in coral-like circular deposits that form a stairstep sequence of turqouise pools. Bathers can catch impromptu rides where the water bubbles over the top (watch out—the 'coral' is sharp!). A trail follows the creek downstream to the Colorado River. Ask around for directions, or call the Havasupai (whose land the creek is on) at 448-2121. You will have to be persistent calling this number, but it's worth it.

INFORMATION
Park office, general information, 638-7888.

TRAVEL
For **bus service** to the South Rim, see Flagstaff. To and from the North Rim, talk to Gray Line in Flagstaff, Phoenix, Las Vegas and other large cities. Surprisingly reasonable tours.
Hitching: 'Save your money by walking 3 miles out of Flagstaff and hitching. Will get a ride easily.' 'Hitching to North Rim is OK—we did it in less than 24 hours from Zion in Sept.'
Within the Canyon: Bus tours from Bright Angel Lodge called 'a waste of money'.
Two free shuttle bus services operate May–Sept every 15 mins, throughout Grand Canyon Village and around South Rim. Get on and off at will. Also to scenic West Rim as far as Hermit's Rest.

LAKE HAVASU CITY If you wanted to hide London Bridge where no one would ever think of looking for it, where would you put it? That's right—in the middle of a big, fat desert! Specifically, at Lake Havasu City, spanning the Colorado river (at least the bridge isn't going to waste). A charmingly ersatz Tudor Village and double-decker bus, fast food restaurants make this a must for the discerning British visitor. Hwy 95 south to Parker traverses a beautiful stretch of scenery; if you continue all the way to **Quartsite**, you can visit the **Hi Jolly Monument**, a tribute to the Middle Easterner who tried to introduce camels to *this* desert, too. Chamber of Commerce, 1930 Mesquite Ave, 855-4115, can direct you. Free guided **Desert Walks**; contact John Kany, 855-7055. Recreationally, the city's lake is described as 'a lake to rent', as all types of **water sports** are available here from paddle boats to jet-skiing and 'wave-runners'.

NEW MEXICO

Travel industry hyperbole aside, New Mexico *does* enchant. It possesses a dramatic landscape heightened by the scalpel-sharp clarity of the desert air; natural wonders like the Navajo's Shiprock and the Carlsbad Caverns; and the finest array of Indian cultures, past and present, in the country. In human terms, New Mexico is incredibly ancient, having been inhabited for over 25,000 years. More significantly, it is the only state that has succeeded in fusing its venerable Spanish, Indian and Anglo influences into a harmonious and singular pattern. You will notice the benign borrowings everywhere, from sensuous adobes tastefully outfitted with solar heating to the distinctive New Mexican cuisine, currently very chic.

New Mexico inspires awe for more than its beauty. On 16 July 1945, at the appropriately named Jornada del Muerto (Journey of the Dead) Desert, the world's first atomic bomb belched its radioactive mushroom into the air. (Physicist Enrico Fermi reportedly took bets on the chances that the test would blow up the state.) Today, the state is a leader in atomic research, testing, uranium mining and related fields. Blithe as locals may be about nuclear materials (the Alamogordo Chamber of Commerce still sponsors a twice-annual outing to Ground Zero the 1st Saturdays in April and October), think twice before visiting the Alamogordo-White Sands region. Your genes may thank you some day. Instead, concentrate on the fascinating and diverse Indian populations: the 19 pueblo villages, each with its own pottery, dance, arts and style; the Navajos, whose capital is at Window Rock; and the Jicarilla and Mescalero Apaches, noted for dancing and coming of age ceremonies. Celebrations open to the public are so numerous that you could plan an itinerary around them.

National Park: Carlsbad Caverns.

The telephone area code for the entire state is 505.

ALBUQUERQUE Named for a ducal viceroy of Mexico, and where Bugs Bunny didn't turn left, Albuquerque is not as pleasing as its euphonious name would lead you to believe. The state's largest city, Albuquerque contains one-quarter of the state's 1.7 million residents and although it has rather more of the state's trash features, from tacky motels to urban sprawl, it has a youthful feeling due in part to the large student population.

However, the setting and the scenery are spectacular and Albuquerque does make a good base for day trips to the Indian pueblos and to the Sandia Mountains. The best times to visit are during the June Arts and Crafts Fair, the September State Fair (the largest in the US), the October Hot-Air Balloon Fiesta and at Christmas, when city dwellings are outlined with thousands of *luminarias* (candles imbedded in sand, their light diffused by paper).

ACCOMMODATION

Central Ave is the north–south divider; railroad tracks divide east–west. 'Cheap hotels on Central SE. Walk to the other side of railroad, right side of Greyhound terminal to Central SE, then straight ahead.'

Albuquerque International AAIH Hostel, 1012 W Central Ave SW, 243-6101. $11; $15 non-members plus $5 key deposit, $2 linen. 'Friendly, no curfew.' Full kitchen. Free coffee, tea, snacks and cereal.
Stardust Inn, 817 Central NE, 243-1321. S–$25, D–$36.
Grand Western Motor Hotel, 918 Central SW, downtown, 243-1773. S–$28, D–$33. 'Very friendly and clean, but not in good side of town.'
Monterey Motel, 2402 Central SW, 243-3554. S–$45, D–$50. 'Small; friendly, helpful people.'
Sandia Mountain AAIH Hostel, 12234 Hwy 14 N in **Cedar Crest**, 20 miles E of Albuquerque (3.5 miles N of I-40 on New Mexico Hwy N), 281-4117. $8, non-members $11. Kitchen, laundry, volleyball, ping-pong!

FOOD
Annie's Soup Kitchen, 3107 Eubank NE, 296-8601 and 3600 Osuria NE, 344-4446. Homemade soups, salads, quiche, crepes.
Capo's Ristorante Italiano, 722 Lomas NW, 242-2007. Inexpensive, attractive place with good Italian food. 11am–8.45pm. $4–$11.
M & J Sanitary Tortilla Factory, 403 2nd SW, 242-4890. Neighbourhood chili parlour; excellent Mexican food, written up in the *New Yorker*; interesting art by locals on walls. Open Mon–Sat 9am–4pm.

OF INTEREST
Old Town, 1 block north of Central NW. Shops, restaurants and occasional live entertainment. The only nugget of Spanishness left in the city. 'Well worth a visit.' On the plaza is the **1706 Church of San Felipe de Neri**.
Albuquerque Museum, 2000 Mountain Rd NW, 243-7255. Permanent and changing exhibits on history of Albuquerque and southwest US. Open Tue–Sun 9am–5pm; free, includes walking tour.
Albuquerque Museum Tours of Historic Old Town, 243-7255. 1-hr walking tours from museum, Tues–Sun, 11am.
Indian Pueblo Cultural Center, 2401 12th St near I-40, 1 mile east of Old Town, 843-7270. Excellent exhibit & sales rooms by the 19 Pueblo Indian groups allow comparison of techniques and styles. High quality, prices to match. 'Only thing of interest in this town.' Open daily 9am–5.30pm, $2.50, students $1. Also **Indian dancing**, Sat & Sun, 11am and 2pm, May–early Oct; free, cameras allowed. Restaurant on premises serves traditional pueblo food—give it a try; 7.30am–3.30pm.
New Mexico Museum of Natural History, 1801 Mountain Rd NW, 841-8837. New hi-tec Dynamax Theater showing 3D movies, and an 'Evolator time machine', unique to the museum, taking you millions of years back through time. 'Fantastic. Don't miss your chance to stand inside an "active" volcano.' Open daily 9am–5pm, $4 adults, $3 students.
National Atomic Museum, Building 358, Wyoming Blvd SE at Kirtland AFB, 845-6670. Free, daily 9am–5pm. Disquieting look at selection of nuclear weapons casings, plus 'oops' items like the A-Bomb the US accidentally dropped on Palomares, Spain, in 1966. Regular screenings of *Ten Seconds that Shook the World*. If driving to the museum, you need to show a driving licence, proof of car ownership, and insurance papers in order to get onto the USAF base.
Indian Pueblos, all over the state. Religious and other dances are held throughout the year. Dances, fiestas and ceremonials are sacred and special to the Pueblo Indians. Tape recording, photography, sketching or painting may not be permissible. Please call ahead to verify dates and to obtain permission to visit the various pueblos.
U of New Mexico, Central NE & University, 277-0111. Pioneer in pueblo revival architecture, has free exhibits, often on Indians, in the **Maxwell Museum**. On campus: **Fine Arts Museum** in Fine Arts Center, 277-4001, has sculptures, photography and paintings. Open Tue–Fri 9am–4pm (Tue also 5pm–8pm), Sun 1pm–4pm. Free.

Maxwell Museum of Anthropology, west end of campus between Grand and Las Lomas, 277-4405, has exhibits on anthropology of Southwest US. Open Mon–Fri 9am–4pm; Sat 10am–4pm, Sun noon–4pm. Free (but donations on the door). Closed hols.

Petroglyph National Monument, 6900 Unser Blvd NW, 873-6620. Formerly the Petroglyph State Park, it became a National Monument late 1990. Open 9am–6pm daily in summer. Parking $1, $2 at w/e.

Sandia Peak Aerial Tramway, NE of town, take Tramway Rd off I-25, 296-5308. At 2.7 miles, the world's longest tramway, climbing to 10,378 ft. Fantastic panorama which sometimes includes hot air balloons and hang gliders in the area. Open daily 9am–10pm. 1.5 hr ride, $12; reduced rate 9am–11am, $9.

American International Rattlesnake Museum, 202 San Felipe, 242-6569. Mon–Sat 10am–6.30pm, Sun 1pm–6pm. $1 for everyone over 3 ft tall! Living and artefact snakes from all over America. Gift shop includes such delights as *Snakebite Salsa* and *Poison Perfume*!

Hot Air Balloon Fiesta, International Balloon Fiesta Field, off I-25, 293-6800. About 650 balloons from around the world assemble for 9 days in early Oct. High points are the mass ascensions on opening and closing weekends: get there 6am–7am. Also balloon rides during fiesta ($145–$185), but cheaper at other times ($125).

Christmas: Convention and Visitors Bureau does free night time bus tours of the outstanding *luminaria* displays, a medieval Spanish custom which began as small bonfires lighting the way to the church for the Christ Child.

INFORMATION

Visitors Information Centers: Albuquerque Convention and Visitors Bureau, 121 Tijeras Ave NE, 243-3696 (main office); Old Town Plaza, 305 Romero NW; Albuquerque International Airport. All open daily 8am–5pm.

TRAVEL

Amtrak, 314 1st St SW, 842-9650.
Greyhound, 300 2nd SW, 243-4435. Clean, safe depot with all-night café.
Sun-Tran Transit, 601 Yale Blvd SE, 843-9200. The city buses, basic fare 75¢.
Albuquerque International Airport, south of downtown, next to the airforce base. Sun-Tran bus #50 from 5th & Central, 75¢, takes about 30 minutes. After bus hours or on Sun, call 883-4888 for a taxi, about $8.

CARLSBAD CAVERNS Eighth deepest and very possibly the most beautiful caves in the world, the Carlsbad Caverns began their stalagtite-spinning activities about 250 million years ago. In contrast, the famous Mexican freetail bat colony has been in residence a mere 17,000 years. Once numbering seven million, give or take a bat, the colony reduced to 250,000, due in part to increased use of insecticides, but is now back to the 1 million mark. It was the eerie sight of bats pouring like smoke from the cave openings that led to Carlsbad's discovery in 1901.

The caves became a National Park in 1930, but the big bucks locally came from the sale of 100,000 tons of prime bat shit ('guano' to the genteel) to California citrus growers. No, the bats don't drink blood— and few harbour rabies, but the superstitious *should* keep the throat and other parts covered while the little boogers are zooming overhead.

Oh yes, the caves. The cross-shaped **Big Room** is 1800 ft by 1100 ft; nearby you'll see a formation called **The Iceberg**, which takes half an hour to circle. The cave's sheer size is not as impressive as the variety of colours and formations and the intricate filigrees (8 percent of which are still living and growing) these caverns house. Don't touch the formations, much as you might like to; a number of them have been turned black by ignorant handling.

ACCOMMODATION

Carlsbad Caverns International AAIH Hostel at Whites City, NM 88268, 785-2291. $10 AYH, + $5 key deposit, non-members not accepted. Pool. Part of **Cavern Inn**, near the caverns in Whites City. Private rooms are pricey, but the campground here is $18 for up to 6 people per site. XP–$3. Seven miles from the caverns.

La Caverna Motel, 223 S Canal, 885-4151. S–$22, D–$24 + $2 key deposit.

Motel 6, 3824 National Parks Hwy, Carlsbad, 885-0011. S–$35, D–$40. 24 miles from caves.

NB: Camping is not permitted in Carlsbad National Park, but there are many good campgrounds nearby.

OF INTEREST

Carlsbad Caverns National Park, 785-2233, is open all year. **Cave tours:** walk in through natural entrance, elevator out; 3 miles, about 2.5 hrs. Elevator in and out: 1.25 miles, about 1 hr. Open summer, 8.30am–6.30pm (access to cave closes at 5pm); winter, 8.30am–5.30pm (last access at 3.30pm). 'Get there early—after 2pm, you'll have to take the shorter 1.25 mile trip. Still worth seeing.' 'Rangers will not let you descend into the caverns unless you are wearing sensible shoes; ie not thongs, sandals, or anything with heels.' 'Free nature walks around cavern entrance at 5pm, something to do while waiting for bats.' Carlsbad costs $5, $6 for **Slaughter Canyon Cave**, more rugged and only for those in good shape. Advance reservations and a flashlight required. Temperature inside the cave is 56 degrees, refreshing in summer but bring a jacket.

Bat facts: bats are in residence spring through mid-Oct only and are at busiest May–Sept. They leave the cave at dusk to fly up to 120 miles, consume an aggregate five tons of insects, return at dawn to spend the day sleeping in cosy bat-fashion, 300 per sq ft. Call Visitor Center, 785-2233, for more bat-data. 'No one should miss the incredible sight of a million bats flying a few feet over one's head. Just like Dracula, in fact.'

Lake Carlsbad & Beach, a three-mile spring-fed water playground with free swimming, boat ramp and docks, water skiing, picnic area, tables, fireplaces, fishing and amusement parks.

Bataan Recreational Area, below Lake Carlsbad is for sail boating, canoeing, picnicking and fishing.

TRAVEL

Texas, New Mexico and Oklahoma Coaches, in El Paso run buses in conjunction with Greyhound, (915) 532-2365. Services Whites City, 8am, 1.45pm & 7.25pm, $29; also between Carlsbad (town) and Whites City, twice daily at 10.45am and 11pm, $3.

Hitching: 'There's about a 15-min wait 7 miles from Caverns while changing bus. Try hitching. If successful, get ticket refund in El Paso.' 'If you hitchhike to Cavern, get in free with whomever gave you a lift.' 'For girls, not worth the risk.'

SANTA FE That rarity of rarities, Santa Fe is a city for walkers, full of narrow, adobe-lined streets that meander round its Spanish heart, the old plaza where the Santa Fe trail ends. Long a crossroads for trade routes and the oldest seat of government in the US, Santa Fe has witnessed a remarkable amount of history. But the age of the place doesn't prepare you for its beauty, the friendliness of its locals, the vitality of its artistic and cultural life. The town has a strict architecture policy that requires that all the buildings must be in 17th century pueblo style and painted in one of 23 varying shades of brown, all of which gives the place a pleasing unity. 'Disappointing—caters too much to rich American tourists.' While here visit **Los Alamos**, where the first A-Bomb was built, and the ghost town of **Madrid**.

ACCOMMODATION

Motel 6, 3007 Cerrillos Rd, 473-1380. S–$35, D–$42. Far from downtown on 'motel row'; other cheapies along Cerrillos, too.

Santa Fe International Hostel AAIH, 1412 Cerrillos Rd, 988-1153 or 983-9896. $11 card-carrying members, $15 non-members; S/D–$30 for private room. 'Excellent hostel; no curfew; friendly people, full of information.' 'More than adequate facilities: cooking, showers.' Also organises occasional tours in summer. Linen $2 per day; use of kitchen $1.

Outlying areas:

Canyon Quarters Hostel, in **Jemez Springs** west of Santa Fe, 867-3294. $8.50 AYH, $12 non-members. S–$22, D–$25 (private room); apartment (up to 6 people) is $32 for 2, XP–$7.50. 'Recommended.'

Circle A Ranch, Box 382, **Cuba**, NM 87013, 289-3350. Adobe hacienda in Sante Fe National Forest near hiking trails and swimming hole; northwest of Sante Fe. Reservations strongly advised. Bunks: $10, D–$20–$30. 'Lovely adobe ranch, friendly people—felt part of the family.' The hostel is 40 miles from **Chaco Culture National Historic Park**, a massive 11th-century ruin, its largest pueblo containing 800 rooms and 39 kivas (sacred chambers). Contemporary with Mesa Verde, possibly more remarkable and certainly less visited.

Camping: Apache Canyon KOA, 11 miles southeast of Santa Fe on I-25, exit 294, 982-1419. Free movies, showers, restrooms, store, laundry, rec room. $15 a night for 2; stay 6 days, 7th free.

Camel Rock, 10 miles north of Santa Fe on Hwy 285, 455-2661. $10/night for 2, XP–$2. 'Clean facilities, very cold at night in Sept.'

FOOD

Santa Fe is the home of southwestern cooking, a current favourite of American palates, and is based on humble indigenous ingredients—beans, corn and chilies, in imaginative combinations with other foods. Sample a bowl of *posole*, the hominy-based stew served with spicy pork that New Mexicans love. If you have a strong stomach and Teflon tastebuds, try the green chili stew. Prepare your mouth for a re-run of the Mt St Helens explosion.

Burrito Company, 111 Washington Ave, 982-4453. 'Tasty; not too chili-infested Mexican food at cheap prices. Varied clientele—many artists.' Open 7.30am–7pm Mon–Sat, Sun 10am–5pm. $2–$5.

Josie's Casa de Comida, 225 E Marcy, 983-5311. 'Very generous helpings of well-cooked Mexican food, $4–$6, popular with locals.' Open Mon–Fri 11am–4pm.

The Shed, 113½ E Palace in *circa* 1692 adobe, 982-9030. Good New Mexican lunches, crowded. Order their blue corn enchiladas and lemon souffle. Mon–Sat 11am–2.30pm.

Woolworth's Luncheonette, an adobe on the plaza, 6062 San Francisco, 982-1062. Breakfast for $3 and up. 'A real anachronism—decor and prices right out of the 19th century. Cheapest place in town; clean.' 'Don't miss the frito pie.'

OF INTEREST

NB: despite its compact size, Santa Fe can wear you out—its altitude is 7000 ft. Pace yourself.

The Plaza: city heart, popular gathering place since 1610, and terminus of both the Santa Fe and El Camino Real trails, the Plaza has seen bullfights, military manoeuvres and fiestas. Billy the Kid was exhibited here in chains after causing much trouble in the area. When the Kid vowed to kill territorial governor Lew

Wallace, the intended victim hid out in the **Palace of the Governors**, fronting the Plaza (while cloistered, Wallace began *Ben-Hur*). The oldest public (1610) building in America and seat of 6 regimes, the Palace, 827-6483, houses historical exhibits; Indian crafts for sale under its portal. Nearby is the **Museum of Fine Arts**, 827-4455. Both open daily 10am–5pm; $4 each.

Museum of International Folk Art, 706 Camino Lejo, 827-6350. See the Girard Collection, miniature displays of cultures from around the world. 'Well worth the walk.' Open daily 10am–5pm, $3.50. Call for special performing arts events.

Museum of Indian Arts and Culture, 710 Camino Lejo, 827-8000. 1st state museum devoted to Pueblo, Navajo, Apache Indians, with exhibits on history and ethnology from the Laboratory of Anthropology. Open daily 10am–5pm, $3.50. NB: At the first of these museums that you visit, pick up a 3-day pass for $5, which gets you entrance into all 4 museums.

Wheelwright Museum of the American Indian, 704 Camino Lejo, 982-4636. This is the best museum in the area, and practically the only one that is still 'free' (donation requested). Designed to resemble a traditional Navajo hogan, the Wheelwright contains the artistry of many Indian cultures. Rotating displays. The gift shop is designed as a replica of a turn-of-the-century Navajo Trading Post. Mon–Sat 10am–5pm, Sun 1pm–5pm.

Santa Fe Opera, 982-3855, one of America's truly great opera companies. Tickets for performances (July & Aug) run $18–$70; standing room, $6–$8. You can also take a 1-hr tour of the open-air **opera house**, set amid hills and white petunias 7 miles north of Santa Fe. Tours run daily at 1pm in July & Aug, $5; call the box office. NB: Unless you have a ticket for a performance or are part of a tour, you won't be allowed in.

A city of **churches** is Santa Fe. Among them: **El Cristo Rey**, noted for its size and stone reredos; the **San Miguel Chapel**, probably the oldest church in the US; the French Romanesque **St Francis Cathedral**, built by Archbishop Lamy (subject of Willa Cather's *Death Comes for the Archbishop*) to house La Conquistadora, a 17th century shrine to the Virgin Mary; the **Loreto Chapel**, a Gothic structure whose so-called 'miraculous' spiral staircase is of mild interest; and the charming **Sanctuario de Guadalupe**, where 18th century travellers stopped to give thanks after their hazardous journeys from Mexico City to Sante Fe.

Interesting neighbourhoods: Canyon Rd for its adobe art galleries, studios and shops; **Barrio de Analco**, across the Sante Fe River and originally settled by Indian labourers; **Sens** and **Prince Plazas**, good shopping areas.

Indian Market, annually every 3rd or 4th weekend in August (1994 20–21 Aug), 983–5220. The largest market of Indian arts and crafts in the world, with 1000 Indian artisans selling handmade jewellery, sculpture, pottery, baskets, beadwork, sand-painting, featherwork et al. Open 8am–6pm, but avoid the initial 8-deep crush in front of the stands by going after 11am. Besides artists' wares there are practical demonstrations, Pueblo dance showcases and a fashion show of traditional and modern Indian dress. NB: Beware the non-authentic tourist-trap vendors who set up stalls in hotels, parking lots and side streets. Free, but $3 to see the dances.

Fiesta de Santa Fe, early- to mid-Sept, begun in 1692, the oldest non-Indian celebration in the US; great community spirit. 'Zozobra or Old Man Gloom, a 40-ft dummy, is burned amidst dancing and fireworks. Most spectacular!' 'Fantastic.'

Los Alamos, 30 miles north of Santa Fe: **Los Alamos National Laboratory**, 667-5061. First atom bomb was built here. Museum, 667-4444, has replicas of 'Fat Man' and 'Little Boy' bombs. Open Tue–Fri 9am–5pm, Sat–Mon 1pm–5pm; free. 'Helpful, friendly staff. Fantastic scenery.'

Bandelier National Monument, ruins of Indian settlement. 'Need a car to get to, but well worth seeing.' Ask for directions in Santa Fe; easy to get to.

INFORMATION

Chamber of Commerce, 510 N Guadolupe, 983-7317. Very helpful with details of Pueblo Indian dances, ceremonials, etc. Good maps, booklets.
Visitors Center, Sweeney Convention Center, 984-6760 or (800) 777-2489.

TRAVEL

Greyhound, 858 St Michaels Dr, 471-0008. NB: bus station is 3 miles outside town.
Gray Line, 983-9491, picks up people where they are staying: Taos Indian Pueblo tour at 9am, $50, and Bandelier National Monument tour at 1pm, $35.
Car rental: Budget Rent-a-Car, 1946 Cerrillos, 984-8028.
Capital Village Cab, 24-hour taxi, 982-9990. Pick up coupons at hostel for discount.

TAOS Set against the rich palette of the crisp, white Sangre de Cristo Mountains, the earth tones of soaring Indian pueblo and the turquoise sky of northern New Mexico, Taos has long been a haven for artists and writers like Georgia O'Keeffe, John Fowles and D H Lawrence. Given its powerful attractions, naturally the town has become a little precious and more than a little expensive. But get to know its traditional Indian and Hispanic communities and you'll glimpse the real Taos still.

ACCOMMODATION

Abominable Snowmansion, PO Box 3271 in **Arroyo Seco**, 10 miles north of Taos, Rte 150, 776-8298. $14 AYH, $16 non-members; at the Teepee Village, several teepees with bunk accommodation ($10 AYH, $11.50 other). D–$38 (private room). Kitchen, pool table, games in main bldg.
Plum Tree, **Pilar** (15 miles south of Taos on Hwy 68), 758-4696. Plenty of diversions—in nature or in the hostel's cafe. Theatre and live music in summer. $9 AYH, $15 non-members; with bfast $12 AYH, $18 non-members. D–$38 (private room).
Camping: various free sites in the Carson National Forest, from 3 to 12 miles away.

OF INTEREST

NB: although Taos is small, its attractions are scattered, making a car very useful.
Kit Carson Museums, 758-0505. Three museums: **Kit Carson Home**, ½ blk E of Taos Plaza on Kit Carson Rd. Period rooms (1850s), Indian, gun and Mountain Man (how the fur-trappers lived) exhibits; **Martinez Hacienda**, 2 miles S of Taos on Ranchitos Rd, Hwy 240. A restored colonial fortress and living museum. Demonstrators show the Spanish way of life in New Mexico over the past 300 yrs; **Blumenschein Home**, 2 blks S of Taos Plaza on Ledoux St. Built circa 1780, the pioneer artist moved here in 1898 where he started Taos' art colony. Furnishings and collectables from around the world; Indian and Taos artists' work. Entry $3 for one museum, $5 for two, $7 for all three.
Art galleries. Best of local artists at **The Stables**, next to Kit Carson Park. For O'Keeffes, go to the **Gallery of the Southwest**. Navajo paintings of R C Gorman at the **Navajo Gallery** on Ledoux St.
Mission of St Francis of Assisi, 4 miles south. A masterpiece of the Spanish Colonial period, the mission has a sculptural quality beloved by painters from O'Keeffe on down. The interior suffers from over-restoration but do see the reredos and Ault's mysterious painting, *The Shadow of the Cross*. Check locally for open hours before setting out.
Millicent Rogers Museum, 4 miles north, 751-0808. $4, $3 students, daily, 9am–5pm, May through Oct, closed Mon other months. Fascinating collection of death carts and *santos* (carved saints) of the Penitentes, New Mexico's fanatical religious brotherhood. Still active, the Penitentes once practised flagellation and other mortifications during Holy Week.

Taos Pueblo, 1½ miles north. Best access via Hwy 64, 758-9593. This eye-satisfying 5-storey pueblo, punctuated with beehive ovens and bright *riatas* of curing corn and chilis, preserves an 1000-year-old architectural tradition. Its 200 families are equally traditional, having banned electricity, piped water, TV and other contrivances. Noted almost solely for their dancing and devotion to ceremonials, the Taos Indians celebrate numerous fiestas, the biggest being the 29–30 Sept Fiesta of San Geronimo (races, dancing). 'Craft market also with good prices.' Also of interest are the ruins of the old **Spanish Mission church**, burned by the Spanish in 1680 and again by the US army in 1847. Guided tours by request (tips).

Today visitors are tolerated 8am–5.30pm; private quarters not open to viewing. $5 per car, $2 per walker. Photography permit is $5 and you must also ask permission to take individuals' portraits. No cameras at ceremonial dances. Faust's Transportation, 758-3410, sends taxis from Taos to the pueblo for $7 one way. 'A spiritual experience—well worth it.'

INFORMATION/TRAVEL

Eight Northern Indian Pueblos Council, 852-4265, Main Church St, San Juan Pueblo, lies between Taos and Santa Fe on Rte 68; for info on all Pueblo activities and regulations.

Taos Chamber of Commerce, 1139 Paseo del Pueblo Sur (Rte 68), 758-3873 or (800) 732-8267.

Greyhound, at the Chevron Food-Mart, 1137 Paseo del Pueblo Sur, 758-1144. Closed from 1pm–4pm for a little siesta.

SILVER CITY Located in the southwest mining country, Silver City also sits in the Gila Wilderness, a wild and lovely terrain of blood-red gorges, ghost towns and Indian ruins. In this region, Geronimo eluded 8000 US Calvary troops for eight years. Amtrak and Greyhound go to Deming; from there take the shuttle to city centre (res. essential: (800) 522-0162), $10.

ACCOMMODATION

Bear Mt Guest Ranch, PO Box 1163, Silver City, NM 88062, 538-2538. A wonderful room/board ranch with a year-round calendar of nature and arts events led by its owners, from wildflower tours to painting expeditions. S–$48, D–$79 (includes 3 meals, private bath). Also housekeeping cottages available. Silver Stage Line comes to ranch.

Carter House Hostel, 101 N Cooper St, 388-5485. $11 AAIH, $14 non-members.

INDIAN GROUPS ELSEWHERE IN NEW MEXICO There are 19 Tewa-speaking Native American groups in all, called collectively the Rio Grande Pueblos. Among the most interesting of the Pueblos' cities is **Acoma**; the 'Sky City', 60 miles west of Albuquerque, occupies a huge and spectacular mesa, the ground so stony that the Indians had to haul soil 430 feet for their graveyard. Inhabited since AD 1075, the pueblo vies with Oraibi in Hopiland as oldest settlement in the US. Noted for high quality pottery with intricate linear designs. Photo fee and restrictions. **Santa Clara**, between Santa Fe and Taos, is famous for its black polished pottery. More outgoing and open to visitors than other Pueblos, the Santa Clarans have fewer restrictions on photography. This is an excellent place to take in the dancing at the late August festival. Furthest west of the pueblos is the **Zuñi**, which figured prominently in the Spanish conquest. Spurred greedily on by the lies of an advance scout, Coronado thought he had 'the seven golden cities of Cíbola' but instead found the Zuñi Pueblo. Renowned as silversmiths, stone craftsmen and dancers, the Zuñis still measure their wealth in horses. Camping available on their lands. One of few places where outsiders can watch the masked dances.

The **Jicarilla Apaches** in the northwest and the **Mescalero Apaches** in the southeast have numerous tourist facilities, including camping on their lands. Their ceremonies are very striking, especially the female puberty rites which take place during Fourth of July week. Non-Indians may respectfully watch the principal activities.

OKLAHOMA

Originally set aside as an Indian Territory, in 1893 Oklahoma was thrown open to settlers in one of the most fantastic landgrabs ever. One hundred thousand homesteaders impatiently lined up on its borders, and at the crack of a gun at noon, 16 September, raced across the prairie in buckboard, buggies, wagons and carts, on bicycles, horseback and afoot to lay claim to the 40,000 allotments drawn up by the federal government.

Some crossed the line ahead of time, giving Oklahoma its nickname, the Sooner State. The territory was admitted to the Union in 1907.

Apart from prairies, the state has generous forests and low rolling mountains in the east. Agriculture, oil and the aviation and aerospace industries bring in most of Oklahoma's revenue. Oklahoma City installed the world's first parking meters way back in 1935.

National Park: Platt

The area code for Oklahoma City and western Oklahoma is 405; for eastern Oklahoma and Tulsa it is 918.

OKLAHOMA CITY Oklahoma City was established in a single day when 10,000 landgrabbers showed up at the only well for miles around in what had till then been scorched prairie-land. The city has become an insurance centre for farming and other enterprises in the area and like other parts of the state got rich on oil. Six oil wells slurp away in the grounds of the capitol building.

ACCOMMODATION

Hotel Cline, 230 NW 10th and Hardy, 239-9632. S/D–$12. Check in before 10pm. 'Neat as a pin.'

Motel 6 West, 820 S Meridian Ave, 946-6662. S–$25, D–$34.

Motel 6, 5th and Walker, 4 blks from Greyhound, 235-7455. S–$25, D–$32.

YMCA, 125 NW 5th St, 232-6101. $13 a night; $53 a week + $5 key deposit. Men only. Pool, AC and full use of facilities.

FOOD

Steaks and cafeterias, that's what Oklahoma City is famous for. The best and cheapest of the former can be had near the stockyards at **Cattlemen's Cafe**, 1309 S Agnew, 236-0416, open 6am–10pm Sun–Thur; Fri–Sat 'til midnight.

Good **cafeterias** in the State Capitol building, the **Furr's** chain, and **Luby's** chain.

OF INTEREST

State Capitol, 2300 N Lincoln Blvd, 521-3356. Six derricks make politics pay; one of them is 'whipstocked' (drilled at an angle) to get at the oil beneath the Capitol, itself an unimpressive structure, one of the few state capitols without a dome. Open daily, 8am–7pm; guided tours 8am–3pm. Free.

National Cowboy Hall of Fame and Western Heritage Center, 1700 NE 63rd, 6 miles north of downtown along I-44, 478-2250. $6, open daily 8.30am–6pm summers, 9am–5pm winter. Sitting right on the Old Chisholm Trail, this complex, a joint venture by the 17 Western states, is magnificent. The art gallery includes many works by Russell, Remington, Schreyrogel, Bierstadt. 'Boring, and not worth $6.'

State Museum of the Oklahoma Historical Society, just south of the capitol at 2100 N Lincoln Blvd, 521-2491. Displays of Oklahoma history, from prehistoric Indians to the present. 'Interesting Indian relics.' Open Mon–Sat, 9am–5pm, both library and museum open till 8pm Mon. Free.

The **Kirkpatrick Omniplex**, 50th and Martin Luther King Ave, 427-5461, houses several museums and galleries: **Oklahoma Air Space Museum** has exhibits on the state's contribution to aviation and space; the **International Photography Hall of Fame Museum**, examples of work by leading photographers around the world. Also the **Center of American Indian**. $6 admission covers all museums; open Mon–Sat 9am–6pm, Sun noon–6pm in summer; slightly shorter hours weekdays in winter.

Only in America: **Enterprise Square, USA**, on the campus of Oklahoma Christian College, 2501 E Memorial Rd, 425-5030. A sort of Disneyland-for-capitalists extolling the virtues of good old fashioned Adam Smith-ism. See the 'World's Largest Functioning Cash Register' with its singing dollar bills, the 'Hall of Achievers' (yay!), the 'Great Talking Face of Government' (boo!) and the 'Time Tunnel' and 'Economic Arcade Game Room,' where you'll find out whether you have the stuff it takes to survive in an open-market economy. Open Mon–Sat 9am–5pm, Sun 1pm–4pm; $5.

Norman, home of **University of Oklahoma** (20,000 students), 30 mins from Oklahoma City. Student life dominates the town, so there's usually plenty to do. The university's housing dept is helpful in finding accommodation during the summer. The University of Oklahoma **Museum of Art**, 410 W Boyd, 325-3272, is worth a visit. Permanent collections of American, European, Oriental and African art. Open Tues–Fri 10am–4.30pm, thurs til 9pm; w/ends 1pm–4.30pm. Free

Oklahoma City Zoo/Aquaticus, 2101 NE 50th St, 424–3344. Open 9am–6pm, $4. Rated one of the top zoos in the nation with over 2000 animals from 500 species. Dolphin shows in the aquaticus $2 extra.

Indian City USA, near Anadarko, 65 miles SW of Oklahoma City on Highway 62, 247-5661. Authentic re-creation of Plains Indian villages, done with help of U Oklahoma Anthropology Dept. Dancing, demonstrations, ceremonies, camping, swimming. Also **Indian Hall of Fame**, etc. $7 for village, including museum. ($1 entry to museum if not on walking tour.)

INFORMATION

Oklahoma City Tourist Information Centers, Oklahoma Tourism and Recreation Dept, 500 Will Rogers Building, 521-2409 at Capitol; and at 5101 N I–35, 427-8491. Both open daily, 8am–5pm.

Oklahoma City Chamber of Commerce, 4 Santa Fe Plaza, 278-8912. Open 8am–4.30pm.

Norman Chamber of Commerce, 115 E Gray St, 321-7260. Open Mon–Fri, 8am–5pm.

Travelers Aid, 412 NW 5th, 232-5507. Also booth at airport.

TRAVEL

Greyhound, 427 W Sheridan, 235-6425. Open 24 hours; crummy area, but station has security guards (until 4am). Also used by MKO; compare schedules and prices.

Oklahoma Metro Area Transit, 300E California Blvd, 235-7433. 75¢ basic fare; runs 6am–7pm.

Yellow Cabs, 232-6161 in Ok. City; 329-3333 in Norman.

Will Rogers International Airport, 7100 Terminal Dr, 681-5311. No buses run directly there. Take the #11 from 10th & Robinson to 29th & Meridian, about 40 mins, from there take a cab, $5–$6; or take a cab from downtown, $14.

TULSA Once known as the 'oil capital of the world', Tulsa has slid technologically sideways to 'aerospace capital of . . . Oklahoma'. Its setting among rolling green hills on the Arkansas River is prettier than OKC but it's just as windy. (The whole state is notorious for wild weather.)

ACCOMMODATION

Motel 6, 5828 Skelly Dr, 445-0223. S–$23, D–$27, XP–$5.
YMCA, 515 S Denver, 583-6201. $11 plus $11 key deposit; full use of facilities. No reservations taken; men only.

FOOD

Williams Center, 2 blocks from Greyhound. 'Amazing shopping centre overlooking ice rink. Cheap breakfasts, better value than Greyhound.'
Both OKC and Tulsa have **Casa Bonitas**, 836-6464, 21st and Sheridan, a crazed mixture of Mexican village and dining area with waterfall, mariachis, puppets, dancers, etc. Open 11am–9.30pm. Good value, all-you-can-eat Mexican dinners; deluxe, $8.
Black-Eyed Pea, family style chain; 3 locations.
Po-Folks, 51st and Peoria in shopping centre, 749-6606. Open 11am–10pm Sun–Thur; Fri–Sat 'til 11pm.
Heritage House, 3637 S Memorial, 663-9410. All-you-can-eat smorgies, $6, $7.25 with unlimited drinks.

OF INTEREST

Creek Council Oak Tree, 1750 S and Cheyenne, 585-1201. Known as 'Tulsa's First City Hall', the site of the Council Fire used by the first group of Creeks to come from Alabama to Oklahoma in 1828.
Tulsa County Historical Society Museum, 1400 N Gilcrease Museum Rd, 585-5520. Collection of historic objects: unique photographs, rare historical books and letters, settlement period furniture. Open Tue–Thur and Sat 11am–4pm; Sun 1pm–4pm. There is another branch downtown with rotating, thematic exhibits: the **Philtower**, 427 S Boston Ave, open 9am–5pm Mon–Fri. Both free.
Thomas Gilcrease Institute of American History and Art, 1400 Gilcrease Museum Rd, 596-2700. The treasurehouse of Western art, plus 250,000 Indian artefacts, interesting maps and documents like the original instructions for Paul Revere's ride, the first letter written from the North American continent by Chris Columbus' son, Aztec codex, etc. Donations encouraged; Mon–Sat 9am–5pm, Sun 1–5pm.
Tsa-La-Gi Village, 70 miles SE of Tulsa near **Tahlequah**, 456-6007. Replica of a 17th century Cherokee village staffed by Cherokee who portray village life of their ancestors, including braves, kids and villagers; 45-min tour $3.50. Open mid-May through late August.
Cherokee National Museum, also in **Tahlequah**, 456-6007. Open Tue–Sat 10am–8pm, Sun 1pm–5pm, Mon 10am–5pm. $2.75. Outdoor drama, the *Trail of Tears*, performed June through August, 8.30pm in a lovely amphitheatre, telling the story of the tragic march 1838–39 in which 4000 of 16000 Cherokees died of hunger, disease and cold, and were forced to begin life anew in the territory that would become the state of Oklahoma. Haunting music and dance. Tickets $9.
Oklahoma in general and Tulsa in particular are in Bible Belt country, and here you'll find **Oral Roberts University**. Founded by the evangelist after a vision from God so specific that he was told what style to build the place in, ORU looks like a fifties version of the future, as seen in those classic B movies.
When you are leaving Oklahoma, go by way of **Quapaw**, in the northeast corner

of the state where Oklahoma cuts a corner with Kansas and Missouri. In this area, which some call the 'Bermuda Triangle of the prairie', is the **Tri-State Spooklight**, described as a 'weird, bobbing light' along State Line Road. Scientific explanations (light refraction from an unknown source, underground quartz crystals) have been given for this phenomenon. But everyone knows the spooklight is really caused by UFOs on their way to North Dakota.

TRAVEL/INFORMATION
Dept of Tourism and Recreation, US 66 and I-44 E of Tulsa nr Will Rogers Turnpike Gate, 256-6748. Open 7.30am–6pm in summer; 8.30am–5pm winter.
Convention and Visitors Bureau, 616 S Boston, 585-1201. Open Mon–Fri 8am- 5pm.
Greyhound, 4th and S Detroit Sts, 584-4428.
Tulsa Transit, 582-2100. Basic fare 75¢, runs 5am–6pm. Has 'ozone alert' days in summer when all buses are free.
Tulsa International Airport, just off Hwy 11, about 6 miles NW of downtown. During the week take #13 'Independence-Barton' bus from 4th & Denver, 75¢. Weekends and after bus hours take a cab, about $12.
Yellow Checker Cabs, 582-6161.

TEXAS

Texans may have had to pass the Stetson of 'biggest state' to Alaska but they haven't lost their talent for beer-drinking, braggadocio, barbeque and making Dallas-sized mountains of money. This state has the size, colour and raw energy of a Texas longhorn steer, and it'll wear you out if you try to cover it. As the old jingle has it, 'the sun is riz, the sun is set, and we ain't out of Texas yet'! Better to focus on its two cities of any charm—San Antonio and Austin—and perhaps the tropical coast around Galveston or Corpus Christi.

Always intensely political, Texas has seen six regimes come and five go, from Spanish, French and Mexican, to a brief whirl as the Republic of Texas and finally Confederate. Through it all, Texas remains good ole boy country, a terrain of hardbitten little towns and hard-edged cities whose icons are Willie Nelson, the Dallas Cowboys and LBJ. In recent years, with the downturn in oil prices, the state's energy-based economy has been depressed.

The Texan scenery may vary from desert to mountains to vast rolling plains but everywhere in the summer months there is one constant—the heat. Temperatures of 90–100 degrees are the norm and in Houston, especially, there is also high humidity—'Gulf weather' it's called.

National Parks: Big Bend
Guadelupe Mountains

Texas telephone area codes: Dallas, 214; El Paso, 915; Ft Worth, 817; Galveston, 409; Houston, 713; San Antonio, 210; Corpus Christi & Austin, 512.

SAN ANTONIO About 75 miles south of Austin sits thoroughly Hispanic San Antonio, the only Texas city to possess a proper downtown, much less one with attractions worth walking to. The action centres round the San Antonio River and its pleasant green Riverwalk, where fiestas, music and fun of one sort or another take place year-round.

This city of 800,000 began in 1691 as an Indian village with the wacky name of 'drunken old man going home at night', which the Spaniards bowdlerised to San Antonio. Despite the early Spanish (and later Mexican) presence in Texas, settlement lagged and authorities began admitting Americans. By the 1830s, six of seven inhabitants were Anglo and the resultant friction caused skirmishes and ultimately the Battle of the Alamo. During its 13-day seige, 200 Americans gallantly fought to the last man against the 5000-man Mexican army of Santa Ana. Afterwards, the rallying cry of 'Remember the Alamo' helped Sam Houston and his troops defeat the Mexicans and establish the Republic of Texas, 1836–1845.

ACCOMMODATION

Motel 6, 5522 N Panam, I-35 and Rittiman, 661-8791. S–$34, D–$41, TV, AC, pool.
B&B Hosts of San Antonio, 166 Rockhill, San Antonio, TX 78209; 824-8036. Finds rooms in private homes, S–$36–$56, D–$59 up.
El Tejas Motel, 2727 Roosevelt Ave, 533-7123. Close to missions, 3 miles from downtown. Bus #42 to door. S/D–$27–$35. AC, TV, swimming pool.
Motel 6, at Starlight Terrace Exit off I-35, 650-4419, and at North WW White Rd off I-10, 333-1850, D–$38.
San Antonio International Hostel/Guest House (AYH), 621 Pierce St, 223-9426. Private rooms with AYH discount, S/D–$33. Dorm rooms $14, $17 non-members. From bus station take #15 bus east from Houston St to Carson St, walk 2 blks west or take #11 to Grayson St at Pierce.
Travelers Hotel, 220 Broadway, 226-4381. Downtown. S–$29, D–$34, +$2 key deposit.

FOOD

NB: San Antonio, with its 52 per cent Latin population, has far better Mexican food than most Mexican border towns.
Along Riverwalk: **El Palenque Mexican Food**, 9300 Wurzbach, 593–0180. Open 24 hrs, specials change weekly. Prices $12 and below.
Henry's Puffy Taco, 3202 W Woodlawn, 432-7341. Open Mon–Sat 8am–8pm, $5–$7, specials $4.
Hung Fong Chinese Restaurant, 3624 Broadway, 822-9211. The oldest Chinese restaurant in San Antonio, $4–$10.
Kangaroo Court, 512 Riverwalk, 224-6821. 'Does Bass ale at $3 for glass of very cold beer!' Seafood and sandwiches. Dinners $8 up.
Maverick Cafe, 6868 San Pedro, 822-9611. Chinese and Mexican food. $4. 'One of a kind.'
Mi Tierra, 218 Produce Row in **El Mercado**, 225-1262. Open 24 hours, dynamite Mexican food. Order the *Chalupa compuesta* and the supercheap *caldo* (soup), $4–$6.

OF INTEREST

The Alamo. Texas' most visited tourist attraction, the restored 1718 presidio-mission is free and open daily 9am–5.30pm, Sun from 10am, 222-1693. Mural inside of heroes Bowie, Crockett and Travis. Pass up the slide show across the way—ear-splitting and redundant. 'Boring—don't bother.'
Also in Old San Antonio: **San Fernando Cathedral**, main Plaza, where Alamo heroes are buried. Behind city hall is the beautiful **Spanish Governor's Palace**, Military Plaza, 224-0601, open daily, Mon–Sat 9am–5pm, Sun 10am–5pm, $1.
La Villita, between Nueva and S Alamo Sts, downtown restoration of the city's early nucleus, with cool patios, banana trees, crafts demos and sales.

Paseo del Rio or **Riverwalk**. The jade green river is echoed by greenery on both sides, cobblestone walks, intimate bridges at intervals, and lined with restaurants and bars with good Happy Hours and late hours. A civic as well as tourist focal point. 'Free lunch, evening concerts in summer.' 'Free dancing along the Riverwalk.'
River Boats—pick up across from the Hilton, and for $2 will take you on a 35–40 minute tour of the river.
Brackenridge Park, 3 miles NE of downtown. Take bus #8. Two art museums, free Japanese sunken gardens, a skyride, riding stables, and the San Antonio Zoo, 734-7184, $6—'worth the money but packed'. Daily 9.30am–6.30pm summers.
Hemisfair Park. The free (donation requested) **Institute of Texan Cultures**, 226-7651, has displays on 26 ethnic groups. The view from the 750 ft **Tower of the Americas**, 299-8617, is worth the $2.50 fee. San Antonio has 5 missions, counting the Alamo. Unless you're mission-mad, skip the others and see **Queen Mission San Jose** (take the hourly S Flores bus marked 'San Jose Mission'). Interesting granary, Indian building, barracks. Try to time your visit for Sun mass when the mariachis play. Free.
El Mercado, typical Mexican market with stalls of fresh fruits and meats, cheap clothes and crafts from Mexico. At junction of Santa Rosa and Commerce Sts.
San Antonio Museum of Art, 200 W Jones Ave, off Broadway, 829-7262. Housed in a restored turn-of-the-century brewery, the museum now exhibits Greek and Roman antiquities, Mexican folk art, 18th–20th century US art and Asian art. $4 adults (NB: steep surcharges on some temporary exhibits). Open Mon–Sat 10am–6pm (through Aug; 'til 5pm in winter), Sun noon–6pm, Tue 'til 9pm and free 3pm–9pm (excluding surcharged exhibitions).
Sea World of Texas, 15 miles NW of downtown, at Ray Ellison Dr and Westover Hills Blvd, (800) 722-2762. $170 million park—aquariums, flamingoes, waterfowl, a 12.5 acre lake for water skiers and, since 1991, two water rides (log flume and river raft). Open daily in summer 10am–10pm, closed Dec–Feb. $26, students 20% off.

ENTERTAINMENT

Mexican Festival, 3rd week in Sept, Riverwalk.
Arneson Theater, 299-8610. Showcases everything from flamenco to jazz to country; river separates you from stage. **Fiesta Noche del Rio** variety show is $8, June–August, Fri, Sat at 8.30pm.
Numerous fiestas, music events and blowouts (most free) throughout the year; during St Patrick's week, San Antonians dye both their beer and their river green!
Floore Country Store, 14464 Old Bandera Rd, btwn Old and New Hwy 16, 695-8827. An old Willie Nelson hangout.
Lerma's, 1602 N Arazmora, 732-0477. Conjunto music (Mexican accordian dance music).

INFORMATION

Visitors Information, 317 Alamo Plaza, 299-8155, or (800) 447-3372, Mon–Fri, 8.30am–6pm; w/ends, 8.30am–5pm.

TRAVEL

Amtrak, 1174 E Commerce St, 223-3326. For *Sunset Limited* LA–New Orleans–Miami and *Texas Eagle* to Chicago routes.
Greyhound, 500 N St Mary's St, 270-5861. Open 24 hours.
San Antonio International Airport, 821-3411. About 5 miles north of downtown; take #12 'Blanco-Airport' bus from Commerce & St Mary's, 40¢. Last bus to airport 8.30pm, last from 9.15pm.
VIA, 227-2020. Runs local buses, basic fare 40¢. Also runs the El Centro old-fashioned trollies that circle downtown, 10¢.

AUSTIN Capital city, named after the state's 'founding father', but Richard Linklater made his film, *Slacker,* here for a reason. With its laidback attitude it doesn't seem like 'real' Texas but it does seem like the most enjoyable city in the state. Truly an oasis, socially and culturally, in the middle of a desert, it has a huge student population that adds a vigour to the place. Austin is *the* place to go to see bands, hang out, drink too much and party hard. It's also, strangely enough, a centre for bats. In summer, a colony of the little critters roosts under the Congress Ave Bridge. Every evening, at around 8pm, a crowd gathers to see them all leave to feed.

ACCOMMODATION

Congress St is cheap hotel/motel row.
Austin International Hostel (AYH), 2200 S Lakeshore, 444-2294. $10, $13 non-members. 'Good facilities.' Nr Barton Springs, pool, laundry.
Motel 6, I-35 N Rundberg Ln Exit, 837-9890. S–$31, D–$36, XP–$3.
The Castilian, 2323 San Antonio St, 478-9811. Dorm-style rooms S–$32, D–$27. 1 June–17 Aug only. Private residence hall, coed, overlooking University. Cafe, AC, pool; very nice. Bus stop ½ blk.
San Jose Motel, 1316 S Congress St, 444-7322. S/D–$25, + $3 key deposit.

FOOD

Great pickings, but you'd better like Texas BBQ, Mexican food and Texas chili. Lots of student hangouts along Guadalupe.
The Filling Station, 801 Barton Springs Rd, 477-1022. Beer from a gas pump; get ethyl-burgers or a gasket platter. 'Try the high-octane speciality drink, the Tune-up, guaranteed to clean out your spark plugs!'
Furr's Cafeteria, 4015 S Lamar, 441-7825. Two other branches in Austin. All-U-Can-Eat, $6.
Hickory Street Bar and Grille, 800 Congress Ave, 477–8968. Array of speciality food bars (salad, soup, potato, bread and sundae); $1–$5, or All-U-Can-Eat for $5.50. 'Austin's best ½ pound hamburgers.'
La Fuentes's Mexican Food, 6507 Circle S Rd, 442–9925. Deli lunch specials, closed Tues. Average plate $5.
Richard Jones Pit, 2304 S Congress, 444-2272, serves best BBQ in town.
Threadgill's, 6416 N Lamar, 451-5440. Run by Eddie Wilson, a founding father of Austin's music scene, this soul-food joint has free seconds on everything and was an early stomping ground of the original screamer, Janis Joplin. Eddie plays the place down, 'I've got easily the best restaurant in the history of the globe'.
GM Steakhouse, 1908 Guadalupe, 476-0755 serves T-bone and sirloin steaks.
Texas Chili Parlor, 1409 Lavaca St, 472-2828. World class chili joint and saloon, also serves $1.50 screwdrivers and Bloody Marys on weekends.
Texas Showdown Saloon, 2610 Guadalupe, 472–2010. Small menu; 'Texas-style' atmosphere; average price $3.

OF INTEREST

Capitol building. Free tours leave from Rotunda, unrestricted entry to public areas, including galleries from which you can observe debates. Unfortunately closed for restoration until '95.
O Henry Museum, 409 E 5th St, 472-1903, free. Personal effects of the popular short-story writer who lived in Austin from 1885–1895. Wed–Sun noon–5pm.
University of Texas, Guadalupe and 24th St, north of Capitol. Huge, rich, highly social school. Has several museums and the **LBJ Library** at 2313 Red River Rd, 482-5279. Free, open daily 9am–5pm. A/V displays, replica of the Oval Office and tapes of LBJ's twang. LBJ's birthplace, home, ranch and grave are west of Austin, in and around Johnson City.
Harry Ransom Center, 21st & Guadalupe on UT campus, 471-8944. Houses a

good art museum, one of the world's four copies of the Gutenburg Bible, lots of Evelyn Waugh and the personal libraries of Virginia Woolf, James Joyce and the devil himself, Aleister Crowley. Open Mon–Sat 9am–5pm, Sun 1am–5pm; free.
Daughters of the Republic of Texas Museum, Anderson Lane, free. Indispensable museum for anyone interested in Texas or Civil War history.
Barton Springs, Zilker Park, 476-9044. Open-air swimming hole (not a chlorinated pool) fed by underground springs. 'Reached by lovely 40-min riverside walk, beautiful setting.' $2.25, $2 during the week, 'but if you smile and ask for the loan of a swimsuit you might get in free'.
Also **Hamilton Pool**—a favourite with Texan students (on Texas 71 West), 264-2740. 60 ft waterfall cascades into a jade green pool. Monitored—closed if bacteria levels are too high. $5 parking fee.

ENTERTAINMENT
Austin is a major music centre; check *The Daily Texan* and the free *Austin Weekly Chronicle* to see who's playing where. Guadalupe Ave, called The Drag, is a hot spot for student and non-student activity; but for clubs it has to be 6th St, wall-to-wall music and a great Halloween street party.
Austin City Limits is an excellent nationwide TV country show broadcast weekly on public television in the US, 471-4811.
Antone's, 2915 Guadalupe, 474-5314. $8–$15 cover charge admits you to a fine blues club.
The Austin Opry House, 200 Academy Dr, 443-7037. Owned by Willie Nelson, gets the top country acts.
Broken Spoke, 3201 S Lamar, 442-6189. Authentic C&W dive with live music, Texas two-step dancing, chicken-fried steaks. Cover, Wed–Fri, $3; w/e, $6.
Continental Club, 1315 S Congress, 441-2444, student dance hangout. Cover $3–$8.
Liberty Lunch, 405 W 2nd, 477-0461. Has all sorts of good touring bands.

INFORMATION
Convention and Visitors Bureau, 201 E 2nd St, 478-0098 or (800) 888-8AUS. Open daily; 125 pieces of free literature on the area. State Tourist Information Center, in Reagan Building, south foyer, Mon–Sat 9am–5pm, Sun noon–5pm, 463–8586 or (800) 452-9292.

TRAVEL
Amtrak, 250 N Lamar Blvd, 476-5684.
Greyhound, 916 E Koenig Lane, 458-3823.
Capital Metro, 474-1200. Local bus company; basic fare 50c. From 6th & Vrazos take #1 bus outbound to reach UT campus.
Robert Mueller Municipal Airport, 4600 Manor Rd. About 5 miles NE of downtown; take bus #20 from 6th & Vrazos, 50¢; last bus out 11.50pm.

DALLAS/FORT WORTH Big D pushes culture but its finest achievements are Neiman-Marcus, the glittering emporium of the conspicuous consumer, and Tolbert's Chili Parlor, where the serious chiliheads go to eat a bowl of red before they die. 'Dallas is a hard-nosed business environment with entertainment geared to the relaxing businessman.' One of the world's largest permanent trade fairs is located here. The city seems to go on forever and attractions are not centralized. If you are not travelling by car, you may want to visit a city more accommodating to the pedestrian.

An airport larger than Manhattan is the umbilical cord linking Dallas with **Forth Worth**, its cattle- and agriculture-based sister city. Fort Worth, surprisingly, has a lot more of interest to see and do, with a number of top-

notch museums and art collections, most free and conveniently clumped in Amon Carter Square. As befits an overgrown cowtown, the honky-tonk country and western scene is alive and well, more cowboy than urban. Forty miles and a heap of freeways separate these two behemoths, so don't plan to lodge in one and visit the other.
Do remember that Dallas (214) and Fort Worth (817) have different telephone area codes. Arlington also uses 817.

ACCOMMODATION

Huge caveat: budget accommodation in either city does not exist in the downtown areas. We suggest you rent a car and schlepp out to one of the 9 Motel 6s ringing the area, or make your visit a brief one.
In Dallas: Allstar Inn, 4220 Independence Dr, 296-3331. S–$26, D–$31, 3 or 4 persons, $37.
B&B Texas Style, 4224 W Red Bird Lane, Dallas, TX 75237; 298-8586. Rooms in private homes S–$45 up, D–$50 up.
Market Center Boulevard Inn, 2026 Market Center Blvd, 748-2243. D–$60, XP–$5, TV, bath, pool.
Red Crown Inn, US 80 at Town East Blvd, 557-1571. S–$30, D–$34.
In Forth Worth: YWCA, 512 W 4th St, (817) 332-6191. Women only, S–$10 + $5 key deposit. 10 blocks from bus station.

FOOD

Farmers' Produce Market, 748-2082, 1010 South Pearl Expressway, downtown, open 6am–7pm. Best places to get fresh produce from local farms.
Mario's Chiquita, 4514 Travis, ground floor of Travis Walk, 521-0092. Mexican food, popular with Dallasites. 'Delicious, excellent service, not costly.' ($3.95–$9.95; specialities change weekly.)
Tolbert's Chili Parlor, 350 N St Paul St, corner of Bryant St, 953-1353. Open Mon–Sat, a primo chili shrine.
In Fort Worth: Paris Coffee Shop, 704 W Magnolia, 335-2041. Home-baking prepared daily, all under $6. 'The best breakfast and lunches in town.'
Under the Tower Restaurant, 5228 Camp Bowie, 731-6051. Chicken-fried steaks, burgers, sandwiches; $2–$6.
Pink Poodle Coffee Shop, 2516 NE 28th St, 624-1027. Homebaked pastries. Meals $4–$10, open 24 hrs.

OF INTEREST

You have probably seen the Zapruder footage so often that there will be no problem in retracing the route that **John F Kennedy** took to his death on 22 Nov 1963. He was driven on Main to Houston and Elm where Lee Harvey Oswald is alleged to have fired the shot from the sixth floor of the **Texas School Book Depository**. Now a museum to the Kennedy life and legacy, it is easily reachable from the Greyhound station during a rest stop. Open Mon–Fri 10am–7pm, w/ends 10am–6pm, $4. 'Very moving and sensitive.' Overlooking the scene is an **obelisk**. A Philip Johnson-designed **Cenotaph** is on Main St at Market. JFK spent his last night on this earth in the **Fort Worth Hyatt Regency**.
Architecture: both the **Hyatt Regency** and **Reunion Tower** at 300 Reunion Blvd get high marks: 'best things in Dallas', 'especially beautiful at sunset.' There is an observation deck on the 50th floor of the Tower, 651-1234, $2, a good way to see the whole city. Also worth a look is the c.1914 **Union rail station**, connected to the tower by underground walkway. The **Adolphus Hotel**, Commerce and Field, was built by a brewer and has a 40-ft beer bottle on top, which serves as a closet for a 19th floor suite.
Neiman-Marcus Dept Store, Main and Ervay. Of it, Lucius Beebe said: 'Dallas, for all its oil, banks, insurance wouldn't exist without Neiman-Marcus. It would be Waco or Wichita, which is to say: nothing.'

West End Market Place, off Houston St. Shops, galleries, eateries, and dance clubs.
Dallas Museum of Art, 1717 N Harwood at Ross, 922-1200. With adjacent sculpture garden. Some pre-Colombian works. Tues–Wed 11am–4pm, Thurs–Fri 11am–9pm, w/ends 11am–5pm.
Sport. Football is the main religion in Dallas. Texas Stadium on the Carpenter Freeway is home to '93 Superbowl champions, the **Cowboys**. Call 579-4800 for ticket availabilities. The **Texas Rangers** play in between the two cities in Arlington.
Six Flags Over Texas, 20 miles west of Dalls in Arlington, 640-8900. Whopping admission fee of $27 includes all rides and shows. Open daily mid-May to mid-Sept; weekends thereafter. The original of this ever expanding chain, the six flags referring to the six regimes that Texas has seen. Especially nauseating is the 'Texas Cliffhanger', a 10 second free-fall from a 128 ft tower and 'Flashback' a looping rollercoaster with fast forward and reverse. The showpiece is a huge wooden frame coaster, the 'Texas Giant', voted by those in the know the world's best. Also 5 hours of air-conditioned shows.
Ft Worth: Amon Carter Square: houses four free museums: the **Amon Carter Museum**, 738-1933, with its splendid Western Art Collection of Russells and Remingtons; the **Kimbell Art Museum**, 332-8451, itself an architectural tour de force by Louis Kahn, housing Oriental, pre-Columbian and late Renaissance works; the **Museum of Modern Art**, 738-9215; includes works by Andy Warhol, and the **Museum of Science and History**, 1501 Montgomery St, 732-1631, with sophisticated exhibits, and science movies in the Omni Theater, $5.50 adults.
Fort Worth Stockyards area, along Exchange Ave and N Main St, on North side. Pungent and still active with Monday cattle auctions (free viewing). 'Original stalls and railway exist, storefronts and boardwalks renovated. Gives a feeling of the past.' Every Fri pm, Sat and Sun, arts and crafts market, Stockyards Market Place, by Coliseum on Plaza.
Billy Bob's Texas, Fort Worth Stockyards, 624-7117, the world's largest honky-tonk, with 42 bars, 3.5 acres of dance floor. Fri and Sat at 9pm and 10pm there is live bull riding. Headliners at weekends; local bands during week, open nightly 11am–2am (Sun noon–2am). You can atone for your hangover at the **Cowboy Church** at the **Stockyards Hotel**, corner of Main and Exchange, Sun at 11am.
Just outside of Fort Worth in **Plano** is **South Fork Ranch**, from the *Dallas* TV series, 442-4868. No longer tours of the house or oil rig, but free to view from outside.
Wet 'n' Wild, I-30 btwn Dallas and Fort Worth, exit Texas 360N, 264-3356. (See 'Amusement Parks' box.)
Frontiers of Flight Museum, Love Field, 2nd floor, 350-1651. Collection of aviation artefacts including the fur parka as worn by Adm Richard E Byrd in 1929 on his first flight to the North Pole. Open Mon–Sat 10am–5pm, Sun 1pm–5pm, $2 adults.

INFORMATION

Dallas Convention and Visitors Bureau, Renaissance Building, 1201 Elm St, 746-6600. Walk-in office at 1303 Commerce St, opposite the Adolphus Hotel.
Fort Worth Convention and Visitors Bureau Information Center, 123 E Exchange, (817) 624-4741. At the Stockyards.

TRAVEL

Dallas: Amtrak, Union Station, 400 S Houston, 653-1101. The bars upstairs in terminal also worth a visit—cheap, and wonderful architecture.'
Greyhound, Commerce at Lamar, (800) 231–2222. Open 24 hours.
DART, 979-1111, The local buses, 75¢.
Dallas-Fort Worth International Airport, between the two cities. Take #26 bus from Hines St downtown; at Parkland Hospital change to #300 'DFW-N Irving'. Free DFW shuttle will do the rest, and all for just 75¢. Or take a Super Shuttle, (817) 329-2000, from one of the main downtown hotels for $10 o/w.

Dallas Lovefield Airport, in the north of the city, take #39 'Lovefield' bus from one of the blue bus stops on Commerce.
Fort Worth: Amtrak, 15th and Jones Sts, 870-1112.
Greyhound, 901 Commerce St, 429-3089. Open 24 hours.
To get to DFW airport, take a Super Shuttle from major hotels, about $12.

HOUSTON The newer skyscrapers that crowd Houston's skyline have sleek skins of black sun-reflecting glass, the same material used for astronaut helmet visors. Seems appropriate, since this city of 1.6 million is inextricably linked with NASA and the first moon landing.

But space money is petty cash compared to Houston's real wealth, which comes from oil refineries and its port activities. A city of scattered satellite nodes, Houston has developed unconstrained by zoning—so it seems to go on for ever. Unless you have an air-conditioned car, ample time and money, skip humid and expensive Houston: ''Houston's wealth has taken a dive as the oil market has gone downhill. It is a huge modern city and has hardly any attractions. It is probably the most boring city I've been to. The tremendous humidity makes it even worse.' 'No car, no roller skates? Forget Houston!' 'Downtown is dead!'

ACCOMMODATION
Houston International AYH Hostel, 5302 Crawford, 523-1009. $10.25 AYH, $13.25 non-members, incl tax. 'Friendly, clean and efficient with AC.' Laundry.
Houston Downtown YMCA, 1600 Louisiana St, Houston, TX 77002, 659-8501. S-$16 + $5 key deposit. 'Basic.' Has cafeteria. 'Usually full by noon.' Must reserve.
Houston Hostel, 5530 Hillman, 926-3444. $7 per night, with lockers and a bike the owner will lend out. Laundry facilities. From downtown bus terminal (4 miles), take bus #36 to Lawndale and Dismuke. Call first.
Space Center AYH, 2242 West Bay Area Blvd, Friendswood, (713) 996-0323. $11, $14 non-members. 3–4 miles from NASA. 'Very friendly and helpful.'

FOOD
Lots of good places, most totally inaccessible without a car.
Downtown: Glatzmaier's Seafood Market, 809 Congress on Old Market Square, 523-6572. Incredible, messy feasts of gumbo, crab, crawfish. Order a 'New Orleans po' boy'—massive bun stuffed with Gulf oysters and shrimp.
J Putty's Pizza, 5 Greenway Plaza, 626-4560 and 500 Dallas, 951-9369.
Otto's BBQ, 5502 Memorial Dr, 864-2573. Serving best ribs in town since 1963. Open 11am-9pm Mon–Sat.

OF INTEREST
NASA-LBJ Space Center, 25 miles south via I-45, 244-2100. Limited bus service (#245), 6 hr Gray Line Tour, 223-8800, costs $29, leaving downtown 10am daily. 'Cheaper to Rent-a-Heap, 977-7771, and take your time.' Also, 'hitching is worst I've ever come across, took us 2 hrs to get a lift'. Centre open daily 9am–7pm, $10. Once there, report at Building 2 for brochure to wander about on your own (see spacecraft, shuttle trainer, moon rocks, NASA films). Or take guided tour: 'No need to book Mission Control tours. First come, first served basis.' 'Very exciting seeing Mission Control in action. We watched a test run for the next shuttle mission.' 'Very informative.'
Astrodome, 799-9500, south of downtown. The first and still one of the largest indoor stadia in the world, modestly called 'Taj Mahal', 'Eighth Wonder', etc, in its literature. Tours $4, 3 times daily (except Sun), obligatory when no event. More worthwhile to combine a visit with a **Houston Astros** baseball game or other

happening (from dog shows to dirt-bike races). Cheapest seats in the pavilion ($4, purchased day of game) but also: 'We recommend $5 Upper Reserve seats, seven levels up, behind home base.' Take #15 bus from Main St.

Astroworld, opposite A-Dome, 799-8404. Six Flags clone with 100 rides, $26, open Apr–Labor Day, varying hours; thereafter w/ends only.

Port of Houston. Now that a deep channel runs 50 miles south to the Gulf of Mexico, Houston is a major port. From the observation platform at Wharf 9 you can watch huge ships in the Turning Basin. 1½-hr boat trips, 670-2416, available Tue–Sun. A free look at the bayou and a stunning perspective of the skyline. Book well ahead in summer.

Museum of Fine Arts, 1001 Bissonet between S Main and Montrose Blvd, 526-1361. Exhibition wing designed by Mies Van der Rohe. Renaissance art plus renowned Hogg collection of 65 paintings, watercolours by Frederick Remington. Open Tue–Sat 10am–5pm, Thur 'til 9pm (free all day Thur), Sun 12.15pm–6pm. $3, $1.50 students.

Hermann Park. Zoo, planetarium and Museums of Natural and Medical Science. **Zoo's** strong suit is a macabre bat colony. You're allowed to see them quaff their daily blood—fascinating, repellant. Entry to Zoo $2.50; 525-3300. **Natural Science Museum** has moon-landing equipment.

Sam Houston Park, downtown at Allen Parkway and Bagby St, 655-1912. Nice melange of historic Greek Revival, Victorian, log cabin and cottage against a canyon of office buildings. Daily guided tours $6, $4 students. Not far away is **Tranquillity Park** at Bagby and Walker, named in honour of lunar landings. 'Truly an oasis in the desert.'

Rothko Chapel, 3900 Yupon, in Montrose area, 524-9839. A multi-faith chapel, its walls bedecked with Rothko's exercises in controlled simplicity. Open daily 10am–6pm.

ENTERTAINMENT

Miller Outdoor Theatre, Hermann Park, 520-3290. Free symphony, ballet, plays, drama and musicals in summer. 'Get there 30 minutes early for good position.'

Astrodome (see Of Interest) also features rock shows. Huge video screens afford a good view. 'During intermission girls often do impromptu strips (really!) when the video camera points at them.' Feb sees the Rodeo and Livestock Show, (naturally) the world's largest.

TRAVEL/INFORMATION

Amtrak, 902 Washington Ave, 224-1577, near to the main post office.

Greyhound, 2121 S Main St, (800) 231-2222. Open 24 hours but not in the greatest area.

Metro Transit Authority, 635-4000. Local buses, basic fare 85¢, express $1.20, free transfers. Pretty good coverage within the 'loop' of I-610.

Houston Intercontinental Airport (HIA), 25 miles north of downtown. Take Metro bus #102 on Travis going north; last bus out 7pm, last into downtown 7.20pm; $1.20. Out of bus hours, catch an Airport Express bus leaving from next door to Hyatt Regency on Louisiana, leaves every half hour, $13.

Convention and Visitors Bureau, 801 Congress across from Market Square, 227-3100. Mon–Fri 8.30am–5pm.

GALVESTON History rich, hurricane prone Galveston was once headquarters for pirate Jean LaFitte, who liked its 32 miles of sandy beaches (so handy for burying bullion). Houston's ship channel eventually siphoned off the big shipping business, leaving Galveston at its architectural peak: a resplendent little city of scarlet oleanders, nodding palms and fine 19th century mansions. Come here to gorge on bay shrimp, and imbibe the placid, slightly decayed Southern feeling of the place.

Unfortunately, the beach here isn't as fine as those further to the south. Nearby oil wells and refineries pollute the water with annoying globs of tar, and the shore is hard and flat. It reminds you of a parking lot by the seashore. Camping is permitted in the state park. Access via causeway and by free ferry from Port Bolivar to the East.

OF INTEREST

Texas Seaport Museum, Pier 21 at end of Kempner (22nd) St, 763-3037. Home to *Elissa*, a Scottish-built square-rigged sailing ship restored to its 1877 condition. Open daily 9.30am–5.30pm, $5.

Some of the **architecture** worth seeing: **Ashton Villa**, 24th and Broadway, 762-3933, an elegantly restored 1859 Italianate mansion. Tour includes slide show about the 1900 hurricane that claimed 5000–7000 lives, $2.50. **The Bishop's Palace**, 762-2475, 1402 Broadway, extravagant 1886 home, $3.50. **The Strand** contains a fine concentration of 19th C iron front buildings.

'Rollerskate', bike rental shops on Seawall Blvd. Useful shower/changing facilities on Stewart beach, $5 entry includes use of shower. Has lockers.

INFORMATION/TRAVEL

Information Center, 2106 Seawall Blvd, 763-4311. Mon–Fri, 8.30am–5pm, Sun, noon–5pm.

Texas Bus Lines, 4913 Broadway, 765-7731. 5 buses daily between Houston and Galveston, $9 each way.

CORPUS CHRISTI and THE SOUTH TEXAS COAST A large port city with a leaping population, **Corpus Christi** makes a good gateway to **Padre Island**, a long lean strip of largely unspoilt National Seashore that points toward the Texas toe. Once inhabited by cannibals, the shifting blond sands of Padre have seen five centuries of piracy and shipwrecks and no doubt conceal untold wealth. The natural wonders of the 110-mile-long island are quite sufficient for most people. However, it's a prime area for bird watching, shelling and beachcombing for glass floats. You can camp free at a number of idyllic and primitive spots. All are at the South Padre end, reached only via Highway 100. Camp on the seaward side of the dunes; the grassy areas may have poisonous rattlesnakes. Besides Galveston and Padre, the South Texas coast has hundreds of miles of coastline and various other islands.

North and east of Padre Island and Corpus Christi is the **Aransas Wildlife Refuge** where you can go by boat from Rockport and see (in season and at a distance) the world's remaining 150 whooping cranes. In **Rockport**, get down to marvellous seafood and gumbo eating at **Charlotte Plummer's**, 729-1185. Corpus Christi, South Padre and the entire area are rich in roadside stands that sell cheap, fresh boiled shrimp and tamales, the local speciality.

South Texas border towns with Mexico are numerous but not particularly appealing. Avoid **Laredo**: 'A dump with ripoff hotels.' **Brownsville/Matamoros** is probably the best and certainly most convenient to South Padre. 'Got free tourist card from Mexican consulate at 10th and Washington Streets in 5 minutes.'

FOOD
Che Bello, 320 C William St, 882-8832. Homemade gelato, sorbets and pastries. Lunch $6, patio.

INFORMATION/TRAVEL
Tourist Bureau, 1201 N Shoreline Blvd, Corpus Christi, 882-5603 or (800) 766-2323.
South Padre Tourist Bureau, 761-6433.
Greyhound, 702 N Chaparral, 882-2516. Open 6am–2pm.

EL PASO Biggest Mexican border city, El Paso feels neither Hispanic nor Texan. Backed by mountains, El Paso's main focus is the Rio Grande River, where early Spanish expeditions used to cross. The river also serves as the border and a casual, non-bureaucratic one it is. Other than sampling the sleazy delights of **Ciudad Juarez**, there's little reason to tarry in El Paso. It can serve as a base for Carlsbad Caverns (in New Mexico) and **Big Bend**, 477-2251, and **Guadalupe Mountains National Parks**, 828-3251. The latter, 110 miles east, includes **El Capitan**, a 8085 ft cliff, and 8749 ft **Guadalupe Peak**, highest in Texas. The park has two main campgrounds; $6, no reservations. 'Unless your journey necessitates going via El Paso, take another route.'

ACCOMMODATION
El Paso International AYH Hostel in the **Gardner Hotel**, 311 E Franklin Ave, 532-3661. Dorm-style rooms for $11, membership required; non-members must stay in the hotel proper, S–$27 up. AC, kitchen, laundry, 24 hr check-in.
Central YMCA, 701 Montana Ave, 533-3941. S–$13.50, $75/wk, includes use of pool, sauna and weight room. Coed. Due to reopen in '94 after renovation.

FOOD
Forti's Mexican Elder Restaurant, 321 Chelsea Dr close to I-10, 772-0066. The fajitas and shrimps are superb. $5–$12. Open Sun–Thur 11am–10pm, Fri–Sat 11am–11pm.
Leo's, 5315 Hondo Pass, 757-0505. 'Good Mexican food. Fast, helpful service.' 4 other locations in El Paso.
Tigua Indian Reservation, 121 Old Pueblo Rd, Ave of America's Exit off I-10, 859-7913. Daily till 5pm. Besides its crafts and rather small restored mission, the reservation has a good eating place, 859-3916, in the museum, with excellent red and green chili, and other traditional dishes. Worth a stop, if only for the food.

OF INTEREST
Americana Museum, Civic Center Plaza, under Performing Arts Bldg, 542-0394. Explores Native American and pre-Columbian America. Open Tue–Fri, 10am–5pm, free.
El Paso Museum of History, I-10 West and Avenue of the Americas, 858-1928. Tells the story of the Indian, Conquistador, Vaquero (Mexican cowboy), cowboy, and the US Cavalryman, all of whom fought and bled to win the Southwest. Tue–Sun 9am–4.50pm, free.
Fort Bliss, in north El Paso, 568-4518, houses several museums on the base exploring the history of the Civil War, the 3rd Armored Cavalry, and air defense, daily from 9am–4.30pm.
Ciudad Juarez. Simply stroll across the bridge, 25¢ toll each way. 'Mexican immigration didn't even give us a glance.' 'You can also ride the bus over but why bother. If you do, hold on to your passport and don't surrender your IAP-66 to the US authorities.'

Ciudad Juarez, 4th largest city in Mexico, is poor by western standards, though wealthy by Mexican standards. The shopping for leather, rugs and clothing is excellent. Drinking Tecate Beer in the **Kentucky Club**, an old western bar, you can pretend you're Papa Hemingway as you wait for the bullfights to begin.
Three bridges span the Rio Grande between El Paso and Ciudad Juarez. The main bridge is Cordova, which is free. Other bridges charge $1 there, $2 back (cars); on foot, 25¢ there and 50¢ back.

INFORMATION
El Paso Visitors Information Center, 1 Civic Center Plaza, 534-0698.
Mexican Consulate General, 910 E San Antonio, 533-3644.

TRAVEL
Amtrak, 700 San Francisco St, 545-2247. On *Texas Eagle* route, open 11am–7pm Sun–Thurs.
Greyhound, 111 San Francisco St, 542-1355. Open 24 hours.
SCAT, 533-3333. Local bus service, basic fare 75¢.
El Paso International Airport, about 5 miles north-east of downtown. Take #33 bus from the Plaza, 75¢; takes about 30 mins, last bus out to airport at 8.45pm.
Omnibus Lines to Chihuahua, Durango (Mex), and Mexico City leave from Juarez.

LUBBOCK The link between Texas' heartland and coastal ports and called 'Chrysanthemum Capital of the World', with over 80,000 plants throughout the city. However, it is perhaps better known as home of the **Red Raiders** (Texas Tech Football Stadium) and site of **Buddy Holly's Memorial and Walk of Fame**, 8th St and Ave A; a collection of plaques commemorating West Texas stars. Lubbock's state park, **Mackenzie**, is the most popular in Texas, off E Broadway and Ave A. BUNACers recommend the **Midnight Rodeo** (745-2813; closed Mon), a huge dance bar in the middle of town, for the traditional Texan two-step. The area code for Lubbock is 806.

THE SOUTH

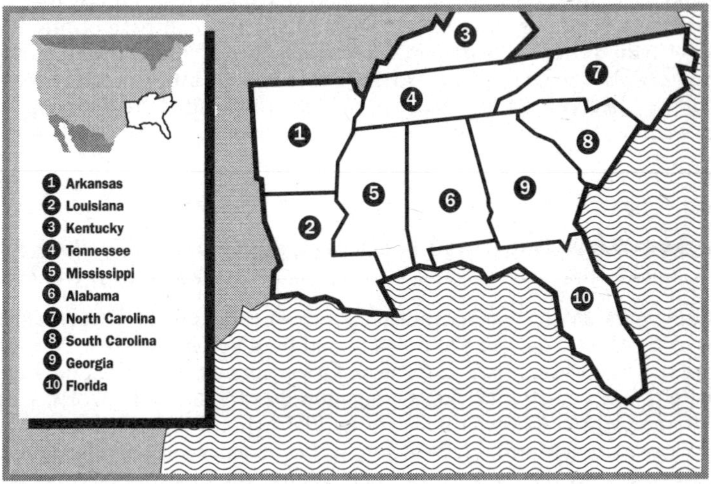

Although Northerners may hate to admit it, the South has given birth to much of the best American music, architecture and literature. The plaintive call of the blues rose up from the Mississippi Delta, and from the hills of Appalachia came the early strains of country music. Exuberant jazz echoed from the alleys of New Orleans; from Memphis burst rock n' roll. In contrast to the pristine architecture of Puritan New England, Spanish and French sensibilities contributed to the refined ante-bellum architecture of the deep South. Together, romantic notions of the plantation, the isolation of agricultural life, and the rigid social stratifications of slavery provided the setting for Southern writers such as Twain, Wright, Faulkner, Williams, Wolfe and Welty.

From a Southern perspective, the Civil War was a Northern attack upon a way of life based upon the misery of millions of slaves, but also upon agriculture and a planters' aristocracy. The passions the war unleashed are difficult to appreciate. The fight was to the death, and most of the old South was in fact destroyed. Although the United States had one-sixth the population in 1860 that it had in 1960, six times as many men died in the Civil War as in Vietnam. In defeat, Virginia General Robert E. Lee and Confederate President Jefferson Davis are still honored with statues and parades in the central square of every Southern city.

Only recently has the South begun to come out from under the economic and racial clouds of the War Between the States. The dream of equal rights, deferred since the Civil War, was won by blacks in a hard fought civil rights movement. Today black mayors run many cities, including Atlanta. High technology in Alabama, banking in Atlanta, and research in North Carolina testify to the growing economic power of the 'New South'.

While you explore its quirks, the South is bound to treat you well. Being polite counts down here. You won't be travelling long before you are introduced to simple, but gracious 'Southern Hospitality'. Perhaps the sultry weather contributes to a slower, more Mediterranean pace of life. If you travel in the summer, be prepared to sweat it out. It will be hot and humid as you never imagined possible. Do make sure you are introduced to Southern cooking—hearty food, like pecan pie, chicken and catfish fried to crisp, juicy perfection. And don't pass up spicy Cajun cooking in New Orleans!

ALABAMA

Thirty years ago the ways of the Old South were dear to the 'Heart of Dixie'. (so called due to the old $10 notes issued here before the Civil War which bore the word 'dix', French for ten). Governors stood in the doorways of white schools barring blacks; segregation was the law. The world's attention focused on Alabama's racism in 1955 when blacks, led by a young minister named Martin Luther King, Jr, began a peaceful revolt against the Jim Crow laws that walled them in. Today, the civil rights struggle has borne fruit in the form of integrated buses and schools and the first elected black officials since reconstruction.

Economic changes have been as far-reaching. Share-cropping and agrarian poverty still exist, but King Cotton no longer rules Alabama's economy as it did before the Civil War. Medical research in Birmingham, aircraft engines in Mobile, and rockets from Huntsville are major industries, closely followed by tourism, thanks to the Gulf Coast, the Tennessee Valley lake country in the north, and graceful touches of the Old South in Mobile and Montgomery. The humble peanut provides the base for another booming industry; there are acres of peanut fields in the southern Wiregrass area of the State, and each autumn the town of Dothan hosts the National Peanut Festival.

'The State of Surprises' is home to many of America's most prominent blacks, including Joe Louis, the boxer, Hank Aaron, the baseball home run king, W C Handy, father of the blues, George Washington Carver, scientist, Booker T Washington, educator, Jesse Owens, Olympic athlete, and Nat King Cole, singer.
The area code for Alabama is 205.

MOBILE The flags of France, Spain, England and the Confederacy have all flown over this attractive port city on the Gulf of Mexico. The town's varied history is best reflected in the old quarter's architecture and is at its most beautiful when the azaleas bloom in March. The people of Mobile have been celebrating Mardi Gras since 1703, longer than anywhere else in the US, and people who have seen it say it is second only to the one in New Orleans, 150 miles west.

The area is not as attractive as it once was. Hurricane Frederick, which struck in 1979, destroyed many charming old buildings, now replaced by papermills and typical highway eyesores. Still, Mobile offers some of the most beautiful streets in the South.

ACCOMMODATION

Economy Inn, 1119 Government St, 433-8800. S-$30, D-$35.
Heart of Mobile, 559 Goldman St, Hwy 90, 433-0590. S-$25, D-$32 up.
Motel 6, 1520 Matzenger Dr, I-10 exit on Dauphin Island Parkway, 473-1603. S-$26, D-$30.
Olsson's Motel, 4137 Government Blvd, 661-5331. S-$29, D-$30.
Holiday Inn Express, 255 Church St, 433-6923. S-$43, D-$52. 'Right downtown. Rooms of a very good standard. Includes breakfast AND there's a swimming pool.'

FOOD

Rousso's, 166 S Royal St, 433-3322. Open 11am–10pm. 'Good food, quite reasonably priced.'
Wintzell's Oyster House, 605 Dauphin St, 433-1004. Lunch under $5, dinner $8 up. 'Very popular place.' Open Mon–Sat, 11am–9pm (Fri 9.45pm).

OF INTEREST

Nice to wander around the old squares and streets, dating back to the 1700s when the French held sway in Mobile. **Bienville Sq, De Tonti Sq** and **Church Street** have been restored. Check with the Mobile Visitors Center for walking maps of the neighbourhoods. Among the houses open to the public are: **Condé Charlotte House**, 104 Theatre St, 432-4722. Open Tues–Sat 10am–4pm; $3. Students $1.
Richards DAR House, 256 N Joachim St, 434-7320. A $3 charge buys a tour of the 1845 period-furnished home as well as tea and cookies with the house staff. Tues–Sat 10am–4pm, Sun 1pm–4pm.
Oakleigh, 350 Oakleigh Place, 432-1281, 1833 antebellum mansion furnished by the Historic Society. $4 adults, $2 students. Admission includes tours of the mansion and the nearby **Creole Cottage**. Mon–Sat 10am–4pm, Sun 1pm–4pm (last tour 3.30pm).
Museum of the History of Mobile, 355 Government St, 434-7569. 17th, 18th, 19th century artefacts. Tue–Sat 10am–5pm, Sun 1pm–5pm. Free.
U.S.S. Alabama Battleship Memorial Park, Mobile Bay, Battleship Pkwy, 432-5951. Visit the historic WWII battleship moored here on the Tensas River along with the submarine U.S.S. Drum. See also the B-52 bomber 'Calamity Jane,' a SR-71 Blackbird spy plane and other military exhibits. The battleship is now a state shrine. 'Can be explored from bow to stern.' $5. Ticket office open 8am-7pm, ship closes 8pm. 'Non-drivers must take a taxi to get there—cannot walk through road tunnel—about $4 each way.'
Cathedral of the Immaculate Conception, 4 S Clairbourne St, 432-6684. Designed by Claude Beroujon in 1835 who supervised construction until 1849. Open daylight hours. 'Worth a look.'
Dauphin Island, 30 miles south of Mobile, is a quiet place where you can camp, swim and wander. Off the highway just before the island, blooms **Bellingrath Gardens**, designed by the founder of Coca-Cola.

INFORMATION

Fort Conde Welcome Center, 150 S Royal St, (800) 252-3862 or 434-7304. Inside reconstructed 1724 fort.
Chamber of Commerce, 451 Government St, 433-6951.

TRAVEL

Greyhound, 2545 Government Blvd, (800) 231 2222.
Mobile Transit Authority, 344-6600, runs Mon–Sat 6am–7pm. 75¢. NB: There is no service to the airport. For a taxi call 476-7711, around $22 o/w.

BIRMINGHAM Once known as the steel town of the South, Birmingham is now a major centre for biomedical research, finance, manufacturing, wholesale/retail industries and engineering (it has the largest population of engineers in the south outside Houston, Texas). The city scored a double in 1989 when it was named 'America's Most Livable City' by the US Conference of Mayors, and one of 'America's Hot Cities' by *Newsweek Magazine*. 'Hot' certainly describes Birmingham in summer, when temperatures are regularly over the 100 degree mark.

The great civil rights marches of 1963 began here—protests that threw Martin Luther King, Jr. into the city's jail. Sixteen years later, Birmingham elected its first black mayor. Although the population is predominantly white, the city retains an ethnic diversity from the days when immigrants came to work in the steel industry. Birmingham stretches for 15 miles along the Jones Valley, and the best views are from the top of nearby Shades and Red Mountains.

ACCOMMODATION

Economy Inn, 2224 5th Ave N, 324-6688, nr downtown. TV, pool. S/D-$30.
Tourway Inn, 1101 6th Avenue N, 252-3921. S-$34, D-$39. TV, pool. Downtown.
YWCA, for women only, 309 23rd St N, 322-9922, $10/night, $1.50 for use of pool.

FOOD

Ollie's, 515 University Blvd, 324-9485. Famous for barbecued dishes. Meals under $5. Mon–Sat 8am–8pm.
Milo's, 509 18th St S, 933-5652. Unique hamburgers and fries. Mon–Sat 10am–9pm, Sun 11am–9pm.

OF INTEREST

Antebellum Arlington, the birthplace of Birmingham, is at 331 Cotton Ave SW, 780-5656. Home features period furniture. $2 students. Open Tue–Sat 10am–4pm, Sun 1pm–4pm. 'Something out of old Dixie.'
The **Vulcan Statue**, which dominates Red Mountain, is the largest cast iron statue in the world, and, in the US, is second only to the Statue of Liberty in height. Erected to honour the steel industry, Vulcan is 55 feet tall and stands on a 124-foot pedestal; his massive head alone weights 6 tonnes. He carries a torch in his hand which burns green unless there has been a traffic fatality in the area, in which case the flame turns red: the world's largest traffic safety reminder! Elevator to observation deck at top; $1. 328-2863.
The Red Mountain Museum and Discovery Place, 1421 22nd St S, 933-4153. The former offers mineral and fossil displays as well as a free self-guided tour of the geology supporting Vulcan's craft. Don't miss the 14 ft mosasaur fossil or the solar telescope—the only one of its kind in the country. **Discovery Place** next door invites children of all ages to explore body mechanics and the myths of modern technology. Open Mon–Fri 9am–5pm, Sat 10am–4pm, Sun 1pm–4pm. $2.
Birmingham Civil Rights Institute, 520 16th St N, 328-9696, documents the Civil Rights Movement since the 1920's. More than just a museum as it promotes ongoing research and discourse on human rights issues. Open Tues–Sat 10am–6pm, Sun 1am–5pm. Free.
Alabama Sports Hall of Fame, 2150 Civic Center Blvd, 323-6665, pays tribute to all-time greats such as Jesse Owens and Birmingham's own prize hitter, Willie Mays. Open Mon–Fri 9am–5pm, Sun 1am–5pm. $5, $3 students. 'Arrive early.'
Sloss Furnaces, 32nd St by 2nd Ave, 324-1911. Exhibits of iron and steel making. Free. Tue–Fri 10am–4pm, Sat 10am–5pm, Sun 12pm–4pm.
Botanical Gardens, 2612 Lane Park Road, 879-1227. Rose Garden, Japanese Garden with tea house and the largest conservatory in the Southeast. Open sunrise to sunset daily. Free.

Across the road is **Birmingham Zoo**, 879-0408, the largest zoo in the Southeast which houses nearly 1000 mammals, birds and reptilea over 100 acres. Open 9.30am–5pm daily. $4.
Alabama Museum of the Health Science, Lister Hill Library, University Of Alabama Campus, 934-4475. Exhibits relating to history of medicine in the State. The adjoining **Reynolds Historical Library**, one of the top historical science libraries in the nation, has original letters from George Washington and Florence Nightingale.

INFORMATION/TRAVEL
Visitors Info Center, University and 12th, 254-1654, (800) 962-6453. Mon–Fri 8.30am–5pm, Sun 1–5pm.
Travelers Aid, 3600 8th Ave S, 322-5426. Mon–Fri 8am–4.30pm.
Chamber of Commerce, 2027 1st Ave N, 323-5461.
Greyhound, 619 N 19th St, (800) 231-2222.
For a taxi to the airport call 788-8294, $8–$11.

MONTGOMERY The capital of Alabama, Montgomery was capital of the entire Confederacy until the honour was transferred to Richmond. The Senate Chamber is kept just as it was the day secession was voted, and the tree-shaded streets lined with ante-bellum homes help carry you back a hundred and more years.

It was not until 1955, almost 100 years after the Civil War, that Rosa Parks, a black woman of tremendous courage, dragged Montgomery into the 20th Century when she refused to give up her bus seat to a white passenger. Parks was arrested, and Montgomery blacks voted to stage a bus boycott on Dec 2, 1955. A young preacher named King helped organize the boycott.

ACCOMMODATION
Motel 6, 1051 Eastern Bypass, I-85 to East Blvd Exit 6, 277-6748. S–$30, D–$35.
Ranch House Motel, 2127 7th Ave S, 322-0691. Pleasant motel rooms with baths in a happening area. Lounge and pool. S–$31, D–$38.
Capital Inn, 205 N Goldthwaite St, 265-0541. Nr Civic Center, in historic district. AC, pool, TV. S–$35, D–$38.
Town Plaza, 743 Madison Avenue, 269-1561, S–$22, D–$25.

FOOD
Chris's Dogs, 138 Dexter Avenue, 265-6850. Famous for its chili sauce.
Montgomery Curb Market, 1004 Madison Ave, 263-6445. Sells home-made pies, fresh produce. Tue, Thur, Sat am. Also try **Montgomery State Farmers' Market**, 1655 Federal Dr, 242-5350, a 28-acre complex including cafe serving breakfast and lunch, garden centre and stalls selling farm produce, home baking, preserves and crafts. Open 7 days, 7am–7pm.

OF INTEREST
State Capitol, Brainbridge St and Dexter Ave. A gold star marks the spot where Jefferson Davis was inaugurated as president of the Confederacy in February 1861. Note also the impressive murals depicting state history and the graceful hanging spiral staircases. Recently renovated and restored.
First White House of the Confederacy, across the street from the Capitol, 242-1861, contains memorabilia of Confederate President Jefferson Davis and family. Mon–Fri 8.30am–4.30pm, weekends 9am–4.30pm. Free. 'Worthwhile.'
Designed by the architect of the Vietnam War Memorial in Washington, DC, the **Civil Rights Memorial** was unveiled during the fall of 1989. Visitors can view the outdoor memorial at the corner of Washington Ave and Hull St, 264-0286.

Dexter Ave King Memorial Baptist Church, 454 Dexter Ave. Where Martin Luther King, Jr. was pastor for 6 years. Open Mon–Fri, 9.30am–12pm and 1pm–4pm, 263-3970. Free.

Montgomery Museum of Fine Arts, in W M Blount Cultural Park off Woodmere Blvd, 244-5700. Tues–Sat 10am–5pm, Thur 10am–9pm, Sun 12–5pm. Free.

W A Gayle Space Transit Planetarium, 1010 Forest Ave in Oak Park, 241-4799. Simulated space journeys. Shows year round at weekends, 2pm, $2.

The **Alabama Shakespeare Festival**. Renaissance-style theatre houses performances running from Oct–Aug. 1 Festival Drive, 271-5353.

Scott and Zelda Fitzgerald Museum, 919 Felder Ave, 264-4222. Home to novelist F Scott and wife Zelda from October 1931 to April 1932, during which time Scott worked on *Tender is the Night*. Works of both writers on display. Open Wed–Fri 10am–2pm; Sat, Sun 1pm–5pm. Free.

Northeast of Montgomery about 40 miles is the noted **Tuskegee University**, a co-ed university founded in 1881 by former slave Booker T Washington. One of the University's alumni was George Washington Carver, who became famous for his research on peanuts. **Grey Columns**, the historical site's visitor center, is open Mon–Fri 9am–5pm with weekend hours during the summer, 727-3200.

INFORMATION

Montgomery Visitor Information Center, 41 Madison Ave, 262-0013. Open Mon–Fri 8.30am–5pm, Sat 9am–4pm, Sun 10am–4pm.

TRAVEL

Greyhound, 210 S Court St, (800) 231-2222. 'Don't turn right out of the terminal. Bad area.'

Montgomery Area Transit System, 262-7321, buses run daily 6am–6pm. $1. For a bus to the airport take the #11 from downtown which runs daily 5.25am–6.15pm. Taxis will cost around $11–$12 o/w; call 834-9944.

HUNTSVILLE Founded by John Hunt in 1805 and the site of the first English settlement in Alabama, this one-time sleepy town has become rather more 'spaced out' as it is today host to one of the state's biggest attractions. The **US Space and Rocket Center** was established here in 1960 and, thanks to the late German scientist, Wernher von Braun and his pioneering work on the Saturn V Moon Rocket, the Center is now the nation's focal point for the research and development of the NASA Space Program. Among its many public attractions is the only full-size model of the space shuttle and a 67ft domed theatre screen showing breathtaking films of space flight. Open 8am–7pm, 9am–6pm after Labor Day. $11.95 includes the Spacedome Theater and NASA bus tour, 837-3400.

Back on earth, however, and for those seeking alternative and more cultural stimulation, Hunstville offers two historic areas downtown and east of Court House Square. Many of the 19th century houses are inhabited by descendants of the original owners. Located just north of the Tennessee River and its numerous adjoining lakes, the area provides scope for watersport enthusiasts and is beautified with many parks such as Big Spring International.

An hour's drive west of Huntsville is **Muscle Shoals**, a town known to few people except the big names in the music business. *Time's better there* according to Deep River Blues. Several recording studios are in and around the town, and musicians ranging from WC Handy to Elton John to Doc Watson have come here to play. Studio tours available, call Muscle Shoals Sound, 381-2060.

ARKANSAS

Arkansas was named after the native Quapaw Indians, called 'Akansea' by other tribes, the name (meaning 'South Wind') was misspelled by early French explorers—hence its present form. The Land of Opportunity, as Arkansas calls itself, was admitted to the Union in 1836 as the 25th state.

Eastern Arkansas, with its long hot summers and rich alluvial soil well suited for the cultivation of tobacco, corn and cotton, became prime plantation country. Also known as 'The Natural State', Arkansas has always drawn its income from agriculture; only in the last two decades has industrial production increased substantially. A predominantly Democratic domain, and home state of course of President Bill Clinton, Arkansas has only elected 4 Republican governors in its history—against 37 Democrats.

Western Arkansas, with its hills and forests, and the colourful Ozark Mountains to the north, smacked more of the frontier, and settler opinion caused the state to hesitate before seceding from the Union. The Ozark and Ouachitas areas retain a strong folksy flavour with a distinct mountain culture which has left its mark on national folk art, legend and music. Although Little Rock is the geographical, legislative and commercial centre of the state, look to Hot Springs National Park and the Ozarks for the truly rustic Arkansas.

National Park: Hot Springs.

The area code for the entire state is 501.

LITTLE ROCK Named after a local landmark on the bank of the Arkansas River, this one-time hunter and trapper outpost is now the state capital. Known to its residents as the 'City of Roses', Little Rock came to the world's attention back in 1957 with the attempt to ban nine black children from the segregated Central High School. It came to everyone's attention again in 1992 with the emergence of Bill Clinton and his run for the White House. Heady days in Little Rock! Don't neglect the surrounding countryside: west of the town is Hot Springs, and to the northwest lie the Ozarks.

ACCOMMODATION

Motel 6, 9525 I-30, 7 miles outside town, 565-1388, S–$27.50, D–$34. Pool, AC.
KOA Campground, in North Little Rock on Crystal Hills Road, 758-4598, $21 for 2, $24.50 w/full hook-up, $4 for extra person.

OF INTEREST

The only city to have three capitol buildings. The hand-hewn, oak-log territorial capitol is in the **Arkansas Territorial Capitol Restoration**, a collection of 14 restored buildings dating to the 1820s, E 3rd and Scott Sts, 324-9351, available for tours, $2. The aristocratic **Old State House**, 300 West Markham St, 324-9685, regarded as one of the most beautiful antebellum structures in the South, was used from 1836 to 1912. Open Mon–Sat 9am–5pm, Sun 1pm–5pm.

The present **State Capitol**, Woodlawn and Capitol Ave, 682-5080, was based on the US Capitol in Washington. Don't miss the beautiful gardens and the brass doors made by Tiffany's of New York. Daily, self-guided tours 10am–6pm.

The Quapaw Quarter, a nine square mile area, is the original Little Rock with many 19th century additions, both business and residential, including the **Gover-**

nor's Mansion; the **Pike Fletcher-Terry Mansion**, home of three colourful and famous Arkansans, and now a part of the **Arkansas Arts Center**, 372-4000. Open Mon–Sat 10am–5pm, Sun noon–5pm; free. Also included in the quarter is the Old Arsenal in **MacArthur Park**, birthplace of Gen Douglas MacArthur and now the **Museum of Science and History**, 324-9231. Open Mon–Sat 9am–4.30pm, Sun 1pm–4pm. $1; free on Mon.

Riverfront Park between the Statehouse Plaza and the Arkansas River has lighted brick walkways, fountains, benches, a pavilion with a pictorial display of the city's history and the 'little rock' that gave the city its name.

INFORMATION/TRAVEL

Little Rock Convention and Visitors Bureau, Markham and Broadway, 376-4781, has maps, information, and a helpful staff. Open Mon–Fri, 8.30am–5pm.

Greyhound, 118 E Washington St in North Little Rock, (800) 231-2222.

Amtrak, Markam and Victory St, 372-6841.

Local Transit Authority, 375-1163. Basic fare 80¢, 10¢ transfer. To reach the airport, take the 'College Station' bus from 4th and Louisiana, 6am–4.30pm. Taxis to the airport cost around $9. Call 374-0333.

HOT SPRINGS NATIONAL PARK Pure and bubbling up from the ground at 143 degrees, the waters of the Hot Springs mix with cool water from natural reservoirs to create the ideal 100 degree bath. The hybrid town-national park is cradled between two peaks in the Ouachita Mountains, about an hour south of Little Rock on US 70. From February to April, lodging and bathing costs rise to match the demand of flocking tourists.

Although actual bathing is prohibited in the park, the Visitors Center does offer a free **Thermal Features Tour** during the summer and information on private bathhouses during the rest of the year. Located at 369 Central, in the middle of Bathhouse Row, the center is open daily 9am–4pm, 623-1433. Elsewhere on the Row, look for baths for about $10 and massages as well as a string of moderately-priced motels. Rooms start at around $20 but the prices double from Feb–April. Cheaper lodging can be had at the motels clustered on Hwys 7 and 88 or at one of several campsites, including two nearby state parks. Call (800) 643-8383 for information.

THE OZARKS Although not especially high as mountains go, the Ozarks offer attractive wooded hills, rocky cliffs, gushing springs and rivers. It's a good area for white water canoeing, fishing, hiking, cycling and camping, or just getting away from it all for a few days. The **Ozark National Forest** is bounded on the east by the **White River** and to the west by the **Buffalo National River**, and includes **Blanchard Springs Cavern, Cove Lake** and **Mount Magazine**, the highest point in the state. Stop at the **Ozark Folk Center** in **Mountain View**, 269-3851, for Ozark music and crafts. Open 10am–5pm daily.

Summers are very hot and you will need mosquito repellent. Best months to visit are August and September when it's cooler, driest and bugless.

The small university town of **Fayetteville** is a good centre for visiting the area. Also worth a stop is the Victorian spa town of **Eureka Springs** in the northwest corner of Arkansas; it looks like a village in the Bavarian Alps and indeed has its own version of an Oberammergau passion play every year from April to October—just look for the 7-story tall Christ that weighs in at 2 million pounds. Ticket info at 253-9200.

FLORIDA

Beautiful, tacky, over-touristed and overflowing with Miami-sized vices, Florida draws sunseekers young and old from around the world. The climate is warm and gentle, the beaches broad and sandy, the citrus plentiful. Students from around the country flock here during Spring Break, making it easy to see why Spanish explorer Ponce de Leon believed the fountain of youth was in Florida. In 1513 he named his newly discovered land after the Spanish for Easter—Pascua Florida.

Although Florida was one of the hard-core Confederate states, this followed from her plantation system along the panhandle; the southern part of the state remained tropical wilderness. During America's revolution, conservative Brits in the northern states began a now-familiar migration south to Florida. The state today dwells little on Dixie, but gets its impetus from tourists who have been piling in from the US and Canada since the Miami land boom of the 1920s, though more especially since the Second World War—and now from across the Atlantic, as Florida competes with Spain for northern Europe's summer holiday-makers.

Florida's youthful draw has given way to distinctly middle-aged problems. Rapacious real estate developers have lined the beaches with bland highrise hotels. The buccaneers who plied the coasts in the 1700s were pussy cats compared to the drug-kings of the 1980's, although authorities have reacted strongly and many localities have ultra-strict drug laws. Spanish is as common as English in Dade County where more than 50 percent of the population is now Hispanic, mainly refugees from Cuba and Haiti. Add to this the fact that most Floridians did not grow up in the state and have no developed sense of community and you have some real problems.

If you try hard, you may be able to ignore all the bronzed beach babes, the klatches of complaining New York retirees, and rowdy confederates. Once you catch a glimpse of Florida's stunning beauty—primeval Everglades, palms, mangroves, tropical vegetation and miles of sandy beaches groomed by warm seas, plus Cape Kennedy Space Center and the vast empire of Walt Disney World . . . well, you'll be hooked.

Note: All hotel prices are for the summer/autumn season. Winter/spring rates are generally double. Shop around for cheap car rental deals, particularly off season, and also good air fares to and from the northern states.
National Park: Everglades, Biscayne.
The Area Code for the Panhandle and the Northern Coast is 904, for the Space Coast and Central Florida is 407; for Ft Lauderdale, Miami and the Keys is 305; and for Tampa and the Western Coast, use 813.

THE NORTHEAST COAST The most popular Florida coast begins unimpressively near the Georgia border in the port city of **Jacksonville**. The only site worth seeing is the **Fort Caroline National Monument**, 12713 Fort Caroline Rd, which marks the demise of the Huguenot Colony begun in 1564, open daily 9am–5pm, free, 641-7155. However, nearby Amelia Island boasts nice quartz, white sand beaches at **Fernandina Beach** and **Fort Clinch State Park** as well as offering a haven for getting away from it all.

St Augustine, 40 miles further south, started as a Spanish colony in 1565, and was the survivor of the rivalry with the French to the north. The place is pointedly aware of being the oldest city in the United States and does much to commercialise its heritage. Try to ignore the billboard signs on the way in ('The Old Jail: Authentic and Educational') and give the history and atmosphere of the city a chance to make its mellow impact on you. By Florida standards, this is a tranquil town, picturesquely set on a quiet bay.

ACCOMMODATION

The different regions of Florida have different tourist seasons and St Augustine's is the hot and humid summer. Inexpensive hotels are difficult to find anytime, in summer especially. Your best bet here (and throughout Florida) may be camping.

St Augustine Hostel (AYH), 32 Treasury St, 829-6163. Near Greyhound Station. Members $10, non-members $13. Bike rental $5.

American Motel, 42 San Marco Ave, 829-2292. S/D–$26, more at weekends.

Monson Motor Lodge, 32 Avenida Menendez, 829-2277. Downtown by historical area and waterfront. $60 for 2, $70 at w/end, XP–$6. Pool, TV, AC, 1 mile from Greyhound.

Cooksey's Camping Resort, 2795 State Rd 3, off A1A south, 471-3171. Sites $17 for two, $18 with hook-up. Walking distance to beach. Pool, laundry facilities.

North Beach Campground, 824-1806, 3 miles north of town, on west side of A1A. $19 per site, $21 with hook-up. 'Best campsite in the USA—jungle-type setting.'

FOOD/ENTERTAINMENT

St George's Pharmacy and Restaurant, 121 St George St, 829-5929. Open 7am–5.30pm daily. Great homemade waffles and pancakes for breakfast; lunch specials $3.25.

Churchill's Attic, 21 Avenida Menendez, 824-3523; popular cafe facing water, menu starts at $2.95. Daily 11.30am–10pm (11pm Fri, Sat). 'Good bands upstairs.'

Scarlet O'Hara's, 70 Hipolita St, 824-6535. Place to go for burgers from 11.30am–12.30am. Live R/B and folk music nightly at 9pm. Karaoke Sundays.

OF INTEREST

Among the old Spanish buildings in the town are the **Castillo de San Marcos**, the **Cathedral of St Augustine**, **Mission of Nombre de Dios**, **Old Spanish Inn**, **Oldest House** and the **Old Slave Market**.

A 208 foot **stainless steel cross** marks the spot where the pioneer Spaniards landed in 1565, although the present mission church dates only from earlier this century.

The Spanish Quarter, 825-6830, is the restored area of the old city. Blacksmiths' shops, crafts shops, and morning cooking demonstrations can be had for the $5.50 admission. 'A lot of it is disappointing, however, since a number of the lovely old buildings are now the home of junk and trash shops.' 9am–5pm daily. Students $2.75.

Cross and Sword, Florida's official state play, is presented from mid-June to mid-August at the St Augustine Amphitheater, 471-1965. $10, $4 students. If you haven't had enough of Spain yet, you'll want to catch the **Days in Spain Fiesta**, held in the heart of the city every August, celebrating its birthday.

Tourist-trap museums abound in St Augustine with the oddest of them all being the **Tragedy in US History Museum**, 7 Williams St, where tabloid followers can find the car Jayne Mansfield was decapitated in and various relics of President Kennedy's assassination. Open daily 9am-dark, $4 adults, $3 students.

Nearby on Hwy A1A to the south is **Alligator Farm**, 824-3337. Established 1893, the farm seems to be trying to change from your standard man-vs-gator wrestling/souvenir stand into a place where people actually learn the difference between a crocodile and alligator. Open daily 9am–6pm, $8.95 adults.
Marineland of Florida, 9507 Ocean Shore Blvd, 471-1111. Open since 1938, this was the world's first oceanarium. Dolphin shows, 3-D movie, and some brave divers who risk life (and limb!) to hand-feed dangerous sharks. Open 9am–5.30pm daily. $12 admission, $9 students.

INFORMATION/TRAVEL
Visitors Information and Preview Center, 10 Castillo Dr, 825-1000, 8am- 7pm daily. Lots of free information and walking tour maps. Free 28 min movie on St Augustine.
Greyhound, 100 Malaga St, 829-6401 or (800) 231-2222.

DAYTONA BEACH Fifty miles south of Saint Augustine, following the old Buccaneers' Trail, Daytona Beach stretches out flat and hard. The fast ships of the buccaneers have been replaced by fast cars and fast romance. The **Daytona International Speedway** draws the best racers in the world, and during 'Spring Break' from mid-February to mid-April the beach draws thousands of students, all looking for a good time.

ACCOMMODATION
Rates are highest in summer and lowest after Labor Day. After Labor Day—'Haggle'. There are many hotels on the beach, among those recommended:
Candlelight Motel, 1305 S Ridgewood Ave, 252-1142. Rooms $30–$40. 'Loves having Brits.'
Daytona Beach Youth Hostel, 140 S Atlantic, 258-6937. Hostellers $14 night, $77 a week. Private rooms $34. 'Two minutes from the beach, very friendly.' 'Not very clean.' Runs trips 3 days a week to private lake, $15.
Fiesta Motel, 1000 N Atlantic Ave, 252-5396. D–$28 with shower, AC, TV and pool. 'Owner did a free BBQ for all his guests.'
Lido Beach Motel, 1217 S Atlantic, 255-2553. $30 double room w/bath, shower, cable TV. 'Basic, clean rooms. Short walk to main pier and few seconds from beach.'
Ocean Court Motel, 2315 S Atlantic, 253-8185. Q-$41. 'Recommended.' 10% discount for BUNACers.
Rip Van Winkle Motel, 1025 N Atlantic Ave, 252-6213. S–$18, D–$23. TV, pool. 'Great location.' Discount for BUNACers staying a week or more.
Skyeway Motel, 906 S Atlantic Ave, 252-7377. S–$18, plus $5 extra person.
Surfview Motel, 401 S Atlantic, 253-1626. From $22.
Camping: Daytona Beach Campground, 4601 Clyde Morris Blvd, 761-2663. From I-95, take exit 86A. Sites $21 for two, XP–$2.20. 5 miles from beach. Also **Tomoka State Park**, 676-4050. **Nova Campground**, 1190 Herbert St in Port Orange, 767-0095; and various grounds at **Flagler Beach**.

FOOD/ENTERTAINMENT
Aunt Catfish, west end Port Orange Causeway, 767-4768. Name says it all, hours vary during year but open for lunch and dinner. Seafood, burgers, BBQ.
Gringo's Mexican Restaurant, 701 Atlantic Ave, 258-0610. Open 5pm–10.30pm daily; combination platters under $5.
Ocean Deck, 127 S Ocean Ave, 253-5224. Reasonably priced menu, live reggae—plus beach volleyball court!
Oyster Pub, 555 Seabreeze Blvd, 255-6348. Sandwiches served all day—or try the raw oysters: 25¢ each from 4pm–7pm daily, 15¢ Sunday all day.
Sweetwaters, 3633 Halifax Dr in Port Orange, 761-6724, also has BBQ. Daily 11.30am–10pm.

OF INTEREST

With major automobile and motocycle races scattered throughout the year, **Daytona International Speedway**, 1801 Volusia Ave, seems to always be on the roar. The **Daytona 500** one of the premier races in the US, caps off 'Speed Week' in mid-February. Tickets to any of the races normally start at $45. Call 253-RACE for race details. To learn more about the area's fast history, see the **Birthplace of Speed Museum**, 160 E Granada Blvd in Ormond Beach, 672-5657, Tues–Sat 1pm–5pm, $1; and the **Halifax Historical Society Museum**, 252 S Beach, 255-6976, Tues–Sat 10am–4pm, $2. Free on Saturday.

But flying sand, not racing wheels, probably brought you to the **'World's Most Famous Beach'**, 23 miles of white sand along the Atlantic Ocean. Downtown Daytona is right in the middle, where the bulk of the crowds congregate, near Main St and Seabreeze Blvd; quieter spots can be found to the north and south. A variety of shops in the commercial district rent surf boards while shops along the community's western boundary, the Halifax River, rent sail boards and jet skis. Although overnight camping on the beach is illegal, drivers can take cars onto the beach and roam its length from sunrise to sunset; the fee is $3 per car.

Ponce de Leon Inlet Lighthouse, 4931 S Peninsula Dr, 10 miles south of Daytona Beach, offers self-guided tours of the second tallest lighthouse on the eastern US at 175 feet. Call 761-1821 for information. Open 10am–8pm, admission $3.

INFORMATION/TRAVEL

Destination Daytona!, 126 E Orange Ave, 255-0415 or (800) 854-1234. Open Mon–Fri 9am–5pm.

Amtrak, 2491 Old New York Ave, (800) 872-7245. Station is in Deland, 24 miles to the west.

Greyhound, 138 S Ridgewood Ave, (800) 231-2222. A long way from the beach.

Voltran Transit Company, 761-7700, bus service around county and trolley through city. Fare 75¢.

SPACE COAST Midway along the Atlantic side of the Florida peninsula is considered America's final frontier, the home of the US space program. Because of its close proximity to Orlando and Daytona Beach, the area from Titusville to Melbourne has become a primary stop for anyone travelling through the state. And because it plays second to the other cities' better known attractions, the Space Coast is one of the better values in the state.

Visits to **Titusville**, where the **John F. Kennedy Space Center** and **Cape Canaveral** are located. Shuttle launches draw masses of people along US 1, some camping out nearly a week in advance to watch lift-off. For an up-to-date launch schedule, call (800) 867-4636.

Spaceport USA, (407) 452-2121, is NASA's tourist centre. Many of the exhibits and attractions are free while a spectacular film on a 5½ storey Imax movie screen costs $4, and an interesting 2-hour tour of the Space Center, which includes the world's largest scientific building—the 525-foot VAB (Vehicle Assembly Building), is $7. From I-95, take Rte 50 exit from N, 407 exit from S. The Spaceport is open daily from 9am–8.30pm. Cocoa Beach is the nearest Greyhound stop.

The rockets blast-off over spectacular wild-life on **Canaveral National Seashore** and **Merritt Island Wildlife Reserve**. The reserve's visitor center, 867-0667, is located on Route 406 north of Titusville and is open Mon–Fri 8am–4.30pm, Sat–Sun 9am–5pm (Sun from Nov–April only). The seashore's southern entrance at **Playalinda Beach** is at the end of Route 406. Primitive backcountry camping is allowed in the seashore. On summer evenings, marvel at the flying fish.

THE SCOOP ON AMERICAN ICE CREAM

There's nothing nicer than quenching the heat of an American summer day with an ice-cream cone or a malted milk shake, an all-natural gastronomic experience you're unlikely to forget, since the choice in the US is almost bewildering. Becoming increasingly popular, on this weight-watching, calorie-counting continent, are frozen yoghurts. Refreshing and not just for dieters! There has also been an explosion of new-fangled, mouth-watering ice cream bars, including **Baskin & Robbins'** Jamoca Almond Fudge, Peanut Butter and Chocolate, and Pralines and Cream, but **Ben & Jerry's** are more imaginative with their 'Peace pops'.

NATIONALLY AVAILABLE: The **Baskin-Robbins** franchise, with its trademark 31 flavours, spearheaded the gourmet ice cream trend. Always new flavours, but standards Rocky Road and Chocolate Fudge are musts.

Ben & Jerry's Ice Cream. The pair of socially-aware Vermonters so famous they were parodied in the film *City Slickers* (remember those two bearded men on the cattle drive?). Their Coffee Heath Bar absolutely must be tried. Also Rainforest Crunch, vanilla ice cream with pecans and brazils, gives new taste to tired nuts; Tuskegee Chunk (in honour of George Washington Carver, who loved peanuts); and Cherry Garcia (the only ice cream named after a rock legend). The Chocolate Chip Cookie Dough is supreme, better than the Häagen-Dazs variety; the New York Super Fudge Chunk is also delicious. Also try their frozen yoghurt, lighter but just as flavoursome as its counterparts.

Häagen-Dazs offers, among other delectables, a decadent, deep, dark Belgian chocolate flavour, which will sate even the most hardened chocoholic. For an obscene treat, try the Triple Brownie Overload, a melange of chocolate ice cream, brownie dough, fudge chunks and pecans—worth the calories. Also try juice-sweetened **Gourmet Ice Cream**, available from health food stores, and **Frujen Gladje's** Chocolate or Pralines and Cream. In Canada, **Laura Secord** is reputed to be the best.

LOCAL PARLOURS: Bob's Famous Ice Cream, Washington DC, (202) 342-7622, makes huge sundaes and an orange chocolate chip ice cream rated #1 in the country by *Washingtonian Magazine*. Their Irish Cream is potent, and their Strawberry tastes almost more genuine than the real fruit. Also in DC: **Cone E.Island**, in Pennsylvania Ave 2000 Mall, which received the *Washingtonian* award for its 'Snapper' variety (butter-based ice cream with pecans, caramel and chocolate chunks), but their Strawberry Cheesecake and Chocolate Marshmallow are also good. **Thomas Sweets**, in Georgetown, has lovely Cinnamon ice cream and lots of others.

CC Brown's Hot Fudge Shop, in **Los Angeles, CA**, (213) 464-9726: creators of the hot fudge sundae, they make their ice cream by hand. **Chinatown Ice Cream, New York City**, (212) 608-4170, delights the imagination and palate with its intriguing flavours, such as green tea, red bean and ginger flavours. **Emack and Bolio's,** in **Cambridge, MA**, (617) 247-8772: **Boston**'s best, serves Grasshopper, Orange Creamsickle and the patented Original Oreo Cookie. In **San Francisco, CA, Gelato Classico**, (415) 989-5884, is unparalleled for Italian ices (this side of the Atlantic) and now has a Double Expresso Bean flavour, not to mention the '94% fat-free fresh Banana Walnut and Mocha Chip' which promises to be more of a mouthful than its title! Also **Gino Gelateria**, (415) 981-4664, is noted for its 40 fresh flavours, produced on the premises. Viva variety! 'Try the Chocolate Balls (choc filled with ice cream and cherries in the centre; also 'Fruit Fills'—fruit peel with ice cream inside).' **Great Midwestern Ice Cream Co, Iowa City, IA**, (319) 337-7423, received the nation's #1 vote in *People* magazine. Try Blueberry and 'Sweet Iowa' (choc-blackberry). **King's Ice Cream, Miami, FL,** (305) 643-1842, blends the cream of the Caribbean crop: banana, pineapple and coconut straight from the shell. The **University of Maryland** in College Park, the **University of Wisconsin in Madison**, and **Cornell University, Ithaca, NY**, produce award-winning ice cream with milk from their own cows.

Cheap accommodation abounds along US 1. Rooms are hard to find in the winter and spring, but are one-half as much in the summer. In **Cocoa Beach**, be sure to stay at **Fawlty Towers**, 100 E Cocoa Beach Causeway, 784-3870, S–$38 and up off-season. Tell Paul you saw the listing in *Moneywise*. For camping, try **Jetty Park Campground**, 400 E Jetty Rd, 868-1108. $15 up to 6 people, XP–$5. $18.50 with hook-up. 'Best location of the campgrounds.'

Further down the coast from Melbourne to Jensen Beach, 700 pound sea turtles lumber ashore. The **Jensen Beach Turtle Watch** offers late night sea turtle egg-laying and hatching tours in June and July, $5 for a guided tour. Call Jensen Beach Chamber of Commerce ahead to see if the turtles are up to it, 334-3444.

More information on the area is available through the Cocoa Beach Area Chamber of Commerce, 400 Fortenberry Road in Merritt Island, 459-2200 and the Titusville Area Chamber of Commerce, 2000 Washington Ave, 267-3036.

FORT LAUDERDALE Midway between Palm Beach and Miami, Fort Lauderdale is a double attraction, with a six mile beach on one side (probably the finest on the Gold Coast), and 250 miles of lagoons, rivers and canals on the other, hence the nickname, 'The Venice of America'.

Each Spring Break, college students from all over America write an American version of *Debauch in Venice*. The students are crazed and local police overwhelmed. Local authorities have cracked down on the revellers in recent years, causing somewhat of an exodus to Daytona Beach and Clearwater. Still, March and April are crazy months.

To the north in the little town of **Palm Beach** it is illegal to own a kangaroo, hang a clothesline, and it is impossible to find cheap lodging. A playground for the rich and merely tacky, Palm Beach is crowded with homes of Kennedys and lesser millionaires. You can look, but if you have to ask the price, you can't afford to shop in the posh stores of **Worth Avenue**. For a real taste of the wealth that circulates here, walk through the **Breakers Hotel** and stroll down **Millionaire's Row**. The home of the man who built Palm Beach is now the **Henry Flagler Museum**, an impressive demonstration of what money can buy.

ACCOMMODATION

All Ft Lauderdale rates are for the off-season. Expect to pay more during winter and spring.

Lodging information: Broward County Hotel and Motel Association, 462-0409, 701C East Broward Blvd, for free directory of budget hotels. Broward County Parks and Recreation, 357-8100, for general information on camping in the county.

International House Hostel, 3811 N Ocean Blvd, 568-1615. $12 AYH members, $16 otherwise. Kitchen, laundry, pool, close to beach. 'Great place to stay.'

Lafayette Motel, 2231 N Ocean Blvd, 563-5892, from $39. 'Bright, simply furnished rooms with very friendly and helpful staff.'

Lamplighter Motel, 2401 N Ocean Blvd, 565-1531. S–$32, D–$48, XP–$5.

Merrimac Hotel, 551 N Atlantic Blvd, 564-2345. Special BUNAC rate of $29 per day for four sharing. Pool, plus right on the beach.

Ocean Way Motel, 1933 N Ocean Blvd, 566-8261, S–$29.50 up, $4 per extra person. Incls bath/shower, fridge, AC, colour TV; 'Beautiful apts just across the road from the beach; owner very helpful.' Will pick up at bus station for stays of 2 days.

Seagate Apt Motel, 2909 Vistamar St, 566-2491. $25 double. All facs incl pool, close to beach. 'Brilliant.'
The Seville, 3020 Seville St, 463-7212. S–$25, $30 for 2, XP–$5. 'Very clean, 5 minutes from beach; ask for Linda.'

FOOD AND ENTERTAINMENT
Fast food joints and expensive restaurants prey on the students who flock to Fort Lauderdale. Lots of bars, discos, along beach-front Atlantic Blvd. Some have happy hours with lots of free food.
Big Louies has the best pizza, 1990 Sunrise, 467-1166. Open daily till midnight (1am weekends).
Chilli's, Powerline Rd, 776-6837. Open 7 days. 'The best burgers ever!'
Pantry Pride, 500 E Las Olas Blvd, 467-7436, best market in the middle of town.
Southport Raw Bar, 1536 Cordova Road, 525-2526. Cheap seafood and sandwiches. Open daily till 1am. Friendly staff: 'Come on down: it's great!'
The Musician's Exchange, 729 W Sunrise, 764-1905, draws national name bands from reggae to blues Thur–Mon. Cover charge ranges from $2–$20. Cafe serves sandwiches, salads, burgers. It's not the best neighbourhood, though.

OF INTEREST
Tacky tours proliferate along the coast. Choose carefully.
Museum of Art, 1 East Las Olas Blvd, 525-5500. Largest collection of Cobra Art—post WWII artists from Northern Europe (Karel Appel, Asger Jorn and Joseph Noiret)—in the US. Tues 11am—9pm; Wed–Sat 10am–5pm and Sun 12pm–5pm, $4, $2 for students.
Everglades Park, 21940 Griffin Road West, 434-8111. Free admission to park. 45-minute airboat tour for $13.25. Open 9am–5pm daily.
To see the waterways through the city, the ***Jungle Queen*** sails twice daily (10am and 2pm) for 3-hour tours, $7.95, at the Bahia Mar Yacht Center on A1A, 462-5596.
Hugh Taylor Birch State Recreation Area, 3109 E Sunrise, 564-4521. One of the few natural sights on the concrete beach, trails, fishing and canoeing. $3.25 per car, pedestrians $1. Open daily 8am–sunset.
Ocean World, 1701 SE 17th St, I-95 exit 28, 525-6611. Marine life shows daily 10am–6pm, $10.95.

INFORMATION/TRAVEL
Chamber of Commerce Visitor Information, 527-8755, 512 NE 3rd Ave, open Mon–Fri 9am–5pm.
Greyhound, 515 NE 3rd St, 764-6551.
Amtrak, 200 SW 21st Terrace, 587-6692.
Broward County Transit (BCT), 357-8400. 85¢.
This stretch of coast is served by airports at Fort Lauderdale and West Palm Beach. The BCT runs regularly to and from Fort Lauderdale airport (#1) and connects with Palm Beach County Transit at the Boca Mall, and Dade County Transit at the Aventura Mall. From West Palm Beach airport, catch the #4 bus to downtown. Call (407) 272-6350 for times.
Tri-Service Commuter Rail, (800) 728-8445. See note under Miami *Travel*.

MIAMI Miami's mayor once called his city 'the Beirut of Latin America'. He meant it as a compliment—Beirut was once the intellectual and economic trade centre for a region, as Miami is for Latin America. Unfortunately, most Americans believed the analogy to Beirut's violence was more appropriate for Miami's legendary crime problems. Boatloads of poor Haitians and Cuban criminals fed the legend. Miami still requires caution but not as much as television would have you believe.

Racial tension exists under the surface, but need not be intrusive: for the most part the Anglos, Hispanics and blacks live peaceably alongside one another. Add Nicaraguans to the list of exiled Hispanics living in Miami—there is quite a sizable population. They and the Cubans give the city a very right-wing political flavour.

The city does sprawl—as one taxi-driver said, it goes out rather than up. While parts of the city are slums, other parts have the appearance of being very modern and high-tech; and other parts exhibit beautiful vegetation. The new high-speed Metrorail, a people mover and excellent bus system, provide access to many areas of the city without the need for a car.

ACCOMMODATION/FOOD

Not many motels within Miami that are safe, clean and cheap. Smarter to stay at Miami Beach and commute to Miami attractions by bus or rail.

Miami Airways Motel, 5001 NW 36th St, 883-4700, S–$39, D–$45, pool, movie channel, restaurant. Pick up at airport.

Kobe Trailer Park, 11900 NE 16th Ave, I-95 exit 14, 893-5121. Sites $25 for 2, XP–$2.

Miami North KOA, 14075 Biscayne Blvd, 940-4141. Sites $25.95 for two.

Read Friday's *Miami Herald* for restaurant and entertainment listings.

Canton Too, 2614 Ponce de Leon Blvd, Coral Gables, 448-3736. Reputedly the best Chinese food in Miami. Open Mon–Thur 11am–11pm, Fri, Sat midnight, Sun 2pm–11pm.

OF INTEREST

Seaquarium, Rickenbacher Causeway on Key Biscayne, 361-5703. Oldest and best: dolphins, sharks and killer whales; home of TV star Flipper, Lolita the 10,000 lb killer whale, Salty the Sea Lion. Also a wildlife sanctuary and rainforest exhibit. Open 9.30am–6pm. Adults $19.50. Ticket office closes at 4.30pm.

Bayside, Biscayne Blvd and 4th St, 577-3344. $95 million complex of shops, restaurants and night spots highlighting downtown. Open Mon–Thurs 10am–10pm, Sun noon–8pm. Fri and Sat till 11pm.

Little Havana, lies between SW 12th and SW 27th Ave with Calle Ocho (SW 8th St) housing most of the restaurants. Cigar and pinata manufacturers also. **Bay of Pigs Memorial** commemorates the failed US-backed invasion of Cuba in 1961, at SW 13th Ave and SW 8th St.

Vizcaya, 3251 S Miami Ave, 579-2708. An Italian-style palace created by millionaire James Deering, now the Dade County Art Museum. Open daily 9.30am–4.30pm. Adults $8 for tour of home and gardens.

St Bernard de Clarrvaux, the Spanish monastery was imported from Spain and reassembled in North Dade. Self-guided tours of the 'biggest jigsaw puzzle in the world', Mon–Sat 10am–5pm, Sun noon–5pm. Call 945-1461 for directions.

For wildlife try **Monkey Jungle**, 14805 SW 216 St, 235-1611. Monkeys run wild, you view them from cages: look smart and they might give you a cream bun. $10.50, daily 9.30am–6pm. Ticket office closes at 5pm. $1 discount with ISIC card.

Also see **Parrot Jungle**, SW 112th St near US 1, 666-7834. A huge cypress and oak jungle filled with exotic birds, some on roller skates. $10.50, daily 9.30am–6pm. Trained bird shows 10.30am–5pm. Ticket office closes 5pm. $1 discount with ISIC card.

Museum of Science and Planetarium, 3280 S Miami Ave, 854-4242. Open daily 10am–6pm; $6 for museum, $5 for planetarium, $8.50 for both. Cosmic Hotline, 854-2222, for recording of everything you ever wanted to know and much more about what's going on in the sky. Laser show weekend nights: $6.

Miami Jai-Alai Fronton, 301 E Dania Beach Blvd, 949-2424, $1 admission, $1.50–$7 for reserved seating. Betting on this fast-paced game is a prime Miami attraction.

Coconut Grove, in the southern suburbs, for a look at a 'Florida-style subtropical Chelsea scene'. Galleries, boutiques, boat hiring. Get there via bus 14 going south to Main Highway. The bulletin boards in Coconut Grove are said to be good for rides going north.
South of Miami in Homestead is **Coral Castle**, US 1 at SW 286th St, 248-6344. Designed by a jilted lover who waited for his fiance by creating a 1,100-ton estate out of coral, the castle stood originally in Florida City; in 1939, it was moved in its entirety to its present location. Open daily 9am–7pm, adults $6 for self-guided tour.
Water Sports: surfing at Haulover Beach Park and South Miami Beach, but beware: the waves are small; good swimming at Cape Florida State Park, Matheson Hammock, Tahiti Beach, Lummus Park, etc. Sailing, jet skiing and windsurfing on Hobie Beach off Rickenbacher Causeway.

INFORMATION
Greater Miami Convention and Visitors Bureau, 701 Brickell Ave # 2700, 539-3000, (800) 283-2707 (out of Fl), Mon–Fri 8.30am–5.30pm.

TRAVEL
Greyhound, 99 NE 4th St, (800) 231-2222.
Amtrak, 8303 NW 37th Ave, 835-1221, (800) 872-7245.
Metro Dade Transportation, 638-6700. Extensive network of buses (Metrobus), subway (Metrorail) and downtown people mover (Metromover). Services airport. Bus and rail fare $1, 25¢ transfer. Metromover 25¢, 'Best tour of the city for a quarter.'
Tri-County Commuter Rail, 728-8445. Established in 1989 and offers rail service as far north as West Palm Beach. $3 each way but trains only run during morning and afternoon rush hours Mon–Fri.

MIAMI BEACH Situated on a long, narrow island, across Biscayne Bay from Miami, Miami Beach came to be regarded as the ultimate in opulence, the dream place for retirement, or a bar mitzvah. Seventy years ago this was a steamy mangrove swamp. Now it's a long strip of hotels of varying degrees of grandness, plus of course the beach.

It's still a favourite retirement spot but the really rich have moved further up the coast. In their wake have come the Cuban refugees and the North European package tours, making it harder to get the good hotel rates which used to be available here during the summer. Still worth bargaining, however. The peak season is from late December to April.

ACCOMMODATION
(Off-season prices given)
Del Rio Hotel, 1100 Collins Ave, 538-9301. 2-bed apts, $140. TV, AC, bathroom, kitchen. 'Negotiable rates—ask for Guy.' '1 block off beach. Safe area.'
Haddon Hall Hotel, 1500 Collins Ave, 531-1251, S–$35, D–$40.
International Travellers Hostel, 236 9th St, 534-5862. $12. Kitchen, laundry and locker facilities. Private rooms from $28. In the heart of the Art Deco district, right on the beach.
James Hotel, 1680 James Ave, 531-1125. Rooms $35 up. AC. 'Manager and wife were very friendly and really helpful.'
Palmer House Hotel, 1119 Collins Ave, 538-7725, Art Deco hotel, S/D–$40.
South Miami Beach YH in Clay Hotel, 1438 Washington Ave, 534-2988. Members $10 (no AC), $11 (AC), non-members $3 extra. $5 key deposit. $2 breakfast served in the renovated kitchen. No reservations, no lights out or curfew time. 'Cheap, with friendly and helpful staff.' 'Not very clean.' Hostel is in heart of Art Deco district, one block from the beach. From Amtrak station, bus L goes within 3 blocks of hostel.

FOOD

La Rumba, 2008 Collins Ave, 534-0522, serves cheap Cuban fare. Open 7.30pm–midnight daily.
Our Place Natural Foods Eatery, 830 Washington Ave, 674-1322. Bookshop and vegetarian hang-out serving salads, pita sandwiches, juice drinks. Menu: $1–$7. Live folk music on weekends, open Mon–Thurs 11am–9am, Fri & Sat 11am–11pm, Sun 1pm–8pm.
Puerto Sagua, 700 Collins, 673-1115. Specializes in seafood and Latin food. Try the paella. $3.95–$19.25.
Wolfie's Restaurant, 2038 Collins Ave, 538-6626, is a New York deli transplanted to Miami Beach. An institution, it is open 24 hrs a day.

OF INTEREST

Whimsical and gaudy, the **Art Deco District** is as close to high art as Miami Beach comes. With the south half of the island designated a National Historic District because of 'Tropical Deco', the truly impressive sights are along Collins Ave and Ocean Dr. The homes are part of a depression-era development, and can be seen on a Preservation League, 672-1836, tour. Only 1 guided tour a week, Sat at 10:30am, $6. League office also has maps for self-guided tour, 661 Washington Ave. Different areas of **The Beach** cater to different groups: punks and surfers stick to the area below 5th St, volleyball players at 14th St, gays to 21st St and the rich and famous to Bal Harbor near 96th St.
Miccosukee Indian Village, mile marker 20, Hwy 41, 223-8386.
Guided tours show Miccosukee craftsmen at work. Museum has Indian artifacts. Open 9am–5pm daily, admission $5. Airboat rides $7.

ENTERTAINMENT

Club Nu, Collins Ave and 22nd St, 672-0068, is becoming a beach mainstay, changes decor often, cover around $5–$10.
If money is tight, try **South Point Park**, which has free concerts on Friday nights through the summer until September. 673-7224.

THE KEYS The only living coral reef in America drapes itself along the Florida Keys, the scimitar-shaped chain of islands curving southwest from Miami to Key West.

You pick up the toll-free Overseas Highway at Key Largo for the 100-mile run down to Key West. Enroute the road hops from island to island and at times you can travel up to 7 miles with only the sea around you. It's worth a brief stop in **Key Largo** to visit the **John Pennekamp Coral Reef State Park** and to pay a brief tribute to Humphrey Bogart. The *African Queen* now sits outside the Holiday Inn here and you can visit the rebuilt Caribbean Club Bar, 451-9970, open all day except 4am–7am, where the movie *Key Largo* was filmed. Locations along the highway are designated by milepost markers.

Key West itself is the southernmost and second oldest town in the United States. Hemingway once lived here and it remains a favourite place for gays, writers and artists—creative or otherwise. Key West is not typical America. Easy to imagine you've somehow made it to a Caribbean island; even the food—turtle steak, conch (pronounced 'conk') chowder, Key lime pie—suggests this.

Don't miss sunset over the Gulf of Mexico—the whole town turns out on Mallory Square to watch the show, both heavenly and earthly, for sundown here is usually accompanied by some kind of people-performance, a waterski display, a magician or a folk singer.

'Key West was virtually deserted when we were there in September and October; very quiet and idyllic.'

ACCOMMODATION

Key Largo: John Pennekamp State Park Campsite, mile marker 102.5, 451-1202, Sites $24–$26 with hook-up. 'Take more mosquito spray than you'll ever believe you need. Nice campsite, good swimming, it's just a shame the bugs spoil it.'
Bahia Honda State Park, mile marker 36.5, 872-2353, $26 site. 'Well worth the stop but be prepared, as it is in the middle of nowhere.' 'White sands and crystal clear water.' Open 8am–sunset.
Jules Undersea Lodge, world's first underwater hotel, 57 Shoreland Drive, Mile 103.5, 451-2353. A diver's dream; a pinch at $195.00 including dinner, unlimited snacking and diving! Worth a peek.
Key West: Boyd's Campground, Stock Island, mile marker 5, 294-1465, $24.50 for two, XP–$4. More for ocean site. Stay 6 nights, 7th night free. 'Worth it if enough people (more than two). Helpful owners, site has washing facilities, pool and TV.' Regular bus service to Key West, 75¢, bus leaves every hour from 6am–10pm; every half hour at rush hour times.
Jabour's Trailer Court, 223 Elizabeth St, 294-5723. $26 for 2 in a tent. XP–$5. 10% discount if you stay 4 days and pay cash.
Angelina Guest House, 302 Angela St, 294-4480. T–$40. 'Clean and simple. Very friendly.'
Caribbean House, 226 Petronia St, 296-1600 or (800) 543-4518. D–$35–$48. 'Excellent.' 'Very friendly and central.' AC, private bathroom. Cable TV & breakfast.
El Rancho Motel, 830 Truman St, 294-8700, $83 for 4. 'Excellent, quiet.'
Key West AYH, 718 South St, 296-5719. $14.25 members, $17.50 non-members (4 people per room, bunk beds). Private rooms available. Bicycles available for $6 a day. 'Clean, good kitchen, plenty of fridges.' 'Highly recommended.' 'Good friendly atmosphere.' Organises snorkelling trips—'a taste of paradise.'
Key West Bed and Breakfast, 415 William St, 296-7274, $65–75 double, with breakfast. 'Feels like home.'

FOOD

In Key West, the more expensive restaurants line Duval St while the side streets offer a more eclectic selection. Don't forget to try authentic Key Lime pie.
El Cacique, 125 Duval St, 294-4000. Cuban fare with daily lunch and dinner specials. Open 7 days.
Sloppy Joe's, 201 Duval, 294-5717. Hemingway's favourite pub. Live entertainment seven days a week. Mon–Sat 9am–4am, Sun noon–4pm. Open 365 days a year! 'Don't miss it.'

OF INTEREST

Hemingway Museum, 907 Whitehead St, 294-1575. Papa left Paris and moved to Key West in 1928. This became his home in 1931 until he left for Cuba in 1940. He wrote *A Farewell to Arms* and *For Whom the Bell Tolls* among others in this 1851 house. On discovering that the house was as Hemingway left it, when he died the present owners decided to turn it into a museum. 'Full of the overfed descendants of Hemingway's cats.' Open daily 9am–5pm, $6.
Conch Tour Train. Takes you about 14 miles in 1½ hours and includes 65 points of interest such as Hemingway's house, **Truman's Little White House**, **Audubon House** where the artist stayed while sketching birdlife over the Keys, the **turtle kraals**, the **shrimp fleet**, etc. Ticket Office, 501 Front St or 3850 N Roosevelt, 9am–4.30pm, 294-5161, $12 for the whole island.
Tours of the area are also available by **glass-bottomed boat**. *Fireball*, 296–6293, Glass Bottom Boat Tour, $14 for 2 hr trip. Leaves 3 times daily, 451-4655. And try snorkelling trips over the coral reefs. 'Well worth splashing out $15 or so—and maybe even buying an underwater camera.' 'Explore the island by foot if you

have more than one day in Key West, or rent a bike.' Try **Bicycle Center**, 523 Truman Ave, US 1, 294-4556. $4 for 24 hrs, $3 for day trip (9am–5pm), $20 for week.

There's an early morning bus from Miami which gives you most of the day at Key West with time for a Conch Train ride before catching the evening bus back again. 'The most amazing bus journey I have made.'

INFORMATION/TRAVEL

Florida Upper Keys Chamber of Commerce, 451-1414, mile 103.4 in Key Largo. Open daily 9am–6pm.

Key West Chamber of Commerce, 294-2587, 402 Wall St, open daily 8.30am–5pm, 9am–5pm w/ends.

Key West Visitors Bureau, telephone information 1-800-FLA-KEYS.

Key West Welcome Center, 296-4444, 3840 N Roosevelt Blvd, open daily 9am–5pm.

Greyhound, 615½ Duval St in Key West, 296-9072.

For a taxi to the airport, call 296-2222, $8–$12 o/w.

EVERGLADES and BISCAYNE NATIONAL PARKS The Everglades lies farther south than any other area of the US mainland and is the last remaining subtropical wilderness in the country.

World famous as a wildlife sanctuary for rare and colourful birds, this unique, aquatic park is characterised by broad expanses of sawgrass marsh, dense jungle growth, prairies interspersed with stands of cabbage palm and moss-draped cypresses, and mangroves along the coastal region. The level landscape gives the impression of unlimited space.

The western entrance to the park is near **Everglades City** on Route 29, but the only auto road leading into the area is Route 9336 from **Florida City**, 11 miles to the east. Admission is $5 paid at the entrance station; the Visitors Center, 247-6211, which offers a free film, is open 8am–5pm daily. You will need to get out and walk along the paths to really understand the place. Try the **Anhinga Trail**, 2 miles past the entrance. The Royal Palm Visitors Center has great displays on the unique Everglades' ecology.

Winter temperatures generally range between 60 and 85 degrees F. The rest of the year, the heat climbs over 90 degrees by mid-morning, and feels much hotter because of the high humidity. You are advised to bring sunglasses, suntan oil and gallons of insect repellent. Accommodation, restaurants, sightseeing and charter boats and other services are found in **Flamingo**, at the end of the main park road, about 50 miles from the park entrance. From the Gulf Coast of Florida, you can enter the park at Everglades City. Call (813) 695-3101.

Biscayne National Park is a jewel for snorkellers and scuba divers as most of the marine park's treasures are underwater in living coral reefs. Above ground, exotic trees, colourful flowers and unique shubbery form dense forests. The main entrance is at the western side of the park at the **Convoy Point** Visitor Center, 9 miles east of **Homestead** on North Canal Drive, 247-7275, open 8.30am–6pm daily. For snorkelling equipment and canoe rental or information on glass-bottomed boat tours, call the Biscayne Aqua Center in Homestead, 247-2400.

ACCOMMODATION

Everglades Motel, 605 S Krome Ave, Homestead, 247-4117. D-$39, XP-$5, summer. AC, colour TV, coin laundry, small pool.

Flamingo Lodge, in Flamingo, inside the park, 253-2241. D–$52, XP–$11, cottages with room for 4, $72. Higher rates at w/ends.
Camping, $8 a site in winter, at **Lone Pine Key** and **Flamingo**. The Park office, (305) 247-6211, doesn't charge for camping in summer because they feel sorry for anyone who would brave the clouds of mosquitoes to do it. For the truly adventurous, 19 backcountry sites are accessible by motorboat or canoe. Just don't try swimming or paddling in the lakes or ponds. You must have a backcountry permit, if you want to do your own canoe trip overnight. Note: in summer you'll need to bring food if you camp.

TOURS

Gray Line Tours from Miami and Miami Beach, but for a group of people it would be better and cheaper to hire a car for a day.
Also available: air-boat rides and ordinary boat rides from various bases in the park. Trips last 1½ hours and cost about $10. Call Sammy Hamilton Boat Tours, (813) 695-2591, for tours in Everglades City.

ORLANDO Standing 35 miles from the east coast in the heart of the Florida lakes area, Orlando—hardly heard of a few years ago—is now perhaps the most visited place in the state owing to its access to the nearby Kennedy Space Center and especially the Walt Disney World complex. A favourite EEC tourist spot, the chances are you'll meet folks from your home town. It has the mayhem atmosphere of a boom town, but choose carefully before you set out to see the sights—so many of them are waste-of-time, money-grabbing parasitical spinoffs. Cheap car rentals may be the best bet to visit these spaced out attractions.

ACCOMMODATION

A hundred zillion hotels have opened here in the last decade to lure the folks visiting all the nearby worlds. Most are expensive, but a few inexpensive chains like Motel 6 and Days Inn have staked their claim to the action. It may prove cheaper to stay in a more expensive motel nearer to Disney, etc and get *free* shuttle to the attractions.
Airport Youth Hostel, 3500 McCoy Rd, 859-3165. $10 per night. $60 per week. 'Cheap, but shabby.' Take #11 bus from town. 'Clean and friendly.' Shuttle to Disney—$10.
Orlando International AYH Hostel, 227 N Eola Dr in downtown, 843-8888, $12.65 members, $14.65 non-members. Also has private rooms, $29 members, $31 non-members. No telephone reservations. 'A 15 min walk from the bus station, but well worth the effort.' 'Very pleasant.' Shuttle to Disney–$10. Some discounts to attractions available. #13 bus from downtown.
Quality Inn Plaza, 9000 International Dr, 345-8585, (800) 999-8585. Rates vary during year but are based on per room, not per person. 4 people can stay in one room for under $15 each during off-peak and $20 each in season. Same applies to **International Inn**, 6327 International Drive, 351-4444, (800) 999-6327.
Travelodge, 409 Magnolia Ave, 423-1671. Free breakfast, pool, laundry room. Shuttles to Disney $15 return. 'Very friendly and helpful.' Also **Travelodge** at 1853 McCoy Rd, 851-1113, nr airport. $42. Free transport to and from airport and to attractions. Pool.
Young Women's Community Club, 107 E Hillcrest St near D-town, 425-2502. $12. For women only. Pool, laundry. 'Very nice.'
Camping: Kissimmee Campground, 2643 Alligator Lane (5 miles from Disney World), 396-6851. $17.75 for two, XP–$2. Call for directions.

KOA Disneyworld, off US 192 in Kissimmee, 396-2400. $42 for 4 in cabin. 'Basic, no electricity' but 'excellent' facilities—pool, store, laundry, showers. Also has tent sites, $19 for two. $25 with hook-up.
KOA Orlando, 12343 Narcoossee Road SE (Hwy 15, 4½ miles S of Hwy 528), 277-5075. $16 for two, XP–$3. $18 for lakeside site.

FOOD

Duffs Smorgasbord, all-you-can eat; all over Orlando.
Fat Boys Bar-B-Q, 1606 W Vine St, Kissimmee, 847-7098. 'Good steak.' Juke Box. Daily 6am–9pm, 10pm Fri.
Fox and Hounds Pub, 3514 W Vine St, Kissimmee, 847-9927. English/Irish decor and beer. Staffed by British. 'Worth a visit.' Mon–Sat 11.30am–2am, Sun 1pm–2am.
Ronnie's Restaurant, 2702 Colonial Plaza, 894-2943. New York-style deli food. Famous breakfast special $4.75. Sun–Thur 7am–11pm, Fri, Sat 7am–1am.
Church St Exchange offers a collection of shops and cheap places to eat from deli's to Mexican and Chinese. 'Fun atmosphere. Great bar downstairs.'

OF INTEREST

Prime your smile, open your wallet because a huge mouse with better name recognition than Bill Clinton is waiting for you at **Walt Disney World**. The huge complex of three theme parks, two water parks, an entertainment complex and thousands of hotel rooms sits glistening at Lake Buena Vista, about 15 miles south of Orlando on I-4. Some hotels and campgrounds offer free transportation to the complex while other commercial choices also are available. A 1-day ticket for one of the major theme parks is $35 + tax, while multi-day tickets are usable for any combination of the parks on any of the days you use the ticket (4-day $132, 5-day $180). Tips to avoid the longest queues include getting to the parks when they open and hitting the most popular attractions first or wait until late afternoon and evening. General information number—824-4321.
Magic Kingdom. The park that's the equivalent to Disneyland in Los Angeles and Tokyo, this is the place to venture on a ride through Space Mountain, to drift through the Pirates of the Caribbean or to watch all 41 US presidents come to life in one room. Exceeds Disneyland as a magnificent architectural, technological and entertainment achievement. 'You definitely need 2 days.' 'Great! I wish I was a child again.' 'Better than it's hyped up to be.' 'We thought the whole place was very artificial and plastic. Enormous queues for everything.' 'Visit after Labor Day to avoid queuing 1 hour for everything.' 'Food expensive, old and pre-packed.' 'Don't miss Space Mountain, but only if you like rollercoasters, 10,000 Leagues Under The Sea, Pirates of the Caribbean, and the amazing 3-D movie at the Kodak pavilion.'
Epcot Center (Experimental Prototype of Community of Tomorrow). Billed by some as an 'adult' amusement park and as 'dull' by others, the $1 billion Epcot is the second jewel in Disney's triple crown. Epcot has two worlds, Futureworld and the World Showcase. The former has exhibits and rides based on science and nature. Don't miss *Captain Eo*, the 3-D film starring Michael Jackson and a host of cuddly, floating creatures. It's all you can do not to reach out and touch them. *Wonders of Life* is a journey through the human body in a simulator designed by George Lucas, the father of *Star Wars*. While some readers call some of the pavilions, like the one by GM, 'mind-boggling boredom', with a future depicted that is already passé, others are 'wonderful', e.g. the incredible dinosaur ride in the Energy Pavilion. The World Showcase features pavilions from 11 lands, the most recent being Norway. All the employees in the showcase including the chefs come from their host countries and work at Disney for 1 year. Epcot has built a reputation as having the best food of any of the parks; visitors should make lunch and dinner reservations as soon as they enter the park at Spaceship Earth. Best bargain is the all-you-can-eat Norwegian smorgasbord. Be sure to view the park's

nightly spectacular laser display, illuminations. 'Not worth the price; very modern and technical, no place to have fun like in Disneyworld.' 'Unique, contemporary—very good.'

Disney/MGM Studios Theme Park. Opened in 1989 to great reviews and huge crowds. The park, designed as a movie set, is inhabited by various Disney characters as well as 'directors' and 'stars'. In addition to the standard rides and attractions, there is a backstage Studio Tour which offers a behind-the-scenes look at film making. Production for some Disney and Touchstone (its adult subsidiary) releases takes place here, but the main goal of the park is to bring in tourists and their dollars. The Great Movie Ride, Catastrophe Canyon, Star Tours, the Animation studio and the Indiana Jones Stunt Spectacular are highlights; recent additions include the Muppets in their own stage show, and those infamous Teenage Mutant Ninja Turtles.

Other Disney Parks. Of the two water parks, **River Country** and **Typhoon Lagoon**, the latter is of the 'traditional' variety with water slides and a wave machine, while River Country bills itself as the land of Tom Sawyer, where visitors can spend a lazy day swinging into lakes. Neither of the parks is covered by the multi-day passports. River Country, $14. Typhoon Lagoon, $21.75. For a taste of Disney nightlife, venture to **Pleasure Island**. Seven distinct nightclubs, as well as numerous shops and restaurants, inhabit the island. Open 7pm–2am, one admission charge of $14.80 allows you to visit all of the clubs.

Sea World, on I-4 between Orlando and Disneyworld, 351-3600. $32.95 adults. 9am–10pm. Features sharks, killer whales, walruses, multimedia fish and naked dolphins. 'One of the most spectacular aquatic animal displays I've ever seen.'

Wet n' Wild Amusement Park, off I-4 10 miles northeast of Disney, 351-3200. Water park with slides of all degrees of daring including two 7-story spectacular slides. 'Brilliant day out.' $22 adults, half-price after 5pm. Open 9am–11pm daily.

Universal Studios Orlando, near I-4 and the Florida Tnpk, 10 miles southwest of downtown, 363-8200. Open since May 1990, the largest movie studios outside Hollywood stretch 444 acres and feature such attractions as *ET Adventure*, King Kong in *Kongfrontation* (no more said), a *Back to the Future* ride with seven-storey high OMNIMAX screens, and *Ghostbusters*. There is also a tour of famous film sets which include Jaws, and the Bates Motel from *Psycho*. Open daily 9am–10pm. 1-day pass $39, 2-day pass $62.

INFORMATION

Orlando-Orange County Visitors and Convention Bureau, 363-5871, several miles southwest of downtown in Mercado, 8445 International Dr. Open daily 8am–8pm.

TRAVEL

Orlando Airport, 825-2001. 'Amazing airport, with fake monorail operated completely automatically.' #11 bus to town, 75¢.

Amtrak, 1400 Sligh Blvd, 843-7611.

Greyhound, 555 N Magruder St, (800) 231-2222.

Tri-County Transit, 841-8240. Bus system serves downtown, airport and Sea World. Fare 75¢.

Orlando Airport Limousine, 423-5566, 324 W Gore St, open 24 hours. $12.50 to airport, one-way. Also runs from most hotels to Disney for around $10 round trip.

THE GULF COAST Broader, blindingly white and generally cleaner than those in the East Coast, the beaches of the West Coast are why many people vacation here. The area between Fort Myers and St Petersburg (St Pete), where the best beaches are found, is growing rapidly, though areas of relative isolation can still be found. The largest concentration of retirees also can be found here.

TAMPA/ST PETERSBURG Tampa, located 22 miles east of St Pete, best known for its cigars, is the area's business centre while **Clearwater** is the most popular beach destination among the under 25-set. But looks are deceiving. Tampa's only real draws are Ybor City, a unique Latin quarter, and Busch Gardens, an amusement park. Clearwater has not-so-pleasant crowds and tall nondescript hotels. The best finds on the Sun Coast, as the area is called, are tucked away and tough to get to. But once there, the beauty and relaxed atmosphere are supreme.

At the other side of the bay is sedate St Pete, the 'Sunshine City', with a reputation for being a retirement community—*Cocoon* was filmed here—which helps obscure several interesting attractions as well as miles of excellent beaches.

ACCOMMODATION

Beach House Motel, Treasure Island, 360-1153. Doubles from $27 off-season. 'Right on the beach.'

Camping: St Petersburg KOA, 5400 95th St N, 392-2233. $21.95. 'Great.'

Clearwater Beach Intl Hostel, at the Sands Hotel, 606 Bay Esplanade Ave, Clearwater Beach, 443-1211. $12 members, $14 non-members. AC, free bikes, pool. 'Excellent, friendly & fun.'

Days Inn, 2901 E Busch Blvd, on Rt 580, 1¾ miles east of jct I-75, exit 33, 933-6471. Rooms $55, up to 4 people. AC, colour TV, coin laundry, pool. 10 minutes from Busch Gardens.

Dunedin Beach Campground, US 19 near Honeymoon Island, 784-3719. $19 a night for up to 4 people. 'Good campsite'.

Fort DeSoto Camp Grounds, 866-2662, near St Pete Beach, follow signs on Pinellas Bayway. Wildlife sanctuary composed of five islands. Sites $16.50. Call for availability but must make reservations in person at camp grounds, or 150 5th St N, #146, in St Pete, or 631 Chestnut St in Clearwater.

Motel 6, I-275 and Fowler Ave Exit, 932-4948. S–$26.50, XP–$6 (up to 4). AC. Pool.

Pass-A-Grille Beach Motel, 709 Gulf Way in St Petersburg Beach, 367-4726. Efficiency doubles from $43 off-season. Hotel overlooks gulf.

St Petersburg AYH Hostel at McCarthy Hotel, 326 1st Ave N, 822-4141. $11 night, $13 non.

St Petersburg/Gulf Beaches: AAIH-St Petersburg International Hostel at Detroit Hotel, 215 Central Ave, 822-4095. $11 night, $55 a week.

Shirley Ann Hotel, 936 1st Ave N, 894-2759. S–$28, D–$35, T–$45 (private bath). 'Clean, comfortable. Owners are lovely people.'

Spanish Main Travel Parkway, 12101 US Hwy 301 N, 986-2415. Tent sites $13.50 for 2, XP–$1.

Tampa: Belmont Motel, 734 S Dale Mabry, on US 92, 1½ miles south of I-275, exit 23, 877-5843. S–$30, D–$33, fridge, colour TV, AC, pool.

FOOD/ENTERTAINMENT

Cha Cha Coconuts, The Pier in St Petersburg, 822-6655. Mon–Thur 11am–mid, Fri–Sat 11am–1am, Sun noon–10pm. Sandwiches and ribs under $5. Live jazz, reggae and rock Wed–Sun nights.

Gold Coffee Shop, 1st Ave N, next to St Pete YHA, 822-4922. Open 6am–4pm. 'Amazing old fashioned lunch counter. Really cheap food—full breakfast for $2, main meal under $4.'

Hurricane Seafood Restaurant, 807 Gulf Way in St Petersburg Beach, 360-9558. Right on Pass-A-Grille beach, famous for its grouper sandwich and other seafood selections from $4. Open daily for lunch and dinner as well as live jazz Wed–Sun 9.30pm–1am.

Carmine's, 1802 7th Ave in Tampa's Ybor City, 248-3834. Italian and Cuban fare under $6 for lunch and dinner. Live music on Sat nights.

Cafe Creole, 1330 9th Ave E in Tampa's Ybor City, 247-6283. Cajun cuisine from $8–$12. Live cajun music and Dixieland jazz Wed–Sat. Also check the music scene at **El Pasaje Plaza** next door, live cajun and zydeco played outdoors on the weekends.

OF INTEREST

St Petersburg: Almost everything worth seeing in St Petersburg is located downtown but take caution after dark and stay in well-lit areas. The city's focal point and the centrepiece of the waterfront is **The Pier**, a recently renovated 5-story upside-down pyramid in the middle of Tampa Bay. The Pier, 2nd Ave NE, 821-6164. Open Mon–Sat 10am–8pm, Sun 12am–6pm; houses a variety of shops, restaurants and the **University of South Florida Aquarium**, 895-7437, free. For miles in both directions of The Pier, you can walk through waterfront parks, beaches and marinas.

The Museum of Fine Arts, 255 Beach Dr NE, 896-2667, is near the entrance to the Pier and boasts of having one of the largest photography collections in the Southeast. Open Tues–Sat 10am–5pm, Sun 1pm–5pm. $4 suggested donation.

Salvador Dali Musuem, 1000 3rd St S, 823-3767. Largest collection of surrealist works by the Spanish master. Adults $5, students $3.50, Tues–Sat 9.30am–5.30pm, Sun 12pm–5.30pm. Across the street at 1120 4th St S is **Great Explorations**, 821-8885, one of the better 'hands-on' museums that appeals to adults. $5. Open Mon–Sat 10am–5pm, Sun noon–5pm.

Sunken Gardens, 1825 4th St N, 896-3186, is a 5-acre sinkhole filled with tropical flora and fauna. Open 9am–5.30pm (last ticket 5pm); $8.95. Also has **Biblical Wax Museum**. Open 10am–4.30pm. Free.

Thirty miles north of St Petersburg off the hellish highway US 19 is **Tarpon Springs**, a small colony of Greek fisherman who have been harvesting sponges for generations. Stroll through the village, dine on Greek fare and soak in **Spongeorama**, the free sponge museum open daily 10am–6pm on Dodecanese Blvd, 942-3771.

On the Beaches: Of the group, **Pass-A-Grille Beach** and **Caladesi/Honeymoon Islands** are 'supreme'. **Pass-A-Grille**, at the southern tip of St Petersburg Beach, combines the dunes, quaint shops, dolphins, and casual sun worshippers into a good mix. Take I-275 to the Bayway exit, the last exit before leaving the peninsula, then head west to the beach.

Caladesi Island State Park and **Honeymoon Island State Recreation Area** have preserved the pristine state of the gulf shore while providing miles of white sand for beach goers. Side-by-side, one admission price admits you to both islands but the only way to get to Caladesi is by ferry, $4. Call 734-5263 for information. Ferry runs hourly 10am–4pm weekdays, half-hourly 10am–5pm weekends. When the gate keeper asks if you're from Florida, say yes—it's cheaper. Located between Tarpon Springs and Clearwater, take US 19 to State Road 586 and head west to the end of the road.

Tampa: Watch the **banana boats** dock and unload at Kennedy Blvd and 13th St. A stroll along Bayshore Blvd brings you a string of southern mansions.

The Tampa Theater, 223-8981, a genuine old-time movie palace from the 1920s, designed in Rococco, Mediterranean and maybe other styles, the theatre shows old movies and art films at good prices, and when the show starts, watch the stars come out on the ceiling above. Franklin St in downtown Tampa. $4.75 admission.

Busch Gardens—The Dark Continent, just off Rt 580, 987-5171. $31.90 adults, open daily in summer 8.45am–8pm, closes 6pm rest of year. Take an African safari to view more than 1000 animals, as well as dolphins and belly dancers, roller-coaster rides, shows, etc.

Adventure Island, 4500 Bougainvillea Ave, 1 mile northeast of Busch Gardens, 987-5660, is one of the better water parks in Florida complete with water slides, rapids, wave pool, etc. $18.85. Open daily in summer, 9am–8pm.

Museum of Science and Industry, 4801 E Fowler Ave, 985-5531, features a simulated hurricane. $5 adults. Open Sun–Thurs 9am–6pm. Till 9pm Fri & Sat.

Museum of Art, 601 Doyle Carlton Drive, 223-8130. Ancient and contemporary art from Impressionism to photography. Open Tue–Sat 10am–5pm (Wed open till 9pm), Sun 1pm–5pm. $3.50. Students $2.50.
Ybor City, which was once the 'cigar manufacturing headquarters of the world', in the process of being gentrified, Ybor retains a stylish Latin influence. Learn of its history and that of the cigar industry at the **Ybor City State Museum**, 1818 9th Ave, 247-6323. Open Tue–Sat 9am–noon, 1pm–5pm. $1. Although several restaurants with live music and dance bars are in the area, take precaution when walking through Ybor at night.

INFORMATION
St Petersburg Chamber of Commerce, 100 2nd Ave N, 821-4069.
St Pete Beach Chamber of Commerce, 6990 Gulf Blvd, 360-6957.
Clearwater Chamber of Commerce, 128 N Osceola Ave, 461-0011.
Greater Tampa Chamber of Commerce, 801 E Kennedy Blvd, 228-7777.

TRAVEL
Tampa: Amtrak, 601 Nebraska Ave, 221-7600.
Greyhound, 610 E Polk St, 229-2112 or (800) 231-2222.
Hillsborough Area Regional Transit, 254-HART, 85¢. #30 between airport and downtown.
St Petersburg: Greyhound, 189 9th St N, (800) 231-2222.
Pinellas Suncoast Transit Authority, 530-9911. Runs 6am–6pm, 90¢ fare.
BATS (bus service through the beaches), 367-3702. $1.25.

THE PANHANDLE The strip of land jabbing into Alabama, the panhandle has more in common with the states of the Deep South than it does with sub-tropical South Florida. Winter is distinctly cooler here and the terrain is broken up with that rarity in Florida, a hill.

Hidden away in the hills and forests is **Tallahassee**, the state capital. Much as the town seems able to resist the invasion of tourists today, it also avoided capture by the Union forces during the Civil War, the only Confederate capital east of Mississippi with that distinction. This is a city of real Floridians, not transplanted northerners, and there's still much of its 19th century architecture to see, and a slower way of life to appreciate.

Moving further west along the Panhandle, you come to **Panama City** and the commercialised resort of **Panama City Beach**. Panama City runs on Central Standard Time and so is one hour behind the rest of Florida. It used to be a peaceful fishing village and it remains quieter than most places along this coast. The developers are moving in, however, in the wake of their triumphs down the road at Panama City Beach. The beach really is lovely and the sea is clear and warm, but everything is over-priced and over-populated.

Further west still, and the last city in Florida, is **Pensacola**. Since the first successful settlement here in 1698, Pensacola has flown the flags of five nations and has changed hands 13 times. The British used it as a trading post in the 18th century and business seems to have been good, for here Scotsman James Panton became America's first recorded millionaire. Here too, in 1821, Andrew Jackson completed the transaction whereby Spain sold Florida to the United States.

The white sand beaches near Pensacola are among the best in Florida; after a dip you're on your way west to **Gulf Islands National Seashore** (see Biloxi, Mississippi) and to New Orleans. Information Center in Gulf Breeze, (904) 932-1500.

GEORGIA

Georgia has seen rough times. Named after George II, the state began as an English debtor's colony, and many died before the swamps were cleared for cotton fields. Just when things were looking up, the final moments of the Civil War saw Union General Sherman break through rebel defenses at Chattanooga and devastate a 60 mile-wide swath to the sea.

But unlike some other states of the Deep South, the Peach State has chosen to look more to the future than to the past, and since the Second World War has been rising on the crest of an industrial boom. Atlanta is now the unchallenged capital of the 'New South'. Peanut farmer Jimmy Carter marched out of the anonymity of Plains to become president in 1976, and Savannah is still a strong rival to Charleston's claim as the most beautiful city in the South.

The area code for Atlanta is 404, for Savannah and Southern Georgia 912.

ATLANTA Host to the forthcoming 1996 Olympic Games, Atlanta's story has so far been one of fast-growing success. Founded in 1837 as a site for the South Western terminal of the Western & Atlantic Railroad, Atlanta was, by the time of the Civil War, the commercial and industrial centre of the South. In 1864, General Sherman 'drove old Dixie down', with his devastating march to the sea, during which Atlanta was bombarded and then burned to the ground, as immortalised in *Gone with the Wind*.

The city rose again, and has shown that progress counts more than prejudice. Atlantans elected their first black mayor in 1973, and it was here that Martin Luther King was raised and first preached.

Its skyscraper skyline, crisscrossing expressway system and ultra-modern airport (one of the 3 busiest in the world), while proclaiming perhaps Atlanta's leadership of the 'New South', tend to be boring and charmless. However, Peachtree Street (be careful, there are 32 Peach Tree Streets in Atlanta), financial hub of the ante-bellum South, still retains some of its presence, and, away from downtown, the city's hills, wooded streets and numerous colleges—Atlanta University, Clark College, Emory University and the Georgia Institute of Technology—create a pleasant atmosphere. The Dogwood Festival here in April is the highlight of the year.

On the debit side, Atlanta has one of the worst murder records of urban America. After working hours, downtown is soulless, even uncomfortable. Tread carefully.

ACCOMMODATION

International Youth Travel Program, run by the Atlanta Visitors Bureau refers students to discount hotel rooms. 'Can cost as little as $15 per night in good hotel.' 'Go there first, very helpful.' Open Mon–Fri 8.30am–5.30pm, 521-6600. Must make reservations at office. On the 20th floor of Harris Tower in Peach Tree Center.

Atlanta Dream Hostel, 222 E Howard Ave, 370-0380. Located in a safe and fun intown neighbourhood, 2 blocks from Decatur metro. $10 per night. 24 hrs, no curfew, kitchen/laundry facilities, TV lounge. Free coffee, local calls and pick-up service (call for availability).

Bed and Breakfast Atlanta, 1801 Piedmont Ave NE, 875-0525, offers rooms in desirable neighbourhoods in and near Atlanta from $42 single, $55 double, but it's advisable to reserve in advance; reservation is free of charge. 'Southern hospitality in the European tradition.'
Villa International, 1749 Clifton Rd NE, 633-6783. 'A ministry of the Christian community.' Situated nr Emory U in a pleasant and safe suburb and next door to the Center for Disease Control. 'Quiet with a very helpful staff, though a little shabby.' S–$26 with shower, $34 small double, $40 double. No TV/tel.
Woodruff AYH Hostel, 223 Ponce de Leon Ave, 875-2882. 5 blocks east of North Avenue MARTA. AYH $13.25, non-members $16.25. 'Clean, safe and friendly.'
YMCA, 22 Butler St NE, 659-8085. Singles from $16 per night, $66 per week. Men only. No AC, 'stuffy and tatty rooms.'
Numerous budget motels, e.g. **Scottish Inns, Red Carpet Inn, Comfort Inn**, in Atlanta area, but you'll need a car and they usually cost more here than elsewhere. Look around Myrtle, Piedmont, Peachtree and Ponce DeLeon.

FOOD

Atlanta's specialties are fried chicken, black-eyed peas, okra and sweet potato pie.
Barkers Red Hots, 136 Marietta St NW, 584-8518. Dinner from $3–$6. Named 'Atlanta's Best Hot Dog'—a city landmark!
Junior's Grill, 124 North Ave NW, 881-8059. Small, friendly reasonably priced restaurant. Good breakfast. Open 6am–1.30pm Mon–Fri.
Mary-Macs, 224 Ponce DeLeon Ave NE, 875-4337. Good, cheap food (try the green turnip soup and corn muffins). Open 11am–3pm daily. 'Where the natives eat!'
Pitty Pat's Porch, 25 International Blvd, 525-8228. 'Great atmosphere.' Prices start at $16.95. Open 5pm–9ish daily. Sat and Sun till 10pm.
P J Haley's Pub, Sage Hill Shopping Center, 1799 Briarcliff Rd, 874-3116. Near Emory U. A lively pub with good food and a wide selection of beers.
The Varsity, North Ave at I-75, 881-1706. World's largest drive-in, next to Georgia Tech campus. Serves 15,000 people with 8,300 Colas, 18,000 hamburgers, 25,000 hotdogs each day. 'Clean, fast, cheap and good.' Mon–Fri 8am–12am, Sat, Sun 8am–2am.
Three large markets with cheap produce, meats, cheeses, etc: **Atlanta Municipal Market**, 209 Edgewood Ave in downtown, 659-1665 (Mon–Thurs 8am–5.45pm; Fri, Sat 6.45pm); **DeKalb Farmer's Market**, 3000 E Ponce de Leon Ave outside Decatur, 377-6400 (Mon–Fri 10am–9pm; Sat, Sun 9am–9pm); and **Atlanta State Farmer's Market** 15 miles south of downtown off I-75, 366-6910, open 24 hours.

OF INTEREST

Memorial & Grave of Martin Luther King Jr, in Ebenezer Baptist Churchyard at 413 Auburn Ave NW, 688-7263. The inscription on the tomb reads: 'Free at last, free at last, thank God Almighty, I'm free at last'. Includes inter-faith Peace Chapel. Open Mon–Fri 9.30am–4pm. 'Be careful in this area.'
Next door is the **ML King Jr. Center for Non Violent Social Change**, 449 Auburn Ave, 524-1956. Free tour of his home and exhibits on the slain civil rights leader. Free film on his life. Open 9am–8pm daily in summer. Tours 10am–6pm.
State Capitol, Washington at Mitchell, 656-2844. Modelled on the Washington DC capitol building and topped with gold from the Georgia goldfield at Dahlonega, brought to Atlanta by special wagon caravan. Houses state **Museum of Science and Industry, Hall of Flags** and **Georgia Hall of Fame**. Open 8am–5.30pm daily. Tours 10am–2pm (exc. noon). Free.
Underground Atlanta, in downtown around Upper Alabama St. 12-acre complex housing more than 130 restaurants, shops and nightclubs. Impressive 10-storey light tower at main entrance. Shops open Mon–Sat 10am–9.30pm, Sun noon–6pm; restaurant/club hours vary.
World of Coca-Cola, 55 Martin Luther King Dr, 676-5151. Adjacent to Underground Atlanta; the pavilion includes historic memorabilia, radio and TV

retrospective, a futuristic soda fountain and an 18 ft coke bottle! 'Watch the film and hear how Coca-Cola helped win World War II! . . . Brilliant museum, brilliant value.' Open 10am–9.30pm, Sun noon–6pm; $2.50.

Science and Technology Museum of Atlanta (Sci Trek), 395 Piedmont Ave, 552-5500. Said to be one of the top ten physical science museums in America; hands-on science exhibits. Open daily 10am–5pm; $6.

The Atlanta Historical Society, 3101 Andrews Dr NW, 814-4000. 34 acres of landscaped gardens and trails. Library, archives, exhibitions and films on Atlanta and its history. 9am–5.30pm Mon–Sat, noon–5.30pm Sun. Admission to gardens $3 or $6 incl guided tours of mansions and grounds.

Atlanta Preservation Center, 84 Peachtree St NW, 876-2040. Guided walking tours of Atlanta's historic districts conducted 3 times weekly. $5; $3 for students.

High Museum of Art, 1280 Peachtree St NE, 892-3600 for general info and 892-4444 for exhibit info. Tue–Sat 10am–5pm, Sun noon–5pm. Adults $4, students $2. Free, Thur 1pm–5pm, Fri open till 9pm. 'Intriguing design. Excellent and varied temporary exhibitions, plus good American 19th century collection.'

Jimmy Carter Presidential Center, Cleburne Ave, off Highland Ave, 331-3942. Museum on the Carter presidency plus presidents old and modern. Mon–Sat 9am–4.45pm, Sun noon–4.45pm, $2.50. 'Well worth it.'

Joel Chandler Harris, author of the Uncle Remus stories, lived at **Wren's Nest**, 1050 Abernathy Blvd, 753-7735. See the briar Brer Rabbit lived in. Entrance $3. Open Tue–Sat 10am–4pm, Sun 1pm–4pm.

Cyclorama, in Grant Park, 658-7625. 100-year-old circular painting (one of the largest in the world) with 3-dimensional diorama complete with lighting and sound effects, depicting the Battle of Atlanta. Don't miss the *Texas*, of the Great Locomotive Chase of the Civil War (immortalised by Buster Keaton in *The General*). Open daily 9.30am–5.30pm: $3.50, $3 students.

Further **Civil War memorabilia** in the area include the breastworks erected for the defence of the town—in Grant Park, Cherokee Ave and Boulevard SE—and Fort Walker, Confederate Battery, set up as during the siege.

Stone Mountain, Grant Park. In massive bas-relief the equestrian figures of Generals Robert E Lee, Stonewall Jackson and Confederate President Jefferson Davis have been cut from a 600-ft-high granite dome, the world's largest exposed mass of granite. Astride this mountain, looking down on Lee and Davis you can understand why King, in his 'I have a dream' speech said 'Let freedom ring from Stone Mountain in Georgia'. A cable car runs to the top, or you can climb it. Also in the 3200-acre historical and recreational park is an ante-bellum plantation, an antique auto and music museum, a game ranch, riverboat cruises, a 5-mile steam railroad and more. Entrance to the park is $5 a car, and then you pay for attractions individually, $3 each. Dazzling nightly laser show at 9.30pm at no extra cost. 'Worth waiting till dark: brilliant effects.' 'Take MARTA bus and you don't pay the $5.' 25 miles east of Atlanta off Hwy 78, 498-5600. Gates open 6am–midnight, attractions open 10am–5.30pm, 8.30pm in summer. One way to get to the park is on the **New Georgia Railroad**, a collection of turn-of-the-century passenger coaches that make Saturday tours to the park. Depot at Zero Mile Post near Underground Atlanta, 656-0769. Stone Mtn trip $39.50 incl. dinner.

Regency Hyatt Hotel, 265 Peachtree St NE, 577-1234. Built like a hollow skyscraper. A spectacular piece of engineering with statutory revolving restaurant at the top. The walls of the building are one suite thick and there's nothing in the middle. After 6pm you'll have to be jacketed and tied if you want to go to the top.

Marriott Marquis, 265 Peachtree Center Ave, 521-0000. Newest of the spectacular genre of hotels featuring a breathtaking atrium. A must-see if you are in Atlanta. Most expensive to construct and largest hotel in the southeast.

CNN Center, Marietta St at Techwood Dr, 827-2400. Tour the studios of this 24-hour all news network. $6. Mon–Fri 10am–5pm, Sat 10am–4pm.

Next door is the **Omni Coliseum**, home of the Atlanta Hawks basketball team. Call 249-6400 for tickets.

The Atlanta Fulton Stadium, 521 Capitol Ave, is the home of the **Braves** baseball team, winners of the National League 2 years running (91-92). Call 249-6400 for tickets. American football is played by the **Falcons** at the new **Georgia Dome** which hosted the 1994 Superbowl and will also host some of the Olympic events in 1996.

ENTERTAINMENT

Read the free, weekly *Creative Loafing*, *Atlanta Gazette* and *Where Magazine* to find out what goes on. 'You should make it clear that Atlanta, especially midtown, is known second only to San Francisco for a large gay community.'

Piedmont Park, free open-air jazz and classical concerts, Atlanta Philharmonic Orchestra, throughout the summer. First week in Sept, Atlanta Jazz Festival. 'Not to be missed. People dance, drink; on a good evening it can be like the last night of the proms. Also watch the fireflies do illuminated mating dances.' Park also has an open-air swimming pool. 'Beautiful; great for a rest and a free shower. Friendly pool attendants.' Open to public 2pm–6.30pm daily, noon–8pm weekends. Free 2pm–5pm Mon–Fri; $1 other times. Keep eyes open at night; not too friendly a neighbourhood.

Six Flags Over Georgia, 12 miles west on I-20. 331-acre entertainment park, home to the 'Georgia Cyclone' rollercoaster and such rides as 'Mind Bender' and 'Splashwater Falls'. Open Sun–Thur 10am–10pm, Fri, Sat 10am–midnight. One day entrance fee $25, $28.50 for two-day pass. Take MARTA to Hightower Station, then bus # 201. 'Don't go on Saturdays as you will spend the whole day in queues.'

The Fox, 660 Peachtree, 881-2100. Second largest movie theatre in America and now a national landmark. One of the last great movie palaces. Built in 1929; Moorish design. Now a venue for concerts, theatre and special film presentations. Call for listings.

INFORMATION

Visitors Center, Harris Tower, 233 Peachtree St NE, Suite 2000, 521-6600. Open Mon–Fri 8.30am–5.30pm. 'Far more helpful than Chamber of Commerce.' Satellite locations in Lenox Square Mall and Underground Atlanta.

Chamber of Commerce, Omni Building, Marietta St, 880-9000. 'Very helpful.'

Travelers Aid, in Greyhound Terminal, 81 International Blvd NW, 527-7411. Open Mon–Fri 8am–8pm, Sat 10am–6pm.

TRAVEL

MARTA (Metropolitan Atlanta Rapid Transit Authority) is the affectionate name given to the city's superb new subway system, 848-4711. Transfers between subway and buses. Basic fare $1, 1 week pass $9 for unlimited travel on MARTA train and buses. Subway runs 5am–1am.

Greyhound, 81 International Blvd NW, (800) 231-2222. Bus station is in bad area.

Amtrak, Peachtree Station, 1688 Peachtree St NW, (800) 872-7245. The NY–New Orleans *Crescent* stops here daily.

Hartsfield International Airport is situated 12 miles south of the city; 530-6600 for general info. MARTA buses can take you downtown, 15 mins rides run every 8 mins. The Atlanta Airport Shuttle (525-2177) also runs a service to mid or downtown ($8–$12). Taxis $15 one-way (530-6698). An impressive, innovative piece of building.

SAVANNAH When Ray Charles sings *Georgia on My Mind*, it's surely Savannah and *not* Atlanta he's mooning over. Laid out in 1733 by English General James Oglethorpe, Savannah was America's first planned city and Georgia's oldest. In one of the earliest evangelical movements, Charles and John Wesley, accompanied Oglethorpe as missionaries, later establishing in the city the Wesleyan Methodist Church. After seeing what Sherman had done to Atlanta in 1864, Savannah wisely decided to surrender, saving her charming gardens, public squares and old homes from certain destruction.

What Sherman spared, however, seemed almost doomed by declining cotton prices. The town was run-down until restoration efforts began on Trustees Garden in the 1950s. Today, the city (which has no less than 21 squares) echoes with reminders of its colonial past. Warehouses once housing stores of cotton and now shops and restaurants, line the cobblestoned River Street which runs along the Savannah River. Here, monthly parades, concerts and other events take place; St Patrick's Day celebrations are said to rival those of New York. The first steamship (the *Savannah*, of course) crossed the Atlantic to Liverpool (in 1819) from here, the 10th largest port in the US. And an old seamen's pub referred to in Robert Louis Stevenson's *Treasure Island* still survives as the Pirate's House.

The telephone area code is 912.

ACCOMMODATION

Bed and Breakfast Inn, 117 W Gordon at Chatham Sq, 233-9481. In the heart of the historic district, an 1853 townhouse. 'Clean and well maintained.' S-$36 up, D-$53 up, incl. breakfast and shared bath.

Thunderbird Inn, 611 West Oglethorpe Ave, 232-2661. S-$31, D-$34 and up. Nr bus station.

Camping: Bellaire Woods Campground, GA Hwy 204, 15 miles northwest from downtown, 748-4000. $19 for 2 people; with water and electricity.

Skidway Island State Park, 6 miles SE of downtown on Waters Ave, 598-2300. $12 for first night, $10 thereafter.

Youth Hostel, 304 E Hall St, 236-7744; $12 AYH members, $13 non. Just open.

FOOD

Faber's, 20 W Broughton St, 232-7859. Subs, sandwiches, salads. 'Good value, generous portions, and their pizza sub is superb!' Open 7.30am–3pm, Mon–Fri.

Crystal Beer Parlour, 301 W Jones St, 232-1153. Hamburgers, chili dogs, seafood, gumbo. Open 11am–9pm Mon–Sat.

Morrison's Cafeteria, 15 Bull St, 232-5264. Good and inexpensive. Closes 8pm.

Shucker's Seafood Restaurant, almost at end of W River St, 236-1427. 'Recommended by the locals, it's casual, with a laid-back atmosphere and good food.' Open 11.30am–10pm daily.

Spanky's Pizza Galley and Saloon, 317 East River St, 236-3009. 'River Street's favourite good-time saloon.' Dinner $5.50–$10.

Wally's Sixpence Pub, 245 Bull St, 233-3151. Mon–Sat 11.30–midnight. 'A haunt of unusual and interesting characters.'

OF INTEREST

Old Savannah offers cobbled streets, charming squares, formal gardens and several beautiful mansions. Among the stately houses of the town is the **Owens-Thomas House**, at 124 Abercorn St, 233-9743, at which Lafayette was a visitor in 1825. Open Tue–Sat 10am–4.30pm, Sun, Mon 2pm–4.30pm; $5; $3 students.

Green-Meldrim House, Madison Sq, 233-3848, is where General Sherman enjoyed his victory, $3. The Green-Meldrim serves as Parish house for the Gothic Revival Style **St John's Episcopal Church**, built 1852. Open Tue–Sat 10am–4pm.

Savannah Waterfront. The old cotton trade buildings, restored, reconstructed and used as restaurants, shops and night spots. 'Beware: it's a tourist trap with masses of souvenir shops and over priced beer.'

In the same vein is **City Market**, four restored warehouses now as shops, restaurants, jazz clubs and artists' studios. At St Julian and Jefferson Sts.

Ships of the Sea Maritime Museum, 503 E River St, 232-1511. Models and maritime memorabilia. Open daily 10am–5pm, $3 adults.
Telfair Academy of Arts and Sciences, 121 Barnard St, 232-1177. The oldest art museum in the southeast and the home of a fine collection of portraits and 18th century masterpieces. Tue–Sat 10am–5pm, Sun 2pm–5pm, closed Mon. $3, $1 students; free on Sun.
Christ Episcopal Church, 28 Bull St, 232-8230. First church in Georgia; the present building was erected in 1840. John Wesley preached here in 1736-37, arousing extraordinary emotions in the congregation. He also founded the first Sunday school here.
Temple Mickve Israel, 20 E Gordon, 233-1547. Seeking religious freedom, a group of Sephardic Jews from England were among the first to settle here in 1733. The oldest congregation practicing reform Judaism. The synagogue looks like a church, complete with a steeple, choir loft, and gothic design. No one is sure why the Orthodox congregation built it this way. Tours in morning, afternoon (10am––noon, 2pm–4pm). Two of the Torahs, the oldest in America, are from the original congregation. Services Friday evening, Saturday morning.

ENTERTAINMENT
Kevin Barry's, 117 W River St, 233-9626, Irish pub immortalised in a song, offering good, cheap Irish food, Guinness on draught (not so cheap!) and Irish folk music. Mon–Sat 11pm–3am, Sun 12.30–2am.

INFORMATION/TRAVEL
Savannah Visitors Center, 301 Martin Luther King Blvd, 944-0460. Literature, maps, a self-guided walking tour leaflet, slide show. Many tours start here. Open Mon–Fri 8.30am–5pm; Sat, Sun 9am–5pm.
Chamber of Commerce, 222 W Oglethorpe Ave, 944-0456.
Gray Line Bus Tours, 236-9604.
Amtrak, 2611 Seaboard Coastline Blvd.
Greyhound, 610 W Oglethorpe, (800) 231-2222.

OKEFENOKEE SWAMP This large swamp area lies in southeast Georgia. Eight miles south of **Waycross** on highways US 1 and US 23, is the **Okefenokee Swamp Park**, 283-0583. This is a private park with an observation tower, 2-mile boat tour (special 2-hour 'Deep Swamp' also available), and walkways enabling you to take in the cypresses, flowers, aquatic birds, bears and alligators without getting your feet wet. There is also a museum telling the story of the 'Land of the Trembling Earth' (the old Indian name for the swamp). Entrance to the park is $8. Open 9am–6.30pm daily. For information on the **Federal Park**, telephone 496-3331. The park offers 2–5 days canoe trips (reserve in advance). Canoe trips range from $11 for a day.

KENTUCKY

A land of country pleasures, Kentucky's bluegrass hills have yielded bourbon whiskey, fried chicken, fast horses and even faster bluegrass music. Since 1769 when Daniel Boone cleared the Wilderness Trail to settle the first lands west of the Allegheny Mountains, Kentuckians have quietly elevated country living into an art form. Bluegrass Music features complex picking on guitars, banjos and fiddles, sometimes tedious in its traditional forms, but exhilarating in its progressive modes. Merle Travis, who initiated the famous Travis-style picking is from the state. Kentucky produces 87% of the world's bourbon (from Bourbon county) and bottles almost half of the nation's whiskey. The abundance of fertile bluegrass, which is not actually blue—it is green and blossoms blue in spring, attracted livestock farmers and in particular, horses. As a consequence the Kentucky equine passion has developed into a refined, multi-million dollar international obsession indulged annually at Louisville's Kentucky Derby.

Hardy country living has bred many proud Kentucky natives, among them Henry Clay, Jefferson Davis, Abraham Lincoln and Muhammed Ali. Kentucky's fighting spirit, important reserves of coal and strategic location made it a decisive factor in the Civil War. Even though the Constitution says nothing about allowing a state to be 'neutral', that is what Kentucky tried to be. A worried Lincoln was said to have remarked that he hoped to have God on his side, but he had to have Kentucky.

National park: Mammoth Caves

The area code for Louisville, Frankfurt and western KY is 502, for Lexington and eastern KY, 606.

LOUISVILLE The most prestigious horse race in the country, the Kentucky Derby, is held here the first week in May amidst a festival atmosphere of parades, concerts and a steamboat race.

Founded by George Rogers Clark as a supply base on the Ohio for his Northwest explorations, Louisville is now a commercial, industrial and educational centre specializing in things that are supposed to be bad for you. Fast food, bourbon whiskey and cigarettes are made here in abundance. This is also the hometown of the Louisville Lip, though the boulevard named after him is called Muhammed Ali.

Keep your eyes on the fountain in the Ohio River directly outside downtown. The tallest computerized floating fountain in the world, a series of 41 jets and 102 coloured lights create some spectacular effects.

Enroute from here to **Mammoth Caves** are various folksy attractions, including Abraham Lincoln's birthplace at Hodgenville, Stephen Foster's original 'My Old Kentucky Home' and the Lincoln Homestead nearby. Note: Louisville is pronounced Loo-AH-ville.

ACCOMMODATION

Motel 6, 3304 Bardstown Rd, 456-2861. Exit 16A off I-264. S–$27.50, D–$34, XP–$6.
Emily Boone Home Hostel AYH, 1027 Franklin St, 585-3430. $6.25, non-members $10, plus 20 minutes of chores around the house. Reservations are essential, make sure you speak with the proprietor directly. 2 miles from bus station, nr Farmers' Market.
Thrifty Dutchman Budget Hotel, 3357 Fern Valley Rd, 968-8124. Off I-65. S–$41.75 up, D–$52.75.

FOOD

BBQ's, burgoo stew and cured ham are all Kentucky delicacies, unlike the famed fried chicken (see the Colonel Sanders Museum below).
Check's Cafe, 1101 Burnett, 637-9515. Local favourite where a full meal runs under $4. Hamburgers from $1.10. Open 8am–9pm Mon–Sat, Sun 1pm–9pm.
The Old Spaghetti Factory, 235 W Market St, 581-1070. Full dinner with pasta, salad, bread and desert $4.95–$6.95. Open 7 days 5pm–10pm. Fri & Sat till 11pm.

Phoenix Hill Tavern, 644 Baxter Ave, 589-4957. Live music every night till 4am plus cheap sandwiches. $2 or $3 cover charge.
The Rudyard Kipling, 422 W Oak St, 636-1311, 7 blks south of downtown in Old Louisville. 'Hearty food and drink from all around the world.' Here you can eat anything from curry to crêpes as well as a variety of national pasties! Try a bowl of Kentucky burgoo (a meat and veg stew) for $3. Mon and Wed nights offer folk and jazz music; theatre is performed on the in-house stage during Sept and Oct. 'If you eat one meal in Louisville, eat it here.' Open Mon–Thurs 11.30am–2pm and 5.30pm–midnight, Fri from 11.30am and Sat from 5.30pm till midnight.

OF INTEREST
Churchill Downs, home of the **Kentucky Derby**, 700 Central Ave, 636-4400. On the morning of Derby Day, the first Saturday in May, arrive around 8am to claim a small piece of the track infield for $20 a person. The big race is in the afternoon, but the partying goes on all day. Potent mint juleps, the drink of the South, are available from vendors. Racing also takes place from the end of April to early July and late October to late November. At gate 1 stands the **Kentucky Derby Museum**, 637-1111, open daily 9am–5pm. $3.50 adults, $1.50 kids. Includes exhibits on horseracing and breeding, and an exciting 360 degree movie theatre that puts you in the middle of the race. Shows every hour.
Each August Louisville hosts the **Kentucky State Fair** which features the World Championship Horse Show for American saddlebreds—Kentucky's native horse breed.
JB Speed Art Museum, 2035 3rd St, 636-2893, Tues–Sat 10am–4pm, Sun noon–5pm free. One of the better mid-South galleries. Medieval, Renaissance and French works, a strong Dutch collection and a spacious sculpture court. The museum boasts an elborately carved, oak-panelled English Renaissance room from 'The Grange', Devon. Thomas Jefferson was the architect of the **John Speed Mansion, Farmington**, 3033 Bardstown Rd, 452-9920. $3. During the summer (mid-June–Aug), Shakespeare falls trippingly off the tongue in Louisville's **Central Park**. You will not have to pay a pound of flesh, it's free, 634-8237 for details. Curtain is 8.30pm, Tue–Sun.
Col Harland Sanders Museum, 1441 Gardiner Lane, 456-8300. Free museum records the life of the 'finger lickin' good' chicken purveyor who helped start the phenomenon of fast food. Open Mon–Thur 8am–5pm, Fri 8am–1pm.
A pleasant way to spend an afternoon is to take a cruise on the Ohio River on the ***Belle of Louisville***, 625-2355, an old sternwheeler. The boat leaves from the landing at 4th at 2pm and 7pm (sunset cruise) Tue–Sun between late May and early Sept. $7.50; Saturday night 'dancing cruise', $12.
The **Corn Island Storytelling Festival**, usually the third weekend in September, 245-0643, uses the *Belle* for a storytelling tour along the river. The most popular festival event is the **Long Run Park** ghost story event. Held near an old graveyard, thousands come out to hear the tales beginning at nightfall. Festival tickets for all the events are $32 for one or $55 for a couple. Individual event tickets also are available. **Howard Steamboat Museum**, 1101 E Market St, (812) 283-3728, Tue–Sat 10am–3pm, Sun 1pm–3pm, $4 adults, $2 students. Billed as the 'only museum of its kind in the US', models of steamboats, tools and pilot wheels are on display. Located across the Ohio River from Louisville in Jeffersonville, Indiana.
Jim Beam's American Outpost has a 10 minute movie and self-guided tour which shows you the joys of bourbon-making. (Bourbon is made using at least 51% corn and must be aged at least two years, preferably in a charred white oak container. Anything less is 'just' whiskey.) The tour is free, Mon–Sat 9am–4.30pm, Sun 1pm–4pm, 543-2221 for details. Follow I-65 22 miles south from Louisville, then east on Rt 245 toward **Clermont**.
America hoards her gold at **Fort Knox**, 25 miles SW of Louisville on US31W-60. Don't expect to see the metal, but if you're in a military frame of mind, visit the **Gen Patton, KB, OBE, Museum of Cavalry and Armor**, Building 4554, Fayette

Ave, in Fort Knox, 624-6350. 200 years of military history, from the old frontier fort to displays of weapons, equipment and uniforms dating back to the Revolutionary War. Also see the 'ivory-handled Patton pistols' and war booty that Old Blood and Guts gathered in WWII. Free. Mon–Fri 9am–4.30pm. Sat–Sun 10am–6pm.
The Coca-Cola Museum, 1201 N Dixie Ave, Elizabethtown, 737-4000. Located 45 miles south of Louisville in the Elizabethtown bottling plant, this museum houses the world's largest collection of Coca-Cola memorabilia. Remnants of forgotten ad campaigns and items dating back to the 1880's, the dawn of the soft-drinks era. Open Mon–Fri 9am–4pm, $1, students 50¢.

INFORMATION
Visitors Information Center, 400 S 1st St, corner of Liberty, 582-3732. Open Mon–Fri 8.30am–5pm, Sat 8.30am–4pm, Sun 10am–4pm. Open later in summer.
Travelers Aid, 1115 Garvin Pl, 584-8186.

TRAVEL
Local bus, TARC, costs 35¢, 65¢ during rush hour. Info: 585-1234. 30 min rides to the airport leave from 1st and Market St throughout the day. Limo service also available from outside the Hyatt and Goldhouse Hotels, $6.
Greyhound, 720 W Muhammed Ali Blvd, (800) 231-2222.
Gray Line Tours, 1601 S Preston St, 636-5664.

MAMMOTH CAVES NATIONAL PARK Halfway between Louisville, Kentucky, and Nashville, Tennessee, above ground this is a preserve of forest, flowers and wildlife, below ground several hundred miles of passages, pits, domes, gypsum and travertine formations, archaeological remains and a crystal lake. The caves rival in size the better-known Carlsbad Caverns and may be explored on foot, or afloat during conducted boat trips. Call the park office for details: (502) 758-2328.

Keep to the caves within the park and do not stray into the trashy/commercial/privately-owned/exploited caves nearby. There are several campgrounds within the park. Various tours leave regularly from the Visitors Center. **Cave City** is the service centre for the Park. Lots of motels here.

A short drive from Cave City north is **Hodgenville** where you can visit the modest **Lincoln Birthplace and National Historic Site**. Nearby Knob Creek Farm was Abe's boyhood home, 549-3741, 9am–7pm in summer, earlier closing rest of year. $1 includes tour.

LEXINGTON Named in honour of its New England counterpart, Lexington was described by one traveller as 'an interesting historical town with a rich economy, not such a 'hillbilly' image as people say'. Sheik Mohammed bin Rashid al-Maktoum would certainly agree. He makes time for the annual horse sales at Keeneland Race Course. He has been known to snatch up prized thoroughbreds for $1 million plus. Lexington horse-traders have a certain shrewdness born of their unique trade. Luckily, the local industry leaves little non-organic pollution to spoil the rolling bluegrass hills of the countryside.

ACCOMMODATION
Phone DIAL-A-CCOMMODATIONS for free assistance Mon–Fri 8.30am–5pm and Sat 10am–5pm, (606) 233-7299 or (800) 845-3959.
Kimball House, 267 S Limestone, 252-9565. Rates start at S–$25, D–$30.

Hojo Inn, 2250 Elkhorn Dr, Exit 110 off I-75, 299-8481. S–$35, D–$37.50.
YMCA, 239 E High St, 255-5651, $20, $85 per week, $10 key deposit. Men only.
The **University of Kentucky** has rooms and apartments available mid-May to August. Call the housing office at 257-3721.

FOOD

Alfalfa Restaurant, 557 S Limestone St, across from University Memorial Hall, 253-0014. Wide variety of seafood, meat and vegetarian dishes from $2. Live music Thur–Sat.
Central Christian Church Cafeteria, 205 E Short St, 255-3087. Filling Southern food; entrees under $3. Open Mon–Fri 11am–2pm.

OF INTEREST

Some of the most magnificent horses in the world have been raised on **Lexington farms**. Seattle Slew and Affirmed are two of the most famous studs hard at work making future Derby winners. You can try to arrange a private barn tour, but with fillies going for up to $10.2 million, many of the farms have decided not to interrupt the horseplay with buses of gawking tourists. **Bluegrass Tours**, 252-5744, provides a $18, 3 hour daily tour of the area which takes you past the paddocks of the famous thoroughbred farms. Famous farms include **Calumet**, **Darby Dan** and **King Ranch**. Reservations required for the two tours on weekdays and one tour Sat and Sun. Also visit the **Kentucky Horse Park**, Iron Works Pike, 6 miles north on I-75, exit 120, 233-4303. 'Well worth a visit, especially for horse lovers. See a film, excellent museum, various shows, many different breeds, horse riding at extra cost.' $10 for 1 hr ride. Open daily 9am–5pm. $8.95. The park includes a 260-site campground.
Ashland, Richmond Rd at Sycamore Rd, 266-8581, was the home of politician Henry Clay, the engineer of the great Missouri compromise on slavery. The compromise allowed slavery below, but not above the 36th parallel. Ultimately proving unworkable, the compromise pushed the war back for years. The $5 admission includes a guided tour. Open Mon–Sat 10am–4.30pm, Sun 1pm–4.30pm.
The **Mary Todd Lincoln House**, 578 W Main St, 233-9999, built 1803, is where Abraham Lincoln's wife lived as a girl; Lincoln himself stayed here several times. Open Tue–Sat 10am–4pm (last tour 3.15pm). $4.
The first college west of the Alleghenies was **Transylvania University**. Folklore has it that the old administration building burned down and 10 students suffered nasty deaths because of a curse placed upon the school. Inside the new administration building at Old Morrison Hall lies the crypt of a professor named Rafinesque, which was placed there to remove the curse. Students celebrate the tale each Halloween. Tours of the crypt and the campus, west of Broadway and north of 3rd St, can be arranged by calling 233-8242.
The **University of Kentucky** gives free campus tours abroad an English double decker bus; daily 10am and 2pm, Mon–Fri. Sat, walking tours only. 257–3595. Also worth seeing is the **University Art Museum**, 257–5716, featuring over 3000 works including drawings, paintings and sculpture. Open Tue–Sun noon–4.30pm; free. The **Museum of Anthropology**, 257–7112, has exhibits ranging from the Native Indians to contemporary cultures. Open Mon–Fri 8am–4.30pm; free.
Outside Lexington: Shaker Village, in **Harrodsburg**, 25 miles southwest of Lexington on US 68, this community was established by the Shaker sect in 1805 and by the middle of that century numbered 500 inhabitants. The Shakers have departed, but their buildings, with the help of some restoration, still stand. The museum preserves Shaker furnishings. Admittance $8.50. To relive the Shaker life, you can stay in one of the buildings, furnished in the Shaker style, for $49 and up single, $59 up for doubles. Inexpensive Shaker meals as well (breakfast from $7, lunch $5–$10, dinner $12–$19). Call (606) 734-5411 for reservations. 7 miles from the original Kentucky settlement at Fort Harrod.

In the southeast corner of the state, the **Cumberland Gap National Historical Park** and the **Daniel Boone National Forest** provide a beautiful retreat into untouched wilderness. The Park Headquarters and Visitors Center, 248-2817 (8am–6pm), has information on tours, camping and hiking in the Gap area. For information on hiking and camping in the Daniel Boone National Forest call 745-3100.

INFORMATION/TRAVEL
Convention and Visitors Bureau, 430 W Vine St, (606) 233-1221, (800) 848-1244.
The Visitors Center is in the same building, Suite 363. 8.30am–5pm weekdays.
Greyhound, 477 New Circle Rd NW, 255-4261.
There are no buses serving the airport. For a cab, call 231-8294, $11 o/w.

LOUISIANA

With its Voodoo, Jazz, Mardi Gras and Cajun cooking, Louisiana is anything but bland. The Creole State has given the United States some of its most varied ethnic cooking, its best party—Mardi Gras, and most flamboyant politicians (depression-era Huey Long vowed to 'Soak the Rich!', former Governor Edwin Edwards claims that losing $1 million in Vegas was part of his hobby).

Louisiana's cultural heritage is a rich gumbo stew. The original French and Spanish settlers brought old world architecture and manners to the state, while their African and Caribbean slaves laid the musical foundations for what became jazz music. And, after the British expelled them from Nova Scotia in 1775, the French Acadians, now called Cajuns, brought fur-trapping, Cajun cooking, dialects and their special music to the bayous.

Caribbean pirates, Mississippi riverboat gamblers and plantation owners, have given way to a more respectable economy based upon offshore oil and trade, but Louisiana still beguiles visitors with a care-free, genteel atmosphere unlike anything else in America.
The telephone area code for New Orleans is 504, for Acadiana, 318.

NEW ORLEANS New Orleans is a party that never ends. First hosted by the French in 1718, followed by the Spanish, and the French again, the party finally passed to the Americans who bought out the last host, Napoleon, for $15 million in the Louisiana Purchase. Each culture has contributed an ingredient to the festivity: Spanish architecture, French joie de vivre, and a Caribbean sense of pace. A limitless supply of alcohol and music have contributed to New Orlean's reputation as the 'city which forgot to care'.

Visitors are drawn by the Vieux Carre above Canal Street, where gracious homes, walled gardens, narrow streets overhung by iron-lace balconies, and delicious Creole food struggle to retain a mellow atmosphere against encroaching plastic America. The 'grandfather' of the impressionists, Edgar Degas, captured the atmosphere of the city during his visit here in 1872–73 (his mother came from Louisiana) with some of his paintings, including *The Cotton Exchange of New Orleans*.

And of course there's jazz, though today Bourbon Street comes out with the wrong notes. The street is an over-commercialised strip of bars, drunks, prostitutes, skin shows, rip-off joints and gawking tourists in bermuda shorts. The locals usually avoid it, and the cognoscenti will at once make for the Jazz Museum and Preservation Hall, the place nonpareil for the traditional sound.

The New Orleans police have gained a reputation for brutality towards, and general ill-treatment of young foreign visitors. Be careful.

ACCOMMODATION

Many of the rates given do not apply during Mardi Gras, the Jazz Festival and the Super Bowl. Check first. Off season rates prevail Memorial Day to Labor Day.
Cairo Pete's Hostel, 4220 Canal St, 488-0341 and **India House**, 124 S. Lopez St, 821-1904. $10 dorm. Both hostels run by same people. Mixed feedback. Not especially recommended.
Friendly Inn, 4861 Chef Menteur Hwy, 800-445-3940 or 283-1531. TV, pool, free transport to and from airport, Greyhound. S–$25, D–$30, XP–$5. 'Excellent.'
LaSalle Hotel, 1113 Canal St, 523-5831, (800) 521-9450 (US). Student rates: S–$45, D–$50. Advanced reservations suggested. 'Absolutely excellent! Near Vieux Carre. Clean, large rooms. TV, AC, laundry, safe-deposit boxes.'
Longpré House, 1726 Prytania St, 581-4540. $10 AYH, S–$35 up. Coffee and donuts in the morning. 'Friendly and helpful.'
Marquette House Youth Hostel, 2253 Carondelet St, 523-3014. $15 non-members, $12 with AYH card. Day use permitted. Greek revival home near Garden District, mile south of Canal St, along St Charles Streetcar line (one block from Jackson Street stop). Arrive early, or send money order for reservation as rooms fill up quickly. Separate m and f dorms. 2 blocks from laundry, supermarket, street car. 'Very helpful and friendly.' 'Excellent.' 'Carondelet St dangerous.'
Prytania Inn, 1415 Prytania St, 566–1515. S–$32–$38, D–$39–$45. 'Excellent; highly recommended.' One block from street car.
Prytania Park Hotel, 1525 Prytania St, 524-0427. S/D–$66.50. AC, TV, incls breakfast. Nr French Quarter. 'Luxury.'
St Charles Guest House, 1748 Prytania St, 523-6556. B&B 10 minutes from French Quarter by streetcar; 'beautiful terrace with palms'. W/prvt bath and AC, $48 for 1, $55 for 2. Without private bath or AC, $42–$48. Pool. 'Near small supermarket and laundry. Excellent free breakfast and newspapers.' 'Owners are friendly and as kind and generous as anyone could be.' Reservations recommended.
YMCA, 920 St Charles Ave, 568-9622. Men and women (co-ed rooms in international dorm). S–$32, D–$38.75 ($5 key deposit). Reservations recommended. Advance $20 deposit required. AC, pool and gym. 'Relatively safe area in French Quarter; helpful travel info in lobby.'
Campus accommodation available during summer; **Tulane U**, 27 McAlister Dr, 865-5426, on streetcar line. Rooms S–$37.50 and apartments for rent through summer. **Loyola U**, 6363 St Charles St, 865-3735. 25 minutes from downtown by streetcar. S–$30, D–$42 includes linen.
Camping: New Orleans KOA West, 11129 Jefferson Hwy, River Ridge, 467-1792. $21.65 site for 2, XP–$3, pool, laundry. On bus route to downtown.
Bayou Segnette State Park, 7777 Westbank Expressway, 736-7140. Bus service runs to park. Site $12, cabin (up to 8 people) $65. Reservations essential for cabins.
St Bernard State Park, 682-2101. Follow I-10 to LA 47 S; left on LA 39. $12 night for up to 6 people; 16 miles from French Quarter. 'Great camping.'

FOOD

Hot, spicy Cajun food abounds, as does old fashioned stick-to-your-ribs Southern cooking. Gumbo, jambalaya, and crawfish are specialities. Try chocolate pecan pie and beignets—a hot, square doughnut without the hole.

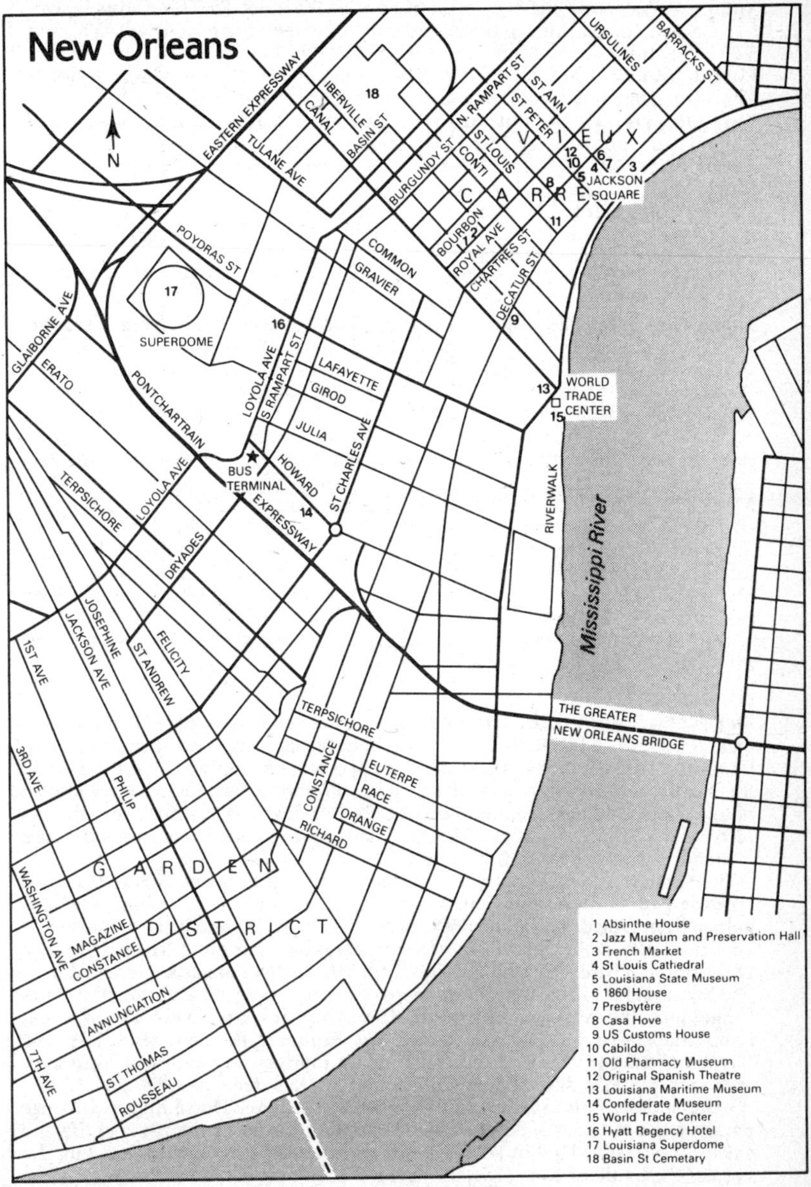
New Orleans
N
EASTERN EXPRESSWAY
TULANE AVE
IBERVILLE
CANAL
BASIN ST
18
BURGUNDY ST
N. RAMPART ST
ST PETER
ST ANN
URSULINES
BARRACKS ST
ST LOUIS
CONTI
VIEUX
CARRE
JACKSON SQUARE
BOURBON
ROYAL AVE
CHARTRES ST
DECATUR ST
COMMON
GRAVIER
POYDRAS ST
17
SUPERDOME
16
GLAIBORNE AVE
ERATO
LOYOLA AVE
S. RAMPART ST
LAFAYETTE
GIROD
JULIA
PONTCHARTRAIN
HOWARD
ST CHARLES AVE
BUS TERMINAL
EXPRESSWAY
14
WORLD TRADE CENTER
RIVERWALK
Mississippi River
TERPSICHORE
DRYADES
JOSEPHINE
JACKSON AVE
1ST AVE
ST ANDREW
FELICITY
THE GREATER NEW ORLEANS BRIDGE
TERPSICHORE
CONSTANCE
EUTERPE
RACE
ORANGE
RICHARD
3RD AVE
PHILIP
GARDEN DISTRICT
WASHINGTON AVE
MAGAZINE
CONSTANCE
ANNUNCIATION
ST THOMAS
ROUSSEAU
7TH AVE
1 Absinthe House
2 Jazz Museum and Preservation Hall
3 French Market
4 St Louis Cathedral
5 Louisiana State Museum
6 1860 House
7 Presbytère
8 Casa Hove
9 US Customs House
10 Cabildo
11 Old Pharmacy Museum
12 Original Spanish Theatre
13 Louisiana Maritime Museum
14 Confederate Museum
15 World Trade Center
16 Hyatt Regency Hotel
17 Louisiana Superdome
18 Basin St Cemetary

K Paul's Kitchen, 416 Chartres St, 524-7394, in the French Quarter, looks like a hole in the wall. It's actually world famous, and if you're there at dinner time, you'll see a looooong line to get in. It's because of the chef, Paul Prudhomme, who has made Cajun cuisine famous worldwide. Excellent, but expensive. A la carte, $20–$28 entrées. Open Mon–Sat 11.30am–2.30pm (lunch), 5.30–10pm (dinner).
Cafe du Monde, 800 Decatur, 525-4544, in the French Market. Open 24 hours. This is the place to get your beignets, 3 for 99¢. 'An experience not to be missed.'
Café Mospero, 601 Decatur, 523-6250. Sandwiches, fried seafood. Open daily 11am–11pm, later at w/end $2–$7. 'Good food—substantial meal $4.'
Coops Place, 1109 Decatur, 525-9053. Cajun food, about $6 dinner. 'The real thing, unpretentious local restaurant.' Open 7 days.
Eddie's Restaurant, 2119 Law St, 945-2207. 'Excellent downhome cooking, gumbo recommended. "Eat as much as you like" buffet every Thursday, 7–11pm, $6'. 'Great atmosphere.'
Fat Harrys, 4330 St Charles, 895-9582, 11am to 3am. Student atmosphere, from $3. Late night spot after the bars, on streetcar line. 'Excellent.'
Fudge Time in **Jax Brewery**, 620 Decatur, 529-3013. Delicious homemade fudge. 'Watch them make it right in front of you—yummy!' Open 7am-10pm daily.
Johnny's Po-Boy, 511 St Louis, 524-8129. 'Good sandwiches; excellent gumbo.' 'Friendly staff.' Open Mon–Fri 7am–4.30pm, Sat 9am–4pm, Sun 9am–3pm.
Kaldi's Coffee House and Coffee Museum, 941 Decatur, 586-8989. 'Alternative hang-out, a change from the tourists.' 'Delicious, real, fresh coffee.' 'Very reasonable; a must for coffee lovers.' Open 7am–midnight weekdays, 7am–2am weekends.
Mena's Place, 622 Iberville, 525-0217. Excellent seafood gumbo runs $3.25, daily specials $3–$5. 'Very friendly.' Open 6.30am–6.45pm Mon–Sat.
Seaport Cafe, on Bourbon St, is a combo cafe and bar; not cheap, but has tasty food and a balcony—'fascinating way of viewing the Bourbon St characters'.
Shoney's, 619 Decatur, 525-2039, and other locations. Breakfast special $3.99, salad bar from $4. 'Superb.' You can learn to cook Cajun food from Chef Joe Cahn at the **New Orleans School of Cooking**, 620 Decatur. Crash courses Mon–Sat, $15. Call 525-2665 for information.

OF INTEREST
French Quarter or **Vieux Carre** (Old Square), the heart and soul of New Orleans, includes about 70 blocks of the old city between the river and Rampart St and Canal and Esplanade Sts. Apart from the pleasure of simply wandering around the streets, and through back alleys, you will find in this area the city's most noteworthy buildings. Caution—do not wander down dark streets at night. As picturesque as they may be, the French Quarter's dark back alleys are good places for the foolish traveller to find trouble.

The Quarter is a National Historic District, within the **Jean LaFitte National Historic Park and Preserve**. Lafitte was a famous New Orleans pirate who also helped defeat the British at the Battle of New Orleans. Legend has it that his most audacious plan was to rescue Napoleon from his British captors. The park service **Folklife and Visitors Center**, 589-2636, 916-918 N Peters St in the French Market (enter through 914 Decatur) offers maps, informed rangers, and different tours throughout the area. A general **History Tour** covering New Orleans and Louisiana leaves at 10.30am each day. The **Faubourg Promenade** explores the Garden District of the city, and the **Tour du Jour** covers a different historic or cultural topic each day, depending on the Ranger's whim.
A good starting point in the Quarter is **Jackson Square**. The old Place d'Armes parade ground, Jackson Square has been the central gathering place in the city since it was first laid out in 1721. The square is named after Andrew Jackson, the hero of the battle of New Orleans. The statue honouring 'Old Hickory', as the scrappy populist was called, was erected in 1856.
St Louis Cathedral, Jackson Sq's exquisite centrepiece was rebuilt in 1794 after a fire destroyed the original and remodeled in 1850. It is a minor basilica and the

oldest active cathedral in the United States. Free guided tours (donations accepted) Mon–Sat 9am–5pm; 1.30pm–5pm Sun. For Sat and Sun mass info, call 525-9585.

The **Louisiana State Museum**, 568-6968, includes several historical buildings in the Quarter which can be toured individually, or for a package rate. Single tickets for one of the museum buildings is $3, $1.50 students. Combination tickets: $5, $2.50 for two houses; $7, $3.50 for three.

Next to the Cathedral is the old Spanish governor's residence, **The Cabildo**, site of the US/French negotiations for the Louisiana Purchase. It was heavily damaged by fire in 1988, restoration work is still in progress—call museum for info. No 2 at the museum is **The Presbytere**, on Chartres St facing the Square. Dates to 1791 and houses portraiture, New Orleans architecture exhibit and changing collections. Tue–Sun 10am–5pm.

The 1850 House, in a portion of the **Pontabla Apartments** (coincidently also damaged by fire in 1989), facing the Square, offers a glimpse of elegant Southern living. Said to be the oldest apartments in the United States, the Pontabla Buildings were built for Baroness Pontabla and are furnished in the traditional antebellum style. Guided tours on the hour Tue–Fri 11am–2pm.

Finally, the **Old US Mint**, 400 Esplanade, houses historical documents and jazz and carnival exhibits. A working mint from 1838–62 and 1879–1920, it's 'O' mintmark is a favourite among coin collectors worldwide. Wed–Sun 10am–5pm.

Other historic buildings of the French Quarter include:

Absinthe House, 240 Bourbon St. The house where the LaFitte brothers, Pierre and Jean, 'plotted against honest shipping'. Now a bar and literary landmark, 523-3181.

US Customs House, 423 Canal St, 589-6353. Dates from 1848; used as headquarters during Civil War Union occupation. Open Mon–Fri 8am–5pm. Free.

The Old French Market, 800, 900, and 1,000 blocks of Decatur St, 522-2621. Built in early 1800's, these old colonnaded buildings have recently been restored and converted to shops and restaurants. The famous old vegetable market is still in operation 24 hours. Other attractions open daily 9am–7pm. Flea Market daily. 'Wonderful. Lots of junk and good jazz in the air.'

Contemporary Arts Center, 900 Camp St, 523-1216. Open Mon–Sat 10am–5pm, Sun 11–5pm. 'Visual arts, music theater; stunning interior to building.' $3, students $2.

Old Pharmacy Museum, 514 Chartres St, 524-9077. Was first used as a pharmacy in 1823 and is now an interesting museum of old apothecary items, voodoo potions, medical instruments and hand-blown pharmacy bottles and 'show globes'. Open Tue–Sun 10am–5pm. $2 donation.

Voodoo Museum, 724 Dumaine St, 523-7685. If you are not too squeamish, learn about the magic and history of this ancient religion. Swamp and ritual tours offered for the strong of stomach and spirit. 'Recommended for the entire family', as advertised by the owner. Open daily 10am–7pm. $5, students $4 with ID.

Historical Wax Museum, 917 Conti St, 525-2605, features a recreation of 'Congo Square', the voodoo center of old New Orleans, as well as the popular Haunted Dungeon. Open 10am–5pm daily, $5.70

Original Spanish Theater, 718 St Peter, built in 1791 was the first Spanish theatre in the US, later a private home, and has housed the well known Pat O'Brien's (of 'hurricane' fame) since 1942.

Of note outside the French Quarter:

Confederate Museum, 929 Camp St, one block off Lee Circle, 523-4522. Has memorabilia of the Civil War. 'Ten out of ten.' Open Mon–Sat 10am–4pm. $3, $2 with student ID.

Take the St Charles St streetcar—one of only 2 remaining in the city—through the fashionable **Garden District** (80¢, 10¢ transfer). The line is an excellent way to get to know the city. Once you reach the Garden District, get out and wander among the sumptuous houses built by rich antebellum whites to rival the Creole dwellings in the Vieux Carre. The District stretches from Jackson to Louisiana Avenues

between St Charles and Magazine Sts. Further down the streetcar line, you reach **Audubon Park** and the **Audubon Zoo**, 6500 Magazine, 861-2537. One of the 'top 10 zoos in the US', open daily 9.30am–4.30pm, closes 5pm at w/end; $7.50.
Another prime attraction outside the French Quarter is **City Park**, at Esplanade and Carrollton Sts, 482-4888, site of the famous **Duelling Oaks**, where New Orleans society settled their differences 'under the Oaks at dawn'. The **New Orleans Museum of Art**, 488-2631, is located in the Park. The collection includes works by the Russian jeweller, Fabergé. Open Tues–Sun 10am–5pm, $6.
For more modern sites there is the **Hyatt Regency Hotel**, Poydras and Loyola, with a free spectacular view. Not free, but still spectacular is the **Louisiana Superdome**, 1500 Poydras St, 587-3808. Opened in 1975, and the world's largest indoor stadium with the largest single room in the history of man. Four tours daily; $6, $5 with student ID. 'The stadium is impressive but the tour is a rip-off; better to pay to see an event. Nothing like it at home.'
Cruises on the Mississippi. A variety of companies offer all kinds of cruises, including buffets and parties, trips to Audubon Zoo, 2-hour port tours ('interesting only if you're into docks and Liberian freighters'), 5-hour explorations of nearby bayous and swamplands, and trips up the Mississippi into the heartland. The **Delta Queen Steamboat Co**, 586-0631, offers expensive cruises up the Mississippi River to Natchez and Memphis. For bayou, harbour, and zoo cruise information, call 586-8777 for the **New Orleans Steamboat Co**. The **Creole Queen**, 524-0814, offers a bayou, plantation, and battlefield cruise. Readership consensus is that the boat rides are generally 'boring' and 'not worth it', but the Bayou trips by bus and boat are highly recommended if you want to see alligators 'au naturel'.
Open since late 1989 is the **Woldenberg Riverfront Park**, 17 acres of parkland down by the Mississippi stretching from Canal Street through the French Quarter to the Moonwalk. You can ride to the top of the **World Trades Center** building ($2), Canal St, for a view of the city and river. The **Old Algiers Ferry** crosses the river from here—and it's free! This is the first time for more than 100 years that residents have had direct access to the river. The **Aquarium of the Americas** on Canal St, 565-3006, recreates the underwater environments of the American continent. Open 9.30am–8pm daily. $8.75.

ENTERTAINMENT

New Orleans *is* entertainment. This is a city that knows how to have a good time, and it's not only during Mardi Gras. The French Quarter, one of the most European areas in the US, is always full of life and has been since Louis Armstrong, Bunk Johnson, Jelly Roll Morton, King Oliver, Kid Ory and other greats of trad jazz stomped in Storyville. **Bourbon St**, though somewhat sleazy, is a perpetual party, and a visit to this city would not be complete without at least one nightly stroll down this crazy stretch of decadence. Although the jazz revival in New Orleans has brought back many good musicians, there are also, on Bourbon St, scores of overpriced nightclubs, flashy restaurants, endless clip joints, and plenty of bad music. Choose carefully (always check prices before you buy a drink, as you are sometimes paying for the band with them) and carry ID. Check *Gambit* and *Wavelength* newspapers for current listings.
New Orleans' temple of jazz is the **Preservation Hall**, 726 St Peter St, 522-2841 (days), 523-8939 (nights), where pioneers of jazz have always performed—and still do. Traditional jazz. 8pm–12am nightly. 'Arrive early.' $3 admission. 'Great atmosphere, the only original jazz bands left in New Orleans; a must.' 'I'd pay $10 to go and see it again—a magical experience. It converted me to jazz—and that's no mean achievement.'
In **Jackson Square**, Saturday jazz concerts are held 2pm–6pm during Oct, Nov, April–Aug. Most shows are free.
Annual Jazz and Heritage Festival. Takes place late April, early May. Includes jazz, dancing, crafts and entertainments. 'A good time was had by all.' Held at New Orleans Fair Grounds. 522-4786 for information.

Check Point, Decatur St past French Market. Bar, cafe and launderette all in one, plus live music and shelves of books. 'Where the alternative crowd hangs out.'
Tipitina's, 501 Napoleon, 895-8477. 'The real thing.' Dixie Cups, good music and cheap drinks. Live music nightly, including Zydeco, cover $4 to $12. Sunday is Cajun dance night. 'We ended up being taught to Cajun dance—best part of our stay!'
Pat O'Brien's, 718 St Peter St, 525-4823. 'Great atmosphere; no cover; closes 5 am.' 'Home of the Hurricane Cocktail. Don't miss it.'
Also try **Snug Harbor** and **Storyville** for music. Uptown New Orleans, around Maple, Oak and Willow Sts, down St Charles from Canal. 'Where the locals go. Good bars and clubs. Better music and cheaper.'
Warehouse Café, 1179 Annunciation St, 586-1282. 'Excellent new bar with live music most nights; Friday nights a must.' $3 cover.

INFORMATION
New Orleans/Louisiana State Office of Tourism, 529 St Anne Street, 568-5661.
Greater New Orleans Tourist Convention Center, 1520 Sugarland Drive, 566-5011.

TRAVEL
New Orleans Regional Transit Authority, 569-2700. City bus and streetcar, some lines run 24 hours. $1, transfers 10¢. All-day visitor pass $4, $8 for 3-day pass.
Louisiana Transit Authority, 737-9611. Bus from airport to downtown, $1.10. Last bus leaves airport at 5.40pm.
Amtrak, 1001 Loyola Ave, 528-1610. *Crescent* to NY, *City of New Orleans* to Chicago and *Sunset Limited* to LA originate here.
Greyhound Terminal, 1001 Loyola in train station, (800) 231-2222. 'Bad neighbourhood.' Accommodation board here has been recommended.
Try Tulane and Loyola for their ride boards.

BATON ROUGE During the first 150 years of its short history, Louisiana experienced considerable difficulty in deciding on a state capital. Opelousas, Alexandria, Shreveport and New Orleans all previously enjoyed such status until 1849 when Baton Rouge was chosen over New Orleans due to concern over the state government being based in such a "careless" city!

Situated in the heart of plantation country, 60 miles northwest of the "Big Easy" on the Mississipi, Baton Rouge was named after the cypress tree used by the Indians to mark hunting boundaries. Today it is the state's second largest city and one of the nations largest ports, profiting mainly from petro-chemical and sugarcane production. However, the abundance of magnolia and cypress trees belies this industrial bias and the city still retains a small-town character. Of special interest are the 34 storey **State Capitol Building** (342-7317); the great white, **Old Governor's Mansion** and the two universities (Louisiana State and Southern). Call (504) 342-8119 for tourist info.

ACADIANA True bayou country—alligators, Spanish moss hanging from trees—begins in the Cajun area called Acadiana. The original French Acadians came to Louisiana after the British overran their native Nova Scotia. The British insisted that the Acadians swear allegiance to the British crown and renounce Catholicism. The Acadians refused, instead moving to Louisiana where they became known as Cajuns. Using their knowledge of fur-trapping, the Cajuns quickly adapted to the ways of the swamp. (One ingenious adaptation was the use of moths for bedding.)

Today's Cajuns still speak some Creole French, and the bayous of Louisiana continue to account for much of the fur-trapping in the United States. Cajun cooking and music are currently in vogue. Paul Simon's *Graceland* was heavily influenced by Cajun Zydeco music, a version of which makes for wonderful rock and roll. Modern Cajun life centers around **Lafayette**, **New Iberia** and **St Martinville**, about 120 miles northwest of New Orleans. **Accommodation** is fairly inexpensive with most lodging centered in Lafayette. Try the **Lafayette Inn**, 2615 Cameron St, 235-9442 (S–$20, D–$25) or the **Lafayette Travel Lodge**, 1101 W Pinnhook Rd, 234-7402 (S–$39, D–$47). **Mulate's Cajun Restaurant**, 325 Mills Ave in Breaux Bridge, 332-4648 (800-42-CAJUN), is arguably the most famous Cajun restaurant in the world. 'Not to be overlooked. Not cheap but meals can be split—worth it.' Open 7 days.

OF INTEREST

In Lafayette: Layfayette Museum, 1122 Lafayette St, 234-2208. With Mardi Gras costumes and LA heirlooms. Open Tues–Sat 9am–5pm, Sun 3–5pm, $3. Just outside Lafayette, the **Acadian Village**, 981-2364, is a good place to learn about Cajun culture. Somewhat touristy, with authentic Cajun houses, tools, and furnishings. Open daily 10am–5pm, $5. Just north of the city lies the **Academy of the Sacred Heart**, 662-5494, the only known exact spot of a miracle in the US. It was here that St John Berchmans, a Jesuit novice, appeared in response to the prayers of a dying woman. She recovered and Berchman returned to heaven. Open Mon–Fri 9am–4pm. Tours Sun 1pm–4pm; other times call for appointment.

In **Eunice**, about 30 miles north on US 190, every Sat night a live Cajun radio show is staged at the Liberty Center for the Performing Arts featuring Cajun music, humourists and recipes. $2 adults. Eunice Chamber of Commerce is 457-2565.

In **New Iberia, St Martinville: Shadows on the Teche**, 317 E Main St, New Iberia, 369-6446, a famous plantation on the banks of the Bayou Teche. HL Mencken stayed here as did Cecil B DeMille. Open daily 9am–4.30pm, $5.

Jungle Gardens, at end of Hwy 329 about 7 miles south of New Iberia, 369-6243, features a 1000 year old Buddha set in a swamp garden. Daily 9am–dusk, $5.

If you doubt that Cajuns like hot food, you should know that tabasco was invented nearby at the **Avery Islands Tabasco Pepper Sauce Factory**, 365-8173, free 20 min tours Mon–Fri 9am–3.45pm, Sat 9am–11.45am.

Evangeline Oak on Port St at Bayou Teche marks the legendary first landing of the Acadians in bayou country. Nearby is statue of **Evangeline** beside **St Martin de Tours Catholic Church**, one of the oldest in Louisiana. Evangeline was one-half of the legendary pair of Acadian lovers immortalised by the Longfellow poem. The reputed home of Evangeline's beau, Gabrielle, is in the **Longfellow-Evangeline Commemorative Area**. A must-see quirk of history is the Roman-era **Statue of Hadrian** standing guard, appropriately, in front of a bank, on the corner of Weeks and Peters Sts.

In the bayou: Louisiana swampland is unique, and tours into the swamps abound. Choose carefully, though, as rip-offs exist. Call **Atchafalaya Delta Wildlife Area**, (504) 395-4905, they can refer you to tours. If you are heading to Texas, try the drive along Hwys 82 and 27 through the **Creole Nature Trail**.

INFORMATION

Lafayette Convention and Visitors Commission, 1400 NW Evangeline Thruway, 232-3808. Open Mon–Fri 8.30am–5pm, 9am–5pm at weekend.

Iberia Tourist Info, 2704 Hwy 14, 365-1540. Open 9am–5pm daily.

MISSISSIPPI

The Blues, King Cotton, southern hospitality, civil rights and riverboat rides—Mississippi *is* the Old South, the embodiment of a myth which, though tarnished, still grips the American imagination. The myth's central character is the Southern Gentleman. A man of breeding (usually a dubious relation to the Marquis de Lafayette), he builds a refined plantation home from which to oversee the works of his slaves, and the harvesting of his cotton. He is braver, more polite, and not at all taken by the Puritan parsimony of his Yankee counterpart.

Like any myth, parts of it are true—Mississippi folk are more polite than their Yankee neighbours. The graceful plantation homes that survived the Civil War do speak eloquently for the sensibilities of a lost time. And in the hot, humid Delta backwoods, the rhythms that once consoled the slaves, have been pressed gradually into the modern blues by such Mississippi giants as John Lee Hooker, John Hurt, Son House, Elmore James and Muddy Waters.

The myth of the Old South itself begat legends in the works of Tennessee Williams and William Faulkner, Mississippi's most famous literary sons. From the last stand of the Southern Gentleman at the Battlefield of Vicksburg, to the blues music of the Delta, Mississippi, the Magnolia State, is the stage upon which an American myth lived and is surely dying. See it and you'll have gained a valuable insight into the history of the United States.

The Natchez Trace Parkway stetches diagonally across Mississippi along the historic highway of bandits, armies and adventurers. You can drive along it, or else explore the old trails on foot. Along Mississippi's Gulf coastline there runs another old trail. This is the old Spanish Trail which ran from St Augustine, Florida, to the missions in California. US 90 from Pascagoula to Bay St Louis follows the trail through the state.
The telephone area code for Mississippi is 601.

JACKSON Set on the west bank of the Pearl River, the capital city of the state began life as a trading post reputedly established by Canadian Louis LeFleur. It was not until early this century that Jackson became Mississippi's largest city. The discovery of natural gas in the area meant that Jackson remained unaffected by the Great Depression.

ACCOMMODATION/FOOD
Admiral Benbow Inn, 905 N State St, 948-4161. S-$39, D-$52.
Primo's, 1016 N State St, 948-4343. Southern cooking; breakfasts under $3. Open daily 7am-9.15pm.
Sun 'n' Sand Motel, 401 N Lamar St, 354-2501. Central location. $38 up, XP-$5.
The Elite Cafe, 141 E Capitol, 352-5606. Homestyle cooking; lunch specials $4.85-$6.

OF INTEREST
Mississippi Crafts Center, Natchez Trace Parkway at Ridgeland, 856-7546. Traditional and contemporary folk arts and crafts. Open 9am-5pm daily.

Mississippi Museum of Art, 201 E Pascagoula, 960-1515. Jackson's first art museum; opened in 1978. Presents as many as 40 exhibitions each year. Tue–Sat 10am–5pm, Sun noon–5pm. $2.
Mississippi State Capitol, 400 High St, 359-3114. Built in 1919; underwent $19 million restoration in 1979. Tours Mon–Fri 9am–3.30pm (open 8am–5pm). Free.
The Oaks, 823 N Jefferson, 353-9339. Jackson's oldest house built 1746, occupied by General Sherman during the Jackson siege in 1863. Open Tue–Sat 10am–3pm. $2.
Old Capitol Museum, 100 S State St, 359-6920. Mississippi's second state house, built 1838, opened as a museum in 1961. Mon–Fri 8am–5pm, Sat 9.30am–4.30pm. Sun 12.30–4.30pm. Free.
Russell C Davis Planetarium, 201 E Pascagoula St, 960-1550. The largest in the Southeast, and one of the best in the world. Shows weekday evenings and weekend afternoons. Call for times. $4.

INFORMATION/TRAVEL
Jackson Visitor Information Center, 1180½ Lakeland Dr, 960-1800.
Amtrak, 300 W Capitol St, 355-6350.
Greyhound, 201 S Jefferson St, 353-6342.
No buses to/from the airport. For a taxi, call 948-4761, $13 o/w.

OXFORD An unpretentious little town set in corn, cotton and cattle country in the north of the state, Oxford nevertheless stands large in the world's great literature. Novelist William Faulkner's Jefferson in his fictitious Yoknapatowpha County corresponds to Oxford and his fictitious home is here, along with several beautiful ante-bellum mansions and the University of Mississippi—Ole Miss. Faulkner, a Nobel and Pulitzer prize winner, wrote about the anguish of a decaying South and the plight of blacks in particular.

ACCOMMODATION/FOOD
Ole Miss Motel, 1517 E University Ave, 234-2424, 3 blocks from city square. S–$25, D–$30, ($38 for up to 4).
The Hoka, 234-3057, just off the city square. Art movie theatre in the back and cafe in the front. Hoka features occasional blues bands and nightly jam sessions on the piano. Sandwiches $3 up (try the cheesecake!). For more mainstream music, try **The Gin**, 234-0024, across the street.
Smitty's Restaurant, 208 S Lamar, 234-9111, just off the square. Southern cooking means fried chicken and catfish from $3.75 to $7.95.

OF INTEREST
Annual Faulkner Festival in the first week of August draws scholars from around the world. 232-5993 for details. If you go, first read *The Sound and the Fury*, *As I Lay Dying* or *The Reivers*.
William Faulkner's Home, called Rowan Oak, Old Taylor Rd, 234-3284. Tucked back in the woods, unmarked from the street, Faulkner's home until 1962 can be reached by walking down S Lamar Street. Free, open Mon–Fri and Sat 10am–noon and 2pm–4pm, Sun 2pm–4pm.
Square Books, 1126 Van Buren on the sq, 236-2262, has impressive collection of Southern writers, and a cafe upstairs. Open Mon–Thur 9am–9pm, Fri, Sat 9am–10pm, Sun 10am–6pm. On the way to Vicksburg is the **Delta Blues Museum**, 624-4461, in the Carnegie Public Library at **Clarksdale**, 114 Delta St. Containing archives, books, records and instruments, the free museum is open Mon–Thurs 9am–5.30pm, Fri and Sat 10am–5pm.

INFORMATION/TRAVEL
Tourist Information Center, in Oxford Square, 232-2419.
Greyhound, 925 Van Buren Ave, 234-1424.

VICKSBURG Lincoln had a simple, but brilliant two-part strategy for the Civil War. First, blockade Southern cotton from reaching European ports. Second, split the South in two by driving a wedge down the Mississippi river. The wedge fell upon Vicksburg, the heart of the South's defense of the Mississippi. After a campaign lasting more than a year and climaxed by 47 days of siege led by Gen. Ulysses S Grant, 'the Gibraltar of the South' fell to Union troops on Independence Day, July 4, 1863. The triumph effectively gave the Union control of the entire Mississippi River. Not surprisingly the city has many Civil War sites, and not a few antebellum mansions.

ACCOMMODATION/FOOD
Hillcrest Motel, 4503 Highway 80 East, 638-1491. S–$20.50, D–$24.75. Pool.
Ramada Hotel, 4216 Washington St, 638-5750. S–$40, D–$50.
Scottish Inn, 3955 Hwy 80 East, ¼ mile from battleground, 638-5511. S–$32, D–$35.
The Dock, 1425 Lum Drive, ¼ mile from National Military Park, 634-0450. All-you-can-eat seafood buffet, $10.95.
Walnut Hills Restaurant, 1214 Adams St, 638-4910. Southern cooking, sandwiches, soup, salads. $2.95 up. Mon–Fri 11am–9pm.

OF INTEREST
Marble monuments, over 1,600 of them, recreate the fury of the battle at **Vicksburg National Military Park**, 636-0583. The Pantheon-like **Illinois monument** is the largest. A Civil War soldier's life is described by actors who dress in period costume and fire muskets and cannons. The park is a mile and a half east of town on I-20. Summer hours are 8am–8.30pm, shorter hours rest of year. Licensed guides provide a two hour tour for $20, or you can hire a cassette, $4.50. There is a $4 auto fee to enter the park. 'Need a whole day if you plan to walk the park. Bring water.' The Civil War gunboat ***Cairo***, sunk by the confederacy, and raised 100 years later, is also on the park grounds.
A climb up to the **Vicksburg Bluffs** yields a great view of the Mississippi. Among several impressive ante-bellum mansions to see are: **Anchuca**, 1010 First E St, 636-4931; **Cedar Grove**, 2200 Oak St, 636-1605; **McRaven House**, 1445 Harrison, 636-1663; **Balfour House**, 1002 Crawford St, 638-3690; and **Martha Vick House**, 1300 Grove St, 638-7036. Most of the homes are open Mon–Sat 9am–5pm, Sun 1pm–5pm, and cost $4.50–$5.
Biedenharn Candy Co Museum, 1107 Washington, 638-6514, 9am–5pm daily, but 1.30pm–4.30pm on Sun. Where Coca-Cola was first bottled in 1894. $1.75. In the summer you can get cokes in antique soda fountain.
To tour the Mississippi around Vicksburg, call *Mississippi Adventure Tours* on (800) 521-4363, two excursions daily in summer, 2pm and 5pm. $15 adults. Pier at end of Clay St. Old Man River is also the site of the Army Corps of Engineers **Waterways Experiment Station**, 3909 Halls Ferry Rd, 634-2502, with working scale models of many of America's rivers, dams, harbours (including Niagara Falls) and tidal waterways. Guided tours at 10am Mon–Fri, self-guided tours daily 7.30am–4.30pm.
South of Vicksburg, beautiful **Port Gibson** was considered by Union General Grant to be 'too beautiful to burn'. A good stop on the way to Natchez.

INFORMATION/TRAVEL
Vicksburg Convention and Visitors Bureau, Clay St and Old Hwy 27 (exit 4B off I-20), 636-9421. Open daily 8am–5.30pm in summer.
Greyhound, 3324 Halls Ferry Rd, 638-8389. Closes 9.30pm.

NATCHEZ Natchez is the Old South. An important cotton trading centre, the port attracted some of the great fortunes of the 1850s. Cotton planters, brokers, and bankers settled in the small town named after the Indian tribes which first settled the area. Non-commercialised, Natchez is one of the finest historical towns in the US.

The favoured architectural style was Classical Greek and Roman as promoted by Palladio, Inigo Jones and Thomas Jefferson. Natchez families have carefully preserved, rather than modernised, their treasures, and for the visitor a block's walk off Main Street is to retreat a century and more back into time.

ACCOMMODATION/FOOD
Days Inn, 109 US Hwy 61 S, 445-8291. S–$45, D–$50, XP–$5.
Fat Mama's Tamales, 500 S Canal St, 442-4548. Mild or spicy tamales.
Natchez Inn, 218 John R Junkin Drive, 442-0221. S–$24 up, D–$32 up.
Camping: Natchez State Park, 363 State Park Road, 10 miles north on Hwy 61, 442-2658. Sites $6–$11.
Traceway Campground, Hwy 61 North, 101 Log Cabin Ln, 8 miles from Natchez, 445–8279. Sites from $10, XP–$2.

OF INTEREST
There are so many truly stunning homes here, that one can easily see how Natchez housed one-sixth of America's pre-war millionaires. 30 homes and gardens are thrown open to visitors during the Pilgrimages each spring and fall while 12 residences are kept open year-round. The most impressive homes are **Dunleith** (Greek Revival style), **D'Evereux** (Greek Revival), **Rosalie** (Brick Federal) and **Longwood** (Moorish style—octagonal with a whimsical cupola). The Pilgrimage Tours Headquarters, 446-6631, at the Canal St Depot offers a package of three homes for $12, but students can get into most homes for $4. Some of the more popular homes may cost a little more. The once notorious **Natchez-Under-the-Hill**, 446-6345, was the old cotton port and steamboat landing and is now an area with shops and a restored saloon.
The Natchez Trace: Natchez is named for the Indian tribe which lived in the area before the white man came. The Trace was the centre of Indian activity from 1682–1729. An archeological site inside the city has uncovered the **Grand Village of the Natchez**. The Indians forged the Natchez Trace which winds its way north to Nashville. A beautiful drive, the trace is also full of history. **Emerald Mound**, one of the largest Indian Burial mounds is 1 mile off the pkwy 11 miles north-east of Natchez. Built in 1300, the mound covers 8 acres and is the third largest such site in the US, 445-4211. Free. Davy Crockett travelled the trace, and the Bowie knife was forged at a campfire along the way. In 1812 Old Hickory (Andrew Jackson) led his troops against the British at New Orleans using the trace. The Visitor's Center Museum at the trace, 842-1572, at marker 266, has artifacts from the site. Free. Elvis Presley was born along the trace in the little town of **Tupelo**. Elvis gave a benefit performance for his home town which raised enough money to create a park out of the King's first 'shotgun' (read hovel) home. Tours through the home, 306 Elvis Presley Dr on Tupelo's east side, 841-1245, Mon–Sat 9am–5.30pm, Sun 1pm–5pm. $1. Fans donated for the construction of a chapel in Presley's honour on the site. (The **Tupelo McDonald**'s, 372 S Gloster, is a temple to the King.)
The **Tupelo City Museum**, Highway 6 West at James A Ball Park, 841-6438, houses a large collection of Elvis memorabilia, as well as Civil War artifacts. Open Tue–Fri 8am–4pm, Sat, Sun 1pm–5pm; $1.

INFORMATION
Adams County Welcome Center, 370 Seargent Prentis Dr, 442-5849, 8am–5pm daily. Provides maps, lists of tours and homes.

Natchez Chamber of Commerce, 205 N Canal, 445-4611. Mon–Fri 8am–5pm.
Tupelo Convention and Visitors Bureau, 712 E President St, 841-6521. Mon–Fri 8am–5pm.
Natchez Convention and Visitors Bureau, 311 Liberty Rd, 446-6345.

BILOXI The town is along the most populated area of the Gulf coast and has commercialised on its white sand beach. Though tourism is important, this has been a shrimping community since the Civil War. In early June, the fleets are ritually blessed; at the harbour front down the end of Main Street, or in the Back Bay area, you can watch the fishermen get on with their lives oblivious to tourism.

At various times in the town's history, Biloxi has been under the flags of France, Spain, Britain, the West Florida Republic, the Confederacy and the US.

ACCOMMODATION

Beach Manor Motel, 662 Beach Bvld, 436-4361. Nr Greyhound. D–$66, weekend rates more expensive.
Sea Gull Motel, 2778 Beach Blvd, about 7m from town, 896-4211. S–$40–$60, AC, TV, pool, nr beach.
Camping: Biloxi Beach Campground, US 90 at 1816 Beach Blvd, 432-2755, 3 miles from town. Sites $15 with hook-up, $14 w/o for two. Across from beach and pier.

FOOD

Mary Mahoney's French House Restaurant, 138 Rue Magnolia, 1 block north of US 90, 374-0163. In a 1737 home, one of the oldest in America, not cheap, but excellent regional cuisine.
McElroy's Harbour House Restaurant, 695 Beach Blvd, 435-5001. Anything from local seafood to steaks and burgers, $5–$13. Breakfast $3. Open 7 days 7am–10pm.

OF INTEREST

Beauvoir. The last home of Jefferson Davis; on US 90 at Beavoir St, 388-1313. See the library where he worked, and the Tomb of the Unknown Soldier of the Confederate States. Open daily 9am–5pm, $4.75. The famous cast iron 65-ft **Biloxi Lighthouse**, built in 1848 and one of the few remaining iron lighthouses, on US 90. Open by appointment only; call 435-6293. Free.

Other than Biloxi's white-sand **beaches**, the most enticing site along the coast is the **Gulf Islands National Seashore**, 875-3962. The seashore stretches into Florida, but there are 4 islands off the Mississippi coast which can be visited—West and East Ship, Petit Bois (pronouned Petty Boy), and **Horn Island**. The islands have a unique ecosystem. They are anchored by sea oats which keep the sand from washing away. The islands are also great places to bird-watch. The *Biloxi* Excursion Boat runs to Ship Island from the Pier four blocks east of the lighthouse. $12 round trip, call 432-2197 for details. The main site there is **Fort Massachusetts**, a linch pin of Lincoln's effort to blockade the south.

Four miles from Biloxi, at the Visitors Center in **Ocean Springs**, 3500 Park Rd, 875-9057, you can see a movie about the islands. Open 9am–6pm daily. Camping is allowed on East Ship, but there is no regular boat service to the island. You can camp out at the grounds near the visitors center in Davis Bayou.

J L Scott Marine Education Center and Aquarium, 115 Beach Blvd (US Hwy 90), 374-5550. The state's largest public aquarium includes the 42,000 gallon 'Gulf of Mexico' tank which houses sharks, sea turtles and eels. Open Mon–Sat 9am–4pm. $3.

INFORMATION/TRAVEL •
Biloxi Visitor Center, 710 Beach Blvd, 374-3105. Open Mon-Fri 8am–5pm, Sat 9am–5pm, Sun noon–5pm.
Greyhound, 166 Main St, 436-4335.

NORTH CAROLINA

American writer H L Mencken once described North Carolina as 'a valley of humility between two mountains of conceit'. Wedged between Virginia and South Carolina and once isolated from them, the 'Tarheel State' has the unhurried, folksy manner you'd expect from its hardworking people. They just don't think it would be polite to boast of all their blessings: unspoiled beaches, rugged mountains, and a stimulating cultural and intellectual life.

However, these blessings have not gone unnoticed by others. The state—first in the US in tobacco, textiles and furniture manufacturing—has attracted so many people that some native North Carolinians are now grumbling about an influx of 'Yankees'. Northern companies have flocked into North Carolina seeking non-union labour and better living conditions for executives. The area around Raleigh-Durham, the so-called 'research triangle', has attracted a flourishing medical research community, much of it financed by tobacco giants such as RJ Reynolds, but powered by Yankee know-how.

In just a few years, the triangle has grown to house more PhD's per capita than anywhere else in the country. Outside of the triangle, especially in the Asheville area, the economy has not benefited from high tech employment. Areas of the Appalachian Mountains are still some of the poorest in the land. In one Blue Ridge town, Deep Gap, lives guitarist-singer Doc Watson, one of America's greatest living folk artists.

The contrast between Yankee and native adds to North Carolina's greatest appeal, its diversity. Here you can enjoy the mountains or the shore, a small town's tranquility or a big town's bustle. And everywhere you will meet friendly, approachable people swollen with pride about their humility.

National Parks: Great Smoky Mountains, Cape Hatteras and Cape Lookout National Seashores

The area code for Asheville and Charlotte is 704, for Raleigh and the Coast, 919.

THE COAST The 'Outer Banks' is the name given to the three curving island strips, **Ocracoke**, **Hatteras** and **Bodie Island**, sheltering the North Carolina mainland from the Atlantic surf. The sandy beaches are relatively unspoiled and offer some of the best surfcasting in the country.

At the northern end of the Banks, fishing gives way to flying. The first power-driven flight was made near **Kitty Hawk** at Kill Devil Hills on 17 December 1903, by Orville Wright. Now in the Smithsonian Institution in Washington, the plane was aloft for 12 seconds and achieved a speed of 35 miles per hour. Orville later explained that he and his brother Wilbur had remained bachelors because they hadn't means to 'support a wife as well as an aeroplane'.

From the relatively crowded and popular sands of Kitty Hawk, the Banks stretch south past the large sand dunes at Jockey's Ridge towards the primitive wildlife refuges of the **Cape Hatteras National Seashore**, the country's first national seashore. The treacherous currents off the Cape earned this strip of land the nickname 'graveyard of the Atlantic'. Frequent hurricanes and strong Gulf Stream currents drove many a ship aground in the shallow waters. The currents were used to great advantage by 18th century pirates. Legend has it that the pirates led unsuspecting ships to their doom by tying a lantern to their horse's neck and then walking up the beach towards Diamond Shoals. Before a navigator realized that the lighthouse he was steering by was moving, he had run aground. The tallest lighthouse in the US (208 feet) now warns ships away.

The hurricanes and strong currents offer the best protection from development for the abundant wildlife on the Banks. **Pea Island National Wildlife Refuge**, 987-2394, shelters great snow geese among others. **Ocracoke Island** was home to America's most famous pirate, Edward Teach. Better known as Blackbeard, Teach enjoyed the protection of several colonial governors until he was done in by the Virginia Militia.

Further south along the coast lies the unsuspecting historical city of **Wilmington** also a good base from which to explore the **Cape Fear River** and coastline. The name supposedly originates from sailors' battles with the strong currents at the river mouth. In any case, do not be put off by the movie!

ACCOMMODATION

Like every other coastline, summer is the most expensive time to stay. The following rates are off-season.

Kitty Hawk: Ocean Inn, Milepost 11 on Admiral St, 441-9973, D–$72, AC, TV, fridge.

Camping: There are 5 National Park Service campgrounds along the 125-mile national seashore. The camp at Ocracoke can only be reserved through TICKETRON or write to PO Box 85705, San Diego, CA 92116-5705 for $12 a night. The other four are on a first-come, first-served basis for $11. For more information contact Cape Hatteras National Seashore, Rte 1, PO Box 675, Manteo, NC 27954. Tel (919) 473-2111.

Ocracoke: The following motels are located off Route 12.

Blackbeard's Lodge, 928-3421, rooms $38–$48; **Sand Dollar Motel**, 928-5571, $40–$58; and the **Pony Island Motel**, 928-4411, $60–$70 (10% discount for stays of a week or more).

Wilmington: The Glenn Hotel, 16 Nathan St on Wrightsville Beach, 256-2645. S–$28, D–$40. Basic, shared bath, no AC.

FOOD

Not far from the Wright Brothers Memorial is **Kelly's Outer Banks Restaurant and Tavern**, Mile 10½, 441-4116. Seafood, steak, chicken, pasta. Open daily; food served till 10pm, bar open till 2am.

At Nag's Head Causeway is **RV's**, 441-4963. Sandwiches, steak, seafood. Open 11.30am–10pm daily.

City Market Café, 118 S Front St, Wilmington, 762-6730. Open daily except Sunday 5.30am–2.30pm, traditional Southern breakfast—tasty, filling and very cheap. $2.75 brkfst special.

OF INTEREST

Just on the mainland side of the Banks, the small town of **Manteo** marks the site of a big mystery. Three hundred Englishmen led by Sir Walter Raleigh built a small fort and settled near here in 1587. When a small expedition set out for the colony three years later, they found that the entire colony had disappeared without a trace. The expedition found only one clue to the colony's fate—the word 'Croatan' scratched onto a tree trunk. Rebuilt **Fort Raleigh**, 473-5772, and **Elizabeth Gardens**, 473-3234, mark the likely site of the lost colony. Both are located at the north end of Roanoke Island on Route 64. Fort open 9am–dusk; free. Gardens open 9am–8pm; admission $2.50. *Lost Colony*, 473-2127, is an outdoor drama which tells the story of the Roanoke Island Colony, $10 nightly exc. Sun. Runs through summer till end of August. The *Elizabeth II*, a representation of the ship which brought the first English settlers to North America, is moored 4 miles south on Route 400, Manteo St across from the waterfront. $3, $1.50 for students, tours 10am–5pm, 473-1144.

Nags Head Woods Preserve, 441-2525, 15 miles north of Manteo, is a nature preserve with two walking trails, open Tue, Thur and Sat 10am–3pm. Nearby in Kitty Hawk, the **Wright Bros Memorial and Museum** on Route 158, 441-7430, pays homage to the great inventors. Open 9am–6pm daily. $4 carload, $2 per person. What better way to celebrate a visit to the place where man first took flight than with an airplane tour from **Kitty Hawk Aerotours**, 441-4460. $19 for a 25 min tour of the island. Icarus fans may want to try the nearby hang-gliding operations: call **Kitty Hawk Kites**, 441-4124. $59 for a 3-hour lesson including training film, ground school and 5 flights.

Ramada Inn organises **dolphin tours**; $22 for one hour, 441-0424.

Lighthouses, at Cape Hatteras, Ocracoke, Corolla and Bodie. Visitors are not permitted to climb up the tower, but are free to wander the grounds. Finally, the **Chicamacomico Life Saving Station**, on Hatteras Island near Rodanthe, records how private rescue companies of the 19th century operated.

Cape Fear Museum, 814 Market St btwn 8th & 9th St, Wilmington, 341-4350. Dive into the background and history of the Lower Cape and learn how North Carolina earned its nickname, 'the Tarheel State'. Open Mon–Sat 9am–5pm, Sun 12–5pm. $4 admission.

INFORMATION

Outer Banks Chamber of Commerce, Collington Rd, 441-8144. Mon–Fri 9am–5pm, Sat 10am–2pm during summer.

Aycock Brown Welcome Center on Bodie Island near Kitty Hawk, 261-4644.

Cape Hatteras Ntl Seashore Information Centers: Bodie Island, 441-5711; Hatteras Island, 995-4474; Ocracoke Island, 928-4531. All open daily 9am–5pm.

TRAVEL

Car Ferry between Cedar Island and Ocracoke Island costs $10, takes 2 hours, and on summer weekends must be booked several days in advance. Call 928-3841 in Ocracoke, 225-3551 in Cedar Island.

Taxis to and from Wilmington airport cost around $6–$7. Call 762-3322.

TOBACCO ROAD A 150-mile-long arc of cities stretching between **Raleigh** and **Winston-Salem** is the backbone of North Carolina. Rolling through a region of gentle hills called the Piedmont, I-40 and I-85 pass the major tobacco growing farms and factories. The state capital is in Raleigh and the **Raleigh/Durham Triangle** area, home to three major universities, has the nation's highest number of PhD's per head of population.

ACCOMMODATION

In Raleigh: Regency Motel, 300 N Dawson, 828-9081. S–$38, D–$41.

YMCA, 1601 Hillsborough St, 832-6601. $17, room with shared bath. Use of pool.

YWCA, 1012 Oberlin Rd, 828-3205. Women only. $18 night. Best make reservations. $90 week, $55 after 4-week stay.

In Durham: Carolina-Duke Motor Inn, I-85 Guess Rd Exit in Durham, 286-0771. S-$31, D-$38, XP $3. Pool, AC, TV.
Duke Motor Lodge, 4144 Chapel Hill Blvd, 489-9111. S-$31, D-$39.
In Winston-Salem: Days Inn, 5218 Germanton Rd, 744-5755. S-$42, D-$51, XP-$5.
Motel 6, 3810 Patterson Ave, 661-1588. I-40 exit to US 52 north, exit Patterson Ave. S-$25, D-$29, XP-$4.

FOOD

In Raleigh: Applebee's Neighborhood Grill & Bar, 4004 Capitol Blvd, 878-4595. American fare (burgers, chicken, steaks) $6.95-$9.95.
Two Guys, 2504 Hillsborough St, 832-2324. Menu includes Italian and Greek dishes.
In Durham: 9th Street Bakery, 776 9th Street, 286-0303. Pastries, breakfast, lunch. Live folk music at weekends. Mon-Thur 7am-7pm, Fri-Sat 8am-11pm, Sun 8am-5pm.
Satisfaction, Lakewood Shopping Center, 682-7397. Big Duke hangout. Pizzas, sandwiches, burgers. Lunch, dinner Mon-Sat 11am-2am.
The Weeping Radish, 115 N Duke St, 682-2337. Restaurant from 5.30pm-9.30pm and wild bar with its own brewery till late. Closed Sun.

OF INTEREST

Raleigh: Mordecai Plantation House Historic Park, 1 Mimosa St, 834-4844. Birthplace of Andrew Johnson and other historic buildings. Tues-Fri 10am-3pm, Sat-Sun 1.30pm-3.30pm. $3.
NC State University, tours Mon-Fri at 12.15pm, 515-2434.
NC Museum of Art, 2110 Blue Ridge Blvd, 833-1935. European paintings from 1300, American 19th century paintings, Egyptian, Greek and Roman art. Open Tue-Sat 9am-5pm (Fri till 9pm), Sun 11am-6pm. Free.
Durham: Duke University, a gothic wonderland built with tobacco money, site of **Duke Chapel** (210 foot tower and 50-bell carillon), **Sarah P Duke Gardens** and **Duke Medical Center**. Daily tours Mon-Sat, 684-3214.
Chapel Hill is a college town 15 miles SW of Durham on US 15-501. Home of the **University of North Carolina**, the first public university in America. Visit the **Moorhead Planetarium** on Franklin St, near campus, 962-1236. Star shows cost $2.50 students, $3 adults. Two-show discount ticket $5, $4 students. **Franklin St** is also the place to find cheap food and student bars and clubs.
Winston-Salem: Reynolda House Museum and Gardens, Reynolda Rd, 725-5325, houses the fine American paintings, sculpture, prints associated with the founder of R J Reynolds Tobacco, including Church's *The Andes of Ecuador*. Tues-Sat 9.30am-4.30pm, Sun 1.30pm-4.30pm, $6 adults and $3 students.
Old Salem and Historic Bethabara reconstruct life of the Moravians who first settled in this area. Old Salem features a 1797 organ in the reconstructed congregation setting, 721-7300. Admission to 7 buildings and the **Museum of Early Southern Decorative Arts**, $13. With a graveyard, and foundations of original settlements, Bethabara is more of an archeological site than Old Salem, and it is also free, 924-8191. Both are open Mon-Sat 9.30am-4.30pm, Sun 1.30pm-4.30pm.
The new art is at the **Southeastern Center for Contemporary Art**, 750 Marguerite Dr, 725-1904. Open Tue-Sat 10am-5pm, Sun 2pm-5pm; $3, $2 for students.

INFORMATION

Raleigh: Capital Area Visitor Center, 301 N Blount, 733-3456.
Durham: Chamber of Commerce, 300 W Morgan St, 682-2133.
Winston-Salem: Chamber of Commerce, 601 W 4th St, 725-2361.
Winston-Salem Visitors Center, 601 N Cherry St, 777-3796.

TRAVEL
Raleigh: Amtrak, 320 West Cabarrus, 833-7594.
Greyhound, 314 W Jones St, 834-8275.
Durham: Greyhound, 820 W Morgan St, 687-4800.
Many hotels offer free shuttles to and from Raleigh-Durham airport to downtown, so ask around. Taxis cost around $25 o/w. Call 832-5811.

ASHEVILLE AND AREA Travellers to this area find a simple, unhurried charm which is fading elsewhere in the busy 'New South'. The crafts and folklore of the Appalachias flourish in the shops and markets here, and the region's natural beauty is protected from overdevelopment. If you put your feet up anywhere in North Carolina, this is the place to do it.

ACCOMMODATION
Down Town Motel, 65 Merriman Ave, 253-9841. S-$33, D-$39.
Intown Motor Lodge, 100 Tunnel Rd, 252-1811, S-$32, D-$37; higher at weekends.
Log Cabin Motor Court, 330 Weaverville Hwy, 645-6546. Some cabins, with fireplaces, kitchens. S-$34 up, with double bed.

FOOD
Boston Pizza, 501 Merriman, 252-9474. Popular student hangout; pizzas $5 up. Try the 'Boston Supreme'! Closed Mon; open Tue–Sat 11am–11.30pm, Sun noon–10pm.
The Hop, 507 Merriman, 252-8362. Homemade ice-cream in 50's style joint.
Three Brothers Restaurant, 183 Haywood St, 253-4971, serves everything, over 40 types of sandwiches. Open 11am–10pm weekdays, Sat 4pm–10pm.

OF INTEREST
The **Thomas Wolfe Memorial**, 48 Spruce St, 253-8304, honours Asheville's most famous son. Wolfe's best known novel, *Look Homeward Angel* (titled after Milton's poem of the same name), was inspired by childhood experiences; his father was the town stonecutter.
Asheville is a prime spot to shop for **local crafts**. Traditions are lovingly preserved. The **Mountain and Dance and Folk Festival**, 258-6111, on the first weekend in August has been going more than 60 years. The annual **World Gee Haw Wimmy Diddle Competition** is held annually in August at the **Folk Arts Center**, 298-7928, and includes demonstrations of this native Appalachian toy, made from laurel wood.
Biltmore House and Gardens, built by the Vanderbilt family, is an opulent exception to the area's humble charms. Peter Sellers' last film *Being There* was filmed at this 250-room mansion, which is built after the style of a European chateau. Includes garden, conservatory, winery, and two restaurants. Take exit 50 or 50B on I-40 south of Asheville, 255-1776. Open 9am–5pm daily; admission $22.95.
For learning, head to **Flat Rock**, once home to Carl Sandburg, and current site of the **Flat Rock Playhouse**, North Carolina's State theatre, 693-0731. Sandburg's home for 22 years, **Connemara**, 693-4178, has books and videos of the writer-poet's life. His championship goat herd lives on. Tours of the home daily 9am–5pm, $2.
Chimney Rock Park lies 25 miles SE of Asheville nr intersection of US 64 and 74. A 26-story elevator runs inside the mountain and ascends to 1200 ft. 'Spectacular views over the Appalachian Mountains.' Also various nature trails through the nearby **Pisgah National Forest**, natural rock slides at **Sliding Rock** and a 404 ft waterfall, 877-3265.

INFORMATION/TRAVEL
Asheville Visitors Information, 151 Haywood St, 258-6111. 'A very helpful staff.'
Greyhound, 2 Tunnel Rd, 253-8451.
City Bus Service, 253-5691. Fare 60¢, 10¢ transfer.

GREAT SMOKY MOUNTAINS NATIONAL PARK The name Great Smokies is derived from the smoke-like haze that envelopes these forest-covered mountains. The Cherokee Indians called this the 'Land of a Thousand Smokes'. Part of the Appalachian Mountains near the southern end of the Blue Ridge Parkway, the popular park has been preserved as a wilderness that includes some of the highest peaks in the eastern US and 68 miles of the Appalachian Trail.

The **Great Smoky Mountain Railway** runs 4 hr trips through Nantahala Gorge and Fontana Lake twice daily at 9.30am and 2.30am, $14. 'Waste of time. What mountains? Telephone cables obscured view of scrap yards.' Nantahala Gorge 4 hr day trips, $16; 7 hr Raft and Rail trips, $45 (includes picnic lunch and guided raft ride). All departures from Bryson City. Call (704) 586-8811 to reserve.

The area near **Cataloochee** affords an excellent impression of the obstacles facing the earliest pioneers on their push into the west. Cabins, cleared acreage and other pioneer remnants dot this section of the park. Perhaps the most fascinating visit is to the **Cherokee Reservation**. There's a recreated Indian village, and a production of *Unto These Hills*, an Indian drama about their land and the meaning it holds for them, and a museum.

The North Carolina entrance to the park is on US 441 at Cherokee with the visitor centre located at **Oconaluftee**, not far from the Indian reservation. Park information, including information of its 900 walking trails can be obtained by calling (615) 436-1200. Cherokee also offers numerous motels and campgrounds. Cheapest lodging is available at **Little John's Efficiencies**, 441 River Rd, (704) 497-3157, from $25; and **Oconaluftee Motel**, US 19 South, (704) 488-2950, D–$53.

SOUTH CAROLINA

In its semi-tropical coastal climate and historical background, the Palmetto State, first to secede from the Union, marks the beginning of the Deep South. South Carolina also typifies the New South. Since the Second World War, booming factories, based on the Greenville area, have replaced sleepy cotton fields and cotton itself has been replaced by tobacco as the major cash crop. Textile manufacturing and chemicals are the state's major industries, but industry has not developed at the expense of the state's traditional charm and lovely countryside.

South Carolina has, however, something of a split personality. Charleston beckons the visitor with its graceful streets and refined architecture. Myrtle Beach entices with all the subtlety of a tourist-howitzer. South Carolina has her slower country charms, but other than Charleston, few

compare favourably with her neighbours. The beaches are less cluttered in North Carolina and the mountains are grander in Tennessee.
The area code for the state is 803.

CHARLESTON The curtain rose here on the Civil War to the cheers of society ladies and the blasts of harbour canon. Charleston's exuberance found a less violent expression in the 1920s when a dance dubbed the *Charleston* became a national obsession.

Dance was better suited to Charleston's nature which epitomises Southern graciousness. Settled by aristocracy, Charleston has always been concerned with architecture, art and the length of the family tree. More recently in 1989, this lovely old town was severely battered when hurricane Hugo roared through. Many of the historic buildings suffered severe damage, so much so that the town will never look the same again.

ACCOMMODATION

Bed, No Breakfast, 16 Halsey St, 723-4450. Guest house in Harleston Village nr College of Charleston, $45 for 1 or 2, $55 for 3. 'Comfortable.' Limited space.
Rutledge Victorian Guest House, 114 Rutledge Ave, 722-7551, also **Periwinkle House**, 4 Halsey St, and **King George Inn**, 32 George St. Located downtown. D-$45-$85. Student rooms: shared, $21 per night or $16 for stays of two nights or more; private from $40 double. AC, TV. Favourite stop for BUNAC travellers. Call to reserve in advance at Rutledge House for all three places.

FOOD

The Gourmetisserie in the City Market is junk food centre—hamburger, pizza stands. 'Great meeting place.'
Olde Towne Restaurant, 229 King St, 723-8170. Despite its name, it turns out to be Greek, with fish and meat specialities. Lunches from $4. Friendly.
Papillion's Pizza Bar, 41 Market, 723-6510. Lunch buffets every day $4.75, dinner buffet Mon and Tues $6.75—all you can eat.

OF INTEREST

A tremendous city pride exists in Charleston, and there are excellent documentaries on the city shown in the downtown area. *Forever Charleston*, a slide show on the city, is shown at the Visitor Reception and Transportation Center, 375 Meeting St, 724-7474, from 9am–5pm daily; $2.50. The **Preservation Society**, 147 King St at Queen, 722-4630, is a useful place to learn about the history of Charleston and the volunteers welcome foreign visitors. Maps, pamphlets and walking books are available. Open Mon–Sat 10am–5pm.
The Old Exchange and Provost Dungeon, 122 East Bay at Broad St, 792-5020. Built between 1767 and 1771; delegates to the first Continental Congress were elected here in 1774. The dungeon was used as a prison by the British during the Revolution. Open daily 9am–5pm, $3. Self-guided tour.
Charleston is famous for its fine houses, squares and cobblestone streets. Start your walk along **Church Street**, the vision Heyward and Gershwin used to create **Catfish Row** in *Porgy and Bess*. The **Battery**, along the Cooper and Ashley rivers, has blocks of attractive old residences. The only **Huguenot church** in the US is at Church and Queen streets while the **Dock Street Theater** is across the street.
Topping the list of restorations is the **Nathaniel Russell House**, 51 Meeting St, 723-1623. Costs $5 but is probably the best house to visit. Dating from 1808, it has a famous 'free-flying' spiral staircase and lavish furnishings. Open daily 10am–5pm. The **Aiken-Rhett Home** at 48 Elizabeth St, 723-1159, boasts a stunning entrance hall. $5 includes tour of home and slave quarters. Open Mon–Sat 10am–5pm, Sun 1pm–5pm (last tour 4.30pm).

The Charleston Museum, 360 Meeting St, 722-2996. Started in 1773, claims to be the oldest museum in the country. Open 9am–5pm, Sun 1pm–5pm. Adults $5. Exhibits include a full-scale replica of the Confederate submarine, *HL Hunley*; you can peer into the open side of the sub.

Gibbes Museum of Art, 135 Meeting St, 722-2706. Displays early art and portraiture of South Carolina and one of the finest collections of miniatures in the world. 'Worthwhile: some quite impressive early American paintings, and some even more impressive modern woodwork.' Open Tues–Sat 10am–5pm; Sun, Mon 1pm–5pm. Adults, $3; students $2.

Basket-weaving traditions inherited from Africa, and handed down by generations of slaves can still be seen at the **Market**, Meeting and Market Sts. Fruit, veggies, masses of junk and some beautiful handicrafts. Watch the ladies making baskets—and then buy one. 'Lively and colourful.' **Daughters of the Confederacy Museum**, 723-1541. 'Rather higgledy-piggledy, but there are some unusual Confederate memorabilia at this place.' Open Sat and Sun 12pm–5pm, $2.

Founded by Sephardic Jews in 1749 with the current temple built in 1841, **Kahal Kadosh Beth Elohim** is the oldest synagogue in continuous use in the US, and an early centre of reform Judaism. Call 723-1090 for weekday morning tours of the Greek Revival building.

Charleston parades with military history: the **Citadel Military College**, 792-5006, is known as the West Point of the South. West Point was stormed and taken by women cadets, but the staunchly conservative Citadel still holds out. The college, at Moultrie Street on banks of Ashley River, offers tours and a free museum, open Sat noon–5pm, Sun–Fri 2pm–5pm. Don't miss the dress parade every Friday at 3.45pm when the cadets are in session.

The Confederate bombardment of Federally-garrisoned **Fort Sumter**, just across the harbour, began the Civil War. Now Fort Sumter is a national monument, 883-3123, with its history depicted through exhibits and dioramas. There are as many as 6 boat tours a day to the fort, $9 adults. Boats leave from City Marina and Patriot's Point, 722-1691. Be careful to take a boat that actually lands on the fort!

Ft Moultrie, on Sullivan's Island but easily reached by car, has served as the bastion of security for Charleston harbour since the revolutionary war.

Also just outside Charleston is **Boone Hall Plantation**, 884-4371, 7 miles north near US 17. Open Mon–Sat 8.30am–6.30pm, Sun 1pm–5pm, $7.50 adults. Beautiful house and gardens; the stunning Avenue of Oaks leading to the mansion inspired the one seen in *Gone With the Wind*.

Charles Towne Landing, 1500 Old Towne Rd, 6 miles outside Charleston, marks the site of the first permanent English speaking settlement in South Carolina. See the *Adventure*, a working reproduction of a 17th century sailing vessel. Also guided tram tours, animal forest, bike paths and walkways. Open 9am–6pm daily; $5.

Summers can be close, but you can cool off at **Folly Beach**, off Rte 171, with public parking and showers. 'Excellent beach, very long, deserted and clean.'

INFORMATION

Charleston Visitor Reception and Transportation Center, 375 Meeting St, 853-8000. Open daily. Good maps available. 'Helpful.'

Even the Chamber of Commerce is historic—it is one of the nation's oldest civic commercial organisations; 81 Mary St, 577-2510.

TRAVEL

Greyhound, 3610 Dorchester Rd, 744-4247.

Local Bus (SCE & G), 747-0922. Fare 50¢.

Amtrak, 4565 Gaynor Ave, 9 miles west of town on Hwy 52, 744-8263. The *Palmetto* and the *Silver Meteor* call here, both from NYC, the first terminating at Savannah, the second at Miami. Taxi from downtown, $8–$11.

Charleston Airport is located 13 miles north of downtown. Taxis $14, 577-6565. Limo shuttle $9, call 767-7111 to reserve.

MYRTLE BEACH AND THE GRAND STRAND The 60 mile stretch of South Carolina's northern coast, known as the Grand Strand, has seen almost frightening growth in the past two decades. It's loaded with countless amusements, fast food joints, and tacky boutiques with merchants selling the inevitable Myrtle Beach T-shirts and trinkets. In summer, the 29,730 population of Myrtle Beach swells to 350,000.

Brookgreen Gardens, on US 17 South, 20 min south of Myrtle Beach, 237-4218, seems out of place here. In a serene setting, the world's largest outdoor collection of American sculpture—over 400 works of art are on show, set against 2000 species of plants. The gardens also feature a wildlife park and avairy. Open daily, 9.30am–4.45pm, $5.

Further south a short distance, is pretty and famous **Pawleys Island**. One of the oldest resorts on the Atlantic coast, this was originally a refuge for colonial rice planters' families fleeing from a malaria epidemic. Residents work hard to preserve its more elegant, less commercialised feeling. The well known Pawleys Island Hammock is hand-woven and sold here—you can watch them being made by local craftsmen.

Georgetown, on Hwy 17 at the southern end of the Grand Strand, was the first settlement in North America, established in 1526 by the Spaniards, and named 200 years later in honour of King George II. It became a thriving port in the 18th century, concentrating on the export of rice and in the early 19th century becoming the biggest exporter of rice in the world. Although this trade has now gone, there are still many signs remaining and things worth seeing, such as the old docks along the waterfront which have been converted into **Harborwalk**, a promenade of restaurants and shops.

ACCOMMODATION/FOOD/ENTERTAINMENT

Although hotels are everywhere, they are generally expensive in season. But you can find bargains.

Mildred Banther Guest House, 201 Oak St, 448-0907. 'She rents twin rooms for the summer, $40 per person; close to the beach; will not find anything cheaper. No AC which is the only downfall.'

Sea Bair, 2307 N Ocean Blvd, 626-9267. S-$41, D-$54, XP-$5. AC, pool, TV.

Sand Dollar, 403 6th Ave N, 448-9329. S-$43, D-$52. Rooms with baths, AC, TV. BUNACers welcome—special rate, $60/wk per person for 4 in a double room. Pool.

For the **Myrtle Beach Reservation Referral Service**, call 626-7477.

Fortunately Myrtle Beach claims 12,000 **campsites** and calls itself the 'Camping Capital of the World'. The Myrtle Beach Chamber of Commerce, 1301 N Kings Highway, 626-7444, has a complete guide to the area's campsites. Try **Myrtle Beach State Park** on Route 17 South, 238-2224, $15 site.

For food try: **Peaches Corner**, 900 Ocean Blvd, 448-7424. 'Best burgers on the beach—try a famous 'Peaches Burger.' Also **Mr Munchies**, 301 11th Ave N, 626-9753. 'Nothing beats a good 2×2×2 breakfast after a night on the town!)

Club Zero on 38th Ave North provides night-time entertainment 11pm–5am, $6 cover, free with local paycheck. 'Best club in Myrtle Beach . . . unless you want Bobby Brown and bikini contests.' 'Decent dance and alternative music.'

COLUMBIA In the middle of South Carolina at the joining of three interstates sits Columbia, the state's largest city and capital since 1786. Although growing rapidly, the city is mild by Charleston or Myrtle Beach standards. Lake Murray, with 520 miles of scenic lakefront, is less than 20 miles away.

ACCOMMODATION/FOOD

Along the interstates are the best places to find cheap and clean rooms.

Budgetel, 911 Bush River off I-26, 798-3222. S–$37.50, D–$45.

Masters Economy, 613 Knox Abbott Drive, 796-4300. S–$26, D–$31. Near the university campus.

Off-Campus Housing Office, Devine St, 777-4174, can direct visitors to people in the university community with rooms to rent. Open 8am–4.30pm.

For food and entertainment, head to Five Points—a business district at Blossom, Devine and Harden Sts—frequented by students.

Yesterday's Restaurant and Tavern, 2030 Devine St, 799-0196, is an institution. Open daily for lunch and dinner, lunch from $3.50, dinner from $4. 'Friendly manager!'

For cheap, filling sandwiches, try **Groucho's**, 611 Harden St, 799-5708, Columbia's renowned New York-style Jewish deli.

Columbia State Farmer's Market, Bluff Road across from the USC stadium, 253-4041. Fresh produce daily. Open Mon–Sat 6am–9pm.

OF INTEREST

Many of the city's attractions are located in or around the **University of South Carolina**. A mall-like area lined with stately buildings built in the early 19th century and called the **Horseshoe** marks the campus centre. On the Horseshoe facing Sumter St is the **McKissick Museum**, 777-7251, which houses the repository of the **20th Century-Fox Movietone News** archives. Open Mon–Fri 9am–5pm, Sat and Sun 1pm–5pm. Free.

Columbia Museum of Art, within walking distance from the McKissick at Senate and Bull Sts, 799-2810, houses Renaissance and baroque art as well as oriental and neoclassical Greek art galleries. Open Tue–Fri 10am–5pm, Sat, Sun 12.30pm–5pm. Free. Adjoining planetarium open at weekend 12pm–5pm. $2.50.

State Capitol, at Main and Gervais Sts, 734-2430, free weekday tours. Built in 1855, the six bronze stars on the outer western wall mark cannon hits scored by the Union during the Civil War. Open Mon–Fri 9am–5pm. Free.

In a renovated textile mill, the **South Carolina State Museum**, 301 Gervais St, 737-4921, focuses on art, history, natural history, and science and technology. Open Mon–Sat 10am–5pm, Sun 1–5pm, $4 adults or $3 students.

INFORMATION/TRAVEL

Greater Columbia Convention and Visitors Bureau, 301 Gervais St, in the State Museum building, 254-0479. Open Mon–Fri 8.30am–5pm, Sat 10am–5pm, Sun 1pm–5pm. Free.

Greyhound, 2015 Gervais St, 256-6465 or (800) 231-2222.

TENNESSEE

Tennessee is music country. Memphis has been fertile ground for blues musicians and rock and roll. Nashville brought country music down from the hills to mainstream America. The difference in music reflects deeper social differences within the state. The east is 'Hill Country', backwoods and fiercely independent. The west is flat and more Southern, drawing life from the Mississippi River. The two cultures clashed violently during the Civil War, and several of the war's most costly battles were decided on Tennessee soil.

Tennessee's evolution from a backwoods state into the 20th century has not been easy. After a famous trial in 1925, a teacher named Scopes was fined for teaching the theory of evolution. The eastern half of the state is less isolated today thanks to the Tennessee Valley Authority (TVA) built by the Franklin Roosevelt Administration. TVA was a massive effort to both tame a river, and to civilise an entire region. People still argue over the proper role of government power in projects such as TVA. With a revitalized Memphis, the location of a major Nissan plant in Smyrna, and GM's billion dollar Saturn plant just south of Nashville, the economic future appears bright.
National Park: Great Smoky Mountains (also in NC)
The area code for Nashville and the east is 615. For Memphis and the west dial 901.

NASHVILLE The Hollywood of the South, Nashville sparkles with the rhinestone successes and excesses of her country music stars. Bulging with moral character, Nashville is a centre of education and has more churches per capita than anywhere else in the country. Country music itself tends to have a patriotic, moral tone to it.

ACCOMMODATION
'Most cheap motels are several miles outside town. Difficult to find cheap accommodation unless you have a car.'
Days Inn, I-65 and W Trinity Lane, exit 87B, 226-4500. 3 miles north of Nashville. S–$42, D–$45, XP–$6. AC, TV.
Motel 6, 311 W Trinity Ln, 227-9696. Junction of I-24 east and I-65 north. AC. S–$31, D–$35.
Travelodge, Exit 209 off I-40, 366-9000. Downtown. S–$43, D–$45.
Camping: Many campgrounds are clustered around Opryland.
Try **Nashville Travel Park**, 889-4225, or **Two Rivers Campground**, 883-8559. Take Briley Parkway north to McGavock Pike and take exit 12B onto Music Valley Drive. Sites $17.50 for two. $24 w/hook-up.

FOOD
Brown's Bar-B-Q Pit and Soul Food, 13 Lafayette, 255-7207, closes 9pm. 'Excellent cheap smoked chicken sandwiches.'
Bluebird Cafe, 4104 Hillsboro Pike, 383-1461. Opens 5.30pm–midnight, live music with cover charge. Sandwiches, french bread pizzas.
Elliston Place Soda Shop, 2111 Elliston Pl, 327-1090. Open Mon–Fri 6am–7.45pm, Sat 7am–7.45pm. Home-cooked food.

OF INTEREST
Number one on any tourist list is the **Country Hall of Fame**, 4 Music Square East, 256-1639. $7.50, includes tour of **RCA studio B**, where Elvis Presley cut 100 records from 1963–71, and the King's solid gold cadillac. Tours 8am–7pm daily. 'Watch out for bogus Hall of Fame on next street.' 'Not worth it.'
Music Row, betwn 16th and 19th Aves South. The recording studios for Columbia, RCA and many others are here.
For the less musical there is **Fort Nashborough**, 1st Ave N between Broadway and Church Sts. A reproduction of the original fort from which the city first grew. For a tour by the river try the *Belle Carol*, leaves daily from the downtown Riverfront Park at 2pm, $11.90. Also Fri–Sat 11pm party cruise with rock bands. Call (800) 342-2355. Nashvillians are hot on reproductions. Their pride and joy is the **Parthenon Pavilion**, the world's only full-sized copy of the original in Centennial Park along West End Ave, 862-8431, Tue–Sat 9am–4.30pm, Sun 12.30pm–4.30pm, $2.50. For some real history, leave town on I-40 (Old Hickory Blvd exit) and head 12 miles east to the **Hermitage**, 4580 Rachel's Lane, 889-2941,

the home of Andrew Jackson, a backwoods orphan who became US president (1829–1837). He is buried on the grounds. Open 9am–5.30pm daily; admission $7.
Belle Meade Mansion, 5025 Harding Rd, 356-0501. Was the largest plantation and thoroughbred nursery in Tennessee. Open Mon–Sat 9am–5pm, Sun 1pm–5pm, $5.50.
Walk through the garish **Opryland Hotel**, 889-1000, where tropical vegetation, southern architecture, a Liberace impersonator and a waterfall all co-exist under one enormous roof.

ENTERTAINMENT
Topping the entertainment list is the show that made Nashville, **The Grand Ole Opry**. Radio WSU and later television broadcast this country music show out to a receptive nation. Tickets are tough to get during **Fan Fair**, the annual jamboree of country music held in June. The rest of the year you stand a decent chance. $13 and $14 admission to the two shows each Friday and Saturday nights with cheaper matinees in summer. You can ask to be on the waiting list. 'If you have up to number 15, you stand a chance.' 'Nothing quite like it.' The Opry's home is in **Opryland**, an entertainment park which offers 12 live music shows as well as rides and glitz. Open 10am–9pm Mon–Fri, Sat 9am–10pm in summer. Closed Nov–March. On Briley Pkwy, 1-day tickets $26, 2-days $39. Opry and Opryland 889-6611.
There are many clubs along 'Printer's Alley', Nashville's standard club strip. Try **Boots Randolph's**, 209 Printer's, between 3rd and 4th, 256-5500 about $9 per show Mon–Sat.
Topping the country list is **Tootsie's Orchid Cafe**, 422 Broadway, 726-3739. Country/Western bar, springboard for future Opry stars. Merle Haggard and other country greats may drop in to see how things are going. Nightly till 3am, no cover.
Also try the **Station Inn**, 402 12th Ave S, 255-3307. The area near Vanderbilt Campus has more student-oriented entertainment.

INFORMATION
Convention and Visitors Division, Chamber of Commerce, 161 4th Ave N, 259-4755. Mon–Fri 8am–5pm.
Tourism Info Center, Interstate Dr between Woodland St and James Robertson Parkway, 259-4747. 8am–8pm.
Travelers Aid, 138 8th Ave S, 780-9471. Open Mon–Fri 8am–4.30pm.

TRAVEL
Greyhound, 8th Ave and Demonbreun St, 2 blocks south of Broadway, 255-3556.
City Bus Info (MATA), 242-4433. Murfreesboro Rd/Airport Bus, $1.15. Runs 6.15am–10.15pm. #18.

EASTERN TENNESSEE AND THE GREAT SMOKIES The **Great Smoky Mountains National Park** is one of the most heavily visited parks in the United States. Named by the Cherokee Indians for the haze which shrouds the mountain peaks, the 900 miles of trails offer an immense variety of wildlife and landscapes. You will have to travel through **Gatlinburg** to reach the park entrance. 'Commercialism at its worst', Gatlinburg specializes in wax museums, Elvis memorabilia, and UFO and Jesus nick-nacks all for sale to the gullible tourist. The only things worth doing, perhaps, are to ride the ski lift or to climb the space needle from where you get a good look at the mountains. 10 miles east of Gatlinburg on US 321 N is the **Wa-Floy Retreat Hostel**, 436-7700, $10 with AYH card, $12 without.

North of Gatlinburg on US Hwy 441 is **Pigeon Forge**, home of **Dollywood**, the only Tennessee attraction to rival Graceland. The theme park is devoted to the life and career of Tennessee's own Queen of Country, Dolly Parton, and includes music shows, restaurants, shops and rides—all with an 'old-time' atmosphere. (615) 428-9488. 'You won't be disappointed!'

Once in the park, stop at the Visitors Center, 436-1200, where you can get maps, and information on the park's unique history and wildlife. You must get a permit at the center in order to stay overnight at any of the 100 back-country campsites which dot the park. For 3 of the 9 drive-in campgrounds you have to make reservations. You can only do this in person at a TICKETRON Office, or call (804) 456-2267 if you have a credit card. The other 6 campgrounds are first-come, first-served. If you decide to stay over in the park, you will need to bring in your own food; there are no restaurants.

Getting around the park requires a car. The best way to see the mountain peaks is to drive along **Foothills Parkway** towards Walland, or along I-40 skirting the park's northeast flank. Only one road, Hwy 441, actually crosses the park, but it sometimes seems more like a superhighway than a drive through the country. Along the way there are numerous turn-outs and trailheads. A ranger can direct you to quiet walkways (trailheads with only one or two parking spaces) which offer more challenging and private trails, or you can stick to the more touristed, but impressive main turn-outs at the well-known vista points. **Cade's Cove** in the western part of the park offers some of the best wildlife, and a collection of historic buildings. Come early if you want to see the animals. Rangers offer guided tours in the evenings from most campgrounds in summer.

CHATTANOOGA In the southestern corner of the state, this was the site of an important Civil War battle. Union troops were pinned down under siege here for two months before reinforcements allowed them to break free from the mountains and down into the plains of Georgia. 'A lovely city. One of the nicest places I visited in the USA.'

OF INTEREST

For both the view and the history, take the incline railway ($6 return) up **Lookout Mountain**, site of the famous Battle Above the Clouds. The mountain was an important signalling point for troops in the field. The gradient is 77.9% at its maximum. There is a **Visitors Center**, 821-7786, at the top which has displays on signalling in the Civil War. Also a 13′ × 30′ painting, *The Battle of Lookout Mountain*. 'Cheaper to pay for bus right to top and back, $1. Bus leaves from near Greyhound.' 'While at the top, follow road to park and see the cannons and memorials, and imagine the battle. The view is still better from up here.'

Just over the border with Georgia, on Hwy 27 is **Chickamauga** and **Chattanooga National Military Park**. The Union forces were driven from here into Chattanooga after a fierce battle. Between here and the battle for Chattanooga, 34,000 men were wounded or killed. (404) 706-9241 for info. The **Visitors Center** has an excellent slide and map show of the battle. Open 8am–5.45pm during summer.

If you are heading to Chattanooga from Nashville, you may want to stop at the **Jack Daniel's Distillery**, Hwy 55 in Lynchburg, 759-4221. Free tours daily 8am–4pm but don't expect free samples, the distillery of the potent whiskey is in a dry county.

MEMPHIS Chuck Berry, WC Handy, Carl Perkins, Jerry Lee Lewis, Elvis Presley and so many others have called Memphis home. Cradled in a bend of the Mississippi River, this city gave birth (via such legends as James Cotton, Howlin' Wolf and Junior Wells) to the urban blues and to rock 'n' roll. U2, Depeche Mode and Paul Simon all have a keen fascination with the place.

After a long spell of urban decay, Memphis has recently reconstructed its downtown waterfront. Beale Street, famous for its blues clubs, is once again worth visiting. And Mud Island, in the Mississippi River, has several river related attractions reached by monorail. The river connects Memphis with the Deep South, giving the city the most southern feeling of Tennessee's large cities. There are excellent views of the Mississippi as she makes a broad sweep away to the southwest just below the city.

Despite attempts to spruce up the city, however, vast sections remain depressed, reminding the visitor that this is a town where dreams have died. The number one attraction in Memphis is Graceland, where rock 'n' roll king Elvis Presley is buried. And in April, 1968, Martin Luther King, Jr was assassinated at the Lorraine Motel.

ACCOMMODATION

Bed and Breakfast in Memphis, 726-5920. Helen Denton provides a listing of hosts who offer B&B services and makes reservations. Prices range from $55 for a double and up. Try to give two weeks advance notice.

Admiral Benbow Inn, 1220 Union Ave, 725-0630. S-$34, D-$40, $5 key deposit. TV, AC, pool. Take bus 13 down Union. 'Cheapest place in expensive city.'

Kings Court Motel, 265 Union Ave, 527-4305. Downtown. S-$32, D-$40. TV, AC. Turn right out of station and it's on the right. Discount for longer stays.

Lowenstein Longhouse International Hostel, 217 N Waldran St, 527-7174. $10 per night, $50 for 7 nights. Kitchen facilities. Check-in 9–10am and 5–8pm.

Super 8 Motel, 6015 Maccon Cove Rd, 373-4888. Exit 12C off I-40, 3m to airport. S-$39, D-$50. Eating places nearby, about 12m to Gracelands.

Motel 6, 1321 Sycamore View Rd, 382-8572. I-40 east exit on Sycamore View Rd South, 25 miles from train station. S-$31, D-$38. AC.

Memphis YMCA, 3548 Walker Ave, near Memphis State University, 323-4505. Weekly rate students $45, non-students $51; refundable $30 key deposit.

Camping available in **TO Fuller State Park**, nr Chucalissa Indian Village, 543-7581. $11 for two, XP–50¢. Open 24 hours. 'Very good.'

FOOD

Memphis is famous for pork BBQ, with over 100 BBQ restaurants.

Near Graceland is **Leonard's Barbecue Pit**, 4560 Elvis Presley, 396-7044. Barbecue, ribs, spaghetti. Open 7 days.

The North End, 346 N Main St, 526-0319. Southern-style cooking; good, cheap vegetarian dishes. Open 11am–1am daily. Live music Wed–Sun.

OF INTEREST

The best sights in Memphis are her many musical shrines, the most holy of which is Elvis Presley's home, **Graceland**, 3734 Elvis Presley Blvd, 10 miles south of town, 332-3322. Open daily 7.30am–6pm. Tour the 23-room, 14-acre mansion, the Lisa Marie, a 96-seat airplane/penthouse in the sky, Elvis' tour bus, a stunning car museum, plus the Meditation Garden where Elvis and family are buried. $17.95 gains entry to everything. You can pay less for a partial tour ($8), but you will not want to miss the costumes, gold-wrapped grand piano, and 'jungle' playroom. Walking through the amazing 80 foot long 'Hall of Gold' lined with the King's gold records is almost breathtaking. Only by walking down this hallway can you

GREAT AMERICAN BREAKFASTS

Breakfasts, and their Sunday cousin, 'brunch', have a special place in American culture. For the great all-American breakfast, try: **Colony Inn, Amana, IA**, (319) 622-6270, offers a plentiful spread of all the traditionals. A spicier wake-up call awaits at **Cisco's Bakery, Austin, TX**, (512) 478-2420. Its Tex-Mex-breax include huevos rancheros, which will open even the most stubborn lids. **Em Lee's** best offerings are the huge blueberry waffles, **Carmel, CA,** (408) 625-6780. **Lou Mitchell's, Chicago, IL,** (312) 939-3111, serves up unforgettable Greek toast. Also in **Chicago** the **West Egg Cafe**, 280-8366, does wonderful things with eggs, from breakfast burritos to the 'veggie benedict' special. Near Chicago in **Willmette, IL, Walker Brothers Original Pancake House**, (708) 251-6000, is noteworthy for pancakes of all kinds, with apple at the top of the list. **Primo's Cafe, Jackson, MS,** (601) 948-4343, is famous for Southern breakfasts, the heartiest anywhere with hominy grits, omelettes and biscuits and gravy. **The Bunnery** in **Jackson, WY,** (307) 733-5474, boasts wonderful buttermilk coffee cake and much more. At **Original Pantry, Los Angeles, CA,** (213) 972-9279 (open 24 hours), try hot cakes or French toast. **Sara Beth's, New York City,** (212) 496-6280, makes its own preserves, homebaked muffins, sticky buns and offers a wide range of other breakfast foods. In **San Francisco, Doidges** serves unique concoctions: peach and walnut chutney omelettes, and a breakfast casserole with meat, cheese, potato, tomato, sour cream and a poached egg. Open till 2pm weekdays and 3pm weekends, (415) 921-2149. For excellent coffee, try **Cafe Trieste** at **North Beach** in **SF**, where Kerouac probably began his day, (415) 392-6739. **Avignone Frères, Washington, DC,** (202) 462-2050, serves continental, English and country breakfasts; great omelettes and good homemade muesli.

North of the border in **Toronto**, **Ottawa** and **Montreal**, look for **Peel's Pubs** where you can still get eggs, toast, juice and a bottomless coffee pot for 99¢.

begin to comprehend the enormity of Elvis's success. 'Can get there by taking # 13 bus just outside Greyhound, 95 cents.' 'Get there by bus, then buy tickets.' 'Amusing and sad. I toured house hurriedly with 15 middle aged fans brought to tears in midst of disgusting bad taste. Plastic souvenirs are everywhere. Still worth it though.'

Memphis Music & Blues Museum and **Hall of Fame**, 97 S 2nd St, 525-4007. $5 admission to each, $9 to both. Open Mon–Sat 10am–6pm, Sun 11am–5pm. 'Rare blues recordings, posters, guitars, video exhibits, photos and general memorabilia.' 'Not worth the money.'

The **Memphis Pink Palace and Planetarium**, 3050 Central Ave, 320-6320, is one of the largest museums in the Southeast, and specializes in science and history. Originally housed in the adjoining pink marble mansion. Tue–Sat 10am–5pm, Thur till 8pm (free 5pm–8pm), Sun 1pm–5pm. $6.50 museum, $3 planetarium. Combo ticket $8.50. **Dixon Gallery and Garden**, 4339 Park Ave, 761-5250. Good collection of French and American Impressionist paintings. Tue–Sun 10am–5pm, Sun 1pm–5pm, $5. $2.50 on Mondays.

Stroll through the **Audubon Gardens**; and the 18 old buildings which make up **Victorian Village**, 680 Adams Ave, 526-1469, are highly recommended, $5, $2 students. Open Mon–Sat 10am–3.30pm, Sun 1pm–3.30pm.

The 32-storey, 6-acre **Great American Pyramid**, which opened in autumn 1991, houses the American Music Hall of Fame, the Memphis Music Experience, College Football Hall of Fame and an arena seating 20,000.

Mud Island, 576-7230, situated offshore from main downtown area and accessible by a monorail, offers attractions relating to the Mississippi River. The park alone costs $2 while the park and the **River Museum** costs $6. Includes a tour of a towboat, a film about the river, and a Mark Twain talking mannequin that tells you about the river's history. More fun is the 5 block long **Mississippi River scale model**, complete with flowing water. Open 10am–6pm (last admission 4.30pm). Concerts in the summer, call 725-4822 or 525-3000 (10am–5pm) for details. Big names who have played in the past include Don Henley and Chicago. Mud Island is also home of the ***Memphis Belle***, the first B-17 bomber to successfully complete 25 missions in WWII, and subject of a recent Hollywood movie. 576-7235.
National Civil Rights Center, 450 Mulberry St, 521-9699. Open since August 1991, it houses exhibits and films on the individuals who led the civil rights movement. Adjoining the centre is the **Lorraine Motel**, site of the 1968 assassination of Martin Luther King, Jr. Open Wed–Mon 10am–6pm; 1pm–6pm Sun; closed Tuesday. $5, $4 student.
Chucalissa Indian Village, Indian Village Drive, TO Fuller State Park, 785-3160. Reconstructed 1000-year-old Indian village. Choctaw Indians live on the site and demonstrate Indian crafts. Guided tours. Open Tue–Sat 9am–4.30pm, Sun 1pm–5pm. Admission $3.

ENTERTAINMENT

Beale St is the place where WC Handy blew the notes to make him 'Father of the Blues'. His house is now a museum, 352 Beale St. At night, a half-dozen clubs start swinging. Read the Friday section of the *Commercial Appeal*. Try **Rum Boogie Cafe**, 182 Beale St, 528-0150, 11.30am–3am, $2–$5 cover. During the day, **Abe Schwab**'s, 163 Beale St, 523-9782, an eclectic and amusing drugstore, sells just about anything. 'Lively and bustling rapping, blues and loud records combine to create a unique atmosphere.' Listen to WDIA, 1070 AM, the famous black radio station where B.B. King used to spin records and an important station for the early growth of the blues, and R&B scene. Try to plan your trip for Elvis Week in August, and the National Blues Amateur Talent Contest, 527-2583.

INFORMATION

Visitor Information Center, 340 Beale St, 543-5333. Open Mon–Sat 9am–6pm, 12–6pm Sun.
Travelers Aid, 46 N 3rd St, Suite 708, 525-5466. Open Mon–Fri 8.30am–4.30pm.

TRAVEL

Greyhound, 203 Union Ave, 523-1184 or (800) 231-2222. 'Good facilities.'
Amtrak, 545 S Main St, 526-0052 for terminal.
City bus, $1, 274-6282 for information.
Gray Line Elvis Tours, 948-8687.
Buses to Memphis International Airport depart from 3rd and Beale, Mon–Fri 6.45am–6.15pm. Take the Showboat bus and transfer to #32 at the fairground. Hotel Express (HTS), 922-8238, is an airport shuttle and will pick you up from any downtown hotel. $8.
For a taxi call 577-7777, $14 o/w.

2 CANADA

BACKGROUND

BEFORE YOU GO

Citizens and legal, permanent residents of the United States do not need passports to enter Canada as visitors although they may be asked for identification (proof of citizenship or Alien Registration card) or proof of funds at the border. All other visitors entering Canada must have valid passports. Since Immigration officials have enormous discretionary powers, it is wise to be well dressed, clean cut, and the possessor of a return ticket if possible. The following persons do not need a visa if entering only as visitors:

1. British citizens and British overseas citizens who are readmissible to the United Kingdom.
2. Citizens of Andorra, Antigua and Barbuda, Argentina, Australia, Austria, Bahamas, Barbados, Belgium, Belize, Bolivia, Botswana, Costa Rica, Cyprus, Denmark, Dominica, Fiji, Finland, France, Federal Republic of Germany, Greece, Grenada, Honduras, Iceland, Ireland, Israel, Italy, Japan, Kenya, Kiribati, Lesotho, Liechtenstein, Luxembourg, Malawi, Malaysia, Malta, Mexico, Monaco, Nauru, The Netherlands, New Zealand, Nicaragua, Norway, Panama, Papua New Guinea, Paraguay, San Marino, Saudi Arabia, Seychelles Republic, Singapore, Solomon Islands, Spain, St. Kitts and Nevis, St. Lucia, St. Vincent, Surinam, Swaziland, Sweden, Switzerland, Tonga, Trinidad and Tobago, Tuvalu, United States, Uruguay, Vanuatu, Venezuela, Western Samoa, Zambia and Zimbabwe.
3. Citizens of the British dependent territories who derive their citizenship through birth, descent, registration or naturalization in one of the British dependent territories of Anguilla, Bermuda, British Virgin Islands, Cayman Islands, Falkland Islands, Gibraltar, Hong Kong, Montserrat, Pitcairn, St. Helena, or the Turks and Caicos Islands.

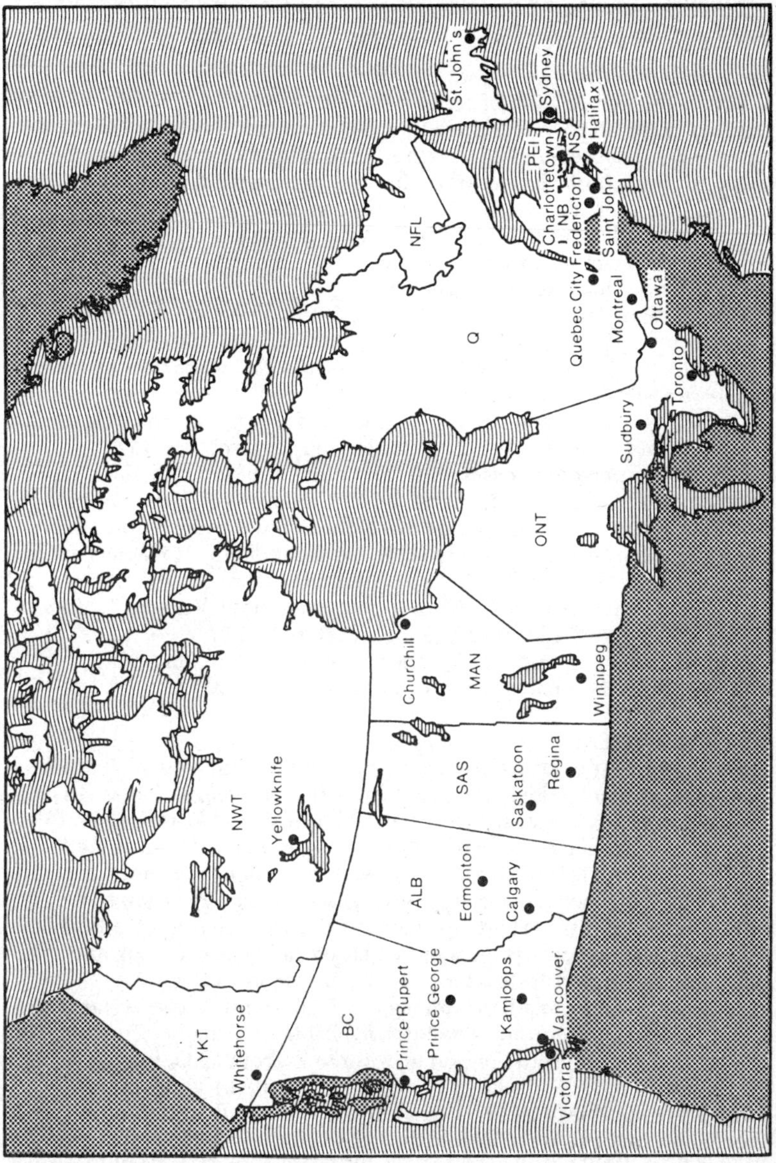
St. John's
Sydney
Halifax
PEI
Charlottetown
NS
NB
Fredericton
Saint John
NFL
Quebec City
Montreal
Ottawa
Q
Toronto
Sudbury
ONT
Churchill
MAN
Winnipeg
SAS
Saskatoon
Regina
NWT
Yellowknife
ALB
Edmonton
Calgary
BC
Prince Rupert
Prince George
Kamloops
Vancouver
Victoria
YKT
Whitehorse

Nationals of all other countries should check their visa requirements with their nearest Canadian consular office. If there is no official Canadian representative in the country, visas are issued by the British embassy or consulate. Those requiring visas must apply before leaving home.

To **work in Canada**, a work visa must be obtained from the Canadian immigration authorities before departure. To qualify you must produce written evidence of a job offer. If you are a student, contact the **BUNAC** London office (071 251-3472) for information about the *Work Canada* programme which gives eligible students (tertiary level or gap year) temporary work authorisation. Similar opportunities are open to students of a few other countries. Check with your nearest consulate. If you plan to **study in Canada** you will need a special student visa, obtainable from any Canadian consulate. You must produce a letter of acceptance from the Canadian college before the visa can be issued.

Visitors who plan to re-enter the United States after visiting Canada must be sure to keep their US visa documentation and passport to regain entry into the US. (*See Background USA chapter for information on the Visa Waiver programme.*)

Customs permit anyone over 16 to import, duty free, up to 50 cigars, 200 cigarettes and 1 kg (2.2 lbs) of manufactured tobacco.

Along with personal possessions, any number of individually wrapped and addressed gifts up to the value of $40 (Canadian) each may be brought into the country. Each visitor who meets the minimum age requirements of the province or territory of entry (19 in Newfoundland, Nova Scotia, New Brunswick, Saskatchewan, British Columbia, Ontario, the Yukon and Northwest Territories; 18 elsewhere) may, in addition, bring in 1.1 litres of liquor or wine or 8.2 litres of beer or ale, duty and tax-free.

Further details on immigration, health or customs requirements may be obtained from the nearest High Commission, embassy or consulate.

GETTING THERE

From Europe. Advanced booking charter (ABC) flights are available from London and other British and European cities, to various Canadian cities including Halifax, Ottawa, Toronto and Montréal, and Winnipeg and Vancouver. Also available are several different types of package deal. Canadian Airlines and Air Canada offer packages including anything from bus passes, hotels, coach tours, rail passes, to car and camper wagon rental. The only way to discover the best fare and route for yourself is to get all available information from your travel agent when you are ready to book and check with airlines directly for current promotions or seat sales.

Air Canada and Canadian Airlines have 7-day and 21-day advance purchase tickets. Student fares are also available to Canada. Currently the return student fare from London to Toronto is about £330; the Air Canada APEX fare is £459. Expect to pay about £120 more to Vancouver.

If you are not able to take advantage of the various advance booking fares, then it may make sense to fly into the USA and continue your journey from there. Using **VUSA fares** and booking before leaving for North America, you could fly on from New York for about $120, or $95 on an Air Canada Youth Standby fare. Again, do your research before paying out your money, and bear in mind that travel from the USA, by bus, rail or air, into Canada is very easy and can be very inexpensive. (See below.) Travellers to Canada via the USA will of course need to obtain a US visa before leaving their home country.

From the USA. You have the choice of bus, train, plane or car, or of course you can simply walk across on foot. It is impossible, within the confines of this Guide, to give all the possible permutations of modes, fares and routes from points within the USA to points within Canada, but, as a rough guide to fares (in $CAN) from New York to the major eastern Canadian cities, the current fares to Toronto are: by train, $134 one-way, $161–$212 round trip depending on when you travel; by air, about $167 one-way, about $280 round-trip, depending on dates of travel, and by bus, about $100 one-way. Don't overlook the aforementioned VUSA fares.

Should you cross the border by car it's a good idea to have a yellow 'Non-resident, Interprovincial Motor Vehicle Liability Insurance Card' (phew!) which provides evidence of financial responsibility by a valid automobile liability insurance policy. This card is available in the US through an insurance agent. Such evidence is required at all times by all provinces and territories. In addition Québec's insurance act bars lawsuits for bodily injury resulting from an auto accident, so you may need some additional coverage should you be planning to drive in Québec. If you're driving a borrowed car it's wise to carry a letter from the owner giving you permission to use the car.

CLIMATE AND WHAT TO PACK

Canada's principal cities are situated between the 43rd and 49th parallels, consequently summer months in the cities, and in the southernmost part of the country in general, are usually warm and sunny. August is the warmest month when temperatures are in the 80s. Ontario and the Prairie Provinces are the warmest places and although it can be humid it is never as bad as the humidity which accompanies high temperatures in the US.

Be warned, however, that nights, even in high summer, can be cool and it's advisable to bring lightweight sweaters or jackets. Naturally as you go north, temperatures drop accordingly. Yellowknife in the North West Territories has an *average* August temperature of 45°F (7°C) for instance, and nights in the mountains can be pretty cold. Snow can be expected in some places as early as September, and in winter Canada is very cold and snowy everywhere.

When you've decided which areas of Canada you'll be visiting, note the local climate and pack clothes accordingly. Plan for a variety of occasions, make a list, and then cut it by half! Take easy-to-care-for garments. Permanent press, non-iron things are best. Laundromats are cheap and readily available wherever you go. Remember too that you'll probably want to buy things while you're in North America. Canadians, as well as Americans, excel at producing casual, sporty clothes, T-shirts, etc. But if you're visiting both countries plan to buy in the US, it's decidedly cheaper. The farther north you plan to go and the more time you intend to spend out of doors, the more weatherproof the clothing will need to be. And don't forget the insect repellent.

It's important too to consider the best way of carrying your clothes. Lugging heavy suitcases is nobody's fun. A lightweight bag or a backpack is possibly best. A good idea is to take a smaller flight-type bag in which to keep a change of clothes and all your most valuable possessions like passport, travellers cheques and air tickets as well, but always hand carry the bag containing your passport and money. For extra safety many travellers like to carry passport documents and travellers cheques in a special neck/waist pouch or wallet. When travelling by bus be sure to keep your baggage within your sights. Make sure it's properly labelled and on the same bus as yourself—at every stop!

TIME ZONES

Canada spans six time zones:

1. Newfoundland Standard Time: Newfoundland, Labrador and parts of Baffin Island.
2. Atlantic Standard Time: The Maritimes, Gaspé Peninsula, Anticosti Island, Québec Province east of Comeau Bay, most of Baffin Island and Melville Peninsula.
3. Eastern Standard Time: Québec Province west of Comeau Bay, and all of Ontario east of 90 degrees longitude.
4. Central Standard Time: Ontario west of 90, Manitoba, Keewatin district of Saskatchewan and southeastern part of the province.
5. Mountain Standard Time: rest of Saskatchewan, Alberta, part of Northwest Territories and northeastern British Columbia.
6. Pacific Standard Time: British Columbia (except northeastern portion) and Yukon Territory.

Newfoundland Standard Time is 3 hours 30 minutes after Greenwich, Atlantic Standard Time, 4 hours, and, moving westwards, each zone is one hour further behind Greenwich, so that the Pacific Zone is 8 hours behind.

From the last Sunday in April through the last Sunday in October, Daylight Saving Time is observed everywhere except Thunder Bay and Essex County, Ontario, and the Province of Saskatchewan.

THE CANADIAN PEOPLE

Although Canada, like its neighbour to the south, is a comparatively young country, Canadians now feel that they have finally emerged as a major world power in their own right, and gone are the days when Canada can only function in the shadow of Great Britain or the United States.

It is only 126 years since the confederation of 1867. At that time Canada petered out into trackless forest to the north of Lake Superior, and no regular communication existed to the isolated settlements of the Red River in the west. The provinces of Ontario, Québec, Nova Scotia and Prince Edward Island made up the confederation. The other six provinces and two territories only gradually joined. Of the last provinces, Saskatchewan and Alberta were formed in 1905 and Newfoundland entered the federation in 1949—all amazingly recent.

The population of Canada is roughly 26 million, a relatively small population spread over a gigantic land mass. Practically everyone lives along the southern strip of Canada, which borders on the United States. Most of

Canada is still wilderness. The majority of the Canadian people are descendants of white European types, either Gallic or Celtic. There are also Native Peoples (Indians and Eskimoes), Chinese, Eastern European immigrants, Tamils, Sikhs and other people from all corners of the world.

Canada is rich in natural resources and rich with money in the bank. There are five banks in Canada, and the influence of the big five is very strong, reaching far beyond banking. The Canadian dollar is for all intents and purposes pegged to the value of the US dollar, although, dollar for dollar, it is worth less (about 75%). All its natural wealth has not, however, prevented Canada from joining the ranks of nations suffering from economic recession; unemployment is high, and the federal debt is large. Such was the economic state of the nation, that it brought an end to the long rule of the Conservative Party at the end of October 1993. Overwhelmingly, Canadians voted to transfer the economic future of Canada to the care of Jean Chretien and the Liberal Party.

The election also brought to centre-stage prominence the perenial problem of Canadian politics—Québec. The Bloc Québecois, led by Lucien Bouchard, whose main pre-election aim was to prepare Canada for Québec's independence, won the second highest number of seats in parliament. In Canada, the values and traditions of the individual provinces are strong and Canadian politics is renowned for its bitter interprovincial and provincial anti-federal rivalries. Ontario, the most wealthy province and the principal seat of the government, is often at the centre of the controversy, and one of the most bitter power struggles has been between Ontario and Québec.

There are more than 6 million French speaking Canadians; the majority live in Québec. You will notice the phrase 'je me souviens' on the license plates in Québec. This phrase (I remember) refers to the defeat of Montcalm on the Plains of Abraham by General Wolfe. This event signalled the end of a French power base in the New World. The French have felt besieged and encroached upon by the English world ever since—hence their sometimes desperate measures to protect their heritage and remain a 'distinct society' within Canada. Constitutional proposals designed to keep Quebec within the federation and everyone else happy as well, have so far failed to gain approval. Though many bitter feelings still stem from the conflict, there is no doubt that this unsubtle blend of French and British influence adds an extra quelque chose to the Canadian cultural picture.

The Canadians have acquired something of a reputation for being puritanical, conformist, humourless and dull! Certainly there's a need there for more than a touch of Gallic charm and chic. Of course this image is largely the face of officialdom and bureaucracy. You will find the Canadian people charming, hospitable and anxious to share their land with you. They will also be most anxious to uphold Canada's uniqueness and to show that Canada is not the same as America—despite the apparent social similarities. Never call a Canadian 'American'!

Try and see something of the *real* Canada. Don't expect to find the stereotypical Mountie on every street corner; Native Indians don't live in teepees, and it doesn't start snowing on September 1st! Visit an Indian reservation, learn about Eskimo native arts and crafts, meet with Canadians as they celebrate at the numerous fairs, rodeos and festivals across the country. (Provincial tourist authorities can supply dates and locations of the various events.) 'Man-made 20th century Canada will impress you, but the Canadian way of life and the natural beauty of the land will really dazzle you.'

HEALTH

Canada does operate a subsidised health service, though on a provincial rather than federal basis. Most provinces will cover most of the hospital and medical services of their inhabitants, although three months' residency is required in Québec and British Columbia. The short-term visitor to Canada, therefore, must be adequately insured *before* arrival.

MONEY

Canadian currency is dollars and cents and comes in the same units as US currency, i.e. penny, nickel, quarter and a dollar, as well as a $2 bill. Canada has now added a new dollar coin with a great name, the 'loonie'. A loon (bird!) is featured on one side.

US coins are often found among Canadian change and are accepted at par. Most people will give you an exchange rate on US dollars. At present one Canadian dollar is worth US $0.75. To avoid exchange rate problems, it is a good idea to change all your money into Canadian currency or travellers cheques. (At the time of writing; £1 equals approximately (CAN$2.10.)

Unless otherwise stated, all prices in this section are in Canadian dollars.

Travellers cheques are probably the safest form of currency and are accepted at most hotels, restaurants and shops. As well as American Express, Thomas Cook and Barclays Bank (Visa) cheques, you can also purchase cheques issued by Canadian banks before you go.

Credit cards—Barclaycard and Visa are reciprocal with Chargex, and Access or Eurocard with MasterCard.

Bank hours are generally 10am to 4pm, Monday to Friday, and often with a later opening on Friday. If you are planning an extensive trip to Canada and the USA, you might consider opening a bank account that offers a cash card which works on both a Canadian and US bank system. The only reference you need to open an account in Canada is cash. It is a simple matter of filling out one form. Since opening an account with a Canadian bank means corresponding with them through the mail, you will want to look into it well in advance of your trip. The Royal Bank of Canada offers a 'client card' that is valid in Canada and at all 'Plus' system machines in the US.

Provincial **sales tax** applies on the purchase of goods and services. In Ontario for instance the rate is eight percent, although there are exceptions such as on shoes under $30, books, groceries, and restaurant meals costing less than $4. On the other hand if your meal costs more than $4, then the tax is ten percent. Canada also has a **VAT tax** of seven percent. Overseas visitors may be able to claim a rebate of this **GST** (Goods and Services Tax) paid on short term accommodation and on consumer goods. Details from: Revenue Canada, Customs & Excise, Visitors' Rebate Program, Ottawa K1A 1J5. Or, once in Canada, phone (800) 66VISIT.

Tipping, as in the USA, is expected in eating places, by taxi drivers, bellhops, baggage handlers and the like. Fifteen percent is standard.

COMMUNICATIONS

Mail. Postage stamps can be purchased at any post office or from vending machines (at par) in hotels, drug stores, stations, bus terminals and some newsstands. At present it costs 49¢ to send a letter to a US address and 86¢ to Europe and other overseas destinations. Within Canada the rate is 43¢. Canada Post is *very* slow. Post offices are not generally open at weekends.

If you do not know where you will be staying, have your mail sent care of 'General Delivery'. You then have 15 days to collect.

Telegrams. Not handled by the post office, but sent via a CP or CN telegraph office.

Telephone. Local calls from coin telephones usually cost 25¢. As in the USA (see earlier section—the two systems are very similar) local calls from private phones are usually free. You can direct dial to most places in Canada and the United States and to Europe from some areas of Canada. To check with the operator dial 0. Check local directories for the cheapest times to place a long distance call.

ELECTRICITY

110v, 60 cycles AC, except in remote areas where cycles vary.

SHOPPING

Stores are generally open until 5.30 or 6pm with late opening on Thursday or Friday. Usually, only shops located in tourist areas will be open on Sundays. Canada is big on shopping malls (the inventor of which was a Canadian). In the large cities there are huge underground shopping malls so that you do not need to go outside at all in the harsh Canadian winter, but can move underground from mall to mall, or mall to subway or train station.

Good buys in Canada include handicrafts and Eskimo products such as carvings, moccasins, etc. Casual, outdoors or winter wear is recommended too, but if you are visiting the USA and Canada you will probably be able to buy more cheaply in the USA.

THE METRIC SYSTEM

As already noted above, Canada has gone metric. Milk, wine and gasoline are sold by the litre; groceries in grams and kilograms; clothing sizes come in centimetres, fabric lengths in metres; and, most important, driving speeds are in kilometres per hour. See the conversion tables in the Appendix.

DRINKING

Liquor regulations come under provincial law, and although it's pretty easy to buy a drink by the glass in a lounge, tavern or beer parlour, it can be be pretty tricky tracking down one of the special liquor outlets which can be few and far between. Beer, wine and spirits can only be bought from a liquor store which will keep usual store hours and be closed on Sundays. The drinking age is 19, except in PEI, Quebec, Manitoba and Alberta, where it is 18.

DRUGS

Narcotics laws in Canada are federal, rather than provincial, and it is illegal to possess or sell such drugs as cannabis, cocaine and heroin. Penalties (up to $1,000 or 6 months in jail for a first offence) are the same for offences involving marijuana as for heroin, etc.

CIGARETTES

Currently cost about $6 (perhaps this is a good time to give up the weed!) for a packet of 25. Foreign brands available.

PUBLIC HOLIDAYS

New Year's Day	1st January
Good Friday/Easter Monday	Variable
Victoria Day	3rd Monday in May
Canada Day	1st July
Labour Day	1st Monday in September
Thanksgiving Day	2nd Monday in October
Remembrance Day	11th November
Christmas Day	25th December
Boxing Day	26th December

INFORMATION

In *Britain* contact Canada House, Trafalgar Square, London SW1, 071 629-9492. In *Canada* tourist information centres abound and are indicated on highway maps. Especially recommended is the information published by the provincial tourist offices. If you plan to spend any length of time in one province it is well worth writing to them and asking for their free maps, guides and accommodation information.

Provincial Tourist Offices

Alberta Economic Development and Tourism, 3rd Floor, 10155 102 St, Edmonton, Alberta T5J 4L6, (403) 427-4321, toll free, (800) 661-8888.

Tourism British Columbia, 387–1428 Parliament Buildings, Victoria, BC V8V 1X4, (800) 663-6000, or (604) 387-1428.

Travel Manitoba, Dept 7036, 7th Floor, 155 Carlton St, Winnipeg, Manitoba R3C 3H8, (204) 945-3777, or toll-free US and Canada (800) 665-0040.

Tourism New Brunswick, PO Box 12345, Fredericton, NB E3B 5C3, toll free in NB (800) 442-4442, or toll free (800) 561-0123.

Newfoundland and Labrador Tourist Branch, Department of *Tourism and Culture*, PO Box 8730, St John's, Newfoundland A1B 4K2, (709) 729-2830 or toll free from US and Canada (800) 563-6353.

Travel Arctic, Governments of the Northwest Territories, Box 1320, Yellowknife, NWT X1A 2L9, (403) 873-7200 or toll free (800) 661-0788.

Nova Scotia Department of Tourism, PO Box 130, Halifax, NS B3J 2M7, (902) 424-4247, toll free from the USA (800) 341-6096, or toll free from Canada (800) 565-0000.

Ontario Travel, 9th floor, 77 Bloor St W, Toronto, Ontario M7A 2R9, (416) 965-4008, or toll-free from Canada and continental US (800) ONTARIO.

Visitor Services Division of *Prince Edward Island*, PO Box 940, Charlotte-

town, PEI C1A 7M5, (902) 368-4444, toll free in US (800) 565-0267, in Maritimes (800) 565-7421.
Tourisme Québec, CP 979, Montréal, QUE H3C 2W3, in New York (212) 397-0200, toll free from US and Canada (800) 363-7777.
Tourism Saskatchewan, 1919 Saskatchewan Dr, Regina, S4P 3V7, (800) 667-7538 in Saskatchewan, (306) 787-2300 in Regina and (800) 667-7191 toll free.
Tourism Yukon, PO Box 2703, Whitehorse, Yukon Y1A 2C6, (403) 667-5340.

THE GREAT OUTDOORS

Hardly surprising with all those wide open spaces, that Canadians are very outdoors minded. Greenery is never far away and the best of it has been preserved in national parks. There are many national parks in Canada ranging in size from less than one to more than 17,000 square miles, and in type from the immense mountains and forests of the west to the steep cliffs and beaches of the Atlantic coastline. In addition there are many fine provincial parks and more than 600 national historic parks and sites.

Entrance to the national parks costs $3 for a one-day pass, $6 for four days, or $20 for the season. All but the most primitive offer camping facilities, hiking trails, and facilities for swimming, fishing, boating and other such diversions. Most of the national parks are dealt with in this Guide. For more detailed information we suggest you write to the individual park or to: Parks Canada, Ottawa, Ontario K1A 1G2, for a copy of the free booklet *National Parks of Canada*. A list of major parks follows.

Banff, Alberta.
Cape Breton Highlands, Nova Scotia.
Elk Island, Alberta.
Forillon, Québec.
Fundy, New Brunswick.
Georgian Bay Islands, Ontario.
Glacier, British Columbia.
Gros Morne, Newfoundland.
Jasper, Alberta.
Kejimkujik, Nova Scotia.
Kootenay, British Columbia.
Mount Revelstoke, British Columbia.
Point Pelee, Ontario.
Prince Albert, Saskatchewan.
Prince Edward, Prince Edward Island.
Riding Mountain, Manitoba.
St Lawrence Islands, Ontario.
Terra Nova, Newfoundland.
Waterton Lakes, Alberta.
Wood Buffalo, Alberta/North Western Territories.
Yoho, British Columbia.

MEDIA AND ENTERTAINMENT

Canada until recently was viewed as a cultural wasteland. Even now, for preference, Canadians watch US or British television programmes and read US or European magazines. Traditionally, talented Canadians in order to achieve fame, have moved from Canada to the USA. However, this has begun to change.

This is partly because the government has legislated a minimum level of Canadian content in radio and television and implemented a strict 'hire Canadian' policy throughout the arts and entertainment business. Canadian culture is also flourishing more as a reflection of newfound Canadian pride. Visitors will be surprised at the high standards in ballet, the theatre and classical music. Folk music thrives too as do the visual arts and Canada boasts a number of exceptional museums and restorations well worth visiting for a glimpse of Canada past.

SPORT AND RECREATION

Both spectator and participatory sports are major activities. Canadians love to camp, fish, hike, ski, canoe, sail and generally enjoy the outdoors. Winter sports (naturally) are very popular from ice-skating to snowmobiling. Ice hockey is the biggie for watching. There is a Canadian version of American football and baseball is also very popular. The Toronto Blue Jays, have won the world championship for the last two years. Surprisingly perhaps, the national game is lacrosse.

ON THE ROAD

ACCOMMODATION

For general hints on finding the right accommodation for you, please read the 'Accommodation' section for the USA. The basic rules are the same.

All the provincial tourist boards publish comprehensive accommodation lists. These are obtainable from Canadian government tourist offices or directly from provincial tourist boards and have details of all approved hotels, motels and tourist homes in each town. These are excellent guides and are highly recommended.

Hotels and Motels. Always plenty to choose from around sizeable towns or cities, but if you're travelling don't leave finding accommodation until too late in the day. In less populated areas distances between motels can be very great indeed. The major difference between the hotel/motel picture here and in the US is that the budget chains like Days Inn and Motel 6 have not yet made it to Canada in force. The exceptions are Friendship Inns, Journey's End Hotels, Days Inns in Ontario, and Relax Inns in Alberta.

Many highway motels will often have restaurants attached. The local tourist bureau will usually have a list of local hotels and motels. However, for the budget traveller, it is likely that a tourist home will nearly always be a less expensive alternative.

Tourist Homes. A bit like bed and breakfast places in Britain and Europe, only without the breakfast. In other words a room in a private home. Usually you share a bathroom and your room will be basic but perfectly adequate. Such establishments are scattered very liberally all over Canada with prices starting around $20. Certainly if hostels are not for you, and your budget doesn't quite stretch to a motel, then these are the places to look for. Again, the local tourist bureau will be able to provide you with a list of possibilities.

Bed and Breakfasts. There is now also the firmly established bed and breakfast circuit. Single it's about $30 and up, double about $35 to $65. Several guides to bed and breakfast establishments (town and country locations) are published in Canada and can be picked up in bookshops everywhere. Otherwise, the local tourist office will provide listings. (See also under *Guest Farms and Ranches*.)

Hostels. The Canadian Youth Hostels Association (CYHA), has adopted the International Youth Hostel Federation blue triangle and become Hostelling International—Canada. The association has over 60 member hostels across the country with at least one hostel in each major city. The National Parks in Alberta are well covered. You can save money with an International Youth Hostel Card from your own country since non-members usually pay about 2 dollars more. There is no limit to a stay.

For detailed information and lists of hostels write to: HI-Canada, 1600 James Naismith Dr, Gloucester, Ontario, K1B 5N4 or phone (613) 748-5638; or else enquire via the association in your own country. Membership is $25 a year.

YM/YWCAs. Y's have weight lifting machines, pools and aerobics classes for those in need of an exercise fix, but standards vary. Cheaper and often better, are tourist homes. Worth considering is the Y's Way travel voucher scheme. Contact the Y's Way, 224 E 47th St, New York, NY 10017 or phone (212) 755-2410 for information. For a complete list and information on Canadian Y's: YMCA National Council, 2160 Yonge St, Toronto, Ontario M4S 2A1.

University Accommodation. There is much campus housing available during the summer. Look particularly for student owned co-operatives in cities such as Toronto which provide a cheapish service, often with cooking facilities. In fact they are only too pleased to have summer visitors since it helps to keep the place going. University housing services and fraternities will often be able to help you also. In general, college housing starts at about $17 single but can be as high as $35 single. Staying on campus usually gives access to all the usual facilities including cafeterias, lounges, etc, and often a pool and gymnasium/athletic fields. The drawback about campus accommodation is that it is usually not available after mid-late August since that is when US and Canadian students begin returning to college. For campus housing listings for both the USA and Canada, consult Peterson's *Directory of College Accommodations*.

Camping. Canadians are very fond of camping and during the summer, sites in popular places will always be very full. Usually, however, campgrounds are not as spacious as those in the USA and less trouble is taken with the positioning of individual sites. Prices are about the same—about $8–$15 per site. There are many provincial park campgrounds, as well as sites in the national parks and the many privately operated grounds usually to be found close to the highways. Campgrounds are marked on official highway maps.

The Rand McNally *Campground and Trailer Park Guide* covers Canada as well as the USA. Also, the Canadian Government Office of Tourism publishes guides on camping across Canada: Canadian Government Office of Tourism, 150 Kent St, Ottawa, Ontario. The much recommended KOA now have about 50 campgrounds in Canada. Details from: KOA, 6A Tilbury Court, Unit No. 4, Brampton, Ontario L6T 3T4. Tel: (416) 453-7080. Both the provincial tourist guides and local tourist bureaux are other sources of information on where to find a campground. The government-run parks tend to have the more scenic tent sites.

For real outdoor camping in Canada you need a tent with a flyscreen. Black flies and mosquitoes are a serious problem in June and July and the further north you go the worse the little darlings are. It gets cold at night too as early as August, so be prepared for colder temperatures and wetter weather than in the US. Other hazards of camping in Canada include bears and 'beaver fever'—a rare intestinal parasite (*giardia lamblia*).

Guest Ranches and Farms. Many farms accept paying guests during the summer. Prices vary and in some cases guests are encouraged to help about the farm. For information write for *Farm, Ranch and Country Vacations*, Farm and Ranch Vacations Inc, PO Box 698, Newfoundland, NJ 07435, USA. For reservations and information (in the US) call (800) 252-7899 (sending US$17 from the UK), or Ontario Farm Vacations, Ontario Travel, 77 Bloor St W, 9th Fl, Toronto, Ontario M7A 2R9.

FOOD

How much you spend per day on food will obviously depend upon your taste and your budget, but you can think in terms of roughly $2–$5 on breakfast, $3 upwards on lunch, and anything from $5 upwards on dinner. It is customary in Canada to eat the main meal of the day in the evening from about 5pm onwards. In small, out-of-the-way towns, any restaurants there are may close as early as 7pm or 8pm. Yes, McDonalds does operate in Canada, as do several other US fast food chains.

Canadian food is perhaps slightly more Europeanised than American and in the larger cities you will find a great variety of ethnic restaurants—anything from Chinese through Swedish and French. In Québec, of course, French-style cooking predominates and in the Atlantic provinces sea food and salmon are the specialities. Remember to try Oka Cheese in Québec and wild, ripe berries everywhere in the summer.

TRAVEL

To be read in conjunction with the USA Background travel section.

Bus. Bus travel is usually the cheapest way of getting around, fares generally being less than half the airfare. Every region in Canada has different bus companies, Gray Coach, Acadian Lines, Greyhound and Voyageur are the largest.

The Greyhound Ameripasses are only valid in Canada on specific routes, e.g. Buffalo or Detroit to Toronto. There are, however, two Greyhound Canadian passes available year-round. The All Canada Pass is valid for the whole of Canada and costs £150 for 15 days. For a 30-day Pass the cost is £200. Daily extensions are not available.

The second pass is simply called the Canada Pass and is also available year-round but just for travel west of Montreal and Toronto. A 7-day version is available for £92. For 15 days the cost is £120, and for 30 days, the pass costs £165 any time of the year. Daily extensions are not available. As with the the Ameripass, the Canada Passes are intended for overseas visitors and so must be purchased before arrival in Canada. Considering the distances it is possible to travel by bus in Canada, the passes represent good value for money.

Always check for the cheapest 'point-to-point' fare or excursion fare when making just one or two journeys without a bus pass. Toronto to the west coast, for instance, could cost about $125 (Canadian) one way. A discount of 25 percent is given for YH membership.

One difference between the US and Canadian Greyhound operations worth noting is in baggage handling. Unlike the USA, the Canadian bus companies will never check baggage through to a destination without its owner. Bags cannot be sent on ahead, for instance, if you are simply seeking a way to dump them for a day or so while you see the sights. Lockers are usually on hand at bus stations, and don't forget to collect your bags from the pavement once they have been off-loaded by the driver.

Car. The Canadian is as attached to his car as is his American cousin. In general roads are better, speed limits are higher and there are fewer toll roads than south of the border. Canadian speed limits have gone metric and are posted everywhere in kilometres per hour. Thus, 100 km/h is the most common freeway limit, 80 km/h is typical on two-lane rural highways, and 50 km/h operates most frequently in towns. Canadians, of course, drive on the right!

When considering **buying a car** for the summer, it may be as well to bear in mind that car prices are higher in Canada than in the US. Anyone planning to visit both countries by car would clearly be well advised to buy in the US first. You'll need to check that the US insurance policy is good for Canada too. It's a help to have a yellow 'Non-Resident Interprovincial Motor Vehicle Liability Insurance Card'. This is obtainable through any US insurance agent.

Note that the wearing of **seat belts** by *all* persons in a vehicle is compulsory in British Columbia, Manitoba, New Brunswick, Newfoundland, Nova Scotia, Ontario, Québec and Saskatchewan.

Car rental will cost from about $36 per day, with free mileage up to a point and a cost per kilometre of about 14¢ thereafter. Or call Rent-A-Wreck, who charge $8.95 per day plus kilometrage. To hire a Volkswagen camper would cost about twice as much, but of course you wouldn't be paying for accommodation. As always, shop around for the best available rates.

Third party **insurance** is compulsory in all Canadian provinces and territories and can be expensive. 'Insurance to cover a VW camper worth $1000 with a driver 24 years of age cost $155 for three months.' British, other European and US drivers licences are officially recognised by the Canadian authorities. Membership of the AA, RAC, other European motoring organisations, or the AAA in the US, entitles the member to all the services of the **Canadian AA** and its member clubs free of charge. This includes travel info, itineraries, maps and tour books as well as emergency road services, weather reports and accommodation reservations. (NB: The US AAA also publishes excellent tour guides for Canada.)

Gas is now sold by the litre and costs up to 50¢ to 60¢ a litre. Gas stations can be few and far between in remoter areas and it is wise to check your gauge in the late afternoon before the pumps shut off for the night.

One **hazard** to be aware of when driving in Canada is the unmarked, and even the marked, railroad crossing. Many people are killed every year on railroad crossings. Trains come and go so infrequently in remote areas that it's simply never possible to know when one will arrive. Be particularly alert at night.

Air. The two major Canadian airlines, Air Canada and Canadian Airlines, offer many different discount fares. There are Youth Standby Fares, 7-day, 14-day and 21-day advance fares, touchdown fares, and late night fares to name a few. Canadian Airlines offer a Europe-Go Canadian ticket which allows from 2–8 coupons (on a confirmed basis only) in a range of £246–£432 for high season fares. The rule is that when you make a stopover, you give up a coupon.

Air Canada participates in the VUSA fares, which offer discounts of 25–30% on fares, however, you must book in advance. Air BC offers the Western Air Pass for one week's travel, £119; for three weeks, £219. Students (with an ISIC card) may be able to get student discounts through Travel CUTS, The Canadian Universities Travel Service Ltd, 171 College St, Toronto, (416) 977-3703 or (800) 268-9044 (in Ontario), or at any of their other offices throughout Canada.

Rail. One of the conditions for the entry of British Columbia into the Confederation was the building of the Canadian Pacific Railway, and with the completion of the track in 1885, Canada as a transcontinental nation finally became a reality. Later came Canadian Northern and the Grand Trunk Pacific, nationalised into Canadian National in 1923 after both companies had gone bankrupt.

Until 1978, Canada possessed two rail systems, the privately operated but viable Canadian Pacific, and the state-owned, often floundering, Canadian National. With the formation of VIA Rail Canada in 1978, the routes and fare structures of both became totally integrated. To cross Canada by train was quite an adventure—one of the world's great railway journeys. Unfortunately, the Canadian government has now scrapped the famous transcontinental track through the Rockies via Banff as part of a mammoth, more than 50 per cent cut in rail services nationwide. However, the more northern route via Jasper still operates but only three times a week. The one way fare coast-to-coast, is about $400.

The service cuts mean that many small, more remote communities can no longer be reached by train.

In the East, VIA Rail runs high speed *Rapido* trains along the so-called Ontario–Québec corridor connecting Montréal with Windsor, Ontario. The Toronto to Montréal trip takes less than 5 hours and costs around $65. System-wide various discount fares are available. These vary according to the time of year, day of the week, length of stay, age of traveller, etc, so always enquire about the 'cheapest possible fare' when planning a trip. If you have a student ID card, be sure to show it.

Then there is the CANRAIL Pass. This gives unlimited travel on VIA trains and is good value for someone planning to do a lot of travelling. Currently, VIA offer just one pass which is valid for 12 days within a 30-day period. During peak travel times (7th June–30th September and 15th

December–5th January) it costs $510 ($460 student) for the entire system. The off-peak fare is $349 ($319 student). The trains are comfortable, civilised, have good eating facilities and are easy to sleep on. A much recommended way to travel. The pass can only be bought overseas and on production of passport. Long Haul Leisurerail, PO Box 113, Peterborough PE1 1LE, (0733-51780), are the main agents in the UK but other travel agents may also stock the pass.

Hitching. Thumbing is illegal on the major transcontinental routes, but it is common to see people hitching along access ramps. Check the 'local rules' before setting out. In some cities there are specific regulations regarding hitching, but in general the cognoscenti say that hitchers are not often hassled and that Canada is one of the best places to get good lifts, largely because rides tend to be long ones—even if you do have to wait a long time on occasions.

The Trans Canada Highway can be rough going during the summer months so look for alternative routes, for example the Laurentian Autoroute out of Montréal, and the Yellowhead Highway out of Winnipeg. Wawa, north of Sault Ste Marie, Ontario, is another notorious spot where it is possible to be stranded for days. The national parks can also be tricky in summer when 'there are too many tourists going nowhere'.

Hiking and Biking. Trail walking is one of Canada's best offers. There is so much wilderness space that it really would be a crying shame to spend any length of time in the country without experiencing something of The Great Outdoors. Some of the best, of course, is in the national parks. A good guide to hiking trails in the national parks is *The Canadian Rockies Trail Guide: A Hiker's Manual to the National Parks,* by Bart Robinson and Brian Patton. Information is also available from the individual parks. For information on the best routes for cyclists, contact the Canadian Cycling Association at 333 River Road, Vanier, Ontario K1L 8H9, tel: (613) 748-5629.

Urban Travel. Town and city bus or subway fares are generally charged at a standard rate. Exact fares are generally required and are around 90¢ to $1.10, and upwards.

MARITIME PROVINCES AND NEWFOUNDLAND

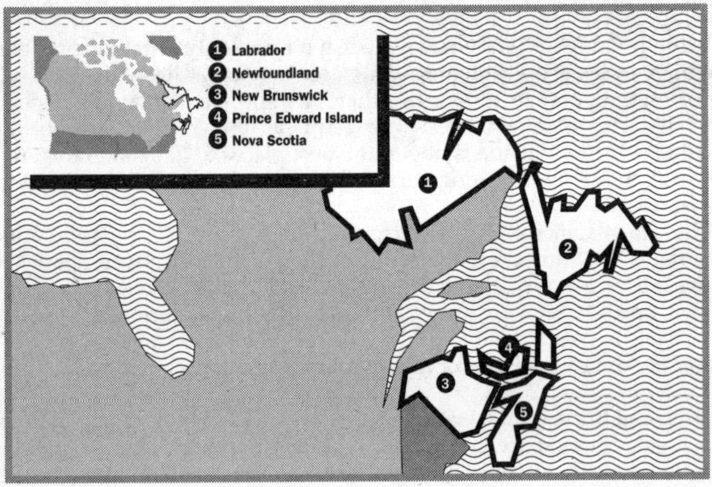

These Atlantic-lapped provinces were the early stop-off points for eager explorers from Europe and subsequently became one of the main battle-grounds for their colonial ambitions. The chief combatants were Britain and France and as a result, strong English, French, and Scottish threads run through Maritime culture and history.

The story of the Maritimes is the story of a people who have fished and travelled and died at sea. The Grand Banks, the huge, shallow continental shelf ranging from Massachusetts to Newfoundland, is the most fertile fishing ground in the world. The economy of the Maritimes is based on the Grand Banks, forestry and tourism.

The Maritimes are beautiful in the summer, filled with swimming in lakes or in the sea, eating excellent seafood and lying in the sun. Winters are long and spring comes late, so it is best to visit in the summer or autumn.

NEW BRUNSWICK

New Brunswick is bounded mostly by water, with over 1300 miles of coast-line—a constant reminder of the importance of the sea in this Maritime province. To the west, it is bordered by Maine, Québec and part of the Appalachian mountain range. Inland, there is rugged wilderness accounting for the popularity of huntin', fishin', campin' and hikin'.

The Vikings are said to have come here some thousand years ago, but when French explorer Jacques Cartier arrived in 1535, the area was occupied by Micmac and Maliseet Indians. Later, the province became a battleground for French Acadian and British Loyalist forces. In 1713, by the Treaty of Utrecht, New Brunswick was ceded to the British along with the rest of Acadia (PEI and Nova Scotia). Many of the French fled south to the United States and settled in Louisiana. There, 'Acadian' was corrupted into 'Cajun', a word still used to describe the French in Louisiana. As a result of this early French influence, New Brunswick today remains 35 per cent Acadian, most in the north and the east of the province.

While in New Brunswick, be sure to sample the great variety of shellfish available, as well as the province's speciality—fiddleheads. Also, try a pint of the local Moosehead beer—although it is now available nationally, the sea air of New Brunswick itself is essential for a successful taste test.

National Parks: Fundy, Kouchibougnac

The telephone area code is 506.

FREDERICTON The City of Elms is the capital city of the province and its commercial and sporting centre. Clean and green, this is 'a good Canadian town' which got started in 1783, when a group of Loyalists from the victorious colonies to the south made their home here, naming the town after the second son of George III. They chose for their new town a spot where there had previously (until the Seven Years War) been a thriving Acadian settlement. During hostilities the settlement was reduced by the British and the inhabitants expelled.

Fredericton's great benefactor was local boy and press baron, Lord Beaverbrook. His legacies include an art gallery, a theatre, and the university library. The latter is named Bonar Law-Bennett Library, after two other famous sons of New Brunswick, one of whom became Prime Minister of Great Britain, and the other Prime Minister of Canada.

The town is situated inland on the broad St John River, the 'Rhine of America', once an Indian highway and a major commercial route to the sea. The whole area is one of scenic river valleys and lakes.

ACCOMMODATION

Elms Tourist Home, 269 Saunders St, 454-3410. S-$35, D-$45. $10-XP.

Fredericton York House Hostel, 193 York St, 454-1233. Only open Jun 1–Aug 31. Members $9, non-members $12. Linen rental, on-site parking, equipment storage area, showers, kitchen facs. Open 7am–10am/4pm–12pm. Reservations not essential. Close to bus station and train station.

Happy Apple Acres Bed & Breakfast, RR4 Fredericton, 458-1819. S-$35, D-$55. Incl. breakfast & private bath. Closed mid-Oct–Nov.

Univ of New Brunswick, Aitken House, Kings College Road, 453-4891. S-$12.50 per person, D-$11.50 per person, $58–$68 weekly. Central.

Camping: Mactaquac Provincial Park, 12 miles west on Hwy 2, 363-3011. $12–$14.

FOOD

Bar-B-Q Barn, 540 Queen St, 455-2742. Inexpensive hot-spot. Open 11am–11pm.

Boyce's Farmers' Market, George St, Sat only 7am–noon. Go to **Goofy Roofy's** for breakfast or early lunch. Then walk around the market and check out the craft stalls.

Crispin's, King's Place Mall, at Brunswick & York. Cafeteria style, where the government types go for lunch.
Student Union Building, UNB campus. Cafeteria in the basement.

OF INTEREST

Beaverbrook Art Gallery, Queen St, 458-8545. Has works of Dali, Reynolds, Gainsborough, Churchill, etc, plus good section on history of English china. A gift to the province from the press baron. Open Sun & Mon 12am–8pm, Tue & Wed 10am–8pm, Thur–Sat 10am–5pm.
Provincial Legislative Buildings, Queen and St John Sts, 453-2527. Includes, in Library, complete set of Audubon bird paintings and copy of 1783 printing of Domesday Book. Library and gallery open in the summer, daily 9am–8pm. Tours available every half hour, starting at 9.15am. Rest of the year, open 9am–4pm.
Christ Church Cathedral, off Queen at Church, 450-8500. Worth a visit for its beautiful stained-glass windows. Open in the summer Mon–Fri 9am–8pm, Sat 9am–8pm, Sun 12pm–6pm. Free tours available. Rest of year open 8.30am–5.30pm.
Kings Landing Historical Settlement, at Prince William, 363-3805, 23 miles west of Fredericton. Re-created pioneer village showing life as it was in the Central Saint John River Valley between 1820 and 1890. Features homes, school, church, theatre, farm, etc. Also restaurant and gift shop. Daily, 10am–5pm; $7.50.
York–Sunbury Historical Museum, 455-6041. In **Officers Square**, this military museum depicts the history of Fredericton and New Brunswick. Open June–Aug, Mon–Sat 10am–6pm, Tue and Thur to 9pm, Sun noon–6pm; Sept and mid-Oct, Mon–Fri 9am–5pm, Sat noon–4pm; rest of year until April 30, Mon, Wed and Fri, 11am–3pm. Students 50¢. 'Kind of neat.'
University of New Brunswick. Founded 1785, making it the third oldest university in Canada. Buildings on campus include the **Brydone Jack Observatory**, Canada's first astronomical observatory. Tours available.

INFORMATION/TRAVEL

Tourism Information Centre, City Hall, Queen St, (800) 651-0123.
Fredericton Chamber of Commerce, Wilmot Park, Woodstock Rd, 458-8006. Open 9am–5pm.
TRIUS Transit, 459-2047. Buses do not serve the airport directly. Airport shuttles run from the Lord Beaverbrook Hotel, $6. Taxis cost around $16 o/w, 459-3366. Airport Info, (506) 451-0555.

MONCTON This unofficial capital of Acadia is a major communications centre, but really has only two tourist sites of any importance: **Magnetic Hill** and the **Tidal Bore**. At Magnetic Hill, go to the bottom of the hill in a car or on a bike, turn off the ignition, and through some freak of nature you'll find yourself drifting up the hill!

The Tidal Bore is at its highest when it sweeps up the Petitcodiac River from the Bay of Fundy, reaching heights of 30 feet along the way. Bore Park is the spot to be when the waters rush in. Check the schedule published in the daily paper for the times when the tide is at its highest. Magnetic Hill is located at the corner of Mountain Road (126) and the Trans Canada. Bore Park is at the east end of Main St.

There is a nice beach with the warmest waters north of Florida at **Shediac** on the Northumberland Straight. This is also the place to catch the annual lobster festival held in July. It's a short bus ride from Moncton and there is plenty of camping space nearby.

ACCOMMODATION

For a list of local Bed & Breakfasts contact the Tourist Office, 581 Main St.
Sunset Hotel, 162 Queen St, 382-1163. S–$36, D–$42.
Univ de Moncton, 858-4008. Residence halls may have accommodation.
YWCA, 35 Highfield St at Campbell, 855-4349. Open year-round, $20 per night. In the summer, there is also a **hostel** here: $8 non-members, $12 with linens. Shared bath. 20 min walk from Bore Park, downtown. Women only.
Camping: Camper's City (384-7867), **Green Acres Tenting and Trailer Park** (384-0191), both close to Magnetic Hill. $14–$17 per site. Open May 1–Oct 31.

CARAQUET Situated on scenic Baie des Chaleurs in the north of the province, Caraquet is the oldest French settlement in the area and just west of town is a monument to the first Acadian settlers who came here following their expulsion by Britain. On St Pierre Boulevard there is an interesting museum of Acadian history, the **Acadian Museum**, and off Highway 11 to the west of town is the **Village Historique Acadien**. The buildings here are all authentic and were brought here and then restored. There are also crafts and demonstrations showing the Acadian lifestyle.

SAINT JOHN Known as the Loyalist City, and proudly boasting a royal charter. Saint John was founded by refugees—among them no less a personage than Benedict Arnold, reputedly disliked by his fellow Loyalists for his sharp business practices—from the rebel New England colonies. The landing place of the Loyalists is marked by a monument at the foot of King Street, and a Loyalist house stands yet at Germain and Union Streets. Before the Seven Years War, however, Saint John was occupied by the French. The first recorded European discovery was in 1604 when Samuel de Champlain entered the harbour on St John's Day—hence the name of the town and the river on which it stands.

Largely as a result of its strategic ice-free position on the Bay of Fundy, Saint John has become New Brunswick's largest city and its commercial and industrial centre. Shipbuilding and fishing are the most important industries and Saint John Dry Dock, at 1150 feet long, is one of the largest in the world. Recently the entire city—the waterfront in particular—underwent a facelift. Good times to visit are during the Festival-by-the-Sea in August and Loyalist Days, the third week in July. (Incidentally, Saint John is never abbreviated, thereby making it easier to distinguish from St John's, Newfoundland.)

ACCOMMODATION

Fundy Ayre Motel, 1711 Manawagonish Rd, 672-1125. S–$50, D–$65 with private bath. 10 mins from downtown, close to ferry to Nova Scotia.
YM-YWCA, 19–25 Hazen Ave, 634-7720. Operates a **youth hostel** year-round. Members $22, non-members $28, plus a $10 refundable deposit. Dorm-style facs with shared washroom. Equipment storage area, limited on-site parking, wheelchair accessible.
Camping: Rockwood Park, off Route 1, 652-4050. In the heart of the city. $12–$50 (weekly rate).

FOOD

Market Square, renovated building with 19th century exterior and modern, trendy interior; on the waterfront. Lots of places to eat and shop. If you're a lover of raw oysters, **Grannan's**, 1 Market Square, 634-1555, is the place where you'll want to eat.

Reggie's Restaurant, 26 Germain St, 657-6270. Imports its smoked meat from Ben's, the famous Montréal deli. Inexpensive but filling meals. Open 6am–9pm Mon–Fri, 6am–7pm Sat.

Saint John Old City Market, Germain St. Fresh produce, crafts, antiques. Browsing and buying. A must. Closed Sundays and holidays.

OF INTEREST

There are four **walking tours** around Saint John: Prince William's Walk, the Loyalist Trail, a Victorian Stroll and the Douglas Avenue Amble. Each takes around an hour and a half, and shows you the highlights of the historic streets of Saint John. Among these are **Loyalist House**, 120 Union St, a Georgian house built in 1816; the **Old Loyalist Burial Ground** opposite King Square; the spiral staircase in the **Old Courthouse**, King Sq; **Barbour's General Store**, fully stocked as in the year 1867, with a barbershop.

New Brunswick Museum, 277 Douglas Ave, 635-5381. This museum, founded in 1842, was the first in Canada. It features a variety of historic exhibits, both national and international, a natural science gallery, artwork and Canadiana. There is also a book store and a tea-room. Open daily, from 10am–5pm. Students $1.

Fort Howe Blockhouse, Magazine St. Replica of blockhouse built during 1777–78 for protection against American privateers and Indian uprisings. Good panoramic view of the city. Daily 10am–dusk. Free.

Carleton–Martello Tower, Lancaster Heights. Fortification erected during and surviving the War of 1812. Now houses a display of firearms and 'antiquities'. Another nice place to view the city.

Reversing Falls Rapids. The town's biggest tourist attraction. Twice a day, at high tide, waters rushing into the gorge where the Saint John River meets the sea force the river to run backwards creating the Reversing Falls Rapids. There are two good lookouts for watching this phenomenon: the Tourist Bureau lounge and the sun deck on King St.

INFORMATION

Visitor and Convention Bureau, City Hall, 658-2990.

3 Info Centres open in summer: Reversing Falls Visitor Centre, 658-2937; City Centre Seasonal, on Hwy 1, 658-2940; and one at Barbour's General Store, 658-2855.

TRAVEL

VIA Rail station, Rothsay Ave, nr Loyalist House, 642-2916.

SMT Bus Lines, 300 Union St, 648-3500.

There's a ferry service from Saint John to Digby, Nova Scotia. Takes cars. About a 2½ hour trip. Nice scenery, but rather pricey. Crowded in the summer. Call 636-4048 for info.

CAMPOBELLO ISLAND Going west on Highway 1 from Saint John, you can catch a ferry from Back Bay which will take you, via Deer Isle and Campobello, to Lubec, Maine. On Campobello is the 3000-acre Roosevelt Campobello International Park. Visitors can see the 34-room 'cottage' occupied by FDR from 1905 to 1921. Open daily 10am–6pm June–Oct. Free. The island is also linked to Maine by the Franklin D Roosevelt Memorial Bridge. Also home of the Herring Cove Provincial Park. For tourist info on the island, call 752-2997. Open daily 9am–7pm in summer, 11am–6pm the rest of the year.

FUNDY NATIONAL PARK The Bay of Fundy boasts the world's highest tides (16 metres). This allows visitors the unique experience of strolling along the ocean floor at low tide. The area offers a variety of impressive maritime scenery from fog-shrouded shores to sun-dappled forests, from steep coastal cliffs to tide-washed beaches, and from bubbling streams to crashing waterfalls. For info call 887-2000.

Centrally located, the park is just over an hour from Moncton and within two hours of Fredericton and Saint John. It is only a few hours from the Maine/New Brunswick border and within a day's drive from Montréal or Boston. Fundy National Park is a spectacular setting.

ACCOMMODATION
Fundy National Park Hostel, Open year-round. A 20-bed facility made up of small, rustic-style cabins located right in the park. $8.50, $10 non-members.

NOVA SCOTIA

Known as the Land of 10,000 Welcomes and the Festival Province, Canada's 'Ocean Playground' is famous for its attractive fishing villages, rocky, granite shores, and historic spots like Louisbourg and Grand Pré. The early Scottish immigration to Nova Scotia is manifested in such events as the annual Highland Games in Antigonish and St Ann's Gaelic College. It is said that there is more Gaelic spoken in Nova Scotia than in Scotland.

Although the French were the first to attempt colonisation of the area, it was James I who first gave Nova Scotia (New Scotland) its own flag and coat-of-arms when he granted the province to Sir William Alexander. The French preferred the name Acadia, after explorer Verrazano's word for Peaceful Land, however, and so the French thereafter became known as Acadians. By the Treaty of Utrecht in 1713, the province was finally ceded to the British for good. Cape Breton Island followed later, after the siege of Louisbourg in 1758.

Many Americans also emigrated to Nova Scotia in the late eighteenth and early nineteenth centuries, among them the Chesapeake Blacks and a group of 25,000 Loyalists—possibly the largest single emigration of cultured families in British history, since their numbers included over half of the living graduates of Harvard. They settled mostly around Sherbourne.

Driving is the best way of discovering Nova Scotia. There are eight specially designated tourist routes throughout the province which cover most of the points of interest. Among these, the Cabot Trail on Cape Breton Island is particularly recommended. Autumn is the most beautiful season; in summer, the ocean breeze always has a cooling effect. Although most people visit Halifax and the South Shore, Cape Breton Island is also worth a visit and has much to offer the nature-loving traveller.
National Parks: Cape Breton Highlands, Kejimkujik.
The telephone area code is 902.

HALIFAX Provincial capital and the largest city and economic hub of the Maritimes. The making of Halifax has been its fine ice-free harbour so that not only does it deal with around 3500 commercial vessels a year but it is also Canada's chief naval base. Halifax was founded by Cornwallis in 1749 as a British military and naval depot and as a British response to the French fort at Louisbourg.

Although a thriving metropolis with the usual tall concrete buildings and expressways, the town does retain a certain charm with many constant reminders of its colourful past. Walk or bicycle around Halifax, and check with the Tourist Office for information on the many festivals that go on in and around the town. **Citadel Hill** in the middle of the town is a good place to start exploring and to get your bearings in relation to both Halifax and its twin across the bay, **Dartmouth**.

Connected to Halifax by two bridges and two ferries (75¢), Dartmouth is known as the 'city of lakes' since there are some 22 lakes within the city boundaries. 'Walk across Macdonald Bridge, free, for a very good view of both cities.' The town is also home to the well-respected Bedford Institute of Oceanography, which collects data on tides, currents and ice formations.

ACCOMMODATION

Halifax Hostel, 1253 Barrington St, 422-3863. Situated near the bridge to Dartmouth, in a neighbourhood where women might not want to walk alone at night. Members $12.75, non-members $15.75. 'Very friendly.'

Inglis Lodge, 5538 Inglis St, 423-7950. S–$30, D–$36, $82 per week. Shared washroom facs. Cooking facs and TV room.

YMCA, 1565 Park St, 423-9622. S–$36.

Dalhousie University residences: Howe Hall, Coburg Rd, 494-2108. Coed for the summer (June–August). S–$20, D–$36. **Shirreff Hall**, 6285 South St, 494-2577.

Fenwick Place (off-campus residence), 5599 Fenwick St, 494-2075. Apartment style. 10 min from Dalhousie. $21 per person per night. Min 2 nights stay. Weekly rate $92 per person. May–mid-Aug, reservations are a must.

The **Halifax Bed & Breakfast Organization**, will set you up with a good place to stay from May to November, 434-7283. Here are a few examples: **Birdland B&B**, 14 Bluejay St, 443-1055. D–$35 per night, with full breakfast incl (fresh raspberries in season!). In residential neighbourhood just outside downtown. 'Very friendly.'

Waken'n Eggs, 2114 Windsor St, 422-4737. From $35–$45 per night. Full breakfast incl. Shared bath. Reservations recommended in the summer. Central.

Camping: **Laurie Prov Park**, 12 mi N of Halifax on old Hwy 2, in Grand Lake, 861-1623. $8 per night for tent site (unserviced). No showers.

FOOD

Athens Restaurant, Barrington & Blowers Sts, 422-1595. Good for breakfast.

Camille's, 2564 Barrington St, 423-8869. English-style pub with fish n' chips and other seafood. Open 11am–11pm.

Juicy Jane's Sandwich Bar, 1576 Argyle St, 422-2814. Sandwiches to go.

Midtown Tavern, Prince & Grafton Sts, 422-5213. Cheap diner-type place.

Satisfaction Feast, 1581 Grafton St, 422-3540. Good vegetarian.

Thirsty Duck, 5472 Spring Garden Rd, 422-1548. Irish and English beer; good music. Open 11am–midnight.

OF INTEREST

The Halifax Citadel National Historic Park. This hilltop fortress surrounded by a moat (now a dry ditch) was built in 1828–56 to defend against the Americans and is now Canada's most visited historic site. There is a magnificent view of the harbour and a free 45-minute guided tour is available. The fort once served as a prisoner-of-war camp and numbered Leon Trotsky among the inmates. 'Staff in uniform, friendly and well-informed.' There is an **Army Museum** recalling the military history of the fort, and a museum featuring pioneer and MicMac Indian artefacts. There is also a tea shop here. The Citadel is open mid-June to mid-Sept, 9am–6pm daily; $2, $1 with student ID.

York Redoubt, Purcell's Cove Rd. Situated 15 miles out of Halifax on a bluff overlooking the harbour, this fortification was used as a lookout to warn against the approaching enemy. Open daily in the summer 10am–6pm; grounds open until 8pm. Picknicking facilities. Free.

Prince of Wales Martello Tower, located in Point Pleasant Park, the tower acted as part of the 'coastal defence network' set up by the British to protect against the French. Open June–Sept 10am–6pm. Free.

Province House, Hollis St, 424-4661. Canada's oldest and smallest parliament house. A handsome Georgian building, built in 1818, called 'a gem of Georgian architecture' by Charles Dickens. Canada's first newspaper, the *Halifax Gazette*, was published here in 1752. 'The house has very detailed plasterwork and carving, very well kept.' Open Mon–Fri 9am–5pm, Sat & Sun 10am–4pm.

Churches: St George's Round Church, Brunswick St and Cornwallis, 421-1705. An example of the very rare round church, built around 1800. In the summer, **Music Royale**, period music in historic settings, is presented. Tours are also available. **St Mary's Basilica**, on Spring Garden Rd, has the highest granite spire in the world. Tours offered daily in the summer, 8.30am–4.30pm. **St Paul's Church**, Barrington and Duke Sts, 429-2240. Oldest Anglican church in Canada. Built in 1750, this is also the oldest building in Halifax. **Old Dutch Church**, Brunswick and Garrish Sts, built in 1756, was the first Lutheran church in Canada.

Maritime Museum of the Atlantic, Lower Water St, 424-7490. Clipper ship and other maritime relics. Don't miss the 'stunning panoramic view' of the harbour. Open May–Oct, Mon–Sat 9.30am–5.30pm, Tues to 9pm, Sun 1pm–5.30pm. Closed on Mon in the winter. $2.25.

Nova Scotia Museum, 1747 Summer St, 424-7353. Featuring the province's natural and human history. Also Micmac Indian artefacts. Open in summer Mon–Sat 9.30am–5.30pm, Wed to 8pm, Sun 1pm–5.30pm. Closed Mon in the winter.

Dalhousie University, Coburg Rd. An attractive campus with the usual facilities and guided tours. **The Art Gallery**, 6101 University Ave, 494-2403, is worth a look.

Halifax Public Gardens, on Spring Garden Rd and South Park St, 421-6550. 16 acres and 400 different varieties of plants and flora. Open 8am–dusk.

Art Gallery of Nova Scotia, 1741 Hollis St, 424-7542. Both local and well-known artists are represented here. Open Tue–Sat 10am–5.30pm, Thur to 9pm; Sun noon–5.30pm. Closed Mon. Adults $2.50, students $1.25. Free on Tue.

Point Pleasant Park is 20 minutes from downtown. A good place to eat lunch.

Nearby: Peggy's Cove, Liverpool, Lunenberg, Bridgewater and the rest. Picturesque fishing villages but overrun by tourists. At Lunenburg you can visit the **Maritime Museum of the Atlantic**, 1675 Lower Water St, 424-7490. Consisting of a main building and three old ships, the museum contains mementoes of the days of wooden ships. There is also an aquarium. June–Sept, open daily 9.30am–5.30pm; Tue 9.30am- 8pm. Adults $2.25.

SHOPPING/ENTERTAINMENT

Barrington Street and the Historic Properties are both good places to shop for crafts and the like. The Scotia Square Complex has the usual shopping mall attractions. Try **Scoundrel's** for evening fun.

There are many festivals held in Halifax throughout the year. Among them, **The Nova Scotia Tattoo**, at the beginning of July, is a popular extravaganza featuring both Canadian and international performers of all kinds. Ask at the tourist office about this and other events going on.

INFORMATION

Nova Scotia Travel Info Centre at the airport, Hwy 102.
City info booths: Tourism Halifax, City Hall, 1749 Duke St, 421-8736.
Provincial info: The Red Store, Historic Properties, Water St, 424-4247.
Check In Nova Scotia, 425-5781, or (800) 565-0000.
YHA, 425-5450 for current hostel location info; The Trail Shop, 6210 Quinpool Rd, 423-8736, for purchase of YH cards, info. Also has bike rentals.

TRAVEL

Acadian Lines Bus station, 6040 Almon St, nr the Forum, 454-9321.
VIA Rail, 429-8421.
Metro Transit, 421-6618. Basic fare: $1.20.
The ***Bluenose II*** sails from Historic Properties for a two-hour cruise around Halifax Harbour. This is the schooner stamped on the back of the Canadian dime. Many other harbour cruises are also available. Contact the tourist office for details.

GRAND PRÉ NATIONAL HISTORIC PARK The restored site of an early Acadian settlement. The nearby dykeland (grand pré–great meadow) is where the French Acadians were deported to in 1766 after failing to take an oath of allegiance to the English king, preferring to remain neutral.

Longfellow immortalized the sad plight of the deported Acadians of Nova Scotia in his narrative poem *Evangeline* (see under Louisiana in USA section). There is a museum in the park with a section on Longfellow and a fine collection of Acadian relics, everything from farm tools to personal diaries. Also in the park is the **Church of the Covenanters**. Built in 1790 by New England planters, this do-it-yourself church was constructed from hand-sawn boards fastened together by square hand-made nails. The similarly homemade pulpit spirals halfway to the ceiling.

The gardens are nice for walking and the whole park is open June to September, 9am–6pm daily. Free. To get there from Halifax take Route 101 going north and the park is three miles east of Wolfville. During the summer, accommodation is available in the residences of Acadia University in Wolfville.

ANNAPOLIS ROYAL Situated in the scenic Annapolis Valley, famous for its apples, this was the site of Canada's oldest settlement. Founded by de Monts and Champlain in 1604, and originally Port Royal, it became Annapolis Royal in honour of Queen Anne, after the final British capture in 1710. The town then served as the Nova Scotian capital until the founding of Halifax in 1749.

The site of the French fort of 1636 is now maintained as **Fort Anne National Historic Park**, and seven miles away, on the north shore of Annapolis River, is the **Port Royal Habitation National Historic Park**. This is a reconstruction of the 1605 settlement based on the plan of a Normandy farm. Here, too, the oldest social club in America was formed. L'Ordre de Bon Temps was organised by Champlain in 1606 and visitors to the province for more than three days can still become members. The park is open daily from May to October, 9am–6pm. Free. Thirty five miles to the south is **Kejimkujik National Park**, an area once inhabited by the Micmac Indians.

The park entrance and information centre is at **Maitland Bridge**. Daily admission is charged. The park is good for canoeing, fishing, hiking, and skiing in winter.

ACCOMMODATION

Sandy Bottom Lake Hostel, Virginia/Bear River Rd, 532-2497. Open until end Oct. $10, $12 non-members. Basic groceries available, canoe rentals, kitchen facs.

YARMOUTH The only place of any size on the western side of Nova Scotia, Yarmouth is the centre of a largely French-speaking area. During the days of sail this was an important shipbuilding centre although today local industry is somewhat more diversified.

A good time to visit is at the end of July when the Western Nova Scotia Exhibition is held here. The festival includes the usual agricultural and equestrian events plus local craft demonstrations and exhibits.

ACCOMMODATION

El Rancho Motel, 214 Lakeside Drive, 742-2408. D–$56, overlooking Milo lake, with cooking facs.

Sophie's Guest House, 20 Chestnut St, 742-7447. S–$20, D–$30. Big full breakfast incl. 'Very helpful and friendly.'

Whittaker's, RR 5, Peterson Rd, Yarmouth, 742-7649. S–$20, D–$30, T–$40, Q–$50. Full breakfast incl. Garden area for barbecuing.

TRAVEL

Ferries go from here to Portland (10-hour trip) and Bar Harbor, Maine (5 hours). For info on the Portland run call (800) 565-7900 (in Canada), (800) 341-7540 (in USA); for Bar Harbor info call (800) 565-9411 (in Canada) or (902) 742-5033 (USA).

SYDNEY Situated on the Atlantic side of the province, Sydney is the chief town on Cape Breton Island and a good centre for exploring the rest of the island. It is a steel and coal town, a grim, but friendly, soot-blackened old place. While here you can visit the second largest steel plant in North America.

Like the whole of Cape Breton Island, Sydney has a history of struggles against worker exploitation and bad social conditions. Since France ceded the island to Britain as part of the package deal Treaty of Utrecht in 1713, hard times and social strife have frequently been the norm.

A ferry goes to Newfoundland from North Sydney across the bay.

ACCOMMODATION

Garden Court Cabins, RR 1, Site 7, Box 11, Sydney Forks, 564-6201; 14 miles west of Hwy 125 on Route 4. $35 up for cabin (sleeps 3 comfortably); communal kitchen.

OF INTEREST

Highland Games, July, Antigonish or St Anne's. Kilts, pipes and drums, sword dancing, caber toss, etc.

Cape Breton School of Crafts, George St., Townsend, 539-7491. Offers classes in art, weaving, pottery, etc, and holds annual crafts fair in July.

Nearby: Baddeck. Alexander Graham Bell National Historic Park. Displays, models, papers, etc, relating to Bell's inventions. Bell had his summer home in the town. Summer open 9am–9pm, otherwise 9am–5pm. Free. 295-2069.

Baddeck. Centre Bras d'Or Festival of the Arts, mid-July through mid-Aug, includes Music Fest with many famous artists, $8+, 295-2787.
Glace Bay, 13 miles east of Sydney and site of the **Miners Museum and Village**, 849-4522. Includes tour of underground mine running out and under the sea, and the village shows the life of a mining community 1850–1900. Museum features weekly concerts of Cape Breton music. June–Sept, daily 10am–6pm. Sept–June, Mon–Fri 9am–4pm, Tue 10am–7pm. Admission $2.75. Mine tour, $5.

INFORMATION/TRAVEL
Visitors Information, 539-9876.
Ferries to Argentia and Porte-aux-Basques, Newfoundland, 794-5700.

FORTRESS OF LOUISBOURG NATIONAL HISTORIC PARK Built by the French between 1717 and 1740 and presently in the process of being restored by the federal government, this fortress was once the biggest built in North America since the time of the Incas. Louisbourg played a crucial role in the French defence of the area and was finally won by Britain in 1760, but not before it had been blasted to rubble.

The restoration project involves the rebuilding of a complete colonial town within the fortifications and it will be several years before it is completely finished. There is a museum and you will be shown around by a French colonial-costumed guide.

Accessible by bus from Sydney, 26 miles to the south, the park is open from 9am to 5pm daily during June and September. During July–August 10am to 6pm daily. Admission $6.50, students ½ price. (Visitors Information Centre, 733-2280.)

CAPE BRETON HIGHLANDS NATIONAL PARK The park lies on the northern-most tip of Cape Breton sandwiched between the Gulf of St Lawrence and the Atlantic Ocean. It covers more than 360 square miles of rugged mountain country, beaches and quiet valleys. The whole is encircled by the 184-mile-long Cabot Trail, an all-weather paved highway on its way round the park climbing four mountains and providing spectacular views of sea and mountains.

In summer, however, it gets very crowded and the narrow, steep roads are jammed with cars. There are camping facilities in the park and good sea and freshwater swimming.

This is an area originally settled by Scots and many of the locals still speak Gaelic. There are park information centres at Ingonish Beach and Cheticamp. Admission to the park is $5 per day. At **Cheticamp**, a rug-making centre, there is also an Acadian Museum with craft demonstrations and French-Canadian antiques and glassware. Open daily during the summer. Visitors Information, 285-2329, 285-2691 off-season.

IONA On the way back across the Strait of Canso, a side trip here to the Nova Scotia Highland Village may be worthwhile. The village includes a museum and other memorabilia of the early Scottish settlers. A highland festival is held here on the first Saturday in August, 725-2272. Summer opening 10am–5pm, Sun 12–6pm. Admission $4. The village is off Highway 105 and 15 miles east on Highway 223 via Little Narrows, overlooking the Bras d'Or lakes.

PRINCE EDWARD ISLAND

Prince Edward Island—known primarily as the home of *Anne of Green Gables* and as a great producer of spuds—is Canada's smallest and thinnest province, being only 140 miles long and averaging a width of just twenty miles. The province has a population of a mere 128,000. Although the Island is separated from the mainland by the Northumberland Strait, there has been increased talk in recent years of building a connecting bridge between the two. PEI was originally named 'Abegweit' by the local Micmac Indians, meaning 'land cradled on the waves'. The French colonised the Island and baptized it Isle St Jean, but when it was utlimately ceded to Britain as a separate colony, the British renamed it after Prince Edward, Duke of Kent. Now known as the 'Garden of the Gulf', PEI is a popular spot for Canadian family vacations because of its great sandy beaches and warm waters, perfect for lazy summer sunning!

Note the colour of the soil in PEI: it's red because it contains iron which rusts on exposure to the air. Limits are put on billboards here: you won't see any along the side of PEI's highways. The full effect of this constraint only hits you when you are bombarded with billboards back on the mainland. A note of caution: only camp in areas that are designated as camping grounds—camping is prohibited everywhere else (including the beach).

Reach this island paradise by ferry, either from Cape Tormentine, New Brunswick, to Borden, west of Charlottetown (45 min. crossing), or from Caribou, Nova Scotia, to Wood Islands, east of the capital (75 min. crossing). Fares are low, but queues are long in the summer, particularly if you're taking a car.

National Park: Prince Edward Island.

The telephone area code is 902.

CHARLOTTETOWN The first meeting of the Fathers of the Confederation took place in Charlottetown in 1864. Out of this meeting came the future Dominion of Canada (hence the nickname, 'The Cradle of Confederation'). In the Confederation Chamber, Province House, where the meeting was held, a plaque proclaims 'Providence Being Their Guide, They Builded Better Than They Knew'. The citizens of PEI were not so convinced however. They waited until 1873 before joining the Confederation. Even then, according to the then Governor General, Lord Dufferin, they came in 'under the impression that it is the Dominion that has been annexed to Prince Edward Island'.

These days things are quieter hereabouts, only livening up in summer when Canadian families descend en masse, and PEI's other tourist attraction, harness racing, gets going out at Charlottetown Driving Park. The restored waterfront section of town, Olde Charlottetown, offers the usual craft shops, eating places and boutiques. You can tour the town in a London double-decker bus, leaving from Confederation Centre.

ACCOMMODATION

Youth Hostel, 153 Mt Edward Rd at Belvedere, 894-9696. Near UPEI campus. $12.50 with student card, $15 without. Kitchen facs. Check-in after 4pm. Accessible to Charlottetown. Open June–Labour Day.

Univ of PEI residences: at University and Belvedere Ave, 566-0442 (aptmts) or 566-0447 (dorms). Aptmts sleep up to 4 people with kitchenette and private bath, $62 p/n (May and June only). Dorms $22 p/n, incl breakfast, with shared bath (July and August). Central.

For a listing and reservations of **Bed and Breakfasts and Tourist Homes**, call 368-5555. Centrally located basic accommodation $30–$40 per night.

FOOD

Cedar's Eatery, 81 University Ave, 892-7377. Canadian and Lebanese cuisine. Daily specials $6.

Olde Dublin Pub, 131 Sydney St, 892-6992. Specializes in seafood, under $5. Live Irish entertainment nightly in the summer. Open 11am–11pm.

OF INTEREST

Confederation Centre of The Arts, Queen and Grafton Sts, 628-1864. Focal point of the town's cultural life, it has an art gallery, museum, library and three theatres. In the main theatre, a musical version of the story of PEI's favourite orphan—Anne of Green Gables—is staged every summer. Tickets range from $17–$30. A summer festival is held here annually.

Province House, Queen Square at Grafton St, 566-7626. The site of Confederation, Canada's founding fathers met here in 1864 at the historical Charlottetown Conference to decide the fate of the Dominion. The provincial Legislature now meets here. Open 1 June to Sept 1 daily 9am–8pm; in Sept daily 9am–5pm; Oct–May, weekdays only 9am–5pm. Free tours available.

Micmac Indian Village, on Route 19, 675-3800. At Rocky Point, across the harbour, 45 min away from Charlottetown. Re-created 16th century Indian village with artefacts and other exhibits. Open June and Sept, daily 9.30am–6pm, $3.25. Also here is the **Fort Amherst National Historic Park**, 675-2220, site of the first European settlement in 1720. Open daily in the summer 10am–6pm. Free.

Pioneer Village, on Rte 11 at Mont-Carmel, in the Acadian region of PEI, 854-2227. A log reproduction of an Acadian settlement with homes, blacksmith's shop, barn, school, general store and church. Approximately 1½ hours from Charlottetown. Open mid-June to Sept, daily, 10am–7pm, $2.

Abegweit Sightseeing Tours operate guided **tours** of both the South and North Shores, covering most points of interest including the Micmac Indian Village, Ft Amherst National Historic Park and Pioneer Village, above. Tours leave daily from Charlottetown, 894-9966.

TRAVEL

'Everyone hitches around here.'

Acadian Bus Lines operate a route via ferry from Nova Scotia. Charlottetown is also accessible by rail from Moncton, New Brunswick and Amherst, Nova Scotia. Island Transit Bus, 566-9962. Crosses the Island east to west once daily.

PRINCE EDWARD ISLAND NATIONAL PARK Situated north of Charlottetown, the Park consists of 25 miles of sandy beaches backed by sandstone cliffs. Thanks to the Gulf Stream the sea is beautifully warm. **Rustico** is one of the quieter beaches.

Ask about good places for clamming. Assuming you pick the right spot, you can just wriggle your toes in the sand and dig up a good meal.

At **Cavendish Beach**, on a golf course, is **Green Gables**, the farmhouse home of the famous Anne. Anne's creator, Lucy Maud Montgomery, was born just west of the park. The visit to Green Gables is free. The beach here, however, is very crowded during summer and probably best avoided. Camping sites and tourist homes abound on the island. Visitor Information, 672-6350.

NEWFOUNDLAND

Officially entitled Newfoundland and Labrador, and with a population of just over 550,000, the province is a bit off the beaten track, but it's worth taking a little time and trouble to get here—some world travellers have described Newfoundland as the most beautiful place they've ever been! It is a province rich in historic associations and, as revealed by recent archaeological excavations, one of the oldest settled regions in North America. The Vikings were here as early as AD 1000, settling on an isolated stretch of shoreline at **L'Anse Aux Meadows** at the tip of the Great Northern Peninsula.

By the time John Cabot 'discovered' Newfoundland and made it England's oldest colony (excepting Ireland) in 1497, the Vikings had long since gone and little remained of their hamlets. Newfoundland is also the youngest Canadian province, having joined the Confederation in 1949. **Labrador**, the serrated northeastern mainland of Canada, was added to Newfoundland in 1763. Until recent explorations and development of some of Labrador's natural resources (iron ore, timber), the area was virtually a virgin wilderness with the small population scattered in rugged little fishing villages and centred around the now all but obsolete airport at Goose Bay.

Newfoundland Island is characterised by a wild and rugged coastline dotted with fjords, picturesque fishing villages (some still with access only from the sea), deep harbours and a society neither wholly North American nor yet European. Fishing is still the main industry, although mining is important and the oil industry has reached here too.

Newfoundlanders' speech is unique: English interspersed with plenty of slang and colloquialisms. The quaintness of Newfoundland is also evident in the names of its towns, like Heart's Content and Blow-Me-Down. The people here are very friendly and helpful—well prepared to take a visitor under a collective wing. Ask about the many folk festivals held every summer. Newfoundland is probably the only Canadian province to celebrate Guy Fawkes Day every November 5th.

There is a daily car and passenger ferry service to Port-aux-Basques from North Sydney, Nova Scotia, and once on the island the Trans Canada Highway goes all the way to the capital, St John's, via Corner Brook and Terra Nova National Park. There is a bus service from the ferry to St John's.

National Parks: Gros Morne, Terra Nova.

The telephone area code is 709.

ST JOHN'S St John's is a gentle though weather-beaten city, overlooking a natural habour situated on the eastern side of the island, 547 miles from

Port-aux-Basques on the southwestern tip. Nearby Cape Spear is just 1640 miles from Cape Clair, Ireland, and the city's strategic position has in the past made it the starting point for transatlantic contests and conflicts of one sort or another.

Bitter struggles between the English and French for domination of the Atlantic coast culminated here in 1762 with the final capture of St John's by the British after the last brief French occupation; the first successful transatlantic cable was landed nearby in 1866; the first transatlantic wireless signal was received by Marconi at St John's in 1901; and the first non-stop transatlantic flight took off from here in 1919. Between 1919 and 1937 the city was involved in more than 40 pioneering transatlantic airplane crossings, hosting, among others, Charles Lindbergh and Amelia Earhart, and the inaugural transatlantic flights of Pan American and British Imperial Airways.

Lately, St John's has begun to develop more after the recent discovery of off-shore oil fields. Take a walk along Gower St to view the rows of historical old houses; Water St is the main thoroughfare for eating, shopping and drinking.

ACCOMMODATION

Seaflow Tourist Home, 57 William St, 753-2425. S–$33, D–$38, linens and towels incl. Private or shared bath, some kitchen facs. Close to harbour. Reservations recommended (1 night deposit).

The Old Inn, 157 LeMarchant Rd, 722-1171. S–$36, D–$48, $10 for every extra person. Breakfast incl, 5 min from downtown. Call to reserve.

Youth Hostel, on the campus of Memorial University of Newfoundland, in Hatcher House, 737-7590. $15 p/n.

Camping: CA Pippy Park, $5–$12. **La Manche Prov Park**, north on Hwy 10.

FOOD

There is a good variety of reasonably priced places to eat on Duckworth St:

Cavendish Café, 73 Duckworth St, 579-8024. Breakfast, lunch and dinner in traditional café-style. $5–$8. Open Mon–Fri 8am–10pm, Thur–Sat till 11.30pm.

Cafée Duckworth, 192 Duckworth St, 772-1444. 'A bit of everything'. Open daily 8am–10pm.

Chess' Snacks, 9 Freshwater Rd, 722-4083. Take-out fish. $4.

Memorial University campus, Thompson Student Centre. Not just for students.

OF INTEREST

Signal Hill National Historic Park. Accessible from Duckworth St. Scene of last battle between the English and the French, and site where Marconi received the first transatlantic wireless signal. Visit **Cabot Tower**, built in 1900 to celebrate both the 400th anniversary of John Cabot's discovery of Newfoundland and Queen Victoria's Diamond Jubilee. 'Million dollar view' of St. John's and the Atlantic, and an interesting visitors centre. Open daily in the summer (June–September) 8.30am–9pm, 772-5367.

Anglican Cathedral, 22 Church Hill. Said to be one of the finest examples of Gothic architecture in North America. Begun in 1816, and following two fires, restored in 1905. Features sculptured arches and carved furnishings. National Historic Site. Open Mon–Sat 10am–6pm, Sun 1pm–5pm. Tours available on an ad hoc basis. 726-5677.

Quidi Vidi Battery, (pronounced Kiddy Viddy). This provincial historic site located just outside St John's, occupies a cliffside position overlooking scenic Quidi Vidi and is now restored to its War of 1812 appearance. Manned by guides dressed in period Royal Artillery costume. Open daily in summer, admission free. Call 729-2977 for info.

Newfoundland Museum, 285 Duckworth St, 576-2460. St John's is rich in history and folklore and this particular museum has the only relics in existence of the vanished Indian tribe, the Beothuks. Open Mon–Fri 9am–5pm, Sat, Sun 2pm–5pm. Free. Tours available on an ad hoc basis, with 48-hr notice.

Newfoundland Museum at the Murray Premises, Water St. These premises house shops, a pub and the second branch of the Newfoundland Museum. Exhibits include the military, naval and marine history of the province. Same hours and phone number as the Duckworth location, above.

INFORMATION/TRAVEL

St John's Tourist Commission, 576-8514.
Canadian National Bus terminal, 495 Water St, 737-5915.
The airport is situated north of town and is reached only by taxi. Call 726-4400, $12.

ENTERTAINMENT/EVENTS/SHOPPING

Newfoundland and Labrador Folk Arts Festival in CA Pippy Park at the end of June. Great music and camping. The annual **regatta** on Quidi Vidi Lake at the beginning of August is the province's event of the year.

TERRA NOVA NATIONAL PARK In the central region of Newfoundland, around three hours away from St John's, this area was once covered by glaciers 750 feet thick which left behind boulders, gravel, sand and grooved rock. The sea filled the valleys, leaving the hills as islands. The result is the incredibly beautiful **Bonavista Bay** with its rugged coastline, fjord-like sounds, and bold headlands. But it's certainly not swimming country. The cold Labrador Current bathes the shores and it's not unusual to see an iceberg.

Inland the park is thickly forested and nature trails are provided by the park service. Moose are common sights in the park, and occasionally a fox or a bear may be spotted. Fishing and canoeing are available inside the park.

Access to the park is easy since the Trans Canada Highway passes right through it for a distance of 25 miles. Terra Nova Transport also provides bus transportation from St John's. Admission to the park is free. There are two campgrounds in the park; the fee is around $8/night. For Park info, call (800) 563-6353.

GROS MORNE NATIONAL PARK This is Newfoundland's second National Park, located on the west coast of the island, 10 hours away from St John's. This park, about 65 miles wide, is the more popular of the two parks because of the rugged beauty of its mountains. The landscape here is very different from that of the eastern coast of the province—rockier and more mountainous: 'fantastic'. Wildlife is abundant, and salmon fishing very popular. There are many campsites within the park; the prices range from $7–$10 per night. For groceries head for **Rocky Harbour**. For more info, call (800) 563-6353. Entry fee $5.

ST PIERRE AND MIQUELON ISLANDS Off the southern coast of Newfoundland, these islands constitute the only remaining holdings of France in North America. Once called the 'Islands of 11,000 Virgins', these granite outcrops total only about 93 square miles. A French territory since 1814, the natives parlent Francais, mangent baguettes and pay for them in francs. You can reach the islands by ferry from **Fortune** on Route 210. Canadians and Americans need to show proof of citizenship (driver's licence or birth certificate) and all other nationalities must have a passport. Tourist information, 011-508-412-222.

L'ANSE AUX MEADOWS At the northern tip of Newfoundland, and believed to be the site of the Viking settlement of AD 1000. According to legend, the Vikings defended this post against Indians until perils became too great and they withdrew to Greenland. No standing ruins of their buildings have survived, but excavations have disclosed the size and location of buildings, and many everyday objects have been found. Guides on site daily. Open from mid-June to August daily 9am–8pm; during the winter, 9am–4pm. Free.

ONTARIO AND QUÉBEC

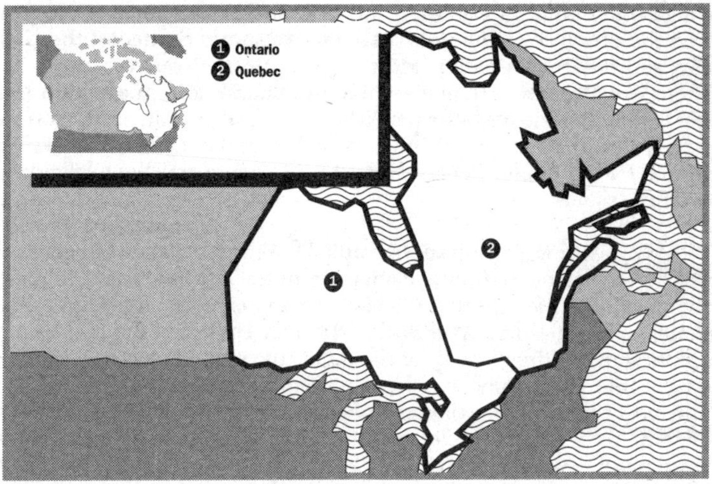

This section is devoted to those old enemies and still rivals, Ontario and Québec. Both provinces evolved out of vast wilderness areas first opened up by Indians and fur traders, only later to become the focus of the bitter rivalry between the French and British in North America as Québec was colonised by the French and Ontario by the British and American Loyalists. In 1791 Québec became Lower Canada and Ontario became Upper Canada. In 1840 the Act of Union united the two and finally brought responsible and stable government to the area.

Cultural differences between the two provinces remain strong, but one thing which is pretty similar is the climate. Summers can be hot and humid but winters long, very cold and snowy. Both Québec and Ontario also offer progressive, modern cities as well as vast regions of wilderness great for getting far away from whatever it is you're getting away from.

ONTARIO

The 'booming heartland' of Canada is the second largest province, claims one-third of the nation's population, half the country's industrial and agricultural resources and accounts for about 40 percent of the nation's income. Since Confederation, Ontario has leapt ahead of its neighbours, becoming highly industrialised and at the same time reaping the benefits of the great forest and mineral wealth of the Canadian Shield which covers most of the northern regions.

Ontario was first colonised, not from Britain, but by Empire Loyalists from the USA. Previously there were only sporadic French settlements and trading posts in what was otherwise a vast wilderness. The ready transportation provided in the past by the Great Lakes, all of which (except Lake Michigan) lap Ontario's shores, and now the St Lawrence Seaway, has linked the province to the industrial and consumer centres of the United States and has been a major factor behind Ontario's success story.

There is water virtually everywhere in Ontario, and in addition to the Great Lakes, Ontario has a further 250,000 small lakes, numerous rivers and streams, a northern coastline on Hudson Bay and of course Niagara Falls.
National Parks: Point Pelee, Pukashwa, Georgian Bay Islands, St Lawrence Islands.

OTTAWA Although the nation's capital has the reputation of being a dull city, Ottawa has perked up considerably in the last few years. It boasts a thriving cultural life, offering the visitor many excellent museums and art galleries, and top-notch theatrical performances. When the bars and restaurants start shutting down for the night, the popular solution is to cross the river into Hull, Québec, where everything is open until 3 am.

The most colourful time of year to visit is during spring when more than a million tulips bloom in the city and Ottawa celebrates its Festival of Spring. The tulip bulbs were a gift to Ottawa from the government of the Netherlands as thanks for the refuge granted to the Dutch royal family during World War II. In summer the city is crowded with visitors and there are many special festivals and activities. A lively, fun atmosphere prevails. Even Ottawa in the winter has its charms. You can enjoy the spectacle of civil servants, with their suits and briefcases, skating to work on the four and a half mile long Rideau Canal. The canal is known as the world's longest skating rink.

Champlain was here first, but didn't stay long and it took a further 200 years and the construction of the Rideau Canal before Ottawa was founded. Built between 1827 and 1831, the Canal provided a waterway for British gunboats allowing them to evade the international section of the St Lawrence where they might be subject to American gun attacks. Queen Victoria chose Ottawa as the capital of Canada in 1857 because it was halfway between the main cities of Upper and Lower Canada—Toronto and Québec City—and therefore a neutral choice.
The telephone area code is 613.

ACCOMMODATION

Bed & Breakfast places are abundant. Information is available at the tourist office in the National Arts Centre. Also, from **Ottawa B&B Organization**, 563-0161, S-$40-$44, D-$50-$54, and **Capital B&B Reservation Service**, 737-4129, S-$45 up, D-$55 and up. Shared bathroom, free parking.

Somerset House Hotel, 352 Somerset St West, 233-7762. Located between bus station and parliament buildings—10min. walk from downtown. S-$34, D-$45. 'Nice, clean rooms and very friendly staff.'

Auberge Nicholas Street Gaol Hostel—CYHA, 75 Nicholas St, 235-2595. Heritage building, jail 1862-1972, hostel since 1973. Members $14, $18 non-members. Laundry, kitchen. 'Fantastic place; unique; friendly people.' 'Sleep in the corridors of a former jail and take a shower in a cell.'

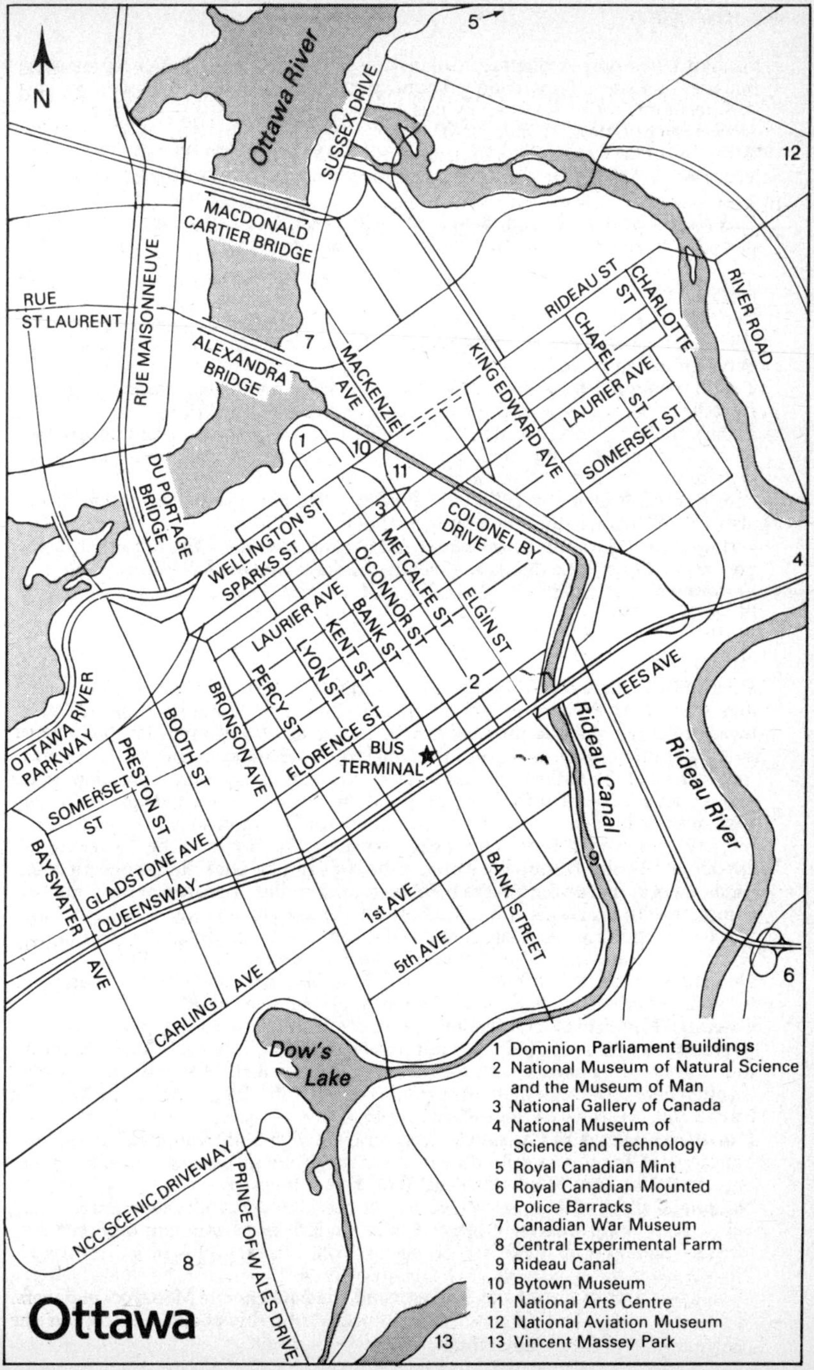
Ottawa
N
Ottawa River
SUSSEX DRIVE
5
12
MACDONALD CARTIER BRIDGE
RUE ST LAURENT
RUE MAISONNEUVE
ALEXANDRA BRIDGE
7
MACKENZIE AVE
KING EDWARD AVE
RIDEAU ST
CHAPEL ST
CHARLOTTE
RIVER ROAD
LAURIER AVE
ST
SOMERSET ST
1
10
11
3
DU PORTAGE BRIDGE
WELLINGTON ST
SPARKS ST
COLONEL BY DRIVE
4
METCALFE ST
O'CONNOR ST
ELGIN ST
LAURIER AVE
BANK ST
KENT ST
LYON ST
PERCY ST
BRONSON AVE
BOOTH ST
PRESTON ST
OTTAWA RIVER PARKWAY
SOMERSET ST
FLORENCE ST
BUS TERMINAL
2
LEES AVE
Rideau Canal
Rideau River
9
BAYSWATER AVE
GLADSTONE AVE
QUEENSWAY
1st AVE
5th AVE
BANK STREET
CARLING AVE
6
Dow's Lake
NCC SCENIC DRIVEWAY
PRINCE OF WALES DRIVE
8
13
1 Dominion Parliament Buildings
2 National Museum of Natural Science and the Museum of Man
3 National Gallery of Canada
4 National Museum of Science and Technology
5 Royal Canadian Mint
6 Royal Canadian Mounted Police Barracks
7 Canadian War Museum
8 Central Experimental Farm
9 Rideau Canal
10 Bytown Museum
11 National Arts Centre
12 National Aviation Museum
13 Vincent Massey Park

Carlton University Residence, Colonel By Drive, 788-5609. S–$30 per person, includes breakfast. Summer only. Laundry, cafeteria. 'Away from downtown but well recommended.' Reached by bus 4 or 7.
University of Ottawa, University Private St, 564-5400. May–Aug, S–$20, D–$38.
Richmond Plaza Motel, 238 Richmond Rd, 722-6591. S–$51, D–$56.
YM/YWCA, 180 Argyle Ave, 237-1320. Shared bath: S–$40, D–$49. AC, gym, TV, pool, cafeteria. 'Clean and bright.'
Camping: Gatineau Park, $10–$14, 827-2020 and **Camp Le Breton**, at Le Breton Flats, Booth and Fleet Sts, 943-0467. Summer $7.50 per night. 'Very convenient.'

FOOD

Byward Market, north of Rideau. Local produce, cheese, meat, fish, fruit, clothing; it's been here since 1846. Daily. 'Great.' The area around the market is good for eating places in general.
Café Bohémien, 89 Clarence, 238-7182. Innovative menu and reasonable prices ($4–$7).
Father and Sons, 112 Osgoode St, 233-6066. Favoured by students and close to the U of O campus. Traditional tavern-style food and a variety of Lebanese specialities. Open daily 7am–2am.
Peel Pub, 62 William St, 562-PEEL. Breakfast 99¢ plus inexpensive other times also. 'Excellent, whether on a budget or not.'
Wringer's Restaurant & Laundromat, 151 Second Ave, 234-9700. Kill 2 birds with one stone. Open Mon–Fri 9am–10.45pm, Sat and Sun 9am–10pm.
Yesterdays, 152 Spark St Mall, 235-1424. 'Good food at reasonable prices ($3–$12).'

OF INTEREST

Dominion Parliament Buildings. The Gothic-style, green copper-roofed buildings stand atop Parliament Hill overlooking the river. Completed in 1921, the three buildings replaced those destroyed by fire in 1916. Conducted tours daily every 10 minutes 9am–8.30pm; July 9am–9pm; weekends 9am–6pm. Go to info tent located at the Parliament Buildings to make same day tour reservations and avoid queues. Free. During the summer there are *son et lumière* displays. When parliament is in session you can visit the House of Commons. For the best view in the city climb the 291-foot-high **Peace Tower** in the Square. The Tower has a carillon of 53 bells. During the summer the bells ring out hour-long concerts four times a week. In true Buckingham Palace tradition, the **Changing of the Guard**—complete with bearskins and red coats—takes place on Parliament Hill at 10am, weather permitting, from late June to late Aug. The flame located in front of the Buildings burns eternally to represent Canada's unity. Info: 992-4793.
Note: Most museums in Ottawa are closed Mondays in fall and winter. A passport to all national museums is available after July 1 and costs $15.
Canadian Museum of Civilisation, Laurier St & St Laurent Blvd, just across the river in Hull, (819) 776-7002. This impressive museum, opened in 1989, explores the history of Canada's cultural heritage. There are IMAX and OMNIMAX theatres here too. Open daily 9am–6pm, Thur to 8pm. Closed Mon after Labour Day. $4.50, $3 students. Free Thur 5–8pm.
Canadian Museum of Caricature, 136 Patrick St, 995-3145. Smirk at cartoon impressions of famous people drawn by artists from all over the world. Open Sat–Tue 10am–6pm, Wed–Fri 10am–8pm. Free admission.
National Gallery of Canada, 380 Sussex Dr, opp Notre Dame Basilica. 10am–6pm daily, Thur to 8pm. Newly opened in a modern glass building designed by Moshie Safdie. Canadian art of all periods. $5, students free, 990-1985. 'Spectacular.'
National Museum of Natural Sciences and the Museum of Man, McLeod and Metcalf Sts, (819) 776-7000. Eskimoes, Indians, natural history, free films. Daily 9.00am- 6pm, Thur to 8pm. $4.50.

National Museum of Science and Technology, 1867 St Laurent. 'A must for those who like to participate.' Recently renovated with updated exhibits. Summer daily, 10am–8pm; winter 9am–5pm, free Thur 5pm–9pm, closed Mon after Labour Day. $4.
Royal Canadian Mint, 320 Sussex Dr. Guided tours every half hour, 8.30–11am, 12.30pm–2.30pm, Mon–Fri. Call 993-5700 to make a reservation.
Canadian War Museum, 330 Sussex Dr, 992-2774. Canada's military history from the early 1600s on. Daily 9.30am–5pm, May–Labour Day, Tue–Sun 10am–5pm, rest of yr. Students $1.25, free Thursdays 5pm–8pm.
Central Experimental Farm, Maple Dr, 995-8963. Established 1886 and HQ for the Canada Dept of Agriculture. Flowers, tropical greenhouse, animals. Great place for a picnic—beautiful site on the canal. Daily 9am–4pm. Horse-drawn wagon tours available. April–Oct, Mon–Fri 10am and 2pm.
Château Laurier Hotel, 2 Rideau St, 232-6411. Guided tours in summer (12.30pm and 2.30pm). A guide in historical costume will take you around this fairytale hotel. Among the many tidbits offered, you will learn that the original furniture bound for the Château Laurier went down with the *Titanic*. 'The art deco pool is wonderful.'
Rideau Canal. The 124-mile waterway which runs to Kingston on Lake Ontario. The 'giant's staircase', a series of eight locks, lifts and drops boats some 80 feet between Ottawa River and Parliament Hill. Cruises on the Canal and river are available. Cost $8. Contact Paul Boat Lines, 225-6781 or 235-8409. Or hire a bike at Dows Lake and ride along the towpath.
Near the locks is the **Bytown Museum,** 234-4570. An interesting look at old Ottawa. Mon–Sat 10am–4pm, Sun 5pm, closed Tues. May–Sept. Students $1.10.
Close by, in Major's Hill Park, is the spot from where the **Noonday Gun** is fired. Everyone in Ottawa sets their watches by it. Can be heard 14 miles away.
National Arts Centre, Confederation Sq, 996-5051. Completed in 1969, the complex includes theatres, concert halls, an opera house and an art gallery. Open all year 9am–5pm, tours available.
National Aviation Museum, Rockcliffe Airport, just off St Laurent Blvd, 993-2010. Offers special exhibitions in the summer. Discover the role played by airplanes in the development of Canada. Open May–Sept, daily 9am–5pm; Sept–Apr, 9am–5pm, Thurs to 9pm. $4 students. Free Thurs 5–9pm.
There is a nice park at Somerset and Lyon and the **Vincent Massey Park**, off Riverside Dr, has free summer concerts. If you have transport, a trip to **Gatineau Park**, five miles beyond Hull, is worth a thought. Good swimming. 'The park gives one an impression of the archetypal Canada; rugged country, timber floating down the Gatineau, etc.'

INFORMATION

Canada's Capital Visitor Information Centre, 14 Metcalfe St (opposite Parliament Buildings). Open Sept–Apr, Mon–Sat 9am–5pm; May–Aug, daily 8.30am–9pm, 239-5000.
Info Kiosk at National Arts Centre, Elgin & Queen. Open daily in summer 9am–9pm, otherwise Mon–Sat 9am–5pm, Sun 10am–4pm, 237-5158.
Capital Visitors and Convention Bureau, 111 Lisgar St, in the Capital Square Building, 237-5150. All have accommodation and sightseeing advice, including *See & Do* brochure, maps, etc. Open Mon–Fri 9am–5pm.
Read *Usually Reliable Source* and *Penny Press* for what's happening.
Post Office at Elgin and Sparks Sts.

ENTERTAINMENT

Read *What's on in Ottawa*. For late entertainment cross the river to Hull where the pubs are open longer. Ottawa has several English style pubs. Recommended are: **Elephant & Castle**, Rideau Centre (fish 'n chips). **Marble Works**, 14 Waller St, and **Earl of Sussex**, 431 Sussex Dr, 14 English beers on tap.
Bon Vivante Brasserie, St Joseph, Hull. French Canadian music.

At the **National Arts Centre**, 53 Elgin St, 996-5051, student standby tickets (2 tickets per person maximum) are available from 4pm–6pm on the day of the performance, certain performances only half price, $12+.
Annual **summer exhibition**, Lansdowne Park. Fair, animals, crafts, concerts, etc. 'Good fun.' Held in August.

SHOPPING
Arthur's Place, Bank, nr Somerset. Second-hand books and records.
For Indian and Eskimo stuff try Four Corners, 93 Sparks St, and Snow Goose on Sparks St.
Sparks Street Mall, 3-block traffic-free section between Elgin and Bank. Fountains, sidewalk cafes, good shopping, etc.
Rideau Centre, on Rideau, 5 min walk from Arts Centre. Ottawa's newest shopping mall. 'There's even a Marks & Spencers.'
If you are in town on Labour Day Weekend, don't miss the **International Hot Air Balloon Festival** which launches itself from the Parc de l'Abée in Gatineau and can be watched from Parliament Hill.

TRAVEL
OCTranspo Bus depot: Kent and Catherine Sts. Rail station is two miles from city centre. To get there catch number 95 bus on Slater St or Mackenzie King Bridge, every 15 minutes. $1.50. For all bus info: 741-4390.
Voyageur Colonial Coach, to many Canadian cities, 238-5900.
VIA Rail, passenger train service throughout Canada, 244-8283.
The airport is six miles out. Buses run from the Château Laurier, and other major hotels, twice every hour. Info: 523-8880. $9.
One of the nicest ways of seeing Ottawa is by bike, and an extensive system of bikeways and routes is there for this purpose. Info from Ottawa Bikeways, on Carling St, 722-4470. Bicycles are available for hire at Château Laurier and on sunny days, at Confederation Sq. Info: 233-0268. $6/hour, $14/half day, $18/day. Open daily 9am–8pm.

MORRISBURG A small town on the St Lawrence whose main claim to fame is **Upper Canada Village**, a re-creation of a St Lawrence Valley community of the 19th century. The village is situated some 11 kms east of Morrisburg on Hwy 2, in Crysler Farm Battlefield Park, 543-3704. The Park serves as a memorial to Canadians who died in the War of 1812 against the United States.

The buildings here were all moved from their previous sites to save them from the path of the St Lawrence Seaway and include a tavern, mill, church, store, etc, all of which are fully operational. Vehicles are not allowed. Open 9.30am–5pm mid-May to mid-Oct; $9 adults, $6 students.

KINGSTON A small, pleasant city situated at the meeting place of the St Lawrence and Lake Ontario. Early Kingston was built around the site of Fort Frontenac, then a French outpost, later to be replaced by the British Fort Henry, the principal British stronghold west of Québec. This was, ever so briefly, the capital of Canada (1841–44) and many of the distinctive limestone 19th century houses still survive.

The town is the home of Queens University, situated on the banks of the St Lawrence. The Kingston Fall Fair, which in fact happens in late summer, is considered 'worth a stop'. Kingston is also a good centre for visiting the picturesque **Thousand Islands** in the St Lawrence.

ACCOMMODATION

Hilltop Motel, 2287 Princess St, 542-3846. D–$47.
Kingston Area Bed & Breakfast Association, 542-0214. S–$38, D–$49. Incl. brkfst.
Kingston International Youth Hostel, 210 Bagot St, 546-7203. $12 per night members, $16 non-members. Shower, lockers and kitchen facs. Closed after Labour Day. 'Super friendly place (hostel), 5 mins from bus route, shops, laundry, lake nearby. Highly recommended.'
Prince George Hotel, 200 Ontario St, 549-5440. D–$73.
Princess Hotel, 720 Princess St, 542-7395. S–$35, D–$47 per room.
Queen's University, 545-2529, has rooms May–Aug. Reservations only. $15.75 per night students. $31.50 non-students.
Camping: Lake Ontario Park Campground, 542-6574, 4 kms west on King St. Open May–Sep. $12 for 2, $2.50 per person extra. **Rideau Acres**, on Hwy 15, north of exit 104, exit 623 on Hwy 401, 546-2711. $17.50 per site.

FOOD

Brew Pub, 34 Clarence St, 542-4978. Produces own lager and Dragon's Breath Ale. Tours of brewery available.
The Farmers' Market, Market Sq, is open Tue, Thur, Sat.
Morrison's, 318 King St E, 542-9483. 'Best value set meals at $4–$7.' Closes 8pm.
Pilot House, 265 King St E, 542-0222. Fish and chips and expensive English beer.

OF INTEREST

Old Fort Henry, east on Hwy 2 at junction Hwy 15. The fort has been restored and during the summer 'hand-picked' college students dressed in Victorian army uniforms give displays of drilling. Open daily 10.00am–6.00pm, Mon, Weds, Sat till 9pm during July and August. Ceremonial retreat takes place Mon, Weds, Sat, $5.85. The fort is also a military museum. For info call 542-7388.
John A MacDonald, Canada's first Prime Minister, lived in **Bellevue House** on Centre St. The century-old house has been restored and furnished in the style of the 1840s. Known locally as the 'Pekoe Pagoda' or 'Tea Caddy Castle' because of its comparatively frivolous appearance in contrast to the more solid limestone buildings of the city. The house is open daily, 9am–6pm. Free. 545-8666.
Fort Frederick, Royal Military College Museum. On RMC grounds, half a mile east of Hwy 2. Canada's West Point, founded in 1876. The museum, in a Martello tower, features pictures and exhibits of Old Kingston and Military College history, and the Douglas collection of historic weapons. Open June through Labour Day. $1.50. 541-6660.
Murney Redoubt. At the foot of Barrie St, 544-9925. Now run by the Kingston Historical Society. 10am–5pm. Open daily. $2.
Pump House Steam Museum, on Ontario St, 546-4696. A restored 1848 pump house now housing a vintage collection of working engines. $3.75, $3.25 students. Open mid-June–Labour Day. Tue–Sun 10am–5pm.
North of the city the **Rideau Lakes** extend for miles and miles. The Rideau Hiking Trail winds its way gently among the lakes. You can take a free ferry to **Wolfe Island** in the St Lawrence. Ferries leave from City Hall. Once on the island it is possible to catch another boat (not free) to the US.
Thousand Islands Boat Tours. From Gananoque Quay, 20 miles from Kingston, on Hwy 2, 382-2144. Trip lasts 3 hours. $15. There is a shorter cruise at $10. Tours 9am–3pm, mid-May–mid-Oct.
Departing from Crawford Dock at the foot of Brock St in downtown Kingston, there are additional tours of the harbour and Thousand Islands. About $15. For info: call Island Queen, 549-5544.

INFORMATION

Visitor & Convention Centre, 209 Ontario St, 548-4415. Open Sun–Wed 9am–7pm, Thur–Sat 9am–9pm.
John Deutsch, University Centre Union, and University Sts. Ride board, shops, post office, laundry, etc.

ENTERTAINMENT
Stages Nightclub, 390 Princess St, 547-3657. Bands and disco.

SPORT
Canadian Olympic Training Regatta. An annual event, held during the last week in August, and one of the largest regattas in North America.
International Hockey Hall of Fame, Alfred and York Sts. Open daily. Small charge.

TRAVEL
Voyageur Colonial Bus Terminal, 175 Counter St, 547-4916. Open 6.30am–11pm.
VIA Rail Station, Princess and Counter St, 544-5600.

ST LAWRENCE ISLANDS NATIONAL PARK The park is made up of 17 small islands in the Thousand Islands area of the St Lawrence between Kingston and Brockville, and Mallorytown Landing on the mainland. The islands can be reached only by water-taxi from Gananoque, Mallorytown Landing and Rockport, Ontario, or from Alexandria Bay and Clayton in New York State. Park is open daily, mid-May to mid-Oct. Free.

It's a peaceful, green-forested area noted chiefly for its good fishing grounds. Camping facilities are available on the islands.

TORONTO 'Trunno', or 'Metro' as the natives call their city, is the most American of the Canadian cities, having many of the characteristics of metropolitan America but without all of the usual problems. It's a brash, cosmopolitan city with some 25 different languages on tap around town, sprawling over 270 square miles, with many fine examples of skyscraper architecture, good shopping areas, excellent theatre, music and arts facilities, a vibrant night life, fast highways, and yet it's a clean city, with markedly few poor areas, and the streets are safe at night.

Perhaps out of envy, Toronto is also nicknamed 'Toronto The Good'; more like Switzerland than North America, remarked one reader. 'Good' in that the city has yearned to be as stylish as New York without the poverty and dirt, and has succeeded. You can get a great haircut, great clothes, great movies, great drinks, great music and a great job here. They also have a great polar bear section at the zoo where you experience a polar bear diving into the water two inches from your face.

Then take a look at the windows of the Royal Bank building. The golden glow emanating from them is real gold dust, mixed with the glass. That also is proof of how rich Canada is, and most of the wealth and power, the envy of the other provinces, is situated right here on Bay Street.

This is also a good centre from which to see other places in Ontario. Niagara Falls and New York State are an hour and a half away down the Queen Elizabeth Way (QEW), to the north there is Georgian Bay and the vast Algonquin Provincial Park, while to the west there are London and Stratford. *The telephone area code is 416.*

ACCOMMODATION
Econo-Lodging Services, 101 Nymark Ave, 494–0541. Provides accommodation referral for hotels, furnished apartments and B&B's. Also **Bed and Breakfast Registry**, 964-2566, and **B&B Homes of Toronto**, 363-6362. \$45–\$75 double occupancy.

Downtown Toronto Association of B&B Guesthouses, PO Box 190, Station B, Toronto M5T 2W1, 690-1724. S–$45–$60, D–$55–$75.
Karabanow Tourist Home, 9 Spadina Rd, at Bloor St W, 923-4004. Rooms with shared bath and free parking: S–$50, D–$56. Private rooms from $55. Cable colour TV, next to subway. Discounts for stays of 7 nights or more. 'Clean and very helpful.'
Leslieville Home Hostel, 185 Leslie St, 461-7258. $15 dorm, S–$35, D–$45. Incls breakfast . 'Fabulous.' 'Downtown.'
Neill-Wycik, 96 Gerrard St E, 977-2320. 14 May–early Sept. S–$33, D–$41, $10 rollaway beds; 10% weekly discount; also 'student standby' rates at 20% discount. Try here first. Good facilities, baggage storage, central, 5 mins from subway. No AC but TV. 'Recommended.'
University of Toronto, Scarborough campus, 1265 Military Trail, 287-7367. $90 pw min 2 wk stay. 'Fantastic student residence.' 'Parties, sports facilities.' 90 mins from downtown.
U of Toronto Housing Service, 214 College St, 978-8045. Has list of accommodation available in student residences in summer only. $25–$45 range.
Toronto International Hostel, 223 Church St, 368-0207. $15 members, $20 non-members. Kitchen, laundry, linen provided, lockers, TV incl. 'Fills quickly.' 'Convenient.' 'Lovely place.' 'Noisy.' Reservations advisable in summer.
University College, 85 St George St, 978-8735. S–$42, D–$31 per person. Summers only. Also suggested are **Trinity** and **Wycliffe Colleges** on Hoskin Ave, and **St Hildas** on Devonshire Place. About $80 pw. 'Pleasant and clean.'
YWCA, 80 Woodlawn Ave, 923-8454. Shared bath: S–$43, D–$58. Dorm $18. Linen incl. Take Yonge-University subway to Summerhill, walk two blocks north. Summer only.

FOOD

Bregman's, on Yonge north of St Clair. Great brownies and cheese danish.
For seafood lovers, **Coasters**, upstairs from the Old Fish Market on Market St near the St Lawrence Market, has inexpensive nightly specials in a cozy bar with a fireplace.
Druxy's Famous Deli Sandwiches, a cafeteria-style eating place with locations all over Toronto, is a good spot for salads and sandwiches.
Fran's Restaurants, 21 St Clair Ave W, 2275 Yonge, 20 College, 923-9867. Spaghetti, fish and chips, burgers. Open 24 hrs. Under $12.
Ginsberg and Wong, McCaul and Dundas. Chinese and Jewish. 'Great food, reasonable prices.'
Hungarian Goulash Party Tavern, 498 Queen St W, 863-6124. Good, cheap Hungarian food. Entrées $8–$12.
Lick's Homeburgers and Ice Cream, on Yonge south of Eglinton and on Queen St E in the Beaches. For the messiest, yummiest burgers around in a fun atmosphere.
Loon Fong Yuen, 393 Spadina. Unpretentious Chinese. $6ish. In fact lots of places in Chinatown (around Dundas & Spadina) offer meals at reasonable prices.
Organ Grinder, Esplanade east of Yonge, 364-6517. 'Noisy but a good laugh.' Pizza, Italian food. Prices range $6–$12. 'Entertainment by the only organ of its kind in the world.'
Old Spaghetti Factory, Esplanade, east of Yonge, 864-9761. About $7 up. 'Very delicious. Excellent value and service.' Huge old warehouse.
Sneaky Dees, 431 College St, 368-5090, serves a bargain of a breakfast for $2.95 from 3am–11am. Doubles as a night-time hot spot.
Swiss Chalet, a chain with numerous outlets, has 'great' barbequed chicken and ribs at very reasonable prices.
Toby's Goodeats. With locations across the city (including Yonge & Bloor, Bloor & Bay, the Eaton Centre, Yonge & St Clair) 925-2171, Toby's serves up some of the best-value meals in the city. Under $10.

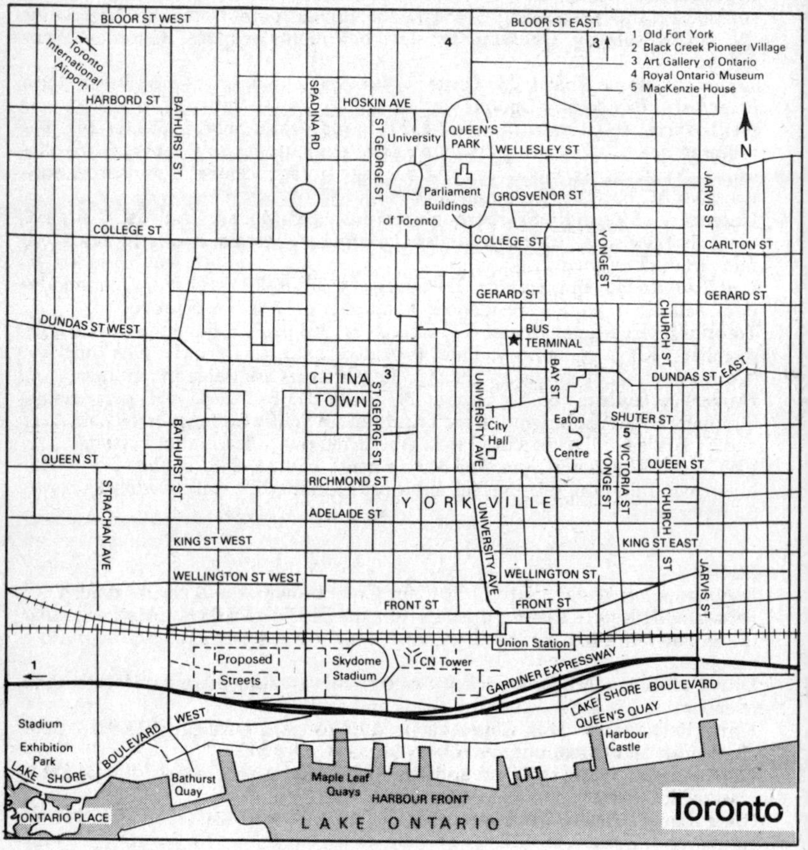

Wheatsheaf Pub, 667 King St West, 364-3996. Toronto's oldest pub—since 1849. 'Excellent burgers & wings!' 'Don't miss.'

Westclair Italian Village (little Italy) along St Clair Ave West between Dufferin and Lansdown. Sidewalk cafes, restaurants.

Don't miss 2 good **markets**, for fresh produce and a wide variety of food:

Kensington Market, Dundas St West to College St, Spadina Ave to Augusta St.

St Lawrence Market, 95 Front St East. Over 40 foodstalls in this historic 1844 building, Toronto's first city hall.

OF INTEREST

Parliament Buildings, Queen's Park, ½ block north of College St, University Ave. Completed in 1892, the Legislative Buildings once provided living accommodation for its elected members. Guided tours Mon to Fri, mid May-

Labour Day, 9am–4pm, including a ½-hr visit to the Public Gallery. Check on 325-7500 for exact schedule at the time of visit.

City Hall, 100 Queen St at Bay St, 392-7341. $30m creation of Finnish architect Viljo Revell, perhaps most impressive when lit at night. The reflecting pool in the centre becomes a skating rink in winter. One free tour daily at 3.15pm, Mon–Fri.

CN Tower, foot of John St. At 1815 ft the tallest free-standing structure in the world. The observation deck is open in summer 9am–midnight, 10am–10pm to 11pm on Fri & Sat. Elevator to observation deck $12 (no student discount); it is $2.25 more to go to the Space Deck. The CN Tower has a great view, but don't eat there unless the Air Show is on, when you can have a front row seat and the planes are so close that the pilots wave to you, 360-8500.

Tour of the Universe, base of the CN Tower, 363-8687. Discover life in the year 2019. Climb aboard a space shuttle for a simulated trip through space, stopping at the planet Jupiter. Hour-long tours leave every 15 min. Sun–Thur 11am–7pm; Fri 10pm; Sat 10am–10pm. $12.

Old Fort York. On Garrison Rd, the Fort was built in 1739 and has been completely restored during the last ten years. It now houses a collection of antique weapons, tools, etc. Guided tours, 10am–4pm, admission $4.75, 392-6907.

Black Creek Pioneer Village, on the northern edge of Toronto at Jane and Steeles Sts. A reconstructed pioneer village of the 18th century. Costumed workers perform daily tasks in the restored buildings. July and Aug open 10am–6pm; mid-March to June, Sept–Oct open 9.30am (10 weekends)–5pm; 9.30am (10)–4pm, Nov–Dec. Closed Jan & Feb. $7, $3 children. If travelling there by subway and streetcar, allow about one hour each way from the city centre. 736-1733.

Casa Loma, Davenport at Spadina, 923-1171. An eccentric chateau-style mansion built by the late Sir Henry Pellatt between 1911 and 1914 at a reported cost of $3m. It was restored in 1967 and the proceeds from the daily tours go to charity. 'Fantastic.' Open daily 9.30am–4pm, year round. $8 adults. No student discount.

Spadina House, next door, is also open to the public. Family mansion. To get there take the subway to Dupont.

Toronto Stock Exchange, The Exchange Tower, 2 First Canadian Place, 947-4670. Visitors Gallery has recorded explanatory guide on tape. Mon–Fri 9am–4.30pm. Free tour daily 2pm.

University of Toronto, just west of Queens Park. The largest educational institution in the British Commonwealth. Free one-hour tours of the campus available, starting from either Hart House or University College. 10.30am, 1pm and 2.30pm Mon–Fri, 978-5000.

Bata Shoe Museum, 131 Bloor St W, the Colonnade (2nd floor), 924-7463. The only shoe museum in North America, displaying over 9000 pairs from Elton's platforms to ancient Egyptian sandals. Open Tues–Sun 11am–6pm. $3, $1 students.

Art Gallery of Ontario, 317 Dundas St at McCaul, 977-0414. Rembrandt, Picasso, Impressionists, large collection of Henry Moore sculptures, plus Oldenburg's 'Hamburger', and collections by Canadian artists. Mon–Sun 10am–5.30pm; Fri & Weds till 10pm. Closed Mon in winter. Adults $7.50; students with ID $4. Wed 5pm–9pm, free.

Ontario Science Centre, 770 Don Mills Rd and Eglinton Ave E. A do-it-yourself-place which is 'part-museum, part fun fair'. 'Breathtaking.' 'An absolute must.' Open 10am–6pm, Fri to 9pm. Cost: adults $7.50. Free admission Fri 5pm–9pm. To get there take Yonge Subway to Eglinton, then 34 bus to Don Mills Rd. 429-4100. Closed on Mon in winter.

Royal Ontario Museum, 100 Queen's Park. 10am–6pm; Tue, Thur to 8pm. Adults $7, students, seniors $4. Free Tue after 4.30pm. Has the largest Chinese art collection outside China and fine natural history section. Next door is the **McLaughlin Planetarium.** Call for showtimes, 586-5736 or 5750. Adults $8.50, students $5. Laser and astronomy shows.

Mackenzie House, 82 Bond St, 392-6915. Mid-Victorian home and print shop of William Lyon Mackenzie, first mayor of Toronto and leader of the Upper Canada rebellion in 1837. Now restored to mid-1800s condition. Open Mon–Sat 9.30am–5pm, Sun 12 noon–5pm; adults $3.25, over 65 and under 13, $2.50.

George R Gardiner Museum of Ceramic Art, 11 Queen's Park, 586-8080. The only museum of its kind in North America, with a vast collection of pottery and porcelain. Open Tue–Sun 10am–5pm. Closed Mon, free on Tue. Adults $7, students $4. Admission gets you into Royal Ontario Museum and vice-versa.

The Sky Dome. Toronto's newest sports and concert venue opened in June 1989. Located at the foot of Peter St, this impressive structure boasts the largest retractable roof in the world and numerous bars and restaurants. Catch a football or baseball game here starring Toronto's Argonauts or the world champion Blue Jays. Tours also available. Info: 341-3663.

Marine Museum of Upper Canada, Exhibition Place, 392-1765. History of shipping and the Great Lakes from fur trading days on. Open Mon–Sat 9.30am–5pm, Suns & hols noon–5pm. $3.25, no student reduction.

Chinatown, along Dundas West and China Court, Spadina, south of Dundas. Usual mixture of tourist and 'real' Chinese. Good place to eat.

Ontario Place on the lakefront. Opened in 1971, Ontario Place is a complex of manmade islands and lagoons, with a marina and some attractive parkland. Free outdoor rock, folk or symphony concerts are given late afternoons and evenings at the Forum; there are films at Cinesphere on the 'largest screen in the world'; and multimedia presentations of Ontario are shown in several unusual pavilions. There's an amazing children's fun village and fairly cheap food is available in several different eating places. Well recommended by previous visitors. $8.50. Take the TTC—bus every 30 mins from Union Station, $1 each way.

Canadian National Exhibition, otherwise known as CNE or 'The Ex', held annually next to Ontario Place during the 18 days before Labour Day. Free admission to Ontario Place from the CNE during this time. A sort of glorified state fair, Canadian style, and the largest annual exhibition in the world. Cheap food in the Food Hall, and site of the Hockey Hall of Fame. Info: 965-7711. 'Fabulous.'

Harbourfront, 235 Queen's Quay West, 930-3000. 92 acres of restaurants, art shows, films, theatre, etc, on Lake Ontario. Free Sun concerts at 1pm. Great place to spend a sunny summer afternoon.

Canada's Wonderland, 30 kms north, Rutherford Rd, off Hwy 400. Ontario's answer to Disney? Includes 5 theme areas, a 150-ft man-made mountain complete with waterfalls, and all the usual rides and entertainments, May–Sept from 10am. For info: 832-2205, 832-7000. $31 for a day pass.

The best of the city's **parks** and open spaces are High Park (free swimming), Edwards Gardens, Don Mills, Forest Hill and Rosedale. The ferry ride to **Centre Island** in the harbour costs $3 return. Or take a stroll along the boardwalk in the Beaches, south of Queen St E, east from Woodbine.

Metro Toronto Zoo, 25 miles northeast of junction Hwy 401 and Meadowvale Rd, 392-5901. Open year round from 9am; closing time varies with season. $9.75. Take bus #86A from Kennedy Subway station.

INFORMATION

Convention and Tourist Bureau, 207 Queen's Quay W, Harbourfront, 203-2500. Open Mon–Fri 9am–5pm. There is a booth at 220 Yonge St, open 7 days a week.

7 Convenient Visitor Info Centres located throughout Toronto late May–Labour Day; open 9am–7pm daily.

Post Office at Front and Bay Sts.

City of Toronto Info: 392-7341.

ENTERTAINMENT

Check the *Globe and Mail, Toronto Star* and *Toronto Sun* for daily entertainments guide, as well as the free weekly guides, *NOW* and *EYE*. Also look for *Key to Toronto,* monthly.

Cineplex Odeon, 1303 Yonge St, 323-6600. One of the largest cineplexes in the world with 17 screens. $8 admission, $5 matinées, $4.25 on Tuesdays. Tickets go fast for the evening performances of new movies so buy early.

The Big Bop, 651 Queen St W, 366-6699. A multi-story dance club with different styles of music on each floor and a sofa-lounge upstairs. Popular with students. Open 8pm–2am most nights, Fri and Sat till 3am.

R.P.M.'s, Queen's Quay, Harbourfront, 869-1461. Dancing, rock. 'Excellent.' Free bus from Union Station. $6 or free Weds, incl free buffet.

The Festival of Festivals—Toronto Film Festival, first Thurs after Labour Day, tickets available at box office, Cumberland Terrace, Bay St entrance, 2nd floor, 968-FILM.

O'Keefe Centre, Front and Yonge Sts. Opera, ballet, concerts, jazz, drama. Student rush seats available on night of performance. Info: 393-7469.

St Lawrence Centre for the Arts, Front and Scott Sts. Was Toronto's project for the Confederation celebrations in 1967. Drama, dance and opera. Info: 366-7723.

The Strip. On Yonge St, running between Dundas and Gerrard Sts. The usual.

Free swimming at **Woodbine Swimming Pool** (subway to Woodbine, bus to Lakeshore), and **Sunnyside Swimming Pool** (subway to Dundas W, streetcar to Queen), and ten other pools. Call Recreation Info: 392-7259.

The Nag's Head, Eaton Centre. Folk music most nights.

Ye Olde Brunswick House, Brunswick and Bloor. 'Good jazz and a lively amateur night.' Bavarian-style long benches and pitchers of beer. Live music upstairs in Albert Hall.

Bourbon St, 180 Queen St W. Jazz, often with top-name appearances.

Harbourfront, 235 Queen's Quay, 973-3000. Concerts, etc, plus movie theatre showing oldies, horror movies, and other classics.

There are many bars situated along Queen St W, some of which feature nightly live entertainment: check out especially the **Bamboo** and the **Rivoli**. Also, **Lee's Palace** on Bloor St W, just east of Bathurst and the **El Mocambo** at College and Spadina.

Yuk Yuk's, at Yonge and Eglinton and Bay and Yorkville, offers a night of amateur stand-up comedians. Dinner available. Also **Second City** at the Old Firehall, 110 Lombard, 863-1111. Features excellent nightly shows. 'Canadian humour at its best.'

Five Star Tickets offers half-price tickets on the day of the performance for many of the music, dance and theatre productions in Toronto. Locations at Eaton Centre, Yonge and Dundas, Mon–Fri noon–7.30pm and Sat 11am–3pm. For Info call 596-8211.

For free tickets to **CBC TV shows**, call 205-3311, open weekdays only 9am–5pm.

Molson Indy, at the Canadian National Exhibition, 260-4639 for tickets. Prices range from $35–$150. It varies every year, but it is usually during the second half of July. 'This race has been on the Indy car circuit since 1986 and has grown more popular each year.'

TRAVEL

Allostop, 323-0874. $24 to Ottawa; $41 to NYC or Québec City. $6 membership.

Grey Coach/Greyhound Bus Terminal, Bay at Dundas, call 367-8747 for info.

Toronto Driveaway Service, 5803 Yonge St, Suite 101, 225-7754. Open 9am–5pm, Sat 10am–1pm.

Bike rentals: Brown's Sport and Cycle Shop, 2447 Bloor St W, 763-4176. $14/day, $32/weekend, $48/week, $100 deposit. Open Mon–Sat 9.30am–6.00pm, Thur–Fri to 8.00pm.

Standard fares operate on the integrated transport system, TTC (bus and subway), and it is cheaper to buy tokens. Current fare is $2, $3 r.t., 10 tokens–$13, monthly pass $67. Transfers, valid between subway and bus lines, are free. Exact fare required for buses and streetcars. Sun and holidays bus pass $5. Bus drivers do not give change. Route maps available from ticket booths. The Toronto Transit Commission (TTC) offers information on 393-4636.
There is an express bus service from Islington, Yorkdale and York Mills Subway Stations to the airport every half hour and costs $7–$11.
Airport buses leave the Royal York Hotel and the Sheraton Centre every 20 mins. City buses run to airport (terminal 2 only) at least every hour from St Lawrence West subway. $2.75.
VIA Rail Canada information: 366-8411. Trains from Union Station to Niagara Falls—about $37 same day return.
The Last Minute Club, at Union Station—ground floor, 441-2582. Open Mon–Fri 9am–9pm; Sat 9am–4pm. $40 membership. 'Best place to get really cheap flights'.

SHOPPING
Queen St west of University Ave. Alternative student shopping area. 'Vibrant.'
Honest Ed, Bloor and Bathurst. 'Just about everything at 40% reduction.'
Sam the Record Man, Yonge and Dundas. 'Huge selection of cheap records.'
Cheap clothes at Hercules, 577 Yonge St. Army surplus store.
Bee Bee's Flea Market Inc, St Lawrence Market, 92 Front St at Jarvis. Most Sundays all year, 10am–5pm. Antiques, crafts. Free coffee or tea.
World's Biggest Bookstore, 20 Edward St at Yonge (one block from Eaton Centre). 17 miles of shelves with over 1 million books. Open daily.
Yorkville, north of Queens Park east of Avenue Rd. 'Lively, open till about 1am on Sat night—street theatre, music, etc.'
Eaton Centre Shopping Mall, Yonge and Dundas. An impressive multi-levelled, glass-domed complex of stores, eating places and entertainments. 'Definitely worth a visit.'
Beneath the Toronto Dominion Bank complex, Bay and King Sts, there is a wealth of shops and restaurants, bustling during the day but closed at night. Interconnects into the subway system, the Royal York Hotel and Union Station.

HAMILTON Situated on the shores of Lake Ontario roughly midway between Toronto and Niagara Falls, Hamilton is Canada's King of Steel. The city is home to the two principal steel companies in the nation, Stelco and Dofasco, and like its US counterpart, Pittsburgh, is in the throes of an urban cleanup and renewal in the wake of the steel giants. The air and the water are cleaner here these days and many new and interesting buildings have gone up around town. Hamilton is working hard to improve its image.

The city is also blessed with one of the largest landlocked harbours on the Great Lakes, as a result handling the third largest water tonnage in the country. Although primarily a shipping and industrial centre, Hamilton does offer a variety of non-related activities to the visitor. It is also within easy reach of Niagara, Brantford, Stratford and London.

ACCOMMODATION
McMaster University, 1280 Main St West, 525-9140, ext 2909. May–Aug. Shared bath, kitchen facs, indoor pool. S–$37, $196 wk, discounts for longer stays.
Pines Motel, 395 Centennial Pkwy, 561-5652. AC and TV. S–$49 up; D–$58 up. Close to Confederation Park, waterslide and wave pool.

YMCA, 79 James St S, 529-7102. Singles only $27 per night + $10 deposit.
YWCA, 75 MacNab St S, 522-9922. S–$26 + $5 deposit. 'Reservations a good idea.'

FOOD
Barangas, 580 Van Wagner's Beach Rd, 544-7122. Open 11am–1am. Recently opened on the beach. Food with an international flavour, $6–$15.
Christopher's Cameo Restaurant, 50 James St N, 529-4214. 'Inexpensive.'
Farmers Market, central Hamilton, and the largest such market in Canada.
McMaster University Common Building Refec. 'During the summer, June through Aug, it is possible to eat here. Meals about $3.'
Texas Border Boot and Grill Bar, 77 King William St, 527-7488. Steaks and tex-mex, $5–$15. Open daily except Sun 11.30am–1am.

OF INTEREST
Dundurn Castle, York St at Dundurn, 546-2872. Restored Victorian mansion of Sir Allen Napier MacNab, Prime Minister of United Canada, 1854–1856. *Son et lumière* performances during summer. Mansion open 10am–4pm June–Labour Day, thereafter 12pm–4pm.Closed Mon & Fri. $4.50, students $2.75.
Art Gallery of Hamilton, 123 King St West, 527-6610. Canadian and American art. Open Wed–Sat 10am–5pm, Thur 10–9pm, Sun 1–5pm. Closed Mon/Tues. $1.
MacMaster University. Has one of Canada's first nuclear reactors and a planetarium. There is also an art gallery on campus in Togo Salmon Hall.
Hamilton Museum of Steam and Technology, 900 Woodward Ave, 549-5225. Open daily 11am–4pm; $2.25 adults, $1.75 students.
Canadian Warplane Heritage Museum, Hamilton Airport Hangar 4, 679-4183. Planes remaining from WWII are kept in flying condition. Daily, year-round 10am–4pm. $3.25.
Canadian Football Hall of Fame, 58 Jackson St W, within City Hall Plaza area, 528-7566. Push button exhibits. Open Mon–Sat 9.30am–4.30pm, Sun 12pm–4.30pm. $2, students and over 64, $1.
Royal Botanical Gardens, York Blvd. Nature parkland and a wildlife sanctuary called 'Cootes Paradise' where trails wind through some 1,200 acres of marsh and wooded ravines. Free from dawn to dusk daily. A maple syrup festival is held here in March.
Hamilton Place, 50 Main St West, an impressive $11m showcase for the performing arts and part of the downtown renewal project. Home of 'Hamilton Philharmonic', one of Canada's finest. Call 546-3100 for schedules.
Hess Village, four blocks between King and Main. Restored Victorian mansions in a 19th century village. Trendy shops, antiques, restaurants, etc.
The Bruce Trail extends more than 700 km along the Niagara escarpment. Good for hiking, pleasant walks. 'Gorgeous.'
African Lion Safari and Game Farm, west off hwy 8, south of Cambridge. 1,500 exotic animals roam this drive-through wild-life park.

INFORMATION/TRAVEL
Convention and Visitors Bureau, 118 King St W, 15th Fl, 546-4222. 'Very helpful.'
Hamilton Street Railway (local transit). Basic fare $1.60. Buses do not serve the airport directly; take #277 to Hwy 53 then a taxi to the airport.

BRANTFORD Chief Joseph Brant brought the Mohawk Indians to settle here at the end of the American Revolution, the tribe having fought with the defeated Loyalist and British North American armies. Her Majesty's Chapel of the Mohawks was built in 1785 and ranks as the oldest church in Ontario and the only royal chapel outside the United Kingdom. King George III himself was pleased to donate money for the cause.

Chief Brant's tomb adjoins the chapel. The annual **Six Nation Indian Pageant**, depicting early Indian history and culture, takes place at the beginning of August. Visit the Six Nations Reserve to see how Native Indians really live.

The town's other claim to fame is **Tutela Heights**, the house overlooking the Grand River Valley where Alexander Graham Bell lived and to which he made the first long distance telephone call, all the way from Paris, Ontario, some eight miles away. The call was made in August 1876, following Bell's first call in Boston.

The telephone area code here and for the area west of Toronto between the lakes is 519.

OF INTEREST

Bell Homestead Museum, 94 Tutela Heights Rd, 756-6220. Bell's birthplace and museum, furnished in style of 1870s. Daily 10am–4.45pm in summer, Tue–Sun rest of yr. Free. (Donations appreciated.)

Brant County Museum, 57 Charlotte St, 752-2483. Indian and pioneer displays. Tue–Fri 9am–5pm, Sat–Sun 1pm–4pm. Closed Mon and Sun outside summer months. $1.50, students $1.

Woodland Indian Cultural Centre and Museum, 184 Mohawk St, 759-2650. Collection of artefacts of Eastern Woodland Indians. Open daily. $3, $2 students.

Brantford Highland Games, held early July. Pipe bands, dancing, caber tossing.

Chiefswood, 8 miles E by Hwy 54, near Middleport, on Indian reservation. 1853 home of 'Mohawk Princess', well-known poetess Pauline Johnson, daughter of Indian Chief Johnson. Her works include *Flint and Feather* and *Legends of Vancouver*. Newly renovated.

INFORMATION

Visitors and Conventions Bureau, 100 Willington Sq, 759-4150. Open 8.30am–4.30pm. Also organises daily tours of town.

NIAGARA FALLS The Rainbow Bridge (25c) which spans the Niagara River connects the cities of Niagara Falls, NY, with Niagara Falls, Ontario, and whichever side of the river you stay on the Canadian side is definitely the better side from which to view the Falls. It's an awe-inspiring sight which somehow manages to remain so despite all the commercial junk and all the jostling crowds you have to fight your way past to get there. Try going at dusk or dawn for a less impeded look, and then again later in the evening when everything is floodlit. Snow and ice add a further grandeur to the scene in winter. (*See Niagara Falls, NY, for further details.*)

ACCOMMODATION

Tourist homes are the best bet here. Beware of taxi drivers who try and take you to motels or the more expensive tourist homes. Suggest you call first, many tourist homes offer a free pick-up service from the bus depot. For accommodation assistance, phone 356-6061.

Mrs J Dick, 5561 McGrail, (416) 354-5569. $25 for one double bed, $36 for two double beds. Open May–Nov. Close to Falls. 'Nice people.'

Henri's Motel, 4671 River Rd, 358-6573. S–$21. 'Very friendly.' 'Decent rooms.'

Maple Leaf Motel, 6163 Buchanan Ave, 354-0841. S–$40, D–$58+. 'Nr Falls and very comfortable.'

Motel Olympia, 5099 Centre St, 356-2614. S–$30, D–$40, less for longer stays. 'They gave us a student discount.'

Niagara Falls Youth Hostel, 4699 Zimmerman Ave, 357-0770. $12 members, $17 non-members, $1 sheet rental. Out by 11am; kitchen facs. Coupons available for local attractions. 'Very cosy and friendly.'
Petersen's Cabins, 11445 Niagara River Pkwy, 295-3517. Cabin $50, sleeps 4. 'Beautiful setting; incls coffee & muffins for breakfast.'
Rainbow View Tourist Home, 4407 John St, 374-1845. S–$40, D–$55. Incls breakfast. Student rooms available—$22 (arrive early). 2 blocks from Falls. 'Great.'
Camping: Riverside Park, 14 kms south on Niagara River Pkwy, on Niagara River banks, 382-2204. $21 for 4, laundry, pool. Open May–mid-Oct.
Oaklands Tent & Trailer Park, 9015 Stanley Ave, 295-8191. 4 miles from Falls. $20 for 4, 'Very friendly, Scottish owner, pool, free showers.' Open May–Oct.

OF INTEREST

***'Maid of the Mist'* boat trip**, 358-5781. The boats pass directly underneath the Falls. Oilskins provided. 'Make sure yours is dry or you'll be miserable.' $8.65. Open 9am–7.45pm. Definitely recommended. 'Most memorable thing I did in North America.' Boats run every 15 mins. Open May–Oct.
Walk under the Falls through tunnels from Table Rock House, $5.25. 'Very amusing.' 'A big con.' 356-7944.
Minolta Tower, 356-1501. 665 ft tall with a restaurant at the top. $5.95, students $4.95.
Skylon Tower, 356-2651. One of the tallest concrete structures in the world. See-through elevator; revolving restaurant at 500 feet. $6.50. Open daily 8am–11pm. 'Arrive first around sunset and see the Falls floodlit by night and then by day.' 'Excellent view.'
Marineland Game Farm, 3657 Portage Rd, 356-8250. Dolphins and sealions. $19.95. 'Rollercoaster, Dragon's Mouth, incredible.' Open 9am–6pm.
Fort George, 468-4257, at Niagara-on-the-Lake. Reconstructed 18th century military post. 10.30am–5.30pm, 9.30am–4.30pm after Labour Day. $2.75, $1.25 with student ID. Whole town of **Niagara-on-the-Lake** is worth a visit. This was the first capital of Ontario and home of the first library, newspaper and law society in Upper Canada. Has a certain 19th century charm. The drive along the Niagara Pkwy from Niagara-on-the-Lake to the Falls is particularly recommended. There is also a bicycle route.
Bright's Winery, 4887 Dorchester Rd, 357-2400. Free tours and samples—Canada's largest winery. Mon–Sat 10.30am–3.30pm, Sun 2.30–3.30pm.
Shaw Festival, Niagara-on-the-Lake. May–Oct, season of Shaw productions. 20 miles from Niagara Falls. Tickets from $20. Box office: 468-2172.
Helicopter rides, 3137 Victoria Ave, 357-5672. $65 for a 9 min tour. 'Expensive, but an amazing experience and impressive views.'
Whirlpool and Rapids, four miles from Falls by sightseeing tour. Aero car and Rapids Broadwalk. 354-4731. 'Not worth the bother.'

INFORMATION

Visitors and Convention Centre, 356-6061. Open 9am–5pm. Weekends 9am–6pm.

TRAVEL

To reach Niagara Falls Airport, USA, (commuter service to Syracuse and connections) catch city bus.
For Buffalo Airport take bus from bus station, $13.
VIA Rail runs 2 trains a day (2 hr journey) from Toronto to the Falls. $37 rt ($22 if bought 1 week in advance). 'A great day trip.' 'Don't catch shuttle bus from station to the Falls. It costs $3.50 and it's only a 10-min. walk.'

KITCHENER-WATERLOO A little bit of Germany lives exiled in Kitchener-Waterloo, a community delighting in beer halls and beer fests. The highlight of the year is the Oktoberfest, a weeklong festival of German bands, beer, parades, dancing, sporting events and more beer.

Waterloo is often referred to as the 'Hartford of Canada' since the town is headquarters of a number of national insurance companies. The best days to visit K-W (a fairly easy 69-mile excursion from Toronto) are Wednesday and Saturday in time for the farmers' market where black-bonneted and gowned Amish and Mennonite farming ladies and their menfolk sell their crafts and fresh-picked produce. Sixteen miles north at **Elmira**, there's the annual Maple Syrup Festival, held in the spring.

ACCOMMODATION
Kitchener Motel, 1485 Victoria St N, 745-1177. D–$40 and up.
The Olde Heidelberg Brewery & Restaurant, S–$40, D–$45.
YWCA, 84 Frederick St, Kitchener, 744-0120. $35, breakfast included.

OF INTEREST
Kitchener is the site of Woodside, boyhood home of **William Lyon Mackenzie King**, Prime Minister from 1921 to 1930 and 1935 to 1948. His former home at 528 Wellington St, is open to the public during the summer, 10am–5pm daily. Free. For info: 742-5273.
Doon Heritage Crossroads, south of town on Huron Rd, 748-1914. Exit 275 (Doon Blair Rd) off Hwy 401. Re-creation of rural Waterloo County village of 1914. Open daily May–Dec 10am–4.30pm. $5, $3 students.

INFORMATION
Kitchener Chamber of Commerce, 576-5000. Open 9am–5pm.

GEORGIAN BAY ISLANDS NATIONAL PARK A good way north of Toronto on the way to Sudbury, this is one of Canada's smallest national parks. It consists of 30 islands or parts of islands in Georgian Bay. The largest of the islands, Beausoleil, is just five miles square, while all the rest combined add only two-fifths of a mile.

The special feature of the park is the remarkable geological formations. The mainly Precambrian rock is more than 600 million years old and there are a few patches of sedimentary rock carved in strange shapes by glaciers.

Midland is the biggest nearby town for services and accommodation but boats to Beausoleil Island go from **Honey Harbour**, a popular summer resort off Route 103. On Beausoleil, once the home of the Chippewa Indians, there are several campsites.

The telephone area code is 705 for Midland, 519 for London and Stratford.

ACCOMMODATION
Park Villa Motel, 751 Yonge St W, adjoining Little Lake Pk, Midland, 526-2219. D–$67 and up. Heated pool. Open year-round.
Chalet Motel, on Little Lake, 748 Yonge St W, 526-6571. $40 and up.

OF INTEREST
Huronia Museum and Indian Village, off King St, in Little Lake Park, 526-2844. Open year-round. Mon–Sat 9am–5.30pm, Sun 10am–5.30pm. $5.
Sainte-Marie Among the Hurons, 3 miles east on Hwy 12, 526-7838. $5.75, $3.50 students. Re-creation of Jesuit mission which stood here 1639–1649 plus Huron

longhouses, cookhouse, blacksmith, etc. Orientation centre offers a colour film about the mission and the excavation work involved in the project. Daily 10am–6pm.
30,000 Island Cruise, at Midland Dock. Two and a half hour trip among the islands of Georgian Bay. 10.45am, 1.45pm, 4.30pm (from June) and 7.15pm (after July 19). $13. Call for reservations and info: 526-0161.
Wye Marsh Wildlife Centre, Hwy 12, 526-7809. Guided tours, animals, exhibits, floating boardwalk. Daily 10am–6pm. $5, $3.50 students.

INFORMATION
Georgian Bay Islands National Park, 756-2415.
Midland Chamber of Commerce, 526-7884. Open Mon–Fri 8am–6pm, Sat–Sun 10am–6pm.

LONDON Not to be outdone by the other London back in Mother Britain, this one also has a River Thames flowing through the middle of the city. London, Ontario, also has its own Covent Garden Market. It's a town of comfortable size, and a commercial and industrial centre. Labatt's Brewery is perhaps the town's most famous industry.

London also offers the visitor a thriving cultural life. It is physically a pleasant spot, known as 'Forest City', and is situated midway between Toronto and Detroit. The University of Western Ontario is here and is said to have the most beautiful campus of any Canadian university. You will find it on the banks of the Thames, in the northern part of the city.

ACCOMMODATION
Univ of Western Ontario, Alumni House, Dept of Housing, 661-3814. May–Aug. Reservations required. S–$27, shared washroom, laundry, pool, continental breakfast.

FOOD
Fatty Patty's, 207 King St, 438-7281. Burgers, fries and salads in huge portions. Open daily 11am–10pm, closed Sunday.
Joe Kool's, 595 Richmond St, 'right in centre—ask a local'. Tortillas, burgers, etc; 'good music'.
Prince Albert's Diner, Richmond St at Prince Albert. 50s-style diner with great cheap meals.
Spageddy Eddy, 428 Richmond St, 673-3213. Copious canneloni, seas of spaghetti with lashings of lasagne. Open 11am–9pm, til later at weekends.

OF INTEREST
Eldon House, 481 Ridout St. London's oldest house and now a historical museum. Noon–5pm, closed Mon. $3.
The Museum of Indian Archaeology and Pioneer Life, 1600 Attawandaron Rd, 473-1360. Open daily 10am–5pm. Adults $4, students, $2.75.
London Regional Art Gallery, 421 Ridout St N, 672-4580. Open daily noon–5pm. Closed Mon.
Fanshawe Pioneer Village, Fanshawe Pk, off Clarke Rd, 457-1296. Re-creation of 19th century pre-railroad village. Log cabins, etc. Daily 10am–4.30pm. Adults $5. Students $4.
Children's Museum, 21 Wharncliffe Road South, 434-5726. World cultures, communications, music and crafts. 'Excellent.' Daily 10am–5pm. Adults $3.50, children $3.
Royal Canadian Regiment Museum, Wolseley, on Canadian Forces Base, London, 660-5102. History of Canadian forces from 1883. Tues–Fri 10am–4pm, Sat, Sun 12pm–4pm. Closed Mon. Free.

Springbank Park, Springbank Dr. Nice for walking or for taking a ride on the mini train in summer. The *London Princess* leaves hourly from 1pm for a 45 min river cruise along the Thames. Adults $6.95, 473-0363.

INFORMATION
Visitors and Convention Services, 300 Dufferin Ave, City Hall, 661-5000. Open 8.30am–4.30pm.
Visitors Center, 360 Wellington Rd S, 681-4047. Open daily 8am–8pm.

ENTERTAINMENT
The Spoke, Somerville House, University of Western Ontario. A popular campus pub.
The Ceeps/Barney's, 671 Richmond St. The local hangout. Cheap draught beer in the Ceeps. Arrive early to get a spot on the patio in the summer.
Call the Office, 216 York St, east of Richmond. Live bands.
Second City, 340 Wellington St, 439-0521. Canadian comedians.
Western Fair, western Fairgrounds. Agricultural show and fair with midway rides and games. Held in mid-September.

TRAVEL
Greyhound, 101 York at Talbot, 434-3250 or (800) 661-8747.
VIA Rail, on York east of Richmond, 672-5722 or (800) 677-1645.

STRATFORD In 1953 this average-sized manufacturing town, on the banks of the River Avon some 50 kilometres north of London, held its first Shakespearian festival. The now world-renowned season has become an annual highlight on the Ontario calendar. The festival lasts for 22 weeks from mid-June, attracting some of the best Shakespearian actors and actresses, as well as full houses every night.

Based on the Festival Theatre, but encompassing several other theatres too, the festival includes opera, original contemporary drama and music, as well as the best of the Bard. In September the town also hosts an international film festival.

There's not much else of interest in Stratford except a walk along the riverside gardens and a look at the swans. Heading west there is Point Pelee National Park before going to Windsor and crossing to the US.

ACCOMMODATION
The Festival Theatre provides an accommodation service during the summer. You are advised to contact them first, 271-4040.
Burnside Guest Home, B&B, 139 William St, 271-7076. S–$45, D–$60. Turn of the century home.
Kent Hotel, 209 Waterloo St S, 271-7805. From S–$50, D–$55.
Rosecourt Motel, 599 Erie St, 271-6005. D–$66; 4 person suite $119.
Camping: Wildwood Conservation Ground, 284-2292. 7 miles W on Hwy 7, $17 per night.

ENTERTAINMENT
Festival Theatre. Tickets from $20–$50, Festival Theatre, Third Stage and Avon Theatre. The Festival Theatre is at 55 Queen St, Avon Theatre on Downie St, Third Stage on Lakeshore. Order from: Festival Box Office, PO Box 520, Stratford, ONT N5A 6V2. Call: 273-1600. Special student matinees in Sept and Oct often swamped by high school parties. 'Get there early on the day of the performance for returns.' $10.50–$12.50.
Stratford Farmers' Market, Coliseum Fairground, Sat mornings.

INFORMATION

Stratford Chamber of Commerce, 88 Wellington St, top floor, 271-5140. Mon–Fri 8.30am–4pm.
Tourist Info Centre, 30 York St, 273-3352. Open April–Oct; daily 9am–8pm (Tue–Fri), Sat–Mon 9am–5pm.

POINT PELEE NATIONAL PARK About 35 miles from Windsor, Point Pelee is a V-shaped sandspit which juts out into Lake Erie. On the same latitude as California, the park is the southernmost area of the Canadian mainland.

Only six square miles in area, Point Pelee is a unique remnant of the original deciduous forests of North America. Two thousand acres of the park are a freshwater swamp and the wildlife found here is unlike anything else to be seen in Canada. On the spring and fall bird migration routes, the park is a paradise for ornithologists. There are also several strange fish to be seen and lots of turtles and small water animals ambling around.

Point Pelee is quite developed as a tourist attraction and there are numerous nature trails, including a one-mile boardwalk trail. Canoes and bicycles can be rented during the summer months and the Visitor Centre has maps, exhibits, slide shows and other displays about the park. Entrance to the park is $5 per day. There is no camping in Point Pelee, although there are two sites in the nearby town of Leamington. For info: 322-2365.

SUDBURY Sudbury is some 247 miles northwest of Toronto and the centre of one of the richest mining areas in the world. The local Chamber of Commerce will tell you that Sudbury enjoys more hours of sunshine per year than any other city in Ontario (and we have no reason to doubt them), but this is not a pretty area. Part of the empty landscape looks so like a moonscape that American astronauts came here to rehearse lunar rock collection techniques before embarking on the real thing.

However away from the immediate vicinity of the town there are scores of lakes, rivers and untracked forests to refresh the soul after witnessing the ravages of civilisation. The city is often referred to as the 'nickel capital of the world'. Be sure to see the lunar landscape of Sudbury basin, a geological mystery that may have been caused by a gigantic meteor or volcanic eruption.

With more than 30 sparkling lakes and thousands of acres of protected woodlands, Sudbury has plenty to offer outdoor lovers as well. In summer enjoy swimming, canoeing, hiking, and cycling. Alpine and cross-country skiing are big in winter.

The telephone area code is 705.

ACCOMMODATION

Cheapest in the Ukrainian District, around Kathleen St. There is usually hostel accommodation available here in summer, but as with other cities in Canada locations change year to year. For current hostel info, call Canadian Hostelling Association, (613) 748-5638.

Laurentian University, Ramsey Lake Rd, 673-6597. They are helpful and provide accommodation in summer.

Plaza Hotel, 1436 Bellevue St, 566-8080. $65 a week, without bath.

Sudbury International Hostel, 302 Cedar St, 674-0104, $10 members, $14 non-members. Open 24 May–Sept 8. Kitchen, laundry facs, on-site parking, TV room and tourist info.

OF INTEREST
Free guided tours are available of the **INCO Smelter** at Copper Cliff, 4 miles west of town on Highway 17. The smelter is the world's largest single smelting operation and is open to visitors. Call 673-5659 for slagpouring info. They'll direct you to the current slagpouring site. Slag is the 2100°F molten waste. 'Hot show.' $7.
Copper Cliff Museum, Sudbury Parks and Recreation Dept, 674-3141 ext 457. Open June–Sept, Mon–Fri 10am–4pm, closed noon–1pm.
Big Nickel Mine and Numismatic Park, at Hwy 17 West & Big Nickel Mine Dr, 673-5659. 3 miles west of Sudbury. Daily 9am–6pm; $6.50, $4.25 students.
Science North, Ramsey Lake Rd and Paris St, 1 mile from Hwy 69 S, 522-3700. Excellent science museum. Open daily, summer 9am–6pm, $7.95, $5.25 students.

INFORMATION/TRAVEL
Chamber of Commerce, 100 Elm St W, 673-7133.
Visitor Info Centre, 200 Brady St, Civic Sq, 674-3141.
Rainbow Country Travel Assoc, 1984 Region's St S, Cedar Pointe Mall, next to Casey's, 522-0104. Open Mon–Fri 8.30am–4.30pm (summer), 9am–5pm (winter).

SAULT STE MARIE First established in 1669 as a French Jesuit mission, Sault Ste Marie later became an important trading post in the heyday of the fur trade. Today 'The Soo', as locals call the town, oversees the great locks and canals that bypass St Mary's Rapids. The **Soo Locks**, connecting Lake Superior with St Mary's River and Lake Huron, allow enormous Atlantic ocean freighters to make the journey 1748 miles inland. From special observation towers visitors can watch the ships rising and falling up to 40 feet.

The town is connected to its US namesake across the river in Michigan by an auto toll bridge. If you're going north from here, 'think twice about hitching'. Lifts are hard to come by, the road is long and empty. It's probably best to get as far beyond **Wawa** as possible. Thunder Bay is 438 miles away to the northwest. Two of the most popular local events are the **Bon Soo Winter Carnival**, which runs from January to February, and the **Northern Triathalon** in August. From late September to mid-October, the foliage colours are spectacular and the weather is perfect for hiking. This is also an excellent time to catch the **Agawa Canyon Train**.

ACCOMMODATION
Algoma Cabins & Motel, 1713 Queen St E, 256-8681. D–$40, $200 weekly.
Ambassador Motel, 1275 17 N, 759-6199. D–$47 up.
Rocky Mountain Ranch Hostel, 2881 Valleyview Road, 897-4931. 10 min north of Sudbury. $12. Situated on a 230-acre horse ranch—an ideal place to enjoy the outdoor life; riding, hiking, volleyball and swimming all available.
Youth Hostel, 864 Queens St E, 253-2311, $21 YH, $23 non-members. Cooking facs. Linen rental, on-site parking, canoe rental.
Camping: Woody's Campsites, Hwy 17 N, 12 kms north, 777-2638. $8.50 for 2.

FOOD
Ernie's Coffee Shop, 13 Queen St. 'Big, cheap meals, excellent value.'

OF INTEREST
Lock Tours. 2-hr round trip cruises through both the Canadian and American (which are the world's busiest) locks. Dep from McLean Dock, Foster Dr, next to the Civic Centre. Also takes in St Mary's River. Daily in summer, $14.50. Info: 253-9850.

Agawa Canyon Wilderness Tours, from Algoma Central Railway Terminal, 129 Bay St. Rail excursion to wilderness, scenic areas. Daily dep 8am, ret 5pm. $44 round trip. For info: 254-4331.
***MS Norgoma* Museum Ship**, Norgoma Dock at Foster Dr. The last of the overnight passenger cruise ships built on the Great Lakes, the ship plied the Owen Sound to Sault Ste Marie route from 1950 to 1963. Daily 10am–6pm June, Sept; July–Aug 9am–8pm. Donations. For info: 759-7278.
The Old Stone House, 831 Queen St E, 759-5443. Completed 1814 and a rare example of early Canadian architecture. Restored. Daily 10am–5pm. Donations.
Lake Superior Provincial Park. A fair ride north of here—some 130 kms—but nonetheless worth the trip to this rugged wilderness park. Includes nature trails, moose hunting in season, Indian rock paintings and a fine beach.

INFORMATION
Sault Ste Marie Chamber of Commerce, 360 Great Northern Rd, 949-7152.
Ministry of Tourism, 120 Huron St. Open daily.
Hospitality and Travel Sault Ste Marie, 99 Foster Dr, 759-5432.

THUNDER BAY On the northern shore of Lake Superior and an amalgam of the towns of Port Arthur and Fort William, Thunder Bay is the western Canadian terminus of the Great Lakes/St Lawrence Seaway system and Canada's third largest port. Port Arthur is known as Thunder Bay North and Fort William is Thunder Bay South. The towns are the main outlet for Prairies grain and have a reputation for attracting swarms of huge, and hungry, black flies during the summer.

The city's new name was selected by plebiscite and is derived from the name of the bay and Thunder Cape, 'The Sleeping Giant', a shoreline landmark. Lake Superior is renowned for its frequent thunderstorms and since in Indian legend the thunderbird was responsible for thunder, lightning and rain, that was how the bay got its name. The city is 450 miles from Winnipeg to the west, and about the same distance from Sault Ste Marie to the southeast.
The telephone area code is 807.

ACCOMMODATION
Circle Inn Motel, 686 Memorial Ave, 344-5744. S–$48, D–$55. 'Reasonably close to the bus terminal.'
Confederation College, Sibley Hall Residence, 960 William St. Rooms available until the end of August. S–$34, D–$28 per person. Call 475-6383 for availability.
Lakehead University Residence, Oliver Rd, 343-8512. May–Aug with student ID S–$12, D–$10 per person. Also weekly rates: single $78, double (per person) $70.
Thunder Bay Backpackers' International Hostel, Lakeshore Dr and McKenzie Stn Rd, 983-2042. $13; tenting, $9. 'Friendly, warm hostel, baths, TV.' 'The best in Canada.'

OF INTEREST
Thunder Bay Historical Society Museum, 219 S May St, 623-0801. Indian artefacts and general pioneering exhibits. Daily, June–Aug 11am–5pm; 1pm–5pm other months. Free.
The Sleeping Giant. He of the Indian folk legends from whom the town derives its name. Impressively visible across the bay in Lake Superior.
Old Fort William. On the banks of the Kaministiquia River, 577-8461. Once a major outpost of the North West Trading Company, now a 'living' reconstruction. Craft shops, farm, dairy, naval yard, Indian encampment, breadmaking, musket firing, etc. Daily 10am–5pm. $7.25, students $3.75.

Amethyst Mine. 35 miles on Trans Canada Highway, then north on E Loon Lake Rd, 622-6908. Open daily 10am–7pm. Admission $1.
Centennial Park, east of Arundel St, 683-6511. Animal farm, a museum and a reproduction of a typical northern Ontario logging camp of the early 1900s. Open daily 8am–dark. Free.
Chippewa Park, south off Hwy 61, 623-8592. A wooded park on Lake Superior with a sandy beach, camping, picnic grounds, a funfair and wildlife exhibit. Open daily, late June–Labour Day.
Hillcrest Park, High St. A lookout point with a panoramic view of Thunder Bay Harbour and the famous Sleeping Giant.

INFORMATION
Convention and Visitors Bureau, Patterson Park Info, 520 Leith St, 625-2149 or (800) 667-8386.
Pagoda Info Centre, Water St, 345-6812, open 8.30am–8.30pm daily in summer.

TOURS/TRAVEL
Harbour cruises, on *Welcome* ship, from Port Arthur Marina, Arthur St, 344-2512. Several cruises, daily, mid-May to Oct, from $12.
Greyhound/Grey Goose, 815 Fort William Rd, by SKAFF, 345-2194. Open daily.

ONTARIO'S NORTHLANDS Going north out of Toronto on the Trans Canada Highway, you can carry on round to Sudbury, Sault Ste Marie and Thunder Bay, or else, at Orillia, you can get on to Route 11 which will take you up to North Bay, and from there to Ontario's little-explored north country. **North Bay** is 207 miles from Toronto and is a popular vacation spot as well as the accepted jumping off point for the polar regions.

There's not much in North Bay itself, but there is ready access to the **Algonquin Provincial Park**, a vast area of woods and lakes good for hiking, canoeing and camping, and also to **Lake Nipissing**. Pressing north, however, there is **Temagami**, a hunting, fishing, lumbering, mining and outfitting centre. The Temagami Provincial Forest was the province's pioneer forest, established in 1901 and providing mile upon mile of sparkling lakes and rugged forests. It's quiet country up here; even with modern communication systems, people are few. It's also mining country. **Cobalt** is the centre of a silver mining area and **Timmins** is the largest silver and zinc producing district in the world. You can visit mines and mining museums in both towns.

At **Cochrane**, 207 miles north of North Bay, the northbound highway runs out, and the rest of the way is by rail. The **Polar Bear Express** runs daily except Friday during the summer (June 27–September 7) up to Moosonee on James Bay, covering the 186 miles in four and a half hours ($47 round trip). After September, the **Little Bear** runs three times a week ($76 r/t). For reservations (required): (800) 268-9281 from 416, 705, 613, 519 or (416) 314-3750 in Toronto. It's a marvellous ride, the train packed with an odd assortment of people, everyone from tourists to miners, missionaries, geologists and adventurers. Before boarding the train for the trip north there is the **Cochrane Railway Museum** to visit. Housed in an engine and four coaches, the museum traces the history of the James Bay Frontier. **Moosonee** counts as one of the last of the genuine frontier towns and is accessible only by rail or air. Since 1673 when the Hudson Bay Company established a post on nearby Moose Factory Island, this has been an important rendezvous for fur traders and Indians. It's also a good place to see the full beauty of the Aurora Borealis.

This is as far north as most people get, but there's still a lot of Ontario lapped by Arctic seas. Over 250 miles north of Moosonee by air, there's **Polar Bear Provincial Park**. This is a vast area of tundra and sub-arctic wilderness. The summer is short and the climate severe. The rewards of a visit here can be great however. There are polar bears, black bears, arctic foxes, wolves, otters, seals, moose and many other varieties of wildlife to be seen in plenty.

ACCOMMODATION

All the towns mentioned above have small hotels or motels, none of them especially cheap however. If planning to come this far off the beaten track, it is advisable to give yourself plenty of time to find places to stay. Remember that if everything is full in one town your next options may be several hours' driving further down the road. There are many campgrounds in this part of Ontario, but again the distances between them are often considerable.

QUÉBEC

Québec is the largest province in Canada—its area is seven times that of the United Kingdom—and it really has a character all its own. The vast majority of French Canadians live here in La Belle Province, and the French culture is apparent in all walks of life—from the French-only street signs in Montréal and Québec City to the smaller, rural towns where the only language you'll hear is French interspersed with expressions in 'joual'—a dialect used mostly in Northern Québec. Some Québecois may seem reluctant to speak English to the visitor; in the bigger cities, however, the shopkeepers will understand enough to serve you, and you may find the younger Québecois eager to practice their English.

The name of the province is derived from the Algonquin Indian word 'Kebec', meaning 'where the river narrows'. This reference to the St Lawrence River indicates both the important role the river played in the development of the province in the 18th and 19th centuries and its continued importance for Québec's economy today. Four-fifths of the province lies within the area of the barren Canadian Shield to the north. The atmosphere in the smaller, unassuming rural towns contrasts sharply with the cosmopolitan sophistication of Montréal and the Old World charm of Québec City.

National Parks: Forillon, La Mauricie, Auguittuq.

MONTRÉAL Canada's largest city is built around the mountain, Mount Royal, from which it derives its name. Located on the archipelago at the junction of the Outaouais and Saint-Laurent Rivers, Montréal is a natural meeting point for overland and water passages.

Jacques Cartier arrived here in 1535 to find a large Indian settlement, Hochelaga, believed to have been where McGill University now stands. When Champlain arrived, nearly 100 years later, the Indians had gone, and the French subsequently settled there. Their city is now one of the world's greatest inland ports, boasting some 14 miles of berthing space. Since the opening of the St Lawrence Seaway in 1959, the city's port-based industries have greatly expanded and increased, making Montréal one of North America's most important commercial, industrial and economic centres.

More than two-fifths of the total population of Québec live in the Montréal metropolitan area. Two-thirds of Montréalers speak French, and as a result their city is second only to Paris in terms of French-speaking population.

Host city for Expo '67 and the 1976 Summer Olympics, Montréal is forever improving, expanding, renovating. Theatre and the arts flourish. There is always something to do here, and Montréalers consider their city to provide the best of everything in Canada—the best restaurants, shopping, nightclubs, the best bagels, and the best smoked-meat sandwiches (the last of which may in fact be true). This is a cosmopolitan vibrant city whose liveliness is epitomized in Vieux Montréal, on Crescent Street, or on Rue St Denis where you can mingle with the French Canadians and discover a part of the culture and joie de vivre that is neither North American, nor European, but unique unto itself.

The telephone area code is 514.

ACCOMMODATION

A L'Américain, 1042 Rue St Denis, 849-0616. S–$39, D–$45. Highly recommended. 'Friendly people, large rooms, and close to Old Montréal.'

Armor Tourist Rooms, 157 Sherbrooke St, 285-0140. S/D from $38. 'Clean and friendly, close to cafés, bus terminal, metro and shops.'

Castel St Denis Tourist Rooms, 2099 Rue St Denis, 842-9719. S–$39, D–$45.

Collège Français, 5155 Rue De Gaspé, 495-2581. $12 dorm. 'Clean and simple.' Take Metro to Laurier.

Maison Kent, 1216 Rue St-Hubert, 845-9835. S–$52, D–$57. Central, 3 mins from bus station. Free parking. AC. TV.

Métro Motel, 9925 Lajeunesse, 382-9780. S/D from $45. TV. 'Car necessary.'

Le Breton, 1609 Rue St Hubert, 524-7273. S–$33, D–$47. AC. TV.

Maison André Tourist Rooms, 3511 Rue University, 849-4092. S–$26, D–$38 up. 'Clean and comfortable'.

B&B à Montréal, 4912 Victoria Ave, 738-9410.

B&B Downtown Network, 3458 Laval Ave, 289-9749. S–$40 up, D–$55 up, incl b/fast.

University Residences: Concordia, 7141 Sherbrooke Ouest, 848-4755. Students $19 per night, D–$38; non-students S–$26, D–$40.

McGill, 3935 University St, 398-6367. Students $26.50 per night, non-students $30, weekly $115. Shared washroom, laundry, kitchenettes.

Université de Montréal, 2350 Edouard Montpetit, 343-6531. Students $23, non-students $35. Weekly rates. Inexpensive cafeteria on campus. Easy access by bus. 'Highly recommended for value, location, ambience and comfort.' Open mid-May–August.

Note: Both Concordia and McGill are English-speaking universities.

Auberge de Montréal (Youth Hostel), 3541 Aylmer, 843-3317. $15 members, $19 non-members. Kitchen facs. 'Clean, safe, friendly.'

YMCA, 1450 Ave Stanley, 849-8393. S–$30, D–$48.

YWCA, 1355 René Lévesque Blvd Ouest, 866-9941. S–$30, D–$54.

Camping: Paul Sauvé State Park, 659-3451, on Lac des Deux Montagnes (about 60 km from Montréal via Routes 13 or 15). $12–$17 for a campsite, depending on amenities. 'Friendly staff, lovely lake, ideal for swimming.' Crowded in summer, make reservations for groups. Guided nature walks, fishing, sleigh rides.

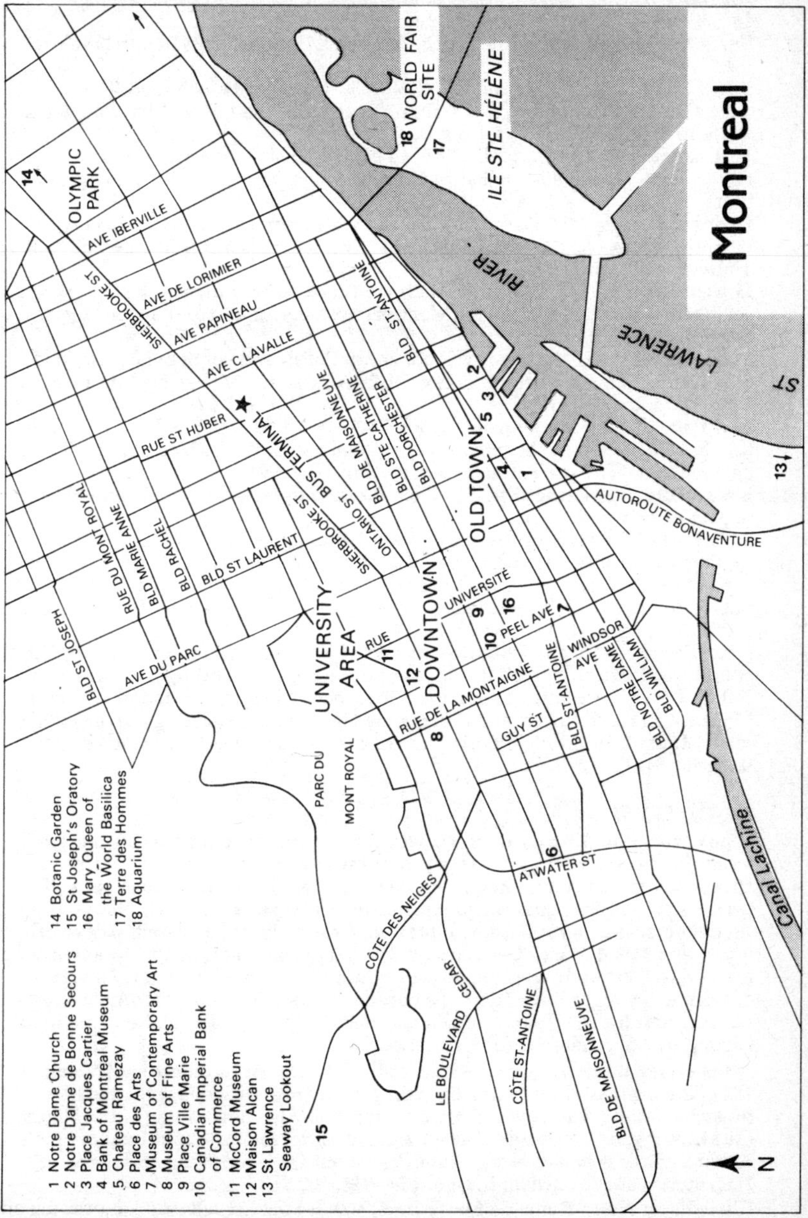
Montreal
1 Notre Dame Church
2 Notre Dame de Bonne Secours
3 Place Jacques Cartier
4 Bank of Montreal Museum
5 Chateau Ramezay
6 Place des Arts
7 Museum of Contemporary Art
8 Museum of Fine Arts
9 Place Ville Marie
10 Canadian Imperial Bank of Commerce
11 McCord Museum
12 Maison Alcan
13 St Lawrence Seaway Lookout
14 Botanic Garden
15 St Joseph's Oratory
16 Mary Queen of the World Basilica
17 Terre des Hommes
18 Aquarium
OLYMPIC PARK
18 WORLD FAIR SITE
ILE STE HÉLÈNE
ST LAWRENCE RIVER
AVE IBERVILLE
AVE DE LORIMIER
AVE PAPINEAU
AVE C LAVALLE
SHERBROOKE ST
RUE ST HUBER
BUS TERMINAL
BLD DE MAISONNEUVE
BLD STE CATHERINE
BLD DORCHESTER
BLD ST-ANTOINE
ONTARIO ST
OLD TOWN
DOWNTOWN
UNIVERSITY AREA
AUTOROUTE BONAVENTURE
RUE DU MONT ROYAL
RUE MARIE ANNE
BLD RACHEL
BLD ST LAURENT
BLD ST JOSEPH
AVE DU PARC
RUE UNIVERSITÉ
PEEL AVE
WINDSOR AVE
BLD NOTRE DAME
BLD WILLIAM
RUE DE LA MONTAIGNE
GUY ST
PARC DU MONT ROYAL
CÔTE DES NEIGES
ATWATER ST
LE BOULEVARD
CEDAR
CÔTE ST-ANTOINE
BLD DE MAISONNEUVE
Canal Lachine
N

FOOD

Amelio's, 3565 Lorne Ave, 845-8396. Italian-style pizza and pasta, average meal $6–$7. McGill 'ghetto', 'intimate atmosphere'.

Ben's, 990 Maisonneuve. Cheap deli, 7am–4am. Famous for its Montréal smoked meat. 'Delightfully tacky decor.'

Boeuf à la Mode, 273 St-Paul Est, 866-0963. 'Excellent French food.'

Café Commun/Commune, 201 Milton. Vegetarian food served by volunteers. Close to McGill. 'Artsy.'

La Cabanne, St Laurent, 843-7283. Cheapish shish-kabob-type food in good atmosphere. Upstairs is the Bar St Laurent where you can play pool and drink beer.

Carlos & Pepe's, 1420 Peel, 288-3090. Spicy assortment of Mexican delicacies—burritos, salsas, sangria plus a live band. Average meal $10–$15. Open till 1am, Thurs–Sat till 3am.

Le Faubourg. Food-hall on St Catherine St filled with various cafes and shops selling fresh produce and serving Montréal cuisine. Home of the famous Montréal Bagel Bakery.

Mazurka, 64 Prince Arthur E. 'Good, cheap Polish and continental style food.'

Sun Heung, La Gauchetiere E, 866-5912. A little seedy, but has the greatest Chinese food.

Peel Pub, 1106 de Maisonneuve Ouest, 845-9002. Old-fashioned tavern, serves fish and chips, beer by the pitcher. Big student hangout. Much recommended by past readers. 'The place if on a budget.' Breakfast 99¢.

L'Anecdote, 801 Rachel Est, 526-7967. Great burgers and vegetarian tofu hot dogs. Open 9am–9.45pm.

La Paryse, 302 Ontario E, 842-2040. 'Best hamburgers in Montreal.'

La Pizzaiolle, 1446A Crescent Est, 845-4158. 'Good, cheap pizza in attractive surroundings. Ceasar salad and dessert (L'*indulgent*) are recommended.'

There are many **Greek** restaurants on Prince Arthur E between St Laurent and Carre St Louis. Definitely worth a try.

Note: Prince Arthur and Duluth Streets both have 'bring your own wine' restaurants (Fr: *apportez vin*) which cool and serve any bottle you bring. Great meals for $10. St-Denis, the centre of numerous clubs, bars, cafes, and restaurants, reflects Montreal's French culture and is frequented by a heterogeneous group including many students from neighbouring universities. A preppier crowd tends to gravitate towards Crescent St.

OF INTEREST

Vieux Montréal. Situated on the Lower Terrace, this area includes business and local government sectors. In recent times the buildings lining the old narrow streets have received facelifts, funds being provided from the public, as well as private, purse. The squares and streets are best explored on foot. **Notre-Dame Bonsecours**, and **St-Paul** make for pleasant strolls. Not to be missed, particularly if you don't plan to visit Québec City. During the summer months Montréalers are avid walkers and there is street activity until all hours of the night. As a result, one can enjoy night-life without the burden of urban paranoia. Pick up excellent walking tour leaflets from the city's information bureaux. To get there: metro to Champ-de-Mars, Place d'Armes or Victoria.

Notre-Dame Basilica, Place d'Armes, 849-1070. The city's oldest parish built in 1829. The wonderful vaulted starry ceiling, extraordinary wood work and beautiful stained-glass windows never fail to impress. Also houses one of the largest Casavant organs ever made. The gilded interior threatens to 'out-Pugin Pugin'. 'Interior decor is breathtaking.' June 25–Labour Day 7am–8pm; rest of the year 7am–6pm. Tours available. Museum $1, 842-2925.

Chapelle de Notre-Dame de Bonsecours, 400 St-Paul Est. Overlooking the harbour and known as the 'sailors' church'. Built in 1771 and the oldest church still standing in the city, it was once an important landmark for helmsmen navigating the river. There is a fine view from the top of the tower. It has been dedicated to sailors since the original chapel was erected in 1657.

Place Jacques Cartier. Once Montréal's farmers' market. The restored Bonsecours Market building is on the south side of the square. This square also features the first monument to Nelson erected anywhere in the world. You can buy food at the stalls or sit at a street cafe and listen to a jazz band. 'Touristy.'

Bank of Montreal Museum, Place d'Armes. Coins, documents and general banking memorabilia tracing Montréal's history as the country's financial centre. 10am–4pm, closed noon–1pm, Mon–Fri, 877-6892. Free admission.

Château Ramezay, 280 Rue Notre-Dame Est, 861-3708. Built in 1705 by Claude de Ramezay, a governor of Montréal, the building is a prime example of the architecture of the time and contains a wealth of furniture, engravings, oil paintings, costumes and other items relating to 18th century life. Open 10am–4.30pm. Closed Mon Sept–May. $5, $3 students.

The Upper Terrace. Flanking the southern edge of the mountain, the area includes a considerable part of the city stretching east and west for several miles. At its heart was the Indian town of Hochelaga, discovered by Cartier in 1535, standing not far from the present site of **McGill**. The high-rise area through which run **Sherbrooke, Maisonneuve, Ste-Catherine Sts** and **Dorchester Blvd** is the urban centre where metro, bus and rail lines converge. It is also where the major hotels and shops are situated. Beyond Blvd St-Laurent, Montréal is entirely French. On the western half of the Upper Terrace is the City of **Westmount**, famous for its stately mansions, fine churches and public buildings.

Place des Arts, Rue Ste-Catherine, 842-2112. Montréal's cultural complex. Features concert, dance and theatrical performances. Free lunchtime concerts, Sat and Sun.

Musée d'Art Contemporain, 185 Ste Catherine W, 847-6226. The only institution of its type in Canada dedicated exclusively to all forms of contemporary art including paintings, sculpture, multi-media and performance art. Call information on special showings. 11am–6pm, closed Mon. Wed 6pm–9pm free, otherwise $4.75, $2.75 students.

Museum of Fine Arts (*Musée des Beaux-arts*), 1379 Sherbrooke St, 285-1600. The oldest established museum in Canada—founded in 1860—housed in a magnificent neoclassical edifice built in 1912. An extensive permanent collection, including many treasures and decorative arts which date from 3,000 BC is found throughout the 34 rooms. Call for information about new displays. Admission $9.50, $4.75 students. Open Tue–Sun, 10am–5pm. Closed Mon.

Maison Alcan, 1184 Rue Sherbrooke Ouest, 848-8000. Base of operations for the world's second largest aluminium manufacturer. Art and architecture. Mid-day choral performances in atrium. Eateries. Métro: Peel.

St Lawrence Seaway Lookout (*Voie maritime du St-Laurent*), Côte Ste Catherine and Beauharnois Locks, 672-4110.

Maisonneuve Park, 4601 Sherbrooke St E, 872-6211. 525-acre park with a botanical garden, golf course, picnic areas and skating rink.

Mount Royal Park. On a fine day the views from the 763 foot slope are spectacular. The view encompasses St Lawrence and Ottawa Rivers, the Adirondacks (New York State), and the Green Mountains (Vermont). It is also an excellent place to admire the nightscape of Montréal. During the summer: open-air concerts, winters: skiing and skating.

St Joseph's Oratory. On the north slope of Westmount Mountain which is separated by a narrow cleft from Mount Royal. The Oratory dome is a marked feature of the Montréal skyline. The world's largest pilgrimage centre, including a remarkable 'way of the cross', the original chapel and two museums containing memorabilia of founder Brother André and religious art. Also famous for its cures said to have been affected through the prayers of the 'Miracle Man of Montréal'. Daily 6.30am–9.30pm. Admission free. 733-8211. Museum is open 10am–5pm. Donations. Saint Joseph is the patron saint of Canada.

Mary, Queen of the World Cathedral, Rue de la Cathedrale on Dominion Sq. Small-scale version of St Peters in Rome. Built 1878.
Nearby: St Helen's Island (*Ile Ste-Hélène*). Beautiful park. 'Take picnic for a quiet day away from the city.' Metro from Berri de Montigny.
Terre des Hommes (*Man and His World*), St Helen's Island. Site of Expo '67, now a permanent cultural and entertainment centre. Many of the Expo buildings survive but the whole place shuts up after Labour Day. 'Well worth a day—lots of free exhibitions and music, fascinating buildings.' Also includes **La Ronde**, an amusement park at the eastern end of the island—'sensational waterskiing shows'. For information on both, 872-6222. Open weekends in May. Starting in June, open daily 11am–11pm. Day passes available. La Ronde, $10.50, unlimited, $19. Roller-coaster, Le Monstre—'very scary'.
Biodôme, 4777 Pierre-De-Coubertin Avenue, 868-3000. This recently opened attraction (June 1992), offers you the chance to explore the 1001 wonders of Naturalia from all remote corners of the planet. Tropical Rainforest, Desert, Polar and Sea Worlds all under one dome. Located next to the Olympic Stadium and Botanical Gardens. Open 9am–6pm (8pm in summer). Admission $8.50.
Canadian Railway Museum, 122 St-Pièrre (alias Rte 209) in St Constant, 632-2410. 28 km from Montréal. Largest railway museum in Canada. 120 vehicles dating from 1863. Streetcar demonstrations daily. Bilingual tours geared to non-specialist. Note: public transport to St Constant is a disaster. Call museum to arrange group transportation. 9am–5pm daily (summer only). $4.50, students $2.50. Reservations: 638-1522.
Insectarium, 4581 Rue Cherbourg E, 872-8753. Unique in North America, it combines science and entertainment and is home to 350,000 insect specimens from 88 countries. Open 9am–8pm. $7. Tickets also give access to the Botanical Garden.
Botanical Garden, Rue Cherbourg, 872-1400. One of the most significant (2nd largest) in the world: 30 specialized gardens spread out over 65 acres, a vast complex of greenhouses, the largest collection of Bonsai and Penjing trees in the western world, a 1700-specie orchid collection, a Japanese Garden and a Chinese Garden opened in June 1991. Open daily 9am–8pm. $7.
Canadian Centre for Architecture, 1820 Rue Baile, Métro Guy, 939-7000. Open Tue–Sun 11am–6pm, Thurs 11am–8pm. Admission $5, students $3. This museum and architecture centre dedicated to the art of architecture is considered to be a world-class institution. Its collection includes 47,000 drawings and master prints, a library with 135,000 books, 45,000 photos as well as important archival finds.
Olympic Park, eastern Montréal. Site of the 1976 Olympic Games, now home to Montréal's baseball (the Expos) and soccer teams. Daily tours (bilingual), $7. Information: 252-4737. 'Better value: savour a sporting event.' 'Very disappointing—certainly not worth the bother.' 'For lovers of modern architecture only.' 'Go and see a baseball game—much better than the tour.' Open Tue–Sun 10am–11pm.
Markets, numerous locations. Include: Atwater, Maisonneuve, and Marche Ouest. Everything from soup to boutiques, handmade articles, produce, fast food. Open daily. Go and haggle.

INFORMATION

Montréal Tourist Bureaux, 1001 Rue de Square Dorchester, 872-4755.
Montréal tourist info. 2 Place Ville Marie, 873-2015; info on provincial activities. Open Mon–Fri 9am–7pm.

ENTERTAINMENT

Read the free *Montreal Mirror* or *Voir* for what's going on.
The Alley, on the McGill campus. Quiet pub and coffee house with live jazz.
Bar St Laurent, 384 St Laurent, 844-4717. 'Very trendy.'
Beef-teque, 3702 St Laurent, 844-6211. 'Sleazy' beer bar, cheap pints and pitchers ($9 during week, $12 at w/end). Open daily 2pm–3am.
Café Campus, student hang-out on Queen Mary Rd near Côte des Neiges, drinking, dancing, French students. Cheap. Free on Wednesday nights.

Club Lezards, 4177 Rue St Denis, 289-9819. Eclectic, arty, lively discothéque situated in the heart of the city. 'Wall and body painting'(!). $3–$5 cover. Open 10pm–3am.
D.J's Pub, 1443 Crescent St, 287-9354. On Thursday nights here you can get 6 mixed drinks for $12. Open till 3am daily, Happy Hour 12–8pm.
Peel Pub Showbar, 1106 de Maisonneuve W, 845-9002, live entertainment nightly.
Peel Pub Tavern, 1107 Ste Catherine W, 844-6769. 99¢ breakfast. McGill hangout.
Thunderdome, 1254 Stanley, 397-1628. Another student place. $3 cover on weekends.
Zoo Bar, Rue St Laurent. $5 entrance. 'Wild & crazy place.'
Be sure to visit a 'bal musette' at the Place d'Armes to hear old Québecois waltzes played on the traditional accordion and guitar.
Montréal International Jazz Festival. 10 days of music and fun throughout the city, more than 90 indoor, and 240 outdoor shows. Sainte-Catherine & Jeanne Mance Streets; Info-Festival: 871-1881. With many top-name performers.
In August try to catch the **World Film Festival**. The largest celebration of film in North America, ranked with that of Cannes, Berlin and Venice. In 1990 300,000 movie goers viewed 580 screenings of 350 films from 52 countries. Place des Arts, Complexe Desjardins, 933-9699.
In September, the **Montréal International Music Festival** features classes and concerts, conferences and recitals for classical music lovers. Place des Arts, Complexe Desjardins, 282-0731.
Montréal is a vibrant theatrical centre with enough performances and styles to suit most tastes. See travelling productions of *Cats* or *Les Miserables* at the **Théâtre Saint-Denis**, 1594 St Denis (849-4211) or for Québecois works (in French), go to the **Théâtre du Rideau Vert**, 4664 Rue St Denis. Check the local papers or call Ticketmaster on 790-2222.

TRAVEL
Metro (built for Expo '67), 288-6287. Fully integrated with the bus system, it whispers along on rubber tyres. Public transit with flair. 'A joy after New York.' Current fare: $1.75, $7 for 6 tickets. Ask for transfers (honoured on both buses and metro). Hours 5.30am–12.30am daily. For information, call: 288-6287. Free maps available at certain stations.
Gray Line City Tours, depart from 1001 Metcalfe St, 934-1222. Prices range from $16.50 to $34.50 depending on tour. Call for info on various tour permutations. Metro stop: Peel.
Murray Hill Tours 871-4733, $23.50 for tour of city.
Central bus terminal, Maisonneuve and Berri, 842-2281.
Central train station (Gare Centrale), under Queen Elizabeth Hotel, info and reservations: 871-1331. Metro: Bonaventure.
Mirabel Airport, 55 km from city centre, international flights (476-3010). Dorval Airport, 21 km from city centre, domestic and US flights. Transportation: Gray Line $8.50 to Dorval, $13 to Mirabel from Queen Elizabeth Hotel. To reach the airport (Dorval) by city bus, take #211 to Dorval Train Station then transfer to #204. The metro system does not extend to the airport.
Auto Driveaways: 1117 Ste-Catherine Ouest, Suite #606, 844-1033. 85 offices in North America. $200–$250 security deposit (takes credit cards). Valid license. Drivers aged 21+, maximum of four riders. Summer: all destinations, fall: mostly Florida-bound. Must average 350 driving miles/day.
Allostop, 4317 St-Denis, 985-3032. Connects travellers with motorists. Membership card $7. 'More reliable than hitchhiking, cheaper than bus or train.' $50 to NYC.
Bike hire: Cycle Tourist, Métro Ile St Hélène, 879-1468. Mountain bikes $20 per day (9.30am–7pm), helmets $2. Passport or credit card deposit required. Rental also available from the information center in Dorchester Square.
River rafting: Lachine Rapid Tours, 284-9607. 'Excellent fun.'

Tour of Montréal Harbour: Miss Olympia Tours, 842-3871. Summers, starting in May through mid-Oct, lasts 2 hrs. $19–$40. 'Outstanding.'

LES LAURENTIDES (THE LAURENTIAN MOUNTAINS) This region of mountains, lakes and forests is located just north and west of Montréal via Autoroute 15 and Route 117. Proximity to Montréal and Québec City ensures that amenities are well developed in this area known for camping, hiking, and skiing, a resort area in both winter and summer.

Ste-Agathe, built on the shore of Lac des Sables, is the major town of the Laurentians. Water sports and cruises are major pastimes here. Other towns of interest include: **St Donat**, the highest point in the area (which consequently attracts both climbers and skiers); **St-Sauveur-des-Monts**, an arts and crafts centre; **Mont Laurier**, a farming area; and **Mont Tremblant**, a year-round sports centre which caters to those interested in fishing, watersports and hiking in the summer. In winter, it's probably the most popular ski resort in the area.

In the hills to the northeast of Montréal, north of Trois-Rivières, and accessible off Highway 55, is the unspoiled **La Mauricie National Park**. The park's rolling hills and narrow valleys are dotted with lakes. Canoeing and cross-country skiing are extremely popular here. Moose, black bear, coyote and a great variety of birds are indigenous to the area. The park is open year-round.

Accommodation is plentiful, although somewhat costly. The area is very busy in the summer and from December to March, so it is wise to book ahead. There are a lot of Bed & Breakfast places, inns and lodges to choose from. It is also possible to make day trips out to the Laurentians from Montréal which is a little over an hour away.

QUÉBEC CITY The pride and focal point of French Canada is in fact two cities. Below Diamond Rock, Lower Town (*Basse Ville*) spreads over the coastal region of Cape Diamond and up the valley of St Charles. Atop rugged Diamond Rock, 333 ft above the St Lawrence River, is Upper or Old Québec. Originally a fortification located in the heart of New France, it remains the only walled city in North America. It's joined to the charming Quartier Petit Champlain by a 200 ft funicular.

In 1759, General Wolfe and his British troops scaled the cliffs in pre-dawn darkness and took Montcalm and his French troops by surprise, thereby securing Canada for the British. The site of this attack, the Plains of Abraham, is now a peaceful public park.

Despite the outcome of that battle, Québec remains quintessentially French. In fact, only five percent of its inhabitants speak English. Walking around narrow, winding streets past the grey-stone walls, sidewalk cafes, and artists on the Rue du Trèsor, it's as if one were transported across the Atlantic to the alleyways of Montmartre. The town is best explored on foot and details of a walking tour are available from the Tourist Bureaux. Montréal is situated 150 miles due west.

The telephone area code is 418.

ACCOMMODATION

Auberge La Paix, 31 Rue Couillard, 694-0735. $15 per night. $2 for bedding or bring a sleeping bag. Kitchen facs. Free breakfast, all you can eat. 'Central location, clean.'

Auberge St Louis, 48 Rue St-Louis, 692-2424. S/D $50 and up.

Château de la Lery, 8 Rue Laporte, 692-2692. $75 and up. Continental breakfast included.

Hôtel Manoir Charest, 448 Rue Dorchester, 647-9320. S-$40, D-$47. 'Clean and friendly.'

Maison du Général, 72 Rue St-Louis, 694-1905. S-$28, D-$33. 'Very well situated.' No reservations taken; call or show up after noon (check out time).

Maison Ste Ursule, 40 Rue Ste Ursule, 694-9794. S-$41, D-$54. 3 rooms with kitchen facs.

Le Manoir Lasalle, 18 Rue Ste Ursule, 692-9953. S-$28, D-$45-$55.

Maison Acadienne, 43 Rue Ste Ursule, 694-0280. S/D-$51. Free continental breakfast.

Bonjour Québec, 3765 Blvd Monaco, 527-1465. A B&B agency that will set you up with a place to stay, S-$42, D-$52-$58.

Centre International de Séjour de Québec (CHYA) 19 Rue St Ursule, 694-0755. Members $13, non-members $18. Laundry facs, limited street parking, linen provided. 'Very nice and well situated.'

YWCA, 855 Holland Ave, 683-2155. S-$30, D-$50. For women and couples only.

Camping: Camping Piscine Turmel, 7000 Blvd Ste Anne, off Rte 138, 824-4311. Open May 15–Sept 15. $18 a night. Showers, laundry, pool, auto mechanics and ice cream parlour. 'Clean and well kept.' **Aéroport Camping**, 2050 Rue de l'Aéroport, also off Rte 138, 871-1574. $14 basic camping with pool.

FOOD

Marché de Vieux Port (open-air market), 160 Rue St-André. Open daily, March through November.

Cafés along **Rue St Jean** and **Rue Buade**. Complete 3-course meals (répas complet), quite economical.

Casse Crêpe Breton, 1136 Rue St Jean. Breakfast special $3, lunch specials (11am–2pm). Open Sun–Thur 8am–1am, Fri–Sat 9.30am–2am. 'Excellent crêpes.'

Café Buade, 31 Rue Buade, 692-3909. Open 7.30am–11pm. Breakfast offered all day long; entrées $5–$12.

Café Ste-Julie, 865 Rue des Zouaves—off St Jean, 647-9368. Open daily 6am–8pm. Big filling breakfast $3.50, burger lunch $4.50.

La Fleur de Lotus, 38 Côte de la Fabrique, across from the Hôtel de Ville, 692-4286. 'A local favourite'. Thai dishes $2.75–$8.75. Open Mon–Fri 11.30am–10.30pm, Sat & Sun 5pm–10.30pm.

Le Picotin, 4 Petit Champlain, 692-1862. Good filling French meals. Prices range for lunch: $6–$12; $15–$20 dinner. Open 11am–midnight. Kitchen closes at 10pm.

OF INTEREST

La Citadelle, on Cap-Diamant promontory. Constructed by the British in the 1820's on the site of the 17th century French defences, the Citadel is the official residence of the Governor-General and the largest fortification in North America still garrisoned by regular troops. Changing of the Guard ceremony by the 'Van Doos' at 10am daily. The **Royal 22nd Regiment Museum** (648-3563) has exhibits of military objects such as firearms, decorations, and uniforms. Museum and Citadelle are open daily from May to Sept 9am–5pm, mid-June to Labour Day until 6pm. With reduced hours thereafter. $4 with tour.

The **Fortifications de Québec** are also worth a visit. This is the stone wall which encircles Vieux Québec (the old city). Frontenac erected this wall in the late 17th century in order to fortify the city and guard against British incursion. Tours available. Open end of June to Sept, daily 10am–5pm, with restricted hours the rest of the year. There are great views of the city from the walkways along the wall.

The Plains of Abraham. Battlefields Park was the scene of the bloody clash between the French and British armies. A Martello Tower, part of the historic defence system of walled Québec, still stands. There are a number of other historic sites in this 250 acre park including the Wolfe Monument and the Jardin Jeanne d'Arc. Also here is the **Musée du Québec** which houses the original hand copy of the surrender by Montcalm and displays Québec art. Since its recent renovation you can visit the jail. Open daily. Thur–Tue 10am–5.45pm, Wed 10am–9.45pm. $4.75, $2.75 students. Free on Wed. Call: 643-2150 regarding temporary exhibits.

Outside the Walls, at the corner of La Grande Allée and Rue Georges VI, stands **L'Assemblée Nationale**, 643-7239. It was completed in 1886. From the visitors gallery you can view debates in French. Free 30-min tours. Daily 9am–5pm; Sept–May, Mon–Fri 9am–5pm.

Musée du Fort, 10 Rue Ste Anne, 692-2175. Diorama sound and light show. Re-live the six sieges of Québec. In summer open daily 10am–6pm. $4.25, $2.75 students.

Château Frontenac, Rue St Pierre. Named for the 'illustrious governor of New France', this hotel is one of Québec City's most prominent landmarks. There is a spectacular view of the St Lawrence from the Promenade des Gouverneurs.

Parliament Buildings, on Grande Allée at Ave Dufferin. The main building built in 1884, is in Second Empire style. The bronze statues in front represent the historical figures of Québec. Open end of June to Labour Day, daily 10am–5.30pm. Free. While in the area, notice the architecture of the buildings on Grand Allé and the sidewalk cafes lining the street.

The Ramparts, Rue des Ramparts. Studded with old iron cannons, probably the last vestiges of the Siege of Québec in 1759.

Notre Dame de Québec, 16 Rue Buade, 692-2533/4. Restored many times, the basilica was first constructed in 1650 when it served a diocese stretching from Canada to Mexico. All the bishops of Québec are buried in the crypt. Open daily 7am–6pm. Get there early. Tours of the basilica and crypt are available 10.30am–5pm, from May to November. Free.

Notre-Dame-Des-Victoires, Place Royale, Basse Ville. Built in 1688. Eighty years before its construction, this is where Champlain established the first permanent white settlement in North America north of Florida. The church itself gets its name in honour of two French military victories. Its main altar resembles the city in that it is shaped like a fortress complete with turrets and battlements.

Place Royale has undergone considerable restoration under its current owner, the Government of Québec. In the summer, the roads are blocked off and restricted to pedestrians only, and many plays and variety shows are put on in the parks of the area. This is one of the oldest districts in North America.

Ile d'Orléans. This island in the St Lawrence is a slice of 17th century France. Wander around the old houses, mills, churches. Also known for its handicrafts, strawberries and home-made treats.

INFORMATION

Information Centre (Ministère du Tourisme), 3005 Blvd Laurier (Ste-Foy branch), 651-2882. 8.30am–5pm, summer until 8pm.

Tourisme Québec, (800) 361-5405 from anywhere in province, (800) 363-7777 from outside.

TRAVEL

Central bus terminal (Gare Centrale d'Autobus), 524-4692. Open 5am–1am.

Ste-Foy bus terminal (west end), 651-7015.

Voyageur Bus Terminus, several locations. Québec City: 225 Charest Est, 524-4692; Ste-Foy: 2700 Blvd Laurier, 651-7015. Hourly service to Montréal.

Québec National Airport, Ste Foy, Blvd Hamel to Blvd de l'Aéroport. 14 miles (23 km) from city centre. For a shuttle to the airport call Visites Touristiques Foy d'Erable, 649-9226, $7.50.
CN train station, 3255 Chemin de la Gare, Ste Foy (west end).
VIA Rail reservations, 692-3940, or 658-8792.
Allostop, 467 Rue St-Jean, Québec, 522-0056. (See Montréal section for description of service.) Open 9am–6pm.
Ferry across the St Lawrence, daily departures from the wharf 6.30am–3am, 644-3704. Fare: $1.25. Nice views of Québec, especially at sunset.

LA GASPESIE (THE GASPÉ PENINSULA) This is the bit of Québec Province jutting out above New Brunswick into the Gulf of St Lawrence. The word Gaspé is derived from the Micmac Indian word meaning Lands End. You'll appreciate this when standing on the shore at Gaspé for there's nothing but sea between you and Europe. Picturesque fishing villages line the Peninsula; slow, pleasant places in summer, rugged in winter. Inland it's farming country although a large area is taken up by the Gaspesian Provincial Park.

The route from Québec City to Gaspé runs along the mighty St Lawrence where the scenery closely resembles that of the Maritime Provinces. The North Shore is a more interesting drive, but at some point, you have to take a ferry to get to the South Shore. (The narrower the river at the point of crossing, the cheaper the ferry ride.) You can, for instance, take Route 138 out of Québec City and pass by the **Chute de Montmorency**, the impressive 250 foot waterfall—higher than Niagara. Then, through **Ste-Anne-de-Beaupré**, destination of millions of pilgrimages yearly since 18th century shipwrecked sailors believed Ste-Anne was their saviour. Next, through **Baie-St-Paul** where there is an interesting museum of old-time French Canadiana, and up to St Simeon where there is a ferry crossing to Rivière du Loup. From here, take Route 132 as far as **Trois Pistoles**.

Long before Canada was 'officially discovered', Basque whale hunters built ovens at Trois Pistoles to reduce whale blubber to oil. The remains of the ovens can still be seen. Carry on along the south shore of the St Lawrence through the fishing villages, catching all the while the ever changing seascapes. From **Rivière A Claude** access to the top of 4160-foot **Mount Jacques Cartier** is 'easy'. The mountain is in the Gaspesian Provincial Park and is the highest point in the province, guaranteeing a great view and perhaps even some caribou.

Or for the moment carry on round the top of the Peninsula coming first to **Gaspé** itself where Jacques Cartier came ashore in 1533 and set up a cross to stake France's claim to Canada. Nearby is **Forillon National Park**.

Forillon scenery is typified by jagged cliffs and fir-covered highlands. The park is criss-crossed by many hiking trails and on the way you may see deer, fox, bear or moose. Large colonies of seabirds such as cormorants, gannets, and gulls nest on the cliff headlands and it is possible to see whales and seals basking offshore.

Naturalists offer talks and slide presentations at the Interpretive Centre on Highway 132 near **Cap-des-Rosiers**. There are **campsites** at Cap Bon Ami, Le Havre, and Petit-Gaspé. All three have good recreational facilities including beaches.

The views around here are fantastic but none better than at **Percé**. The village takes its name from **Rocher Percé**, the Pierced Rock, which is just offshore. You can walk there on a sandbar at low tide.

From Percé boat trips go to nearby **Ile Bonaventure**, where there is a bird sanctuary. Be sure to stop off at the **Gaspesian Provincial Park** before heading down to **Chaleur Bay** on your way back to Québec's urban centres. In the park you may catch a glimpse of the caribou herd which spends its summers here. Mornings are the time you are most likely to see them. It's a good place for fishing and hiking.

ACCOMMODATION

Maison Bérubé, 245 Montée Sandy Beach, Gaspé, 368-6402. S/D-$40. Open year-round.

Motel Fort Ramsay, 254 Blvd Gaspé, 368-5094. Open May–Sept. S–$39, D–$45. Kitchen facs.

Collège de la Gaspésie in Gaspé, 368-2749. Open year round. S–$26, D–$33 (with shared bath). Apt. for 6–8 person, $80.

Youth Hostels: Auberge de Cap-aux-Os, 2095 Blvd Grande-Grève. Gaspé, Forillon National Park, 892-5153. $12, $15 nm. Laundry facs, linen & bike rental, new kitchen. 'Very friendly, bilingual but mostly French.' Voyageur Bus stops at the hostel (June 24–September 30). During the off-season take Grey Coach or train from Québec City to Gaspé (25 kms from hostel).

Auberge du Château, Pointe à la Garde, 788-2048. Auberge with a castle built by the owner, Jean. $17, breakfast incl. Laundry facs. Linen rental. Dinner served in castle, $8. 'Excellent atmosphere, excellent food, excellent host.' 'Phone before going to get exact location.'

THE PRAIRIE PROVINCES

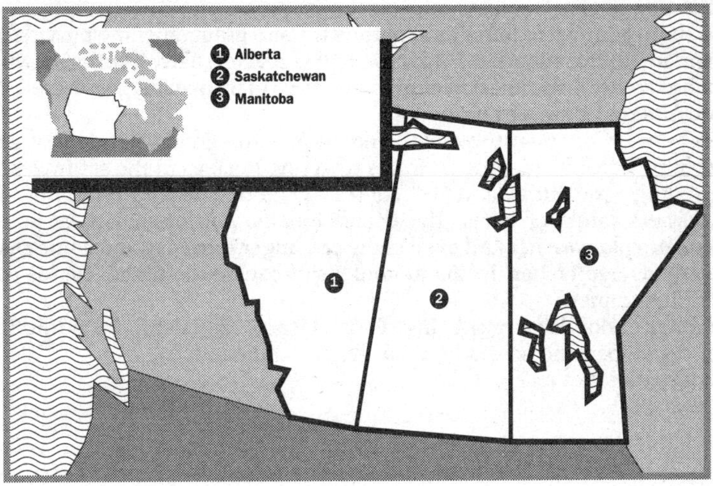

Alberta, Manitoba and Saskatchewan are for the most part wide open prairie country, although western Alberta offers, in contrast, the magnificent scenery of the Rockies. Grain once formed the basis of the economy of these provinces but today mineral wealth and tourism are also the big money spinners.

Although the major cities are fast-growing modern centres of commerce and culture, there remains a touch of the frontier about all three provinces. Vast areas of virgin wilderness are still there for the intrepid to explore and conquer and it is possible to travel for days in some places without ever seeing another human being.

ALBERTA

Once an agricultural backwater with an economy dependent solely on wheat, Alberta is still enjoying the economic boom based on the Province's multi-billion dollar oil and gas industries which took off in the '70s and '80s. The former small-town farming centres of Calgary and Edmonton are now thriving metropolises, their skylines dotted with skyscraping corporate headquarters. With 85 percent of Canada's oil and gas on tap, Albertans are enjoying the lowest taxes, the least unemployment and the highest per capita incomes in the country.

The situation is not without its political implications. The four western provinces and two territories hold less than 30 percent of the seats in the Federal Parliament and westerners feel themselves deprived of power by the more populous East. It is not only in Québec that the language of separation is often spoken.

In sharp contrast to the skyscrapers, cattle and grain ranching provide the other side to the Albertan landscape and character. The Albertan cowboy ranches some of the finest beef in the world. As the saying goes here: 'If it ain't Alberta, it ain't beef.'

Of all the Canadian provinces, Alberta has the greatest variety of geographical features, ranging from the towering Rockies in the southwest to the rolling agricultural land north of the US border, and up north the near wilderness lands of lakes, rivers and forests. Although it gets hot in summer, cold weather and even snow can linger into May and come again as early as September. In the mountains of course the nights can be cool even in summer.

National Parks: Waterton Lakes, Banff, Jasper, Elk Island, Wood Buffalo (not developed, no access by road, no accommodation).

The telephone area code is 403.

EDMONTON The close proximity of the highly productive Leduc, Redwater and Pembiano oilfields to the provincial capital made Edmonton one of the fastest growing cities in Canada. Coal-mining, natural gas, and a couple of throw-backs to Edmonton's origins, fur-trading and wheat, were the other factors behind the boom. However, with the downturn in world oil prices those heady days are over and Edmonton is in the process of re-assessment.

During the Klondike gold rush Edmonton was a stopping place for prospectors enroute to the goldfields. The town remembers this with joy every July during Klondike Days when the place goes wild for a week. Otherwise it's a sober, hard-working spot, the most northerly major city in North America, boasting as well as skyscrapers a progressive university, the only subway system in western Canada and, as a result of hosting the Commonwealth Games a few years back, some of the finest sporting facilities anywhere.

Edmonton is centrally situated within Alberta and it's a good starting point for a northbound trip or for going westwards towards the Rockies. Jasper is 228 miles away, but first there's Elk Island National Park just 30 miles east.

ACCOMMODATION

Cecil Hotel, 10406 Jasper Ave, 428-7001. S/D–$33. Downtown location.

Commercial Hotel, 10329 82nd Ave, 439-3981. S–$28 (no bath), S–$28 (with bath), D–$23 (no bath), D–$32 (with bath). Located south in trendy Strathcona.

Edmonton Hostel, 10422 91 St, 429-0140. $12 members, $17 non-members. 'Easy walk from downtown. Comfortable.' Cooking facs. Also bike hire, $12 per day.

Grand Hotel, 10266 103 St, 422-6365. S–$34, D–$39. Across from Greyhound bus station.

Klondiker Hotel, 153 St and Stony Plain Rd, 489-1906. S–$33, D–$36. West-end location.

Ellerslie Motel, 1304 Calgary Trail SW, 988-6406. S-$36, D-$40. Student discount.
Relax Inn, 10320 45th Ave, 436-9770, and Stony Plain Rd, 483-6031. S-$53, D-$57. $4 for XP.
University of Alberta Residence, Lister Hall, 87th Ave and 116th St, 492-4281. Open to non-students May–Aug. S-$27, D-$40. Cafeteria.
YMCA, 10030 102A Ave, 421-9622. S-$26, $36 w/bath, D-$40, $10 key deposit.
YWCA, 10305 100 Ave, 423-9922. S-$30, $36 w/bath, D-$45.

FOOD

Amandine, 10130 103rd St. Small French cafe. 'Pleasant place with good food.'
Bones, 10220 103rd St. Specialises in ribs.
David's, 8407 Argyll Road—the true taste of Alberta beef.
Earl's, various locations. Generous servings—one on U of A campus.
Hello Deli, 10725 124 St, for sandwiches, bagels, soups.
Smitty's Pancake House, various locations—big breakfasts.
Strathcona Square, 8150 105 St, restored Victorian building, several restaurants.
Whyte Avenue, from 99 St to 109 St; lots of eateries along this stretch—close to U of A campus.
Downtown along 104 St is "Restaurant Row" with over 50 places within walking distance of each other.

OF INTEREST

Legislature Bldg, 97th Ave and 108th St, 427-7362. On the site of the original Fort Edmonton. Built at the beginning of this century. Free tours every half hour.
Fort Edmonton Historical Park, corner of White Mud and Fox Dr, 496-8787. Reconstruction of the original and a replica of a Hudson's Bay Co Trading Post. Open daily 10am–6pm in summer months. Sept–Oct 12 open Sat, Sun and hols 1pm–5pm. $6.25. 'Worth a visit.'
The John Walter Museum, at 10627 93rd Ave, 428-3033, was built of hand-hewn logs in 1874. The house was the district's first telegraph office. Four historic buildings on original site. Open Sun 1–4pm. Admission free. Different activities each Sun.
Edmonton Art Gallery, 2 Sir Winston Churchill Sq, 422-6223. More than 30 exhibitions each year including contemporary and historical art from Canada and around the world. Mon–Wed 10.30am–5pm, Thur & Fri 10.30am–8pm, Sat, Sun, hols 11am–5pm. $3 adults, students $1.50. Thur 4–8pm, free.
Provincial Museum, 12845 102nd Ave, 453-9100. Features displays of Alberta's natural and human history, including native people, pioneers, wildlife, and geology. Open daily 9am–8pm, $3.25.
Edmonton Space Sciences Centre, 11211 142nd St. Over two million dollars worth of exhibits, IMAX film theatre, exhibit gallery and science shop. For info: 452-9100, or recording of events 451-7722.
Muttart Conservatory, 9626-96A St. Four glass pyramids nestled in the city centre feature more than 700 species of plants from arid to temperate climates. Recording: 496-8755. Open Sun–Wed 11am–9pm, Thurs–Sat 11am–6pm, $4.
Ukrainian Canadian Archives and Museum of Alberta, 10611 110 Ave. Traces history of Ukranian pioneers in Alberta. Includes costumes, paintings, folk art. Mon–Fri 10am–4pm. Hours subject to change, phone prior to visit. 424-7580.
West Edmonton Mall, 170 St and 87 Ave. World's largest indoor shopping mall with over 800 stores. Employs 15,000 people, and features waterslides, dolphin tank, full size replica of Santa Maria, skating rink, a petting zoo, 10 aviaries, miniature golf—you name it! 'Mind boggling.' 'A must see.'
Polar Park, 22 kms SE on Hwy 14, 922-3401. Preserve for cold-climate and hardy African animals. Cross country trails and sleigh rides in winter. Daily 8am–dusk, $4 admission.

INFORMATION

Visitors Info Centre, 9797 Jasper Ave, lobby level, 426-4715. Open Mon–Sat, 9am–4.30pm, May–Sept. Rest of year 8.30am–4.30pm, Mon–Fri. Closed Sat, Sun and hols. Another info centre at 2404 Calgary Trail Northbound SW, 496-8400. Open 8am–9pm, 8.30am–4.30pm after Labour Day.

Royal Tours, Ste 600, 1 Thornton Ct, Jasper Ave and 99 St, 488-9040. Gives daily 3 hr tours of Edmonton from $21, includes admission to the Provincial Museum of Alberta. All day tours also include admission to the Historical Park and cost $38.

ENTERTAINMENT

Klondike Days. 'Excellent entertainment' in the style of the 1890s is provided during the nine Klondike Days in mid-July. The show at MacDonald Hotel, Jasper and 98th St, during this time, is 'not to be missed'. Free entrance to the Golden Slipper Saloon. Corona Hotel, bar downstairs. 'Where most students drink; good entertainment.'

The Red Barn, RR1, about 30 miles out of town, 921–3918. 'Largest indoor barbeque in Canada. Worth a visit.' 'Very popular.' Dance on Saturday. Closed Sun.

Jazz City International Festival, late June. Canadian and overseas jazz musicians. Running simultaneously is **The Works**, a celebration of the visual arts.

Edmonton Street Performers Festival, mid-July. Downtown streets come alive with magicians, jugglers, clowns, mime artists, musicians and comics.

Edmonton Folk Music Festival, mid-August, Gallagher Park. Features traditional and bluegrass music, country, blues and Celtic music—all under the bright Alberta sun.

Theatre and Concerts, Edmonton Opera and Symphony, plus many live theatres. Call the LIVE LINE at 436-9955 for performance information.

TRAVEL

Greyhound, 421-4211.

Edmonton Transit System Info, 421-4636. Standard fare: $1.25. Peak hour fare: $1.50.

Red Arrow Express, 425-0820. Coach service between Edmonton and Calgary 4 times daily (8am, 12.15pm, 4.30pm, 6pm) o/w $29.50, r/t $56.70.

CN/VIA Rail Station, (800) 561-8630.

Edmonton International Airport is 15 km south off Hwy 2. The Grey Goose Airporter shuttle runs from 5.30am until 10.45pm and departs every 45 minutes from Macdonald Place, various downtown hotels and the Airport Arrivals Terminal. $11 o/w, call 463-7520 for more info.

ELK ISLAND NATIONAL PARK This 75-square-mile park is the largest fenced wild animal preserve in Canada. Apart from the elk, moose, mule deer and numerous smaller animals who live here, there is a herd of some 600 buffalo. Once roaming the North American continent in their millions, the buffalo were hunted almost to extinction by the end of the 19th century. The herd here at Elk Island has been built up from about 40 animals since 1907.

It is possible to observe the buffalo from close proximity, but on the other side of a strong fence. Walking on the buffalo range itself is discouraged! North America's largest buffalo herd, 12,000 strong, is contained in **Wood Buffalo National Park** in the far north of Alberta. This area, however, remains relatively undeveloped.

Elk Island is open throughout the year and the daily admission is $5 per vehicle. There is a Visitor Centre just north of Hwy 16, 922-5790, which features exhibits and displays. Walks, hikes, campfire talks and theatre programmes are also offered by the park rangers. Recreation facilities are available on the east shore of Astotin Lake including swimming, golf and hiking trails. There are camping facilities in the park.

OF INTEREST
Ukrainian Cultural Heritage Village, on Hwy 16, 662-3640. Russian immigrants played an important role in taming western Canada and this open-air museum portrays pre-1930s life of the Ukrainian settlers. The buildings are authentic and have been moved here and then restored. Daily 10am–6pm. $5.50. Tues free.

JASPER NATIONAL PARK Jasper National Park is 4200 square miles of lofty, green-forested, snow-capped mountains, canyons, dazzling lakes, glaciers and hot mineral springs. In sharp contrast to one another, within the park are the Miette Hot Springs, one of which gushes forth at a temperature of 129°F, and the huge Columbia Icefields which send their melting waters to three oceans, the Atlantic, the Pacific and the Arctic.

Reached by Route 16 (The Yellowhead Highway) from Edmonton, Jasper lies along the eastern slopes of the Canadian Rockies running south until the park meets Banff National Park. This vast mountainous complex of national parkland is an extremely popular resort area throughout the year. Jasper National Park takes its name from one Jasper Hawes who was clerk in the first trading-post at Brulé Lake in about 1813.

One of the park's biggest attractions is the 17-mile-long **Maligne Lake**. This is the largest of several beautiful glacial lakes in the area and the tour to the lake from the township of Jasper has been much recommended by previous visitors.

Within the park it is possible to drive through some of the West's most spectacular mountain scenery. **Mount Edith Cavell** (11,033 feet) and **Whistler's Peak** (7350 feet) are two of the more accessible points from Jasper township and the aerial tramway has put Whistler's Peak within reach of even the most nervous would-be mountaineers. In the cablecar at the highest point above the ground you will be 450 feet in the air and once atop the Peak the view is tremendous. In winter this is a favourite skiing spot.

Sixty-five miles from Jasper on the Icefield Highway between Jasper and Banff (Route 93) is the **Columbia Icefield**. This is 130 square miles of impressive glacial ice. You can walk across parts of the glacier but it is perhaps best seen by snowmobile. Even on a very hot day take a sweater with you. Also to be seen along this most beautiful of highways are the several glaciers creeping down from the Icefields. **Athabasca Glacier** is but a mile from the road and snowmobile trips are available on the glacier.

The resort village of **Jasper** is the Jasper National Park Headquarters and also an important CN railroad junction. Should you arrive by train, take note of the 70-foot Raven Totem Pole at the railway depot. The totem was carved by Simeon Stiltae, a master carver of the Haida Indians of the Queen Charlotte Islands, and gives its name to a famous annual golf tournament held here.

ACCOMMODATION
Chamber of Commerce, 632 Connaught Dr, 852-3858. Has list of hotels in the area.
Parks Canada Information Office, Town Info Centre, 852-6176. Provides list of approved tourist homes.

Athabasca Hotel, 510 Patricia St, 852-3386. S–$51, D–$54, shared bath.
Youth Hostels: General info, 10926 88th Ave, Edmonton, T6G 0Z1, (403) 439-3089. $8–$15. The Pika Shuttle Company runs a shuttle service between hostels in Alberta; (800) 363-0096 for info. Fares vary according to distance.
Hostels: Maligne Canyon, 15 km from Jasper. $9 member, $14 non-member.
Mount Edith Cavell, 14 km from Jasper (10½ km straight uphill, not accessible by car in winter or spring). $8, $13 non-members.
Athabasca Falls, 28 km from Jasper on Hwy 93. $9 member, $14 non-member.
Beauty Creek, 81 km from Jasper on Hwy 93. $8 member, $13 non-member. Winter: pick up key, call (403) 439-3089.
Whistler's Hostel, 8 km from Jasper by Skytram. $13 member, $18 non-member.
Camping: there are several campgrounds in the area, the nearest ones to Jasper being at **Whistler's** on Icefield Pkwy S (852-3963), and **Wapiti**, also on Icefield Pkwy (852-3992). $12–$16 per site. Gets very cold at night. Open May–Oct.

OF INTEREST
Columbia Icefield. Snowmobile trips available daily mid-Apr to mid-Nov, weather permitting, $18.50, ages 6–15, $6. Open 9am–5pm Mon–Sun. Info: 762-2241.
Jasper Skytram. 2 miles south via Hwy 93 and Whistler Mountain Rd. Daily mid-May to early Oct, 8.00am–9.30pm July through August. $9. Bus connections from RR station, 10.15am, 1.45pm, 3.15pm, or walk there. 852-3093.
Jasper Raft Tours. 3-hr trips on Athabasca River. Twice a day. June–Sept. $30.50. Tkts available at the Brewster Bus Depot and Jasper Park Lodge. For info: 852-3613 or 852-4721.
Maligne Lake Boat Tours. 1½ hr tour ($27), 852-3370. Views of Maligne Narrows. Open May–August.

INFORMATION/TRAVEL
Jasper National Park Interpretive Centre, 852-6161. Guided walks, info. Daily June–Sept. Free.
Jasper Chamber of Commerce, 632 Connaught Dr, 852-4919. Open Mon–Fri 9am–5pm. Travel Alberta (same office) open Mon–Sun 8am–8pm.
Brewster Transportation and Tours, 852-3332. Provides local transportation and sightseeing. Open June–Sept, two tours daily.

BANFF NATIONAL PARK Banff, Canada's oldest national park, was established in 1885 after hot springs were seen gushing from the side of Sulphur Mountain. It takes in an area of 2546 square miles of the Rockies and the area's dry, equable climate, alpine-style grandeur, hot mineral springs and pools, have brought Banff fame and fortune as a summer health and winter ski resort. **Banff** and **Lake Louise** are the main resort towns. The park gets its name from Banffshire in Scotland, the birthplace of Lord Strathcona, a past president of the Canadian Pacific Railroad.

Operating all year round are the cable cars which take the visitor high into the mountains. Both the **Sulphur Mountain Gondola Lift** and the **Mount Norquay Chair Lift** offer fantastic views. There are many trails winding up and around the mountains but it's tough going and the inexperienced should acquire a guide before venturing forth.

It is possible to walk up **Mount Rundle** or **Cascade Mountain** in a day, but you must first register with a park ranger. If you're on Mount Rundle, make sure that you're on the right trail, since it's easy to mistake the trail and get on to the less scenic one along the river valley.

The trail up Sulphur Mountain takes one and a half hours from Upper Hot

Springs. You can ride the cable car down for free. At **Upper Hot Springs** there is a pool fed by sulphur springs at 100 degrees; great for swimming although it will cost you $3. If you need to hire a towel this will be a further $1. Hitching up here from Banff town is said to be 'easy'.

If you don't have much time in Banff, there is a nice trail walk along the glacial green Bow River to **Bow Falls** near the Banff Springs Hotel. The hotel, the pride of Canadian Pacific, is built in the style of a Scottish baronial mansion. The scenery, however, really is spectacular and the area is not overrun by tourists. An alternative short walk is the trail up Tunnel Mountain which should take about an hour and a quarter from bus station to summit.

Glacial lakes are one of the most attractive features of Banff. **Peyto Lake** (named after Bill Peyto, famous explorer and guide of the 1890s) changes from being a deep blue colour in the early summer to an 'unbelievably beautiful turquoise' later in the year as the glacier melts into it. Tourists have been known to ask the locals whether the lake is drained each year to paint the bottom blue! The glacier which feeds the lake is receding at 70 feet a year.

'The jewel of the Rockies', **Lake Louise**, lies in a hanging valley formed during the Ice Age and is one of the loveliest spots in the world. It is a placid green lake in a terrific setting. Not for swimming in however. The water is a chilly 10 degrees centigrade. The town of Lake Louise is 36 miles from Banff on the Jasper highroad. From the town suggested trips are the 9 miles to the incredibly blue **Moraine Lake**, and the **Valley of the Ten Peaks** and back through Larth Valley and over Sentinel Peak, or a walk out to the **Plain of the Six Glaciers** via Lake Agnes. You will need lots of time and a pair of stout shoes.

Be careful of the black and grizzly bears who live in the park. You may also see moose, elk, cougars, coyotes and Rocky Mountain goats. The lakes and rivers of the park are excellent for trout and Rocky Mountain Whitefish fishing.

BANFF Situated 81 miles west of Calgary and 179 miles south of Jasper, the village of Banff is always buzzing with activity. With downhill skiing in the winter, and hiking, cycling, golfing, and mountain climbing in the summer, this little town is rarely at a loss for anything to do. Banff is also a lively arts centre and is home to the Banff School of Fine Arts, as well as hosting a Festival of the Arts from May until late August.

Over recent years Banff has become the favourite playground of Japanese tourists, whose multitude is so great that many of the town's signs are bilingual: Japanese and English. This sudden interest in Banff partly stems from a Japanese soap opera that uses the famous Banff Springs Hotel as its backdrop. As a result, the hotel is constantly full of honeymooners from the Pacific Rim. 'Banff was seriously disappointing. Expensive and unfriendly'.

ACCOMMODATION

Accommodation options in and around Banff are generally expensive. However, there are many hostels in the area and for the budget traveller they are undoubtedly the best bet.

Central Reservations, (800) 661-1676, will find accommodation for a fee of $10. Not advisable to arrive in Banff on Sunday evening without reservation.
Kudzin's, 337 Big Horn St, 762-3491. D–$10 per person. No linens, must bring sleeping bag. 'Very reasonable, no-smoking.' Close to railway station.
Tan-Y-Bryn, Mrs Cowan, 118 Otter St, 762-3696. S–$12–$45, D–$34–$49. Continental breakfast incl. 'Super guest house.'
YM/YWCA, Springs Mountain Hostel, 762-3560. $17 bunk (bring sleeping bag), S–$47, D–$53.
Youth Hostels: Reservations: 283-5551. **Banff Intl Hostel**, Tunnel Mtn Rd, 762-4122. $16 members, $21 non-members. N on Banff Ave to Wolf St, L on Otter, up hill on left hand side. 2 km from downtown. 45 min walk from train or bus station. 'Excellent.' Pika Shuttle between Alberta hostels can be reserved from here. Or call: (800) 363-0096.
Castle Mtn, Hwy 1A and 93 South, 762-2367. 1.5 km east of junction of Trans Canada and 93S. 25km east of Lake Louise. $9 members, $14 non-members.
Corral Creek, 4.5 km east of Lake Louise on Hwy 1A. Greyhound to 1A-Trans Canada junction. Ask to disembark 1.6 km up Trans Canada. $8 members, $13 non-members. 'Basic.'
Ramparts Creek, on Hwy 93. 20 km north of Saskatchewan River Crossing. 34 km south of Columbia Icefields. $8 members, $13 non-members.
Mosquito Creek, on Hwy 93, 26 km north of Lake Louise next to Mosquito Campground. $8 members, $13 non-members.
Hilda Creek, 8.5 km south of Columbia Icefields Visitors Centre, 120 km north of Lake Louise on Hwy 93. $8 members, $13 non-members.
Lake Louise Intl Hostel. Villagee Rd, 522-2200. Opened in 1992. $15, $19.50 non-members. Kitchen/laundry facilities, café, library, guided hikes.

FOOD

Athena Pizza, Banff Ave. 'Large deep pan pizza $15–enough for 4.'
Guido's, Banff Ave, 762-4002. 'Generous 3-course meal $7.50–$14.50. One of the best eating places in Canada.' Open 4.30pm–7.30pm.
Joe's Diner, 221 Banff Ave, 762-5529. 50's style decor & music. 'Good and cheap.'
Melissa's, 218 Lynx St, 762-5511. Varied menu, large portions, nice atmosphere.
Smitty's, 227 Banff Ave, 762-2533; and **Sam** on Mall, Lake Louise. Great for breakfast.

OF INTEREST

The Park Museum, 93 Banff Ave, 762-1558. The museum deals with the flora, fauna and geography of the park. Admission free. Open 10am–6pm daily, during the summer.
Natural History Museum, 762-4747, 112 Banff Ave. Geology, archaeology and plantlife of Rockies plus films. Open 9am–10pm, July, Aug; 10am–7pm, May, June, Sept. $2.
Peter White Foundation and Archives of Canadian Rockies, 111 Bear St. Library, art gallery, history of Rockies. Daily 10am–6pm in summer. 762-2291. $3, students $1.
The Indian Trading Post, 762-2456. A museum-like store which sells everything on display. Indian crafts and furs. Open daily 9am–9pm (summer).
Buffalo Paddock. On the Trans Canada Highway half a mile west of the eastern traffic circle. A 300-acre buffalo range. No entrance fee charged. You have to stay in your car.
Sulphur Mt Gondola Lift. 2½ miles south of Banff. Daily May–Oct. $8, ages 5–12 $3.75. Info: 762-2523.
Lake Louise Gondola, off Trans Canada Hwy. Daily 8.30am–6pm June-Labour Day. $8 roundtrip, one-way hikers' special $5.50. Skiing Nov–May. Info: 522-3555.
Upper Hot Springs, 4 km south via Mountain Ave, 762-1515. Pool has temp of 38°–41°C. 10am–11pm in summer, 9am–9pm in winter. $3.
Icefields Snowmobile trips. See under Jasper.

INFORMATION
Banff-Lake Louise Chamber of Commerce, 762-3777.
Parks Info Bureau, 224 Banff Ave, 762-4256. Open daily 8pm–8pm.
Banff National Park Interpretive Centre, Banff Ave, 762-3229. Lake Louise Info Centre, 522-3833.

TRAVEL
Brewster Transportation, 762-2241. Banff to Jasper, about $44; to Yoho Valley and Emerald Lake (much recommended, fantastic scenery) from Lake Louise, or from Banff; 5-hour express bus, $37.
'Unless you have a car, forget trying to see both parks.' Tilden Rent-a-Car has an office in town at Lynx and Caribou Sts, 762-2688. On the other hand: 'hitching between the beauty spots is easy'.
Bike Hire: Park 'n Pedal Bike Shop, 226 Bear St, 762-3191. Open 9am–8pm (summer). Bactrax, 339 Banff Ave at the Ptarmigan Inn, 762-8177. Mountain bikes available from $3.75 per hour and $17 per day 8am–8pm. Also Peak Experience on Bear St, 762-0581.
Canoes and rowing boats are on hire at Banff and Lake Louise; and at Lake Minniewanka and Bow River motor boats are available. Motor boats are not allowed on Lake Louise. Youth hostel and the Y run rafting trips. About $40.
Saddle horses from Martins Stables, Banff, Banff Springs Hotel and Chateau Lake Louise. Hired horses cannot be ridden in the park without a guide escort.

KANANASKIS COUNTRY Tucked away between Banff and Calgary, Kananaskis Country is a provincial recreation area, containing sections of three provincial parks (Bow Valley, Peter Lougheed and Bragg Creek). This 4,000 sq km backcountry area offers skiing, snowmobiling and windsurfing. There are excellent hiking trails and plenty of unpaved roads and trails for mountain biking.

Canmore, an old pioneer town, is situated at the north-western tip of Kananaskis Country. Still retaining the haunting presence of the early settlers, this picturesque town has much to offer, including a legacy of the XVth Olympic Winter Games, the Canmore Nordic Centre.

ACCOMMODATION
Ribbon Creek Hostel, (403) 591-7333, 70 km W of Calgary on Hwy 1 (Trans-Canada Hwy), then 25 km south on Hwy 40, turn right at Nakiska Skill Hill access, cross the Kananaskis River and left 1.5 km to the Hostel. $9.

CALGARY This fast growing city of 683,000 enjoys a friendly rivalry with Edmonton, 186 miles to the north. Known as the oil capital of Canada, Calgary, like Edmonton, went through a massive boom during the late seventies when growth in the city was astounding. More recently, however, Calgary's growth has stabilized and those gleaming office towers put up during the boom years, are now the Canadian headquarters of the world's largest oil and gas exploration companies.

At one time the city's only claim to fame was the internationally known Calgary Stampede, a ten day revelry devoted to the city's homesteading, steer wrestling, and bull riding heritage. But in 1988 Calgary busted out of its cowboy breeches into a city of international standing as a result of hosting the Winter Olympic Games. The games have left behind various facilities including 70 and 90 metre ski jumps, bobsleigh and luge tracks, and an impressive indoor speedskating oval. (If you are adventurous, you can rent a pair of speedskates and try your luck.)

Geographically, the city is huge. Once annexation plans are complete, Calgary will be the largest city in Canada. Roads are good, however, and the city also has over 100 km of bicycle paths that span the length and width of the city. In addition, Calgary has a fast light-rail transit (train) system.

Despite its northerly location, Calgary gets less snow than New York City and it hardly ever rains here either. Local weather is determined by the chinook, a mass of warm air rushing in from the Pacific which can instantly send the temperature from minus 10°C to plus 15°C.

ACCOMMODATION

Circle Inn Motel, 2373 Banff Tr NW, 289-0295. S–$41, D–$36–38.
Elbow River Inn, 1919 Macleod Trail S, 269-6771. S/D–$66.
Relax Inn South, 9206 Macleod Trail S, 253-7070. D–$66.
St Louis Hotel, 430 8th Ave, 262-6341. S–$18, D–$33, cheapest rooms no bath.
YWCA, 320 5th Ave SE, 263-1550. S–$25 no bath, D–$30 w/bath, D–$40 w/bath; $15 dorm.
Youth Hostel, 520 7th Ave SE, 269-8239. $13 members, $18 non-members. 'Excellent facilities.'
U of Calgary, Kananaskis Hall and **Rundle Hall**, 220-7243. S–$21. Students only. Monthly rates also available. 'Good facilities, gym, cheap meals.'
Camping: KOA Calgary W, 288-0411, 1.6 km west on Hwy 1, and **Langdon Park**, about 20 miles east.

FOOD

Earl's, various locations. 'Great burgers, great prices.'
Joey's Only, 1411 17th Ave SW. Fish & chips and seafood. All you can eat chips. Inexpensive, good food.
Kensington's Delicafe, 1414 Kensington Rd NW. Earthy atmosphere, live entertainment, Weds–Sat.
Nick's Steak House and Pizza, 2430 Crowchild Trail NW. Close to U of Calgary across from McMahon Stadium.
North Hill Diner, 80216 Ave NW.
Smitty's Pancake House, various locations—big breakfasts.
Kensington—Louise Crossing area—Memorial Dr. and 10th Ave NW. Several restaurants to choose from, all reasonably priced.
Electric Avenue, 11 Ave SW between 4th & 6th Sts—trendy nightclub area with lots of eateries.
17th Ave SW, between 1st and 14th Sts. Lots of places sandwiched among interesting shops.

OF INTEREST

Calgary Tower, 101 9th Ave at Centre St S, 266-7171. Offers fantastic views of the city and the Rockies. Open 7.30am–11pm daily. $4.25.
Canada Olympic Park, Hwy 1 W, 247-5404. Bus tour of bobsleigh, luge runs, 70 and 90 metre ski jumps. In the winter the public can try bobsleigh and luge. Call for prices. Also the **Olympic Hall of Fame** with a heartstopping audiovisual ski-jump simulator that allows visitors to experience the sensations felt by the athletes. 10am–5pm $8. Bus tour $8.50, students $4.50.
Calgary Zoo and Dinosaur Park, Memorial Dr and 12th St E on George's Island, 232-9372. Has a fine aviary and a large display of cement reptiles and prehistoric monsters including one 120-ton dinosaur. Mon–Fri 9am–6pm; 8.30pm Sat, Sun during rest of year. $7.50, ages 10–17 $4.50. Tue, half price.
Centennial Planetarium and Alberta Science Centre, Mewata Pk, 11th St and 7th Ave SW, 221-3700. Phone to check times of shows in planetarium. Museum has vintage aircraft, model rockets and a weather station, $5.50, $2.50 extra for planetarium, open daily 10am–8pm. Fri & Sat till 10.30pm.

Energeum, 640 5th Ave, 297-4293. Hands-on science centre about energy resources, oil and gas, coal, and hydroelectricity. Free. Open Sun–Fri 10.30am–4.30pm.
Fort Calgary Interpretive Centre, 750 9th Ave SE, 290-1875. Calgary's birthplace. Traces early NorthWest Mounted Police life and prairie natural history. Daily 9am–5pm. Donations.
Glenbow Museum, 130 9th Ave SE, 264-8300. Art and artefacts of the west with a large collection of Canadian art and native artefacts. Daily 10am–6pm, $4.50, students $3. Sat $1.
Heritage Park, 1900 Heritage Dr, 259-1900. Calgary was once the Northwest Mountie outpost and this and other aspects of the city's past are dealt with in the park. The reconstructed frontier village includes a Hudson's Bay Co. trading post, an Indian village, trapper's cabin, ranch, school, and a blacksmiths. $6, ages 3–15 $3. Open daily 10am–6pm.
Prince's Island Park, on the northern edge of downtown has special events and is just nice for sunbathing, etc.

INFORMATION
Calgary Hospitality Centre, 1300 6 Ave SW. Open June–Sept daily, 8am–9pm; Sept–June Mon–Fri, 9am–5pm.
Calgary Tourist and Convention Bureau, 9th Ave, Centre St, 262-2766/263-8510. Open Mon–Fri 8.30am–5pm.
Calgary International Airport, at the 'Chuckwagon' on Arrivals level. Open 364 days a year, 7am–10pm.

ENTERTAINMENT
Calgary Stampede. Second week in July. Calgary returns to its wild cowboy past. Rodeo events, chuckwagon races, free pancake breakfasts, bands, parties and tons of Texas two-steppin'. For info on tickets, call 261-0101; for ticket orders only, call (800) 661-1260. '10 days of fun and enjoyment.'
Ranchman's, 9615 Macleod Tr S, 253-1100. A Honkytonk, saloon, restaurant, nightclub and rodeo cowboy museum. Boot stompin' country music and western dance hall.
Electric Ave, 11th Ave SW (see under *Food*). An action packed strip of real estate that comes alive at night. 'Try **The Warehouse** and **Tasmanian Ballroom**.'
Calgary Centre for Performing Arts, 205 8th Ave. Calgary Symphony Orchestra and live theatre. Call the 24hr Show Information Line, 294-7444.

TRAVEL
Greyhound Bus Station: 850 16th St SW, 265-9111. Leave terminal by 9th Ave exit and take #79, 103, 10, 102 bus to town, $1.50.
'The only bus south out of Calgary to the USA leaves at 7am, arriving Butte, Montana, at 7pm.' $87.
Hitchhiking is illegal within city limits.
Calgary International Airport is located 12 miles north of the city. The Airporter bus leaves every 30 minutes from major downtown hotels, $7.50, 6.30am–11.30pm. A taxi will cost about $20–$25, call 250-8311. Airport info—292-8477.

DRUMHELLER In the Drumheller Badlands, northwest of Calgary, the 30-mile **Dinosaur Trail** leads to the mile-wide valley where more than 30 skeletons of prehistoric beasts have been found. Everything from yard-long bipeds to the 40-foot-long Tyrannosaurus Rex.

As well as dinosaur fossils, petrified forests and weird geological formations such as hoodoos, dolomites and buttes are to be seen in the valley. Another survivor of prehistory is the yucca plant found here, also in fossil

form. The **Tyrell Museum** (823-7707) in Midland Provincial Park on Hwy 838 is one of the largest paleontology museums in the world. Daily 9am–9pm, $5.50. Free on Tues.
Drumheller Big Country Tours Association, 823-5885.

ACCOMMODATION
Alexandra International Hostel, 30 Railway Avenue N, Drumheller, 823-6337. Located inside a refurbished hotel built in the 30's. $10 members, $15 non-members.

WATERTON LAKES NATIONAL PARK The other bit of the Waterton/Glacier International Peace Park (see also under Montana). Mountains rise abruptly from the prairie in the southwestern corner of the province to offer magnificent jagged alpine scenery, several rock-basin lakes, beautiful U-shaped valleys, hanging valleys and countless waterfalls.

There are more than 100 miles of trails within the park which is a great place for walking or riding. It's also a good spot for fishing and canoeing and has four campsites. Several cabins and hotels are provided within the park. Most of Waterton's lakes are too cold for swimming but a heated outdoor pool is open during the summer in Waterton township.

A drive north on Route 6 will take you close to a herd of plains buffalo. Go south on the same road and you cross the border on the way to Browning, Montana. You can also reach the US by boat. The *International* sails daily between Waterton Park townsite and Goathaunt Landing in Glacier National Park. Park admission $5 daily. **Waterton Park** townsite, on the west shore of Upper Waterton Lake, is the location of the park headquarters. The park information office is open daily during the summer and park rangers arrange guided walks and tours, and give talks and campfire programmes, etc, about the flora and fauna of the area. Park Info: 859-2224.

MEDICINE HAT A town whose best claim to fame is its unusual name. Legend has it that this was the site of a great battle between the Cree and Blackfeet Indians. The Cree fought bravely until their medicine man deserted them, losing his headdress in the middle of the nearby river. The Cree warriors believed this to be a bad omen, laid down their weapons and were immediately annihilated by the Blackfeet. The spot became known as 'Saamis', meaning 'medicine man's hat'.

ACCOMMODATION
Assiniboia Inn, 680 3rd St SE, 526-2801. S-$31, D-$36.
El Bronco Motel, 1177 1 St SW, 526-5800. S/D-$45.
Trans Canada Motel, 780 8th St, 526-5981. S-$24, D-$32.

OF INTEREST
Medicine Hat Museum and Art Gallery, 1302 Bomford Cr, 527-6266. Indian artefacts, pioneer items and national and local art exhibits. Mon-Fri 9am–5pm, Sat and Sun 1pm–5pm. Donations. Closed 1–2pm daily.

INFORMATION
Information Center, 8 Gehing Rd SE, 527-6422. Open 8am–9pm in summer, 9am–5pm after Labour Day.
Chamber of Commerce, 577 2nd St SE, 527-5214.

WRITING-ON-STONE PROVINCIAL PARK In the south of the province, 40 kilometres from the small town of Milk River on Highway 501, is this park which is of great biological, geological and cultural interest. The site, overlooking the Milk River, contains one of North America's largest concentrations of pictographs and petroglyphs. Inscribed on massive sandstone outcrops, these examples of plains rock art were carved by nomadic Shoshoni and Blackfoot tribes.

This site is open year round but access is only on the one and a half hour guided tours daily from May through beginning of Sept. Call for info on special events, 647-2364. Camping $11.

HEAD-SMASHED-IN BUFFALO JUMP If the name isn't enough to pique your curiosity, then the fact that this historical interpretive centre is a UNESCO World Heritage site may. The Plains Indians who once inhabited this area, hunted buffalo by driving herds of the massive beasts over the huge sandstone cliffs to certain death below. According to legend, a young Indian brave tried to watch one of the hunts from a sheltered ledge below (somewhat like standing underneath a waterfall). So many animals were driven over the cliff, that his people found him after the hunt with his skull crushed by the weight of the buffalo, hence the rather startling name.

The centre is located 18 km northwest of Fort Macleod on secondary Highway 875 and is 175 km south of Calgary. Open 7 days a week 9am–8pm (9am–5pm in the winter). $5.50, 553-2731.

MANITOBA

Situated in the heart of the North American continent, Manitoba extends 760 miles from the 49th to the 60th parallel; from the Canada–United States border to the Northwest Territories. Surprisingly then the province has a 400-mile-long coastline. This is on Hudson Bay where the important port of Churchill is located.

The first European settlers reached Hudson Bay as early as 1612 although the Hudson's Bay Company was not formed until 1670. You cannot travel far in Canada without becoming aware of the power of the Hudson's Bay Company and its influence in the settlement of the country. At one time its territory included almost half of Canada, its regime only ending in 1869 when its lands became part of Canada. These days the company is relegated back to its origins—you will see the name on a chain of department stores across Canada.

By 1812 both French and British traders were well established along the Red and Assiniboine Rivers and in that year a group of Scottish crofters settled in what is now Winnipeg. The present population of Manitoba includes a large percentage of German and Ukrainian immigrants although the English, Scots and French still predominate. Manitoba became a province in 1870, although only after the unsuccessful rising of the Metis (half Indian/half trapper stock) had been quashed. After the rail link to the east reached here in 1881, settlers flocked here to clear the land and grow wheat. Winnipeg became the metropolis of the Canadian west.

Though classed as a Prairie Province, three-fifths of Manitoba is rocky forest land, but even this area is pretty flat. If you're travelling across the province the landscape can get pretty tedious, prairies in the west and endless forests and lakes in the east. More than 100,000 lakes in all, the largest of which is Lake Winnipeg at 9320 square miles.

National Park: Riding Mountain.

The telephone area code is 204.

WINNIPEG A stop here is almost a necessity if you're travelling across Canada. The provincial capital of Manitoba, Canada's fourth largest city, has plenty to offer, especially if you can time a visit to coincide with one of the many festivals happening in and around Winnipeg in the summer months. Among these are the Winnipeg Folk Festival, held annually at Birds Hill Park in July and Folklorama, Winnipeg's cultural celebration, held every year in early August.

Winnipeg (from the Cree word 'Winnipee' meaning 'muddy waters') is very 'culture-conscious', with good theatre, a symphony orchestra, the world-renowned Royal Winnipeg Ballet, and a plethora of museums and art galleries. It's also a major financial and distribution centre for western Canada: hence the chains of vast grain elevators, railway yards, stockyards, flour mills and meat packaging plants.

The Red River divides the city roughly north to south. Across the river from downtown Winnipeg is the French-Canadian suburb, St Boniface. This community retains its own culture while mixing well with the Anglophones in Winnipeg. Many services are, therefore, offered in both languages. Winnipeg is known for its very long and cold winters, but in the summer, the temperatures are comfortably in the high 70s and 80s. Cool in the evenings though.

ACCOMMODATION

Backpackers Guest House Intl, 168 Maryland St, 772-1272. 'Clean and friendly.'

Ivey House Int'l Hostel, 210 Maryland St (Broadway & Sherbrooke), 772-3022. Members $12, non-members $16. Central bath. Bicycle rentals. Open for check-in 8–9.30am and after 5pm. Reservations recommended. 'Very friendly.' Central.

McLaren Hotel, 514 Main St (across from the Centennial Centre), 943-8518. Room with double bed, wash basin–$30. With full bath, $35. Very central.

Winnipeg Hotel, 214 S Main St, 942-7762. S–$21, D–$27, with private bath.

University of Manitoba Residence, 26 MacLean Cr, 474-9942. May–Aug, co-ed, $17 single. Small fee gives access to pool and other sports facilities on the campus. Call during the day for information.

There are many **Bed & Breakfast** places in Winnipeg. The tourist office has a complete listing, or call 783-9797 for reservations. Open daily 8am–8pm.

FOOD

Basil's, 117 Osborne, 453-8440. Trendy, studenty.

Blue Boy Café, 911 Main St, 943-1308. Cheap breakfast and lunch, $2.50 up. Open 7am–10pm, afternoon closing on the w/end.

Kelekis, 1100 Main St N, 582-1786. Renowned deli. Good and cheap.

Old Market Café, Old Market Square. Good in the summer. Outdoor patio. Next to it is **King's Head**, a British-style pub.

Mamma Mia Pizzeria, 631 Corydon Ave, 453-9210. The name says it all.

OF INTEREST

A 1-hour **walking tour** of historic Winnipeg is available from Museum of Man and Nature, 190 Rupert St. For info call 774-3514. $4 July & Aug only.

Legislative Building, Broadway and Osborne. Built of native stone, this fine neo-classical building houses, as well as the legislative chambers, an art gallery, a museum and a tourist office. It is set in a 30-acre landscaped park. Tours available. For info call 945-3700. Note the Golden Boy on the top of the building, and also the totem pole nearby which was a gift to the people of Manitoba from the people of British Columbia to commemorate BC's centennial in 1971.

Centennial Centre, on Main St across from City Hall. This new cultural complex houses many sources of entertainment. There is a concert hall, 956-1360, free tours of which are given daily in the summer. The **Museum of Man and Nature**, 555 Main St, 956-2830, features provincial history and natural history of the Manitoba grasslands. Includes dioramas depicting Indian and urban Manitoban history and a replica of the 17th century sailing ship *Nonsuch*. Open daily in summer, 10am–6pm. Tues–Sun 10am–4pm in winter.

Winnipeg Art Gallery, 300 Memorial Blvd, 786-6641. One of the world's largest Inuit art collections. Traditional and contemporary Canadian, American, and European works. Open Tues–Sun 10am–5pm and on Wed and Thurs 'till 9pm. Closed Mon (winter). On Thursday afternoons in the summer there are free jazz concerts on the rooftop of the gallery. $3, students $2 (includes Ukrainian Exhibition).

Ukrainian Cultural and Education Centre, 184 Alexander Ave E, 942-0218. Folk art, documents, costumes, and history. Open Tues–Sat 10am–4pm, Sun 2pm–5pm. Free.

Assiniboine Park, Corydon Ave W at Shaftsbury. On the Assiniboine River with miniature railway and an English garden. This park is very popular in the summer and there is always some sort of production here, be it Shakespeare, the symphony, or the ballet. In the winter there is skating, sleigh rides and tobogganning. Call 942-4576 for performance info.

Lower Fort Garry, on the banks of the Red River 19 miles north of Winnipeg on Hwy 9. This National Historic Park is the only stone fort of the fur-trading days in North America still intact. The fort has been used at different times for various purposes. Originally the fortified headquarters of the ubiquitous Hudson's Bay Company, it has also been used as a garrison for troops, a Governor's Residence, a meeting place for traders and Indians, and the first treaty with the Indians was signed here. The park is open daily from May–Sept, 9.30am–6pm. Tours are available. There is also a museum with nice displays of pioneer and Indian goods, maps and clothes. To reach the fort take a Beaver Bus Line bus from downtown Winnipeg (Beaver Bus Lines—237-3989) or by boat tour, 947-6843.

Upper Fort Garry Gate, the only bit remaining of the original Fort stands in a small park opposite the CN station on Main St. This stone structure was Manitoba's own 'Gateway to the Golden West'. A plaque outlines the history of several forts which stood in the vicinity. Free.

Riel House, 330 River Rd, 257-1783. This house is a good example of a Metis dwelling of the nineteenth century. Louis Riel was the leader of the Metis revolt in 1870. His mother lived here, and this is where his coffin lay in state. Open daily, 10am–6pm May–Aug; weekends only in Sept.

Royal Canadian Mint, 520 Lagimodiere Blvd, 257-3359. One of the largest coin producing mints in the world. Free tours available every half hour, Mon–Fri 9am–3pm; until 3.30pm July & Aug. $2 admission.

Living Prairie Museum and Nature Preservation Park, 2795 Ness Ave, 832-0167. See what the prairie looked like before the settlers came. Open daily July–Aug, 10am–5pm. Free. Tours available. The prairie is open 24 hrs. 'Take insect repellent!'

St Boniface. Across the Red River, this French Canadian suburb is the site of the largest stockyards in the British Commonwealth. The **St Boniface Museum**, 494 Taché, 237-4500, is interesting, as is the **St Boniface Cathedral** next door.

Steinbach Mennonite Village Museum, 40 miles outside Winnipeg. Go east on Hwy 1 and south on Hwy 12. This re-creation of a turn-of-the-century Mennonite village comes complete with mill, store, school, and costumes of the day. There is also a good restaurant. Open May 1–Sept 30. Admission charged. Accessible by Greyhound or Grey Goose Bus Lines.

INFORMATION
Manitoba Visitors Reception Centre, Room 101, Legislative Building, 450 Broadway at Osborne, 945-3777. Maps and literature. Open in summer Mon–Fri 8am–7pm, 8.30am–4.30pm rest of year. Pick up a copy of *Passport to Winnipeg* for up-to-date information.

TRAVEL
River Cruises on the Red and the Assiniboine Rivers leave from Louise Bridge or Redwood Bridge. Also paddlewheel trips from 2285 Main St N to Fort Garry. From about $12. Info: 947-6843.
Bus station, 487 Portage Ave, 783-8840, for Greyhound and 301 Burnell St, 786-8891, for Grey Goose Bus Lines.
VIA Rail station is at Broadway and Main, (800) 561-8630. The train to Churchill takes over 2 days and costs $150 rt (if bought 14 days in advance).
Bike hire: several locations in Assiniborne Park: ask at Visitors Centre.
Winnipeg International Airport, 20 minutes west of downtown, is served by the local transit buses, 986-5700. Take 15 (Sargent Airport) from Vaughn and Portage, $1.30. A taxi will cost around $10 o/w, call 925-3131.

SHOPPING/EVENTS
Osborne Village, between River and Corydon Junction. Boutiques, craft and speciality shops and eating places. Look out for the Medea, a co-op art gallery found in the Village.
The Exchange District and Old Market Square are also interesting places to shop. Portage Ave is the main downtown shopping area. Portage Place has shops, restaurants, and a new IMAX theatre.
The **Winnipeg Folk Festival** takes place annually at the beginning of July in Birds Hill Provincial Park. This internationally renowned festival features the best in bluegrass, jazz, and gospel music. The park is accessible from Hwy 59 north of Winnipeg or through Winnipeg Transit.
Folklorama is Winnipeg's multi-cultural celebration held in early August. This two week-long festival highlights the ethnic diversity of Winnipeg with over 40 pavilions featuring the food, dance, and culture of different nations. Day passports are available.
The Fringe Festival. Canada's answer to the Edinburgh version, held in mid-July, welcomes the talents of 65 performing companies from around the world to the streets of Winnipeg. Shows are presented in seven venues in Old Market Square and each one costs less than $5. Mime, improv, drama, cabarets.

RIDING MOUNTAIN NATIONAL PARK In western Manitoba, the park occupies the vast plateau of Riding Mountain, which rises to 2200 feet, offering great views of the distant prairie lands.

The total area of Riding Mountain Park is about 1200 square miles and although parts of it are fairly commercialised there are still large tracts of untamed wilderness to be explored by boat or on the hiking and horse trails. Deer, elk, moose and bear are all common and at **Lake Audy** there is a herd of bison. Also good for fishing.

Clear Lake is the part most exploited for and by tourists and the township of **Wasagaming** (an Indian term meaning 'clear water') has campsites, lodges, motels and cabins as well as many other resort-type facilities, right down to a movie theatre built like a rustic log cabin.

The park is reached from Winnipeg via Route 4 to Minnedosa, and then on Route 10. Daily admission $5, $10 (4 day pass). 848-2811.

CHURCHILL Known as the 'Polar Bear Capital of the World', Churchill has been a trading port since 1689 and is still the easiest part of the 'frozen north' to see. During the short July to October shipping season, this sub-artic seaport handles vast amounts of grain and other goods for export. The west's first settlers came to Manitoba via Churchill.

The partially-restored **Prince of Wales Fort**, the northernmost fort in North America, was built by the British in 1732. It took 11 years to build and has 42-foot-thick walls. Despite this insurance against all-comers, the garrison surrendered to the French without firing a single shot in 1782.

Churchill is a great place to view some of the wonders of nature. From September to April, the beautiful **Aurora Borealis** (northern lights) are visible and good for picture-taking. The summer daylight, however, doesn't provide the best viewing conditions. To make up for it, whale watching is best in the summer months, from July to early September. The beluga whales come in and out with the tides. Polar bears are most frequently seen roaming around the city in September and October and are periodically airlifted to other regions.

Note that Churchill is only accessible by plane or train (no automobiles). Look into the package deals put together by VIA Rail (see Winnipeg).

ACCOMMODATION
Churchill Motel, 675-8853. D–$80. Double bed with bath, TV and telephone. Free transportation from airport and train station.
Polar Hotel, 15 Franklin St, 675-8878, D–$80.

OF INTEREST
The **Eskimo Museum**, next to the Catholic Church on LaVerendrye St, is worth visiting. Fur trade memorabilia, kayaks, Indian and Eskimo art and utensils. Open Tues–Sat 9am–noon, 1pm–5pm, Mon 1pm–5pm. Free. 675-2030.
Fort Prince of Wales National Historic Park, at west bank of mouth of Churchill River. After its partial destruction by the French in 1782, it was never again occupied. Now partially restored. Open daily. Entrance to the Fort is free but it is only accessible by boat (weather permitting). $38. 'Recommended early summer for the whales.'

INFORMATION/TRAVEL
Parks Canada, Manitoba North Historic Sites, Bayport Plaza, 675-8863. Open 8am–5pm daily.
North Star Bus station, 203 LaVerendrye, 675-2629. Local bus company offering 4 hr tours of the town, $30.
Sea North Tours, 675-2195. Tours of Fort Prince of Wales, the harbour plus whales and bears. June–Sept.

SASKATCHEWAN

Cornflakes country. Known as the 'Wheat Province', Saskatchewan, wedged between Alberta and Manitoba, is the prairie keystone. Although the black ribbon of the Trans Canada Highway takes the traveller through seemingly endless, flat expanses of wheat fields in southern Saskatchewan, the province does have a more diverse geography. From the scenic hills of the Qu'Appelle Valley to the Cypress Hills in the southwest and the badlands in the southeast, Saskatchewan is anything but wholly flat.

In the south, where visibility can be up to 20 miles, watch the sky—sunsets and rises are beautiful, and cloud formations during a wild prairie storm can be spectacular. As you travel north of the prairies, north of Highway 16, the yellow landscape gives way to green rolling hills, and, still further north, to rugged parkland—lakes, rivers and evergreen forests.

Saskatchewan derives its name from 'Kisiskatchewan', a Cree word meaning 'the river that flows swiftly', a reference no doubt to the South Saskatchewan River. The Hudson's Bay Company began the exploitation of the province's natural resources when it started fur trading here in the late 1700s. Recently, oil exploration in the south has led to the discovery of helium and potash, in addition to large quantities of 'bubbling crude'. In the summer, the weather is hot and dry while the winters are long, cold and snowy.

National Park: Prince Albert.

The telephone area code is 306.

REGINA Provincial capital, situated in the heart of the wheatlands, and the accepted stopping place between Winnipeg and Calgary. Regina became capital of the entire Northwest Territories in 1883 just one year after its founding. Situated on the railroad the town served as a government outpost and headquarters for the Northwest Territories Mounted Police until the formation of Saskatchewan as a separate province.

The town was founded and christened Regina after Queen Victoria in 1882 when the first Canadian Pacific Railway train arrived. Its earlier, more picturesque name of Pile O'Bones, referring to the Indian buffalo killing mound at the site, was considered inappropriate for a capital city.

ACCOMMODATION

B & J Bed and Breakfast, 2066 Ottawa St, 522-4575. S–$22, D–$33.
Empire Hotel, 1718 McIntyre St, 522-2544. S–$24, D–$36. Central bath.
Georgia Hotel, 1927 Hamilton St, 569-3226. S–$26, D–$28. A/C, TV, shower/bath. Close to downtown and night clubs.
Turgeon Hostel, 2310 McIntyre (at College), 791-8165. Members $10, non-members $15. Cooking facs, laundry, common room, library. 'Great place—clean, convenient.'
University of Regina—College West Residence, Wascana Pkwy & Kramer Blvd, 585-4111. $17, bath, TV. Available May–Aug only. Call ahead for reservations.
YMCA, 2400 13th Ave, 757-9622. $18.50 per night. $5 key deposit. Men only.
YWCA, 1940 McIntyre St, 525-2141. $33 per night plus $2 refundable key deposit. $255 monthly. Rooms have basin, fridge, shared kitchen facs, showers, laundry.
Camping: Fifty Plus Campground, 8 mi east on Hwy 1, 781-2810.

FOOD

Geno's Pizza and Pasta, Albert St N at Ring Rd and Gordon Rd at Rae St. Inexpensive Italian.
The Novia Cafe, 2158 12th Ave. A trendy Regina tradition. 'Don't miss the cream pie.' Open 'til 8.30pm.
City Hall Cafeteria, 359-3989, on main floor, McIntyre and Victoria. 'Best lunch bargains in town.'

OF INTEREST

Wascana Park, built around Wascana Lake, this 2500-acre chunk of parkland in the southern end of the city is home to a great many of the tourist sites in Regina. The provincial **legislative buildings** are here and tours are offered on the half-hour. You should also visit the **The Saskatchewan Museum of Natural History**, 787-2815, a walk-through museum with Eskimo carvings and exhibits on the bird and animal life of Saskatchewan and local geology. Open daily 9am–8.30pm, 9am–4.30pm in winter. Donations.

The new **Saskatchewan Science Centre**, 791-7900, in the park features many 'hands-on' type exhibits and is said to be 'quite fun'. Open Tue–Sat 9am–6pm, Fri till 9pm, Sun 10am–7.30pm. $7. Hours change after Labour Day.

Part of the **University of Regina** campus is also located here; campus tours are available. The **MacKenzie Art Gallery**, specializing in European and American art is found on the old University of Regina campus, on College Ave, 522-4242. Open Tue–Sun 11pm–6pm, Wed & Thurs till 9.30pm. Tours Sun 2–4pm.

Finally, the **Diefenbaker Homestead**, 522-3661, the boyhood home of the former Prime Minister, is also in the Park. Open daily 10am–7pm. Free.

Bicycle rentals are available in the park at the Marina. Or tour the entire centre in a double-decker bus, boarded at the **Wascana Centre**. Also here are a water-fowl sanctuary on Willow Island, a restaurant and a concert hall.

RCMP Barracks and Museum, Dewdney Ave on the western edge of town, 780-5838. HQ and training school. The Centennial Museum is open daily, 8am–6.45pm. Free. Every Tuesday in July and August the Sunset Ceremony takes place at Depot Division at 6.45pm. There is also the daily Sergeant Major's Parade at 1pm which includes a drill display and inspection of the troops. Tours of the training facility available.

Government House, corner of Dewdney Ave and Pasque St, 787-5726, is the restored home of the former Lieutenant Governor of Saskatchewan. Open daily 1pm–4pm, Sun till 5pm. Closed Mon. Free. Guided tours available.

Buffalo Days are held in Regina at the end of July or beginning of August. A celebration of Saskatchewan traditions such as chuckwagon races, logging contest, agricultural fair and exhibition. Also midway rides, grandstand shows and casino. At the Agridome Star theatre. Entrance around $8. 'Great fun.'

There is also a three day **Folk Festival** held at the University of Regina in June.

One of Saskatchewan's biggest attractions is the **Big Valley Jamboree** in **Craven**, 26 miles north of Regina. During the third week of July the population of this small town swells by nearly one hundred times as thousands congregate for free unserviced camping and North America's largest Country and Western festival, featuring many top names. This is followed by Saskatchewan's largest rodeo, the last weekend in July.

INFORMATION/TRAVEL

Regina Convention and Visitors Bureau, Hwy 1E, 789-5099. Open Mon–Fri 8am–7pm, Sat/Sun 10am–6pm.

Greyhound Station, 2041 Hamilton St, 787-3340.

Regina Airport is reachable by cab only. Call 586-6555, $6–$8.

SASKATOON Saskatoon got going in 1883 as the proposed capital of a temperance colony. An Ontario organisation acquired 100,000 acres of land and settlement began at nearby Moose Jaw. It seems that Saskatchewantonians were unwilling to go without drink. The population of Saskatoon failed to increase, so plans for the temperance colony were essentially scrapped, and the city continued to develop as a trading centre. Some establishments remain dry, however.

CANADIAN WILDLIFE

With so much remote and relatively uninhabited land, Canada is also rich in wildlife. These are some of the more common and/or interesting types the visitor to the backwoods or mountains may come across.

Bears—the dangerous **grizzly**, to be found in BC, Alberta and the Yukon, is very fast but doesn't see well, can't climb trees and runs slowest downhill; the smaller **black and brown bears** are found all over and often visit campgrounds and dumps—keep your food locked away and never in the tent! Largest of all is the **polar bear**—that's the white one . . . only in the far north however. The **beaver** is one of Canada's symbols and is found all across the country. Most likely to be seen chewing its way through a log or having a wash in the very early morning or early evening.

The massive, mean-looking **buffalo**, still exists, but only in government-run parks. Not to be tampered with—don't climb that fence. When out in the prairie or bush you may hear the howl of a **wolf** or **coyote** at night. The coyote is a small, timid animal, more of a scavanger than a hunter. The larger, silver grey wolf has been getting a better press of late. Previously vilified as being fierce and a danger to humans, current rethinking says that the wolf just *looks* fierce (probably because they hunt in packs) and seldom harms humans.

The **lynx** is a large grey cat with mainly nocturnal habits. It hunts small animals and is found all over. **Deer** of many kinds can likewise be found everywhere. Moose too are found across Canada but more commonly in northern woods and around swamps. A large brown, shy animal, the moose is a popular target for hunters. Their distant cousins, **caribou** (or reindeer) live in herds only in the far north. Overhunting and radioactive fallout had severely reduced the numbers of the caribou herds so they are now more carefully monitored. Some Inuit still use caribou for food and for their hides. The more usual smaller animals such as the **squirrel**, **chipmunk**, **raccoon** and **skunk** are common everywhere in Canada and may well be seen around campsites.

If on either the Pacific or Atlantic, or Hudson's Bay coastline, **whale-watching** may appeal. Canada is a fisherman's paradise, northern **pike**, **bass** and **trout** are the most common **freshwater fish**, while the highly prized **salmon** can be found on the east and west coasts, that of British Columbia being the best.

One of the most mournful and memorable bird calls heard in Canada is that of the **loon**. Once heard over a northern Ontario lake in the late evening, and never again forgotten.

The South Saskatchewan River cuts right through the middle of the town and the parklands along its bank make Saskatoon a really pretty place, especially in the summer; it's an easy-going town with friendly residents. Saskatoon is 145 miles north of Regina, in the heart of the parklands.

ACCOMMODATION

Patricia Hotel, 345 2nd Ave N, 242-8861. With private bath: S–$31, D–$39. Central. Reservations recommended. Also, the hotel runs a year-round **Hostel**: Members $12, non-members–$15. Bunkbeds.

The Senator, 3rd Ave S at 21 St E, 244-6141. S–$38, D–$43. Includes TV, A/C and private bath. Hotel fills up quickly so call in advance. Very central.

YWCA, 510 25th St E, 244-0944. $38 nightly, $120 per wk, $285 per month. With $10 key deposit. Sports facilities available for use at a minimal charge. Women only. Call to reserve.

FOOD

David's Lounge and Restaurant, 294 Venture Cr off Circle Drive North, 664-1133. Good for big hearty breakfasts.
Louis' Campus Pub, on the University of Saskatchewan campus. Named after the rebellious Louis Riel. A favourite summertime haunt. Lunch on the patio.
Saint Tropez Bistro, 243 3rd Ave S, 652-1250. 'Nice light meals downtown.'

OF INTEREST

Stretching along both sides of the South Saskatchewan River, near Spadina Cres, the **Meewasin Valley Trail** is the perfect place to go for a long walk or to have a picnic in the hot summer sum. The **Meewasin Valley Centre**, an interpretive centre, is open Mon–Fri 9am–5pm and weekends & hols 10.30am–6pm. Also in and around the park is the **Mendel Art Gallery**, 950 Spadina Cres, open daily 10am–10pm, featuring soapstone carvings, a Rembrandt and lots of Canadiana. The campus of the **University of Saskatchewan** borders on the park and tours are available there. For a change from the ordinary, try Shakespeare prairie-style at the **Shakespeare on the Saskatchewan Festival**, held during July and the first two weeks of August in the park. Advance tickets recommended.
Ukrainian Museum of Canada, 910 Spadina Cres E, 244-3800. Folk art, photographs and exhibits depicting the history of Ukrainian immigrants in Saskatchewan. Summer, Mon–Sat 10am–5pm, Sun 1pm–5pm. $2.
Museum of Ukrainian Culture, 202 Ave M South, 244-4212. History of Ukrainian heritage exhibited. Open daily, June–Aug, 2pm–5pm daily. $1 students.
The Western Development Museum, 2610 Lorne Ave, 931-1910. Turn of the century 'Pioneer Street'—family life, transportation, industry, agriculture, etc. The museum's collection is 'said to be the best of its kind in North America'. 'Good.' Open daily 11am–5pm, Sun 1–5pm. $4.
Saskatchewan Jazz Festival, along the riverbank of the South Saskatchewan. Takes place on the first weekend in July.
Harvest Fest, held in conjunction with the **Saskatchewan Exhibition** in early Sept. Midway, casino, grandstand, tractor pulls and other contests. The town's biggest event of the year. At Exhibition Grounds south of Lorne Ave.

INFORMATION/TRAVEL

Visitors and Convention Bureau, 102–310 Idylwyld Dr N, 242-1206.
Greyhound Bus Terminal, 50 23rd St E, 933-8000.
W W Northcote River Cruises from bandstand in Kiwanis Park and from behind Mendel Art Gallery. $6. 244-1975, 665-1818.
Saskatoon airport is reachable by taxi only. Call 653-3333, $10–11.

PRINCE ALBERT NATIONAL PARK This 1496-square-mile park typifies the lake and woodland wilderness country lying to the north of the prairies. It's an excellent area for canoeing with many connecting rivers between the lakes. From 1931–8 it was home to Grey Owl, one of the world's most famous park naturalists and imposters. Born Archibald Belaney, old Grey was an Englishman who came to Canada to fulfil a boyhood dream of living in the wilderness. Donning traditional clothing, he presented himself as the son of an Apache woman and carried out valuable research work for the park.

Accommodation in the park includes campsites, hotels and cabins. **Waskesiu** is the main service centre. Saskatoon is 140 miles south. For Park information: Prince Albert National Park, 663-5322; or Prince Albert Convention and Visitors Bureau, 764-6222.
Waskesiu International Hostel, Montréal Rd near Waskesiu Lake, 663-5450. $12, $15 non-members. Kitchen facs, laundry, linen (50¢).

THE PACIFIC

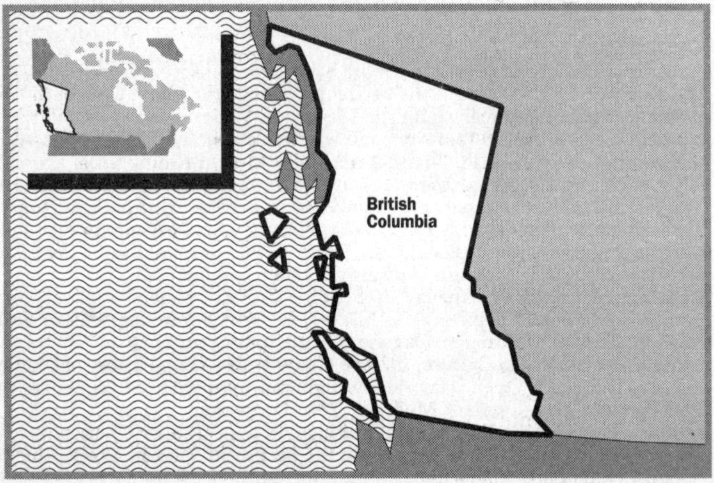

BRITISH COLUMBIA

Sandwiched between the Pacific Ocean and the Rocky Mountains to the west and east and bordered to the south by Washington State and to the north by the Yukon Territory, British Columbia is Canada's most westerly province and arguably the most scenic as well. This is an almost storybook land of towering snow-topped mountains, timbered foothills, fertile valleys, great lakes and mightier rivers, plus a spectacular coastline. The coast has long deep fjords dotted with many islands, and rising out of the coastline are ranges of craggy mountain peaks, in some cases exceeding 13,000 feet.

Inland there is a large plateau that provides British Columbia's ranching country. This is bounded on the east by a series of mountain ranges extending to the Rocky Mountain Trench. From this valley flow the Fraser, Columbia and Peace Rivers. The southwestern corner of British Columbia is considered one of the world's best climatic regions having mild winters and sunny, temperate summers and is consequently popular with Canadian immigrants.

This vast and beautiful province, which is about four times the size of the United Kingdom, was, however, a late developer. As recently as the 1880s there was no real communication and no railroad link with the east. Then as now the Rockies formed a natural barrier between British Columbia and the rest of the Confederation. Although both Sir Francis Drake, while searching for the mythical Northwest Passage, and Captain James Cook came this way, there was no real development and exploration on the Pacific coast until the mid-1800s. Vancouver Island was not designated a colony until 1849 and the mainland not until 1866. British Columbia became a province in 1871.

The whole province still only has a population of three million people, but in recent years has enjoyed one of the highest standards of living in Canada thanks to the rapid development of British Columbia's abundance of natural resources. About 50 percent of provincial monies comes from timber-related products and industries but BC also has an amazing diversity of minerals on tap as well as oil and natural gas. Fishing and tourism are the other major money-makers.

National Parks: Yoho, Glacier, Kootenay, Mount Revelstoke, Pacific Rim.
The telephone area code is 604.

VANCOUVER This rapidly-growing West Coast city rivals San Francisco for the sheer physical beauty of its setting. Behind the city sit the snow-capped Blue Mountains of the Coast Range; lapping its shores are the blue waters of Georgia Strait and English Bay; across the bay is Vancouver Island; and to the south is the estuary carved out by its magnificent Fraser River.

Metropolitan Vancouver now covers most of the peninsula between the Fraser River and Burrard Inlet. Towering bridges link the various suburbs to the city and downtown area which occupies a tiny peninsula jutting into Burrard Inlet with the harbour to the east and English Bay to the west. Once downtown you are within easy reach of fine sandy beaches (or ski slopes in winter) and within the city limits there are several attractive parks. Most notable of these are the Queen Elizabeth Park, from which there is a terrific view of the whole area, and the thickly wooded 1000-acre Stanley Park.

Again like San Francisco, Vancouver is a melting-pot. English, Slavs, mid-Europeans, Italians, Americans, and the second largest Chinatown in North America. The politics are very west coast, some people are rabidly right wing, and some are rabidly left wing.

Canada's 'Gateway to the Pacific' has a harbour frontage of 98 miles but the railroads too have an important part to play in Vancouver's communications system; one of the most spectacular rides is that into Fraser Canyon, once the final heartbreak of the men pushing their way north to the gold-fields with only mules and camels to help them. If you're heading back east from here, this is the route to take.

Vancouver's climate is mild, but it does rain a fair amount. January is the coldest month although temperatures then are only about 11° Centigrade cooler than in July. Snow is rare and roses frequently bloom at Christmas. Altogether a great place to visit.

In 1986 Vancouver was host to the world for Expo '86 with the theme of transportation and related communications and technology. You can visit the site and the buildings down at the harbour. Vancouver has now become the city of choice for many American filmmakers. This 'Hollywood to the north' (as it has been nicknamed) provides a diverse backdrop for all types of movie sets and at lower costs than on US locations.

ACCOMMODATION

Globetrotters Inn, 170 W Esplanade, 968-5141. Dorm $13, S–$27, $38 with bath, D–$33 (twin beds). 'It's a good idea to book ahead as it gets busy here in summer.'

Hazelwood Hotel, 344 E Hastings St, 688-7467, in Chinatown. Weekly rates only: S–$110 shared bath, $159 with bath.
Kingston Hotel, 757 Richards St, 684-9024. $41 single up, $47 double up, continental breakfast included. B&B. Very European. Swedish sauna. Cafe outside, TV lounge, laundry. 'Nice place.' 'Good people.' 'Gives student discount.'
Niagara Hotel, 435 W Pender, 688-7574. $38 up single, no TV, no bath, $42 single with TV, $55 single with bath. $61 and up double. 'Comfortable and close to stores and bus station.'
Patricia Hotel, 403 E Hastings, 255-4301. $38 up single, $58 double. 'Close to downtown facilities.'
Regent Hotel, 160 E Hastings St, 681-7435. S–$30 with a $10 deposit. 'Basic but clean and safe.' Chinatown. 'Not for a girl on her own.'
Vancouver International Hostel, 1515 Discovery St, 224-3208. $13.50 CYH, $19 non-members. At foot of Jericho Beach. Take bus #4 UBC from Granville Station to 4th & Northwest Marine Drive, then a 5-min walk downhill to Discovery St. Big hostel with excellent facilities. Book ahead in summer. 'A great place but arrive early' (before 11pm). Bike rental $20 per day.
Vincents Backpackers Hostel, 927 Main St, 682-2441, near to VIA Rail & Greyhound stations. Dorm $10, S–$20, D–$25. $10 key deposit. 'Friendly and safe.' Turn right out of the bus station and walk for 10 mins downhill.
YMCA, 955 Burrard St, 681-0221. Single from $32, double from $52. Co-ed. 'Conveniently situated, friendly staff.'
YWCA, 580 Burrard St, 662-8188 or (800) 663-1424 from Alberta, BC, Washington, Oregon, Montana and Idaho. $49 single, $71 double, $82 quad. Women, couples, co-ed groups. 'Pool, quite nr bus station.'
University residence: Simon Fraser University, McTaggart Hall, Burnaby, 291-4503. $18 1 or 2 people (no linens), $30 single with linens. May–end Aug.
UBC Conference Centre, Gage Tower Residence, 5961 Student Union Blvd, 228-2963. S–$30, D–$80, dorm $20. Shared kitchen, washroom, 15 min to downtown and close to Wreck Beach.
Harbourfront Hostel, 209 Heatley Ave, 254-0733. $15 dorm-style, D-$35. Kitchen. 5 minutes to Chinatown and Gastown.
Camping: Surrey Timberland Campsite, 3418 King George Hwy, 531-1033. $12 per site. Store and laundry.

FOOD

Granville Public Market, Granville Island underneath the Granville St Bridge. 9am–6pm except Mon. Exceptional quality fresh produce, fish and other edibles. An excellent place to stop and have lunch. You can browse the market and be entertained, and then enjoy your meal of Fukomaki (sushi, under $3), Indian Candy (smoked salmon, about $2), fresh fruit, or any of a rainbow of other varied and exotic choices while your eyes feast on a difficult to beat view of sailboats, the city of Vancouver and the mountains rising up to snow-capped heights in the background.
Heavenly Muffins, 1025 House St, 'Italian crepe, $4, is delicious.'
JJ's, 644 Bute St, 682-2068. 'Products of cooking school sold to public. Good main course about $4.50.' Breakfast 7am–8am, lunch 11.30am–3pm.
Keg Restaurants, several locations. Inexpensive; salad bar, sea food, burgers. 'Keg-sized drinks.'
McLeans, 4530 Fraser St, 873-5636. Great for breakfast.
Milestones All Star Cafe, 2966 W 4th Ave, 734-8616. Burgers.
Old Spaghetti Factory, 53 Water St. Gastown. Large portions and reasonable prices.
Saigon Restaurants, 4 locations, Vietnamese food. 'Order combination D only.'
Subway, Univ of BC, Students' Union Bldg. Cafeteria style.
Taf's Cafe, 829 Granville St. 'Arty atmosphere cafe. Reasonably priced. You can leave messages and luggage here.' 684-8900.

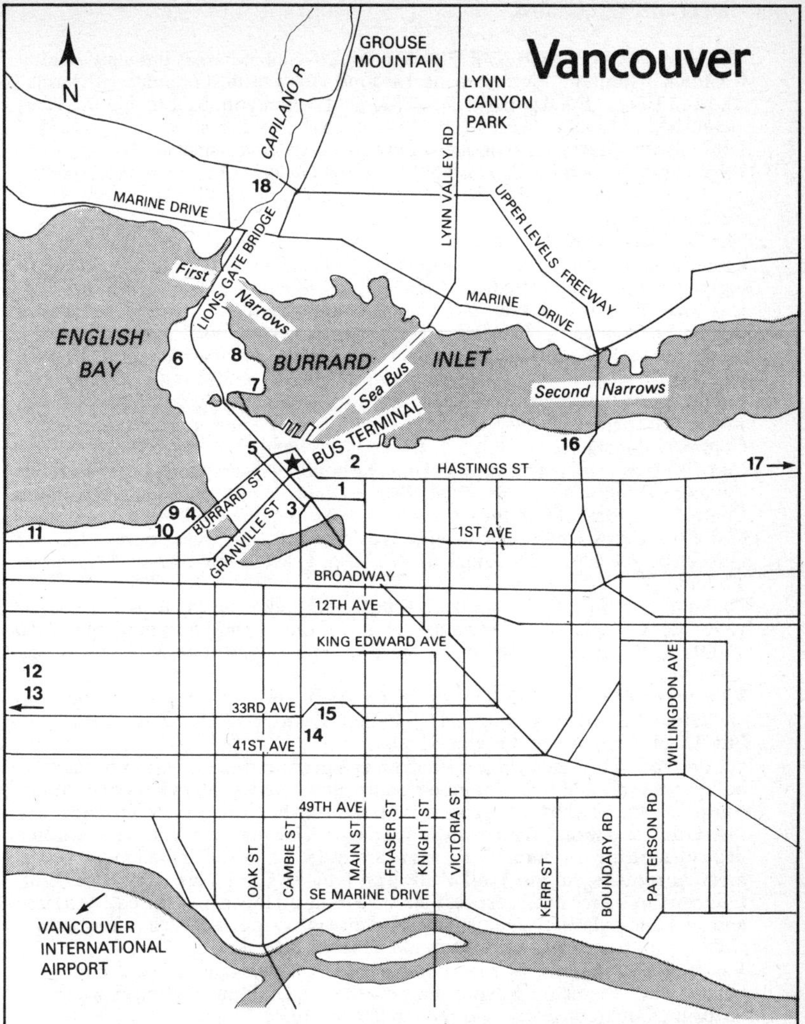

1 Chinatown
2 Gastown
3 Robson St
4 Canada Harborplace
5 Vancouver Art Gallery
6 Stanley Park
7 Seawall Walk
8 Vancouver Public Aquarium
9 Vancouver Museum and Macmillan Planetarium
10 Maritime Museum
11 Old Hastings Mill Store
12 University of British Columbia
13 Anthropological Museum, Nitobe Japanese Garden and Totem Park
14 Queen Elizabeth Gardens, Little Mountain
15 Bloedel Conservatory
16 Exhibition Park
17 Simon Fraser University
18 Capilano Suspension Bridge

The Only Cafe, 681-6546, 20 E Hastings. Meals from $6. 'Basic but tasty meal. A Gastown institution.' Complete meal around $10. 'Queues, popular with locals.'
The Tea House, Stanley Park, 669-3281. Only when you want to splurge. Very expensive, but really lovely.
UBC Campus Pizza, 2136 Western Pkway. Close to university.
White Spot Restaurants, 731-2434. Good and cheap.

OF INTEREST
The Downtown area
Chinatown, on Pender St, between Gore and Abbott Sts. Gift and curio shops, oriental imports, night clubs and many Chinese restaurants.
Gastown, in the area of Water, Alexander, Columbia and Cordova Sts. The original heart of Vancouver. In 1867 'Gassy Jack' Deighton set up a hotel in the shanty town on the banks of the Burrard Inlet. His establishment became so popular that the whole town was dubbed 'Gastown'. Now an area of trendy boutiques, good restaurants, antique shops, and pubs.
Robson St, between Howe St and Broughton St. European import stores and Continental restaurants. 'Vibrant. Great at weekends.'
Canada Place, at foot of Burrard St. Unusual building resembling a cruise ship; the Canadian Pavilion during Expo '86, it's now Vancouver's Trade and Convention Centre. A 5-storey IMAX theatre is also housed here (682-4629). For the domed OMNIMAX experience, go to **Science World**, a 4 min SkyTrain ride away at 1455 Quebec St, 268-6363. 40 min film, *To The Limit*, tickets $9 (film only), $11 combo, students $7.
Lookout!, 555 Hastings St, 689-0421. Ride the glass elevator 167m up to the observation deck of this tower for a superb view of the city and surroundings. $5.50 adults, $3.75 students, tickets last all day. Free if you dine at the revolving restaurant!
Vancouver Art Gallery, 750 Hornby St, 682-5621. Look out for special exhibitions and lunchtime poetry readings, etc. Sat–Wed 10am–5pm, Thur & Fri 10am–9pm, Sun 12pm–5pm, $4.75, students $2.50.
Stanley Park. This, the largest of Vancouver's parks, occupies the peninsula at the harbour mouth and has swimming pools, golf courses, a cricket pitch, tennis courts, several beaches, a free zoo, an aquarium, an English rose garden, and many forest trails and walks. A nice way to see the park is by bicycle. You can hire a bike just outside the park entrance. Rates are around $5 ph. If you're walking, a recommended route is the **Sea Wall Walk** past Nine O'Clock Gun, Brockton Point, Lumberman's Arch and Prospect Point. Near the eastern rim of the park is a large and very fine collection of totem poles. Admission to the park itself is free but you will have to pay for the aquarium. 681-1141 for info.
Vancouver Aquarium, Stanley Park, 682-1118. Open daily 9.30am–8pm until Labour Day. Thereafter 5.30pm. Entrance $9.50. Dolphins and killer whales. 'Brilliant. Could have watched the whales for hours.'
Vancouver West
Vancouver Museum, 1100 Chestnut St, 736-4431. Traces the development of the Northwest Coast from the Ice Age through pioneer days to the present. Entrance $5, $2.50 students. Daily 10am–5pm. Closed Mon in winter.
Macmillan Planetarium, 1100 Chestnut St. 'Essential to arrive early and book. Very popular.' Summer daily 1pm, 2.30pm, 4pm, 8pm. Winter 2.30pm, 8pm Tues–Sun with additional shows at 1pm and 4pm weekends and hols. Also laser shows. Around $6. Info: 736-3656.
Maritime Museum, foot of Cypress St, 737-2211. Exhibits include the RCMP ship *St Roch*, the first ship to navigate the Northwest Passage in both directions and to circumnavigate the continent of North America. Open daily. 10am–5pm, $5, $2.50 students.
Hastings Mill Museum, 1575 Alma Rd, 228-1213. One of the few buildings remaining after the Great Fire of 13 June 1886, this is now a museum with Indian

artefacts, mementoes of pioneer days and pictures of the city's development. Open daily 11am–4pm. Sept 16–May 31, Sat and Sun only, 1pm–4pm.
University of British Columbia, at Point Grey, has a population of some 23,000 students. There is a good swimming pool, cafeteria and bookshop. Also an **Anthropological Museum**, the **Nitobe Japanese Garden** and **Totem Park** which has carvings and buildings representing a small segment of a Haida Indian village. To get to the campus take a #10 bus from Granville and Georgia.
Queen Elizabeth Gardens, Little Mountain. When you enter the park keep left for the side with the views overlooking the North Shore mountains and harbour. There is a good view from the Lookout above the sunken gardens. Also, **Bloedel Conservatory**, 872-5513, on top of the mountain has a fine collection of tropical plants. Entrance $3. To get to and return from Little Mountain, take a #15 Cambie bus from Granville and Pender Sts and get off at 33rd and Cambie. Open Mon–Fri 9am–8pm, Sat–Sun 10am–9pm.

Vancouver East, Burnaby

Exhibition Park, bounded by Renfrew, Hastings and Cassiar Sts, is the home of the **Pacific National Exhibition**, **Stadia** and a **Sports Hall of Fame**. The PNE takes place at the end of August. $9.50 for a day's admission. 'Fantastic. Includes lumberjack competition, rodeo, demolition derby, exhibitions, fair, etc.' Open August–September. Call 253-2311 for info.
Simon Fraser University, atop Burnaby Mountain. Constructed in only 18 months, the giant module design of this ultra-modern seat of learning makes it possible to move around the university totally under cover. The views from up here are superb. To reach the campus catch a #10 bus on Hastings east, change at Kooteney Loop to the 135 SFU. Hitching is said to be easy.

Vancouver North

Capilano Suspension Bridge, 985-7474. Going north, the bridge is on the left hand side of Capilano Rd. The swinging 137-metre long bridge spans a spectacular 70-metre-deep gorge. Entrance to the rather commercialised park costs $6.50, $5 students. 'Not worth it unless you have time to walk one of the trails.'
Grouse Mountain. The skyride is located at the top of Capilano Rd and you can ride it to the top of the mountain for incredible views, a cup of coffee or a quick hike. Make sure the weather is clear before you go. 'Take food with you and make a day of it'. 'Spectacular. Not to be missed. Best thing I did in North America.' The gondola costs $15.50, $13.50 students and operates daily 9am–10pm. 984-0661.
Lynn Canyon Park, 987-5922. Less exploited than Capilano and free. The bridge swings high above Lynn Canyon Creek. Swimming in the creek is nice too and there is an 'excellent' ecology centre by the park entrance. To get there: catch the Seabus at bottom of Granville. At Grouse Mountain take a 228 bus to Peters St and then walk. By car, take the Upper Levels Hwy to Lynn Valley Rd and follow the signs. 'Peaceful and uncrowded.' Open 10am–5pm summer. Winter weekdays.
Beaches. Near UBC there is Wreck Beach, free and nude; other recommended spots are English Bay, Tower Beach (also naturist), Spanish Banks (watch the tides), Locarno and Kitsilano.
Whistler Mountain, lies just north of Vancouver and is easily accessible from the city by bus or train. This area of incredible natural beauty is ideal for hiking, biking, rafting or horse-riding and boasts skiing conditions ranking among the best in the world. Even in summer it is possible to ski on the glacier. Trains leave from North Vancouver Rail Station daily at 7am, take 2½ hours and cost $16 o/w. Maverick Coach Lines run a 2 hr bus service 5 times a day from Vancouver depot, $13 o/w. **Whistler Hostel** (932-5492) is a timber cabin on picturesque Alta Lake and a good base from which to explore the area. $13.50 per night with great facilities and just 10 mins from the main resort.

INFORMATION

Vancouver Travel Information Centre, Pavilion Plaza, 4 Bentall Centre, 1055 Dunsmuir St. Open daily 9am–5.30pm. Call 683-2000.

Chamber of Commerce, Ste #400, 999 Canada Place, 681-2111.
Tourism BC, (800) 663-6000. Info kiosks at airport, Gastown and Eaton's department store.
Read *Georgia Straight* and the *Westender*, free from the Tourist Info Centres, for what goes on generally.

ENTERTAINMENT

Arts Hotline, for information on all arts and theatre events call 684-ARTS.
Jazz Hotline, offers the latest on current and upcoming jazz events. Call 682-0706.
Punchlines Comedy Theatre, 15 Water St (Gastown), 684-3015.
Yuk Yuk's Comedy Club, 750 Pacific Blvd S, 687-LAFF.
Sea Festival, second week in July. A week long celebration on the shores of English Bay featuring bathtub races, sandcastle competition, parades, parties, and the city's biggest fireworks display.
Vancouver Folk Music Festival. Held in mid-July at Jericho Beach Park, 879-2931, features over 50 acts from across Canada and around the world.
Vancouver International Comedy Festival. From street theatre to cabaret to stand-up, it's all there during the first week of August at Granville Island, 683-0883. Some performances are free, $6–$25 for ticketed events.
Jolly Taxpayer Pub, 828 W Hastings St, 681-3574.
The Luv Affair, 1275 Seymour St, 685-3288. Downtown Vancouver. Vancouver's hottest club. 'As radical as the Canadians can get. Black, gothic, hi-energy atmosphere, favourite haunt of visiting celebrities in the past.' Cover charge $3–$6. Open 9pm–2am. Sun 'till midnight.
The Roxy, 932 Granville St, 684-ROXY. Downtown Vancouver. 'Good atmosphere, extremely popular with locals'. 'Great in-house band.' Cover $3–$6. Sun free. Open 7pm–2am.

TRAVEL

Hitching is legal and usual in Vancouver but no safer than anywhere else in North America.
Exact-fare buses (currently $1.50–$2.75) operate in the city. The Skytrain, a light rapid transit system runs between downtown and New Westminster and connects to the bus system. The Seabus also connects to the bus system. A Daypass costs $4.50. You can ride anywhere, all day, after 9.30am. The passes can be bought from the stores like 7-Eleven or from the Youth Hostel. Take the ultra-modern Seabus from the bottom of Granville St to N Van, for stunning views enroute. Catch bus #236 to Grouse Mountain.
BC Transit Info: 261-5100. Schedules change every 3 months so call first. There is a free, direct line to BC Transit in the Skytrain stations.
Greyhound Bus Terminal, 1150 Station St, 662-3222.
VIA Rail Info: 669-3050. Train terminals located at 1150 Station St, at 200 Granville St, and 1311 West 1st in North Van.
Gray Line Tours, 681-8687, leave at 9.15am and 1.45pm daily for 3½ hour city tours in a double-decker red London bus. They will pick you up from any downtown hotel as long as you call the day before to reserve. $32.
Vancouver International Airport is reached via Hwy 99, Grant McConachie Way. Take city bus #20 from Granville St to 70th Ave. Change to the Airport #100 bus which takes about 45 mins. Perimeter Airport Shuttles run 25 min services every ½ hour from the Sandman Inn, Skytrain and Seabus stations, Canada Place and other downtown locations. $8.25 o/w.
'Downtown to Downtown' Vancouver to Victoria bus service (via ferry) on Pacific Coach Lines, 662-3222. Cost: about $31 rt. However, it is much cheaper to go by public transport all the way using the ferry services. Take 601 bus, change at Ladner Exchange to 640 or 404 bus to Tsawassen ferry terminal. Ferry costs $6. From Swartz Bay take 70 PAT bus to Victoria.

VANCOUVER ISLAND The island, and the Gulf Islands which shelter on its leeward side, are invaded annually by thousands of tourists attracted by the temperate climate and the seaside and mountain resorts. Vancouver Island is a 'fisherman's paradise', with mining, fishing, logging and manufacturing the chief breadwinners. There are good ferry and air connections with the mainland. (See under Vancouver and Victoria.)

Victoria, the provincial capital, is situated on the southern tip of the Island. **Nootka**, on the western coast, was the spot where Captain Cook landed in 1778, claiming the area for Britain. In the ensuing years, despite strong Spanish pressure, Nootka became a base for numerous exploratory voyages into the Pacific. The Spaniards were finally dispersed as a result of the Nootka Convention of 1790 but a strong sprinkling of Spanish names on the lower coast bear witness to the past.

Long Beach, 12 miles of white sand west of **Port Alberni** on the Pacific Coast, is recommended for a bit of peace. To get there take Route 4 from Port Alberni across the mountains towards **Tofino**, the western terminus of the Trans Canada Highway. The beach is part of the new, and as yet not fully developed, national park, **Pacific Rim**. Also in the park is the Broken Island Group in Barkley Sound and the 45-mile-long Lifesaving Trail between Bamfield and Port Renfrew. There are campsites in the Long Beach area and on the Ucluelet access road, as well as at Tofino.

The Pacific Ocean is too cold for swimming here, though it's great for surfing or beachcombing. But at **Hot Springs Cove** there are reputed to be the best hot springs in Canada. The least known too, for you can only reach the springs by boat from Tofino and then walk a one-mile trail. The springs bubble up at more than 85° Centigrade and flow down a gully into the ocean. The highest pool is so hot that you can only bathe in winter when cooler run-off waters mix with the springs. Sneakers (as protection against possible jagged rocks underfoot) are the only dress worn while bathing.

Back over on the southeastern side of the Island there is a superb drive from Victoria north to **Duncan**, and at Duncan itself the Forest Museum offers a long steam-train ride and a large open forestry museum. Going further north you come to **Nanaimo**, the fastest growing town on the island. (By ferry to Vancouver $6.25.) Lumbering and fish-canning are the main occupations in town and it's worth taking a look at Petroglyph Park with its preserved Indian sandstone carvings of thousands of years ago. Nanaimo is also a bungee jumping centre (the only real place to do it in N America) and the starting point for the annual Vancouver Bathtub race across the Georgia Strait in mid-July. There are 'mini hostels' in Duncan and Nanaimo.

ACCOMMODATION

Port Hardy: Betty Hamilton's B&B, 9415 Mayors Way—Box 1926, BC VON 2PO, 949-6638. $30–$35. 'Really nice after all my hostels and Betty certainly looked after you.'

Nanaimo: Nichol St Mini Hostel, 65 Nichol St, 753-1188. On bus route, communal kitchen, laundry facilities, showers. Registration 4pm–11pm. Open May 1st to Sept 1st only. $12 YH members, $14 non-members. Camping $6.

Verdun Thomson Mini Hostel, take the #11 bus from the Island Depot and ask the driver to drop you off. Free pick-up between 6–9pm and ride into town in the morning. Comfortable shared rooms, kitchen, pool table. $12 per night in the hostel, $5 on the campsite.

VICTORIA Former Hudson's Bay Company trading post and fort and now provincial capital, Victoria is noted for its mild climate and beautiful gardens. This small, unassuming little town is located at the southern tip of Vancouver Island on the Juan de Fuca Strait. As a result of its attractive climate, it's a popular retirement spot as well as being popular with British immigrants. Victoria has the largest number of British-born residents anywhere in Canada, and likes to preserve its touch of Olde Englande for the benefit of the year-round tourist industry.

Afternoon tea, fish n' chips, British souvenir shops, tweed and china and double-decker buses all have their place, but if you can get beyond all that, you will find Victoria a pleasant place to be for a time with plenty to explore around the town and out on the rest of the island. From August 18–28, Victoria will host the 1994 Commonwealth Games. Events will be held at various locations around town and the opening ceremony will take place on the university campus. There are ferry connections from here to Vancouver and Prince Rupert as well as to Anacortes and Port Angeles, Washington.

ACCOMMODATION

Difficult to find in summer. Book ahead if possible.

Victoria Backpackers International Hostel, 1418 Fernwood, 386-4471. $15 per night, breakfast included. 'Very spacious rooms, lovely place and clean.'

Cherry Bank Hotel, 825 Burdett Ave, 385-5380. Singles from $46, doubles from $54 (without bath). Includes breakfast. 'Comfortable, central, recommended by locals.'

Craigmyle Guest Home, 1037 Craigdarrock Rd, 595-5411. S–$50, D–$65–$70.

Hotel Douglas, 1450 Douglas St, 383-4157, D–$64 and up. City centre, close to City Hall.

James Bay Inn, 270 Government St, 384-7151. S/D without bath, $61. Nr Parliament buildings. 'Friendly.'

Selkirk Guest House, 934 Selkirk Ave, 389-1213. $13.50 for a shared dorm, $15 non-members. Private rooms available. Kitchen/laundry facs, boat/kayak rental.

Univ of Victoria Residence, 721-8395. May–Aug, students and non-students, $33 incl full breakfast. No rooms during Jul, Aug 94 due to Commonwealth Games.

Victoria Visitors Bureau, 1117 Wharf St, 387-6417 or 387-1642, can help find accommodation for you.

Victoria International Hostel, 516 Yates St, 385-4511. $13.50 members, $18 non-members. Kitchen, laundry facs, linen rental, lockers, hostel-based programmes. Reservations essential: families, groups, summer. Close to bus station and the train station. 'Priority given to members; if you are not one, you'll have to wait until 8pm to see if there is a bed.'

YWCA, 880 Courtney St, 386-7511. $36 single. 'New building with coffee shop.'

FOOD

Butchart Gardens, 800 Benvenuto Ave. For afternoon tea English-style, in winter served in front of open fire. Tea, scones, crumpets, etc. Info: 652-5256 or 652-4422.

Chinatown. Fishgard St and Government. Inexpensive Chinese eateries.

Fisherman's Wharf, St Lawrence and Erie Sts. Great place to buy seafood when the fleet's in.

London Fish & Chips, 5142 Cordova Bay Rd, 658-1921. Has the great British 'chippy' successfully crossed the Atlantic? Decide for yourself—but you'll still have to order 'french fries'.

Scotts, 650 Yates St. Open 24 hr. Meals from $5.

The Empress Hotel, 721 Government St. Also serves afternoon tea in the lobby. Includes scones with Devonshire cream—of course. 'Not cheap but très elegant!'

OF INTEREST

Parliament Buildings, Government and Belleville Sts. The seat of British Columbia's government is a palatial, many-turreted Victorian building with a gilded seven-foot figure of Captain George Vancouver, the first British navigator to circle Vancouver Island, on top. Conducted tours available daily throughout summer months.

BC Provincial Museum of Natural History and Anthropology, next door at 675 Belleville St. British Columbia flora and fauna, Indian arts and crafts and a reconstructed 1920s BC town. In summer daily 9.30am–7pm. $5, students $3, 387-3014. 'Great museum.'

Bastion Square overlooks the harbour. There is a **Maritime Museum** in the square (open daily 9.30am–4.30pm, $9) also a number of other renovated 19th-century buildings housing curio shops and boutiques. 'Nice place for just sitting, sometimes there is free entertainment around noon.' Info: 385-4222.

Beacon Hill Park, 'Nice for walking and having a peaceful time by the lake.'

Thunderbird Park, Douglas and Belleville. The park contains 'the world's largest collection of totem poles', a Kwakiutl Tribal Long House, its entrance shaped like a mask, and a flotilla of canoes fashioned from single logs of red cedar.

Butchart Gardens, 14 miles north of the city off Hwy 17. An English Rose Garden, a Japanese Garden and a formal Italian garden, are the chief features of Victoria's most spectacular park. Floodlit in the evening in summer. 9am–10.30pm July and Aug; 9am–9pm May, June, Sept; otherwise 9am–4pm or dusk. $11. For info: 652-4422. 'Definitely worthwhile.' 'Don't take the special tour bus.'

The Undersea Gardens, Inner Harbour, 382-5717. You can look through glass at a large collection of sea plants, octopi, crabs, and other sea life. Also scuba diving shows with Armstrong the giant octopus. Daily 9am–9pm May–Sept; rest of year 10am–5pm. $6.

Anne Hathaway's Thatched Cottage, 429 Lampson St, 388-4353. 'Authentic' replicas of things English, plus 16th and 17th century armour and furniture. Tours daily 9am–9pm in summer, 10am–4pm rest of year, $6.

Market Square, off Douglas St. Attractive pedestrian mall with shops, fine restaurants and bars.

Christ Church Cathedral, Quadra and Rockland Sts, 383-2714. One of Canada's largest cathedrals, built in Gothic style. Started 1920s and completed in 1991. The bells are replicas of those at Westminster Abbey in London, England.

Art Gallery of Greater Victoria, 1040 Moss St. Includes contemporary and oriental sections. Mon–Sat 10am–5pm, Thur until 9pm, Sun 1pm–5pm. $4, $2 students with ID. Thurs 5pm–9pm free. Call 384-4101.

Craigdarroch Castle, 1050 Joan Crescent St. Sandstone castle built in late 1880s by Scottish immigrant Robert Dunsmuir as a gift for his wife, Joan. Now a museum with stained glass windows, Gothic furnishings, original mosaics and paintings. 9am–7.30pm. $5.50, $4.50 students. 592-5323.

INFORMATION

Tourism Victoria Info Centre, 812 Wharf St on the Inner Harbour, 382-2127. Open daily in summer 9am–9pm.

TRAVEL

BC Transit, 261-5100. New schedule every 3 months so call first. (There is a free, direct line phone to BC Transit in the Skytrain station.)

Double decker bus tours of Victoria and Butchart Gardens depart the Empress Hotel. 1½ hr city tours; buses depart every 30 mins. For rates and info call Gray Line Tours, 388-5248.

Island Coach—Pacific Coach—Greyhound, 385-4411, for buses and connections to and from Victoria and other cities.

Victoria Regional Transit, local bus, 382-6161.

VIA Rail, (800) 665-8630 for reservations, 383-4324 for arrivals, departures and baggage.

BC Clipper, catamaran service to Seattle, 382-8100. One way $61, return $85. Takes 2½ hrs.
Ferry Services: for 24 hour recorded BC/Victoria ferry schedule information: 656-0757.
From Victoria to Courtenay: the train journey is beautiful—in a small-one car including engine train—spectacular scenery, high bridges. The train stops over Nanaimo's bridge so you can watch the bungee-jumpers.
From Courtenay to Port Hardy, you can only go by bus. $43. Ferry goes from here to Prince Rupert.

KELOWNA Going east out of Vancouver, Route 3 takes you over the Cascade Mountains and down into the Okanagan Valley. One-third of apples harvested in Canada come from this area. Good therefore for summer jobs, if you're looking for such work, or, if you're taking it slow, for a nice holiday, just lying by the lake in the sun. The **Kelowna Regatta** is held during the second weekend in August, with accompanying traditional festivities.

Beware of the local lake monster. It goes by the name of Ogopogo, and is like the Loch Ness Monster but with a head like a sheep, goat or horse.

Not to be missed are the two local wineries. **Mission Hill Vineyards, Westbank and Calona Wines**, in Kelowna, both offer free tours, with sampling daily: 10am–4pm. The **Kelowna Centennial Museum** on Queensway Avenue has nice displays of Indian arts and crafts. Tue–Sat 10am–5pm. Free. Info: 763-2417.

ACCOMMODATION
CYA Hostel, Gospel Mission, 251 Leon Ave, 763-3737. $19, includes meals.
Kelowna Backpackers Hostel, 2343 Pandosy St, 763-6024. $10 dorms, $2 linen. Kitchen/laundry facs, bike rental available.
Willow Inn, 235 Queensway, 762-2122. S–$48, D–$59 incl breakfast. Downtown, close to lake and park.
Hiawatha Park Campground, 3787 Lakeshore Rd, 862-8222. $20–$22 for 2, additional person $3. Laundry, store, pool, hotdogs.

INFORMATION/TRAVEL
Kelowna Tourist Info, 544 Harvey Ave, 861-1515. Open daily, 8am–8pm in summer; 9am–5pm winter.
Greyhound, 2366 Leckie Rd, 860-3835.
Kelowna City Bus Transit, 860-8121. $1 fare.

KAMLOOPS The Trans Canada Highway takes the Fraser Canyon/ Kamloops/Revelstoke route through the province. The Highway, incidentally, at 5000 miles long, is the longest paved highway in the world, and Kamloops, situated at the point where Route 5 crosses it, is a doubly important communications centre, for the railroad also takes this route through the mountains.

Kamloops is useful perhaps as a halfway stopover point between Vancouver and Banff or else a possible jumping-off point for visits to the Revelstoke, Yoho, Glacier, and Kootenay National Parks. The **Kamloops Museum** on Seymour Street deals with the region's agricultural and Indian history. Kamloops is a popular place for skiers and trout fishermen.

ACCOMMODATION/FOOD
Bambi Motel, 1084 Battle St, 3 blks W of Yellowhead Bridge, 372-7626. Single $36 up, double $48 up; kitchen available at extra cost.
Kamloops Old Courthouse Hostel, 7 W Seymour St, 828-7991. $13.50. Downtown location. Kitchen, laundry, TV.
Thrift Inn, 2459 East Trans Canada Hwy, 374-2488. S–$46, D–$49, pool, AC, TV.
Mr Mike's Broiler Restaurant, 2121 E Trans Canada Hwy. 'A place for a pig-out. Don't be put off by the exterior.'

INFORMATION/TRAVEL
Tourist Bureau, 1290 W Trans Canada Hwy, 828-0151. Open 8am–8pm.
Greyhound, 725 Notre Dame, 374-1212. Open 8.30am–9pm.
Kamloops City Bus Transit, 376-1216. Open 8.30am–4.30pm.
VIA Rail, reservations (800) 561-8630, arrivals and departures 374-3935.

MOUNT REVELSTOKE NATIONAL PARK The park, midway between Kamloops and Banff, Alberta, is situated in the Selkirk Range. The Selkirks are more jagged and spikey than the Rockies and are especially famous for the excellent skiing facilities available on their slopes. The summit drive to the top of **Mount Revelstoke** is a 26 km parkway with scenic views. At the summit there is a 9 km trail winding through forests and meadows with fantastic views of distant peaks, glaciers and mountain lakes.

The Trans Canada runs along the southern edge of the park following the scenic **Illecillewaet River** and there are 2 self-guiding tours available. One is a tour of the rain forest, with its huge cedar trees, and the other of the rare skunk cabbage plants. You can see it all without ever getting out of the car. Park services are provided in the town of **Revelstoke**, a quiet, pretty place set amidst the mountains.

ACCOMMODATION
In **Revelstoke**:
Frontier Motel, at jct of Hwys 1 & 23 N, 837-5119. S/D–$45.
King Edward Hotel, 112 E 2nd St, 837-2104. $25 single, $29 double/triple. 'Good value.'
Mountain View Motel, 1017 First St W, 837-4900. $44 up single, $57 up double, $50 up triple, $5 addt'l person; kitchen $5. Central. AC, cable TV.
R Motel, 1200 1st St W, 837-2164. S–$41, D–$44.
Camping: Canada West Campground, 2½ miles west of Revelstoke, 837-4420. $12 for 2, addt'l person $1; laundry, showers, outdoor heated pool.

OF INTEREST
Canyon Hot Springs, about 15 miles east of town. 39°C mineral waters, or a swim in a pool of 26°C. $4.50, daypass $6.50. 837-2420.
Three Valley Gap Ghost Town, about 10 miles west on Trans Canada Hwy 1. Nr site of original mining town of Three Valley with historical buildings moved here from various places in BC. Open daily 8am–dusk in summer. $6.50. Also has accommodation from $72 double. Info: 837-2109.
Revelstoke Museum and Art Gallery, 837-3067. Mon–Fri 10am–5pm, Sat 1–5pm. Donations accepted.
Revelstoke Dam, free, self-guided tours. March 18–June 16 9am–5pm; June 17–Sept 10 8am–8pm; Sept 11–Oct 29 9am–5pm. 837-6515 for Info.

INFORMATION
Tourist Info, 837-3522. Open 9am–5pm.
Chamber of Commerce, 837-5345. Open 9am–5pm.
Mount Revelstoke National Park, 837-5155. Open 8am–4.30pm.

GLACIER NATIONAL PARK From Revelstoke carry on eastwards along the Trans Canada and you very quickly come to this park. As its name tells you, Glacier is an area of icefields and glaciers with deep, awesome canyons and caverns, alpine meadows and silent forests. There are many trails within the park and, like Revelstoke, this too is a touring skiers' paradise. The Alpine Club of Canada holds summer and winter camps here.

The annual total snowfall in the park averages 350 inches and sometimes exceeds 600 inches. With the deep snow and the steep terrain, special protection is necessary for the railway and highway running through Glacier. Concrete snowsheds and manmade hillocks at the bottom of avalanche chutes slow the cascading snow, while artillery fire is used to bring down the snow before it accumulates to critical depths. Travellers through Rogers Pass in winter may feel more secure in the knowledge that they are passing through one of the longest controlled avalanche areas in the world.

Admission to the park is $5 daily and climbers and overnight walkers must register with the wardens at **Rogers Pass**. Park services and accommodation are available at Rogers Pass. The Information Centre here has displays and exhibits on the history and national resources of Glacier National Park.

ACCOMMODATION
See also under Revelstoke.
Golden Municipal Park, in Golden on Kicking Horse River, 344-5412. $12 per site. Hot showers, outdoor pool, rollerskating.
There are **National Park sites** at Illecillewaet River, Loop Creek, Mountain Creek and Rogers Pass.

INFORMATION
Golden Chamber of Commerce, Caboose, 344-7125. Open 9am–7pm.
Glacier National Park, 837-6274. Open 7am–9pm.

YOHO NATIONAL PARK Still going east, Yoho National Park is on the British Columbia side of the Rockies adjoining Banff National Park on the Alberta side. It gets its name from the Indian, meaning 'how wonderful'.

Yoho is a mountaineer's park with some 250 miles of trails leading the walker across the roof of the Rockies. Worth looking at are the beautiful alpine **Emerald** and **O'Hara Lakes**, the curtain of mist at **Laughing Falls**, the strangely shaped pillars of **Hoodoo Valley**, and **Takakkaw Falls**, at 800 meters one of the highest in North America. The spectacular, rushing **Kicking Horse River** flows across the park from east to west.

ACCOMMODATION
There are 5 **campgrounds** and various cabins within the park. The campgrounds are at **Chancellor Peak, Hoodoo Creek, Kicking Horse, Takakkaw Falls** and **Lake O'Hara**. Reservations taken for Lake O'Hara, 343-6433. Alternatively, Yoho is

easily visited from either Lake Louise or Banff. Tours of the park are available from both places.

Whiskey Jack Hostel, 13 kms west along the Yoho Valley road (which begins at the Kicking Horse Campground) and 22 kms west of Lake Louise on Highway 1 (Trans-Canada Highway). $10, $15 non-members. No phone.

INFORMATION

Yoho National Park, 343-6324. Open 8am–4.30pm.

KOOTENAY NATIONAL PARK Lying along the Vermilion-Sinclair section of the Banff-Windermere Parkway (Highway 93), going south from Castle Junction, Kootenay is rich in canyons, glaciers and ice fields as well as wild life. Bears, moose, elk, deer and Rocky Mountain goats all live here. The striking **Marble Canyon**, just off the highway, is formed of grey limestone and quartzite laced with white and grey dolomite and is one of several canyons in Kootenay.

The western entrance to the park is near the famous **Radium Hot Springs**. There are two pools with water temperatures at almost 60°C. Springs are open daily in summer and entrance is $2. Admission to the park is $6 daily; visitors must obtain a park motor vehicle license at the entrance before driving through. There are campgrounds and motel accommodation within the park (beside the springs and another location) and accommodation is available in the town of Radium Hot Springs. Park Info: 347-9615.

PRINCE GEORGE This fairly uninteresting town has become the takeoff point for development schemes in the wilderness Northwest. Travellers en route to Alaska from Jasper use the Yellowhead Hwy (Route 16). At Prince George change to Route 97 to Dawson Creek and the Alaska Hwy or Hwy 37 for Alaska or continue on Hwy 16 winding over the Hazelton Mountains to Prince Rupert on the coast. If you are travelling north from Kamloops, Route 5 picks up the 16 at Tete Jaune Cache.

ACCOMMODATION

Nechako Inn, 1915 3rd Ave, 563-7106. $41 up single, $51 up double, $60 up triple. Waterbeds available. TV, phones, whirlpool.

Prince George Hotel, 487 George St, 564-7211. S–$36, D–$38, T–$49, $6 each addt'l person. English pub, TV.

Municipal Campground, 18th Ave, 563-2313. $11 up to 3 people a site, $1 addt'l person. Hot showers. Free firewood.

BARKERVILLE The boom town story that triggered off the settlement of British Columbia started here on 21 August 1862 when Billy Barker, a broke, bearded Cornishman and a naval deserter, struck the pay dirt that, within a short time, earned him $800,000, and all from a strip of land only 600 feet long. As a result of his find Barkerville became a boom town.

The shaft that started it all is now a part of the restored gold rush town at **Barkerville Historic Park** located 55 miles east of Quesnel and 130 miles south of Prince George. You will need a car to get there.

In Barkerville you can do some panning, call in at the Gold Commissioner's office, visit Trapper Dan's cabin in Chinatown, have your photograph taken in period clothes and visit the same type of shows the miners once enjoyed at the Theatre Royal. A fine museum in the park tells the whole saga of Barkerville with photos, exhibits and artefacts. For info call 994-3332. Open 8am–dusk.

There is a camp ground near the park or alternatively there is fairly inexpensive motel accommodation in nearby **Wells**. Park admission is $5. The park is open year-round with reduced opening hours and no guided tours after Labour Day.

DAWSON CREEK A small, but rapidly growing town northeast of Prince George on Highway 97 which marks the start of the Alaska Highway (see also under Alaska). The Zero Milepost for the Highway is the centre of town.

Dawson Creek was settled as recently as 1912 when the railroad was built to ship wheat from the area. A much older settlement, **Fort St John**, about 50 miles north, was established in 1793 as a fur trading outpost and mission. Today the community thrives on the expanding gas and oil industries in the area.

ACCOMMODATION

Cedar Lodge Motel, 801 110th Ave, 782-8531. S/D–$35.
Windsor Hotel, 1100 102nd Ave, 782-3301. S/D–$35. Coffee shop, TV.
Camping: Mile 0 Campsite, 1 mile west of jnct Alaska Hwy next to golf course. $10 per site. Hot showers, laundry. 782-2590.

OF INTEREST

South Peace Pioneer Village, 1 mile southeast on Hwy 2. Turn of the century village incl log schoolhouse, trapper's cabin, blacksmith's shop, etc. Daily 10am–6pm, June–Sept. Donations. Call 782-7144 for info.
Historical Society Museum, 900 Alaska Ave, 782-9595. In renovated 1931 railway station; local wildlife and history exhibits. Open in summer, daily 8am–8pm; Tue–Sat 9am–5pm in winter. $1.

INFORMATION

Tourist Info, 900 Alaska Ave, 782-9595. Open in summer, daily 8am–8pm.

FORT ST JAMES NATIONAL HISTORICAL PARK Back on Highway 16 (the Yellowhead Hwy) and heading from Prince George to Prince Rupert, it is perhaps worth a small detour at **Vanderhoof** to the shores of **Stuart Lake** to visit this former Hudson's Bay Company trading post. The 19th century post features restored and reconstructed homes, warehouses and stores. The park is open daily, 9.30am–5.30pm, May to October, and entrance is free. It must have been an isolated, strange existence for the Hudson's Bay men here in the middle of nowhere 100 years ago. For info call 996-7191.

PRINCE RUPERT Known as the 'Halibut Capital of the World', Prince Rupert is the fishing centre of the Pacific Northwest. The season's peak is reached in early August and this is the time to visit the canneries.

This area was a stronghold of the Haida and Tsimpsian Indians and the **Museum of North British Columbia** on First Avenue contains a rare collection of Indian treasures. In front of the building stands a superb totem pole. Inside, there are more totems, masks, carvings and beadwork.

Prince Rupert is marvellously situated among the fjords of Hecate Strait and at the mouth of the beautiful Skeena River. There is also a reversing tidal stream fit to rival the falls at Saint John, New Brunswick. You get a good view of the Butz Rapids from Highway 16, enroute from Prince George. The town is also a major communications centre being the southernmost port of the Alaska Ferry System, the northern terminus of the British Columbia Ferry Authority and the western terminus of VIA Rail.

ACCOMMODATION

Accommodation hereabouts tends to be expensive. The Visitors Information Bureau may be able to help.

Aleeda Motel, 900 3rd Ave, 627-1367. $57 single up, $68 double up, $82 triple up, $5 addt'l person. Courtesy coffee, TV, 10% student discount. Newly renovated.

Pioneer Rooms, 167 E 3rd Ave, 624-2334. S–$20, D–$30. 'Friendly.' 'Small, clean and cosy.'

Raffles Inn, 1080 3rd Ave W, 624-9161. $84 for 4. 'Comfortable and clean.' Nr ferries & bus station.

Park Ave Campground, 1750 Park Ave, 624-5861, $13 per night. 1km from ferry terminal. Covered areas for cooking and eating.

OF INTEREST

Museum of Northern British Columbia, 1st Ave and McBride St, 624-3207. Mon–Sat 9am–9pm, Sun 9am–5pm, May–Sept; 10am–5pm Mon–Sat rest of year.

North Pacific Cannery, Port Edward. Old, original cannery buildings, wooden fishing boats, fishing exhibits. Free.

Queen Charlotte Islands, west of Prince George. Miles of sandy beaches. A place for taking it easy and doing some boating. Accessible from Prince Rupert by plane or boat.

Hazelton. A village northwest of Prince Rupert off Highway 16, Hazelton is worth a stop for the interesting **Ksan Indian Village and Museum**. This is an authentic village and consists of a carving house and four communal houses. The houses are decorated with carvings and painted scenes in classic West Coast Indian style. Tours daily May–Oct.

Prince Rupert Grain Elevator, tours of the most modern grain elevator in the world. Reserve through Visitors Info Bureau.

INFORMATION/TRAVEL

Visitors Information Bureau, 1st Ave and McBride, 624-5637.

The nicest way to approach Prince Rupert is undoubtedly by sea. A ferry calls here from Port Hardy on Vancouver Island, making the trip on odd days of the month. $90. One-way it takes about 15 hrs. Leaves 7.30am–arrives 10.30pm. The scenery is magnificent and if you can afford it, it's a great trip, well worth taking. Ferries also leave here for Haines, Alaska. If you want a shorter trip, take the one to Ketchikan, passing through glaciers and fjords enroute. 'Very beautiful.'

THE TERRITORIES

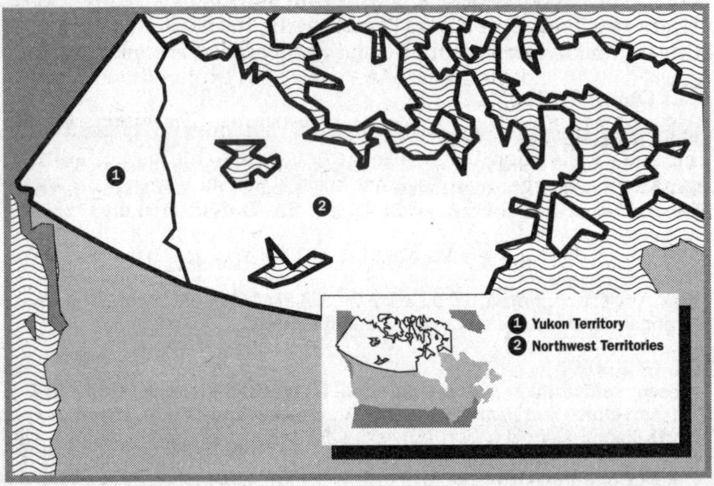

Both the Northwest Territories and the Yukon were originally fur-trading areas of the Hudson's Bay Company, only becoming part of Canada in 1870. If planning a trip to either the Yukon or the Northwest Territories, be sure to contact the tourist office in advance. They can send you more detailed information so that you can take advantage of the many package tours available. Or call the Arctic Hotline: (800) 661-0788.

NORTHWEST TERRITORIES

Canada's Arctic is larger than half of the continental USA. It's a vast, mostly unexplored, lonesome area, with a population of 57,000, scattered over 1,300,000 square miles. The territories are not, however, entirely perpetual ice and snow. Although half the mainland and all the islands lie within the Arctic zone, the land varies from flat, forested valleys, to never-melting ice peaks; from blossom-packed meadows to steep, bleak cliffs and from warm, sandy shores to frigid, glacial banks.

A final settlement between the Canadian government and the Inuit people on the splitting of The Northwest Territories was reached at the end of 1992. This was the first adjustment to Canadian boundaries since 1949 and gives the Inuit people outright ownership of 135,000 square miles of the eastern half of the territory, to be called **Nunavut**. They also received financial 'compensation' as well as the right to hunt, fish and trap across 740,000 square miles of the eastern part of the present territory. The western part of the Northwest Territories will be renamed.

For their part of the deal the 17,500 or so Eskimos living in Nunavut surrendered their claim to own the entire Northwest Territories. Both the House of Commons and the Inuit people had to ratify the agreement before it could become binding.

European explorers looking for a water route to the Orient came here as early as the 16th century. Sir Martin Frobisher sailed here in 1576 and founded the first settlement on what is now called Frobisher Bay in 1578. Henry Hudson and Alexander Mackenzie both explored the area in search of greater trading outlets and profits.

With the more recent discoveries of rich mineral deposits and the promised exploitation of the oil and gas fields, life in the Territories is beginning to change, many believe, for the worse. Fur trapping is still the principal occupation of the natives while the Inuit rely on the white fox and seal for their chief source of income. In many areas the native peoples are fighting hard against encroaching modernisation but continued development of the area's natural resources could threaten their traditional ways of survival.

It's a long long way North but once you've decided to go there are various alternatives. There are regular scheduled air services from Edmonton, Winnipeg and Montréal into the Territories. Once within the Territories flights are available to the remoter parts of the Arctic. By road, the Mackenzie Highway starts 250 miles inside the Alberta boundary travelling up to **Hay River** on the Great Slave Lake before striking west to **Fort Simpson**. From Hay River it's a further 600 miles to the capital, Yellowknife, on the north shore of the lake. There are daily buses to Hay River and three buses a week as far as Yellowknife from Edmonton, Alberta. When travelling in the Territories, always carry ample supplies of food and fuel since it can be hundreds of miles between towns with few, if any, services enroute.

The **Mackenzie** is one of the world's greatest rivers, twisting and turning for 1200 miles from the Great Slave Lake to the Arctic Ocean, and offering access to more hundreds of navigable miles on the Slave River, the Nahanni, Liard, the Peel and Arctic Red Rivers, and on Great Bear Lake. During the ice-free months (end of May to October) tugs and barges ply up and down the river. The hardiest canoeists and trailer-boaters can join them for one of the loneliest, loveliest trips in the world.

The **Great Slave Lake** is the jumping-off point for the vast developments underway to the north. **Hay River** is a vital freight transportation centre being the transshipment point between rail and river barges.

Yellowknife, the territorial capital, and less than 300 miles from the Arctic Circle on Great Slave Lake, has 'a wild frontier atmosphere' and two gold mines. Accommodation and food are expensive but new suburbs are springing up and business is booming. In June you can take part in a 24-hour golfing marathon made possible since the sun doesn't set here for the whole of the summer. It is also possible to visit the underground gold mines. Tourist information is available from the Chamber of Commerce, 48th Street and 50th Avenue, and from Yellowknife Tourist Information, 52nd Street and 49th Avenue. One other place to visit is the **Prince of Wales Northern Heritage Centre**, 48th St, (403) 873-7551, which has exhibits and crafts on the history and cultural developments in the Northwest Territories. Open daily 10.30am–5.30pm. Free.

Fort Smith, just across from the Albertan frontier, and once the Territorial capital, is a sprawling mixture of shacks, log cabins and more modern government-built establishments. The Hudson Bay Company established a trading post here in 1874, the town later becoming a stopping place for goldseekers on their way to the Yukon.

Trips to **Wood Buffalo National Park** depart from the Fort Smith Federal Bldg, MacDougall Street. For info call (403) 872-2349. Wood Buffalo straddles the Alberta/Northwest Territories line and was established to protect the only remaining herd of wood bison. In the park there are also plains bison, moose, caribou, black bear and a great variety of birds and fish. There are several trails within the park and rangers sponsor guided nature hikes in summer. Camping is permitted: May to Sept, $6.50 per site.

Two other national parks are under development in the Territories, although neither is accessible by road. **Auyuittuq National Park** is near the Inuit settlement of Pangnirtung on Baffin Island and is notable for its fjords, glacial valleys and mountains. For info call: (819) 473-8829. The second new park, **Nahanni**, is northwest of Fort Simpson and is a wilderness area of hot springs, waterfalls, canyons and river rapids. For info call: (403) 695-3151.

The third largest city in the Northwest Territories is **Inuvik**, way up in the northernmost corner. A boom town, ever alert for news of oil strikes, it is an interesting mixture of old timers, traders, delta Eskimos, Indians, oilmen and entrepreneurs. There are three hotels, all expensive, but camping is also possible. Even in summer it gets very cold however.

The town of **Frobisher Bay**, way up north on Baffin Island, is the administrative, education and economic centre of the eastern Arctic region of Canada. Frobisher Bay has also, since 1954 and the establishment of the Distant Early Warning Line, become an important defence and strategic site and a refuelling stop for military and commercial planes.

National Parks: Auyuittuq, Nahanni, Wood Buffalo.

THE YUKON TERRITORY

Fur-trading brought the Hudson's Bay Company into the Yukon in the mid-1800s but it was the Klondike Gold Rush of 1898 that really put the area on the map. Thousands of gold-seekers climbed the forbidding Chilkoot and White Passes and pressed on down the Yukon River to Dawson City. In two years **Dawson City**, at the junction of the Klondike and Yukon Rivers, grew from a tiny hamlet to a settlement of nearly 30,000.

There's not much gold around anymore, however. Instead there's silver, copper, zinc, open-pit mining and a big hunt for oil. In fact following the Gold Rush the Yukon practically settled back into its pre-gold hunting and trapping days, once again a remote spot on a map in northwestern Canada until the Japanese occupied the Aleutian Islands in the Second World War.

Then another rush to the Yukon was on, this time of army engineers who constructed the **Alaska Highway** as a troop route in 1942, passing right through the Yukon and up to Alaska.

The 1523-mile Highway begins at Dawson Creek, British Columbia, and winds its way, via **Whitehorse**, the Yukon capital, and a mining and construction centre, to **Fairbanks, Alaska**. Services are provided at regular intervals along the route. Anyone heading up this way by car is advised to get a copy of the *Alaska Milepost*, a mile-by-mile guide to the Alaskan wilderness published by Northwest Publishing Company, 130 2nd Ave S, Edmonds, WA 98020. Also available are the *Wilderness Milepost* and the *Northwest Milepost*. Each book is US $14.95 and postage is US $9.71 air mail overseas per book. Also recommended is *Alaska-Yukon Handbook* by D. Stanley, Moon Publications.

Above Whitehorse, many prospectors lost their lives in the dangerous Whitehorse Rapids. Later, the White Pass and Yukon narrow gauge railway now in restored operation, took the prospectors as far as **Skagway**. For info call: (800) 343-7373 or (907) 983-2217. Round trip excursions from Skagway, and through connections to Whitehorse.

You can also fly into Dawson City or Whitehorse, or else travel by cruise ship as far as Skagway, Alaska, and from there drive on a year round highway to Whitehorse. Hitching is said to be reasonable.

Whitehorse is also the headquarters of the Territory Mounties. A visit here should include a stop at the **WD McBride Museum** on First Avenue and Wood Street, 667-2709, to look at Gold Rush and Indian mementoes including a steam locomotive, a sleigh wagon, guns, shovels, etc. Audio-visual presentations on Yukon history are offered. Adult $3.25, $2.25 students. Open daily, 12pm–4pm May 15–Sept 30 (summer); Sunday, 1pm–4pm (winter). You can also ride the Yukon River through turbulent **Miles Canyon** on the *MV Schwatka* (named after the explorer) and visit the Whitehorse Power Dam to see the salmon leap in August.

ACCOMMODATION

In Whitehorse: Fourth Avenue Residence, 4051 4th Ave, 667-4471. Cooking and laundry facs; public showers. Shared accommodation: $18 per person, single accommodation: $37. Open 24 hours, year round.

98 Hotel, 110 Wood St, 667-2641. S–$30, D–$45. 16 units (w/out private bath). Open 24 hours, year round.

At **Dawson City** many of the buildings hurriedly thrown up in 1898 still stand. At the height of the Gold Rush more than 30,000 people lived in Dawson, in the settlement at the meeting point of the Yukon and Klondike Rivers. The now declining population capitalises on the tourist trade with things like an old time music hall and gold panning for $5 a pan. Food and accommodation prices are high. Picks, pans, and even bags of unrefined gold are all on view.

ACCOMMODATION

Gold Rush Campground, 5th Ave and York St, 993-5247. Has full facilities (showers, laundrymat, TV, store) in a convenient downtown location. $17 per site. Open 7.30am–10.30pm, June–Aug; 9am–9pm, May & Sept.

OF INTEREST

The Dawson City Museum, 5th Avenue, 993-5291. The Yukon's first museum, was established in Dawson City in 1901 in conjunction with the local library. The museum has the largest single collection of recovered artefacts in the Yukon. Its collection of early narrow-gauge locomotives includes a 'Vauclain-type' Baldwin engine, the last one in existence. Historic films and slides are shown nightly during the peak season. Open daily, 10am–6pm, June 1 to Sept 3; by appointment only in the winter. $3.25.

In the southwestern corner of the Yukon is the mountainous **Kluane National Park**. The park has extensive icefields and Canada's highest peak, Mt Logan (19,850 feet), as well as a great variety of animals, fishes and birds. The rugged, snowy mountains of Kluane typify the storybook picture one has of the Yukon. In fact the territory is not entirely a land of perpetual ice and snow. Summers here are warm with almost total daylight during June and although winters are cold, they are generally no more so than in many Canadian provinces. 'This is Big Country to beat Montana.'

The Yukon government provides and maintains more than 50 **campgrounds** throughout the territory, mostly in scenic places along the major highways. Hotel/motel accommodation is available in all the towns mentioned above but it's on the expensive side.

3 MEXICO

BACKGROUND

BEFORE YOU GO

Mexico is anxious to keep formalities to a minimum for the border hopper with dollars to spend. Anyone content with a visit of three days or less to a border town (by land) or seaport (by sea) need only present a passport at the crossing point.

For trips further afield, a **tourist card** is needed. If you try to leave the border area without one, you may be stopped and sent back at customs posts 20 miles inland. Cards are issued by Mexican embassies, consulates and tourist offices, by certain travel agencies and at the border itself: if you are flying in, the airline will handle the formalities. All you need is a valid passport, or for US and Canadian nationals, other proof of citizenship. Travellers under 18 also require an authorisation signed by both parents and witnessed by a Commissioner for Oaths or Notary Public. The card suffices for citizens of the UK, most other European countries, the US and Canada, but nationals of Australia and New Zealand are required to obtain full visas. Those in doubt should refer to their nearest consulate. At the port of entry, both card and passport must be shown, together with a cholera certificate if you have been in an infected area during the preceding five days. No other vaccinations are required.

European visitors receive a card valid for 90 days from the date of entry. US citizens are given 180 days, but in both cases *Migracion* officials can vary the duration at whim, often stamping the card with a 30 day limit, as well as charging for the privilege on occasion. The card must be used to enter Mexico within 90 days of the issuing date. So if planning to spend several months in the US first you should obtain the card there at the end of your stay, rather than from the home country. There are Mexican Consulates in most US cities and border towns.

If you are likely to need an extension, request a longer validation when first applying; doing it within Mexico is time-consuming and may involve a trip back to the border to get a new card. In Mexico City you can try your luck at the Visa Renewal office, located at Insurgentes Sur 1768, half a block south of the Liverpool department store—be prepared for a long wait. The card is issued in duplicate: one part is taken from you on entry, the other as you leave. Once in Mexico you are obliged by law to carry it with you at all times, and you can be fined quite heavily for overstaying the expiry date, particularly if you have a car.

If you are on an Exchange Programme Visa, do not let US officials take your IAP-66, or any other visa documentation, when you cross into Mexico. You need it to get back into the US!

In London, the Mexican Consulate is at 8 Halkin Street, SW1, tel: 253-6393; and the Mexican National Tourist Council is at 7 Cork Street, W1X 1PB, tel: 734-1058. In the US the Mexican Embassy is at 1911 Pennsylvania Ave NW, Washington DC 20006, tel: (202) 728-1600.

GETTING THERE

Most travellers (and certainly the overwhelming majority using this guide) will be visiting Mexico via the US. Major American, Mexican and international carriers fly from Los Angeles, Chicago, New York, Miami, San Antonio and other US and Canadian cities to Mexico City and elsewhere in Mexico. It is usually cheaper to fly to the US and shop around there for a flight to Mexico, rather than fly direct from Europe. But because of the continuing devaluation of Mexican currency it is usually cheaper to cross into Mexico by land and then travel on domestic flights purchased in pesos.

The most popular (and often fully booked) flight, at present costing about $320 one-way, $420 r.t., is Mexicana's flight from Los Angeles to Mexico City. From Ciudad Juarez, just over the Texas border, to Mexico City the current one way fare is about $220. Tijuana to Mexico City costs about the same although it may be possible to find a cheaper fare by shopping around closer to the time of departure. For brief round-trips from the US it is worth checking with the various airlines as they all offer competitive (and, at press time, totally unpredictable) fares. Major US carriers flying to Mexico include American, Delta and Continental.

Special deals offering percentage discounts on internal flights for those with international return tickets are of limited interest, since they apply only to trips originating in Europe, not the US, and carry time and other restrictions. Mexicana has offices in most US cities: for up to date information in the UK contact Mexicana House, 61 High Street, Barnet, Herts EN5 5UR; (081) 440-7830. NB. Airlines impose a US$10 departure tax on passengers leaving Mexico.

There are 12 major and a number of minor crossing points along the US–Mexico border. The most important are Tijuana (12 miles south of San Diego), Calexico-Mexicali, Nogales (south of Tucson), Douglas/Agua Prieta, El Paso/Ciudad Juarez, Eagle Pass/Piedras Negras, Laredo/Nuevo Laredo, Hidalgo/Reynosa and Brownsville/Matamoros. If you have a car, the smaller border crossings (such as Tecate, 40 miles east of San Diego) are often less bureaucratic. Car travellers should avoid Tijuana, especially on

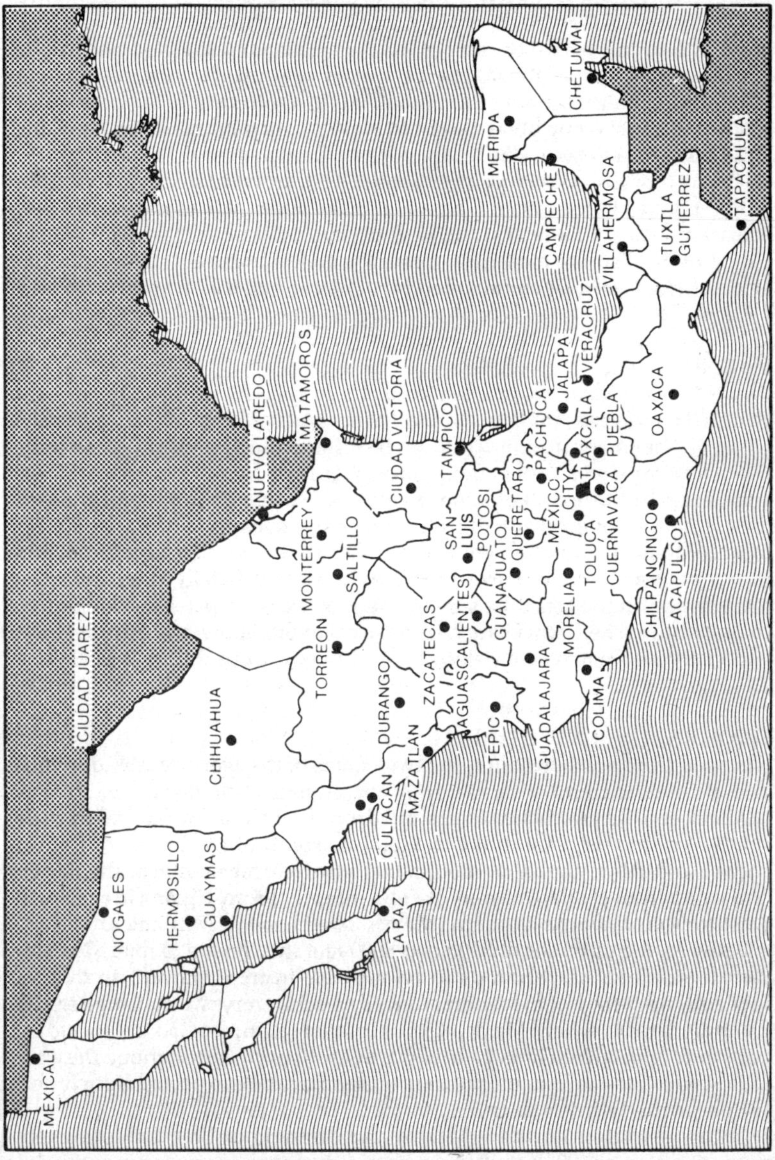
MEXICALI
NOGALES
HERMOSILLO
GUAYMAS
LA PAZ
CULIACAN
MAZATLAN
CIUDAD JUAREZ
CHIHUAHUA
DURANGO
TORREON
ZACATECAS
TEPIC
AGUASCALIENTES
GUADALAJARA
GUANAJUATO
MONTERREY
SALTILLO
NUEVO LAREDO
MATAMOROS
CIUDAD VICTORIA
SAN LUIS POTOSI
TAMPICO
QUERETARO
MEXICO CITY
MORELIA
COLIMA
TOLUCA
CUERNAVACA
PACHUCA
TLAXCALA
PUEBLA
JALAPA
VERACRUZ
CHILPANCINGO
ACAPULCO
OAXACA
VILLAHERMOSA
CAMPECHE
MERIDA
CHETUMAL
TUXTLA GUTIERREZ
TAPACHULA

weekends. There are generally long delays caused by extensive searches for drugs and aliens. El Paso/Ciudad Juarez border is often mentioned by readers as the easiest crossing: 'Mexican officials didn't pay any attention to us'. Matamoros may be the most corrupt: 'We refused to pay a bribe and were kicked out of the country'. Bribees are usually satisfied with US$5; principles notwithstanding, paying a *mordida* is usually cheaper and certainly less time-consuming than travelling to another crossing point. Matamoros is the crossing point closest to Mexico City (622 miles/996 kms); first class bus fare is about US$80. Even from Ciudad Juarez, a much greater distance, first class bus fare is only about US$120. Amtrak goes to the border at El Paso and Laredo from where you make your own arrangements with Mexican National Railways. Trains also leave daily from Mexicali to Mexico City, but the distance makes it a dreadful trip. It's relatively cheap at around US$50 for a seat in air conditioned first class or half that if you can tolerate second class.

CAR RENTALS

Reservations for car rentals can be made in the US with the major companies (Hertz, Avis, Budget, Dollar, Thrifty and National, etc) for a rental in Mexico. The major international car hire companies, plus of course many Mexican companies, have offices throughout the country. In theory all the companies in Mexico charge the same rates for any given car type, as rates are set by the Government, but shopping around, especially among smaller local companies, can often get you significant savings. The official rates are based on time + kilometres at inland towns and daily rates including 200 km/day on the coast. Be sure to check on extra costs for insurance, and to determine whether you are dealing in miles or kilometres. Car hire is not especially inexpensive in Mexico. Expect to pay around US$40–US$65 per day.

GEOGRAPHY AND CLIMATE

Running from north to south, the two chains of the Sierra Madre dominate and dictate the country's geography and climate. The vast central plateau lies between the mountain ranges and drops to the Rio Grande valley in the north. Around the area of the capital, just south of the Tropic of Cancer, there is a further jumble of mountains, finally petering out in the narrow and comparatively flat Isthmus of Tehuantepec. From Tijuana in the northwest to Merida in the Yucatan, Mexico stretches for 2750 miles.

Between the altitudes of 5000 and 8000 feet the climate is mild. The descent to sea level corresponds to an increase in temperature, so that the lowlands are very hot in summer as well as being very warm in winter. The Central Plateau, where Mexico City is located (altitude 7350 feet), enjoys a pleasant, springlike climate. It is warm and sunny throughout the year, although regular afternoon showers or storms can be expected from June to October—the Rainy Season.

In the deserts of northern Mexico and throughout Baja California temperatures of over 100°F are to be expected during the summer months. It is similarly hot on the coast, although the sea breezes are cooling. But in the lush tropical jungle lands to the south of the Tropic of Cancer, humidity is high and the annual rainfall is nearly as great as anywhere else in the world. On the northern side of the Isthmus of Tehuantepec, rainfall reaches a staggering 10 feet a year. The large numbers of rivers and the frequency with which they become rushing, swollen torrents, make the land impassable by permanent rail or road systems.

WHAT TO WEAR

Light clothing made of natural fibres (cotton, etc) is recommended. Bring a jacket or something warmer for Mexico City and the Central Plateau's cool evenings, plus raingear for the rainy season. Shoes, rather than sandals, are a necessity for uneven streets and climbing up pyramids.

Lavenderías automáticas (laundromats) and *tintorerías* (dry cleaners) can be found in larger towns and cities. Many hotels also offer their own laundry service. In smaller places you'll have to rely on two stones and the washing powder you have remembered to pack along with the spare plug for the sink.

TIME ZONES

Virtually all of Mexico, from the Yucatan to the Pacific due west of Mexico City, falls within the zone corresponding to Central Standard Time in the US. The west coast from Tepic up to the border, and including the southern half of Baja California, is an hour earlier, while the northern half of Baja is an hour earlier still and corresponds to Pacific Standard Time in the US. The Mexicans stay on Standard Time throughout the year.

MEXICO AND ITS PEOPLE

Modern Mexico is the product of three distinct historical phases: pre-Columbian (or pre-Cortes) Indian, three centuries of Spanish colonial rule, and since 1821 independent Mexican government. The Revolution of 1910 was followed by ten years of near-anarchy during which one in every eight Mexicans was killed, and although the peasants played a crucial role in overthrowing the corrupt aristocracy, in the end it was (and is) the middle classes who have benefited from the uninterrupted tenure of the Institutional Revolutionary Party (PRI) since 1929. There is at present a higher percentage of landless peasants than when the Revolution began, and the poor live in overcrowded slums where illiteracy is common, malnutrition rampant and basic services often non-existent.

There are however some indications of improvement, albeit very slow improvement. The country is not as desperately poor as it was and the government appears to be making real efforts to root out some of the social ills. Until now the benefits of industrial and agricultural development have been defeated by the explosive population growth. Although the area of harvestable land has doubled since 1940, the population has risen from 20 million to over 80 million in the same period, and half of these are under fifteen years of age.

Despite relatively successful efforts made to increase earnings from tourism and manufacturing industries, Mexico's economy still relies heavily on oil exports. Mexico is the world's second largest debtor with its external debt at a level of over US$100 billion. It is, however, considered a model debtor by the International Monetary Fund and the international financial community in general, as it has not declared a moratorium on its debt and has implemented a series of economic austerity programmes.

Despite gestures of independence—most notably the nationalisation of the oil industry in 1938—Mexico seeks foreign investment and to a great extent is economically dependent on its neighbour to the north. At the time of writing, hopes are pinned on the acceptance of NAFTA - North American Free Trade Association - which would give Mexican business direct access to the US, and vice versa. Until then, the relationship remains epitomised by the ceaseless flow of undocumented immigrants across the US border, and by the steady growth of *maquiladora* (in-bond manufacturing) industries on the Mexican side whereby US companies can take advantage of cheap Mexican labour to produce US products.

POLITICS

At first glance, Mexican politics appears to be an alphabet soup of letters with the parties known as PAN, PRD, PDM, PRT, PARM and of course, PRI. PRI is the Partido Revolucionario Institucional. The party is not very revolutionary but is certainly institutional since it is the most popular and largest party in Mexico, having ruled the Country since 1929. The participation and activity of the opposition parties has increased considerably in recent years but as yet they have been unable to topple the PRI's domination. President Carlos Salinas de Gortari took office in December 1988 for a six year term (Mexican presidents cannot be re-elected) and made an aggressive start to solving several of the Country's problems including union and police corruption and runaway inflation.

CULTURE

Mexico is a fascinating and colourful country, physically and culturally, bridging the gap between America North and South. It is a feast of art and history, with more than 11,000 archaeological sites, temples, pyramids and palaces of bygone civilisations, and many museums which are generally regarded as being among the best in the world. Although Mexico City and resort towns like Acapulco have their share of tall buildings, expensive hotels and general North American glitter, rural Mexico is something else again and the whole pace of life visibly alters the moment you cross the border from the United States.

Three centuries of Spanish rule have left their mark not only on the lifestyle of the country but also on its appearance. The fusion of Spanish baroque with the intricate decorative style of the Indians produced the distinctive and dramatic style called Mexican Colonial. A number of towns rich in Mexican Colonial buildings are preserved as national monuments and new building is forbidden. The most important colonial towns are: Guadalajara, Léon, Guanajuato, San Miguel de Allende, Morelia, Taxco, Cholula, Puebla and Mérida.

Despite its Spanish architectural and linguistic overtones, Mexico has a distinctly Indian soul: fatalistic, taciturn, reflective and strong on tradition and folklore. You will notice this most sharply in the villages, where it is easy to misinterpret the dignified shyness of the villagers as coldness. Various towns stand out as being Indian in character: Queretaro (where the Mexican constitution was drafted in 1917), Patzcuaro, Oaxaca, Tehuantepec and San Cristobal de las Casas. Not to be missed are Indian market days and festivals. Toluca, an hour's drive from Mexico City, has an outstanding Indian market.

There were six major pre-Columbian cultures in Mexico: the Olmec, Mixtec, Maya, Zapotec, Toltec and Aztec. Among the most important archaeological sites are the following. In the Mexico city area: Pyramid of Cuicuilco, Teotihuacán, Tepoztlán near Cuernavaca, Tula, Pyramid of Tenayuca, and Tzintzúntzan on Lake Patzcuaro. Near Zacatecas in central Mexico: La Quemada. Near Oaxaca south of Mexico City: Mitla and Monte Albán. On the Yucatan peninsula in southeast Mexico: Palenque, Chichen Itza, Uxmal and Tulum.

MONEY

In 1993, Mexico introduced the 'new peso'. One new peso equals 1,000 'old' pesos and the old and new currencies will circulate together until the old currency is phased out. The 'Nuevo Pesos' are denoted by the symbol N$. In this guide, prices are quoted either in US dollars–US$, or in new pesos.

The exchange rate with the U.S. dollar is now about 3.1. New coins in units of 1, 2, 5 and 10 new pesos are now in circulation, and 100 old centavos equal 1 new peso. New bills resemble the old ones but are designated N$ and have 3 zeros fewer. The currency change is aimed at simplifying calculations.

Mexico uses the $ sign for the peso, unfortunately the same as the US dollar sign; where necessary the two are distinguished by the addition of the suffixes MN (*Moneda Nacional*) pesos and US or 'dls' for dollars. Important note: all peso prices in this section are written as—pesos. US dollar prices are given as US$.

Shop around for the best exchange rates, especially in the large cities and resort areas. Generally the best rates can be obtained at the casas de cambio (money exchanges). Try to avoid the hotels for changing money if possible. Many larger stores and some market vendors will accept dollars but check carefully on the rates they are using.

Banks. Banking hours are 9am–1.30pm Monday–Friday. (The casas de cambio are usually open till around 5pm.) The larger banks (Banamex, Bancomer) are the best bets for changing money if there are no casas de cambio around in the provinces. The major credit cards are accepted in most places but the cheaper hotels and restaurants may not take them. Don't take it for granted—always ask first.

Tipping and Tax. 10–15 percent is the standard tip. Service charges are very rarely added to the bill when you receive it so they must be determined by the total before tax. Almost everything you have to buy or pay for, including hotels and restaurant food, has IVA (*Impuesto al valor agregado*)—value added tax—on it which may be included or shown separately.

HEALTH

Medical services are good, and in Mexico City it's easy to find an English-speaking doctor. Fees are reasonable compared to the US, and some hospitals will examine you and give prescriptions free. Nevertheless, where a fee is likely you should ask for a quote beforehand, and insurance is advisable.

'If you travel in the US before Mexico, you'll hear many ghastly tales of internal infections and uncontrollable bacteria. It's not true. Almost everywhere the water is so chlorinated that you're more likely to kill off your own bacteria than find any new ones.'

However, this is a minority view. For the long term traveller acclimatisation is the best policy, but it can take from three days to four weeks. You can stop *turista* spoiling a brief trip by using Lomotil (which delays the symptoms but will not remove the cause), or Pepto-Bismol, the antibiotic Bactrim, or Kaomycin. Entero-Vioform may still sometimes be on sale, despite being banned everywhere else. It makes you go blind.

If you have decided *not* to 'get used to it', then be cautious. Drink only bottled water; if you are not sure about the water, boil it for 30 minutes or use purification tablets. Be careful when buying food from street vendors: is the fat rancid? Beware ice cream, salads, unpeeled fruit and vegetables washed in impure water. Eating plenty of garlic, onions and lime juice (which act as natural remedies and preventatives) may help, but need to be taken in large quantities. *Pero te* (dog tea), fresh coconut juice and plain boiled white rice are the native Mexican recommendations.

Anti-malarial drugs are advisable in tropical and southern coastal areas—but as Mexico denies (perhaps rightly) that it has malaria, it's difficult to get any drugs for it there, so bring them with you. It wouldn't hurt to have inoculations against yellow fever, cholera, typhoid and polio, especially if you travel to coastal areas in the south.

'It helps to warn people—but hopefully they won't be frightened off.'

LANGUAGE

The more alert among you will have guessed by now that it's Spanish although in some areas Indian languages are still spoken—e.g. Mayan in The Yucatan. The point is, you should learn some Spanish, especially the words for numbers, food and directions. 'Well worth learning some Spanish if you can: don't expect too many Mexicans to know English.' Your efforts in Spanish will normally be encouraged and appreciated by the local people.

COMMUNICATIONS

Mail. Do not have mail sent Lista de Correos (Poste Restante) unless you are sure of being able to collect it within 10 days. After that time it is likely to be 'lost'. Letters or postcards to North America are 1.50 pesos; to Europe, 2 pesos; to Australia and New Zealand, 2.30 pesos. Important mail should be sent registered mail from a post office, and never put in an ordinary letter box. 'Send mail only from post offices—letter boxes not reliable.'

Chances are that packages sent in or out of the Country will not make it to their destination. There are telegraph offices (Telegrafos Nacionales) in all cities and towns and many villages too. Domestic cables are cheap and a good way to communicate with other travellers. International cable service is also good and the 'night letter' service, sent after 7pm, is good value. Public telex and fax facilities can be found in the larger cities.

Telephones. Public phone booths are to be found in most cities and larger towns. Elsewhere make use of telephones in stores, tobacco stands, hotels, etc. Public phones with direct dial long distance service (national and international), identified as 'Ladatel' are now being installed in the larger cities. To make a call from one city to another in Mexico, dial 91 + the city code + the number. Note that the number of digits in phone numbers is not standardized across Mexico. From other public phones dial 02 for the long distance operator for calls within Mexico or 09 for the international operator. In smaller towns look for the 'Larga distancia' sign outside a store or cafe in the centre of town. Collect calls (reverse charges) are called *llamadas a cobrar*.

Some important phone numbers used throughout Mexico are: emergency assistance—915-250-0123/915-250-0151; local information 04; countrywide information 01.

For calls to the UK, Ireland or other European countries the code is: 98. For the US or Canada the code is: 95.

PUBLIC HOLIDAYS

Mexico's religious and political calendar supplies many excuses for public holidays. Expect everything to close down on the following dates:

January 1	New Year's Day
February 5	Constitution Day
March 21	Juárez Birthday
March–April*	Holy Thursday
March–April*	Good Friday
May 1	Labor Day
May 5	Battle of Puebla Day
September 15**	Declaration of Independence
September 16	Independence Day
October 12	Dia de la Raza
November 1**	All Saints' Day
November 2	All Souls' Day (or Day of the Dead)
November 20	Revolution Day
December 12**	Our Lady of Guadalupe Day
December 24**	Christmas Eve
December 25	Christmas Day
December 31**	New Year's Eve

*Date varies with year.
**Usually working half a day.

On top of these, every town has its own festival and fiesta days, with processions, fireworks, and dancing in the streets. Local tourist authorities will fill you in on the details.

ELECTRICITY

All Mexico is on 110V, 60 cycles AC—in common with the rest of North America. It's a good idea to take a small torch as electricity can be uncertain, especially in small towns.

SHOPPING

The favourable rate of exchange and colourful markets will tempt even those who hate to shop. Mexico is famous for its arts and crafts and the markets guarantee some of the best entertainment anywhere. Look for woven goods, baskets, pottery, jewellery, leather goods, woodcarving, metalwork and lacquerware. A number of towns or states specialize in a particular craft or style. The government-run FONART shops feature some of the best local works and will give a general idea of price variations. FONART shops are generally a bit higher and will not bargain, but sometimes the quality is superior to what is available in the market. Prices and quality vary. Be sure to look over everything carefully. The vendor may guarantee that the sarape you're holding is *'pura lana'* but you know acrylic when you see and touch it. Bargaining is a fine art and expected.

'The cheapest market by far for sarapes, ponchos and embroidery is Mitla, near Oaxaca. Knock them down to one-third the asking price, and make rapid decisions in order to keep the price down.'

THE METRIC SYSTEM

Mexico is metric. See appendix.

INFORMATION

There are Mexican Government tourist offices in most US cities and border towns. Here are the main addresses:
New York: 405 Park Ave, Suite 1002, New York, NY 10022, (212) 755-7261. *Houston:* 2707 North Loop West, #450, Houston, TX 77008, (713) 880-5153. *Los Angeles:* 10100 Santa Monica Blvd, #224, Los Angeles, CA 90067, (213) 203-8343/8350. *Washington, DC:* 1911 Pennsylvania Ave NW, Washington, DC 20006, (202) 728-1600. *Toronto:* 2 Bloor St W, Suite 1801, Toronto, Ontario M4W 3E7, (416) 925-0704.

Once in Mexico itself, tourist information is provided at federal, state and local levels and most towns on the tourist track have at least one information office. Bear in mind that the level of service provided is extremely variable, and in particular do not presume that English will be spoken.

NATIONAL PARKS

'Both Mexican and foreign visitors are admitted from 8am–5pm throughout the year', according to the official tourism handbook, but most National Parks are without visible regulation and either merge imperceptibly with the surrounding farmland or are undeveloped and inaccessible wilderness. Don't expect the services of Yosemite or Yellowstone.
NB: all beaches in Mexico are federally owned and free.

ON THE ROAD

ACCOMMODATION

The range of **hotel accommodation** in Mexico is wide, from ultra-modern marble skyscrapers, and US-style motels along the major highways, to colonial inns and haciendas to modest guesthouses, called pensiones or casas de huespedes. There is also a marked difference between north and south Mexico. In the north of the country hotels tend to be older, often none too clean with bad plumbing, and large noisy ceiling fans to hum you to sleep. In southern Mexico hotels 'are a joy'. They are rarely full and often offer a high standard of comfort and cleanliness at low rates. It is fairly common to find hotels which are converted old aristocratic residences built around a central courtyard. Hoteliers will probably offer you their most expensive room first. A useful phrase in the circumstances is: *Quisiera algo mas barato, por favor* (I'd like something cheaper, please). Ask to see the room first: *Quiero ver el cuarto, por favor*. Of course a double room always works out cheaper per person than two singles, but also one double bed—*cama matrimonial*—is cheaper than two beds in a room. On the other hand, cheaper hotels often don't mind how many people take a room. 'Travelling in a group of four, considerable savings are possible. Most hotel beds are big enough for two people; therefore a double-bedded room can accommodate four.'

Prices are fixed, and should be prominently displayed by law; though inflation is moving so fast you should not be surprised if your bill bears little relation to the posted rate. In general you should expect to pay about US$8–12 per person per night in a basic but tolerable hotel a few blocks from the centre of town. An intermediate standard hotel should cost US$20–$28. It should rarely be *necessary* to pay more than this, though if you want to pay US$120 for a US-style resort hotel, that's possible too.

Hotel rates may vary between high and low season. High season extends from mid-December to Easter or the beginning of May, the remaining months being low season. Seasonal variations will be more marked at coastal resorts. *As most travellers using this Guide tour North America, including Mexico, in the summer months, low season rates have been quoted.*

'We notice that cockroaches are mentioned by people assessing places to stay. Even the best hotels are full of them—they are part of the scene and should not be regarded as unusual.'

'As it is rare indeed for Mexican wash basins to have plugs, I would recommend travellers to be equipped with this useful item.'

Hostels. There are two youth hostel organisations, the Mexican 'Villas Deportivas' chain and the International YHA-backed SETEJ establishments. The hostels offer cheap dormitory accommodation and we list them here only when a viable option for the tourist.

In general, however, hostels tend to cater more to a Mexican high school clientele, are some distance from town centres, and are rarely worth the small amount saved compared with a cheap hotel room in a better location. For details contact Agencia Nacional de Turismo Juvenil, Glorieta Metro Insurgentes, Local C-11 col Juárez, CPO6600, Mexico DF; 525-25-48.

Camping. Hotels are so cheap it is difficult to justify taking a tent. Where campsites exist, they tend to double as trailer parks and be some distance from areas of interest. Camping independently in the middle of nowhere is definitely pushing your luck, though in some of the beach resorts, nights under the stars are a feasible option. Those who insist on doing things the hard way should get *The People's Guide to Camping in Mexico,* by Carl Franz (John Muir, $11.95.) The Secretaria de Turismo publishes a detailed state-by-state guide to campsites (in Spanish), available from tourist offices or from Direccion de Turismo Social, Mariano Escobedo 726, 11590 Mexico DF; 211-0099.

FOOD AND DRINK

Because high altitude slows digestion, it's customary to eat a large, late, lingering lunch and a light supper. (You may be wise to eat less than usual until your stomach adjusts.) Do not eat unpeeled fruit and avoid drinking tap water, unprocessed milk products and ice cubes.

Stick to bottled mineral water, bottled juices, soft drinks or the excellent Mexican beer. Mexican milkshakes or *licuados* are made with various fruits and are delicious; probably best to avoid *licuados con leche* (those made with milk). Go to a *jugos and licuados* shop for *lu uados*, and home-made fruit ice creams.' 'The most important thing is to eat plenty of limes, garlic and onions—all "natural disinfectants"—we didn't have any stomach troubles.'

Mexican cuisine is much more than tacos and beans but the basic menu revolves around ground maize (first discovered by the Mayans), cheese, tomatoes, beans, rice and a handful of flavourings: garlic, onion, cumin and chilies of varying temperatures. The ground maize flour is made into pancake-shaped *tortillas*, which appear in a variety of dishes and also on their own to be eaten like bread. *Tortillas* are also made with wheat flour: restaurants will customarily ask, *'De maíz o de harina?'* (Do you want corn or flour tortillas?) Enchiladas are tortillas rolled and filled with cheese, beef, etc, baked and lightly sauced. *Tacos, tostadas, flautas* and *chalupas* all use fried tortillas, which are either stacked or filled with cheese, beans, meat, chicken, sauce, etc. *Tamales* use softer corn dough, filled with spicy meat and sauce and wrapped in corn husks to steam through. Other dishes to sample: *pollo con mole* (chicken in a sauce containing chocolate, garlic and other spices), fresh shrimp and fish (often served Veracruz style with green peppers, tomatoes, etc). Beans and rice accompany every meal, even breakfast. A good breakfast dish is *huevos rancheros*, eggs in a spicy tomato-based sauce. Mexico is also noted for its pastries, honey and chocolate drinks.

There are over 80 types of chilies in Mexico ranging in taste from sweet to steamroller hot. The different sauces are served from little containers found on tabletops so the diner can determine how mild or hot the dish will be. Best bargain for lunch is *comida corrida* or *menu de hoy*. This can be a filling four-course meal and cost as little as US$3.

breakfast: *desayuno*
coffee and a roll: *cafe con panes*
lunch: *almuerzo* (lighter) or *comida*
dinner/supper: *cena*
fixed-price meal: *menu corrida*
eggs: *huevos*
fish: *pescado*
meat: *carne*
salad: *ensalada*
fruit: *fruta*
beer: *cerveza*
soft drink: *refresco*
mineral water: *agua mineral*
bread: *pan*
potatoes: *papas*
vegetables (greens): *verduras*
bacon: *tocino*
ham: *jamón*
cheese: *queso*

I want something not too spicy, please: *Quiero algo no muy picante, por favor.*

The best-known hard liquor is tequila, a potent clear drink made from the maguey plant tasting 'similar to kerosene.' The sharp-spiked maguey is also the source for other highly-intoxicating liquors such as aguamiel, pulque, and mezcal. Look for the fat worm at the bottom of mezcal. It guarantees that you have the real thing. If you don't drink it (and by the time you reach the bottom of the bottle you won't know or care), some people like to fry them for snacks. Margarita cocktails are made with tequila but are primarily popular with turistas. The Mexicans prefer to take their tequila neat with a little salt and lime on the back of the hand. Mexico produces some decent wines but is famous for its beer; don't pass up Dos Equis dark.

TRAVEL

Now for your basic Spanish travel vocabulary: bus—*autobús;* train—*tren* or *ferrocarril;* plane—*avión;* auto—*carro;* ticket—*boleto;* second class—*segunda clase;* first class—*primera clase;* first class reserved seat (on trains)—*primera especial;* sleeping car—*coche dormitorio;* which platform?—*cúal anden?* which departure door/gate?—*cúal puerta?* What time?—*qué hora?* And inevitably: How many hours late are we?—*Cuántas horas de retraso tenemos?* Street—*calle;* arrival—*llegada;* departure—*salida;* detour—*desviación;* north—*norte;* south—*sur;* east—*este* or *oriente* (and abbreviated *Ote*); west—*oeste* or *poniente* (abbreviated *Pte*). Junction—*empalme;* indicates a route where one must change buses/trains; avoid *empalmes* at all costs.

Bus. Bus travel is the most popular means of transportation for Mexicans. Buses cost a bit more than trains, but will cut travelling times by anything from a quarter to a half and in any case are absurdly inexpensive by American or European standards: Tijuana to Mexico City (1871 miles/2995 kms) costs about US$40. All seats are reserved on first class (*primera*) buses, but 'beware of boarding a bus where there are no seats left—you may be standing for several hours for first class fare'. Sometimes it's advisable to book for second class also although in southern Mexico a reader advises: 'Normally there are no standby passengers on first class and you get a reserved seat; on second class buses this is rarely the case'. Standards of comfort, speed, newness of buses, etc, vary more between bus lines than between first and second class, although second class will invariably be slower (sometimes days slower with attendant expenses) and cheaper on longer runs. 'Mexico City to Mazatlan, on a second class bus, took 24 hours. Scenery superb, driving horrifying. Great journey.' Travellers generally recommend deluxe or first class buses: 'By far the best—quite exciting, cheap, fast'. Most towns have separate terminals for first and second class buses. Always take along food, a sweater (for over-air-conditioned vehicle) and toilet paper.

When making reservations you are always allotted a particular seat on a particular bus so if you want a front seat book a couple of days ahead. No refunds are made if you miss the bus; and be careful of buying a ticket for a bus which is just pulling out of the bus station! No single carrier covers the whole country and in some areas as many as 20 companies may be in competition, and while this doesn't mean much variation in fares, it can mean a big difference in service. Greyhound passes are not valid in Mexico, though by waving a student card you can sometimes get a substantial discount—though really this is only for Mexican students during vacations.

Though you shouldn't have too much faith in the precision of its contents, ask for *un horario*—a timetable—showing all bus lines and issued free.

Rail. The trains are operated by Mexican National Railways ('N de M' or simply 'Ferrocarriles'). There has been a marked improvement in the quality and speed of the main passenger services—Servicio Estrella—in the last few years although in most cases trains are still slower than the buses. The food on board is generally inexpensive and the scenery always magnificent once you are out of the cities. Students can sometimes get a discount. You should avoid travelling on or around any of the main public holidays as the trains get packed. The Servicio Estrella trains generally have *Primera Especial*, air-conditioned coaches which are to be recommended whenever available. Overnight trains have sleeping cars with two types of accommodation, *camarín*—berth for 1 and *alcoba* for 2. Reservations should be made in advance for these services at the station of departure (Central reservations in Mexico City, Tel. 597.61.77). Other trains have *Primera Regular* and *Segunda Clase*—much cheaper, no air conditioning and no reserved seats. The toilets are generally dreadful and vendors pass frequently through the coaches selling food, soft drinks and other items. If you travel in *Primera Regular* or *Segunda*, it's best to take your own food, however, and water for drinking and washing. 'If possible choose a carriage far from the station entrance and get a seat in the middle of the carriage, away from the loos and women with screaming babies.' 'Despite discomforts, second-class was great fun—marketplace for parakeets, avocados, tequila, lugubrious serenades by buskers at 2am for which the Mexicans—incredibly—gave money.' 'Very useful rail timetable for all of Mexico from Mexican Tourist Office in New Orleans.'

'You dismiss second class rail travel, but huge savings can be made this way for starvation budget travellers who are prepared to rough it. And rough it is the word. You are not guaranteed a seat (they are terribly uncomfortable), toilet facilities are awful, and nighttime finds people bedding down on the floors. My journey from Mexicali to Mexico City took three nights and two days (24 hours longer than by bus) with a five-hour stopover at Guadalajara. But you become totally immersed in Mexican life. The train stops about every 10 miles and this brings all the villagers to the trackside to sell cooked food, fruit and juices. The further you travel southwards the more people board the train to sell their wares.' 'Second class is fine. Lots of room, seats reasonable, loos, as always, revolting. Definitely recommended as a cheap, fun way of travelling.'

Particularly recommended routes are: through the northern desert between Monterrey and San Luis Potosí (10 hours); and from Chihuahua through the spectacular Tarahumara (or Copper) Canyon (four times wider than the Grand Canyon) and down to the west coast at Los Mochis. Enroute the train passes through 89 tunnels, crosses over 30 bridges, crosses the Continental Divide three times, and climbs to 8071 feet at the track's highest point. The Canyon is the home of the semi-nomadic Tarahumara Indians. Stop off at Creel if you want to visit them.

Air. If time is short you may well want to consider city hopping by air. Although obviously more expensive than bus or train, the plane wins hands down for comfort and will give you more time in the places you really want to visit. Mexicana operates the largest number of domestic services (see the 'Getting There' section). Other destinations are served by Aeromexico (which also flies to Paris and Madrid as well as several US cities), Aero-California and Aeromar.

Car. Taking a car to Mexico offers the prospect of unlimited freedom of movement, but also of unlimited hassles if you fall foul of Mexican bureaucracy. Firstly, you need a car permit, which is issued with your tourist card, and the card itself is specially stamped. (The permit is not strictly necessary for Baja-only trips.) You cannot then leave Mexico without your car; if called away in an emergency, you must pay Mexican customs to look after it until your return, and in theory if the vehicle is written off in an accident it must be hauled back to the border at your expense. Airlines are not allowed to sell international tickets to visitors with the special card, without proof that the vehicle has been lodged with the authorities.

At the border you must produce a valid licence and registration certificate. A UK licence is likely to produce incomprehension in the average Mexican traffic cop: an international one is recommended.

Only Mexican **insurance** is valid in Mexico. You can get it at the border where 24-hour insurance brokers exist for the purpose. It is advisable to increase public liability and property damage coverage beyond the minimum. If you are involved in an accident, the golden rule is to get out of the way as quickly as possible before the police arrive: they tend to keep all parties concerned—whether responsible or not—in jail until claims are settled. A convincing level of insurance may assist your quick release.

Some practical concerns: do not try to deliver your Driveaway Cadillac or BMW to Los Angeles via Oaxaca. Choose a rugged vehicle and take plenty of spares: basic VWs, Dodges and Fords are manufactured in Mexico and are most easily repairable. VW buses are a favourite for small groups. All main roads are patrolled by the Green Angels (*Angeles Verdes*) fleet, radio coordinated patrol cars with English speaking two man crews. They are equipped to handle minor repairs, give first aid and supply information: a raised hood will convey your need of assistance.

Garage repairs are reported as 'often incredibly cheap, particularly if you avoid 'authorised dealers', where you should expect to pay through the nose. Get a quote first!' Although you are not permitted to sell your car in Mexico, in theory you can do so in Guatemala and Belize, though these days purchasers are hard to find.

Pemex, the nationalised gasoline supplier, produces two grades of petrol. 'Don't buy cheap gas. Pemex Nova caused our car to shudder and stall. A mixture of Nova and the (better quality) Extra was a vast improvement.' Extra is however hard to find outside the larger towns, and some travellers detune their vehicles to take low-grade fuel.

It's important to note that all US cars manufactured after 1975 require unleaded gasoline. Outside the big cities unleaded petrol is undependable or not to be found and the use of anything else may damage the catalytic converter and ruin the entire engine. Garage attendants are notorious for swindling tourists: watch the dial carefully. Fuel itself is very cheap, at about US$0.25 per litre. 'Never let the gas level go low, and fill up at every opportunity. Gas stations are few and far between in remoter areas.'

Mexico has good main highways. Petrol stations (Pemex) are infrequent on the road, but most villages will have a 'vendor de gasolina', who will sell you a can-full and syphon it into your tank. Ask: *Dónde se vende gasolina acui, per favor?* Once off major highways, be on the alert. Branches or rocks strewn across the road are an indication of a hazard ahead. Watch for potholes, rocks and narrow bridges (*puente angosto*), and slow down in advance of the sometimes vicious 'speed bumps' (*topes*) near roadside communities. Unless absolutely necessary, *do not drive at night*: many Mexican drivers rarely use headlights, and wandering cattle, donkeys, hens and pedestrians never do.

Car theft is a frequent occurrence: it is worth paying extra for a hotel with a secure car park. And US plates tend to attract the meticulous attention of traffic police. 'You are considered fair game for police along the road, who will stop you and fine you for 'speeding'. Haggle with them—they always come down to five to ten dollars. One man was asleep in his car in Nuevo Laredo when he was arrested for speeding: the car was parked at the time.'

'Drivers should be warned that after entering the country there is a 'free zone' of about 100 miles, with three or four customs stations along the road. You will have to bribe at least one official in order not to have your car ripped apart. But once you leave the 'free zone' you will have no more problems with customs and hardly see any police.'

Mexico's principal highways lead from Nogales, Juarez, Piedras Negras, Nuevo Laredo, Reynosa and Matamoros, all on the border, to Mexico City. The most expensive road in the world is the new toll highway from Mexico City to the Pacific coast resorts, including Acapulco. It costs $82 to drive the full length.

The most scenic road in Mexico is the well-maintained 150D which sweeps through the Puebla Valley past the volcanic peaks of Popocatepetl and Orizaba, climbs into lush rain forests and down through foothills covered with flowers and coffee plantations, to end up in the flat sugarcane country around Veracruz. Note, however, that wherever a car is a definite advantage over the comprehensive bus network, a pretty sturdy vehicle is often needed: this is particularly true in Baja, where a four wheel drive is a major asset.

Some signs: *Alto*—Stop; *No se estacione*—no parking; *bajada frene con motor*—steep hill, use low gear; *vado a 70 metros*—ford 70 metres; *cruce de peatones*—pedestrian crossing; *peligro*—danger; *camino sinuoso*—winding road; (*tramo de*) *curvas peligrosas*—(series of) dangerous curves; *topes a 150 metres*—speed bumps 150 metres; *Ote* (abbr.)—east; *Pte* (abbr.)—west.

Urban Travel. Most cities of any size have a good public transport service on buses, minibuses or converted vans. The flat fare is usually about US$0.50. When choosing a destination note that *Centro* is the centre of town and *Central* is the bus station.

Hitching. Can be hazardous with long waits (not just for a lift but for a car to come along) in high temperatures. However . . . 'found hitching pretty easy in northern Mexico. If you don't speak Spanish at all (like me) show a sign saying *estudiante* and giving your destination. Plan your trip with a map and accept rides only to places you know, unless the driver can make it clear to you in any other language.' 'Water in the desert, I never realised how important it was. Anyone hitching should take a water canteen.' *Not* recommended for women.

For Women Alone For better or worse, *machismo* is alive and well in Mexico. The causes and results of *machismo* are frequently discussed and written about but it still doesn't make things any easier for women. Males from 8 to 80 feel compelled to remark on a woman's (and especially a foreigner's) legs, arms, breasts, hair, eyes, etc. In a country of dark-haired people, light or blonde hair has come to symbolize sexiness or higher status. Bare arms and legs, no bra and a casual manner signify that a woman is free and easy. Use common sense—don't hitchhike or enter cantinas. The best way to deal with hassles is to say nothing and continue walking. If possible, travel with a male friend (although *machos* will still try to pick you up) or a couple of women friends.

'I travelled alone and despite many warnings (mostly from US citizens!) I felt very safe. Mexicans seem more curious and friendly than anything else. Not at all like southern Europe.'

FURTHER READING

For anyone planning more than a brief trip to Mexico the following are recommended for additional information.

Let's Go: Mexico. Annually updated, group-researched 560 page guide, full of detailed background and essential practical information. Pan 1993. Price £13.99.

The Rough Guide to Mexico, by John Fisher. More personal guide covering roughly the same ground; slightly less detailed but a smoother read. Harrap-Columbus. Price £9.99.

Mexico: a travel survival kit. A high quality, thorough updating of this excellent guide. Lonely Planet 1992 (3rd Edition). Price £12.95.

Insight Guide to Mexico. Interestingly written and illustrated combination of travel guide and historical/sociological portrait. APA Publications 1991. Price £11.95.

Baedeker's Mexico. Thorough, concise, with good maps, colour plates, etc, and a free map of Mexico. Very good for a short stay or tour. AA 1992. Price about £9.95.

Mexico: American Express Pocket Guide. James Tickell. A genuine pocket book, well edited to provide essential facts, colour items, and town & country maps. Mitchell Beazley 1991. Price £7.99.

The People's Guide to Mexico, by Carl Franz. More than a travel guide, this book also tells about the people, the culture, the land and living in a foreign country. Described with wit and wisdom. John Muir Publications. $14.95 in the USA.

NORTHWEST MEXICO

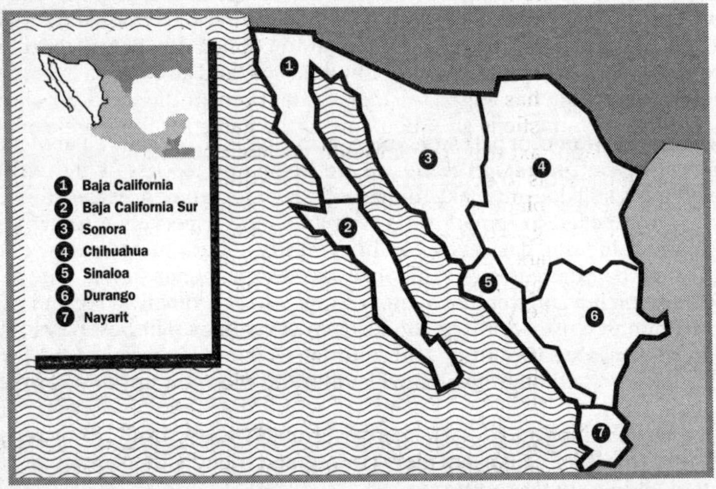

This vast arid region of stark desert, sharp mountains, deep valleys and canyons contains the states of Baja California, Sonora, Chihuahua, Durango, Nayarit and Sinaloa.

The nearness of Mexico to the US is deceptive once you learn that one way or another, you must cross many miles of thinly populated and largely dull terrain in this northern sector in order to get anywhere more interesting.

The coastline offers some relief, especially from Hermosillo southward as it gradually becomes greener, until you reach the lush and humid jungle around Tepic and San Blas.

Baja California has its own peninsula to the west; poorest of Mexican states, beautiful in a bare-bones sort of way, especially on its eastern coast on the warm Sea of Cortez (also called the Gulf of California).

BAJA CALIFORNIA

TIJUANA Previous editions of this guide have dismissed Tijuana and the other border towns; yet more of its readers visit 'TJ' than anywhere else in Mexico,numbering themselves among the millions of day trippers passing through the city each year. You will do Mexico an injustice if you judge it by the border towns, but you will do yourself an injustice if you fail to take the opportunity provided by a free day in San Diego, El Paso or Laredo to experience an abrupt cultural discontinuity available in few other places on the planet. The most cursory trip across puts into sudden perspective everything the traveller has taken for granted in the course of a trip round the US.

Tourist trap, home of cheap assembly plants, staging post for illegal immigrants en route to El Norte—Tijuana's every aspect depends on its proximity to the border. Possessing few Mexican virtues but pandering to most American vices, the town has long functioned as a commercial and sexual bargain basement for southern California, and although a municipal clean-up campaign has edged the more blatant prostitution and sex shows to the outskirts, hustle is still the name of the game for the storekeepers, street traders and taxi drivers competing for your attention.

There are bargains to be had if you bargain ruthlessly: good deals likely for leather goods, blankets and non-Mexican items such as cameras and name brand clothing. 'You can knock all goods down to a third of the asking price. Take US dollars.' 'Some great buys if you enjoy haggling.' 'If you go in a spirit of sociological enquiry, remember to have fun—well worth a day visit.' 'I enjoyed every minute of it.'

ACCOMMODATION

Tijuana has over a hundred hotels: those in the south-east section of the city are reputedly the quietest and most salubrious. Expect to pay US$20–$30, and be prepared to haggle. 'Lower prices possible if you don't mind sleaze. There are several small, inexpensive hotels on Ave Madero, to the left as you leave the old Tres Estrellas de Oro bus station.

Hotel Caesar, Revolución and Calle 5, 85-16-06, 85-16-67, S-US$30, D-US$38.
Villa Deportiva Youth Hostel, Via Oriente y Puente Cuauhtemoc, 82-90-67, Zona del Río, near the bridge, about US$5 for dormitory bed.
Hotel Nelson, Revolución 721, 85-43-02. 'Clean, decent bathrooms, relatively expensive. Good restaurant.' US$25.

FOOD

Nelson (see Hotel Nelson). Reasonable prices for full-scale Mexican meals, and for breakfasts. Open 24 hours during summer, 7am–11pm rest of the year.
Caesar (see Hotel Caesar). Supposedly home of the Caesar salad.
Bol Corona Cantina and Restaurant (opposite Hotel Nelson). Mexican food and drink.
Carnitas Uruapuana, Blvd. Díaz Ordaz 550, 81-61-81. Deep-fried pork (carnitas) in various combinations. Popular with locals and tourists. One order US$6.
Rio Rita Bar, Revolución 744 between Calles 3 and 4, 85-57-45. Mon–Sun 9am–2am. 'We found the best Margaritas we've ever tasted here. Two drinks for the price of one.'
Cheapest food will be purchased from street vendors catering to locals—but same warnings apply as elsewhere in Mexico.

OF INTEREST

Centro Cultural FONART, Paseo de los Héroes & Calle Mina, Zona Rio, 84-11-11. New cultural museum of striking modern design with archeological, historical and handicrafts displays. Auditorium with multimedia show in English (afternoons) and Spanish (evenings), also theatre, art shops, and restaurant. Open daily 11am–8pm. Museum admission US$1.25. Show admission US$5.50—includes free pass to museum.

ENTERTAINMENT

Jai Alai. At 7pm every night except Wednesday, in Fronton Palacio (Revolucíon and Calle 7, 85-16-12). Fast and furious version of squash using arm baskets to hurl hard rubber ball against walls of court. Betting on every game. Reserved seats

US$6, general admission $2. 'A whole evening's entertainment for $2—a small bet can earn you a few extra dollars.'
Bullfighting. Every Sunday, May–Sept, in one of two rings. Tickets (US$6) sold in advance at Revolución 921 (Calles 5 and 6, 85-22-10) or at gate. 'Amazing and disgusting.'
Racetrack (*Hippodromo*), Ave Agua Caliente, 61-81-78-11. Moorish-influenced building containing enclosed and open-air stands. Horse racing Sundays at noon, greyhounds at 8pm Wed–Sun.

INFORMATION

State Tourism Office, Via Oriente 1, Government Centre, Suite 208, tel 82-33-47 or 82-33-48.

TRAVEL

To Tijuana: see section on San Diego, California. From SD AMTRAK terminal, the San Diego Trolley will take you to US border suburb of San Ysidro (cost about US$6); then 20 minute walk to centre, or catch local bus. 'Taxi from border should cost no more than US$7.' If passing straight through, get either the shuttle bus from AMTRAK or the Greyhound service from LA and San Diego: these both take you to the new so-called 'central' bus station on the eastern edge of town. The old Tres Estrellas terminal near the border has poor connecting service and a 3 new peso taxi ride is the only other option. Mexicoach offers an excessively expensive centre-to-centre service from San Diego.
Onward: frequent bus services to Ensenada (2 hrs), Mexicali (3 hrs), Santa Ana (11 hrs), Los Mochis (22 hrs), Mazatlán (28 hrs), Guadalajara (40 hrs), Mexico City and points between. Six buses daily to La Paz (22 hrs).

MEXICALI The next border town inland, and departure point for bus and rail routes to West Coast destinations. One of the hottest places in Mexico, with few concessions to tourists or to anyone else: accommodation choice is between three hotels priced at US levels or Zona Rosa sleaze. However, for even the short stay border-hopper the trip from Tijuana (the new terminal) is recommended: the three hour ride gives an acceptably brief taste of the starkness of Northern Mexico, and the descent on the eastern side of the mountains towards Mexicali is both hair-raising and dramatic.

ACCOMMODATION

Hotel Plaza, Av Madero 366, tel 52-97-57 or 52-97-59, S–US$20, D–US$30.
Hotel Riviera. Marmoliras 313, US$15–25 per night.
Hotel Del Norte, Av Madero 205, 52-81-01, S–US$32, D–US$36.

ENTERTAINMENT

Desert Biking. Behind Hotel Riviera, quarter-mile down road on right. US$15 per hour, plus US$20 deposit. 'Three wheeler fat tyre motorcycles for desert tracks and sand dunes. Great fun for novices.'
Bodegas de Santo Tomás, Mexico's largest winery, tours and tastings offered Mon–Sat.

TRAVEL

Bus and rail stations are near Mateos and Independencia, a mile south of the border: no need to enter the town itself. Buses every half hour to Tijuana, hourly to the South. Trains depart at 9am, tickets available from 6.30am. 'From Calexico border to station is 5 minute journey. Not worth waiting for a bus: get a taxi and don't pay more than US$2 per person.'
San Felipe: A two-hour, 125 mile drive from Mexicali, through desert and beautifully harsh mountains, San Felipe is a likeable, ramshackle fishing village with

miles of white sand beaches and superb fishing. After this an unpaved road continues South to join Route 1 from Ensenada.

ENSENADA Slightly hipper version of Tijuana, 70 miles south via a new toll road. A thriving fishing industry fails to impart authenticity to anything but the cheap and tasty seafood. The town is full of Californians, especially at weekends, and is one of the few towns where you will get better value from US dollars than from pesos. But 'the drive to Ensenada along the coast is beautiful—well worth crossing the border just to experience the complete change of environment'.

ACCOMMODATION

'Reservations vital for Saturdays. We didn't have one and spent the night on the streets.'

In general expect to pay US$15–25 single and US$20–35 double.

Hotel Plaza, 540 Ave Lopez at Mateos, 8-27-15. S–US$25, D–US$30. 'Central location, cockroach-free rooms, flashy bathroom.'

Motel Presidente, Mateos and Rayon, 6-14-76. S–US$28, D–US$33. Restaurant and pool.

Hotel Ramirez, Mateos and Ryerson. 'Cheap.'

Many US-style motels, with some cheaper hotels at south end of Calle Mateos.

FOOD

Hussong's Cantina, Ruíz and Mateos. Famous for T-shirts, bumper stickers and Margaritas.

Casamar No. 1, Costero 499, 8-18-96. **Casamar No. 2**, Mucheros and Costero, 8-25-40. Both open 7am to 12 midnight. Recommended.

Las Brasas, Mateos 486, 8-11-95. Open grill, hectic, big portions. 8am–9pm.

Smitty Gonzales Restaurant and Bar, Lopez Mateos Ave. 'Excellent breakfast. Good value.' Open 8am–midnight.

OF INTEREST

Shopping: FONART store, next to tourist office, Mateos 885, 8-24-11. Open 9am-7pm. High quality textiles, silver, ceramics, etc. No bargaining. Most goods from southern Mexico: a good place to buy if not going further. El Nuevo Nopal, on northern edge of Ensenada, offers similar range. BS Beauty Supply (Calle 4 and Ruíz) and La Joya (Calle 5 and Ruíz) specialise in tax-free imported goods.

La Bufadora. Spectacular natural geyser, shooting water into the air from underground cavern. 20 miles south of town, and off the main road: own transport needed.

Agua Caliente Hot Springs. 22 miles east on Route 3. Unpaved but navigable road.

BAJA BEYOND ENSENADA After Ensenada the paved but narrow and variable quality Transpeninsular Highway (Mexico 1) leads the bus traveller to the tip of Baja at the resort center of **Cabo San Lucas**, 1,000 dusty miles and 20 hours further on. Known for its sport fishing and beautiful beaches, this is where the Gulf of California and the Pacific Ocean meet. To explore most areas of interest en route you need a car, and often a four-wheel drive: buses do not prolong their rest stops at the roadside towns, which in most cases is no great loss. Expect visions of desolate beauty and long passages of tedium, especially when the road loses sight of the coast.

OF INTEREST

The mountains, forest and trout streams of **San Pedro Martir National Park** lie two hours away from **Colonet**, 74 miles from Ensenada. Superb hiking and climbing but check at the turnoff that the dirt road is open all the way. Further down the Highway the agricultural town of **San Quintin** offers good markets and restaurants, and **Bahia San Quintin**, five miles away by dirt road, has fine beaches, expensive motels and excellent seafood.

The next 250 miles or so consist of bleak inland desert. Those with an interest in salt evaporation plants will enjoy **Guerro Negro**, at the border of Baja California Sur: otherwise its only virtue lies in proximity to Scammon's Lagoon, breeding ground for grey whales and an unmissable spectacle during the breeding period of late December–February. Four wheel drive needed for the 20 mile track.

San Ignacio is a delightful oasis village with date palms imported by its Jesuit founders in the eighteenth century, a reconstructed Mission, and its own wine. But more and cheaper accommodation will be found 50 miles further on at **Santa Rosalia**, a copper mining town of interest for its friendly inhabitants, ugly galvanised steel church, and thrice-weekly ferry to Guaymas on the mainland, the shortest and cheapest crossing. Boats leave (subject to change): Mon, Weds and Sat at 11pm from Transboradores Terminal (2-01-09). The seven hour trip costs 40 pesos salon class, 80 turista, and 200 for cars. See below for further details.

The desert oasis of **Mulegé** has hotels and restaurants and—two hours away by four wheel drive—Baja's best cave paintings. Between Mulegé and **Loreto** are a number of beaches accessible by car. Loreto itself was founded in 1697, but most in evidence now is work-in-progress on the Government-sponsored tourist resort.

La Paz follows after another 200 miles of boring inland desert. For years an isolated pearl-fishing centre, the ferry service and completion of Highway 1 have turned La Paz into a major tourist town, but the centre at least preserves a relaxed charm. Not much to see except the famous sunsets, some good beaches and snorkelling, but many good restaurants and hotels, and the zócalo (main plaza) is spectacularly lit at night. Tourist Information Office, Obregón and 16 de Septiembre, 2-59-39. Open 8am–8pm.

Ferries Sematur is located at Guilhermo Prieto and 5 de Mayo, tel 5-38-33. Daily services at 3pm for **Mazatlan** (18 hours, US$20 salon class, US$40 for a bunk). Also daily, except Tuesday, to **Topolobampo (Los Mochis)**—10 hour trip, US$12 salon class and US$25 bunk.

Cabo San Lucas lies 120 miles further south at the tip of the peninsula, and is a purpose-built tourist town with little time for the budget-conscious, who will have better luck at **San José del Cabo**. The whole southern tip has beautiful and—so far—unspoilt beaches, a couple of which, on Route 9 out of San Lucas, are accessible to campers. **Sierra de la Laguna National Park**, reached by dirt road from Pescadero, offers pine forests and the occasional puma. The San Lucas-Puerto Vallarta ferry, a gruelling 20-hour trip, is currently suspended. In any case the La Paz-Mazatlán route, followed by the bus, is the more tolerable alternative.

Ferries: The Baja-Mainland routes make few concessions to tourist convenience or comfort. You must queue for tickets several hours before they go on sale, and be prepared for long waits and customs hassles. Salon class is incredibly cheap, but involves a long and rowdy voyage with two hundred or so others crowded together on bus seats. Tourist class cabins are still a bargain, but frequent air conditioning breakdowns often make them unendurable. Taking a car across demands a willingness to wait several *days* (commercial vehicles always get priority) and pay substantial bribes. As if all this wasn't enough, the food is awful too. The ferry service has recently been privatised—hopefully it will improve. Remember that flights duplicate most ferry routes and are definitely a less exhausting, albeit more expensive, option.

OTHER BORDER TOWNS

CIUDAD JUAREZ Over the bridge from El Paso, and seemingly part of the same urban sprawl, this is the city about which Bob Dylan wrote his most depressing song ever (*Just Like Tom Thumb's Blues*). Souvenirs, gambling, racetracks and brothels, and it's easy to get lost in the rain. But still worth a quick visit (the market is recommended), rather than cowering on the other side of the border: 'it's easy to make the crossing for a much, much cheaper hotel room than you'll find in El Paso'.

ACCOMMODATION
Singles average US$15, doubles US$20.
Hotel Impala, Ave Lerdo N 670, 15-04-31. S/D–US$35, with bath, TV.
Hotel Juárez, Ave Lerdo N 143, 15-02-98, 15-04-18, S–US$15, D–US$20.
Hotel Koper, Juárez N124 and Ave 16 de Septiembre, 15-03-24, 15-03-84, S–US$17, D–US$20.

TRAVEL
By bus to Chihuahua, Mexico City or most other destinations. Instead of direct route to Chihuahua it is possible to go via **Nuevo Casas Grandes**, impressive ruins (pyramids, ball courts) of 1000 AD agricultural community. 'Get up early to squeeze this trip into a day.' 'Beware of low flying taxi drivers.'
NB: Mexican buses to Chihuahua and Mexico City also depart from El Paso Greyhound terminal. By train to Chihuahua and to Mexico City (about US$25 first class). By air, Gonzalez Airport to Mexico City, about US$150 one-way.

CHIHUAHUA The first major town on the route down from El Paso, Chihuahua is a prosperous industrial and cattle-shipping centre, once famous for breeding tiny, hairless and bad-tempered dogs of the same name. The city is of interest primarily as the inland terminus for the dramatic *Al Pacífico* train ride from Los Mochis on the coast through the Barranca del Cobre (Copper Canyon). This is one of the world's most spectacular train rides.

ACCOMMODATION
Singles average US$15, doubles US$18.
Hotel Reforma, Victoria 814, 12-58-08. 'Clean rooms with hot water.' US$12 single, US$18 double.
Hotel San Juan, Calle Victoria 823, 2-81-67. Off the Plaza Principal. 'Clean and friendly.' 'Lovely patio.' US$10 single, US$15 double.
Casa de Huespedes, Calle Libertad 1404, 10-09-69. US$10. 'Inexpensive, clean and quiet.'

OF INTEREST
A crumbling **Cathedral** in Colonial style overlooks the Plaza Principal.
The Palacio de Gobierno, where Miguel Hidalgo, the 'Father of Mexico', was executed at 7am 30 July 1811, is decorated with 'lovely lurid murals'.
Quinta Luz, The Museum of Pancho Villa is a fortresslike 50-rm mansion, Villa's home and hideout. At Calle 10, number 3014, tel 16-29-68. Take bus from Plaza Principal to Parque Lerdo. Calle 10 (unmarked so ask for Calle Diez) is opposite the park, running SE of Paseo Bolivar. Open 9am–1pm, 3pm–7pm, closed Sun. Now state-run, after being in the hands of Villa's 'official' widow for many years:

see Villa memorabilia including weapons and the bullet-scarred car in which he was assassinated in 1923.

TRAVEL

The 12-hr *Al Pacífico* train to Los Mochis (US$26 First Class) passes through Copper Canyon, 1500 ft deeper and 4 times wider than the Grand Canyon. At **Divisadero Barrancas** it stops to allow passengers to see and photograph the spectacular view on foot. 'I'd recommend the night train; the day train invariably runs late, and you just get past the canyon before it gets dark.' 'A wonderful trip—but the 7am departure is better.'

The Tarahumara Indians who live in the canyon can be seen enroute; despite the tourism the train brings, they live in largely traditional ways and are known for their basketry and long distance running abilities. You can break your journey in the old lumber town of **Creel** (Cre-ehl), 30 miles beyond Divisadero. Best bet for accommodation is **Hotel Korachi**, opposite the station: 'spartan but clean and central'. Also dearer **Hotel Nuevo** and rock-bottom **Hotel Ejido**. **Hotel del Cobre**, Calle san Juanito. 'Nice and affordable.' **Pensione Margarita**, Ave Lopez Mateaos y Parroquia 11, (145) 6-00-45. 'The highlight of my whole trip. $28 for 4. B&B including dinner. Daniel, Margarita's husband, runs local tours of the Canyon, horseback rides, and trips to the waterfalls, including an all day trip to the second highest falls in the world. Worth 2 days in Creel.' Call ahead to ensure reservations. **Camping** also possible but bring a tent (summer is rainy season).

Three services: (schedules subject to change) Vistadome trains leave daily at 7.00am for 12 hr trip to Los Mochis. Good dining car. Autovía (railbus) leaves 8am: return trip to Creel and back Mon, Thurs, Sat; to Los Mochis Tues and Fri (12½ hrs). Overnight trains depart Tues, Fri, 10.30pm: 16 hr trip. 'Leaves fabulous canyon and mountains for early morning but check sunrise times first.' Not recommended in winter. Choose train over Autovía given the chance. Buy tickets at the station of Ferrocarril de Chihuahua al Pacífico, near intersection of Paseo Bolivar and Blvd Diaz Ordaz, call 13-09-03. Also ask at the Tourism Office of major hotels. Buy your ticket at least an hour before departure; 'for 1st class, I recommend reserving the day before'. 'Breath-taking journey—2nd class was quite comfortable and the people inside the train were just as interesting as the scenery outside.' See Los Mochis for return journey.

LOS MOCHIS A dull agricultural city of interest only as the southern terminus for the *Al Pacífico* rail journey and its ferry connections with La Paz in nearby Topolobampo.

ACCOMMODATION

Hotel Beltrán, Hidalgo, 281 Poniente, 2-07-10. Showers, TV, AC. 'Clean.' 'Bus to Los Mochis station leaves from front.' US$20 single, US$25 double.
Hotel Lorena, Av Obregón, 186 Poniente, 2-02-39. 2 blocks from bus station. Shower, AC. 'Clean: what a relief after a long bus trip.' US$25 single, US$30 double.
Hotel Monte Carlo, Flores and Independencia, 2-18-18. Colonial-style, good value, with restaurant and bar, US$25 single, US$30 double.

TRAVEL

Al Pacifico train to Los Mochis: the journey takes at least 18 hours and often up to 24. The train is slow, stops frequently, and is hot and crowded. 'Not worth doing unless you have a lot of time and are really bored.'
Trains leave Los Mochis at 7am. Tickets (see under Chihuahua for prices) on sale from 5.45am: buy from station, as agents in town can be unreliable. Call 5-08-53 for information. Starting from Los Mochis end reportedly gives best views: sit on

the right. Station is 3 miles out of town: allow plenty of time for local bus or take rip-off taxi: 'It took ages to haggle him down from 5 to 1.50 pesos.' Note: FCP line from Nogales has different station 30 miles away in San Blas, Sinaloa: it is possible to transfer to Pacifico line here, but at risk of being stranded. Also be aware that Los Mochis station uses Chihuahua time, one hour earlier than local time.
Ferry for La Paz, if operating (see Baja section), leaves from **Topolobampo** for the 8 hour trip, Mon and Thur at 10am. Salon class 35,000 pesos. Often sold out 24 hours ahead. Nowhere to stay in Topolobampo, but 'a night out under the stars is fun. Fishermen cook freshly caught fish and shrimp over wood fires and invite you to partake. But buying even basics is difficult—don't count on it for food for the ferry'.
Going straight from the ferry to the Al Pacifico, or vice versa, is logistically difficult and an exhausting trip: a stopover in Los Mochis is recommended.

MAZATLAN Big, boisterous and a major gringo tourist town, Mazatlan offers a ten mile strip of international hotels and some superb game fishing: to the south of this, the old section of the town has more affordable hotels, local colour and an element of risk. The El Cid Hotel rents out windsurfers, sailboats, catamarans and snorkel gear. A 10–12 minute parachute/sail along the beach averages US$15. *Piedra Isla,* a tiny island just offshore, has good beaches, diving and camping possibilities: very congenial after the last boat leaves at 4.30pm.

ACCOMMODATION/INFORMATION
Singles average US$10–15, doubles US$20–25. Best value around the bus station and in Old Mazatlan on Aves Juarez, Aquiles Serdan and Azueta.
Hotel del Río, Canizales Nte 18, 82-46-54. Town centre near Juárez intersection. 'Spotless'. US$10–20.
Hotel Fiesta, opposite bus station, 81-78-88. 'Clean'. US$14 single, US$25 double.
Tourism Office, Av. Olas Altas 1300, tel. 85-12-20 or 85-12-21. Open weekdays 8am–8.30pm.

TRAVEL
Local bus, 'Zaragoza', 5 pesos from bus station into town. Ferry leaves 5pm, daily to La Paz, a 16 hour trip. Be at terminal before 8am to get ticket.
'The route (Mexico 40) from Mazatlán to Durango is absolutely breath-taking. Although it's just over 300 miles, it took us a long time to cover as the road twists and turns up to 7,000 ft where it crosses the Continental Divide. A part of Mexico that should not be missed.' Take Transportes Monterrey-Saltillo bus for the 6 hour trip.

SAN BLAS An hour's drive off the highway just north of Tepic takes you through increasingly lush tropical country to San Blas, once a sleepy seaside village, but no longer. 'Signs advertising granola and yogurt, expensive hotels and food, dirty beaches and medium surfing.' 'Very hippified but nice with a good swimming beach.' 'Bring lots of insect repellent – famous for its gnats.' 'We really liked it here. The beach is lovely and the town is small but pretty with nice places to sit and eat.'

ACCOMMODATION
Hotel Bucanero, Juarez 75, near plaza: 'Clean, popular with young people'. 5-01-01.

Hotel Casa Mar, Batallon 26. 'Mosquito-proofed rooms, showers, clean.'
Hotel Flamingo, Juarez 105. 'Clean, shabby, cell-like rooms, twin beds with shower.'
Hotel Playa Hermosa, dirt road from Batallón. Isolated 'brokendown palace' with big, decrepit rooms and an ocean view. Bar and restaurant. Around US$10 for two.
Posada Portola, Parades 118, off the plaza, 5-03-86. US$14 single, US$20 double. 'Clean mosquito-proofed with shower, stove and fridge. Excellent value.'

FOOD

Try the little cafes along the beach for inexpensive fish, oyster meals. Also check to see if the pool in the bar of the Torino restaurant still has 4 crocodile residents.
Restaurant–Bar **La Familia**, Av. H. Batallón 16, 5-02-58. Open 5pm–10pm. 'Brilliant.'

INFORMATION/TRAVEL

Tourist Info, opposite plaza, has useful booklet with maps, lodgings, etc.
Buses from Tepic to San Blas run fairly regularly. 'Interesting jungle scenery enroute.' The bus station is on Calle Sinaloa, tel 5-00-43.
Take a small boat trip into the jungle lagoons and creeks behind the town. Dawn is the best time for you to catch the animals (or vice versa).

NORTHEAST MEXICO

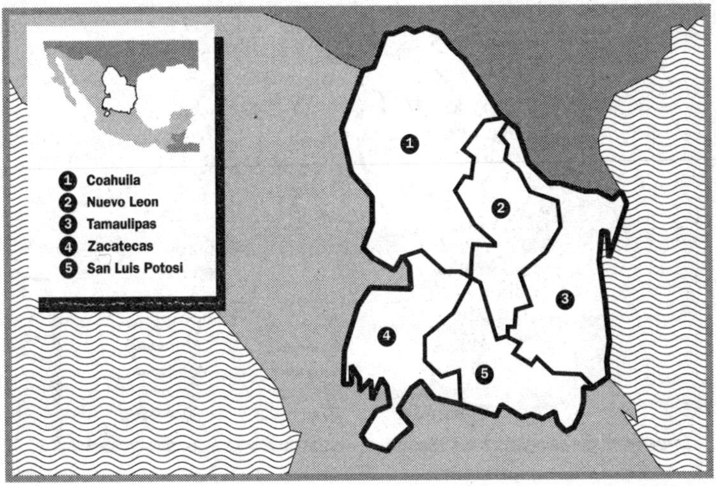

The northeast states offer little worth tarrying for. The border towns east of Juárez—Nuevo Laredo, Reynosa and Matamoros—provide similar experiences to the others, and are worth a quick visit but no more. 'Nuevo Laredo is a corrupt dump and an insult to Mexico'; Matamoros has either exceptionally friendly or unbelievably officious and venal *Migracion* people, depending on whom you listen to. All three offer flights to Mexico City (about US$80 one way), and bus and train routes via Monterrey.

From Nuevo Laredo you can catch the *Regiomontano,* leaving daily at 3.15pm and arriving in Mexico City at 10am the following day. This is one of the faster and more comfortable Mexican trains.

The best route south is the Pan American highway, Mexico 85, taking you from Nuevo Laredo to **Monterrey**, a sprawling and expensive industrial city; **Saltillo**, 50 miles up in the hills to the west, is preferable if you need to break your journey. Further on towards Mexico City, **San Luis Potosí** is a gold and silver mining town of considerable historical interest and with a distinctive regional cuisine.

Zacatecas is the capital city of the state of the same name and is built on the side of a 7,000 ft mountain. It's still a silvermining centre and is famous for its baroque cathedral and the Quemada ruins. Yes, those are rattlesnake skins for sale in the market. For 'marvellous views' of the area take a ride on the cablecar (*teleferíco*) north of the plaza. US$2 r/t.

If you cross by car at Reynosa or Matamoros, it is advisable to travel inland to Route 85 rather than taking the coastal road: while this is the shortest trip to the Yucatán if bypassing Mexico City, the road is in poor repair and the journey offers only unbearable temperatures and polluted beaches.

CENTRAL MEXICO

Mexico seems to save itself scenically, culturally and every other way, in order to burst upon you in central Mexico in a rich outpouring of volcanic mountains, pre-Columbian monuments, luxuriant flowers, exuberant people and picturesque architecture. This is the region where the Mexican love of colour manifests itself and the air is cool and fresh on the high Central Plateau. Be prepared for mugginess on either coast around Acapulco and Veracruz, however.

Mexico City lies in the centre of this region, surrounded by a dozen tiny states from Tlaxcala to Guanajuato. Northwest of Mexico City is the orbit of Guadalajara, second largest city and home to the largest colony of American expatriates. That fact makes its outlying satellite towns of Tlaquepaque, Chapala, Ajijic and so on quite expensive.

PUERTO VALLARTA Now pushing 100,000 residents, PV has lost its small-village charm in the traffic and the singles bars but its emerald green setting on a perfect crescent of beach still pleases the eye if not the pocketbook. Come here to enjoy the tremendous breakers and the carefully non-maintained cobblestone streets, to dance and drink margaritas and eat Gulf shrimp and oysters. (The big ones from Guaymas are called *zapatos*—'shoes'—for their strapping size.)

If the town itself palls: try **Mismaloya**, 7 miles away, with good beach, waterfall and natural swimming pool, plus film set for 1964 movie *Night of the Iguana*, publicity from which put PV on tourist map. Also boat trip to **Yelapa**, fishing village of dubious authenticity but with all mod cons.

ACCOMMODATION
Cheapest lodgings on south side of Rio Cuale, especially Basilio Vadillo and Av Madero near the bus station. Singles average US$10, doubles US$15.
Hotel Ana Liz, Calle Francisco Madero 429, 2-17-57. 'Cheap and clean.' S–US$10, D–US$14.
Hotel Azteca, Madero 473, 2-27-50. S–US$9, D–US$11.
Hotel Central, Calle Juárez 70, 2-49-66. 'Very plain, decent, probably cheapest on north side of river.' S–US$5, D–US$10.
Hotel Mexico 70 Venustiano Carranza 466, 2-21-90. 'Cheap, basic.' S–US$10, D–US$12.
Posada Roger, Basilio Badillo 237, 2-08-36/2-06-39. Popular, young crowd. Has own ride board. S–US$15, D–US$22.
El Oceano, 31 de Mayo and Galeana, 2-13-22. Downtown on ocean.

FOOD/ENTERTAINMENT
La Hacienda, Aguacate 274, 2-05-90. Open 6pm to midnight. '*The* restaurant in PV. We had oysters, octopus, wine and dessert for US $10 each. Service out of this world. The best!'
Try **El Ostión Feliz** on Calle Libertad for good *ceviche* (marinated fish) and oysters.
Impromptu music and dancing on the beach at night. Lots of Europeans, Yanks and Canadians, all trying to score.

TRAVEL/INFORMATION
Several buses a day from Tepic (3 hrs) and Guadalajara (7 hrs).
Flights from Guadalajara, Mexico City and several US cities.
Ferry to Cabo San Lucas is suspended at time of going to press. Check locally.
Tourism office: 2-02-42. Entrance on Calle Juarez. Open weekdays 9am–7pm, Sat 9am–1pm.

MANZANILLO Located 150 miles south of Puerto Vallarta and currently enlarging its harbour facilities in order be the *numero uno* port on Mexico's Pacific coast. It earned its reputation as a jet set resort when Bo Derek was filmed romping along the beach for the movie *10*. The beaches are among the best in Mexico but in order to avoid the resort crowd head to the nearby smaller towns of **Barra de Navidad**, **Cuyutlan**, **Melaque Bay** or **Bahía de Tenacatita** for lower prices and easier living, though these are now also being rapidly developed.

There is a daily train service from Guadalajara (US$9) leaving 9am and arriving at Manzanillo at 4pm. Return train leaves at 1pm. Tourist information: in the Palacio Municipal, tel 2-00-00. Open weekdays 8am to midnight, closed weekends.

IXTAPA/ZIHUATANEJO Ixtapa is another planned resort with lots of high rise hotels and burned turistas. However, its 16 mile beach is open to the public. Try to stay in the less pretentious town of Zihuatanejo where smaller hotels are more plentiful. Zihuatanejo used to be a tranquil fishing town but is growing fast. However, its four main beaches are easily accessible. A cheap boat trip will take you to an offshore wildlife refuge for the day. Basic food at reasonable prices at Neuva Zealanda coffee shops in Ixtapa and downtown Zihuatanejo. Tourist information: 4-22-07, open weekdays 9am–3pm and 6pm–8pm. Saturday 9am–2pm.

ACAPULCO A thin rind of elegance round a beautiful palm-fringed bay, Acapulco's phalanx of tall hotels gives way four blocks back to some of

Mexico's worst slums. This extraordinary mix of haves and have-nots means that thievery and every sort of scam are endemic, so watch your wallet, passport and camera ALL the time.

The summers get very hot and humid, occasionally enlivened by summer rainstorms in June, September and October, but these factors are balanced by the fall in hotel prices and the blissfulness of the water. High season is mid-December to mid-April.

ACCOMMODATION

Note: rates fall considerably in summer; always make sure you're being quoted *precios de verano* (summer prices). Hotels are plentiful and cheap: don't be afraid to haggle or ask for student discounts. Calle La Quebrada has best range of low-budget places.

Singles average US$12–25, doubles US$20–40. Don't sleep on the beaches!

Bali Hai Motel, Ave Costera Miguel Alemán, 4-11-11, S–US$20, D–US$25.

Casa Mireva, Quebrada 42. 'Basic but clean.'

Hotel Avenida, Costera Miguel Alemán y Palmas, 3-45-23, S–US$18, D–US$22.

Hotel Bonanza, Lopez Mateos 14, 3-77-65. Basic but has a pool, S–US$15, D–US$18.

La Mama Helen, Calle Benito Juarez 12. Close to the zócalo, 3-86-97/2-23-96. 'The French hostess who has been living in Mexico for more than 20 years will fix for you her famous *chausson aux pommes or au poulet*. Clean and pleasant place.'

Motel La Jolla, Costera Alemán 506, 2-58-62. 'Spacious rooms with fridge, a/c, shower and big pool.' US$42

Villas Deportívas Youth Hostel, Ardillas 121, 6 kms from corner of Carretera Pie de la Cuesta.

FOOD

Cheapest restaurants for both Mexican and American food are found around the Zócalo.

100% Natural Restaurant, Costera Alemán, past Hertz towards Bali Hai Motel, tel 85-39-83. 'Huge sandwiches and shakes: try cococabana, guava, orange, oat-meal.'

OF INTEREST

The famous **high-dive act** takes place nightly off the rocks at the far end of La Quebrada: 7.15pm, 8.15pm, 9.15pm, 10.30pm. The floodlit drop is 130ft into 5ft deep water, and the diver hits the water at about 60 miles an hr, timing his dive to meet the incoming surf. You can either sit in the lounge of the Mirador Hotel to watch, in which case you'll have to buy an (expensive) drink, or you can go down the steps from the hotel to a public platform overlooking the cliff, paying a modest 'contribution' (20 pesos).

Beaches: Playas Caleta and **Caletilla** are known as 'morning beaches', **Playas Hornos** and **Hornitos** are 'afternoon' ones, because of the movement of the sun and tides. Lots of other less crowded beaches to try, though, such as **Playa Guitarrón** on the east bay.

For the rest, there's fishing, boating, water skiing, para-sailing and underwater diving. If you're good enough, you can explore sunken wrecks and the underwater shrine of **Our Lady of Guadalupe** off La Roqueta Island.

ENTERTAINMENT

Generally sky-high; the only sure way to hold onto your pesos is to grab a table around the Zocálo and watch the goings-on: organ players, gigolos, chewing-gum salesmen, old ladies flogging flowers—they're all selling it. Best discos are **Baby O**, Costera Miguel Alemán, near Nelson, tel 84-74-74, and **Magic**, Costera Miguel Alemán, near Yucatán, tel 84-88-15. About US$10 cover-expensive drinks. The 'best bar' is **Mimi's** on the bay. 'Where all the Brits hang out. US$2 for beer.'

INFORMATION
Dept of Tourism, Costera Miguel Alemán 187, 85-10-41. Open weekdays 8am–8pm, weekends 10am–6pm. They suggest contacting them if you need help finding lodgings; you should not accept 'guidance' from bus station and taxi driver hustlers who may tell you (sometimes by pretending to phone) that your hotel is full and that you should go where they suggest.

TRAVEL
Buses to Acapulco from Mexico City leave from Terminal Central de Autobuses del Sur, near the Metro Taxquena; trip is 7 hrs. Cost: about US$10 one way. 'Go first class; you arrive at a much better place in Acapulco.'
Numerous flights from Mexico City; daily flights from several other Mexican and US cities.

A new, very expensive, toll road now runs between Acapulco and Mexico City. It's now possible to do the trip in half the time but tolls for the length of the road amount to $US82!

CUERNAVACA Located 58 miles south of Mexico City, Cuernavaca is one of Mexico's most charming cities and boasts a year round spring-like climate, pastel coloured houses and lush vegetation. Summer homes have been maintained here by everyone from the Aztec nobles to Maximilian and Carlotta to the late Shah of Iran.
Tourist Information: Morelos Sur 802, tel 14-39-20. Open weekdays 9am–8pm.

OF INTEREST
Borda Gardens. On Morelos—behind the Palacio Municipal. Semi-ruins of the magnificent estate built by a Frenchman José de la Borda and occupied by the ill-fated Maximilian. 'Atmospheric.'
Palace of Cortes. This was the conquistador's favourite city and he built his headquarters here. Diego Rivera had his revenge when he painted the murals around the courtyard and depicted the Spaniards as rapacious caricatures burning the Aztec cities and enslaving the native population. Now a museum, admission: US$3, open Tues–Sun 10.30am–6pm. Closed Mon.
Xochicalco Ruins, 37 kms SW of the city. Still a mystery to archeologists, the pyramids, temples and other buildings are believed to have been a major ceremonial and communications center for several different civilizations. Entrance: 9 pesos.
Caves of Cacahuamilpo, 46 miles south. Mexico's largest and most beautiful caverns. Guided tours. Entrance fee.

MEXICO CITY The Aztec city of Tenochtitlán had a population of 300,000 by 1521, when stout Cortes demolished it to build Mexico City from the remains. Today that figure represents the number of new residents the city acquires *each year*, making it likely that total population will reach 20 million during the lifetime of this guide.

Mexico DF (pronounced 'day effy', for Distrito Federal) is the nation's cultural, economic and transportation hub, with most of the country's people living on the surrounding plateau. As well as being the largest city in the world, it is probably the most polluted, with a smog level to make LA seem positively bracing and a crime level to make New York City seem like the Garden of Eden on a Sunday afternoon: be alert, especially away from the centre. The altitude—7,400 feet—together with the crowds, suicidal traffic and incessant din, can quickly exhaust the unacclimatised traveller.

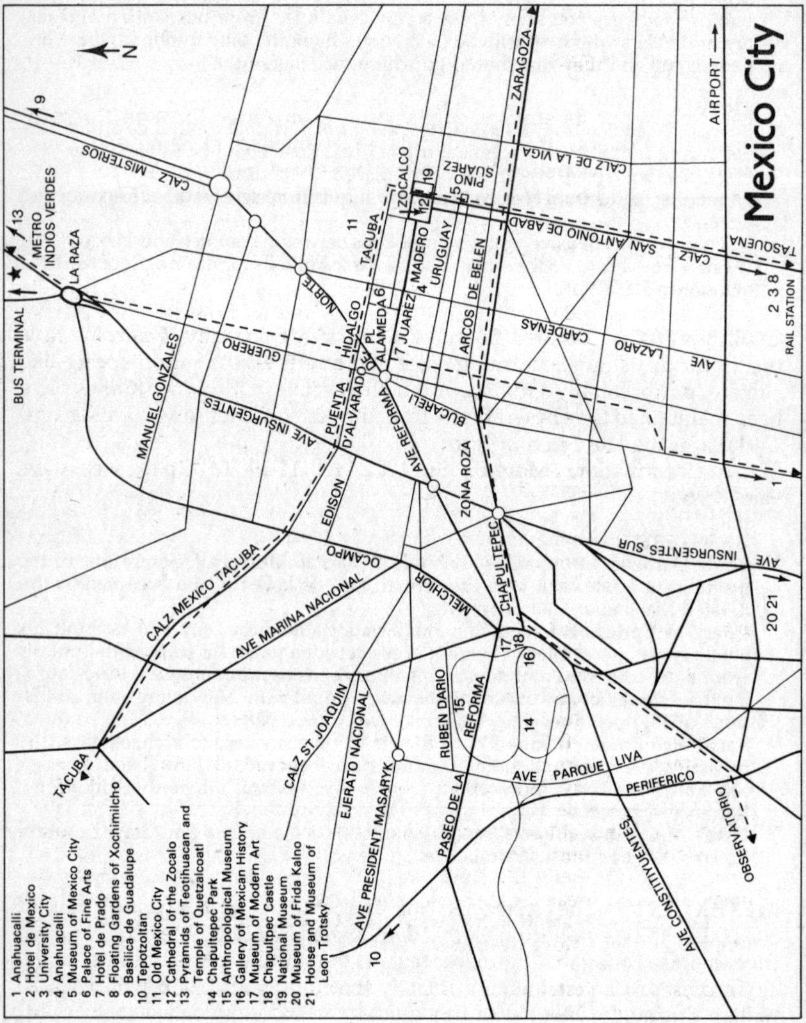
Mexico City
1 Anahuacalli
2 Hotel de Mexico
3 University City
4 Anahuacalli
5 Museum of Mexico City
6 Palace of Fine Arts
7 Hotel de Prado
8 Floating Gardens of Xochimilcho
9 Basilica de Guadalupe
10 Tepotzoltan
11 Old Mexico City
12 Cathedral of the Zocalo
13 Pyramids of Teotihuacan and Temple of Quetzalcoatl
14 Chapultepec Park
15 Anthropological Museum
16 Gallery of Mexican History
17 Museum of Modern Art
18 Chapultpec Castle
19 National Museum
20 Museum of Frida Kalno
21 House and Museum of Leon Trotsky
N
BUS TERMINAL
METRO INDIOS VERDES
LA RAZA
CALZ MISTERIOS
ZARAGOZA
AIRPORT
CALZ DE LA VIGA
PINO SUAREZ
ZOCALO
TACUBA
MADERO
URUGUAY
SAN ANTONIO DE ABAD
CALZ TASQUENA
RAIL STATION
NORTE
HIDALGO
ALAMEDA
JUAREZ
ARCOS DE BELEN
CARDENAS
AVE LAZARO
GUERRERO
PL
MANUEL GONZALES
AVE INSURGENTES
PUENTA D'ALVARADO
AVE REFORMA
BUCARELI
ZONA ROZA
EDISON
CHAPULTEPEC
AVE INSURGENTES SUR
OCAMPO
MELCHIOR
CALZ MEXICO TACUBA
AVE MARINA NACIONAL
TACUBA
CALZ ST JOAQUIN
EJERATO NACIONAL
AVE PRESIDENT MASARYK
RUBEN DARIO
REFORMA
PASEO DE LA
AVE PARQUE LIVA
PERIFERICO
OBSERVATORIO
AVE CONSTITUYENTES

The earthquake of September 1985 overshadowed these problems. In addition to the thousands of deaths, 250 major buildings were toppled and the whole country's communication network was seriously disrupted. The city has now fully recovered from the destruction caused by the earthquakes, except for a few damaged buildings still in the process of demolition and clearance.

Visit the city for its striking architecture from Aztec through Spanish Colonial to modern, from pyramids to enamelled skyscrapers, from modern subways to archeological finds preserved *in situ* at Metro stops. Great wealth and poverty exist side by side but residents at all economic levels tend to be the most hospitable of Mexicans. 'North America is incomplete without a visit to this vast and fascinating city.'

ACCOMMODATION

Singles average US$20, doubles US$15–35. Best area for low price accommodation is around Alameda Park, especially Revillagigedo Street, Plaza San Fernando, Zarazoga, and (further West just before Insurgentes) Bernal Diaz and Bernadino de Sahagun. Also try the area immediately surrounding the zócalo. Be prepared to add 25% to these prices during summer: during this period pressure on a diminishing reserve of low cost hotels is intense, and a room in Cuernavaca, about an hour away by bus, may be the only viable option.

Asociacion Cristiana Femenina, Humboldt 62 and Artículo 123, near Alameda and Juárez metro, 585-06-55. Mexican version of YWCA. Women only; safe and well-located.

Hotel Atlanta, B Dominguez 31 at Allende, 518-12-00. Nr Zócalo, close to sights in old town. 'Clean, comfortable.' S–US$15, D–US$20.

Hotel Avenida, 38 Eje Lázaro Cárdenas, 518-10-07. D–US$18, shower, 'Really good.' 1 block from Torre Latinoamericano.

Hotel Cosmos, Lazaro Cardemas 12, 521-98-89. Metro Bellas Artes. 'Central, D-Q room with or without bath. Ask for a room with a patio.' S–US$15, D–US$20.

Hotel Doral, Sullivan 9, 592-28-66. 'Small rm but very clean and good tourist info in hotel. V good English spoken.' S–US$16, D–US$22.

Hotel Guadalupe, Revillagigedo 36, 747-20-07. AC, shower, TV. Also **Fleming**, next door. 'Both no-frills but comfortable.'

Hotel Montecarlo, Uruguay 69, 521-25-59. 'Clean and friendly.' Built in 1772 as an Augustine monastery. DH Lawrence briefly lived here. S–US$15, D–US$20.

Hotel Rioja, Ave 5 de Mayo 45, 521-82-73, Metro Allende or Zócalo. S–US$10, D–US$15. 'Congenial, clean, a nice place.'

Villa Deportiva Youth Hostel, Insurgentes Sur, 573-77-40. Take bus to Universidad, then another to Olympic Village. Bit of a way from city centre, but safe and comfortable. Breakfast and dinner available.'

Also recommended are **Hotel Paraiso**, Calle I. Mariscal (S–US$12), and **Hotel Metropol**, on Luis Moya (D–US$22), 521-49-13/521-49-10.

Outside Mexico City:

Tlamacas Youth Hostel at Popocatepetl, (dorms). 'Near snow line, with magnificent views. Bus from Mexico City (San Lázaro Metro) to Amecameca, then taxi to Tlamacas.' 'Well worth the trip.' US$3 per bed. Reservations and information in Mexico City, 553-62-86.

FOOD

Mexico City is a good place to taste frothy Mexican hot chocolate, a drink once so prized that only the Aztec and Mayan nobility drank it, to the tune of 50 tiny cups a day. A dish invented locally and now popular all over Mexico is *carne asada a la tampiqueña* (grilled beef Tampico style).

Due to reports of rude waiters and rapacious mariachis, Plaza Garibaldi is no longer recommended as 'best and cheapest'. 'Good cheap eating at small restaur-

ants around Glorieta Insurgentes situated where Insurgentes crosses Avenida Chapultepec. Fewer mariachis than Garibaldi but you can sit in greater comfort to hear them.'
Cafe Paris, Plaza San Fernando and elsewhere, is good for breakfast.
Fleming Hotel Restaurant, 35 Revillagigedo. 'Good food at reasonable prices', 50 pesos and up.
Las Cazuelas, Av San Antonio 143E, open 8am–midnight daily. Savoury home cooking, lots of choice: try their *chiles rellenos* or *pollo en pipian* (chicken in pumpkin-seed sauce). Mariachi-filled but non-touristy.
Taqueria Beatriz, Londres 190, 521-42-13. 'All kinds of tacos. Try the tepache.'
'**Zona Rosa** is a pleasant place to go strolling and there are some cheap restaurants among the plush sidewalk cafes. **Las Tortugas** on Hamburgo is cheap and good.' For real Mexican tacos (not to be confused with the Tex-Mex variety found in most parts of the US), try **Beatriz** (several branches downtown and near the Zona Rosa) or **El Caminero** (Río Lerma, just behind the Sheraton Hotel).

OF INTEREST

Anahuacalli (Diego Rivera Museum), Calle 150, near Division del Norte, tel 677-29-84. Diego Rivera-designed black lava building housing his large collection of Aztec, pre-Columbian artefacts. Open Tue–Sun 10am–2pm, 3pm–6pm. Free, closed Mon.
Polyforum Cultural Siqueiros, Av Insurgentes Sur in the Hotel de Mexico. A monument designed by and in honour of the artist. 'The March of Humanity mural is indescribably wonderful—like being inside an opium dream.' Open 10am–9pm. Sound and light show in the evening.
University City, home of UNAM, the Universidad Nacional Autónoma de México. 11 miles south, reached by buses 17 or 19 from downtown or trolley bus from Eje Cent Lázaro Cárdenas. Famous for its modern design and colourful murals, mosaics and bas-reliefs by Rivera, Juan O'Gorman, Siqueiros and others.
Torre Latinoamericano, corner of Cárdenas and Madero. A miniature Empire State building that floats, with a magnificent view (smog and weather permitting) from its 44th floor. Open 10am–midnight. Small admission charge (100 pesos).
Museum of Mexico City, Pino Suárez 30, three blocks south of Zócalo, tel 542-83-56. Built and rebuilt on site of razed Aztec temple (only cornerstone remains), museum provides excellent introduction to city's history with models, murals, photographs. Good background at the start of your visit. Tues–Sat 9.30am–7pm, Sun 9.30am–4pm. Closed Mon.
Palace of Fine Arts, S Juan de Letrán and Juárez. This heavy white opera house contains Mexico's finest art collection. Upstairs are some of the best murals by Orozco, Siqueiros, Rivera and Tamayo. 'Worth every centavo.' Open Tues–Sun, 10am–7pm. Small admission fee.
Floating Gardens of Xochimilco (so-chee-meel-coh), 15 miles south. Cheapest to catch 31 or 59 bus from downtown. If you get on, you almost certainly won't get a seat. Very crowded weekends, boats take you around lake, other boats sell food, drink. 'A complete waste of time—muddy canals and gardens.' 'Smelly canals full of refuse.' Boat prices: 'Take one-third off first price quoted.'
Basilica de la Virgin de Guadalupe. Take bus to La Villa, on Reforma, or Metro to Basilica. The holiest of Mexican shrines, it honours the nation's patron saint, The Virgin of Guadalupe. Legend has it that she appeared to an Indian, Juan Diego, in 1531. Devout visitors show their faith by walking on their knees across the vast, cement courtyard. Indians dress in national costume, dance, and parade by on her feast day, December 12. The old cathedral leans in all directions and is slowly sinking into the soft lakebed soil. The new basilica was designed by Pedro Ramirez Vasquez, architect of the National Museum of Anthropology.
Tepotzotlán, 25 miles north by *auto-pista* (expressway). Buses from Terminal del Norte, or Metro to Indios Verdes then local bus. Has a magnificent 18th century **church**, possibly Mexico's finest, with a monastery and an interesting collection of colonial religious art. Open Tue–Sun 10am–6pm.

Alameda. A park since 1592, it lies west of the Palace of Fine Arts between Avs. Juárez and Hidalgo. Originally the site of executions for those found guilty by the Spanish Inquisition, it is now the scene of popular Sunday concerts and family outings. On June 13, Mexico's single women line up at the Church of San Juan de Dios and plead with St Anthony to find a husband for them.
Zócalo, or Plaza de la Constitución, has been the centre of the country from Aztec times. Second only in size to Red Square, vehicular traffic is restricted. The Cathedral, National Palace, Templo Mayor, and much more, are all within 5 minutes of each other.
The Cathedral at the Zócalo is the oldest church edifice on the North American continent (1573–1667) and was built on the ruins of the Aztec temple. On the east side of the Zócalo is the **National Palace**, begun in 1692, interesting on its own and for its enormous and impressive murals by Diego Rivera.
Templo Mayor. Just off the corner of the Zócalo, between the Cathedral and the National Palace, is the excavated site of the Aztec Templo Mayor—really twin temples and several associated buildings. Although only the lower and internal parts remain, the ruins are extremely impressive. At the rear of the site is the recently inaugurated Museo del Templo Mayor which houses many of the artefacts recovered during the excavations, tel 542-06-06. Open Tues–Sun 9am–6pm. Admission US$4 except Sun. Guided Tours available. Not to be missed.
The **Pyramids of Teotihuacán** and **Temple of Quetzalcoatl**. Take Metro to Indios Verdes (last station on north end of line 3), then take bus (50 pesos) marked 'Pyramids'. (NB: no backpackers on Metro.) Frequent buses from Terminal del Norte direct to site, 1½ hrs each way. US$1.10. The temples are part of the ruins of the once-great city built even before the Aztecs. The Pyramid of the Sun is 216 ft high (248 steps to the top where the sacrifices were made) and the older Pyramid of the Moon, ¼ mile away, although less vast, is just as impressive. The Temple of Quetzalcoatl is about ½-mile from the pyramids and has some superb Toltec carvings. Open daily 8am–5pm. Admission US$4 except holidays and Sunday. When climbing pyramids, take care—they're very steep. Traders everywhere—even at the top of the pyramids selling fake artefacts that 'they made at home'. *Son et lumière* six nights per week, in English at 7pm. (Not June-Sept.)
Chapultepec Park. Most of the city's important **museums** are in the Park, but it is also an attraction in its own right, especially on Sun when all the families in the city seem to parade there. 'Should be a compulsory visit—very colourful.' Free **zoo** contains the first captive pandas to be born outside China. Metroline 1 to Chapultepec or line 7 to Auditorium.
Anthropological Museum, tel 553-62-66. The claim that this is the finest museum in the world is well-founded; 'certainly one of the world's top ten.' Contains Mexico past and present. The Museum has recovered some of its most prized treasures which were stolen in December, 1985, but they are not displayed yet. 'Deserves every accolade thrown at it. Worth going here *before* you visit the pyramids at Teotihuacán.' Cameras but no tripods allowed, so bring fast film or flash. 'Worth taking your own photos, since postcards of exhibits are very poor and few (as in all Mexican museums I've visited).' Open Tue-Sat 9am–7pm, Sun 10am–6pm. Closed Mon. Admission US$4, free Sun. Take Metro to Chapultepec or yellow and brown bus #76 on Reforma Paseo.
Gallery of Mexican History, a cleverly designed building within Chapultepec Castle, with a first-rate presentation of Mexican history since 1500. Open 9am–6pm daily.
Museum of Modern Art. Has Mexico's more recent masterpieces. 'Excellent collection, not only of Orozco, Rivera, etc, but some charming primitive paintings.' Be sure to see *La Revolución* by Lozano. Open 10am–6pm daily except Mon. Fee 5 pesos. At the entrance of Chapultepec park, corner of Reforma and Ghandhi Calle, 553-62-11. Metro Line 1: Chapultepec. Admission US$4, Sun free. Open Tues–Sun 10am–6pm, closed Mon.

Chapultepec Castle, old castle with original furnishings and objets d'art. Found fame in 1848 when young Mexican cadets fought off invading Americans here. Rather than surrender, the final 6 wrapped themselves in Mexican flags and jumped from the parapets to their death. Unless you want to copy them 'beware stone parapets and banisters, both very unsafe. Castle not impressive but worth visiting for the murals.'
Museo Rufino Tamayo. Exhibitions of modern art and sculpture, including the personal collection of Mexico's best known living artist, Rufino Tamayo. The building itself is worth a visit. Located opposite the Museum of Modern Art. Open Tue–Sun 10am to 6pm. Free Tue. 286-58-39.

Two museums in the southern suburb of **Coyoacán**. Take 23A bus south on Burcareli marked 'Coyoacán' or 'Col del Valle' and the journey takes an hour.

House and Museum of Leon Trotsky, Viena 45, tel 658-87-32. Ring door buzzer to be let in. This is where Trotsky was pickaxed to death in 1940; his tomb is in the garden. His house is preserved as he left it. Open Tue–Sun 10am–5pm, closed Mon. Admission US$4. 'Really interesting museum.'
Museo Frida Kahlo, 5 min from Trotsky house, corner of Allende and Londres 127, tel 554-59-99. Metro Coyoacán (or sometimes called Bancomer), line 3. Open Tues–Sun 10am–12pm, 3pm–6pm. Closed Mon. Admission is free. Guided tours at 11am. Frida was Diego Rivera's wife and a prominent artist in her own right. Their colonial style house is filled with their effects and many of Frida's works.
The **volcanoes of Popocatepetl and Iztaccihuatl** can be seen on a clear day in the east, although 'for good views take bus to Amecameca from ADO Terminal'. The peaks are some 3000 ft higher than Mts Rainier or Whitney in the USA. 'Mind-blowing view when sitting on the right-hand side of bus from Mexico City to Puebla.'
Mexican **Independence Day celebrations**, 15 Sept at 11am. President gives traditional cry of liberty to crowd in the Zócalo amid churchbells ringing, fireworks firing, confetti floating, much rejoicing. **Military parade** 16 Sept down Reforma.

ENTERTAINMENT

Jai Alai, the fastest game in the world, nightly at 6pm except Mon and Fri at Fronton Mexico, on Plaza de la Republica. Fee. Jacket preferred. Complex betting system; stick to the pre-game parimutual.
Bullfight season runs Nov to March; other times of year, you can see *novilladas* (younger bullfighters, younger bulls) which are cheaper and may please you just as well if you know nothing of bullfighting. Fights Sun at 4pm; booking in advance recommended. Take 17 bus down Insurgentes Sur to Plaza California, 1 block from the Plaza. Monumental (also known as Plaza Mexico) is at 50,000 seats the biggest in the world; buy *'sol'* seats in *barrera* or *tendido* sections to see anything, tel 563-39-59. Tickets from US$2 to US$12.
Ballet Folklorico at the Palace of Fine Arts, Sun at 9.30am and 9pm; Wed at 9pm. 'A real must—not classical ballet but a series of short dances representing Spanish, Indian and Mexican cultures.' Incredible costumes! Reserve in advance, tel 529-93-20. Tickets from US$10 to US$25.
Casa del Canto, Plaza Insurgentes. Music from all over Latin America, cover charge about 12 pesos. 'Terrific.'
Plaza de Garibaldi. Nightly after 9pm, mariachi music, sometimes free, sometimes not. Can be dangerous—be careful.
Danceteria 200, 598-00-55. Nightclub—about 500 pesos (US$16) for double ticket but drinks inside are all free. Has an eating place inside and plays lots of good music.

SHOPPING

Many good markets including the Saturday market at *Plaza San Jacinto* in the suburb of San Angel; **San Juan market** on Ayuntamiento is a city-run market with

many Mexican handicrafts and a good place to practice haggling; the **Handicrafts Museum** is on the Plaza de la Cuidadela at Avenida Balderas and has lots of trash and treasures; the **Thieves Market** (adjoining the Mercado La Lagunilla on Rayón between Allende and Commonfort) is open on Sundays. **La Lagunilla** is also especially interesting on Sundays when vendors come from all over the city to set up booths.
Books, guidebooks, American mags: American Bookstore, Madero 25.

INFORMATION
Post Office on Lázaro Cárdenas and Tacuba, has a *poste-restante* section where letters are held up to 10 days for you. Tel 521-73-94. Open weekdays 8.30am–11.30pm, Sat 8.30–7pm, Sun 8.30–4pm.
Mexico City News is an all-English paper with good travel section.
Mexican Government Tourist Bureau, Presidente Masaryk 172, 250-86-01, north of Chapultepec Park—rather out of the way. Otherwise phone 250-01-23 for English-language tourist information. Open Mon–Fri, 8am–7pm. 'Go there in the morning.'
Tourist Police are seen along Reforma and Juárez wearing light blue uniforms with US/Canadian/British flag badges indicating that they speak English. Friendly, well-informed, they provide on-the-spot information.
Radio VIP—CBS Affiliate Station, 88.1 FM.

MEDICAL SERVICES
American-British Cowdray Hospital, Observatorio and Calle Sur 136. Call 207-50-00 or in emergencies, 515-83-59. Open 24 hours.

EMBASSIES
Britain: Calle Rio Lerma 71. 207-21-86, 207-20-89.
US: Reforma 305. 211-00-42.
Canada: Schiller 529. 254-32-88.

TRAVEL
Taxis: 4 types, drivers described as '99.9% cheats—best to find out roughly how much the journey should cost before taking it. Wherever possible, fight to the death!' Regular taxis (yellow) have meters, and you pay 10% more at night. Jitney or 'pesero' taxis (green) cruise the main streets; the driver's finger held aloft indicates that he has space among the other passengers, who fill the taxi like a bus. Sitio taxis (red) operate from ranks on street corners; agree on fare beforehand if possible. Outside hotels, etc, you'll find unmetered taxis; always agree on fare beforehand. 'Taxi meter or not, arrange price beforehand. Hard to bargain, you get overcharged all the time.'
Trolleys and buses; buses cost about 5 pesos. If time is short, Gray Line Tours do a day tour: 533-15-40. If staying any length of time it is suggested that you get a street map and a metro guide.
The Mexico City Metro, opened in 1970, now carries some 8 million passengers daily at a ridiculously low price. 'The world's best transport bargain.' 'Use wherever possible, the streets are choked with traffic.' But avoid during rush hours (7.30–9am, 7–9pm) and be prepared to jostle with the rest of them at other times. Work out connections in advance—no overall plans inside stations. Backpacks, suitcases and large packages are *banned* during rush hours (7am–10am, 5pm–8pm)—this can be strictly applied. Women and children should take advantage of separate queues and cars provided at worst times, and everyone should beware endemic bag-snatching and slashing. Some stops have artefacts uncovered during excavation: Aztec pyramid foundation at Pino Suárez, more artefacts at Bellas Artes and Zócalo. 'Clean, fast and incredibly simple to use.' When leaving the city, it is best to consult the Tourist Office for info.
Rail: Estación Buenavista, Insurgentes and Mosqueta, 4 blocks from Guerro Metro. Bus on Insurgentes Norte to downtown.

Train information 547-10-84, 547-65-93, daily 6am–9.30pm.
Air: Benito Juárez International Airport, 571-36-00. Flights to all Mexican destinations. For international flights remember US$10 departure tax (pesos only). From the airport take the official yellow taxis, buying a fixed price ticket to your destination from desks at the end of the arrivals building. You can also call this service for transport to the airport, but it costs the same or more than a regular taxi. Or Metro to 'Terminal Aerea line 5'—but transfers involved and remember baggage limitations.
For buses getting into or out of Mexico City: 4 terminals, each located near a Metro stop. North arrivals/departures at Terminal Central del Norte, tel 587-59-67, change at La Raza and go to Autobuses del Norte, line 5. (Also get there by bus, Insurgeantes Norte then Cien Metros.) South: Terminal Sur, at the Taxqueña Metro stop, southern end of line 2, tel 544-21-01, West: Terminal Poniente, at Observatorio Metro station, west end of line 1. East: Terminal Central del Oriente (also known as ADO), tel 762-59-77, at the San Lazaro Metro station, to the east on line 1.
Mexico City travel and tourist info from DF tourist office, Amberes and Londres in the Zona Rosa, 525-93-80/525-93-81. Open daily 9am–9pm.

GUADALAJARA With a population touching four million, Guadalajara is Mexico's second largest city and capital of the state of Jalisco. Located 370 miles northwest of the capital city, it has undergone a major facelift and the mile-long Plaza Tapatía, completed in 1982, blends seamlessly into the older city, where vehicle-less malls provide shopping reputedly better than that of Mexico City. Residents are called *Tapatíos* and lay claim to originating tequila, charros (a type of cowboy), mariachis and the Mexican hat dance.

Despite a huge gringo population of retired expatriates and international students, Guadalajara remains cosmopolitan only in the best of senses, and is still a good city for strolling and for sidewalk cafe idling, especially around the Plaza de Mariachis.

ACCOMMODATION
The bus and train stations are at the south end of Calzada Independencia; to reach downtown, head north past 2 roundabouts (called *glorietas* in Spanish).
Cheapest places near bus station on Calzada Independencia Sur, but noisy and polluted.
Singles average US$10–16, doubles US$12–20.
Hotel Central, 28 de Enero, opposite bus station. 'Not luxurious but clean and convenient.'
Hotel Las Americas, Hidalgo 76, between C Independencia past 2nd *glorieta*, 13-96-22. S–US$17, D–US$22.
Hotel Occidental, Huerto and Villa Gomez, left of C Independencia past 2nd *glorieta*, 13-84-06. 'Excellent value, very clean, central.' S–US$10, D–US$13.
Hotel San José, 25 de Febrero 116, opposite bus station, 19-27-26. 'Very nice place, clean and friendly.' S–US$10–$12.
Morales Hotel, 243 Av Corona, overlooking San Francisco Park, downtown. Colonial mansion, charming patio and rooms. 13-29-62. About US$10–15.
Nuevo Hotel Calzada, C Independencia Sur 808, tel 14-67-28. S-US$9, D-US$13. 'Clean, safe and within easy walking distance of bus station and centre.'
Villa Deportiva Youth Hostel, Av Prolongación Alcalde 1360, Barranquitas. No phone—messages can be left at tel 24-65-15. Beds US$6 each, 11pm curfew.

FOOD
The huge **Libertad Market** at Calzada Independencia and Mina is good for cheap food and indeed cheap anything: it's the biggest open market in the Western

Hemisphere, more than 1000 stalls covering 4 square blocks. 'A whole day could easily be spent here.'
Reasonably priced cafes, restaurants along both Av Vallarta and Av Juárez. **Cafe Madrid**, on Av Juarez, is recommended for breakfast.

OF INTEREST
Palacio de Gobierno, facing Plaza de Armas between Morelos and Pedro Moreno. The 17th-C palace of the governor of Jalisco has early Orozco murals including one of Hidalgo brandishing a flaming sword against the Nazis. Open daily 9am–9pm.
The cathedral at Liberation Plaza off Morelos was built in the same century and has fine views from its twin towers.
The **painter/muralist Jose Orozco** lived in Guadalajara and the house in which he did some of his work, at Aurelio Aceves 27, is now a **museum**. Open 10am–2pm, 4–6pm: closed Sun pm and all day Mon. Paintings, murals, personal effects. Orozco died in Mexico City in 1949. The street runs off Juárez at the beautiful Glorieta Minerva fountain.
Hospicio Cabañas. 'Museum with many of Orozco's most important works. Try to find English-speaking guide. Fascinating.' Calle Cagnas and Hospicio. Open daily 9am–7pm.
Regional Museum, 1 block north of the Palacio de Gobierno. An 18th C seminary with Murillo's *Assumption of the Virgin*, 10 others from the school of Murillo plus Spanish, Mexican art. Open Tues–Sun 9am–4pm. Closed Mon. Small admission fee, students with ID free.
Tequila Sauza bottling plant, Av Vallarta. Open to public during working hours: cheap tequila cocktails for lunch.
Nearby and beautiful **Lake Chapala** is famous for its fish. On its shores are dotted Indian villages as well as American retirement communities, such as Chapala itself. Buses leave the Central Camionera every 15 minutes from 6am–10pm. US$1. Stay at the Casa de Huéspedes **Las Palmitos**, Juárez 531, tel 5-30-70, US$8. 'Cheap, pleasant, not far from lake shore.'
Ajijic, 4 miles from Chapala, is more bohemian: Lawrence wrote *The Plumed Serpent* here, Ken Kesey followed later. Third lake community is **Jocotepec**, bigger and less touristy.
Tlaquepaque. Suburb noted for glass and ceramics, though both available more cheaply elsewhere. Central plaza (El Parián) is effectively one enormous bar, with food and mariachis. Further on is **Tonala**, a most interesting village which is entirely given over to family arts and crafts workshops; their specialties are papier-mache, pottery and brass, of good quality, subtle workmanship. Take the bus from C Independencia and Juan Manuel that's marked 'Ruta 110, Seccion 6' to get there. Tonala is 10 miles away and the trip takes about 40 minutes.
Tequila, some 30 miles from Guadalajara, offers tours round Sauza, Cuervo and other distilleries. The surrounding fields of maguey, from which the fiery liquid is distilled, may seem more beautiful on the trip back. No other reason to go.
'SE of Guadalajara and SW of Morelia is **Uruapan**. Nearby is the **Paricutin volcano** which first erupted in 1943 and destroyed a whole village except for a church. In the village of **Angahuan** you can hire a horse and ride to the church or walk (2½–3 hrs round trip) or you can go up to the crater (6–7 hrs there and back). It's a fantastic trip. Take the Los Reyes bus from Uruapan: 1½ hrs over a bumpy track, 2 pesos each way. Nowhere to stay at Angahuan: at Uruapan we stayed at the **Hotel Tivoli** on the plaza, US$9 double with bath. We ate in the **Hotel Progreso** on Calle 5 de Febrero, a good comida corrida for about 40 pesos. Hotel looked lovely with patio, fountain, bright and airy—didn't look expensive.'
Patzcuaro is 125 miles SE of Guadalajara as the *cuervo* flies and 24 miles east beyond Uruapan. About half-way between Guadalajara and Mexico City (near Morelia), and could be visited enroute. The town overlooks Lake Patzcuaro, highest in Mexico. 'An old colonial town rather than a colonial city, it's an agreeable place with interesting corners. Frequent ferries cross to Janitzio Island rising steeply from the lake with lovely views from its highest point. Indian fishermen

living on the island are famous for their butterfly nets (now used for photogenic rather than practical matters).' **Posada de la Salud**, Av Serrato 9, 2-00-58, S–US$10, D–US$13. 'Clean and pleasant. One of the best values'.

Wide choice of hotels in Patzcuaro; **Meson del Gallo** at 20 Dr Cross, has singles from US$6, D–US$10, pool, bars, English-speaking staff. Buses from Guadalajara via Uruapan, or from Mexico City via Toluca and Morelia. Food: 'try street stalls—excellent value.' **Lake Patzcuaro** is famous for its whitefish.

INFORMATION

State Tourist Office, Morelos 102, 58-22-22. 'Best month to visit is Oct for their festivals. Pick up details from tourist office.' Open weekdays 9am–9pm, weekends 9am–1pm.

Federal Tourist Office, Paseo Degollado 50, 14-86-55, open weekdays 9am–3pm.

MORELIA Morelia is the capital city of Michoacan, considered to be the most naturally beautiful state in Mexico. A university city, Morelia is known for its colonial architecture, arts and crafts and candies. Most of the latter are too sticky sweet for conventional tastes, although chocoholics will be in heaven. Spend some time sitting in the tree shaded plazas or at the outdoor cafes lining the main plaza. The twin-towered **Cathedral** took over a century to build and has a honey/pink-coloured facade. The **Casa de las Artesanías** is in the cloister of the Church of San Francisco and has displays of arts and crafts from around the state as well as a good crafts shop. 'Ask about guitars.'

Tourist office: Nigromante 79, 3-26-54. Open weekdays 9am–2pm and 4–8pm, weekends 9am–8pm.

QUERETARO One hundred and thirty-seven miles northwest of Mexico City, Queretaro is a lovely and lively town with a fascinating history. Hidalgo launched Mexico's fight for independence here in 1810; the Treaty of Guadalupe Hidalgo, ending the Mexican War with the US was signed here; the Emperor Maximilian was executed here in 1866; and the present Mexican Constitution was drafted here in 1916.

Tucked away off main streets are numerous little plazas and cobblestoned by-ways, hidden pools and streams of tranquillity. Queretaro is often given a miss or visited only cursorily by tourists in a rush to get to Guanajuato or San Miguel and thereby preserves a freshness of atmosphere. 'This town is the best I've been to in Mexico. Clean, beautiful and very friendly. So nice after Mexico City. People open and spontaneous—I was dragged into a bar by the market, fervently embraced, and regaled with tequila.'

ACCOMMODATION

Hotel Hidalgo, Madero Ote 11, Phone 12-00-81. Nr main square. 'Looks a bit posh from outside but backpackers welcome. Clean and comfortable old colonial style building.' S–US$12, D–US$18.

Hotel Plaza, Av Juarez Norte 23, 12-11-38. 'Clean, reasonable price.' About US$ 12–20.

Motel Azteca, Kilometre 155, Highway 57 (need car). 12-20-60.

Villa Deportiva Youth Hostel, Av Ejército Republicano, ex-convento de la Cruz, tel 14-30-50, US$3 for a bed.

FOOD

La Flor de Queretaro, Juarez Norte 5. A large selection of inexpensive dishes. Full meal 40 pesos.

Molino Rojo, Clata Passage, behind Hotel Plaza in the gallery. 'Excellent food and cheap.'

OF INTEREST

The **Cerro de las Campanas** (Hill of Bells) just outside town is topped by a large statue of Juárez, just below which is the spot where Maximilian, ruler of a briefly dreamed Empire of Mexico, was shot by firing squad. An Expiatory Chapel, built by the Austrian government, contains portraits of Max and Carlotta, and engravings of the execution scene.

Regional **museum** at Corregidora 3, tel 12-20-36, contains further Max-memorabilia including his coffin. Also has interesting comparative displays of Mexican and European paintings matched period for period. Admission US$3.50, free on Sun. Open Tues–Sat 10am–6pm, Sun 10am–3.30pm.

The Church of Santa Rosa de Viterbo was built in the 18th C by Mexico's greatest religious architect, Eduardo Tresguerras.

Aqueduct, built 1726–35, 6 miles in length, some arches 55 ft high. It ends in the cloisters of the **Convent of Santa Cruz**. The convent and its church are open to visitors. Here in 1693 was established the first college for missionaries in the Americas. In 1863 the convent was HQ and then, briefly, the prison of Maximilian. Admission: small donation. Open Mon–Sat 9am–2pm, Sun 9am–3pm.

Teatro de la República at Angela Peralta, near Juarez, where Mexico's constitution was signed in 1917.

INFORMATION

Tourist Office: Calle 5 de Mayo 61. Tel 14-01-79. Open weekdays 9am–3pm and 5pm–8pm, weekends 10am–1pm. Queretaro is a gem cutting centre, particularly amethysts, opals and topaz. The Tourist Office recommends that you buy only from qualified dealers. Be wary of sidewalk vendors.

SAN MIGUEL DE ALLENDE

One of three Mexican towns declared a National Monument, San Miguel is a treasurehouse of art, past and present, from its Colonial palaces built by silver-rich aristocrats to its Instituto Allende, which draws art students and painters from all over the world. Its setting is one of great beauty, with steep cobblestoned streets climbing a mountainside. Despite the high proportion of American students, writers and artists, the village maintains an engaging, slightly Bohemian air. However the large gringo population does make San Miguel comparatively expensive.

ACCOMMODATION

Singles average US$10–15, doubles US$15–20.

Hotel Hidalgo, Hidalgo 22, 2-02-75. 'Still clean, pleasant and cheap.' S–US$10, D–US$20.

Hotel La Huerta, at the end of Barrera, follow Mesones to the east, from the Plaza. 2-03-60. 'Difficult to find, but inexpensive.' S–US$12, D–US$18.

Quinta Loreto, Calle Loreto 15, 2-00-42. 'Really excellent place. Beautiful garden, swimming pool. It's paradise.' 'Best value hotel in Mexico.' Book in advance. S–US$20, D–US$25.

Hotel Sautto, Hernandez Macías 59, 2-00-51. 'Clean, quaint—rooms open out onto courtyard with gardens and parrots in cages.' US$18.

FOOD

Cafe Colón, San Francisco 21. 'Good food, reasonable prices, quick, friendly service.'

Lonchera Alejandra, Calle del Reloj 21. 'Comida corrida at low prices.' 'Clean. Open all night long.'

OF INTEREST

The Parroquía, unique among Mexican churches for being designed by an untutored Indian architect in French Gothic style.
Instituto Allende, Calle de Ancha San Antonio 20, tel 2-01-90. Office open weekdays 9am–noon and 3pm–6pm. Founded in 1938, this has become a well-known arts and crafts school, which also draws many foreigners (especially Americans) to its writing classes and Spanish language studies. The number of students in town keeps long-term rents low but demand high.
'A road from San Miguel to Guanajuato passes through **Dolores Hidalgo**, where a plaque in the parish church marks the spot where Miguel Hidalgo rang the bell to start the fight for independence.'

INFORMATION

Tourist Office, Plaza Mayor, 2-17-47. Open weekdays 10am–3pm and 5pm–7pm, weekends 10am–2pm.

GUANAJUATO Just west of San Miguel and 250 miles north of Mexico City, Guanajuato is another Spanish colonial town whose mines once supplied one-third of all the silver in the world in the 16th–18th centuries. Its picturesque site is a canyon so steep that auto traffic is confined to one street. The city is best explored on foot through the maze of streets, plazas and alleyways known as callejones. Known for its cultural activities, especially the International Cervantes music and drama festival in October and November. Guanajuato also has the ghoulish pleasures of mummy-viewing, a collection of local citizens preserved in an extraordinary fashion by the climate.

ACCOMMODATION/FOOD

Singles average US$10–20, doubles US$15–30.
Casa Kloster, Calle de Alonzo 32, 2-00-88. US$10 per person.
Also try the **Hostería del Fraile**, Sopena 3, 2-11-79, S–US$30, D–US$40; and **San Diego**, Jardín de la Unión 1, 2-13-00, S–US$7, D–US$9. Information pillars along Av Juárez give prices and locations of local hotels. Avoid festival times here unless you have a booking.
The **cafeteria at the University of Guanajuato** on Pocitos is cheap and congenial.
Hotel Molino del Rey, Calle Belaunzaran, stairway Campanero, 2-22-23. 'Very charming and quiet.' 'Clean with cheap and excellent menu.'

OF INTEREST

For a great **view of the town**, walk up Calle Sopena from the Jardín de la Unión, turn right up the Callejón del Calvario and up the steep winding path to the **statue of José Barajas**, also known as El Pipila. Barajas was the young miner who on Hidalgo's order set fire to a strategically-positioned grain warehouse in which royalists were hiding during the War of Independence. The restored warehouse, the **Alhondiga de Granaditas**, is now a museum. On Calle Canitos, it contains exhibits on Hidalgo, pre-Columbian relics and samples of local crafts, small admission fee. Closed Mon. 'If your only day in Guanajuato is Mon, go and look at least at the courtyard and the lovely colours in the stone.' For great views climb the narrow stairs behind Pipila's shoulder. Admission US$3.50. Open Tues–Sat 10am–2pm and 4pm–6pm, Sun 10am–3.30pm, tel 2-11-12.
The **Museo del Pueblo de Guanajuato**, Pocitos 7, tel 3-29-90, next to the University, was opened in 1983 and contains the work of local artists, including a new historical mural by Morado. Closed Mon.
Interesting buildings include: the **Church of la Compañía**; the **Church of San Cayetano**, called La Valenciana, after the silver mine across the street; **Teatro Juárez**, where some of the world's greatest artists once played and sang; the

ruined **Teatro Principal** and **Placita de Mexiamora**, enclosing a haven of green-lawned tranquillity. **Diego Rivera** was born in the house (now museum) at Calle de Pocitos 47. Tel 2-11-97. Open Tues–Sat 10am–6.30pm, Sun 10am–2.30pm.
Mummies. Over 100 of the local citizenry are on display as *momías*, preserved by the climate. Their mummified state was first discovered when the town ran out of cemetery space and dug up those folks whose families had failed to pay maintenance costs for 5 years. Guanajuatans quickly agreed that there's nothing like a mummy for paying the bills, thus the display which costs you 3 pesos to view mummies with and without clothing, some with mouths soundlessly agape. Deliciously spooky. In basement cavern at El Panteón cemetery, 1½ kms SW of the main plaza. Daily 9am–6pm, tel 2-06-39. Admission US$1. If locked, wait around until someone shows up and lets you in. 'Not for the squeamish.'
There are many old **silver mines** around the town, only one reachable by public transport at **La Valenciana**, two miles north of the city by bus. The mine has been operating for several hundred years and still does so on a reduced scale: visitors can wander round the machinery and workings. Nearby is the lopsided but beautiful Churrigueresque church, partly financed in the 1780s by the silver miners: sumptuous filigree decoration and gold-covered altars.

INFORMATION
Tourist Information at Plaza de la Paz 14. Tel 2-00-86. Open weekdays 8.30am–7.30pm. Weekends 10am–2pm.

TOLUCA At 8760 feet, Toluca is the highest city in Mexico. This capital of the State of Mexico lies about an hour's drive west of Mexico City with magnificent scenery in-between.

The main attraction is the Friday market, the stall-keepers mostly Indians, the regional specialties straw goods, papier mache figures and sweaters. The last might come in handy as summers are mild and winters often downright chilly. Before risking the shirt off your back in bargaining, go to the Museum of Popular Arts and Crafts where an adjoining Government store sells many of the goodies you'll see at the market at very reasonable prices. If you can't knock the stall-keepers lower than the Government, you'll know you're being screwed.

Three miles north of town on the Queretaro road is the **Calixtlahuaca** archaeological zone where digging is still in progress. 'Beware unofficial 'guides'—the visit is usually free.' 'Not worth the hassle.'

OF INTEREST
Museum of Popular Arts and Crafts, ¼ mile east of bus station. Contains regional crafts, replicas of Mexican kitchens, a cool airy place to take a breather. Open 9am–2.30pm weekdays, 10am–1pm, 4pm–6pm Sun. Closed Sat.
Calixtlahuaca is best reached by taxi though accessible by local bus; the most interesting structure unearthed is the circular pyramid.
Nevado de Toluca is nearby volcano with magnificent views of crater lakes, Toluca Valley and the Sierra Madres. 14,000 feet up and accessible by rough dirt road.

TRAVEL
In Mexico City: take Metro line 1 to Observatorio station, then bus from Observatorio to Toluca, about 1 hr, 15 pesos. Or direct bus from Terminal Poniente.

TAXCO Beyond Cuernavaca and about 130 miles from Mexico City, Taxco sits high in the Sierra Madres and is Mexico's silver centre. It is best seen from high up on the mountainside. Views in any direction are marvellous, and the town itself charmingly enbalmed in the colonial period by order of the Government, which in making it a National Monument has prevented the construction of modern buildings.

The narrow streets are roughly cobbled, the roofs tiled red, the twin-spired ornate Santa Prisca church illuminated at night. 'One of the prettiest towns in Mexico, set in magnificent countryside. Be sure to climb up to the top of the town for the view below.'

ACCOMMODATION

Singles average US$30–US$35, doubles US$40–US$45.

Hotel Agua Escondida, Plaza Borda 4 nr the Zócalo. 2-07-26. 'Good food at the Hacienda.' 'Very comfortable, nice situation, good views.' 'Clean and luxurious, with own pool.' S–US$30, D–US$40.

Hotel Santa Prisca, Plazuela de San Juan, 2-00-80. Small rooms giving onto patio, good location, unpretentious and very Mexican. Expensive at S–US$35, D–US$45.

OF INTEREST/TRAVEL

In the 1930s an American named William Spratling revived the silver industry and craftsmanship in Taxco. Today there are at least 300 silver shops in town, many of them fascinating one-man design factories. Shop around, there are no real bargains, even Mexico City may sell silver jewellery cheaper. The national silver fair is in December.

From Mexico City: take Metro to Taxqueña and Terminal Sur, from where you catch the bus to Taxco.

PUEBLA Eighty miles east of Mexico City, Puebla is approached over a route recommended for its varied, sometimes wild and mountainous scenery. As you draw nearer, the volcanoes of Popocatapetl (dormant) and Iztaccihuatl (extinct) rise snow-capped into view.

Nine miles west of Puebla, just off the main road, is **Cholula**, a pre-Columbian religious centre second only in importance to Teotihuacán with over 400 shrines and temples. The Spaniards destroyed most of them and built Christian edifices on their ruins. 'Spent 2 days camping in the hills near Cholula. Beautiful and peaceful: saw one shepherd in 2 days.' The Pyramid of Tepanapa here is the largest in Mexico; a Spanish shrine and marvellous view are met at the top. 'In the nearby villages of Tonantzintla and Acatepec are churches with beautifully tiled walls and richly decorated interiors.' 'Don't camp on top of the pyramid: obnoxious guards. But definitely worth visiting. We climbed it at dawn and watched the volcanoes becoming clearly illuminated. Spectacular.'

Puebla itself is renowned for its ceramics, which decorate fountains, houses and patios, and for its 60 churches, the more noteworthy of which have their facades or domes completely covered with locally made polychrome faience. Puebla is also the home of a succulent dish called *mole* (that's *mo*-lay), made of chocolate, chilis and other puzzling but delicious things and served over turkey or chicken.

ACCOMMODATION

Singles average US$15–20, doubles US$25–30.

Hotel Colonial, 4 Sur 105, 46-41-99, 1 block from bus station. 'Full of character.' S–US$30, D–US$40.

Hotel Latino, 6 Norte 8, 41-23-25. On same block as bus station. S–US$10.
Hotel del Portal, Maximino Avila Camacho 205, 46-02-11. Opposite zócalo. S–US$25, D–US$30.
In Cholula:
Hotel Villa Arqueologicas, 47-19-66. Near historic sites. Expensive at US$50.

OF INTEREST/INFORMATION
The Cathedral of the Immaculate Conception. 'Second only to St Peters in Rome. Magnificent Mexican baroque carvings and numerous beautiful chapels.' Begun in 1562 at the command of Spain's Phillip II and completed just over 100 years later. Admission free. Open daily 10.30am–noon and 4pm–6pm.
Santa Monica Convent, 18 Poniente 103. Mexican law once forbad convents and monasteries but this one operated secretly from 1857 to 1935, when it was discovered by government officials. Kept as found, it's now a museum, open Tues–Sun 10am–5pm, closed Mon. Admission US$1.
In the vicinity of Santa Monica is the **onyx workshop area**.
The best **market** is along Av 8 Poniente, from Calle 7 Norte to Calle 5 de Mayo.
On the hill NE of Puebla, about 2 miles from the zócalo, are **Forts Loreto and Guadalupe**. Here on 5 May 1862, 2000 Mexican troops defeated a French force of 6000 (part of Maximilian's attempt to establish an empire in Mexico), a date recalled with great national pride and responsible for all the '5 de Mayo' streets in Mexico. Admission US$3, free Sun. Open Tues–Sun 10am–5pm, closed Mon.
Tourist Office, Av 5 Oriente 3, 46-12-85. Open Mon–Sat 10am–8pm.

VERACRUZ Ever since Cortes put ashore on Good Friday 1519, the Rich City of the True Cross has been the main point of invasion and principal port of Mexico. The Spanish shipped most of their gold and silver out of here, an activity that did not escape the attention of pirates. These, as well as the regular forces of France and the United States, invaded and sometimes ransacked the port on half a dozen occasions. A producer of fine seafood, cigars and sugarcane, Veracruz shows echoes of Havana in the old days, a humid, sometimes rough and raucous city with a strong Mardi Gras tradition. The Afro-Caribbean influence is evident in the marimba music and dances.

ACCOMMODATION
Hotel Central, Av Diaz Mirón 1612, 37-22-54. Next to Central Camionera bus station. Not at all central as the bus station is south of downtown, but perhaps convenient for the weary. S–US$17, D–US$30.
Hotel Sevilla, Morales 359, 32-42-46. Good views of zócalo and city. S–US$17, D–US$20.
Hotel Santillana, Landero y Coss 209, at Dehesa, 32-31-36. In the market area. S–US$17, D–US$30.
Hotel Veracruz, Av Independencia 89, Plaza de Armas, 31-24-91. More expensive but near city centre.
Villa Deportiva Youth Hostel. Paso Doña Juana, Municipio de Ursulo Galván.

OF INTEREST/INFORMATION
El Tajín. The ruins of this Totonac holy city surround the 7-storey Pyramid of the Niches, whose name derives from the 366 niches believed to be linked to the Toltec calendar. The Veracruz Indians were obsessed with ball games and from this area came the rubber to make the balls. Engravings at El Tajín clearly show that games were no light matter; some of the losers were ritually decapitated (just as at Mayan and other sites).
Castle of San Juan de Ulúa. 'Impregnable' fortress on Gallega Island in Veracruz harbour, surrendered without a shot to the US in 1847 after the city itself had

fallen. Subsequently used as prison, with punishment cells partially submerged at high tide. Run down, gloomy and fascinating: take a torch. By bus from zócalo, or 40 min walk. Admission US$3.50. Free on Sun. Open Tues–Sun 9am–4.30pm.
Beaches: The best are Mocambo and Boca del Río, both reached by bus which runs along the sea front. Somewhat muddy, beaches here have shark-infested waters. Wise to enquire *Hay tiburón?* before plunging in.
Tourism Office, Palacio Municipal, on the Zócalo, tel 2-16-13. Open daily 9am–9pm.

ENTERTAINMENT

Mardi Gras in Veracruz could well be the best in the hemisphere. 'Friendlier than New Orleans.'

TRAVEL

Frequent buses to, and from Mexico City (7–8 hour trip), twice daily to Oaxaca, 3 times daily to Mérida. The main bus terminal is at Av Diaz Miron 1698, tel 37-57-44.
Train station is downtown on the harbour. Terminal ferrocarriles, tel 32-25-69. The overnight train to Mexico City leaves at 9.30pm. Also services to Mérida and other parts of the south-east but with bad connections.

OAXACA (pronounced wa-HA-cah) Located about 330 winding miles south of Mexico City, the principal city in south Mexico lies in a semitropical valley surrounded by beautiful jagged peaks. For over 2000 years, this region has been the domain of the Zapotec Indians, who in 1806 produced Benito Juárez, Mexico's Abraham Lincoln. The city still has an Indian atmosphere and is noted for a variety of crafts made there, ranging from leather goods to cottons to hand-carved knives, all of which you can see at the Saturday market. But six miles from the city is the greatest attraction: the Zapotec religious centre and necropolis of **Monte Albán**, towering 1300 feet above Oaxaca. This is one of the best large archaeological sites in Mexico.

A beautiful, narrow mountain road zigzags up to Monte Albán, suddenly opening out onto the great square of this religious acropolis. The summit of the mountain was levelled to provide a platform for pyramids, sanctuaries, observatories and palaces. The magnificent perspectives along the north–south axis are broken only by Building J, looking curiously like the prow of a ship and in fact a great astral observatory used to work out the Zapotec calendar.

Mitla, at a further distance from Oaxaca, was the centre of the Mixtec world. Between AD 900 and 1200, the Mixtecs moved in on Zapotec territory, consolidating their conquest by diplomatic intermarriage with the Zapotecs. Consummate artists, the Mixtecs had no peer in ceramics, turquoise mosaics and goldwork. When the conquistadores came this way, Mixtec princes were living in numerous palaces, although only one remains well-preserved today. Each facade is decorated with tiny mosaics forming diamond, coil and key-like patterns symbolising, in highly stylised form, the Plumed Serpent.

Many of the treasures of both Mitla and Monte Albán are on view in the **Oaxaca Regional Museum** in town. Be sure to see the treasure of Tomb Seven, an immense quantity of gold and turquoise jewellery, quartz and pottery found in the grave of a prince and rivalling in splendour the Tutankhamun find.

ACCOMMODATION

Oaxaca sometimes bursts at the seams with tourists: if you arrive late in the day, don't be too picky. Cheapest hotels are in the market area (Aldama and 20 de Noviembre).

Singles average US$10–15, doubles US$20–25.

Hotel Roma, Aldama 500, 6-41-13. Bargain by any standards. S–US$10, D–US$15.

Hotel Pasaje, Calle Mina 302, 1 block south of Aldama, 6-42-13. 'Friendly, clean with a talking parrot named Lorenzo.' S–US$10, D–US$15.

Hotel Veracruz, Héroes de Chapultepec 1020, 5-05-11. Next door to 1st class bus station; turn left out of station. 'Excellent value.' S–US$25, D–US$30.

FOOD

'In the market (mercado) are hot food stalls where dishes are prepared before your eyes. Similar to Plaza Garibaldi.'

'**The Restaurant Colonial**, nr Zócalo, can be recommended.'

Mercado 20 de Noviembre, on Aldama near church. Department-store-style food market with dozens of small restaurants.

OF INTEREST/INFORMATION

Oaxaca Regional Museum, Calle Macedonia Alcalar 202. Open 10am–2pm, 5pm–8pm, Tue to Sun. Closed Monday. Admission US$1.50. Former convent setting for archeological and cultural exhibits including Mixtec hallucinogenic mushrooms and other treasure from Monte Albán. 'Don't fail to see (adjacent) church of Santo Domingo as well.'

Rufino Tamayo Museum of Pre-Hispanic Art, Av Morelos 503, tel 6-47-50, nr Zócalo. Open 10am–2pm, 4pm–7pm daily, closed Tue. Small admission fee. 'Well displayed collection of exceptional and striking pre-Columbian art. Much more impressive than the archaeological exhibits at the Oaxaca Museum as it is primarily artistic in intent.'

Monte Albán. Six miles from Oaxaca, 'the best site in SW Mexico.' Parts of the city date from 500 BC, and excavations are still under way. Open 8am–5pm daily: small entrance fee. At least four buses per day from Hotel Mesón del Angel, Calle Mina 518, tel 6-53-27: the excursion (with fixed return time) allows only an inadequate two hours to explore. Pay double to come back on later bus, take a taxi, or a two hour walk to town. 'Buses book up quickly—be there early.'

Mitla, 24 miles to the southeast, only partly excavated. Buses (2nd class) from terminal at the end of Calle Trujano, takes 1hr. 'Mitla is not very impressive, but you can stop along the way at the Tree of Tula, 2500 years old with a 43-yard girth, and at the crossroad to Yagul (1½ mile walk), a lately discovered ruin in magnificent surroundings with long, beautiful views.'

Tourist Office, Morelos 200 at 5 de Mayo, tel 6-48-28. Open daily 9am–6pm.

SHOPPING

'There's a small market by the cathedral where you can see Indians weaving things you'll see done nowhere else.' In villages around Oaxaca you can buy wares directly from the Indians cheaper than at the market, e.g. serapes at Teotitlán del Valle, left off the road enroute to Mitla; dresses and blouses at San Antonio Ocotlán, south of Oaxaca. The whole area is renowned for weaving.

TRAVEL

The train from Mexico City leaves at 7pm and arrives 9.20am. Same times for return journey. 'Be careful when buying ticket: the Mexicans try to fit three people in a berth designed for one.'

The 1st class bus allows you to do it by day, 9 hrs, 'nice scenery'. About 400 pesos.

The train station is at Calzada Madero, tel 6-22-53.

Both train and bus stations are outside the downtown area; easiest to take a taxi, about 15 pesos to the Zócalo. Otherwise, catch buses marked 'Col America' or 'Col Reforma' left out of the bus station, to get to the centre. The first class bus station is on Calzada Héroes de Chapultepec, tel 5-17-03; the second class bus station is off Periferico, tel 6-53-23. From the train station, take the bus marked 'Estación', which runs along Av Hidalgo to the Zócalo, or 'Centro', which runs along Aldama.

SOUTHEAST MEXICO

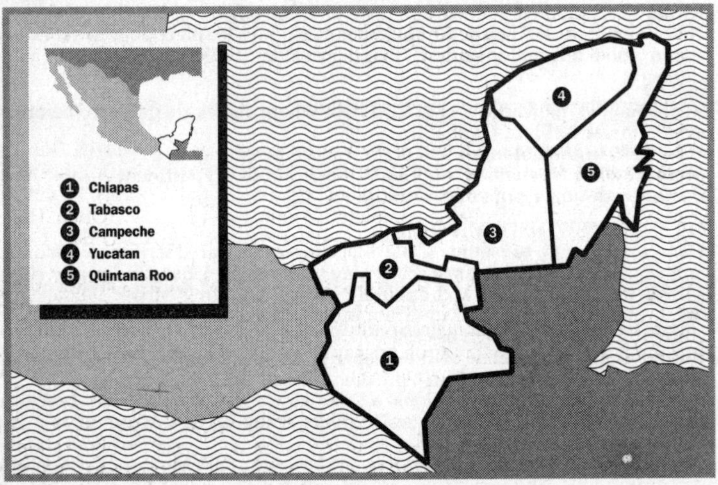

The five states making up southeast Mexico contain some of the most beautiful, varied and untouched territory in all of Mexico: lush orchid jungles, cool mountain highlands, arcing waterfalls, bone-white beaches, delta river country, tiny offshore islands. But the great Mayan ruins and the artistry and colour of their present-day descendants are the chief draws of the region.

From the isthmus, you can either make the coast-run down into Guatemala via Highway 200, or choose the superlative uplands route that takes you through bustling oil city Tuxtla Gutierrez and picturesque San Cristobal de las Casas on Highway 190 (the Pan-American Highway).

Not all of the enormous region is worth exploring, however; the Tabasco coastline, Villahermosa and environs are full of oil fields. Further south, large portions of the Yucatan peninsula have little to interest the eye, a monochromatic sameness of low tropical brushland.

SAN CRISTOBAL DE LAS CASAS Spanish colonial in appearance, San Cristobal's position in the lovely green Jovel Valley has made it a major trading centre for numerous Indian tribes of Chiapas. Every day is market day here and you'll see Tenejapas in black serapes, Chamulas in white wool tunics, Zincantan Indians in red-striped gowns, together with some of the finest crafts and the most luscious produce to be found anywhere. A very fine spot, and, at the beginning of 1994, the scene of a peasants' revolution fuelled largely by fear of the effects of NAFTA.

ACCOMMODATION

Casa de Huéspedes Margarita, Real de Guadalupe 34, 8-09-57. Former mansion, with cafe: near Zócalo. S–US$11, D–US$14.

Hotel Capri, Insurgentes 54 near 1st class bus station, 8-00-15. S–US$10, D–US$12. 'Clean.'
Casa de Huéspedes Pola, Calle Insurgentes 77, and Pino Suáres, opposite Hotel Capri.
Casa de Huéspedes Santa Lucía, opposite 2nd-class bus station. 'Clean.'

FOOD

La Olla Podrida in Diego Mazariegos, off the south side of Zócalo. Variety and good quality, including 'magnificent vegetable soup which is a meal in itself'.

OF INTEREST

Na Bolom Museum, NE end of Av Vincente Guerrero 33, 8-14-18. 'Remarkable place run by local 'hero', Frau Gertrude Blom from Switzerland. Life's work has been study of Lacandon Indians (remote tribe of Mayan descent). Fascinating . . . no visit to San Cristobal is complete without coming here.' Open Tues–Sun, 4–6pm. Serious students of subject can stay here, S–US$30, D–US$40. Call in first to reserve.
Rent horses and guides for day treks to surrounding villages and nearby caves. Ask at Casa Margarita, tel 8-09-57, or Hotel Real del Valle, tel 8-06-80. Or take local buses. Show respect for *indigena* culture: a recurring cautionary tale concerns two tourists stoned to death for photographing the inside of a village church. Photo permit and further information from Tourist Office.

INFORMATION

If you take a fancy to the area, go to the Librería El Recoveco bookshop on the Zócalo and get the guidebook to San Cristobal, which contains much useful info and is written by an Englishman.
Tourist Office: Plaza 31 de Marzo, 8-04-14. Open Mon–Sat 8am–8pm, Sun 9am–2pm.

TRAVEL

The bus terminal is 5 minutes outside town, tel 8-02-91. Buses to Palenque leave at 8am, 9am, take about 7½ hrs, from 2nd-class depot. Buses are much in demand: book well in advance and arrive early.
Airport is for light planes only. No regular services but charters possible to Tuxtla, Palenque and elsewhere.
'The road is mostly unpaved through superb and lush mountains.' 'Take Ocosingo route for really fantastic scenery.' 'The road via San Cristobal is the nicest way to go to Guatemala.'

VILLAHERMOSA The area around Villahermosa marked the westernmost limits of the Maya Empire. Today the Gulf Highway (180) running from Mexico City out to the Yucatan passes through here. Located inland by a river, the city is nearly at sea level and consequently quite hot in summer. The local oil boom has made this a busy, increasingly sprawling and expensive place where budget accommodation is now hard to come by. A pause but not a stay is recommended.

ACCOMMODATION

Casa de Huéspedes Mary, Calle Juárez 225, nr the market. 'A friendly place.'
Hotel Aurora, Calle 27 Frebrero 633. 'One of the least expensive.'
Hotel Madero, Madero 301, 2-05-16. S–US$15, D–US$20.
Hotel San Miguel, Lerdo 315, downtown. 2-15-00. S–US$12, D–US$15. 'Clean and inexpensive.'

OF INTEREST

La Venta, 84 miles west, was the home of the Olmecs, generally considered the originators of pre-Columbian civilisation in Mexico. In the 1950s, the archaeological finds at the site were transferred *in toto* to escape destruction from oil drilling. The colossal Olmec heads of basalt can now be seen at the archaeological museum in Mexico City, at the Tabasco Museum in Villahermosa, and at Parque Museo La Venta, on Rt 180 nr the airport. Apart from the 3 heads, the site has stelae, altars, mosaics and a model of the original site. Self-guiding tour map. Admission US$2, open daily 8am–4.30pm, tel 5-22-28. Take a Tabasco 2000 bus from Parque Juarez to the site.

Regional Museum of Anthropology, 20 min walk along river. Part of newly-opened Olmec and Mayan Research Centre complex, and a valuable introduction to the area's archaeological sites. Same building houses theatre, bookshop and restaurant. Av Carlos Pellicer 511, tel 2-18-03. Museum admission US$4, open daily 9am–8pm.

INFORMATION

Tourist Office: Passeo Tabasco 1504, tel 5-06-93. Open daily 9am–3pm and 6pm–8pm.

PALENQUE About 80 miles inland from Villahermosa are the jungle ruins of the classic Mayan sacred city of Palenque, which flourished AD 300–700. Built on the first spurs of the Usumacinta Mountains, the gleaming white palaces, temples and pyramids rise from the high virgin jungle. Its visually compelling site, its compact size (the excavated portion is about three-quarters of a mile by half a mile, out of the 20-square-mile extent of the city) and its dramatic burial chamber make Palenque, to many minds, more outstanding than Chichen Itza. The 1950 discovery of an ornate crypt containing fantastically jade-bedecked remains of a Mayan priest-king revised archaeologists' theories about Mayan pyramids, which were earlier believed to be mere supports for the temples on top. Although it's a hot, steep and slippery journey, you should climb the Temple of the Inscriptions, descend the 80 feet into its crypt to view the bas-reliefs: chilling and wonderful. NB: here you'll see the relief of *Chariot of the Gods* notoriety. Tomb contents are in Mexico City museum, however.

ACCOMMODATION

Bargain over rates to avoid arbitrary 'tourist taxes'. Singles average US$6–15, doubles US$10–25.

Camping Maria del Mar. About 2 miles from downtown, on the road to the ruins. It has a pool and a restaurant.

Camping Mayabel, 4 miles from town on road to ruins. 23 sites from US$10 double.

Posada Alicia, outside centre, 10 minutes walk from bus. 'Reasonable rates for room and board which in Palenque is rare. The cognoscenti stay at Alicia's.'

OF INTEREST

The ruins—'most spectacular we saw in Mexico'—are 5 miles from town and served by local bus, leaving from main street several times daily. Jeep taxis to the Zone are available at the city plaza with some bargaining. Admission: US$3.50. The ruins are open daily 8am–5pm.

TRAVEL
Train station is about 3 miles outside town. There are 2 trains to Merida: 2nd-class cheapo taking 20 hrs and a 'rapido', with both 1st and 2nd class, taking 14 hrs. Delays common. The 2nd-class bus leaves at 5pm and takes about 8 hrs.
Air connections: daily flights from Mexico City.
Tourist information: Palacio Municipal, tel 5-01-14. Open Mon–Sat 8am–2pm, 5–8pm.

MÉRIDA Called the 'white city', partly for its tidiness, more so for the striking regional dress worn by both men and women, Mérida is the Yucatan capital and bustles at 500,000. Built upon the remains of Tiho, a Mayan settlement, Mérida looks Spanish colonial (lots of fine churches and homes) but still sounds and tastes Mayan. Don't fail to sample Yucateco cooking: *sopa de lima* (chicken with lime soup), *huachinango* (red snapper fish), *panuchos* (Yucatan version of a taco) Carta Clara beer and the traditional Mayan liquor *x-tabentún*.

A delightful city for strolling, which will enable you to see details such as the clay animal sculptures sometimes placed at street corners in lieu of signposts. Local crafts include all items made from sisal fibre—hammocks, shoes, baskets and panama hats (here, not Panama, is where they come from). Mérida makes a good base for exploring the Yucatan peninsula, most especially the ruins of Uxmal and Chichen Itza. However: 'Mérida is not in the least bit delightful. Most people we met were very glad to get out of the place.'

ACCOMMODATION
Singles average US$8–12, doubles US$12–25.
NB: Mérida is laid out on a grid system. All streets are numbered *calles*, whether north–south or east–west; the N–S ones are even-numbered, the E–W ones, odd.
Hotel América, Calle 67, 500. 21-51-33. 4 blocks from ADO terminal. 'Central, clean and very friendly.' US$12.
Hotel Caribe, Calle 59, 500. 24-90-22. 'Clean, friendly, helpful. Central, with pool.' S–US$22, D–US$25.
Hotel Casa Bowen, Calle 66 nr Calle 65. D–US$12. Built around a cool, leafy courtyard. Nr the bus station (3 blocks). Friendly service. Restaurant next door. Mon–Sat. Order preceding day. Cost about US$2 full meal.
Hotel Chac-Mool, Calle 54, 474 at Calle 55. Has pool. 'Marvellous after the train journey from Palenque.' 23-07-20, US$12–15.
Hotel San-Luis, Calle 68, 534, 24-76-29. AC rooms, central.

FOOD
Los Almendros, Calle 59, 434 (between Calles 50 and 52). 'Try this for inexpensive Yucatan specialties—excellent!'
Hotel Flamingo Restaurant, Calle 57, 485. Tasty 4-course meals.
Cafe Alameda, Calle 56, 518. 'Very inexpensive Lebanese.' Closes around 7.30pm. 'Try poc-chuc, a sort of pork cutlet.'

OF INTEREST
Casa de Montejo, main plaza on Calle 63. Built in 1546 by Don Francisco de Montejo, Merida's founder, and occupied until recently by his descendants. Open on weekdays 9am–1pm. Admission free. The plateresque doors are its best feature.
Mérida Market, junction of Calles 60 and 65, sells embroidered shirts, blouses, leather goods, hammocks, etc. 'Knock them down to at least half their asking price.' 'Good market, very friendly people.' Haggle, and don't be palmed off with

a loose-woven 'basura' job: for quality, feel the width and the closest-packed weave.' The market is open daily from 6am–5pm.

Free **outdoor concerts** Sun eves at Parque de las Américas and Thur eves at Parque Santa Lucia on Calle 60.

Place Merida, on Calle 60, North of the Cathedral. On Sundays the streets are closed to traffic and local families come out to enjoy street entertainers and browse through craft stalls.

Calle 56A, Junc. with Calle 43. 'Smallish Museum of Anthropology, good display of Mayan life in colonial mansion.' Admission US$3.50. Free Sun and holidays. Open Tues–Sat 8am–6pm, Sun 8am–2pm.

INFORMATION/TRAVEL

Tourist Office, Calle 60, 470. 24-93-69/24-92-90. Open daily 8am–8pm.

Yucatan Weekly Bulletin, English info on local events, customs, sights; available free in hotels.

Flights from Mexico City and from Miami and elsewhere in the US.

To and from Mexico City, there are trains (30 hrs) and buses (22 hrs).

UXMAL and CHICHEN ITZA Along with Palenque, Uxmal was one of the chief Mayan cities and the showpiece of that civilisation's finest architectural accomplishments. Chichen Itza, on the other hand, was first a Mayan city and later occupied and built on by the belligerent Toltecs, becoming in the process the most stupendous city in the Yucatan.

Fifty miles of good road lead from Mérida to **Uxmal**, where the clean, open lines of the ancient city create an impression of serenity and brilliant organisation on a par with the greatest cities of either Eastern or Western civilisation at that time. As white as marble and gilded by the sunshine, the limestone complex of the Nunnery Quadrangle, the Palace of the Governor and the Pyramid of the Soothsayer has a fascinating and almost modern beauty. The friezes of the palaces are decorated with stone mosaics in intricate geometric designs. Open daily 9am–5pm. Admission US$4.50, free on Sundays.

In the 10th century the peaceful Mayan world was disturbed by the warlike Toltecs, who came down from their northern plateau capital of Tula to conquer the Yucatan cities and make **Chichen Itza** their southern capital. The monumental constructions you see are both Mayan (e.g. El Caracol, the circular observatory) and Toltec (e.g. the Court of a Thousand Columns). The city is dominated by the Great Pyramid, the Temple of Kukulcán, with its stairways of 91 steps on each of four sides, making a total of 364. That figure plus one step round the top totals the days in the year. Other points of interest include the Ball Court and its inscriptions and the Sacred Well into which human sacrifices were hurled. 'Chichen Itza is an amazing place. You need at least a day, preferably two days, to see it properly.' Open 6am–5pm.

ACCOMMODATION

You'll probably make Mérida your overnight base, but there are a few cheap digs at Chichen and nearby **Valladolid** as well. At Uxmal you can try **Misión Inn**, 99-247-308. Pool and AC.

Misión Inn, 99-239-500, in Pisté. About a mile from the ruins at Chichen Itza. 'Moderate prices.'

Posada Novello, at Pisté, a mile before the ruins at Chichen when coming from Mérida on main road. 'Friendly, with fan and shower.'

INFORMATION/TRAVEL

Admission fee for each site. English-language books on sale.
Buses to Uxmal, Chichen Itza leave from Mérida depot at Calles 68 and 69. Several buses, both 1st and 2nd class, starting from 8am, go to Chichen and/or Uxmal, some of them tours taking in other sites in the area as well.
'Don't get afternoon buses to site as it closes at 5pm. If you want to see the evening *son et lumière*, you won't be able to get back by bus.'
'It's possible to get an early bus from Campeche, spend several hours at Uxmal, and then continue to Mérida on a bus leaving the ruins at about 2.30pm.'

ISLA MUJERES Off the northeast corner of the Yucatan peninsula, this 'island of women' got its name when the first Spaniards found a large number of Mayan stone goddesses here. The beaches are excellent, the foliage semi-tropical, the island beautiful, the pace relaxed and informal. Don't expect an undiscovered paradise, however. Granted, the big bucks go to **Cancun** and **Cozumel**, but Isla Mujeres is getting the overflow and the purple prose in US travel mags, with attendant hotel-building and price-climbing.

ACCOMMODATION

Singles average US$10–15, doubles US$12–25.
Hotel Caracol, Av Matamoros 5, off Av Madero, 2-01-50. 'Spartan.' 'Inexpensive restaurant in lobby.' US$14–16.
Posado San Jorge, Calle Juarez between Mateos and Matamoros, 2-01-55. S–US$15, D–US$20. 'Basic, but clean with noisy, necessary fan. 5 mins from beach.'
Poc-Na Hostel, Matamoros 91, Playa Norte, 2-00-90. US$3.50 per person per night. 'Beautiful place, clean and safe. 'Not beautiful, but cheap, friendly and good fun.' Room deposit also required.
Rocamar Hotel, Av Nicolas Bravo y Guerrero, 2-01-01. On cliff. 'One of the few cheap places on Isla.' US$18.
Camping: on North Beach. 'Take your own tent and hammock—cheaper. Or rent hammock on spot.'

FOOD/OF INTEREST

Be sure to sample *caracol* (conch meat), either grilled or made into marinated *ceviche;* turtle steak: barbequed barracuda; and good local beer—León Negro is a full-bodied ale.
Bicycle Rental, from Auto Carmelina, Calle Guerrero 9. About US$3 an hour.
Fishing, swimming and snorkelling are the things to do; you can rent equipment locally. Snorkelling is magnificent. 'Best snorkelling in **El Garrafón** at southern end of island. Get there early before the rich tourists from the El Presidente Hotel come to trample on the coral and frighten the fish. Amazing to see such colourful life so close to shore. Swim 50 yards north to pond with giant green turtles and (harmless) shark: didn't see any sharks outside the pond!' Experienced divers might like to visit the **Caves of the Sleeping Sharks** where you can stroke the sharks as they 'sleep'!

INFORMATION

Tourist Office: Calle Hidalgo 6, tel 2-03-16. Open weekdays 8am–2pm, 5–8pm.

TRAVEL

For Isla Mujeres, take the bus from Mérida to **Puerto Juárez**, where it connects with a ferry costing US$2. (Usually a wait.) Last ferry leaves at 7.30pm.
To get to Cancun from Isla take the ferry to **Playa Luda** or Puerto Juárez.

CANCUN AND COZUMEL Twenty years ago **Cancun Island** was deserted jungle and swamp. It was then selected by Fonatur as the spot for Mexico's premier Caribbean resort and development has proceeded apace ever since. Some of the hotels are magnificent and it is a beautiful resort. However, prices are Manhattan level—even McDonalds costs more here! But the beaches are free and open to all and the sea is warm and inviting.

Further south, on the island of **Cozumel**, life moves at a slower pace. Cozumel is best known for its excellent diving, being a favourite haunt of Jacques Cousteau. **Palancar**, the main coral reef, is the second largest natural coral formation in the world. Ferries to Cozumel go from **Playa del Carmen**. Continuing south on the mainland, there are the Mayan ruins at **Tulum** and **Coba** to explore. The whole coastline is quite beautiful and is excellent for snorkelling and other water sports.

ACCOMMODATION

Cancun—cheaper hotels to be found in Cancun City on the mainland. Best buy is the **CREA Youth Hostel**, Av Kukulkán km 3.2, 3-13-37, right on the beach near Hotel Los Playos. US$8 for dorm bunks. Take bus from downtown.

On **Cozumel**, cheapest (about US$15) hotels are in **San Miguel**. Try **Jose Leon** or **Posada Cozumel** at Calle y Norte 5, tel 2-02-14, S–US$18, D–US$23.

INFORMATION/TRAVEL

Pick up a copy (free) of *Cancun Tips* for up to the minute information on the area.

Cancun Tourist Office, Av Tulum 29, tel 4-80-73. Open daily 9am–9pm.

Cozumel Tourist Office is Av Juarez and 10 Avenida, tel 2-02-18. Open weekdays 8am–3pm.

There are good local and regional bus services, and many tours to everywhere up and down the coast!

From Cancun airport you can fly to New York, Mexico City, etc.

'For anyone wishing to cross from Mexico into Belize, the bus leaves the border town of Chetumal at 10am on Tue, Thur and Sat, arriving Belize City about 4pm.'

Appendix I TABLE OF WEIGHTS AND MEASURES

Conversion to and from the metric system

Mexico employs the metric system. **Canada** has almost completed the changeover to metric, and the **United States** as yet uses it only sporadically and within its National Parks.

Temperature

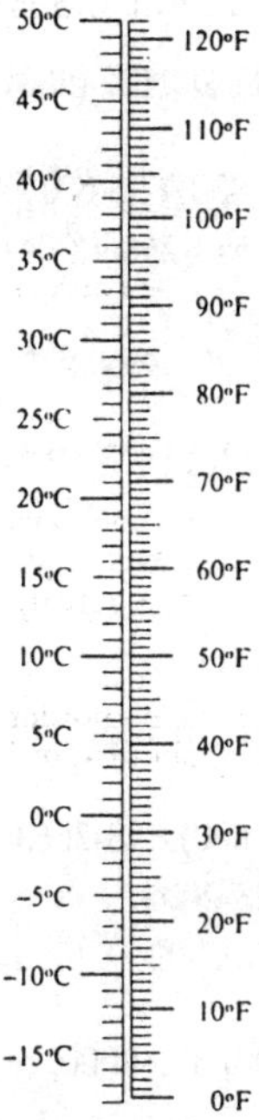

Fahrenheit into Centigrade/Celsius: subtract 32 from Fahrenheit temperature, then multiply by 5, then divide by 9. *Centigrade/Celsius into Fahrenheit:* multiply Centigrade/ Celsius by 9, then divide by 5 then add 32.

Linear Measure	0.3937 inches	1 centimetre
	1 inch	2.54 centimetres
	1 foot (12 in)	0.3048 metres
	1 yard (3 ft)	0.9144 metres
	39.37 inches	1 metre
	0.621 miles	1 kilometre
	1 mile (5280 ft)	1.6093 kilometres
	3 miles	4.8 kilometres
	10 miles	16 kilometres
	60 miles	98.6 kilometres
	100 miles	160.9 kilometres
Weight	0.0353 ounces	1 gram
	1 ounce	28.3495 grams
	1 pound (16 oz)	453.59 grams
	2.2046 pounds	1 kilogram
	1 ton (2000 lbs)	907.18 kilograms
Liquid Measure	1 US fluid ounce	0.0296 litres
	1 US pint (16 US fl oz)	0.4732 litres
	1 US quart (2 US pints)	0.9464 litres
	1.0567 US quarts	1 litre
	1 US gallon (4 US quarts)	3.7854 litres
	3 US gallons	11.3 litres
	4 US gallons	15.1 litres
	10 US gallons	37.8 litres
	15 US gallons	56.8 litres

The British imperial gallon (used in Canada) has 20 fluid ounces and 4 imperial quarts and is equal to 4.546 litres.

Speed

25 km/h equals (approx.) 15 m.p.h.
40 km/h equals (approx.) 25 m.p.h.
50 km/h equals (approx.) 30 m.p.h.
60 km/h equals (approx.) 37 m.p.h.
80 km/h equals (approx.) 50 m.p.h.
100 km/h equals (approx.) 60 m.p.h.
112 km/h equals (approx.) 70 m.p.h.

Appendix II SOME BUDGET MOTEL CHAINS IN THE US

Budget Host Inns, PO Box 10656, Ft Worth, TX 76114. (817) 626-7064/(800) 283-4678.

Chalet Susse International, Chalet Dr, Wilton, NH 03086. (800) 258-1980.

Days Inn, 339 Jefferson Rd, PO Box 278, Parsippany, NJ 07054. (800) 325-2525.

E–Z 8 Motels, 2484 Hotel Circle Place, San Diego, CA 92108. (800) 32M-OTEL

Econo-Lodges of America, 505 Clanton Rd, Charlotte, NC 28217. (800) 553-2666/(704) 523-1404.

Exel Inns, 4706 E Washington Avenue, Madison, WI 53704. (800) 856-8013.

Friendship Inns, Address as Econo-Lodges (above). (800) 553-2666/(704) 523-1404.

Hampton Inn, 6800 Poplar Ave, Suite 200, Memphis, TN 38138. (800) 426-7866.

Interstate Inns, PO Box 760, Kimball, NE 69145. (308) 235-4616, (800) 462-4667.

Knights Inn, 26650 Emery Pkwy, Cleveland, OH 44128. (216) 464-5055/(800) 722-7220.

Motel 6, 14651 Dallas Pkway, Dallas, TX 75240. (505) 891-6161.

Quality Inns (Choice Hotels), 10750 Columbia Pike, Silver Spring, MD 20901. (800) 424-6423.

Red Roof Inns, 4355 Davidson Road, Hilliard, OH 43026. (800) 843-7663.

Rodeway Inns, Address as Econo-Lodges (above). (800) 228-2000.

Scottish Inns of America, 1152 Spring St, Suite A, Atlanta, GA 30309. (800) 251-1962.

Super 8 Motels, PO Box 4090, Aberdeen, SD 57402-4090. (800) 800-8000, or (800) 848-8888.

Travelodge Forte Hotels, 5700 Broodmoor, Suite 500, Mission, KS 66202. 800-255-3050.

Write to any of the above for their directories of motels, containing full information on rates, facilities, locations and often small maps pinpointing each motel.

INDEX

CORRECTIONS AND ADDITIONS

The detail, accuracy and usefulness of future editions of this Guide depends greatly on your help. Share the benefit of your experiences with other travellers by sending us as much information on accommodation, eating places, places of interest, entertainment, events, travel, etc, as you can.

These printed forms are supplied to get you started. Additional information should be sent on separate sheets of paper. *Please do not write on the back of these forms, nor on the back of your own sheets*. When making remarks, bear in mind that a comment on a hotel like 'Quite good' or 'OK' conveys little to anyone—be as descriptive and as quotable as you can, but please also be concise. If suggesting new hotels, eating places etc, please give full information: ie. **correct name, address, phone numbers, price** etc. **This is very important**. Without complete information your special 'hot' tip may not get published.

Please use these slips *only* for this guidebook information and not for any other BUNAC publications. Completed slips and other information should be sent to: General Editor, *The Moneywise Guide to North America*, BUNAC, 16 Bowling Green Lane, London EC1R 0BD.
In the USA: BUNAC, PO Box 49, South Britain, CT 06487.

The deadline for information to be included in the 1994 edition of the Guide is 10th October, 1994.

EXAMPLE

Place: LONE PINE, CALIFORNIA	Date: 10 Sept 1994
Subject: ACCOMMODATION	Page no: 244
~~Correction~~/Addition	Comments
Redwood Hotel, 123 Spruce Ave. (209) 976-5432 $28 single, $32 with bath. $35 double, $40 with bath.	Clean, bright, though simply furnished. Vibrating water bed. Friendly and helpful. Turn left out of bus station and walk two blocks.

Place: Date:

Subject: Page no:

Correction/Addition
(*Please give complete information*)

Comments

Place: Date:

Subject: Page no:

Correction/Addition
(*Please give complete information*)

Comments

Place: Date:

Subject: Page no:

Correction/Addition
(*Please give complete information*)

Comments

Place: Date:

Subject: Page no:

Correction/Addition
(*Please give complete information*) Comments

Place: Date:

Subject: Page no:

Correction/Addition
(*Please give complete information*) Comments

Place: Date:

Subject: Page no:

Correction/Addition
(*Please give complete information*) Comments

Place:	Date:
Subject:	Page no:
Correction/Addition (*Please give complete information*)	Comments

Place:	Date:
Subject:	Page no:
Correction/Addition (*Please give complete information*)	Comments

Place:	Date:
Subject:	Page no:
Correction/Addition (*Please give complete information*)	Comments